www.wadsworth.com

www.wadsworth.com is the World Wide Web site for Wadsworth and is your direct source to dozens of online resources.

At *www.wadsworth.com* you can find out about supplements, demonstration software, and student resources. You can also send email to many of our authors and preview new publications and exciting new technologies.

www.wadsworth.com
Changing the way the world learns®

Psychology

Psychology
A Journey

Second Edition

Dennis Coon

THOMSON
WADSWORTH™

Australia • Canada • Mexico • Singapore • Spain • United Kingdom • United States

THOMSON
WADSWORTH

Publisher: Vicki Knight
Psychology Editor: Marianne Taflinger
Development Editor: Jeremy Judson
Assistant Editor: Jennifer Keever
Editorial Assistant: Justin Courts
Technology Project Manager: Erik Fortier
Marketing Manager: Chris Caldeira
Marketing Assistant: Laurel Anderson
Advertising Project Manager: Brian Chaffee
Project Manager, Editorial Production: Jerilyn Emori
Art Director: Vernon Boes
Print/Media Buyer: Karen Hunt

Permissions Editor: Joohee Lee
Production Service: Carol O'Connell, Graphic World Publishing
    Services
Text Designer: Lisa Buckley
Photo Researcher: Kathleen Olson
Illustrator: Graphic World Illustration Studio
Cover Designer: Denise Davidson
Cover Image: © Peter Lavery/Masterfile
Cover Printer: Phoenix Color Corp
Compositor: Graphic World, Inc.
Printer: Courier Corporation/Kendallville

Printed in the United States of America
1   2   3   4   5   6   7   08   07   06   05   04

For more information about our products, contact us at:
Thomson Learning Academic Resource Center
1-800-423-0563
For permission to use material from this text or product, submit a
request online at http://www.thomsonrights.com.
Any additional questions about permissions can be submitted by
email to thomsonrights@thomson.com.

Library of Congress Control Number: 2004104601

Student Edition: ISBN 0-534-63264-5

Instructor's Edition: ISBN 0-534-63270-X

Thomson Wadsworth
10 Davis Drive
Belmont, CA 94002-3098
USA

Asia
Thomson Learning
5 Shenton Way #01-01
UIC Building
Singapore 068808

Australia/New Zealand
Thomson Learning
102 Dodds Street
Southbank, Victoria 3006
Australia

Canada
Nelson
1120 Birchmount Road
Toronto, Ontario M1K 5G4
Canada

Europe/Middle East/Africa
Thomson Learning
High Holborn House
50/51 Bedford Row
London WC1R 4LR
United Kingdom

Latin America
Thomson Learning
Seneca, 53
Colonia Polanco
11560 Mexico D.F.
Mexico

Spain/Portugal
Paraninfo
Calle Magallanes, 25
28015 Madrid, Spain

About the Author

After earning a doctorate in psychology from the University of Arizona, Dennis Coon taught for 22 years at Santa Barbara City College, California. Throughout his career, Dr. Coon has especially enjoyed the challenge of teaching introductory psychology. He and his wife Sevren now live in Tucson, where he continues to teach, write, edit, and consult.

Dr. Coon is the author of **Introduction to Psychology,** as well as **Essentials of Psychology.** Together, these texts have been used by over 2 million students. Dr. Coon frequently serves as a reviewer and consultant to publishers, and he edited the best-selling trade book, **Choices.** He also helped design modules for **PsychNow!,** Wadsworth's interactive CD-ROM.

In his leisure hours, Dr. Coon enjoys hiking, photography, painting, woodworking, and music. He also designs, builds, and plays classical and steel string acoustic guitars. He has published articles on guitar design and occasionally offers lectures on this topic, in addition to his more frequent presentations on psychology. His return to Arizona has made it possible for him to fulfill a lifelong dream of using operant conditioning to teach scorpions to tap dance.

My first psychology course was taught by a woman whose intellect, warmth, and wisdom had a lot to do with my decision to major in psychology. In the years that followed, I was inspired and challenged by other gifted teachers. Their voices, as well as my own, can be heard throughout this book.

Brief Contents

Contents

CHAPTER 2   **Brain and Behavior**   51

CHAPTER 6   **Conditioning and Learning**   216

CHAPTER 8   **Cognition, Intelligence, and Creativity** 293

Preface

TO THE STUDENT—THE JOURNEY BEGINS

Psychology is an exciting field. It is at once familiar, exotic, surprising, and challenging. Most of all, psychology is changing. Indeed, this book is just a "snapshot" of a colorful passing scene. Yet, change makes psychology especially fascinating: What, really, could be more intriguing than our evolving understanding of human behavior?

Psychology is about each of us. Psychology asks, "How can we step outside of ourselves to look objectively at how we live, think, feel, and act?" Psychologists believe the answer is through careful thought, observation, and inquiry. As simple as that may seem, it is the guiding light for all that follows in this text.

Each chapter of this book will take you into a different realm of psychology, such as personality, abnormal behavior, memory, consciousness, or child development. Each realm is complex and fascinating in its own right, with many pathways, landmarks, and interesting detours to discover. The title of this book, *Psychology: A Journey,* reflects the fact that learning is an adventure. Like any journey of discovery, your "tour" of psychology will help you to better understand yourself, others, and the world around you. It's definitely a trip worth taking.

I sincerely hope you will find human behavior as fascinating as I do. In the pages that follow, I have done all that I could imagine to make your first journey through psychology enjoyable and worthwhile.

Getting Started

To help you get off to a good start, a short Introduction precedes Chapter 1. The Introduction describes study skills you can use to get the most out of this text and your psychology course. It also tells how you can explore psychology through the Internet, electronic databases, and interactive CDs.

Psychology: A Journey is your passport to an adventure in learning. Please view this book as a long letter from me to you. It is, in a very real sense, written about you, for you, and to you.

TO THE INSTRUCTOR—A CONCISE SURVEY OF PSYCHOLOGY

Psychology: A Journey was written to provide a concise, but complete, first course in psychology. It is organized into 14 chapters so that the entire field can be covered in a single term, at a pace of one chapter per week. *Journey's* brevity prompted me to select only the very "best" material from the many topics that could be presented. Nevertheless, *Journey* covers not only the heart of psychology, but also many topics at the cutting edge of current knowledge. New information, anecdotes, perspectives, and narratives appear throughout the Second Edition. The result is a concise text that is readable, manageable, informative, and motivating.

Readability and Narrative Emphasis

Selecting a textbook is half the battle in teaching a successful course. A good text does much of the work of informing students. This frees class time for discussion, extra topics, or media presentations. It also leaves students asking for more. When a book overwhelms students or cools their interest, teaching and learning suffer.

Many introductory psychology students are reluctant readers. No matter how interesting a text may be, its value is lost if students fail to read it. That's why I've worked hard to make this a clear, readable, and engaging text. I want students to read with genuine interest and enthusiasm, not merely as an obligation.

To encourage students to read, I made a special effort to weave narrative threads through every chapter. Everyone loves a good story, and the story of psychology is among the best. Throughout *Psychology: A Journey,* I have used intriguing anecdotes and examples to encourage reading and sustain interest. As students explore concepts, they are asked to think about ideas and relate them to their own experiences. For example, the September 11, 2001, terrorist attacks on the World Trade Center are used to illustrate flashbulb memories and the impact of traumatic stressors.

Practical Applications

Psychology: A Journey is designed to give students a clear grasp of major concepts, without burying them in details. At the same time, it offers a broad overview that reflects psychology's rich heritage of ideas. I think students will find this book informative and intellectually stimulating. Moreover, I have emphasized the many ways that psychology relates to daily life.

A major feature of this book is the *Psychology in Action* section found in each chapter. These high-interest discussions bridge the gap between theory and practical applications. I believe it is fair for students to ask, "Does this mean anything to me? Can I use it? Why should I learn it if I can't?" The information found in Psychology in Action shows students how to solve practical problems and manage their own behavior. This allows them to see the benefits of adopting new ideas, and it breathes life into psychology's concepts.

An Integrated Study Guide

The chapters of this text are divided into short segments by features called *Study Breaks.* Each Study Break challenges students to relate concepts to their own experiences, to quiz themselves, and to think critically about the principles they are learning. In addition, each chapter concludes with a self-assessment called *Test Your Knowledge.* The multiple-choice questions in Test Your Knowledge provide a way for students to judge how well they are doing in their studies, by taking a sample test. These tests now include 20 questions that are comparable in difficulty to in-class exams.

If students would like more feedback and practice, a great new printed supplement, *Practice Exams with Visual Guides and "Try It!" Exercises* is bundled with this text, a traditional *Study Guide* is available, and students can use a Web-based course management tool called *Web Tutor Toolbox* to practice with electronic flashcards or take online quizzes.

Electronic Resources

To encourage further explorations, students will find a section called *Interactive Learning* at the end of each chapter. The Web sites described there offer a wealth of information on topics related to psychology. Students are also directed to relevant articles in *InfoTrac® College Edition,* Wadsworth's exclusive online college library. All chapters include a list of relevant modules in *PsychNow!* This excellent CD-ROM from Wadsworth provides students with a rich assortment of interactive learning experiences, animations, and simulations.

Human Diversity

Today's students reflect the multicultural, multifaceted nature of contemporary society. In *Psychology: A Journey,* students will find numerous discussions of human diversity, including differences in race, ethnicity, culture, gender, abilities, sexual orientation, and age. Too often, such differences needlessly divide people into opposing groups. My aim throughout this text is to discourage stereotyping, prejudice, discrimination, and intolerance. I've tried to make this book gender neutral and sensitive to diversity issues. All pronouns and examples involving females and males are equally divided by gender. In artwork, photographs, and examples, I have tried to portray the rich diversity of humanity. Many topics and examples encourage students to appreciate social, physical, and cultural differences and to accept them as a natural part of being human.

Positive Psychology

Over the past 100 years, psychologists have paid ample attention to the negative side of human behavior. This is easy to understand because we urgently need to find remedies for human problems. However, Martin E. P. Seligman and Mihaly Csikszentmihalyi have urged us to also study optimal functioning or "positive psychology." What do we know, for instance, about love, happiness, creativity, well being, self-confidence, and achievement? Throughout this book, I have attempted to answer such questions for students. My hope is that students who read *Journey* will gain an appreciation for the potential we all have for optimal functioning. Also, of course, I hope that they will leave introductory psychology with emotional and intellectual tools they can use to enhance their lives.

How Chapter Features Support the SQ4R Method

Psychology: A Journey uses an SQ4R, active-learning format to make studying psychology a rewarding experience. Notice how the steps of the SQ4R method—*survey, question, read, recite, relate,* and *review*—are incorporated into the chapter design.

Survey

At the front of each chapter, several features help students build cognitive maps of upcoming topics. A short preview called *Journey Into Psychology* arouses interest, provides an entry point into the main topic of the chapter, and focuses attention. Next, a list of *Survey Questions* provides a focused overview of the chapter. These same Survey Questions appear in the main body of the chapter to help students structure their learning. Later, the Survey Questions are used to organize the chapter Summary, and they also appear in the *Study Guide*. In this way, students are given a consistent framework for studying and learning.

Question

Throughout each chapter, italicized dialogue questions serve as advance organizers that prompt students to look for important ideas as they read. Guide Questions also establish a dialogue in which the questions and reactions of students are anticipated. This dialogue clarifies difficult points—in a lively give-and-take between questions and responses.

Read

I've made every effort to make this a clear, readable text. To further aid comprehension, I've used a full array of traditional learning aids. These include: boldface terms (with phonetic pronunciations), bullet summaries, a robust illustration program, summary tables, a name index, a subject index, and a detailed Glossary. As an additional aid, figure and table references are marked with small geometric shapes. These "place-holders" make it easier for students to return to reading after they have paused to view a table or figure.

An integrated glossary aids reading comprehension by providing precise definitions directly in context. When important terms first appear, they are immediately defined. In this way, students get clear definitions when and where they need them—in the general text itself. In addition, a parallel Running Glossary defines key terms in the page margins. The Running Glossary makes it easier for students to find, study, and review important terms.

In each chapter, several boxed highlights discuss recent research, personal applications, critical thinking, clinical issues, and human diversity. Highlights are stimulating but non-intrusive supplements to the main text. They enrich the presentation and encourage students to think about the ideas they are learning.

Recite

Every few pages, a Study Break gives students a chance to test their understanding and recall of preceding topics. The Study Breaks are small, built-in study guides that include a Learning Check (a short, noncomprehensive quiz). Learning Checks help students actively process information and assess their progress. However, Learning Check questions are not as difficult as in-class tests, so students who miss any items are asked to backtrack and clarify their understanding before reading more. Completing Learning Checks serves as a form of recitation to enhance learning.

Relate

Cognitive psychology tells us that elaborative rehearsal is one of the best ways to form lasting memories. Through elaborative rehearsal we make new information more meaningful by relating it to existing, familiar knowledge. To help students practice elaborative rehearsal, each Study Break includes a series of "Relate" questions. These questions encourage students to associate new concepts with personal experiences and prior knowledge.

A course in psychology naturally contributes to critical thinking abilities. To further facilitate critical thinking, each Study Break also includes one or more Critical Thinking questions. These stimulating questions challenge students to think critically and analytically about psychology. Each is followed by a brief answer with which students can compare their own thoughts. Many of these answers cite research findings and are informative in their own right.

Review

As noted above, all important terms appear in a Running Glossary throughout the book, which aids review. As also noted, a Psychology in Action section shows students how psychological concepts relate to practical problems, including problems in their own lives. The information found in Psychology in Action helps reinforce learning by illustrating psychology's practicality.

To help students consolidate their learning, the Chapter in Review section restates all of the major ideas presented earlier in the chapter. This section begins with a list of Major Points that summarize the "take home" concepts every student should be able to remember 10 years after reading this text. Next, a point-by-point Summary provides a detailed synopsis of the chapter. As mentioned before, the Summary is organized around the same Survey Questions found at the beginning of the chapter. This brings the SQ4R process full-circle and reinforces the learning objectives for the chapter. Every chapter concludes with Test Your Knowledge, the brief multiple-choice test described earlier. Students who miss any questions on this test are urged to review further, using various supplements available with this text.

Critical Thinking

The active, questioning nature of the SQ4R method is, in itself, an inducement to think critically. Many of the Guide Questions that introduce topics in the text act as models of critical thinking. More important, Chapter 1 contains a discussion of critical thinking skills and a rational appraisal of pseudo-psychologies. In addition, the discussion of research methods in Chapter 1 is actually a short course on how to think clearly about behavior. It is augmented by suggestions about how to critically evaluate claims in the popular media. Chapter 8, "Cognition, Intelligence, and Creativity," includes many topics that focus on thinking skills. Throughout the text, many boxed highlights promote critical thinking about specific topics that students should approach with healthy skepticism. As mentioned earlier, every Study Break includes Critical Thinking questions. Taken together, these features will help students gain thinking skills of lasting value.

PSYCHOLOGY: A JOURNEY—WHAT'S NEW IN THE SECOND EDITION?

Thanks to psychology's vitality and suggestions from professors, this edition has improved in many ways. A notable change is a new feature called *Clinical File*. Many students enter the introductory course expecting to learn about clinical psychology (therapies, disorders, mental health, and personal adjustment). However, they typically have to wait until the course is nearly over before these topics are discussed. In view of this, the Second Edition features new clinical content in every chapter. In addition to infusing interesting topics from clinical psychology into every chapter, Clinical Files enhance the relevance of topics in nonclinical chapters.

The Second Edition of *Journey* features some of the most recent and interesting information in psychology. The following annotations highlight some of the new topics and features that appear in this edition.

Introduction: The Psychology of Studying

In the Introduction, which is new to this edition, students will find a collection of highly useful strategies for improving their study habits. The Introduction shows students how to read effectively, study more efficiently, take good notes, prepare for tests, perform well on various types of tests, create study schedules, and avoid procrastination. In addition, I have moved the discussion of self-regulated learning here. (It was formerly in Chapter 6.) My goal is to help students apply active learning principles to the entire course, not just the second half.

Chapter 1: Introduction to Psychology and Research Methods

This chapter received a light update. The psychology of gender and evolutionary psychology are now included in the list of research specialties. New art provides a better example of a perceptual Gestalt. A discussion of the pros and cons of Internet surveys has been added to the section on the survey method. Ten more questions have been added to sample test at the end of the chapter ("Test Your Knowledge"). (This improvement applies to all chapters.)

Clinical File: The Genain Sisters—Trouble Times Four
This new highlight describes a long-running classic study of four identical quadruplets who became schizophrenic. The chances of four identical quads all becoming schizophrenic are about one in 1.5 billion. Thus, the Genain sisters show students why clinical studies sometimes provide insights that can't be obtained by any other means.

Chapter 2: The Brain, Biology, and Behavior

This chapter has been rewritten for greater human interest and clarity. Improved art clarifies the events that take place during an action potential. Art illustrating the lobes of the cerebral cortex and the limbic system has also been improved. Recent findings update what we know about the origins of right- and left-handednesss.

Clinical File: A Stroke of Bad Luck
This new highlight describes some of the neurological soft signs that psychologists look for when they suspect a brain injury, disease, or malfunction.

Chapter 3: Child Development

In this chapter the discussion of ethnic differences in child-rearing practices has been updated and enlarged. A new highlight, "To Spank or not to Spank?," discusses empirical evidence that provides the rationale for minimizing or avoiding the use of spanking to discipline children. Also, research updates enhance discussions of sensitive periods and language, the Mozart effect, toilet training, secure attachment, and day care.

Clinical File: Beyond Homesickness

This new highlight discusses separation anxiety disorder in children and helps students distinguish it from attachment, clinging, and shyness.

Chapter 4: Sensation and Perception

The basic organization of this chapter remains unchanged. Revisions mostly involve research updates and new information, where appropriate. This chapter has always appeared to be long (in pages) because it is heavily illustrated. To avoid intimidating students, I have condensed the text, while retaining the art. As a result, the chapter is more approachable and the time required to read it is comparable to other chapters. Additional revisions are listed below.

- New art clarifies the structures and functions of the retina and the ear.
- Recent research findings are used to update the discussion of olfaction.
- A brief new discussion examines the causes of the "other-race effect" in facial recognition.
- Brief new coverage of inattentional blindness has been added.
- "Miss Cleo" and similar TV frauds are debunked in the discussion of ESP.
- An updated discussion of perceptual accuracy includes a table (based on recent research) that summarizes major factors that affect eyewitness perceptions.

Clinical File: Doctor, Can't You Hear Them?

This new highlight explains why hallucinations are regarded as a symptom of mental disorders and it tells how "sane hallucinations" can occur.

Chapter 5: States of Consciousness

As detailed below, information about psychoactive drugs has been significantly updated and improved. Also, research updates improve discussions of a variety of topics throughout the chapter.

- A brief new section explains synaptic mechanisms underlying drug effects.
- A new discussion examines the effects and dangers of using methamphetamine and MDMA ("Ecstasy").
- Another new section discusses the effects of GHB and its potential risks.
- "Street" names are now listed for some commonly abused drugs.
- More information is provided about the damaging effects of binge drinking and alcohol abuse.
- Research updates address SIDS and its prevention, the effects of hypnosis, mediation as an antidote to stress, the nature of addiction, nicotine, and the residual cognitive effects of marijuana use.

Clinical File: Teenage Sleep Zombies

This new highlight documents the connection between chronic teenage sleep deprivation and adolescent moodiness.

Chapter 6: Conditioning and Learning

This chapter needed few changes. Nevertheless, I have found ways to make some of the discussions shorter and clearer. In addition, three new highlights and some worthwhile research updates enhance this chapter. The topic of self-regulated learning has been moved to the Introduction, where it adds to the presentation of helpful study skills.

- A new highlight, "Conditioning and Conservation" explains how operant principles have been used to encourage energy conservation and recycling.
- A new highlight, "Violent Video Games—Toxic Kombat?" reviews recent evidence that indicates violent video games increase aggressive behavior.

Clinical File: Blink If Your Brain Is Healthy

This new highlight describes recent research suggesting that eye-blink conditioning (classical conditioning) may be useful for identifying very early stages of dementia.

Chapter 7: Memory

Research updates improve discussions of short-term memory, state dependent memory, suppression/repression, and brain mechanisms of memory.

Clinical File: The Recovered Memory/False Memory Debate

This highlight offers a revised discussion of the recovered memory epidemic and helps students recognize both the reality of early sexual abuse and the risk of making false accusations.

Chapter 8: Cognition, Language, and Creativity

This chapter covers the new Fifth Edition of the Stanford-Binet Intelligence Scale (the SB5), published in 2003. The SB5 now measures five cognitive factors (rather than four) and it can be scored for verbal and performance intelligence. In addition:

- A brief new discussion draws a distinction between intelligence and wisdom.
- Research updates have been added to discussions of gestural languages and evolution, the characteristics of creative people, and techniques for promoting creative problem solving.

Clinical File: Madness and Creativity

This new highlight documents that many of history's renowned artists, writers, poets, and composers suffered from mood disorders. In doing so, it provides a fascinating look at the question, "Is genius next to insanity?".

Chapter 9: Motivation and Emotion

This chapter has been streamlined for greater interest and readability. It includes a new highlight and a variety of small updates and enhancements as described next.

- An updated version of Robert Plutchik's theory of emotions is presented, along with updated and improved art.
- New art clarifies connections between emotions and activity in the autonomic system.
- A revised discussion of emotional intelligence describes the skills that comprise emotional maturity.
- Research updates improve discussions of hunger, obesity and external eating cues, behavioral dieting, eating disorders, sex drive and aphrodisiacs, sudden death related to intense emotion, sensitivity to threatening facial expressions, and the facial feedback hypothesis.

Clinical File: Sexual Problems—When Pleasure Fades
This new highlight identifies the most common sexual problems and provides an example of how they are treated.

Chapter 10: Personality

In this chapter:

* Social learning theory is now more clearly differentiated from behavioral theories of personality. Also, Bandura's concept of self-efficacy has been added.
* A brief report describes an interesting study that relates personality traits to musical tastes.
* This chapter also benefits from brief research updates on self-esteem, the consistency of traits, the Big Five, situational determinants of behavior, the accuracy of personality tests, honesty testing, and shyness.

Clinical File: Near-Death Experiences—A Fresh Look at Life
This new highlight examines the effects that near-death experiences can have on the personalities of persons who reach the brink of death and survive to tell about it.

Chapter 11: Health, Stress, and Coping

In addition to detailed research updates, this chapter has a new highlight, as described in the list that follows. Also, suggestions for coping with conflict and frustration have been moved into the chapter. This places the suggestions in context and it shortens the Psychology in Action feature, which was disproportionately long in the prior edition.

* Information about HIV and AIDS has been revised to reflect the latest data.
* This chapter includes updates on behavioral risk factors, the disease-prone personality, refusal skills and life skills training, unpredictability and stress, job burnout, the nature of threat, daily hassles, hostility and the Type A personality, hardiness and happiness, psychoneuroimmunology, and stress management.

Clinical File: September 11 and Traumatic Stress
Examines the nature of traumatic stress and discusses some helpful ways of managing initial reactions to highly stressful events.

Chapter 12: Psychological Disorders

The section of this chapter that discusses anxiety disorders is more concise and it includes updated information about stress disorders. Post-traumatic stress disorders are specifically related to the September 11 terrorist attacks in New York. The section on hospitalization has been moved to Chapter 13, where it complements a discussion of medical approaches to mental disorders. Other revisions include:

* An updated discussion of biochemical explanations of schizophrenia now includes the influence of glutamate levels on dopamine systems.
* This chapter also has brief updates on borderline personality, antisocial personality, multiple personality disorder, mental illness and violence, Alzheimer's disease, the causes of schizophrenia, the causes of depression, and seasonal affective disorder.

Chapter 13: Therapies

Mental hospitalization, which was formerly discussed in Chapter 12, is now presented here. This allows students to gain a better perspective on the range of medical therapies available, and the differences between psychological and somatic approaches.

Some types of distance therapy are starting to produce good results. I have revised the discussion of distance therapy to reflect this progress and the greater acceptance that telephone counseling is receiving. However, students are still cautioned about the questionable value of commercial telephone counseling "services" and counseling offered via the Internet. The list that follows describes other improvements in this chapter.

- Additional studies are reported showing that virtual reality exposure can be used to successfully treat phobias.
- The discussion of eye movement desensitization and reprocessing (EMDR) presents recent evidence for and against the effectiveness of this controversial therapy.
- A brief new section discusses the future of psychotherapy, as predicted by a panel of experts.
- Research updates are found in discussions of psychoanalysis, desensitization, group therapy, the therapeutic alliance, ECT, deinstitutionalization, and the use of paraprofessionals.

Chapter 14: Social Behavior

This chapter has been distilled without a loss of content. The section titled "Forced Attitude Change—Brainwashing and Cults," has been revised to reflect the role of cults in terrorism. Updated information is presented about homogamy, role conflicts, intergroup conflict, symbolic prejudice, and the unconscious origins of discrimination. I have also updated the section on the causes of human aggression, including the impact of media violence. New information in Psychology in Action shows students that "race" is a matter of social labeling, not a biological reality.

Clinical File: School Violence—Warning Signs and Remedies
In the wake of the school shootings at Columbine and similar tragedies, this new highlight presents warning signs that may help identify persons at risk for violence. It also suggests steps that parents can take to reduce the likelihood of violence.

A COMPLETE COURSE—TEACHING AND LEARNING SUPPLEMENTS

A rich array of supplements accompanies *Psychology: A Journey,* including several that make use of the latest technologies. These supplements are designed to make teaching and learning more effective. Many are available free to professors or students. Others can be packaged with this text at a discount. For more information on any of the listed resources, please call the Thomson Learning™ Academic Resource Center at 800-423-0563.

Student Support Materials

Introductory students must learn a multitude of abstract concepts, which can make a first course in psychology difficult. The materials listed here will greatly improve students' chances for success.

Practice Exams with Visual Guides and "Try It!" Exercises
This free booklet is included with every copy of *Journey* (ISBN: 0-534-63268-8). The Visual Guides present important topics from each chapter in an easy-to-use flow chart. The Visual Guides were created by Art VanDeventer of Thomas Nelson Community College to help students connect ideas and build cognitive maps of key concepts. In the "Try It!" exercises, students apply concepts to real-world examples through a mixture of mini-application games and demonstrations. The "Try It!" exercises, written by Britton Mace of Southern Utah University, are a fun and creative way to bring concepts to life. The Practice Exams,

also written by Britton Mace, consist of 20 multiple-choice questions that students can use to evaluate their understanding and prepare for classroom tests.

Study Guide

To facilitate learning, the *Study Guide* provides abundant opportunities for practice, self-testing, and rehearsal. The *Study Guide* is structured around the SQ4R method and is closely coordinated with this text. Each chapter includes the following sections: Chapter Overview (a concise chapter summary), Learning Objectives (a detailed list of what students need to know), Recite and Review (a survey of major terms and concepts), Connections (matching items), Check Your Memory (true-false items), Final Survey and Review (fill-in-the-blank questions) and a Mastery Test (multiple-choice questions similar to in-class test items). (*Study Guide,* by Dennis Coon, ISBN: 0-534-63267-X.)

Language Development Guide

For some students, language and culture can be major barriers to comprehension. The *Language Development Guide* (ISBN: 0-534-61264-4), prepared by Robert Moore, of Marshalltown Community College, helps clarify idioms and special phrases, cultural and historic allusions, and tricky vocabulary. Much of this information would be difficult or impossible to look up in a dictionary. All terms and phrases in the manual are page-referenced to the text and followed by concise definitions. Like a helpful tutor, the *Language Development Guide* can answer questions about the meaning of unfamiliar terms and expressions. Contact your Wadsworth/Thomson Learning™ Representative for ordering information.

Careers in Psychology: Opportunities in a Changing World

This informative new booklet, written by Tara L. Kuther, is a Wadsworth exclusive. The pamphlet describes the field of psychology, as well as how to prepare for a career in psychology. Career options and resources are also discussed. *Careers in Psychology* can be packaged with this text at no additional cost to students (ISBN 0-534-61776-X).

Multimedia CD-ROMs

Interactive CD-ROMs make it possible for students to directly experience some of the phenomena they are studying. The following CDs from Wadsworth provide a wealth of engaging modules and exercises.

PsychNow! Interactive Experiences in Psychology 2.0

This exciting CD-ROM was created by Joel Morgovsky, Lonnie Yandell, Elizabeth Lynch, and project consultant Dennis Coon. An updated and enlarged *PsychNow!* (ISBN: 0-534-59046-2) is perfectly matched to *Psychology: A Journey*. At the end of each chapter of this text, students will find a list of *PsychNow!* modules they can access for additional, "hands-on" learning.

PsychNow! provides a multimedia experience that allows students to explore psychology like never before. Stunning graphics and animations, interesting video clips, interactive exercises, and Web links bring psychology to life. With *PsychNow!*, students can do more than just read about a topic—they can read, watch, listen, react, and reflect on the meaning of their own responses. *PsychNow!*, which is available for Macintosh and Windows, contains 39 fully interactive modules that will enhance their understanding. Students can also conduct 15 different "Interactive Research Experiments" in areas such as neurocognition, perception, memory, concepts, and imagery. The latest edition includes eight new "Interact Now" Collaborative Labs and new "Quiz Game Now" quizzes.

Although *PsychNow!* can be used alone, it is also available in a discount bundle for students when packaged with this text. Contact your sales representative for ordering information, or for a demonstration.

Sniffy™ the Virtual Rat, Lite Version 2.0

There's no better way to master the basic principles of learning than working with a real laboratory rat. However, this is usually impractical in introductory psychology courses. *Sniffy the Virtual Rat* offers a fun, interactive alternative to working with lab animals. This innovative and entertaining software teaches students about operant and classical conditioning by allowing them to condition a virtual rat. Users begin by training Sniffy to press a bar to obtain food. Then they progress to studying the effects of reinforcement schedules and simple classical conditioning. In addition, special "Mind Windows" enable students to visualize how Sniffy's experiences in the Skinner Box produce learning. The Sniffy CD-ROM includes a Lab Manual that shows students how to set up various operant and classical conditioning experiments. *Sniffy™ the Virtual Rat, Lite Version 2.0* may be packaged with this text for a discount (ISBN: 0-534-63357-9).

Internet Resources

The Internet is providing new ways to exchange information and enhance education. In psychology, Wadsworth is at the forefront in making use of this exciting technology.

Book Companion Web Site

As users of this text, you and your students will have access to the *Psychology: A Journey* section of the Wadsworth Psychology Resource Center (http://psychology.wadsworth.com). Access is free and no pincode is required. The site includes chapter outlines, learning objectives, chapter summaries, a glossary, flashcards, crossword puzzles, exercises that use the *InfoTrac College Edition* online database, and extensive Web links. It also offers chapter quizzing—multiple-choice and short-answer—as well as *Self-Study Assessments,* written by Britton Mace.

The new Self-Study Assessments work in tandem with this text's SQ4R learning system. For every Study Break in the text, the Self-Study Assessment program offers a *Pre-Test* (about 35 questions) that students can complete to determine what they know. A second *Post-Test* (with about 35 different questions) lets students see what they've learned after further study. Then, personalized *Integrated Study Plans* (with page numbers) are generated automatically, based on their responses to the *Pre-Tests* and *Post-Tests.*

The Book Companion Web Site features over 30 *MediaWorks* demonstrations and narrated simulations (with critical thinking questions). These presentations allow students to experience key concepts interactively.

The Book Companion Web Site also includes a free passcode to *iLrn* that gives you exclusive access to a grade book for tracking student progress, and gives your students a version of the *Integrated Study Plans* with learning modules that include simulations and animations.

PsychStudy

This valuable new study aid is available free to students. After they read a text chapter, students can access a Pre-Test from the book Companion Web site using the free Pin Code that came with their text. (Please note: This Pin Code is not automatically packaged with *Journey,* it must be requested as a bundle.)

After submitting the Pre-Test, a Personalized Study Plan is created, which directs students to specific topics (and specific page references) they need to review. For convenience, students can print the Personalized Study Plan to use as a guide. Students are also given access to numerous digital resources, such as CNN videos, simulations, narrated animations, glossary terms, and Web links, all of which are tied to specific topics in the text. Extensive, media-rich Learning Modules with strong pedagogy are also available for key concepts.

Following their review of specific topics in *Psychology: A Journey,* students take a Post-Test to verify their understanding of the chapter. PsychStudy also includes a gradebook for instructors to track students' progress through the Pre-Test and Post-Test process (ISBN: 0-534-63277-7).

InfoTrac College Edition

InfoTrac College Edition is a powerful online learning resource, consisting of thousands of full-text articles from hundreds of journals and periodicals. Students using *Psychology: A Journey* receive four months of free access to InfoTrac College Edition. This fully searchable database offers over 20 years' worth of full-text articles from thousands of scholarly and popular sources—updated daily, and available 24 hours a day from any computer with Internet access. By doing a simple keyword search, students can quickly generate a list of relevant articles from thousands of possibilities. Then they can select full-text articles to read, explore, and print for reference or further study. InfoTrac College Edition's collection of articles can be useful for doing reading and writing assignments that reach beyond the pages of this text. Students also have access to *InfoWrite,* which provides extensive resources for writing papers, including suggested topics, APA guidelines, and more. (InfoTrac College Edition is at http://www.infotrac-college.com.)

Thomson Learning *Web Tutor Toolbox*

This online supplement helps students succeed by taking them into an environment rich with study and mastery tools, communication aids, and additional course content. For students, *Web Tutor* offers real-time access to a full array of study tools, including flashcards (with audio), practice quizzes and tests, online tutorials, exercises, asynchronous discussion, a whiteboard, and an integrated e-mail system. Students will also have integrated access to InfoTrac College Edition, the online library, as well as to the *Newbury House Online Dictionary,* an interactive dictionary that gives users instant access to definitions (including audio pronunciations).

Professors can use *Web Tutor Toolbox* to offer virtual office hours, to post syllabi, to set up threaded discussions, to track student progress on quizzes, and more. You can customize the content of *Web Tutor* in any way you choose, including uploading images and other resources, adding Web links, and creating course-specific practice materials. (*Web Tutor Toolbox* on *WebCT,* ISBN: 0-534-27490-0; *Toolbox* on *Blackboard,* ISBN: 0-534-27491-9.)

Essential Teaching Resources

As every professor knows, teaching an introductory psychology course is a tremendous amount of work. The supplements listed here should not only make life easier for you, they should also make it possible for you to concentrate on the more creative and rewarding facets of teaching.

Instructor's Resource Manual

The *Instructor's Resource Manual* (ISBN: 0-534-63271-8) was prepared by Wanda McCarthy, of the University of Cincinnati–Raymond Walters College. For every chapter in the text, this manual includes: learning objectives and detailed chapter outlines; discussion topics, classroom activities, and handouts; Web links with activities; video suggestions; InfoTrac College Edition search terms and articles with activities; and grading rubrics. The manual also includes questions and activities that apply to the recently revised *PsychNow!* CD-ROM, as well as a detailed *Resource Integration Guide* that shows, at a glance, how each of this text's supplements correlates to each chapter of the text.

Test Bank

The *Test Bank* was prepared by Jeannette Murphey of Meridian Community College. It includes over 2,000 multiple-choice questions organized by chapter and by Learning Objectives. All items, which are classified as factual, conceptual, or applied, include correct answers and page references from the text. To encourage students to study, 15 items per chapter in the *Test Bank* are drawn from the printed *Study Guide,* and 10 items are taken from online Web quizzes. Every chapter of the *Test Bank* also includes 15–20 fill-in-the-blank and 5 essay questions that tie into the learning objectives (ISBN: 0-534-63272-6).

Multimedia Manager Instructor's Resource CD-ROM

This CD-ROM includes PowerPoint® lecture outline slides with video clips, animations, and art from the book—as well as the complete *Instructor's Resource Manual* and *Test Bank* in Word® format (ISBN: 0-534-63275-0).

ExamView Computerized Testing

This software helps you create, deliver, and customize tests and study guides (both in print and online). In just minutes, this easy-to-use system can generate the assessment and tutorial materials your students need. *ExamView* offers both a Quick Test Wizard and an Online

Test Wizard that guide you step-by-step through the process of creating tests. *ExamView* shows the test you are creating on the screen exactly as it will print or display online. Using a database prepared by Sandra Madison, you can build tests of up to 250 questions using up to 12 question types. *ExamView's* complete word processing capabilities also allow you to enter an unlimited number of new questions or edit existing questions (ISBN: 0-534-63273-4).

Transparency Acetates

If you customarily use transparencies in class, a nice set is available to illustrate and enliven your lectures. Approximately 135 text-specific transparencies make it easy to display tables, graphs, charts, and drawings from this text (ISBN: 0-534-63274-2).

Videotapes and Films

Wadsworth offers a variety of videotapes and films to enhance classroom presentations. Many video segments in the Wadsworth collection pertain directly to major topics in this text, making them excellent lecture supplements.

Wadsworth Film and Video Library for Introductory Psychology

Adopters can select from a variety of continually updated film and video options. The Wadsworth Film and Video Library includes selections from the *Discovering Psychology* series, the *Annenberg* series, and *Films for Humanities*. It also includes the exclusive CNN offerings described below. Contact your local sales representative or Wadsworth Marketing at 877-999-2350 for details.

CNN® Today Videos for Introductory Psychology

These one- to four-minute video clips, a Wadsworth exclusive, allow you to integrate the newsgathering and programming power of CNN into the classroom to show students the relevance of psychology to daily life. Organized by course topics, these compelling clips are ideal for launching lectures and encouraging discussion. Adopters receive one new, updated video each year. A Wadsworth/Thomson Learning Exclusive!

Topics covered in the videos include: the brain, genetic mapping, sensation and perception, variations in consciousness, learning, human memory, language and thought, intelligence and psychological testing, gender and sexuality, diversity, human development, stress, health, psychological disorders, mental health, therapies, social behavior, and more. Volumes I through IV are now available on CD-ROM and DVD. Contact your sales representative to order.

> *CNN Today: Introductory Psychology, Volume I* (ISBN: 0-534-36634-1)
> *CNN Today: Introductory Psychology, Volume II* (ISBN: 0-534-50420-5)
> *CNN Today: Introductory Psychology, Volume III* (ISBN: 0-534-50749-2)
> *CNN Today: Introductory Psychology, Volume IV* (ISBN: 0-534-50751-4)
> *CNN Today: Introductory Psychology,* Volume V (ISBN: 0-534-54905-5)

Psychology Digital Video Library Version 2.0 CD-ROM

This CD-ROM contains a diverse selection of more than 100 classic and contemporary clips, including "Little Albert," the "Action Potential of a Neuron," "Parts of the Brain," and many more! The digital library offers a convenient way to access an appropriate clip for every lecture. An accompanying *Digital Video Handbook* offers a detailed description, approximate running time, and references to related media clips. It also offers objective quizzing and critical-thinking questions for each clip, as well as instructions on how to embed clips into your *PowerPoint®* presentations. Available exclusively to instructors who adopt Wadsworth psychology texts (ISBN: **0-534-57671-0).**

Wadsworth Media Guide for Introductory Psychology

This essential instructor resource, edited by Russell J. Watson, contains hundreds of video and feature film recommendations for all major topics in Introductory Psychology (ISBN: 0-534-17585-6).

Supplementary Books

No text can cover all of the topics that might be included in an introductory psychology course. If you would like to enrich your course, or make it more challenging, the Wadsworth titles listed here may be of interest.

Challenging Your Preconceptions: Thinking Critically about Psychology, Second Edition

This paperbound book (ISBN: 0-534-26739-4), written by Randolph Smith, helps students strengthen their critical thinking skills. Psychological issues such as hypnosis and repressed memory, statistical seduction, the validity of pop psychology, and other topics arc used to illustrate the principles of critical thinking.

Writing Papers in Psychology: A Student Guide

The Sixth Edition of *Writing Papers in Psychology* (ISBN: 0-534-52395-1), by Ralph L. Rosnow and Mimi Rosnow, is a valuable "how to" manual for writing term papers and research reports. This new edition has been updated to reflect the latest APA guidelines. The book covers each task with examples, hints, and two complete writing samples. Citation ethics, how to locate information, and new research technologies are also covered.

College Survival Guide: Hints and References to Aid College Students

This Fourth Edition of Bruce Rowe's *College Survival Guide* (ISBN: 0-534-35569-2) is designed to help students succeed. Rowe provides valuable tips on how to finance an education, how to manage time, how to study for and take exams, and more. Other sections focus on maintaining concentration, credit by examination, use of the credit/ no credit option, cooperative education programs, and the importance of a liberal arts education.

Cross-Cultural Perspectives in Psychology

How well do the concepts of psychology apply to various cultures? What can we learn about human behavior from cultures different from our own? These questions lie behind a collection of original articles written by William F. Price and Rich Crapo. The Fourth Edition of *Cross-Cultural Perspectives in Psychology* (ISBN: 0-534-54653-6) contains articles on North American ethnic groups as well as cultures from around the world.

Culture and Psychology: People Around the World, Second Edition

David Matsumoto's unique book (ISBN: 0-534-35436-X) discusses similarities and differences in research findings in the United States and other cultures. By doing so, it helps students see psychology and their own behavior from a broader, more culturally-aware perspective.

The 'Net, the Web, and You

This paperback by Daniel Kurland offers a brief, comprehensive, easy-to-understand introduction to the Internet. It is useful for any course that requires students to use the Internet for research or inquiry (ISBN: 0-534-51281-X).

Summary

I sincerely hope that teachers and students will consider this book and its supporting materials a refreshing change from the ordinary. Creating it has been quite an adventure. In the pages that follow, I think students will find an attractive blend of the theoretical and the practical, plus many of the most exciting ideas in psychology. Most of all, I hope that students using this book will discover that reading a college textbook can be entertaining and enjoyable.

ACKNOWLEDGMENTS

Psychology is a cooperative effort requiring the talents and energies of a large community of scholars, teachers, researchers, and students. Like most endeavors in psychology, this book reflects the efforts of many people. I deeply appreciate the contributions of all those who have supported this text's evolution, including the following psychologists:

Jean Brown, Cambrian College

Anice Bullock, Tomball College

Lisa Clark, Clark Atlanta University

Eric Comstock, Heald College, Concord

David Das, Elgin Community College

Michael Gardner, California State University, Northridge

Dorothy Gomez, Bunker Hill Community College

Frank Hager, Allegany College of Maryland

John Haworth, Florida Community College at Jacksonville

John S. Klein, Castleton State College

Patricia Lanzon, Henry Ford Community College

Denis Laplante, Lambton College

Laura Madson, New Mexico State University

Errol Magidson, Richard J. Daley College

Horace Marchant, Westfield State College

Richard Mascolo, El Camino Community College

Shawn Mikulay, Elgin Community College

Pike Nelson, Chicago State University

Alysia Ritter, Murray State University

Moises Salinas, Central Connecticut State University

Matthew Westra, Longview Community College

I especially wish to thank the following professors, whose sage advice helped improve the Second Edition of *Psychology: A Journey.*

Dana Albright, Clovis Community College

Saundra Ciccarelli, Gulf Coast Community College

Ellen Cotter, Georgia Southwestern State University

Keith Davis, University of South Carolina

Mary Ellen Dello Stritto, Ball State University

Mylo Egipciaco, Los Angeles Pierce College

Richard Epro, Nassau County Community College

Sabra Jacobs, Prestonsburg Community College

Thuy Karafa, Ferris State University

Jimi Leopold, Tarleton State University

Feleccia Moore-Davis, Houston Community College

Todd Nelson, California State University, Stanislaus

Randall Osborne, Southwest Texas State University

Sandra Phipps, Hazard Community College

Robert Wellman, Fitchburg State College

Matthew Zagumny, Tennessee Tech University

Producing *Psychology: A Journey* and its supplements was a formidable task. I am especially indebted to each of the following individuals, for supporting this book: Susan Badger, Sean Wakely, and Eve Howard.

I also wish to thank the individuals at Wadsworth who so generously shared their knowledge and talents over the past year. These are the people who made it happen: Vernon Boes, Chris Caldeira, Brian Chaffee, Jerilyn Emori, Jeremy Judson, Jennifer Keever, Margaret Parks, Joohee Lee, and Laura Stowe. It has been a pleasure to work with such a gifted group of professionals and many others at Wadsworth.

I would like to express my gratitude to Marianne Taflinger for plotting a new course for *Journey*. Your editorial guidance will make life easier for professors and students who use this book. Special thanks also to Jeremy Judson for helping to bring the itinerary into sharper focus.

Last of all, I would like to thank my wife Sevren for making the journey worthwhile.

Psychology

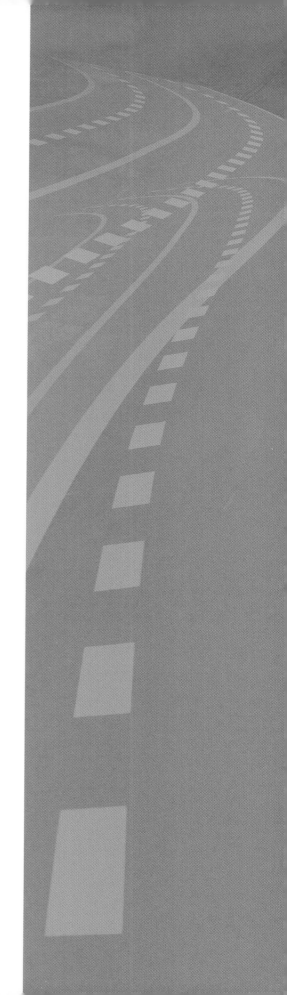

The Psychology of Studying

Even if you're an excellent student, you may be able to improve your study skills. Students who get good grades tend to work *smarter,* not just longer or harder (Hill, 1990). To help you get a good start, let's look at several ways to improve studying.

THE SQ4R METHOD—HOW TO TAME A TEXTBOOK

How much do you typically remember after you've read a textbook chapter? If the answer is "Nada," "Zip minus 1," or simply "Not enough," it may be time to try the **SQ4R method.** SQ4R stands for *survey, question, read, recite, relate,* and *review.* These six steps can help you grasp ideas quickly, learn as you read, remember more, and review effectively:

S = *Survey.* Skim through a chapter before you begin reading it. Start by looking at topic headings, figure captions, and the chapter summary. Try to get an overall picture of what lies ahead.

Q = *Question.* As you read, turn each topic heading into one or more questions. For example, when you read the heading "Stages of Sleep," you might ask: "Is there more than one stage of sleep?" "What are the stages of sleep?" "How do they differ?" Asking questions helps you read with a purpose.

R1 = *Read.* The first R in SQ4R stands for *read.* As you read, look for answers to the questions you asked. Read in short "bites," from one topic heading to the next, then stop. For difficult material, you may want to read only a paragraph or two at a time.

R2 = *Recite.* After reading a small amount, you should pause and recite or rehearse. That is, try to mentally answer your questions and summarize what you read. Or better yet, summarize by making brief notes (Lahtinen, Lonka, & Lindbloom-Ylaenne, 1997).

If you can't summarize the main ideas, skim over each section again. Until you can remember what you just read, there's little point to reading more.

After you've studied a short "bite" of text, turn the next topic heading into questions. Then read to the following heading. Remember to look for answers as you read and to recite or take notes before moving on. Ask yourself repeatedly, "What is the main idea here?" Repeat the question-read-recite cycle until you've finished an entire chapter.

R3 = *Relate.* You've probably noticed that it is easier to remember ideas that are personally meaningful. When you study a chapter, try to link new facts, terms, and concepts to your own experiences or to information you already know well. This may be the most important step in the SQ4R method. The more genuine interest you can bring to your reading, the more you will learn (Hartlep & Forsyth, 2000).

R4 = *Review.* When you're done reading, skim back over the chapter or read your notes. Then check your memory by reciting and quizzing yourself again. Try to make frequent, active review a standard part of your study habits (see ◆Fig. I.1).

Effective studying is planned and systematic. The number of hours you spend studying is less important than the quality and efficiency of your learning strategies (Woehr & Cavell, 1993).

SQ4R method An active study-reading technique based on these steps: survey, question, read, recite, relate, and review.

*✦FIGURE I.1 The SQ4R method pro-
motes active learning and information
processing. You should begin with a survey
of the chapter; proceed through cycles of
questioning, reading, reciting, and relating;
and conclude with a review of the chapter.*

Does this really work?   Yes. Using a reading strategy improves learning and course grades (Chastain & Thurber, 1989; Taraban, Rynearson, & Kerr, 2000). Simply reading straight through a chapter can give you "intellectual indigestion." That's why it's better to stop often to think, question, recite, relate, review, and thoroughly "digest" information as you read.

How to Use *Psychology: A Journey*

You can apply the SQ4R method to any text. However, this book is specifically designed to help you actively learn psychology.

Survey

Each chapter opens with a preview called *Journey into Psychology* and a list of *Survey Questions.* You can use these features to identify important ideas as you begin reading. The previews should help you get interested in the topics you will be reading about, and Survey Questions are a good guide to the kinds of information you should look for as you read. After you've studied these features, take a few minutes to do your own survey of the chapter. Doing so will help you build a "mental map" of upcoming topics.

Question

How can I use the SQ4R method to make reading more interesting and effective?   One of the key steps is to ask yourself lots of questions while you read. The Survey Questions are repeated throughout each chapter to help you recognize key topics. In addition, questions like the one that began this paragraph appear throughout each chapter. They will help you focus on seeking information as you read. However, be sure to ask your own questions, too. Try to actively interact with your textbooks as you read.

Read

As an aid to reading, important terms are printed in **boldface type** and defined where they first appear. (Some are followed by pronunciations—capital letters show which syllables are accented.) You'll also find a *margin glossary* beside the text you are reading, so you never have to guess about the meaning of technical terms. If you need to look up a term from lecture or another chapter, check the main *Glossary.* This "mini-dictionary" is located near the end of the book. Perhaps you should take a moment to find it now.

Recite and Relate

Every few pages, a learning guide called a *Study Break* provides chances to think, rehearse, relate, and test your memory. (Don't forget to also take notes or recite on your own.) If you want to study chapters in smaller "bites," Study Breaks make good stopping points. Near the end of each chapter, you'll find a section called *Psychology in Action.* These discussions are filled with practical ideas you can put to use in your own life.

Review

Each chapter of this book concludes with a final summary, called *Chapter in Review,* that will help you identify key ideas to remember. Each Chapter in Review begins with a list of *Major Points* that make up the most important concepts or "big ideas" of the chapter. Then, a point-by-point *Summary* reviews the chapter in greater detail. These summaries are organized around the same Survey Questions you read at the beginning of the chapter. You can also return to the glossary items throughout each chapter for further review.

On the last page of every chapter you will find a brief quiz called *Test Your Knowledge.* You can use this quiz to get a preliminary idea about how well you remember ideas and concepts from your reading. But don't stop studying just because you do well on one of these quizzes. Additional review and practice will add greatly to your understanding—not to mention your test scores.

△ Table I.1 summarizes how this text helps you apply the SQ4R method. Even with all this help, there is still much more you can do on your own.

▲*TABLE I.1*	Using the SQ4R Method

SURVEY
Preview
Survey Questions
Figure captions
Chapter in Review

QUESTION
Topic headings
Survey Questions
In-text dialogue questions

READ
Topic headings
Boldface terms
Margin glossary
Figures and tables

RECITE
Learning Check Questions (in Study Breaks)
Practice Quizzes (online)
Notes (make them while reading)

RELATE
Relate Questions (in Study Breaks)
Critical Thinking Questions (in Study Breaks)

REVIEW
Chapter in Review
Boldface terms
Margin glossary
Tables
Test Your Knowledge
Practice Quizzes (online)
Study Guide

EFFECTIVE NOTE TAKING— GOOD STUDENTS, TAKE NOTE!

Reading strategies may be good for studying, but what about taking notes in class? Sometimes it's hard to know what's important.   Like effective reading, good notes come from actively seeking information. People who are **active listeners** avoid distractions and skillfully gather ideas from lectures. Here's a listening/note-taking plan that works for many students. The letters LISAN, pronounced like the word *listen,* will help you remember the steps.

L = *Lead. Don't follow.* Try to anticipate what your teacher will say by asking yourself questions. Questions can come from study guides, reading assignments, or your own curiosity.

I = *Ideas.* Every lecture is based on a core of ideas. Usually, an idea is followed by examples or explanations. Ask yourself often, "What is the main idea now? What ideas support it?"

S = *Signal words.* Listen for words that tell you what direction the instructor is taking. For instance, here are some signal words:

There are three reasons why . . .   Here come ideas
Most important is . . .   Main idea
On the contrary . . .   Opposite idea
As an example . . .   Support for main idea
Therefore . . .   Conclusion

A = *Actively listen.* Sit where you can get involved and ask questions. Bring questions you want answered from the previous lecture or from your text. Raise your hand at the beginning of class or approach your professor before the lecture. Do anything that helps you stay active, alert, and engaged.

N = *Note taking.* Students who take accurate lecture notes tend to do well on tests (Williams & Eggert, 2002). However, don't try to be a tape recorder. Listen to everything, but be selective and write down only key points. If you are too busy writing, you may not grasp what your professor is saying. When you're taking notes, it might help to think of yourself as a reporter who is trying to get a good story (Ryan, 2001).

Actually, most students take reasonably good notes—and then don't use them! Most students wait until just before exams to review their notes. By then, their notes have lost much of their meaning. If you don't want your notes to seem like hieroglyphics or "chicken scratches," it pays to review them every day (Luckie & Smethurst, 1998).

Using and Reviewing Your Notes

When you review, you will learn more if you take the extra steps listed here (Kiewra et al., 1991; King, 1992, 1995; Luckie & Smethurst, 1998).

- As soon as you can, improve your notes by filling in gaps, completing thoughts, and looking for connections among ideas.
- Remember to link new ideas to what you already know.
- Summarize your notes. Boil them down and *organize* them.
- After each class session, write down at least seven major ideas, definitions, or details that are likely to become test questions. Then, make up questions from your notes and be sure you can answer them.

 Active listener A person who knows how to maintain attention, avoid distractions, and actively gather information from lectures.

Summary

The letters LISAN are a guide to active listening, but listening and good note taking are not enough. You must also review, organize, relate, extend, and think about new ideas. Also, remember that teachers almost always know the names of the best listeners in their classes. Get involved and you will undoubtedly learn more (Luckie & Smethurst, 1998).

STUDY STRATEGIES—MAKING A HABIT OF SUCCESS

Grades depend nearly as much on effort as they do on "intelligence." However, don't forget that good students work more *efficiently,* not just harder. Many study practices are notoriously poor, such as recopying lecture notes, studying class notes but not the textbook (or the textbook but not class notes), outlining chapters, answering study questions with the book open, and "group study" (which often becomes a party). The best students emphasize *quality:* They study their books and notes in depth and attend classes regularly. It's a mistake to blame poor grades on events "beyond your control." Students who are motivated to succeed usually get better grades (Perry et al., 2001). Let's consider a few more things you can do to improve your study habits.

Study in a Specific Place

Ideally, you should study in a quiet, well-lighted area free of distractions. If possible, you should also have at least one place where you *only study.* Do nothing else at that spot: Keep magazines, CD players, friends, pets, posters, video games, puzzles, food, lovers, sports cars, elephants, pianos, televisions, hang gliders, kazoos, and other distractions out of the area. In this way, the habit of studying will become strongly linked with one specific place. Then, rather than trying to force yourself to study, all you have to do is go to your study area. Once there, you'll find it is relatively easy to get started.

Use Spaced Study Sessions

It is reasonable to review intensely before an exam. However, you're taking a big risk if you are only "cramming" (learning new information at the last minute). Spaced practice is much more efficient (Naveh-Benjamin, 1990). **Spaced practice** consists of a large number of relatively short study sessions. Long, uninterrupted study sessions are called **massed practice.** (If you "massed up" your studying, you probably messed it up, too.)

Cramming places a big burden on memory. Usually, you shouldn't try to learn anything new about a subject the day before a test. It is far better to learn small amounts every day and review frequently (Luckie & Smethurst, 1998).

Try Mnemonics

Mnemonics make new information more familiar and memorable. Forming an image of a duck wearing a pot for a hat might help you remember that *pato* is the Spanish word for "duck."

Learning has to start somewhere, and memorizing is often the first step. Many of the best ways to improve memory are covered in Chapter 7. Let's consider just one technique here.

A **mnemonic** (pronounced nee-MON-ik) is a memory aid. Most mnemonics link new information to ideas or images that are easy to remember. For example, what if you want to remember that the Spanish word for "duck" is *pato* (pronounced POT-oh)? To use a mnemonic, you could picture a duck in a pot or a duck wearing a pot for a hat. Likewise, to remember that the cerebellum controls coordination, you might picture someone named "Sarah Bellum" who is very coordinated. For best results, make your mnemonic images exaggerated or bizarre, vivid, and interactive (Campos & Perez, 1997). There are many ways to create mnemonics. If you would like to learn more about memory strategies, see Chapter 7.

Test Yourself

A great way to improve grades is to take several practice tests before the real one in class. In other words, studying should include **self-testing** in which you pose questions to yourself. You can use flash cards, "Learning Check" questions, "Test Your Knowledge" questions, a

Spaced practice Practice spread over many relatively short study sessions.
Massed practice Practice done in a long, uninterrupted study session.
Mnemonic A memory aid or strategy.
Self-testing Evaluating learning by posing questions to yourself.

study guide, or other means. As you study, ask many questions and be sure you can answer them. Studying without self-testing is like practicing for a basketball game without shooting any baskets.

To make self-testing more convenient, your professor may make a *Study Guide* or a separate booklet of *Practice Quizzes* available. You can use either to review for tests. Practice quizzes are also available on the Internet, as described later. However, don't use practice quizzes as a substitute for studying your textbook and lecture notes. Trying to learn course material from practice quizzes alone will probably *lower* your grades. It is best to use quizzes to identify gaps in your knowledge. Then, you can restudy any topics that need more attention (Brothen & Wambach, 2001).

Overlearn

Many students *underprepare* for exams, and most *overestimate* how well they will do. A solution to both problems is **overlearning,** in which you continue studying beyond your initial mastery of a topic. In other words, plan to do extra study and review after you think you are prepared for a test.

Here's another reason for overlearning: Students who expect to take an essay test (usually the hardest kind) do better on essay, multiple-choice, and short-answer tests (Foos & Clark, 1984). Before tests, students ask, "Will it be essay or multiple choice?" But as you can see, *it is best to approach all tests as if they will be essays.* That way, you will learn more completely, so you really "know your stuff."

SELF-REGULATED LEARNING— ACADEMIC ALL-STARS

Think of a topic you are highly interested in, such as music, sports, fashion, automobiles, cooking, politics, or movies. Whatever the topic, you have probably learned a large amount of information about it—painlessly. How could you make your college work more like voluntary learning? An approach known as self-regulated learning might be a good start. **Self-regulated learning** is active, self-guided study. In addition to the specific strategies already described, you can use self-regulated learning to change passive studying into more active, goal-oriented learning (Zimmerman, 1996). Follow these steps to get the most from your self-guided study:

1. *Set specific, objective learning goals.* Try to begin each learning session with specific goals in mind. What knowledge or skills are you trying to master? What do you hope to accomplish? (Schunk, 1990).
2. *Plan a learning strategy.* How will you accomplish your goals? Make daily, weekly, and monthly plans for learning. Then put them into action.
3. *Be your own teacher.* Effective learners silently give themselves guidance and ask themselves questions. For example, as you are learning, you might ask yourself, "What are the important ideas here? What do I remember? What don't I understand? What do I need to review? What should I do next?"
4. *Monitor your progress.* Self-regulated learning depends on self-monitoring. Exceptional learners keep records of their progress toward learning goals (pages read, hours spent studying, assignments completed, and so forth). They quiz themselves, use study guides, and find other ways to check their understanding while learning.
5. *Reward yourself.* When you meet your daily, weekly, or monthly goals, reward your efforts in some way, such as going to a movie or buying a new CD. Be aware that self-praise also rewards learning. Being able to say "Hey, I did it!" or "Good work!" and know that you deserve it can be very rewarding. In the long run, success, feelings of accomplishment, and personal satisfaction provide the real payoffs for learning.
6. *Evaluate your progress and goals.* It is a good idea to frequently evaluate your performance records and goals. Are there specific areas of your work that need im-

Overlearning Continuing to study and learn after you first think you've mastered a topic.

Self-regulated learning Active, self-guided learning.

provement? If you are not making good progress toward your long-range goals, do you need to revise your short-term targets?

7. *Take corrective action.* If you fall short of your goals you may need to adjust how you budget your time. You may also need to change your learning environment to deal with distractions such as watching TV, daydreaming, talking to friends, or testing the structural integrity of the walls with your stereo system.

If you discover that you lack necessary knowledge or skills, ask for help, take advantage of tutoring programs, or look for sources of information beyond your courses and textbooks. Knowing how to regulate and control learning can be a key to lifelong enrichment and personal empowerment.

PROCRASTINATION—AVOIDING THE LAST-MINUTE BLUES

All these study techniques are fine. But what can I do about procrastination?   A tendency to procrastinate is almost universal. (When campus workshops on procrastination are offered, many students never get around to signing up!) Even when procrastination doesn't lead to failure, it can cause much suffering. Procrastinators work only under pressure, skip classes, give false reasons for late work, and feel ashamed of their last-minute efforts (Burka & Yuen, 1990). They also tend to feel stressed and are ill more often (Tice & Baumeister, 1997).

Why do so many students procrastinate?   Many students equate grades with their *personal worth.* That is, they act as if their grades tell whether they are good, smart people who will succeed in life. By procrastinating they can blame poor work on a late start, rather than a lack of ability (Beck, Koons, & Milgrim, 2000). After all, it wasn't their best effort, was it?

Perfectionism is a related problem. If you expect the impossible, it's hard to start an assignment. Students with high standards often end up with all-or-nothing work habits (Onwuegbuzie, 2000).

Time Management

Most procrastinators must eventually face the self-worth issue. Nevertheless, most can improve by learning study skills and better time management. We have already discussed general study skills, so let's consider time management in a little more detail.

A **weekly time schedule** is a written plan that allocates time for study, work, and leisure activities. To prepare your schedule, make a chart showing all the hours in each day of the week. Then fill in times that are already committed: sleep, meals, classes, work, team practices, lessons, appointments, and so forth. Next, fill in times when you will study for various classes. Finally, label the remaining hours as open or free times.

Each day, you can use your schedule as a checklist. That way you'll know at a glance which tasks are done and which still need attention (Luckie & Smethurst, 1998).

You may also find it valuable to make a **term schedule** that lists the dates of all quizzes, tests, reports, papers, and other major assignments for each class.

The beauty of sticking to a schedule is that you know you are making an honest effort. It will also help you avoid feeling bored while you are working or guilty when you play.

Be sure to treat your study times as serious commitments, but respect your free times, too. And remember, students who study hard and practice good time management *do* get better grades (Britton & Tesser, 1991; Leeming, 1997).

Goal-Setting

As mentioned earlier, students who are active learners set **specific goals** for studying. Such goals should be clear-cut and measurable (Schunk, 1990). If you find it hard to stay motivated, try setting goals for the semester, the week, the day, and even for single study sessions.

Weekly time schedule A written plan that allocates time for study, work, and leisure activities during a one-week period.

Term schedule A written plan that lists the dates of all major assignments for each of your classes for an entire semester or quarter.

Specific goal A goal with a clearly defined and measurable outcome.

Also, be aware that more effort early in a course can greatly reduce the "pain" and stress you will experience later (Brown, 1991). If your professors don't give frequent assignments, set your own day-by-day goals. That way, you can turn big assignments into a series of smaller tasks that you can actually complete (Ariely & Wertenbroch, 2002). An example would be reading, studying, and reviewing 8 pages a day to complete a 40-page chapter in 5 days. Remember, many small steps can add up to an impressive journey.

Make Learning an Adventure

A final point to remember is that you are most likely to procrastinate if you think a task will be unpleasant (Pychyl et al., 2000). Learning can be hard work. Nevertheless, many students find ways to make schoolwork interesting and enjoyable. Try to approach your schoolwork as if it is a game, a sport, an adventure, or simply a way to become a better person. The best educational experiences are challenging, yet fun (Ferrari & Scher, 2000).

Virtually every topic is interesting to someone, somewhere. I'm not particularly interested in the sex life of South American tree frogs. However, a biologist might be fascinated. (Another tree frog might be, too.) If you wait for teachers to "make" their courses interesting, you are missing the point. Interest is a matter of *your attitude*. (See ✦Fig. I.2 for a summary of study skills.)

TAKING TESTS—ARE YOU "TEST WISE"?

If I read and study effectively, is there anything else I can do to improve my grades? You must also be able to show what you know on tests. Here are some suggestions for improving your test-taking skills.

General Test-Taking Skills

You'll do better on all types of tests if you observe the following guidelines (Wood & Willoughby, 1995):

1. Read all directions and questions carefully. They might give you good advice or clues.
2. Quickly survey the test before you begin.
3. Answer the easy questions before you spend time on the more difficult ones.
4. Be sure to answer all questions.
5. Use your time wisely.
6. Ask for clarification when necessary.

Several additional strategies can help you do better on objective tests.

Objective Tests

Objective tests (multiple-choice and true-false items) require you to recognize a correct answer among wrong ones or a true statement versus a false one. Here are some strategies for taking objective tests:

1. First, relate the question to what you know about the topic. Then, read the alternatives. Does one match the answer you expected to find? If none match, reexamine the choices and look for a *partial* match.
2. Read *all* the choices for each question before you make a decision. Here's why: If you immediately think that *a* is correct and stop reading, you might miss seeing a better answer such as "both *a* and *d*."
3. Read rapidly and skip items you are unsure about. You might find "free information" in later questions that will help you answer difficult items.
4. Eliminate certain alternatives. With a four-choice multiple-choice test, you have one chance in four of guessing right. If you can eliminate two alternatives, your guessing odds improve to 50-50.

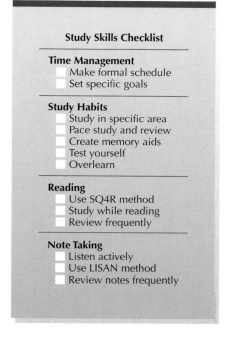

Study Skills Checklist

Time Management
☐ Make formal schedule
☐ Set specific goals

Study Habits
☐ Study in specific area
☐ Pace study and review
☐ Create memory aids
☐ Test yourself
☐ Overlearn

Reading
☐ Use SQ4R method
☐ Study while reading
☐ Review frequently

Note Taking
☐ Listen actively
☐ Use LISAN method
☐ Review notes frequently

✦**FIGURE I.2** *Study skills checklist.*

5. Unless there is a penalty for guessing, be sure to answer any questions you skipped earlier before finishing the exam. Even if you are not sure of the answer, you might be right. If you leave a question blank, it is automatically wrong. When you are forced to guess, don't choose the longest answer or the letter you've used the least. Both strategies lower scores more than random guessing does.

6. There is a bit of folk wisdom that says "Don't change your answers on a multiple-choice test. Your first choice is usually right." Careful study of this idea has shown it is *false*. If you change answers, you are three times more likely to gain points than to lose them (Geiger, 1991). This is especially true if you feel *very* uncertain of your first answer. ("When in doubt, scratch it out!") When you have doubts, your second answer is more likely to be correct (Harvil & Davis, 1997).

7. Remember, you are searching for the one *best* answer to each question. Some answers may be partly true yet flawed in some way. If you are uncertain, try rating each multiple-choice alternative on a 1-to-10 scale, with 1 being the answer you feel most uncertain about and 10 being the most certain. The answer with the highest rating is the one you are looking for.

8. Few circumstances are *always* or *never* present. Answers that include superlatives such as *most, least, best, worst, largest,* or *smallest* are often false (Luckie & Smethurst, 1998).

Essay Tests

Essay questions are a weak spot for students who lack organization, don't support their ideas, or don't directly answer the question. When you take an essay exam, try the following:

1. Read the question carefully. Be sure to note key words, such as *compare, contrast, discuss, evaluate, analyze,* and *describe.* These words all demand a certain emphasis in your answer.

2. Think about your answer for a few minutes and list the main points you want to make. Just write them as they come to mind. Then rearrange the ideas in a logical order and begin writing. Elaborate plans or outlines are not necessary (Torrance, Thomas, & Robinson, 1991).

3. Don't beat around the bush or pad your answer. Be direct. Make a point and support it. Get your list of ideas into words.

4. Look over your essay for errors in spelling and grammar. Save this for last. Your *ideas* are of first importance. You can work on spelling and grammar separately if they affect your grades.

Short-Answer Tests

Tests that ask you to fill in a blank, define a term, or list specific items can be difficult. Usually, the questions themselves contain little information. If you don't know the answer, you won't get much help from the questions.

The best way to prepare for short-answer tests is to overlearn the details of the course. As you study, pay special attention to lists of related terms.

Again, it is best to start with the questions you're sure you know. Follow that by completing items you think you probably know. Questions you have no idea about can be left blank (Luckie & Smethurst, 1998).

Again, for your convenience, Figure I.2 provides a checklist summary of the main study skills we have covered.

USING ELECTRONIC MEDIA— NETTING NEW KNOWLEDGE

The Internet and electronic media are providing exciting new ways to explore topics ranging from affection to zoophobia. Let's see how you can use these technologies to learn more about psychology.

Electronic Journeys

The **Internet** is a network of computers that communicate through the phone system and other electronic links. An important subpart of the Internet is the **World Wide Web,** an interlinked system of information "sites" or "pages." A Web site is a collection of information stored on a computer. Through the Internet, you can retrieve Web pages from other computers and display them on your own screen. Thus, if you know the electronic "address" of a Web site, you can view the information it contains.

Many Web pages also have links to other Web sites. These **links** let you "jump" from one site to the next to find more information. In seconds you can connect with university computers, search engines that scan the Internet for specific topics, electronic journals, and even virtual libraries, where all the books are available in electronic form.

Using the Net

To find psychological information on the Internet you'll need a computer and a modem. If you don't own a computer, you can usually use one on campus to access the Internet. Various software browsers make it easier to navigate around the Internet and receive information over the telephone connection. A **browser** enables you to see text, images, sounds, video, and other information stored in formats used on the Internet. Browsers also keep lists of your favorite Internet addresses so you can return to them later.

The Psychology Resource Center

Once I have access to the Internet, how would I find information about psychology? Your first stop on the Internet should be the Psychology Resource Center. This specialized site is designed to support students who are using Wadsworth textbooks to learn psychology. Here's what you'll find there:

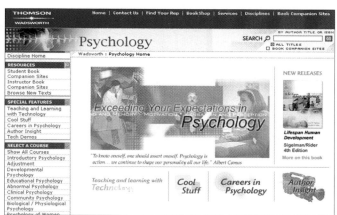

Online Quizzes. You can use these chapter-by-chapter multiple-choice quizzes to practice for tests and check your understanding of the material.

Interactive Activities. The demonstrations and mini-experiments in this feature enable you to directly experience various psychological principles.

Internet Resources. This area is a "launching pad" that will take you to other psychology-related sites on the Internet. If a site sounds interesting, a click of the mouse will link you to it.

Online Flash Cards. These online flash cards enable you to practice terms and concepts interactively.

Hot Topics. This section features a news item or current event that is explored from a psychological perspective. After you've thought about a topic, you can share your opinions with others in an online discussion.

Discussion Forum. In the Discussion Forum, you'll have a chance to share your ideas with psychology students from all over the country.

Research and Teaching Showcase. Here you'll find regularly updated summaries of presentations, articles, or other teaching and research materials.

Archives. Using the Archives, you can quickly search for current and past articles from Hot Topics and the Research and Teaching Showcase.

Meet the Author. Here you can meet the author of your text in an interactive, multimedia presentation.

The Psychology Resource Center is located at **http://www.psychology.wadsworth.com.** Be sure to visit this site for valuable information about how to improve your grades and enhance your appreciation of psychology. You can follow the "Find Companion Sites" link to locate quizzes and other materials related to this text.

Wadsworth's Psychology Resource Center gives you online access to a variety of valuable learning aids and interesting materials.

Internet An electronic network that enables computers to communicate with one another, usually through the telephone system.

World Wide Web A system of information "sites" accessible through the Internet.

Links Connections built into Internet sites that let you "jump" from one site to the next.

Browser Software that facilitates access to text, images, sounds, video, and other information stored in formats used on the Internet.

Psych Sites

At the end of each chapter in this book, you'll find a list of interesting Internet sites you might want to explore. The best way to reach these sites is through the Psychology Resource Center. I have not included Web site addresses here because they often change or may become inactive. At the Psychology Resource Center you'll find up-to-date links for Web sites listed in this book. The sites I've listed are generally of high quality. However, be aware that information on the Internet is not always accurate. It is wise to approach all Web sites with a healthy dose of skepticism.

InfoTrac College Edition

InfoTrac College Edition is an online university library of articles from more than 700 publications. These articles cover a multitude of topics in psychology. You can read them online or print complete articles right from InfoTrac College Edition. InfoTrac College Edition is a great source for writing reports, doing research, or just reading more about psychology.

InfoTrac College Edition is located at **http://www.infotrac-college.com/wadsworth.** You will need a password to use this service. If InfoTrac was included with this textbook, you already have a password. Otherwise, you can buy a subscription at the campus bookstore.

PsycINFO

Psychological knowledge can also be found in specialized online databases. One of the best is **PsycINFO,** offered by the American Psychological Association (APA), provides summaries of the scientific and scholarly literature in psychology. Each record in PsycINFO consists of an abstract (short summary), plus notes about the author, title, source, and other details (◆Fig. I.3). All entries are indexed using key terms, so you can search for various topics by entering words such as *drug abuse, postpartum depression,* or *creativity.*

You can gain access to PsycINFO in several ways. Many colleges and universities subscribe to PsycINFO or to a related CD-ROM version called *PsycLIT*. If this is the case at your school, you can usually search PsycINFO from a terminal in the college library or computer center—for free. PsycINFO can also be accessed through the Internet, either directly or through the APA's PsycDIRECT service. For more information on how to gain access to PsycINFO, check this Web site: **http://www.apa.org/psycinfo.**

TITLE   Combat exposure and adult psychosocial adjustment among U.S. Army veterans serving in Vietnam, 1965-1971.

ABSTRACT   (from the journal abstract) This study investigated the relationship between combat exposure and adult antisocial behavior in a sample of 2,490 male Army veterans of the Vietnam War who completed questionnaires about their psychological functioning. After adjustment for history of childhood behavior problems, posttraumatic stress disorder diagnosis, and demographic and military characteristics, it was found that veterans who experienced high and very high levels of combat were twice as likely to report adult antisocial behavior as veterans with no or low levels of combat and were also more likely to meet criteria for antisocial personality disorder. The results indicate that exposure to traumatic events during late adolescence or early adulthood is associated with multiple adult adjustment problems in vocational, interpersonal, and societal functioning. Treatment focusing on the effects of the trauma is likely to be necessary but not sufficient for improving affected veterans' behavior. (PsycINFO Database Record (c) 2002 APA, all rights reserved)

AUTHOR   Barrett, Drue H.; Resnick, Heidi S.; Foy, David W.; Dansky, Bonnie S.; Flanders, W. Dana; Stroup, Nancy E.

AFFILIATION   Barrett, D. H.: Ctrs for Disease Control & Prevention, National Ctr for Environmental Health, Atlanta, GA, US

SOURCE   Journal of Abnormal Psychology. 1996 Nov Vol 105(4) 575-581

◆**FIGURE I.3** *This is a sample abstract from the PsycINFO database. If you search for the term* antisocial behavior, *you will find this article and many more in PsychINFO. (From Abstract on Combat Exposure,* Journal of Abnormal Psychology, *November 1996, 575–581. Copyright © 1996 APA. Reprinted by permission of the publisher.)*

PsycINFO A searchable online database that provides brief summaries of the scientific and scholarly literature in psychology.

The APA Web Site

The APA maintains an online library of general interest articles on aging, anger, children and families, depression, divorce, emotional health, kids and the media, sexuality, stress, testing issues, women and men, and other topics. These articles are available to the public for free. They are well worth consulting when you have questions about psychological issues. You'll find them at **http://www.apa.org.** For links to recent articles in newspapers and magazines, be sure to check the APA's PsycPORT page at **http://www.psycport.com.**

Please do take some of the "electronic journeys" described here. You might be surprised by the fascinating information that awaits you. Investigating psychology on your own is one of the best ways to enrich an already valuable course.

Multimedia CD-ROMs

Multimedia CD-ROMs are an exciting recent development in education. A single CD can store reams of text and thousands of pieces of art. All the information contained in traditional print textbooks can easily fit on a CD for display on a computer screen. In addition, CDs are capable of presenting animations, audio clips, film clips, and interactive exercises. A CD you may be interested in trying is *PsychNow!*, offered by Wadsworth to complement this textbook.

PsychNow!

Using this dynamic multimedia CD enables you to actively explore the world of psychology. Full audio and video presentations will help you discover interesting principles—often by observing your own behavior (◆Fig. I.4). *PsychNow!* includes many interactive demonstrations, experiments, games, and activities, all designed to expand your understanding. Rather than just reading about concepts, *PsychNow!* makes it possible to experience them directly. With the click of a mouse you can call up a large variety of helpful materials that make learning psychology more exciting than ever.

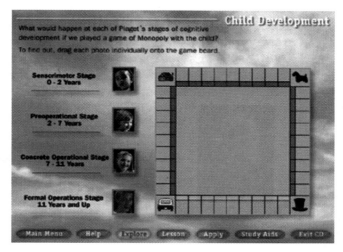

◆FIGURE I.4 *A sample screen from* PsychNow!

Using Multimedia CD-ROMs

PsychNow! and similar CD-ROMs can be used alone or in conjunction with a textbook. At the end of each chapter in this book you'll find a list of *PsychNow!* modules. Using these materials will enable you to see psychology come to life in ways that are not possible in a printed text. If you would like to be part of the electronic revolution in psychology, give *PsychNow!* a try.

A Final Word

In Zen, there is a distinction between "live words" and "dead words." Live words come from personal experience; dead words are "about" a subject. This book can only be a collection of dead words unless you accept the challenge of making an intellectual journey. You will find many helpful, useful, and exciting ideas in the pages that follow. To make them yours, you must set out to *actively* learn as much as you can. The ideas presented here should get you off to a good start. Good luck!

For more information, consult any of the following books:

Burka, J. B. & Yuen, L. M. (1990). *Procrastination: Why You Do It; What to Do About It*. Cambridge, MA: Perseus Books.

Campanelli, J. F. & Price, J. L. (1991). *Write in Time: Essay Exam Strategies*. Ft. Worth, TX: Holt, Rinehart & Winston.

Hettich, P. I. (1998). *Learning Skills for College and Career.* Belmont, CA: Wadsworth.

Luckie, W. & Smethurst, W. (1998). *Study Power.* Cambridge, MA: Brookline.

Rosnow, R. L. & M. Rosnow. (2002). *Writing Papers in Psychology: A Student Guide.* Belmont, CA: Wadsworth.

Rowe, B. (1998). *College Survival Guide: Hints and References to Aid College Students.* Belmont, CA: Wadsworth.

STUDYBREAK Y *Study Skills*

RELATE

Which study skills do you think would help you the most? Which techniques do you already use? Which do you think you should try? How else could you improve your performance as a student?

LEARNING CHECK

1. The four R's in SQ4R stand for *read, recite, relate,* and *review.* T or F?

2. When using the LISAN method, students try to write down as much of a lecture as possible so that their notes are complete. T or F?

3. Spaced study sessions are usually superior to massed practice. T or F?

4. According to recent research, you should almost always stick with your first answer on multiple-choice tests. T or F?

5. To use the technique known as overlearning, you should continue to study after you feel you have begun to master a topic. T or F?

6. Setting learning goals and monitoring your progress are important parts of _____ learning.

7. Procrastination is related to seeking perfection and equating self-worth with grades. T or F?

8. An Internet browser is typically used to search CD-ROM databases for articles on various topics. T or F?

Critical Thinking

9. How are the SQ4R method and the LISAN method related?

ANSWERS

1. T 2. F 3. T 4. F 5. T 6. self-regulated 7. T 8. F 9. Both encourage students to actively seek information as a way of learning more effectively.

Interactive Learning

Internet addresses frequently change. To find the sites listed here, visit **http://www.psychology. wadsworth.com/coon_journey2e** *for an updated list of Internet addresses and direct links to relevant sites.*

PSYCHOLOGY: A JOURNEY COMPANION WEB SITE On-line quizzes, flash cards, and other helpful study aids for this text.

http://www.psychology.wadsworth.com/coon_journey2e

HOW TO SUCCEED AS A STUDENT Advice on how to be a college student. Topics from studying to housing to preparation for work are included.

LIBRARY RESEARCH IN PSYCHOLOGY Hints on how to do library research in psychology.

PSYCHOLOGY GLOSSARY You can use this glossary to get additional definitions for common psychological terms.

STUDY SKILLS More information on SQ4R, taking tests, note taking, and time management.

INFOTRAC COLLEGE EDITION For recent articles on studying, use the Subject Guide and search for STUDY SKILLS.

PSYCHNOW! 1a. Study skills.

Introducing Psychology and Research Methods

The Mysteries of Human Behavior

When I first meet someone, they often ask, "Why did you become a psychologist?" Because you and I are just getting acquainted, let me answer this way:

You are a universe, a collection of worlds within worlds. Your brain is possibly the most complicated system in existence. Through its action you are capable of art, music, science, philosophy, love, hatred, and charity. You are the most challenging riddle ever written, a mystery even to yourself at times. Your thoughts, emotions, and actions—and those of your family and friends—are the most fascinating subject I can imagine. I chose to study psychology because everything of interest and importance in the world is ultimately related to human behavior.

Look around you: Newspapers, radio, magazines, television, and the Internet are brimming with psychological topics. Psychology is an ever-changing panorama of people and ideas. You really can't call yourself educated without knowing something about it. And although we might envy those who have walked on the moon or explored the ocean's depths, the ultimate frontier still lies close to home. What could be more fascinating than a journey of self-discovery?

As you read this book, think of it as a travel guide. Ultimately, each person's path through life is unique. Nonetheless, psychology can show you much about human behavior and help you better understand yourself and others. Your guide awaits you. I hope you enjoy the journey.

PSYCHOLOGY—SPOTLIGHT ON BEHAVIOR

] SURVEYQUESTION *What is psychology? What are its goals?*

Psychology touches our lives in many ways. Psychology is about memory, stress, therapy, love, persuasion, hypnosis, perception, death, conformity, creativity, learning, personality, aging, intelligence, sexuality, emotion, happiness, and much more.

Psychology is both a *science* and a *profession*. As scientists, some psychologists do research to discover new knowledge. Others are teachers who pass this knowledge on to students. Still others apply psychology to solve problems in mental health, education, business, sports, law, and medicine. Later we will return to the profession of psychology. For now, let's focus on how knowledge is created. Whether they work in a lab, classroom, or clinic, all psychologists rely on information from scientific research.

Psychologists are highly trained professionals who have specialized skills in counseling and therapy, measurement and testing, research and experimentation, statistics, diagnosis, treatment, and many other areas.

Defining Psychology

The word *psychology* comes from the roots *psyche*, which means "mind," and *logos*, which means "knowledge" or "study." However, when did you last see or touch a "mind"? Because the mind can't be studied directly, **psychology** is now defined as the scientific study of behavior and mental processes.

What does behavior refer to in the definition of psychology? Anything you do—eating, sleeping, talking, or sneezing—is a behavior. So are dreaming, gambling, watching television, learning Spanish, basket weaving, and reading this book. Naturally, we are interested

Psychology The scientific study of behavior and mental processes.

in *overt behaviors* (observable actions and responses). But psychologists also study *covert behaviors.* These are private, internal activities, such as thinking, remembering, and other mental events (Kelly & Saklofske, 1994).

Empiricism

At various times in the last 100 years, experts have stated that "Heavier-than-air flying machines are impossible," "Radio has no future," "X-rays are a hoax," and "Computers will never serve any practical purpose." Obviously, all these ideas proved to be wrong.

Self-appointed "authorities" are also often wrong about human behavior. Because of this, psychologists have a special respect for *empirical evidence* (information gained from direct observation). We study behavior directly and collect data (observed facts) so we can draw valid conclusions. Would you say it's true, for instance, that "You can't teach an old dog new tricks"? Why argue about it? As a psychologist, I would simply get 10 "new" dogs, 10 "used" dogs, and 10 "old" dogs and then try to teach them all a new trick to find out!

Basically, the empirical approach says, "Let's take a look" (Stanovich, 2001). Have you ever wondered if drivers become more hostile when it's blazing hot outside? Douglas Kenrick and Steven MacFarlane (1986) decided to find out. They parked a car at a green light in a one-lane intersection in Phoenix, Arizona, in temperatures ranging from 88° to 116°F. Then they recorded the number of times other frazzled drivers (in cars without air-conditioning) honked at the stalled car as well as how long they honked. The results are shown in ✦Figure 1.1. Notice that when it was very hot, drivers spent more time leaning on the horn (which may be why cars have horns instead of cannons).

Isn't the outcome of this study fairly predictable? The results of many studies are surprising or unexpected. In this instance, you may have guessed how drivers would react. You would also be right to predict that riots and assaults increase when it's hot. However, hostile actions that require physical exertion, such as a fist fight, become *less* likely at very high temperatures. Without gathering data, we don't know if overheated drivers become more lethargic or more aggressive. Thus, the study tells us something interesting about frustration, discomfort, and aggression.

Psychological Research

Many fields, such as history, law, art, and business, are interested in human behavior. How is psychology different? Psychology's great strength is that it uses **scientific observation** to answer questions about behavior (Stanovich, 2001). For instance, some parents believe that the music of Mozart increases babies' intelligence. Is this true? Many popular magazines and books say yes. Scientific testing says no. (See "The Mozart Effect—Smart Music?" in Chapter 3 to learn why.)

Of course, some topics can't be studied because of ethical or practical concerns. More often, questions go unanswered for lack of a suitable **research method** (a systematic process for answering scientific questions). In the past, for example, we had to take the word of people who say they never dream. Then the EEG (electroencephalograph, or brain-wave machine) was invented. Certain EEG patterns along with the presence of eye movements can reveal that a person is dreaming. People who "never dream," it turns out, dream frequently. If they are awakened during a dream they vividly remember it. Thus, the EEG helped make the study of dreaming more scientific.

✦FIGURE 1.1 *Results of an empirical study. The graph shows that horn honking by frustrated motorists becomes more likely as air temperature increases. This suggests that physical discomfort is associated with interpersonal hostility. (Data from Kenrick & MacFarlane, 1986.)*

The scientific study of dreaming was made possible by use of the EEG, a device that records the tiny electrical signals generated by the brain as a person sleeps. The EEG converts these electrical signals to a written record of brain activity. Certain shifts in brain activity, coupled with the presence of rapid eye movements, are strongly related to dreaming. (See Chapter 5 for more information.)

Scientific observation An empirical investigation that is structured to answer questions about the world.

Research method A systematic approach to answering scientific questions.

Research Specialties

What kinds of topics do psychologists study? Here's a sample of what various psychologists might say about their work.

"In general, *developmental psychologists* study the course of human growth and development, from conception until death. I'm especially interested in how young children develop the ability to think, speak, perceive, and act."

"I'm also interested in how people get to be the way they are. Like other *learning theorists,* I study how and why learning occurs in humans and animals. Right now I'm investigating how patterns of reward affect learning."

"I'm a *personality theorist.* I study personality traits, motivation, and individual differences. I am especially interested in the personality profiles of highly creative college students."

"As a *sensation and perception psychologist,* I investigate how we discern the world through our senses. I am using a perceptual theory to study how we are able to recognize faces."

"*Comparative psychologists* study and compare the behavior of different species, especially animals. Personally, I'm fascinated by the communication abilities of porpoises."

"*Biopsychologists* are interested in how behavior relates to biological processes, especially activities in the nervous system. I've been doing some exciting research on how the brain controls hunger."

"*Cognitive psychologists* are primarily interested in thinking. I want to know how reasoning, problem solving, memory, and other mental processes relate to human behavior."

"*Gender psychologists* study differences between females and males. I want to understand how gender differences are influenced by biology, child-rearing, education, and stereotypes."

The variety and complexity of human behavior make psychological investigation challenging. How would you explain the behaviors shown here?

"*Social psychologists* explore human social behavior, such as attitudes, persuasion, riots, conformity, leadership, racism, and friendship. My own interest is interpersonal attraction. I place two strangers in a room and analyze how strongly they are attracted to each other."

"*Cultural psychologists* study the ways in which culture affects human behavior. The language you speak, the foods you eat, how your parents disciplined you, what laws you obey, who you regard as 'family,' whether you eat with a spoon or your fingers—these and countless other details of behavior are strongly influenced by culture."

"*Evolutionary psychologists* are interested in how our behavior is guided by patterns that evolved during the long history of humankind. I am studying some interesting trends in male and female mating choices that don't seem to be merely learned or based on culture."

This small sample should give you an idea of the diversity of psychological research. It also hints at some of the kinds of information we will explore in this book.

Animals and Psychology

Research involving animals was mentioned in some of the preceding examples. Why is that? You might be surprised to learn that psychologists are interested in the behavior of *any* living creature—from flatworms to humans. Indeed, some comparative psychologists spend their entire careers studying rats, cats, dogs, turtles, or chimpanzees.

Some psychologists use **animal models** to discover principles that apply to humans. For instance, animal studies have helped us understand stress, learning, obesity, aging, sleep,

Animal model In research, an animal whose behavior is used to discover principles that may apply to human behavior.

and many other topics. Psychology also benefits animals. For example, caring for endangered species in zoos relies on behavioral studies. Overall, about 8 percent of all psychological research is done with animals (McCarty, 1998).

Some of the most interesting research with animals has focused on attempts to teach primates to communicate with sign language. Such research has led to better methods for teaching language to aphasic children (children with serious language impairment). (See Chapter 8 for more information.)

Psychology's Goals

What do psychology's goals mean in practice? Imagine that we would like to answer questions such as these: What happens when the right side of the brain is injured? Is there more than one type of memory? Do autistic children react abnormally to their parents?

Description

Answering psychological questions requires a careful description of behavior. **Description,** or naming and classifying, is typically based on making a detailed record of behavioral observations.

But a description doesn't explain anything, does it? Right. Useful knowledge begins with accurate description, but descriptions fail to answer the important "why" questions. *Why* do more women attempt suicide, and *why* do more men complete it? *Why* are people more aggressive when they are uncomfortable? *Why* are bystanders often unwilling to help in an emergency?

Understanding

We have met psychology's second goal when we can explain an event. That is, **understanding** usually means we can state the causes of a behavior. Take our last "why" question as an example: Research on "bystander apathy" reveals that people often fail to help when *other* possible helpers are nearby. Why? Because a "diffusion of responsibility" occurs. Basically, no one feels personally obligated to pitch in. As a result, the more potential helpers there are, the less likely it is that anyone will help (Darley & Latané, 1968). Now we can explain a perplexing problem.

Prediction

Psychology's third goal, **prediction,** is the ability to forecast behavior accurately. Notice that our explanation of bystander apathy makes a prediction about the chances of getting help. If you've ever been stranded on a busy freeway with car trouble, you'll recognize the accuracy of this prediction: Having many potential helpers nearby is no guarantee that anyone will stop to help.

Some psychologists specialize in administering, scoring, and interpreting psychological tests, such as tests of intelligence, creativity, personality, or aptitude. This specialty, which is called psychometrics, is an example of using psychology to predict future behavior. For instance, psychological tests are frequently used to select people for jobs and admission to colleges.

Control

Description, explanation, and prediction seem reasonable, but is control a valid goal? Control might seem like a threat to personal freedom. However, to a psychologist, **control** simply refers to altering conditions that affect behavior. If I suggest changes in a classroom that help children learn better, I have exerted control. If a clinical psychologist helps a person overcome a terrible fear of heights, control is involved. Control is also involved in designing airplanes to keep pilots from making fatal errors. Clearly, psychological control must be used wisely and humanely.

In summary, psychology's goals are a natural outgrowth of our desire to understand behavior. Basically, they boil down to asking the following questions:

What is the nature of this behavior? (description)
Why does it occur? (understanding and explanation)
Can we forecast when it will occur? (prediction)
What conditions affect it? (control)

Description In scientific research, the process of naming and classifying.

Understanding In psychology, understanding is achieved when the causes of a behavior can be stated.

Prediction An ability to accurately forecast behavior.

Control Altering conditions that influence behavior.

STUDYBREAK **Y** *The Science of Psychology*

RELATE

At first, many students think psychology is primarily about abnormal behavior and psychotherapy. Did you? How would you describe the field now?

LEARNING CHECK

To check your memory, see if you can answer these questions. If you miss any, skim over the preceding material before continuing, to be sure you understand what you just read.

1. Psychology is the _____ study of _____ and _____ processes.
2. Information gained through direct observation and measurement is called _____ evidence.
3. In psychological research, animal _____ may be used to discover principles that apply to human behavior.
4. Which of the following questions relates most directly to the goal of *understanding* behavior?
   a. Do the scores of men and women differ on tests of thinking abilities?
   b. Why does a blow to the head cause memory loss?
   c. Will productivity in a business office increase if room temperature is raised or lowered?
   d. What percentage of college students suffer from test anxiety?

Match the following research areas with the topics they cover.

5. _____ Developmental psychology
6. _____ Learning
7. _____ Personality
8. _____ Sensation and perception
9. _____ Biopsychology
10. _____ Social psychology
11. _____ Comparative psychology

A. Attitudes, groups, leadership
B. Conditioning, memory
C. The psychology of law
D. Brain and nervous system
E. Child psychology
F. Individual differences, motivation
G. Animal behavior
H. Processing sensory information

Critical Thinking

12. All sciences are interested in controlling the phenomena they study. True or false?

ANSWERS

1. scientific, behavior, mental 2. empirical 3. models 4. b 5. E 6. B 7. F 8. H 9. D 10. A 11. G 12. False. Astronomy and archaeology are examples of sciences that do not share psychology's fourth goal.

A BRIEF HISTORY OF PSYCHOLOGY— PSYCHOLOGY'S FAMILY ALBUM

] **SURVEYQUESTION** *How did psychology emerge as a field of knowledge?*

Psychology began long ago as a part of philosophy, the study of knowledge, reality, and human nature. In contrast, psychology's short history as a science dates back only about 120 years. Of course, to some students any history is "not short enough"! Nevertheless, to understand psychology now, we need to explore its past.

Wilhelm Wundt, 1832–1920. Wundt is credited with making psychology an independent science, separate from philosophy. Wundt's original training was in medicine, but he became deeply interested in psychology. In his laboratory, Wundt investigated how sensations, images, and feelings combine to make up personal experience.

Archives of the History of American Psychology, University of Akron

Psychology's history as a science began in 1879 in Leipzig, Germany. There, the "father of psychology," Wilhelm Wundt (VILL-helm Voont), set up the first psychological laboratory to study conscious experience. What happens, he wondered, when we have sensations, images, and feelings? To find out, Wundt observed and measured stimuli of various kinds (lights, sounds, and weights). A **stimulus** is any physical energy that affects a person and evokes a response (stimulus: singular; stimuli [STIM-you-lie]: plural). Wundt then used **introspection**, or "looking inward," and careful measurement to probe his reactions to various stimuli. (If you carefully examine your thoughts, feelings, and sensations for a moment, you will have done some introspecting.) Over the years, Wundt studied vision, hearing, taste, touch, memory, time perception, and many other topics. By insisting on careful observation and measurement, he answered some interesting questions and got psychology off to a good start.

Stimulus Any physical energy that has some effect on an organism and that evokes a response.

Introspection To look within; to examine one's own thoughts, feelings, or sensations.

Structuralism The school of thought concerned with analyzing sensations and personal experience into basic elements.

Structuralism

A man named Edward B. Titchener (TICH-in-er) carried Wundt's ideas to the United States. Titchener called Wundt's ideas **structuralism** and tried to study the structure of mental life. Essentially, the structuralists hoped to analyze their experiences into basic "elements" or "building blocks."

How could they do that? You can't analyze experience like a chemical compound, can you? Perhaps not, but the structuralists tried, mostly by using introspection. For instance, an observer might heft an apple and decide that she had experienced the elements "hue" (color), "roundness," and "weight." Another example of a question that might have interested a structuralist is, What basic tastes mix together to create complex flavors as different as liver, lime, bacon, and burnt-almond fudge?

Introspection proved to be a poor way to answer many questions. Why? Because the structuralists frequently *disagreed.* And when they did, there was no way to settle differences. If two people came up with different lists of basic taste sensations, for example, who could say which was right? Despite such limitations, "looking inward" is still used in studies of hypnosis, meditation, problem solving, moods, and many other topics (Mayer & Hanson, 1995).

Functionalism

William James, an American scholar, broadened psychology to include animal behavior, religious experience, abnormal behavior, and other interesting topics. James's brilliant first book, *Principles of Psychology* (1890), helped establish the field as a separate topic (Simon, 1998).

The term **functionalism** comes from James's interest in how the mind functions to help us adapt to our environment. James regarded consciousness as an ever-changing stream or flow of images and sensations— not a set of lifeless building blocks, as the structuralists claimed.

The functionalists admired Charles Darwin, who deduced that creatures evolve in ways that favor survival. According to Darwin's principle of **natural selection**, physical features that help animals adapt to their environments are retained in evolution. Similarly, the functionalists wanted to find out how the mind, perception, habits, and emotions help us adapt and survive.

William James, 1842–1910. William James was the son of philosopher Henry James, Sr., and the brother of novelist Henry James. During his long academic career, James taught anatomy, physiology, psychology, and philosophy at Harvard University. James believed strongly that ideas should be judged in terms of their practical consequences for human conduct.

Behaviorism

Functionalism was soon challenged by **behaviorism,** the study of observable behavior. Behaviorist John B. Watson objected strongly to the study of the "mind" or "conscious experience." "Introspection," he said, "is unscientific." Watson realized that he could study the behavior of animals even though he couldn't ask them questions or know what they were thinking (Watson, 1994). He simply observed the relationship between **stimuli** (events in the environment) and an animal's **responses** (any muscular action, glandular activity, or other identifiable behavior). Why not, he asked, apply the same objectivity to human behavior?

Watson soon adopted Russian physiologist Ivan Pavlov's (ee-VAHN PAV-lahv) concept of *conditioning* to explain most behavior. (A *conditioned response* is a learned reaction to a particular stimulus.) Watson eagerly claimed, "Give me a dozen healthy infants, well-formed, and my own special world to bring them up in and I'll guarantee to take any one at random and train him to become any type of specialist I might select—doctor, lawyer, artist, merchant-chief, and yes, beggarman and thief" (Watson, 1913).

Would most psychologists agree with Watson's claim? No. Today it is regarded as an overstatement. Just the same, behaviorism helped make psychology a natural science, rather than a branch of philosophy (Richelle, 1995).

One of the best-known behaviorists, B. F. Skinner (1904–1990), believed that our actions are controlled by rewards, or positive reinforcers. To study learning, Skinner created his famous conditioning chamber, or "Skinner box." With it, he could present stimuli to animals and record their responses (see "Operant Conditioning" in Chapter 6). Many of Skinner's ideas about learning grew out of his work with rats and pigeons. Nevertheless, he believed that the same laws of behavior apply to humans. As a "radical behaviorist," Skinner also believed

John B. Watson, 1878–1958. Watson's intense interest in observable behavior began with his doctoral studies in biology and neurology. Watson became a psychology professor at Johns Hopkins University in 1908 and advanced his theory of behaviorism. He remained at Johns Hopkins until 1920, when he left for a career in the advertising industry!

Functionalism School of psychology concerned with how behavior and mental abilities help people adapt to their environments.

Natural selection Darwin's theory that evolution favors those plants and animals best suited to their living conditions.

Behaviorism School of psychology that emphasizes the study of overt, observable behavior.

Response Any muscular action, glandular activity, or other identifiable aspect of behavior.

B. F. Skinner, 1904–1990. Skinner studied simple behaviors under carefully controlled conditions. The "Skinner box" you see here has been widely used to study learning in simplified animal experiments. In addition to advancing psychology, Skinner hoped his radical brand of behaviorism would improve human life.

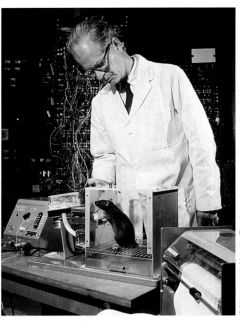

© Nina Leen/Life Magazine/Timepix

that mental events, such as thinking, are not needed to explain behavior (Richelle, 1995).

Skinner was convinced that a "designed culture" based on positive reinforcement could encourage desirable behavior. (Skinner disliked the use of punishment because it doesn't teach correct responses.) Too often, he believed, misguided rewards lead to destructive actions that create problems such as overpopulation, pollution, and war.

Cognitive Behaviorism

Strict behaviorists can be criticized for ignoring the role that thinking plays in our lives. One critic even charged that Skinnerian psychology had "lost consciousness"! However, many criticisms have been answered by **cognitive behaviorism,** a view that combines cognition (thinking) and conditioning to explain behavior (Sperry, 1995). As an example, let's say you frequently visit a particular Web site because it offers free games. A behaviorist would say that you visit the site because you are rewarded by the pleasure of game playing each time you go there. A cognitive behaviorist would add that, in addition, you *expect* to find free games at the site. This is the cognitive part of your behavior.

✦FIGURE 1.2 *The design you see here is entirely made up of broken circles. However, as the Gestalt psychologists discovered, our perceptions have a powerful tendency to form meaningful patterns. Because of this tendency, you will probably see a triangle in this design, even though it is only an illusion. Your whole perceptual experience exceeds the sum of its parts.*

Gestalt Psychology

Imagine that you just played "Happy Birthday" on a tuba. Next, you play it on a high-pitched violin. None of the tuba's sounds are duplicated by the violin. Yet, we notice something interesting: The melody is still recognizable—as long as the *relationship* between notes remains the same.

Now, what would happen if you played the notes of "Happy Birthday" in the correct order, but at a rate of one per hour? What would we have? Nothing! The separate notes would no longer be a melody. Perceptually, the melody is somehow more than the individual notes that define it.

It was observations like these that launched the Gestalt school of thought. **Gestalt psychologists** studied thinking, learning, and perception as whole units, not by analyzing experiences into parts. Their slogan was, "The whole is greater than the sum of its parts" (see ✦Fig. 1.2).

In Germany, Max Wertheimer (VERT-hi-mer) was the first psychologist to advance the Gestalt viewpoint. It is a mistake, he said, to analyze psychological events into pieces, or "elements," as the structuralists did. Like a melody, many experiences cannot be broken into smaller units. For this reason, studies of perception and personality have been especially influenced by the Gestalt viewpoint.

Were all the early psychologists men? So far, no women have been mentioned. For the most part, men dominated science at the beginning of the twentieth century. Nevertheless, women have contributed to psychology from the beginning (Minton, 2000). Take a moment and read "Women in Psychology" for more information.

Archives of the History of American Psychology, University of Akron

Max Wertheimer, 1880–1941. Wertheimer first proposed the Gestalt viewpoint to help explain perceptual illusions. He later promoted Gestalt psychology as a way to understand not only perception, problem solving, thinking, and social behavior, but also art, logic, philosophy, and politics.

Cognitive behaviorism An approach that combines behavioral principles with cognition (perception, thinking, anticipation) to explain behavior.

Gestalt psychology A school of psychology emphasizing the study of thinking, learning, and perception in whole units, not by analysis into parts.

Psychoanalytic Psychology

As American psychology grew more scientific, an Austrian doctor named Sigmund Freud was developing his own theories. Freud believed that mental life is like an iceberg: Only a small part is exposed to view. He called the area of the mind that lies outside of personal

HUMAN DIVERSITY   Women in Psychology

Women were actively discouraged from seeking advanced degrees in the late 1800s. Even so, by 1906 in America, about 1 psychologist in every 10 was a woman. Who were these "foremothers" of psychology? Three who became well known are Mary Calkins, Christine Ladd-Franklin, and Margaret Washburn.

Mary Calkins did valuable research on memory. She was also the first woman president of the American Psychological Association, in 1905. Christine Ladd-Franklin studied color vision. In 1906, she was ranked among the 50 most important psychologists in America. In 1908, Margaret Washburn published an influential textbook on animal behavior titled *The Animal Mind.*

The first woman to be awarded a Ph.D. in psychology was Margaret Washburn, in 1894. Over the next 15 years many more women followed her pioneering lead. Today, two of three graduate students in psychology are women. And in recent years, nearly 75 percent of all college graduates with a major in psychology have been women. Clearly, psychology has become fully open to both men and women (sources: Furumoto & Scarborough, 1986; Howard et al., 1986; Madigan & O'Hara, 1992; Martin, 1995).

Mary Calkins, 1863–1930.

Christine Ladd-Franklin, 1847–1930.

Margaret Washburn, 1871–1939.

awareness the **unconscious.** According to Freud, our behavior is deeply influenced by unconscious thoughts, impulses, and desires—especially those concerning sex and aggression. Freud's ideas opened new horizons in art, literature, and history, as well as psychology (Robins, Gosling, & Craik, 1998).

Freud theorized that many unconscious thoughts are *repressed* (held out of awareness) because they are threatening. But sometimes, he said, they are revealed by dreams, emotions, or slips of the tongue. ("Freudian slips" are often humorous, as when a student who is tardy for class says, "I'm sorry I couldn't get here any later.")

Freud believed that all thoughts, emotions, and actions are *determined.* In other words, nothing is an accident: If we probe deeply enough we will find the causes of every thought or action. Freud was also among the first to appreciate that childhood affects adult personality ("The child is father to the man"). Most of all, perhaps, Freud is known for creating **psychoanalysis,** the first "talking therapy." Freud's method of psychotherapy explores unconscious conflicts and emotional problems (see Chapter 13). Today, his ideas have been altered so much that few strictly psychoanalytic psychologists are left. However, Freud's legacy is still evident in various **psychodynamic theories,** which emphasize internal motives, conflicts, and unconscious forces (Westen, 1998).

Sigmund Freud, 1856–1939. For more than 50 years, Freud probed the unconscious mind. In doing so, he altered modern views of human nature. His early experimentation with a "talking cure" for hysteria is regarded as the beginning of psychoanalysis. Through psychoanalysis, Freud added psychological treatment methods to psychiatry.

Unconscious Contents of the mind that are beyond awareness, especially impulses and desires not directly known to a person.

Psychoanalysis A Freudian approach to psychotherapy emphasizing the exploration of unconscious conflicts.

Psychodynamic theory Any theory of behavior that emphasizes internal conflicts, motives, and unconscious forces.

▲TABLE 1.1	The Early Development of Psychology	
PERSPECTIVE	**DATE**	**NOTABLE EVENTS**
Experimental psychology	1875	• First psychology course offered by William James
	1878	• First American Ph.D. in psychology awarded
	1879	• Wilhelm Wundt opens first psychology laboratory in Germany
	1883	• First American psychology lab founded at Johns Hopkins University
	1886	• First American psychology textbook written by John Dewey
Structuralism	1898	• Edward Titchener advances psychology based on introspection
Functionalism	1890	• William James publishes *Principles of Psychology*
	1892	• American Psychological Association founded
Psychodynamic psychology	1895	• Sigmund Freud publishes first studies
	1900	• Freud publishes *The Interpretation of Dreams*
Behaviorism	1906	• Ivan Pavlov reports his research on conditioned reflexes
	1913	• John Watson presents behavioristic view
Gestalt psychology	1912	• Max Wertheimer and others advance Gestalt viewpoint
Humanistic psychology	1942	• Carl Rogers publishes *Counseling and Psychotherapy*
	1943	• Abraham Maslow publishes "A theory of human motivation"

Humanistic Psychology

Humanism is a view that focuses on subjective human experience. Humanistic psychologists are interested in human problems, potentials, and ideals.

How is the humanistic approach different from others? Carl Rogers, Abraham Maslow, and other humanists rejected the Freudian idea that we are ruled by unconscious forces. They were also uncomfortable with the behaviorist emphasis on conditioning. Both views have a strong undercurrent of **determinism** (the idea that behavior is determined by forces beyond our control). Instead, the humanists stress **free will,** our ability to make voluntary choices. Of course, past experiences do affect us. Nevertheless, humanists believe that people can freely *choose* to live more creative, meaningful, and satisfying lives.

Abraham Maslow, 1908–1970. As a founder of humanistic psychology, Maslow was interested in studying people of exceptional mental health. Such self-actualized people, he believed, make full use of their talents and abilities. Maslow offered his positive view of human potential as an alternative to the schools of behaviorism and psychoanalysis.

Ted Polumbaum

Humanists are interested in psychological needs for love, self-esteem, belonging, self-expression, creativity, and spirituality. Such needs, they believe, are as important as our biological urges for food and water. For example, newborn infants deprived of human love may die just as surely as they would if deprived of food.

How scientific is the humanistic approach? Initially, humanists were less interested in treating psychology as a science. They stressed more subjective factors, such as one's self-image, self-evaluation, and frame of reference. (*Self-image* is your perception of your own body, personality, and capabilities. *Self-evaluation* refers to appraising yourself as good or bad. A *frame of reference* is a mental perspective used to interpret events.) Today, humanists still seek to understand how we perceive ourselves and experience the world. However, most now do research to test their ideas, just as other psychologists do (Schneider, Bugental, & Pierson, 2001).

Humanism An approach to psychology that focuses on human experience, problems, potentials, and ideals.

Determinism The idea that all behavior has prior causes that would completely explain one's choices and actions if all such causes were known.

Free will The idea that human beings are capable of freely making choices or decisions.

Self-actualization The process of fully developing one's personal potentials.

Maslow's concept of self-actualization is a special feature of humanism. **Self-actualization** refers to developing one's potential fully and becoming the best person possible. According to humanists, everyone has this potential. Humanists seek ways to help it emerge. (Return to ▲Table 1.1 for a summary of psychology's early development.)

▲*TABLE 1.2*	**Five Ways to Look at Behavior**
CONSCIOUS / UNCONSCIOUS	**PSYCHODYNAMIC VIEW** *Key Idea: Behavior is directed by forces within one's personality that are often hidden or unconscious.* Emphasizes internal impulses, desires, and conflicts—especially those that are unconscious; views behavior as the result of clashing forces within personality; somewhat negative, pessimistic view of human nature.
S ▶ R	**BEHAVIORISTIC VIEW** *Key Idea: Behavior is shaped and controlled by one's environment.* Emphasizes the study of observable behavior and the effects of learning; stresses the influence of external rewards and punishments; neutral, scientific, somewhat mechanistic view of human nature.
Self / Self-image / Self-evaluation	**HUMANISTIC VIEW** *Key Idea: Behavior is guided by one's self-image, by subjective perceptions of the world, and by needs for personal growth.* Focuses on subjective, conscious experience, human problems, potentials, and ideals; emphasizes self-image and self-actualization to explain behavior; positive, philosophical view of human nature.
(brain)	**BIOPSYCHOLOGICAL VIEW** *Key Idea: Human and animal behavior is the result of internal physical, chemical, and biological processes.* Seeks to explain behavior through activity of the brain and nervous system, physiology, genetics, the endocrine system, biochemistry, and evolution; neutral, reductionistic, mechanistic view of human nature.
INPUT / Processing / OUTPUT	**COGNITIVE VIEW** *Key Idea: Much human behavior can be understood in terms of the mental processing of information.* Concerned with thinking, knowing, perception, understanding, memory, decision-making, and judgment; explains behavior in terms of information processing; neutral, somewhat computer-like view of human nature.

PSYCHOLOGY TODAY—FIVE VIEWS OF BEHAVIOR

] SURVEYQUESTION *What are the major trends and specialties in psychology?*

At one time, loyalty to each school of thought was fierce, and clashes were common. Today, viewpoints such as functionalism and Gestalt psychology have blended into newer, broader perspectives. Also, some early systems, such as structuralism, have disappeared entirely. Certainly, loyalties and specialties still exist. But today, many psychologists are *eclectic* (ek-LEK-tik; they draw from a variety of perspectives). Even so, five major views shape modern psychology. These are the *psychodynamic, behavioristic,* and *humanistic* views, plus modern *cognitive* and *biopsychological* perspectives (▲Table 1.2) (Robins, Gosling, & Craik, 1999).

Biopsychology is a fast-growing area. Eventually, biopsychologists expect to explain all behavior in terms of physical mechanisms, such as brain activity and genetics. Their optimism is based on exciting new insights about how the brain relates to thinking, feelings, perception, abnormal behavior, and other topics.

Cognitive science is another rapidly expanding area. In fact, over the last 10 years, a "cognitive revolution" has taken place. *Cognition* means "thinking" or "knowing." As mentioned earlier, cognitive psychologists study thoughts, expectations, memory, language, perception, problem solving, consciousness, creativity, and other mental processes. With all this renewed interest in thinking, it can be said that psychology has finally "regained consciousness" (Robins, Gosling, & Craik, 1999).

Positive Psychology

Psychologists have always paid attention to the negative side of human behavior. This is easy to understand because of the pressing need to solve human problems. However, psychologists have recently begun to ask, What do we know about love, happiness, creativity, well-being, self-confidence, and achievement? Together, such topics make up **positive psychology**,

Positive psychology The study of human strengths, virtues, and effective functioning.

the study of human strengths, virtues, and optimal behavior (Seligman & Csikszentmihalyi, 2000). Many topics from positive psychology can be found in this book. Ideally, they will help make your own life more positive and fulfilling.

Summary

As you can see, it is helpful to view human behavior from more than one perspective. This is also true in another sense. We are rapidly becoming a multicultural society, made up of people from many different nations. How has this affected psychology? The next section explains why it is important for all of us to be aware of cultural differences.

HUMAN DIVERSITY—APPRECIATING SOCIAL AND CULTURAL DIFFERENCES

Jerry, who is Japanese American, is married to an Irish Catholic American. Here is what Jerry, his wife, and their children did on New Year's Day:

> We woke up in the morning and went to Mass at St. Brigid's, which has a black gospel choir. . . . Then we went to the Japanese-American Community Center for the Oshogatsu New Year's program and saw Buddhist archers shoot arrows to ward off evil spirits for the year. Next, we ate traditional rice cakes as part of the New Year's service and listened to a young Japanese-American storyteller. On the way home, we stopped in Chinatown and after that we ate Mexican food at a taco stand. (Njeri, 1991)

Jerry and his family reflect a new social reality: Cultural diversity is becoming the norm. About one third of the population in the United States is now African American, Hispanic, Asian American, Native American, or Pacific Islander. In some large cities "minority" groups are already the majority (Schmitt, 2001).

To fully understand human behavior, personal differences based on age, race, culture, ethnicity, gender, and sexual orientation must be taken into account.

Cultural relativity The idea that behavior must be judged relative to the values of the culture in which it occurs.

Social norms Unspoken rules that define acceptable and expected behavior for members of a group.

The Impact of Culture

In the past, psychology was based mostly on the cultures of North America and Europe. Now, we must ask, Do the principles of Western psychology apply to people in all cultures? Are some psychological concepts invalid in other cultures? Are any universal? As psychologists have probed such questions, one thing has become clear: Most of what we think, feel, and do is influenced in one way or another by the social and cultural worlds in which we live (Segall, Lonner, & Berry, 1998).

Cultural Relativity

Imagine that you are a psychologist. Your client, Linda, who is a Native American, tells you that spirits live in the trees near her home. Is Linda suffering from a delusion? Is she abnormal? Obviously, you will misjudge Linda's mental health if you fail to take her cultural beliefs into account. **Cultural relativity** (the idea that behavior must be judged relative to the values of the culture in which it occurs) can greatly affect the diagnosis of mental disorders (Alarcon, 1995). Cases like Linda's teach us to be wary of using narrow standards when judging others or comparing groups.

A Broader View of Diversity

In addition to cultural differences, age, ethnicity, gender, religion, disability, and sexual orientation all affect the **social norms** that guide behavior. Social norms are rules that define acceptable and expected behavior for members of various groups. All too often, the unstated standard for judging what is "average," "normal," or "correct" is the behavior of white, middle-class males (Reid, 2002). To fully understand human behavior, psychologists need to know how people differ, as well as the ways in which we are all alike. For the same reason, an appreciation of human diversity can enrich your life, as well as your understanding of psychology.

In a moment, we will further explore what psychologists do. First, here's a chance to improve your next test score.

STUDYBREAK ✱ *History and Major Perspectives*

RELATE

Which school of thought most closely matches your own view of behavior? Do you think any of the early schools offers a complete explanation of why we behave as we do? What about the five contemporary perspectives? Can you explain why so many psychologists are eclectic?

LEARNING CHECK

Match:

1. _____ Philosophy
2. _____ Wundt
3. _____ Structuralism
4. _____ Functionalism
5. _____ Behaviorism
6. _____ Gestalt
7. _____ Psychodynamic

8. _____ Humanistic
9. _____ Cognitive
10. _____ Washburn
11. _____ Biopsychology

A. Against analysis; studied whole experiences
B. "Mental chemistry" and introspection
C. Emphasizes self-actualization and personal growth
D. Interested in unconscious causes of behavior
E. Interested in how the mind aids survival
F. First woman Ph.D. in psychology
G. Studied stimuli and responses and conditioning
H. Part of psychology's "long past"
I. Concerned with thinking, language, and problem solving
J. Used introspection and careful measurement
K. Relates behavior to the brain, physiology, and genetics
L. Also known as engineering psychology

12. Universal norms exist for judging the behavior of people in various cultural and social groups. T or F?

Critical Thinking

13. Modern sciences such as psychology are built on observations that can be verified by two or more independent observers. Did structuralism meet this standard? Why or why not?

ANSWERS

1. H 2. J 3. B 4. E 5. G 6. A 7. D 8. C 9. I 10. F 11. K 12. F 13. No, it did not. The downfall of structuralism was that each observer examined the contents of his or her own mind, which is something no other person can observe.

PSYCHOLOGISTS—GUARANTEED NOT TO SHRINK

QUESTION: What is the difference between a psychologist and a psychiatrist?

ANSWER: About $30 an hour. (And going up.)

What are the differences among various kinds of mental health professionals? Certainly, they're not all "shrinks." Each has a specific blend of training and skills.

A **psychologist** is highly trained in the methods, knowledge, and theories of psychology. Psychologists usually have a master's degree or a doctorate. These degrees typically require from 3 to 8 years of postgraduate training. Psychologists may teach, do research, give psychological tests, or serve as consultants to business, industry, government, or the military.

Public impressions of psychologists are often inaccurate. Perhaps this occurs because so many stereotyped images appear in movies and on television. For example, in the film *Good Will Hunting*, a psychologist angrily chokes his rebellious young patient. No ethical therapist would ever engage in such behavior, yet it is not unusual in the movies. Such scenes may be dramatic and entertaining, but they seriously distort public perceptions of responsible and hard-working psychologists (Sleek, 1998). Real psychologists follow an ethical code that stresses respect for people's privacy, dignity, confidentiality, and welfare ("Ethical," 2002; Sullivan et al., 1998).

© Miramax/The Kobal Collection

In the film *Good Will Hunting*, Robin Williams plays a psychologist who physically assaults a defiant patient, played by Matt Damon. Such dramatic scenes are typical of the way the media misrepresent psychologists and psychotherapy.

Psychologist A person highly trained in the methods, factual knowledge, and theories of psychology.

▲TABLE 1.3 | Kinds of Psychologists and What They Do

SPECIALTY		TYPICAL ACTIVITIES
Biopsychology	B*	Does research on the brain, nervous system, and other physical origins of behavior
Clinical	A	Does psychotherapy; investigates clinical problems; develops methods of treatment
Cognitive	B	Studies human thinking and information processing abilities
Community	A	Promotes community-wide mental health through research, prevention, education, and consultation
Comparative	B	Studies and compares the behavior of different species, especially animals
Consumer	A	Researches packaging, advertising, marketing methods, and characteristics of consumers
Counseling	A	Does psychotherapy and personal counseling; researches emotional disturbances and counseling methods
Cultural	B	Studies the ways in which culture, subculture, and ethnic group membership affect behavior
Developmental	A, B	Conducts research on infant, child, adolescent, and adult development; does clinical work with disturbed children; acts as consultant to parents and schools
Educational	A	Investigates classroom dynamics, teaching styles, and learning; develops educational tests, evaluates educational programs
Engineering	A	Does applied research on the design of machinery, computers, airlines, automobiles, and so on, for business, industry, and the military
Environmental	A, B	Studies the effects of urban noise, crowding, attitudes toward the environment, and human use of space; acts as a consultant on environmental issues
Forensic	A	Studies problems of crime and crime prevention, rehabilitation programs, prisons, courtroom dynamics; selects candidates for police work
Gender	B	Does research on differences between males and females, the acquisition of gender identity, and the role of gender throughout life
Health	A, B	Studies the relationship between behavior and health; uses psychological principles to promote health and prevent illness
Industrial-organizational	A	Selects job applicants, does skills analysis, evaluates on-the-job training, improves work environments and human relations in organizations and work settings
Learning	B	Studies how and why learning occurs; develops theories of learning
Medical	A	Applies psychology to manage medical problems, such as the emotional impact of illness, self-screening for cancer, compliance in taking medicine
Personality	B	Studies personality traits and dynamics; develops theories of personality and tests for assessing personality traits
School	A	Does psychological testing, referrals, emotional and vocational counseling of students; detects and treats learning disabilities; improves classroom learning
Sensation and perception	B	Studies the sense organs and the process of perception; investigates the mechanisms of sensation and develops theories about how perception occurs
Social	B	Investigates human social behavior, including attitudes, conformity, persuasion, prejudice, friendship, aggression, helping, and so forth

*Research in this area is typically applied (A), basic (B), or both (A, B).

Even without media distortions, misconceptions about psychologists are common. For instance, most psychologists are not therapists in private practice. Instead, they are employed by schools, businesses, and social agencies. Likewise, only 16 percent work in clinics or hospitals.

One perception of psychologists is accurate: Most do help people in one way or another. Psychologists interested in emotional problems specialize in clinical or counseling psychology (see ▲Table 1.3). **Clinical psychologists** treat psychological problems or

Clinical psychologist A psychologist who specializes in the treatment of psychological and behavioral disturbances or who does research on such disturbances.

do research on therapies and mental disorders. In contrast, **counseling psychologists** tend to treat milder problems, such as poor adjustment at work or school. However, such differences are fading, and many counseling psychologists now work full-time as therapists.

To enter the profession of psychology, it is best to have a doctorate (Ph.D., Psy.D., or Ed.D.). Most clinical psychologists have a Ph.D. degree and follow a scientist-practitioner model. That is, they are trained to do either research or therapy. Many do both. Other clinicians earn the Psy.D. (Doctor of Psychology) degree, which emphasizes therapy skills rather than research.

Other Mental Health Professionals

A **psychiatrist** is a medical doctor who treats mental disorders, usually by doing psychotherapy. However, psychiatrists can also prescribe drugs, which is something a psychologist cannot do. This might change, however. Psychologists in New Mexico can now legally prescribe drugs. Psychologists in other states are seeking similar privileges. It will be interesting to see whether lawmakers agree that psychologists should have this option (Daw, 2002).

To be a psychoanalyst, you must have a moustache and goatee, spectacles, a German accent, and a well-padded couch—or so the TV and movie stereotype goes. Actually, to become a **psychoanalyst,** you must have an M.D. or Ph.D. degree plus further training in Freudian psychoanalysis. In other words, either a physician or a psychologist may become an analyst by learning a specific type of psychotherapy.

In many states, counselors also do mental health work. A **counselor** is an adviser who helps solve problems with marriage, career, school, work, or the like. To be a licensed counselor (such as a marriage and family counselor, a child counselor, or a school counselor) typically requires a master's degree plus 1 or 2 years of full-time supervised counseling experience. Counselors learn practical helping skills and do not treat serious mental disorders.

Psychiatric social workers play an important role in many mental health programs. **Psychiatric social workers** apply social science principles to help patients in clinics and hospitals. Most hold an M.S.W. (Master of Social Work) degree. Often, they assist psychologists and psychiatrists as part of a team. Their typical duties include evaluating patients and families; conducting group therapy; or visiting a patient's home, school, or job to alleviate problems.

Specialties in Psychology

Do all psychologists do therapy and treat abnormal behavior?   No. Only about 58 percent are clinical and counseling psychologists. The rest are found in other specialties. At present, the American Psychological Association (APA) consists of more than 50 divisions, each reflecting special skills or areas of interest. Some of the major specialties are listed in Table 1.3 (also see ◆Fig. 1.3). Nearly 30 percent of all psychologists are employed full-time at colleges or universities, where they teach and do research, consulting, or therapy. Some do *basic research,* in which they seek knowledge for its own sake. For example, a psychologist might study memory simply to understand how it works. Others do *applied research* to solve immediate practical problems, such as finding ways to improve the memory of eyewitnesses to crimes. Some do both types of research.

In a moment we'll take a closer look at how research is done. Before that, here's a chance to do a little research on how much you've learned.

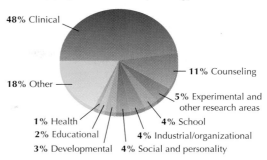

(a) Specialties in Psychology

48% Clinical
11% Counseling
5% Experimental and other research areas
18% Other
1% Health
2% Educational
3% Developmental
4% School
4% Industrial/organizational
4% Social and personality

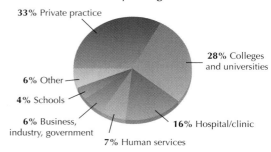

(b) Where Psychologists Work

33% Private practice
28% Colleges and universities
6% Other
4% Schools
6% Business, industry, government
7% Human services
16% Hospital/clinic

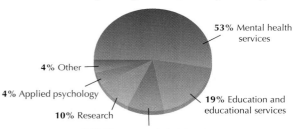

(c) What Psychologists Do (Primary Activity)

53% Mental health services
4% Other
4% Applied psychology
19% Education and educational services
10% Research
10% Management/administration

◆**FIGURE 1.3**   (a) *Specialties in psychology. Percentages are approximate.* (b) *Where psychologists work.* (c) *This chart shows the main activities psychologists do at work. Any particular psychologist might do several of these activities during a work week (APA, 1998). As you can see, most psychologists specialize in applied areas and work in applied settings.*

Counseling psychologist A psychologist who specializes in the treatment of milder emotional and behavioral disturbances.

Psychiatrist A medical doctor with additional training in the diagnosis and treatment of mental and emotional disorders.

Psychoanalyst A mental health professional (usually a medical doctor) trained to practice psychoanalysis.

Counselor A mental health professional who specializes in helping people with problems not involving serious mental disorder; for example, marriage counselors, career counselors, or school counselors.

Psychiatric social worker A mental health professional trained to apply social science principles to help patients in clinics and hospitals.

RELATE

You're going to meet four psychologists at a social gathering. How many would you expect to be therapists in private practice? Odds are that only two will be clinical (or counseling) psychologists and only one of these will work in private practice. On the other hand, at least one of the four (and probably two) will work at a college or university.

LEARNING CHECK

See if you can answer these questions before continuing.

1. Which of the following can prescribe drugs?
   a. a psychologist   b. a psychiatrist   c. a psychotherapist
   d. a counselor

2. A psychologist who specializes in treating human emotional difficulties is called a _____ psychologist.

3. Roughly 40 percent of psychologists specialize in counseling psychology. T or F?

4. Who among the following would most likely be involved in the detection of learning disabilities?
   a. a consumer psychologist   b. a forensic psychologist
   c. an experimental psychologist   d. a school psychologist

Critical Thinking

5. If most psychologists work in applied settings, why is basic research still of great importance?

ANSWERS

1. b 2. clinical or counseling 3. F 4. d 5. Because practitioners benefit from basic psychological research in the same way that physicians benefit from basic research in biology. Discoveries in basic science form the knowledge base that leads to useful applications.

SCIENTIFIC RESEARCH—HOW TO THINK LIKE A PSYCHOLOGIST

] **SURVEYQUESTIONS** *Why is the scientific method important to psychologists? How do psychologists collect information?*

Drawing valid conclusions in psychology is more challenging than you might think. In the course of a day, you probably hear dozens of false statements about human behavior. How

Applying the scientific method to the study of behavior requires careful observation. Here, a psychologist videotapes a session in which a child's thinking abilities are being tested.

Scientific method Testing the truth of a proposition by careful measurement and controlled observation.

Hypothesis The predicted outcome of an experiment or an educated guess about the relationship between variables.

can you separate fact from fiction and reality from fantasy? Psychologists have found that the tools of science provide an elegant way to investigate human and animal behavior.

Carefully recording facts and events is the heart of all sciences. To be *scientific,* our observations must be *systematic,* so that they reveal something about behavior (Stanovich, 2001). To use an earlier example, if you are interested in heat and aggression, you will learn little by driving around and making haphazard observations of aggressive horn honking. To be of value, your observations must be planned and systematic.

The Scientific Method

The **scientific method** is based on careful collection of evidence, accurate description and measurement, precise definition, controlled observation, and repeatable results (Schick & Vaughn, 2001). In its ideal form the scientific method has six elements:

1. Making observations
2. Defining a problem
3. Proposing a hypothesis
4. Gathering evidence/testing the hypothesis
5. Publishing results
6. Building a theory

Let's take a closer look at some elements of the scientific method.

Hypothesis Testing

Yes, what exactly is a hypothesis?   A **hypothesis** (hi-POTH-eh-sis) is a tentative explanation of an event or relationship. In common terms, a hypothesis is a *testable* hunch or educated guess about behavior. For example, you might hypothesize that "Frustration encourages aggression." How could you test this hypothesis? First you would have to decide how you are going to frustrate people. (This part might be fun.) Then you will need to find a way to measure whether or not they become more aggressive. (Not so much fun if you plan to be nearby.) Your observations would then provide evidence to confirm or disconfirm the hypothesis.

Operational Definitions

Because we cannot see or touch frustration, it must be defined operationally. An **operational definition** states the exact procedures used to represent a concept. Operational definitions allow abstract ideas to be tested in real-world terms (see ✦Fig. 1.4). For example, you might define frustration as "interrupting an adult before he or she can finish a puzzle and win a $100 prize." And aggression might be defined as "the number of times a frustrated individual insults the person who prevented work on the puzzle."

Clever Hans

Several steps of the scientific method can be illustrated with the story of Clever Hans, a famous "wonder horse" (Rosenthal, 1965). Clever Hans seemed to solve difficult math problems, which he answered by tapping his hoof. If you asked Hans, "What is 12 times 2, minus 18," Hans would tap his hoof six times. This was so astonishing that a scientist decided to find out if Hans really could do arithmetic. Assume you are the scientist and you are just itching to discover how Hans *really* does his trick.

CAN A HORSE ADD?

Your investigation of Hans's math skills would probably begin with careful *observation* of both the horse and his owner. Assume that these observations fail to reveal any obvious cheating. Then the *problem* becomes more clearly *defined:* What signals Hans to start and stop tapping his hoof? Your first *hypothesis* might be that the owner is giving Hans a signal. Your proposed *test* would be to make the owner leave the room. Then someone else could ask Hans questions. Your test would either confirm or deny the owner's role. This *evidence* would support or eliminate the cheating hypothesis. By changing the conditions under which you observe Hans, you have *controlled* the situation to gain more information from your observations.

Incidentally, Hans could still answer when his owner was out of the room. But a brilliant series of controlled observations revealed Hans's secret. If Hans couldn't see the questioner, he couldn't answer. It seems that questioners always *lowered their heads* (to look at Hans's hoof) after asking a question. This was Hans's cue to start tapping. When Hans had tapped the correct number, a questioner would always *look up* to see if Hans was going to stop. This was Hans's cue to stop tapping!

Theories

What about theory formulation? Because Clever Hans's ability to do math was an isolated problem, no theorizing was involved. However, in actual research, a **theory** acts as a map of knowledge. Good theories summarize observations, explain them, and guide further research (see ✦Fig. 1.5). Without theories of forgetting, personality, stress, mental illness, and the like, psychologists would drown in a sea of disconnected facts (Stanovich, 2001).

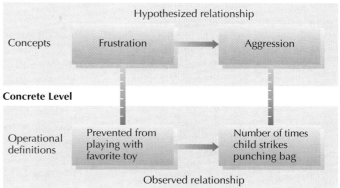

✦FIGURE 1.4 *Operational definitions are used to link concepts with concrete observations. Do you think the examples given are reasonable operational definitions of frustration and aggression? Operational definitions vary in how well they represent concepts. For this reason, many different experiments may be necessary to draw clear conclusions about hypothesized relationships in psychology.*

✦FIGURE 1.5 *Psychologists use the logic of science to answer questions about behavior. Specific hypotheses can be tested in a variety of ways, including naturalistic observation, correlational studies, controlled experiments, clinical studies, and the survey method. Psychologists revise their theories to reflect the evidence they gather. New or revised theories then lead to new observations, problems, and hypotheses.*

Operational definition Defining a scientific concept by stating the specific actions or procedures used to measure it. For example, "hunger" might be defined as "the number of hours of food deprivation."

Theory A system of ideas designed to interrelate concepts and facts in a way that summarizes existing data and predicts future observations.

▲*TABLE 1.4*	**Outline of a Research Report**

- **Abstract** Research reports begin with a very brief summary of the study and its findings. The abstract allows you to get an overview without reading the entire article.
- **Introduction** The introduction describes the question to be investigated. It also provides background information by reviewing prior studies on the same or related topics.
- **Method** This section tells how and why observations were made. It also describes the specific procedures used to gather data. That way, other researchers can repeat the study to see if they get the same results.
- **Results** The outcome of the investigation is presented. Data may be graphed, summarized in tables, or statistically analyzed.
- **Discussion** The results of the study are discussed in relation to the original question. Implications of the study are explored and further studies may be proposed.

Publication

Scientific information must always be *publicly available.* The results of psychological studies are usually published in professional journals (see ▲Table 1.4). That way, anyone willing to make appropriate observations can see whether or not a claim is true (Schick & Vaughn, 2001).

Summary

Now let's summarize more realistically. All the basic elements of the scientific method are found in the example that follows.

Observation: Suzanne, a psychologist, observes that some business managers seem to experience less work-related stress than others do.

Defining a Problem: Suzanne's problem is to identify the ways in which high-stress and low-stress managers are different.

Observation: Suzanne carefully questions managers about how much stress they experience. These additional observations suggest that low-stress managers feel they have more control over their work.

Proposing a Hypothesis: Suzanne hypothesizes that having control over difficult tasks reduces stress.

Gathering Evidence/Testing the Hypothesis: Suzanne designs an experiment in which people must solve a series of very difficult problems. In one group, people solve the problems at a forced pace, dictated by Suzanne. In another group, they are allowed to set the pace themselves. While working, the second group reports lower stress levels than the first did. This suggests that Suzanne's hypothesis is correct.

Publishing Results: In a scholarly article, Suzanne carefully describes the question she investigated, the methods she used, and the results of her experiment. The article is published in the *Journal of Clinical Psychology.*

Building Theories: Drawing on the results of similar experiments, Suzanne and other psychologists create a theory to explain why having control over a task helps reduce stress.

Research Methods

Psychologists gather evidence and test hypotheses in many ways: They observe behavior as it unfolds in natural settings (**naturalistic observation**); they make measurements to discover relationships between events (**correlational method**); they use the powerful technique of controlled experimentation (**experimental method**); they study psychological problems and therapies in clinical settings (**clinical method**); and they use questionnaires to poll large groups of people (**survey method**). Let's see how each of these is used to advance psychological knowledge.

NATURALISTIC OBSERVATION— PSYCHOLOGY STEPS OUT!

Psychologists sometimes actively observe behavior in a *natural setting* (the typical environment in which a person or animal lives). The work of Jane Goodall provides a good example. She and her staff have been observing chimpanzees in Tanzania since 1960. A quote from her book, *In the Shadow of Man,* captures the excitement of a scientific discovery:

Quickly focusing my binoculars, I saw that it was a single chimpanzee, and just then he turned my direction. . . . He was squatting beside the red earth mound of a termite nest, and as I watched I saw him carefully push a long grass stem into a hole in the mound. After a moment he withdrew it and picked something from the end with his mouth. I was too far away to make out what he was eating, but it was obvious that he was actually using a grass stem as a tool (◆Fig. 1.6). (Van Lawick-Goodall, 1971)

Naturalistic observation Observing behavior as it unfolds in natural settings.

Correlational method Making measurements to discover relationships between events.

Experimental method Investigating behavior through controlled experimentation.

Clinical method Studying psychological problems and therapies in clinical settings.

Survey method Using questionnaires and surveys to poll large groups of people.

✦FIGURE 1.6 *A special moment in Jane Goodall's naturalistic study of chimpanzees: A chimp uses a grass stem to extract a meal from a termite nest. Goodall's work also documented the importance of long-term emotional bonds between chimpanzee mothers and their offspring, as well as fascinating differences in the behavior and "personalities" of individual chimps (Goodall, 1990). (Photo by Baron Hugo van Lawick. © National Geographic Society.)*

Notice that naturalistic observation only provides *descriptions* of behavior. To *explain* observations, we may need information from other research methods. Just the same, Goodall's discovery showed that humans are not the only tool-making animals (Lavallee, 1999).

Chimpanzees in zoos use objects as tools. Doesn't that demonstrate the same thing? Not necessarily. Naturalistic observation allows us to study behavior that hasn't been tampered with or altered by outside influences. Only by observing chimps in their natural environment can we tell if they use tools without human interference.

Limitations

Doesn't the presence of human observers affect the animals' behavior? Yes. The observer effect is a major problem. The **observer effect** refers to changes in a subject's behavior caused by an awareness of being observed. Naturalists must be very careful to keep their distance and avoid "making friends" with the animals they are watching. Likewise, if you are interested in schoolyard bullying, you can't simply stroll onto a playground and start taking notes. As a stranger, your presence would probably change children's behavior. When possible, this problem can be minimized by concealing the observer. Another solution is to use hidden recorders. For example, a naturalistic study of playground aggression was done with video cameras and remote microphones (Pepler, Craig, & Roberts, 1998).

Observer bias is a related problem in which observers see what they expect to see or record only selected details. For instance, teachers in one study were told to watch normal elementary school children who had been labeled (for the study) as "learning disabled," "mentally retarded," "emotionally disturbed," or "normal." Sadly, teachers gave the children very different ratings, depending on the labels used (Foster & Ysseldyke, 1976). In some situations, observer bias can have serious consequences. For example, psychotherapists tend to get better results with the type of therapy they favor (Lambert, 1999).

The Anthropomorphic Error

A special mistake to avoid while observing animals is the **anthropomorphic** (AN-thro-po-MORE-fik) **error.** This is the error of attributing human thoughts, feelings, or motives to animals—especially as a way of explaining their behavior (Blumberg & Wasserman, 1995). The temptation to assume that an animal is "angry," "jealous," "bored," or "guilty" can be strong, but it can lead to false conclusions. If you have pets at home, you probably already know how difficult it is to avoid anthropomorphizing.

Recording Observations

Psychologists doing naturalistic studies make a special effort to minimize bias by keeping an *observational record*, or detailed summary of data and observations. As suggested by the study of playground aggression, videotaping often provides the best record of all (Pepler & Craig, 1995).

Despite its problems, naturalistic observation can supply a wealth of information and raise many interesting questions. In most scientific research it is an excellent starting point.

Observer effect Changes in behavior brought about by an awareness of being observed.
Observer bias The tendency of an observer to distort observations or perceptions to match his or her expectations.
Anthropomorphic error The error of attributing human thoughts, feelings, or motives to animals, especially as a way of explaining their behavior.

CORRELATIONAL STUDIES—IN SEARCH OF THE PERFECT RELATIONSHIP

Let's say a psychologist notes an association between the IQs of parents and their children, or between beauty and social popularity, or between anxiety and test performance, or even between crime and the weather. In each case, two observations or events are **correlated** (linked together in an orderly way).

A **correlational study** finds the degree of relationship, or correlation, between two existing traits, behaviors, or events. First, two factors are measured. Then a statistical technique is used to find their degree of correlation. (See the "Statistics" appendix near the end of this book for more information.) For example, we could find the correlation between the number of hours slept at night and afternoon sleepiness. If the correlation is large, knowing how long a person sleeps at night would allow us to predict his or her degree of sleepiness in the afternoon. Likewise, afternoon sleepiness could be used to predict the duration of nighttime sleep.

Correlation Coefficients

How is the degree of correlation expressed?   The strength and direction of a relationship can be expressed as a **coefficient of correlation.** This is simply a number falling somewhere between $+1.00$ and -1.00 (see the "Statistics" appendix). If the number is zero or close to zero, the association between two measures is weak or nonexistent. For example, the correlation between shoe size and intelligence is zero. (Sorry, size 12 readers.) If the correlation is $+1.00$, a perfect positive relationship exists; if it is -1.00, a perfect negative relationship has been discovered.

Correlations in psychology are rarely perfect. But the closer the coefficient is to $+1.00$ or -1.00, the stronger the relationship. For example, identical twins tend to have almost identical IQs. In contrast, the IQs of parents and their children are only generally similar. The correlation between the IQs of parents and children is .35; between identical twins it's .86.

What do the terms "positive" and "negative" correlation mean?   A *positive correlation* shows that increases in one measure are matched by increases in the other (or decreases correspond with decreases). For example, there is a positive correlation between high school grades and college grades; students who do well in high school tend to do well in college (and the reverse). In a *negative correlation,* increases in the first measure are associated with decreases in the second (◆Fig. 1.7). We might observe, for instance, that students who watch many hours of television get lower grades than those who watch few hours. (This is the well-known TV zombie effect.)

Would that show that watching TV too much causes lower grades?   It might seem so, but we cannot be sure without performing an experiment.

Correlation and Causation

Correlational studies help us discover relationships and make predictions. However, correlation *does not* demonstrate *causation* (a cause-effect relationship) (Meltzoff, 1998). It could be, for instance, that students who aren't interested in their classes have more time for TV. If so, their lack of study and lower grades would *both* result from disinterest, not from excess TV watching. Just because one thing *appears* to be related to another does not mean that a cause-and-effect connection exists.

◆**FIGURE 1.7** *The correlation coefficient tells how strongly two measures are related. These graphs show a range of relationships between two measures, A and B. If a correlation is negative, increases in one measure are associated with decreases in the other. (As B gets larger, A gets smaller.) In a positive correlation, increases in one measure are associated with increases in the other. (As B gets larger, A gets larger.) The center-left graph ("medium negative relationship") might result from comparing anxiety level (B) with test scores (A): Higher anxiety is associated with lower scores. The center graph ("no relationship") would result from plotting a person's shoe size (B) and his or her IQ (A). The center-right graph ("medium positive relationship") could be a plot of grades in high school (B) and grades in college (A) for a group of students: Higher grades in high school are associated with higher grades in college.*

Correlation
Strength of relationship

| Perfect −1.00 | Very large −.75 | Large −.50 | Medium −.30 | Small −.10 | Zero 0.0 | Small +.10 | Medium +.30 | Large +.50 | Very large +.75 | Perfect +1.00 |

Perfect negative relationship

Medium negative relationship

No relationship

Medium positive relationship

Perfect positive relationship

Correlation The existence of a consistent, systematic relationship between two events, measures, or variables.

Correlational study A non-experimental study designed to measure the degree of relationship (if any) between two or more events, measures, or variables.

Coefficient of correlation A statistical index ranging from −1.00 to +1.00 that indicates the direction and degree of correlation.

Here is another example of mistaking correlation for causation: What if a psychologist discovers that the blood of patients with schizophrenia contains a certain chemical not found in the general population? Does this show that the chemical *causes* schizophrenia? It might seem so, but schizophrenia could cause the chemical to form. Or both schizophrenia and the chemical might be caused by some unknown third factor, such as the typical diet in mental hospitals. Just because one thing *appears* to cause another does not *confirm* that it does. The best way to be confident that a cause-and-effect relationship exists is to perform a controlled experiment. You'll learn how in the next section.

STUDYBREAK *Research Methods, Naturalistic Observation, and Correlation*

RELATE

You probably hypothesize daily about why people act the way they do. Do you seek to verify your hypotheses? Usually we closely observe others to determine if our "educated guesses" about them are correct. But casual observation can be misleading. To really test a hypothesis, systematic observation and formal research methods are necessary.

LEARNING CHECK

1. Most of psychology can rightfully be called common sense because psychologists prefer naturalistic observation to controlled observation. T or F?
2. A hypothesis is any careful observation made in a controlled experiment. T or F?
3. Two major problems in naturalistic observation are the effects of the observer and observer bias. T or F?
4. The _____ error involves attributing human feelings and motives to animals.

5. Correlation typically does not demonstrate causation. T or F?
6. Which correlation coefficient represents the strongest relationship?
   a. −0.86   b. +0.66   c. +0.10   d. +0.09

Critical Thinking

7. Can you think of some "common-sense" statements that contradict each other?
8. Attributing mischievous motives to a car that is not working properly is a thinking error similar to anthropomorphizing. T or F?
9. Adults who often ate Frosted Flakes cereal as children now have half the cancer rate seen in adults who never ate Frosted Flakes. What do you think explains this strange correlation?

ANSWERS

1. F 2. F 3. T 4. anthropomorphic 5. T 6. a 7. There are many examples. Here are more to add to the ones you thought of: "You can't make a silk purse out of a sow's ear" versus "Clothes make the man (or woman)." "He (or she) who hesitates is lost" versus "Haste makes waste." "Birds of a feather flock together" versus "Opposites attract." 8. True. It appears to be difficult for humans to resist thinking of other species and even machines in human terms. 9. The correlation is related to an age bias in the group of people studied. Older adults have higher cancer rates than younger adults, and Frosted Flakes weren't available during the childhoods of older people. Thus, Frosted Flakes appear to be related to cancer, when age is the real connection (Tierny, 1987).

THE PSYCHOLOGY EXPERIMENT—WHERE CAUSE MEETS EFFECT

] **SURVEYQUESTION** *How is an experiment performed?*

The most powerful research tool is an **experiment** (a formal trial undertaken to confirm or disconfirm a hypothesis). Psychologists carefully control conditions in experiments to identify cause-and-effect relationships. To perform an experiment you would do the following:

1. Directly vary a condition you think might affect behavior.
2. Create two or more groups of subjects. These groups should be alike in all ways *except* the condition you are varying.
3. Record whether varying the condition has any effect on behavior.

Assume you want to find out if hunger affects memory. First, you would form two groups of people. Then you could give the members of one group a memory test while they are hungry. The second group would take the same test after eating a meal. By comparing average memory scores for the two groups, you could tell if hunger affects memory.

As you can see, the simplest psychological experiment is based on two groups of *subjects* (animals or people whose behavior is investigated). One group is called the *experimen-*

Experiment A formal trial undertaken to confirm or disconfirm a fact or principle.

tal group; the other becomes the *control group.* The control group and the experimental group are treated exactly alike except for the condition you intentionally vary. This condition is called the *independent variable.*

Variables and Groups

A *variable* is any condition that can change and that might affect the outcome of the experiment. Identifying causes and effects in an experiment involves three types of variables:

1. **Independent variables** are conditions altered or varied by the experimenter, who sets their size, amount, or value. Independent variables are suspected *causes* for differences in behavior.
2. **Dependent variables** measure the results of the experiment. That is, they reveal the *effects* that independent variables have on *behavior.* Such effects are often revealed by measures of performance, such as test scores.
3. **Extraneous variables** are conditions that a researcher wishes to prevent from affecting the outcome of the experiment.

We can apply these terms to our hunger/memory experiment in this way: Hunger is the independent variable—we want to know if hunger affects memory. Memory (defined by scores on the memory test) is the dependent variable—we want to know if the ability to memorize depends on how hungry a person is. All other conditions that could affect memory scores are extraneous. Examples are the number of hours slept the night before the test, intelligence, or difficulty of the questions.

As you can see, an **experimental group** consists of subjects exposed to the independent variable (hunger in the preceding example). Members of the **control group** are exposed to all conditions except the independent variable.

Let's examine another simple experiment. Suppose you notice that you seem to study better while listening to music. This suggests the hypothesis that music improves learning. We could test this idea by forming an experimental group that studies with music. A control group would study without music. Then we could compare their scores on a test.

Is a control group really needed? Can't people just study with music on to see if they do better? Without a control group it would be impossible to tell if music had any effect on learning. The control group provides a *point of reference* for comparison with the scores in the experimental group. If the average test score of the experimental group is higher than the average of the control group, we can conclude that music improves learning. If there is no difference, it's obvious that the independent variable had no effect on learning.

In this experiment, the amount learned (indicated by scores on the test) is the *dependent variable.* We are asking, Does the independent variable *affect* the dependent variable? (Does music affect or influence learning?)

Experimental Control

How do we know that the people in one group aren't more intelligent than those in the other group? It's true that personal differences might affect the experiment. However, they can be controlled by randomly assigning people to groups. **Random assignment** means that a subject has an equal chance of being in either the experimental group or the control group. Randomization evenly balances personal differences in the two groups. In our musical experiment, this could be done by simply flipping a coin for each subject: Heads, and the subject is in the experimental group; tails, it's the control group. This would result in few differences in the number of people in each group who are geniuses or dunces, hungry, hung over, tall, music lovers, or whatever.

Other *extraneous,* or outside, variables—such as the amount of study time, the sex of subjects, the temperature in the room, the time of day, the amount of light, and so forth—

Courtesy of Peter S. Mueller

CONTROL GROUP   OUT OF CONTROL GROUP

Independent variable In an experiment, the condition being investigated as a possible cause of some change in behavior. The values that this variable takes are chosen by the experimenter.

Dependent variable In an experiment, the condition (usually a behavior) that is affected by the independent variable.

Extraneous variables Conditions or factors excluded from influencing the outcome of an experiment.

Experimental group In a controlled experiment, the group of subjects exposed to the independent variable or experimental condition.

Control group In a controlled experiment, the group of subjects exposed to all experimental conditions or variables *except* the independent variable.

Random assignment The use of chance (for example, flipping a coin) to assign subjects to experimental and control groups.

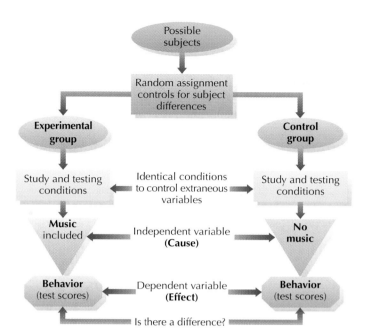

✦**FIGURE 1.8** *Elements of a simple psychological experiment to assess the effects of music during study on test scores.*

must also be prevented from affecting the outcome of an experiment. But how? Usually this is done by making all conditions (except the independent variable) *exactly* alike for both groups. When all conditions are the same for both groups—*except* the presence or absence of music—then a difference in the amount learned *must* be caused by the music (✦Fig. 1.8).

Cause and Effect

Now let's summarize. In an experiment two or more groups of subjects are treated differently with respect to the independent variable. In all other ways they are treated the same. That is, extraneous variables are equalized for all groups. The effect of the independent variable (or variables) on some behavior (the dependent variable) is then measured. In a carefully controlled experiment, the independent variable is the only possible *cause* for any *effect* noted in the dependent variable. This allows clear cause-and-effect connections to be identified (✦Fig. 1.9).

Placebo Effects, Sugar Pills, and Saltwater

Now let's do an experiment to see if the drug amphetamine (a stimulant) affects learning: Before studying, members of our experimental group take an amphetamine pill. Control group members get nothing. Later, we assess how much each subject learned. Does this experiment seem valid? Actually, it is seriously flawed.

Why? The experimental group took the drug and the control group didn't. Differences in the amount they learned must have been caused by the drug, right? No, because the drug wasn't the only difference between the groups. People in the experimental group swallowed a pill, and control subjects did not. Without using a placebo (plah-SEE-bo), it is impossible to tell if the drug affects learning. It could be that those who swallowed a pill *expected* to do better. This alone might have affected their performance, even if the pill didn't.

What is a placebo? Why would it make a difference? A *placebo* is a fake drug. Inactive substances such as sugar pills and saline (saltwater) injections are commonly used as place-

Dependent Variable

A B C — A B C

Experimental Group   Control Group

☐ Extraneous Variables
☐ Independent Variable

✦**FIGURE 1.9** *Experimental control is achieved by balancing extraneous variables for the experimental group and the control group. For example, the average age (A), education (B), and intelligence (C) of group members could be made the same for both groups. Then we could apply the independent variable to the experimental group. If their behavior (the dependent variable) changes (in comparison with the control group), the change must be caused by the independent variable.*

The placebo effect is a major factor in medical treatments. Would you also expect the placebo effect to occur in psychotherapy? (It does, which complicates studies on the effectiveness of new psychotherapies.)

bos. If a placebo has any effect, it must be based on suggestion, rather than chemistry (Quitkin, 1999).

The **placebo effect** (changes in behavior caused by belief that one has taken a drug) can be powerful. For instance, a saline injection is 70 percent as effective as morphine in reducing pain. That's why doctors sometimes prescribe placebos—especially for complaints that seem to have no physical basis. Placebos have been shown to affect pain, anxiety, depression, alertness, tension, sexual arousal, cravings for alcohol, and many other processes (Kirsch & Lynn, 1999).

How could an inert substance have any effect?   Placebos alter people's expectations about their own emotional and physical reactions. These expectancies, in turn, influence bodily functions. For example, placebos relieve pain by causing the pituitary gland to release *endorphins*. These powerful chemicals are similar to painkilling opiate drugs such as morphine (ter Riet et al., 1998). (See Chapter 2 for more information.) Placebos also gain some of their effect through learning. Because we associate taking medicine with feeling better, inert placebos can often make us feel better, too (Brody & Brody, 2000).

Controlling Placebo Effects

To control for placebo effects, we could use a **single-blind experiment.** In this case, subjects do not know if they are receiving a real drug or a placebo. All subjects get a pill or injection. People in the experimental group get a real drug and the control group gets a placebo. Because subjects are *blind* as to whether they received the drug, their expectations are the same. Any difference in their behavior must be caused by the drug.

Keeping subjects "blind" is not necessarily enough, however. In a **double-blind experiment** neither subjects nor experimenters know who has received a drug and who has taken a placebo. This keeps researchers from unconsciously influencing subjects. Typically, someone else prepares the pills or injections so that experimenters don't know until after testing who got what. Double-blind testing has shown that about 50 percent of the effectiveness of antidepressant drugs, such as the "wonder drug" Prozac, is due to the placebo effect (Kirsch & Sapirstein, 1998). It's very likely that much of the current popularity of herbal health remedies is also based on the placebo effect (Seidman, 2001).

Sometimes, researchers themselves affect experiments by influencing the behavior of their subjects. Let's see how this occurs.

The Experimenter Effect

How could a researcher influence subjects?   The **experimenter effect** (changes in behavior caused by the unintended influence of an experimenter) is a common problem in psychological research. In essence, experimenters run the risk of finding what they expect to find. This occurs because humans are very sensitive to hints about what is expected of them (Rosenthal, 1994).

The experimenter effect even applies outside the laboratory. Psychologist Robert Rosenthal (1973) reports an example of how expectations can influence people: At the U.S. Air Force Academy Preparatory School, 100 airmen were randomly assigned to 5 different math classes. Their teachers did not know about this random placement. Instead, each teacher was told that his or her students had unusually high or low ability. Students in the classes labeled "high ability" improved much more in math scores than those in "low-ability" classes. Yet initially, all the classes had students of equal ability.

Apparently, the teachers subtly communicated their expectations to students. Most likely, they did this through tone of voice, body language, and by giving encouragement or criticism. Their "hints," in turn, created a self-fulfilling prophecy that affected the students. A *self-fulfilling prophecy* is a prediction that prompts people to act in ways that make the prediction come true. In short, people sometimes become what we prophesy for them. It is wise to remember that others tend to live *up* or *down* to our expectations for them (Jussim & Eccles, 1992; Madon, Jussim, & Eccles, 1997).

Placebo effect Changes in behavior due to expectations that a drug (or other treatment) will have some effect.

Single-blind experiment An arrangement in which subjects remain unaware of whether they are in the experimental group or the control group.

Double-blind experiment An arrangement in which both subjects and experimenters are unaware of whether subjects are in the experimental group or the control group.

Experimenter effect Changes in subjects' behavior caused by the unintended influence of an experimenter's actions.

STUDYBREAK ⓨ *The Psychology Experiment*

RELATE

In a sense, we all conduct little experiments to detect cause-and-effect connections. If you are interested in gardening, for example, you might try adding plant food to one bed of flowers but not another. The question then becomes, Does the use of plant food (the independent variable) affect the size of the flowers (the dependent variable)? By comparing unfed plants (the control group) to those receiving plant food (the experimental group), you could find out if plant food is worth using. Can you think of at least one informal experiment you've run in the last month? What were the variables? What was the outcome?

LEARNING CHECK

1. To understand cause and effect, a simple psychological experiment is based on creating two groups: the _____ group and the _____ group.
2. There are three types of variables to consider in an experiment: _____ variables (which are manipulated by the experimenter), _____ variables (which measure the outcome of the experiment), and _____ variables (factors to be excluded in a particular experiment).

3. A researcher performs an experiment to learn if room temperature affects the amount of aggression displayed by college students under crowded conditions in a simulated prison environment. In this experiment, the independent variable is which of the following?
   a. room temperature   b. the amount of aggression
   c. crowding   d. the simulated prison environment
4. A procedure used to control both the placebo effect and the experimenter effect in drug experiments is the
   a. correlation method   b. extraneous prophecy   c. double-blind technique   d. random assignment of subjects

Critical Thinking

5. There is a loophole in the statement, "I've been taking vitamin C tablets, and I haven't had a cold all year. Vitamin C is great!" What is the loophole?
6. How would you determine if sugary breakfasts affect children's activity levels and their ability to learn in school?
7. People who believe strongly in astrology have personality characteristics that actually match, to a degree, those predicted by their astrological signs. Can you explain why this occurs?

ANSWERS

1. experimental, control 2. independent, dependent, extraneous 3. a 4. c 5. The statement implies that vitamin C prevents colds. However, not getting a cold could just be a coincidence. A controlled experiment with a group given vitamin C and a control group not taking vitamin C would be needed to learn if vitamin C actually has any effect on susceptibility to colds. 6. An actual experiment on this question used a double-blind design in which children were given a breakfast drink containing either 50 grams of sucrose (sugar), a placebo (aspartame), or only a very small amount of sucrose. Observed changes in activity levels and in scores on a learning task did not support the view that sugar causes major changes in children's behavior (Rosen et al., 1988). 7. Belief in astrology can create a self-fulfilling prophecy in which people alter their behaviors and self-concepts to match their astrological signs (van Rooij, 1994).

THE CLINICAL METHOD—DATA BY THE CASE

] SURVEYQUESTION *What other research methods do psychologists use?*

It can be difficult or impossible to use the experimental method to study mental disorders, such as depression or psychosis. Many experiments are impractical, unethical, or impossible to do. In such instances, a **case study** (an in-depth focus on a single subject) may be the best source of information. Clinical psychologists rely heavily on case studies, especially as a way to investigate rare or unusual problems.

Case studies may sometimes be thought of as **natural clinical tests** (accidents or other natural events that provide psychological data). Gunshot wounds, brain tumors, accidental poisonings, and similar disasters provide much information about the human brain. One remarkable case from the history of psychology is reported by Dr. J. M. Harlow (1868). Phineas Gage, a young foreman on a work crew, had a 13-pound steel rod blown through the front of his brain by a dynamite explosion (◆Fig. 1.10). Amazingly, he survived the accident. Within 2 months, Gage could walk, talk, and move normally. But the injury forever changed his personality. Instead of the honest and dependable worker he had been before, Gage became a surly, foulmouthed liar. Dr. Harlow carefully recorded all the details of what was perhaps the first in-depth case study of an accidental frontal lobotomy (the destruction of front brain matter).

When a Los Angeles carpenter named Michael Melnick suffered a similar injury, he recovered completely, with no sign of lasting ill effects. Melnick's very different reaction to a

Case study An in-depth focus on all aspects of a single person.

Natural clinical test A natural event that provides data on a psychological phenomenon.

The Genain Sisters—Trouble Times Four

A classic case study in psychology concerns four identical quadruplets known as the Genain sisters. In addition to having identical genes, all four women became schizophrenic before age 25. By the time they were in high school, the sisters began to act strangely. Hester broke light bulbs and tore buttons off her clothes. By age 20, Nora moaned at meals and complained that the bones in her neck were slipping. At night she stood on her knees and elbows in bed until they bled. At age 22, Iris complained "I am pinned down. Someone wants to fight and I don't want to." Soon after, she "went to pieces." She screamed, drooled at meals, and talked of hearing voices. Myra, who was the fourth identical quad, panicked easily but did not actually break down until age 24 (Rosenthal & Quinn, 1977).

The Genains, who are now in their late 60s, have been in and out of mental hospitals all their lives. The fact that they share identical genes suggests that mental disorders are influenced by heredity. The fact that some of the sisters are more disturbed than others suggests that environmental conditions are also a factor in mental illness. Indeed, Myra, the least ill of the four, was the only sister who was able to avoid her father, an alcoholic who terrorized, spied on, and sexually molested the girls. (See Chapter 12 for more information about the causes of schizophrenia.)

The Genain sisters have been studied for 40 years. The chances of four identical quads all becoming schizophrenic are about 1 in 1.5 billion. Thus, cases such as theirs provide insights that can't be obtained by any other means (Edwards, 1998; Mirsky et al., 2000).

◆FIGURE 1.10 *Some of the earliest information on the effects of damage to frontal areas of the brain came from a case study of the accidental injury of Phineas Gage.*

similar injury shows why psychologists prefer controlled experiments and often use lab animals for studies of the brain. Case studies lack formal control groups. This, of course, limits the conclusions that can be drawn from clinical observations. Nonetheless, case studies are especially valuable for studying rare events, such as unusual mental disorders, childhood "geniuses," or "rampage" school shootings (Harding, Fox, & Mehta, 2002). (See "The Genain Sisters—Trouble Times Four.") Also, case studies of psychotherapy have provided many useful ideas about how to treat emotional problems (Hersen, 2002).

SURVEY METHOD—HERE, HAVE A SAMPLE

Sometimes psychologists would like to ask everyone in the world a few well-chosen questions: "Do you drink alcoholic beverages? How often per week?" "What form of discipline did your parents use when you were a child?" "What is the most creative thing you've done?" The answers to such questions can reveal much about behavior. But because it is impossible to question everyone, doing a survey is often more practical.

In the **survey method,** public polling techniques are used to answer psychological questions. Typically, people in a representative sample are asked a series of carefully worded questions. A **representative sample** is a small group that accurately reflects a larger population. A good sample must include the same proportion of men, women, young, old, professionals, blue-collar workers, Republicans, Democrats, whites, African Americans, Latinos, Asians, and so on, as found in the population as a whole.

A *population* is an entire group of animals or people belonging to a particular category (for example, all college students or all married women). Ultimately, we are interested in entire populations. But by selecting a smaller sample, we can draw conclusions about the larger group without polling each and every person. Representative samples are often obtained by *randomly* selecting who will be included (◆Fig. 1.11). (Notice that this is similar to randomly assigning subjects to groups in an experiment.)

How accurate is the survey method? Modern surveys such as the Gallup and Harris polls are quite accurate. The Gallup poll has erred in its election predictions by only 1.5 percent since 1954. However, if a survey is based on a biased sample, it might paint a false picture. A *biased sample* does not accurately reflect the population from which it was drawn. Surveys done by magazines, Web sites, and online information services can be quite biased. Surveys on the use of illicit drugs done by *Cosmopolitan* and *Rolling Stone* magazines would probably produce very different results—neither of which would represent the general population. That's why psychologists using the survey method go to great lengths to ensure that their samples are representative. Fortunately, people can often be polled by telephone, which makes it easier to obtain large samples. Even if one person of three refuses to answer survey questions, the results are still likely to be valid (Krosnick, 1999).

Survey method The use of public polling techniques to answer psychological questions.

Representative sample A small, randomly selected part of a larger population that accurately reflects characteristics of the whole population.

Nonrandom Sample

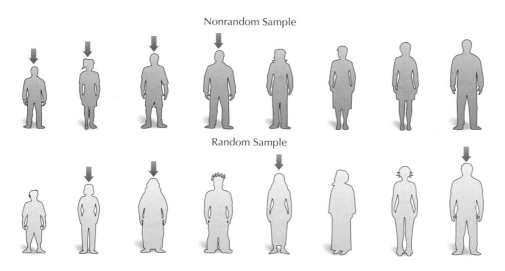

Random Sample

✦FIG. 1.11 *If you were conducting a survey in which a person's height might be an important variable, the non-random sample would be very unrepresentative. The random sample, selected using a table of random numbers, better represents the group as a whole.*

Internet Surveys

Recently, psychologists have started doing surveys and experiments on the Internet. Web-based research has the advantage of low cost and it can reach very large groups of people. However, psychologists are well aware that samples obtained through Web sites are not representative. Nevertheless, Internet studies have provided interesting information about topics such as anger, decision-making, religion, racial prejudice, what disgusts people, sexual attitudes, and much more. It is very likely that in the future many studies will be done online and that some of the limitations of Internet research will be overcome (Birnbaum, 2000).

Social Desirability

Even well-designed surveys may be limited by another problem. If a psychologist were to ask you detailed questions about your sexual history and current sexual behavior, how accurate would your replies be? Would you exaggerate? Would you be embarrassed? Replies to survey questions are not always accurate or truthful. Many people show a distinct *courtesy bias* (a tendency to give "polite" or socially desirable answers). For example, answers to questions concerning sex, drinking or drug use, income, and church attendance tend to be less than truthful. Likewise, the week after an election, more people will say they voted than actually did (Krosnick, 1999).

Summary

Despite their limitations, surveys frequently produce valuable information. For instance, the survey method was used to find out how often sexual harassment occurs and to raise public awareness about the problem (Janus & Janus, 1993). To sum up, the survey method can be a powerful research tool. Like other methods, it has limitations, but new techniques and strategies are providing valuable information about our behavior (Krosnick, 1999).

SCIENCE AND CRITICAL THINKING— HEALTHY SKEPTICISM

] SURVEYQUESTION *What is critical thinking?*

Is so much emphasis on research really necessary in psychology?   In a word, yes. As we have seen, science is a powerful way of asking questions about the world and getting trustworthy answers. Your awareness of this fact should help make you a more critical observer of human behavior. ▲Table 1.5 summarizes many of the important ideas we have covered.

Most of us would be skeptical when buying a used car. But all too often, we may be tempted to "buy" outrageous claims about topics such as dowsing for water, the Bermuda Triangle, the occult, UFOs, Tarot cards, healing crystals, herbal remedies, and so forth. Likewise,

▲TABLE 1.5	Comparison of Psychological Research Methods	
	Advantages	*Disadvantages*
NATURALISTIC OBSERVATION	Behavior is observed in a natural setting; much information is obtained, and hypotheses and questions for additional research are formed	Little or no control is possible; observed behavior may be altered by the presence of the observer; observations may be biased; causes cannot be conclusively identified
CORRELATIONAL METHOD	Demonstrates the existence of relationships; allows prediction; can be used in lab, clinic, or natural setting	Little or no control is possible; relationships may be coincidental; cause-and-effect relationships cannot be confirmed
EXPERIMENTAL METHOD	Clear cause-and-effect relationships can be identified; powerful controlled observations can be staged; no need to wait for natural event	May be somewhat artificial; some natural behavior not easily studied in laboratory (field experiments may avoid these objections)
CLINICAL METHOD	Takes advantage of "natural clinical trials" and allows investigation of rare or unusual problems or events	Little or no control is possible; does not provide a control group for comparison, subjective interpretation is often necessary, a single case may be misleading or unrepresentative
SURVEY METHOD	Allows information about large numbers of people to be gathered; can address questions not answered by other approaches	Obtaining a representative sample is critical and can be difficult to do; answers may be inaccurate; people may not do what they say or say what they do

most of us easily accept our ignorance of sub-atomic physics. But because we deal with human behavior every day, we tend to think that we already know what is true in psychology.

For these and many more reasons, learning to think critically is one of the lasting benefits of a college education. **Critical thinking** refers to an ability to evaluate, compare, analyze, critique, and synthesize information. Critical thinkers are willing to ask the hard questions, including those that challenge conventional wisdom. For example, many people believe that punishment (a spanking) is a good way to reinforce learning in children. Actually, nothing could be farther from the truth (Gershoff, 2002). That's why a critical thinker would immediately ask: "Does punishment work? If so, when? Under what conditions does it not work? What are its drawbacks? Are there better ways to guide learning?"

Thinking about Behavior

The core of critical thinking is a willingness to actively *evaluate* ideas. Critical thinkers analyze the evidence supporting their beliefs and probe for weaknesses in their reasoning. They question assumptions and look for alternate conclusions. True knowledge, they recognize, comes from constantly revising our understanding of the world. As Susan Blackmore (2001) said when her studies caused her to abandon some long-held beliefs, "Admitting you are wrong is always hard—even though it's a skill that every psychologist has to learn."

Critical thinking is built upon four basic principles (Gill, 1991; Shore, 1990):

1. *Few "truths" transcend the need for empirical testing.* It is true that religious beliefs and personal values may be held without supporting evidence. But most other ideas can be evaluated by applying the rules of logic and evidence.
2. *Judging the quality of evidence is crucial.* Imagine you are a juror in a courtroom, judging claims made by two battling lawyers. To decide correctly, you can't just weigh the amount of evidence. You must also critically evaluate the *quality* of the evidence. Then you can give greater weight to the most credible facts.
3. *Authority or claimed expertise does not automatically make an idea true.* Just because a teacher, guru, celebrity, or authority is convinced or sincere doesn't mean you should automatically believe them. Always ask, "What evidence convinced her or him? How good is it? Is there a better explanation?"
4. *Critical thinking requires an open mind.* Be prepared to consider daring departures and go wherever the evidence leads. However, don't become so "open-minded" that you are simply gullible. Critical thinkers strike a balance between open-mindedness and healthy skepticism. They are ready to change their views when new evidence arises (Bartz, 2002).

Critical thinking An ability to evaluate, compare, analyze, critique, and synthesize information.

To put these principles into action, here are some questions to ask over and over again as you evaluate new information (Bartz, 1990):

1. What claims are being made?
2. What test (if any) of these claims has been made?
3. Who did the test? How good is the evidence?
4. What were the nature and quality of the tests? Are they credible? Can they be repeated?
5. How reliable and trustworthy were the investigators? Do they have conflicts of interest? Do their findings appear to be objective? Has any other independent researcher duplicated the findings?
6. Finally, how much credibility can the claim be given? High, medium, low, provisional?

A course in psychology naturally enriches thinking skills. To add to the process, all upcoming chapters include Critical Thinking questions like the ones you have seen here. Tackling these questions will sharpen your thinking abilities and make learning more lively. For an immediate thinking challenge, let's take a critical look at several non-scientific systems that claim to explain behavior.

PSEUDOPSYCHOLOGIES—PALMS, PLANETS, AND PERSONALITY

] SURVEYQUESTION *How does psychology differ from false explanations of behavior?*

A **pseudopsychology** (SUE-doe-psychology) is any unfounded system that resembles psychology. Many pseudopsychologies give the appearance of science but are actually false. (*Pseudo* means "false.") Pseudopsychologies change little over time because their followers avoid evidence that contradicts their beliefs (Kelly & Saklofske, 1994). Scientists, in contrast, actively look for contradictions as a way to advance knowledge. They are skeptical critics of their own theories (Woodward & Goodstein, 1996).

Can you give some examples of false psychologies? *Palmistry* is a pseudopsychology that claims lines on the hand reveal personality traits and predict the future. Despite the overwhelming evidence against this, palmists can still be found separating the gullible from their money in many cities. A similar false system is *phrenology,* which claims that personality traits are revealed by the shape of the skull. Phrenology was popularized in the nineteenth century by Franz Gall, a German anatomy teacher. Modern research has long since shown that bumps on the head have nothing to do with talents or abilities. In fact, the phrenologists were so far off that they listed the part of the brain that controls hearing as a center for "combativeness"!

At first glance, a pseudopsychology called *graphology* might seem more reasonable. Graphologists claim that personality traits are revealed by handwriting. Based on such claims, some companies use graphologists to select job candidates. This is troubling because graphologists score close to zero on tests of accuracy in rating personality (Ben-Shakhar et al., 1986). In fact, graphologists do no better than untrained college students in rating personality and job performance (Neter & Ben-Shakhar, 1989; Rafaeli & Klimoski, 1983). (By the way, graphology's failure at revealing personality should be separated from its value for detecting forgeries.)

Graphology might seem harmless enough. However, this false system has been used to determine who is hired, given bank credit, or selected for juries. In these and similar situations, pseudopsychologies do, in fact, harm people (Barker, 1993; Beyerstein & Beyerstein, 1992).

If pseudopsychologies have no scientific basis, how do they survive and why are they popular? There are several reasons, all of which can be demonstrated by a critique of astrology.

Phrenology was an attempt to assess personality characteristics by examining various areas of the skull. Phrenologists used charts such as the one shown here as guides. Like other pseudopsychologists, phrenologists made no attempt to empirically verify their concepts.

Would you hire this man? Here's a sample of your author's handwriting. What do you think it reveals? Your interpretations are likely to be as accurate (or inaccurate) as those of a graphologist.

Pseudopsychology Any false and unscientific system of beliefs and practices that is offered as an explanation of behavior.

Problems in the Stars

Astrology is probably the most popular pseudopsychology. Astrology holds that the positions of the stars and planets at the time of one's birth determine personality traits and affect behavior. Like other pseudopsychologies, astrology has repeatedly been shown to have no scientific validity (Kelly, 1998, 1999; Stewart, 1996). The objections to astrology are numerous and devastating:

1. The zodiac has shifted in the sky by one full constellation since astrology was first set up. However, most astrologers simply ignore this shift. (In other words, if astrology calls you a Scorpio you are really a Libra, and so forth.)
2. There is no connection between the "compatibility" of couples' astrological signs and their marriage and divorce rates.
3. Studies have found no connection between astrological signs and leadership, physical characteristics, career choices, or personality traits.
4. Astrologers have failed to explain why the moment of birth should be more important than the moment of conception.
5. A study of more than 3,000 predictions by famous astrologers found that only a small percentage were fulfilled. These "successful" predictions tended to be vague ("There will be a tragedy somewhere in the east in the spring") or easily guessed from current events.
6. If astrologers are asked to match people with their horoscopes, they do no better than would be expected by chance (Kelly, 1999).
7. A few astrologers have tried to test astrology. Their results have been just as negative as those obtained by critics. (Sources: Kelly, 1998, 1999; Martens & Trachet, 1998; Stewart, 1996.)

In short, astrology doesn't work.

Then why does astrology often seem to work?   The following discussion tells why.

Uncritical Acceptance

If you have ever had your astrological chart done, you may have been impressed with its apparent accuracy. However, such perceptions are typically based on **uncritical acceptance** (the tendency to believe positive or flattering descriptions of yourself). Many astrological charts are made up of mostly flattering traits. Naturally, when your personality is described in *desirable* terms, it is hard to deny that the description has the "ring of truth." How much acceptance would astrology receive if a birth sign read like this:

> **Virgo:** You are the logical type and hate disorder. Your nitpicking is unbearable to your friends. You are cold, unemotional, and usually fall asleep while making love. Virgos make good doorstops.

Positive Instances

Even when an astrological description contains a mixture of good and bad traits, it might seem accurate. To find out why, read the following personality description:

> *YOUR PERSONALITY PROFILE*
>
> You have a strong need for other people to like you and for them to admire you. You have a tendency to be critical of yourself. You have a great deal of unused energy which you have not turned to your advantage. While you have some personality weaknesses, you are generally able to compensate for them. Your sexual adjustment has presented some problems for you. Disciplined and controlled on the outside, you tend to be worrisome and insecure inside. At times you have serious doubts as to whether you have made the right decision or done the right thing. You prefer a certain amount of change and variety and become dissatisfied when hemmed in by restrictions and limitations. You pride yourself on being an independent thinker and do not accept other opinions without satisfac-

Uncritical acceptance The tendency to believe generally positive or flattering descriptions of oneself.

tory proof. You have found it unwise to be too frank in revealing yourself to others. At times you are extroverted, affable, sociable, while at other times you are introverted, wary, and reserved. Some of your aspirations tend to be pretty unrealistic.*

Does this describe your personality? A psychologist read this summary individually to college students who had taken a personality test. Only 5 students out of 79 felt that the description was inaccurate. Another study found that people rated this "personality profile" as more accurate than their actual horoscopes (French et al., 1991).

Reread the description and you will see that it contains both sides of several personality dimensions ("At times you are extroverted . . . while at other times you are introverted"). Its apparent accuracy is an illusion based on the **fallacy of positive instances,** in which we remember or notice things that confirm our expectations and forget the rest. The pseudopsychologies thrive on this effect. For example, you can always find "Leo characteristics" in a Leo. If you looked, however, you could also find "Gemini characteristics," "Scorpio characteristics," or whatever.

The fallacy of positive instances is used by various "psychic mediums" who pretend to communicate with the deceased friends and relatives of audience members. An analysis of their performances shows that the number of "hits" (correct statements) made by these fakes tends to be very low. Nevertheless, many viewers are impressed because of the natural tendency to remember apparent hits and ignore misses. Also, embarrassing misses are edited out before the shows appear on television (Nickell, 2001).

Non Sequitur, © 1993. Reprinted by permission of Universal Press Syndicate.

The Barnum Effect

Pseudopsychologies also take advantage of the **Barnum effect,** which is a tendency to consider personal descriptions accurate if they are stated in general terms. P. T. Barnum, the famed circus showman, had a formula for success: "Always have a little something for everybody." Like the all-purpose personality profile, palm readings, fortunes, horoscopes, and other products of pseudopsychology are stated in such general terms that they can hardly miss. There is always "a little something for everybody." To observe the Barnum effect, read *all 12* of the daily horoscopes found in newspapers for several days. You will find that predictions for other signs fit events as well as those for your own sign do.

Astrology's popularity shows that many people have difficulty separating valid psychology from systems that seem valid but are not. The goal of this discussion, then, has been to make you a more critical observer of human behavior and to clarify what is, and what is not, psychology. Here is what the "stars" say about your future:

> Emphasis now on education and personal improvement. A learning experience of lasting value awaits you. Take care of scholastic responsibilities before engaging in recreation. The word *psychology* figures prominently in your future.

Pseudopsychologies might seem like no more than a nuisance, but they can do harm. For instance, people seeking treatment for psychological disorders may become the victims of self-appointed "experts" who offer ineffective, pseudoscientific "therapies" (Kalal, 1999). Valid psychological principles are based on observation and evidence, not fads, opinions, or wishful thinking.

---

*Reprinted with permission of author and publisher from: R. E. Ulrich, T. J. Stachnik, and N. R. Stainton, "Student acceptance of generalized personality interpretations," *Psychological Reports,* 13, 1963, 831–834. © 1963 Southern Universities Press.

Fallacy of positive instances The tendency to remember or notice information that fits one's expectations while forgetting discrepancies.

Barnum effect The tendency to consider a personal description accurate if it is stated in very general terms.

A Look Ahead

Now that you have an overview of psychology, I'd like to let psychologists Gary VandenBos and Brenda Bryant summarize:

> Psychologists are explorers and discoverers. They explore the reactions of human beings to small frustrations and great successes, to pleasing colors and the aftermath of disaster, always looking for answers to how and why people think, feel, and behave as they do. . . . The psychologist, regardless of where she or he may work, is always applying what is known in an effort to resolve the unknown. The psychologist, no matter how small the question being asked may appear to be, is looking for the larger answer (VandenBos & Bryant, 1987).

To help you get the most out of psychology, each chapter of this text includes a "Psychology in Action" section like the one that follows. There you will find ideas you can actually use, now or in the future. To complete our discussion, let's take a critical look at information reported in the popular press. You should find this an interesting way to conclude our first tour of psychology and its methods.

STUDYBREAK   *Clinical and Survey Methods, Critical Thinking*

RELATE

It is nearly impossible to get through a day without encountering people who believe in pseudopsychologies or who make unscientific or unfounded statements. How stringently do you evaluate your own beliefs and the claims made by others? Critical thinking requires effort and discipline, but high-quality information is the reward.

LEARNING CHECK

1. Case studies can often be thought of as natural tests and are frequently used by clinical psychologists. T or F?
2. For the survey method to be valid, a representative sample of people must be polled. T or F?
3. Amnesia would most likely be investigated by use of
   a. a representative sample   b. field experiments   c. the double-blind procedure   d. case studies
4. _____ is the out-dated theory that personality is revealed by the skull. It was popularized by Franz _____.

5. The fallacy of positive instances refers to graphology's accepted value for the detection of forgeries. T or F?
6. Personality descriptions provided by pseudopsychologies are stated in general terms that provide "a little something for everybody." This fact is the basis of the
   a. palmist's fallacy   b. uncritical acceptance pattern   c. fallacy of positive instances   d. Barnum effect

Critical Thinking

7. A psychologist conducting a survey at a shopping mall (The Gallery of Wretched Excess) flips a coin before stopping passersby. If the coin shows heads, he interviews the person; if it shows tails, he skips that person. Has the psychologist obtained a random sample?

ANSWERS

1. T 2. T 3. d 4. Phrenology, Gall 5. F 6. d 7. The psychologist's coin flips *might* produce a reasonably good sample of people *at the mall.* The real problem is that people who go to the mall may be mostly from one part of town, from upper income groups, or from some other non-representative group. The psychologist's sample is likely to be seriously flawed.

Psychology in Action

Psychology in the News—Separating Fact from Fiction

] SURVEYQUESTION *How good is psychological information found in the popular media?*

Psychology is a popular topic in magazines and newspapers. Unfortunately, much of what you will read is based on wishful thinking rather than science. Here are some suggestions for separating high-quality information from misleading fiction.

Suggestion 1

Be skeptical.

Reports in the popular press tend to be made uncritically and with a definite bias toward reporting "astonishing" findings. Remember, saying, "That's incredible" means, "That's not believable"—which is often true.

Example 1: Some years ago, news articles described an amazing new "sixth sense" called "dermo-optical perception." A few gifted people, the articles claimed, could use their fingertips to identify colors and read print while blindfolded.

In reality, such "abilities" are based on what stage magicians call a "nose peek." It is impossible to prepare a blindfold (without damaging the eyes) that does not leave a tiny space on each side of the nose. Were the people who claimed to have "x-ray eyes" taking nose peeks? Apparently they were, because "dermo-optical abilities" disappeared as soon as the opportunity to peek was controlled.

Example 2: The *National Enquirer* once reported that "Top University Researchers Reveal . . . 8 million Americans may have been abducted by UFOs." However, one of the researchers cited in the article actually concluded "the public can rest assured that there is no evidence that millions of Americans are being abducted." In other words, the *Enquirer* story completely *reversed* the real findings. You'll find similar misinformation and sensationalism throughout the popular media. Be on guard.

Example 3: The Internet is awash with rumors, hoaxes, half-truths, and urban legends. One recent classic was a story about the health department in Oregon seeking a Klingon interpreter for mental health patients who only speak in the fictional language used on the *Star Trek* TV series.

This tale started when a newspaper reported that Klingon was on a list of languages that some psychiatric patients claimed they could speak. The article specifically noted that "in reality, no patient has yet tried to communicate in Klingon." Nevertheless, as the story spread around the Web, the idea that Oregon was looking for someone fluent in Klingon had become a "fact" (O'Neill, 2003).

Suggestion 2

Consider the source of information.

It should come as no surprise that information used to sell a product often reflects a desire for profit rather than the objective truth. Here is a typical advertising claim: "Government tests prove that no pain reliever is stronger or more effective than Brand X aspirin." A statement like this usually means that there was *no difference* between the products tested. No other pain reliever was stronger or more effective. But none was weaker, either.

Keep the source in mind when reading the claims of makers of home biofeedback machines, sleep-learning devices, subliminal tapes, and the like. Remember that psychological services may be merchandised as well. Be wary of expensive courses that promise instant mental health and happiness, increased efficiency, memory, ESP or psychic ability, control of the unconscious mind, an end to smoking, and so on. Usually they are promoted with a few testimonials and many unsupported claims (Lilienfeld, 1998).

Psychic claims should be viewed with special caution. Stage mentalists make a living by deceiving the public. Understandably, they are highly interested in promoting belief in their nonexistent powers. Psychic phenomena, when (and if) they do occur, are quite unpredictable. It would be impossible for a mentalist to do three shows a night, six nights a week without consistently using deception. The same is true of the so-called "psychic advisors" promoted in TV commercials. These charlatans make use of the Barnum effect to create an illusion that they know private information about the people who call them (Nickell, 2001).

Suggestion 3

Ask yourself if there was a control group.

The key importance of a control group in any experiment is frequently overlooked by the unsophisticated—an error to which you are no longer susceptible! The popular press is full of reports of "experiments" performed without control groups: "Talking to Plants Speeds

Firewalking is based on simple physics, not on any form of supernatural psychological control. The temperature of the coals may be as high as 1,200°F. However, coals are like the air in a hot oven: They are very inefficient at transferring heat during brief contact.

© John Nordell/The Image Works

Growth"; "Special Diet Controls Hyperactivity in Children"; "Food Shows Less Spoilage in Pyramid Chamber"; "Graduates of Firewalking Seminar Risk Their Soles."

Consider the last example for a moment. In recent years, expensive commercial courses have been promoted to teach people to walk barefoot on hot coals. (Why anyone would want to do this is itself an interesting question.) Firewalkers supposedly protect their feet with a technique called "neurolinguistic programming." Many people have paid good money to learn the technique, and most do manage a quick walk on the coals. But is the technique necessary? And is anything remarkable happening? We need a comparison group!

Fortunately, physicist Bernard Leikind has provided one. Leikind showed with volunteers that anyone (with reasonably callused feet) can walk over a bed of coals without being burned. The reason is that the coals, which are light, fluffy carbon, transmit little heat when touched. The principle involved is similar to briefly putting your hand in a hot oven. If you touch a pan, you will be burned because metal transfers heat efficiently. But if your hand stays in the heated air you'll be fine because air transmits little heat (Mitchell, 1987). Mystery solved.

Suggestion 4

Look for errors in distinguishing between correlation and causation.

As you now know, it is dangerous to presume that one thing *caused* another just because they are correlated. In spite of this, you will see many claims based on questionable correlations. Here's an example of mistaking correlation for causation: Jeanne Dixon, an astrologer, once answered a group of prominent scientists—who had declared that there is no scientific foundation for astrology—by saying, "They would do well to check the records at their local police stations, where they will learn that the rate of violent crime rises and falls with lunar cycles." Dixon, of course, believes that the moon affects human behavior.

If it is true that violent crime is more frequent at certain times of the month, doesn't that prove her point? Far from it. Increased crime could be due to darker nights, the fact that many people expect others to act crazier, or any number of similar factors. More important, direct studies of the alleged "lunar effect" have shown that it doesn't occur (Simon, 1998; Wilkinson et al., 1997). Moonstruck criminals, along with "moon madness," are a fiction (Raison, Klein, & Steckler, 1999).

Suggestion 5

Be sure to distinguish between observation and inference.

If you see a person *crying,* is it correct to assume that she or he is *sad?* Although it seems reasonable to make this assumption, it is actually quite risky. We can observe objectively that the person is crying, but to *infer* sadness might be in error. It could be that the individual has just peeled 5 pounds of onions. Or maybe he or she just won a million-dollar lottery or is trying contact lenses for the first time.

Psychologists, politicians, physicians, scientists, and other experts often go far beyond the available facts in their claims. This does not mean that their inferences, opinions, and interpretations have no value; the opinion of an expert on the causes of mental illness, criminal behavior, learning problems, or whatever can be revealing. But be careful to distinguish between fact and opinion.

Suggestion 6

Beware of over-simplifications, especially those motivated by monetary gain.

Courses or programs that offer a "new personality in three sessions," "six steps to love and fulfillment in marriage," or newly discovered "secrets of unlocking the powers of the mind" should be immediately suspect.

An excellent example of over-simplification is provided by a brochure titled "Dr. Joyce Brothers Asks: How Do You Rate as a 'Superwoman'?" Dr. Brothers, a "media" psychologist who has no private practice and is not known for research, wrote the brochure as a consultant for the Aerosol Packaging Council of the Chemical Specialties Manufacturers Association. A typical suggestion in this brochure tells how to enhance a marriage: "Sweep him off to a weekend hideaway. Tip: When he's not looking spray a touch of your favorite *aerosol* cologne mist on the bed sheets and pillows" (italics added). Sure, Joyce.

Suggestion 7

Remember, "for example" is no proof.

After reading this chapter you should be sensitive to the danger of selecting single examples. If you read, "Law student passes state bar exam using sleep-learning device," don't rush out to buy one. Systematic research has shown that these devices are of little or no value (Druckman & Bjork, 1994; Wood et al., 1992). A corollary to this suggestion is to ask, Are the reported observations important or widely applicable?

Examples, anecdotes, single cases, and testimonials are all potentially deceptive. Unfortunately, *individual cases* tell nothing about what is true *in general* (Stanovich, 2001). For instance, studies of large groups of people show that smoking increases the likelihood of lung cancer. It doesn't matter if you know a lifelong heavy smoker who is 94 years old. The general finding is the one to remember.

Summary

We are all bombarded daily with such a mass of new information that it is difficult to absorb it. The available knowledge, even in a limited area such as psychology, biology, medicine, or contemporary rock music, is so vast that no single person can completely know and comprehend it. With this situation in mind, it becomes increasingly important that you become a critical, selective, and informed consumer of information.

STUDYBREAK **Y** *Psychology in the Media*

RELATE

Do you tend to assume that a statement must be true if it is in print, on television, or made by an authority? How actively do you evaluate and question claims found in the media? Could you be a more critical consumer of information? *Should* you be a more critical consumer of information?

LEARNING CHECK

1. Newspaper accounts of dermo-optical perception have generally reported only the results of carefully designed psychological experiments. T or F?
2. Stage mentalists and psychics often use deception in their acts. T or F?

3. Blaming the lunar cycle for variations in the rate of violent crime is an example of mistaking correlation for causation. T or F?
4. If a law student uses a sleep-learning device to pass the bar exam, it proves that the device works. T or F?

Critical Thinking

5. Many parents believe that children become "hyperactive" when they eat too much sugar, and some early studies seemed to confirm this connection. However, we now know that eating sugar rarely has any effect on children. Why do you think that sugar appears to cause hyperactivity?

ANSWERS

1. F 2. T 3. T 4. F 5. This is another case of mistaking correlation for causation. Children who are hyperactive might eat more sugar (and other foods) to fuel their frenetic activity levels.

CHAPTER IN REVIEW

Major Points

- Psychology is the science of behavior and mental processes. Psychology provides objective answers to questions about human behavior.
- Psychologists gather scientific data in order to describe, understand, predict, and control behavior.
- The scientific method consists of highly refined procedures for observing the natural world, testing hypotheses, and drawing valid conclusions.
- Psychologists use several specialized research methods. Each has strengths and weaknesses, so all are needed to fully investigate human behavior.
- Experimentation is the most powerful way to identify cause-and-effect relationships.
- Critical thinking is central to the scientific method, to psychology, and to effective behavior in general.
- The popular media are rife with inaccurate information. It is essential to critically evaluate information, no matter what its source may be.

Summary

What is psychology? What are its goals?

- Psychology is the scientific study of behavior and mental processes.
- Some major areas of research in psychology are comparative, learning, sensation, perception, personality, biopsychology, motivation and emotion, social, cognitive, developmental, the psychology of gender, cultural psychology, and evolutionary psychology.
- Psychologists may be directly interested in animal behavior, or they may study animals as models of human behavior.
- As a science, psychology's goals are to describe, understand, predict, and control behavior.

How did psychology emerge as a field of knowledge?

- Historically, psychology is an outgrowth of philosophy.
- The first psychological laboratory was established in Germany by Wilhelm Wundt, who tried to study conscious experience.
- The first school of thought in psychology was structuralism, a kind of "mental chemistry" based on introspection and analysis.
- Structuralism was followed by functionalism, behaviorism, and Gestalt psychology.
- Psychodynamic approaches, such as Freud's psychoanalytic theory, emphasize the unconscious origins of behavior.

- Humanistic psychology accentuates subjective experience, human potentials, and personal growth.

What are the major trends and specialties in psychology?

- Five main streams of thought in modern psychology are behaviorism, humanism, the psychodynamic approach, biopsychology, and cognitive psychology.
- Although psychologists, psychiatrists, psychoanalysts, and counselors all work in the field of mental health, their training and methods differ considerably.
- Clinical and counseling psychologists, who do psychotherapy, represent only two of dozens of specialties in psychology.
- Psychological research may be basic or applied.

Why is the scientific method important to psychologists?

- Important elements of a scientific investigation include observing, defining a problem, proposing a hypothesis, gathering evidence/testing the hypothesis, publishing results, and forming a theory.
- Before they can be investigated, psychological concepts must be given operational definitions.

How do psychologists collect information?

- Naturalistic observation is a starting place in many investigations.
- Three problems with naturalistic observation are the effects of the observer on the observed, observer bias, and an inability to explain observed behavior.
- In the correlational method, relationships between two traits, responses, or events are measured.
- A correlation coefficient is computed to gauge the strength of the relationship. Correlations allow prediction, but they do not demonstrate cause-and-effect connections.
- Cause-and-effect relationships are best identified by controlled experiments.

How is an experiment performed?

- In an experiment, two or more groups of subjects are formed. These groups differ only with regard to the independent variable (condition of interest as a cause in the experiment).
- Effects on the dependent variable are then measured. All other conditions (extraneous variables) are held constant.
- In experiments that involve drugs, a placebo must be given to control for the effects of expectations. If a

double-blind procedure is used, neither subjects nor experimenters know who received a drug.

- A related problem is the experimenter effect (a tendency for experimenters to unconsciously influence the outcome of an experiment). Expectations can create a self-fulfilling prophecy, in which a person changes in the direction of the expectation.

What other research methods do psychologists use?

- The clinical method employs case studies, which are in-depth records of a single subject. Case studies provide important information on topics that cannot be studied any other way.
- In the survey method, people in a representative sample are asked a series of carefully worded questions.

What is critical thinking?

- Critical thinking is the ability to evaluate, compare, analyze, critique, and synthesize information.
- To judge the validity of a claim, it is important to gather evidence for and against the claim and to evaluate the *quality* of the evidence.

How does psychology differ from false explanations of behavior?

- Numerous pseudopsychologies exist. These false systems are frequently confused with valid psychology. Belief in pseudopsychologies is based in part on uncritical acceptance, the fallacy of positive instances, and the Barnum effect.

How good is psychological information found in the popular media?

- Information in the mass media varies greatly in quality and accuracy.
- It is wise to approach such information with skepticism and caution. This is especially true with regard to the source of information, uncontrolled observation, correlation and causation, inferences, oversimplification, single examples, and unrepeatable results.

Interactive Learning

Internet addresses frequently change. To find the sites listed here, visit http://www.psychology.wadsworth.com/coon_journey2e for an updated list of Internet addresses and direct links to relevant sites.

PSYCHOLOGY: A JOURNEY COMPANION WEB SITE Online quizzes, flash cards, and other helpful study aids for this text. http://www.psychology.wadsworth.com/coon_journey2e

AMERICAN PSYCHOLOGICAL ASSOCIATION Home page of the APA, with links to PsychNET, student information, member information, and more.

AMERICAN PSYCHOLOGICAL SOCIETY Home page of the APS, with links to information, services, and Internet resources.

ETHICAL PRINCIPLES OF PSYCHOLOGISTS AND CODE OF CONDUCT The full text of the ethical principles that guide professional psychologists.

PSYCHWEB This award-winning page provides a multitude of services and links.

PSYCOLOQUY An online journal with short articles on all areas of psychology.

PSYCPORT This site is a large database of psychological information, including daily updates on news related to psychology.

THE JANE GOODALL INSTITUTE Information about Goodall's work at Gombe, in Tanzania, where she has studied and protected wild chimpanzees for more than 40 years.

THE PSYCHOLOGY STUDY CENTER From the publishers of this book, this site offers a study center for this text, online activities, links to multimedia brochures, catalogues, software demos, and more.

TODAY IN THE HISTORY OF PSYCHOLOGY Events in the history of psychology by the date.

INFOTRAC COLLEGE EDITION For recent articles related to the pseudopsychologies discussed in this chapter, use Key Words search for PHRENOLOGY and ASTROLOGY. You can also use a Key Words search for PSYCHOLOGICAL RESEARCH.

PSYCHNOW! 1b. Psychology and Its History, 1c. Research Methods, 1d. Critical Thinking in Psychology.

Test Your Knowledge: Psychology and Research Methods

The questions that follow are only a sample of what you need to know. If you miss any of the items, you should review the entire chapter and get more practice with *WebTutor* or the *Practice Quizzes* that came with this book. Another way to prepare for tests is to use the printed *Study Guide* that is available for this text.

1. Psychology is the _____ of _____ and mental processes.
   A. study, the mind   B. knowledge, philosophy   C. study, personality   D. science, behavior

2. The best psychological information is typically based on
   A. proven theories   B. opinions of experts and authorities   C. anthropomorphic measurements   D. empirical evidence

3. Who among the following is most interested in the growth of young children?
   A. learning theorist   B. personality theorist   C. comparative psychologist   D. developmental psychologist

4. Cognitive psychologists are primarily interested in
   A. thinking and information processing   B. the behavior of various species   C. attitudes, persuasion, riots, conformity, and leadership   D. how the brain evolved to produce human intelligence

5. Research that can explain why people remember better if they relate new information to familiar ideas meets which of psychology's goals?
   A. describe   B. understand   C. predict   D. control

6. Introspection was especially important to which school of thought in psychology?
   A. structuralism   B. functionalism   C. behaviorism   D. Gestalt

7. Which two schools of thought have largely disappeared from contemporary psychology?
   A. behaviorism, Gestalt   B. humanism, cognitive behaviorism   C. functionalism, structuralism   D. structuralism, humanism

8. Who among the following was NOT an historic woman psychologist?
   A. Calkins   B. Ladd-Franklin   C. Washburn   D. Watson

9. Who among the following is LEAST likely to treat serious behavioral and emotional disturbances?
   A. psychologist   B. counselor   C. psychiatrist   D. psychoanalyst

10. Modern psychodynamic theories owe much to the work of
    A. Titchener   B. Freud   C. Darwin   D. Wertheimer

11. A psychotherapist is working with a person from an ethnic group other than her own. She should be aware of how cultural relativity and _____ affect behavior.
    A. the anthropomorphic error   B. operational definitions   C. biased sampling   D. social norms

12. After you identify an interesting problem or question about behavior, you will need to establish _____ of important variables before you begin to make controlled observations.
    A. correlations   B. operational definitions   C. double-blind controls   D. a theory

13. A psychologist does a study to see if having control over difficult tasks reduces stress. In the study he will be testing an
    A. experimental hypothesis   B. operational definition   C. empirical definition   D. anthropomorphic theory

14. Because correlation does not demonstrate causation, psychologists often use _____ to answer questions about behavior.
    A. experimentation   B. naturalistic observation   C. the survey method   D. the clinical method

15. Observer bias and the observer effect are problems in using
    A. naturalistic observation   B. the correlational method   C. the experimental method   D. naturalistic experiments

16. The outcome of a psychology experiment is revealed by measuring changes in behavior. Such measures are the _____ variable of the experiment.
    A. independent   B. correlational   C. dependent   D. extraneous

17. Double-blind experiments are designed to control for the
    A. placebo effect   B. anthropomorphic fallacy   C. unintended influence of operational definitions   D. courtesy bias

18. Obtaining a representative sample is especially important in psychological research involving
    A. the placebo effect   B. hypothesis testing   C. the experimenter effect   D. the clinical method

19. Belief in astrology is based on the fallacy of positive instances, which is a failure to
    A. collect relevant correlations   B. make use of introspection   C. distinguish between observation and inference   D. engage in critical thinking

20. An article in a magazine claims that "Special Diet Controls Hyperactivity in Children." This claim is meaningless unless
    A. the author is an authority on hyperactivity   B. the diet has been tested empirically   C. an animal model was used   D. the author knows of a specific child who benefited from the diet

Brain and Behavior

Finding Music in Tofu

When I watch the movements of a gifted musician, I often think about the brain. I recently saw Yo-Yo Ma, a master cellist, play a Bach suite with such skill that I was utterly amazed. If Ma had been an athlete, you would say he was "in the zone." His performance was unforgettable. Of course, in everything from rock to rap, musicians regularly make music that no machine could duplicate. A virtual Carlos Santana? A mechanical Tori Amos? A synthetic Bono or Bon Jovi? I don't think so. That's why music is a good example of the central role the brain plays in all that is human.

Your brain is about the size of a grapefruit. It weighs around 3 pounds and looks a lot like tofu. The next time you are in a market that sells beef brains, stop and have a look. What you will see is similar to your own brain, only smaller. How could such a squishy little blob of tissue allow us to make music of exquisite beauty? To seek a cure for cancer? To fall in love? Or read a book like this one?

Each nerve cell in your brain is linked to as many as 15,000 others. This network makes it possible to process immense amounts of information. In fact, there may be more *possible* pathways between the neurons in your brain than there are atoms in the entire universe! Undeniably, the human brain is the most amazing of all computers.

Scientists use the power of the brain to study the brain. Yet even now we must wonder if the brain will ever completely understand itself. Nevertheless, answers to many age-old questions about the mind, consciousness, and knowledge lie buried within the brain. Let's visit this fascinating realm.

Cameron/Curtis

Survey Questions

- How do nerve cells operate and communicate?
- What are the functions of major parts of the nervous system?
- How do we know how the brain works?
- How is the brain organized, and what do its higher structures do?
- Why are the brain's association areas important? What happens when they are injured?
- What kinds of behaviors are controlled by the subcortex?
- Does the glandular system affect behavior?
- How do right- and left-handed individuals differ?

NEURONS—BUILDING A "BIOCOMPUTER"

] **SURVEYQUESTION** *How do nerve cells operate and communicate?*

The brain consists of some 100 billion **neurons** (NOOR-ons; individual nerve cells). Neurons carry and process information. They also activate muscles and glands. Thus, everything you do, think, or feel can be traced back to these tiny cells. A single neuron is not very smart—it would take at least several just to make you blink. Yet when neurons form vast networks, they produce intelligence and consciousness. Neurons link to one another in tight clumps and long "chains." Each neuron receives messages from many others and sends its own message on. Millions of neurons must send messages at the same time to produce even the most fleeting thought (Carter, 1998). When Carlos Santana plays a guitar riff, literally billions of neurons may be involved.

Parts of a Neuron

What does a neuron look like? What are its main parts?   No two neurons are exactly alike, but most have four basic parts (◆Fig. 2.1). The **dendrites** (DEN-drytes), which look like tree roots, receive messages from other neurons. The **soma** (SOH-mah; cell body) does the same. In addition, the soma sends messages of its own (nerve impulses) down a thin fiber called the **axon** (AK-sahn).

Most axons end in **axon terminals.** These "branches" link up with the dendrites and somas of other neurons. This link allows information to pass from neuron to neuron. Some axons are only 0.1 millimeter long. (That's about the width of a pencil line.) Others stretch up to a meter through the nervous system. (From the base of your spine to your big toe, for instance.) Like miniature cables, axons carry messages through the brain and nervous system. Altogether, your brain has about 3 million miles of axons in it (Hyman, 1999b).

Now let's summarize with a metaphor. Imagine you are standing in a long line of people who are holding hands. A person on the far right end of the line wants to silently send a message to the person on the left end. She does this by pressing the hand of the person to her left, who presses the hand of the person to his left, and so on. The message arrives at your right hand (your dendrites). You decide whether to pass it on (you are the soma). The message goes out through your left arm (the axon). With your left hand (the axon terminals), you squeeze the hand of the person to your left, and the message moves on.

The Nerve Impulse

Electrically charged molecules called *ions* (EYE-ons) are found inside each neuron (◆Fig. 2.2). Other ions lie outside the cell. Some ions have a positive electrical charge, and some are negative. Different numbers of these "plus" and "minus" charges exist inside and

Neuron An individual nerve cell.
Dendrites Neuron fibers that receive incoming messages.
Soma The main body of a neuron or other cell.
Axon Fiber that carries information away from the cell body of a neuron.
Axon terminals Branching fibers at the ends of axons.

◆FIGURE 2.1 *A neuron, or nerve cell. In the right foreground you can see a nerve cell fiber in cross section. The upper left photo gives a more realistic picture of the shape of neurons. Nerve impulses usually travel from the dendrites and soma to the branching ends of the axon. The nerve cell shown here is a motor neuron. The axons of motor neuron stretch from the brain and spinal cord to muscles or glands of the body.*

◆FIGURE 2.2 *Electrical probes placed inside and outside an axon measure its activity. (The scale is exaggerated here. Such measurements require ultra-small electrodes, as described later in this chapter.) The inside of an axon at rest is about −60 to −70 millivolts, compared with the outside. Electrochemical changes in a neuron generate an action potential. When positively charged sodium ions (Na⁺) rush into the cell, its interior briefly becomes positive. This is the action potential. After the action potential, positive potassium ions (K⁺) flow out of the axon and restore its negative charge (see Fig. 2.3 for further explanation).*

outside of nerve cells. As a result, the inside of each neuron in your brain has an electrical charge of about minus 70 millivolts. (A millivolt is one thousandth of a volt.) This charge allows each neuron in your brain to act like a tiny biological battery.

The electrical charge of an inactive neuron is called its **resting potential.** But neurons seldom get much rest: Messages arriving from other neurons raise and lower the resting potential. If the electrical charge rises to about minus 50 millivolts, the neuron will reach its *threshold,* or trigger point for firing (see Fig. 2.2). It's as if the neuron says "Ah ha! It's

Resting potential The electrical charge of a neuron at rest.

◆FIGURE 2.3 *The electrical charge inside an axon is normally negative. The fluid surrounding an axon is normally positive. As an action potential passes along the axon, these charges reverse so that the interior of the axon briefly becomes positive. This process is described in more detail in Figure 2.4.*

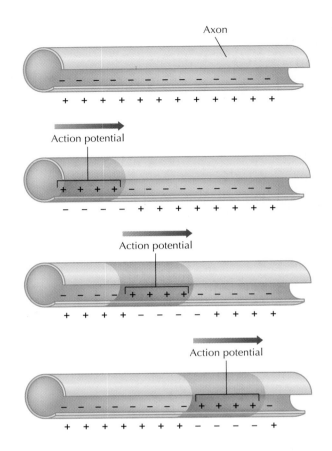

1. In its resting state, the axon has a negatively charged interior.

2. During an action potential, positively charged atoms (ions) rush into the axon. This briefly changes the electrical charge inside the axon from negative to positive. Simultaneously, the charge outside the axon becomes negative.

3. The action potential advances as positive and negative charges reverse in a moving zone of electrical activity that sweeps down the axon.

4. After an action potential passes, positive ions rapidly flow out of the axon to quickly restore its negative charge. An outward flow of additional positive ions returns the axon to its resting state.

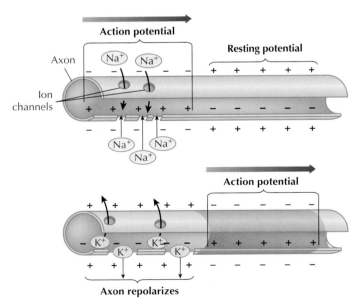

◆FIGURE 2.4 *The interior of an axon. The right end of the top axon is at rest. Thus, it has a negative charge inside. An action potential begins when ion channels open and sodium ions (Na^+) rush into the axon. In this drawing, the action potential would travel from left to right along the axon. In the lower axon, the action potential has moved to the right. After it passes, potassium ions (K^+) flow out of the axon. This quickly renews the negative charge inside the axon, so it can fire again. Sodium ions that enter the axon during an action potential are pumped out more slowly. Removing them restores the original resting potential.*

time to send a message to my neighbors." When a neuron reaches −50 millivolts, an **action potential,** or nerve impulse, sweeps down the axon at up to 200 miles per hour (◆Fig. 2.3). That may seem fast, but it still takes at least a split second to react. That's one reason why hitting a 95-mile-per-hour major league fastball is among the most difficult feats in all of sports.

What happens during an action potential? The axon membrane is pierced by tiny tunnels or "holes," called *ion channels.* Normally, these tiny openings are blocked by molecules that act like "gates" or "doors." During an action potential, the gates pop open. This allows sodium ions (Na^+) to rush into the axon (Carlson, 2001). The channels first open near the soma. Then, gate after gate opens down the length of the axon as the action potential zips along (◆Fig. 2.4).

Each action potential is an *all-or-nothing event* (a nerve impulse occurs completely or not at all). You might find it helpful to picture the axon as a row of dominoes set on end. Tipping over the dominoes is an all-or-nothing act. Once the first domino drops, a wave of falling blocks will zip rapidly to the end of the line. Similarly, when a nerve impulse is trig-

Action potential The nerve impulse.

gered near the soma, a wave of activity (the action potential) travels down the length of the axon. This is what happens in long chains of neurons as Yo-Yo Ma's brain tells his hands what to do next, note after note.

After each nerve impulse, the cell briefly drops below its resting level, and it becomes less willing to fire. This **negative after-potential** occurs because potassium ions (K^+) flow out of the neuron while the membrane gates are open (Fig. 2.4). After a nerve impulse, ions flow both into and out of the axon, recharging it for more action. In our model, the row of dominoes is quickly set up again. Soon, the axon is ready for another wave of activity.

Synapses and Neurotransmitters

How does information move from one neuron to another?   The nerve impulse is primarily electrical. That's why electrically stimulating the brain affects behavior. To prove the point, researcher José Delgado once entered a bullring with a cape and a radio transmitter. The bull charged. Delgado retreated. At the last instant, the speeding bull stopped short. Why? Because Delgado's radio activated electrodes (metal wires) placed deep within the bull's brain. These, in turn, stimulated "control centers" that brought the bull to a halt.

In contrast to the nerve impulse, communication between neurons is chemical. The microscopic space between two neurons, over which messages pass, is called a **synapse** (SIN-aps) (◆Fig. 2.5). When an action potential reaches the tips of the axon terminals, **neurotransmitters** (NOOR-oh-TRANS-mit-ers), chemicals that alter activity in neurons, are released into the synaptic gap.

Let's return to the people standing in a line. To be more accurate, you and the others shouldn't be holding hands. Instead, each person should have a toy squirt gun in his or her left hand. To pass along a message, you would squirt the right hand of the person to your left. When that person notices this "message," he or she would squirt the right hand of the person to the left, and so on.

When chemical molecules cross over a synapse, they attach to special receiving areas on the next neuron (Fig. 2.5). These tiny *receptor sites* on the cell membrane are sensitive to neurotransmitters. The receptor sites exist in large numbers on nerve cell bodies and on dendrites. Muscles and glands have receptor sites, too.

Do neurotransmitters always trigger an action potential in the next neuron?   No. Some transmitters *excite* the next neuron (move it closer to firing). Others *inhibit* it (make firing less likely). At any instant, a single neuron may receive hundreds or thousands of messages. Does it fire an impulse? It depends: If several "exciting" messages arrive close in time, the neuron will fire—but only if it doesn't get too many "inhibiting" messages that push it *away* from its trigger point. In this way, messages are *combined* before a neuron "decides" to fire its all-or-nothing action potential. Multiply these events by 100 billion neurons and 100 trillion synapses, and you have an amazing computer—one that could easily fit inside a shoe box.

More than 100 transmitter chemicals are found in the brain. Some examples are acetylcholine, epinephrine, norepinephrine, serotonin, dopamine, histamine, and various amino acids. Disturbances of any of these substances can have serious consequences. For example, too little dopamine can cause the muscle tremors of Parkinson's disease. Too much dopamine may cause schizophrenia.

Many drugs imitate, duplicate, or block neurotransmitters. For example, *acetylcholine* (ah-SEET-ul-KOH-leen) normally activates muscles. Without acetylcholine, our musical friend Yo-Yo Ma couldn't even move, much less play Bach. That's exactly why the drug curare (cue-RAH-ree) causes paralysis. By attaching to receptor sites on muscles, curare competes with acetylcholine. This prevents acetylcholine from activating muscle cells. As a result, a person or animal given curare cannot move—a fact known to South American Indians of the Amazon River Basin, who use curare as a poison on their hunting arrows.

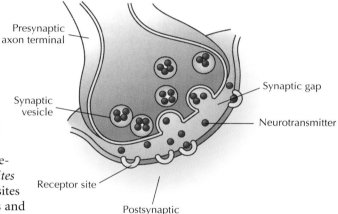

Presynaptic axon terminal

Synaptic vesicle

Synaptic gap

Neurotransmitter

Receptor site

Postsynaptic dendrite

◆**FIGURE 2.5** *A highly magnified view of a synapse. Neurotransmitters are stored in tiny sacs called synaptic vesicles (VES-ih-kels). When a nerve impulse reaches the end of an axon, the vesicles move to the surface and release neurotransmitters. These molecules cross the synaptic gap to affect the next neuron. The size of the gap is exaggerated here; it is actually only about one millionth of an inch. Some transmitter molecules excite the next neuron, and some inhibit its activity.*

Negative after-potential A drop in electrical charge below the resting potential.

Synapse The microscopic space between two neurons over which messages pass.

Neurotransmitter Any chemical released by a neuron that alters activity in other neurons.

Neural Regulators

More subtle brain activities are affected by chemicals called **neuropeptides** (NOOR-oh-PEP-tides). Neuropeptides do not carry messages directly. Instead, they *regulate* the activity of other neurons. By doing so, they affect memory, pain, emotion, pleasure, moods, hunger, sexual behavior, and other basic processes. For example, when you touch something hot, you jerk your hand away. Neurotransmitters carry the messages for this action. At the same time, pain may cause the brain to release *enkephalins* (en-KEF-ah-lins). These opiate-like neural regulators relieve pain and stress. Related chemicals called *endorphins* (en-DORF-ins) are released by the pituitary gland. Together, these chemicals reduce the pain so it is not too disabling (Drolet et al., 2001).

Such discoveries help explain the painkilling effect of placebos (fake pills or injections), which raise endorphin levels (Lipman et al., 1990). A release of endorphins also seems to underlie "runner's high," masochism, acupuncture, and the euphoria sometimes associated with childbirth and painful initiation rites, and even sport parachuting (Janssen & Arntz, 2001; Sternberg et al., 1998). In each case, pain and stress cause the release of endorphins. These in turn induce feelings of pleasure or euphoria similar to being "high" on morphine. People who say they are "addicted" to running or eating hot chilies may be closer to the truth than they realize. And more important, we may at last know why some hardy souls take hot saunas followed by cold showers! Ultimately, brain regulators may help explain depression, schizophrenia, drug addiction, and other puzzling topics. For example, women who suffer from severe premenstrual pain and distress have unusually low endorphin levels (Straneva et al., 2002).

THE NERVOUS SYSTEM—WIRED FOR ACTION

] SURVEYQUESTION *What are the functions of major parts of the nervous system?*

Jamal and Vicki are playing catch with a Frisbee. This may look fairly simple. However, to merely toss the Frisbee or catch it, a huge amount of information must be sensed, interpreted, and directed to countless muscle fibers. As they play, Jamal and Vicki's neural circuits are ablaze with activity. Let's explore the "wiring diagram" that makes their Frisbee game possible.

Neurons and Nerves

Are neurons the same as nerves? No. Neurons are tiny cells. You would need a microscope to see one. **Nerves** are large bundles of axons and dendrites. You can easily see nerves without magnification.

Many nerves are white because they contain axons coated with a fatty layer called *myelin* (MY-eh-lin). Small gaps in the myelin help nerve impulses move faster. Instead of passing down the entire length of the axon, the action potential leaps from gap to gap. Without the added speed this allows, it would probably be impossible to brake in time to avoid many automobile accidents, for example. When the myelin layer is damaged, a person may suffer from numbness, weakness, or paralysis. That, in fact, is what happens in multiple sclerosis, a disease that occurs when the immune system attacks and destroys the myelin in a person's body.

A thin layer of cells called the *neurilemma* (NOOR-rih-LEM-ah) is also wrapped around most axons outside the brain and spinal cord. (Return to Figure 2.1.) The neurilemma forms a "tunnel" that damaged fibers can follow as they repair themselves.

Until only a few years ago, it was widely believed that we are born with all the brain cells we will ever have. This led to the depressing idea that we all slowly go downhill, as the brain loses thousands of neurons every day. However, we now know that a healthy 75-year-old brain has just as many neurons as it did when it was careening through life in the body of a 25-year-old. Although it is true that the brain loses cells daily, it simultaneously grows

Neuropeptides Brain chemicals, such as enkephalins and endorphins, that regulate the activity of neurons.

Nerve A bundle of neuron fibers.

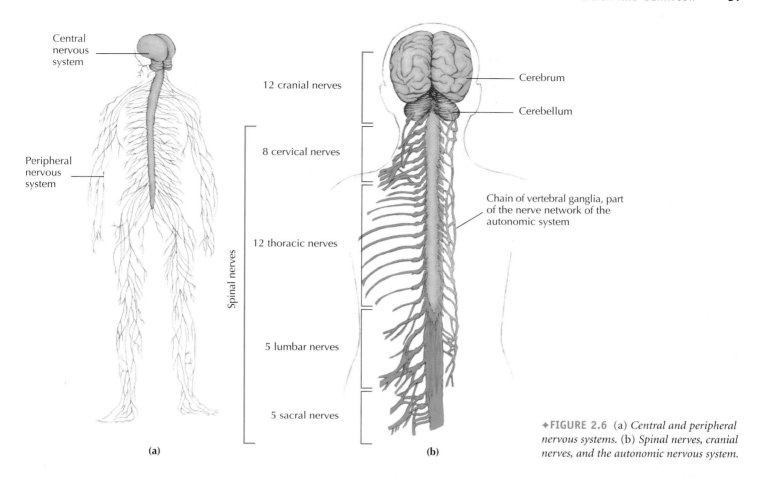

Central nervous system

Peripheral nervous system

12 cranial nerves

8 cervical nerves

12 thoracic nerves

5 lumbar nerves

5 sacral nerves

Spinal nerves

Cerebrum

Cerebellum

Chain of vertebral ganglia, part of the nerve network of the autonomic system

(a)

(b)

✦**FIGURE 2.6** (a) *Central and peripheral nervous systems.* (b) *Spinal nerves, cranial nerves, and the autonomic nervous system.*

new neurons to replace them. This process is called **neurogenesis** (noor-oh-JEN-uh-sis; the production of new brain cells) (Gould et al., 1999). Each day, thousands of new cells originate deep within the brain, move to the surface, and link up with other neurons to become part of the brain's circuitry. This is stunning news to brain scientists, who must now figure out what the new cells do. Most likely they are involved in learning, memory, and our ability to adapt to changing circumstances (Gould & Gross, 2002).

Brain Repair

The discovery of neurogenesis in adult brains has raised new hopes that some types of brain damage can be repaired. For example, doctors are testing a new method to treat strokes by injecting millions of immature nerve cells into damaged areas of the brain. If the technique is successful, the new cells will link up with existing neurons and repair some of the stroke damage (Borlongan, Sanberg, & Freeman, 1999). Researchers are also trying to nudge immature brain cells to develop into particular types of neurons. If they succeed, cures for blindness, Parkinson's disease, and other problems might follow (Kolb & Whishaw, 1998).

Subparts of the Nervous System

As you can see in ✦Figures 2.6 and 2.7, the **central nervous system** (**CNS**) consists of the brain and spinal cord. The brain is the central "computer" of the nervous system. Jamal must use this "computer" to anticipate when and where the Frisbee will arrive. Jamal's brain communicates with the rest of his body through a large "cable" called the spinal cord. From there, messages flow through the **peripheral nervous system** (**PNS**). This intricate network of nerves carries information to and from the CNS.

Neurogenesis The production of new brain cells.

Central nervous system The brain and spinal cord.

Peripheral nervous system All parts of the nervous system outside the brain and spinal cord.

◆FIGURE 2.7 *Subparts of the nervous system.*

A serious injury to the brain or spinal cord is usually permanent. However, as just noted, scientists are starting to make progress in repairing damaged neurons in the CNS. For instance, they have been able to partially repair cut spinal cords in rats. First they closed the gap with nerve fibers from outside the spinal cord. Then they biochemically coaxed the severed spinal nerve fibers to grow through the "tunnels" provided by the implanted fibers. Within 2 months, the rats had regained some use of their hind legs (Cheng, Cao, & Olson, 1996). Imagine what that could mean to a person confined to a wheelchair. Although it is unwise to raise false hopes, solutions to such problems are beginning to emerge. In fact, medical researchers recently began the first human trials in which nerve grafts will be used to repair damaged spinal cords (Levesque & Neuman, 1999). Nevertheless, it is wise to take good care of your own CNS. That means using seatbelts when you drive, wearing a helmet if you ride a motorcycle or bicycle, wearing protective gear for sports, and avoiding activities that pose a risk to the head or spinal cord.

The Peripheral Nervous System

The peripheral nervous system can be divided into two major parts (see Fig. 2.7). The **somatic system** carries messages to and from the sense organs and skeletal muscles. In general, it controls voluntary behavior, such as when Vicki tosses the Frisbee or B. B. King plays the blues. In contrast, the **autonomic system** serves the internal organs and glands of the body. The word *autonomic* means "self-governing." Activities governed by the autonomic nervous system (ANS) are mostly "vegetative" or automatic, such as heart rate, digestion, or perspiration. Thus, messages carried by the somatic system can make your hand move, but they cannot cause your eyes to dilate. Likewise, messages carried by the ANS can stimulate digestion, but they cannot help you carry out a voluntary action, such as writing a letter. If Jamal feels a flash of anger when he misses a catch, a brief burst of activity will spread through his autonomic system.

The ANS can be divided into the sympathetic and parasympathetic branches. Both are related to emotional responses, such as crying, sweating, heart rate, and other involuntary behavior (◆Fig. 2.8). The ANS and the somatic system work together to coordinate the body's internal reactions with events in the world outside. For example, if a snarling dog lunges at you, the somatic system will control your leg muscles so you can run. At the same time, the autonomic system will raise your blood pressure, quicken your heart, and so forth.

How do the branches of the autonomic system differ? The **sympathetic branch** is an "emergency" system. It prepares the body for "fight or flight" during times of danger or high emotion. In essence, it arouses the body for action. (Yo-Yo Ma once left his $2 million cello in a taxi. No doubt his sympathetic nervous system was quite active when he first noticed his error.)

The **parasympathetic branch** quiets the body and returns it to a lower level of arousal. It is most active soon after an emotional event. The parasympathetic branch also helps keep vital processes such as heart rate, breathing, and digestion at moderate levels.

Of course, both branches of the ANS are always active. At any given moment, their combined activity determines if your body is relaxed or aroused.

The Spinal Cord

As mentioned earlier, the spinal cord acts like a cable connecting the brain to other parts of the body. If you were to cut through this "cable," you would see columns of *white matter* in areas that have lots of myelin. This tissue is made up of axons that eventually leave the spinal cord. Outside the cord, they are bundled together into nerves. Return to Figure 2.6 *b* and you will see that 30 pairs of **spinal nerves** leave the sides of the spinal cord. Another pair (not shown) leaves the tip. The 31 spinal nerves carry sensory and motor messages to and from the spinal cord. In addition, 12 pairs of **cranial nerves** leave the brain directly. Together, these nerves keep your entire body in communication with your brain.

How is the spinal cord related to behavior? The simplest behavior pattern is a **reflex arc,** which occurs when a stimulus provokes an automatic response. Such reflexes occur within the spinal cord, without any help from the brain (see ◆Fig. 2.9). Imagine that Vicki

Each year spinal cord injuries rob many thousands of people, such as actor Christopher Reeve, of the ability to move. Yet there is growing hope that nerve grafting techniques may someday make it possible for some of these people to walk again.

Somatic system The system of nerves linking the spinal cord with the body and sense organs.

Autonomic system The system of nerves carrying information to and from the internal organs and glands.

Sympathetic system A branch of the ANS that arouses the body.

Parasympathetic system A branch of the ANS that quiets the body.

Spinal nerves Major nerves that carry sensory and motor messages in and out of the spinal cord.

Cranial nerves Major nerves that leave the brain without passing through the spinal cord.

Reflex arc The simplest behavior, in which a stimulus provokes an automatic response.

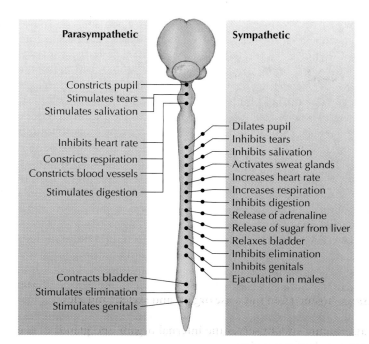

Parasympathetic

Constricts pupil
Stimulates tears
Stimulates salivation

Inhibits heart rate
Constricts respiration
Constricts blood vessels
Stimulates digestion

Contracts bladder
Stimulates elimination
Stimulates genitals

Sympathetic

Dilates pupil
Inhibits tears
Inhibits salivation
Activates sweat glands
Increases heart rate
Increases respiration
Inhibits digestion
Release of adrenaline
Release of sugar from liver
Relaxes bladder
Inhibits elimination
Inhibits genitals
Ejaculation in males

◆FIGURE 2.8 *Sympathetic and parasympathetic branches of the autonomic nervous system. Both branches control involuntary actions. The sympathetic system generally activates the body. The parasympathetic system generally quiets it. The sympathetic branch relays its messages through clusters of nerve cells outside the spinal cord.*

Cell body of
sensory neuron
Sensory
nerve
Sensory neuron
Connector
neuron
Spinal cord
(cross section)
Motor neuron
Muscle cell responds
by contracting
Sensory
receptor
in skin
Stimulus to skin

steps on a thorn. (Yes, they're still playing Frisbee.) Pain is detected in her foot by a *sensory neuron* (a nerve cell that carries messages from the senses toward the CNS). Instantly, the sensory neuron fires off a message to Vicki's spinal cord.

Inside the spinal cord, the sensory neuron synapses with a *connector neuron* (a nerve cell that links two others). The connector neuron activates a *motor neuron* (a cell that carries commands from the CNS to muscles and glands). The muscle fibers are made up of *effector cells* (cells capable of producing a response). The muscle cells contract and cause Vicki's foot to withdraw. Note that no brain activity is required for a reflex arc to occur. Vicki's body will react automatically to protect itself.

In reality, even a simple reflex usually triggers more complex activity. For example, muscles of Vicki's other leg must contract to support her as she shifts her weight. Even this can be done by the spinal cord, but it involves many more cells and several spinal nerves. Also, the spinal cord normally informs the brain of the actions it has taken. As her foot pulls away from the thorn, Vicki will feel the pain and think "Ouch, what was that?"

Perhaps you have realized how adaptive it is to have a spinal cord capable of responding on its own. Such automatic responses leave the brains of our Frisbee aces free to deal with more important information—such as the location of trees, lampposts, and attractive onlookers—as they take turns making grandstand catches.

In a few moments, we will probe more deeply into the brain. Before we do, it might be wise to explore some of the research tools biopsychologists use while working with the brain. Uncovering the brain's mysteries has not been easy. Let's consider some of the basics.

◆FIGURE 2.9 *A sensory-motor arc, or reflex, is set in motion by a stimulus to the skin (or other part of the body). The nerve impulse travels to the spinal cord and then back out to a muscle, which contracts. Such reflexes provide an "automatic" protective device for the body.*

RESEARCH METHODS—CHARTING THE BRAIN'S INNER REALMS

] SURVEYQUESTION *How do we know how the brain works?*

Biopsychology is the study of how biological processes, the brain, and the nervous system relate to behavior. Many of the functions of the brain have been identified by **clinical studies.** Such studies examine changes in personality, behavior, or sensory capacity caused by brain diseases or injuries. A related experimental technique is based on **ablation** (ab-LAY-shun;

Clinical study A detailed investigation of a single person, especially one suffering from some injury or disease.

Ablation Surgical removal of tissue.

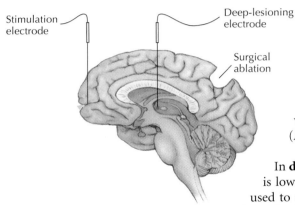

Stimulation electrode

Deep-lesioning electrode

Surgical ablation

✦FIGURE 2.10 *The functions of brain structures are explored by selectively activating or removing them. Brain research is often based on electrical stimulation, but chemical stimulation is also used at times.*

surgical removal) of parts of the brain (✦Fig. 2.10). When ablation causes changes in behavior or sensory capacity, biopsychologists gain insight into the purpose of the missing "part." An alternate approach is to use electrical stimulation to "turn on" brain structures. For example, the surface of the brain can be activated by touching it with a small electrified wire called an *electrode.* When this is done during brain surgery, the patient can tell what effect the stimulation had. (The brain has no pain receptors, so surgery can be done while a patient is awake. Only local painkillers are used for the scalp and skull.) (Any volunteers?)

Even structures below the surface of the brain can be activated or removed. In **deep lesioning** (LEE-zhun-ing), a thin wire electrode, insulated except at the tip, is lowered into a target area inside the brain (Fig. 2.10). An electric current is then used to destroy a small amount of brain tissue. Again, changes in behavior give clues about the function of the affected area. Using a weaker current, it is also possible to *activate* target areas, rather than remove them. This is called ESB, for **electrical stimulation of the brain.** ESB can call forth behavior with astonishing power. Instantly, it can bring about aggression, alertness, escape, eating, drinking, sleep, movement, euphoria, memories, speech, tears, and more. By using ESB, researchers are creating a three-dimensional brain map. This "atlas" shows the sensory, motor, and emotional responses that can be elicited from various parts of the brain. It promises to be a valuable guide for medical treatment, as well as for exploring the brain (Carter, 1998; Yoshida, 1993).

Could ESB be used to control a person against his or her will? It might seem that ESB could be used to control a person like a robot. But the details of emotions and behaviors elicited by ESB are modified by personality and circumstances. Sci-fi movies to the contrary, it would be impossible for a ruthless dictator to enslave people by "radio controlling" their brains.

To find out what individual neurons are doing, we need to do a micro-electrode recording. A *micro-electrode* is an extremely thin glass tube filled with a salty fluid. The tip of a micro-electrode is small enough to detect the electrical activity of a *single* neuron. Watching the action potentials of just one neuron provides a fascinating glimpse into the true origins of behavior. (The action potential shown in Figure 2.2 was recorded with a micro-electrode.)

What about the bigger picture? Is it possible to record what the brain is doing as a whole? Yes, it is, with *electroencephalography* (ee-LEK-tro-in-SEF-ah-LOG-ruh-fee). This technique measures the waves of electrical activity produced by the brain. Small, disk-shaped metal plates are placed on a person's scalp. These electrodes detect electrical impulses from the brain and send them to an **electroencephalograph** (**EEG**). The EEG amplifies these very weak signals (brain waves) and records them on a moving sheet of paper or a computer screen (✦Fig. 2.11). Various brain-wave patterns can identify the presence of tumors, epilepsy, and other diseases. The EEG also reveals changes in brain activity during sleep, daydreaming, hypnosis, and other mental states.

New Images of the Living Brain

Many of the brain's riddles have been solved with the methods just described, plus others based on drugs and brain chemistry. Yet each technique lets us see only a part of the whole picture. What if we could "peek" inside an intact brain while a person is thinking, perceiving, and reacting? Rather than seeing individual musical notes or small musical phrases, what if we could see the brain's entire ongoing symphony? Computer-enhanced images are now making this age-old dream possible. Let's look through some of these newly opened "windows" into the human biocomputer.

Deep lesioning Removal of tissue within the brain by use of an electrode.

Electrical stimulation of the brain (ESB) Direct electrical stimulation and activation of brain tissue.

Electroencephalograph (EEG) A device that detects, amplifies, and records electrical activity in the brain.

Charles Gupton/Stock Boston, Inc.

✦FIGURE 2.11 *An EEG recording.*

CT Scan

Computerized scanning equipment has virtually revolutionized the study of brain diseases and injuries. At best, conventional x-rays produce only shadowy images of the brain. **Computed tomographic** (CT) **scanning** is a specialized type of x-ray that does a much better job of making the brain visible. In a CT scan, x-ray information is collected by a computer and formed into an image of the brain. A CT scan can reveal the effects of strokes, injuries, tumors, and other brain disorders. These, in turn, can be related to a person's behavior.

MRI Scan

Magnetic resonance imaging (**MRI**) uses a very strong magnetic field, rather than x-rays, to produce an image of the body's interior. During an MRI scan, the body is placed inside a magnetic field. Processing by a computer then creates a three-dimensional model of the brain or body. Any two-dimensional plane, or slice, of the body can be selected and displayed as an image on a computer screen. This allows us to peer into the living brain almost as if it were transparent. In ✦Figure 2.12, an MRI scan reveals a brain tumor (see arrow).

A **functional MRI** (**fMRI**) goes one step further by making brain *activity* visible. For example, when Yo-Yo Ma bowed his cello, the motor areas on the surface of his brain would be highlighted in an fMRI image. Such images allow scientists to pinpoint areas in the brain responsible for thoughts, feelings, and actions.

✦FIGURE 2.12 *An MRI scan of the brain reveals a tumor (arrow).*

Huntington Magnetic Resonance Center, Pasadena, CA

Is it true that most people use only 10 percent of their brain capacity? This is one of the lasting myths about the brain. Brain scans show that all parts of the brain are active during waking hours. Obviously, some people make better use of their innate brain power than others do. Nevertheless, there are no great hidden or untapped reserves of mental capacity in a normally functioning brain.

PET Scan

Positron emission tomography (PET) images of the brain are perhaps the most remarkable of all. A **PET scan** detects positrons (subatomic particles) emitted by weakly radioactive glucose (sugar) as it is consumed by the brain. Because the brain runs on glucose, a PET scan shows which areas are using more energy. Higher energy use corresponds with higher activity. Thus, by placing positron detectors around the head and sending data to a computer, it is possible to create a moving, color picture of changes in brain activity. As you can see in ✦Figure 2.13, PET scans reveal that very specific brain areas are active when you are reading a word, hearing a word, saying a word, or thinking about the meaning of a word. It is just a matter of time until even brighter beacons are flashed into the shadowy inner world of thought (see ✦Fig. 2.14).

Washington University School of Medicine, St. Louis

✦FIGURE 2.13 *PET scans.*

Washington University School of Medicine, St. Louis

✦FIGURE 2.14 *The bright spots you see here were created by a PET scan. They are similar to the spots in Figure 2.13. However, here they have been placed over an MRI scan so that the brain's interior is visible. The three bright spots are areas of the left brain related to language. The spot on the right is active during reading. The top-middle area is related to speech. The area to the left, in the frontal lobe, is linked with thinking about a word's meaning (Montgomery, 1989).*

CT scan Computed tomography scan; a computer-enhanced x-ray image of the brain or body.

MRI scan Magnetic resonance imaging; a three-dimensional image of the brain or body, based on its response to a magnetic field.

fMRI scan Functional magnetic resonance imaging that records brain activity.

PET scan Positron emission tomography; a computer-generated image of brain activity based on glucose consumption in the brain.

STUDYBREAK *Neurons, the Nervous System, and Brain Research*

RELATE

To cope with all the technical terms in this chapter, it might help to think of neurons as strange little creatures. How do they act? What excites them? How do they communicate? To remember the functions of major branches of the nervous system, think about what you *couldn't* do if each part were missing.

You suspect that a certain part of the brain is related to memory. How could you use clinical studies, ablation, deep lesioning, and ESB to study the structure? You are interested in finding out how single neurons in the optic nerve respond when the eye is exposed to light. What technique will you use? You want to know which areas of the brain's surface are most active when a person sees a face. What methods will you use?

LEARNING CHECK

1. The _____ and _____ are receiving areas where information from other neurons is accepted.
2. Nerve impulses are carried down the _____ to the _____ _____.
3. The _____ potential becomes an _____ potential when a neuron passes the threshold for firing.
4. Neuropeptides are transmitter substances that help regulate the activity of neurons. T or F?

5. The somatic and autonomic systems are part of the _____ nervous system.
6. Sodium and potassium ions flow through ion channels in the synapse to trigger a nerve impulse in the receiving neuron. T or F?
7. The simplest behavior sequence is a _____ _____.
8. The parasympathetic nervous system is most active during times of high emotion. T or F?
9. Which of the following research techniques has the most in common with clinical studies of the effects of brain injuries? a. EEG recording   b. deep lesioning   c. micro-electrode recording   d. PET scan

Critical Thinking

10. What effect would you expect a drug to have if it blocked passage of neurotransmitters across the synapse?
11. Deep lesioning is used to ablate an area in the hypothalamus of a rat. After the operation, the rat seems to lose interest in food and eating. Why would it be a mistake to conclude that the ablated area is a "hunger center"?

ANSWERS

1. dendrites, soma 2. axon, axon terminals 3. resting, action 4. T 5. peripheral 6. F 7. reflex arc 8. F 9. b 10. Such a drug could have wide-ranging effects. If the drug blocked excitatory synapses, it would depress brain activity. If it blocked inhibitory messages, it would act as a powerful stimulant. 11. Because other factors might explain the apparent loss of appetite. For example, the taste or smell of food might be affected, or the rat might simply have difficulty swallowing. It is also possible that hunger originates elsewhere in the brain and the ablated area merely relays messages that cause the rat to eat.

THE CEREBRAL CORTEX—MY, WHAT A BIG BRAIN YOU HAVE!

] SURVEYQUESTION *How is the brain organized, and what do its higher structures do?*

Many parts of your brain are surprisingly similar to corresponding brain areas in lower animals, such as lizards. Superior human intelligence is related to the fact that our brains have a large cerebrum. The wrinkled surface of the cerebrum can be divided into smaller areas known as lobes. Parts of various lobes are responsible for the ability to see, hear, move, think, and speak. Thus, a map of the cerebrum is in some ways like a map of human behavior, as we shall see.

Cerebrum

In many ways, we humans are pretty unimpressive creatures. Animals surpass humans in almost every category of strength, speed, and sensory sensitivity. The one area in which we excel is intelligence.

Do humans have the largest brains?   Surprisingly, no. Elephant brains weigh 13 pounds, and whale brains, 19 pounds. At 3 pounds, the human brain seems puny—until we compare brain weight to body weight. We then find that an elephant's brain is 1/1,000 of its weight; the ratio for sperm whales is 1 to 10,000. The ratio for humans is 1 to 60. If someone tells you that you have a "whale of a brain," be sure to find out if they mean size or ratio!

The *cerebrum* consists of the two large hemispheres that cover the upper part of the brain. Its outer layer is known as the **cerebral** (seh-REE-brel or ser-EH-brel) **cortex.** Although the cortex is only 3 millimeters thick (1/10 of an inch), it contains 70 percent of the neurons in the central nervous system. It is largely responsible for our ability to use language, make tools, acquire complex skills, and live in complex social groups (Gibson, 2002). Without the cortex, humans wouldn't be much smarter than toads.

Corticalization

The cerebral cortex looks a little like a giant, wrinkled walnut. It covers most of the brain with a mantle of *gray matter* (spongy tissue made up mostly of cell bodies). The cortex in lower animals is small and smooth. In humans it is twisted, folded, and the largest structure of the brain. The fact that humans are more intelligent than other animals is related to this **corticalization** (KORE-tih-kal-ih-ZAY-shun), or increase in the size and wrinkling of the cortex (see ✦Fig. 2.15).

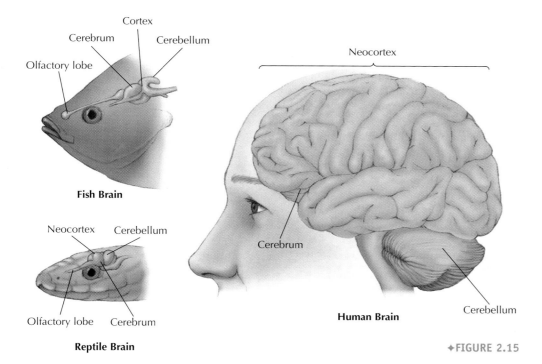

Fish Brain

Reptile Brain

Human Brain

✦FIGURE 2.15

According to folklore, a person with a large head and a high forehead is likely to be intelligent. But brain efficiency has as much to do with intelligence as brain size does (Gazzaniga, 1995).

Psychologist Richard J. Haier and his colleagues found that the brains of people who perform well on mental tests consume less energy than those of poor performers (Haier et al., 1988). Haier measured brain activity with a PET scan. Recall that a PET scan records the amount of glucose (sugar) used by brain cells. The harder neurons work, the more sugar they use. By using harmless radioactively labeled glucose, it is possible to record an image of how hard the brain is working (✦Fig. 2.16).

What did PET scans reveal when subjects took a difficult reasoning test? Surprisingly, the brains of those who scored lowest on the test used the most glucose. Although we might assume that smart brains are hard-working brains, the reverse appears to be true. Brighter subjects actually used less energy than poor performers did. Haier believes this shows that intelligence is related to brain efficiency: Less-efficient brains work harder and still accomplish less. We've all had days like that!

Cerebral cortex The outer layer of the cerebrum.

Corticalization An increase in the relative size of the cerebral cortex.

✦FIGURE 2.16 *In the images you see here, red, orange, and yellow indicate high consumption of glucose; green, blue, and pink show areas of low glucose use. The PET scan of the brain on the left shows that a man who solved 11 out of 36 reasoning problems burned more glucose than the man on the right, who solved 33.*

Courtesy of Richard Haier, University of California, Irvine

Corpus callosum   Cerebral cortex

✦FIGURE 2.17

Cerebral Hemispheres

The cortex is composed of two sides, or half-globes called *cerebral hemispheres*. The two hemispheres are connected by a thick band of fibers called the *corpus callosum* (KORE-pus kah-LOH-sum) (✦Fig. 2.17). The left side of the brain mainly controls the right side of the body. Likewise, the right side of the brain mainly controls left body areas. When my friend Marge had a stroke, her right hemisphere suffered damage. (A stroke occurs when an artery carrying blood to the brain becomes blocked, causing some brain tissue to die.) In Marge's case, the stroke caused some paralysis and loss of sensation on the left side of her body. (See "A Stroke of Bad Luck" for more information.)

CLINICAL FILE   A Stroke of Bad Luck

Strokes and other brain injuries can hit like a thunderbolt. Almost instantly, victims realize that something is wrong. You would, too, if you suddenly found that you couldn't move or feel parts of your body, or see, or speak. However, some brain injuries are not so obvious. Psychologists also look for more subtle signs that the brain is not working properly. "Soft signs" of damage include clumsiness, an awkward gait, poor hand-eye coordination, and other problems with perception and movement. These tell-tale signs are "soft" in the sense that they aren't direct tests of the brain. Nevertheless, they often reveal brain damage (Borod et al., 2002).

Even more subtle changes in behavior may follow brain injuries. For example, damage to the right hemisphere can cause a curious problem called *spatial neglect*. Affected patients pay no attention to the left side of visual space (see ✦Fig. 2.18). Often, the patient will not eat food on the left side of a plate. Some even refuse to acknowledge a paralyzed left arm as their own (Springer & Deutsch, 1998). If you point to the "alien" arm, the patient is likely to say, "Oh, that's not my arm. It must belong to someone else."

Model   Patient's copy

✦FIGURE 2.18 *Spatial neglect. A patient with right-hemisphere damage was asked to copy three model drawings. Notice how he neglected the left side in his drawings. Similar neglect occurs in other patients with right-hemisphere damage. (From* Left Brain, Right Brain, *Fifth Edition, by S. P. Springer and G. Deutsch, copyright 1981, 1985, 1989, 1993, 1998. Used with the permission of W. H. Freeman and Company.)*

Hemispheric Specialization

In 1981, Roger Sperry (1914−1994) won a Nobel prize for his remarkable discovery that the right and left brain hemispheres perform differently on tests of language, perception, music, and other capabilities.

How is it possible to test only one side of the brain?   One way is to work with people who've had a **"split-brain" operation.** In this rare type of surgery, the corpus callosum is cut to control severe epilepsy. The result is a person with essentially two brains in one body. After the surgery, it is a simple matter to send information to one hemisphere or the other (see ◆Fig. 2.19).

"Split Brains"

After the right and left brain are separated, each hemisphere will have its own separate perceptions, concepts, and impulses to act.

How does a split-brain person function after the operation?   Having two "brains" in one body can create some interesting dilemmas. When one split-brain patient dressed himself, he sometimes pulled his pants down with one hand and up with the other. Once, he grabbed his wife with his left hand and shook her violently. Gallantly, his right hand came to her aid and grabbed the aggressive left hand (Gazzaniga, 1970). However, such conflicts are actually rare. That's because both halves of the brain normally have about the same experience at the same time. Also, if a conflict arises, one hemisphere usually overrides the other.

Split-brain effects are easiest to see in specialized testing. For example, we could flash a dollar sign to the right brain and a question mark to the left brain of a patient named Tom. (Figure 2.19 shows how this is possible.) Next, Tom is asked to draw what he saw, using his left hand, out of sight. Tom's left hand draws a dollar sign. If Tom is then asked to point with his right hand to a picture of what his hidden left hand drew, he will point to a question mark (Sperry, 1968). In short, for the split-brain person, one hemisphere may not know what is happening in the other. This has to be the ultimate case of the "right hand not knowing what the left hand is doing"! ◆Figure 2.20 provides another example of split-brain testing.

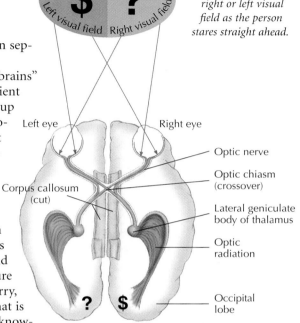

◆**FIGURE 2.19** *Basic nerve pathways of vision. Notice that the left portion of each eye connects only to the left half of the brain; likewise, the right portion of each eye connects to the right brain. When the corpus callosum is cut, a "split brain" results. Then visual information can be sent to just one hemisphere by flashing it in the right or left visual field as the person stares straight ahead.*

Left Brain
- Language
- Speech
- Writing
- Calculation
- Time sense
- Rhythm
- Ordering of complex movements

Right Brain
- Nonverbal
- Perceptual skills
- Visualization
- Recognition of patterns, faces, melodies
- Recognition and expression of emotion
- Spatial skills
- Simple language comprehension

I see a circle.

Left Hemisphere

I see nothing.

Right Hemisphere

◆**FIGURE 2.20** *A circle is flashed to the left brain of a split-brain patient, and he is asked what he saw. He easily replies, "A circle." He can also pick out the circle by merely touching shapes with his right hand, out of sight behind a screen. However, his left hand can't identify the circle. If a triangle is flashed to the patient's right brain, he can't say what he saw (speech is controlled by the left hemisphere). He also can't identify the triangle by touch with the right hand. Now, however, the left hand has no difficulty picking out the triangle. In other tests, the hemispheres reveal distinct skills, as listed above the drawing.*

"Split-brain" operation Cutting the corpus callosum.

When a ✓

Right Brain/Left Brain

Earlier it was stated that the hemispheres differ in abilities; in what ways are they different? The brain divides its work in interesting ways. Roughly 95 percent of us use our left brain for language (speaking, writing, and understanding). In addition, the left hemisphere is superior at math, judging time and rhythm, and coordinating the order of complex movements, such as those needed for speech.

In contrast, the right hemisphere can produce only the simplest language and numbers. Working with the right brain is like talking to a child who can say only a dozen words or so. To answer questions, the right hemisphere must use non-verbal responses, such as pointing at objects (see Fig. 2.20).

Although it is poor at producing language, the right brain has it own talents. The right brain is especially good at perceptual skills, such as recognizing patterns, faces, and melodies; putting together a puzzle; or drawing a picture. It also helps you express emotions and detect the emotions that other people are feeling (Borod et al., 1998; Christianson et al., 1995).

One Brain, Two Styles

In general, the left hemisphere is mainly involved with *analysis* (breaking information into parts). It also processes information *sequentially* (in order, one item after the next). The right hemisphere appears to process information *simultaneously* and *holistically* (all at once) (Springer & Deutsch, 1998).

To summarize further, you could say that the right hemisphere is better at assembling pieces of the world into a coherent picture; it sees overall patterns and general connections. The left brain focuses on small details (see ◆Fig. 2.21). The right brain sees the wide-angle view; the left zooms in on specifics. The focus of the left brain is local, the right is global (Heinze et al., 1998; Hellige, 1993; Huebner, 1998).

Do people normally do puzzles or draw pictures with just the right hemisphere? Do they do other things with only the left? Numerous books have been written about how to use the right brain to manage, teach, draw, ride horses, learn, cook, and even make love (Carter, 1998). But such books drastically oversimplify right- and left-brain differences. People normally use both sides of the brain at all times. It's true that some tasks may make *more* use of one hemisphere or the other. But in most "real world" activities, the hemispheres share the work. Each does the parts it does best and shares information with the other side. Popular books and courses that claim to teach "right-brain thinking" ignore the fact that everyone already uses the right brain for thinking (Hellige, 1990; Ornstein, 1997). To do anything well requires the talents and processing abilities of both hemispheres. A smart brain is one that grasps both the details and the overall picture at the same time (Ornstein, 1997). For example, during a concert, Yo-Yo Ma will use his left brain to judge time and rhythm and coordinate the order of his hand movements. At the same time, he will use his right brain to recognize and organize melodies.

Left hemisphere
DETAILS

"A bunch of Ds"

DDDD
DDDDD

"It's about sewing."

A stitch in time saves nine.

"Dots and blobs"

Ronald C. James

Right hemisphere
OVERALL PATTERN

"The letter L"

"A small effort now saves time later."

"A dog"

◆**FIGURE 2.21** *The left and right brain have different information-processing styles. The left brain focuses on the small details; the right gets the big pattern. (Photograph by R. C. James.)*

Lobes of the Cerebral Cortex

In addition to the two big hemispheres, the cerebral cortex can be divided into several smaller *lobes* (areas bordered by major grooves or fissures or defined by their functions). Many of the lobes of the cerebral cortex are defined by larger fissures on the surface of the cerebrum. Others are regarded as separate areas because their functions are quite different (see ◆Fig. 2.22).

The Occipital Lobes

At the back of the brain, we find the **occipital lobes** (awk-SIP-ih-tal), the primary visual area of the cortex. Patients with tumors (cell growths that interfere with brain activity) in the occipital lobes experience blind spots in their vision.

Occipital lobes Portion of the cerebral cortex where vision registers in the brain.

Do the visual areas of the cortex correspond directly to what is seen? Images are mapped onto the cortex, but the map is greatly stretched and distorted (Carlson, 2001). It is important to avoid thinking of the visual area as being like a little TV screen in the brain. Visual information creates complex patterns of activity in nerve cells; it does *not* make a TV-like image.

The Parietal Lobes

Bodily sensations register in the **parietal lobes** (puh-RYE-ih-tal), located just above the occipital lobes. Touch, temperature, pressure, and other somatic sensations flow into the **somatosensory area** (SO-mat-oh-SEN-so-ree) on the parietal lobes. Again, we find that the map of bodily sensations is distorted. The drawing in ◆Figure 2.23 shows that the cortex reflects the *sensitivity* of body areas, not their size. For example, the lips are large in the drawing because of their great sensitivity, while the back and trunk, which are less sensitive, are much smaller. Notice that the hands are also large in the map of body sensitivity—which is obviously an aid to musicians, typists, watchmakers, massage therapists, lovers, and brain surgeons.

Frontal lobe
(sense of smell, motor control, and higher mental abilities such as reasoning and planning)

Parietal lobe
(sensation such as touch, temperature, and pressure)

Occipital lobe
(vision)

Temporal lobe
(hearing and language)

Cerebellum
(posture, coordination, muscle tone, and memory of skills and habits)

◆FIGURE 2.22

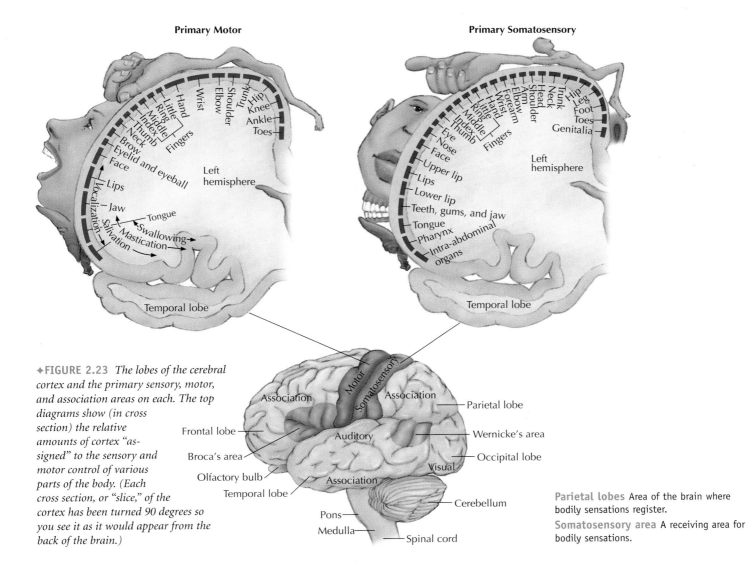

◆**FIGURE 2.23** *The lobes of the cerebral cortex and the primary sensory, motor, and association areas on each. The top diagrams show (in cross section) the relative amounts of cortex "assigned" to the sensory and motor control of various parts of the body. (Each cross section, or "slice," of the cortex has been turned 90 degrees so you see it as it would appear from the back of the brain.)*

Parietal lobes Area of the brain where bodily sensations register.

Somatosensory area A receiving area for bodily sensations.

The Temporal Lobes

The temporal lobes are located on each side of the brain. Auditory information projects directly to the **temporal lobes,** making them the main site where hearing registers. If we did a PET scan of your brain and then started your favorite musical CD, your temporal lobes would light up. Likewise, if we could stimulate the auditory area of your temporal lobe, you would "hear" a series of sound sensations.

For most people, the left temporal lobe also contains a language "center." (For 5 percent of all people, the area is on the right temporal lobe.) Damage to the temporal lobe can severely limit ability to use language. (More on this later.)

The Frontal Lobes

The **frontal lobes** are associated with higher mental abilities. This area is also responsible for the control of movement. Specifically, an arch of tissue over the top of the brain, called the **motor cortex,** directs the body's muscles. If this area is stimulated with an electrical current, various parts of the body will twitch or move. Like the somatosensory area, the motor cortex corresponds to the importance of bodily areas, not to their size. The hands, for example, get more area than the feet (see Fig. 2.23). If you've ever wondered why your hands are more dextrous than your feet, it's partly because more motor cortex is devoted to the hands.

The frontal lobes are also related to more complex behaviors. If the frontal lobes are damaged, a patient's personality and emotional life may change dramatically. (Remember Phineas Gage, the railroad foreman described in Chapter 1?) Reasoning or planning may also be affected. Patients with frontal lobe damage often get "stuck" on mental tasks and repeat the same wrong answers over and over (Goel & Grafman, 1995). PET scans suggest that much of what we call intelligence is related to increased activity in the frontal areas of the cortex (Duncan et al., 2000). Sadly, drug abuse is one way in which this important area of the brain may be damaged (Liu et al., 1998).

] SURVEYQUESTION *Why are the brain's association areas important? What happens when they are injured?*

Association Areas

Only a small part of the cerebral cortex directly controls the body and receives information from the senses. All the surrounding areas, which are called the **association cortex,** combine and process information from the senses. If you see a rose, the association areas will help you recognize it and name it. The association cortex also contributes to higher mental abilities. For example, a person with damage to association areas on the left hemisphere may suffer an **aphasia** (ah-FAZE-yah; impaired ability to use language).

One type of aphasia is related to **Broca's area** (BRO-cahs), a "speech center" on the left frontal lobe (Leonard, 1997). Damage to Broca's area causes great difficulty in speaking or writing. Typically, a patient's grammar and pronunciation are poor and speech is slow and labored. For example, the person may say "bife" for bike, "seep" for sleep, or "zokaid" for zodiac. Generally, the person knows what she or he wants to say but can't seem to utter the words (Geschwind, 1979).

If Broca's area is damaged, the amount of language loss a person suffers may relate to his or her sex. "His and Her Brains?" explains why.

A second language site, called **Wernicke's area** (VER-nick-ees; see Fig. 2.23), lies on the left temporal lobe. If it is damaged, the person has problems with the *meaning* of words, not their pronunciation. Someone with Broca's aphasia might say "tssair" when shown a picture of a chair. In contrast, a Wernicke's patient might say "stool" (Leonard, 1997).

In summary, the bulk of our daily experience and all our understanding of the world can be traced to the sensory, motor, and association areas of the cortex. The human brain is among the most advanced and sophisticated of the brain-bearing species on Earth. This, of course, is no guarantee that this marvelous "biocomputer" will be put to full use. Still, we must stand in awe of the potential it represents.

Temporal lobes Areas that include the sites where hearing registers in the brain.

Frontal lobes A brain area associated with movement, the sense of smell, and higher mental functions.

Motor cortex A brain area associated with control of movement.

Association cortex All areas of the cerebral cortex that are not primarily sensory or motor in function.

Aphasia A speech disturbance resulting from brain damage.

Broca's area A language area related to grammar and pronunciation.

Wernicke's area An area related to language comprehension.

HUMAN DIVERSITY His and Her Brains?

A patient has had a stroke, and it looks like Broca's area was damaged. As expected, the patient's speech is impaired. Will the patient recover any language skills? It may depend on his or her sex.

When Broca's area is damaged, women typically regain more of their lost abilities than men do. Why should this be so? Let's look at some male and female brains for an answer.

Researchers used brain imaging to observe brain activity while people did language tasks. As they worked, both men and women showed increased activity in Broca's area, on the left side of the brain. This is exactly what we would expect. However, to the scientists' surprise, both the left *and the right* brain were activated in more than half the women tested. Apparently, male and female brains tend to differ in ways that can affect speech and language (see ◆Fig. 2.24) (Rossell et al., 2002; Shaywitz & Gore, 1995; Skrandies, Reik, & Kunze, 1999).

Using both sides of the brain for language may be a big advantage. When Broca's area is damaged, some women can use the right side of their brains to compensate for the loss (Hochstenbach et al., 1998). Men with similar damage have little chance of improving. Thus, when a man says, "I have half a mind to tell you what I think," he may be stating a curious truth. The same is true for listening to words, which tends to occur on the left side of male brains and both sides of female brains (Phillips et al., 2001).

◆FIGURE 2.24 *Language tasks activate both sides of the brain in many women but only the left side in men.*

Shaywitz et al., 1995 NMR Research/Yale Medical School

STUDYBREAK Y *Cerebral Cortex and Lobes of the Brain*

RELATE

Learning the functions of the brain lobes is like learning areas on a map. Try drawing a map of the cortex. Can you label all the different "countries" (lobes)? Can you name their functions? Where is the motor cortex? The somatosensory area? Broca's area? Keep redrawing the map until it becomes more detailed and you can do it easily.

LEARNING CHECK

See if you can match the following:

1. _____ Corpus callosum
2. _____ Occipital lobes
3. _____ Parietal lobes
4. _____ Temporal lobes
5. _____ Frontal lobes
6. _____ Association cortex
7. _____ Aphasias
8. _____ Corticalization

9. _____ Left hemisphere
10. _____ Right hemisphere
11. _____ "Split brain"

A. Visual area
B. Language, speech, and writing
C. Motor cortex and abstract thinking
D. Spatial skills, visualization, and pattern recognition
E. Speech disturbances
F. Causes sleep
G. Increased ratio of cortex in brain
H. Bodily sensations
I. Treatment for severe epilepsy
J. Hearing
K. Fibers connecting the cerebral hemispheres
L. Cortex that is not sensory or motor in function

Critical Thinking

12. If you wanted to increase the surface area of the cerebrum so that more cerebral cortex would fit within the skull, how would you do it?
13. What would be some of the possible advantages and disadvantages to having a "split brain"?
14. If your brain were removed, moved into another body, and another brain was inserted into your body, which would you consider to be yourself, your old body with the new brain, or your new body with the old brain?

ANSWERS

1. K 2. A 3. H 4. J 5. C 6. L 7. E 8. G 9. B 10. D 11. I 12. One solution would be to gather the surface of the cortex into folds, just as you might if you were trying to fit a large piece of cloth into a small box. This, in fact, is probably why the cortex is more convoluted (folded or wrinkled) in higher animals. 13. If information were properly routed to each brain hemisphere, it would be possible to have both hands working simultaneously on conflicting tasks. However, such possible benefits would only apply under highly controlled conditions. 14. Although there is no "correct" answer to this question, your personality, knowledge, personal memories, and self-concept all derive from brain activity—which makes a strong case for your old brain in a new body being more nearly the "real you."

THE SUBCORTEX—AT THE CORE OF THE (BRAIN) MATTER

] SURVEYQUESTION *What kinds of behaviors are controlled by the subcortex?*

You could lose large portions of your cerebrum and still survive. Not so with the brain areas below the cortex, however. Serious damage to the subcortex (lower brain) can be fatal. Hunger, thirst, sleep, attention, sex, breathing, and many other vital functions are controlled by parts of the subcortex. Let's take a quick tour of these brain areas.

The **subcortex** lies immediately below the cerebral hemispheres. This area can be divided into the brainstem (or hindbrain), the midbrain, and the forebrain. (The forebrain also includes the cerebral cortex, which we have already discussed because of its size and importance.) For our purposes the midbrain can be viewed as a link between the forebrain and the brainstem. Therefore, let us focus on the rest of the subcortex (see ✦Fig. 2.25).

The Hindbrain

Why are the lower brain areas so important?   As the spinal cord joins the brain, it widens into the brainstem. The **brainstem** consists mainly of the medulla (meh-DUL-ah) and the cerebellum (ser-ah-BEL-uhm). The **medulla** contains centers important for the reflex control of vital life functions, including heart rate, breathing, swallowing, and the like. Various drugs, diseases, and injuries can disrupt the medulla and end or endanger life. That's why a karate chop to the back of the neck can be extremely dangerous.

The **pons,** which looks like a small bump on the brainstem, acts as a bridge between the medulla and other brain areas. In addition to connecting with many other locations, including the cerebellum, the pons influences sleep and arousal.

The cerebellum, which looks like a miniature cerebral cortex, lies at the base of the brain. The **cerebellum** primarily regulates posture, muscle tone, and muscular coordination. The cerebellum also stores memories related to skills and habits (Thompson, 1991).

What happens if the cerebellum is injured?   Without the cerebellum, tasks such as walking, running, or playing catch would be impossible. The first symptoms of a crippling disease called *spinocerebellar degeneration* are tremor, dizziness, and muscular weakness. Eventually, victims have difficulty merely standing, walking, or feeding themselves.

Reticular Formation

A network of fibers and cell bodies called the **reticular** (reh-TICK-you-ler) **formation** (**RF**) lies inside the medulla and brainstem. As messages flow into the brain, the RF gives priority to some while turning others aside. By doing so, the RF influences *attention*. The RF doesn't fully mature until adolescence, which may be why children have such short attention spans. The RF also modifies outgoing commands to the body. In this way the RF affects muscle tone, posture, and movements of the eyes, face, head, body, and limbs. At the same time, the RF controls reflexes involved in breathing, sneezing, coughing, and vomiting.

Keeping us vigilant, alert, and awake is another important task of the reticular formation. Incoming messages from the sense organs branch into a part of the RF called the **reticular activating system** (**RAS**). The RAS bombards the cortex with stimulation, keeping it active and alert. For instance, let's say a sleepy driver rounds a bend and sees a deer standing in the road. The driver snaps to attention and applies the brakes. She can thank her RAS for arousing the rest of her brain and averting an accident. If you're getting sleepy while reading this chapter, try pinching your ear—a little pain will cause the RAS to momentarily arouse your cortex.

The Forebrain

Like hidden gemstones, two of the most important parts of your body lie buried deep within your brain. The thalamus (THAL-uh-mus) and an area just below it called the hypothalamus (HI-po-THAL-uh-mus) are key parts of the forebrain (see Fig. 2.25).

Subcortex All brain structures below the cerebral cortex.

Brainstem The lowest portions of the brain, including the cerebellum, medulla, pons, and reticular formation.

Medulla The structure that connects the brain with the spinal cord and controls vital life functions.

Pons An area on the brainstem that acts as a bridge between the medulla and other structures.

Cerebellum A brain structure that controls posture and coordination.

Reticular formation A network within the medulla and brainstem; associated with attention, alertness, and some reflexes.

Reticular activating system (RAS) A part of the reticular formation that activates the cerebral cortex.

[Handwritten margin note: mind brain- connects the hind + fore bran]

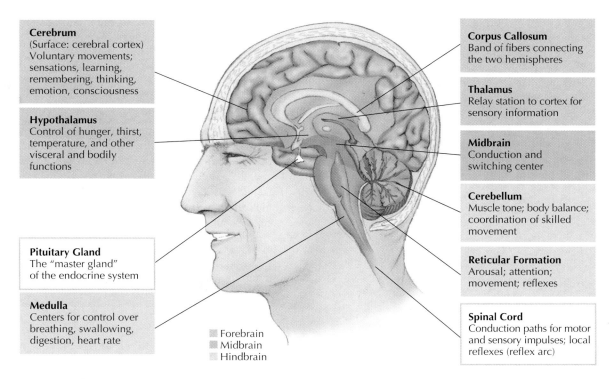

Cerebrum
(Surface: cerebral cortex)
Voluntary movements;
sensations, learning,
remembering, thinking,
emotion, consciousness

Hypothalamus
Control of hunger, thirst,
temperature, and other
visceral and bodily
functions

Pituitary Gland
The "master gland"
of the endocrine system

Medulla
Centers for control over
breathing, swallowing,
digestion, heart rate

Corpus Callosum
Band of fibers connecting
the two hemispheres

Thalamus
Relay station to cortex for
sensory information

Midbrain
Conduction and
switching center

Cerebellum
Muscle tone; body balance;
coordination of skilled
movement

Reticular Formation
Arousal; attention;
movement; reflexes

Spinal Cord
Conduction paths for motor
and sensory impulses; local
reflexes (reflex arc)

■ Forebrain
■ Midbrain
■ Hindbrain

✦**FIGURE 2.25** *This simplified drawing shows the main structures of the human brain and describes some of their most important features. (You can use the color code in the foreground to identify which areas are part of the forebrain, midbrain, and hindbrain.)*

The **thalamus** acts as a final "switching station" for sensory messages on their way to the cortex. Vision, hearing, taste, and touch all pass through this small, football-shaped structure. Thus, injury to even small areas of the thalamus can cause deafness, blindness, or loss of any sense, with the exception of smell (which connects directly to the cortex).

The human hypothalamus is about the size of a small grape. Small as it may be, the **hypothalamus** is a kind of master control center for emotion and many basic motives (Carlson, 2001). The hypothalamus affects behaviors as diverse as sex, rage, temperature control, hormone release, eating and drinking, sleep, waking, and emotion. The hypothalamus is basically a "crossroads" that connects many areas of the brain. It is also the final pathway for many kinds of behavior. That is, the hypothalamus is the last place where many behaviors are organized or "decided on" before messages leave the brain, causing the body to react.

The Limbic System

As a group, the hypothalamus, parts of the thalamus, the amygdala, the hippocampus, and other structures make up the limbic system (✦Fig. 2.26). The **limbic system** has a major role in producing emotion and motivating behavior. Rage, fear, sexual response, and intense arousal can be obtained from various points in the limbic system.

Scientists used to think that all emotions are processed by the cerebral cortex. However, this is not always the case. Imagine this test of willpower: Go to a zoo and place your face close to the glass in front of a rattlesnake display. Suddenly, the rattlesnake strikes at your face. Do you flinch? Even though you know you are safe, researcher Joseph LeDoux predicts that you will recoil from the snake's attack (LeDoux, 1999).

LeDoux and other researchers have found that an area of the brain called the **amygdala** (ah-MIG-duh-la) specializes in producing fear. The amygdala receives sensory information very directly and quickly, bypassing the cortex. As a result, it allows us to respond to potentially dangerous stimuli before we really know what's happening. This primitive fear response is not under the control of higher brain centers. The role of the amygdala in emotion may explain why people who suffer from phobias and disabling anxiety often feel afraid without knowing why (LeDoux, 1999).

People who suffer damage to the amygdala become "blind" to emotion. An armed robber could hold a gun to the person's head and the person wouldn't feel fear. Such people are

The limbic system is responsible for many of our emotional responses. The amygdala, in particular, produces rapid fear, which can help protect us from danger. If you unexpectedly saw a rattlesnake, it is likely that you would jump back instantly in fear, without having to first think about whether you were in danger.

Thalamus A brain structure that relays sensory information to the cerebral cortex.
Hypothalamus A small area of the brain that regulates emotional behaviors and motives.
Limbic system A system in the forebrain that is closely linked with emotional response.
Amygdala A part of the limbic system associated with fear responses.

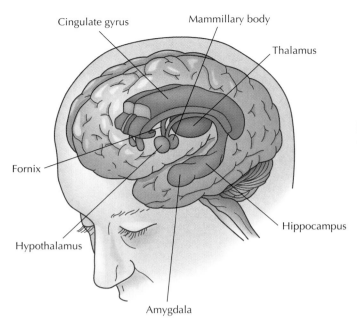

Cingulate gyrus   Mammillary body

Thalamus

Fornix

Hypothalamus

Amygdala

Hippocampus

◆FIGURE 2.26 *Parts of the limbic system. Although only one side is shown here, the hippocampus and the amygdala extend out into the temporal lobes at each side of the brain. The limbic system is a sort of "primitive core" of the brain strongly associated with emotion.*

also unable to "read" or understand other people's emotions. Many lose their ability to relate normally to friends, family, and co-workers (Goleman, 1995).

Some parts of the limbic system have taken on additional, higher-level functions. A part called the **hippocampus** (HIP-oh-CAMP-us) is important for forming lasting memories (Bigler et al., 1996). The hippocampus lies inside the temporal lobes, which is why stimulating the temporal lobes can produce memory-like or dream-like experiences. The hippocampus also helps us navigate through space. Your right hippocampus will become more active, for instance, if you mentally plan a drive across town (Maguire et al., 1997).

Psychologists have discovered that animals will learn to press a lever to deliver a rewarding dose of electrical stimulation to the limbic system. The animals act like the stimulation is satisfying or pleasurable. Indeed, several areas of the limbic system act as reward, or "pleasure," pathways. Many are found in the hypothalamus, where they overlap with areas that control thirst, sex, and hunger. Commonly abused drugs such as cocaine, amphetamine, heroin, nicotine, marijuana, and alcohol activate many of the same pleasure pathways. This appears to explain, in part, why these drugs are so powerfully rewarding (Wise & Rompre, 1989). You might also be interested to know that music you would describe as "thrilling" activates pleasure systems in your brain. This may explain some of the appeal of music that can send shivers down your spine (Blood & Zatorre, 2001). (It may also explain why people will pay so much for concert tickets!)

Punishment, or "aversive," areas have also been found in the limbic system. When these locations are activated, animals show discomfort and will work hard to turn off the stimulation. Because much of our behavior is based on seeking pleasure and avoiding pain, these discoveries continue to fascinate psychologists.

The Brain in Perspective

Given the amount of information covered in our journey through the brain, a short review is in order. We have seen that the human brain is an impressive assembly of billions of sensitive cells and nerve fibers. The brain controls vital bodily functions, keeps track of the external world, issues commands to the muscles and glands, responds to current needs, creates the magic of consciousness, and regulates its own behavior—*all* at the same time.

A final note of caution is now in order: For the sake of simplicity, we have assigned functions to each "part" of the brain as if it were a computer. This is only a half-truth. In reality, the brain is a vast information-processing system. Incoming information scatters all over the brain and converges again as it goes out through the spinal cord to muscles and glands. The overall system is much, much more complicated than our discussion of separate "parts" implies.

We began our exploration of the brain with a virtuoso musician. Imagine the other extreme of being completely unable to move or speak. Even though you would remain alert and intelligent, you would be unable to communicate your simplest thoughts and feelings to others. Each year, this is the fate of thousands of people who are paralyzed by stroke, disease, or injury. In a very real sense, these people become prisoners in their own bodies (Christensen, 1999). What if they could "will" a computer to speak for them?

In pioneering studies, doctors Roy Bakay and Philip Kennedy have inserted special electrodes into the motor cortex of paralyzed patients. When the patient thinks certain thoughts, the implanted wires detect bursts of activity. Instantly, these signals are transmitted to a computer, where they control the movements of a cursor on the screen. Patients are now learning to select icons on the screen that tell the computer to say phrases such as, "Please turn the light on," or "See you later, nice talking to you." (Kennedy & Bakay, 1998).

Neuroscientists realize that they have only taken baby steps toward freeing "locked-in" patients. Nevertheless, what was merely science fiction a few years ago is starting to become reality. The human brain is just beginning to understand itself. What an adventure the next decade of brain research will be.

Hippocampus A part of the limbic system associated with storing memories.

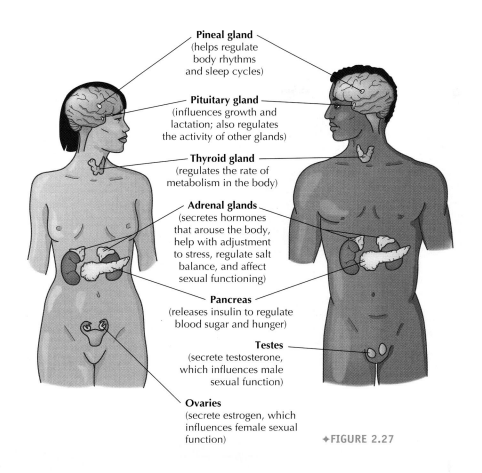

Pineal gland
(helps regulate
body rhythms
and sleep cycles)

Pituitary gland
(influences growth and
lactation; also regulates
the activity of other glands)

Thyroid gland
(regulates the rate of
metabolism in the body)

Adrenal glands
(secretes hormones
that arouse the body,
help with adjustment
to stress, regulate salt
balance, and affect
sexual functioning)

Pancreas
(releases insulin to regulate
blood sugar and hunger)

Testes
(secrete testosterone,
which influences male
sexual function)

Ovaries
(secrete estrogen, which
influences female sexual
function)

✦FIGURE 2.27

THE ENDOCRINE SYSTEM—HORMONES AND BEHAVIOR

] SURVEYQUESTION *Does the glandular system affect behavior?*

Our behavior is not solely a product of the nervous system. The endocrine glands (EN-duh-krin) serve as a second great communication system in the body. The **endocrine system** is made up of glands that pour chemicals directly into the bloodstream or lymph system (see ✦Fig. 2.27). These chemicals, called **hormones,** are carried throughout the body, where they affect both internal activities and visible behavior. Hormones are related to neurotransmitters. Like other such chemicals, hormones activate cells in the body. To respond, the cells must have receptor sites for the hormone. Hormones can affect everything from puberty to personality, giantism to jet lag.

How do hormones affect behavior?   Although we are seldom aware of them, hormones affect us in many ways. Here is a brief sample: Hormone output from the adrenal glands rises during stressful situations; androgens ("male" hormones) are related to the sex drive in both males and females; hormones secreted during times of high emotion intensify memory formation; at least some of the emotional turmoil of adolescence is due to elevated hormone levels; different hormones prevail when you are angry, rather than fearful. These are just samples; let's consider some additional effects hormones have on the body and behavior.

The pituitary is a pea-sized globe hanging from the base of the brain (return to Fig. 2.27). One of the pituitary's more important roles is to regulate growth. During childhood, the pituitary secretes a hormone that speeds body development. If too little **growth hormone** is released, a person may remain far smaller than average. If this condition is not treated, a child may be 6 to 12 inches shorter than age-mates. As adults, some will have *hypopituitary dwarfism* (HI-po-pih-TU-ih-ter-ee). Such individuals are perfectly proportioned

Endocrine system Glands whose secretions pass directly into the bloodstream or lymph system.

Hormone A glandular secretion that affects bodily functions or behavior.

Growth hormone A hormone, secreted by the pituitary gland, that promotes bodily growth.

Dan McCoy/Rainbow

Keystone/The Image Works

Underactivity of the pituitary gland may produce a dwarf; overactivity, a giant.

but tiny. Regular injections of growth hormone can raise a hypopituitary child's height by several inches, usually to the short side of average. Treatment, however, can last from 3 to 7 years and cost from $45,000 to $105,000.

Too much growth hormone produces *giantism* (excessive bodily growth). Secretion of too much growth hormone late in the growth period causes *acromegaly* (AK-row-MEG-uh-lee), a condition in which the arms, hands, feet, and facial bones become enlarged. Acromegaly produces prominent facial features, which some people have used as a basis for careers as character actors, wrestlers, and the like.

The pituitary also governs the functioning of other glands (especially the thyroid, adrenal glands, and ovaries or testes). These glands, in turn, regulate such bodily processes as metabolism, responses to stress, and reproduction. In women, the pituitary controls milk output during pregnancy.

The **pituitary** is often called the "master gland" because it influences other endocrine glands. But the master has a master: The pituitary is directed by the hypothalamus, which lies directly above it. In this way, the hypothalamus can affect glands throughout the body. This, then, is the major link between the brain and hormones (Carlson, 2001).

The pineal gland (pin-EE-ul) was once considered a useless remnant of evolution. However, its function in humans is now coming to light (so to speak). The **pineal gland** releases a hormone called **melatonin** (mel-ah-TONE-in) in response to daily variations in light. Melatonin levels in the bloodstream rise at dusk and peak around midnight. They fall again as morning approaches. This light-driven cycle helps control body rhythms and sleep cycles. As far as the brain is concerned, it's bedtime when melatonin levels rise (Attenburrow, Cowen, & Sharpley, 1996).

Studies of flight crews show that melatonin can be used to minimize jet lag. To reset the body's clock in a new time zone, a small amount of melatonin can be taken about an hour before bedtime. This dose is continued for as many days as necessary to ease jet lag. The same treatment can be used for rotating work shifts (Arendt, 1994; Brown, 1994; Comperatore et al, 1996).

The **thyroid gland**, located in the neck, regulates metabolism. As you may re-

Pituitary gland The "master gland" whose hormones influence other endocrine glands.
Pineal gland Gland in the brain that helps regulate body rhythms and sleep cycles.
Melatonin Hormone released by the pineal gland in response to daily cycles of light and dark.
Thyroid gland Endocrine gland that helps regulate the rate of metabolism.

Flight crews often suffer severe disruptions in their sleep cycles. For example, a crew that leaves Los Angeles at 4 P.M., bound for London, will arrive in 8 hours. Crew members' bodies, which are on California time, will act as if it is 12 A.M. Yet in London, it will be 8 A.M. Recent studies confirm that melatonin can help people adjust more rapidly to such time-zone changes.

Tom McCarthy/PhotoEdit

member from a biology course, *metabolism* is the rate at which energy is produced and expended in the body. By altering metabolism, the thyroid can have a sizable effect on personality. A person suffering from *hyperthyroidism* (an overactive thyroid) tends to be thin, tense, excitable, and nervous. An underactive thyroid (*hypothyroidism*) in an adult can cause inactivity, sleepiness, slowness, and obesity. In infancy, hypothyroidism limits development of the nervous system, leading to severe mental retardation.

When you are frightened or angry, some important reactions prepare your body for action: Your heart rate and blood pressure rise, stored sugar is released into the bloodstream for quick energy, your muscles tense and receive more blood, and your blood is prepared to clot more quickly in case of injury. As we discussed earlier, these changes are controlled by the autonomic nervous system. Specifically, the sympathetic branch of the ANS causes the hormones *epinephrine* and *norepinephrine* to be released by the adrenal glands. (Epinephrine is also known as adrenaline, a term that might be more familiar to you.) **Epinephrine** (ep-eh-NEF-rin), which is associated with fear, tends to arouse the body. **Norepinephrine** also tends to arouse the body, but it is linked with anger.

The **adrenal glands** are located just under the back of the rib cage, atop the kidneys. The *adrenal medulla,* or inner core of the adrenal glands, is the source of epinephrine and norepinephrine. The *adrenal cortex,* or outer "bark" of the adrenal glands, produces a set of hormones called *corticoids* (KOR-tih-coids). One of their jobs is to regulate salt balance in the body. A deficiency of certain corticoids in humans can evoke a powerful craving for the taste of salt. The corticoids also help the body adjust to stress, and they are a secondary source of sex hormones.

An oversecretion of the adrenal sex hormones can cause *virilism* (exaggerated male characteristics). For instance, a woman may grow a beard or a man's voice may become so low it is difficult to understand. Oversecretion early in life can cause *premature puberty* (full sexual development during childhood). One of the most remarkable cases on record is that of a 5-year-old Peruvian girl who gave birth to a son.

While we are on the topic of sex hormones, there is a related issue worth mentioning. One of the principal androgens, or "male" hormones, is testosterone, which is supplied in small amounts by the adrenal glands. (The testes are the main source of testosterone in males.) Perhaps you have heard about the use of anabolic steroids by athletes who want to "bulk up" or promote muscle growth. Most of these drugs are synthetic versions of testosterone.

Although many athletes believe otherwise, there is no evidence that steroids improve performance, and they may have serious side effects. Problems include voice deepening or baldness in women and shrinkage of the testicles, sexual impotence, or breast enlargement in men. When steroids are used by younger adolescents, an increased risk of heart attack and stroke, liver damage, or stunted growth are common (Bahrke, Yesalis, & Brower, 1998). Understandably, all major sports organizations ban the use of anabolic steroids.

During his bid for the major league homerun record, baseball star Mark McGwire admitted to using a steroid drug banned by the NFL and the Olympics but not by major league baseball. Many athletes have been disqualified, banned from competing, or stripped of metals for steroid use.

Epinephrine An adrenal hormone that tends to arouse the body; epinephrine is associated with fear. (Also known as adrenaline.)

Norepinephrine An adrenal hormone that tends to arouse the body; norepinephrine is associated with anger. (Also known as noradrenaline.)

Adrenal glands Endocrine glands that arouse the body, regulate salt balance, adjust the body to stress, and affect sexual functioning.

In this brief discussion of the endocrine system we have considered only a few of the more important glands. Nevertheless, this should give you an appreciation of how completely behavior and personality are tied to the ebb and flow of hormones in the body.

A Look Ahead

In the upcoming Psychology in Action section, we will return to the brain to see how hand preference relates to brain organization. You'll also find out if being right- or left-handed affects your chances of living to a ripe old age.

STUDYBREAK *Subcortex and Endocrine System*

RELATE

If Mr. Medulla met Ms. Cerebellum at a party, what would they say their roles are in the brain? Would a marching band in a "reticular formation" look like a network? Would it get your attention? If you were standing in the final path for behavior leaving the brain, would you be in the thalamus? Or in the hy-**path**-alamus (please forgive the misspelling)? When you are emotional, do you wave your limbs around (and does your limbic system become more active)?

Name as many of the endocrine glands as you can. Which did you leave out? Can you summarize the functions of each of the glands?

LEARNING CHECK

1. Three major divisions of the brain are the brainstem or
_____, the _____, and
the _____.
2. Reflex centers for heartbeat and respiration are found in the
a. cerebellum   b. thalamus   c. medulla   d. RF
3. A portion of the reticular formation, known as the RAS, serves
as an _____ system in the brain.
a. activating   b. adrenal   c. adjustment   d. aversive

4. The _____ is a final relay, or "switching station," for sensory information on its way to the cortex.
5. "Reward" and "punishment" areas are found throughout the _____ system, which is also related to emotion.
6. Undersecretion from the thyroid can cause
a. dwarfism   b. tgiantism   c. obesity
d. mental retardation
7. The body's ability to resist stress is related to the action of the adrenal _____.

Critical Thinking

8. Subcortical structures in humans are quite similar to corresponding lower brain areas in animals. Why would knowing this allow you to predict, in general terms, what functions are controlled by the subcortex?
9. Where in all the brain's "hardware" do you think the mind is found? What is the relationship between mind and brain?

ANSWERS

1. hindbrain, forebrain, midbrain 2. c 3. a 4. thalamus 5. limbic 6. c, d (in infancy) 7. cortex 8. Because the subcortex must be related to basic functions common to all higher animals: motives, emotions, sleep, attention, and vegetative functions such as heartbeat, breathing, and temperature regulation. The subcortex also routes and processes incoming information from the senses and out-going commands to the muscles. 9. This question, known as the mind-body problem, has challenged thinkers for centuries. One recent view is that mental states are "emergent properties" of brain activity. That is, brain activity forms complex patterns that are, in a sense, more than the sum of their parts. Or to use a rough analogy, if the brain were a musical instrument, then mental life would be like music played on that instrument.

Psychology in Action

Handedness—If Your Brain Is Right, What's Left?

] SURVEYQUESTION *How do right- and left-handed individuals differ?*

In the English language, "what's right is right," but what's left may be wrong. We have left-handed compliments, people with "two left feet," those who are left out, and the left-handed. On the other hand (so to speak), we have the right way, the right angle, the "right-hand man" (or woman), righteousness, and the right-handed.

What causes **handedness** (a preference for the right or left hand)? Why are more people right-handed than left-handed? How do left-handed and right-handed people differ? Does being left-handed create any problems—or benefits? The answers to these questions lead us back to the brain, where handedness begins. Let's see what research has revealed about handedness, the brain, and you.

Handedness A preference for the right or left hand in most activities.

Hand Dominance

Take a moment and write your name on a sheet of paper, first using your right hand and then your left. You were probably much more comfortable writing with your dominant hand. This is interesting because there's no real difference in the strength or dexterity of the hands themselves. The agility of your dominant hand is an outward expression of superior motor control on one side of the brain. If you are right-handed, there is literally more area on the left side of your brain devoted to controlling your right hand. If you are left-handed, the reverse applies (Volkmann et al., 1998).

The preceding exercise implies that you are either entirely right- or left-handed. But handedness is a matter of degree (Coren, 1992). To better assess your handedness, circle an answer for each of the questions that follow.

ARE YOU RIGHT- OR LEFT-HANDED?

1. Which hand do you normally use to write?   Right Left Either
2. Which hand would you use to throw a ball at a target?   Right Left Either
3. Which hand do you use to hold your toothbrush?   Right Left Either
4. Which hand do you use to hold a knife when cutting food?   Right Left Either
5. With which hand do you hold a hammer when hitting a nail?   Right Left Either
6. When you thread a needle, which hand holds the thread?   Right Left Either

To find your score, count the number of "Rights" you circled and multiply by 3. Then multiply the number of "Eithers" by 2. Next count the number of "Lefts" you circled. Now add all three totals and compare the result with the following scale (adapted from Coren, 1992).

17−18 Strongly right-handed
15−16 Moderately right-handed (mixed)
13−14 Mildly right-handed (mixed)
12 Ambidextrous
10−11 Mildly left-handed (mixed)
8−9 Moderately left-handed (mixed)
6−7 Strongly left-handed

A majority of people (about 77 percent) are strongly right- or left-handed. The rest show some inconsistency in hand preference. As you can see in the following list, such differences can affect performance in some sports (Coren, 1992).

SPORT	HANDEDNESS ADVANTAGE
Boxing	Left
Fencing	Left
Basketball	Mixed and ambidextrous
Ice hockey	Mixed and ambidextrous
Field hockey	Mixed and ambidextrous
Tennis	Strong left or strong right
Squash	Strong left or strong right
Badminton	Strong left or strong right

Away from sports, left-handedness has an undeserved bad reputation. The supposed clumsiness of lefties is merely a result of living in a right-handed world: If it can be gripped, turned, or pulled, it's probably designed for the right hand. Even toilet handles are on the right side.

If a person is strongly left-handed, does that mean the right hemisphere is dominant?   Not necessarily. It's true that the right hemisphere controls the left hand, but a left-handed person's language-producing, **dominant hemisphere** may be on the opposite side of the brain.

Left-handers have an advantage in sports such as fencing and boxing. Most likely, their movements are less familiar to opponents, who usually face right-handers (Coren, 1992).

Bob Daemmrich/The Image Works

Brain Dominance

About 97 percent of right-handers process speech in the left hemisphere and are left-brain dominant (♦Fig. 2.28). A good 68 percent of left-handers produce speech from the left hemisphere, just as right-handed people do. About 19 percent of all lefties and 3 percent of

Dominant hemisphere A term usually applied to the side of a person's brain that produces language.

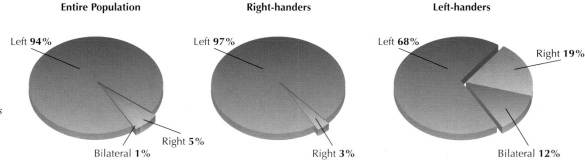

Entire Population   **Right-handers**   **Left-handers**

Left **94%**   Left **97%**   Left **68%**   Right **19%**

✦FIGURE 2.28 *Language is controlled by the left side of the brain in the majority of right- and left-handers.*

Right **5%**   Right **3%**

Bilateral **1%**   Bilateral **12%**

righties use their right brain for language. Some left-handers (approximately 12 percent) use both sides of the brain for language processing. In total, 94 percent of the population uses the left brain for language (Coren, 1992).

Is there any way for a person to tell which of his or her hemispheres is dominant? One interesting clue is based on the way you write. Right-handed individuals who write with a straight hand, and lefties who write with a hooked hand, are usually left-brain dominant for language. Left-handed people who write with their hand below the line, and righties who use a hooked position, are usually right-brain dominant (Levy & Reid, 1976). Another hint is provided by hand gestures. As you talk, if you gesture mostly with your right hand, you probably process language in your left hemisphere. Gesturing with your left hand is associated with right-brain language processing (Hellige, 1993). Are your friends right brained or left brained (see ✦Fig. 2.29)?

Before you leap to any conclusions, be aware that writing position is not a foolproof method of determining which hemisphere is dominant. The only sure way to check is to do a medical test that involves briefly anesthetizing one cerebral hemisphere at a time (Springer & Deutsch, 1998).

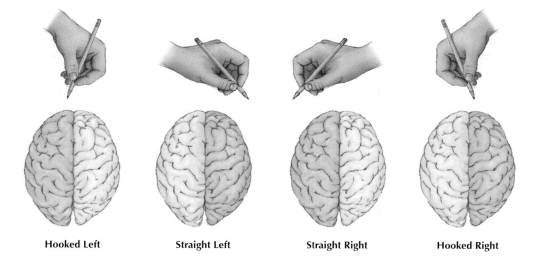

✦FIGURE 2.29 *Research suggests that the hand position used in writing may indicate which brain hemisphere is used for language. (Redrawn from an illustration by M. E. Challinor.)*

Hooked Left   **Straight Left**   **Straight Right**   **Hooked Right**

Handedness

How common is left-handedness, and what causes it? Ninety percent of all humans are right-handed; 10 percent are left-handed. In the past, many left-handed children were forced to use their right hand for writing, eating, and other skills. But as fetal ultrasound images show, clear hand preferences are apparent even before birth (Hepper, McCartney, & Shannon, 1998) (see ✦Fig. 2.30). This suggests that handedness cannot be dictated. Parents should never try to force a left-handed child to use the right hand. To do so may create speech or reading problems.

Is handedness inherited from parents?   Studies of twins show that hand preferences are not directly inherited like eye color or skin color (Reiss et al., 1999; Ross et al., 1999). Yet two left-handed parents are more likely to have a left-handed child than two right-handed parents are (McKeever, 2000). This suggests that handedness is influenced by heredity, at least to a degree. The best evidence to date shows that handedness is influenced by a single gene on the X (female) chromosome (Jones & Martin, 2001). However, learning, birth traumas, and social pressure to use the right hand can also affect which hand you end up favoring (McKeever et al., 2000; Provins, 1997).

Are there any drawbacks to being left-handed?   A minority of lefties owe their hand preference to birth traumas such as prematurity, low birth weight, and breech birth. These individuals have a higher incidence of allergies, learning disorders, and other problems (Betancur et al., 1990). But in most instances, left-handedness is unrelated to intelligence or the overall rate of illness and accidental injury (McManus et al., 1988; Porac et al., 1998).

Then why do right-handed people seem to live longer than left-handed people?   It is true that there is a shortage of very old lefties. However, this does not mean that the left-handed die early. It just reflects the fact that, in the past, more left-handed children were forced to become right-handed. That makes it look like many lefties don't survive to old age. In reality, they do, but many of them are masquerading as righties (Martin & Freitas, 2002)!

✦**FIGURE 2.30** *In this ultrasound image, a 4-month-old fetus sucks her right thumb. A study by psychologist Peter Hepper suggests that she will continue to prefer her right hand after she is born and that she will be right-handed as an adult.*

Advantage Left

Throughout history, a notable number of artists have been lefties, from Leonardo da Vinci and Michelangelo to Pablo Picasso and M. C. Escher. Conceivably, because the right hemisphere is superior at imagery and visual abilities, there is some advantage to using the left hand for drawing or painting (Springer & Deutsch, 1998). At the least, lefties are definitely better at visualizing three-dimensional objects. This may be why there are more left-handed architects, artists, and chess players than would be expected (Coren, 1992).

Lateralization refers to specialization in the abilities of the brain hemispheres. One striking feature of lefties is that they are generally less lateralized than the right-handed. In fact, even the physical size and shape of lefties' cerebral hemispheres are more alike. If you are a lefty, you can take pride in the fact that your brain is less lopsided than most! In general, left-handers are more symmetrical on almost everything, including eye dominance, fingerprints—even foot size (Polemikos & Papaeliou, 2000).

In some situations, less lateralization may be a real advantage. For instance, individuals who are moderately left-handed or ambidextrous seem to have better than average pitch memory, which is a basic musical skill. Correspondingly, more musicians are ambidextrous than would normally be expected (Springer & Deutsch, 1998).

Math abilities may also benefit from fuller use of the right hemisphere. Students who are extremely gifted in math are much more likely to be left-handed or ambidextrous (Benbow, 1986). Even where ordinary arithmetic skills are concerned, lefties seem to excel (Annett & Manning, 1990).

The clearest advantage of being left-handed shows up when there is a brain injury. Because of their milder lateralization, left-handed individuals typically experience less language loss after damage to either brain hemisphere, and they recover more easily (Geschwind, 1979). Maybe having "two left feet" isn't so bad after all.

Lateralization Differences between the two sides of the body; especially, differences in the abilities of the brain hemispheres.

STUDYBREAK *Handedness and Brain Lateralization*

RELATE

Think for a moment about what you "knew" about handedness and left-handed people before you read this section. Which of your beliefs were correct? How has your knowledge about handedness changed?

LEARNING CHECK

1. About 97 percent of left-handed people process language on the left side of the brain, the same as right-handed people do. T or F?
2. Left-handed individuals who write with their hand below the line are likely to be right-brain dominant. T or F?

3. People basically learn to be right- or left-handed. T or F?
4. In general, left-handed individuals show less lateralization in the brain and throughout the body. T or F?

Critical Thinking

5. News reports that left-handed people tend to die younger have been flawed in an important way: The average age of people in the left-handed group was younger than that of subjects in the right-handed group. Why would this make a difference in the conclusions drawn?

ANSWERS

1. F 2. T 3. F 4. T 5. Because we can't tell if handedness or average age accounts for the difference in death rates. For example, if we start with a group of 20- to 30-year-old people, in which some die, the average age of death has to be between 20 and 30. If we start with a group of 30- to 40-year-old people, in which some die, the average age of death has to be between 30 and 40. Thus, the left-handed group might have an earlier average age at death simply because members of the group were younger to start with.

CHAPTER IN REVIEW

Major Points

- Biopsychologists study how processes in the body, brain, and nervous system relate to behavior.
- Ultimately, all behavior can be traced to the activity of nerve cells.
- To map the brain, researchers activate or disable specific areas and observe changes in behavior.
- Bioelectrical recordings and computer-generated images of brain activity provide further insights into how the brain works.
- Sensations, thoughts, feelings, motives, actions, memories, and all other human capacities are associated with brain activities and structures.
- Endocrine glands serve as a chemical communication system within the body. Behavior is greatly influenced by the ebb and flow of hormones in the bloodstream.
- Brain dominance and brain activity determine if you are right-handed, left-handed, or ambidextrous.

Summary

How do nerve cells operate and communicate?

- The nervous system is made up of linked neurons that pass information from one to another through synapses.
- The basic conducting fibers of neurons are axons, but dendrites, the soma, and axon terminals are also involved in communication.
- The firing of an action potential (nerve impulse) is basically electrical. Communication between neurons is chemical.

- Neurotransmitters cross the synapse, attach to receptor sites, and excite or inhibit the receiving cell.
- Chemicals called neuropeptides appear to regulate activity in the brain.
- Nerves are made of axons and associated tissues. Neurons and nerves in the peripheral nervous system can often regenerate. At present, damage in the central nervous system is usually permanent, although scientists are working on ways to repair damaged neural tissue.

What are the functions of major parts of the nervous system?

- The nervous system can be divided into the central nervous system and the peripheral nervous system, which includes the somatic (bodily) and autonomic (involuntary) nervous systems.
- The autonomic system has a sympathetic branch and a parasympathetic branch.

How do we know how the brain works?

- Brain research relies on clinical studies, electrical stimulation, ablation, deep lesioning, electrical recording, micro-electrode recording, and EEG recording.
- Computer-enhanced images are providing three-dimensional pictures of the living human brain and its activity. Examples of such techniques are CT scans, MRI scans, and PET scans.

How is the brain organized, and what do its various areas do?

- The human brain is marked by advanced corticalization, or enlargement of the cerebral cortex.

- The left cerebral hemisphere contains speech or language "centers" in most people. It also specializes in writing, calculating, judging time and rhythm, and ordering complex movements.
- The right hemisphere is largely non-verbal. It excels at spatial and perceptual skills; visualization; and recognition of patterns, faces, and melodies.
- "Split brains" have been created in animals and humans by cutting the corpus callosum. The split-brain individual shows a remarkable degree of independence between the right and left hemispheres.
- The most basic functions of the lobes of the cerebral cortex are as follows: occipital lobes—vision; parietal lobes—bodily sensation; temporal lobes—hearing and language; frontal lobes—motor control, speech, and abstract thought. Damage to any of these areas will impair the named functions.

Why are the brain's association areas important? What happens when they are injured?

- Association areas on the cortex are neither sensory nor motor in function. They are related to more complex skills such as language, memory, recognition, and problem solving.
- Damage to either Broca's area or Wernicke's area causes speech and language problems known as aphasias.

What kinds of behaviors are controlled by the subcortex?

- The brain can be subdivided into the forebrain, midbrain, and hindbrain. The subcortex includes several crucial brain structures found at all three levels, below the cortex.
- The medulla contains centers essential for reflex control of heart rate, breathing, and other "vegetative" functions.
- The cerebellum maintains coordination, posture, and muscle tone.
- The reticular formation directs sensory and motor messages, and part of it, known as the RAS, acts as an activating system for the cerebral cortex.
- The thalamus carries sensory information to the cortex. The hypothalamus exerts powerful control over eating, drinking, sleep cycles, body temperature, and other basic motives and behaviors.
- The limbic system is strongly related to emotion. It also contains distinct reward and punishment areas and an area known as the hippocampus that is important for forming memories.

Is behavior affected by the glandular system?

- The endocrine system provides chemical communication in the body by releasing hormones into the bloodstream. Endocrine glands influence moods, behavior, and personality.

- Many of the endocrine glands are influenced by the pituitary (the "master gland"), which is, in turn, influenced by the hypothalamus. Thus, the brain controls the body through the fast nervous system and the slower endocrine system.

In what ways do right- and left-handed individuals differ?

- Hand dominance ranges from strongly left- to strongly right-handed, with mixed handedness and ambidexterity in between. Ninety percent of the population is basically right-handed and 10 percent left-handed.
- The vast majority of people are right-handed and, therefore, left-brain dominant for motor skills. Ninety-seven percent of right-handed persons and 68 percent of the left-handed also produce speech from the left hemisphere.
- In general, the left-handed are less strongly lateralized in brain function than are right-handed persons.

 Interactive Learning

Internet addresses frequently change. To find the sites listed here, visit www.psychology.wadsworth.com/coon_journey2e for an updated list of Internet addresses and direct links to relevant sites.

PSYCHOLOGY: A JOURNEY COMPANION WEB SITE Online quizzes, flash cards, and other helpful study aids for this text. *www.psychology.wadsworth.com/coon_journey2e*

BRAIN BRIEFINGS Articles on a variety of topics in neuroscience.

BRAIN CONNECTION Explains brain research to the public, including common myths about the brain, the effects of various chemicals, how brain research applies to education, and more.

LORIN'S LEFT-HANDEDNESS SITE Answers to common questions about left-handedness.

PROBE THE BRAIN Explore the motor homunculus of the brain interactively.

THE BRAIN QUIZ Answer questions about the brain and get instant feedback.

THE BRAIN: A WORK IN PROGRESS A set of related articles about the brain.

THE HUMAN BRAIN: DISSECTIONS OF THE REAL BRAIN Detailed photographs and drawings of the human brain.

THE ENDOCRINE SYSTEM Describes the endocrine system and hormones.

INFOTRAC COLLEGE EDITION For recent articles related to brain mapping, use Key Words search for MAGNETIC RESONANCE IMAGING and ELECTROENCEPHALOGRAPHY.

PSYCHNOW! 3a. Neurons and Synaptic Transmission, 3b. Brain and Behavior.

Test Your Knowledge: Brain and Behavior

The questions that follow are only a sample of what you need to know. If you miss any of the items, you should review the entire chapter and get more practice with *WebTutor* or the *Practice Quizzes* that came with this book. Another way to prepare for tests is to use the printed *Study Guide* that is available for this text.

1. The point at which information is passed from one neuron to another links the
   A. neurilemma and myelin   B. soma and ion channels
   C. axon terminals and dendrites   D. enkephalin and myelin

2. The activity of neurons is regulated by _____, which affect memory, pain, moods, hunger, and other processes.
   A. neuropeptides   B. neurilemmas   C. resting potentials
   D. dendrites

3. Muscles are activated by a transmitter substance called
   A. neuropeptide   B. acetylcholine   C. enkephalin
   D. endorphin

4. The brain grows new neurons to replace those that are lost. This process is known as
   A. neurogenesis   B. neuileminal regeneration
   C. autonomic regeneration   D. neuropeptosis

5. Nerves are made up of bundles of dendrites and
   A. action potentials   B. neurotransmitters   C. synapses
   D. axons

6. The somatic nervous system is part of the
   A. PNS   B. ANS   C. sympathetic branch
   D. axon terminal

7. Quieting the body and returning it to a lower level of arousal after an emotional event is a specialty of the
   A. parasympathetic system   B. peripheral nervous system
   C. spinal nerves   D. effector cells

8. To record the electrical activity of a single neuron, you would need to use
   A. an EEG   B. ESB   C. a micro-electrode   D. surface ablation

9. Which research technique provides an image of ongoing brain activity?
   A. ESB   B. deep lesioning   C. PET   D. surface ablation

10. Among animals and humans, greater corticalization is associated with increased
   A. muscular coordination   B. intelligence   C. fight-or-fight responses   D. conduction speed in the axon

11. The left hemisphere of the brain processes information sequentially, and it is superior at
   A. recognizing patterns   B. holistic thinking
   C. expressing and detecting emotions   D. analysis

12. In a "split-brain" operation, the _____ is cut, thereby separating the two cerebral _____.
   A. corpus callosum, hemispheres   B. chiasm, medullas
   C. motor cortex, lobes   D. occipital region, reticulums

13. Impaired hearing could result from damage to the _____ lobes of the brain.
   A. frontal   B. temporal   C. occipital   D. parietal

14. Damage to Broca's area causes
   A. a loss of coordination   B. disturbed sleep patterns
   C. aphasia   D. an inability to remember recent events

15. Structures in the brain that play a major role in producing emotion and motivating behavior are called the
   A. thalamic branch of the RAS   B. cerebellar activating system   C. medial brainstem   D. limbic system

16. Which of the following parts of the brain is most involved in forming lasting memories?
   A. amygdala   B. hippocampus   C. thalamus
   D. hypothalamus

17. The endocrine gland that most influences the activities of other glands is the
   A. pituitary   B. adrenal   C. pineal   D. thyroid

18. Dwarfism and giantism can be caused by problems in the
   A. pituitary gland   B. adrenal glands   C. pineal gland
   D. thyroid gland

19. A majority of both right-handed and left-handed people produce speech from the
   A. right brain hemisphere   B. corpus callosum
   C. left brain hemisphere   D. hippocampus

20. One consistent finding about left-handed people is that they are
   A. less lateralized   B. more likely to die at an early age
   C. unable to use the right brain to produce language
   D. usually also ambidextrous

ANSWERS   1. c 2. a 3. b 4. a 5. d 6. a 7. a 8. c 9. c 10. b 11. d 12. a 13. b 14. c 15. d 16. b 17. a 18. a 19. c 20. a

Human Development

A Star Is Born—Here's Amy!

Olivia has just given birth to her first child, Amy. Frankly, at the moment Amy looks something like a pink prune, with pudgy arms, stubby legs, and lots of wrinkles. She also has the face of an angel—at least in her parents' eyes. As Olivia and her husband Tom look at Amy they wonder, "How will her life unfold? What kind of a person will she be?"

What if we could skip ahead through Amy's childhood and observe her at various ages? What could we learn? Seeing the world through her eyes would be fascinating and instructive. A child's viewpoint can make us more aware of things we take for granted. For example, younger children are very literal in their use of language. When she was 3, Amy thought her bath was too hot and said to Tom, "Make it warmer, Daddy." At first, Tom was confused. The bath was already fairly hot. But then he realized that what she really meant was, "Bring the water closer to the temperature we call *warm*." It makes perfect sense if you look at it that way.

Today we can merely guess about Amy's future. However, psychologists have studied many thousands of children. Their findings tell a fascinating story about human growth and development. Let's let Olivia, Tom, and Amy represent parents and children everywhere, as we see what psychology can tell us about the challenges of growing up. Tracing Amy's development might even help you answer the question, How did I become the person I am today?

Photodisc/Corbis

Survey Questions

- How do heredity and environment affect development?
- What can newborn babies do?
- What influence does maturation have on early development?
- Of what significance is a child's emotional bond with parents?
- How important are parenting styles?
- How do children acquire language?
- How do children learn to think?
- How do we develop morals and values?
- What are the typical tasks and dilemmas through the life span?
- How do effective parents discipline their children?

HEREDITY AND ENVIRONMENT—THE NURTURE OF NATURE

] SURVEYQUESTION *How do heredity and environment affect development?*

Children are the heart of **developmental psychology,** the study of progressive changes in behavior and abilities. However, be aware that human development involves every stage of life from conception to death (or "the womb to the tomb"). Heredity and environment also affect us throughout life. Some events, such as achieving sexual maturity, are mostly governed by heredity. Others, such as learning to swim, read, or drive a car, are primarily a matter of environment. But which is more important, heredity or environment? Let's explore some arguments on both sides of the nature-nurture debate.

◆FIGURE 3.1 *This image, made with a scanning electron microscope, shows several pairs of human chromosomes. (Colors are artificial.)*

Heredity

Heredity ("nature") refers to the genetic transmission of physical and psychological characteristics from parents to their children. An incredible number of personal features are set at conception, when a sperm and an ovum (egg) unite.

How does heredity operate? The nucleus of every human cell contains 46 **chromosomes.** (The word *chromosome* means "colored body.") These thread-like structures hold the coded instructions of heredity (◆Fig. 3.1). A notable exception is sperm cells and ova, which contain only 23 chromosomes. Thus, Amy received 23 chromosomes from Olivia and 23 from Tom. This is her genetic heritage.

Chromosomes are made up of **DNA,** deoxyribonucleic acid (dee-OX-see-RYE-bo-new-KLEE-ik). DNA is a long, ladder-like chain of chemical molecules (◆Fig. 3.2). The order of these molecules, or organic bases, acts as a code for genetic information. The DNA in each cell contains 3 billion base pairs. That's enough to record all the instructions needed to make a human—with room left over to spare.

Genes are small areas of the DNA code. Each of the 40,000 genes in your cells affects a particular process or personal feature. Sometimes, a single gene is responsible for an inherited trait, such as Amy's eye color. Most characteristics, however, are **polygenic** (pol-ih-JEN-ik), or controlled by many genes working in combination.

Genes may be dominant or recessive. When a gene is **dominant,** the feature it controls will appear every time the gene is present. When a gene is **recessive,** it must be paired with a second recessive gene before its effect will be expressed. For example, if Amy got a blue-eye gene from Tom and a brown-eye gene from Olivia, Amy will be brown-eyed, because brown-eye genes are dominant.

Developmental psychology The study of progressive changes in behavior and abilities from conception to death.

Heredity ("nature") The transmission of physical and psychological characteristics from parents to offspring through genes.

Chromosomes Thread-like "colored bodies" in the nucleus of each cell that are made up of DNA.

DNA Deoxyribonucleic acid, a molecular structure that contains coded genetic information.

Genes Specific areas on a strand of DNA that carry hereditary information.

Polygenic characteristics Personal traits or physical properties that are influenced by many genes working in combination.

Dominant gene A gene whose influence will be expressed each time the gene is present.

Recessive gene A gene whose influence will be expressed only when it is paired with a second recessive gene.

Sugar-phosphate backbone

Organic bases

DNA

Cell

Nucleus

Chromosome

✦**FIGURE 3.2** (Top left) *Linked molecules (organic bases) make up the "rungs" on DNA's twisted "molecular ladder." The order of these molecules serves as a code for genetic information. The code provides a genetic blueprint that is unique for each individual (except identical twins). The drawing shows only a small section of a DNA strand. An entire strand of DNA is composed of billions of smaller molecules. (Bottom left) The nucleus of each cell in the body contains chromosomes made up of tightly wound coils of DNA. (Don't be misled by the drawing: Chromosomes are microscopic in size, and the chemical molecules that make up DNA are even smaller.)*

If brown-eye genes are dominant, why do two brown-eyed parents sometimes have a blue-eyed child? If each parent has two brown-eye genes, the couple's children can only be brown-eyed. But what if each parent has one brown-eye gene and one blue-eye gene? In that case, both parents would have brown eyes. Yet there is 1 chance in 4 that their children will get two blue-eye genes and have blue eyes (✦Fig. 3.3). Along the same lines, genetics can sometimes be used to predict the chances that a child will be born with various inherited problems, such as sickle cell anemia, hemophilia, cystic fibrosis, muscular dystrophy, albinism, and some forms of mental retardation.

Genetic Programming

Heredity influences the *human growth sequence,* or overall pattern of physical development (see ▲Table 3.1). Heredity also determines eye color, skin color, and susceptibility to some diseases. To a degree, genetic instructions affect body size and shape, height, intelligence, athletic potential, personality traits, sexual orientation, and a host of other details (Hamer & Copeland, 1998). Score 1 for those who favor heredity as the more important factor in development!

Temperament

How soon do hereditary differences appear? Some appear right away. For instance, newborn babies differ noticeably in **temperament.** This is the physical core of personality. It includes sensi-

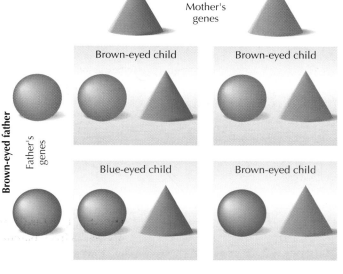

Brown-eyed mother

Mother's genes

Brown-eyed father — Father's genes

Brown-eyed child | Brown-eyed child

Blue-eyed child | Brown-eyed child

✦**FIGURE 3.3** *Gene patterns for children of brown-eyed parents, where each parent has one brown-eye gene and one blue-eye gene. Because the brown-eye gene is dominant, one child in four will be blue-eyed. Thus, there is a significant chance that two brown-eyed parents will have a blue-eyed child.*

Myrleen Ferguson/PhotoEdit

Identical twins, who share identical genes, demonstrate the powerful influence of heredity. Even when they are reared apart, identical twins are strikingly alike in motor skills, physical development, and appearance. At the same time, twins are less alike as adults than they were as children, which shows environmental influences are at work (McCartney, Bernieri, & Harris, 1990).

Temperament The physical core of personality, including emotional and perceptual sensitivity, energy levels, typical mood, and so forth.

▲TABLE 3.1	**Human Growth Sequence**	
PERIOD	**DURATION**	**DESCRIPTIVE NAME**
Prenatal Period	From conception to birth	
Germinal period	First 2 weeks after conception	Zygote
Embryonic period	2–8 weeks after conception	Embryo
Fetal period	From 8 weeks after conception to birth	Fetus
Neonatal Period	From birth to a few weeks after birth	Neonate
Infancy	From a few weeks after birth until child is walking securely; some children walk securely at less than a year, while others may not be able to until age 17–18 months	Infant
Early Childhood	From about 15–18 months until about 2–2½ years	Toddler
	From age 2–3 to about age 6	Preschool child
Middle Childhood	From about age 6 to age 12	School-age child
Pubescence	Period of about 2 years before puberty	
Puberty	Point of development at which biological changes of pubescence reach a climax marked by sexual maturity	
Adolescence	From the beginning of pubescence until full social maturity is reached (difficult to fix duration of this period)	Adolescent
Adulthood	From adolescence to death; sometimes subdivided into other periods as shown at left	Adult
Young adulthood (19–25)		
Adulthood (26–40)		
Maturity (41 plus)		
Senescence	No defined limit that would apply to all people; extremely variable; characterized by marked physiological and psychological deterioration	Adult (senile), "old age"

*Note: There is no exact beginning or ending point for various growth periods. The ages are approximate, and each period may be thought of as blending into the next. (Table courtesy of Tom Bond.)

tivity, irritability, distractibility, and typical mood (Braungart et al., 1992). About 40 percent of all newborns are *easy children* who are relaxed and agreeable. Ten percent are *difficult children* who are moody, intense, and easily angered. *Slow-to-warm-up children* (about 15 percent) are restrained, unexpressive, or shy. The remaining children do not fit neatly into a single category (Chess & Thomas, 1986). (Perhaps we should call them "generic" children?)

Imagine that we start with some infants who are very shy and some who are very bold. By the time they are 4 or 5 years old, most of these children will be only moderately shy or bold. This suggests that inherited temperaments are modified by learning (Kagan, 1999). In other words, nurture immediately enters the picture.

Environment

Environment ("nurture") refers to the sum of all external conditions that affect a person. The environments in which a child grows up can have a powerful impact on development. Humans today are genetically very similar to cave dwellers who lived 30,000 years ago. Nevertheless, a bright baby born today could learn to become almost anything—a ballet dancer, an engineer, a gangsta rapper, or a biochemist who likes to paint in watercolors. But an Upper Paleolithic baby could have only become a hunter or food gatherer. Score 1 for the environmentalists!

Early experiences can have very lasting effects. For example, children who are abused may suffer life-long emotional problems (Rutter, 1995). At the same time, extra care can sometimes reverse the effects of a poor start in life (Bornstein, 1995). In short, environmental forces guide human development, for better or worse, throughout life.

Sensitive Periods
Why do some experiences have more lasting effects than others?   Part of the answer lies in **sensitive periods.** These are times when children are more susceptible to certain environmental influences. Often, certain events must occur during a sensitive period for a person

Environment ("nurture") The sum of all external conditions affecting development, including especially the effects of learning.

Sensitive period During development, a period of increased sensitivity to environmental influences. Also, a time during which certain events must take place for normal development to occur.

to develop normally (Bornstein, 1989). For example, forming a loving bond with a caregiver early in life seems to be crucial for optimal development. Likewise, babies who don't hear normal speech during their first year may have impaired language abilities (Thompson & Nelson, 2001).

Prenatal Influences

The impact of nurture actually starts before birth. Although the intrauterine environment (interior of the womb) is highly protected, environmental conditions can affect the developing child. For example, when Olivia was pregnant, Amy's fetal heart rate and movements increased when loud sounds or vibrations penetrated the womb (Kisilevsky & Low, 1998).

If Olivia's health or nutrition had been poor; if she had German measles, syphilis, or HIV; if she used drugs or was exposed to x-rays or atomic radiation, Amy might have been harmed. In such cases, babies can suffer from **congenital problems** or "birth defects." These problems affect the developing fetus and become apparent at birth. In contrast, **genetic disorders** are inherited from parents. Examples are sickle-cell anemia, hemophilia, cystic fibrosis, muscular dystrophy, albinism, and some forms of mental retardation.

Because of the rapid growth of basic structures, the developing fetus is sensitive to a variety of diseases, drugs, and sources of radiation. This is especially true during the first trimester (3 months) of gestation (pregnancy).

Fetal Vulnerability

How is it possible for the embryo or the fetus to be harmed? No direct intermixing of blood takes place between a mother and her unborn child. Yet some substances—especially drugs—do reach the fetus. If a mother is addicted to morphine, heroin, or methadone, her baby may be born with an addiction. Repeated heavy drinking during pregnancy causes *fetal alcohol syndrome (FAS)*. Affected infants have low birth weight, a small head, bodily defects, and facial malformations. Many also suffer from emotional, behavioral, and mental handicaps (Mattson et al., 1998; Steinhausen & Spohr, 1998).

Tobacco is also harmful. Smoking during pregnancy greatly reduces oxygen to the fetus. Heavy smokers risk miscarrying or having premature, underweight babies who are more likely to die soon after birth (Slotkin, 1998). Children of smoking mothers score lower on tests of language and mental ability (Fried et al., 1992). In other words, an unborn child's future can go "up in smoke."

Some of the typical features of children suffering from fetal alcohol syndrome (FAS) include a small non-symmetrical head, a short nose, a flattened area between the eyes, oddly shaped eyes, and a thin upper lip. Many of these features become less noticeable by adolescence. However, mental retardation and other problems commonly follow the FAS child into adulthood. The child shown here represents a moderate example of FAS.

Teratogens

Anything capable of causing birth defects is called a **teratogen** (teh-RAT-uh-jen). Sometimes women are exposed to powerful teratogens, such as radiation, lead, pesticides, or PCBs, without knowing it (Eliot, 1999). But pregnant women can control their exposure to many teratogens. For example, a woman who takes cocaine runs a serious risk of injuring her fetus (Espy, Kaufmann, & Glisky, 1999; Singer et al., 1999; Swanson et al., 1999). In short, when a pregnant woman takes drugs, her unborn child does, too.

Congenital problems Problems or defects that originate during prenatal development in the womb.

Genetic disorders Problems caused by defects in the genes or by inherited characteristics.

Teratogen Radiation, a drug, or other substance capable of altering fetal development in ways that cause birth defects.

Deprivation In development, the loss or withholding of normal stimulation, nutrition, comfort, love, and so forth; a condition of lacking.

Enrichment Deliberately making an environment more novel, complex, and perceptually or intellectually stimulating.

Deprivation and Enrichment

After a child is born, the effects of environment can be clearly seen when conditions of deprivation or enrichment exist. **Deprivation** refers to a lack of normal stimulation, nutrition, comfort, or love. **Enrichment** exists when an environment is deliberately made more complex and intellectually stimulating.

What happens when children suffer severe deprivation? Tragically, a few mistreated children have spent their first years in closets, attics, and other restricted environments.

Children who grow up in poverty run a high risk of experiencing many forms of deprivation. There is evidence that lasting damage to social, emotional, and cognitive development occurs when children must cope with severe early deprivation.

When first discovered, these children are usually mute, retarded, and emotionally damaged. Fortunately, such extreme deprivation is unusual. Nevertheless, milder levels of perceptual, intellectual, or emotional deprivation occur in many families, especially those that must cope with poverty. By the age of 5, children who grow up in poor homes tend to have lower IQs. They are also more fearful, unhappy, and prone to hostile or aggressive behavior (Carnegie Corporation, 1994; McLoyd, 1998). Later in childhood, damage may result from a lack of intellectual stimulation, or parents who are cold, neglectful, or rejecting. In light of this, it is wise to view all of childhood as a *relatively sensitive period* (Barnet & Barnet, 1998; Nelson, 1999a).

Enriched Environments

Can an improved environment enhance development?   To answer this question, psychologists have created *enriched environments* that are especially novel, complex, and stimulating. Enriched environments may be the "soil" from which brighter children grow. To illustrate, let's consider the effects of raising rats in a sort of "rat wonderland." The walls of their cages were decorated with colorful patterns, and each cage was filled with platforms, ladders, and cubbyholes. As adults, these rats were superior at learning mazes. In addition, they had larger, heavier brains, with a thicker cortex (Benloucif, Bennett, & Rosenzweig, 1995). Of course, it's a long leap from rats to people, but an actual increase in brain size is impressive. If extra stimulation can enhance the "intelligence" of a lowly rat, it's likely that human infants also benefit from enrichment. Many studies have shown that enriched environments improve abilities or enhance development. It would be wise for Tom and Olivia to make a point of nourishing Amy's mind, as well as her body (Dieter & Emory, 1997).

What can parents do to enrich a child's environment?   They can encourage exploration and stimulating play by paying attention to what holds the baby's interest. It is better to "child-proof" a house than to strictly limit what a child can touch. There is also value in actively enriching sensory experiences. Babies should be surrounded by colors, music, people, and things to see, taste, smell, and touch. Infants are not vegetables. It makes perfect sense to take them outside, to hang mobiles over their cribs, to place mirrors nearby, to play music for them, or to rearrange their rooms now and then. (However, see "The Mozart Effect—Smart Music?" for another perspective on enrichment.) Children progress most rapidly when they have responsive parents and stimulating play materials at home (Bradley et al., 1989; Luster & Dubow, 1992).

 CRITICAL THINKING   The Mozart Effect—Smart Music?

Frances Rauscher and Gordon Shaw reported that after college students listened to a Mozart piano sonata they scored higher on a spatial reasoning test (Rauscher & Shaw, 1998; Shaw, 1999). Soon after this observation made the news, doting parents were playing Mozart for their babies around the clock. Obviously, they hoped that, like the college students, their babies would become smarter. However, parents should be suspicious of *any* practice that claims to offer such "magical" benefits. Because the original experiment was done with adults, it tells us nothing about infants.

Then does the Mozart effect actually exist?   A few studies have found small increases in spatial intelligence after exposure to Mozart's music (Rideout, Dougherty, & Wernert, 1998; Rideout & Taylor, 1997). However, most researchers have been unable to duplicate the effect (Bridgett & Cuevas, 2000; Chabris et al., 1999;

McCutcheon, 2000; Steele, Bass, & Crook, 1999; Steele, Brown, & Stoecker, 1999; Wilson & Brown, 1997).

Why do some studies support the effect and others disconfirm it?   Most studies have compared students who heard music to students who rested in silence. However, Kristin Nantais and Glenn Schellenberg found that listening to a narrated story also improves test scores. This is especially true for students who like hearing stories. Thus, students who scored higher after listening to Mozart were probably just more alert or in a better mood (Nantais & Schellenberg, 1999; Thompson, Schellenberg, & Husain, 2001).

As wonderful as Mozart's music may be, it doesn't appear to be magical, at least where children's intelligence is concerned (McKelvie & Low, 2002).

Nature-Nurture Interactions

As Amy passes through life she will have to learn countless bits of information: how to eat with a fork, the names of animals, proper etiquette at a wedding, how to use a computer. This knowledge reflects billions of connections in the brain. No conceivable amount of genetic programming could make it possible. With this fact in mind, the outcome of the nature-nurture debate is clear: Heredity and environment are both important. Heredity gives each of us a variety of potentials and limitations. These, in turn, are affected by environmental influences, such as learning, nutrition, disease, and culture. Thus, the person you are today reflects a constant *interaction,* or interplay, between the forces of nature and nurture (Gopnik, Meltzoff, & Kuhl, 1999).

Reciprocal Influences

Because of differences in temperament, some babies are more likely than others to smile, cry, vocalize, reach out, or pay attention. As a result, babies rapidly become active participants in their own development. Growing infants alter their parents' behavior at the same time they are changed by it. For example, Amy is an easy baby who smiles frequently and is easily fed. This encourages Olivia to touch, feed, and sing to Amy. Olivia's affection rewards Amy, causing her to smile more. Soon, a dynamic relationship blossoms between mother and child.

A person's **developmental level** is his or her current state of physical, emotional, and intellectual development. To summarize, three factors combine to determine your developmental level at any stage of life. These are *heredity, environment,* and your *own behavior,* each tightly interwoven with the others.

STUDYBREAK Ⓨ *Heredity and Environment*

RELATE

Do you think heredity or environment best explains who you are today? Can you think of clear examples of the ways in which heredity and environmental forces have affected your development?

What kind of temperament did you have as an infant? How did it affect your relationship with your parents or caregivers?

What advice would you give a friend who has just become pregnant? Be sure to consider the prenatal environment and sensitive periods.

LEARNING CHECK

1. Areas of the DNA molecule called genes are made up of dominant and recessive chromosomes. T or F?
2. Most inherited characteristics can be described as polygenic. T or F?

3. Which of the following represents a correct sequence?
   a. zygote, fetus, embryo, neonate, infant
   b. zygote, embryo, neonate, fetus, infant
   c. embryo, zygote, fetus, neonate, infant
   d. zygote, embryo, fetus, neonate, infant
4. "Slow-to-warm-up" children can be described as restrained, unexpressive, or shy. T or F?
5. A _____ _____ is a time of increased sensitivity to environmental influences.
6. As a child develops there is a continuous _____ between the forces of heredity and environment.

Critical Thinking

7. Environmental influences can interact with hereditary programming in an exceedingly direct way. Can you guess what it is?

ANSWERS

1. F 2. T 3. d 4. T 5. sensitive period 6. interaction 7. Environmental conditions sometimes turn specific genes on or off, thus directly affecting the expression of genetic tendencies (Gottlieb, 1998).

THE NEWBORN BABY—THE BASIC MODEL COMES WITH OPTIONS

] **SURVEYQUESTION** *What can newborn babies do?*

Infants have mental capacities that continue to surprise researchers and delight parents. The emergence of a baby's mental life, physical abilities, and emotions is closely related to maturation of the brain, nervous system, and body. Let's see how the infant's world unfolds.

At birth the human *neonate* (NEE-oh-NATE; newborn infant) will die if not cared for by adults. Newborn babies cannot lift their heads, turn over, or feed themselves. Does this mean they are inert and unfeeling? Definitely not! Neonates like Amy can see, hear, smell, taste, and

Developmental level An individual's current state of physical, emotional, and intellectual development.

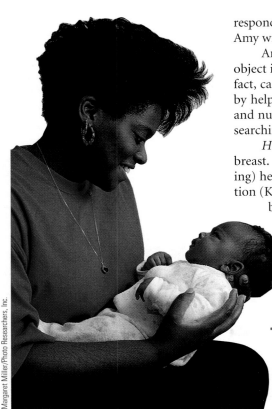

Margaret Miller/Photo Researchers, Inc.

Newborn babies display a special interest in the human face. A preference for seeing their mother's face develops rapidly and encourages social interactions between mother and baby.

respond to pain and touch. Although their senses are less acute, babies are very responsive. Amy will follow a moving object with her eyes and will turn in the direction of sounds.

Amy also has a number of adaptive infant reflexes. To elicit the *grasping reflex,* press an object in the neonate's palm and she will grasp it with surprising strength. Many infants, in fact, can hang from a raised bar, like little trapeze artists. The grasping reflex aids survival by helping infants avoid falling. You can observe the *rooting reflex* (reflexive head turning and nursing) by touching Amy's cheek. Immediately, she will turn toward your finger, as if searching for something.

How is such turning adaptive? The rooting reflex helps infants find a bottle or a breast. Then, when a nipple touches the infant's mouth, the *sucking reflex* (rhythmic nursing) helps her obtain needed food. Like other reflexes, this is a genetically programmed action (Koepke & Bigelow, 1997). At the same time, food rewards nursing. Because of this, babies quickly learn to nurse more actively. Again, we see how nature-nurture interactions alter a baby's behavior.

The *Moro reflex* is also interesting. If Amy's position is changed abruptly or if she is startled by a loud noise, she will make a hugging motion. This reaction has been compared to the movements baby monkeys use to cling to their mothers. (It is left to the reader's imagination to decide if there is any connection.)

The World of the Neonate

Thirty years ago, many people thought of newborn babies as mere bundles of reflexes, like the ones just described. But infants are capable of much more. For example, Andrew Meltzoff and Keith Moore (1983) found that babies are born mimics. ✦Figure 3.4 shows Meltzoff as he sticks out his tongue, opens his mouth, and purses his lips at a 20-day-old girl. Will she imitate him? Videotapes of babies confirm that they imitate adult facial gestures. As early as 9 months of age, infants can imitate actions a day after seeing them (Heimann & Meltzoff, 1996). Such mimicry obviously aids rapid learning in infancy.

How intelligent are neonates? Babies are smarter than many people think. From the earliest days of life, babies seem to be trying to learn how the world works. They immediately begin to look, touch, taste, and otherwise explore their surroundings. From an evolutionary perspective, a baby's mind is designed to soak up information, which it does at an amazing pace (Gopnik, Meltzoff, & Kuhl, 1999).

In the first weeks and months of life, babies are increasingly able to think, learn from what they see, make predictions, and search for explanations. For example, Jerome Bruner (1983) observed that 3- to 8-week-old babies seem to understand that a person's voice and body should be connected. If a baby hears his mother's voice coming from where she is standing, the baby will remain calm. If her voice comes from a loudspeaker several feet away, the baby will become agitated and begin to cry.

Another look into the private world of infants can be drawn from testing their vision. However, such testing is a challenge because infants cannot talk. Robert Fantz invented a device called a *looking chamber* to find out what infants can see and what holds their attention (✦Fig. 3.5 *a*). Imagine that Amy is placed on her back inside the chamber, facing a lighted area above. Next, two objects are placed in the chamber. By observing the movements of Amy's eyes and the images they reflect, we can tell what she is looking at. Such tests show that adult vision is about 30 times sharper, but babies can see large patterns, shapes, and edges.

Fantz found that 3-day-old babies prefer complex patterns, such as checkerboards and bull's-eyes, to simpler colored rectangles. Other researchers have learned that infants are excited by circles, curves, and bright lights (Fig. 3.5 *b*) (Brown, 1990). Immediately after birth, Amy will be aware of changes in the position of objects (Slater et al., 1991). When she is 6 months old, she will be able to recognize categories of objects that differ in shape or color. By 9 months of age, she will be able to tell the difference between dogs and birds or other groups of animals (Mandler & McDonough, 1998). So there really is a person inside that little body!

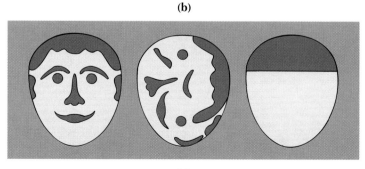

✦FIGURE 3.4 *Infant imitation. In the top row of photos, Andrew Meltzoff makes facial gestures at an infant. The bottom row records the infant's responses. Videotapes of Meltzoff and of tested infants helped ensure objectivity. (Photos courtesy of Andrew N. Meltzoff.)*

(a)

(b)

(c)

✦FIGURE 3.5   (a) *Eye movements and fixation points of infants are observed in Fantz's "looking chamber." (b) Thirteen-week-old infants prefer concentric and curved patterns like those on the left to non-concentric and straight-line patterns like those on the right. (c) Infants tested in a looking chamber look at the normal face longer than at the scrambled face and at both faces longer than at the design on the right. (Photo courtesy of David Linton. Drawing from "The Origin of Form Perception" by Robert L. Fantz, Copyright © 1961 by Scientific American, Inc. All rights reserved.)*

1. Fetal posture (newborn)   2. Holds chin up (1 month)   3. Holds chest up (2 months)   4. Sits when supported (4 months)   5. Sits alone (7 months)

6. Stands holding furniture (9 months)   7. Crawls (10 months)   8. Walks if led (11 months)   9. Stands alone (11 months)   10. Walks alone (12 months)

✦**FIGURE 3.6** *Motor development. Most infants follow an orderly pattern of motor development. Although the order in which children progress is similar, there are large individual differences in the ages at which each ability appears. The ages listed are averages for American children. It is not unusual for many of the skills to appear 1 or 2 months earlier than average or several months later (Frankenberg & Dodds, 1967; Harris & Liebert, 1991). Parents should not be alarmed if a child's behavior differs some from the average.*

Neonates can most clearly see objects about a foot away from them. It is as if they are best prepared to see the people who love and care for them (Gopnik, Meltzoff, & Kuhl, 1999). Perhaps that's why babies have a special fascination with human faces. Just *hours* after they are born, babies begin to prefer seeing their mother's face, rather than a stranger's (Walton, Bower, & Bower, 1992).

In a looking chamber, most infants will spend more time looking at a human face pattern than a scrambled face or a colored oval (Fig. 3.5 *c*). When real human faces are used, infants prefer familiar faces to unfamiliar faces. However, this reverses at about age 2. At that time, unusual objects begin to interest the child. For instance, Jerome Kagan (1971) showed face masks to 2-year-olds. Kagan found that the toddlers were fascinated by a face with eyes on the chin and a nose in the middle of the forehead. He believes the babies' interest came from a need to understand why the scrambled face differed from what they had come to expect. Such behavior is further evidence that babies actively try to make sense of their surroundings (Gopnik, Meltzoff, & Kuhl, 1999).

MATURATION

] **SURVEYQUESTION** *What influence does maturation have on early development?*

The emergence of many basic abilities is closely tied to **maturation** (physical growth and development of the body, brain, and nervous system). Amy's maturation will be especially evident as she learns motor skills such as crawling and walking. Of course, the *rate* of maturation varies from child to child. Nevertheless, the *order* of maturation is almost universal. For instance, Amy will be able to sit without support before she has matured enough to crawl. Indeed, infants around the world typically sit before they crawl, crawl before they stand, and stand before they walk (✦Fig. 3.6).

What about my weird cousin Emo who never crawled?   Like cousin Emo, a few children substitute rolling, creeping, or shuffling for crawling. A very few move directly from sitting

Maturation The physical growth and development of the body and nervous system.

to standing and walking (Robson, 1984). Even so, their motor development is orderly. In general, muscular control spreads in a pattern that is *cephalocaudal* (SEF-eh-lo-KOD-ul; from head to toe) and *proximodistal* (PROK-seh-moe-DIS-tul; from the center of the body to the extremities). Even if cousin Emo flunked Elementary Crawling, his motor development followed the standard top-down, center-outward pattern.

Motor Development

Although maturation has a big impact, motor skills don't simply "emerge." Amy must learn to control her actions. When babies are beginning to crawl or walk, they actively try new movements and select those that work. Amy's first efforts might be flawed—a wobbly crawl or some shaky first steps. However, with practice, babies "tune" their movements to be smoother and more effective. Such learning is evident from the very first months of life (see ✦Fig. 3.7) (Adolph, 1997; Thelen, 1995).

Readiness

At what ages will Amy be ready to feed herself, walk alone, or say good-bye to diapers? Such milestones tend to be governed by a child's **readiness** for rapid learning. That is, a certain level of maturation must occur before some skills can be learned. It is impossible, for instance, to teach children to walk or use a toilet before they have matured enough to control their bodies. Parents are asking for failure when they try to force a child to learn skills too early. Doing so just frustrates children (Luxem & Christophersen, 1994).

Much needless grief can be avoided by respecting a child's personal rate of growth. Consider the eager parents who toilet-trained an 18-month-old child in 10 trying weeks of false alarms and "accidents." If they had waited until the child was 24 months old, they might have succeeded in just 3 weeks. Parents may control when toilet training starts, but maturation tends to dictate when it will be completed (Luxem & Christophersen, 1994). The average age for *completed* toilet training is about 3 years (girls a little earlier; boys a little later) (Schum et al., 2001). So why fight nature? (The wet look is in.)

✦FIGURE 3.7 *Psychologist Carolyn Rovee-Collier has shown that babies as young as 3 months old can learn to control their movements. In her experiments, babies lie on their backs under a colorful crib mobile. A ribbon is tied around the baby's ankle and connected to the mobile. Whenever babies spontaneously kick their legs, the mobile jiggles and rattles. Within a few minutes, infants learn to kick faster. Their reward for kicking is a chance to see the mobile move (Hayne & Rovee-Collier, 1995).*

Emotional Development

Early emotional development also follows a pattern closely tied to maturation. Even the basic emotions of *anger, fear,* and *joy*—which appear to be unlearned—take time to develop. General *excitement* is the only emotion newborn infants clearly express. However, as Tom and Olivia can tell you, a baby's emotional life blossoms rapidly. One researcher (Bridges, 1932) observed that all the basic human emotions appear before age 2. Bridges found that emotions appear in a consistent order and that the first basic split is between pleasant and unpleasant emotions (✦Fig. 3.8).

Many experts continue to believe that emotions unfold slowly, as the nervous system matures (Camras, Sullivan, & Michel, 1993; Matias & Cohn, 1993). However, psychologist Carroll Izard thinks that infants can express several basic emotions as early as 10 weeks of age. When Izard looks carefully at the faces of babies, he sees abundant signs of emotion (see ✦Fig. 3.9). The most common infant expression, he found, is not excitement, but *interest*—followed by *joy, anger,* and *sadness* (Izard et al., 1995).

If Izard is right, then emotions are "hard-wired" by heredity and related to evolution. Perhaps that's why smiling is one of a baby's most common reactions. Smiling probably helps babies survive by inviting parents to care for them (Izard et al., 1995).

At first, a baby's smiling is haphazard. By the age of 2 months, however, most infants smile more frequently when another person is nearby (Jones, Collins, & Hong, 1991). This **social smile** is especially rewarding to parents. On the other hand, when new parents see

Readiness A condition that exists when maturation has advanced enough to allow the rapid acquisition of a particular skill.
Social smile Smiling elicited by social stimuli, such as seeing a parent's face.

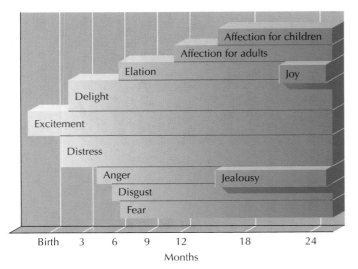

✦**FIGURE 3.8** *The traditional view of infancy holds that emotions are rapidly differentiated from an initial capacity for excitement. (After K. M. B. Bridges, 1932. Reprinted by permission of the Society for Research in Child Development, Inc.)*

and hear a crying baby, they feel annoyed, irritated, disturbed, or unhappy. Babies the world over, it seems, rapidly become capable of letting others know what they like and dislike. (Prove this to yourself sometime by driving a baby buggy.)

With dazzling speed, human infants are transformed from helpless babies to independent persons. Early growth is extremely rapid. By her third year, Amy will have a unique personality, and she will be able to stand, walk, talk, and explore. At no other time after birth does development proceed more rapidly. During the same period, Amy's relationships with other people will expand as well. Before we explore that topic, here's a chance to review what you've learned.

Interest   Joy   Anger   Sadness

✦**FIGURE 3.9** *Infants display many of the same emotional expressions as adults do. Carroll Izard believes such expressions show that distinct emotions appear within the first months of life. Other theorists argue that specific emotions come into focus more gradually, as an infant's nervous system matures. Either way, parents can expect to see a full range of basic emotions by the end of a baby's first year.*

STUDYBREAK Ⓨ *The Neonate and Maturation*

RELATE

What infant reflexes have you observed? How would maturation affect the chances of teaching an infant to eat with a spoon? Can you give an example of how heredity and environment interact during motor development?

To know what a baby is feeling, would it be more helpful to be able to detect delight and distress (Bridges) or joy, anger, and sadness (Izard)?

LEARNING CHECK

1. If an infant is startled, it will make movements similar to an embrace. This is known as the
   a. grasping reflex   b. rooting reflex   c. Moro reflex
   d. adaptive reflex
2. During infancy, a capacity for imitating others first becomes evident at about 9 months of age. T or F?

3. After age 2, infants tested in a looking chamber show a marked preference for familiar faces and simpler designs. T or F?
4. The orderly sequence observed in the unfolding of many basic responses can be attributed to _____.
5. General excitement or interest is the clearest emotional response present in newborn infants, but meaningful expressions of delight and distress appear soon after. T or F?
6. Neonates display a social smile as early as 10 days after birth. T or F?

Critical Thinking

7. If you were going to test newborn infants to see if they prefer their mother's face to that of a stranger, what precautions would you take?

ANSWERS

1. c 2. F 3. F 4. maturation 5. T 6. F 7. In one study of the preferences of newborns, the hair color and complexion of strangers was matched to that of the mothers. Also, only the mother's or stranger's face was visible during testing. And finally, a scent was used to mask olfactory (smell) cues so an infant's preference could not be based on the mother's familiar odor (Bushnell, Sai, & Mullin, 1989).

SOCIAL DEVELOPMENT— BABY, I'M STUCK ON YOU

] SURVEYQUESTION *Of what significance is a child's emotional bond with parents?*

Like all humans, babies are social creatures. Their early **social development** lays a foundation for relationships with parents, siblings, friends, and relatives. A first basic step into the social world involves becoming aware of oneself as a person. When you look in a mirror, you recognize the image staring back as your own—except, perhaps, early on Monday mornings. Would Amy recognize herself at age 1? At age 2? As with many such events, initial self-awareness depends on maturation of the nervous system. In a typical test of self-recognition, infants are shown images of themselves on a TV. Most infants have to be 15 months old before they recognize themselves (Lewis & Brooks-Gunn, 1979).

A sense of self, or self-awareness, develops at about age 18 months. Before children develop self-awareness, they do not recognize their own image in a mirror. Typically, they think they are looking at another child. Some children hug the child in the mirror or go behind it, looking for the child they see there (Lewis, 1995).

Attachment

The real core of social development is found in the **emotional attachment,** or close emotional bond, that babies form with their primary caregivers. There is a sensitive period (roughly the first year of life) during which this must occur for optimal development. Returning to Amy's story, we find that attachment keeps her close to Olivia, who provides safety, stimulation, and a secure "home base" from which Amy can go exploring.

Mothers usually begin to cultivate a parent-child bond within hours of giving birth. For example, they touch their own infants more and hold them closer than they do other babies (Kaitz et al., 1995). A direct sign that an emotional bond has formed appears around 8 to 12 months of age. At that time, Amy will display **separation anxiety** (crying and signs of fear) when she is left alone or with a stranger. (Mild separation anxiety is normal. When it is more intense, it may reveal a problem. See "Beyond Homesickness" for details.)

You may have heard that bonding is especially powerful during the first few hours after birth (Klaus & Kennell, 1995). However, careful studies have generally failed to support a "superglue" version of bonding. Long-term infant attachments are a reality, but "instant bonding" appears to be a myth (Eyer, 1994). Ultimately, it is less important *when* secure attachment occurs, than *if* it occurs.

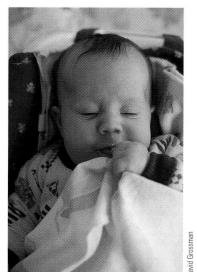

Most parents are familiar with the storm of crying that sometimes occurs when babies are left alone at bedtime. Bedtime distress can be a mild form of separation anxiety. As many parents know, it is often eased by the presence of "security objects," such as a stuffed animal or favorite blanket (Morelli et al., 1992).

Attachment Quality

According to psychologist Mary Ainsworth (1913–1999), the quality of attachment is revealed by how babies act when their mothers return after a brief separation. Infants who are **securely attached** have a stable and positive emotional bond. They are upset by the mother's absence and seek to be near her when she returns. **Insecure-avoidant** infants have an anxious emotional bond. They tend to turn away from the mother when she returns.

Social development The development of self-awareness, attachment to parents or caregivers, and relationships with other children and adults.

Emotional attachment An especially close emotional bond that infants form with their parents, caregivers, or others.

Separation anxiety Distress displayed by infants when they are separated from their parents or principal caregivers.

Secure attachment A stable and positive emotional bond.

Insecure-avoidant attachment An anxious emotional bond marked by a tendency to avoid reunion with a parent or caregiver.

CLINICAL FILE Beyond Homesickness

Camp counselors know the look: Doleful eyes, anxious, and forlorn, a homesick child is easy to spot. But such distress can be more serious than the "summer-camp blues." At some point in their lives, about 5 percent of all children (1 in 20) suffer from *separation anxiety disorder*. These children are miserable when they are separated from their parents, whom they cling to or constantly follow. Some fear that they will get lost and never see their parents again. They are reluctant to leave home, sleep over at a friend's house, or go on errands. Seventy-five percent refuse to go to school, which can be a serious handicap.

What causes separation anxiety disorder?   The problem may begin after a child faces such stresses as illness, the death of a relative or pet, moving to a new neighborhood, or changing schools. Whatever the triggering event, separation anxiety should not be ignored. It can seriously impair emotional development. If separation anxiety is intense or lasts for more than a month, parents should seek professional help for their child (*DSM-IV*-TR, 2000; Masi, Mucci, & Millepiedi, 2001).

Attachment Category

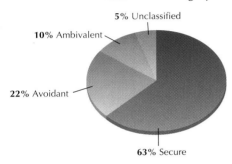

5% Unclassified
10% Ambivalent
22% Avoidant
63% Secure

✦**FIGURE 3.10** *In the United States, about two thirds of all children from middle-class families are securely attached. About one child in three is insecurely attached. (Percentages are approximate. From Kaplan, 1998.)*

Insecure-ambivalent attachment is also an anxious emotional bond. In this case, babies have mixed feelings: They both seek to be near the returning mother and angrily resist contact with her (see ✦Fig. 3.10).

Attachment can have lasting effects. Infants who are securely attached at the age of 1 year show more resiliency, curiosity, problem-solving ability, and social skill in preschool (Collins & Gunnar, 1990). In contrast, attachment failures can be quite damaging. Consider, for example, the plight of children raised in severely overcrowded Romanian orphanages. These children got almost no attention from adults for the first year or two of their lives. Some have now been adopted by American and Canadian families, but many are poorly attached to their new parents. Some, for instance, will readily wander off with strangers, they are anxious and remote, they don't like to be touched, and they refuse to make eye contact with others. In short, for some children, a lack of affectionate care early in life leaves lasting emotional scars (O'Conner et al., 2003).

Promoting Attachment

The key to secure attachment is a mother who is accepting, and sensitive to her baby's signals and rhythms. Poor attachment occurs when a mother's actions are inappropriate, inadequate, intrusive, overstimulating, or rejecting. An example is the mother who tries to play with a drowsy infant or who ignores a baby who is looking at her and vocalizing. The link between sensitive caregiving and secure attachment appears to apply to all cultures (Posada et al., 2002).

What about attachment to fathers?   Fathers of securely attached infants tend to be outgoing, agreeable, and happy in their marriage. In general, a warm family atmosphere—one that includes sensitive mothering *and* fathering—produces secure children (Belsky, 1996).

Day Care

Does commercial child care interfere with the quality of attachment?   A study done by the National Institute of Child Health and Human Development (1999) has finally answered some nagging questions about day care. Overall, *high-quality* day care does not adversely affect attachment to parents. This finding offers some reassurance to working parents, but the quality of day care is extremely important. Children in high-quality day care tend to have better relationships with their mothers and fewer behavior problems. Children receiving high-quality day care also have better cognitive skills and language abilities (Burchinal et al., 2000).

Thus, high-quality day care can actually improve children's social and mental skills (Scarr, 1998). However, all the positive effects just noted are *reversed* for low-quality day care (✦Fig. 3.11). Parents should carefully evaluate and monitor the quality of day care their children receive. Poor-quality day care can actually create behavior problems that didn't exist beforehand (Pierrehumbert et al., 2002).

Insecure-ambivalent attachment An anxious emotional bond marked by both a desire to be with a parent or caregiver and some resistance to being reunited.

Quality

What should parents look for when they evaluate the quality of child care? Low-quality day care *is* risky, and it *may* weaken attachment. Parents seeking quality should insist on *at least* the following: (1) a small number of children per caregiver; (2) small overall group size (12 to 15); (3) trained caregivers; (4) minimal staff turnover; and (5) stable, consistent care (Howes, 1997). (Also, avoid any child-care center with the words *zoo, menagerie,* or *stockade* in its name.)

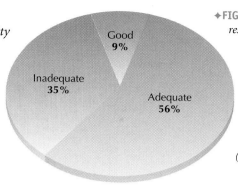

◆FIGURE 3.11 *This graph shows the results of a study of child care in homes other than the child's. In most cases, parents paid for this care, although many of the caregivers were unlicensed. As you can see, child care was "good" in only 9 percent of the homes. In 35 percent of the homes, it was rated as inadequate (Mehren, 1994).*

Attachment and Affectional Needs

A baby's **affectional needs** (needs for love and affection) are every bit as important as more obvious needs for food, water, and physical care. All things considered, creating a bond of trust and affection between the infant and at least one other person is a key event during the first year of life. Parents are sometimes afraid of "spoiling" babies with too much attention, but for the first year or two, this is nearly impossible. In fact, a later capacity to experience warm and loving relationships may depend on it.

STUDYBREAK *Social Development*

RELATE

Think of a child you know who seems to be securely attached and one who seems to be insecurely attached. How do the children differ? Do their parents treat them differently?

Do you think you were securely or insecurely attached as a child? Are there any parallels in your relationships today?

LEARNING CHECK

1. Clear signs of self-awareness or self-recognition are evident in most infants by the time they reach 8 months of age. T or F?
2. The development of separation anxiety in an infant corresponds to the formation of an attachment to parents. T or F?

3. In Mary Ainsworth's system for rating the quality of attachment, secure attachment is revealed by a lack of distress when an infant is left alone with a stranger. T or F?
4. High-quality day care can actually improve children's social and mental skills. T or F?

CRITICAL THINKING

5. Can you think of another way to tell if infants have self-awareness?
6. Can emotional bonding begin before birth?
7. Attachment quality is usually attributed to the behavior of parents or caregivers. How might infants contribute to the quality of attachment?

ANSWERS

1. F 2. T 3. F 4. T 5. Another successful method is to secretly rub a spot of rouge on an infant's nose. The child is then placed in front of a mirror. The question is, Will the child touch the red spot, showing recognition of the mirror image as his or her own? The probability that a child will do so jumps dramatically during the second year. 6. It certainly can for parents. When a pregnant woman begins to feel fetal movements she becomes aware that a baby is coming to life inside of her. Likewise, prospective parents who hear a fetal heartbeat at the doctor's office or see an ultrasound image of the fetus begin to become emotionally attached to the unborn child (Konner, 1991). 7. An infant's behavior patterns, temperament, and emotional style may greatly influence parents' behavior. As a result, infants can affect attachment as much as parents do (Oatley & Jenkins, 1992).

MATERNAL AND PATERNAL INFLUENCES—LIFE WITH MOM AND DAD

] SURVEYQUESTION *How important are parenting styles?*

For the first few years of life, caregivers are the center of a child's world. This makes the quality of mothering and fathering very important. For example, one classic study focused on **maternal influences** (all the effects a mother has on her child). Researchers began by selecting children who were very competent (A children) or low in competence (C children). As they observed younger and younger children, it soon became apparent that A and C pat-

Affectional needs Emotional needs for love and affection.

Maternal influences The aggregate of all psychological effects mothers have on their children.

terns were already set by age 3. To learn how this was possible, psychologists visited homes and observed **caregiving styles** (White & Watts, 1973). What they saw ranged from the "super mother" to the "zoo-keeper mother." Super mothers went out of their way to provide educational experiences and let their children initiate activities. This style produced highly competent "A children." At the other end of the scale, zoo-keeper mothers gave their children good physical care but interacted with them very little. Their rigid child care resulted in "C children" who approached problems inflexibly.

Optimal Caregiving

More recent studies mirror the earlier findings: Optimal caregiving involves *proactive educational interactions* with a child (Olson, Bates, & Kaskie, 1992). For example, Olivia is a proactive mother who talks to Amy and helps her explore her surroundings. This speeds Amy's mental growth and minimizes behavior problems.

Optimal caregiving also depends on the *goodness of fit,* or compatibility, of parent and child temperaments (Chess & Thomas, 1986). For instance, Damion is a slow-to-warm-up child who has impatient parents. Damion will probably have more problems than he would with easygoing parents.

A third ingredient of caregiving is *parental responsiveness* to a child's feelings, needs, rhythms, and signals. When Amy is a month old, Olivia should focus on touching, holding, feeding, and stimulating her. When Amy is a year old, give-and-take interactions that promote Amy's social skills will be more important. Thus, effective mothers adjust their behavior to meet children's changing needs (Heermann, Jones, & Wikoff, 1994).

Paternal Influences

Aren't you overlooking the effects of fathering?   Yes. In fact, fathers make a unique contribution to parenting. Studies of **paternal influences** (the sum of all effects a father has on his child) reveal that fathers typically act as playmates for infants (Parke, 1995). In many homes, fathers spend 4 or 5 times more hours playing with infants than they do in caregiving. It's true that fathers are beginning to get more involved in child care. Just the same, mothers still spend much more time feeding, dressing, grooming, disciplining, teaching, and caring for children (de Luccie & Davis, 1991).

It might seem that the father's role as a playmate makes him less important. Not so. From birth onward, fathers pay more visual attention to children than mothers do. Fathers are much more tactile (lifting, tickling, and handling the baby), more physically arousing (engaging in rough-and-tumble play), and more likely to engage in unusual play (imitating the baby, for example) (Crawley & Sherrod, 1984). In comparison, mothers speak to infants more, play more conventional games (such as peek-a-boo) and, as noted, spend much more time in caregiving (◆Fig. 3.12). Amy's playtime with Tom is actually very valuable. Young children who spend a lot of time playing with their fathers tend to be more competent in many ways (Pettit et al., 1998).

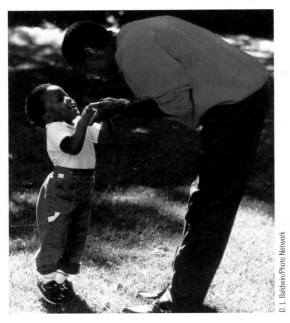

D. L. Baldwin/Photo Network

Fathering typically makes a contribution to early development that differs in emphasis from mothering.

Caregiving styles Identifiable patterns of parental caretaking and interaction with children.

Paternal influences The aggregate of all psychological effects fathers have on their children.

Overall, fathers can be as affectionate, sensitive, and responsive as mothers are. Nevertheless, infants tend to get very different views of males and females. Females, who offer comfort, nurturance, and verbal stimulation, tend to be close at hand. Males come and go, and when they are present, action, exploration, and risk-taking prevail. It's no wonder, then, that the caregiving styles of mothers and fathers have a major impact on children's sex role development (Lindsay, Mize, & Pettit, 1997).

As children mature and become more independent, parents must find ways to control the child's behavior. ("No, you may not smear pudding on Daddy's face.") Such attempts can have a variety of effects, as described next.

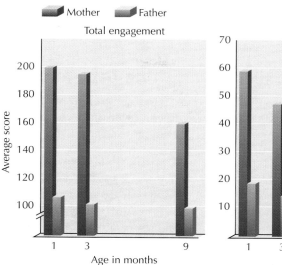

Parenting Styles

Psychologist Diana Baumrind (1991) has studied the effects of three major styles of parenting. See if you recognize the styles she describes.

Authoritarian parents enforce rigid rules and demand strict obedience to authority. Typically they view children as having few rights but adult-like responsibilities. The child is expected to stay out of trouble and to accept, without question, what parents regard as right or wrong. ("Do it because I say so.") The children of authoritarian parents are usually obedient and self-controlled. But they also tend to be emotionally stiff, withdrawn, apprehensive, and lacking in curiosity.

Overly permissive parents give little guidance, allow too much freedom, or don't hold children accountable for their actions. Typically, the child has rights similar to an adult's but few responsibilities. Rules are not enforced, and the child usually gets his or her way. ("Do whatever you want.") Permissive parents tend to produce dependent, immature children who misbehave frequently. Such children are aimless and likely to "run amok."

Baumrind describes **authoritative parents** as those who supply firm and consistent guidance, combined with love and affection. Such parents balance their own rights with those of their children. They control their children's behavior in a caring, responsive, non-authoritarian way. ("Do it for this reason.") Effective parents are firm and consistent, not harsh or rigid. In general, they encourage the child to act responsibly, to think, and to make good decisions. This style produces children who are competent, self-controlled, independent, assertive, and inquiring (Baumrind, 1991).

Culture

Do ethnic differences in parenting affect children in distinctive ways? Diana Baumrind's work provides a good overall summary of the effects of parenting. However, her conclusions are probably most valid for families whose roots lie in Europe. Child-rearing in other ethnic groups often reflects different customs and beliefs. Cultural differences are especially apparent with respect to the meaning attached to a child's behavior. Is a particular behavior "good" or "bad"?

◆**FIGURE 3.12** *Mother-infant and father-infant interactions. These graphs show what occurred on routine days in a sample of 72 American homes. The graph on the left records the total amount of contact parents had with their babies, including such actions as talking to, touching, hugging, or smiling at the infant. The graph on the right shows the amount of caregiving (diapering, washing, feeding, and so forth) done by each parent. Note that in both cases mother-infant interactions greatly exceed father-infant interactions. (Adapted from Belsky et al., 1984.)*

"All right now, give Mommy the super-glue."

Authoritarian parents Parents who enforce rigid rules and demand strict obedience to authority.

Overly permissive parents Parents who give little guidance, allow too much freedom, or do not require the child to take responsibility.

Authoritative parents Parents who supply firm and consistent guidance combined with love and affection.

Should it be encouraged or discouraged? The answer will depend greatly on parents' cultural values (Rubin, 1998).

Ethnic Differences: Four Flavors of Parenting

Making generalizations about groups of people is always risky. Nevertheless, some typical differences in child-rearing patterns have been observed in North American ethnic communities (Kaplan, 1998).

African-American Families

Traditional African-American values emphasize loyalty and interdependence among family members, security, developing a positive identity, and not giving up in the face of adversity. African-American parents typically stress obedience and respect for elders. Child discipline tends to be fairly strict, but many African-American parents see this as a necessity, especially if they live in urban areas where safety is a concern. Self-reliance, resourcefulness, and an ability to take care of oneself in difficult situations are also qualities that African-American parents seek to promote in their children.

Hispanic Families

Like African-American parents, Hispanic parents tend to have relatively strict standards of discipline. They also place importance on family values, family pride, and loyalty. Hispanic families are typically affectionate and indulgent toward younger children. However, as children grow older, they are expected to learn social skills and to be calm, obedient, courteous, and respectful. In fact, such social skills may be valued more than cognitive skills (Delgado & Ford, 1998). In addition, Hispanic parents tend to stress cooperation more than competition. Such values can put Hispanic children at a disadvantage in highly competitive, Anglo-American culture.

Asian-American Families

Asian cultures tend to be group-oriented, and they emphasize interdependence among individuals. In contrast, Western cultures value individual effort and independence (Markus & Kitayama, 1991). This difference is often reflected in Asian-American child-rearing practices. Asian-American children are taught that their behavior can bring either pride or shame to the family. Therefore, they are obliged to set aside their own desires when the greater good of the family is at stake. Parents tend to act as teachers who encourage hard work, moral behavior, and achievement. For the first few years, parenting is lenient and permissive. However, after about age 5, Asian-American parents begin to expect respect, obedience, self-control, and self-discipline from their children.

Arab-American Families

In Middle Eastern cultures, children are expected to be polite, obedient, disciplined, and conforming. Punishment generally consists of spankings, teasing, or shaming in front of others. Arab-American fathers tend to be strong authority figures who demand obedience so the family will not be shamed by a child's bad behavior. Success, generosity, and hospitality are highly valued in Arab-American culture. The pursuit of family honor encourages hard work, thrift, conservatism, and educational achievement. The welfare of the family is emphasized over individual identity. Thus, Arab-American children are raised to respect their parents, members of their extended family, and other adults as well (Erickson & Al-Timimi, 2001; Medhus, 2001).

Implications

Child-rearing is done in a remarkable variety of ways around the world. In fact, many of the things we do in North America, such as forcing young children to sleep alone, would be considered odd or wrong in other cultures. In the final analysis, parenting can only be judged if we know what culture or ethnic community a child is being prepared to enter (Bornstein et al., 1998).

USING PSYCHOLOGY   To Spank or Not to Spank?

Should parents spank their children?

For years, various "experts" have argued for and against spanking. But what does the *evidence* say? After reviewing many studies, psychologist Elizabeth Gershoff concludes that parents should minimize spanking or avoid it entirely (Gershoff, 2002).

Many parents spank their children. Could it be all that bad?

Actually, most children show no signs of long-term damage from spanking—*if* spanking is backed up by supportive parenting (Baumrind, Larzelere, & Cowan, 2002). However, emotional damage does occur if spankings are severe, frequent, or coupled with harsh parenting. In addition, frequent spanking tends to increase aggression, and it leads to *more* problem behaviors, not fewer (McLoyd, & Smith, 2002; Saadeh, Rizzo, & Roberts, 2002).

Even if spanking does briefly halt unwanted actions, it doesn't stop future misbehavior or teach the child better ways to act. Let's say a child is spanked for kicking his little sister. Does spanking teach him that hurting others is bad? Probably not. Instead, the boy learns that it's not a good idea to attack when someone is watching! When possible, parents should use other more positive ways to manage a child's behavior (Gershoff, 2002). This chapter's Psychology in Action section suggests some helpful alternatives.

Side Effects of Child Discipline

When parents fail to provide *discipline* (guidance regarding acceptable behavior), children become antisocial, aggressive, and insecure. Effective discipline is fair but loving, authoritative yet sensitive. It socializes a child without destroying the bond of love and trust between parent and child.

Types of Discipline

Parents typically discipline children in one of three ways. **Power assertion** refers to physical punishment or a show of force, such as taking away toys or privileges. As an alternative, some parents use **withdrawal of love** (withholding affection) by refusing to speak to a child, threatening to leave, rejecting the child, or otherwise acting as if the child is temporarily unlovable. **Management techniques** combine praise, recognition, approval, rules, reasoning, and the like to encourage desirable behavior. Each of these approaches can control a child's behavior, but their side effects differ considerably.

What are the side effects?   Power-oriented techniques—particularly harsh or severe physical punishment—are associated with fear, hatred of parents, and a lack of spontaneity and warmth. Severely punished children also tend to be defiant, rebellious, and aggressive (Patterson, 1982). Despite its drawbacks, power assertion is the most popular mode of discipline (see "To Spank or Not To Spank?") (Papps et al., 1995).

Withdrawal of love produces children who tend to be self-disciplined. You could say that such children have developed a good conscience. Often, they are described as "model" children or as unusually "good." But as a side effect, they are also frequently anxious, insecure, and dependent on adults for approval.

Management techniques also have limitations. Most important is the need to carefully adjust to a child's level of understanding. Younger children don't always see the connection between rules, explanations, and their own behavior. Nevertheless, management techniques receive a big plus in another area. Psychologist Stanley Coopersmith (1968) found a direct connection between discipline and a child's self-esteem.

Self-Esteem

If you regard yourself as a worthwhile person, you have **self-esteem.** High self-esteem is essential for emotional health. Individuals with low self-esteem don't think much of themselves as people. In elementary school, children with high self-esteem tend to be more popular, cooperative, and successful in class. Children with low self-esteem are more withdrawn and tend to perform below average (Hay, Ashman, & Van Kraayenoord, 1998).

How does discipline affect self-esteem?   Coopersmith found that low self-esteem is related to physical punishment and the withholding of love. And why not? What message do children receive if a parent beats them or tells them they are not worthy of love?

Power assertion The use of physical punishment or coercion to enforce child discipline.

Withdrawal of love Withholding affection to enforce child discipline.

Management techniques Combining praise, recognition, approval, rules, and reasoning to enforce child discipline.

Self-esteem Regarding oneself as a worthwhile person; a positive evaluation of oneself.

High self-esteem is promoted by management techniques. Thus, it is best to minimize physical punishment and avoid withdrawal of love. Children who feel that their parents support them emotionally tend to have high self-esteem (Hay, Ashman, & Van Kraayenoord, 1998; Nielsen & Metha, 1994).

STUDYBREAK ⅄ *Parental Influences*

RELATE

Picture a mother you know who seems to be a good caregiver. Which of the optimal caregiving behaviors does she engage in?

Do you know any parents who have young children and who are authoritarian, permissive, or authoritative? What are their children like?

What do you think are the best ways to discipline children? How would your approach be classified? What are its advantages and disadvantages?

LEARNING CHECK

1. Three important elements of effective mothering are _____ maternal involvement; parental _____ to a child's feelings, needs, rhythms, and signals; and compatibility between parent and child _____.

2. Fathers are more likely to act as playmates for their children, rather than caregivers. T or F?

3. According to Diana Baumrind's research, effective parents are authoritarian in their approach to their children's behavior. T or F?

4. Authoritarian parents view children as having few rights but many responsibilities. T or F?

5. Coopersmith found that high self-esteem in childhood is related to discipline based on either management techniques or withdrawal of love. T or F?

Critical Thinking

6. Why is it risky to make generalizations about child-rearing differences for various ethnic groups?

7. If power assertion is a poor way to discipline children, why do so many parents use it?

ANSWERS

1. proactive, responsiveness, temperaments 2. T 3. F 4. T 5. F 6. Because there may be as much variation within ethnic groups as there is between them. For example, there are sizable differences in the child-rearing styles of Hispanic parents from Puerto Rico, Argentina, and Guatemala. 7. Most parents discipline their children in the same ways that they themselves were disciplined. Parenting is a responsibility of tremendous importance, for which most people receive almost no training.

LANGUAGE DEVELOPMENT—
FAST-TALKING BABIES

] **SURVEYQUESTION** *How do children acquire language?*

There's something almost miraculous about a baby's first words. As infants, how did we manage to leap into the world of language? As will soon be apparent, social development provides a foundation for language learning. But before we probe that connection, let's begin with a quick survey of language development.

How We Acquire Language

Language development is closely tied to maturation. As every parent knows, babies can cry from birth on. By 1 month of age they use crying to gain attention. Typically, parents can tell if an infant is hungry, angry, or in pain from the tone of the crying. Around 6 to 8 weeks of age, babies begin *cooing* (the repetition of vowel sounds such as "*oo*" and "*ah*").

By 7 months of age, Amy's nervous system will mature enough to allow her to grasp objects, smile, laugh, sit up, and *babble*. In the babbling stage, the consonants *b, d, m,* and *g* are combined with the vowel sounds to produce meaningless language sounds: *dadadadada* or *bababa*. At first, babbling is the same around the world. But soon, the language spoken by parents begins to have an influence. That is, Chinese babies start to babble in a way that sounds like Chinese, Mexican babies babble in Spanish-like sounds, and so forth (Gopnik, Meltzoff, & Kuhl, 1999).

At about 1 year of age, children can stand alone for a short time and respond to real words such as *no* or *hi*. Soon afterward, the first connection between words and objects forms, and children may address their parents as "Mama" or "Dada." By age 18 months to

© Baby Blues Partnership. Reprinted with special permission of King Features Syndicate.

2 years, Amy will have learned to stand and walk alone. By then, her vocabulary may include from 24 to 200 words. At first there is a *single-word stage,* during which children use one word at a time, such as "go," "juice," or "up." Soon after, words are arranged in simple two-word sentences called *telegraphic speech:* "Want-Teddy," "Mama-gone."

Language and the Terrible Twos

At about the same time that children begin to put together two or three words, they become much more independent. Two-year-olds understand some of the commands parents make, but they are not always willing to carry them out. A child like Amy may assert her independence by saying "No drink," "Me do it," "My cup, my cup," and the like. It can be worse, of course. A 2-year-old may look at you intently, make eye contact, listen as you shout "No, no," and still pour her juice on the cat.

During their second year, children become increasingly capable of mischief and temper tantrums. Thus, calling this time "the terrible twos" is not entirely inappropriate. One-year-olds can do plenty of things parents don't want them to do. However, it's usually 2-year-olds who do things *because* you don't want them to (Gopnik, Meltzoff, & Kuhl, 1999).

Perhaps parents can take some comfort in knowing that a stubborn, negative 2-year-old is simply becoming more independent. When Amy is 2, Olivia and Tom would be wise to remember that "This, too, shall pass." After age 2, a dramatic leap forward occurs in the child's comprehension and use of words (Reznick & Goldfield, 1992). From this point on, vocabulary and language skills grow at a phenomenal rate. By first grade, Amy will be able to understand around 8,000 words and use about 4,000. She will have truly entered the world of language.

The Roots of Language

In a fascinating study, researchers William Condon and Louis Sander (1974) filmed newborn infants as the babies listened to various sounds. A frame-by-frame analysis of the films showed something astonishing: Infants move their arms and legs to the rhythms of human speech. Random noise, rhythmic tapping, or disconnected vowel sounds will not produce a "language dance." Only natural speech has this effect.

Why do day-old infants "dance" to speech but not other sounds? One possibility is that language recognition is innate. Linguist Noam Chomsky (1975, 1986) has long claimed that humans have a **biological predisposition** or hereditary readiness to develop language. According to Chomsky, language patterns are inborn, much like a child's ability to coordinate walking. If such inborn language recognition does exist, it may explain why children around the world use a limited number of patterns in their first sentences. Typical patterns include (Mussen et al., 1979):

Identification:	"See kitty."
Nonexistence:	"Allgone milk."
Possession:	"My doll."
Agent-action:	"Mama give."
Negation:	"Not ball."
Question:	"Where doggie?"

Biological predisposition The presumed hereditary readiness of humans to learn certain skills, such as how to use language, or a readiness to behave in particular ways.

◆**FIGURE 3.13** *Infant engagement scale. These samples from a 90-point scale show various levels of infant engagement, or attention. Babies participate in prelanguage "conversations" with parents by giving and withholding attention and by smiling, gazing, or vocalizing. (From Beebe et al., 1982.)*

85	50	20
Medium high positive	Neutral attention	Avert

Does Chomsky's theory explain why language develops so rapidly?   Perhaps. But many psychologists feel that Chomsky underestimates the importance of learning. Psycholinguists (specialists in the psychology of language) have shown that language is not magically "switched on" by adult speech. Imitation of adults and rewards for correctly using words (as when a child asks for a cookie) are an important part of language learning. Also, babies actively participate in language learning by asking questions, such as "What dis?" (Domingo & Goldstein-Alpern, 1999).

When a child makes a language error, parents typically repeat the child's sentence, with needed corrections (Bohannon & Stanowicz, 1988). More important, still, is the fact that parents and children begin to communicate long before the child can speak. Months of shared effort precede a child's first word. From this point of view, an infant's "language dance" reflects a readiness to interact *socially* with parents, not innate language recognition. The next section explains why.

Early Communication

How do parents communicate with infants before they can talk?   Parents go to a great deal of trouble to get babies to smile and vocalize (◆Fig. 3.13). In doing so, they quickly learn to change their actions to keep the infant's attention, arousal, and activity at optimal levels. A familiar example is the "I'm-Going-to-Get-You Game." In it, the adult says, "I'm gonna getcha . . . . I'm gonna getcha . . . . I'm gonna getcha . . . . Gotcha!" Through such games, adults and babies come to share similar rhythms and expectations (Stern, 1982). Soon a system of shared **signals** is created, including touching, vocalizing, gazing, and smiling. These help lay a foundation for later language use. Specifically, signals establish a pattern of "conversational" *turn-taking* (alternate sending and receiving of messages).

OLIVIA	AMY
	(smiles)
"Oh what a nice little smile!"	
"Yes, isn't that nice?"	
"There."	
"There's a nice little smile."	(burps)
"Well, pardon you!"	
"Yes, that's better, isn't it?"	
"Yes."	(vocalizes)
"Yes."	(smiles)
"What's so funny?"	

Signal In early language development, any behavior, such as touching, vocalizing, gazing, or smiling, that allows non-verbal interaction and turn-taking between parent and child.

From the outside, such exchanges may look meaningless. In reality, they represent real communication. Amy's vocalizations and attention provide a way of interacting emotionally with Olivia and Tom. Infants as young as 4 months engage in vocal turn-taking with adults (see ◆Fig. 3.14) (Jaffe et al., 2001). The more children interact with parents, the faster

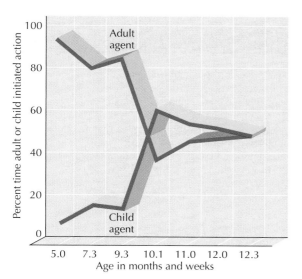

◆**FIGURE 3.14** *This graph shows the development of turn-taking in games played by an infant and his mother. For several months, Richard responded to games such as peek-a-boo and "hand-the-toy-back" only when his mother initiated action. At about 9 months, however, he rapidly began to initiate action in the games. Soon, he was the one to take the lead about half the time. Learning to take turns and to direct actions toward another person underlie basic language skills. (From Bruner, 1983.)*

they learn to talk and the faster they learn thinking abilities (Hart & Risley, 1999; Tamis-LeMonvda & Bornstein, 1994). A recent study found that 6-week-old babies gaze at an adult's face in rhythm with the adult's speech (Crown et al., 2002). Unmistakably, social relationships contribute to early language learning.

Parentese

When they talk to infants, parents use an exaggerated pattern of speaking called **motherese** or **parentese.** Typically, they raise their tone of voice, use short, simple sentences, and repeat themselves more. They also slow their rate of speaking and use exaggerated voice inflections: "Did Amy eat it A-L-L UP?"

What is the purpose of such changes? Parents are apparently trying to help their children learn language. When a baby is still babbling, parents tend to use long, adult-style sentences. But as soon as the baby says its first word they switch to parentese. By the time babies are 4 months old, they prefer parentese to normal speech (Cooper et al., 1997).

In addition to being simpler, parentese has a distinct "musical" quality (Fernald & Mazzie, 1991). No matter what language mothers speak, the melodies, pauses, and inflections they use to comfort, praise, or give warning are universal. Psychologist Anne Fernald has found that mothers of all nations talk to their babies with similar changes in pitch. For instance, we praise babies with a rising, then falling pitch ("BRA-vo!" "GOOD girl!"). Warnings are delivered in a short, sharp rhythm ("Nein! Nein!" "Basta! Basta!" "Not! Dude!"). To give comfort, parents use low, smooth, drawn-out tones ("Oooh, poor baaa-by." "Oooh, pobrecito.") A high-pitched, rising melody is used to call attention to objects ("See the pretty BIRDIE?") (Fernald, 1989).

Motherese helps parents get babies' attention, communicate with them, and teach them language (Kaplan et al., 1995). Later, as a child's speaking improves, parents tend to adjust their speech to the child's language ability. Especially from 18 months to 4 years of age, parents seek to clarify what a child says and prompt the child to say more.

In summary, some elements of language are innate. Nevertheless, our inherited tendency to learn language does not determine if we will speak English or Vietnamese, Spanish or Russian. Environmental forces also influence whether a person develops simple or sophisticated language skills. The first 7 years of life are a sensitive period in language learning (Eliot, 1999). Clearly, a full flowering of speech requires careful cultivation.

As with motherese, parents use a distinctive style when singing to an infant. Even people who speak another language can tell if a tape-recorded song was sung to an infant or an adult. Likewise, lullabies remain recognizable when electronic filtering removes words (Trehub et al., 1993a, 1993b).

Gary Conner/Index Stock Imagery

Motherese (or parentese) A pattern of speech used when talking to infants, marked by a higher-pitched voice; short, simple sentences; repetition; slower speech; and exaggerated voice inflections.

COGNITIVE DEVELOPMENT—HOW DO CHILDREN LEARN TO THINK?

] **SURVEYQUESTION** *How do children learn to think?*

Now that Amy's talking, let's move on to a broader view of intellectual development. Swiss psychologist and philosopher Jean Piaget (Jahn pea-ah-ZHAY) provided some of the first great insights into how children develop thinking abilities.

How different is a child's understanding of the world from an adult's? Generally speaking, a child's thinking is less abstract. Children use fewer generalizations, categories, and principles. They also tend to base their understanding on particular examples and objects they can see or touch.

Before the age of 6 or 7, thinking is very concrete. Younger children cannot make **transformations** in which they must mentally change the shape or form of a substance (such as clay or water). Let's visit Amy at age 5: If you show her a short, wide glass full of milk and a tall, narrow glass (also full), she will tell you that the taller glass contains more milk. Amy will tell you this even if she watches you pour milk from the short glass into an empty, tall glass. She is not bothered by the fact that the milk appears to be transformed from a smaller to a larger amount. Instead, she responds only to the fact that *taller* seems to mean *more* (see ✦Fig. 3.15). After about age 7, children are no longer fooled by this situation. Perhaps that's why 7 has been called the "age of reason." From age 7 on, we see a definite trend toward more logical, adult-like thought (Flavell, 1992).

Is there any pattern to the growth of intellect in childhood? According to Piaget (1951, 1952) there is.

✦FIGURE 3.15 *Children under age 7 intuitively assume that a volume of liquid increases when it is poured from a short, wide container into a taller, thinner one. This boy thinks the tall container holds more than the short one. Actually, each holds the same amount of liquid. Children make such judgments based on the height of the liquid, not its volume.*

Piaget's Theory of Cognitive Development

Jean Piaget believed that all children pass through a series of distinct stages in intellectual development. Many of his ideas came from observing his own children as they solved various thought problems. (It is tempting to imagine that Piaget's illustrious career was launched one day when his wife said to him, "Watch the children for a while, will you, Jean?")

 Transformation The mental ability to change the shape or form of a substance (such as clay or water) and to perceive that its volume remains the same.

Mental Adaptations

Piaget was convinced that intellect grows through processes he called assimilation and accommodation. **Assimilation** refers to using existing mental patterns in new situations. Let's say that a plastic hammer is the favorite toy of a boy named Benjamin. Benjamin holds the hammer properly and loves to pound on blocks with it. For his birthday Benjamin gets an oversize toy wrench. If he uses the wrench for pounding, it has been assimilated to an existing knowledge structure.

In **accommodation,** existing ideas are modified to fit new requirements. For instance, a younger child might think a dime is worth less than a (larger) nickel. However, as children begin to spend money, they must alter their ideas about what "more" and "less" mean. Thus, new situations are assimilated to existing ideas, and new ideas are created to accommodate new experiences.

Piaget's ideas have deeply affected our view of children (Beilin, 1992). The following is a brief summary of what he found.

The Sensorimotor Stage (0–2 Years)

In the first 2 years of life, Amy's intellectual development will be largely non-verbal. She will be mainly concerned with learning to coordinate her movements with information from her senses. Also, **object permanence** (an understanding that objects continue to exist when they are out of sight) emerges at this time. Sometime during their first year, babies begin to actively pursue disappearing objects. By age 2, they can anticipate the movement of an object behind a screen. For example, when watching an electric train, Amy will look ahead to the end of a tunnel, rather than staring at the spot where the train disappeared.

In general, developments in this stage indicate that the child's conceptions are becoming more *stable*. Objects cease to appear and disappear magically, and a more orderly and predictable world replaces the confusing and disconnected sensations of infancy.

The Preoperational Stage (2–7 Years)

During this period, children begin to think *symbolically* and use language. But the child's thinking is still very **intuitive** (it makes little use of reasoning and logic). (Do you remember thinking as a child that the sun and the moon followed you when you took a walk?) In addition, the child's use of language is not as sophisticated as it might seem. Children have a tendency to confuse words with the objects they represent. If Benjamin calls a toy block a "car" and you use it to make a "house," he might get upset. To children, the name of an object is as much a part of the object as its size, shape, and color. This seems to underlie a preoccupation with name-calling. To the preoperational child, insulting words may really hurt. Consider one rather protected youngster who was angered by her older brother. Searching for a way to retaliate against her larger and stronger foe, she settled on "You panty-girdle!" It was the worst thing she could think of saying.

During the preoperational stage, the child is also quite **egocentric** (unable to take the viewpoint of other people). The child's ego seems to stand at the center of his or her world. To illustrate, show Amy a two-sided mirror. Then hold it between you and her, so she can see herself in it. If you ask her what she thinks *you* can see, she imagines that you see *her* face reflected in the mirror, instead of your own. Such egocentrism explains why children can seem exasperatingly selfish or uncooperative at times. If Benjamin

Jean Piaget—philosopher, psychologist, and keen observer of children.

Crossing a busy street can be dangerous for the preoperational child. Because their thinking is still egocentric, younger children cannot understand why the driver of a car can't see them if they can see the car. Children under the age of 7 also cannot consistently judge speeds and distances of oncoming cars. Adults can easily overestimate the "street smarts" of younger children. It is advisable to teach children to cross with a light, in crosswalks, or with assistance.

Assimilation In Piaget's theory, the application of existing mental patterns to new situations (that is, the new situation is assimilated to existing mental schemes).

Accommodation In Piaget's theory, the modification of existing mental patterns to fit new demands (that is, mental schemes are changed to accommodate new information or experiences).

Sensorimotor stage Stage of intellectual development during which sensory input and motor responses become coordinated.

Object permanence The concept, gained in infancy, that objects continue to exist even when they are hidden from view.

Preoperational stage Period of intellectual development during which children begin to use language and think symbolically, yet remain intuitive and egocentric in their thought.

Intuitive thought Thinking that makes little or no use of reasoning and logic.

Egocentric thought Thought that is self-centered and fails to consider the viewpoints of others.

blocks your view by standing in front of the TV, he assumes that you can see it if he can. If you ask him to move so you can see better, he may move so *he* can see better! Benjamin is not being selfish in the ordinary sense. He just doesn't realize that your view differs from his.

The Concrete Operational Stage (7–11 Years)

An important development during this stage is mastery of **conservation** (the concept that mass, weight, and volume remain unchanged when the shape of objects changes). Children have learned conservation when they understand that rolling a ball of clay into a "snake" does not increase the amount of clay. Likewise, pouring liquid from a tall, narrow glass into a shallow dish does not reduce the amount of liquid. In each case, the volume remains the same despite changes in shape or appearance. The original amount is *conserved* (see Fig. 3.15).

During the concrete operational stage, children begin to use concepts of time, space, and number. The child can think logically about very concrete objects or situations, categories, and principles. Such abilities explain why children stop believing in Santa Claus when they reach this stage. Because they can conserve volume, they realize that Santa's sack couldn't possibly hold enough toys for millions of girls and boys.

Another important development at this time is the ability to *reverse* thoughts or mental operations. A conversation with a 4-year-old boy in the preoperational stage shows what happens when a child's thinking *lacks* reversibility (Phillips, 1969).

> "Do you have a brother?"
> "Yes."
> "What's his name?"
> "Jim."
> "Does Jim have a brother?"
> "No."

Reversibility of thought allows children in the concrete operational stage to recognize that if $4 \times 2 = 8$, then 2×4 does, too. Younger children must memorize each relationship separately. Thus, a preoperational child might know that $4 \times 9 = 36$ without being able to tell you what 9×4 equals.

The Formal Operations Stage (11 Years and Older)

Sometime after about the age of 11, children begin to break away from concrete objects and specific examples. Thinking is based more on abstract principles, such as "democracy," "honor," or "correlation." Children who reach this stage can think about their thoughts, and they become less egocentric. Older children and young adolescents also gradually become able to consider hypothetical possibilities (suppositions, guesses, or projections). For example, if you ask a younger child, "What do you think would happen if it suddenly became possible for people to fly?" the child might respond, "People can't fly." Older children are able to consider such possibilities.

Full adult intellectual ability is attained during the stage of formal operations. Older adolescents are capable of inductive and deductive reasoning, and they can comprehend math, physics, philosophy, psychology, and other abstract systems. They can learn to test hypotheses in a scientific manner. Of course, not everyone reaches this level of thinking. Also, many adults can think formally about some topics, but their thinking becomes concrete when the topic is unfamiliar. This implies that formal thinking may be more a result of culture and learning than maturation. In any case, after late adolescence, improvements in intellect are based on gaining knowledge, experience, and wisdom, rather than on any leaps in basic thinking capacity.

How can parents apply Piaget's ideas? Piaget's theory suggests that the ideal way to guide intellectual development is to provide experiences that are only slightly novel, unusual, or challenging. Remember, a child's intellect develops mainly through accommodation. It is usually best to follow a *one-step-ahead strategy,* in which your teaching efforts are aimed just beyond the child's current level of comprehension (Heckhausen, 1987).

For your convenience, ▲ Table 3.2 briefly summarizes each Piagetian stage. To help you remember Piaget's theory, the table describes what would happen at each stage if we played a game of *Monopoly* with the child. You'll also find brief suggestions about how to relate to children in each stage.

Concrete operational stage Period of intellectual development during which children become able to use the concepts of time, space, volume, and number, but in ways that remain simplified and concrete, rather than abstract.

Conservation In Piaget's theory, mastery of the concept that the weight, mass, and volume of matter remain unchanged (are conserved) even when the shape or appearance of objects changes.

Formal operations stage Period of intellectual development characterized by thinking that includes abstract, theoretical, and hypothetical ideas.

▲*TABLE 3.2*	Piaget—A Guide for Parents	
PIAGET	*MONOPOLY* **GAME**	**GUIDELINES FOR PARENTS**
Sensorimotor Stage The stage during which sensory input and motor responses become coordinated.	The child puts houses, hotels, and dice in her mouth and plays with "Chance" cards.	Active play with a child is most effective at this stage. Encourage explorations in touching, smelling, and manipulating objects. Peek-a-boo is a good way to establish the permanence of objects.
Preoperational Stage The period of cognitive development when children begin to use language and think symbolically, yet remain intuitive and egocentric.	The child plays *Monopoly* but makes up her own rules and cannot understand instructions.	Specific examples and touching or seeing things continue to be more useful than verbal explanations. Learning the concept of conservation may be aided by demonstrations with liquids, beads, clay, and other substances.
Concrete Operational Stage The period of cognitive development during which children begin to use concepts of time, space, volume, and number, but in ways that remain simplified and concrete.	The child understands basic instructions and will play by the rules but is not capable of hypothetical transactions dealing with mortgages, loans, and special pacts with other players.	Children are beginning to use generalizations, but they still require specific examples to grasp many ideas. Expect a degree of inconsistency in the child's ability to apply concepts of time, space, quantity, and volume to new situations.
Formal Operations Stage The period of intellectual development marked by a capacity for abstract, theoretical, and hypothetical thinking.	The child no longer plays the game mechanically; complex and hypothetical transactions unique to each game are now possible.	It is now more effective to explain things verbally or symbolically and help children master general rules and principles. Encourage the child to create hypotheses and imagine how things could be.

Piaget Today

Piaget's theory is a valuable "road map" for understanding how children think. However, many psychologists are convinced that Piaget gave too little credit to the effects of learning. For example, children who grow up in villages where pottery is made can correctly answer questions about the conservation of clay at an earlier age than Piaget would have predicted. According to learning theorists, children continuously gain specific knowledge; they do not undergo stage-like leaps in general mental ability. Thus, the truth may lie somewhere between Piaget's stage theory and modern learning theory.

On a broad scale, many of Piaget's *observations* have held up well. However, his *explanations* of childhood thinking abilities continue to be debated. Where early infancy is concerned, even Piaget's observations may need updating. It looks like Piaget greatly underestimated the mental abilities of infants.

Infant Cognition

What evidence is there that Piaget underestimated infant abilities?   Piaget believed that infants under the age of 1 year cannot think. Babies, he said, have no memory of people and objects that are out of sight. Yet we now know that infants begin forming representations of the world very early in life. For example, babies as young as 3 months of age appear to know that objects are solid and do not disappear when out of view (Baillargeon & DeVos, 1992; Johnson & Nanez, 1995).

Why did Piaget fail to detect the thinking skills of infants?   Most likely, he mistook babies' limited *physical* skills for *mental* incompetence. Piaget's tests required babies to search for objects or reach out and touch them. Newer, more sensitive methods are uncovering abilities Piaget missed. One such method takes advantage of the fact that babies, like adults, act surprised when they see something "impossible" or unexpected occur. To use this effect, psychologist Renee Baillargeon (1991) puts on little "magic shows" for infants. In her "the-

✦**FIGURE 3.16** *The panels on the left show a possible event, in which an infant watches as a toy is placed behind the right of two screens. After a delay of 70 seconds, the toy is brought into view from behind the right screen. In the two panels on the right, an impossible event occurs. The toy is placed behind the left screen and retrieved from behind the right. (A duplicate toy was hidden there before testing.) Eight-month-old infants react with surprise when they see the impossible event staged for them. Their reaction implies that they remember where the toy was hidden. Infants appear to have a capacity for memory and thinking that greatly exceeds what Piaget claimed is possible during the sensorimotor period. (Adapted from Baillargeon et al., 1989.)*

ater," babies watch as possible and impossible events occur with toys or other objects. Some 3-month-old infants act surprised and gaze longer at impossible events. An example is seeing two solid objects appear to pass through each other. By the time they are 8 months old, babies can remember where objects are (or should be) for at least 1 minute (✦Fig. 3.16).

Piaget believed that abilities such as those described in Figure 3.16 emerge only after a long sensorimotor period of development. However, it's clear that babies quickly acquire the capacity to form concepts about the world (Eimas, Quinn, & Cowan, 1994). It looks as if further study is likely to refine and amend the ideas that grew from Piaget's fateful decision to "watch the children for a while."

Another criticism of Piaget is that he underestimated the impact of culture on mental development. The next section tells how Amy will master the intellectual tools valued by her culture.

Vygotsky's Sociocultural Theory

Recently, psychologists have become interested in the *sociocultural theory* of Russian scholar Lev Vygotsky (1896–1934). Vygotsky's key insight is that children's thinking develops through dialogues with more capable persons (Vygotsky, 1962, 1978).

How does that relate to intellectual growth?   So far, no one has ever published *A Child's Guide to Life on Earth.* Instead, children must learn about life from various "tutors," such as parents, teachers, and older siblings. Even if *A Child's Guide to Life on Earth* did exist, we would need a separate version for every culture. It is not enough for children to learn how to think. They must also learn specific intellectual skills valued by their culture.

Like Piaget, Vygotsky believed that children actively seek to discover new principles. However, Vygotsky emphasized that many of a child's most important "discoveries" are guided by skillful tutors. Psychologist David Shaffer (1999) offers the following example:

> Annie, a 4-year-old, has just received her first jigsaw puzzle as a birthday present. She attempts to work the puzzle but gets nowhere until her father comes along, sits down beside her, and gives her some tips. He suggests that it would be a good idea to put together the corners first, points to the pink area at the edge of one corner piece and says, "Let's look for another pink piece." When Annie seems frustrated, he places two interlocking pieces near each other so she will notice them, and when Annie succeeds, he offers her words of encouragement. As Annie gradually gets the hang of it, he steps back and lets her work more and more independently. (p. 260)

Zone of proximal development Refers to the range of tasks a child cannot yet master alone, but that she or he can accomplish with the guidance of a more capable partner.

Interactions like this are most helpful when they take place within a child's **zone of proximal development.**

What did Vygotsky mean by that?   The word *proximal* means "close" or "nearby." Vygotsky realized that, at any given time, some tasks are just beyond a child's reach. The child is close to having the mental skills needed to do the task, but it is a little too complex to be mastered alone. However, children working within this zone can make rapid progress if they receive sensitive guidance from a skilled partner.

Vygotsky also emphasized a process he called **scaffolding.** A scaffold is a framework or temporary support. Vygotsky believed that adults help children learn how to think by "scaffolding," or supporting, their attempts to solve problems or discover principles. To be most effective, scaffolding must be responsive to a child's needs. For example, as Annie's father helped her with the puzzle, he tailored his hints and guidance to match her evolving abilities. The two of them worked together, step by step, so Annie could better understand how to assemble the puzzle. In a sense, Annie's father set up a series of temporary bridges that helped her move into new mental territory. As predicted by Vygotsky's theory, the cognitive skills of 3- to 6-year-old children are closely related to the amount of scaffolding their mothers provide (Smith, Landry, & Swank, 2000).

During their collaborations with others, children learn important cultural beliefs and values. For example, imagine that a boy wants to know how many Yu-Gi-Oh! cards he has. His mother helps him stack and count the cards, moving each card to a new stack as they count it. She then shows him how to write the number on a slip of paper so he can remember it. This teaches the child not only about counting, but also that writing is valued in our culture. In other parts of the world, a child learning to count might be shown how to make notches on a stick or tie knots in a cord.

Summary

Vygotsky saw that grown-ups play a crucial role in what children know. As they try to decipher the world, children rely on adults to help them understand how things work. Vygotsky further noticed that adults unconsciously adjust their behavior to give children the information they need to solve problems that interest the child. In this way, children use adults to learn about their culture and society (Gopnik, Meltzoff, & Kuhl, 1999).

MORAL DEVELOPMENT— GROWING A CONSCIENCE

] SURVEYQUESTION *How do we develop morals and values?*

A person with a terminal illness is in great pain. She is pleading for death. Should extraordinary medical efforts be made to keep her alive? A friend of yours desperately needs to pass a test and asks you to help him cheat. Will you do it? These are *moral* questions, or questions of conscience. **Moral development** starts in childhood and continues into adulthood. Through this process, we acquire values, beliefs, and thinking patterns that guide responsible behavior. Let's take a brief look at this interesting aspect of personal development.

Moral Dilemmas

How are moral values acquired?   Psychologist Lawrence Kohlberg (1981a) held that we learn moral values through thinking and reasoning. Thus, emerging cognitive abilities, like those we have just described, help children develop a "moral compass." To study moral development, Kohlberg posed dilemmas to children of different ages. The following is one of the moral dilemmas he used (Kohlberg, 1969, adapted):

> A woman was near death from cancer, and there was only one drug that might save her. It was discovered by a druggist who was charging 10 times what it cost to make the drug. The sick woman's husband could only pay $1,000, but the druggist wanted $2,000. He asked the druggist to sell it cheaper or to let him pay later. The druggist said no. So the husband became desperate and broke into the store to steal the drug for his wife. Should he have done that? Was it wrong or right? Why?

Scaffolding The process of adjusting instruction so it is responsive to a beginner's behavior and supports the beginner's efforts to understand a problem or gain a mental skill.

Moral development The development of values, beliefs, and thinking abilities that act as a guide regarding what is acceptable behavior.

Each child was asked what action the husband should take. Kohlberg classified the reasons given for each choice and identified three levels of moral development. Each is based not so much on the choices made, but on the reasoning used to arrive at a choice (Kohlberg, 1981b).

At the lowest, **preconventional level,** moral thinking is guided by the consequences of actions (punishment, reward, or an exchange of favors). For example, a person at this level might reason that "The man shouldn't steal the drug because he could get caught and sent to jail" (avoiding punishment) or "It won't do him any good to steal the drug because his wife will probably die before he gets out of jail" (self-interest).

At the second, or **conventional level,** reasoning is based on a desire to please others or to follow accepted authority, rules, and values. For example, a person at this intermediate level might say, "He shouldn't steal the drug because others will think he is a thief. His wife would not want to be saved by thievery" (avoiding disapproval) or "Although his wife needs the drug, he should not break the law to get it. Everyone has to obey the law. His wife's condition does not justify stealing" (traditional morality of authority).

At the highest, or **postconventional level,** moral behavior is directed by self-chosen ethical principles that tend to be general, comprehensive, or universal. People at this level place high value on justice, dignity, and equality. For example, a highly principled person might say, "He should steal the drug and then inform the authorities that he has done so. He will have to face a penalty, but he will have saved a human life" (self-chosen ethical principles).

Does everyone eventually reach the highest level? People advance at different rates, and many fail to reach the postconventional level of moral reasoning. In fact, many do not even reach the conventional level. For instance, a survey in England revealed that 11 percent of men and 3 percent of women would commit murder for $1 million if they could be sure of getting away with the crime ("They'd kill," 1991).

The preconventional level is most characteristic of young children and delinquents (Nelson, Smith, & Dodd, 1990). Conventional, group-oriented morals are typical of older children and most adults. Kohlberg estimated that only about 20 percent of the adult population achieves postconventional morality, representing self-direction and higher principles. (It would appear that few of these people enter politics!)

Moral development is an important part of growing up. Many of the choices we make every day involve fundamental questions of right and wrong. Being able to think clearly about such questions is essential to becoming a responsible adult.

Preconventional moral reasoning Moral thinking based on the consequences of one's choices or actions (punishment, reward, or an exchange of favors).

Conventional moral reasoning Moral thinking based on a desire to please others or to follow accepted rules and values.

Postconventional moral reasoning Moral thinking based on carefully examined and self-chosen moral principles.

STUDYBREAK   *Cognitive Development and Moral Development*

RELATE

You are going to make cookies with children of various ages. See if you can name each of Piaget's stages and give an example of what a child in that stage might be expected to do.

You have been asked to help a child learn to use a pocket calculator to do simple addition. How would you go about identifying the child's zone of proximal development for this task? How would you scaffold the child's learning?

At what stage of moral development was former U.S. President Bill Clinton functioning in his well-publicized affair with Monica Lewinsky?

LEARNING CHECK

Match each item with one of the following stages:

A. Sensorimotor B. Preoperational C. Concrete operational
D. Formal operations

1. _____ egocentric thought
2. _____ abstract or hypothetical thought
3. _____ purposeful movement
4. _____ intuitive thought
5. _____ conservation
6. _____ reversibility of thought
7. _____ object permanence
8. _____ non-verbal development

9. Assimilation refers to applying existing thought patterns or knowledge to new situations. T or F?
10. Newer methods for testing infant thinking abilities frequently make note of whether an infant is _____ by seemingly _____ events.
11. Vygotsky called the process of providing a temporary framework of supports for learning new mental abilities _____.
12. According to Kohlberg, the conventional level of moral development is marked by a reliance on outside authority. T or F?
13. Self-interest and avoiding punishment are elements of postconventional morality. T or F?

Critical Thinking

14. Using Piaget's theory as a guide, at what age would you expect a child to recognize that a Styrofoam cup has weight?

ANSWERS

1. B 2. D 3. A 4. B 5. C 6. C 7. A 8. A 9. T 10. surprised, impossible 11. scaffolding 12. T 13. F 14. Seventy-five percent of 4- to 6-year-olds say that a Styrofoam cup has no weight! Most children judge weight intuitively (by the way an object feels) until they begin to move into the concrete operational stage (Smith, Carey, & Wiser, 1985).

THE STORY OF A LIFETIME—ROCKY ROAD OR GARDEN PATH?

] **SURVEYQUESTION** *What are the typical tasks and dilemmas through the life span?*

At the beginning of this chapter we noted that developmental psychologists are interested in every phase of life from the womb to the tomb. Thus far, we have concentrated on Amy's early years because development during childhood can have a large impact on a person's life. It is not possible here to satisfy Olivia and Tom's curiosity about Amy's future. Nevertheless, we can at least sketch the general outlines of her life to come. Every life is marked by a number of *developmental milestones.* These are notable events, markers, or turning points in personal development. Some examples include graduating from school, voting for the first time, getting married, watching a child leave home (or move back!), the death of a parent, becoming a grandparent, retirement, and one's own death.

Perhaps the best way to get a preview of Amy's life is to consider some of the major psychological challenges she is likely to encounter. Broad similarities can be found in the life stages of infancy, childhood, adolescence, young adulthood, middle adulthood, and old age. Each stage confronts a person with new **developmental tasks** that must be mastered for optimal development. Examples are learning to read in childhood, adjusting to sexual maturity in adolescence, and establishing a vocation as an adult.

In an influential book titled *Childhood and Society* (1963), personality theorist Erik Erikson (1903–1994) suggests that we face a specific *psychosocial dilemma,* or "crisis," at each stage of life. A **psychosocial dilemma** is a conflict between personal impulses and the social world. Resolving each dilemma creates a new balance between a person and society. A string of "successes" produces healthy development and a satisfying life. Unfavorable outcomes throw us off-balance, making it harder to deal with later crises. Life becomes a "rocky road," and personal growth is stunted. ▲ Table 3.3 lists Erikson's dilemmas.

What are the major developmental tasks and life crises? A brief description of each psychosocial dilemma follows.

Stage One, First Year of Life: Trust versus Mistrust

During the first year of life, children are completely dependent on others. Erikson believed that a basic attitude of trust or mistrust is formed at this time. **Trust** is established when babies are given adequate warmth, touching, love, and physical care. **Mistrust** is caused by inadequate or unpredictable care and by parents who are cold, indifferent, or rejecting. Basic mistrust might later cause insecurity, suspiciousness, or an inability to relate to others. Notice that trust comes from the same conditions that help babies become securely attached to their parents.

Stage Two, 1–3 Years: Autonomy versus Shame and Doubt

In stage two, children express their growing self-control by climbing, touching, exploring, and trying to do things for themselves. Tom and Olivia can foster Amy's sense of **autonomy** by encouraging her to try new skills. However, her first efforts may be crude, involving spilling, falling, wetting, and other "accidents." If Tom and Olivia ridicule or overprotect Amy, they may cause her to **doubt** her abilities and feel **shameful** about her actions.

Stage Three, 3–5 Years: Initiative versus Guilt

In stage three, children move beyond simple self-control and begin to take initiative. Through play, children learn to make plans and carry out tasks. Parents reinforce **initiative** by giving children freedom to play, ask questions,

Personality theorist Erik Erikson (1903–1994) is best known for his life-stage theory of human development.

▲TABLE 3.3	Erikson's Psychosocial Dilemmas
AGE	**CHARACTERISTIC DILEMMA**
Birth to 1 year	Trust versus mistrust
1 to 3 years	Autonomy versus shame and doubt
3 to 5 years	Initiative versus guilt
6 to 12 years	Industry versus inferiority
Adolescence	Identity versus role confusion
Young adulthood	Intimacy versus isolation
Middle adulthood	Generativity versus stagnation
Late adulthood	Integrity versus despair

Developmental task Any skill that must be mastered, or personal change that must take place, for optimal development.

Psychosocial dilemma A conflict between personal impulses and the social world.

Trust versus mistrust A conflict early in life about learning to trust others and the world.

Autonomy versus shame and doubt A conflict created when growing self-control (autonomy) is pitted against feelings of shame or doubt.

Initiative versus guilt A conflict between learning to take initiative and overcoming feelings of guilt about doing so.

According to Erikson, children aged 3 to 5 learn to plan and initiate activities through play.

◆FIGURE 3.17 *Dramatic differences in physical size and maturity are found in adolescents of the same age. The girls pictured are all 13, the boys 16. Maturation that occurs earlier or later than average can affect the "search for identity." (Adapted from "Growing Up" by J. M. Tanner. Copyright © September 1973 by Scientific American, Inc. All rights reserved.)*

use imagination, and choose activities. Feelings of **guilt** about initiating activities are formed if parents criticize severely, prevent play, or discourage a child's questions.

Stage Four, 6–12 Years: Industry versus Inferiority

Many events of middle childhood are symbolized by that fateful day when you first entered school. With dizzying speed, your world expanded beyond your family, and you faced a whole series of new challenges.

The elementary-school years are a child's "entrance into life." In school, children begin to learn skills valued by society, and success or failure can affect a child's feelings of adequacy. Children learn a sense of **industry** if they win praise for productive activities, such as building, painting, cooking, reading, and studying. If a child's efforts are regarded as messy, childish, or inadequate, feelings of **inferiority** result. For the first time, teachers, classmates, and adults outside the home become as important as parents in shaping attitudes toward oneself.

Stage Five, Adolescence: Identity versus Role Confusion

Adolescence is often a turbulent time. Caught between childhood and adulthood, the adolescent faces some unique problems. Erikson considered a need to answer the question "Who am I?" the primary task during this stage of life. As Amy matures mentally and physically, she will have new feelings, a new body, and new attitudes (◆Fig. 3.17). Like other adolescents, she will need to build a consistent **identity** out of her talents, values, life history, relationships, and the demands of her culture (Douvan, 1997). Her conflicting experiences as a student, friend, athlete, worker, daughter, lover, and so forth must be integrated into a unified sense of self (see "Ethnic Diversity and Identity"). Persons who fail to develop a sense of identity suffer from **role confusion,** an uncertainty about who they are and where they are going.

Stage Six, Young Adulthood: Intimacy versus Isolation

What did Erikson believe is the major conflict in early adulthood? In stage six, the individual feels a need for *intimacy* in his or her life. After establishing a stable identity, a person is prepared to share meaningful love or deep friendship with others. By **intimacy,** Erikson meant an ability to care about others and to share experiences with them. In line with Erikson's view, 75 percent of college-age men and women rank a good marriage and family life as important adult goals (Bachman & Johnson, 1979). And yet marriage or sexual involvement is no guarantee of intimacy: Many adult relationships remain superficial and unfulfilling. Failure to establish intimacy with others leads to a deep sense of **isolation** (feeling alone and uncared for in life). This often sets the stage for later difficulties.

Industry versus inferiority A conflict in middle childhood centered on lack of support for industrious behavior, which can result in feelings of inferiority.

Identity versus role confusion A conflict of adolescence, involving the need to establish a personal identity.

Intimacy versus isolation The challenge of overcoming a sense of isolation by establishing intimacy with others.

HUMAN DIVERSITY Ethnic Diversity and Identity

For adolescents of ethnic descent, the question is often not just "Who am I?" Rather, it is "Who am I at home? Who am I at school? Who am I with friends from my neighborhood?"

Ethnic heritage can have a powerful influence on personal identity. Yet at a time when teens are trying to find their place in society, they may feel rejected or excluded because of their ethnic heritage. For example, popular culture is loaded with images that dismiss anyone who doesn't look like Britney Spears or Matt Damon. Also, ethnic adolescents often face degrading stereotypes concerning their intelligence, sexuality, social status, manners, and so forth. The result can be lowered self-esteem and confusion about roles, values, and personal identity (de las Fuentes & Vasquez, 1999).

In forming an identity, adolescents of ethnic descent face the question of how they should think of themselves. Is Lori an American or a Chinese American? Is Jaime a Chicano, a Mexicano, or a Mexican American? The answer typically depends on how strongly adolescents identify with their family and ethnic community. Teens who take pride in their ethnic heritage have higher self-esteem, a better self-image, and a stronger sense of personal identity (Roberts et al., 1999; Tse, 1999; Verkuyten & Lay, 1998). Group pride, positive models, and a more tolerant society could do much to keep a broad range of options open to *all* adolescents (Vasquez & de las Fuentes, 1999).

Stage Seven, Middle Adulthood: Generativity versus Stagnation

According to Erikson, an interest in guiding the next generation is the main source of balance in mature adulthood. Erikson called this quality **generativity.** It is expressed by caring about oneself, one's children, and future generations. Generativity may be achieved by guiding one's own children or by helping other children (as a teacher, clergyman, or coach, for example). Productive or creative work can also express generativity. In any case, a person's concerns and energies must broaden to include the welfare of others and society as a whole. Failure to do this is marked by a **stagnant** concern with one's own needs and comforts. Life loses meaning, and the person feels bitter, dreary, and trapped (Peterson & Klohnen, 1995).

Stage Eight, Late Adulthood: Integrity versus Despair

What did Erikson see as the conflicts of old age?   Old age is a time of reflection. According to Erikson, when Amy grows old, she must be able to look back over her life with acceptance and satisfaction. People who have lived richly and responsibly develop a sense of **integrity** (self-respect), which allows them to face aging and death with dignity. If previous life events are viewed with regret, the elderly person experiences **despair** (heartache and remorse). In this case, life seems like a series of missed opportunities. The person feels like a failure and knows it's too late to reverse what has been done. Aging and the threat of death then become sources of fear and depression.

To squeeze a lifetime into a few pages, we had to ignore countless details. Although much is lost, the result is a clearer picture of an entire life cycle. Is Erikson's description, then, an exact map of Amy's future—or your own? Probably not. Still, psychosocial dilemmas are major events in many lives. Knowing about them may allow you to anticipate typical trouble spots in your own life. You may also be better prepared to understand the problems and feelings of friends and relatives at various points in the life cycle.

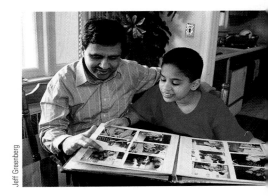

According to Erikson, an interest in future generations characterizes optimal adult development.

Midlife and Old Age

Erikson's dilemmas are not the only challenges of adulthood. Others are all too familiar: marital strife, divorce, career difficulties, unemployment, health problems, financial pressures, legal conflicts, and personal tragedies—to name but a few. How do people maintain a state of well-being as they run the gauntlet of modern life? Psychologist Carol Ryff (1995) believes that well-being during adulthood has six elements:

- Self-acceptance
- Positive relations with others
- Autonomy (personal freedom)
- Environmental mastery
- A purpose in life
- Continued personal growth

Generativity versus stagnation A conflict of middle adulthood in which self-interest is countered by an interest in guiding the next generation.

Integrity versus despair A conflict in old age between feelings of integrity and the despair of viewing previous life events with regret.

At age 77, John Glenn became the oldest person to fly into space, in October 1998. Glenn was also the first American astronaut to orbit Earth, in 1962. As Glenn's space adventure shows, aging does not inevitably bring an end to engaging in challenging activities.

Ryff found that for many older adults, age-related declines are offset by positive relationships and greater mastery of life's demands (Ryff & Keyes, 1995). Thus, sharing life's joys and sorrows with others, coupled with a better understanding of how the world works, can help carry people through midlife and into their later years (Ryff & Singer, 2000). Despite the emphasis on youth in our culture, middle age and beyond can be a rich period of life in which people feel secure, happy, and self-confident (Rubenstein, 2002).

After the late fifties, physical aging complicates personal development. However, it is wrong to believe that most elderly people are sickly, infirm, or senile. Only about 5 percent of those older than 65 are in nursing homes.

Psychologist Bernice Neugarten (1916–2001) examined the lives of people between the ages of 70 and 79 and identified several myths about aging (Neugarten, 1971). Contrary to popular belief:

- Old persons generally do not become isolated and neglected by their families. Most *prefer* to live apart from their children.
- Old persons are rarely placed in mental hospitals by uncaring children.
- Old persons who live alone are not necessarily lonely or desolate.
- Few elderly persons ever show signs of senility or mental decay, and few ever become mentally ill.

In short, most of the elderly studied by Neugarten were integrated, active, and psychologically healthy.

Mentally, many elderly persons are at least as capable as the average young adult. On intellectual tests, top scorers over the age of 65 match the average for men younger than 35. What sets these silver-haired stars apart? Typically, they are people who have continued to work and remain intellectually active (Weintraub et al., 1994). You are most likely to stay mentally sharp in old age if (Schaie, 1994):

- You remain healthy.
- You live in a favorable environment (you are educated and have a stimulating occupation, above-average income, and an intact family).
- You are involved in intellectually stimulating activities (reading, travel, cultural events, continuing education, clubs, professional associations).
- You have a flexible personality.
- You are married to a smart spouse.
- You maintain your perceptual processing speed.
- You were satisfied with your accomplishments in midlife.

A shorter summary of this list is "Those who live by their wit die with their wits."

Aging and Ageism

You have almost certainly encountered ageism in one way or another. **Ageism,** which refers to discrimination or prejudice based on age, can oppress the young as well as the old. For instance, a person applying for a job might just as well be told "You're too young" as "You're too old." In some societies, ageism is expressed as respect for the elderly. In Japan, for instance, aging is seen as positive, and greater age brings more status and respect. In most Western nations, however, ageism tends to have a negative impact on older individuals. Popular stereotypes of the "dirty old man," "meddling old woman," "senile old fool," and the like help perpetuate myths about aging. But such stereotypes are clearly wrong: A tremendous diversity exists among the elderly—ranging from the infirm to aerobic-dancing grandmothers.

In many occupations, older workers perform well in jobs that require *both* speed and skill. Of course, people do experience a gradual slowing as they age. But often this can be offset by experience, skill, or expertise (Schaie, 1988). Overall, very little loss of job performance occurs as workers grow older. In the professions, wisdom and expertise can usually more than compensate for any loss of mental quickness (Ericsson, 2000). Basing retirement solely on a person's age makes little sense (Baltes, Staudinger, & Lindenberger, 1999).

Ageism Discrimination or prejudice based on a person's age.

Successful Aging

What are the keys to successful aging?   They are not unlike the elements of well-being at midlife. Four psychological characteristics shared by the healthiest, happiest older people are (Vaillant, 2002):

• Optimism, hope, and an interest in the future
• Gratitude and forgiveness; an ability to focus on what is good in life
• Empathy; an ability to share the feelings of others and see the world through their eyes
• Connection with others; an ability to give and receive social support

Actually, these are excellent guidelines for well-being at any stage of adulthood.

In summary, enlightened views of aging call for an end to the forced obsolescence of the elderly. As a group, older people represent a valuable source of skill, knowledge, and energy we can't afford to cast aside. As we face the challenges of this planet's uncertain future, we need all the help we can get!

STUDYBREAK ⟨Y⟩ *Psychosocial Dilemmas, Midlife, and Aging*

RELATE

See if you can think of a person you know who is facing one of Erikson's psychosocial dilemmas. Now see if you can think of specific people who seem to be coping with each of the other dilemmas.

See if you can describe three instances of ageism you have witnessed.

LEARNING CHECK

As a way to improve your memory, you might find it helpful to summarize Erikson's eight life stages. Complete this do-it-yourself summary and compare your answers to those given below.

Stage	Crisis	Favorable Outcome
First year of life	1. _____ vs. 2. _____	Faith in the environment and in others
Ages 1–3	Autonomy vs. 3. _____	Feelings of self-control and adequacy
Ages 3–5	4. _____ vs. guilt	Ability to begin one's own activities
Ages 6–12	Industry vs. 5. _____	Confidence in productive skills, learning how to work

Adolescence	6. _____ vs. role confusion	An integrated image of oneself as a unique person
Young adulthood	Intimacy vs. 7. _____	Ability to form bonds of love and friendship with others
Middle adulthood	Generativity vs. 8. _____	Concern for family, society, and future generations
Late adulthood	9. _____ vs. 10. _____	Sense of dignity and fulfillment, willingness to face death

11. After age 65, a large proportion of older people show significant signs of mental disability, and most require special care. T or F?
12. Job performance tends to decline rapidly in older workers. T or F?

Critical Thinking

13. Trying to make generalizations about development throughout life is complicated by at least one major factor. What do you think it is?

ANSWERS

1. Trust 2. mistrust 3. shame or doubt 4. Initiative 5. inferiority 6. Identity 7. isolation 8. stagnation 9. Integrity 10. despair 11. F 12. F 13. Different *cohorts* (groups of people born in the same year) live in different historical times. People born in various decades may have very different life experiences. This makes it difficult to identify universal patterns (Stewart & Ostrove, 1998).

Psychology in Action

Effective Parenting—Raising Healthy Children

] **SURVEYQUESTION** *How do effective parents discipline their children?*

When parents fail to give children a good start in life, everybody suffers—the child, the parents, and society as a whole. Children need to grow up with a capacity for love, joy, fulfillment, responsibility, and self-control. Most people discipline their children in the same way they were disciplined. Unfortunately, this means many parents make the same mistakes their parents did (Covell, Grusec, & King, 1995).

Two key ingredients of effective parenting are communication and discipline. In each area, parents must strike a balance between freedom and guidance.

Parenting with Consistency

How can parents strike a healthy balance? Children should feel free to express their deepest feelings through speech and actions. However, this does not mean they can do whatever they please. Rather, the child is allowed to move freely within well-defined boundaries for acceptable behavior. Of course, individual parents may choose limits that are more "strict" or less "strict." But this choice is less important than **consistency** (maintaining stable rules of conduct). Consistent discipline gives a child a sense of security and stability. Inconsistency makes the child's world seem insecure and unpredictable.

What does consistent discipline mean in practice? To illustrate the errors parents often make, let's consider some examples of inconsistency (Fontenelle, 1989). The following are mistakes to avoid:

- Saying one thing and doing something else. You tell the child, "Bart, if you don't eat your Brussels sprouts you can't have any dessert." Then you feel guilty and offer him some dessert.
- Making statements you don't mean. "If you don't quiet down, I'm going to stop the car and make you walk home."
- Overstating consequences. "Look what you did to the flower bed. You can't ever ride your bike again."
- Changing *no* to *yes,* especially to quiet a nagging child. A good example is the parent who first refuses to buy the child a toy and later gives in and buys it.
- Not checking to see if the child has actually done something you requested, such as picking up clothes or making a bed.
- Contradicting the rules your spouse has set for the child. Parents need to agree on guidelines for child discipline and not undermine each other's efforts.
- Not meaning what you say the first time. Children quickly learn how many times they can be warned before they are actually about to be punished.
- Responding differently to the same misbehavior. One day a child is sent to his room for fighting with his sister. The next day the fighting is overlooked.

Random discipline makes children feel angry and confused because they cannot control the consequences of their own behavior. Inconsistency also gives children the message "Don't believe what I say because I usually don't mean it."

Using Constructive Discipline

At one time or another, most parents use power assertion, withdrawal of love, or management techniques to control their children. Each mode of discipline has its place. However, physical punishment and withdrawal of love should always be used with caution. Here are some guidelines:

1. Parents should separate disapproval of the act from disapproval of the child. Instead of saying, "I'm going to punish you because *you are bad,*" say, "I'm upset about *what you did.*"
2. State specifically what misbehavior you are punishing. Explain why you have set limits on this kind of conduct.
3. Punishment should never be harsh or injurious. Don't physically punish a child while you are angry. Also remember that the message "I don't love you right now" can be more painful and damaging than any spanking.

Consistency With respect to child discipline, the maintenance of stable rules of conduct.

4. Punishment, such as a scolding or taking away privileges, is most effective when done immediately. This statement is especially true for younger children.
5. Spanking and other forms of physical punishment are not particularly effective for children younger than age 2. The child will only be confused and frightened. Spankings also become less effective after age 5 because they tend to humiliate the child and breed resentment.
6. As discussed earlier, many psychologists believe that children should never be spanked. If you do use physical punishment, reserve it for situations that pose an immediate danger to younger children; for example, when a child runs into the street.
7. Remember, too, that it is usually more effective to reward children when they are being good than it is to punish them for misbehavior.

After age 5, management techniques—especially techniques that emphasize communication and the relationship between parent and child—are the most effective form of discipline.

Maintaining a Positive Relationship

The heart of child management is the relationship between parents and their children. Parenting experts Don Dinkmeyer and Gary McKay (1997) believe that there are four basic ingredients of positive parent-child interactions:

- **Mutual respect.** Effective parents try to avoid nagging, hitting, debating, and talking down to their children. They also avoid doing things for their children that the children can do for themselves. (Constantly stripping children of opportunities to learn and take responsibility prevents them from becoming independent and developing self-esteem.)
- **Shared enjoyment.** Effective parents spend some time each day with their children, doing something that both the parent and child enjoy.
- **Love.** This goes almost without saying, but many parents assume their children know that they are loved. It is important to show them you care—in words and by actions such as hugging.
- **Encouragement.** Children who get frequent encouragement come to believe in themselves. Effective parents don't just praise their children for success, winning, or good behavior. They also recognize a child's *progress and attempts to improve.* Show you have faith in your children by letting them try things on their own and by encouraging their efforts.

Communicating Effectively with Children

Creative communication is another important ingredient of successful child management (Bath, 1996). Child expert Haim Ginott (1965) believed that making a distinction between feelings and behavior is the key to clear communication. Because children (and parents, too) do not choose how they feel, it is important to allow free expression of feelings.

Accepting Feelings

The child who learns to regard some feelings as "bad," or unacceptable, is being asked to deny a very real part of his or her experience. Ginott encouraged parents to teach their children that all feelings are appropriate; it is only actions that are subject to disapproval. Many parents don't realize how often they block communication and the expression of feelings in their children. Consider this typical conversation excerpted from Ginott's book (1965):

SON: I am stupid, and I know it. Look at my grades in school.
FATHER: You just have to work harder.
SON: I already work harder and it doesn't help. I have no brains.
FATHER: You are smart, I know.
SON: I am stupid, I know.
FATHER: (loudly) You are not stupid!
SON: Yes, I am!
FATHER: You are not stupid. Stupid!

By debating with the child, the father misses the point that his son *feels* stupid. It would be far more helpful for the father to encourage the boy to talk about his feelings. For instance, he might say, "You really feel that you are not as smart as others, don't you? Do you feel this way often? Are you feeling bad at school?" In this way, the child is given a chance to express his emotions and to feel understood. The father might conclude by saying, "Look, son, in my eyes you are a fine person. But I understand how you feel. Everyone feels stupid at times."

Encouragement

Again, it is valuable to remember that supportive parents encourage their children. In terms of communication, encouragement sounds like this (Dinkmeyer, McKay, & Dinkmeyer, 1997):

"It looks like you enjoyed that."
"I have confidence in you; you'll make it."
"It was thoughtful of you to _____."
"Thanks. That helped a lot."
"You really worked hard on that."
"You're improving. Look at the progress you've made."

I-Messages

Communication with a child can also be the basis of effective discipline. Child psychologist Thomas Gordon (1970) offers a useful suggestion. Gordon believes that parents should send *I-messages* to their children, rather than *you-messages.*

What's the difference? **You-messages** take the form of threats, name-calling, accusing, bossing, lecturing, or criticizing. Generally, you-messages tell children what's "wrong" with them. An **I-message** tells children what effect their behavior had on you. For example, after a hard day's work, Susan wants to sit down and rest a while. She begins to relax with a newspaper when her 5-year-old daughter starts banging loudly on a toy drum. Most parents would respond with a you-message:

"You go play outside this instant." (bossing)
"Don't ever make such a racket when someone is reading." (lecturing)
"You're really pushing it today, aren't you?" (accusing)
"You're a spoiled brat." (name-calling)
"You're going to get a spanking!" (threatening)

Gordon suggests sending an I-message such as, "I am very tired, and I would like to read. I feel upset and can't read with so much noise." This forces the child to accept responsibility for the effects of her actions.

To summarize, an I-message states the behavior to which you object. It then clearly tells the child the consequence of his or her behavior and how that makes you feel. Here's a "fill-in-the-blanks" I-message: "When you [state the child's behavior], I feel [state your feel-

You-message Threatening, accusing, bossing, lecturing, or criticizing another person.

I-message A message that states the effect someone else's behavior has on you.

ings] because [state the consequences of the child's behavior]." For example, "When you go to Jenny's without telling me, I worry that something might have happened to you because I don't know where you are" (Dinkmeyer, McKay, & Dinkmeyer, 1997).

Using Natural and Logical Consequences

Sometimes events automatically discourage misbehavior. For example, a child who refuses to eat dinner will get uncomfortably hungry. A child who throws a temper tantrum may gain nothing but a sore throat and a headache if the tantrum is ignored (Fontenelle, 1989). In such instances, a child's actions have **natural consequences** (intrinsic effects). In situations that don't produce natural consequences, parents can set up **logical consequences** (rational and reasonable effects). For example, a parent might say, "We'll go to the zoo when you've picked up all those toys," or "You can play with your dolls as soon as you've taken your bath," or "You two can stop arguing or leave the table until you're ready to join us."

The concept of logical, parent-defined consequences can be combined with I-messages to handle many day-to-day instances of misbehavior. The key idea is to use an I-message to set up consequences and then give the child a choice to make: "Michelle, we're trying to watch TV. You can settle down and watch with us or go play elsewhere. You decide which you'd rather do" (Dinkmeyer, McKay, & Dinkmeyer, 1997).

How could Susan have dealt with her 5-year-old—the one who was banging on a drum? A response that combines an I-message with logical consequences would be, "I would like for you to stop banging on that drum; otherwise, please take it outside." If the child continues to bang on the drum inside the house, then she has caused the toy to be put away. If she takes it outside, she has made a decision to play with the drum in a way that respects her mother's wishes. In this way, both parent and child have been allowed to maintain a sense of self-respect and a needless clash has been averted.

After you have stated consequences and let the child decide, be sure to respect the child's choice. If the child repeats the misbehavior, you can let the consequences remain in effect longer. But later, give the child another chance to cooperate.

With all child management techniques, remember to be firm, kind, consistent, respectful, and encouraging. And most of all, try every day to live the message you wish to communicate.

Natural consequences The effects that naturally tend to follow a particular behavior.
Logical consequences Reasonable consequences that are defined by parents.

CHAPTER IN REVIEW

Major Points

- You are a product of both your genetic heritage and the environments in which you have lived.
- Infant development is strongly influenced by heredity. However, environmental factors such as nutrition, parenting, and learning are also important.
- Forming an emotional bond with a caregiver is a crucial event during infancy.
- Learning to use language is a cornerstone of early intellectual development.
- Piaget's stage theory provides a valuable map of how thinking abilities unfold.
- Vygotsky's theory reminds us that a child's mind is shaped by culture and human relationships.
- Acquiring moral standards depends, in part, on the development of thinking and reasoning abilities.
- Erik Erikson identified a series of challenges that occur across the life span. These range from a need to gain trust in infancy to the need to live with integrity in old age.
- Effective child discipline is consistent, humane, encouraging, and based on respectful communication.

Summary

How do heredity and environment affect development?

- The nature-nurture controversy concerns the relative contributions to development of heredity (nature) and environment (nurture).
- Hereditary instructions are carried by the chromosomes and genes in each cell of the body. Most characteristics are polygenic and reflect the combined effects of dominant and recessive genes.
- Temperament is hereditary. Most infants fall into one of three temperament categories: easy children, difficult children, and slow-to-warm-up children.
- During sensitive periods in development, infants are more sensitive to specific environmental influences.
- Prenatal development influenced by environmental factors, such as diseases; drugs; radiation; various teratogens; and the mother's diet, health, and emotions.
- Early perceptual, intellectual, or emotional deprivation seriously retards development.
- Deliberate enrichment of the environment has a beneficial effect on infants.
- Heredity and environment are interacting forces. A child's developmental level reflects heredity, environment, and the effects of the child's own behavior.

What can newborn babies do?

- The human neonate has a number of adaptive reflexes, including the grasping, rooting, sucking, and Moro re-

flexes. Neonates begin to learn immediately, and they appear to be aware of the effects of their actions.
- Testing with a looking chamber reveals that neonates prefer bright lights and circular or curved designs.
- Infants prefer human face patterns, especially familiar faces. In later infancy, interest in the unfamiliar emerges.

What influence does maturation have on early development?

- Maturation of the body and nervous system underlies the orderly development of motor skills, cognitive abilities, emotions, and language.
- The rate of maturation varies from person to person. Also, learning contributes greatly to the development of basic motor skills.
- Emotions develop in a consistent order, starting with generalized excitement in newborn babies. Three of the basic emotions—fear, anger, and joy—may be unlearned.
- Many early skills are subject to the principle of readiness.

Of what significance is a child's emotional attachment to parents?

- Emotional attachment of human infants is a critical early event.
- Infant attachment is reflected by separation anxiety. The quality of attachment can be classified as secure, insecure-avoidant, or insecure-ambivalent.
- High-quality day care does not appear to harm children. Low-quality care can be risky.
- Meeting a baby's affectional needs is as important as meeting needs for physical care.

How important are parenting styles?

- Studies suggest that caregiving styles have a substantial impact on emotional and intellectual development.
- Whereas mothers typically emphasize caregiving, fathers tend to function as playmates for infants.
- Optimal caregiving includes proactive maternal involvement, responsiveness to a child's needs and signals, and a good fit between parent and child temperaments.
- Three major parental styles are authoritarian, permissive, and authoritative (effective). Authoritative parenting appears to benefit children the most.
- Effective parental discipline tends to emphasize child management techniques (especially communication), rather than power assertion or withdrawal of love.

How do children acquire language?

- Language development proceeds from crying, to cooing, then babbling, the use of single words, then to telegraphic speech.

- The underlying patterns of telegraphic speech suggest a biological predisposition to acquire language. This innate tendency is augmented by learning.
- Prelanguage communication between parent and child involves shared rhythms, non-verbal signals, and turn-taking.
- Motherese or parentese is a simplified, musical style of speaking that parents use to help their children learn language.

How do children learn to think?

- Jean Piaget theorized that intellectual growth occurs through a combination of assimilation and accommodation.
- Piaget also held that children go through a fixed series of cognitive stages. The stages and their approximate age ranges are: sensorimotor (0–2), preoperational (2–7), concrete operational (7–11), and formal operations (11–adult).
- Learning principles provide an alternate explanation that assumes cognitive development is continuous; it does not occur in stages.
- Recent studies of infants under the age of 1 year suggest that they are capable of thought well beyond that observed by Piaget.
- Lev Vygotsky's sociocultural theory emphasizes that a child's mental abilities are advanced by interactions with more competent partners. Mental growth takes place in a child's zone of proximal development, where a more skillful person may scaffold the child's progress.

How do we develop morals and values?

- Lawrence Kohlberg identified preconventional, conventional, and postconventional levels of moral reasoning.
- Most people function at the conventional level of morality, but some never get beyond the selfish, precoventional level. Only a minority of people attain the highest, or postconventional level, of moral reasoning.

What are the typical tasks and dilemmas through the life span?

- According to Erik Erikson, each life stage provokes a specific psychosocial dilemma.
- In addition to the dilemmas identified by Erikson, we recognize that each life stage requires successful mastery of certain developmental tasks.
- Well-being during adulthood consists of six elements: self-acceptance, positive relations with others, autonomy, environmental mastery, having a purpose in life, and continued personal growth.

- Intellectual declines associated with aging are limited, at least through one's seventies. This is especially true of individuals who remain mentally active.
- Ageism refers to prejudice, discrimination, and stereotyping on the basis of age. It affects people of all ages but is especially damaging to older people. Most ageism is based on stereotypes, myths, and misinformation.

How do effective parents discipline their children?

- Responsibility, mutual respect, consistency, love, encouragement, and clear communication are features of effective parenting.
- Much misbehavior can be managed by use of I-messages and the application of natural and logical consequences.

 Interactive Learning

Internet addresses frequently change. To find the sites listed here, visit www.psychology.wadsworth.com/coon_journey2e for an updated list of Internet addresses and direct links to relevant sites.

PSYCHOLOGY: A JOURNEY COMPANION WEB SITE Online quizzes, flash cards, and other helpful study aids for this text. *www.psychology.wadsworth.com/coon_journey2e*

CHOOSING QUALITY CHILD CARE Provides information on issues related to quality child care.

DEPRESSION AFTER DELIVERY A site devoted to providing information about postpartum depression.

DIVING INTO THE GENE POOL From the Exploratorium, teaches about modern genetics.

HUMAN RELATIONS PUBLICATIONS Covers more than 50 topics spanning the entire range of human development.

I AM YOUR CHILD Information for parents of children up to 3 years of age.

JEAN PIAGET ARCHIVES: BIOGRAPHY The life of Jean Piaget, plus five photos from birth to old age.

PARENTHOOD WEB A comprehensive site for parents.

SESAME STREET PARENTS An expert description of physical development from birth to age 11.

THE PARENT S PAGE Comprehensive site full of links for expectant couples and new parents.

INFOTRAC COLLEGE EDITION For recent articles related to Piaget and Vygotsky, use Key Words search for COGNITION IN INFANTS.

PSYCHNOW! 2a. Infant Development, 2b. Child Development, 2c. Adolescent Development, 2d. Adult Development, Aging, and Death

Test Your Knowledge: Human Development

The questions that follow are only a sample of what you need to know. If you miss any of the items, you should review the entire chapter and get more practice with *WebTutor* or the *Practice Quizzes* that came with this book. Another way to prepare for tests is to use the printed *Study Guide* that is available for this text.

1. In the "nature-nurture" debate, the term *nature* primarily refers to
   A. senescence   B. the existence of sensitive periods
   C. prenatal teratogens   D. heredity

2. If a personal trait is controlled by a single dominant gene, the trait cannot be
   A. hereditary   B. related to DNA sequences
   C. influenced by chromosomes   D. polygenic

3. The influence of heredity on early child development is most clearly shown by
   A. differences in temperament   B. the existence of sensitive periods   C. congenital problems   D. the effects of teratogens

4. Deprivation has an especially strong impact on development during
   A. the reciprocal stage   B. sensitive periods   C. the polygenic stage   D. the social play phase

5. Cephalocaudal and proximodistal patterns show the effects of _____ on motor development.
   A. enriched environments   B. maturation   C. scaffolding   D. sensitive periods

6. Early in life, the learning of basic skills is most effective when parents respect the
   A. Mozart effect   B. value of reactive maternal involvement   C. principle of readiness   D. fact that babies cannot imitate adult actions until they are 18 months old

7. In infancy, an early step toward social development is revealed by the emergence of
   A. self-awareness   B. cephalodistal attachment
   C. the Moro reflex   D. the congenital period

8. A clear sign that infant attachment is beginning to occur is found in the presence of
   A. a social smile   B. separation anxiety   C. social scaffolding   D. affectional needs

9. A baby who turns away from his mother when she returns after a brief separation shows signs of having which type of attachment?
   A. insecure-avoidant   B. insecure-ambivalent
   C. solitary-ambivalent   D. maternal-disaffectional

10. Which of the following is NOT an element of optimal caregiving?
    A. you-messages   B. proactive involvement   C. goodness of fit   D. responsiveness

11. Psychologist Diana Baumrind describes parents who enforce rigid rules and demand strict obedience as
    A. authoritative   B. permissive-repressive   C. proactive-reactive   D. authoritarian

12. Which form of child discipline tends to make children insecure, anxious, and hungry for approval?
    A. withdrawal of love   B. management techniques
    C. power assertion   D. authoritative techniques

13. Turn-taking with non-verbal signals is a first step toward
    A. secure attachment   B. motor development   C. using language   D. an ability to make transformations

14. Parents talk to young children with a raised tone of voice and an exaggerated pattern of speaking that is called
    A. transformational grammar   B. telegraphic speech
    C. signal switching   D. parentese

15. Piaget believed that a child's understanding of the world grows through the mental processes of assimilation and
    A. intuition   B. accommodation   C. egocentricism
    D. reversibility

16. According to Piaget, a child's mastery of conservation occurs during the
    A. formal operations stage   B. preoperational stage
    C. concrete operational stage   D. sensorimotor stage

17. Vygotsky believed that adults help children learn how to think by using a process he called
    A. reversible thinking   B. scaffolding   C. accommodation   D. moral reasoning

18. According to Erikson, the dilemma faced by most 3- to 5-year-olds is
    A. autonomy versus shame and doubt   B. initiative versus guilt   C. trust versus mistrust   D. industry versus inferiority

19. Erikson's theory states that mature adults are best able to avoid stagnation when they express
    A. integrity   B. generativity   C. intimacy   D. preconventional moral reasoning

20. Which type of child discipline take the form of threats, name-calling, accusing, bossing, lecturing, or criticizing?
    A. I-messages   B. you-messages   C. logical consequences   D. natural consequences

Sensation and Perception

Murder on Aisle Nine

I was in a supermarket when an 8-year-old girl ran around a corner, screaming, "Stop! Stop! You're killing my father!" Naturally I was interested! I retraced her path and saw two men on the floor, struggling violently. The guy on top had his victim by the throat. There was blood everywhere. It was a murder in progress!

As a witness, I would have told a jury what I just told you, were it not for an important fact: No murder ever took place that day at the supermarket. When the police arrived, they quickly discovered that the "guy on the bottom" had passed out and hit his head. That caused the cut (actually quite minor) that explained the "blood everywhere." The "guy on top" saw the first man fall and was trying to loosen his collar. Obviously, the girl had misunderstood what was happening to her father. As a psychologist, I still find it fascinating that her words so dramatically influenced what I saw.

Without the senses, we would live in a void of darkness and silence. The next time you drink in the beauty of a sunset, a flower, or a friend, remember this: Sensation makes it all possible. Yet, sensing the world is not enough. As my murder-in-the-supermarket experience shows, sensory information can be interpreted in various ways. In this chapter, we will begin with a look at how the senses operate. Then we will discuss how we assemble sensations into a meaningful "picture" or model of the world. Our perceptions create faces, melodies, works of art, illusions, and on occasion, "murders" out of the raw material of sensation. Let's see how this takes place.

Jay Dickmann/Corbis

SENSORY SYSTEMS—WHAT YOU SEE IS WHAT YOU GET

] SURVEYQUESTION *In general, how do sensory systems function?*

Vision gives us amazingly wide access to the world. In one instant you can view a star light-years away, and in the next, you can peer into the microscopic universe of a dewdrop. Yet, vision also narrows what we observe. Like the other senses, vision acts as a *data reduction system.* It selects, analyzes, and filters information until only the most important data remain.

How does data reduction take place?   Some selection occurs because sensory receptors are biological transducers. A *transducer* is a device that converts one kind of energy into another. For example, an electric guitar converts string vibrations into electrical signals, which are amplified and fed to a speaker. Pluck a string and the speaker will blast out sound. However, stimuli that don't cause the string to move will have no effect. For instance, if you shine a light on the string or pour cold water on it, the speaker will remain silent. (The owner of the guitar, however, might get quite loud at this point!) Similarly, each sensory organ is most sensitive to a select type and range of energy that it converts to nerve impulses.

What we experience is also influenced by **sensory analysis.** As they process information, the senses divide the world into important **perceptual features** (basic stimulus patterns). For vision, such features include lines, shapes, edges, spots, colors, and other patterns. Look at ✦Figure 4.1 and notice how eye-catching the single vertical line is among a group of slanted lines. This effect, which is called *pop-out,* occurs because your visual system is highly sensitive to perceptual features (Ramachandran, 1992b).

In some instances, the senses act as *feature detectors* that are attuned to very specific stimuli. Frog eyes, for example, are highly sensitive to small, dark, moving spots. In other words, they are basically "tuned" to detect bugs flying nearby (Lettvin, 1961). But the insect (spot) must be moving, or the frog's "bug detectors" won't work. A frog could starve to death surrounded by dead flies.

After they have selected and analyzed information, sensory systems must *code* it. **Sensory coding** refers to converting important features of the world into neural messages understood by the brain (Hubel & Wiesel, 1979). To see coding at work, try closing your eyes for a moment. Then take your fingertips and press firmly on your eyelids. Apply enough pressure to "squash" your eyes slightly. Do this for about 30 seconds and observe what happens. (Readers with eye problems or contact lenses should not try this.)

Did you "see" stars, checkerboards, and flashes of color? These are called *phosphenes* (FOSS-feens: visual sensations caused by mechanical excitation of the retina). They occur

✦FIGURE 4.1 *Visual pop-out. (Adapted from Ramachandran, 1992b.) Pop-out is so basic that babies as young as 3 months respond to it (Quinn & Bhatt, 1998).*

Sensory analysis Separation of sensory information into important elements.
Perceptual features Basic elements of a stimulus, such as lines, shapes, edges, or colors.
Sensory coding Codes used by the sense organs to transmit information to the brain.

◆FIGURE 4.2 *An artificial visual system.*

because the eye's receptor cells, which normally respond to light, are also somewhat sensitive to pressure. Notice though, that the eye is only prepared to code stimulation—including pressure—into visual features. As a result, you experience light sensations, not pressure. Also important in producing this effect is *sensory localization* in the brain.

Sensory localization means that the type of sensation you experience depends on which brain area is activated. Some brain areas receive visual information, others receive auditory information, and still others receive taste or touch (see Chapter 2). Knowing which brain areas are active tells us, in general, what kinds of sensations you are feeling. Sensory localization may someday make it possible to artificially restore sight, hearing, or other senses. In fact, researchers have already used a miniature television camera to send electrical signals to the brain (Dobelle, 2000; Normann et al., 1999). As you can see in ◆Figure 4.2, a grid of tiny electrodes stimulates the visual cortex. One man who has an implant of this type can "see" 100 dots of light. Like a sports scoreboard, these lights can be used to form crude letters (Dobelle, 2000). Eventually, a larger number of dots could make reading and "seeing" large objects, such as furniture and doorways, possible (Normann et al., 1999).

It is fascinating to realize that "seeing" and "hearing" take place in your brain, not in your eyes or ears. Information arriving from the sense organs creates **sensations.** When the brain organizes sensations into meaningful patterns, we speak of **perception,** which we will discuss later. For now, let's begin with vision, the most magnificent sensory system of all.

VISION—CATCHING SOME RAYS

] SURVEYQUESTION *How is vision accomplished?*

What are the basic dimensions of light and vision? Various wavelengths of light make up the *visible spectrum* (entire spread of electromagnetic energies to which the eyes respond). Visible light starts at "short" wavelengths of 400 *nanometers* (nan-OM-et-er: one billionth of a meter), which we sense as purple or violet. Longer light waves produce blue, green, yellow, orange, and red, which has a wavelength of 700 nanometers (◆Fig. 4.3).

The term *hue* refers to the basic color categories of red, orange, yellow, green, blue, indigo, and violet. As just noted, various hues (or color sensations) correspond to the wavelength of the light that reaches our eyes. White light, in contrast, is a mixture of many wavelengths. Hues (colors) from a narrow band of wavelengths are very *saturated,* or "pure." (An intense "fire-engine" red is more saturated than a muddy "brick" red.) A third dimension of vision, *brightness,* corresponds roughly to the amplitude, or height of light waves. Waves of

Sensation A sensory impression; also, the process of detecting physical energies with the sensory organs.

Perception The mental process of organizing sensations into meaningful patterns.

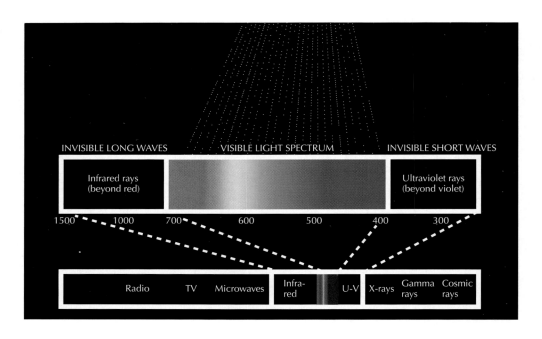

◆FIGURE 4.3 *The visible spectrum.*

greater amplitude are "taller," carry more energy, and cause the colors we see to appear brighter or more intense. For example, the same "brick" red would look bright under intense, high-energy illumination and drab under dim light.

◆FIGURE 4.4 *The human eye, a simplified view.*

Retina The light-sensitive layer of cells at the back of the eye.
Accommodation Changes in the shape of the lens of the eye.
Hyperopia Difficulty focusing nearby objects (farsightedness).
Myopia Difficulty focusing distant objects (nearsightedness).
Astigmatism Defects in the cornea, lens, or eye that cause some areas of vision to be out of focus.
Presbyopia Farsightedness caused by aging.

Structure of the Eye

Is it true that the eye is like a camera? In some ways, it is. Both cameras and eyes have a *lens* to focus images on a light-sensitive layer at the back of a closed space. In a camera, this layer is the film. In the eye, it is a layer of *photoreceptors* (light-sensitive cells) in the **retina,** an area about the size and thickness of a postage stamp (◆Fig. 4.4). Theoretically, the eye could be used as a primitive camera. If you bathe the retina in alum solution, the last image to strike it will appear like a tiny photograph, a fact that might make for a great murder mystery.

How does the eye focus? Most focusing is done at the front of the eye by the *cornea,* a clear membrane that bends light inward. The lens makes additional, smaller adjustments. Your eye's focal point changes when muscles attached to the lens alter its shape. This process is called **accommodation.** In cameras, focusing is done more simply—by changing the distance between the lens and the film.

Visual Problems

The shape of the eye also affects focusing. If your eye is too short, nearby objects will be blurred, but distant objects will be sharp. This is called **hyperopia** (HI-per-OPE-ee-ah: farsightedness). If your eyeball is too long, the image will fall short of the retina, and distant objects cannot be focused. This results in **myopia** (my-OPE-ee-ah: nearsightedness). When the cornea or the lens is misshapen, part of vision will be focused and part will be fuzzy. In this case, the eye has more than one focal point, a problem called **astigmatism** (ah-STIG-mah-tiz-em). All three visual defects can be corrected by placing glasses (or contact lenses) in front of the eye to change the path of light (◆Fig. 4.5).

As people age, the lens becomes less flexible and less able to accommodate. The result is **presbyopia** (prez-bee-OPE-ee-ah: old vision, or farsightedness due to aging). Perhaps you have seen a grandparent or older friend reading a newspaper at arm's length because of presbyopia. If you now wear glasses for nearsightedness, you may need bifocals as you age. (Unless your arms grow longer.) Bifocal lenses correct near vision *and* distance vision.

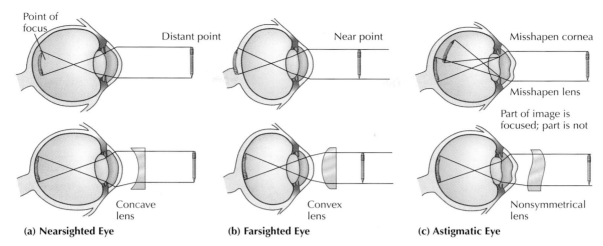

(a) Nearsighted Eye   **(b) Farsighted Eye**   **(c) Astigmatic Eye**

✦FIGURE 4.5 *Visual defects and corrective lenses:* (a) *A myopic (longer than usual) eye. The concave lens spreads light rays just enough to increase the eye's focal length.* (b) *A hyperopic (shorter than usual) eye. The convex lens increases refraction (bending), to focus light on the retina.* (c) *An astigmatic (lens or cornea not symmetrical) eye. In astigmatism, parts of vision are sharp and parts are unfocused. Lenses that correct astigmatism are non-symmetrical.*

✦FIGURE 4.6 *Anatomy of the retina. Note that light does not fall directly on the rods and cones. It must first pass through the cornea, the lens, the vitreous humor (a jelly-like substance that fills the eyeball) and the outer layers of the retina. Only about one half of the light at the front of the eye reaches the rods and cones— testimony to the retina's amazing sensitivity. The lower left photograph shows rods and cones as seen through an electron microscope. In the photograph, the cones are colored green and the rods blue.*

Rods and Cones

The eye has two types of "film," consisting of receptor cells called *rods* and *cones*. The 6.5 million **cones** in each eye work best in bright light. They also produce color sensations and fine details. In contrast, the **rods,** numbering about 100 million, can't detect colors (✦Fig. 4.6). Pure rod vision is black and white. However, the rods are much more sensitive to light than the cones are. The rods, therefore, allow us to see in very dim light.

Cones Visual receptors for colors and daylight visual acuity.

Rods Visual receptors for dim light that produce only black-and-white sensations.

✦FIGURE 4.7 *Experiencing the blind spot. (a) With your right eye closed, stare at the upper right cross. Hold the book about 1 foot from your eye and slowly move it back and forth. You should be able to locate a position that makes the black spot disappear. When it does, it is on your blind spot. With a little practice you can learn to make people or objects you dislike disappear too! (b) Repeat the procedure described, but stare at the lower cross. When the white space falls on the blind spot, the black lines will appear to be continuous. This may help you understand why you do not usually notice a blind spot in your visual field.*

✦FIGURE 4.8 *Tests of visual acuity. Here are some common tests of visual acuity. In (a), sharpness is indicated by the smallest grating still seen as individual lines. The Snellen chart (b) requires that you read rows of letters of diminishing size until you can no longer distinguish them. The Landolt rings (c) require no familiarity with letters. All that is required is a report of which side has a break in it.*

Surprisingly, the retina has a "hole" in it: Each eye has a *blind spot* because there are no receptors where the optic nerve leaves the eye (✦Fig. 4.7 *a*). The blind spot shows that our ability to see depends greatly on the brain. If you close one eye, part of what you see will fall on the blind spot of your open eye. Why isn't there a gap in your vision? The answer is that the visual cortex of the brain actively fills in the gap with patterns from surrounding areas (Fig. 4.7 *b*). By closing one eye, you can visually "behead" other people by placing their images on your blind spot. (Just a hint for some classroom fun.) The brain can also "erase" distracting information. Roll your eyes all the way to the right and then close your right eye. You should clearly see your nose in your left eye's field of vision. Now, open your right eye again and your nose will nearly disappear as your brain disregards its presence.

Visual Acuity

The rods and cones also affect **visual acuity,** or sharpness. The cones lie mainly at the center of the eye. In fact, the *fovea* (FOE-vee-ah: a small cup-shaped area in the middle of the retina) contains only cones—about 50,000 of them. Like a newspaper photograph made of many small dots, the tightly packed cones in the fovea produce the sharpest images. Normal acuity is designated as 20/20 vision: At 20 feet in distance, you can distinguish what the average person can see at 20 feet (✦Fig. 4.8). If your vision is 20/40, you can only see at 20 feet what the average person can see at 40 feet. If your vision is 20/200, everything is a blur and you need glasses! Vision that is 20/12 would mean that you can see at 20 feet what the average person must be 8 feet nearer to see, indicating better than average acuity. American astronaut Gordon Cooper, who claimed to see railroad lines in northern India from 100 miles above, had 20/12 acuity.

Peripheral Vision

What does the rest of the retina do?   Light also falls outside the fovea, creating a large area of **peripheral** (side) **vision.** The greatest number of rods lie about 20 degrees from the center of the retina, where they provide much of our peripheral vision. Although rod vision is not very sharp, it is highly sensitive to *movement*. To experience the rods' radar-like scan, look straight ahead and hold your hand beside your head, at about 90 degrees. Wiggle your finger and slowly move your hand forward until you can detect motion. You will become aware of the movement before you can actually "see" your finger.

The rods are also highly responsive to dim light. Because most rods are 20 degrees to each side of the fovea, the best night vision comes from looking *next to* an object you wish to see. Test this yourself some night by looking at, and next to, a very dim star.

Visual acuity The sharpness of visual perception.
Peripheral vision Vision at the edges of the visual field.

Color Vision

How do the cones produce color sensations? The **trichromatic theory** (TRY-kro-MAT-ik) of color vision holds that there are three types of cones, each most sensitive to either red, green, or blue. Other colors result from combinations of these three. Black and white sensations are produced by the rods.

A basic problem with the trichromatic theory is that four colors of light—red, green, blue, and yellow—seem to be primary (you can't get them by mixing other colors). Also, why is it impossible to have a reddish green or a yellowish blue? These problems led to the development of a second view, known as the **opponent-process theory,** which states that vision analyzes colors into "either-or" messages. That is, the visual system can produce messages for either red or green, yellow or blue, black or white. Coding one color in a pair (red, for instance) seems to block the opposite message (green) from coming through. As a result, a reddish green is impossible, but a yellowish red (orange) can occur.

According to opponent-process theory, fatigue caused by making one response produces an afterimage of the opposite color as the system recovers. *Afterimages* are visual sensations that persist after a stimulus is removed—like seeing a spot after a flashbulb goes off. To see an afterimage of the type predicted by opponent-process theory, look at ✦Figure 4.9 and follow the instructions there.

Which color theory is correct? Both! The three-color theory applies to the retina, where three different types of *visual pigments* (light-sensitive chemicals) have been found. As predicted, each pigment is most sensitive to light in roughly the red, green, or blue region. The three types of cones fire nerve impulses at different rates to produce various color sensations (✦Fig. 4.10).

In contrast, the opponent-process theory better explains what happens in optic pathways and the brain *after* information leaves the eye. For example, some nerve cells in the brain are excited by the color red and inhibited by the color green. So both theories are "correct." One explains what happens in the eye itself. The other explains how colors are analyzed after messages leave the eye.

✦**FIGURE 4.9** *Negative afterimages. Stare at the dot near the middle of the flag for at least 30 seconds. Then look immediately at a plain sheet of white paper or a white wall. You will see the American flag in red, white, and blue. Reduced sensitivity to green, black, and yellow in the visual system, caused by prolonged staring, produces the complementary colors.*

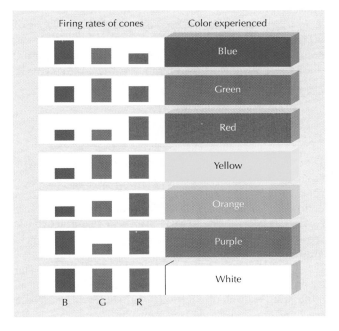

✦**FIGURE 4.10** *Firing rates of blue, green, and red cones in response to different colors. The taller the colored bar, the higher the firing rates for that type of cone. As you can see, colors are coded by differences in the activity of all three types of cones in the normal eye. (Adapted from Goldstein, 2003.)*

Trichromatic theory Theory of color vision based on three cone types: red, green, and blue.

Opponent-process theory Theory of color vision based on three coding systems (red or green, yellow or blue, black or white).

(a)   (b)   (c)

✦**FIGURE 4.11** *Color blindness and color weakness.* (a) *Photograph illustrates normal color vision.* (b) *Photograph is printed in blue and yellow and gives an impression of what a red-green color-blind person sees.* (c) *Photograph simulates total color blindness. If you are totally color-blind, all three photos will look nearly identical.*

Color Blindness

Do you know anyone who regularly draws hoots of laughter by wearing clothes of wildly clashing colors? Or someone who sheepishly tries to avoid saying what color an object is? If so, you probably know someone who is color-blind.

What is it like to be color-blind? What causes color blindness?   A person who is **color-blind** cannot perceive colors. It is as if the world is a black-and-white movie. The color-blind person either lacks cones or has cones that do not function normally (Hsia & Graham, 1997). Such total color blindness is rare. In **color weakness,** or partial color blindness, a person can't see certain colors. Approximately 8 percent of all males (but less than 1 percent of women) are red-green color-blind. These people see reds and greens as the same color, usually a yellowish brown (✦Fig. 4.11). Another form of color weakness, involving yellow and blue, is quite rare (Hsia & Graham, 1997).

How can color-blind individuals drive? Don't they have trouble with traffic lights?   Red-green color-blind individuals have normal vision for yellow and blue, so the main problem is telling red lights from green. In practice, that's not difficult. The red light is always on top, and the green light is brighter than the red. Also, "red" traffic signals have yellow light mixed in with the red and a "green" light that is really blue-green.

How can I tell if I am color-blind?   The *Ishihara test* is a common measure of color blindness and weakness. In the test, numbers and other designs made of dots are placed on a background also made of dots (✦Fig. 4.12). The background and the numbers are of different colors (red and green, for example). A person who is color-blind sees only a jumble of dots. The person with normal color vision can detect the presence of the numbers or designs (Birch & McKeever, 1993).

Adapting to Darkness

What happens when the eyes adjust to a dark room?   **Dark adaptation** is the dramatic increase in retinal sensitivity to light that occurs after a person enters the dark. Consider walking into a theater. If you enter from a brightly lighted lobby, you practically need to be led to your seat. After a short time, however, you can see the entire room in detail (including the couple kissing over in the corner). It takes about 30 to 35 minutes of complete darkness to reach maximum visual sensitivity (✦Fig. 4.13). At that point, your eye will be 100,000 times more sensitive to light (Goldstein, 2003).

What causes dark adaptation?   Like the cones, the rods contain a light-sensitive pigment. When struck by light, visual pigments *bleach,* or break down chemically. (The afterimages you have seen after looking at a flashbulb are a result of this bleaching.) Visual pigments must recombine to restore light sensitivity, which takes time. Night vision is due mainly to an increase in *rhodopsin* (row-DOP-sin), the rod pigment.

Color blindness A total inability to perceive colors.
Color weakness An inability to distinguish some colors.
Dark adaptation Increased retinal sensitivity to light.

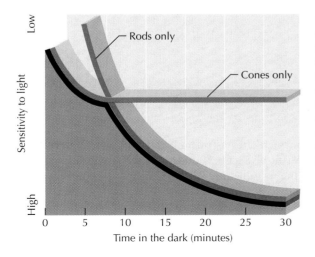

◆**FIGURE 4.13** *Typical course of dark adaptation. The black line shows how the threshold for vision lowers as a person spends time in the dark. (A lower threshold means that less light is needed for vision.) The green line shows that the cones adapt first, but they soon cease adding to light sensitivity. Rods, shown by the red line, adapt more slowly. However, they continue to improve night vision long after the cones are fully adapted.*

Red light allows dark adaptation to occur because it provides little or no stimulation to the rods.

Jon L. Barkerl/Index Stock Imagery

Is there any way to speed up dark adaptation? The rods are *insensitive* to extremely red light. That's why submarines, airplane cockpits, and ready rooms for fighter pilots are illuminated with red light. In each case, people can move quickly into the dark without having to adapt. Because the red light doesn't stimulate the rods, it is as if they had already spent time in the dark. In contrast, a few seconds of exposure to bright white light can completely wipe out dark adaptation. That's why you should be sure to avoid looking at oncoming headlights when you are driving at night—especially the new bluish-white zenon lights.

STUDYBREAK *Sensory Systems and Vision*

RELATE

How does sensation affect what you are experiencing right now? What if data reduction didn't occur? What if you could transduce other energies? What if your senses were tuned to detect different perceptual features? How would the sensory world you live in change?

Pretend you are a beam of light. What will happen to you at each step as you pass into the eye and land on the retina? What will happen if the eye is not perfectly shaped? How will the retina know you've arrived? How will it tell what color of light you are? What will it tell the brain about you?

LEARNING CHECK

1. Sensory receptors are biological _____, or devices for converting one type of energy to another.
2. Lettvin found that a frog's eyes are especially sensitive to phosphenes. T or F?
3. Important features of the environment are transmitted to the brain through a process known as
   a. phosphenation   b. coding   c. detection   d. programming

4. Match:
   _____ Myopia   A. Farsightedness
   _____ Hyperopia   B. Elongated eye
   _____ Presbyopia   C. Farsightedness due to aging
   _____ Astigmatism   D. Lack of cones in the fovea
                           E. Misshapen cornea or lens
5. In dim light, vision depends mainly on the _____. In brighter light, color and fine detail are produced by the _____.
6. The fovea has the greatest visual acuity due to the large concentration of rods found there. T or F?
7. The eyes become more sensitive to light at night because of a process known as _____ _____.

Critical Thinking

8. William James once said, "If a master surgeon were to cross the auditory and optic nerves, we would hear lightning and see thunder." Can you explain what James meant?
9. Sensory transduction in the eye takes place first in the cornea, then in the lens, then in the retina. True or false?

ANSWERS

1. transducers 2. F 3. b 4. B, A, C, E 5. rods, cones 6. F 7. dark adaptation 8. The explanation is based on sensory localization: If a lightning flash caused re-routed messages from the eyes to activate auditory areas of the brain, we would experience a sound sensation. Likewise, if the ears transduced a thunderclap, and sent impulses to the visual area, a sensation of light would occur. 9. False. The cornea and lens bend and focus light rays, but they do not change light from one form of energy to another form of energy. No change in the *type* of energy takes place until the retina converts light to nerve impulses.

HEARING—GOOD VIBRATIONS

] **SURVEYQUESTION** *What are the mechanisms of hearing?*

Rock, classical, jazz, rap, country, hip-hop—whatever your musical taste, you have probably been moved by the riches of sound. Hearing also gathers information from all sides, such as alerting a cyclist that a car is approaching from behind. Vision, in all its glory, is limited to stimuli in front of the eyes (unless, of course, your "shades" have rearview mirrors attached).

What is the stimulus for hearing? If you throw a stone into a quiet pond, a circle of waves will spread in all directions. In much the same way, sound travels as a series of invisible waves of *compression* (peaks) and *rarefaction* (RARE-eh-fak-shun: valleys) in the air.

Any vibrating object—a tuning fork, a musical instrument, or the vocal cords—will produce sound waves (rhythmic movement of air molecules). Other materials, such as fluids or solids, can also carry sound. But sound does not travel in a vacuum or the airless realm of outer space. Movies that show characters reacting to the "roar" of starships in deep space are in error.

The *frequency* of sound waves (the number of waves per second) corresponds to the perceived *pitch* (higher or lower tone) of a sound. The *amplitude* or physical "height," of a sound wave tells how much energy it contains. Psychologically, amplitude corresponds to sensed *loudness* (sound intensity) (✦Fig. 4.14).

How We Hear Sounds

How are sounds converted to nerve impulses? Hearing begins with the *pinna* (PIN-ah: the visible, external part of the ear). In addition to being a good place to hang earrings or balance pencils, the pinna acts like a funnel to concentrate sounds. After they are guided into the ear canal, sound waves collide with the *tympanic membrane* (eardrum), setting it in motion. This, in turn, causes three small bones (the *auditory ossicles*) (OSS-ih-kuls) to vibrate (✦Fig. 4.15). The ossicles are the malleus (MAL-ee-us), incus, and stapes (STAY-peas). Their common

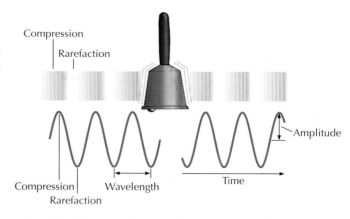

✦**FIGURE 4.14** *Waves of compression in the air, or vibrations, are the stimulus for hearing. The frequency of sound waves determines their pitch. The amplitude determines loudness.*

✦**FIGURE 4.15** *Anatomy of the ear. The inset in the foreground (Cochlea "Unrolled") shows that as the stapes moves the oval window, the round window bulges outward, allowing waves to ripple through fluid in the cochlea. The waves move membranes near the hair cells, causing cilia or "bristles" on the tips of the cells to bend. The hair cells then generate nerve impulses carried to the brain. (See an enlarged cross section of cochlea in Figure 4.16.)*

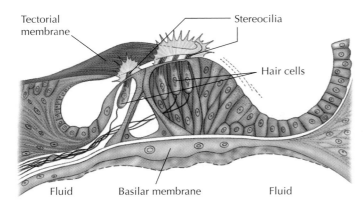

Tectorial membrane
Stereocilia
Hair cells
Fluid
Basilar membrane
Fluid

✦FIGURE 4.16 *A closer view of the hair cells shows how movement of fluid in the cochlea causes the bristling "hairs" or cilia to bend, generating a nerve impulse.*

names are the hammer, anvil, and stirrup. The ossicles link the eardrum with the *cochlea* (KOCK-lee-ah: a snail-shaped organ that makes up the inner ear). The stapes is attached to a membrane on the cochlea called the *oval window*. As the oval window moves back and forth, it makes waves in a fluid inside the cochlea.

Inside the cochlea tiny **hair cells** detect waves in the fluid. The hair cells are part of the **organ of Corti** (KOR-tee), which makes up the center part of the cochlea (✦Fig. 4.16). A set of *stereocilia* (STER-ee-oh-SIL-ih-ah) or "bristles" atop each hair cell brush against the tectorial membrane as waves ripple through the surrounding fluid. Bending the stereocilia triggers nerve impulses, which flow to the brain. (Are your ears "bristling" with sound?)

How are higher and lower sounds detected?   The **frequency theory** of hearing states that as pitch rises, nerve impulses of the same frequency flow into the auditory nerve. That is, an 800 hertz tone produces 800 nerve impulses per second. (*Hertz* refers to the number of vibrations per second.) This explains how sounds up to about 4,000 hertz reach the brain. But what about higher tones? **Place theory** states that higher and lower tones excite specific areas of the cochlea. High tones register most strongly at the base of the cochlea (near the oval window). Lower tones, on the other hand, mostly move hair cells near the outer tip of the cochlea (✦Fig. 4.17). Pitch is therefore signaled by the area of the cochlea most strongly activated. Place theory also explains why hunters sometimes lose hearing in a narrow pitch range. "Hunter's notch," as it is called, occurs when hair cells are damaged in the area affected by the pitch of gunfire.

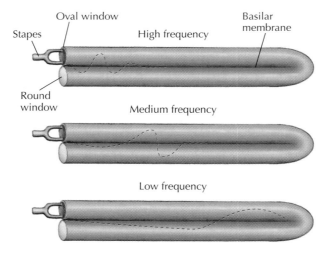

Stapes
Oval window
High frequency
Basilar membrane
Round window
Medium frequency
Low frequency

✦FIGURE 4.17 *Here we see a simplified side view of the cochlea "unrolled." Remember that the basilar membrane is the elastic "roof" of the lower chamber of the cochlea. The organ of Corti, with its sensitive hair cells, rests atop the basilar membrane. The colored line shows where waves in the cochlear fluid cause the greatest deflection of the basilar membrane. (The amount of movement is exaggerated in the drawing.) The area of greatest movement helps identify sound frequency.*

Hair cells Receptor cells within the cochlea that transduce vibrations into nerve impulses.
Organ of Corti Center part of the cochlea, containing hair cells, canals, and membranes.
Frequency theory Holds that tones up to 4,000 hertz are converted to nerve impulses that match the frequency of each tone.
Place theory Theory that higher and lower tones excite specific areas of the cochlea.
Conduction deafness Poor transfer of sounds from the eardrum to the inner ear.

Deafness

What causes other types of deafness?   There are two main types of deafness. In **conduction deafness,** sounds are poorly transferred from the eardrum to the inner ear. For example, the eardrums or ossicles may be damaged or immobilized by disease or injury. In many cases, conduction deafness can be overcome by a hearing aid, which makes sounds louder and clearer.

USING PSYCHOLOGY Artificial Hearing

In many cases of "nerve" deafness, the nerve is actually intact. This finding has spurred development of cochlear implants that bypass hair cells and stimulate the auditory nerves directly (◆Fig. 4.18).

As you can see, wires from a microphone carry electrical signals to an external coil. A matching coil under the skin picks up the signals and carries them to one or more areas of the cochlea. The latest implants make use of place theory to separate higher and lower tones. This has allowed some formerly deaf persons to hear human voices and other higher-frequency sounds. About 60 percent of all multi-channel implant patients can understand some spoken words, and some children learn to speak (Tye-Murray et al., 1995).

At present, artificial hearing remains crude. All but the most successful implant patients describe the sound as "like a radio that isn't quite tuned in." In fact, 30 percent of all adults who have tried implants have given up on them. But the implants are improving. And even now it is hard to argue with enthusiasts like Kristen Cloud. Shortly after Kristen received an implant, she was able to hear a siren and avoid being struck by a speeding car. She says simply, "The implant saved my life."

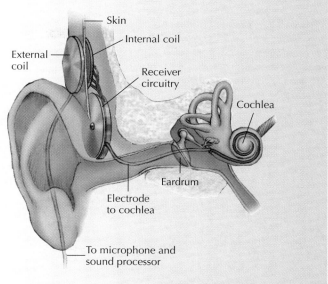

◆FIGURE 4.18 *A cochlear implant, or "artificial ear."*

Nerve deafness results from damage to the hair cells or the auditory nerve. Hearing aids can't help in this case, because auditory messages are blocked from reaching the brain. However, artificial hearing systems are making it possible for some persons with nerve deafness to break through the wall of silence. (See "Artificial Hearing.")

Many jobs, hobbies, and pastimes can cause **stimulation deafness,** which occurs when very loud sounds damage hair cells in the cochlea (as in hunter's notch). The hair cells, which are about as thin as a cobweb, are very fragile (◆Fig. 4.19). By the time you are 65, more than 40 percent of them will be gone. If you work in a noisy environment or enjoy loud music, motorcycling, snowmobiling, hunting, or similar pursuits, you may be risking stimulation deafness. Dead hair cells are never replaced: When you abuse them you lose them.

How loud must a sound be to be hazardous? Daily exposure to 85 decibels or more may cause permanent hearing loss. Decibels are a measure of sound intensity. Every 20 decibels increases the sound pressure by a factor of 10. In other words, a rock concert at 120 decibels is 1,000 times stronger than a voice at 60 decibels. Even short periods at 120 decibels can cause temporary deafness. Brief exposure to 150 decibels (a jet airplane nearby) may cause permanent deafness. You might find it interesting to check the decibel ratings of some of your activities in ◆Figure 4.20. Be aware that amplified musical concerts, stereo headphones, and "boom-box" car stereos can also damage your hearing.

◆FIGURE 4.19 *A highly magnified electron microscope photo of the cilia (orange bristles) on the top of human hair cells. (Colors are artificial.)*

Dr. G. Oran Bredberg/SPL/Photo Researchers, Inc.

Nerve deafness Deafness caused by damage to the hair cells or auditory nerve.
Stimulation deafness Damage caused by exposing the hair cells to excessively loud sounds.

◆FIGURE 4.20 *The loudness of sound is measured in decibels. Zero decibels is the faintest sound most people can hear. Sounds of 110 decibels are uncomfortably loud. Prolonged exposure to sounds above 85 decibels may damage the inner ear. Rock music, which may be 120 decibels, has caused hearing loss in musicians and may affect audiences as well. Sounds of 130 decibels pose an immediate danger to hearing.*

SMELL AND TASTE—THE NOSE KNOWS WHEN THE TONGUE CAN'T TELL

] SURVEYQUESTION *How do the chemical senses operate?*

Unless you are a wine taster, a perfume blender, a chef, or a gourmet, you may think of **olfaction** (smell) and **gustation** (taste) as minor senses. Certainly you could survive without these *chemical senses* (receptors that respond to chemical molecules). Just the same, smell and taste occasionally prevent poisonings, and they add pleasure to our lives. Let's see how they operate.

The Sense of Smell

Smell receptors respond to airborne molecules. As air enters the nose, it flows over roughly 5 million nerve fibers in the upper nasal passages (◆Fig. 4.21). Receptor proteins on the surface of the fibers are sensitive to various airborne molecules. When a fiber is stimulated it sends signals to the brain.

How are different odors produced? This is still an unfolding mystery. One hint comes from a problem called *anosmia* (an-OZE-me-ah: defective smell), a sort of "smell blindness" for a single odor. Anosmia suggests there are receptors for specific odors. Indeed, molecules having a particular odor are quite similar in shape. Specific shapes produce the following types of odors: floral (flower-like), camphoric (camphor-like), musky (have you ever smelled a sweaty musk ox?), minty (mint-like), and etherish (like ether or cleaning fluid). This does not mean, however, that there are just five different olfactory receptors. In humans, 300 to 400 types of smell receptors are believed to exist (Herz, 2001).

Does the existence of 400 different types of receptors mean that we can sense only 400 different odors? No, molecules trigger activity in different *combinations* of odor receptors. Thus, humans can detect at least 10,000 different odors. Just as you can make many thou-

Olfaction The sense of smell.
Gustation The sense of taste.

(c)

Richard Costana, *Discover Magazine*, 1993

✦**FIGURE 4.21** (a) *Olfactory nerve fibers respond to gaseous molecules. Receptor cells are shown in cross section to the left.* (b) *Olfactory receptors are located in the upper nasal cavity.* (c) *On the right, an extreme close-up of an olfactory receptor shows fibers that sense gaseous molecules of various shapes.*

sands of words from the 26 letters of the alphabet, many combinations of receptors are possible, resulting in many different odors. The brain uses the distinctive patterns of messages it gets from the olfactory receptors to recognize particular scents (Malnic, Hirono, & Buck, 1999; Mombaerts, 1999).

It appears that different-shaped "holes," or "pockets," exist on the surface of olfactory receptors. Like a piece fits in a puzzle, chemicals produce odors when part of a molecule matches a hole of the same shape. This is the **lock and key theory.** Scents are also identified, in part, by the *location* of the receptors in the nose that are activated by a particular odor. And finally, the *number of activated receptors* tells the brain how strong an odor is (Freeman, 1991).

What causes anosmia? Risks include infections, allergies, and blows to the head (which may tear the olfactory nerves). Exposure to chemicals such as ammonia, photo-developing chemicals, and hair-dressing potions can also cause anosmia. If you value your sense of smell, be careful what you breathe (Herz, 2001).

Taste and Flavors

There are at least four basic tastes: *sweet, salt, sour,* and *bitter.* We are most sensitive to bitter, less sensitive to sour, even less sensitive to salt, and least sensitive to sweet. This order may have helped prevent poisonings when most humans foraged for food, because bitter and sour foods are more likely to be inedible.

Many experts now believe that a fifth taste quality exists. The Japanese word *umami* (oo-MAH-me) describes a pleasant savory or "brothy" taste associated with certain amino acids in chicken soup, some meat extracts, kelp, tuna, human milk, cheese, and soy beans. The receptors for *umami* are sensitive to glutamate, a substance found in MSG (Lindemann, 2000). Perhaps MSG's reputation as a "flavor enhancer" is based on the pleasant *umami* taste (Bellisle, 1999). At the very least, we may finally know why chicken soup is such a "comfort food."

If there are only four or five tastes, how can there be so many different flavors? Flavors seem more varied because we tend to include sensations of texture, temperature, smell, and even pain ("hot" chili peppers) along with taste. Smell is particularly important in determining flavor. Small bits of apple, potato, and onion "taste" almost exactly alike when the nose is plugged. So do gourmet jelly beans! It is probably fair to say that subjective flavor is one half smell. This is why food loses its "taste" when you have a cold.

Taste buds (taste-receptor cells) are mainly located on the top side of the tongue, especially around the edges. However, a few are found elsewhere inside the mouth

Lock and key theory Holds that odors are related to the shapes of chemical molecules.
Taste bud The receptor organ for taste.

Circular papilla   Filamentous papilla

Omikron/Photo Researchers, Inc.

(a)

Taste bud

Hairlike ending of taste receptor

(b)   (c)   (d)   Sensory nerve

+FIGURE 4.22 *Receptors for taste:*
(a) The tongue is covered with small protrusions called papillae. *(b) Most taste buds are found around the top edges of the tongue (shaded area). However, some are located elsewhere, including under the tongue. Stimulation of the central part of the tongue causes no taste sensations. All four primary taste sensations occur anywhere that taste buds exist. (c) An enlarged drawing shows that taste buds are located near the base of papillae. (d) Detail of a taste bud. These receptors also occur in other parts of the digestive system, such as the lining of the mouth.*

(+Fig. 4.22). As food is chewed, it dissolves and enters the taste buds, where it sets off nerve impulses. Much like smell, sweet and bitter tastes appear to be based on a lock-and-key match between molecules and intricately shaped receptors. Saltiness and sourness, however, are triggered by a direct flow of charged atoms into the tips of taste cells (Lindemann, 2001).

STUDYBREAK ◆ *Hearing, Smell, and Taste*

RELATE

Close your eyes and listen to the sounds around you. As you do, try to mentally trace the events necessary to convert vibrations in the air into the sounds you are hearing. Review the discussion of hearing if you leave out any steps.

What is your favorite food odor? What is your favorite taste? Can you explain how you are able to sense the aroma and taste of foods?

LEARNING CHECK

1. The frequency of a sound wave corresponds to how loud it is. T or F?
2. Which of the following is not a part of the cochlea?
   a. ossicles   b. pinna   c. tympanic membrane
   d. all of the above
3. According to the place theory of hearing, higher tones register most strongly near the base of the cochlea. T or F?

4. Nerve deafness occurs when the auditory ossicles are damaged. T or F?
5. Daily exposure to sounds with a loudness of _____ decibels may cause permanent hearing loss.
6. Cochlear implants have been used primarily to overcome
   a. conduction deafness   b. stimulation deafness   c. nerve deafness   d. hunter's notch
7. Olfaction appears to be at least partially explained by the _____ _____ _____ theory of molecule shapes and receptor sites.
8. *Umami* is a type of "smell blindness" for a particular odor. T or F?

Critical Thinking

9. Why do you think your voice sounds so different when you hear a tape recording of your speech?
10. Smell and hearing differ from vision in a way that may aid survival. What is it?

ANSWERS

1. F 2. d 3. T 4. F 5. 85 6. c 7. lock and key 8. F 9. The answer lies in another question: How else might vibrations from the voice reach the cochlea? Other people hear your voice only as it is carried through the air. You hear not only that sound, but also vibrations conducted by the bones of your skull. 10. Both smell and hearing can detect stimuli (including signals of approaching danger) around corners, behind objects, and behind the head.

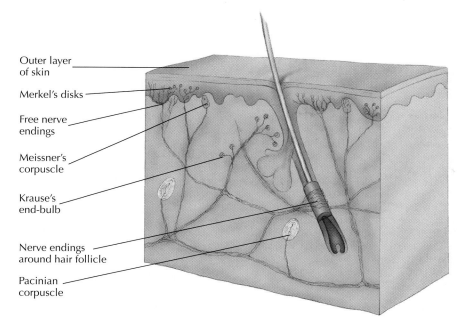

Outer layer of skin

Merkel's disks

Free nerve endings

Meissner's corpuscle

Krause's end-bulb

Nerve endings around hair follicle

Pacinian corpuscle

◆FIGURE 4.23 *The skin senses include touch, pressure, pain, cold, and warmth. This drawing shows different forms the skin receptors can take. The only clearly specialized receptor is the Pacinian corpuscle, which is highly sensitive to pressure. Free nerve endings are receptors for pain and any of the other sensations. For reasons that are not clear, cold is sensed near the surface of the skin, and warmth is sensed deeper (Carlson, 1998).*

THE SOMESTHETIC SENSES—FLYING BY THE SEAT OF YOUR PANTS

] SURVEYQUESTION *What are the somesthetic senses and why are they important?*

A gymnast "flying" through a routine on the uneven bars may rely as much on the **somesthetic senses** as on vision (*soma* means "body," *esthetic* means "feel"). Even the most routine activities, such as walking, running, or passing a sobriety test, would be impossible without the **skin senses** (touch), the **kinesthetic senses** (receptors in muscles and joints that detect body position and movement), and the **vestibular senses** (receptors in the inner ear for balance, gravity, and acceleration). Because of their importance, let's begin with the skin senses.

Skin Senses

It's difficult to imagine what life would be like without the sense of touch, but the plight of Ian Waterman gives a hint. After an illness, Waterman permanently lost all feeling below his neck. Now, in order to know what position his body is in he has to be able to see it. If he closes his eyes, he can't move. If the lights go out in a room, he's in big trouble (Cole, 1995).

Skin receptors produce at least five different sensations: *light touch, pressure, pain, cold,* and *warmth*. Receptors with particular shapes appear to specialize somewhat in various sensations (◆Fig. 4.23). However, free nerve endings alone can produce all five sensations (Carlson, 2001). Altogether, the skin has about 200,000 nerve endings for temperature, 500,000 for touch and pressure, and 3 million for pain.

Does the number of receptors in an area of skin relate to its sensitivity? Yes. We could "map" your skin by applying heat, cold, touch, pressure, or pain to points all over your body. This would show that the number of skin receptors varies, and that sensitivity generally matches the number of receptors in a given area. Generally speaking, important areas such as the lips, tongue, face, hands, and genitals have a higher density of receptors.

Pain

Does the number of pain receptors also vary? Yes, like the other skin senses, pain receptors vary in their distribution. About 230 pain points per square centimeter (about a half inch) are found behind the knee, 180 per centimeter on the buttocks, 60 on the pad of the thumb, and 40 on the tip of the nose. (Is it better then, to be pinched on the nose or behind the knee? It depends on what you like!)

Somesthetic senses Sensations produced by the skin, muscles, joints, viscera, and organs of balance.

Skin senses The senses of touch, pressure, pain, heat, and cold.

Kinesthetic senses The senses of body movement and positioning.

Vestibular senses The senses of balance, position in space, and acceleration.

USING PSYCHOLOGY   How to Control Pain

In some cultures, people endure tattooing, stretching, cutting, and burning with little apparent pain. How do they do it? Very likely the answer lies in three factors that anyone can use to reduce pain. These are: (1) anxiety, (2) control, and (3) attention.

The basic sensory message of pain can be separated from our emotional reactions to it. Fear or high levels of anxiety almost always increase pain. (Anxiety is a feeling of apprehension or uneasiness similar to fear, but based on an unclear threat.) A dramatic reversal of this effect is the surprising lack of pain displayed by soldiers wounded in battle. Being excused from further combat apparently produces a flood of relief. This emotional state leaves many soldiers insensitive to wounds that would agonize a civilian (Melzack & Wall, 1996). In general, unpleasant emotions increase pain and pleasant emotions decrease it (Meagher, Arnau, & Rhudy, 2001).

Fear and anxiety almost always increase pain. Anytime you can anticipate pain (such as a trip to the doctor, dentist, or tattoo parlor), you can lower anxiety by making sure you are *fully informed*. Be sure everything that will happen is explained. Also, be sure to fully discuss any fears you have.

People who are allowed to regulate, avoid, or control painful stimuli suffer less. In general, the more control you *feel* you have over a painful stimulus, the less pain you will experience (Wells, 1994). To apply this principle, you should arrange a signal so your doctor, dentist, or body piercer will know when to start and stop a painful procedure.

Distraction also reduces pain. Subjects in one experiment who were exposed to intense pain got significant relief when they were distracted by watching for signal lights to come on (Johnson et al., 1998). Concentrating on pleasant, soothing images can be especially helpful. Instead of listening to the whirr of a dentist's drill, for example, you might imagine that you are lying in the sun at a beach, listening to the roar of the surf. Or, take a Walkman along and crank up your favorite band. At home, music can be a good distractor from chronic pain (Good, 1995; Michel & Chesky, 1995).

An interesting way of combining these techniques is to *mask* one pain with a second painful stimulus that is under your control. The pain won't seem too bad because you can control it and it is predictable. For instance, if you are having a tooth filled, try pinching yourself or digging a fingernail into a knuckle while the dentist is working. Focus your attention on the pain you are creating, and increase it anytime the dentist's work becomes more painful. This strategy may seem strange, but it works. Generations of children have used it to take the edge off a spanking.

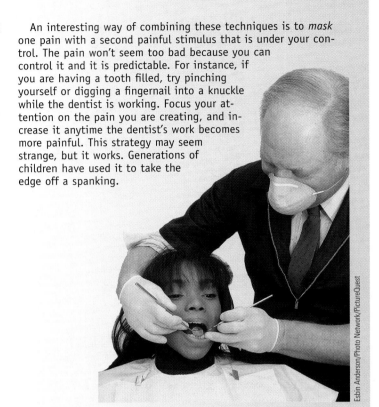

In addition to producing a physical sensation, pain messages activate areas of the brain associated with emotion. If you are fearful or anxious, the emotional part of pain will be magnified, and you will feel more intense pain. Reducing fear and anxiety are two things you can do to diminish pain.

Pain carried by *large nerve fibers* is sharp, bright, fast, and seems to come from specific body areas. This is the body's **warning system.** Give yourself a small jab with a pin and you will feel this type of pain. As you do, notice that warning pain quickly disappears. Much as we may dislike warning pain, it is usually a signal that the body has been, or is about to be, damaged. Without warning pain, we would be unable to detect or prevent injury. Children who are born with a rare insensitivity to pain repeatedly burn themselves, break bones, bite their tongues, and become ill without knowing it (Larner et al., 1994).

A second type of somatic pain is carried by *small nerve fibers.* This type is slower, nagging, aching, widespread, and very unpleasant. It gets worse if the pain stimulus is repeated. This is your body's **reminding system.** It reminds the brain that the body has been injured. For instance, lower back pain often has this quality. Sadly, the reminding system can cause agony long after an injury has healed, or in terminal illnesses, when the reminder is useless. (If you got carried away with the earlier pin demonstration, maybe you should look at "How to Control Pain" now!)

Warning system Pain based on large nerve fibers; warns that bodily damage may be occurring.

Reminding system Pain based on small nerve fibers; reminds the brain that the body has been injured.

The Vestibular System

Space flight might look like fun. But if you ever get a ride into space, it is about 70 percent likely that your first experience in orbit will be throwing up. Weightlessness and space flight affect the vestibular system, often causing severe motion sickness. Within the vestibular sys-

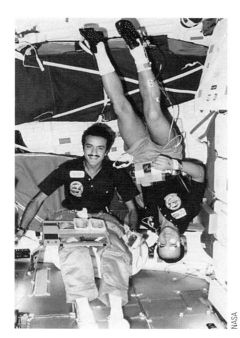

Weightlessness presents astronauts with a real challenge in sensory adaptation.

tem, fluid-filled sacs called *otolith organs* (OH-toe-lith) are sensitive to movement, acceleration, and gravity (✦Fig. 4.24). The otolith organs contain tiny crystals in a soft, gelatin-like mass. The tug of gravity or rapid head movements can cause the mass to shift. This, in turn, stimulates hair-like receptor cells, allowing us to sense gravity, acceleration, and movement through space.

Three fluid-filled tubes called the *semicircular canals* are the sensory organs for balance. If you could climb inside these tubes, you would find that head movements cause the fluid to swirl about. As the fluid moves, it bends a small "flap," or "float," called the *crista*, that detects movement. The bending of each crista stimulates hair cells and again signals head rotation.

What causes motion sickness? According to **sensory conflict theory,** dizziness and nausea occur when sensations from the vestibular system don't match sensations from the eyes and body (Warwick-Evans et al., 1998). On solid ground, information from the vestibular system, vision, and kinesthesis usually matches. However, in a heaving, pitching boat, car, or airplane, a serious mismatch can occur—causing disorientation and heaving of another kind.

Why would sensory conflict cause nausea? You can probably blame (or thank) evolution. Many poisons disturb the vestibular system, vision, and the body. Therefore, we may have evolved so that we react to sensory conflict by vomiting to expel poison. The value of this reaction, however, may be of little comfort to anyone who has ever been "green" and miserable with motion sickness. To minimize such conflicts, try to keep your head still, fix your vision on a distant immobile object, and lie down if you can.

Many people become nauseated the first time they experience virtual reality. Why? Because virtual reality also creates a sensory conflict: Computer-generated visual images change as if the viewer's body is in motion, but the vestibular system tells viewers that they are standing still. The result? The scenery may not be real but the nausea is.

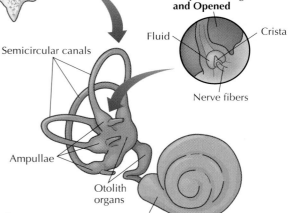

ADAPTATION, ATTENTION, AND GATING— TUNING IN AND TUNING OUT

] **SURVEYQUESTION** *Why are we more aware of some sensations than others?*

You are surrounded by sights, sounds, odors, tastes, and touch sensations. Which are you aware of? Each of the senses is continuously active. Even so, many sensory events never reach awareness because of *sensory adaptation, selective attention,* and *sensory gating.* Let's see how information is filtered by these processes.

✦**FIGURE 4.24** *The vestibular system. (See text for explanation.)*

Sensory Adaptation

Think about walking into a house where fried fish, sauerkraut, and head cheese were prepared for dinner. (Some dinner!) You would probably pass out at the door, yet people who had been in the house for some time wouldn't be aware of the food odors. Why?

Sensory conflict theory Explains motion sickness as the result of a mismatch between information from vision, the vestibular system, and kinesthesis.

Because sensory receptors respond less to unchanging stimuli, a process called **sensory adaptation.**

Fortunately, the olfactory (smell) receptors adapt quickly. When exposed to a constant odor, they send fewer and fewer nerve impulses to the brain until the odor is no longer noticed. Adaptation to pressure from a wristwatch, waistband, ring, or glasses is based on the same principle. Sensory receptors generally respond best to *changes* in stimulation. No one wants or needs to be reminded 16 hours a day that his shoes are on.

Selective Attention

As you sit reading this page, receptors for touch and pressure in the seat of your pants are sending nerve impulses to your brain. Although these sensations have been present all along, you were probably not aware of them until just now. This "seat-of-the-pants phenomenon" is an example of **selective attention** (voluntarily focusing on a specific sensory input). We are able to "tune in on" a single sensory message while excluding others. For example, if you are listening to someone talk, another person nearby can talk *backward* and you will not notice it (Wood & Cowan, 1995). However, no matter how interesting your companion may be, your attention will probably shift if you hear your own name spoken somewhere in the room (Conway, Cowan, & Bunting, 2001). We do find what others say about us to be very interesting, don't we?

Selective attention is based on the brain's ability to give some messages priority while putting others on hold (Mangun, 1995). You might find it helpful to think of selective attention as a *bottleneck,* or narrowing in the information channel linking the senses to perception. When one message enters the bottleneck, it seems to prevent others from passing through (see ◆Fig. 4.25). Imagine, for instance, that you are a pilot preparing to land a jumbo jet. You need to be sure the flaps are down. Just as you are about to check them, your copilot says something to you. If you then fail to notice the flaps are still up, an air disaster is just seconds away.

Are some stimuli more attention getting than others? Yes. Very *intense* stimuli usually command attention. Stimuli that are brighter, louder, or larger tend to capture attention: A gunshot in a library would be hard to ignore. If a brightly colored hot-air balloon ever lands at your college campus, it will almost certainly draw a crowd.

Repetitious stimuli, repetitious stimuli, repetitious stimuli, repetitious stimuli, repetitious stimuli, repetitious stimuli are also attention getting. A dripping faucet at night makes little noise by normal standards, but because of repetition, it may become as attention getting as a single sound many times louder. This effect is used repeatedly, so to speak, in television and radio commercials.

ATTENTION IS ALSO **FREQUENTLY** RELATED TO contrast OR *change* IN STIMULATION. The contrasting type styles in the preceding sentence draw attention because they are *unexpected.* Norman Mackworth and Geoffrey Loftus (1978) found that people who look

In many sports, expert players are much better than beginners at paying attention to key information. Compared with novices, experts scan actions and events more quickly, and they focus on only the most meaningful information. This allows experts to make decisions and react more quickly (Bard, Fleury, & Goulet, 1994).

◆FIGURE 4.25 The attentional "spotlight" can be widened or narrowed. If you focus on local details in this drawing you will see the letter A repeated 13 times. If you broaden your field of attention to encompass the overall pattern, you will see the letter H. (After Lamb & Yund, 1996.)

Sensory adaptation A decrease in sensory response to an unchanging stimulus.
Selective attention Giving priority to a particular incoming sensory message.

at drawings like ✦Figure 4.26 focus first and longest on unexpected objects (the octopus, in this case).

Sensory Gating

Are sensory messages ever blocked before they reach the brain? Yes, a process called *sensory gating* blocks some incoming nerve impulses while allowing others to pass through (Melzack, 1993; Melzack & Wall, 1996). A fascinating example of sensory gating is provided by Ronald Melzack and Patrick Wall, who study "pain gates" in the spinal cord (Melzack & Wall, 1996). Melzack and Wall noticed (as described earlier) that one type of pain will sometimes cancel another. Their **gate control theory** suggests that pain messages from different nerve fibers pass through the same neural "gate" in the spinal cord. If the gate is "closed" by one pain message, other messages may not be able to pass through (Humphries, Johnson, & Long, 1996).

How is the gate closed? Messages carried by large, fast nerve fibers seem to close the spinal pain gate directly. Doing so can prevent slower, "reminding system" pain from reaching the brain. As a pain control technique, this is called *counterirritation.* Pain clinics use it by applying a mild electrical current to the skin. This causes only a mild tingling that can greatly reduce more agonizing pain (Long, 1991). Counterirritation is also evident in some of the oldest pain control methods, such as applying ice packs, hot-water bottles, or massage to the body.

Messages from small, slow fibers seem to take a different route. After going through the pain gate, they pass on to a "central biasing system" in the brain. Under some circumstances, the brain then sends a message back down the spinal cord, closing the pain gates (✦Fig. 4.27). Melzack and Wall believe that gate control theory explains the painkilling effects of acupuncture.

Acupuncture is the Chinese medical art of relieving pain and illness by inserting thin needles into the body. As the acupuncturist's needles are twirled, heated, or electrified, they activate small pain fibers. These relay through the biasing system to close the gates to intense or chronic pain (Melzack & Wall, 1996). Studies have shown that acupuncture produces short-term pain relief for 50 to 80 percent of patients tested (Ernst, 1994; Murray, 1995). (However, its ability to cure illness is much more debatable.)

The senses supply raw data to the brain, but the information remains mostly meaningless until it is interpreted. It's as if the senses provide only the jumbled pieces of a complex puzzle. In the remainder of this chapter we will explore how we put the puzzle together.

✦**FIGURE 4.26** *One of the drawings used by Mackworth and Loftus (1978) to investigate attention. Observers attend to unexpected objects longer than they do to expected objects. In this drawing, observers looked longer at the octopus than they did at a tractor placed in the same spot. What do you think would happen if a tractor were shown upside down or on the roof of the barn?*

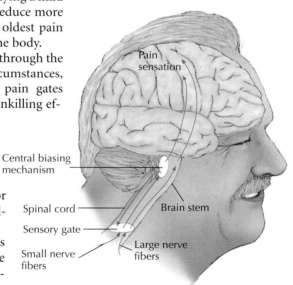

✦**FIGURE 4.27** *Diagram of a sensory gate for pain. A series of pain impulses going through the gate may prevent other pain messages from passing through. Or pain messages may relay through a "central biasing mechanism" that exerts control over the gate, closing it to other impulses.*

(Left) An acupuncturist's chart. *(Right)* Thin stainless steel needles are inserted into areas defined by the chart. Modern research has begun to explain the painkilling effects of acupuncture (see text). Acupuncture's claimed ability to cure diseases is more debatable.

Gate control theory Proposes that pain messages pass through neural "gates" in the spinal cord.

STUDYBREAK *Somesthetic Senses, Adaptation, Attention, and Gating*

RELATE

Stand on one foot with your eyes closed. Now touch the tip of your nose with your index finger. Which of the somesthetic senses did you use to perform this feat?

Imagine you are on a boat ride with a friend who starts to feel queasy. Can you explain to your friend what causes motion sickness and what she or he can do to prevent it?

As you sit reading this book, which sensory inputs have undergone adaptation? What new inputs can you become aware of by shifting your focus of attention?

Think about a strategy you have used for reducing pain at the doctor, dentist, or some other painful situation. Did you alter anxiety, control, or attention? Can you think of any ways in which you have used counterirritation to lessen pain?

LEARNING CHECK

1. Which of the following is a somesthetic sense?
   a. gustation   b. olfaction   c. rarefaction   d. kinesthesis
2. Warning pain is carried by _____ nerve fibers.
3. Head movements are detected primarily in the semicircular canals, gravity by the otolith organs. T or F?

4. Sensory conflicts appear to explain nausea caused by poisoning, but not the nausea associated with motion sickness. T or F?
5. Sensory adaptation refers to an increase in sensory response that accompanies a constant or unchanging stimulus. T or F?
6. The brain-centered ability to influence what sensations we will receive is called
   a. sensory gating   b. central adaptation   c. selective attention   d. sensory biasing
7. The painkilling effects of acupuncture appear to result from _____ _____.
8. Like heightened anxiety, increased control tends to increase subjective pain. T or F?

Critical Thinking

9. Drivers are less likely to become car-sick than passengers are. Why do you think drivers and passengers differ in susceptibility to motion sickness?
10. What special precautions would you have to take to test the ability of acupuncture to reduce pain?
11. What measures would you take to ensure that an experiment involving pain is ethical?

ANSWERS

1. d 2. large 3. T 4. T 5. F 6. c 7. sensory gating 8. F 9. Drivers experience less sensory conflict because they control the car's motion. This allows them to anticipate the car's movements and to coordinate their head and eye movements with those of the car. 10. At the very least, you would have to control for the placebo effect by giving fake acupuncture to control group members. However, a true double-blind study would be difficult to do. Acupuncturists would always know if they were giving a placebo treatment or the real thing, which means they might unconsciously influence subjects. 11. Experiments that cause pain must be handled with care and sensitivity. Participation must be voluntary, the source of pain must be non-injurious, and subjects must be allowed to quit at any time.

PERCEPTUAL CONSTANCIES— TAMING AN UNRULY WORLD

] **SURVEYQUESTION** *How do perceptual constancies affect our perceptions?*

What would it be like to have your vision restored after a lifetime of blindness? Actually, a first look at the world can be disappointing. Newly sighted persons must *learn* to identify objects; to read clocks, numbers, and letters; and to judge sizes and distances (Senden, 1960). Learning to "see" can be quite frustrating. For instance, a cataract patient named Mr. S. B. had been blind since birth. After an operation restored his sight at age 52, Mr. S. B. struggled to use his vision. At first, he could only judge distance in familiar situations (Gregory, 1990). One day he was found crawling out of a hospital window to get a closer look at traffic on the street. It's easy to understand his curiosity, but he had to be restrained. His room was on the fourth floor!

Why would Mr. S. B. try to crawl out of a fourth-story window? Couldn't he at least tell distance from the size of the cars? No, you must be familiar with objects to use their size to judge distance. Try holding your left hand a few inches in front of your nose and your right hand at arm's length. Your right hand should appear to be about half the size of your left hand. Still, you know your right hand did not suddenly shrink, because you have seen it many times at various distances. We call this **size constancy:** The perceived size of an object remains the same, even though the size of its image on the retina changes.

To perceive your hand accurately, you had to draw on past experience. Some perceptions are so basic they seem to be *native* (inborn). An example is the ability to see a

Size constancy The perceived size of an object remains constant, despite changes in its retinal image.

Visual perception involves finding meaningful patterns in complex stimuli. If you look closely at this painting by the artist Yvaral, you will see that it is entirely made up of small, featureless squares. An infant or newly sighted person would see only a jumble of meaningless colors. But because the squares form a familiar pattern, you should easily see Marilyn Monroe's face. (Or is that Madonna?) (© Yvaral, "Marilyn Numerisee #420," © Yvaral 1990, courtesy of Circle Gallery.)

line on a piece of paper. Likewise, even newborn babies show some evidence of size constancy (Slater, Mattock, & Brown, 1990). However, many of our perceptions are *empirical,* or based on prior experience. For instance, cars, houses, and people look like toys when seen from an unfamiliar perspective, such as from the top of a skyscraper. This suggests that while some size constancy is innate, it is also affected by learning.

In **shape constancy,** the shape of an object remains stable, even though the shape of its retinal image changes. You can demonstrate shape constancy by looking at this page from directly overhead and then from an angle. Obviously, the page is rectangular, but most of the images that reach your eyes are distorted. Yet, while the book's image changes, your perception of its shape remains constant. (For additional examples, see ✦Fig. 4.28.) On the highway, alcohol intoxication impairs size and shape constancy, adding to the accident rate among drunk drivers (Farrimond, 1990).

Let's say that you are outside in bright sunlight. Beside you, a friend is wearing a gray skirt and a white blouse. Suddenly a cloud shades the sun. It might seem that the blouse would grow dimmer, but it still appears to be bright white. This happens because the blouse continues to reflect a larger *proportion* of light than nearby objects. **Brightness constancy** refers to the fact that the brightness of objects appears to stay the same as lighting conditions change. However, this holds true only if the blouse and other objects are all illuminated by the same amount of light. You could make an area on your friend's gray skirt look whiter than the shaded blouse by shining a bright spotlight on the skirt.

(a) (b)

✦**FIGURE 4.28** *Shape constancy. (a) When a door is open, its image actually forms a trapezoid. Shape constancy is indicated by the fact that it is still perceived as a rectangle. (b) With great effort you may be able to see this design as a collection of flat shapes. However, if you maintain shape constancy, the distorted squares strongly suggest the surface of a sphere. (From* Spherescapes-1 *by Scott Walter and Kevin McMahon, 1983.)*

Almost everyone's family album has at least one photo like this. Extreme viewing angles can make maintaining size constancy difficult, even for familiar objects.

Shape constancy The perceived shape of an object is unaffected by changes in its retinal image.
Brightness constancy The apparent (or relative) brightness of objects remains the same as long as they are illuminated by the same amount of light.

To summarize, the energy patterns reaching our senses are constantly changing, even when they come from the same object. Size, shape, and brightness constancy rescue us from a confusing world in which objects would seem to shrink and grow, change shape as if made of rubber, and light up or fade like neon lamps. Gaining these constancies was only one of the hurdles Mr. S. B. faced in learning to see. In the next section, we will consider some others.

PERCEPTUAL ORGANIZATION— GETTING IT ALL TOGETHER

] **SURVEYQUESTION** *What basic principles do we use to group sensations into meaningful patterns?*

We have seen that Mr. S. B. had to *learn* to understand his visual sensations. He was soon able to tell time from a large clock and to read block letters he had known only from touch. At a zoo, he recognized an elephant from descriptions he had heard. However, handwriting meant nothing to him for more than a year after he regained sight, and many objects were meaningless until he touched them. Thus, while Mr. S. B. had visual *sensations,* his ability to *perceive* remained limited.

How are sensations organized into meaningful perceptions?   The simplest organization involves grouping some sensations into an object, or figure, that stands out on a plainer background. **Figure-ground organization** is probably inborn, since it is the first perceptual ability to appear after cataract patients regain sight. In normal figure-ground perception, only one figure is seen. In *reversible figures,* however, figure and ground can be switched. In ✦Figure 4.29 it is equally possible to see either a wineglass figure on a dark background or two face profiles on a light background. As you shift from one pattern to the other, you should get a clear sense of what figure-ground organization means.

Gestalt Principles

How do we separate a figure from its background?   The Gestalt psychologists (see Chapter 1) studied this question in detail. Even if you were seeing for the first time, they concluded, several factors would bring some order to your perceptions (✦Fig. 4.30).

1. **Nearness.** All other things being equal, stimuli that are near each other tend to be grouped together (Kubovy & Holcombe, 1998). Thus, if three people stand near each other and a fourth person stands 10 feet away, the adjacent three will be seen as a group and the distant person as an outsider (see Fig. 4.30 *a*).
2. **Similarity.** "Birds of a feather flock together," and stimuli that are similar in size, shape, color, or form tend to be grouped together (see Fig. 4.30 *b*). Picture two bands marching side by side. If their uniforms are different colors, the bands will be seen as two separate groups, not as one large group.
3. **Continuation, or continuity.** Perceptions tend toward simplicity and continuity. In Figure 4.30 *c* it is easier to visualize a wavy line on a squared-off line than it is to see a complex row of shapes.
4. **Closure.** Closure refers to the tendency to *complete* a figure, so that it has a consistent overall form. Each of the drawings in Figure 4.30 *d* has one or more gaps, yet each is perceived as a recognizable figure. Our tendency to form shapes—even with minimal cues—is powerful.
5. **Contiguity.** A principle that can't be shown in Figure 4.30 is contiguity, or nearness in time *and* space. Contiguity is often responsible for the perception that one thing has *caused* another (Michotte, 1963). A psychologist friend of the author's demonstrates this principle in class by knocking on his head with one hand while knocking on a wooden table (out of sight) with the other. The knocking sound is

✦**FIGURE 4.29** *A reversible figure-ground design. Do you see two faces in profile or a wineglass?*

Figure-ground organization Part of a stimulus appears to stand out as an object (figure) against a less prominent background (ground).

✦FIGURE 4.30 *How we organize perceptions.*

(a) Principle of nearness
Notice how differently a group of six objects can be perceptually organized, depending on their spacing.

(b) Principle of similarity
In these examples, organization depends on similarity of color.

Similarity and nearness can be combined to produce a new organization.

(c) Principle of continuity

This?
plus
or
This?

(d) Principle of closure

(e) Principle of common region

perfectly timed with the movements of his visible hand. This leads to the irresistible perception that his head is made of wood.

6. **Common region.** As you can see in Figure 4.30 *e*, stimuli that are found within a common area tend to be seen as a group (Palmer, 1992). On the basis of similarity and nearness, the stars in Figure 4.30 *e* should be one group and the dots another. However, the colored backgrounds define regions that create three groups of objects (four stars, two stars plus two dots, and four dots). Perhaps the principle of common region explains why we tend to mentally group together people from a particular country, state, province, or geographic region.

Clearly, the Gestalt principles shape our day-to-day perceptions. But, again it is important to remember that learning and past experience do, too. Take a moment and look for the camouflaged animal pictured in ✦Figure 4.31. (Camouflage patterns break up figure-ground organization). If you had never seen similar animals before, could you have located this one? Mr. S. B. would have been at a total loss to find meaning in such a picture.

In a way, we are all detectives, seeking patterns in what we see. In this sense, a meaningful pattern represents a **perceptual hypothesis,** or initial guess about how to organize sensations. Have you ever seen a "friend" in the distance, only to have the person turn into

✦FIGURE 4.31 *A challenging example of perceptual organization. Once the camouflaged insect (known as a giant walking-stick) becomes visible, it is almost impossible to view the picture again without seeing the insect.*

Perceptual hypothesis An initial guess regarding how to organize (perceive) a stimulus pattern.

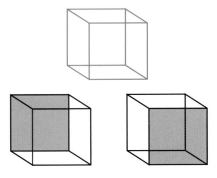

◆FIGURE 4.32 *Necker's cube.*

a stranger as you drew closer? Pre-existing ideas and expectations *actively* guide our interpretation of sensations (Mack & Rock, 1998).

The active nature of perception is perhaps most apparent for *ambiguous stimuli* (patterns allowing more than one interpretation). If you look at a cloud, you may discover dozens of ways to organize its contours into fanciful shapes and scenes. Even clearly defined stimuli may permit more than one interpretation. Look at Necker's cube in ◆Fig. 4.32 if you doubt that perception is an active process. Visualize the top cube as a wire box. If you stare at the cube, its organization will change. Sometimes it will seem to project upward, like the lower left cube; other times it will project downward. The difference lies in how your brain interprets the same information. In short, we actively *construct* meaningful perceptions, we do not passively record the events and stimuli around us (Hoffman, 1999).

In some instances, a stimulus may offer such conflicting information that perceptual organization becomes impossible. For example, the tendency to make a three-dimensional object out of a drawing is frustrated by the "three-pronged widget" (◆Fig. 4.33), an *impossible figure*. Such patterns cannot be organized into stable, consistent, or meaningful perceptions. If you cover either end of the drawing in Fig. 4.33, it makes sense perceptually. However, a problem arises when you try to organize the entire drawing. Then, the conflicting information it contains prevents you from forming a stable perception.

One of the most amazing perceptual feats is our capacity to create three-dimensional space from flat retinal images. We'll explore that topic in a moment, but first here's a chance to rehearse what you've learned.

◆FIGURE 4.33 (Left) *An impossible figure—the "three-pronged widget."* (Right) *It might seem that including more information in a drawing would make perceptual conflicts impossible. However, Japanese artist Shigeo Fukuda has shown otherwise.* (Disappearing Column, © Shigeo Fukuda, 1985.)

STUDYBREAK ⓨ *Perceptual Constancies and Perceptual Organization*

RELATE

If you needed to explain the perceptual constancies to a friend, what would you say? Why are the constancies important for maintaining a stable perceptual world?

As you look around the area in which you are now, how are the Gestalt principles helping to organize your perceptions? Try to find a specific example for each principle.

LEARNING CHECK

1. Which among the following are subject to basic perceptual constancy?
   a. figure-ground organization e. continuity
   b. size f. closure
   c. ambiguity g. shape
   d. brightness h. nearness

2. The first and most basic perceptual organization to emerge when sight is restored to a blind person is
   a. continuity b. nearness constancy c. recognition of numbers and letters d. figure-ground

3. At times, meaningful perceptual organization represents a _____, or "guess," held until the evidence contradicts it.

4. The design known as Necker's cube is a good example of an impossible figure. T or F?

Critical Thinking

5. People who have taken psychedelic drugs, such as LSD or mescaline, often report that the objects and people they see appear to be changing in size, shape, and brightness. This suggests that such drugs disrupt what perceptual process?

ANSWERS 1. b, d, g 2. d 3. hypothesis 4. F 5. Perceptual constancies (size, shape, and brightness).

DEPTH PERCEPTION— WHAT IF THE WORLD WERE FLAT?

] **SURVEYQUESTION** *How is it possible to see depth and judge distance?*

Close one of your eyes, hold your head very still, and stare at a single point across the room. If you don't move your head or eyes, your surroundings will appear to be almost flat, like a painting or photograph. But even under these conditions you will still have some sense of depth. Now, open both eyes and move your head and eyes as usual. Suddenly, the "3-D" perceptual world returns. How are we able to perceive depth and space?

Depth perception is the ability to see three-dimensional space and to accurately judge distances. Without depth perception, you would be unable to drive a car or ride a bicycle, play catch, shoot baskets, thread a needle, or simply navigate around a room. The world would look like a flat surface.

Mr. S. B. had trouble with depth perception after his sight was restored. Is depth perception learned? Studies done with a *visual cliff* suggest that depth perception is partly learned and partly innate. Basically, a visual cliff is a glass-topped table (◆Fig. 4.34). On one side, a checkered surface lies directly beneath the glass. On the other side, the checkered surface is 4 feet below. This makes the glass look like a tabletop on one side and a cliff, or drop-off, on the other.

To test for depth perception, 6- to 14-month-old infants were placed in the middle of the visual cliff. This gave them a choice of crawling to the shallow side or the deep side. (The glass prevented them from doing any "skydiving" if they chose the deep side.) Most infants chose the shallow side. In fact, most refused the deep side even when their mothers tried to call them toward it (Gibson & Walk, 1960).

If the infants were at least 6 months old when they were tested, isn't it possible that they learned to perceive depth? Yes, it is, so let's consider another test. Psychologist Jane Gwiazda fitted infants with goggles that make some designs stand out three-dimensionally while others remain flat. By watching head movements, Gwiazda could tell when babies first became aware of the "3-D" designs. As in other tests, this occurred at age 4 months. The nearly universal emergence of depth perception at this time suggests that it depends more on brain maturation than on individual learning (Aslin & Smith, 1988). It is very likely that at least a basic level of depth perception is innate.

We also learn to use a variety of *depth cues* as aids to perceiving three-dimensional space. **Depth cues** are features of the environment and messages from the body that supply information about distance and space. Some cues will work with just one eye (*monocular cues*), while others require two eyes (*binocular cues*).

Muscular Cues

As their name implies, muscular cues come from the body. One such cue is accommodation, the bending of the lens to focus on nearby objects. Sensations from muscles attached to each lens are channeled back to the brain. Changes in these sensations help us judge distances within about 4 feet of the eyes. This information is available even if you are just using one eye, so accommodation is a monocular cue. Beyond 4 feet, accommodation has limited value. Obviously, it is more important to a watchmaker or a person trying to thread a needle than it is to a basketball player or someone driving an automobile.

A second bodily source of information about depth is *convergence,* a binocular cue. When you look at a distant object, the lines of vision from your eyes are parallel. However,

◆**FIGURE 4.34** *Human infants and newborn animals refuse to go over the edge of the visual cliff.*

Depth perception The ability to see three-dimensional space and to accurately judge distances.
Depth cues Perceptual features that impart information about distance and three-dimensional space.

FIGURE 4.35 *The eyes must converge, or turn in toward the nose, to focus on close objects.*

when you look at something 50 feet or less in distance, your eyes must converge (turn in) to focus the object (◆Fig. 4.35).

You are probably not aware of it, but whenever you estimate a distance under 50 feet (as when you play catch or zap flies with your personal laser), you are using convergence. How? Convergence is controlled by muscles attached to the eyeball. These muscles feed information on eye position to the brain to help it judge distance. You can feel convergence by exaggerating it: Focus on your fingertip and bring it toward your eyes until they almost cross. At that point you can feel the sensations from the muscles that control eye movement.

Stereoscopic Vision

The most basic source of depth perception is *retinal disparity* (a discrepancy in the images that reach the right and left eyes). Retinal disparity, which is a binocular cue, is based on the fact that the eyes are about 2.5 inches apart. Because of this, each eye receives a slightly different view of the world. When the two images are fused into one overall image, **stereoscopic vision** (three-dimensional sight) occurs. The result is a powerful sensation of depth (◆Fig. 4.36 and ◆Fig. 4.37).

If disparity is so important, can a person with one eye perceive depth?   A one-eyed person lacks convergence and retinal disparity, and accommodation only helps us judge short distances. That means a person with only one eye will have limited depth perception. Try driving a car or riding a bicycle with one eye closed. You will find yourself braking too soon or too late, and you will have difficulty estimating your speed. ("But officer, my psychology text said to . . ..") Despite this, you will be able to drive, although it will be more difficult than usual. A person with one eye can even successfully land an airplane—a task that depends strongly on depth perception. Overall, stereoscopic vision is 10 times better for judging depth than perception based on just one eye (Rosenberg, 1994).

Stereoscopic: optic nerve transmissions from each eye are relayed to both sides of brain

Binocular: both eyes have overlapping fields of vision

Allows depth perception with accurate distance estimation

Stereoscopic vision Perception of space and depth caused chiefly by the fact that the eyes receive different images.

FIGURE 4.36 (a) *Stereoscopic vision.* (b) *The photographs show what the right and left eyes would see when viewing a plant. Hold the page about 6 to 8 inches from your eyes. Allow your eyes to cross and focus on the overlapping image between the two photos. Then try to fuse the leaves into one image. If you are successful the third dimension will appear like magic.*

✦**FIGURE 4.37** *This computer-generated art creates a 3-D illusion by superimposing two patterns. There are mismatches between some areas of the two patterns. This simulates retinal disparity and creates a sensation of depth. To get the 3-D effect, hold the stereogram about 8 inches from the end of your nose. Relax your eyes and look* through *the art, as if you were focusing on something in the distance. If you're patient, you may see a 3-D globe. (Stereogram © Anything Enterprises, 1994.)*

Pictorial Cues for Depth

A good movie, painting, or photograph can create a convincing sense of depth where none exists. And, as noted, a one-eyed person can learn to gauge depth.

How is the illusion of depth created on a two-dimensional surface, and how is it possible to judge depth with one eye? The answers lie in the pictorial depth cues, all of which are monocular (they will work with just one eye). **Pictorial depth** cues are features found in paintings, drawings, and photographs that supply information about space, depth, and distance. To understand these cues, imagine that you are looking outdoors through a window. If you trace everything you see onto the glass, you will have an excellent drawing, with convincing depth. Then, if we analyze what is on the glass, we will find the following features.

1. **Linear perspective.** This cue is based on the apparent convergence of parallel lines in the environment. If you stand between two railroad tracks, they appear to meet near the horizon. Because you know they are parallel, their convergence implies great distance (✦Fig. 4.38 *a*).
2. **Relative size.** If an artist wishes to depict two objects of the same size at different distances, the artist makes the more distant object smaller (Fig. 4.38 *b*). Films in the *Star Wars* series created sensational illusions of depth by rapidly changing the image size of planets, space stations, and starships. (Also see ✦Figure 4.39.)
3. **Height in the picture plane.** Objects that are placed higher (closer to the horizon line) in a drawing tend to be perceived as more distant. In the upper frame of Figure 4.38 *b* the black columns look like they are receding into the distance partly because they become smaller, but also because they move higher in the drawing.
4. **Light and shadow.** Most objects are lighted in ways that create clear patterns of light and shadow. Copying such patterns of light and shadow can give a two-dimensional design a three-dimensional appearance (Fig. 4.38 *c*). (Also, look ahead to ✦Figure 4.40 for more information on light and shadow.)
5. **Overlap.** Overlap (also known as *interposition*) occurs when one object partially blocks another object. Hold your hands up and ask a friend across the room which is nearer. Relative size will give the answer if one hand is much nearer to your friend than the other. But if one hand is only slightly closer than the other, your friend may not be able to see it—until you slide one hand in front of the other. Overlap then removes any doubt (Fig. 4.38 *d*).

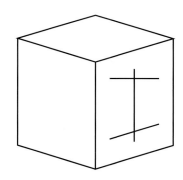

Linear perspective is a very powerful cue for depth. Because of the depth cues implied in this drawing, the upper cross on the vertical line appears to be diagonal. It is actually a right angle. The lower cross, which appears to be a right angle, is actually diagonal to the vertical line. (After Enns & Coren, 1995.)

Pictorial depth cues Features found in paintings, drawings, and photographs that impart information about space, depth, and distance.

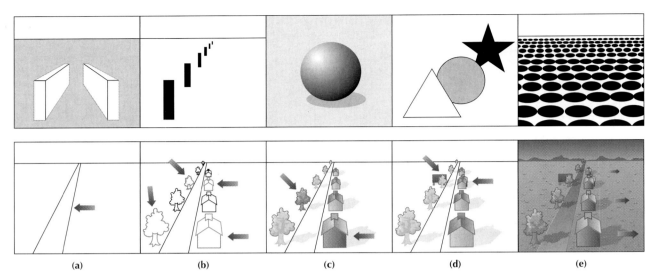

✦FIGURE 4.38 (a) *Linear perspective.* (b) *Relative size.* (c) *Light and shadow.* (d) *Overlap.* (e) *Texture gradients. Drawings in the top row show fairly "pure" examples of each of the pictorial depth cues. In the bottom row, the pictorial depth cues are used to assemble a more realistic scene.*

✦FIGURE 4.39 *On a dry lake bed, relative size is just about the only depth cue available for judging the camera's distance from this vintage aircraft. What do you estimate the distance to be? For the answer, look ahead to* ✦*Figure 4.43.*

6. **Texture gradients.** Changes in texture also contribute to depth perception. If you stand in the middle of a cobblestone street, the street will look coarse near your feet. However, its texture will get smaller and finer if you look into the distance (Fig. 4.38 *e*).

7. **Aerial perspective.** Smog, fog, dust, and haze add to the apparent distance of an object. Because of aerial perspective, distant objects tend to be hazy, washed out in color, and lacking in detail. Aerial haze is often most noticeable when it is missing. If you have traveled the wide-open spaces of the United States or Canada, you may have seen mountain ranges that seemed to be only a few miles away. In reality, you could have been viewing them through 50 miles of crystal-clear air.

8. **Relative motion.** Relative motion, also known as *motion parallax* (PAIR-ah-lax), can be seen by looking out a window and moving your head from side to side. Notice that nearby objects appear to move a sizable distance as your head moves. Trees, houses, and telephone poles that are farther away appear to move slightly in relation to the background. Distant objects like hills, mountains, or clouds don't seem to move at all.

✦FIGURE 4.40 (Left) *When judging depth, we usually assume that light comes mainly from one direction, usually from above. Squint a little to blur the image you see here. You should perceive a collection of globes projecting outward. If you turn this page upside down, the globes should become cavities. (After Ramachandran, 1995.)* (Right) *The famed Dutch artist M. C. Escher violated our assumptions about light to create the dramatic illusions of depth found in his 1955 lithograph* Convex and Concave. *In this print, light appears to come from all sides of the scene. (Courtesy of the Collection Haags Gemeente Museum, The Hague.* © 1994 M. C. Escher/Cordon Art, Baarn, The Netherlands. All rights reserved.)

← Direction of travel

✦FIGURE 4.41 *The apparent motion of objects viewed during travel depends on their distance from the observer. Apparent motion can also be influenced by an observer's point of fixation. At middle distances, objects closer than the point of fixation appear to move backward; those beyond the point of fixation appear to move forward. Objects at great distances, such as the sun or moon, always appear to move forward.*

▲TABLE 4.1	Summary of Visual Depth Cues

BINOCULAR CUES
- **Convergence**
- **Retinal disparity**

MONOCULAR CUES
- **Accommodation**
- **Pictorial depth cues** (listed below)
  Linear perspective
  Relative size
  Height in the picture plane
  Light and shadow
  Overlap
  Texture gradients
  Aerial perspective
  Relative motion (motion parallax)

When combined, pictorial cues can create a powerful illusion of depth. (See ▲Table 4.1 for a summary of all the depth cues we have discussed.)

Is motion parallax really a pictorial cue? Strictly speaking it is not, except in movies, television, or animated cartoons. However, when parallax is present, we almost always perceive depth. Much of the apparent depth of a good movie comes from relative motion captured by the camera. ✦Figure 4.41 illustrates an interesting feature of motion parallax. Imagine that you are in a bus and watching the passing scenery (with your gaze at a right angle to the road). Under these conditions, nearby objects will appear to rush *backward*. Those farther away, such as distant mountains, will seem to move very little or not at all. Objects that are more remote, such as the sun or moon, will appear to move in the *same* direction you are traveling. (That's why the moon appears to "follow" you when you take a stroll at night.)

The Moon Illusion

How do the depth perception cues relate to daily experience? We constantly use both pictorial cues and bodily cues to sense depth and judge distances. Depth cues also produce an intriguing effect called the *moon illusion* (perceiving the moon as larger when it is low in the sky). When the moon is on the horizon, it tends to look like a silver dollar. When it is directly overhead, it looks more like a dime. Contrary to what some people believe, the moon is not magnified by the atmosphere. But the moon *looks* nearly twice as large when it's low in the sky (Plug & Ross, 1994). This occurs, in part, because the moon's *apparent distance* is greater when it is near the horizon than when it is overhead (Kaufman & Kaufman, 2000).

But if it seems farther away, shouldn't it look smaller? No. When the moon is overhead, few depth cues surround it. In contrast, when you see the moon on the horizon, it is behind houses, trees, telephone poles, and mountains. These objects add numerous depth cues, which cause the horizon to seem more distant than the sky overhead. Picture two balloons, one 10 feet away and the second 20 feet away. Suppose the more distant balloon is inflated until its image matches the image of the nearer balloon. How do we know the more distant balloon is larger? Because its image is the same size as a balloon that is closer. Similarly, the moon makes the same-size image on the horizon as it does overhead. However, the horizon seems more distant because more depth cues are present. As a result, the horizon moon must be perceived as larger (Kaufman & Kaufman, 2000) (✦Fig. 4.42).

✦FIGURE 4.42 *The Ponzo illusion may help you understand the moon illusion. Picture the two white bars as resting on the railroad tracks. In the drawing, the upper bar is the same length as the lower bar. However, because the upper bar appears to be farther away than the lower bar, we perceive it as longer. The same logic applies to the moon illusion.*

Dennis Coon

◆FIGURE 4.43 *Before you can use familiar size to judge distance, objects must actually be the size you assume they are. Either these men are giants, or the model airplane was closer than you may have thought when you looked at Figure 4.39.*

This explanation is known as the **apparent-distance hypothesis** (the horizon seems more distant than the night sky). You can test it by removing depth cues while looking at a horizon moon. Try looking at the moon through a rolled-up paper tube, or make your hands into a "telescope" and look at the next large moon you see. It will immediately appear to shrink when viewed without depth cues (Plug & Ross, 1994).

STUDYBREAK   *Depth Perception*

RELATE

Part of the rush of excitement produced by action movies and video games is based on the sense of depth they create. Return to the list of pictorial depth cues. What cues have you seen used to portray depth? Try to think of specific examples in a movie or game you have seen recently.

LEARNING CHECK

1. The visual cliff is used to test for infant sensitivity to linear perspective. T or F?
2. Write an *M* or a *B* after each of the following to indicate if it is a monocular or binocular depth cue.

   accommodation _____   convergence _____
   retinal disparity _____   linear perspective _____
   motion parallax _____   overlap _____ relative size _____

3. Which of the depth cues listed in Question 2 are based on muscular feedback? _____
4. Interpretation of pictorial depth cues requires no prior experience. T or F?
5. The moon's image is greatly magnified by the atmosphere near the horizon. T or F?

Critical Thinking

6. What hearing ability would you say is most closely related to stereoscopic vision?

ANSWERS

Answers: 1. F 2. accommodation (M), convergence (M), retinal disparity (B), linear perspective (B), motion parallax (M), overlap (M), relative size (M) 3. accommodation or convergence 4. F 5. F 6. If you close your eyes, you can usually tell the direction and perhaps the location of a sound source, such as a hand-clap. Locating sounds in space is heavily dependent on having two ears, just as stereoscopic vision depends on having two eyes.

PERCEPTION AND OBJECTIVITY— BELIEVING IS SEEING

] **SURVEYQUESTION** *How is perception altered by learning, expectations, and motives?*

At the beginning of this chapter I described an apparent murder that turned out to be something quite different. If I had never returned to "the scene of the crime," I would have sworn that I had seen a homicide. The girl's description completely shaped my own perceptions. This perhaps is understandable. But I'll never forget the added shock I felt when I met the "murderer"—the man I had seen a few moments before as huge, vicious, and horrible-looking. The man was not a stranger. He was a neighbor of mine. I had seen him dozens of times before. I know him by name. He is a rather small man. Stories such as this show that our experiences are **perceptual reconstructions** or mental models of external events. Perceptions are filtered through our needs, expectations, attitudes, values, and beliefs (◆Fig. 4.44). Clearly, we don't just believe what we see. We also see what we believe. Let's review some factors that alter or distort our perceptions.

Apparent-distance hypothesis An explanation of the moon illusion stating that the horizon seems more distant than the night sky.

Perceptual reconstruction A mental model of external events.

Perceptual Learning

England is one of the few countries in the world where people drive on the left side of the road. In view of this reversal, it is not unusual for visitors to step off curbs in front of cars—after carefully looking for traffic in the *wrong* direction. As this example suggests, learning has a powerful impact on perception.

How does learning affect perception? The term **perceptual learning** refers to changes in the brain that alter how we process sensory information (Ahissar, 1999). For example, to use a computer, you must learn to pay attention to specific stimuli, such as icons, commands, and signals. We also learn to tell the difference between stimuli that seemed identical at first. An example is the novice chef who discovers how to tell the difference between dried basil, oregano, and tarragon. In other situations, we learn to focus on just one part of a group of stimuli. This saves us from having to process all of the stimuli in the group. For instance, a linebacker in football may be able to tell if the next play will be a run or a pass by watching one or two key players, rather than the entire opposing team (Goldstone, 1998).

Perceptual Habits

In general, learning creates *perceptual habits* (ingrained patterns of organization and attention) that affect our daily experience. Stop for a moment and look at ✦Figure 4.45. The left face looks somewhat unusual, to be sure. But the distortion seems mild—until you turn the page upside down. Viewed normally, the face looks quite grotesque. Why is there a difference? Apparently, most people have little experience with upside-down faces. Perceptual learning, therefore, has less impact on our perceptions of an upside-down face. With a face in the normal position, you know what to expect and where to look. Also, you tend to see the entire face as a recognizable pattern. When a face is inverted, we are forced to perceive its individual features separately (Bartlett & Searcy, 1993).

Magicians rely on perceptual habits when they use sleight of hand to distract observers while performing tricks. Another kind of "magic" is related to consistency. It is usually safe to assume that a room is shaped roughly like a box. This need not be true, however. An *Ames room* (named for the man who designed it) is a lopsided space that appears square when viewed from a certain point (✦Fig. 4.46). This illusion is achieved by carefully distorting the proportions of the walls, floor, ceiling, and windows. Because the left corner of the Ames room is farther from a viewer than the right, a person standing in that corner looks very small; one standing in the nearer, shorter right corner looks very large. A person who walks from the left to the right corner, will seem to "magically" grow larger.

✦FIGURE 4.44 *It is difficult to look at this simple drawing without perceiving depth. Yet, the drawing is nothing more than a collection of flat shapes. Turn this page counterclockwise 90 degrees, and you will see three C's, one within another. When the drawing is turned sideways, it seems nearly flat. However, if you turn the page upright again, a sense of depth will reappear. Clearly, you have used your knowledge and expectations to construct an illusion of depth. The drawing itself would only be a flat design if you didn't invest it with meaning.*

✦FIGURE 4.45 *The effects of prior experience on perception. The doctored face looks far worse when viewed right side up because it can be related to past experience.*

Perceptual learning Changes in perception that can be attributed to prior experience; a result of changes in how the brain processes sensory information.

◆**FIGURE 4.46** *The Ames room. From the front, the room looks normal; actually, the right-hand corner is very short, and the left-hand corner is very tall. In addition, the left side of the room slants away from viewers. The diagram shows the shape of the room and reveals why people appear to get bigger as they cross the room toward the nearer, shorter right corner.*

As mentioned earlier, the brain is especially sensitive to perceptual features such as lines, shapes, edges, spots, and colors. At least some of this sensitivity appears to be learned. Colin Blakemore and Graham Cooper of Cambridge University raised kittens in a room with only vertical stripes on the walls. Another set of kittens saw only horizontal stripes. When returned to normal environments, the "horizontal" cats could easily jump onto a chair, but when walking on the floor, they bumped into chair legs. "Vertical" cats, on the other hand, easily avoided chair legs, but they missed when trying to jump to horizontal surfaces. The cats raised with vertical stripes were "blind" to horizontal lines, and the "horizontal" cats acted as if vertical lines were invisible. Other experiments show that there is an actual decrease in brain cells tuned to the missing features (Grobstein & Chow, 1975).

Perceptual features might seem removed from daily experience. Nevertheless, they can have a profound effect on human behavior. In recognizing faces, for example, a consistent *other-race effect* occurs. This is a sort of "They all look alike to me" bias in perceiving persons from other racial and ethnic groups. In tests of facial recognition, people are much better at recognizing faces of their own race than others. One reason for this difference is that we typically have more experience with people from our own race. As a result, we become very familiar with the features that help us recognize different persons. For other groups, we lack the perceptual expertise needed to accurately separate one face from another (Sporer, 2001).

Illusions

Illusion A misleading or distorted perception.
Hallucination An imaginary sensation—such as seeing, hearing, or smelling something that does not exist in the external world.

Perceptual learning is responsible for a number of *illusions.* In an **illusion,** length, position, motion, curvature, or direction is consistently misjudged. Note that illusions are distorted perceptions of stimuli that actually exist. In a **hallucination,** people perceive objects or events that have no external reality (Lepore, 2002). For example, they hear voices that are not there (see "Doctor, Can't You Hear Them?"). If you think you see a 3-foot-tall butterfly,

CLINICAL FILE Doctor, Can't You Hear Them?

The voices scream, swear, criticize, and tell you how worthless you are. Often, and without warning, a voice shouts "Buckets of blood!" It startles you every time. If you had experiences like these, you almost certainly would be mentally disturbed. Hallucinations are one of the clearest signs that a person has "lost touch with reality." They are a major symptom of psychosis, dementia, epilepsy, migraine headaches, alcohol withdrawal, and drug intoxication. The most common hallucinations are auditory, such as hearing voices.

Do disturbed people also have visual hallucinations? Although they are less common, hallucinations can involve vision, touch, smell, or taste. For instance, patients might see "insects crawling

everywhere," feel that people are touching them, or smell "poisons" in their food. Such hallucinations seem completely "real" to the person who has them. Yet, they obviously arise in the brain, rather than the world outside (Lepore, 2002).

As you can imagine, it would be very disturbing to be the only person who could hear a voice shrieking "Buckets of blood!" However, it is important to note that "sane hallucinations" also occur. For example, people who are partially blind may "see" people, animals, buildings, plants, and other objects appear and disappear in front of their eyes. However, they can easily tell that their hallucinations aren't real. Such "sane hallucinations" merely show how powerfully the brain seeks meaningful patterns in sensory input.

(a) Which of the horizontal lines is longer?

(b) Is the diagonal a single straight line? Check it with a ruler.

(c) Is this a drawing of a staircase descending from upper left to lower right . . . or is it the view of the underneath of a staircase from lower right to upper left?

(d) Are these lines parallel? Cover some of the slash marks to see.

(e) Which line is longer, horizontal or vertical?

(f) Notice how the background distorts the square.

(g) Which quadrilateral is larger?

(h) Which column is shortest? Which is longest?

✦FIGURE 4.47 *Some interesting perceptual illusions. Such illusions are a normal part of visual perception.*

you can confirm you are hallucinating by trying to touch its wings. To detect an illusion, you may have to measure a drawing or apply a straight-edge to it.

Can illusions be explained? Not in all cases, or to everyone's satisfaction. In general, size and shape constancy, habitual eye movements, continuity, and perceptual habits combine in various ways to produce the illusions in ✦Figure 4.47. Rather than attempt to explain all of them, let's focus on one deceptively simple example.

Figure 4.47 *a* shows the familiar **Müller-Lyer illusion** (MEOO-ler-LIE-er). Note that the horizontal line with arrowheads appears shorter than the line with V's. If you measure the lines, you'll find that they are the same length. How can we explain this illusion? Evidence suggests it is based on a lifetime of experience with the edges and corners of rooms and buildings. Richard Gregory (1990) believes you see the horizontal line with the V's as if it were the corner of a room viewed from inside (✦Fig. 4.48). The line with arrowheads, on the other hand, suggests the corner of a room or building seen from outside. In other words, cues that suggest a 3-D space alter our perception of a two-dimensional design (Enns & Coren, 1995).

Earlier, to explain the moon illusion, we said that if two objects make images of the same size, the more distant object must be larger. This is known formally as *size-distance invariance* (the size of an object's image is precisely related to its distance from the eyes). Gregory believes the same concept explains the Müller-Lyer illusion. If the V-tipped line looks farther away than the arrowhead-tipped line, you must compensate by seeing the V-tipped line as longer. This explanation presumes that you have had years of experience with straight lines, sharp edges, and corners—a pretty safe assumption in our culture.

Is there any way to show that past experience causes the illusion? If we could test someone who saw only curves and wavy lines as a child, we would know if experience with a "square" culture is important. Fortunately, a group of people in South Africa, the Zulus, live in a "round" culture. In their daily lives, Zulus rarely encounter a straight line: Their houses are shaped like rounded mounds and arranged in a circle, tools and toys are curved, and there are no straight roads or square buildings.

Müller-Lyer illusion Two equal-length lines tipped with inward or outward pointing V's appear to be of different lengths.

✦**FIGURE 4.48** *Why does line (b) in the Müller-Lyer illusion look longer than line (a)? Probably because it looks more like a distant corner than a nearer one. Because the vertical lines form images of the same length, the more "distant" line must be perceived as larger. As you can see in the drawing on the right, additional depth cues accentuate the Müller-Lyer illusion. (After Enns & Coren, 1995.)*

What happens if a Zulu looks at the Müller-Lyer design?   The typical Zulu villager does not experience the illusion. At most, she or he sees the V-shaped line as *slightly* longer than the other (Gregory, 1990). This seems to confirm the importance of past experience and perceptual habits in determining our view of the world.

Attention and Perception

As we take in information, attention is the key that unlocks the door to perception. The reverse is also true: At times, we all suffer from *inattentional blindness* (Mack & Rock, 1998). That is, we may not see something that is plainly before our eyes when our attention is narrowly focused (Mack 2002).

Inattentional blindness is vividly illustrated by the work of psychologists Daniel Simons and Christopher Chabris. In one study, Simons and Chabris showed people a film of two basketball teams, one wearing black shirts and the other wearing white. Observers watched the film and tried to count how many times a basketball passed between members of one of the teams. They were told to ignore the other team. As observers counted, a person wearing a gorilla suit walked into the middle of the basketball game, faced the camera, thumped its chest, and walked out of view. Half the observers failed to notice this rather striking event (Simons & Chabris, 1999). By the way, using a cell phone while driving—even a hands-free phone—can cause inattentional blindness. Instead of not seeing a gorilla, you might miss seeing another car, a motorcyclist, or a pedestrian while your attention is focused on the phone (Strayer, Drews, & Johnson, 2003).

Motives

Motives also play a role in perception. For example, if you are hungry, food-related words are more likely to gain your attention than non-food words (Mogg et al., 1998). Advertisers, of course, know that their pitch will be more effective if it gets your attention. That's why ads are loud, repetitious, and often intentionally irritating. They also take advantage of two motives that are widespread in our society: *anxiety* and *sex*. Everything from mouthwash to automobile tires is merchandised by using sex to gain attention. Other ads combine sex with anxiety. Deodorant, soaps, toothpaste, and countless other articles are pushed in ads that play on desires to be attractive, to have "sex appeal," or to avoid embarrassment.

In addition to directing attention, motives may alter what is perceived. As part of a supposed study of "the dating practices of college students," male volunteers were shown a

CRITICAL THINKING | The Boiled Frog Syndrome

Until something surprising happens, like the "murder" I saw that wasn't a murder at all, we tend to take perception for granted. But make no mistake, the world as we know it is created from sensory impressions. In fact, it takes about 50 milliseconds for a visual signal to move from the retina to the brain. Therefore, our perceptions always lag slightly behind the "real world." An event that happens quickly, like the pop of a flashbulb, may be over by the time we perceive it.

On the other end of the time scale, perception can blind us to very slow events and gradual changes. Humans evolved to detect sharp changes, such as the sudden appearance of a lion, a potential mate, or sources of food. However, many of the threats facing us today develop very slowly. Examples include the stockpiling of nuclear warheads, degradation of the environment, global defor-

estation, global warming, erosion of the ozone layer, and runaway human population growth.

Robert Ornstein, a psychologist, and Paul Ehrlich, a population biologist, believe that many of the large-scale threats we face are similar to the "boiled frog syndrome." Frogs placed in a pan of water that is slowly heated cannot detect the gradual rise in temperature. They will sit still until they die. Like the doomed frogs, many people seem unable to detect gradual but deadly trends in modern civilization. To avoid disasters, it may take a conscious effort by large numbers of people to see the "big picture" and reverse lethal but easily overlooked patterns (Ornstein & Ehrlich, 1989). Understanding how perception shapes "reality" may ultimately prove to be a matter of life or death. Are *you* paying attention?

picture of a female student and asked to give a first impression of how attractive she was. Before making these ratings, each person read one of two short written passages: One was sexually arousing and the other was not. The important finding was that men who read the more arousing passage rated the female as more attractive (Stephan et al., 1971). This result may come as no surprise if you have ever been infatuated with someone and then fallen out of love. A person who once seemed highly attractive may look quite different when your feelings change.

An emotional stimulus can shift attention away from other information. In an experiment, members of a Jewish organization watched as pictures like ✦Figure 4.49 were flashed on a screen for a split second. People were less likely to recognize symbols around the drawing's edge when the center item was an emotional symbol like the swastika (Erdelyi & Appelbaum, 1973). This effect probably explains why fans of opposing sports teams often act as if they had seen two completely different games. (Also see "The Boiled Frog Syndrome.")

✦**FIGURE 4.49** *Emotionally significant stimuli influence attention. (Erdelyi & Appelbaum, 1973, p. 50. Reprinted by permission.)*

Perceptual Expectancies

On a piece of paper, draw a circle about 3 inches in diameter. Inside the circle, above and to the left of center, make a large black dot, about one-half inch in diameter. Make another dot inside the circle above and to the right of center. Now, still inside the circle, draw an arc, curved upward and about 2 inches long just below the center of the circle. If you followed these instructions, your reaction might now be, "Oh! Why didn't you just say to draw a happy face?"

Like the happy face drawing, perception seems to proceed in two major ways. In **bottom-up processing,** we analyze information starting at the "bottom" with small sensory units (features) and build upward to a complete perception. The reverse also seems to occur. In **top-down processing** pre-existing knowledge is used to rapidly organize features into a meaningful whole. Bottom-up processing is like putting together a picture puzzle you've never seen before: You must assemble small pieces until a recognizable pattern appears. Top-down processing is like putting together a puzzle you have solved many times: After only a few pieces are in place you begin to see outlines of the final picture.

Bottom-up processing Organizing perceptions by beginning with low-level features.

Top-down processing Applying higher level knowledge to rapidly organize sensory information into a meaningful perception.

◆FIGURE 4.50 *This painting by abstract artist Al Held is 9 feet by 9 feet. If you process the painting "bottom-up," all you will see is two small dark geometric shapes. Would you like to try some top-down processing? Knowing the painting's title will allow you to apply your knowledge and see the painting in an entirely different way. The title? It's* The Big N. *Can you see it now? (Courtesy The Museum of Modern Art, New York. © Held, Al, "The Big N" (1965) synthetic polymer paint on canvas 9' 3/8" × 9'. Collection, The Museum of Modern Art, New York, Mrs. Armand P. Bartos fund.)*

Perceptual expectancy (or set) A readiness to perceive in a particular manner, induced by strong expectations.

Both types of processing are illustrated by ◆Figure 4.50. Also, return to Figure 4.31, the giant walkingstick. The first time you saw the photo you probably processed it bottom-up, picking out features until the insect was recognizable. This time, because of top-down processing, you should see the insect instantly. Another good example of top-down processing is found in perceptual expectancies.

Perceptual Set

What is a perceptual expectancy? A runner in the starting blocks at a track meet is *set* to respond in a certain way. Likewise, past experience, motives, context, or suggestions may create a **perceptual expectancy** (or **set**) that prepares you to perceive in a certain way. If a car backfires, runners at a track meet may jump the gun. As a matter of fact, we all frequently jump the gun when perceiving. In essence, an expectancy is a perceptual hypothesis we are *very likely* to apply to a stimulus—even if applying it is inappropriate.

Perceptual sets often lead us to see what we *expect* to see. I thought I saw a murder in the supermarket because I had just heard the girl's description of what was happening. Here's a more familiar example: Let's say you are driving across the desert and you're very low on gas. Finally, you see a sign approaching. On it are the words FUEL AHEAD. You relax, knowing you will not be stranded. But as you draw nearer, the words on the sign become FOOD AHEAD. Most people have had similar experiences in which expectations altered their perceptions. To observe perceptual expectancies firsthand, perform the demonstration described in ◆Figure 4.51.

Perceptual expectancies are frequently created by *suggestion*. This is especially true of perceiving other people. In one classic experiment, a psychology professor arranged for a guest lecturer to teach his class. Half the students in the class were given a page of notes that described the lecturer as a "rather *cold* person, industrious, critical, practical, and determined." The other students got notes describing him as a "rather *warm* person, industrious, critical, practical, and determined" (Kelley, 1950; italics added). Students who received the "cold" description perceived the lecturer as unhappy and irritable and didn't volunteer in class discussion. Those who got the "warm" description saw the lecturer as happy and good natured, and they actively took part in discussion with him. In the same way, labels such as "punk," "mental patient," "queer," "illegal immigrant," "bitch," and so on, are very likely to distort perceptions.

Those are extremes. Does it really make that much difference what you call someone or something? Perceptual categories, especially those defined by labels, do make a difference. This is especially true in perceiving people, where even trained observers may be influenced. For example, in one study, psychotherapists were shown a videotaped interview. Half of the therapists were told that the man being interviewed was applying for a job. The rest were told that the man was a mental patient. Therapists who thought the man was a job appli-

View I

View II

View III

◆FIGURE 4.51 *"Young woman/old woman" illustrations. As an interesting demonstration of perceptual expectancy, show some of your friends view I and some view II (cover all other views). Next show your friends view III and ask them what they see. Those who saw view I should see the old woman in view III; those who saw view II should see the young woman in view III. Can you see both? (After Leeper, 1935.)*

cant perceived him as "realistic," "sincere," and "pleasant." Those who thought he was a patient perceived him as "defensive," "dependent," and "impulsive" (Langer & Abelson, 1974).

In the next section, we will go beyond normal perception to ask, Is extrasensory perception possible? Before we do that, here's a chance to answer the question, Is remembering the preceding discussion possible?

STUDYBREAK ⟨Y⟩ *Perception and Objectivity*

RELATE

How has perceptual learning affected your ability to safely drive a car? For example, what do you pay attention to at intersections? Where do you habitually look as you are driving?

If you spent a year hiking the Amazon River Basin, what effect might it have on your perception of the Müller-Lyer illusion?

You have almost certainly misperceived a situation at some time because of a perceptual expectancy or the influence of motives. How were your perceptions influenced?

LEARNING CHECK

1. Perceptual habits may become so ingrained that they lead us to misperceive a stimulus. T or F?
2. Perceptual learning seems to program the brain for sensitivity to important _____ of the environment.
3. The Ames room is used to test infants for depth perception. T or F?

4. Size-distance relationships appear to underlie which two illusions? _____ and _____
5. Research shows that heightened sexual arousal can cause a person to perceive members of the opposite sex as more physically attractive. T or F?
6. In top-down processing of information, individual features are analyzed and assembled into a meaningful whole. T or F?
7. When a person is prepared to perceive events in a particular way, it is said that a perceptual expectancy or _____ exists.

Critical Thinking

8. What size object do you think you would have to hold at arm's length to cover up a full moon?
9. Cigarette advertisements in the United States are required to carry a warning label about the health risks of smoking. How have tobacco companies made these labels less visible?

ANSWERS

1. T 2. features 3. F 4. moon illusion, Müller-Lyer illusion 5. T 6. T 7. set 8. The most popular answers range from a quarter to a softball. Actually, a pea held in the outstretched hand will cover a full moon (Kunkel, 1993). If you listed an object larger than a pea, be aware that perceptions, no matter how accurate they seem, may distort reality. 9. Advertisers place health warnings in the corners of ads, where they attract the least possible attention. Also, the labels are often placed on "busy" backgrounds so that they are partially camouflaged. Finally, the main images in ads are designed to strongly attract attention. This further distracts readers from seeing the warnings.

EXTRASENSORY PERCEPTION— DO YOU BELIEVE IN MAGIC?

] **SURVEYQUESTION** *Is extrasensory perception possible?*

Uri Geller, a self-proclaimed "psychic," once agreed to demonstrate his claimed paranormal abilities. During testing, it seemed that Geller could sense which of ten film canisters contained a hidden object, he correctly guessed the number that would come up on a die shaken in a closed box, and he reproduced drawings sealed in envelopes.

Was Geller cheating, or was he using some ability beyond normal perception?   There is little doubt that Geller was cheating (Randi, 1980). But how? The answer lies in a discussion of **extrasensory perception** (**ESP**)—the purported ability to perceive events in ways that cannot be explained by known sensory capacities.

Parapsychology is the study of ESP and other **psi phenomena** (events that seem to defy accepted scientific laws). (Psi is pronounced like "sigh.") Parapsychologists seek answers to the questions raised by three basic forms that ESP could take. These are:

1. **Clairvoyance.** The purported ability to perceive events or gain information in ways that appear unaffected by distance or normal physical barriers.
2. **Telepathy.** Extrasensory perception of another person's thoughts, or more simply, the purported ability to read someone else's mind.
3. **Precognition.** The purported ability to perceive or accurately predict future events. Precognition may take the form of prophetic dreams that foretell the future.

Extrasensory perception The purported ability to perceive events in ways that cannot be explained by known capacities of the sensory organs.

Psi phenomena Events that seem to lie outside the realm of accepted scientific laws.

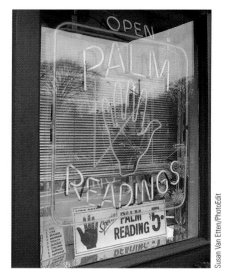

Most so-called psychics are simply keen observers. The "psychic" begins a "reading" by making general statements about a person. The "psychic" then plays "hot and cold" by attending to the person's facial expressions, body language, or tone of voice. When the "psychic" is "hot" (on the right track) the "psychic" continues to make similar statements about the person. If the person's reactions signal that the "psychic" is "cold" the "psychic" drops that topic or line of thought and tries another (Schouten, 1994).

◆FIGURE 4.52 *ESP cards used by J. B. Rhine, an early experimenter in parapsychology.*

Run of luck A statistically unusual outcome (as in getting 5 heads in a row when flipping a coin) that could still occur by chance alone.

While we are at it, we might as well toss in another purported psi ability:

4. **Psychokinesis.** The purported ability to exert influence over inanimate objects by willpower ("mind over matter"). (Psychokinesis cannot be classed as a type of ESP, but it is frequently studied by parapsychologists.)

An Appraisal of ESP

Psychologists as a group are highly skeptical about psi abilities. If you've ever had an apparent clairvoyant or telepathic experience, you might be convinced that ESP exists. However, the difficulty of excluding *coincidence* makes such experiences less conclusive than they might seem. Consider a typical "psychic" experience: During the middle of the night, a woman away for a weekend visit suddenly had a strong impulse to return home. When she arrived she found the house on fire with her husband asleep inside (Rhine, 1953). An experience like this is striking, but it does not confirm the reality of ESP. If, by coincidence, a hunch turns out to be correct, it may be *reinterpreted* as precognition or clairvoyance (Marks & Kammann, 1979). If it is not confirmed, it will simply be forgotten. Most people don't realize it, but such coincidences occur quite often.

Formal investigation of psi events owes much to the late J. B. Rhine, who tried to study ESP objectively. Many of Rhine's experiments made use of the *Zener cards* (a deck of 25 cards, each bearing one of five symbols) (◆Fig. 4.52). In a typical clairvoyance test, people tried to guess the symbols on the cards as they were turned up from a shuffled deck. Pure guessing in this test will produce an average score of 5 "hits" out of 25 cards.

Fraud and Skepticism

Unfortunately, some of Rhine's most dramatic early experiments used badly printed Zener cards that allowed the symbols to show faintly on the back. It is also very easy to cheat by marking cards with a fingernail or by noting marks on the cards caused by normal use. Even if this were not the case, there is evidence that early experimenters sometimes unconsciously gave people cues about cards with their eyes, facial gestures, or lip movements. In short, none of the early studies in parapsychology were done in a way that eliminated the possibility of fraud or "leakage" of helpful information (Alcock, 1990).

Modern parapsychologists are now well aware of the need for double-blind experiments, security and accuracy in record keeping, meticulous control, and repeatability of experiments (Milton & Wiseman, 1997). In the last 10 years, hundreds of experiments have been reported in parapsychological journals. Many of them seem to support the existence of psi abilities.

Then why do most psychologists remain skeptical about psi abilities? For one thing, fraud continues to plague the field. It is remarkable, for instance, that many parapsychologists chose to ignore a famous "psychic's" habit of peeking at ESP cards during testing (Cox, 1994). As one critic put it, positive ESP results usually mean "Error Some Place" (Marks, 1990). The more closely psi experiments are examined, the more likely it is that claimed successes will evaporate (Hyman, 1996b; Stokes, 2001).

The need for skepticism is especially great anytime there's money to be made from purported psychic abilities. For example, the owners of the "Miss Cleo" TV-psychic operation were convicted of felony fraud in 2002. "Miss Cleo," supposedly a Jamaican-accented psychic, was really just an actress from Los Angeles. People who paid $4.99 a minute for a "reading" from "Miss Cleo" actually reached one of several hundred operators. These people were hired through ads that read "No experience necessary." Despite being entirely faked, the "Miss Cleo" scam brought in more than $1 billion before it was shut down.

Statistics and Chance

Inconsistency is a major problem in psi research. For every study with positive results, there are others that fail (Hansel, 1980; Hyman, 1996b). It is rare—in fact, almost unheard of—for a person to maintain psi ability over any sustained period of time (Jahn, 1982). ESP researchers believe this "decline effect" shows that parapsychological skills are very fragile. But critics argue that a person who only temporarily scores above chance has just received credit for a **run of luck** (a statistically unusual outcome that could occur by chance alone). When the run is over, it is not fair to assume that ESP is temporarily gone. We must count *all* attempts.

To understand the run-of-luck criticism, imagine that you flip a coin 100 times and record the results. You then flip another coin 100 times, again recording the results. The two lists are compared. For any 10 pairs of flips, we would expect heads or tails to match 5 times. Let's say that you go through the list and find a set of 10 pairs where 9 out of 10 matched. This is far above chance expectation. But does it mean that the first coin "knew" what was going to come up on the second coin? The idea is obviously silly.

Now, what if a person guesses 100 times what will come up on a coin. Again, we might find a set of 10 guesses that matches the results of flipping the coin. Does this mean that the person, for a time, had precognition—then lost it? Parapsychologists tend to believe the answer is yes. Skeptics assume that nothing more than random matching occurred, as in the two-coin example.

Inconclusive Research

Unfortunately, many of the most spectacular findings in parapsychology simply cannot be replicated (reproduced or repeated) (Hyman, 1996a). Even the same researchers using the same experimental subjects typically can't get similar results every time (Schick & Vaughn, 1995). More importantly, improved research methods usually result in fewer positive results (Hyman, 1996b).

Reinterpretation is also a problem in psi experiments. For example, ex-astronaut Edgar Mitchell claimed he did a successful telepathy experiment from space. Yet news accounts never mentioned that on some trials Mitchell's "receivers" scored above chance, while on others they scored *below* chance. The second outcome, Mitchell decided, was also a "success" because it represented intentional "psi missing." But, as skeptics have noted, if both high scores and low scores count as successes, how can you lose?

Of course, in many ESP tests the outcome is beyond debate. A good example is provided by recent ESP experiments done through newspapers, radio, and television. In these mass media studies, people attempted to identify ESP targets from a distance. Such studies allow large numbers of people to be tested. The results of over 1.5 million ESP trials recently done through the mass media are easy to summarize: There was no significant ESP effect (Milton & Wiseman, 1999b). Zero. Zip. Nada. Clearly, state lottery organizers have nothing to fear!

Stage ESP

If psychic phenomena do occur, they certainly can't be controlled well enough to be used by entertainers. **Stage ESP** simulates ESP for the purpose of entertainment. Like stage magic, it is based on sleight of hand, deception, and patented gadgets (✦Fig. 4.53). A case in point is Uri Geller, a former nightclub magician who "astounded" audiences—and some scientists—with apparent telepathy, psychokinesis, and precognition.

Stage ESP The simulation of ESP for the purpose of entertainment.

(a)

(b)

(c)

Dennis Coon

✦**FIGURE 4.53** *Fake psychokinesis. (a) The performer shows an observer several straight keys. While doing so, he bends one of the keys by placing its tip in the slot of another key. Normally, this is done out of sight, behind the "psychic's" hand. It is clearly shown here so you can see how the deception occurs. (b) Next, the "psychic" places the two keys in the observer's hand and closes it. By skillful manipulation, the observer has been kept from seeing the bent key. The performer then "concentrates" on the keys to "bend them with psychic energy." (c) The bent key is revealed to the observer. "Miracle" accomplished! (Adapted from Randi, 1983.)*

It's now clear that tests of Geller's performance were incredibly sloppy. For instance, Geller reproduced sealed drawings in a room next to the one where the drawings were made. Original reports failed to mention that there was a hole in the wall between the rooms, through which Geller could have heard descriptions of the pictures as they were being drawn. Likewise, in the "die in the box" tests, Geller was allowed to hold the box, shake it, and have the honor of opening it (Randi, 1980; Wilhelm, 1976).

Why weren't such details reported?   Sensational and uncritical reporting of apparent paranormal events is widespread. Hundreds of books, articles, and television programs are produced each year by people who are getting rich by promoting unsupported claims. If a person did have psychic powers, he or she would not have to make a living by entertaining others. A quick trip to a casino would allow the person to retire for life.

Implications

After close to 130 years of investigation, it is still impossible to say conclusively whether psi events occur. As we have seen, a close look at psi experiments often reveals serious problems of evidence, procedure, and scientific rigor (Alcock, 1990; Hyman, 1996b; Marks, 2000; Stokes, 2001). It is also interesting to note that a survey of leading parapsychologists and skeptics found that almost all in both camps said their belief in psi had decreased (Blackmore, 1989). Yet, being a skeptic does not mean a person is against something. It means that you are unconvinced. The purpose of this discussion, then, has been to counter the *uncritical* acceptance of psi events that is rampant in the media.

What would it take to scientifically demonstrate the existence of ESP?   Quite simply, a set of instructions that would allow any competent, unbiased observer to produce a psi event under standardized conditions that rule out any possibility of fraud (Schick & Vaughn, 1995). Undoubtedly, some intrepid researchers will continue their attempts to supply just that. Others remain skeptics and consider 130 years of inconclusive efforts reason enough to abandon the concept of ESP (Marks, 2000). At the least, it seems essential to be carefully skeptical of evidence reported in the popular press or by researchers who are uncritical "true believers." (But then, you already knew I was going to say that, didn't you!)

A Look Ahead

In this chapter we have moved from basic sensations to the complexities of perceiving people and events. We have also probed some of the controversies concerning ESP. In the Psychology in Action section, we will return to "everyday" perception, for a look at perceptual awareness.

STUDYBREAK *Extrasensory Perception*

RELATE

Let's say that a friend of yours is an avid fan of TV shows that feature paranormal themes. See if you can summarize for her or him what is known about ESP. Be sure to include evidence for and against the existence of ESP and some of the thinking errors associated with non-skeptical belief in the paranormal.

LEARNING CHECK

1. Four purported psi events investigated by parapsychologists are clairvoyance, telepathy, precognition, and _____.
2. The _____ cards were used by J. B. Rhine in early tests of ESP.
3. Natural, or "real-life," occurrences are regarded as the best evidence for the existence of ESP. T or F?

4. Skeptics attribute positive results in psi experiments to statistical runs of luck. T or F?
5. Replication rates are very high for ESP experiments. T or F?

Critical Thinking

6. What would you estimate is the chance that two people in a group of 30 will have the same birthday (day and month, but not year)?
7. A "psychic" on television offers to fix broken watches for viewers. Moments later, dozens of viewers call the station to say that their watches miraculously started running again. What have they overlooked?

ANSWERS

1. psychokinesis 2. Zener 3. F 4. T 5. F 6. Most people assume that this would be a relatively rare event. Actually there is a 71 percent chance that two people will share a birthday in a group of 30. Most people probably underestimate the natural rate of occurrence of many seemingly mysterious coincidences (Alcock, 1990). 7. When psychologists handled watches awaiting repair at a store, 57 percent began running again, with no help from a "psychic." Believing the "psychic's" claim also overlooks the impact of big numbers: If the show reached a large audience, at least a few "broken" watches would start working merely by chance.

Psychology in Action

Becoming a Better Eyewitness to Life

] **SURVEYQUESTION** *How can I learn to perceive events more accurately?*

In the courtroom, the claim "I saw it with my own eyes" carries a lot of weight with a jury. Most jurors (unless they have taken a psychology course) tend to assume that eyewitness testimony is nearly infallible (Durham & Dane, 1999). But to put it bluntly, eyewitness testimony is frequently wrong. Recall, for instance, that I would have sworn in court that I had seen a murder taking place at the supermarket—*if* I hadn't received more information to correct my misperceptions.

What about witnesses who are certain that their perceptions were accurate? Should juries believe them?   Actually, having confidence in your testimony has almost no bearing on its accuracy (Wells, 1993)! Psychologists are gradually convincing lawyers, judges, and police that eyewitness errors are common. Even so, thousands of people have been wrongfully convicted (Scheck, Neufeld, & Dwyer, 2000). In one typical court case, a police officer testified that he saw the defendant shoot the victim as both stood in a dimly lit doorway. When a psychologist arranged for a juror to stand in the doorway under identical lighting conditions, none of the other jurors could identify him. The defendant was acquitted (Buckhout, 1974).

Unfortunately, perception rarely provides an "instant replay" of events. Impressions formed when a person is surprised, threatened, or under stress are especially prone to distortion. A recent study of eyewitness cases found that the *wrong person* was chosen from police lineups 25 percent of the time (Levi, 1998).

Wouldn't the victim of a crime remember more than a mere witness?   Not necessarily. A revealing study found that eyewitness accuracy is virtually the same for witnessing a crime (seeing a pocket calculator stolen) as it is for being a victim (seeing one's own watch stolen) (Hosch & Cooper, 1982). Placing more weight on the testimony of victims may be a serious mistake. In many crimes, victims fall prey to *weapon focus.* Understandably, they fix their entire attention on the knife, gun, or other weapon used by an attacker. In doing so, they fail to notice details of appearance, dress, or other clues to identity (Steblay, 1992). Additional factors that consistently lower eyewitness accuracy are summarized in ▲Table 4.2 (Kassin et al., 2001).

Even in broad daylight, eyewitness testimony is untrustworthy. In 2001 an airliner crashed near Kennedy International Airport in New York. Hundreds of people saw the plane go down. Half of them said the plane was on fire. Flight recorders showed there was no fire. One witness in five saw the plane make a right turn. An equal number saw it make a left turn! As one investigator noted, the best witness may be a "kid under 12 years old who doesn't have his parents around." Adults, it seems, are easily swayed by their expectations.

▲TABLE 4.2	Factors Affecting the Accuracy of Eyewitness Perceptions
SOURCES OF ERROR	**SUMMARY OF FINDINGS**
1. Wording of questions	An eyewitness's testimony about an event can be affected by how the questions put to that witness are worded.
2. Postevent information	Eyewitness testimony about an event often reflects not only what was actually seen but also information obtained later on.
3. Attitudes, expectations	An eyewitness's perception and memory for an event may be affected by his or her attitudes and expectations.
4. Alcohol intoxication	Alcohol intoxication impairs later ability to recall events.
5. Cross-racial perceptions	Eyewitnesses are better at identifying members of their own race than they are at identifying people of other races.
6. Weapon focus	The presence of a weapon impairs an eyewitness's ability to accurately identify the culprit's face.
7. Accuracy-confidence	An eyewitness's confidence is not a good predictor of his or her accuracy.
8. Exposure time	The less time an eyewitness has to observe an event, the less well she or he will perceive and remember it.
9. Unconscious transference	Eyewitnesses sometimes identify as a culprit someone they have seen in another situation or context.
10. Color perception	Judgments of color made under monochromatic light (such as an orange street light) are highly unreliable.
11. Stress	Very high levels of stress impair the accuracy of eyewitness perceptions.

Adapted from Kassin et al., 2001.

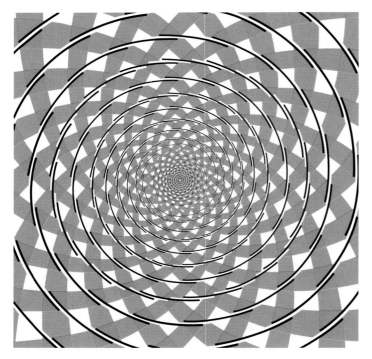

✦**FIGURE 4.54** *The limits of pure perception. Even simple designs are easily misperceived. Fraser's spiral is actually a series of concentric circles. The illusion is so powerful that people who try to trace one of the circles sometimes follow the illusory spiral and jump from one circle to the next. (After Seckel, 2000.)*

Implications

Now that DNA testing is available, more than 100 people who were convicted of murder, rape, and other crimes in the United States have been exonerated. Each of these innocent people was convicted mainly on the basis of eyewitness testimony. Each also spent *years* in prison before being cleared (Foxhall, 2000). How often are everyday perceptions as inaccurate or distorted as those of an emotional eyewitness? The answer we have been moving toward is, very frequently. Bearing this in mind may help you be more tolerant of the views of others and more cautious about your own objectivity. It may also encourage more frequent *reality testing* on your part.

What do you mean by reality testing? In any situation having an element of doubt or uncertainty, **reality testing** involves obtaining additional information to check your perceptions. ✦Figure 4.54 shows a powerful illusion called Fraser's spiral. What appears to be a spiral is actually made up of a series of closed circles. Most people cannot spontaneously see this reality. Instead, they must carefully trace one of the circles to confirm what is "real" in the design.

Psychologist Sidney Jourard once offered a prime example of reality testing. One of Jourard's students believed her roommate was stealing from her. The student gradually became convinced of her roommate's guilt but said nothing. As her distrust and anger grew, their relationship turned cold and distant. Finally, at Jourard's urging, she confronted her roommate. The roommate cleared herself immediately and expressed relief when the puzzling change in their relationship was explained (Jourard, 1974). With their friendship reestablished, the true culprit was soon caught. (The cleaning woman did it!)

If you have ever concluded that someone was angry, upset, or unfriendly without checking the accuracy of your perceptions, you have fallen into a subtle trap. Personal objectivity is an elusive quality, requiring frequent reality testing to maintain. At the very least, it pays to ask a person what she or he is feeling when you are in doubt. Clearly, most of us could learn to be better "eyewitnesses" to daily events.

Perceptual Awareness

Do some people perceive things more accurately than others? Humanistic psychologist Abraham Maslow (1969) believed that some people perceive themselves and others with unusual accuracy. Maslow characterized these people as especially alive, open, aware, and mentally healthy. He found that their perceptual styles were marked by immersion in the present; a lack of self-consciousness; freedom from selecting, criticizing, or evaluating; and a general "surrender" to experience. The kind of perception Maslow described is like that of a mother with her newborn infant, a child at Christmas, or two people in love.

In daily life, we quickly **habituate** (respond less) to predictable and unchanging stimuli. Habituation is a type of learning—basically, we learn to cease paying attention to familiar stimuli. For instance, when you buy a new CD, the music initially holds your attention all the way through. But when the CD becomes "old," all the songs may play without your really attending to them. When a stimulus is repeated *without change,* our response to it habituates, or decreases. Interestingly, creative people habituate *more slowly* than average. We might expect that they would rapidly become bored with a repeated stimulus. Instead, it seems that creative people actively attend to stimuli, even those that are repeated (Colin, Moore, & West, 1996).

Attention

Whereas the average person has not reached perceptual restriction of the "if you've seen one tree, you've seen them all" variety, the fact remains that most of us tend to look at a tree and classify it into the perceptual category of "trees in general" without really appre-

Reality testing Obtaining additional information to check on the accuracy of perceptions.
Habituation A decrease in perceptual response to a repeated stimulus.

ciating the miracle standing before us. How, then, can we bring about **dishabituation** (a reversal of habituation) on a day-to-day basis? Does perceptual clarity require years of effort? Fortunately, a more immediate avenue is available. The deceptively simple key to dishabituation is: Pay attention. The following quote summarizes the importance of attention:

> One day a man of the people said to Zen Master Ikkyu: "Master, will you please write for me some maxims of the highest wisdom?"
> Ikkyu immediately took his brush and wrote the word "Attention."
> "Is that all?" asked the man. "Will you not add something more?"
> Ikkyu then wrote twice running: "Attention. Attention."
> "Well," remarked the man rather irritably, "I really don't see much depth or subtlety in what you have just written."
> Then Ikkyu wrote the same word three times running: "Attention. Attention. Attention."
> Half angered, the man demanded, "What does that word 'Attention' mean anyway?"
> And Ikkyu answered gently: "Attention means attention." (Kapleau, 1966)

To this we can add only one thought, provided by the words of poet William Blake: "If the doors of perception were cleansed, man would see everything as it is, infinite."

How to Become a Better "Eyewitness" to Life

Here's a summary of ideas from this chapter to help you maintain and enhance perceptual awareness and accuracy.

1. *Remember that perceptions are reconstructions of reality.* Learn to regularly question your own perceptions. Are they accurate? Could another interpretation fit the facts? What assumptions are you making? Could they be false? How might your assumptions be distorting your perceptions?
2. *Break perceptual habits and interrupt habituation.* Each day, try to do some activities in new ways. For example, take different routes when you travel to work or school. Do routines, such as brushing your teeth or combing your hair, with your non-preferred hand. Try to look at friends and family members as if they are persons you just met for the first time.
3. *Shift adaptation levels and broaden frames of reference by seeking out-of-the-ordinary experiences.* The possibilities here range from trying foods you don't normally eat, to reading opinions very different from your own. Experiences ranging from a quiet walk in the woods to a trip to an amusement park may be perceptually refreshing.
4. *Beware of perceptual sets.* Anytime you pigeonhole people, objects, or events, there is a danger that your perceptions will be distorted by expectations or pre-existing categories. Be especially wary of labels and stereotypes. Try to see people as individuals and events as unique, one-time occurrences.
5. *Be aware of the ways in which motives and emotions influence perceptions.* It is difficult to avoid being swayed by your own interests, needs, desires, and emotions. But be aware of this trap, and actively try to see the world through the eyes of others. Taking the other person's perspective is especially valuable in disputes or arguments. Ask yourself, "How does this look to her or him?"
6. *Make a habit of engaging in reality testing.* Actively look for additional evidence to check the accuracy of your perceptions. Ask questions, seek clarifications, and find alternate channels of information. Remember that perception is not automatically accurate. You could be wrong—we all are frequently.
7. *Pay attention.* Make a conscious effort to pay attention to other people and your surroundings. Don't drift through life in a haze. Listen to others with full concentration. Watch their facial expressions. Make eye contact. Try to get in the habit of approaching perception as if you are going to have to testify later about what you saw and heard.

Dishabituation A reversal of habituation.

STUDYBREAK *Perceptual Awareness and Accuracy*

RELATE

Because perceptions are reconstructions or models of external events, we should all engage in more frequent reality testing. Can you think of a recent event when a little reality testing would have saved you from misjudging a situation?

In order to improve your own perceptual awareness and accuracy, which strategies would you emphasize first?

LEARNING CHECK

1. Most perceptions can be described as active reconstructions of external reality. T or F?
2. Inaccuracies in eyewitness perceptions obviously occur in "real life," but they cannot be reproduced in psychology experiments. T or F?

3. Accuracy scores for facts provided by witnesses to staged crimes may be as low as 25 percent correct. T or F?
4. Victims of crimes are more accurate eyewitnesses than are impartial observers. T or F?
5. *Reality testing* is another term for dishabituation. T or F?

Critical Thinking

6. Return for a moment to the incident described at the beginning of this chapter. What perceptual factors were involved in the first version of the "murder"? How did the girl affect what I saw?

ANSWERS

1. T 2. F 3. T 4. T 5. F 6. The girl's misperception, communicated so forcefully to me, created a powerful expectancy that influenced what I perceived. Also, the event happened quickly (the exposure time was brief), and the stressful or emotional nature of the incident encouraged my own misperception.

CHAPTER IN REVIEW

Major Points

- Sensory systems select, analyze, and transduce information from the surrounding world.
- All of the senses rely on a complex series of mechanical, chemical, and neural events to generate messages understood by the brain.
- Sensory adaptation, selective attention, and sensory gating significantly modify our experiences.
- Perception is an active process of assembling sensations into meaningful patterns.
- We unconsciously use Gestalt principles to organize sensations into meaningful patterns.
- Our wondrous ability to perceive three-dimensional space is based on retinal disparity, bodily cues, and pictorial cues.
- Perception is greatly affected by learning, expectations, and motives.
- Perceptual accuracy can be improved by conscious effort and an awareness of factors that contribute to erroneous perceptions.

Summary

In general, how do sensory systems function?

- Because of transduction, selectivity, limited sensitivity, feature detection, and coding patterns, the senses act as data reduction systems.

- Sensation can be partially understood in terms of sensory localization in the brain.

How is vision accomplished?

- The eye is a visual system, not a photographic one. The entire visual system is structured to analyze visual information.
- Four common visual defects are myopia, hyperopia, presbyopia, and astigmatism.
- The rods and cones are photoreceptors in the retina of the eye.
- The rods specialize in peripheral vision, night vision, seeing black and white, and motion detection. The cones specialize in color vision, acuity, and daylight vision.
- Color vision is explained by the trichromatic theory in the retina and by the opponent-process theory in the visual system beyond the eyes.
- Total color blindness is rare, but 8 percent of males and 1 percent of females are red-green color-blind or color-weak.
- Dark adaptation is caused mainly by an increase in the amount of rhodopsin in the rods.

What are the mechanisms of hearing?

- Sound waves are the stimulus for hearing. They are transduced by the eardrum, auditory ossicles, oval window, cochlea, and ultimately, the hair cells.

- The frequency theory and place theory of hearing together explain how pitch is sensed.
- Three basic types of deafness are nerve deafness, conduction deafness, and stimulation deafness.

How do the chemical senses operate?

- Olfaction (smell) and gustation (taste) are chemical senses responsive to airborne or liquefied molecules.
- The lock and key theory partially explains smell. In addition, the location of the olfactory receptors in the nose helps identify various scents.
- Sweet and bitter tastes are based on a lock-and-key coding of molecule shapes. Salty and sour tastes are triggered by a direct flow of ions into taste receptors.

What are the somesthetic senses, and why are they important?

- The somesthetic senses include the skin senses, vestibular senses, and kinesthetic senses (receptors that detect muscle and joint positioning).
- The skin senses are touch, pressure, pain, cold, and warmth. Sensitivity to each is related to the number of receptors found in an area of skin.
- Distinctions can be made between warning pain and reminding pain.
- Pain is greatly affected by anxiety, attention, and control over a stimulus. Pain can be reduced by controlling these factors.
- Various forms of motion sickness are related to messages received from the vestibular system, which detects gravity and movement.

Why are we more aware of some sensations than others?

- Incoming sensations are affected by sensory adaptation, selective attention, and sensory gating.
- Selective gating of pain messages takes place in the spinal cord, as explained by gate control theory.

How do perceptual constancies affect our perceptions?

- Perception is the process of assembling sensations into a usable mental representation of the world.
- In vision, the image projected on the retina is constantly changing, but the external world appears stable and undistorted because of size, shape, and brightness constancy.

What basic principles do we use to group sensations into meaningful patterns?

- Separating figure and ground is the most basic perceptual organization.
- The following factors help organize sensations: nearness, similarity, continuity, closure, contiguity, and common region.
- A perceptual organization may be thought of as a hypothesis held until evidence contradicts it.

How is it possible to see depth and judge distance?

- A basic capacity for depth perception is present soon after birth.
- Depth perception depends on the muscular cues of accommodation and convergence. Stereoscopic vision is created mainly by retinal disparity.
- Pictorial cues also underlie depth perception. These include linear perspective, relative size, height in the picture plane, light and shadow, overlap, texture gradients, aerial haze, and motion parallax.
- The moon illusion can be explained by the apparent distance hypothesis, which emphasizes that many depth cues are present when the moon is on the horizon.

How is perception altered by learning, expectations, and motives?

- Perception is an active reconstruction of events.
- Perceptual learning influences the ways in which we organize and interpret sensations.
- One of the most familiar of all illusions, the Müller-Lyer illusion, seems to be related to perceptual learning, linear perspective, and size-distance invariance relationships.
- Personal motives and values often alter perceptions by changing the evaluation of what is seen or by altering attention to specific details.
- Perceptions may be based on top-down or bottom-up processing of information.
- Attention, prior experience, suggestion, and motives combine in various ways to create perceptual sets, or expectancies.

Is extrasensory perception possible?

- Parapsychology is the study of purported psi phenomena, including clairvoyance, telepathy, precognition, and psychokinesis.
- Research in parapsychology remains controversial because of a variety of problems and shortcomings. The bulk of the evidence to date is against the existence of ESP.
- Stage ESP is based on deception and tricks.

How can I learn to perceive events more accurately?

- Eyewitness testimony is surprisingly unreliable. Eyewitness accuracy is further damaged by weapon focus and a number of similar factors.
- When a stimulus is repeated without change, our response to it undergoes habituation.
- Perceptual accuracy is enhanced by reality testing, dishabituation, and conscious efforts to pay attention.
- It is also valuable to break perceptual habits, to broaden frames of reference, to beware of perceptual sets, and to be aware of the ways in which motives and emotions influence perceptions.

Interactive Learning

Internet addresses frequently change. To find the sites listed here, visit www.psychology. wadsworth.com/coon_journey2e for an updated list of Internet addresses and direct links to relevant sites.

PSYCHOLOGY: A JOURNEY COMPANION WEBSITE Online quizzes, flash cards, and other helpful study aids for this text. *www.psychology.wadsworth.com/coon_journey2e*

HEARNET A page that promotes ear protection for rock musicians.

ILLUSIONWORKS A large collection of visual illusions.

QUESTIONS AND ANSWERS ABOUT PAIN CONTROL Answers common questions about pain control.

SMELL AND TASTE DISORDERS FAQ Questions and answers about smell and taste disorders.

STEREOGRAM LINKS Provides links to stereograms and information about stereograms, including how to create your own.

THE JOY OF VISUAL PERCEPTION An online book about visual perception.

VESTIBULAR DISORDERS ASSOCIATION Provides links to sites concerned with vestibular problems.

VISION TEST An on-screen vision test.

INFOTRAC COLLEGE EDITION For recent articles related to pain control, use Key Words search for ANXIETY and COUNTERIRRITATION. You can also use a Key Words search for EXTRASENSORY PERCEPTION.

PSYCHNOW! 4a. Vision and Hearing, 4b. Chemical and Somesthetic Senses, 4c. Perception.

Test Your Knowledge: Sensation and Perception

The questions that follow are only a sample of what you need to know. If you miss any of the items, you should review the entire chapter and get more practice with *WebTutor* or the *Practice Quizzes* that came with this book. Another way to prepare for tests is to use the printed *Study Guide* that is available for this text.

1. The senses divide the world into basic perceptual features and sensory patterns, a process known as
   A. sensory localization   B. sensory analysis
   C. accommodation   D. phosphenation

2. If you press on your closed eyelids you will experience phosphenes. This illustrates the concept of
   A. visual saturation   B. sensory coding
   C. accommodation   D. hyperopia

3. People who become farsighted as they get older have the condition known as
   A. hyperopia   B. myopia   C. astigmatism
   D. presbyopia

4. The greatest visual acuity is associated with the _____ and the _____.
   A. trichromat, rods   B. itreous humor, cones   C. fovea, cones   D. nanometer, cones

5. Black and white vision and a high degree of sensitivity to movement are characteristic of
   A. rod vision   B. cone vision   C. the blind spot
   D. the fovea

6. Colored afterimages are best explained by
   A. trichromatic theory   B. the effects of astigmatism
   C. sensory localization   D. opponent-process theory

7. Dark adaptation is directly related to an increase in
   A. rhodopsin   B. astigmatism   C. accommodation
   D. saturation

8. The loudness of a sound is determined by the _____ of sound waves.
   A. frequency   B. amplitude   C. rarefaction   D. ossicle

9. Sounds are ultimately transduced by movements of the
   A. pinna   B. malleus   C. chochlea   D. hair cells

10. The term *umami* refers to
    A. smell blindness   B. temporary damage to the hair cells
    C. secondary olfaction   D. a taste quality

11. The lock-and-key model appears to partly explain
    A. motion sickness   B. olfaction and gustation   C. dark adaptation   D. color blindness

12. Which of the following is NOT a somesthetic sense?
    A. taste   B. touch   C. balance   D. kinesthesis

13. As time passes, nerve endings in the skin under your wristwatch send fewer signals to the brain and you become able to feel the watch. This process is called
    A. sensory gating   B. the sensory bottleneck   C. reverse attention   D. sensory adaptation

14. The fact that a mild surface pain can greatly reduce more agonizing pain is consistent with
    A. gate control theory   B. the concept of sensory adaptation
    C. sensory conflict theory   D. perceptual constancy theory

15. Which of the following is LEAST likely to contribute to the formation of a perceptual figure?
    A. continuity   B. closure   C. similarity   D. separation

16. The clearest example of a binocular depth cue is
    A. linear perspective   B. retinal disparity   C. aerial perspective   D. motion parallax

17. The apparent distance hypothesis provides a good explanation of the
    A. moon illusion   B. horizontal-vertical illusion
    C. Zulu illusion   D. effects of inattentional blindness

18. Top-down perceptual processing is closely related to
    A. perceptual expectancies   B. the Müller-Lyer illusion
    C. size-distance invariances   D. precognition

19. The Zener cards were used in early studies of
    A. psi phenomena   B. inattentional blindness
    C. the Müller-Lyer illusion   D. top-down processing

20. A good antidote to perceptual habituation can be found in conscious efforts to
    A. reverse sensory gating   B. pay attention   C. achieve visual accommodation   D. counteract shape constancy

ANSWERS   1. b 2. b 3. d 4. c 5. a 6. d 7. a 8. b 9. d 10. d 11. b 12. a 13. d 14. a 15. d 16. b 17. a 18. a 19. a 20. b

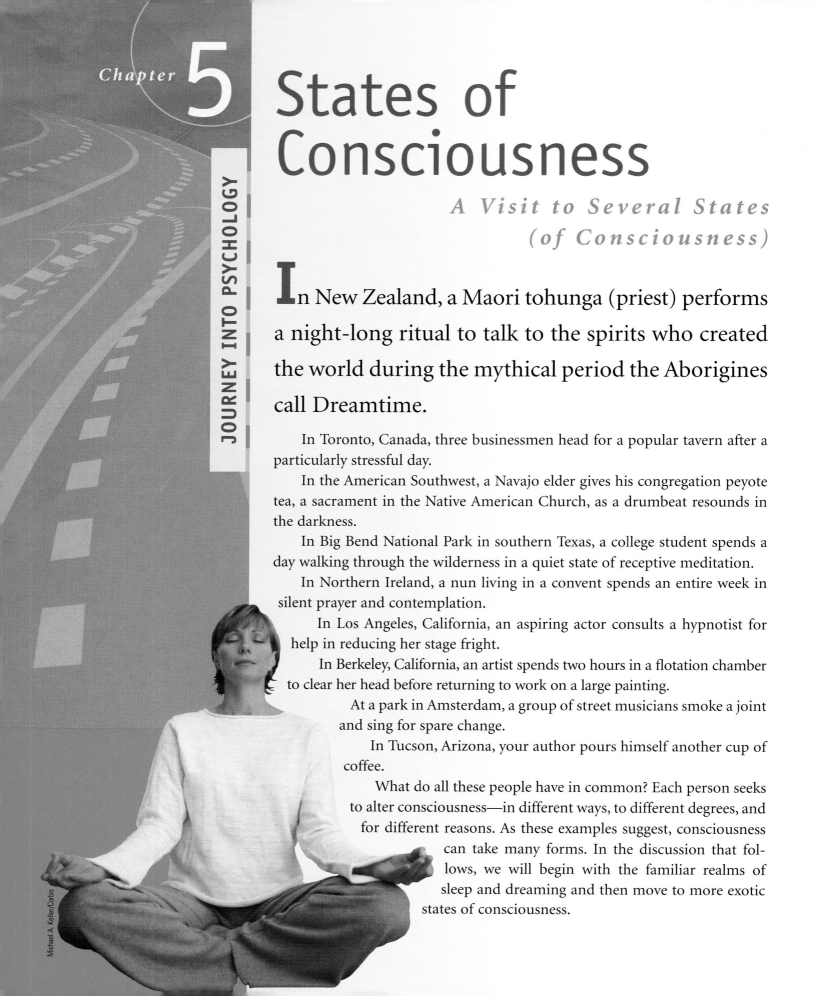

States of Consciousness

A Visit to Several States (of Consciousness)

In New Zealand, a Maori tohunga (priest) performs a night-long ritual to talk to the spirits who created the world during the mythical period the Aborigines call Dreamtime.

In Toronto, Canada, three businessmen head for a popular tavern after a particularly stressful day.

In the American Southwest, a Navajo elder gives his congregation peyote tea, a sacrament in the Native American Church, as a drumbeat resounds in the darkness.

In Big Bend National Park in southern Texas, a college student spends a day walking through the wilderness in a quiet state of receptive meditation.

In Northern Ireland, a nun living in a convent spends an entire week in silent prayer and contemplation.

In Los Angeles, California, an aspiring actor consults a hypnotist for help in reducing her stage fright.

In Berkeley, California, an artist spends two hours in a flotation chamber to clear her head before returning to work on a large painting.

At a park in Amsterdam, a group of street musicians smoke a joint and sing for spare change.

In Tucson, Arizona, your author pours himself another cup of coffee.

What do all these people have in common? Each person seeks to alter consciousness—in different ways, to different degrees, and for different reasons. As these examples suggest, consciousness can take many forms. In the discussion that follows, we will begin with the familiar realms of sleep and dreaming and then move to more exotic states of consciousness.

Michael A. Keller/Corbis

Survey Questions

- What is an altered state of consciousness?
- What are the effects of sleep loss or changes in sleep patterns?
- Are there different stages of sleep?
- What are the causes of sleep disorders and unusual sleep events?
- Do dreams have meaning?
- How is hypnosis done, and what are its limitations?
- What is meditation? Does it have any benefits?
- What are the effects of the more commonly used psychoactive drugs?
- How are dreams used to promote personal understanding?

STATES OF CONSCIOUSNESS—THE MANY FACES OF AWARENESS

] SURVEYQUESTION *What is an altered state of consciousness?*

To be conscious means to be aware. **Consciousness** consists of all the sensations, perceptions, memories, and feelings you are aware of at any instant (Farthing, 1992). We spend most of our lives in waking consciousness, a state of clear, organized alertness. In waking consciousness we perceive times, places, and events as real, meaningful, and familiar. But states of consciousness related to fatigue, delirium, hypnosis, drugs, and ecstasy may differ markedly from "normal" awareness. Everyone experiences at least some altered states, such as sleep, dreaming, and daydreaming. In everyday life, changes in consciousness may also accompany long-distance running, listening to music, making love, or other circumstances.

Altered States of Consciousness

How are altered states distinguished from normal awareness?   During an **altered state of consciousness** (**ASC**), changes take place in the *quality* and *pattern* of mental activity. Typically there are distinct shifts in perceptions, emotions, memory, time sense, thinking, feelings of self-control, and suggestibility (Tart, 1986). Definitions aside, most people know when they have experienced an ASC.

Are there other causes of ASCs?   In addition to those already mentioned, we could add: sensory overload (for example, a rave, Mardi Gras crowd, or mosh pit), monotonous stimulation (such as "highway hypnotism" on long drives), unusual physical conditions (high fever, hyperventilation, dehydration, sleep loss, near-death experiences), restricted sensory input, and many other possibilities. In some instances, altered states of awareness have important cultural significance. (See "Consciousness and Culture" for more information.)

In this chapter we will focus on sleep, dreaming, hypnosis, meditation, sensory deprivation, and the effects of drugs. Let's begin with questions about sleep, the most familiar ASC.

SLEEP—A NICE PLACE TO VISIT

] SURVEYQUESTION *What are the effects of sleep loss or changes in sleep patterns?*

Each of us will spend some 25 years of life asleep. Contrary to common belief, you are not totally unresponsive during sleep. For instance, you are more likely to awaken if you hear your own name spoken instead of another. Likewise, a sleeping mother may ignore a siren

Consciousness Mental awareness of sensations, perceptions, memories, and feelings.

Altered state of consciousness (ASC) A condition of awareness distinctly different in quality or pattern from waking consciousness.

HUMAN DIVERSITY Consciousness and Culture

Throughout history, people have found ways to alter consciousness. A dramatic example is the sweat lodge ceremony of the Sioux Indians. During the ritual, several men sit in total darkness inside a small chamber heated by coals. Cedar smoke, bursts of steam, and sage fill the air. The men chant rhythmically. The heat builds. At last they can stand it no more. The door is thrown open. Cooling night breezes rush in. And then? The cycle begins again—often to be repeated four or five times more.

The ritual "sweats" of the Sioux are meant to cleanse the mind and body. When they are especially intense, they bring altered awareness and personal revelation.

People seek some altered states for pleasure, as is often true of drug intoxication. Yet as the Sioux illustrate, many cultures regard

altered consciousness as a pathway to personal enlightenment. Indeed, all cultures and most religions recognize and accept some alterations of consciousness. However, the meaning given to these states varies greatly—from signs of "madness" and "possession" by spirits, to life-enhancing breakthroughs. Thus, cultural conditioning greatly affects what altered states we recognize, seek, consider normal, and attain (Heath, 2001; Metzner, 1998).

In many cultures, rituals of healing, prayer, purification, or personal transformation are accompanied by altered states of consciousness.

SLEEP QUIZ

1. People can learn to sleep for just a few hours a night and still function well. T or F?
2. Everyone dreams every night. T or F?
3. The brain rests during sleep. T or F?
4. Resting during the day can replace lost sleep. T or F?
5. As people get older, they sleep more. T or F?
6. Alcohol may help a person get to sleep, but it disturbs sleep later during the night. T or F?
7. If a person goes without sleep long enough, death will occur. T or F?
8. Dreams mostly occur during deep sleep. T or F?
9. A person prevented from dreaming would soon go crazy. T or F?
10. Sleepwalking occurs when a person acts out a dream. T or F?

ANSWERS

1.F 2.T 3.F 4.F 5.F 6.T 7.T 8.F 9.F 10.F

outside, but wake at the slightest whimper of her child. It's even possible to do simple tasks while asleep. In one experiment, people learned to avoid an electric shock by touching a switch each time a tone sounded. Eventually, they could do it without waking. (This is much like the basic survival skill of turning off your alarm clock without waking.) Of course, sleep does impose limitations. Don't expect to learn math, a foreign language, or other complex skills while asleep—especially if the snooze takes place in class (Druckman & Bjork, 1994; Wood et al., 1992).

Because sleep is familiar, many people think they know all about it. Before reading more, test your knowledge with the Sleep Quiz you see here. Were you surprised by any of the answers? Let's see what we know about our "daily retreat from the world."

The Need for Sleep

How strong is the need for sleep? Sleep is an innate **biological rhythm** that can never be entirely ignored (Webb, 1994). Of course, sleep will give way temporarily, especially at times of great danger. As one comic put it, "The lion and the lamb shall lie down together, but the lamb will not be very sleepy." However, there are limits to how long humans can go without sleep. A rare disease that prevents sleep always ends the same way: The patient falls into a stupor, followed by coma, followed by death (Oliwenstein, 1993) (◆Fig. 5.1).

Imagine placing an animal on a moving treadmill, over a pool of water. This is not a good way to sleep! Even so, sleep will always win. Under these conditions, animals soon drift into repeated microsleeps (Goleman, 1982). A **microsleep** is a brief shift in brain activity to the pattern normally recorded during sleep. When you drive, remember that microsleeps can lead to macro-accidents. Even if your eyes are open, you can fall asleep for a few sec-

---

Biological rhythm Any repeating cycle of biological activity, such as sleep and waking cycles or changes in body temperature.

Microsleep A brief shift in brain-wave patterns to those of sleep.

◆FIGURE 5. 1 *Not all animals sleep, but like humans, those that do have powerful sleep needs. For example, dolphins must voluntarily breathe air, which means they face the choice of staying awake or drowning. The dolphin solves this problem by sleeping on just one side of its brain at a time! The other half of the brain, which remains awake, controls breathing (Jouvet, 1999).*

CLINICAL FILE Teenage Sleep Zombies

Did you ever have to fight to stay awake in a high school class? Hypersomnia (hi-per-SOM-nee-ah: excessive daytime sleepiness) is a common problem during adolescence. The reason? Rapid physical changes during puberty increase the need for sleep. However, sleep time tends to *decrease* during the teen years. At a time when they need more sleep, many adolescents get less.

If teenagers are sleep deprived, why don't they just sleep more? As children enter puberty, they begin to stay up later at night. However, they must get up early to attend school, regardless of when they went to bed. As a result, many teens are seriously sleep deprived during the week. Then, on the weekend, they sleep longer and get up late in the morning. After sleeping extra amounts for 2 days, many teens have difficulty falling asleep Sunday night. On Monday, they have to get up early for school, and the sleep loss cycle begins again.

What can be done about teenage sleep deprivation? Psychologists have persuaded some school districts to start classes later so that high school students can sleep longer. Preliminary studies suggest that this schedule improves learning and reduces behavior problems. It looks like some of the "storm and stress" of adolescence may be ordinary grouchiness caused by sleep loss. (Sources: Fukuda & Ishihara, 2001; Laberge et al., 2001; Mitru, Millrood, & Mateika, 2002.)

---

onds. Roughly 2 out of every 100 highway crashes are caused by sleepiness (Lyznicki et al., 1998). By the way, if you are struggling to stay awake while driving, you should stop, quit fighting it, and take a short nap. Coffee helps too, but briefly giving in to sleep helps more (Horne & Reyner, 1996).

Sleep Deprivation

How long could a person go without sleep? With few exceptions, 4 days or more without sleep becomes hell for everyone. For example, a disc jockey named Peter Tripp once stayed awake for 200 hours to raise money for charity. After 100 hours, Tripp began to hallucinate: He saw cobwebs in his shoes and watched in terror as a tweed coat became a suit of "furry worms." By the end of 200 hours, Tripp was unable to distinguish between his waking nightmares, hallucinations, and reality (Luce, 1965). Despite Tripp's breakdown, longer sleepless periods are possible. The world record is held by Randy Gardner— who at age 17 went 268 hours (11 days) without sleep. Surprisingly, Randy needed only 14 hours of sleep to recover. It is not necessary to completely replace lost sleep. As Randy found, most symptoms of **sleep deprivation** (sleep loss) are reversed by a single night's rest.

What are the costs of sleep loss? Age and personality make a big difference. Although Peter Tripp's behavior became quite bizarre, Randy Gardner was less impaired. However, make no mistake: Sleep is a necessity. At various times, Randy's speech was slurred, and he couldn't concentrate, remember clearly, or name common objects (Coren, 1996). Sleep loss also typically causes trembling hands, drooping eyelids, inattention, irritability, staring, increased pain sensitivity, and general discomfort (Naitoh et al., 1989).

Most people who have not slept for 2 or 3 days can still do interesting or complex mental tasks (Binks, Waters, & Hurry, 1999). But they have trouble paying attention, staying alert, and following simple or boring routines. For a driver, pilot, or machine operator, this can spell disaster (Fairclough & Graham, 1999). If a task is monotonous (such as factory work or air traffic control), no amount of sleep loss is safe (Gillberg & Akerstedt, 1998). In fact, if you lose just 1 hour a night of sleep, it can affect your mood, memory, ability to pay attention, and even your health (Everson, 1998; Maas, 1999). (See "Teenage Sleep Zombies.")

Calvin and Hobbes. Copyright © Watterson. Reprinted with permission of Universal Press Syndicate. All rights reserved.

Sleep deprivation Being prevented from getting desired or needed amounts of sleep.

Time of Day

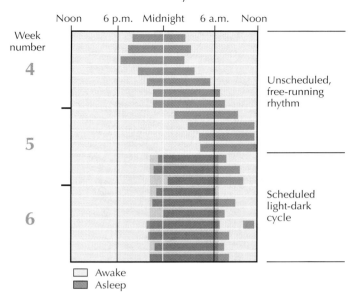

◆ **FIGURE 5.2** *Sleep rhythms. Bars show periods of sleep during the fourth, fifth, and sixth weeks of an experiment with a human subject. During unscheduled periods, the subject was allowed to select times of sleep and lighting. The result was a sleep rhythm of about 25 hours. Notice how this free-running rhythm began to advance around the clock as they fell asleep later each day. When periods of darkness (shaded area) were imposed during the fifth week, the rhythm quickly resynchronized with 24-hour days. (Adapted from Czeisler, 1981.)*

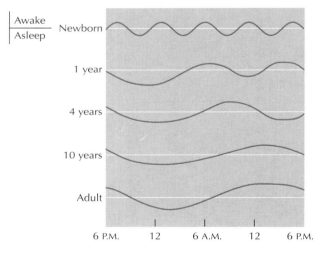

◆ **FIGURE 5.3** *Development of sleep patterns. Short cycles of sleep and waking gradually become the night-day cycle of an adult. While most adults don't take naps, midafternoon sleepiness is a natural part of the sleep cycle. (After Williams et al., 1964.)*

Sleep-deprivation psychosis A major disruption of mental and emotional functioning brought about by sleep loss.

How can I tell how much sleep I really need? Pick a day when you feel well rested. Then sleep that night until you wake without an alarm clock. If you feel rested when you wake up, that's your natural sleep need. If you're sleeping fewer hours than you need, you're building up a sleep debt every day (Maas, 1999).

Severe sleep loss can cause a temporary **sleep-deprivation psychosis** (loss of contact with reality) like Peter Tripp suffered. Confusion, disorientation, delusions, and hallucinations are typical of this reaction. Fortunately, such "crazy" behavior is uncommon. Hallucinations and delusions rarely appear before 60 hours of wakefulness (Naitoh et al., 1989).

Sleep Patterns

Sleep was described as an innate biological rhythm. What does that mean? Daily sleep and waking periods create a variety of sleep patterns. Rhythms of sleep and waking are so steady that they continue for many days, even when clocks and light-dark cycles are removed. However, under such conditions, humans eventually shift to a sleep-waking cycle that averages slightly more than 24 hours (24 hours and 10 minutes, to be exact) (Czeisler et al., 1999). This suggests that external time markers, especially light and dark, help tie our sleep rhythms to days that are exactly 24 hours long (◆Fig. 5.2). Otherwise, many of us would drift into our own unusual sleep cycles (Lavie, 2001).

What is the normal range of sleep? A few individuals can get by on only an hour or two of sleep a night—and feel perfectly fine. However, this is rare. Only 8 percent of the population are *short sleepers,* averaging 5 hours of sleep or less per night. On the other end of the scale we find *long sleepers,* who doze 9 hours or more (and tend to worry a lot during the day) (McCann & Stewin, 1988). The majority of us sleep on a familiar 7- to 8-hour-per-night schedule. For a few people, however, it is quite normal to sleep as little as 5 hours per night or as much as 11. Urging everyone to sleep 8 hours would be like advising everyone to wear medium-size shoes.

Do elderly people need more sleep? Sleep needs actually remain fairly constant as people age. However, older people rarely get the sleep they need. Total sleep time declines throughout life. Those over the age of 50 average only 6 hours of sleep a night. In contrast, infants spend up to 20 hours a day sleeping, usually in 2- to 4-hour cycles.

As they mature, most children go through a "nap" stage and eventually settle into a steady cycle of sleeping once a day (◆Fig. 5.3). Some people, of course, maintain the afternoon "siesta" as an adult pattern. Perhaps we all should: Midafternoon sleepiness is a natural part of the sleep cycle. Brief, well-timed naps can help maintain alertness in people like truck drivers and hospital interns, who often must fight drowsiness (Batejat & Lagarde, 1999).

It is very tempting to try to reduce sleep time. However, people on *shortened* cycles—for example, 3 hours of sleep to 6 hours awake—often can't get to sleep when the cycle calls for it. That's why astronauts continue to sleep on their normal Earth schedule while in space. Adapting to *longer* than normal days is more promising. Such days can be tailored to match natural sleep patterns, which have a ratio of 2 to 1 between time awake and time asleep. For instance, one study showed that 28-hour "days" work for some people. Overall, however, sleep is a "gentle tyrant." Sleep patterns may be bent and stretched, but they rarely yield entirely to human whims (Akerstedt et al., 1993).

STAGES OF SLEEP—THE NIGHTLY ROLLER-COASTER RIDE

] SURVEYQUESTION *Are there different stages of sleep?*

What causes sleep? Early sleep experts thought that something in the bloodstream must cause sleep. But Siamese twins, whose bodies are joined at birth, show that this is false. It's not unusual for one twin to be asleep while the second is awake (◆Fig. 5.4). During waking hours, a **sleep hormone** (sleep-promoting chemical) collects in the brain and spinal cord, *not* in the blood. If this substance is extracted from one animal and injected into another, the second animal will sleep deeply for many hours (Cravatt et al., 1995).

Whether you are awake or asleep right now depends on the *balance* between separate sleep and waking systems. Brain circuits and chemicals in one of the systems promote sleep. A network of brain cells in the other system responds to chemicals that inhibit sleep. The two systems see-saw back and forth, switching the brain between sleep and wakefulness (Lavie, 2001). Note that the brain does not "shut down" during sleep. Rather, the *pattern* of activity changes. The total amount of activity remains fairly constant (Steriade & McCarley, 1990).

◆ **FIGURE 5.4** *These Siamese twins share the same blood supply, yet one sleeps while the other is awake. (Photo by Yale Joel, Life Magazine. © 1954 Time, Inc.)*

Stages of Sleep

How does brain activity change when you fall asleep? The changes that come with sleep can be measured with an **electroencephalograph** (eh-LEK-tro-en-SEF-uh-lo-graf) or **EEG**. The brain generates tiny electrical signals (brain waves) that can be amplified and recorded. When you are awake and alert, the EEG reveals a pattern of small fast waves called **beta** (◆Fig. 5.5). Immediately before sleep, the pattern shifts to larger and slower waves called **alpha**. (Alpha waves also occur when you are relaxed and allow your thoughts to drift.) As the eyes close, breathing becomes slow and regular, the pulse rate slows, and body temperature drops. Soon after, four separate **sleep stages** occur.

Stage 1

As you lose consciousness and enter **light sleep** (stage 1 sleep), your heart rate slows even more. Breathing becomes more irregular. The muscles of your body relax. This may trigger a reflex muscle twitch throughout the body called a *hypnic jerk* (HIP-nik: sleep). (This is

Sleep hormone A sleep-promoting substance found in the brain and spinal cord.
Electroencephalograph (EEG) A device designed to detect, amplify, and record electrical activity in the brain.
Beta waves Small, fast brain waves associated with being awake and alert.
Alpha waves Large, slow brain waves associated with relaxation and falling asleep.
Sleep stages Levels of sleep identified by brain-wave patterns and behavioral changes.
Light sleep Stage 1 sleep, marked by small, irregular brain waves and some alpha waves.

(a)

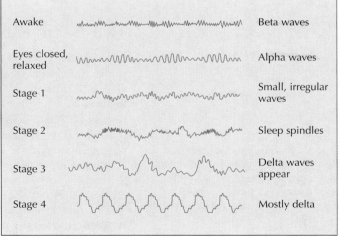
(b)

◆**FIGURE 5.5** (a) *Photograph of an EEG recording session. The man in the background is asleep.* (b) *Changes in brain-wave patterns associated with various stages of sleep. Actually, most wave types are present at all times, but they occur more or less frequently in various sleep stages.*

✦**FIGURE 5.6** (a) *Average proportion of time adults spend daily in REM sleep and NREM sleep. REM periods add up to about 20 percent of total sleep time.* (b) *Typical changes in stages of sleep during the night. Notice that dreams mostly coincide with REM periods.*

quite normal, so have no fear about admitting to your friends that you fell asleep with a hypnic jerk.) In stage 1 sleep the EEG is made up mainly of small, irregular waves with some alpha. Persons awakened at this time may or may not say they were asleep.

Stage 2

As sleep deepens, body temperature drops further. Also, the EEG begins to include **sleep spindles,** which are short bursts of distinctive brain-wave activity. Spindles seem to mark the true boundary of sleep. Within 4 minutes after spindles appear, most people will say they were asleep.

Stage 3

In stage 3, a new brain wave called delta begins to appear. **Delta waves** are very large and slow. They signal a move to deeper sleep and a further loss of consciousness.

Stage 4

Most people reach **deep sleep** (the deepest level of normal sleep) in about an hour. Stage 4 brain waves are almost pure delta, and the sleeper is in a state of oblivion. If you make a loud noise during stage 4, the sleeper will wake up in a state of confusion and may not remember the noise. After spending some time in stage 4, the sleeper returns (through stages 3 and 2) to stage 1. Further shifts between deeper and lighter sleep occur throughout the night (✦Fig. 5.6).

Two Basic Kinds of Sleep

If you watch a person sleep, you will soon notice that the sleeper's eyes occasionally move under the eyelids. These **rapid eye movements** (or **REMs**) are associated with dreaming (Fig. 5.6). Roughly 85 percent of the time, people awakened during REMs report vivid dreams. In addition to rapid eye movements, **REM sleep** is marked by a return to fast, irregular EEG patterns similar to stage 1 sleep. In fact, the brain is so active during REM sleep that it looks as if the person is awake (Hobson et al., 1998). REM sleep is easy to observe in pets, such as dogs and cats. Watch for eye and face movements and irregular breathing. (You can forget about your pet iguana, though. Reptiles show no signs of REM sleep.)

REM and NREM Sleep

The two most basic states of sleep are REM sleep with its associated dreaming and **non-REM** (**NREM**) **sleep,** which occurs during stages 1, 2, 3, and 4 (Jouvet, 1999). NREM sleep is dream free about 90 percent of the time. Your first period of stage 1 sleep usually lacks REMs and dreams. Each later return to stage 1 is usually accompanied by rapid eye movements. Dreams during REM sleep tend to be longer, clearer, more detailed, more bizarre, and more "dream-like" than thoughts and images that occur in NREM sleep (Hobson, Pace-Schott, & Stickgold, 2000). Also, brain areas associated with imagery and emotion become

Sleep spindles Distinctive bursts of brain-wave activity that indicate a person is asleep.

Delta waves Large, slow brain waves that occur in deeper sleep (stages 3 and 4).

Deep sleep Stage 4 sleep; the deepest form of normal sleep.

Rapid eye movements (REMs) Swift eye movements during sleep.

REM sleep Sleep marked by rapid eye movements and a return to stage 1 EEG patterns.

NREM sleep Non-rapid eye movement sleep characteristic of stages 2, 3, and 4.

more active during REM sleep. This may explain why REM dreams tend to be more vivid than NREM dreams (Braun, Balkin, & Herscovitch, 1998).

What is the function of NREM sleep?   NREM sleep increases after physical exertion. This suggests that it helps us recover from bodily fatigue. In comparison, daytime stress tends to increase REM sleep. REM sleep totals only about 90 minutes per night (about the same as a feature movie). Yet, its link with dreaming makes it as important as NREM sleep. REM sleep may rise dramatically when there is a death in the family, trouble at work, a marital conflict, or other emotionally charged events.

Dreaming

What happens to the body when a person dreams?   REM sleep is a time of high emotion. The heart beats irregularly. Blood pressure and breathing waver. Both males and females appear to be sexually aroused: Males usually have an erection, and genital blood flow increases in women. This occurs for all REM sleep, so it is not strictly related to erotic dreams (Jouvet, 1999).

During REM sleep your body becomes quite still, as if you were paralyzed. Imagine acting out some of your recent dreams. Very likely, REM-sleep paralysis prevents some hilarious—and even dangerous—nighttime escapades. A lack of muscle paralysis during REM sleep is called *REM behavior disorder.* People with this problem may thrash violently, leap out of bed, or attack their bed partners. One patient tied himself to his bed every night. That way, he couldn't jump up and crash into furniture or walls (Shafton, 1995).

In a moment, we will survey some additional sleep problems—if you are still awake. First, here are a few questions to check your memory of our discussion so far.

STUDYBREAK **Y** *Altered States and Sleep*

RELATE

Make a quick list of some altered states of consciousness you have experienced. What do they have in common? How are they different? What conditions caused them?

Imagine that you are a counselor at a sleep clinic. You must explain the basics of sleep and dreaming to a new client who knows little about these topics. Can you do it?

LEARNING CHECK

1. Altered states of consciousness are defined mainly by changes in patterns of alertness. T or F?
2. A momentary shift in brain activity to a pattern characteristic of sleep is referred to as
   a. delta sleep b. light sleep c. microsleep
   d. deprivation sleep

3. Delusions and hallucinations typically continue for several days after a sleep-deprived individual returns to normal sleep. T or F?
4. Older adults, and particularly the elderly, sleep more than children do because the elderly are more easily fatigued. T or F?
5. Most studies of sleep patterns show a consistent ratio of 2 to 1 between time awake and time asleep. T or F?
6. Rapid eye movements (REMs) indicate that a person is in deep sleep. T or F?
7. Alpha waves are to presleep drowsiness as _____ _____ are to stage 4 sleep.

Critical Thinking

8. Why might it be better for the unscheduled human sleep-waking cycle to average more than 24 hours, instead of less?
9. Biologically, what advantages might sleeping provide?

ANSWERS

1. F 2. c 3. F 4. F 5. F 6. T 7. delta waves 8. Sleep experts theorize that the 25-hour average leaves a little "slack" in the cycle. External time markers can then retard the bodily cycle slightly to synchronize it with light-dark cycles. If the bodily cycle were shorter than 24 hours, we might all have to "stretch" every day to adjust. 9. Lowering bodily activity and metabolism during sleep may help conserve energy and lengthen life. Also, natural selection may have favored sleep because animals that remained active at night probably had a higher chance of being killed. (I'll bet they had more fun, though.)

SLEEP DISTURBANCES—SHOWING NIGHTLY: SLEEP WARS!

] SURVEYQUESTION *What are the causes of sleep disorders and unusual sleep events?*

Sleep quality has taken a beating in North America. Artificial lighting, frenetic schedules, exciting pastimes, smoking, drinking, over-stimulation, and many other factors have contributed to a near epidemic of sleep problems. Sleep disturbances are a serious risk to health and happiness. Sleep clinics treat thousands of people each year who suffer from sleep dis-

▲ *TABLE 5.1*	**Sleep Disturbances—Things That Go Wrong in the Night**

HYPERSOMNIA Excessive daytime sleepiness. This can result from depression, insomnia, narcolepsy, sleep apnea, sleep drunkenness (a very slow transition to waking), periodic limb movements, drug abuse, and other problems.

INSOMNIA Difficulty in getting to sleep or staying asleep; also, not feeling rested after sleeping.

NARCOLEPSY Sudden, irresistible, daytime sleep attacks that may last anywhere from a few minutes to a half hour. Victims may fall asleep while standing, talking, or even driving.

NIGHTMARE DISORDER Vivid, recurrent nightmares that significantly disturb sleep.

PERIODIC LIMB MOVEMENT SYNDROME Muscle twitches (primarily affecting the legs) that occur every 20 to 40 seconds and severely disturb sleep.

REM BEHAVIOR DISORDER A failure of normal muscle paralysis, leading to violent actions during REM sleep.

RESTLESS LEGS SYNDROME An irresistible urge to move the legs in order to relieve sensations of creeping, tingling, prickling, aching, or tension.

SLEEP APNEA During sleep, breathing stops for 20 seconds or more until the person wakes a little, gulps in air, and settles back to sleep; this cycle may be repeated hundreds of times per night.

SLEEP DRUNKENNESS A slow transition to clear consciousness after awakening; sometimes associated with irritable or aggressive behavior.

SLEEP TERROR DISORDER The repeated occurrence of night terrors that significantly disturb sleep.

SLEEP-WAKE SCHEDULE DISORDER A mismatch between the sleep-wake schedule demanded by a person's bodily rhythm and that demanded by the environment.

SLEEPWALKING DISORDER Repeated incidents of leaving bed and walking about while asleep.

(Bond & Wooten, 1996; DSM-IV-TR, 2000; Hauri & Linde, 1990.)

orders or complaints. (See ▲ Table 5.1.) Let's explore some of the more interesting problems these people face, starting with insomnia.

Insomnia

Staring at the ceiling at 2 AM is pretty low on most people's list of favorite pastimes. Yet, about 30 percent of all adults have had insomnia. Roughly 9 percent have a serious or chronic problem. **Insomnia** includes difficulty in going to sleep, frequent nighttime awakenings, waking too early, or a combination of these problems. Insomnia can harm people's work, health, and relationships (Walsh & Uestuen, 1999).

The citizens of North America will spend well over one-half billion dollars this year on sleeping pills. There is real irony in this expense. Nonprescription sleeping pills such as *Sominex, Nytol,* and *Sleep-Eze* have little sleep-inducing effect. Even worse are barbiturates. These prescription sedatives decrease both stage 4 sleep and REM sleep, drastically lowering sleep quality. In addition, many users become "sleeping-pill junkies" who need an ever-greater number of pills to get to sleep. The end result is *drug-dependency insomnia* (sleep loss caused by withdrawal from sleeping pills). Victims must be painstakingly weaned from their sleep medicines. Otherwise, terrible nightmares and "rebound insomnia" may drive them back to drug use. It's worth remembering that although alcohol and other depressant drugs may help a person get to sleep, they greatly reduce sleep quality (Lobo & Tufik, 1997).

If sleeping pills are a poor way to treat insomnia, what can be done? Sleep specialists now prefer to treat insomnia with lifestyle changes and behavioral techniques, like those described in "Behavioral Remedies for Insomnia" (Walsh & Scweitzer, 1999).

Types and Causes of Insomnia

Worry, stress, and excitement can cause temporary insomnia and a self-defeating cycle. First, excess mental activity ("I can't stop turning things over in my mind") and heightened arousal block sleep. Then, frustration and anger over not being able to sleep cause more worry and arousal. This further delays sleep, which causes more frustration, and so on (Espie, 2002). A good way to beat this cycle is to avoid fighting it. It is usually best to get up

Insomnia Difficulty in getting to sleep or staying asleep.

Behavioral Remedies for Insomnia

All of the approaches discussed here are helpful for treating insomnia (Hopson, 1986). Experiment a little and find out what works for you. Of the methods listed, sleep restriction and stimulus control are the most effective (Chesson et al., 1999).

STIMULANTS

Avoid stimulants such as coffee and cigarettes. Also remember that alcohol, while not a stimulant, impairs sleep quality.

WORRIES

Schedule time in the early evening to write down worries or concerns. Plan what you will do about them the next day. Then put them out of mind until morning.

RELAXATION

Learn a physical or mental strategy for relaxing, such as progressive muscle relaxation (see Chapter 17), meditation, or blotting out worries with calming images. Strenuous exercise during the day promotes sleep. It is best if done about 6 hours before bedtime (Maas, 1999). Exercise in the evening is helpful only if it is very light.

SLEEP RESTRICTION

Even if you miss an entire night's sleep, do not sleep late in the morning, nap more than an hour, sleep during the evening, or go to bed early the following night. Try to restrict sleep to your normal bedtime hours. That way, you will avoid fragmenting your sleep rhythms (Lacks & Morin, 1992).

STIMULUS CONTROL

Link only sleep with your bedroom so that it does not trigger worrying: (1) Go to bed only when you are feeling sleepy. (2) Awaken at the same time each morning. (3) Avoid non-sleep activities in bed. (4) Always leave the bedroom if sleep has not occurred within 10 minutes. (5) Do something else when you are upset about not being able to sleep (Bootzin & Epstein, 2000).

PARADOXICAL INTENTION

To remove the pressures of trying to get to sleep, try instead to keep your eyes open (in the dark) and stay awake as long as possible (Horvath & Goheen, 1990). This allows sleep to overtake you unexpectedly and lowers performance anxiety. Never try to go to sleep. Arrange to let it happen (Espie, 2002).

and do something useful or satisfying when you have difficulty sleeping. (Reading a textbook might be a good choice of useful activities.) Return to bed only when you begin to feel that you are struggling to stay awake.

What you eat can also affect how easily you get to sleep. Eating starchy foods increases the amount of *tryptophan* (TRIP-tuh-fan: an amino acid) reaching the brain. More tryptophan, in turn, increases the amount of serotonin in the brain. Serotonin is associated with relaxation, a positive mood, and sleepiness. Thus, to promote sleep, try eating a snack that is nearly all starch. Good sleep-inducing snacks are cookies, bread, pasta, oatmeal, pretzels, bagels, and dry cereal. If you really want to drop the bomb on insomnia, try eating a baked potato (which may be the world's largest sleeping pill!) (Sahelian, 1998).

What about more serious cases of insomnia? Chronic insomnia exists if sleeping problems last for more than 3 weeks. Treatment for chronic insomnia usually begins with a careful analysis of a patient's sleep habits, lifestyle, stress levels, and medical problems. The first thing patients should do is consume less caffeine, alcohol, and tobacco. Some insomniacs use relaxation training to lower arousal before sleep. Stimulus control strategies also help. **Stimulus control** refers to linking a response with specific stimuli. For example, patients are told to avoid doing anything but sleeping when they are in bed. They are not to study, eat, watch TV, read, pay the bills, worry, or even think in bed. (Lovemaking is okay, however.) In this way, only sleeping and relaxation become associated with going to bed (Bootzin & Epstein, 2000).

One of the best ways to combat insomnia is also the simplest. Many insomniacs have scattered sleep habits. For these people, adopting a regular schedule helps establish a firm body rhythm, greatly improving sleep. Patients are told to get up and go to sleep at the same time each day, including weekends (Bootzin & Epstein, 2000). (As noted earlier regarding adolescent sleep loss, many people upset their sleep rhythms by staying up late on weekends.) (Again, see "Behavioral Remedies for Insomnia.")

Sleepwalking and Sleeptalking

Sleepwalking is eerie and fascinating. **Somnambulists** (som-NAM-bue-lists: those who sleepwalk) avoid obstacles, descend stairways, and on rare occasions may step out of windows or in front of automobiles. The sleepwalker's eyes are usually open, but a blank face and shuffling feet reveal that the person is still asleep. A parent who finds a child sleepwalk-

Stimulus control Linking a particular response with specific stimuli.
Somnambulism Sleepwalking; occurs during NREM sleep.

ing should gently guide the child back to bed. Awakening a sleepwalker does no harm, but it is not necessary.

Does sleepwalking occur during dreaming?   No. Remember that people are normally immobilized during REM sleep. EEG studies have shown that somnambulism occurs during NREM stages 3 and 4. **Sleeptalking** also occurs mostly in NREM stages of sleep. The link with deep sleep explains why sleeptalking makes little sense and why sleepwalkers are confused and remember little when awakened (DSM-IV-TR, 2000).

Nightmares and Night Terrors

Stage 4 sleep is also the realm of night terrors. These frightening episodes are quite different from ordinary nightmares. A **nightmare** is simply a bad dream that takes place during REM sleep. Nightmares, which occur about twice a month, are usually brief and easily remembered (Wood & Bootzin, 1990). During stage 4 **night terrors,** a person suffers total panic and may hallucinate frightening dream images into the bedroom. An attack may last 15 or 20 minutes. When it is over, the person awakens drenched in sweat but only vaguely remembers the terror. Since night terrors occur during NREM sleep (when the body is not immobilized), victims may sit up, scream, get out of bed, or run around the room. Victims remember little afterward. (Other family members, however, may have a story to tell.) Night terrors are most common in childhood, but they continue to plague about 2 out of every 100 adults (Ohayon et al., 1999).

How to Eliminate a Nightmare

Is there any way to stop a recurring nightmare?   A bad nightmare can be worse than any horror movie. You can leave a theater, but we often remain trapped in terrifying dreams. Nevertheless, most nightmares can be banished by following three simple steps. First, write down your nightmare, describing it in detail. Next, change the dream any way you wish, being sure to spell out the details of the new dream. The third step is *imagery rehearsal,* in which you mentally rehearse the changed dream before you fall asleep again (Krakow & Neidhardt, 1992). Imagery rehearsal may work because it makes upsetting dreams familiar while a person is awake and feeling safe. Or perhaps it mentally "re-programs" future dream content. In any case, the technique has helped many people (Krakow et al., 1996).

Sleep Apnea

Some sage once said, "Laugh and the whole world laughs with you; snore and you sleep alone." Nightly "wood sawing" is often harmless, but it can signal a serious problem. A person who snores loudly, with short silences and loud gasps or snorts, may suffer from apnea (AP-nee-ah: interrupted breathing). In **sleep apnea,** breathing stops for periods of 20 seconds to 2 minutes. As the need for oxygen becomes intense, the person wakes a little and gulps in air. She or he then settles back to sleep. But soon, breathing stops again. This cycle is repeated hundreds of times a night. As you might guess, apnea victims are extremely sleepy during the day (DSM-IV-TR, 2000).

What causes sleep apnea?   Some cases occur because the brain stops sending signals to the diaphragm to maintain breathing. Another cause is blockage of the upper air passages. Anyone who snores loudly should seek treatment at a sleep clinic (Koenig, 1996).

SIDS

Sleep apnea is suspected as one cause of **sudden infant death syndrome** (**SIDS**), or "crib death." Each year 1 out of every 500 babies is a victim of SIDS. In the "typical" crib death, a slightly premature or small baby with some signs of a cold or cough is bundled up and put to bed. A short time later, parents find the child has died. A baby deprived of air will normally struggle to begin breathing again. However, SIDS babies seem to have a weak arousal reflex. This prevents them from changing positions and resuming breathing after an episode of apnea (Horne et al., 2001).

Sleeptalking Speaking that occurs during NREM sleep.

Nightmare A bad dream that occurs during REM sleep.

Night terror A state of panic during NREM sleep.

Sleep apnea Repeated interruption of breathing during sleep.

Sudden infant death syndrome (SIDS) The sudden, unexplained death of an apparently healthy infant.

Babies at risk for SIDS must be carefully watched for the first 6 months of life. To aid parents in this task, a special monitor may be used that sounds an alarm when breathing or pulse becomes weak (✦Fig. 5.7). The list that follows gives some danger signals for SIDS.

- The mother is a teenager.
- The baby is premature.
- The baby has a shrill, high-pitched cry.
- The baby engages in "snoring," breath-holding, or frequent awakening at night.
- The baby breathes mainly through an open mouth.
- The baby remains passive when its face rolls into a pillow or blanket.
- The baby's bed contains soft objects such as pillows, quilts, comforters, or sheepskins.
- Parents or other adults in the home are smokers.

"Back to Sleep"

Pop quiz: Should babies be placed face down or face up in bed? Sleeping position is another major risk factor for SIDS. Healthy infants are better off sleeping on their backs or sides. (Premature babies, those with respiratory problems, and those who often vomit may need to sleep face down. Ask a pediatrician for guidance.) At least one third of all SIDS cases involve babies who were placed face down. Remember, "*back* to sleep" is the safest position for most infants (Hauck et al., 2002).

✦**FIGURE 5.7** *Infants at risk for SIDS are often attached to devices that monitor breathing and heart rate during sleep. An alarm sounds to alert parents if either pulse or respiration falters. SIDS rarely occurs after an infant is 1 year old. Babies at risk for SIDS should be placed on their sides or on their backs. (Photo courtesy of Healthdyne, Inc.)*

DREAMS—A SEPARATE REALITY?

] **SURVEYQUESTION** *Do dreams have meaning?*

When REM sleep was discovered in 1952, it ushered in a "Golden Era" of dream inquiry. To conclude our discussion of sleep, let's consider some age-old questions about dreaming.

Does everyone dream? Do dreams occur in an instant? Most people dream four or five times a night, but not all people remember their dreams. "Non-dreamers" are often surprised by their dreams when first awakened during REM sleep. Dreams are usually spaced about 90 minutes apart. The first dream lasts only about 10 minutes; the last averages 30 minutes and may run as long as 50. Dreams, therefore, occur in real time, not as a "flash" (Shafton, 1995).

REM Sleep Revisited

How important is REM sleep? Is it essential for normal functioning? To answer these questions, sleep expert William Dement awakened volunteers each time they entered REM sleep. Soon, their need for "dream time" grew more urgent. By the fifth night, many had to be awakened 20 or 30 times to prevent REM sleep. When the volunteers were finally allowed to sleep undisturbed, they dreamed extra amounts. This effect, called a **REM rebound,** explains why alcoholics have horrible nightmares after they quit drinking. Alcohol suppresses REM sleep and sets up a powerful rebound when it is withdrawn. It's worth remembering that while alcohol and other depressant drugs may help a person get to sleep, they greatly reduce sleep quality (Lobo & Tufik, 1997).

Dement's volunteers complained of memory lapses, poor concentration, and daytime anxiety. For a while, it was thought that people deprived of REM sleep might go crazy. But this is now known as the "REM myth." Later experiments showed that missing *any* sleep stage can cause a rebound for that stage. In general, daytime disturbances are related to the *total amount* of sleep lost, not to the *type* of sleep lost (Devoto et al., 1999).

Dr. John Herman of the University of Texas may look like he just stepped out of the movie *Star Wars,* but he is actually involved in dream research. Dr. Herman is wearing goggles that electronically monitor eye movements during sleep. Use of such devices has greatly extended our understanding of dreaming.

REM rebound The occurrence of extra rapid eye movement sleep following REM sleep deprivation.

Functions of REM Sleep

What then, is the purpose of REM sleep? Early in life, REM sleep may stimulate the developing brain. Newborn babies spend a hearty 8 or 9 hours a day in REM sleep. That's about 50 percent of their total sleep time. In adulthood, REM sleep may prevent sensory deprivation during sleep, and it may help us process emotional events. REM sleep also seems to help us sort and integrate memories, especially memories about strategies that help us solve problems (Stickgold et al., 2001). Speaking very loosely, it's as if the dreaming brain were reviewing messages left on a telephone answering machine, to decide which are worth keeping. During the day, when information is streaming in, the brain may be too busy to efficiently select useful memories. When the conscious brain is "off-line" we are better able to build new memories. Although we have much to learn, it's clear that REM sleep and dreaming are valuable for keeping the brain in good working order (Stickgold et al., 2001).

Dream Worlds

Calvin Hall, a noted dream expert, collected and analyzed over 10,000 dreams (Hall, 1966; Hall et al., 1982). Hall found that most dreams reflect everyday events. The favorite dream setting is a familiar room in a house. Action usually takes place between the dreamer and two or three other emotionally important people—friends, enemies, parents, or employers. Dream actions are also mostly familiar: running, jumping, riding, sitting, talking, and watching. About half of all dreams have sexual elements. Dreams of flying, floating, and falling occur less frequently.

What kinds of emotions are most typical in dreams? If you ask people in the morning what they dreamed about, they mention more unpleasant emotions than pleasant emotions (Merritt et al., 1994). However, it may be that dreams of fear, anger, or sadness are easier to remember. When people are awakened during REM sleep, they report equal numbers of positive and negative emotions (Fosse, Stickgold, & Hobson, 2001).

Dream Theories

How meaningful are dreams? Most theorists agree that dreams reflect our waking thoughts, fantasies, and emotions (Cartwright & Lamberg, 1992; Domhoff, 1999). Thus, the real question might be, How deep should we dig in interpreting dreams? Some theorists believe that dreams have deeply hidden meanings. Others regard dreams as no more meaningful than ordinary thinking. Let's examine both views.

Psychodynamic Dream Theory

Sigmund Freud's landmark book, *The Interpretation of Dreams* (1900), first advanced the idea that many dreams are based on *wish fulfillment* (an expression of unconscious desires). Thus, a student who is angry at a teacher might dream of embarrassing the teacher in class; a lonely person may dream of romance; or a hungry child may dream of food.

Freud's **psychodynamic theory** of dreaming emphasizes internal conflicts and unconscious forces. While many of his ideas may seem persuasive, there is evidence against them. For example, volunteers in a study of starvation showed no particular increase in dreams about food and eating. In general, dreams show few signs of directly expressing hidden wishes (Fischer & Greenberg, 1996).

Freud's response to critics, no doubt, would have been that dreams rarely express needs so directly. Freud believed that dreams express unconscious desires and conflicts as disguised **dream symbols** (images that have deeper symbolic meaning) (Globus, 1987). For instance, death might be symbolized by a journey, children by small animals, or sexual intercourse by horseback riding or dancing. Similarly, a woman sexually attracted to her best friend's husband might dream of taking her friend's wedding ring and placing it on her own hand, an indirect symbol of her true desires.

Do all dreams have hidden meanings? Probably not. Even Freud realized that some dreams are trivial "day residues" or carryovers from ordinary waking events. On the other hand, dreams do tend to reflect a person's current concerns, so Freud wasn't entirely wrong (Nikles et al., 1998).

According to Freudian theory, dream imagery often has symbolic meaning. How would you interpret this dream-like image? The fact that dreams don't have a single unambiguous meaning is one of the shortcomings of Freudian dream theory. (Painting by French artist Rene Magritte.)

AKG Berlin/SuperStock

Psychodynamic theory Any theory of behavior that emphasizes internal conflicts, motives, and unconscious forces.

Dream symbols Images in dreams that serve as visible signs of hidden ideas, desires, impulses, emotions, relationships, and so forth.

The Activation-Synthesis Hypothesis

Psychiatrists Allan Hobson and Robert McCarley have a radically different view of dreaming. Hobson and McCarley believe that dreams are made in this way: During REM sleep, brain cells are activated that normally control eye movements, balance, and actions. However, messages from the cells are blocked from reaching the body, so no movement occurs. Nevertheless, the cells continue to tell higher brain areas of their activities. Struggling to interpret this information, the brain searches through stored memories and manufactures a dream (Hobson, 1999).

How does that help explain dream content?   Let's use the classic chase dream as an example. In such dreams we feel we are running but not going anywhere. This occurs because the brain is told the body is running, but it gets no feedback from the motionless legs. To make sense of this information, the brain creates a chase drama. A similar process probably explains dreams of floating or flying.

Hobson and McCarley call their view of dreaming the **activation-synthesis hypothesis.** Hobson explains that several parts of the brain are "turned on" (activated) during REM sleep. This triggers sensations, motor commands, and memories. The cortex of the brain, which also becomes more active during REM sleep, synthesizes this activity into stories and visual images. However, frontal areas of the cortex, which control higher mental abilities, are mostly shut down during REM sleep. This explains why dreams are more primitive and more bizarre than daytime thoughts (Hobson, 1999). Viewed this way, dreams are merely a different type of thinking that occurs during sleep (McCarley, 1998).

Then does the activation-synthesis hypothesis rule out the idea that dreams have meaning?   No, because dreams are created from memories and past experiences, they can tell us quite a lot about each person's mental life, emotions, and concerns (Hobson, 1999). However, many psychologists continue to believe that dreams have deeper meaning (Cartwright & Lamberg, 1992; Globus, 1987; Shafton, 1995).

There seems to be little doubt that dreams can make a difference in our lives: Veteran sleep researcher William Dement once dreamed that he had lung cancer. In the dream, a doctor told Dement he would die soon. At the time, Dement was smoking two packs of cigarettes a day. He says, "I will never forget the surprise, joy, and exquisite relief of waking up. I felt reborn." Dement quit smoking the following day. (For more information about dreaming, see Psychology in Action, later in this chapter.)

Activation-synthesis hypothesis An attempt to explain how dream content is affected by motor commands in the brain that occur during sleep, but are not carried out.

STUDYBREAK *Sleep Disturbances and Dreaming*

RELATE

Almost everyone suffers from insomnia at least occasionally. Are any of the techniques for combating insomnia similar to strategies you have discovered on your own?

How many sleep disturbances can you name (including those listed in Table 5.1)? Are there any that you have experienced? Which do you think would be most disruptive?

Do you think the activation-synthesis theory provides an adequate explanation of your own dreams? Have you had dreams that seem to reflect Freudian wish fulfillment? Do you think your dreams have symbolic meaning?

LEARNING CHECK

1. Night terrors, sleepwalking, and sleeptalking all occur during stage 1, NREM sleep. T or F?
2. Sleep _____ is suspected as one cause of SIDS.
3. Which of the following is *not* a behavioral remedy for insomnia?
   a. daily hypersomnia   b. stimulus control   c. progressive relaxation   d. paradoxical intention

4. The favored setting for dreams is
   a. work   b. school   c. outdoors or unfamiliar places
   d. familiar rooms
5. People generally report that unpleasant emotions such as fear, anger, and sadness occur more frequently in their dreams than pleasant emotions. T or F?
6. According to the activation-synthesis model of dreaming, dreams are constructed from _____ to explain messages received from nerve cells controlling eye movement, balance, and bodily activity.
7. REM sleep seems to contribute to the formation of _____ that aid survival or coping.

Critical Thinking

8. Even without being told that somnambulism is an NREM event, you could have predicted that sleepwalking doesn't occur during dreaming. Why?

ANSWERS

1. F 2. apnea 3. a 4. c 5. T 6. T 7. memories 8. Because people are immobilized during REM sleep and REM sleep is strongly associated with dreaming. This makes it unlikely that sleepwalkers are acting out dreams.

HYPNOSIS—LOOK INTO MY EYES

] SURVEYQUESTION *How is hypnosis done, and what are its limitations?*

"Your body is becoming heavy. You can barely keep your eyes open. You are so tired you can't move. Relax. Let go. Relax. Close your eyes and relax." These are the last words a textbook should ever say to you, and the first a hypnotist might say.

Hypnosis is an altered state of consciousness, characterized by narrowed attention and an increased openness to suggestion (Kosslyn et al., 2000). Not all psychologists accept this definition. To them, hypnosis is merely a blend of conformity, relaxation, imagination, obedience, suggestion, and role-playing (Braffman & Kirsch, 1999). Either way, hypnosis can be explained by normal principles. It is not mysterious or "magical."

Interest in hypnosis began in the 1700s with Franz Mesmer, whose name gave us the term *mesmerize* (to hypnotize). Mesmer, an Austrian physician, believed he could cure disease with magnets. Mesmer's strange "treatments" are related to hypnosis because they were actually based on the power of suggestion, not magnetism. For a time, Mesmer enjoyed quite a following. In the end, however, his theories of "animal magnetism" were rejected and he was recognized as a fraud.

The term *hypnosis* was coined by an English surgeon named James Braid. The Greek word *hypnos* means "sleep," and Braid used it to describe the hypnotic state. Today we know that hypnosis is *not* sleep. Confusion about this point remains because some hypnotists give the suggestion, "Sleep, sleep." However, EEG records made during hypnosis differ from those seen when a person is asleep or pretending to be hypnotized (Barabasz, 2000).

Hypnotic Susceptibility

Can everyone be hypnotized?   About 8 people out of 10 can be hypnotized, but only 4 out of 10 will be good hypnotic subjects. People who are imaginative and prone to fantasy are often highly responsive to hypnosis (Silva & Kirsch, 1992). But people who lack these traits may also be hypnotized. If you are willing to be hypnotized, chances are good that you could be. Hypnosis depends more on the efforts and abilities of the hypnotized person than the skills of the hypnotist (Kirsch & Lynn, 1995). But make no mistake, people who are hypnotized are not merely faking their responses (Perugini et al., 1998).

Hypnotic susceptibility refers to how easily a person can become hypnotized. It can be measured by giving a series of suggestions and counting the number to which a person responds. A typical hypnotic test is the *Stanford Hypnotic Susceptibility Scale* shown in ▲ Table 5.2. In the test, various suggestions are made to see if a person responds to them. For instance, you might be told that your left arm is becoming more and more rigid and that it

▲*TABLE 5.2*	**Stanford Hypnotic Susceptibility Scale**
SUGGESTED BEHAVIOR	**CRITERION OF PASSING**
1. Postural sway	Falls without forcing
2. Eye closure	Closes eyes without forcing
3. Hand lowering (left)	Lowers at least 6 inches by end of 10 seconds
4. Immobilization (right arm)	Arm rises less than 1 inch in 10 seconds
5. Finger lock	Incomplete separation of fingers at end of 10 seconds
6. Arm rigidity (left arm)	Less than 2 inches of arm bending in 10 seconds
7. Hands moving together	Hands at least as close as 6 inches after 10 seconds
8. Verbal inhibition (name)	Name unspoken in 10 seconds
9. Hallucination (fly)	Any movement, grimacing, acknowledgment of effect
10. Eye catalepsy	Eyes remain closed at end of 10 seconds
11. Posthypnotic (changes chairs)	Any partial movement response
12. Amnesia test	Three or fewer items recalled

Adapted from Weitzenhoffer & Hilgard, 1959.

Hypnosis An altered state of consciousness characterized by narrowed attention and increased suggestibility.

Hypnotic susceptibility One's capacity for becoming hypnotized.

◆FIGURE 5.8 *In one test of hypnotizability, subjects attempt to pull their hands apart after hearing suggestions that their fingers are "locked" together.*

will not bend. If you can't bend your arm during the next 10 seconds, you have shown a degree of susceptibility to hypnotic suggestions. (Also see ◆Figure 5.8.) If you were to score high on the scale today, you probably would do the same years from now. Hypnotizability is very stable over time (Piccione et al., 1989).

Inducing Hypnosis

How is hypnosis done? Could I be hypnotized against my will? Hypnotists use many different methods. Still, all techniques encourage a person (1) to focus attention on what is being said, (2) to relax and feel tired, (3) to "let go" and accept suggestions easily, and (4) to use vivid imagination (Druckman & Bjork, 1994). Basically, you must cooperate to become hypnotized. Many theorists believe that all hypnosis is really self-hypnosis (autosuggestion). From this perspective, a hypnotist merely helps another person to follow a series of suggestions. These suggestions, in turn, alter sensations, perceptions, thoughts, feelings, and behaviors (Druckman & Bjork, 1994; Kirsch & Lynn, 1995).

What does it feel like to be hypnotized? You might be surprised at some of your actions during hypnosis. You also might have mild feelings of floating, sinking, anesthesia, or separation from your body. Personal experiences vary widely. A key element in hypnosis is the **basic suggestion effect** (a tendency of hypnotized persons to carry out suggested actions as if they were involuntary). Hypnotized persons feel like their actions and experiences are *automatic*—they seem to happen without effort (Kihlstrom, 1985). Here is how one person described his hypnotic session:

> I felt lethargic, my eyes going out of focus and wanting to close. My hands felt real light. . . . I felt I was sinking deeper into the chair. . . . I felt like I wanted to relax more and more. . . . My responses were more automatic. I didn't have to *wish* to do things so much or *want* to do them. . . . I just did them. . . . I felt floating . . . very close to sleep (Hilgard, 1968).

Contrary to the way hypnosis is portrayed in movies, hypnotized people generally remain in control of their behavior and aware of what is going on. For instance, most people will not act out hypnotic suggestions that they consider immoral or repulsive (such as disrobing in public or harming someone) (Kirsch & Lynn, 1995).

Effects of Hypnosis

What can (and cannot) be achieved with hypnosis? Many abilities have been tested during hypnosis, leading to the following conclusions (Burgess & Kirsch, 1999; Kihlstrom, 1985; Kirsch & Lynn, 1995):

1. **Superhuman acts of strength.** Hypnosis has no more effect on physical strength than instructions that encourage a person to make his or her best effort.
2. **Memory.** There is some evidence that hypnosis can enhance memory. However, it frequently increases the number of false memories as well. For this reason, many states now bar persons from testifying in court if they were hypnotized to improve their memory of a crime they witnessed.

Basic suggestion effect The tendency of hypnotized persons to carry out suggested actions as if they were involuntary.

3. **Amnesia.** A person told not to remember something heard during hypnosis may claim not to remember. In some instances this may be nothing more than a deliberate attempt to avoid thinking about specific ideas. However, brief memory loss of this type actually does seem to occur (Bowers & Woody, 1996).

4. **Pain relief.** Hypnosis can relieve pain (Mauer et al., 1999). It can be especially useful when chemical painkillers are ineffective. For instance, hypnosis can reduce phantom limb pain (Oakley, Whitman, & Halligan, 2002). (Amputees sometimes feel phantom pain that seems to come from a missing limb.)

5. **Age regression.** Given the proper suggestions, some hypnotized people appear to "regress" to childhood. However, most theorists now believe that "age-regressed" subjects are only acting out a suggested role.

6. **Sensory changes.** Hypnotic suggestions concerning sensations are among the most effective. Given the proper instructions, a person can be made to smell a small bottle of ammonia and respond as if it were a wonderful perfume. It is also possible to alter color vision, hearing sensitivity, time sense, perception of illusions, and many other sensory responses.

Hypnosis is a valuable tool. It can help people relax, feel less pain, and make better progress in therapy (Kirsch, Montgomery, & Sapirstein, 1995). Generally, hypnosis is more successful at changing subjective experience than it is at modifying behaviors such as smoking or overeating. In short, hypnotic effects are useful but seldom amazing (Druckman & Bjork, 1994; Gibson & Heap, 1991).

Stage Hypnosis

On stage the hypnotist intones, "When I count to three, you will imagine that you are on a train to Disneyland and growing younger and younger as the train approaches." Responding to these suggestions, grown men and women begin to giggle and squirm like children on their way to a circus.

How do stage entertainers use hypnosis to get people to do strange things?   They don't. Little or no hypnosis is needed to do a good hypnosis act. **Stage hypnosis** is often merely a simulation of hypnotic effects. T. X. Barber, an authority on hypnosis, says that stage hypnotists make use of several features of the stage setting to perform their act (Barber, 1970).

1. **Waking suggestibility.** We are all more or less open to suggestion, but on stage people are unusually cooperative because they don't want to "spoil the act." As a result, they will readily follow almost any instruction given by the entertainer.

2. **Selection of responsive subjects.** Participants in stage hypnotism (all *volunteers*) are first "hypnotized" as a group. Thus, anyone who doesn't yield to instructions is eliminated.

3. **The hypnosis label disinhibits.** Once a person has been labeled "hypnotized," she or he can sing, dance, act silly, or whatever without fear or embarrassment. On stage, being "hypnotized" takes away personal responsibility for one's actions.

4. **The hypnotist as a "director."** After volunteers loosen up and respond to a few suggestions, they find that they are suddenly the stars of the show. Audience response to the antics on stage brings out the "ham" in many people. All the "hypnotist" needs to do is direct the action.

5. **The stage hypnotist uses tricks.** Stage hypnosis is about 50 percent taking advantage of the situation and 50 percent deception. One of the more impressive stage tricks is to rigidly suspend a person between two chairs. This is astounding only because the audience does not question it. Anyone can do it, as is shown in the photographs and instructions in ✦Figure 5.9. Try it!

To summarize, hypnosis is real, and it can significantly alter private experience. Hypnosis is a useful tool that has been applied in a variety of settings. The TV or nightclub stage, however, is not one of these settings. Stage "hypnotists" entertain; they rarely hypnotize.

Stage hypnosis Use of hypnosis to entertain; often, merely a simulation of hypnosis for that purpose.

✦FIGURE 5.9 *Arrange three chairs as shown. Have someone recline as shown. Ask him to lift slightly while you remove the middle chair. Accept the applause gracefully! (Concerning hypnosis and similar phenomena, the moral, of course, is "Suspend judgment until you have something solid to stand on.")*

MEDITATION—THE 20-MINUTE VACATION

] SURVEYQUESTION *What is meditation? Does it have any benefits?*

Meditation is a mental exercise used to alter consciousness. In general, meditation focuses attention and interrupts the typical flow of thoughts, worries, and analysis (Druckman & Bjork, 1994). EEG recordings take on unique patterns during meditation, which suggests that it is a distinct state of consciousness (Dunn, Hartigan, & Mikulas, 1999). People who use meditation to reduce stress often report less daily physical tension and anxiety (Andresen, 2000).

Meditation takes two major forms. In **concentrative meditation,** you attend to a single focal point, such as an object, a thought, or your own breathing. In contrast, **receptive meditation** is "open," or expansive. In this case, you widen your attention to embrace a total, non-judgmental awareness of the world. An example is losing all self-consciousness while walking in the wilderness with a quiet and receptive mind. Although it may not seem so, receptive meditation is more difficult to attain than concentrative meditation. For this reason, we will discuss concentrative meditation as a practical self-control method.

Performing Concentrative Meditation

How is concentrative meditation done? The basic idea is to sit still and quietly focus on some external object or on a repetitive internal stimulus, such as your own breathing (Wilson, 1986). As an alternative, you can silently repeat a *mantra* (a word used as the focus of attention in concentrative meditation). Typical mantras are smooth, flowing sounds that are easily repeated. A widely used mantra is the word *om*. A mantra could also be any pleasant word or a phrase from a familiar song, poem, or prayer. If other thoughts arise as you repeat a mantra, just return attention to it as often as necessary to maintain meditation.

The Relaxation Response

Commercial meditation courses claim to offer mantras tailored to each individual. But medical researcher Herbert Benson found that the physical benefits of meditation are the same no matter what word is used. They include lowered heart rate, blood pressure, muscle tension, and other signs of stress (Lazar et al., 2000).

Benson believes that the core of meditation is the **relaxation response**—an innate physiological pattern that opposes your body's fight-or-flight mechanisms. Benson feels, quite simply, that most of us have forgotten how to relax deeply. People in his experiments have learned to produce the relaxation response by following these instructions:

Sit quietly in a comfortable position. Close your eyes. Deeply relax all your muscles, beginning at your feet and progressing up to your face. Keep them deeply relaxed.

Meditation A mental exercise for producing relaxation or heightened awareness.
Concentrative meditation Mental exercise based on attending to a single object or thought.
Receptive meditation Mental exercise based on widening attention to become aware of everything experienced at any given moment.
Relaxation response The pattern of internal bodily changes that occurs at times of relaxation.

Breathe through your nose. Become aware of your breathing. As you breathe out, say the word "one" silently to yourself.

Do not worry about whether you are successful in achieving a deep level of relaxation. Maintain a passive attitude and permit relaxation to occur at its own pace. Expect distracting thoughts. When these distracting thoughts occur, ignore them and continue repeating "one." (Adapted from Benson, 1977.)

Effects of Meditation

What effects does meditation have, other than producing relaxation? Many extravagant claims have been made about meditation. For example, members of the Transcendental Meditation (TM) movement have stated that 20 minutes of meditation is as restful as a full night's sleep. This, however, is simply not true. In fact, one study found that merely "resting" for 20 minutes produces the same bodily effects as meditation (Holmes, 1984; Holmes et al., 1983). (The relaxation response can also be produced by brief sensory restriction—see "Sensory Deprivation.")

In defense of meditation, it is important to remember that relaxation can be mental as well as physical. As a stress-control technique, meditation may be a good choice for people who find it difficult to "turn off" upsetting thoughts when they need to relax. For example, college students who tried meditation felt happier, less anxious, and less depressed after just two weeks of twice-a-day meditation (Smith, Compton, & West, 1995). Another group of college students that received just 90 minutes of training in the relaxation response experienced greatly reduced stress levels (Deckro et al., 2002). A third study suggests that meditation may also improve physical health. A group of people who completed an 8-week meditation program showed signs of improved immune system activity—a change that could help them avoid getting sick (Davidson et al., 2003).

Sensory deprivation Any major reduction in the amount or variety of sensory stimulation.

REST Restricted Environmental Stimulation Therapy.

 USING PSYCHOLOGY Sensory Deprivation—Getting a Little REST

Throughout history, sensory deprivation has been one of the most widely used means of altering consciousness. **Sensory deprivation (SD)** refers to any major reduction in the amount or variety of sensory stimulation.

What happens when stimulation is greatly reduced? A hint comes from reports by prisoners in solitary confinement, arctic explorers, high-altitude pilots, long-distance truck drivers, and radar operators. When faced with limited or monotonous stimulation, people sometimes have bizarre sensations, dangerous lapses in attention, and distorted perceptions. However, psychologists have also explored the possible benefits of sensory restriction. Much of this work has involved small isolation tanks like the one pictured in ◆Figure 5.10.

Oddly enough, brief periods of sensory restriction can be very relaxing (Forgays & Belinson, 1986). An hour or two spent in a flotation tank, for instance, causes a large drop in blood pressure, muscle tension, and other signs of stress. Of course, it could be argued that a warm bath has the same effect. Nevertheless, brief sensory deprivation appears to be one of the surest ways to induce deep relaxation (Suedfeld & Borrie, 1999).

Psychologists have also found that mild sensory deprivation can help people quit smoking, lose weight, and reduce their use of alcohol and drugs (Borrie, 1990–91; Cooper, Adams, & Scott, 1988; Suedfeld, 1990). Psychologist Peter Suedfeld calls such benefits Restricted Environmental Stimulation Therapy, or **REST.** Deep relaxation makes people more open to suggestion, and SD interrupts habitual behavior patterns. As a result, REST can "loosen" belief

systems and make it easier to change bad habits (Suedfeld & Borrie, 1999).

REST also shows promise as a way to stimulate creative thinking (Norlander et al., 1998). Other researchers have reported that REST sessions can enhance performance in skilled sports, such as gymnastics, tennis, basketball, darts, and marksmanship (Druckman & Bjork, 1994; Norlander et al., 1999). There is also evidence that REST can relieve chronic pain and reduce stress (Kjellgren et al., 2001). Clearly, there is much yet to be learned from studying "nothingness."

◆**FIGURE 5.10** *A sensory isolation chamber. Small flotation tanks like the one pictured have been used by psychologists to study the effects of mild sensory deprivation. Subjects float in darkness and silence. The shallow body-temperature water contains hundreds of pounds of Epsom salts, so that subjects float near the surface. Mild sensory deprivation produces deep relaxation.*

Summary

To summarize, research suggests that concentrative meditation is only one of several ways to elicit the relaxation response. For many people, sitting quietly and "resting" can be as effective. Similar stress reduction occurs when people set aside time daily to engage in other restful activities, such as muscle relaxation, positive daydreaming, and even leisure reading. However, if you are the type of person who finds it difficult to ignore upsetting thoughts, then concentrative meditation might be a good way to promote relaxation. Meditation and similar techniques provide a valuable, stress-lowering "time-out" from the normal clamor of thoughts and worries—something almost everyone could use in our fast-paced society.

STUDYBREAK *Hypnosis, Meditation, and Sensory Deprivation*

RELATE

How have your beliefs about hypnosis changed after reading the preceding section? Can you think of specific examples in which hypnosis was misrepresented? For example, in high school assemblies, stage acts, movies, or TV dramas?

Various activities can produce the relaxation response. When do you experience states of deep relaxation, coupled with a sense of serene awareness? What similarities do these occurrences have to meditation?

Have you experienced any form of sensory restriction or sensory deprivation? How did you react? Would you be willing to try REST in order to break a bad habit?

LEARNING CHECK

1. The term *hypnotism* was coined by a British surgeon named
   a. Franz Mesmer b. James Stanford c. T. A. Kreskin
   d. James Braid
2. Only 4 out of 10 people can be hypnotized. T or F?
3. Which of the following can most definitely be achieved with hypnosis?
   a. unusual strength b. pain relief c. improved memory
   d. sleep-like brain waves

4. The focus of attention in concentrative meditation is "open," or expansive. T or F?
5. Mantras are words said silently to oneself to end a session of meditation. T or F?
6. Research conducted by Herbert Benson indicates that careful selection of a mantra is necessary to obtain the physical benefits of meditation. T or F?
7. The most immediate benefit of meditation appears to be its capacity for producing the relaxation response. T or F?
8. Prolonged periods of extreme sensory deprivation lower anxiety and induce deep relaxation. T or F?

Critical Thinking

9. What kind of control group would you need in order to identify the true effects of hypnosis?
10. Regular meditators report lower levels of stress and a greater sense of well-being. What other explanations must we eliminate before this effect can be regarded as genuine?

ANSWERS

1. d 2. F 3. b 4. F 5. F 6. F 7. T 8. F 9. Most experiments on hypnosis include a control group in which people are asked to simulate being hypnotized. Without such controls, the tendency of subjects to cooperate with experimenters makes it difficult to identify true hypnotic effects. 10. Studies on the effects of meditation must control for the placebo effect and the fact that those who choose to learn meditation may not be a representative sample of the general population. Studies controlling for such factors still show that meditation is beneficial (Pagano & Warrenburg, 1983).

DRUG-ALTERED CONSCIOUSNESS— THE HIGH AND LOW OF IT

] SURVEYQUESTION *What are the effects of the more commonly used psychoactive drugs?*

The surest way to alter human consciousness is to administer a **psychoactive drug** (a substance capable of altering attention, judgment, memory, time sense, self-control, emotion, or perception) (Julien, 1998). Most psychoactive drugs can be placed on a scale ranging from stimulation to depression. A **stimulant** is a substance that increases activity in the body and nervous system. A **depressant** does the reverse. ✦Figure 5.11 shows various drugs and their approximate effects. A more complete summary of frequently abused psychoactive drugs is given in ▲ Table 5.3.

Psychoactive drug A substance capable of altering attention, memory, judgment, time sense, self-control, mood, or perception.

Stimulant A substance that increases activity in the body and nervous system.

Depressant A substance that decreases activity in the body and nervous system.

▲TABLE 5.3	**Comparison of Psychoactive Drugs**			
NAME	CLASSIFICATION	MEDICAL USE	USUAL DOSE	DURATION OF EFFECT
Alcohol	Sedative-hypnotic	Solvent, antiseptic	Varies	1–4 hours
Amphetamines	Stimulant	Relief of mild depression, control of narcolepsy and hyperactivity	2.5–5 milligrams	4 hours
Barbiturates	Sedative-hypnotic	Sedation, relief of high blood pressure, anticonvulsant	50–100 milligrams	4 hours
Benzodiazepines	Anxiolytic (antianxiety drug)	Tranquilizer	2–100 milligrams	10 minutes–8 hours
Caffeine	Stimulant	Counteract depressant drugs, treatment of migraine headaches	Varies	Varies
Cocaine	Stimulant, local anesthetic	Local anesthesia	Varies	Varied, brief periods
Codeine	Narcotic	Ease pain and coughing	30 milligrams	4 hours
GHB	Sedative-hypnotic	Experimental treatment of narcolepsy, alcoholism	1–3 grams (powder)	1–3 hours
Heroin	Narcotic	Pain relief	Varies	4 hours
LSD	Hallucinogen	Experimental study of mental function, alcoholism	100–500 milligrams	10 hours
Marijuana (THC)	Relaxant, euphoriant; in high doses, hallucinogen	Treatment of glaucoma and side effects of chemotherapy	1–2 cigarettes	4 hours
MDMA	Stimulant/hallucinogen	None	125 milligrams	4–6 hours
Mescaline	Hallucinogen	None	350 micrograms	12 hours
Methadone	Narcotic	Pain relief	10 milligrams	4–6 hours
Morphine	Narcotic	Pain relief	15 milligrams	6 hours
PCP	Anesthetic	None	2–10 milligrams	4–6 hours, plus 12-hour recovery
Psilocybin	Hallucinogen	None	25 milligrams	6–8 hours
Tobacco (nicotine)	Stimulant	Emetic (nicotine)	Varies	Varies

Question marks indicate conflict of opinion. It should be noted that illicit drugs are frequently adulterated and thus pose unknown hazards to the user.

How Drugs Affect the Brain

How do drugs alter consciousness?   Psychoactive drugs influence the activity of brain cells. Typically, drugs imitate or alter neurotransmitters, the chemicals that carry messages between brain cells. Some drugs cause more neurotransmitters to be released, increasing the activity of brain cells. Ecstasy, amphetamine, and some antidepressants are examples of drugs that have this effect. Other drugs slow the removal of neurotransmitters after they are released. This prolongs the action of transmitter chemicals and typically has a stimulating effect (cocaine works in this way). Other drugs, such as nicotine and opiates, directly stim-

EFFECTS SOUGHT	LONG-TERM SYMPTOMS	PHYSICAL DEPENDENCE POTENTIAL	PSYCHOLOGICAL DEPENDENCE POTENTIAL	ORGANIC DAMAGE POTENTIAL
Sense alteration, anxiety reduction, sociability	Cirrhosis, toxic psychosis, neurologic damage, addiction	Yes	Yes	Yes
Alertness, activeness	Loss of appetite, delusions, hallucinations, toxic psychosis	Yes	Yes	Yes
Anxiety reduction, euphoria	Addiction with severe withdrawal symptoms, possible convulsions, toxic psychosis	Yes	Yes	Yes
Anxiety relief	Irritability, confusion, depression, sleep disorders	Yes	Yes	No, but can affect fetus
Wakefulness, alertness	Insomnia, heart arrhythmias, high blood pressure	No?	Yes	Yes
Excitation, talkativeness	Depression, convulsions	Yes	Yes	Yes
Euphoria, prevent withdrawal discomfort	Addiction, constipation, loss of appetite	Yes	Yes	No
Intoxication, euphoria, relaxation	Anxiety, confusion, insomnia, hallucinations, seizures	Yes	Yes	No?
Euphoria, prevent withdrawal discomfort	Addiction, constipation, loss of appetite	Yes	Yes	No*
Insightful experiences, exhilaration, distortion of senses	May intensify existing psychosis, panic reactions	No	No?	No?
Relaxation; increased euphoria, perceptions, sociability	Possible lung cancer, other health risks	No	Yes	Yes?
Excitation, euphoria	Personality change, hyperthermia, liver damage	No	Yes	Yes
Insightful experiences, exhilaration, distortion of senses	May intensify existing psychosis, panic reactions	No	No?	No?
Prevent withdrawal discomfort	Addiction, constipation, loss of appetite	Yes	Yes	No
Euphoria, prevent withdrawal discomfort	Addiction, constipation, loss of appetite	Yes	Yes	No*
Euphoria	Unpredictable behavior, suspicion, hostility, psychosis	Debated	Yes	Yes
Insightful experiences, exhilaration, distortion of senses	May intensify existing psychosis, panic reactions	No	No?	No?
Alertness, calmness, sociability	Emphysema, lung cancer, mouth and throat cancer, cardiovascular damage, loss of appetite	Yes	Yes	Yes

*Persons who inject drugs under non-sterile conditions run a high risk of contracting AIDS, hepatitis, abscesses, or circulatory disorders.

ulate brain cells by mimicking neurotransmitters. Another possibility is illustrated by alcohol and tranquilizers. These drugs affect certain types of brain cells that cause relaxation and relieve anxiety. Some drugs fill receptor sites on brain cells and block incoming messages. Other possibilities also exist, which is why drugs can have such a wide variety of effects on the brain (Julien, 1998).

All addictive drugs stimulate the brain's reward circuitry, producing feelings of pleasure. As one expert put it, addictive drugs fool brain-reward pathways: "As a result, the reward pathway signals, 'That felt good. Let's do it again. Let's remember exactly how we did it.'" This creates a compulsion to repeat the drug experience. It's the hook that eventually

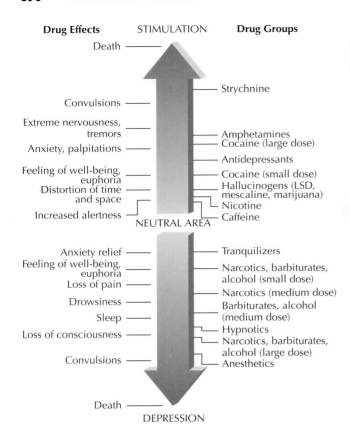

Drug Effects — STIMULATION — **Drug Groups**

Death

Strychnine

Convulsions

Extreme nervousness, tremors

Anxiety, palpitations

Amphetamines
Cocaine (large dose)
Antidepressants
Cocaine (small dose)
Hallucinogens (LSD, mescaline, marijuana)
Nicotine
Caffeine

Feeling of well-being, euphoria
Distortion of time and space
Increased alertness

NEUTRAL AREA

Anxiety relief

Tranquilizers

Feeling of well-being, euphoria

Loss of pain

Narcotics, barbiturates, alcohol (small dose)
Narcotics (medium dose)
Barbiturates, alcohol (medium dose)
Hypnotics
Narcotics, barbiturates, alcohol (large dose)
Anesthetics

Drowsiness

Sleep

Loss of consciousness

Convulsions

Death

DEPRESSION

◆**FIGURE 5.11** *Spectrum and continuum of drug action. Many drugs can be rated on a stimulation-depression scale according to their effects on the central nervous system. Although LSD, mescaline, and marijuana are listed here, the stimulation-depression scale is less relevant to these drugs. The principal characteristic of such hallucinogens is their mind-altering quality.*

snares the addict (Restak, 2001). Adolescents are especially susceptible to addiction because brain systems that restrain risk-taking are not as mature as those that reward pleasure-seeking (Chambers, Taylor, & Potenza, 2003).

Dependence

Drug dependence falls into two broad categories. When a person compulsively uses a drug to maintain bodily comfort, a **physical dependence** (addiction) exists. Addiction occurs most often with drugs that cause **withdrawal symptoms** (physical illness that follows removal of a drug) (Julien, 1998). Withdrawal from drugs such as alcohol, barbiturates, and opiates can cause violent flu-like symptoms of nausea, vomiting, diarrhea, chills, sweating, and cramps (Feldman & Meyer, 1996). Addiction is often accompanied by a **drug tolerance** (reduced response to a drug). This leads users to take larger and larger doses to get the desired effect.

Persons who develop a **psychological dependence** feel that a drug is necessary to maintain feelings of comfort or well-being. Usually, they intensely crave the drug and its rewarding qualities (Feldman & Meyer, 1996). Psychological dependence can be just as powerful as physical addiction. That's why some psychologists define addiction as any compulsive habit pattern. By this definition, a person who has lost control over drug use, for whatever reason, is addicted. In fact, most people who answer yes to both of the following questions have an alcohol or drug problem and should seek professional help (Brown et al., 1997):

- In the last year, did you ever drink or use drugs more than you meant to?
- Have you felt you wanted or needed to cut down on your drinking or drug use in the last year?

Drugs of Abuse

Note in Table 5.3 that the drugs most likely to lead to physical dependence are alcohol, amphetamines, barbiturates, cocaine, codeine, heroin, methadone, morphine, and tobacco (nicotine). Using *any* of the drugs listed in Table 5.3 can result in psychological dependence. Note too that people who take drugs intravenously are at high risk for developing hepatitis and HIV (see Chapter 11). The discussion that follows focuses on the drugs most often abused by students.

Physical dependence Physical addiction, as indicated by the presence of drug tolerance and withdrawal symptoms.

Withdrawal symptoms Physical illness and discomfort following the withdrawal of a drug.

Drug tolerance A reduction in the body's response to a drug.

Psychological dependence Drug dependence that is based primarily on emotional or psychological needs.

UPPERS—AMPHETAMINES, COCAINE, CAFFEINE, NICOTINE

Amphetamines are synthetic stimulants. Common street names for amphetamine are "speed," "bennies," "dex," "go," and "uppers." These drugs were once widely prescribed for weight loss or depression. Today, the only fully legitimate medical use of amphetamines is to treat narcolepsy, childhood hyperactivity, and overdoses of depressant drugs. Illicit use of amphetamines is widespread, especially by people seeking to stay awake and by those who think drugs can improve mental or physical performance.

Methamphetamine is a more potent variation of amphetamine. It can be snorted, injected, or eaten. Of the various types of amphetamine, methamphetamine has created the largest drug problem. "Crank," "speed," "meth," or "crystal," as it is known on the street, can be made cheaply in backyard labs and sold for massive profits. In addition to ruining lives through addiction, it has fueled a violent criminal subculture.

Amphetamines rapidly produce a drug tolerance. Most abusers end up taking ever larger doses to get the desired effect. Eventually, some users switch to injecting methamphetamine directly into the bloodstream. True speed freaks typically go on binges lasting several days, after which they "crash" from lack of sleep and food.

Abuse

How dangerous are amphetamines?   Amphetamines pose many dangers. Large doses can cause nausea, vomiting, extremely high blood pressure, fatal heart attacks, and disabling strokes. It is important to realize that amphetamines speed up the use of bodily resources; they do not magically supply energy. After an amphetamine binge, people suffer from crippling fatigue, depression, confusion, uncontrolled irritability, and aggression. Repeated amphetamine use damages the brain. Amphetamines can also cause a loss of contact with reality known as amphetamine psychosis. Affected users have paranoid delusions that someone is out to get them. Acting on these delusions, they may become violent, resulting in suicide, self-injury, or injury to others (Kratofil, Baberg, & Dimsdale, 1996).

A potent smokable form of crystal methamphetamine has added to the risks of stimulant abuse. This drug, known as "ice" on the street, is highly addictive. Like "crack," the smokable form of cocaine, it produces an intense high. But also like crack (discussed in a moment), crystal methamphetamine leads very rapidly to compulsive abuse and severe drug dependence.

Cocaine

Cocaine ("coke," "snow") is a powerful central nervous system stimulant extracted from the leaves of the coca plant. Cocaine produces feelings of alertness, euphoria, well-being, power, boundless energy, and pleasure (Julien, 1998). Cocaine has a long history of misuse. At the turn of the twentieth century, dozens of nonprescription potions and cure-alls contained cocaine. It was during this time that Coca-Cola was indeed the "real thing." From 1886 until 1906, when the U.S. Pure Food and Drug Act was passed, Coca-Cola contained cocaine (which has since been replaced with caffeine).

How does cocaine differ from amphetamines? The two are very much alike in their effects on the central nervous system. The main difference is that amphetamine lasts several hours; cocaine is snorted and quickly metabolized, so its effects last only about 15 to 30 minutes.

Cocaine was the main ingredient in many nonprescription elixirs before the turn of the twentieth century. Today, cocaine is recognized as a powerful and dangerous drug. Its high potential for abuse has damaged the lives of countless users.

Abuse

How dangerous is cocaine?   Cocaine is one of the most dangerous drugs of abuse. Even casual or first-time users risk having convulsions, a heart attack, or a stroke (Cregler & Mark, 1985; Lacayo, 1995). The highly publicized death of all-American basketball star Len Bias is a case in point.

A person who stops using cocaine does not experience heroin-like withdrawal symptoms. But cocaine can be highly addictive. The brain adapts to cocaine abuse in ways that upset its chemical balance, causing depression when cocaine is withdrawn. First, there is a

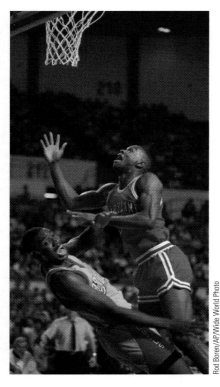

Rod Boren/AP/Wide World Photo

The future looked bright when college basketball star Len Bias was chosen to play for the Boston Celtics. Thrilled by his hard-earned achievement, and perhaps feeling invincible, Bias tried cocaine, probably for the first time. Hours later his dream perished. Bias was dead from cardiac arrest at age 22.

jarring "crash" of mood and energy. Within a few days, the person enters a long period of fatigue, anxiety, paranoia, boredom, and **anhedonia** (an-he-DAWN-ee-ah: an inability to feel pleasure). Before long, the urge to use cocaine becomes intense. So although cocaine does not fit the classic pattern of addiction, it is ripe for compulsive abuse. Even a person who gets through withdrawal may crave cocaine months or years later (Withers et al., 1995). If cocaine were cheaper, 9 out of 10 users would progress to compulsive abuse. In fact, rock cocaine ("crack," "rock," or "*roca*"), which is cheaper, produces very high abuse rates. Here are some signs of cocaine abuse (Pursch, 1983):

- *Compulsive use.* If cocaine is available—say, at a party—you will undoubtedly use it. You can't say no to it.
- *Loss of control.* Once you have had some cocaine, you will keep using it until you are exhausted or the cocaine is gone.
- *Disregarding consequences.* You don't care if the rent gets paid, your job is endangered, your lover disapproves, or your health is affected, you'll use cocaine anyway.

Clearly, cocaine's capacity for abuse and social damage rivals that of heroin. Anyone who thinks she or he has a cocaine problem should seek advice at a drug clinic or a Cocaine Anonymous meeting. Quitting cocaine is extremely difficult. Nevertheless, three out of four cocaine abusers who remain in treatment do succeed in breaking their coke dependence (Simpson et al., 1999).

MDMA ("Ecstasy")

The drug MDMA (methylenedioxymethamphetamine, or "Ecstasy") is also chemically similar to amphetamine. In addition to producing a rush of energy, users say it makes them feel closer to others and heightens sensory experiences. Ecstasy causes brain cells to release extra amounts of serotonin. The physical effects of MDMA include dilated pupils, elevated blood pressure, jaw clenching, loss of appetite, and elevated body temperature (Braun, 2001). Some users believe that Ecstasy increases sexual pleasure. However, it impairs erection in 40 percent of men, and it can retard orgasm in both men and women. Overall, MDMA appears to *diminish* sexual performance (Zemishlany, Aizenberg, & Weizman, 2001).

Abuse

The use of Ecstasy has doubled in North America in the last 5 years. At least 1 in 20 college students has tried Ecstasy. What are the consequences of such widespread use? Serious problems are beginning to surface. Every year, emergency room doctors see more MDMA cases, including a steady increase in MDMA-related deaths. Some of these incidents are caused by elevated body temperature (hyperthermia) or heart arrhythmias, which can lead to collapse. Ecstasy users at "rave" parties try to prevent overheating by drinking water to cool themselves. This may help to a small degree, but the risk of fatal heat exhaustion is real. MDMA can also cause severe liver damage, which can be fatal (Braun, 2001). In addition, Ecstasy users are more likely to abuse alcohol and other drugs, to neglect studying, to party excessively, and to engage in risky sex (Strote, Lee, & Wechsler, 2002).

It may take another 10 years before Ecstasy's full impact on health emerges. For now, we know that repeated use of MDMA damages serotonergic brain cells. This damage lasts for years. It leads to feelings of anxiety or depression that can persist for months after a person stops taking Ecstasy. In addition, heavy users typically do not score well on tests of mental functioning or memory (Morgan, 2000; Zakzanis & Young, 2001). Many of the drugs sold as "Ecstasy" are impure or adulterated with other substances. Despite its street name, Ecstasy may be a ticket to agony for many users (Kuhn & Wilson, 2001).

Caffeine

Caffeine is the most frequently used psychoactive drug in North America. (And that's not counting Seattle!) Caffeine stimulates the brain by blocking chemicals that normally inhibit or slow nerve activity (Julien, 1998). Its effects become apparent with doses as small as 50 mil-

Anhedonia An inability to feel pleasure.

ligrams, the amount found in about one-half cup of brewed coffee. Physically, caffeine causes sweating, talkativeness, tinnitus (ringing in the ears), and hand tremors. Psychologically, caffeine suppresses fatigue or drowsiness and increases feelings of alertness (Smith et al., 1999). Some people have a hard time starting a day (or writing another paragraph) without it.

How much caffeine did you consume today? It is common to think of coffee as the major source of caffeine, but there are many others. Caffeine is found in tea, many soft drinks (especially colas), chocolate, and cocoa (▲Table 5.4). More than 2,000 nonprescription drugs also contain caffeine, including stay-awake pills, cold remedies, and many name-brand aspirin products.

Abuse

Are there any serious drawbacks to using caffeine? Serious abuse may result in an unhealthy dependence on caffeine known as **caffeinism.** Insomnia, irritability, loss of appetite, chills, racing heart, and elevated body temperature are all signs of caffeinism. Many people with these symptoms drink 15 or 20 cups of coffee a day. However, even at lower doses, caffeine can intensify anxiety and other psychological problems (Larson & Carey, 1998).

Caffeine has a variety of health risks. Caffeine encourages the growth of breast cysts in women, and it may contribute to bladder cancer, heart problems, and high blood pressure. Pregnant women should consider giving up caffeine entirely because of a suspected link between caffeine and birth defects. Pregnant women who consume 6 or more cups of coffee a day double the risk of having a miscarriage (Klebanoff et al., 1999).

It is customary to think of caffeine as a non-drug. But as few as 2.5 cups of coffee a day (or the equivalent) can be a problem. People who consume even such modest amounts may experience anxiety, depression, fatigue, headaches, and flu-like symptoms during withdrawal (Silverman et al., 1992). About half of all caffeine users show some signs of dependence (Hughes et al., 1998). It is wise to remember that caffeine *is* a drug and should be used in moderation.

Nicotine

Nicotine is a natural stimulant found mainly in tobacco. Next to caffeine, it is the most widely used psychoactive drug (Julien, 1998).

How does nicotine compare with other stimulants? Nicotine is a potent drug. It is so toxic that it is sometimes used to kill insects! In large doses it causes stomach pain, vomiting and diarrhea, cold sweats, dizziness, confusion, and muscle tremors. In very large doses, nicotine may cause convulsions, respiratory failure, and death. For a non-smoker, 50 to 75 milligrams of nicotine taken in a single dose could be lethal. (Chain-smoking about 17 to 25 cigarettes will produce this dosage.) Most first-time smokers get sick on one or two cigarettes. In contrast, a heavy smoker may inhale 40 cigarettes a day without feeling ill. This indicates that regular smokers build a tolerance for nicotine (Perkins, 1995; Stolerman & Jarvis, 1995).

Abuse

Is it true that nicotine can be addicting? A vast array of evidence confirms that nicotine is addictive (Henningfield & Heishman, 1995). Among regular smokers who are 15 to 24 years old, 60 percent are addicted (Breslau et al., 2001). For many smokers, withdrawal from nicotine causes headaches, sweating, cramps, insomnia, digestive upset, irritability, and a sharp craving for cigarettes (Killen & Fortmann, 1997). These symptoms may last from 2 to 6 weeks and may be worse than heroin withdrawal. Indeed, relapse patterns are nearly identical for alcoholics, heroin addicts, cocaine

Actress Lily Tomlin took up smoking for a role in the movie *Shadows and Fog* and developed a four-pack-a-day habit. As Tomlin's experience shows, the best way to avoid developing a nicotine addiction is to not begin smoking in the first place.

▲TABLE 5.4	Average Caffeine Content of Various Foods
Instant coffee (5 ounces or 1 cup), 64 milligrams	
Percolated coffee (5 ounces or 1 cup), 108 milligrams	
Drip coffee (5 ounces or 1 cup), 145 milligrams	
Decaf. coffee (5 ounces or 1 cup), 3 milligrams	
Black tea (5 ounces or 1 cup), 42 milligrams	
Canned ice tea (17 ounces), 30 milligrams	
Cocoa drink (6 ounces or 1 cup), 8 milligrams	
Chocolate drink (8 ounces or 1 carton), 14 milligrams	
Sweet chocolate (1 ounce square), 20 milligrams	
Colas (12 ounces or 1 can), 50 milligrams	
Soft drinks (12 ounces or 1 can), 0–52 milligrams	

Caffeinism Excessive consumption of caffeine, leading to dependence and a variety of physical and psychological complaints.

THE FAR SIDE® BY GARY LARSON

The real reason dinosaurs became extinct

abusers, and smokers who try to quit (Stolerman & Jarvis, 1995). A staggering 8 out of 10 people who quit smoking relapse within 1 year (Jarvik, 1995).

Impact on Health

How serious are the health risks of smoking?   A burning cigarette releases a large variety of potent *carcinogens* (car-SIN-oh-jins: cancer-causing substances). Lung cancer and other cancers caused by smoking are now considered the single most preventable cause of death in the United States and Canada. Among men, 97 percent of lung cancer deaths are caused by smoking. For women, 74 percent of all lung cancers are due to smoking. Here are some sobering facts about smoking:

Smoking Facts
- Every cigarette reduces a smoker's life expectancy by 7 minutes.
- Smoking is the number one cause of deaths in the United States and Canada—more than the number of deaths from alcohol, drugs, car accidents, and AIDS combined.
- Worldwide, smoking kills 5 million people every year.
- In the United States alone, smoking-related medical costs total $50 billion a year. Taxpayers pick up the bill for 43 percent of this total.
- Forty percent of all smokers who develop throat cancer try smoking again.
- Each year, only 1 out of 5 smokers who tries to quit smoking succeeds.
- Some tobacco companies manipulate nicotine levels in their cigarettes to keep smokers addicted.
- Daily exposure to second-hand smoke at home or work causes a 24 to 39 percent increase in cancer risk to non-smokers.

If you think smoking is harmless, or that there's no connection between smoking and cancer, you're kidding yourself. The scientific link between tobacco smoking and cancer is undeniable. Skeptics please note: Wayne McLaren, who portrayed the rugged "Marlboro Man" in cigarette ads, died of lung cancer at age 51.

Smokers don't just risk their own health, they also endanger those who live and work nearby. Secondary smoke causes 20 percent of all lung cancers. Non-smoking women who are married to smokers suffer a 30 percent increase in their risk of developing lung cancer. It is particularly irresponsible of smokers to expose young children to second-hand smoke (Abramson, 1993).

Quitting Smoking

Is it better for a person to quit smoking abruptly or taper down gradually?   For many years, smokers were advised to quit cold turkey. The current view is that quitting all at once isn't as effective as tapering off. Going cold turkey makes quitting an all-or-nothing proposition. Smokers who smoke even one cigarette after "quitting forever" tend to feel they've failed. Many figure they might just as well resume smoking. Those who quit gradually accept that success may take many attempts, spread over several months. "New Strategies to Stop Smoking" summarizes several ways to quit smoking.

A study of 5th- through 12th-graders found that those who smoke are less likely than non-smokers to believe the health warning labels on cigarette packs (Cecil, Evans, & Stanley, 1996). Smokers in general are less likely to believe that smoking poses a serious risk to health.

New Strategies to Stop Smoking

If you smoke and would like to quit, here are some basic steps you can take: (1) Delay having a first cigarette in the morning. Then try to delay a little longer each day. (2) Gradually reduce the total number of cigarettes you smoke each day. (3) Quit completely, but for just 1 week. Then quit again, a week at a time, for as many times as necessary to make it stick (Pierce, 1991).

You will probably be most successful at strategy number 2 if you *schedule* a gradual reduction in smoking. To begin, count the number of cigarettes you smoke per day. For the first week, your goal will be to smoke only two thirds of that "baseline" number each day. In addition, you should divide the 16 waking hours in each day by the number of cigarettes you will smoke that day. For example, if you plan to smoke 16 cigarettes per day, then you get to smoke only 1 per hour. When a scheduled "smoking time" arrives,

smoke only for 5 minutes, whether you finish the cigarette or not. Don't smoke any "missed" cigarettes later.

During the second week, you should smoke only one third as many cigarettes as you did during your baseline. Again, divide each 16-hour day by the number of cigarettes, so you can plan how much time to allow between smoking periods.

During week 3, reduce your cigarette allowance to 20 percent of the original baseline number.

In the fourth week, stop smoking entirely.

Gradually stretching the time periods between cigarettes is a key part of this program. Scheduled smoking apparently helps people learn to cope with the urge to smoke. As a result, people using this method are more likely to succeed. Also, they more often remain permanent non-smokers than people using other approaches (Cincirpini et al., 1997).

Whatever approach is taken, quitting smoking is not easy. Many people find that using nicotine patches or gum helps them get through the withdrawal period. Also, as we have noted, anyone trying to quit should be prepared to make several attempts before succeeding. But the good news is tens of millions of people have quit.

DOWNERS—SEDATIVES, TRANQUILIZERS, AND ALCOHOL

How do downers differ from the stimulant drugs? The most widely used downers, or depressant drugs, are alcohol, barbiturates, gamma-hydroxybutyrate (GHB), and benzodiazepine (ben-zoe-die-AZ-eh-peen) tranquilizers. These drugs are much alike in their effects. In fact, barbiturates and tranquilizers are sometimes referred to as "solid alcohol." Let's examine the properties of each.

Barbiturates

Barbiturates are sedative drugs that depress brain activity. Common barbiturates include amobarbital, pentobarbital, secobarbital, and tuinal. On the street they are known as "downers," "blue heavens," "yellow jackets," "purple hearts," "goof balls," "reds," "pink ladies," "rainbows," or "tooies." Medically, barbiturates are used to calm patients or to induce sleep. At mild dosages, barbiturates have an effect similar to alcohol intoxication. Higher dosages can cause severe mental confusion or even hallucinations. Overdoses can easily cause coma or death. Barbiturates are often taken in excess amounts because a first dose may be followed by others as the user becomes uninhibited or forgetful. Overdoses first cause a loss of consciousness. Then they severely depress brain centers that control heartbeat and breathing. The result is death (McKim, 1997).

GHB

Would you swallow a mixture of degreasing solvent and drain cleaner to get high? Apparently, a lot of people would. A mini-epidemic of GHB (gamma-hydroxybutyrate) use has taken place in recent years, especially at nightclubs and raves. GHB ("goop," "scoop," "max," "Georgia Home Boy") is a central nervous system depressant that relaxes and sedates the body. Users describe its effects as being similar to alcohol. Mild GHB intoxication tends to produce euphoria, a desire to socialize, and a mild loss of inhibitions. GHB's intoxicating effects typically last 3 to 4 hours, depending on the dosage.

Abuse

At lower dosages, GHB can relieve anxiety and produce relaxation. However, as the dose increases, its sedative effects may result in nausea, a loss of muscle control, and either sleep or a loss of consciousness. Higher dosages can cause coma, breathing failure, and death. GHB inhibits the gag reflex, so some users choke to death on their own vomit. Potentially fatal doses of GHB are only three times the amount typically taken by users. This narrow margin of safety has led to numerous overdoses, especially when GHB was combined with alcohol. An overdose causes sleep or deep sedation from which the person cannot be awakened.

In March 2000, the U.S. government classified GHB as a controlled substance, making its possession a felony crime. Clinical evidence increasingly suggests that GHB is addictive and a serious danger to users. Two out of three frequent users have lost consciousness after taking GHB. Heavy users who stop taking GHB have withdrawal symptoms that include anxiety, agitation, tremor, delirium, and hallucinations (Miotto et al., 2001).

As if the preceding weren't enough reason to be leery of GHB, here's one more to consider: GHB is often manufactured in homes with recipes and ingredients purchased on the Internet. As mentioned earlier, it can be produced by combining degreasing solvent with drain cleaner (Falkowski, 2000). If you want to degrease your brain, GHB will do the trick.

Tranquilizers

A **tranquilizer** is a drug that lowers anxiety and reduces tension. Doctors prescribe benzodiazepine tranquilizers to alleviate nervousness and stress. Valium is the best-known drug in this family; others are Xanax, Halcion, and Librium. Even at normal dosages these drugs can cause drowsiness, shakiness, and confusion. When used at too high a dosage or for too long a time, benzodiazepines have strong addictive potential (McKim, 1997).

A drug sold under the trade name Rohypnol (ro-HIP-nol) has added to the problem of tranquilizer abuse. This drug, which is related to Valium, is cheap and 10 times more potent. It lowers inhibitions and produces relaxation or intoxication. Large doses induce short-term amnesia and sleep. "Roofies," as they are known on the street, are odorless and tasteless. They have been used to spike drinks, which are given to the unwary as a "date-rape drug." Victims are then sexually assaulted or raped while they are unconscious (Navarro, 1995). (Be aware, however, that drinking too much alcohol is by far the most common prelude to rape.)

Abuse

Repeated use of barbiturates can cause physical dependence. Some abusers suffer severe emotional depression that may end in suicide. Similarly, when tranquilizers are used at too high a dosage or for too long a time, addiction can occur. Many people have learned the hard way that their legally prescribed tranquilizers are as dangerous as many illicit drugs (McKim, 1997).

Combining barbiturates or tranquilizers with alcohol is extremely risky. When mixed, the effects of both drugs are multiplied by a **drug interaction** (one drug enhances the effect of another). Drug interactions are responsible for many hundreds of fatal drug overdoses every year. All too often, depressants are gulped down with alcohol or added to a spiked punch bowl. This is the lethal brew that left a young woman named Karen Ann Quinlan in a coma that lasted 10 years, ending with her death. It is no exaggeration to restate that mixing depressants with alcohol can be deadly.

Alcohol

Alcohol is the common name for ethyl alcohol, the intoxicating element in fermented and distilled liquors. Contrary to popular belief, alcohol is not a stimulant. The noisy animation at drinking parties is due to alcohol's effect as a *depressant*. As ✦Figure 5.12 shows, small

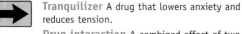

Tranquilizer A drug that lowers anxiety and reduces tension.

Drug interaction A combined effect of two drugs that exceeds the addition of one drug's effects to the other.

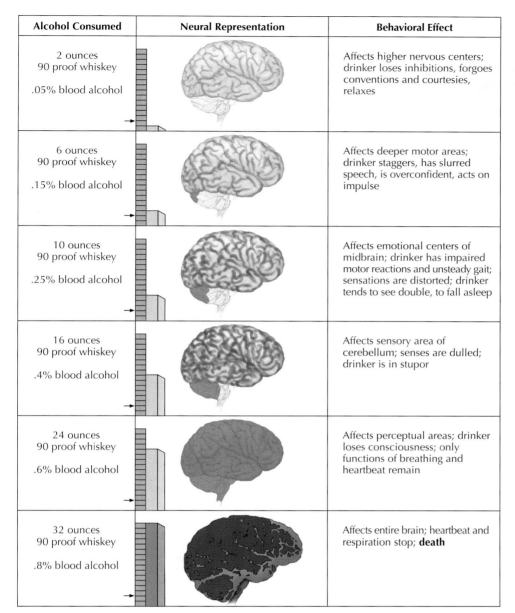

Alcohol Consumed	Neural Representation	Behavioral Effect
2 ounces 90 proof whiskey .05% blood alcohol		Affects higher nervous centers; drinker loses inhibitions, forgoes conventions and courtesies, relaxes
6 ounces 90 proof whiskey .15% blood alcohol		Affects deeper motor areas; drinker staggers, has slurred speech, is overconfident, acts on impulse
10 ounces 90 proof whiskey .25% blood alcohol		Affects emotional centers of midbrain; drinker has impaired motor reactions and unsteady gait; sensations are distorted; drinker tends to see double, to fall asleep
16 ounces 90 proof whiskey .4% blood alcohol		Affects sensory area of cerebellum; senses are dulled; drinker is in stupor
24 ounces 90 proof whiskey .6% blood alcohol		Affects perceptual areas; drinker loses consciousness; only functions of breathing and heartbeat remain
32 ounces 90 proof whiskey .8% blood alcohol		Affects entire brain; heartbeat and respiration stop; **death**

◆FIGURE 5.12 *The behavioral effects of alcohol are related to blood alcohol content and the resulting suppression of higher mental function. Arrows indicate the typical threshold for legal intoxication in the United States. (From Jozef Cohen,* Eyewitness Series in Psychology, *p. 44. Copyright © by Rand McNally and Company. Reprinted by permission.)*

amounts of alcohol reduce inhibitions and produce feelings of relaxation and euphoria. Larger amounts cause ever-greater impairment of the brain until the drinker loses consciousness. Alcohol is also not an aphrodisiac. Rather than enhancing sexual arousal, it usually impairs performance, especially in males. As William Shakespeare observed long ago, drink "provokes the desire, but it takes away the performance."

Abuse

Alcohol, the world's favorite depressant, breeds our biggest drug problem. An estimated 25 million people in the United States and Canada have serious drinking problems. The level of alcohol abuse among adolescents and young adults is alarming. Seventy percent of college students have engaged in binge drinking. For fraternity and sorority members, the figure jumps to 84 percent. **Binge drinking** is defined as downing 5 or more drinks in a short time (4 drinks for women). Apparently, many students think it's entertaining to get completely wasted and throw up on their friends. However, binge drinking is a serious sign of alcohol abuse. It is responsible for numerous deaths and thousands of trips to the ER (Wechsler et al., 2002).

Binge drinking Consuming 5 or more drinks in a short time.

Binge drinking and alcohol abuse have become serious problems among college students. Many alcohol abusers regard themselves as "moderate" drinkers, which suggests that they are in denial about how much they actually drink (Grant & Dawson, 1997).

Creasource/Series/PictureQuest

Binge drinking is of special concern because the brain continues to develop into the early twenties. Research has shown that teenagers and young adults who drink too much may lose as much as 10 percent of their brain power—especially their memory capacity (Brown et al., 2000). Such losses can have a long-term impact on a person's chances for success in life. In short, getting drunk is a slow but sure way to get stupid (Obernier et al., 2002; Wechsler & Wuethrich, 2002).

Positive reinforcement—drinking for pleasure—motivates most people who consume alcohol. What sets alcohol abusers apart from other drinkers is that they also drink to cope with negative emotions, such as anxiety and depression. That's why alcohol abuse increases with the level of stress in people's lives. People who drink to cope with bad feelings run a great risk of becoming alcoholics (Kenneth, Carpenter, & Hasin, 1998).

Recognizing Problem Drinking

What are the signs of alcohol abuse? Because alcohol abuse is such a common problem, it is important to recognize the danger signals of growing dependency. The path from a social drinker to an alcohol abuser to an alcoholic is often subtle. Jellinek (1960) gives these typical steps in the development of a drinking problem:

1. **Initial phase.** At first, the social drinker begins to turn more often to alcohol to relieve tension or to feel good. Four danger signals in this period that signal excessive dependence on alcohol are:
   Increasing consumption. The individual drinks more and more and may begin to worry about his or her drinking.
   Morning drinking. Morning drinking is a dangerous sign, particularly when it is used to combat a hangover or to "get through the day."
   Regretted behavior. The person engages in extreme behavior while drunk that leaves her or him feeling guilty or embarrassed.
   Blackouts. Abusive drinking may be revealed by an inability to remember what happened during intoxication.
2. **Crucial phase.** A crucial turning point comes as the person begins to lose control over drinking. At this stage, there is still some control over when and where a first drink is taken. But one drink starts a chain reaction leading to a second and a third, and so on.
3. **Chronic phase.** At this point, the person is alcohol dependent. Victims drink compulsively and continuously. They rarely eat, they become intoxicated from far less alcohol than before, and they crave alcohol when deprived of it. Work, family ties, and social life all deteriorate. The person's self-drugging is usually so compulsive that when given a choice, the bottle comes before friends, relatives, employment, and self-esteem. The person is an addict.

The Development of a Drinking Problem

To add to this summary, the following lists will help you form a more detailed picture of how alcohol abuse develops.

Early Warnings
- You are beginning to feel guilty about your drinking.
- You drink more than you used to and tend to gulp your drinks.
- You try to have a few extra drinks before or after drinking with others.
- You have begun to drink at certain times or to get through certain situations.
- You drink to relieve feelings of boredom, depression, anxiety, or inadequacy.
- You are sensitive when others mention your drinking.
- You have had memory blackouts or have passed out while drinking.

Signals Not To Be Ignored
- There are times when you need a drink.
- You drink in the morning to overcome a hangover.
- You promise to drink less and are lying about your drinking.
- You often regret what you have said or done while drinking.
- You have begun to drink alone.
- You have weekend drinking bouts and Monday hangovers.
- You have lost time at work or school because of drinking.
- You are noticeably drunk on important occasions.
- Your relationship to family and friends has changed because of your drinking.

Moderated Drinking

Many social-recreational drinkers could do a far better job of managing their use of alcohol. Almost everyone has been to a party spoiled by someone who drank too much too fast. Those who avoid overdrinking have a better time, and so do their friends. But how do you avoid drinking too much? After all, as one wit once observed, "The conscience dissolves in alcohol." Psychologists Roger Vogler and Wayne Bartz (1982, 1992) have observed that it takes skill to regulate drinking in social situations, where the temptation to drink can be strong. If you choose to drink, here are some guidelines that may be helpful. (Adapted from Vogler & Bartz, 1992.)

Paced Drinking
1. Think about your drinking beforehand, and plan how you will manage it.
2. Drink slowly, eat while drinking, and make every other drink (or more) a non-alcoholic beverage.
3. Limit drinking primarily to the first hour of a social event or party.
4. Practice how you will politely but firmly refuse drinks.
5. Learn how to relax, meet people, and socialize without relying on alcohol.

Treatment

Treatment for alcohol dependence begins with sobering up the person and cutting off the supply. This phase is referred to as **detoxification** (literally, "to remove poison"). It frequently produces all the symptoms of drug withdrawal and can be extremely unpleasant. The next step is to try to restore the person's health. Heavy abuse of alcohol usually causes severe damage to body organs and the nervous system. After alcoholics have "dried out" and some degree of health has been restored, they may be treated with tranquilizers, antidepressants, or psychotherapy. Unfortunately, the success of these procedures has been limited.

One mutual-help approach that has been fairly successful is Alcoholics Anonymous (AA). AA acts on the premise that it takes a former alcoholic to understand and help a current alcoholic. Participants at AA meetings admit that they have a problem, share feelings, and resolve to stay "dry" one day at a time. Other group members provide support for those struggling to end dependency. (Cocaine Anonymous and Narcotics Anonymous use the same approach.)

Eighty-one percent of those who remain in AA for more than 1 year get through the following year without a drink. However, AA's success rate may simply reflect the fact that members join voluntarily, meaning they have admitted they have a serious problem (Morgenstern et al., 1997). Sadly, it seems that alcohol abusers will often not face their problems until they have "hit rock bottom." If they are willing, though, AA presents a practical approach to the problem.

Two newer groups offer a rational, non-spiritual approach to alcohol abuse that better fits the needs of some people. These are Rational Recovery and Secular Organizations for Sobriety (SOS). Other alternatives to AA include medical treatment, group therapy, and individual psychotherapy (Institute of Medicine, 1990). There is a strong tendency for abusive drinkers to deny they have a problem. The sooner they seek help, the better.

Detoxification In the treatment of alcoholism, the withdrawal of the patient from alcohol.

MARIJUANA AND HALLUCINOGENS— WHAT'S IN THE POT?

Marijuana and hashish are derived from the hemp plant *Cannabis sativa.* Marijuana ("pot," "herb," "weed") consists of the leaves and flowers of the hemp plant. Hashish is a resinous material scraped from Cannabis leaves. The main active chemical in marijuana is tetrahydrocannabinol (tet-rah-hydro-cah-NAB-ih-nol), or THC, for short. THC is a mild **hallucinogen** (hal-LU-sin-oh-jin: a substance that alters sensory impressions).

LSD and PCP

The drug LSD (lysergic acid diethylamide or "acid") is perhaps the best-known hallucinogen. Even when taken in tiny amounts, LSD can produce hallucinations and psychotic-like disturbances in thinking and perception. Two other common hallucinogens are mescaline (peyote) and psilocybin ("magic mushrooms"). Incidentally, the drug PCP (phencyclidine or "angel dust") can have hallucinogenic effects. However, PCP, which is an anesthetic, also has stimulant and depressant effects. This potent combination can cause extreme agitation, disorientation, violence—and too often, tragedy. All of the hallucinogens, including marijuana, typically affect neurotransmitter systems that carry messages between brain cells (Julien, 1998).

Marijuana

Marijuana's psychological effects include a sense of euphoria or well-being, relaxation, altered time sense, and perceptual distortions. At high dosages, however, paranoia, hallucinations, and delusions can occur (Palfai & Jankiewicz, 1991). All considered, marijuana intoxication is relatively subtle by comparison to drugs such as LSD or alcohol (Kelly et al., 1990). Despite this, driving a car while high on marijuana can be extremely hazardous. As a matter of fact, driving under the influence of any intoxicating drug is dangerous.

No overdose deaths have been reported from marijuana. However, marijuana cannot be considered harmless. Particularly worrisome is the fact that THC accumulates in the body's fatty tissues, especially in the brain and reproductive organs. Even if a person smokes marijuana just once a week, the body is never entirely free of THC. Scientists have located a specific receptor site on the surface of brain cells where THC binds to produce its effects (◆Fig. 5.13). These receptor sites are found in large numbers in the cerebral cortex, which is the seat of human consciousness (Matsuda et al., 1990).

Does marijuana produce physical dependence? Studies of long-term heavy users of marijuana in Jamaica, Greece, and Costa Rica failed to find any physical dependence (Carter, 1980; Rubin & Comitas, 1975; Stefanis et al., 1977). Marijuana's potential for abuse lies pri-

Artists have tried at times to capture the effects of hallucinogens. Here, the artist depicts visual experiences he had while under the influence of LSD.

"Marijuana and the Brain," *Science News,* vol 143

◆**FIGURE 5.13** *This thin slice of a rat's brain has been washed with a radioactive THC-like drug. Yellowish areas show where the brain is rich in THC receptors. In addition to the cortex, or outer layer of the brain, THC receptors are found in abundance in areas involved in the control of coordinated movement. Naturally occurring chemicals similar to THC may help the brain cope with pain and stress. However, when THC is used as a drug, high doses can cause paranoia, hallucinations, and dizziness (Julien, 1998).*

Hallucinogen A substance that alters or distorts sensory impressions.

marily in the realm of psychological dependence, not addiction. Nevertheless, frequent users of marijuana find it very difficult to quit, so dependence is a risk (Budney et al., 1999; Haney et al., 1999).

Dangers of Marijuana Use

There have been very alarming reports in the press about the dangers of marijuana. Are they accurate?   As one pharmacologist put it, "Those reading only *Good Housekeeping* would have to believe that marijuana is considerably more dangerous than the black plague." Unfortunately, an evaluation of marijuana's risks has been clouded by emotional debate. Let's see if we can make a realistic appraisal.

In the past, it was widely reported that marijuana causes brain damage, genetic damage, and a loss of motivation. Each of these charges can be criticized for being based on poorly done or inconclusive research. But that doesn't mean that marijuana gets a clean bill of health. For about a day after a person smokes marijuana, his or her attention, coordination, and short-term memory are impaired (Pope, Gruber, & Yurgelun-Todd, 1995). Frequent marijuana users show small declines in learning, memory, attention, and thinking abilities (Solowij et al., 2002).

People who smoke five or more joints a week score 4 points lower on IQ tests. This is enough to dull their learning capacity. In fact, many people who have stopped using marijuana say they quit because they were bothered by short-term memory loss and concentration problems. Fortunately, IQ scores and other cognitive measures rebound in about a month after a person quits using marijuana (Fried et al., 2002; Grant et al., 2001). In other words, people who smoke dope may act like dopes, but if they quit, there's a good chance they will regain their mental abilities.

An outdated anti-marijuana poster demonstrates the kind of misinformation that has long been attached to this drug. Research has finally begun to sort out what risks are associated with use of marijuana.

Health Risks

After many years of conflicting information, some of marijuana's health hazards are also being clarified. Marijuana's long-term effects include the following health risks.

1. In regular users, marijuana causes pre-cancerous changes in lung cells. At present, no direct link between marijuana and lung cancer has been proved, but it is suspected. Marijuana smoke contains 50 percent more cancer-causing hydrocarbons and 16 times more tar than tobacco smoke does. Thus, smoking several "joints" a week may be the equivalent of smoking a dozen cigarettes a day (Barsky et al., 1998).

2. Marijuana temporarily lowers sperm production in males, and users produce more abnormal sperm. This could be a problem for a man who is marginally fertile and wants to have a family (Schuel et al., 1999).

3. In experiments with female monkeys, THC causes abnormal menstrual cycles and disrupts ovulation. Other animal studies show that THC causes a higher rate of miscarriages and that it can reach the developing fetus. As is true for so many other drugs, it appears that marijuana should be avoided during pregnancy.

4. THC can suppress the body's immune system, increasing the risk of disease.

5. In animals, marijuana causes genetic damage within cells of the body. It is not known to what extent this happens in humans, but it does suggest that marijuana can be detrimental to health.

6. Activity levels in the cerebellum are lower than normal in marijuana abusers. This may explain why chronic marijuana users tend to show some loss of coordination (Volkow et al., 1996).

7. There is some evidence that THC damages parts of the brain important for memory (Chan et al., 1998).

8. Children whose mothers smoked marijuana during pregnancy show lowered ability to succeed in challenging, goal-oriented activities (Fried & Smith, 2001).

When the preceding findings are compared with the studies of veteran marijuana users, it is clear that no one can say with certainty that marijuana is extremely harmful or completely safe. Although much is still unknown, marijuana appears to be in a class with two other potent drugs—tobacco and alcohol. Only future research will tell for sure "what's in the pot."

Summary

Why is drug abuse such a common problem?   People seek drug experiences for many reasons, ranging from curiosity and a desire to belong to a group, to a search for meaning or an escape from feelings of inadequacy. The best predictors of adolescent drug use and abuse are drug use by peers, parental drug use, delinquency, parental maladjustment, poor self-esteem, social nonconformity, and stressful life changes. A recent study found that adolescents who abuse drugs tend to be maladjusted, alienated, impulsive, and emotionally distressed (Masse & Tremblay, 1997). Antisocial behavior, school failure, and risky sexual behavior are also commonly associated with drug abuse (Ary et al., 1999). Such patterns make it clear that taking drugs is a symptom, rather than a cause, of personal and social maladjustment (Derzon & Lipsey, 1999; Welte et al., 1999).

Many abusers turn to drugs in a self-defeating attempt to cope with life. All of the frequently abused drugs produce immediate feelings of pleasure. The negative consequences follow much later. This combination of immediate pleasure and delayed punishment allows abusers to feel good on demand. In time, of course, most of the pleasure goes out of drug abuse, and the abuser's problems get worse. But if an abuser merely feels better (however briefly) after taking a drug, drug taking can become compulsive (Barrett, 1985). In contrast, people who stop using drugs often say that they quit because the drawbacks had come to exceed the benefits (Toneatto et al., 1999).

Although billions of dollars have been spent on drug enforcement in recent years, there has been an increase in the overall level of drug use in the United States. Most drug use begins in early adolescence (Chen & Kandel, 1995). Given this fact, some experts believe that prevention through education and early intervention is the answer to drug problems (Julien,1998). What do you think?

A Look Ahead

Of the many states of consciousness we have discussed, dreaming remains one of the most familiar—and the most surprising. Are there lessons to be learned from dreams? What personal insights lie hidden in the ebb and flow of your dream images? Let's find out.

Well-crafted information and education can discourage drug use. This billboard is part of California's anti-smoking campaign. It emphasizes the dangers of second-hand smoke. Research has shown that this is one of several issues that motivates children and adolescents to resist pressures to begin smoking.

STUDYBREAK ⅄ *Psychoactive Drugs*

RELATE

What legal drugs did you use in the last year? Did any have psychoactive properties? How do psychoactive drugs differ from other substances in their potential for abuse?

LEARNING CHECK

1. Which of the drugs listed below are known to cause a physical dependence?
   a. heroin
   b. morphine
   c. codeine
   d. methadone
   e. barbiturates
   f. alcohol
   g. caffeine
   h. amphetamines
   i. nicotine
   j. cocaine
   k. GHB
2. Amphetamine psychosis is similar to extreme _____, in which the individual feels threatened and suffers from delusions.
3. Cocaine is very similar to which of the following in its effects on the central nervous system?
   a. Seconal   b. codeine   c. *Cannabis*   d. amphetamine

4. The combination of _____ or _____ and alcohol can be fatal.
5. One drink starts a chain reaction leading to a second and a third in the crucial phase of problem drinking. T or F?
6. This country's biggest drug problem centers on abuse of
   a. marijuana   b. alcohol   c. tobacco   d. cocaine
7. MDMA and GHB are classified as depressants. T or F?

Critical Thinking

8. The U.S. government, which helps fund anti-smoking campaigns and smoking-related health research, also continues to subsidize tobacco growers. Can you explain this contradiction?
9. Why do you think there is such a contrast between the laws regulating marijuana and those regulating alcohol and tobacco?

ANSWERS

1. All but g 2. paranoia 3. d 4. barbiturates, tranquilizers 5. T 6. b 7. F 8. Neither can 1. 9. Drug laws in Western societies reflect cultural values and historical patterns of use. Inconsistencies in the law often cannot be justified on the basis of pharmacology, health risks, or abuse potential.

Psychology in Action

Exploring and Using Dreams

] SURVEYQUESTION *How are dreams used to promote personal understanding?*

At one time or another almost everyone has had a dream that seemed to have deep meaning. What strategies do psychologists use to interpret dreams? Let's start with Sigmund Freud's approach.

To unlock dreams, Freud identified four **dream processes,** or mental filters, that disguise the meanings of dreams. The first is **condensation,** in which several people, objects, or events are combined into a single dream image. A dream character that looks like a teacher, acts like your father, talks like your mother, and is dressed like your employer might be a condensation of authority figures in your life.

Displacement is a second way of disguising dream content. Displacement may cause important emotions or actions of a dream to be redirected toward safe or seemingly unimportant images. Thus, a student angry at his parents might dream of accidentally wrecking their car instead of directly attacking them.

A third dream process is **symbolization.** As mentioned earlier, Freud believed that dreams are often expressed in images that are symbolic rather than literal. That's why it helps to ask what feelings or ideas a dream image might symbolize. Let's say, for example, that a student dreams of coming to class naked. A literal interpretation would be that the student is an exhibitionist! A more likely symbolic meaning is that the student feels vulnerable or unprepared in the class.

Secondary elaboration is the fourth method by which dream meanings are disguised. **Secondary elaboration** is the tendency to make a dream more logical and to add details when remembering it. The fresher a dream memory is, the more useful it is likely to be.

Looking for condensation, displacement, symbolization, and secondary elaboration may help you unlock your dreams. But there are other techniques that may be more effec-

Dream processes Mental filters that hide the true meanings of dreams.
Condensation Combining several people, objects, or events into a single dream image.
Displacement Directing emotions or actions toward safe or unimportant dream images.
Symbolization The non-literal expression of dream content.
Secondary elaboration Making a dream more logical and complete while remembering it.

Courtesy of Maryanne Mott

How would you try to find the meaning of dream? A traditional approach is to look for symbolic messages, as well as literal meanings. If you find yourself wearing a mask in a dream, for instance, it could relate to important roles that you play at school, work, or home. It could also mean that you want to hide or that you are looking forward to a costume party. However, to accurately interpret a dream, it is important to learn your own "vocabulary" of dream images and meanings. Keeping a dream diary is the first step toward gaining valuable insights.

▲TABLE 5.5	Effects of Selected Drugs on Dreaming
DRUG	**EFFECT ON REM SLEEP**
Alcohol	Decrease
Amphetamines	Decrease
Barbiturates	Decrease
Caffeine	None
Cocaine	Decrease
LSD	Slight increase
Marijuana	Slight decrease or no effect
Opiates	Decrease
Valium	Decrease

tive. Dream theorist Calvin Hall (1974) preferred to think of dreams as plays and the dreamer as a playwright. Hall admitted that dream images and ideas tend to be more primitive than waking thoughts. Nevertheless, much can be learned by simply considering the *setting, cast of characters, plot,* and *emotions* portrayed in a dream.

Another dream theorist, Rosalind Cartwright, suggests that dreams are primarily "feeling statements." According to her, the overall *emotional tone* (underlying mood) of a dream is a major clue to its meaning. Is the dream comical, threatening, joyous, or depressing? Were you lonely, jealous, frightened, in love, or angry? Cartwright believes that exploring everyday dream life can be a source of personal enrichment and personal growth (Cartwright & Lamberg, 1992).

In many ways, dreams can be thought of as a message *from* yourself *to* yourself. Thus, the way to understand dreams is to remember them, write them down, look for the messages they contain, and become deeply acquainted with *your own* symbol system. Here's how.

How to Catch a Dream

1. Before going to sleep, plan to remember your dreams. Keep a pen and paper or a tape recorder beside your bed.
2. If possible, arrange to awaken gradually without an alarm. Natural awakening almost always follows soon after a REM period.
3. If you rarely remember your dreams, you may want to set an alarm clock to go off an hour before you usually awaken. Although less desirable than awakening naturally, this may let you catch a dream.
4. Upon awakening, lie still and review the dream images with your eyes closed. Try to recall as many details as possible.
5. If you can, make your first dream record (whether by writing or by tape) with your eyes closed. Opening your eyes will disrupt dream recall.
6. Review the dream again and record as many additional details as you can remember. Dream memories disappear quickly. Be sure to describe feelings as well as the plot, characters, and actions of the dream.
7. Put your dreams into a permanent dream diary. Keep dreams in chronological order, and review them periodically. This procedure will reveal recurrent themes, conflicts, and emotions. It almost always produces valuable insights.
8. Remember, a number of drugs suppress dreaming (see ▲Table 5.5).

Dream Work

Because each dream has several possible meanings or levels of meaning, there is no fixed way to work with it. Telling the dream to others and discussing its meaning can be a good start. Describing it may help you relive some of the feelings in the dream. Also, family members or friends may be able to offer interpretations to which you would be blind. Watch for verbal or visual puns and other playful elements in dreams. For example, if you dream that you are in a wrestling match and your arm is pinned behind your back, it may mean that you feel someone is "twisting your arm" in real life.

The meaning of most dreams will yield to a little detective work. Rosalind Cartwright suggests asking a series of questions about dreams you would like to understand (Cartwright & Lamberg, 1992).

Probing Dreams

1. Who was in the dream? Do you recognize any of the characters?
2. What was happening? Were you active in the dream or watching it transpire? Did someone else do something to you?
3. Where did the action of the dream take place? Have you seen the setting or any part of it in real life, or was it a fantasy scene?
4. What was the time frame? What was your age in the dream?
5. Who is responsible for what happened in the dream?
6. Who are you in your dreams? Are you someone you would like to be or someone you'd rather not be?

If you still have trouble seeing the meaning of a dream, you may find it helpful to use a technique developed by Fritz Perls. Perls, the originator of Gestalt therapy, considered most dreams a special message about what's missing in our lives, what we avoid doing, or feelings that need to be "re-owned." Perls believed that dreams are a way of filling in gaps in personal experience (Perls, 1969).

An approach that Perls found helpful is to "take the part of" or "speak for" each of the characters and objects in the dream. In other words, if you dream about a strange man standing behind a doorway, you would speak aloud to the man, then answer for him. To use Perls' method, you would even speak for the door, perhaps saying something like, "I am a barrier. I keep you safe, but I also keep you locked inside. The stranger has something to tell you. You must risk opening me to learn it."

A particularly interesting dream exercise is to continue a dream as waking fantasy so that it may be concluded or carried on to a more meaningful ending. As the world of dreams and your personal dream language become more familiar, you will doubtless find many answers, paradoxes, intuitions, and insights into your own behavior.

Using Your Dreams

Creative people tend to remember more dreams (Schredl, 1995). It could be that such people just pay more attention to their dreams. But dream theorist Gordon Globus (1987) believes that dreams make a major contribution to creativity. Globus points out that some of our most creative moments take place during dreaming. Even unimaginative people may create amazing worlds each night in their dreams. For many of us, this rich ability to create is lost in the daily rush of sensory input. How might we tap the creative power of dreams that is so easily lost during waking?

Dreams and Creativity

History is full of cases where dreams have been a pathway to creativity and discovery. A striking example is provided by Dr. Otto Loewi, a pharmacologist and winner of a Nobel prize. Loewi had spent years studying the chemical transmission of nerve impulses. A tremendous breakthrough in his research came when he dreamed of an experiment 3 nights in a row. The first 2 nights he woke up and scribbled the experiment on a pad. But the next morning, he couldn't tell what the notes meant. On the third night, he got up after having the dream. This time, instead of making notes he went straight to his laboratory and performed the crucial experiment. Loewi later said that if the experiment had occurred to him while awake he would have rejected it.

Loewi's experience gives some insight into using dreams to produce creative solutions. Inhibitions are reduced during dreaming, which may be especially useful in solving problems that require a fresh point of view.

Being able to take advantage of dreams for problem solving is improved if you "set" yourself before retiring. Before you go to bed, try to think intently about a problem you wish to solve. Steep yourself in the problem by stating it clearly and reviewing all relevant information. Then use the suggestions listed in the previous section to catch your dreams. Although this method is not guaranteed to produce a novel solution or a new insight, it is certain to be an adventure. About half of a group of college students using the method for 1 week recalled a dream that helped them solve a personal problem (Barrett, 1993).

Lucid Dreaming

If you would like to press further into the territory of dreams, you may want to learn lucid dreaming, a relatively rare, but fascinating experience. During a **lucid dream,** a person feels as if she or he is fully awake within the dream world and capable of normal thought and action. If you ask yourself, "Could this be a dream?" and answer "Yes," you are having a lucid dream (Blackmore, 1991a).

Stephen LaBerge and his colleagues at the Stanford University Sleep Research Center have used a unique approach to show that lucid dreams are real and that they occur during REM sleep. In the sleep lab, lucid dreamers agree to make prearranged signals when they become aware they are dreaming. One such signal is to look up abruptly in a dream, causing a distinct upward eye movement. Another signal is to clench the right and left fists (in the

Lucid dream A dream in which the dreamer feels awake and capable of normal thought and action.

dream) in a prearranged pattern. In other words, lucid dreamers can partially overcome REM sleep paralysis. Such signals show very clearly that lucid dreaming and voluntary action in dreams is possible (La Berge, 1981, 1985; Moss, 1989).

How would a person go about learning to have lucid dreams? Dream researcher Stephen LaBerge found he could greatly increase lucid dreaming by following this simple routine: When you awaken spontaneously from a dream, take a few minutes to try to memorize it. Next, engage in 10 to 15 minutes of reading or any other activity requiring full wakefulness. Then while lying in bed and returning to sleep, say to yourself, "Next time I'm dreaming, I want to remember I'm dreaming." Finally, visualize yourself lying in bed asleep while in the dream you just rehearsed. At the same time, picture yourself realizing that you are dreaming. Follow this routine each time you awaken (substitute a dream memory from another occasion if you don't awaken from a dream). Researchers have also found that stimulation from the vestibular system tends to increase lucidity. Thus, sleeping in a hammock, a boat, or on a waterbed might increase the number of lucid dreams you have (Leslie & Ogilvie, 1996).

Why would anyone want to have more lucid dreams?   Researchers are interested in lucid dreams because they provide a tool for understanding dreaming. Using subjects who can signal while they are dreaming makes it possible to explore dreams with firsthand data from the dreamer's world itself.

On a more personal level, lucid dreaming can convert dreams into a nightly "workshop" for emotional growth. Consider, for example, a recently divorced woman who kept dreaming that she was being swallowed by a giant wave. Rosalind Cartwright asked the woman to try swimming the next time the wave engulfed her. She did, with great determination, and the nightmare lost its terror. More important, her revised dream made her feel that she could cope with life again. For reasons such as this, people who have lucid dreams tend to feel a sense of emotional well-being (Wolpin et al., 1992). Dream expert Allan Hobson believes that learning to voluntarily enter altered states of consciousness (through lucid dreaming or self-hypnosis, for example) has allowed him to have enlightening experiences without the risks of taking mind-altering drugs (Hobson, 2001). So, day or night, don't be afraid to dream a little.

STUDYBREAK Y *Exploring and Using Dreams*

RELATE

Some people are very interested in remembering and interpreting their dreams. Others pay little attention to dreaming. What importance do you place on dreams? Do you think dreams and dream interpretation can increase self-awareness?

LEARNING CHECK

1. In secondary elaboration, one dream character stands for several others. T or F?
2. Calvin Hall's approach to dream interpretation emphasizes the setting, cast, plot, and emotions portrayed in a dream. T or F?

3. Rosalind Cartwright stresses that dreaming is a relatively mechanical process having little personal meaning. T or F?
4. Both alcohol and LSD cause a slight increase in dreaming. T or F?
5. "Taking the part of" or "speaking for" dream elements is a dream interpretation technique originated by Fritz Perls. T or F?
6. Recent research shows that lucid dreaming occurs primarily during NREM sleep or micro-awakenings. T or F?

Critical Thinking

7. The possibility of having a lucid dream raises an interesting question: If you were dreaming right now, how could you prove it?

ANSWERS 1. F 2. T 3. F 4. F 5. F 6. F 7. In waking consciousness, our actions have consequences that produce immediate sensory feedback. Dreams lack such external feedback. Thus, trying to walk through a wall or doing similar tests would reveal if you were dreaming.

CHAPTER IN REVIEW

Major Points

- Consciousness and altered states of awareness are core features of mental life.
- Sleep is necessary for survival; dreaming appears to contribute to memory consolidation and perhaps to general mental and emotional health.
- Sleep loss and sleep disorders are serious health problems that should be corrected when they persist.
- Dreams are at least as meaningful as waking thoughts. Whether they have deeper, symbolic meaning is still debated.
- Hypnosis is useful but not "magical." Hypnosis can change private experiences more readily than behaviors or habits.
- Meditation can be used to alter consciousness, as well as to reliably produce deep relaxation.
- Psychoactive drugs, which alter consciousness, are highly prone to abuse.
- Collecting and interpreting your dreams can promote self-awareness.

Summary

What is an altered state of consciousness?

- States of awareness that differ from normal, alert, waking consciousness are called altered states of consciousness (ASCs). Altered states are especially associated with sleep and dreaming, hypnosis, sensory deprivation, and psychoactive drugs.
- Cultural conditioning greatly affects what altered states a person recognizes, seeks, considers normal, and attains.

What are the effects of sleep loss and changes in sleep patterns?

- Sleep is an innate biological rhythm essential for survival. Higher animals and people deprived of sleep experience involuntary microsleeps.
- Moderate sleep loss mainly affects vigilance and performance on routine or boring tasks. Extended sleep loss can (somewhat rarely) produce a temporary sleep-deprivation psychosis.
- Sleep patterns show some flexibility, but 7 to 8 hours remains average. The amount of daily sleep decreases steadily from birth to old age. Once-a-day sleep patterns, with a 2-to-1 ratio of waking and sleep, are most efficient for most people.

Are there different stages of sleep?

- Sleep occurs in four stages. Stage 1 is light sleep, and stage 4 is deep sleep. The sleeper alternates between stages 1 and 4 (passing through stages 2 and 3) several times each night.

How does dream sleep differ from dreamless sleep?

- There are two basic sleep states, rapid eye movement (REM) sleep and non-REM (NREM) sleep. REM sleep is much more strongly associated with dreaming than non-REM sleep is.
- Dreaming and REMs occur mainly during light sleep, similar to stage 1. Dreaming is accompanied by emotional arousal but relaxation of the skeletal muscles.
- People deprived of dream sleep show a REM rebound when allowed to sleep without interruption. However, total sleep loss seems to be more important than loss of a single stage.
- In addition to several other possible functions, REM sleep appears to aid the processing of memories.

What are the causes of sleep disorders and unusual sleep events?

- Sleepwalking and sleeptalking occur during NREM sleep. Night terrors occur in NREM sleep, whereas nightmares occur in REM sleep. Narcolepsy (sleep attacks) and cataplexy are caused by a sudden shift to stage 1 REM patterns during normal waking hours.
- Sleep apnea (interrupted breathing) is one source of insomnia and daytime hypersomnia (sleepiness).
- Apnea is suspected as one cause of sudden infant death syndrome (SIDS). Exposure to secondhand smoke is a major risk factor for SIDS. With only a few exceptions, healthy infants should sleep face up or on their sides.
- Insomnia may be temporary or chronic. When it is treated through the use of drugs, sleep quality is often lowered and drug-dependency insomnia may develop.
- Behavioral approaches to managing insomnia, such as sleep restriction and stimulus control, are quite effective.

Do dreams have meaning?

- Most dream content is about familiar settings, people, and actions. Dreams more often involve negative emotions than positive emotions.
- The Freudian, or psychodynamic, view is that dreams express unconscious wishes, frequently hidden by dream symbols.
- Many theorists have questioned Freud's view of dreams. For example, the activation-synthesis model portrays dreaming as a physiological process.

How is hypnosis done, and what are its limitations?

- Hypnosis is an altered state characterized by narrowed attention and increased suggestibility. (Not all psychologists agree that hypnotic effects require an alteration of consciousness.)

- Hypnosis appears capable of producing relaxation, controlling pain, and altering perceptions. Stage hypnotism takes advantage of typical stage behavior and uses deception to simulate hypnosis.

What is meditation? Does it have any benefits?

- Concentrative meditation can be used to focus attention, alter consciousness, and reduce stress. Major benefits of meditation are its ability to interrupt anxious thoughts and to elicit the relaxation response.
- Brief exposure to sensory deprivation can also elicit the relaxation response. Under proper conditions, sensory deprivation may help break long-standing habits.

What are the effects of the more commonly used psychoactive drugs?

- A psychoactive drug is a substance that affects the brain in ways that alter consciousness. Most psychoactive drugs can be placed on a scale ranging from stimulation to depression.
- Drugs may cause a physical dependence (addiction) or a psychological dependence, or both. The physically addicting drugs are alcohol, amphetamines, barbiturates, cocaine, codeine, GHB, heroin, methadone, morphine, nicotine, and tranquilizers. All psychoactive drugs can lead to psychological dependence.
- Drug use can be classified as experimental, recreational, situational, intensive, and compulsive. Drug abuse is most often associated with the last three.
- Stimulant drugs are readily abused because of the period of depression that often follows stimulation. The greatest risks are associated with amphetamines (especially methamphetamine), cocaine, MDMA, and nicotine, but even caffeine can be a problem. Nicotine includes the added risk of lung cancer, heart disease, and other health problems.
- Barbiturates and tranquilizers are depressant drugs whose action is similar to that of alcohol. The overdose level for barbiturates and GHB is close to the intoxication dosage, making them dangerous drugs. Mixing barbiturates, tranquilizers, or GHB and alcohol may result in a fatal drug interaction.
- Alcohol is the most heavily abused drug in common use today. The development of a drinking problem is usually marked by an initial phase of increasing consumption, a crucial phase, in which a single drink can set off a chain reaction, and a chronic phase, in which a person lives to drink and drinks to live.
- Marijuana is subject to an abuse pattern similar to alcohol. Studies have linked chronic marijuana use with lung cancer, various mental impairments, and other health problems.

How can dreams be used to promote personal understanding?

- Dreams may be used to promote self-understanding. Freud held that the meaning of dreams is hidden by condensation, displacement, symbolization, and secondary elaboration.
- Hall emphasizes the setting, cast, plot, and emotions of a dream. Cartwright's view of dreams as feeling statements and Perls' technique of speaking for dream elements are also helpful.
- Dreams may be used for creative problem solving, especially when dream awareness is achieved through lucid dreaming.

Interactive Learning

Internet addresses frequently change. To find the sites listed here, visit www.psychology. wadsworth.com/coon_journey2e for an updated list of Internet addresses and direct links to relevant sites.

PSYCHOLOGY: A JOURNEY COMPANION WEB SITE Online quizzes, flash cards, and other helpful study aids for this text. *www.psychology.wadsworth.com/coon_journey2e*

ALCOHOLICS ANONYMOUS (AA) Home page of Alcoholics Anonymous.

CIRCADIAN RHYTHMS Basic information about circadian rhythms and jet lag.

COCAINE ANONYMOUS Offers advice and information on how to quit cocaine addiction.

DRUGS AND BEHAVIOR LINKS Comprehensive links to topics in drugs and behavior.

MARIJUANA ANONYMOUS Offers advice and information on how to quit smoking marijuana.

SELF-SCORING ALCOHOL CHECK UP A short quiz for identifying drinking problems.

SLEEPNET Information about sleep and sleep disorders, with many links to other sites.

SUDDEN INFANT DEATH AND OTHER INFANT DEATH Information about SIDS, with links to related topics.

THE ANTIDRUG.COM Advice to parents and other adults about how to help children resist drug use.

THE REALITY OF HYPNOSIS An extended discussion of hypnosis.

INFOTRAC COLLEGE EDITION For recent articles related to the Psychology in Action feature, use Key Words search for DREAMS.

PSYCHNOW! 3c. Sleep and dreaming, 3d. Psychoactive drugs.

Test Your Knowledge: States of Consciousness

The questions that follow are only a sample of what you need to know. If you miss any of the items, you should review the entire chapter and get more practice with *WebTutor* or the *Practice Quizzes* that came with this book. Another way to prepare for tests is to use the printed *Study Guide* that is available for this text.

1. Changes in the quality and pattern of mental activity define
   A. an EEG   B. an REM   C. SIDS   D. an ASC

2. Alyssa experiences a microsleep while driving. Most likely, this indicates that she
   A. was producing mostly beta waves   B. had high levels of sleep hormones in her bloodstream   C. switched from delta waves to alpha waves   D. was sleep deprived

3. A person in deep sleep produces mostly
   A. beta waves   B. alpha waves   C. delta waves
   D. REMs

4. Which of the following would normally be most incompatible with moving your arms and legs while asleep?
   A. REM sleep   B. sleep spindles   C. delta waves
   D. NREM sleep

5. People who suffer from sudden daytime sleep attacks have which sleep disorder?
   A. narcolepsy   B. REM behavior disorder   C. somnambulism   D. sleep spindling

6. Eating a snack that is nearly all starch can promote sleep because it increases _____ in the brain.
   A. beta waves   B. tryptophan   C. EEG activity
   D. hypnic cycling

7. Sleep restriction and stimulus control are techniques used to treat
   A. sleep apnea   B. sleep talking   C. night terrors
   D. insomnia

8. Sorting and integrating memories is one function of
   A. activation-synthesis cycles   B. REM sleep   C. deep sleep   D. NREM sleep

9. Wish fulfillment and dream symbols are important concepts in which explanation of dream content?
   A. activation-synthesis   B. the REST hypothesis
   C. imagery rehearsal   D. psychodynamic

10. Tests of hypnotic susceptibility measure a person's tendency to respond to
    A. suggestion   B. imagery rehearsal   C. stimulus control techniques   D. the activation-synthesis effect

11. Research has shown that hypnosis cannot produce
    A. unusual strength   B. improved memory   C. pain relief   D. sensory changes

12. Which terms DO NOT belong together?
    A. concentrative meditation—relaxation response
    B. sensory deprivation—relaxation response   C. receptive meditation—mantra   D. sensory deprivation—REST

13. Addictive drugs stimulate the brain's reward circuitry by affecting
    A. neurotransmitters   B. alpha waves   C. tryptophan levels   D. delta spindles

14. Drug tolerance is most closely associated with
    A. psychological dependence   B. marijuana
    C. withdrawal symptoms   D. anhedonia

15. Cocaine is most similar to _____ in its effects on the nervous system.
    A. marijuana   B. benzodiazepine   C. serotonin
    D. amphetamine

16. Hyperthermia, heart arrhythmias, and severe liver damage are major risks in the use of
    A. marijuana   B. benzodiazepine   C. MDMA   D. GHB

17. Drug interaction is a special danger when a person combines
    A. marijuana and amphetamine   B. barbiturates and alcohol   C. alcohol and cocaine   D. marijuana and THC

18. Treatment for alcohol dependence begins with sobering up the person and cutting off the supply. This is referred to as
    A. "hitting bottom"   B. the crucial phase   C. detoxification
    D. clinical anhedonia

19. Drug abuse is partly explained by the fact that psychoactive drugs produce immediate pleasure and
    A. somnambulism   B. enhanced self-esteem   C. delayed punishment   D. brain carcinogens

20. Which is NOT one of the four dream processes identified by Freud?
    A. condensation   B. lucidity   C. displacement
    D. symbolization

ANSWERS   1. d 2. d 3. c 4. a 5. a 6. b 7. d 8. b 9. d 10. a 11. a 12. c 13. a 14. c 15. d 16. c 17. b 18. c 19. c 20. b

Conditioning and Learning

What Did You Learn in School Today?

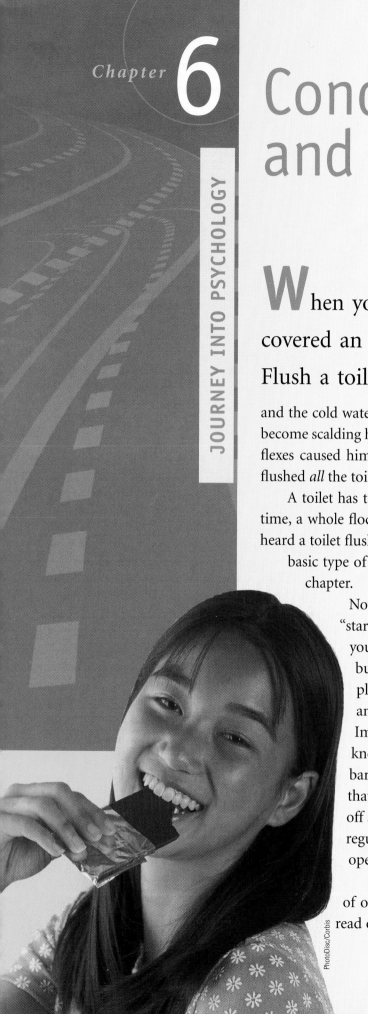

When your aging author was in college we discovered an intriguing flaw in the dorm plumbing: Flush a toilet while someone was taking a shower, and the cold water pressure would suddenly drop. This caused the shower to become scalding hot. Naturally, the shower victim screamed in terror as his reflexes caused him to leap backward in pain. Soon we discovered that if we flushed *all* the toilets at once, the effects were multiplied many times over!

A toilet has to be one of the world's most uninspiring stimuli. But for a time, a whole flock of college students twitched involuntarily whenever they heard a toilet flush. Their reactions were the result of classical conditioning, a basic type of learning. Classical conditioning is one of the topics of this chapter.

Now, let's say that you are at school and you feel like you are "starving to death." You locate a vending machine and deposit your last two quarters to buy a candy bar. Then you press the button, and . . . nothing happens. Being civilized and in complete control, you press the other buttons, try the coin return, and look for an attendant. Still nothing. Your stomach growls. Impulsively, you give the machine a little kick (just to let it know how you feel). Then, as you turn away, out pops a candy bar plus 25 cents change. Once this happens, chances are good that you will repeat the "kicking response" in the future. If it pays off several times more, kicking vending machines may become a regular feature of your behavior. In this case, learning is based on operant conditioning (also called instrumental learning).

Classical and operant conditioning reach into every corner of our lives. Are you ready to learn more about learning? If so, read on!

PhotoDisc/Corbis

Survey Questions

- What is learning?
- How does classical conditioning occur?
- Does conditioning affect emotions?
- How does operant conditioning occur?
- Are there different kinds of operant reinforcement?
- How are we influenced by patterns of reward?
- What does punishment do to behavior?
- What is cognitive learning?
- Does learning occur by imitation?
- How does conditioning apply to practical problems?

WHAT IS LEARNING—DOES PRACTICE MAKE PERFECT?

] SURVEYQUESTION *What is learning?*

Most behavior is learned. Imagine if you suddenly lost all you had ever learned. What could you do? You would be unable to read, write, or speak. You couldn't feed yourself, find your way home, drive a car, play the bassoon, or "party." Needless to say, you would be totally incapacitated. (Dull, too!)

Learning is obviously important. What's a formal definition of learning? **Learning** is a relatively permanent change in behavior due to experience. Notice that this definition excludes temporary changes caused by motivation, fatigue, maturation, disease, injury, or drugs. Each of these can alter behavior, but none qualifies as learning.

Isn't learning the result of practice? It depends on what you mean by practice. Merely repeating a response will not necessarily produce learning. You could close your eyes and swing a tennis racket hundreds of times without learning anything about tennis. Reinforcement is the key to learning. **Reinforcement** refers to any event that increases the probability that a response will occur again. A response is any identifiable behavior. Responses may be observable actions, such as blinking, eating a piece of candy, or turning a doorknob. They can also be internal, such as having a faster heartbeat.

To teach a dog a trick, I could reinforce correct responses by giving the dog some food each time it sits up. Similarly, you could teach a child to be neat by praising her for picking up her toys. Learning can also occur in other ways. For instance, if a girl gets stung by a bee, she may learn to associate pain with bees and to fear them. In this case, the girl's fear is reinforced by the discomfort she feels immediately after seeing the bee. Later, you'll discover how such varied experiences lead to learning.

Antecedents and Consequences

Unlocking the secrets of learning begins with noting what happens before and after a response. Events that precede a response are called **antecedents.** For example, Ashleigh, who is three, has learned that when she hears a truck pull into the driveway, it means that Daddy is home. Ashleigh runs to the front door to get a hug. Effects that follow a response are **consequences.** The hug that Ashleigh receives from her father reinforces her tendency to run to the door. As this suggests, paying careful attention to the "before and after" of learning is a key to understanding it.

Learning Any relatively permanent change in behavior that can be attributed to experience.

Reinforcement Any event that increases the probability that a particular response will occur.

Antecedents Events that precede a response.

Consequences Effects that follow a response.

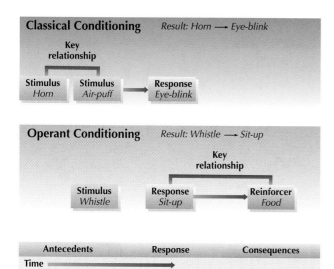

◆FIGURE 6.1 *In classical conditioning, a stimulus that does not produce a response is paired with a stimulus that does elicit a response. After many such pairings, the stimulus that previously had no effect begins to produce a response. In the example shown, a horn precedes a puff of air to the eye. Eventually, the horn alone will produce an eye-blink. In operant conditioning, a response that is followed by a reinforcing consequence becomes more likely to occur on future occasions. In the example shown, a dog learns to sit up when it hears a whistle.*

Reflex An innate, automatic response to a stimulus; for example, an eye-blink.

Classical conditioning A form of learning in which reflex responses are associated with new stimuli.

Operant conditioning Learning based on the consequences of responding.

Classical Conditioning

Classical conditioning is based on what happens before a response. We begin with a stimulus that reliably triggers a response. Imagine, for example, that a puff of air (the stimulus) is aimed at your eye. The air puff will make you blink (a response) every time. The eye-blink is a **reflex** (automatic, non-learned response).

Now, assume that we sound a horn (another stimulus) just before each puff of air hits your eye. If the horn and the air puff occur together many times, what happens? Soon, the horn alone will make you blink. What took place? Clearly, you've learned something. Before, the horn didn't make you blink. Now it does. Similarly, if your mouth waters each time you eat a cookie, you may learn to salivate when you merely *see* a cookie, a picture of cookies, a cookie jar, or other stimuli that preceded salivation.

In **classical conditioning,** antecedent events become associated with one another: An antecedent stimulus that does not produce a response is linked with one that does (a horn is associated with a puff of air to the eye, for example). We can say that learning has occurred when the new stimulus will also elicit (bring forth) responses (◆Fig. 6.1).

Operant Conditioning

In **operant conditioning,** learning is based on the consequences of responding. A response may be followed by a reinforcer (such as food). Or by punishment. Or by nothing. These results determine whether a response is likely to be made again (Fig. 6.1). For example, if you wear a particular hat and get lots of compliments (reinforcement), you are likely to wear it more often. If people snicker, insult you, call the police, or scream (punishment), you will probably wear it less often.

Now that you have an idea of what happens in the two basic kinds of learning, let's look at classical conditioning in more detail.

CLASSICAL CONDITIONING—DOES THE NAME PAVLOV RING A BELL?

] SURVEYQUESTION *How does classical conditioning occur?*

How was classical conditioning discovered? At the beginning of the twentieth century, something happened in the lab of Russian physiologist Ivan Pavlov that brought him lasting fame. The event now seems so trivial that a lesser man might have ignored it: Pavlov's subjects drooled at him.

Actually, Pavlov was studying digestion. To observe salivation, he placed meat powder or some tidbit on a dog's tongue. After doing this many times, Pavlov noticed that his dogs were salivating *before* the food reached their mouths. Later, the dogs even began to salivate when they saw Pavlov enter the room. Was this misplaced affection? Pavlov knew better. Salivation is normally a reflex. For the animals to salivate at the mere sight of food, some type of learning had to have occurred. Pavlov called it conditioning (◆Fig. 6.2). Because of its importance in psychology's history, it is now called classical conditioning (also known as *Pavlovian conditioning* or *respondent conditioning*).

Pavlov's Experiment

How did Pavlov study conditioning? After Pavlov observed that meat powder made his dogs salivate, he began his classic experiments (Fig. 6.2). To begin, he rang a bell. At first, the bell was a neutral stimulus (it did not evoke a response). Immediately after Pavlov rang the bell,

◆**FIGURE 6.2** *An apparatus for Pavlovian conditioning. A tube carries saliva from the dog's mouth to a lever that activates a recording device (far left). During conditioning, various stimuli can be paired with a dish of food placed in front of the dog. The device pictured here is more elaborate than the one Pavlov used in his early experiments.*

he placed meat powder on the dog's tongue, which caused reflex salivation. This sequence was repeated many times: bell, meat powder, salivation; bell, meat powder, salivation. Eventually (as conditioning took place), the dogs began to salivate when they heard the bell (◆Fig. 6.3). By association, the bell, which before had no effect, began to evoke the same response as food. This was shown by sometimes ringing the bell alone. Pavlov then observed that the dog salivated even when no food was present.

Psychologists use several terms to describe these events. The bell in Pavlov's experiment starts out as a **neutral stimulus (NS)**. In time, the bell becomes a **conditioned stimulus (CS)** (a stimulus that, because of learning, will evoke a response). The meat powder is an **unconditioned stimulus (US)** (a stimulus innately capable of eliciting a response). Notice that the dog did not have to learn to respond to the US. Such stimuli naturally elicit reflexes or emotional reactions.

Because a reflex is innate, or "built in," it is called an **unconditioned** (non-learned) **response (UR)**. Reflex salivation was the UR in Pavlov's experiment. When Pavlov's bell also produced salivation, the dog was making a new response. Thus, salivation had become a **conditioned** (learned) **response (CR)** (Fig. 6.3). ▲Table 6.1 summarizes the important elements of classical conditioning.

Neutral stimulus A stimulus that does not evoke a response. *bell*

Conditioned stimulus A stimulus that evokes a response because it has been repeatedly paired with an unconditioned stimulus. *bell*

Unconditioned stimulus A stimulus innately capable of eliciting a response. *meat pow*

Unconditioned response An innate reflex response elicited by an unconditioned stimulus. *saliv*

Conditioned response A learned response elicited by a conditioned stimulus. *saliv*

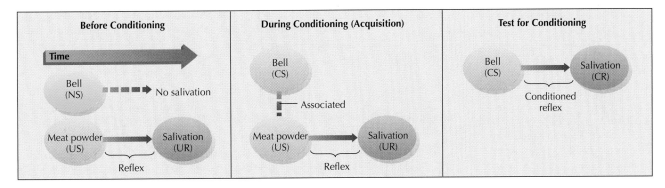

◆**FIGURE 6.3** *The classical conditioning procedure.*

▲*TABLE 6.1*	**Elements of Classical Conditioning**		
ELEMENT	**SYMBOL**	**DESCRIPTION**	**EXAMPLE**
Neutral stimulus	NS	A stimulus that does not evoke a response	Bell
Unconditioned stimulus	US	A stimulus innately capable of eliciting a response	Meat powder
Conditioned stimulus	CS	A stimulus that evokes a response because it has been repeatedly paired with an unconditioned stimulus	Bell
Unconditioned response	UR	An innate reflex response elicited by an unconditioned stimulus	Reflex salivation
Conditioned response	CR	A learned response elicited by a conditioned stimulus	Salivation

Are all these terms really necessary? Yes, because they help us recognize similarities in various instances of learning. Let's summarize the terms using an earlier example:

BEFORE CONDITIONING	EXAMPLE
US → UR	Puff of air → eye-blink
NS → no effect	Horn → no effect

AFTER CONDITIONING	EXAMPLE
CS → CR	Horn → eye-blink

Now let's see if we can explain the shower and flushing toilet example described earlier. The unconditioned, or non-learned, response was a reflex jump from the hot water. The unconditioned stimulus was the hot water (or the pain it caused). The conditioned stimulus was the sound of a flushing toilet. That is, the flushing sound was at first neutral. But as a result of conditioning, it became capable of eliciting a reflex.

PRINCIPLES OF CLASSICAL CONDITIONING— TEACH YOUR LITTLE BROTHER TO SALIVATE

To observe conditioning, you could ring a bell, squirt lemon juice into a child's mouth, and condition salivation to the bell. The child's reactions might then be used to explore other aspects of classical conditioning. Let's see how conditioning occurs.

Acquisition

During **acquisition,** or training, a conditioned response must be reinforced (strengthened) (◆Fig. 6.4). Classical conditioning is **reinforced** when the CS is followed by, or paired with, an unconditioned stimulus. For our child, the bell is the CS, salivating is the UR, and the sour lemon juice is a US. To reinforce salivating to the bell, we must link the bell with the lemon juice. Conditioning will be most rapid if the US (lemon juice) follows *immediately* after the CS (the bell). With most reflexes, the optimal delay between CS and US is from one-half second to about 5 seconds (Schwartz & Robbins, 1995).

◆FIGURE 6.4 *Acquisition and extinction of a conditioned response. (After Pavlov, 1927.)*

◆FIGURE 6.5 *Higher order conditioning takes place when a well-learned conditioned stimulus is used as if it were an unconditioned stimulus. In this example, a child is first conditioned to salivate to the sound of a bell. In time, the bell will elicit salivation. At that point, you could clap your hands and then ring the bell. Soon, after repeating the procedure, the child would learn to salivate when you clapped your hands.*

Acquisition The period in conditioning during which a response is reinforced.

Respondent reinforcement Reinforcement that occurs when an unconditioned stimulus closely follows a conditioned stimulus.

Higher order conditioning Classical conditioning in which a conditioned stimulus is used to reinforce further learning; that is, a CS is used as if it were a US.

Higher Order Conditioning

Once a response is learned, it can bring about **higher order conditioning.** In this case, a well-learned CS is used to reinforce further learning. That is, the CS has become strong enough to be used like an unconditioned stimulus. Let's illustrate again with our salivating child.

As a result of earlier learning, the bell now makes the boy salivate. (No lemon juice is needed.) To go a step further, you could clap your hands and then ring the bell. (Again, no lemon juice would be used.) Through higher order conditioning, the child would soon learn to salivate when you clapped your hands (◆Fig. 6.5). (This little trick could be a real hit with friends and neighbors.)

Higher order conditioning extends learning one or more steps beyond the original conditioned stimulus. Many advertisers use this effect by pairing images that evoke good feelings (such as people smiling and having fun) with pictures of their products. Obviously, they hope that you will learn, by association, to feel good when you see their products (Johnsrude et al., 1999).

Expectancies

Many psychologists believe that classical conditioning is related to information that might aid our survival. According to this **informational view,** we look for associations among events. Doing so creates new mental **expectancies,** or expectations about how events are interconnected.

How does classical conditioning alter expectancies?   Notice that the conditioned stimulus reliably precedes the unconditioned stimulus. Because it does, the CS *predicts* the US (Rescorla, 1987). During conditioning, the brain learns to *expect* that the US will follow the CS. As a result, the brain prepares the body to respond to the US. Here's an example: When you are about to get a shot with a hypodermic needle, your muscles tighten and there is a catch in your breathing. Why? Because your body is preparing for pain. You have learned to expect that getting poked with a needle will hurt. This expectancy, which was acquired during classical conditioning, changes your behavior.

Extinction and Spontaneous Recovery

After conditioning has occurred, what would happen if the US no longer followed the CS? If the US never again follows the CS, conditioning will extinguish, or fade away. Let's return to the boy and the bell. If you ring the bell many times and do not follow it with lemon juice, the boy's expectancy that "bell precedes lemon juice" will weaken. As it does, he will lose his tendency to salivate when he hears the bell. Thus, we see that classical conditioning can be weakened by removing reinforcement (see Fig. 6.4). This process is called **extinction.**

If conditioning takes a while to build up, shouldn't it take time to reverse?   Yes. In fact, it may take several extinction sessions to completely reverse conditioning. Let's say that we ring the bell until the child quits responding. It might seem that extinction is complete. However, the boy will probably respond to the bell again on the following day, at least at first. The reappearance of a response following apparent extinction is called **spontaneous recovery.** It explains why people who have had terrifying automobile accidents may need many slow, calm rides before their fears extinguish.

Generalization

After conditioning, other stimuli similar to the CS may also trigger a response. This is called **stimulus generalization.** For example, we might find that our child salivates to the sound of a ringing telephone or doorbell, even though they were never used as conditioning stimuli.

It is easy to see the value of stimulus generalization. Consider the child who burns her finger while playing with matches. Most likely, lighted matches will become conditioned fear stimuli for her. But will she fear only matches? Because of stimulus generalization, she should also have a healthy fear of flames from lighters, fireplaces, stoves, and so forth. It's fortunate that generalization extends learning to related situations. Otherwise, we would all be far less adaptable.

As you may have guessed, stimulus generalization has limits. As stimuli become less like the original CS, responding decreases. If you condition a person to blink each time you play a particular note on a piano, blinking will decline as you play higher or lower notes. If the notes are *much* higher or lower, the person will not respond at all (◆Fig. 6.6). Stimulus generalization explains why many stores carry imitations of nationally known products. For

Informational view Perspective that explains learning in terms of information imparted by events in the environment.

Expectancy An anticipation concerning future events or relationships.

Extinction The weakening of a conditioned response through removal of reinforcement.

Spontaneous recovery The reappearance of a learned response after its apparent extinction.

Stimulus generalization The tendency to respond to stimuli similar to, but not identical to, a conditioned stimulus.

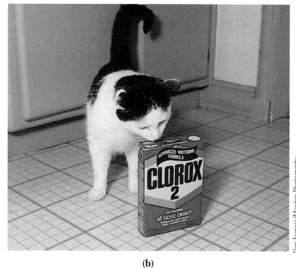

✦FIGURE 6.6 (a) *Stimulus generalization. Stimuli similar to the CS also elicit a response.* (b) *This cat has learned to salivate when it sees a cat food box. Because of stimulus generalization, it also salivates when shown a similar-looking detergent box.*

many customers, positive attitudes conditioned to the real products tend to generalize to the cheaper knockoffs (Till & Priluck, 2000).

Discrimination

Let's consider one more idea with our salivating child (who by now must be ready to hide in the closet). Suppose the child is again conditioned with a bell as the CS. As an experiment, we occasionally sound a buzzer instead of the bell, but never follow it with the US (lemon juice). At first, the buzzer produces salivation (because of generalization). But after hearing the buzzer several times more, the child will stop responding to it. The child has now learned to *discriminate,* or respond differently, to the bell and the buzzer. In essence, the child's generalized response to the buzzer has extinguished.

Stimulus discrimination is the ability to respond differently to various stimuli. As an example, you might remember the feelings of anxiety or fear you had as a child when your mother's or father's voice changed to its you're-about-to-get-swatted tone. (Or the dreaded give-me-that-Game-Boy tone.) Most children quickly learn to discriminate voice tones associated with pain from those associated with praise or affection.

CLASSICAL CONDITIONING IN HUMANS— AN EMOTIONAL TOPIC

] SURVEYQUESTION *Does conditioning affect emotions?*

How much human learning is based on classical conditioning? At its simplest, classical conditioning depends on reflex responses. As mentioned earlier, a reflex is a dependable, inborn stimulus-and-response connection. For example, your hand reflexively draws back from pain. Bright light causes the pupil of the eye to narrow. A puff of air directed at your eye will make you blink. (See "Blink If Your Brain Is Healthy.") Various foods elicit salivation. Any of these reflexes, and others as well, can be associated with a new stimulus. At the very least, you have probably noticed how your mouth waters when you see or smell a bakery. Even pictures of food may make you salivate (a photo of a sliced lemon is great for this).

Stimulus discrimination The learned ability to respond differently to similar stimuli.

CLINICAL FILE Blink If Your Brain Is Healthy

Dementia is a terrifying mental disorder. Imagine how it would feel to lose your ability to read, think, recognize family members, or do ordinary tasks. Dementia (duh-MEN-sha) is caused by various brain diseases, including many associated with aging. Eventually, people with dementia suffer major declines in memory, judgment, language, and thinking abilities. Yet, in its early stages dementia may be nearly invisible.

It is important to detect dementia as soon as possible so that treatment can begin early, possibly slowing mental losses. However, most screening tests for dementia are based on higher mental abilities, such as memory or reasoning. By the time a person has problems in these areas, dementia is already fairly advanced.

How else could dementia be detected?   Psychologist Diana Woodruff-Pak believes she has found a new way to tell if a person is in the early stages of dementia. Woodruff-Pak noticed that eye-blink conditioning was slowed in a patient 6 years before other tests showed any signs of trouble. As a very basic form of learning, classical conditioning appears to be quite sensitive to changes in the brain.

Eye-blink conditioning is simple to do and non-threatening to patients. In the future, it may be a valuable addition to standard mental tests. In fact, it may eventually be possible to detect dementia "in the blink of an eye" (Woodruff-Pak, 2001).

Conditioned Emotional Responses

In addition to simple reflexes, more complex *emotional,* or "gut," responses may be linked to new stimuli. For instance, if your face reddened when you were punished as a child, you may blush now when you are embarrassed or ashamed. Or think about the effects of associating pain with a dentist's office during your first visit. On later visits, did your heart pound and your palms sweat *before* the dentist began?

Many *involuntary,* autonomic nervous system responses ("fight-or-flight" reflexes) are linked with new stimuli and situations by classical conditioning. For example, learned reactions worsen many cases of hypertension (high blood pressure). Traffic jams, arguments with a spouse, and similar situations can become conditioned stimuli that trigger a dangerous rise in blood pressure (Reiff, Katkin, & Friedman, 1999).

Of course, emotional conditioning also applies to animals. One of the most common mistakes people make with pets (especially dogs) is hitting them if they do not come when called. Calling the animal then becomes a conditioned stimulus for fear and withdrawal. No wonder the pet disobeys when called on future occasions. Parents who belittle, scream at, or physically abuse their children make the same mistake.

Learned Fears

Some phobias (FOE-bee-ahs) are also based on emotional conditioning. A *phobia* is a fear that persists even when no realistic danger exists. Fears of animals, water, heights, thunder, fire, bugs, elevators, and the like are common. Psychologists believe that many phobias begin as **conditioned emotional responses** (**CERs**). (A CER is a learned emotional reaction to a previously neutral stimulus.) People who have phobias can often trace their fears to a time when they were frightened, injured, or upset by a particular stimulus. Many spider phobias, for example, start in childhood. Just one bad experience in which you were frightened or disgusted by a spider may condition fears that last for years (de Jong & Muris, 2002; Merckelbach & Muris, 1997).

Stimulus generalization and higher order conditioning can spread CERs to other stimuli (Gewirtz & Davis, 1998). As a result, what began as a limited fear may become a disabling phobia (◆Fig. 6.7). However, a therapy called *desensitization* is now widely used to extinguish fears, anxieties, and phobias. This is done by gradually exposing the phobic person to feared stimuli while she or he remains calm and relaxed. Incidentally, desensitization works on animals, too. For example, dogs have been desensitized for fears of fireworks, thunder, airplanes, bees, hot-air balloons, and other frightening stimuli (Rogerson, 1997).

Undoubtedly, we acquire many of our likes, dislikes, and fears as conditioned emotional responses. For example, in one study, college students developed CERs when colored geometric shapes were paired with the theme music from the movie *Star Wars.* The colored shapes were the CS, and the music, which made the students feel good, was the US. When

Conditioned emotional response An emotional response that has been linked to a previously non-emotional stimulus by classical conditioning.

◆FIGURE 6.7 *Hypothetical example of a CER becoming a phobia. Child approaches dog* (a) *and is frightened by it* (b). *Fear generalizes to other household pets* (c) *and later to virtually all furry animals* (d).

tested later, the students gave higher ratings to shapes paired with the pleasant music than to shapes associated with silence (Bierly et al., 1985). As noted before, advertisers try to achieve the same effect by pairing products with pleasant images and music. So do many students on a first date.

Vicarious, or Secondhand, Conditioning

Conditioning also occurs indirectly, which adds to its impact on us. Let's say, for example, that you watch another person get an electric shock. Each time, a signal light comes on before the shock is delivered. Even if you don't receive a shock yourself, you will soon develop a CER to the light (Bandura & Rosenthal, 1966). Children who learn to fear thunder by watching their parents react to it have undergone similar conditioning.

Vicarious classical conditioning occurs when we learn to respond emotionally to a stimulus by observing another person's emotional reactions. Such "secondhand" learning affects feelings in many situations. For example, "horror" movies filled with screaming actors probably add to fears of snakes, caves, spiders, heights, and other terrors. If movies can affect us, we might expect the emotions of parents, friends, and relatives to have even more impact. How, for instance, does a city child learn to fear snakes and respond emotionally to mere pictures of them? Being told that "snakes are dangerous" may not explain the child's *emotional* response. More likely, the child has observed others reacting fearfully to the word *snake* or to snake images on television (Ollendick & King, 1991).

The emotional attitudes we develop toward foods, political parties, ethnic groups, escalators—whatever—are probably conditioned not only by direct experiences, but vicariously as well. No one is born prejudiced—all attitudes are learned. Parents may do well to look in a mirror if they wonder how or where a child "picked up" a particular fear or emotional attitude (Mineka & Hamida, 1998).

Vicarious classical conditioning Classical conditioning brought about by observing another person react to a particular stimulus.

STUDYBREAK   *Classical Conditioning*

RELATE

US, CS, UR, CR—How will you remember these terms? First, you should note that we are interested in either a stimulus (S) or a response (R). What else do we need to know? Each S or R can be either conditioned (C) or unconditioned (U).

Can a stimulus provoke a response before any learning has occurred? If it can, then it's a US. Do you have to learn to respond to the stimulus? Then it's a CS.

Does a response occur without being learned? Then it's a UR. If it has to be learned, then it's a CR.

LEARNING CHECK

1. In learning, antecedents are the effects that follow the making of a response. T or F?
2. Classical conditioning, studied by the Russian physiologist _____, is also referred to as _____ conditioning.
3. Classical conditioning is strengthened or reinforced when the _____ follows the _____.
   a. CS, US   b. US, CS   c. UR, CR   d. CS, CR

4. The informational view says that classical conditioning is based on changes in mental _____ about the CS and US.
5. Training that inhibits (or weakens) a conditioned response is called _____.
6. When a conditioned stimulus is used to reinforce the learning of a second conditioned stimulus, higher order conditioning has occurred. T or F?
7. Psychologists theorize that many phobias begin when a CER generalizes to other, similar situations. T or F?
8. Conditioning brought about by observing pain, joy, or fear in others is called _____ conditioning.

Critical Thinking

9. Lately you have been getting a shock of static electricity every time you touch a door handle. Now there is a hesitation in your door-opening movements. Can you analyze this situation in terms of classical conditioning?

ANSWERS

1. F 2. Pavlov, respondent 3. b 4. expectancies 5. extinction 6. T 7. T 8. vicarious 9. Door handles have become conditioned stimuli that elicit the reflex withdrawal and muscle tensing that normally follows getting a shock. This conditioned response has also generalized to other handles.

OPERANT CONDITIONING—CAN PIGEONS PLAY PING-PONG?

] SURVEYQUESTION *How does operant conditioning occur?*

Operant conditioning applies to all living creatures, and it explains much of our day-to-day behavior. The principles of operant learning are among the most powerful tools in psychology. You won't regret learning how to use them. Operant conditioning can be used to alter the behavior of pets, children, other adults, and your own behavior, too.

As stated earlier, in **operant conditioning** (or instrumental learning) we associate responses with their consequences. The basic principle is simple: Acts that are reinforced tend to be repeated. Pioneer learning theorist Edward L. Thorndike called this the **law of effect** (the probability of a response is altered by the effect it has). Learning is strengthened each time a response is followed by a satisfying state of affairs. Think of the earlier example of the vending machine. Because kicking the machine had the effect of producing food and money, the odds of repeating the "kicking response" increased.

Classical conditioning is passive. It simply "happens to" the learner when a US follows a CS. In operant conditioning, the learner actively "operates on" the environment. Thus, operant conditioning refers mainly to learning *voluntary* responses. For example, pushing buttons on a TV remote control is a learned operant response. Pushing a particular button is reinforced by gaining the result you desire, such as changing channels. (See ▲Table 6.2 for a further comparison of classical and operant conditioning.)

Positive Reinforcement

The idea that reward affects learning is certainly nothing new to parents (and other trainers of small animals). However, parents, as well as teachers, politicians, supervisors, and even you may use reward in ways that are inexact or misguided. A case in point is the term

Operant conditioning Learning based on the consequences of responding.

Law of effect Responses that lead to desirable effects are repeated; those that produce undesirable results are not.

▲*TABLE 6.2*	**Comparison of Classical and Operant Conditioning**	
	CLASSICAL CONDITIONING	**OPERANT CONDITIONING**
Nature of response	Involuntary, reflex	Spontaneous, voluntary
Reinforcement	Occurs *before* response (CS paired with US)	Occurs *after* response (response is followed by reinforcing stimulus or event)
Role of learner	Passive (response is *elicited* by US)	Active (response is emitted)
Nature of learning	Neutral stimulus becomes a CS through association with a US	Probability of making a response is altered by consequences that follow it
Learned expectancy	US will follow CS	Response will have a specific effect

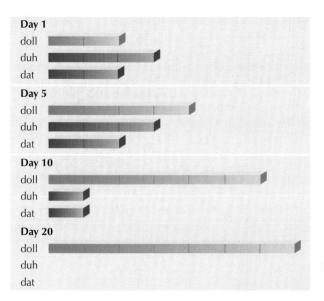

◆FIGURE 6.8 *Assume that a child who is learning to talk points to her favorite doll and says either "doll," "duh," or "dat" when she wants it. Day 1 shows the number of times the child uses each word to ask for the doll (each block represents one request). At first, she uses all three words interchangeably. To hasten learning, her parents decide to give her the doll only when she names it correctly. Notice how the child's behavior shifts as operant reinforcement is applied. By day 20, saying "doll" has become the most probable response.*

reward. To be correct, it is better to say *reinforcer.* Why? Because rewards do not always increase responding. If you try to give licorice candy to a child as a "reward" for good behavior, it will work only if the child likes licorice. What is reinforcing for one person may not be for another. As a practical rule of thumb, psychologists define an **operant reinforcer** as any event that follows a response and increases its probability of occurring again (◆Fig. 6.8).

Acquiring an Operant Response

Many studies of instrumental learning have been done in a conditioning chamber, an apparatus designed to study operant conditioning in animals. This device is also sometimes called a Skinner box, after B. F. Skinner, who invented it (◆Fig. 6.9). A look into a typical Skinner box will clarify the process of operant conditioning.

THE ADVENTURES OF MICKEY RAT

A hungry rat is placed in a small cage-like chamber. The walls are bare except for a metal lever and a tray into which food pellets can be dispensed (see Fig. 6.9).

Frankly, there's not much to do in a Skinner box. This increases the chances that our subject will make the response we want to reinforce, which is pressing the bar. Also, hunger

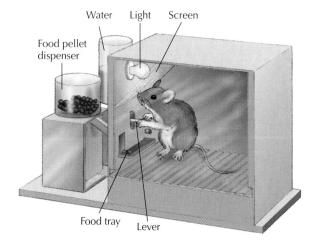

Water   Light   Screen

Food pellet dispenser

Food tray   Lever

◆FIGURE 6.9 *The Skinner box. This simple device, invented by B. F. Skinner, allows careful study of operant conditioning. When the rat presses the bar, a pellet of food or a drop of water is automatically released. (A photograph of a Skinner box appears in Chapter 1.)*

Operant reinforcer Any event that reliably increases the probability or frequency of responses it follows.

keeps the animal motivated to seek food and actively *emit*, or freely give off, a variety of responses. Now let's take another look at our subject.

FURTHER ADVENTURES OF MICKEY RAT

For a while our subject walks around, grooms, sniffs at the corners, or stands on his hind legs—all typical rat behaviors. Then it happens. He places his paw on the lever to get a better view of the top of the cage. *Click!* The lever depresses, and a food pellet drops into the tray. The rat walks to the tray, eats the pellet, then grooms himself. Up and exploring the cage again, he leans on the lever. *Click!* After a trip to the food tray, he returns to the bar and sniffs it, then puts his foot on it. *Click!* Soon the rat settles into a smooth pattern of frequent bar pressing.

Notice that the rat did not acquire a new skill in this situation. He was already able to depress the bar. Reinforcement only alters how *frequently* he presses the bar. In operant conditioning, new behavior patterns are molded by increasing the probability that various responses will be made.

Information

Like classical conditioning, operant learning is based on information and expectancies. In operant conditioning, *we learn to expect that a certain response will have a certain effect at certain times* (Bolles, 1979). That is, we learn that a particular stimulus is associated with a particular response that is associated with reinforcement (Dragoi & Staddon, 1999). From this point of view, a reinforcer tells a person or an animal that a response was "right" and worth repeating.

◆Figure 6.10 shows how operant reinforcement can change behavior. The results are from an effort to teach a severely disturbed 9-year-old child to say "Please," "Thank you," and "You're welcome." As you can see, during the initial, baseline period, the child rarely used the word *please*. Typically, he just grabbed objects and became angry if he couldn't have them. However, when he was reinforced for saying "Please," he soon learned to use the word nearly every time he wanted something. When the child said "Please," he was reinforced in three ways: He received the object he asked for (a crayon, for example); he was given a small food treat, such as a piece of candy, popcorn, or a grape; and he was praised for his good behavior (Matson et al., 1990).

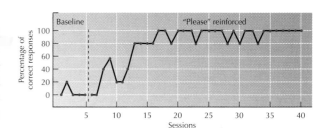

◆**FIGURE 6.10** *Reinforcement and human behavior. The percentage of times that a severely disturbed child said "Please" when he wanted an object was increased dramatically by reinforcing him for making a polite request. Reinforcement produced similar improvements in saying "Thank you" and "You're welcome," and the boy applied these terms in new situations as well. (Adapted from Matson et al., 1990.)*

Contingent Reinforcement

Operant reinforcement works best when it is *response contingent* (kon-TIN-jent). That is, it must be given only after a desired response has occurred. If the disturbed child received reinforcers haphazardly, his behavior wouldn't have changed at all. In situations ranging from studying to working hard on the job, contingent reinforcement also affects the *performance* of responses. For example, ◆Figure 6.11 shows the performance of 38 major league pitchers who signed multi-year contracts for large salaries. When salary was no longer contingent on good performance, there was a rapid decline in innings pitched and in the number of wins. During the same 6-year period, the performance of pitchers on 1-year contracts remained fairly steady. In similar ways, operant principles greatly affect behavior in homes, schools, and businesses. It is always worthwhile to arrange reinforcers so that they encourage productive and responsible behavior.

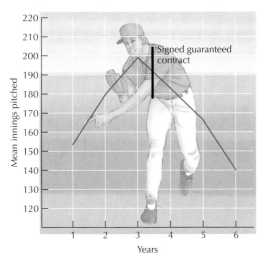

◆**FIGURE 6.11** *Average number of innings pitched by major league baseball players before and after signing long-term guaranteed contracts. (Data from O'Brien et al., 1981.)*

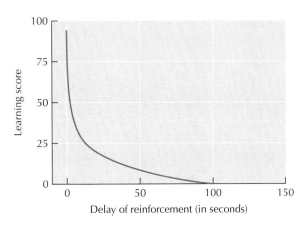

The Timing of Reinforcement

Operant reinforcement is most effective when it rapidly follows a correct response. For rats in a Skinner box, very little learning occurs when the delay between bar pressing and receiving food reaches 50 seconds. If the food reward is delayed more than about a minute and a half, no learning occurs (Perin, 1943) (◆Fig. 6.12). In general, you will be most successful if you present a reinforcer *immediately* after a response you wish to change. Thus, a child who is helpful or courteous should be praised immediately for her good behavior.

Let's say I work hard all semester in a class to get an A grade. Wouldn't the delay in reinforcement keep me from learning anything? No, for several reasons. First, as a human you can anticipate future reward. Second, you get reinforced by quiz and test grades all through the semester. Third, a single reinforcer can often maintain a long **response chain** (a linked series of actions that lead to reinforcement). For instance, the long series of events necessary to prepare a meal is rewarded by the final eating. A violin maker may carry out thousands of steps for the final reward of hearing a first musical note. Tying a shoe is a short but familiar response chain.

Superstitious Behavior

Reinforcers affect not only the response they follow but also other responses that occur shortly before. This helps explain many human superstitions. If a golfer taps her club on the ground three times and then hits an unusually fine shot, what happens? The successful shot reinforces not only the correct swing but also the three taps. During operant training, animals often develop similar unnecessary responses. If a rat scratches its ear just before its first bar press, it may continue to scratch before every bar press. Pressing the bar is all that is required to produce food, but the animal may continue to "superstitiously" scratch its ear, as if this were necessary.

Superstitious behaviors are repeated because they appear to produce reinforcement, even though they are actually unnecessary (Pisacreta, 1998). If you get the large half of a wishbone and have good fortune soon after, you may credit your luck to the wishbone. If you walk under a ladder and then break a leg, you may avoid ladders in the future. Each time you avoid a ladder and nothing bad happens, your superstitious action is reinforced. Belief in magic can also be explained along such lines. Rituals to bring rain, ward off illness, or produce abundant crops very likely earn the faith of participants because they occasionally appear to succeed. Besides, better safe than sorry!

Shaping

How is it possible to reinforce responses that rarely occur? Even in a barren Skinner box, it could take a long time for a rat to accidentally press the bar and get a food pellet. We might wait forever for more complicated responses to occur. For example, you would have to wait a long time for a duck to accidentally walk out of its cage, turn on a light, play a toy piano, turn off the light, and walk back to its cage. If this is what you wanted to reward, you would never get the chance.

Then how are the animals on TV and at amusement parks taught to perform complicated tricks? The answer lies in **shaping,** which is the gradual molding of responses to a desired pattern. Let's look again at our subject, Mickey Rat.

MICKEY RAT SHAPES UP

Assume that the rat has not yet learned to press the bar. He also shows no signs of interest in the bar. Instead of waiting for the first accidental bar press, we can shape his behavior. At first, we settle for just getting him to face the bar. Any time he turns toward the bar, he is reinforced with a bit of food. Soon Mickey spends much of his time facing the bar. Next, we reinforce him every time he takes a step toward the bar. If he turns toward the bar and walks away, nothing happens. But when he faces the bar and takes a step forward, *click!* His responses are being shaped.

Response chaining The assembly of separate responses into a series of actions that lead to reinforcement.

Superstitious behavior A behavior repeated because it seems to produce reinforcement, even though it is actually unnecessary.

Shaping Gradually molding responses to a final desired pattern.

By changing the rules about what makes a successful response, we can gradually train the rat to approach the bar and press it. In other words, *successive approximations* (ever-closer matches) to a desired response are reinforced during shaping. B. F. Skinner once taught two pigeons to play Ping-Pong in this way (✦Fig. 6.13). Shaping applies to humans, too. Let's say you want to study more, clean the house more often, or exercise more. In each case, it would be best to set a series of gradual, daily goals. Then you can reward yourself for small steps in the right direction (Watson & Tharp, 2001).

✦**FIGURE 6.13** *Operant conditioning principles were used to train these pigeons to play Ping-Pong.*

Operant Extinction

Would a rat stop bar pressing if no more food arrived? Yes, but not immediately. Learned responses that are not reinforced gradually fade away. This process is called **operant extinction.** Just as acquiring an operant response takes time, so does extinction. For example, if a TV program repeatedly bores you, watching the program will probably extinguish over time.

Even after extinction seems complete, the previously reinforced response may return. If a rat is removed from a Skinner box after extinction and given a short rest, the rat will press the bar again when returned to the box. Similarly, a few weeks after they give up on buying state lottery tickets, many people are tempted to try again.

Does extinction take as long the second time? If reinforcement is still withheld, a rat's bar pressing will extinguish again, usually more quickly. The brief return of an operant response after extinction is another example of spontaneous recovery (mentioned earlier regarding classical conditioning). Spontaneous recovery is very adaptive. After a rest period, the rat responds again in a situation that produced food in the past: "Just checking to see if the rules have changed!"

Marked changes in behavior occur when reinforcement and extinction are combined. For example, parents often unknowingly reinforce children for *negative attention seeking* (using misbehavior to gain attention). Children are generally ignored when they are playing quietly. They get attention when they become louder and louder, yell "Hey, Mom!" at the top of their lungs, throw tantrums, show off, or break something. Granted, the attention they get is often a scolding, but attention is a powerful reinforcer, nevertheless. Parents report dramatic improvements when they *ignore* their children's disruptive behavior and praise or attend to a child who is quiet or playing constructively.

Negative Reinforcement

Until now, we have stressed **positive reinforcement,** which occurs when a pleasant or desirable event follows a response. How else could operant learning be reinforced? The time has come to consider **negative reinforcement,** which occurs when making a response removes an unpleasant event. Don't be fooled by the word *negative*. Negative reinforcement also increases responding. However, it does so by ending discomfort.

Let's say that you have a headache and take an aspirin. Your aspirin taking will be negatively reinforced if the headache stops. Likewise, a rat could be taught to press a bar to get food (positive reinforcement), or the rat could be given a continuous mild shock (through the floor of its cage) that is turned off by a bar press (negative reinforcement). Either way, bar pressing would increase. Why? Because it leads to a desired state of affairs (food or an end to pain). Often, positive and negative reinforcement combine. If you are uncomfortably hungry, eating a meal is reinforced by the good-tasting food (positive reinforcement) and by an end to nagging hunger (negative reinforcement).

Punishment

Many people mistake negative reinforcement for punishment. However, **punishment** refers to following a response with an **aversive** (unpleasant) consequence. Punishment *decreases* the likelihood that the response will occur again. As noted, negative reinforcement *increases* responding.

Operant extinction The weakening or disappearance of a non-reinforced operant response.

Positive reinforcement Occurs when a response is followed by a reward or other positive event.

Negative reinforcement Occurs when a response is followed by an end to discomfort or by the removal of an unpleasant event.

Punishment Any event that follows a response and *decreases* its likelihood of occurring again.

▲TABLE 6.3	Behavioral Effects of Various Consequences		
	CONSEQUENCE OF MAKING A RESPONSE	EXAMPLE	EFFECT ON RESPONSE PROBABILITY
Positive reinforcement	Positive event begins	Food given	Increase
Negative reinforcement	Negative event ends	Pain stops	Increase
Punishment	Negative event begins	Pain begins	Decrease
Punishment (response cost)	Positive event ends	Food removed	Decrease
Non-reinforcement	Nothing	_____	Decrease

The difference can be seen in a hypothetical example. Let's say you live in an apartment and your neighbor's stereo is blasting so loudly that your ears hurt. If you pound on the wall and the volume suddenly drops (negative reinforcement), future wall pounding will be more likely. But if you pound on the wall and the volume increases (punishment) or if the neighbor comes over and pounds on you (more punishment), wall pounding becomes less likely.

As another example, consider a drug addict undergoing withdrawal. Taking the drug will temporarily end painful withdrawal symptoms. Drug taking is therefore negatively reinforced. If the drug made the pain worse (punishment), the addict would quickly stop taking it.

Isn't it also punishing to have privileges, money, or other positive things taken away for making a particular response? Yes. Punishment also occurs when a reinforcer or positive state of affairs is removed, such as losing privileges. This second type of punishment is called **response cost**. Parents who "ground" their teenage children for misbehavior are applying response cost. Parking tickets and other fines are also based on response cost. For your convenience, ▲ Table 6.3 summarizes four basic consequences of making a response.

OPERANT REINFORCERS— WHAT'S YOUR PLEASURE?

] SURVEYQUESTION *Are there different kinds of operant reinforcement?*

For humans, learning may be reinforced by anything from an M&M candy to a pat on the back. In categorizing reinforcers, useful distinctions can be made between *primary reinforcers, secondary reinforcers,* and *feedback.* Operant reinforcers of all types have a large impact on our lives. Let's examine them in more detail.

Primary Reinforcers

Primary reinforcers are natural, non-learned, and rooted in biology: They produce comfort, end discomfort, or fill an immediate physical need. Food, water, and sex are obvious examples. Every time you open the refrigerator, walk to a drinking fountain, turn up the heat, or order a double latte, your actions reflect primary reinforcement.

In addition to obvious examples, there are other less natural primary reinforcers. One of the most powerful is *intra-cranial stimulation* (ICS). ICS involves direct electrical activation of "pleasure centers" in the brain (Olds & Fobes, 1981) (◆Fig. 6.14).

WIRING A RAT FOR PLEASURE

Use of brain stimulation for reward requires the permanent implantation of tiny electrodes in specific areas of the brain. A rat "wired for pleasure" can be trained to press the bar in a Skinner box to deliver electrical stimulation to its own brain. Some rats will press the bar thousands of times per hour to obtain brain stimulation. After 15 or 20 hours of constant pressing, animals sometimes collapse from exhaustion. When they revive, they begin pressing again. If the reward circuit is not turned off, an animal will ignore food, water, and sex in favor of bar pressing.

Response cost Removal of a positive reinforcer after a response is made.

Primary reinforcers Non-learned reinforcers; usually those that satisfy physiological needs.

Many natural primary reinforcers activate the same pleasure pathways in the brain that make ICS so powerful (McBride, Murphy, & Ikemoto, 1999).

One shudders to think what might happen if brain implants were easy and practical to do. (They are not.) Every company from *Playboy* to Microsoft would have a device on the market, and we would have to keep a closer watch on politicians than usual!

Secondary Reinforcers

In some traditional societies, learning is still strongly tied to food, water, and other primary reinforcers. Most of us, however, respond to a much broader range of rewards and reinforcers. Money, praise, attention, approval, success, affection, grades, and the like all serve as learned or **secondary reinforcers.**

How does a secondary reinforcer gain its ability to promote learning? Some secondary reinforcers are simply associated with a primary reinforcer. For example, if you would like to train a dog to follow you ("heel") when you take a walk, you could reward the dog with small food treats for staying near you. If you praise the dog each time you give it a treat, praise will become a secondary reinforcer. In time, you will be able to skip giving treats and simply praise your pup for doing the right thing. The same principle applies to children. One reason that parents' praise becomes a secondary reinforcer is because it is frequently associated with food, candy, hugs, and other primary reinforcers.

Tokens

Secondary reinforcers that can be *exchanged* for primary reinforcers gain their value more directly. Printed money obviously has little or no value of its own. You can't eat it, drink it, or sleep with it. However, it can be exchanged for food, water, lodging, and other necessities.

A **token reinforcer** is a tangible secondary reinforcer, such as money, gold stars, poker chips, and the like. In a series of classic experiments, chimpanzees were taught to work for tokens. The chimps were first trained to put poker chips into a "Chimp-O-Mat" vending machine. Each chip dispensed a few grapes or raisins. Once the animals had learned to exchange tokens for food, they would learn new tasks to earn the chips. To maintain the value of the tokens, the chimps were occasionally allowed to use the "Chimp-O-Mat" (♦Fig. 6.15) (Cowles, 1937; Wolfe, 1936).

A major advantage of tokens is that they don't lose reinforcing value as quickly as primary reinforcers do. For instance, if you use candy to reinforce a mentally retarded child for correctly naming things, the child might lose interest once he is satiated (fully satisfied) or no longer hungry. It would be better to use tokens as immediate rewards for learning. Later, the child could exchange his tokens for candy, toys, or other treats.

Tokens have been used in similar ways with troubled children and adults in special programs, and even in ordinary elementary school classrooms (Spiegler & Guevremont, 2003) (♦Fig. 6.16). In each case the goal is to provide an immediate

♦**FIGURE 6.14** *In the apparatus shown in* (a), *the rat can press a bar to deliver mild electric stimulation to a "pleasure center" in the brain. Humans also have been "wired" for brain stimulation, as shown in* (b). *However, in humans, this has been done only as an experimental way to restrain uncontrollable outbursts of violence. Implants have not been done merely to produce pleasure.*

♦**FIGURE 6.15** *Poker chips normally have little or no value for chimpanzees, but this chimp will work hard to earn them once he learns that the "Chimp-O-Mat" will dispense food in exchange for them.*

Secondary reinforcer A learned reinforcer; often one that gains reinforcing properties by association with a primary reinforcer.

Token reinforcer A tangible secondary reinforcer such as money, gold stars, poker chips, and the like.

◆FIGURE 6.16 *Reinforcement in a token economy. This graph shows the effects of using tokens to reward socially desirable behavior in a mental hospital ward. Desirable behavior was defined as cleaning, making the bed, attending therapy sessions, and so forth. Tokens earned could be exchanged for basic amenities such as meals, snacks, coffee, game-room privileges, or weekend passes. The graph shows more than 24 hours per day because it represents the total number of hours of desirable behavior performed by all patients in the ward. (Adapted from Ayllon & Azrin, 1965.)*

reward for learning. Typically, tokens may be exchanged for food, desired goods, special privileges, or trips to movies, amusement parks, and so forth. Many parents find that tokens greatly reduce discipline problems with younger children. For example, children can earn points or gold stars during the week for good behavior. If they earn enough tokens, they are allowed on Sunday to choose one item out of a "grab bag" of small prizes.

Social Reinforcers

As we have noted, learned desires for attention and approval, which are called **social reinforcers,** often influence human behavior. This fact can be used in a classic, if somewhat mischievous, demonstration.

SHAPING A TEACHER

For this activity, about one half (or more) of the students in a classroom must participate. First, select a target behavior. This should be something like "lecturing from the right side of the room." (Keep it simple, in case your teacher is a slow learner.) Begin training in this way: Each time the instructor turns toward the right or takes a step in that direction, participating students should look *really* interested. Also, smile, ask questions, lean forward, and make eye contact. If the teacher turns to the left or takes a step in that direction, participating students should lean back, yawn, check out their split ends, close their eyes, or generally look bored. Soon, without being aware of why, the instructor should be spending most of his or her time each class period lecturing from the right side of the classroom.

This trick has been a favorite of psychology graduate students for decades. For a time, one of my professors delivered all of his lectures from the right side of the room while toying with the cords on the window shades. (We added the cords the second week!) The point to remember from this example is that attention and approval can change the behavior of children, family members, friends, roommates, and co-workers. Be aware of what you are reinforcing.

Feedback

His eyes, driven and blazing, dart from side to side. His left hand twitches, dances, rises, and strikes, hitting its target again and again. At the same time, his right hand furiously spins in circular motions. Does this describe some strange neurological disorder? Actually, it depicts 10-year-old Mark as he plays his favorite video game, an animated skateboarding adventure!

How did Mark learn the complex movements needed to excel at virtual skateboarding? After all, he was not rewarded with food or money. The answer lies in the fact that Mark's favorite video game provides two key elements that underlie learning: *a responsive environment* and *information*.

Every time a player moves, a video game responds instantly with sounds, animated actions, and a higher or lower score. The machine's responsiveness and the information flow it provides can be very motivating if you want to win. The same principle applies to many other learning situations: If you are trying to learn to use a computer, to play a musical instrument, to cook, or to solve math problems, reinforcement comes from knowing that you achieved a desired result.

The adaptive value of information helps explain why much human learning occurs in the absence of obvious reinforcers, such as food or water. Humans readily learn responses that merely have a desired effect or that bring a goal closer. Let's explore this idea further.

Social reinforcers Reinforcers, such as attention and approval, provided by other people.

USING PSYCHOLOGY   Conditioning and Conservation

As a psychologist, I enjoy seeing behavioral principles used to solve practical problems. One area of behavior very much in need of attention is our "throw-away" society. We burn fossil fuels, destroy forests, use chemical products, and strip, clear, and farm the land. In doing so, we alter the very face of the earth. What can be done? One approach involves changing the *consequences* of wasteful energy use, polluting, and the like. For example, energy taxes can be used to increase the cost of using fossil fuels (response cost). On the reinforcement side of the equation, rebates can be offered for installing insulation, or buying energy-efficient appliances or cars, and tax breaks can be given to companies that take steps to preserve the environment.

On a daily level, people can help recycle materials such as paper, steel, glass, aluminum, and plastic. Again, behavioral principles come into play. For instance, people who set their own goals for recycling tend to meet them. Likewise, when families, work groups, factories, and dorms receive feedback, on a weekly basis, about how much they recycled, they typically recycle more. We also know that people are most likely to continue recycling if they feel a sense of satisfaction from helping protect the environment (Werner & Makela, 1998). Is such satisfaction sufficiently reinforcing to encourage more people to reduce, reuse, and recycle? I certainly hope so.

Knowledge of Results

Imagine that you are asked to throw darts at a target. Each dart must pass over a screen that prevents you from telling if you hit the target. If you threw 1,000 darts, we would expect little improvement in your performance because no *feedback* is provided. **Feedback** (information about the effect a response had) is particularly important in human learning. Mark's video game did not explicitly reward him for correct responses. Yet, because it provided feedback, rapid learning took place.

How can feedback be applied?   Increased feedback (also called **knowledge of results, or KR**) almost always improves learning and performance (Lee & Carnahan, 1990). If you want to learn to play a musical instrument, to sing, to speak a second language, or to deliver a speech, tape-recorded feedback can be very helpful. In sports, videotapes are used to improve everything from tennis serves to pick-off moves in baseball. (Taped replays of this kind are most helpful when a skilled coach directs attention to key details.) Whenever you are trying to learn a complex skill, it pays to get more feedback (Wulf, Shea, & Matschiner, 1998). (Also, see "Conditioning and Conservation.")

Learning Aids

How do these techniques make use of feedback?   Feedback is most effective when it is *frequent, immediate,* and *detailed.* A method called *programmed instruction* teaches students in a format that presents information in small amounts, gives immediate practice, and provides continuous feedback to learners. Frequent feedback keeps learners from practicing errors. It also lets students work at their own pace. (A small sample of programmed instruction is shown in ✦Figure 6.17 so that you can see what the format looks like.) Programmed learning can be done in book form or presented by a computer (Mabry, 1998).

In *computer-assisted instruction (CAI),* learning is aided by computer-presented information and exercises. In addition to giving learners immediate feedback, the computer can give hints about why an answer was wrong and what is needed to correct it (Light, 1997). Although the final level of skill or knowledge gained is not necessarily higher, CAI can save much time and effort. In addition, people often do better with feedback from a computer because they can freely make mistakes and learn from them (Schneider & Shugar, 1990). For example, CAI can give medical students unlimited practice at diagnosing diseases from symptoms, such as "acute chest pain" (Papa et al., 1999).

Some CAI programs make use of instructional games in which stories, competition with a partner, sound effects, and game-like graphics increase interest and motivation

Types of Conditioning
classical reflex — Much _____ conditioning involves involuntary _____ responses. In contrast, operant conditioning affects spontaneous, or _____ , responses.
voluntary
response CS — Reinforcement occurs before the _____ in classical conditioning as the _____ is paired with the US.
reinforcement after reinforcer — In operant conditioning, _____ occurs _____ the response. In this case, the response is followed by a _____ .
passive elicited — In classical conditioning, the learner is _____ because responses are _____ by the US.
learner emits — In operant conditioning, the _____ actively _____ responses that are affected by reinforcement.

✦FIGURE 6.17 *To sample a programmed instruction format, try covering the terms on the left with a piece of paper. As you fill in the blanks, uncover one new term for each response. In this way, your correct (or incorrect) responses will be followed by immediate feedback.*

Feedback Information returned to a person about the effects a response has had; also known as knowledge of results.

Knowledge of results (KR) Informational feedback.

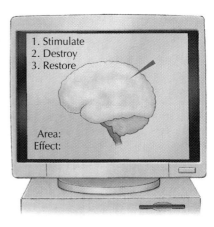

✦**FIGURE 6.18** *Computer-assisted instruction. The screen on the left shows a typical drill-and-practice math problem, in which students must find the hypotenuse of a triangle. The center screen presents the same problem as an instructional game to increase interest and motivation. In the game, a child is asked to set the proper distance on a ray gun in the hovering space ship to "vaporize" an attacker. The screen on the right depicts an educational simulation. Here, students place a "probe" at various spots in a human brain. They then "stimulate," "destroy," or "restore" areas. As each area is altered, it is named on the screen and the effects on behavior are described. This allows students to explore basic brain functions on their own.*

(✦Fig. 6.18) (Stoney & Wild, 1998). Educational simulations go a step further by allowing students to explore an imaginary situation or "microworld" that simulates real-world problems. By seeing the effects of their choices, students discover basic principles of physics, biology, psychology, or other subjects (Cordova & Lepper, 1996).

Psychologists are only now beginning to fully explore the value and limits of computer-assisted instruction. Nevertheless, it seems likely that their efforts will improve not only education but our understanding of human learning as well.

Let's pause now for some learning exercises so that you can get some feedback about your mastery of the preceding ideas.

STUDYBREAK ⓨ *Operant Conditioning*

RELATE

How have your thoughts about the effects of "rewards" changed now that you've read about operant conditioning? Can you explain the difference between positive reinforcement, negative reinforcement, and punishment? Can you give an example of each concept from your own experience?

A friend of yours punishes his dog all the time. What advice would you give him about how to use reinforcement, extinction, and shaping, instead of punishment?

LEARNING CHECK

1. Responses in operant conditioning are _____, whereas those in classical conditioning are passive, _____ responses.
2. Changing the rules in small steps so that an animal (or person) is gradually trained to respond as desired is called _____.
3. Extinction in operant conditioning is also subject to _____ of a response.
   a. successive approximations b. shaping c. automation
   d. spontaneous recovery

4. Positive reinforcers increase the rate of responding and negative reinforcers decrease it. T or F?
5. Primary reinforcers are those learned through classical conditioning. T or F?
6. Tokens are basically _____ reinforcers.
7. Superstitious responses are those that are
   a. shaped by secondary reinforcement b. extinguished
   c. prepotent d. unnecessary to obtain reinforcement
8. Knowledge of results, or KR, is also known as

   _____.
9. Branching programs are a basic feature of CAI. T or F?

Critical Thinking

10. How might operant conditioning principles be used to encourage people to pick up litter? (What rewards could be offered, and how might the cost of rewards be kept low?)

ANSWERS

1. voluntary or emitted, involuntary or elicited 2. shaping 3. d 4. F 5. F 6. secondary 7. d 8. feedback 9. T 10. A strategy that has been used with some success is to hold drawings for various prizes, such as movie or concert passes. Each time a person turns in a specific amount of litter, he or she receives one chance (a token) to enter in the drawing. Giving refunds for cans and bottles is another way to reinforce recycling of litter.

PARTIAL REINFORCEMENT—LAS VEGAS, A HUMAN SKINNER BOX?

] SURVEYQUESTION *How are we influenced by patterns of reward?*

Anyone wishing to influence operant learning would be ill-equipped to do so without knowing how various patterns of reinforcement affect behavior. Imagine, for example, that a mother wants to reward her child for turning off the lights when he leaves a room. Contrary to what you might think, she would be well advised to reinforce only some of her son's correct responses. Why should this be so? You'll find the answer in the following discussion.

B. F. Skinner, so the story goes, was studying operant conditioning when he ran short of food pellets. In order to continue, he arranged for a pellet to reward every other response. Thus began the formal study of **schedules of reinforcement** (plans for determining which responses will be reinforced). Until now, we have treated operant reinforcement as if it were continuous. *Continuous reinforcement* means that a reinforcer follows every correct response. This is fine for the lab, but it has little to do with the real world. Most of our responses are more inconsistently rewarded. In daily life, learning is usually based on **partial reinforcement,** in which reinforcers do not follow every response.

Partial reinforcement can be given in several patterns. Each has a distinct effect on behavior. In addition to these (which will be explored in a moment), there is a general effect: Responses acquired by partial reinforcement are highly resistant to extinction. For some obscure reason, lost in the lore of psychology, this is called the **partial reinforcement effect.**

How does getting reinforced part of the time make a habit stronger? If you have ever visited Las Vegas or a similar gambling mecca, you have probably seen row after row of people playing slot machines. To gain insight into partial reinforcement, imagine that you are making your first visit to Las Vegas. You put a dollar in a slot machine and pull the handle. Ten dollars spills into the tray. Using one of your newly won dollars, you pull the handle again. Another payoff! Let's say this continues for 15 minutes. Every pull is followed by a payoff. Suddenly each pull is followed by nothing. Obviously, you would respond several times more before giving up. However, when continuous reinforcement is followed by extinction, the message soon becomes clear: no more payoffs.

Contrast this with partial reinforcement. Again, imagine that this is your first encounter with a slot machine. You put a dollar in the machine five times without a payoff. You are just about to quit, but decide to play once more. Bingo! The machine returns $20. After this, payoffs continue on a partial schedule; some are large, and some are small. All are unpredictable. Sometimes you hit 2 in a row, and sometimes 20 or 30 pulls go unrewarded.

Now let's say the payoff mechanism is turned off again. How many times do you think you would respond this time before your handle-pulling behavior extinguished? Since you have developed the expectation that any play may be "the one," it will be hard to resist just one more play . . . and one more . . . and one more. Also, because partial reinforcement includes long periods of non-reward, it will be harder to discriminate between periods of reinforcement and extinction. It is no exaggeration to say that the partial reinforcement effect has left many people penniless. Even psychologists visiting Las Vegas may get "cleaned out"—and they should know better!

Christoph Wilhelm/Getty Images

The one-armed bandit (slot machine) is a dispenser of partial reinforcement.

Schedules of Partial Reinforcement

Partial reinforcement can be given in many different patterns. Let's consider the four most basic, which have some interesting effects on us. Typical responses to each pattern are shown in ◆Figure 6.19. Results such as these are obtained when a cumulative recorder is connected to a Skinner box. The device consists of a moving strip of paper and a mechanical pen that jumps upward each time a response is made. Rapid responding causes the pen to draw a steep line; a horizontal line indicates no response. Small tick marks on the lines show when a reinforcer was given.

Schedule of reinforcement A rule or plan for determining which responses will be reinforced.

Partial reinforcement A pattern in which only a portion of all responses are reinforced.

Partial reinforcement effect Responses acquired with partial reinforcement are more resistant to extinction.

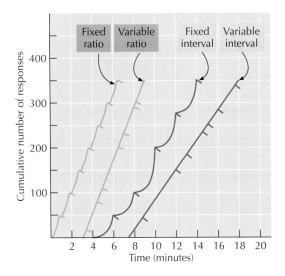

←FIGURE 6.19 *Typical response patterns for reinforcement schedules.*

Fixed Ratio (FR)

What would happen if a reinforcer followed only every other correct response? Or what if we followed every third, fourth, fifth, or other number of responses with reinforcement? Each of these patterns is a **fixed ratio (FR) schedule** (a set number of correct responses must be made to obtain a reinforcer). Notice that in an FR schedule the ratio of reinforcers to responses is fixed: FR-2 means that every other response is rewarded; FR-3 means that every third response is reinforced; in an FR-10 schedule, exactly 10 responses must be made to obtain a reinforcer.

Fixed ratio schedules produce *very high response rates* (Fig. 6.19). A hungry rat on an FR-10 schedule will quickly run off 10 responses, pause to eat, and then run off 10 more. A similar situation occurs when factory or farm workers are paid on a piecework basis. When a fixed number of items must be produced for a set amount of pay, work output is high.

Variable Ratio (VR)

In a **variable ratio (VR) schedule** a varied number of correct responses must be made to get a reinforcer. Instead of reinforcing every fourth response (FR-4), for example, a person or animal on a VR-4 schedule gets rewarded *on the average* every fourth response. Sometimes 2 responses must be made to obtain a reinforcer; sometimes it's 5, sometimes 4, and so on. The actual number varies, but it averages out to 4 (in this example). Variable ratio schedules also produce high response rates.

VR schedules seem less predictable than FR. Does that have any effect on extinction?   Yes. Because reinforcement is less predictable, VR schedules tend to produce greater resistance to extinction than fixed ratio schedules. Playing a slot machine is an example of behavior maintained by a variable ratio schedule. Another would be a child asking for a "treat" at the supermarket. The number of times the child must ask before getting reinforced varies, so the child becomes quite persistent. Golf, tennis, and many other sports are also reinforced on a variable ratio basis: An average of perhaps 1 good shot in 5 or 10 may be all that's needed to create a sports fanatic.

Fixed Interval (FI)

In another pattern, reinforcement is given only when a correct response is made after a fixed amount of time has passed. This time interval is measured from the last reinforced response. Responses made during the time interval are not reinforced. In a **fixed interval (FI) schedule** the first correct response made after the time period has passed is reinforced. Thus, a rat on an FI-30-second schedule has to wait 30 seconds after the last reinforced response before a bar press will pay off again. The rat can press the bar as often as it wants during the interval, but it will not be rewarded.

Fixed interval schedules produce *moderate response rates*. These are marked by spurts of activity mixed with periods of inactivity. Animals working on an FI schedule seem to develop a keen sense of the passage of time (Eckerman, 1999). For example:

MICKEY RAT TAKES A BREAK

Mickey Rat, trained on an FI-60-second schedule, has just been reinforced for a bar press. What does he do? He saunters around the cage, grooms himself, hums, whistles, reads magazines, and polishes his nails. After 50 seconds, he walks to the bar and gives it a press—just testing. After 55 seconds, he gives it two or three presses, but there's still no payoff. Fifty-eight seconds, and he settles down to rapid pressing, 59 seconds, 60 seconds, and he hits the reinforced press. After one or two more presses (unrewarded), he wanders off again for the next interval.

Is getting paid weekly an FI schedule?   Pure examples of fixed interval schedules are rare, but getting paid each week at work does come close. Notice, however, that most people do not work faster just before payday, as an FI schedule predicts. A closer parallel would be having a report due every 2 weeks for a class. Right after turning in a paper, your work would probably drop to zero for a week or more. Then, as the next due date draws near, a

Fixed ratio schedule A set number of correct responses must be made to get a reinforcer. For example, a reinforcer is given for every four correct responses.

Variable ratio schedule A varied number of correct responses must be made to get a reinforcer. For example, a reinforcer is given after three to seven correct responses; the actual number changes randomly.

Fixed interval schedule A reinforcer is given only when a correct response is made after a set amount of time has passed since the last reinforced response. Responses made during the time interval are not reinforced.

work frenzy occurs. Another fixed interval example is checking a Thanksgiving turkey in the oven. Typically, the frequency of checking increases as the time for the turkey to be done draws near (Schwartz & Robbins, 1995).

Variable Interval (VI)

Variable interval (VI) schedules are a variation on fixed intervals. Here, reinforcement is given for the first correct response made after a varied amount of time. On a VI-30-second schedule, reinforcement is available after an interval that *averages* 30 seconds.

VI schedules produce *slow, steady response rates* and tremendous resistance to extinction (Lattal et al., 1998). When you dial a phone number and get a busy signal, reward (getting through) is on a VI schedule. You may have to wait 30 seconds or 30 minutes. If you are like most people, you will doggedly dial over and over again until you get a connection. Success in fishing is also on a VI schedule—which may explain the bulldog tenacity of many anglers (Schwartz & Robbins, 1995).

STIMULUS CONTROL—RED LIGHT, GREEN LIGHT

When you are driving, your behavior at intersections is controlled by the red or green light. In similar fashion, many of the stimuli we encounter each day act like stop or go signals that guide our behavior. To state the idea more formally, stimuli that consistently precede a rewarded response tend to influence when and where the response will occur. This effect is called **stimulus control.** Notice how it works with our friend Mickey Rat.

LIGHTS OUT FOR MICKEY RAT

While learning the bar-pressing response, Mickey has been in a Skinner box illuminated by a bright light. During several training sessions, the light is alternately turned on and off. When the light is on, a bar press will produce food. When the light is off, bar pressing goes unrewarded. We soon observe that the rat presses vigorously when the light is on and ignores the bar when the light is off.

In this example, the light signals what consequences will follow if a response is made. Evidence for stimulus control could be shown by turning the food delivery *on* when the light is *off*. A well-trained animal might never discover that the rules had changed. A similar example of stimulus control would be a child learning to ask for candy when her mother is in a good mood, but not asking at other times.

Generalization

Two important aspects of stimulus control are generalization and discrimination. Let's return to the example of the vending machine (from the chapter preview) to illustrate these concepts. First, generalization.

Is generalization the same in operant conditioning as it is in classical conditioning? Basically, yes. **Operant stimulus generalization** is the tendency to respond to stimuli similar to those that preceded operant reinforcement. That is, a reinforced response tends to be made again when similar antecedents are present. Assume, for instance, that you have been reliably rewarded for kicking one particular vending machine. Your kicking response tends to occur in the presence of that machine. It has come under stimulus control. Now let's say that there are three other machines on campus identical to the one that pays off. Because they are similar, your kicking response will very likely transfer to them. If each of these machines also pays off when kicked, your kicking response may *generalize* to other machines only mildly similar to the original. Similar generalization explains why children may temporarily call all men *daddy*—much to the embarrassment of their parents.

Discrimination

Meanwhile, back at the vending machine . . . . As stated earlier, to discriminate means to respond differently to varied stimuli. Because one vending machine reinforced your kicking response, you began kicking other identical machines (generalization). Because these

Variable interval schedule A reinforcer is given for the first correct response made after a varied amount of time has passed since the last reinforced response. Responses made during the time interval are not reinforced.

Stimulus control Stimuli present when an operant response is acquired tend to control when and where the response is made.

Operant stimulus generalization The tendency to respond to stimuli similar to those that preceded operant reinforcement.

Stimulus control. Operant shaping was used to teach this whale to "bow" to an audience. Fish were used as reinforcers. Notice the trainer's hand signal, which serves as a discriminative stimulus to control the performance.

also paid off, you began kicking similar machines (more generalization). If kicking these new machines has no effect, the kicking response that generalized to them will extinguish because of non-reinforcement. Thus, your response to machines of a particular size and color is consistently rewarded, whereas the same response to different machines is extinguished. Through **operant stimulus discrimination** you have learned to differentiate between antecedent stimuli that signal reward and non-reward. As a result, your response pattern will shift to match these **discriminative stimuli** (stimuli that precede reinforced and non-reinforced responses).

A discriminative stimulus that most drivers are familiar with is a police car on the freeway. This stimulus is a clear signal that a specific set of reinforcement contingencies applies. As you have probably observed, the presence of a police car brings about rapid reductions in driving speed, lane changes, tail-gating, and in Los Angeles, gun battles. Another familiar example is the beep on telephone answering machines. The beep is a signal that speaking will pay off (your message will be recorded). Most of us are well conditioned to "wait for the beep" before talking.

The role of discriminative stimuli may be clarified by an interesting feat achieved by Jack, a psychologist friend of mine. Jack decided to teach his cat to say its name. Here is how he proceeded. First he gave the cat a pat on the back. If the cat meowed in a way that sounded anything like its name, Jack immediately gave the cat a small amount of food. If the cat made this unusual meow at other times, it received nothing. This process was repeated many times each day.

By gradual shaping, the cat's meow was made to sound very much like its name. Also, this peculiar meow came under stimulus control: When it received a pat on the back, the cat said its name; without the pat, it remained silent or meowed normally. Psychologists symbolize a stimulus that precedes reinforced responses as an S+. Discriminative stimuli that precede unrewarded responses are symbolized as S– (Schwartz & Robbins, 1995). Thus, ◆Figure 6.20 summarizes the cat's training.

I should add at this point that I was unaware that Jack had a new cat or that he had trained it. I went to visit him one night and met the cat on the front steps. I gave the cat a pat on the back and said, "Hi kitty, what's your name?" Imagine my surprise when the cat immediately replied, "Ralph"!

Stimulus discrimination is also aptly illustrated by the "sniffer" dogs who locate drugs and explosives at airports and border crossings. Operant discrimination is used to teach these dogs to recognize contraband. During training, they are reinforced only for approaching containers baited with drugs or explosives.

Stimulus discrimination clearly has a tremendous impact on human behavior. Learning to recognize different automobile brands, birds, animals, wines, types of music, and even the answers on psychology tests all depends, in part, on operant discrimination learning.

Operant stimulus discrimination The tendency to make an operant response when stimuli previously associated with reward are present and to withhold the response when stimuli associated with non-reward are present.

Discriminative stimuli Stimuli that precede rewarded and non-rewarded responses in operant conditioning.

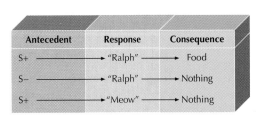

Antecedent	Response	Consequence
S+ ——————→	"Ralph" ——————→	Food
S– ——————→	"Ralph" ——————→	Nothing
S+ ——————→	"Meow" ——————→	Nothing

◆**FIGURE 6.20** *A diagram of Ralph the cat's discrimination training.*

STUDYBREAK *Partial Reinforcement and Stimulus Control*

RELATE

Think of something you do that is reinforced only part of the time. Do you pursue this activity persistently? How have you been affected by partial reinforcement?

See if you can think of at least one everyday example of the four basic schedules of reinforcement.

Doors that are meant to be pushed outward have metal plates on them. Those that are meant to be pulled inward have handles. Do these discriminative stimuli affect your behavior? (If they don't, how's your nose doing?)

LEARNING CHECK

1. Two aspects of stimulus control are _____ and _____.

2. Responding tends to occur in the presence of discriminative stimuli associated with reinforcement and tends not to occur in the presence of discriminative stimuli associated with non-reinforcement. T or F?

3. Stimulus generalization refers to making an operant response in the presence of stimuli similar to those that preceded reinforcement. T or F?

4. When a reward follows every response, it is called
   a. continuous reinforcement b. fixed reinforcement c. ratio reinforcement d. controlled reinforcement

5. Partial reinforcement tends to produce slower responding and reduced resistance to extinction. T or F?

6. The schedule of reinforcement associated with playing slot machines and other types of gambling is
   a. fixed ratio b. variable ratio c. fixed interval
   d. variable interval

Critical Thinking

7. A business owner who pays employees an hourly wage wants to increase productivity. How could the owner make more effective use of reinforcement?

8. How could you use conditioning principles to teach a dog or a cat to come when called?

ANSWERS

1. generalization, discrimination 2. T 3. T 4. a 5. F 6. b 7. Continuing to use fixed interval rewards (hourly wage or salary) would guarantee a basic level of income for employees. To reward extra effort, the owner could add some fixed ratio reinforcement (such as incentives, bonuses, commissions, or profit sharing) to employees' pay. 8. An excellent way to train a pet to come when you call is to give a distinctive call or whistle each time you feed the animal. This makes the signal a secondary reinforcer and a discriminative stimulus for reward (food). Of course, it also helps to directly reinforce an animal with praise, petting, or food for coming when called.

PUNISHMENT—PUTTING THE BRAKES ON BEHAVIOR

] SURVEYQUESTION *What does punishment do to behavior?*

Spankings, reprimands, fines, jail sentences, firings, failing grades, and the like are commonly used to control behavior. Clearly, the story of learning is unfinished without a return to the topic of punishment. Recall that **punishment** lowers the probability that a response will occur again. To be most effective, punishment must be given contingently (only after an undesired response occurs).

Punishers, like reinforcers, are defined by observing their effects on behavior. A **punisher** is any consequence that reduces the frequency of a target behavior. It is not always possible to know ahead of time what will act as a punisher for a particular person. For example, when Jason's mother reprimanded him for throwing toys, he stopped doing it. In this instance, the reprimand was a punisher. However, Chris is starved for attention of any kind from his parents, who both work full-time. For Chris, a reprimand, or even a spanking, might actually reinforce toy throwing. Remember, too, that a

Tony Freeman/PhotoEdit

Punishers are consequences that lower the probability that a response will be made again. Receiving a traffic citation is directly punishing because the driver is delayed and reprimanded. Paying a fine and higher insurance rates add to the punishment in the form of response cost.

Punishment The process of suppressing a response.

Punisher Any event that decreases the probability or frequency of responses it follows.

punisher can be either the onset of an unpleasant event or the removal of a positive state of affairs (response cost).

Variables Affecting Punishment

How effective is punishment?   Many people assume that punishment stops unacceptable behavior. Is this always true? Actually, the effectiveness of punishers depends greatly on their *timing, consistency,* and *intensity.* Punishment works best when it occurs as the response is being made, or *immediately* afterward (timing), and when it is given *each time* a response occurs (consistency). Thus, you could effectively (and humanely) punish a dog that barks incessantly by spraying water on its nose each time it barks. About 10 to 15 such treatments are usually enough to greatly reduce barking. This would not be the case if you applied punishment haphazardly or long after the barking stopped. If you discover that your dog dug up a tree and ate it while you were gone, punishing the dog hours later will do little good. Likewise, the commonly heard childhood threat, "Wait 'til your father comes home, then you'll be sorry," just makes the father a feared brute; it doesn't effectively punish an undesirable response.

Severe punishment (following a response with an intensely aversive or unpleasant stimulus) can be extremely effective in stopping behavior. If 3-year-old Beavis sticks his finger in a light socket and gets a shock, that may be the last time he *ever* tries it. More often, however, punishment only temporarily *suppresses* a response. If the response is still reinforced, punishment may be particularly ineffective. Responses suppressed by mild punishment usually reappear later. If 7-year-old Alissa sneaks a snack from the refrigerator before dinner and is punished for it, she may pass up snacks for a short time. But because snack sneaking was also rewarded by the sneaked snack, she will probably try sneaky snacking again, sometime later (the sneaky little devil).

This fact was demonstrated by slapping rats on the paw as they were bar pressing in a Skinner box. Two groups of well-trained rats were placed on extinction. One group was punished with a slap for each bar press, while the other group was not. It might seem that the slap would cause bar pressing to extinguish more quickly. Yet, this was not the case, as you can see in ◆Figure 6.21. Punishment temporarily slowed responding, but it did not cause more rapid extinction. Slapping the paws of rats or children has little permanent effect on a reinforced response. It is worth stating again, however, that intense punishment may permanently suppress responding, even for actions as basic as eating. Animals severely punished while eating may never eat again (Bertsch, 1976).

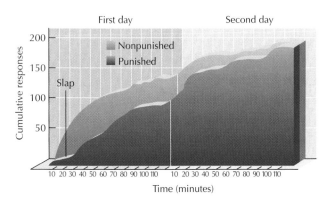

◆**FIGURE 6.21** *The effect of punishment on extinction. Immediately after punishment, the rate of bar pressing is suppressed, but by the end of the second day, the effects of punishment have disappeared. (After B. F. Skinner,* The Behavior of Organisms. *© 1938. D. Appleton-Century Co., Inc. Reprinted by permission of Skinner Foundation.)*

Using Punishment Wisely

In light of its drawbacks, should punishment be used to control behavior?   Parents, teachers, animal trainers, and the like have three basic tools to control simple learning: (1) Reinforcement strengthens responses; (2) non-reinforcement causes responses to extinguish; (3) punishment suppresses responses. (Consult ◆Figure 6.22 to refresh your memory about the different types of reinforcement and punishment.) These tools work best in combination.

If punishment is used at all, it should always be mild. But remember that mild punishment will be ineffective if reinforcers are still available in the situation. That's why it is best to also reward an alternate, desired response. For example, a child who has a habit of taking toys from her sister should not just be reprimanded for it. She should also be praised for cooperative play and sharing her toys with others. Punishment tells a person or an animal that a response was "wrong." However, it does not say what the "right" response is, so it *does not teach new behaviors.* If reinforcement is missing, punishment becomes less effective (Gershoff, 2002).

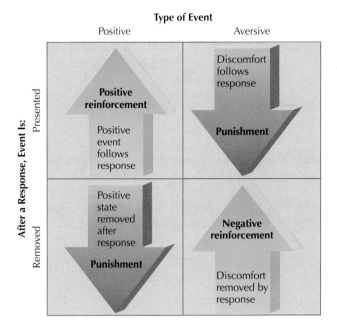

Type of Event

◆**FIGURE 6.22** *Types of reinforcement and punishment. The impact of an event depends on whether it is presented or removed after a response is made. Each square defines one possibility: Arrows pointing upward indicate that responding is increased; downward-pointing arrows indicate that responding is decreased. (Adapted from Kazdin, 1975.)*

In a situation that poses immediate danger, such as when a child reaches for something hot or a dog runs into the street, mild punishment may prevent disaster. Punishment in such cases works best when it produces actions *incompatible* with the response you want to suppress. Let's say a child reaches toward a stove burner. Would a swat on the bottom serve as an effective punisher? Probably so. It would be better, however, to slap the child's outstretched hand so that it will be *withdrawn* from the source of danger. See "If You Must Punish, Here's How" for some additional tips on using punishment.

USING PSYCHOLOGY If You Must Punish, Here's How

There are times when punishment may be necessary to manage the behavior of an animal, child, or even another adult. If you feel that you must punish, here are some tips to keep in mind.

1. *Don't use punishment at all if you can discourage misbehavior in other ways.* Make liberal use of positive reinforcement, especially praise, to encourage good behavior. Also, try extinction first: See what happens if you ignore a problem behavior; or shift attention to a desirable activity and then reinforce it with praise.

2. *Apply punishment during, or immediately after, misbehavior.* Of course, immediate punishment is not always possible. With older children and adults, you can bridge the delay by clearly stating what act you are punishing. If you cannot punish an animal *immediately,* wait for the next instance of misbehavior.

3. *Use the minimum punishment necessary to suppress misbehavior.* Often, a verbal rebuke or a scolding is enough. Avoid harsh physical punishment. (Never slap a child's face, for instance.) Taking away privileges or other positive reinforcers (response cost) is usually best for older children and adults. Frequent punishment may lose its effectiveness, and harsh or excessive punishment has serious negative side effects (discussed in a moment).

4. *Be consistent.* Be very clear about what you regard as misbehavior. Punish every time the misbehavior occurs. Don't punish for something one day and ignore it the next. If you are usually willing to give a child three chances, don't change the rule and explode without warning after a first offense. Both parents should try to punish their children for the same things and in the same way.

5. *Expect anger from a punished person.* Briefly acknowledge this anger, but be careful not to reinforce it. Be willing to admit your mistake if you wrongfully punish someone or if you punished too severely.

6. *Punish with kindness and respect.* Allow the punished person to retain self-respect. For instance, do not punish a person in front of others, if possible. A strong, trusting relationship tends to minimize behavior problems. Ideally, others should *want* to behave well to get your praise, not because they fear punishment.

7. *Be sure to reinforce positive behaviors.* Remember, it is much more effective to strengthen and encourage desirable behaviors than it is to punish unwanted behaviors (Gershoff, 2002).

Side Effects of Punishment

What are the drawbacks of using punishment?   The basic problem with punishment is that it is *aversive* (painful or uncomfortable). As a result, people and situations associated with punishment tend, through classical conditioning, to become feared, resented, or disliked. The aversive nature of punishment makes it especially poor to use when teaching children to eat politely or in toilet training.

Escape and Avoidance

A second major problem is that aversive stimuli encourage escape and avoidance learning. In **escape learning** we learn to make a response in order to end an aversive stimulus. For example, if you work with a loud and obnoxious person, you may at first escape from conversations with him to obtain relief. (Notice that escape learning is based on negative reinforcement.) Later you may dodge him altogether. This is an example of **avoidance learning** (making a response in order to postpone or prevent discomfort). Each time you sidestep him, your avoidance is again reinforced by a sense of relief. In many situations involving frequent punishment, similar desires to escape and avoid are activated. For example, children who run away from punishing parents (escape) may soon learn to lie about their behavior (avoidance) or to spend as much time away from home as possible (also an avoidance response).

Aggression

A third problem with punishment is that it can greatly increase *aggression.* Animals react to pain by attacking whomever or whatever else is around (Azrin et al., 1965). A common example is the faithful dog that nips its owner during a painful procedure at the veterinarian's office. Likewise, humans who are in pain have a tendency to lash out at others.

We also know that one of the most common responses to frustration is aggression. Generally speaking, punishment is painful, frustrating, or both. Punishment, therefore, sets up a powerful environment for learning aggression. When a child is spanked, the child may feel angry, frustrated, and hostile. What if the child then goes outside and hits a brother, a sister, or a neighbor? The danger is that aggressive acts may feel good because they release anger and frustration. If so, aggression has been rewarded and will tend to occur again in other frustrating situations.

A recent study found that children who are physically punished are more likely to engage in aggressive, impulsive, antisocial behavior (Straus & Mouradian, 1998). Another study of angry adolescent boys found that they were severely punished at home. This suppressed their misbehavior at home but made them more aggressive elsewhere. Parents were often surprised to learn that their "good boys" were in trouble for fighting at school (Bandura & Walters, 1959). Yet another study of classroom discipline problems found that physical punishment, yelling, and humiliation are generally ineffective. Positive reinforcement, in the form of praise, approval, and reward, is much more likely to quell classroom disruptions, defiance, and inattention (Tulley & Chiu, 1995).

Should You Punish or Not?

To summarize, the most common error in using punishment is to rely on it alone for training or discipline. The overall emotional adjustment of a child or pet disciplined mainly by reward is usually superior to one disciplined mainly by punishment. Frequent punishment makes a person or an animal unhappy, confused, anxious, aggressive, and fearful (Gershoff, 2002).

Parents and teachers should be aware that using punishment can be "habit forming." When children are being noisy, messy, disrespectful, or otherwise misbehaving, the temptation to punish them can be strong. The danger is that punishment often works. When it does, a sudden end to the adult's irritation acts as a negative reinforcer. This encourages the adult to use punishment more often in the future (Alberto & Troutman, 1998). Immediate silence may be "golden," but its cost can be very high in terms of a child's emotional health. "Sparing the rod" will not spoil a child. In fact, the reverse is true: Two studies found that young children with behavior problems were harshly punished at home (Brenner & Fox, 1998; DeKlyen et al., 1998).

Escape learning Learning to make a response in order to end an aversive stimulus.

Avoidance learning Learning to make a response in order to postpone or prevent discomfort.

STUDYBREAK ◆ *Punishment*

RELATE

Think of how you were punished as a child. Was the punishment immediate? Was it consistent? What effect did these factors have on your behavior? Was the punishment effective? Which of the side effects of punishment have you witnessed or experienced?

LEARNING CHECK

1. Negative reinforcement increases responding; punishment suppresses responding. T or F?
2. Three factors that greatly influence the effects of punishment are timing, consistency, and _____.
3. Mild punishment tends to only temporarily _____ a response that is also reinforced.
   a. enhance   b. aggravate   c. replace   d. suppress

4. Three undesired side effects of punishment are (1) conditioning of fear and resentment, (2) encouragement of aggression, and (3) the learning of escape or _____ responses.
5. Using punishment can be "habit forming" because putting a stop to someone else's irritating behavior can _____ _____ the person who applies the punishment.

Critical Thinking

6. Using the concept of partial reinforcement, can you explain why inconsistent punishment is especially ineffective?
7. Escape and avoidance learning have been applied to encourage automobile seat belt use. Can you explain how?

ANSWERS

1. T 2. intensity 3. d 4. avoidance 5. negatively reinforce 6. An inconsistently punished response will continue to be reinforced on a partial schedule, which makes it even more resistant to extinction. 7. Many automobiles have an unpleasant buzzer that sounds if the ignition key is turned before the driver's seat belt is fastened. Most drivers quickly learn to fasten the belt to stop the annoying sound. This is an example of escape conditioning. Avoidance conditioning is evident when a driver learns to buckle up before the buzzer sounds.

COGNITIVE LEARNING—BEYOND CONDITIONING

] **SURVEYQUESTION** *What is cognitive learning?*

Is all learning just a connection between stimuli and responses?   Much learning can be explained by classical and operant conditioning. But, as we have seen, even basic conditioning has "mental" elements. As a human, you can anticipate future reward or punishment and react accordingly. (You may wonder why this doesn't seem to work when a doctor or dentist says, "This won't hurt a bit." Here's why: They lie!) There is no doubt that human learning includes a large *cognitive*, or mental, dimension. As humans, we are greatly affected by information, expectations, perceptions, mental images, and the like.

Loosely speaking, **cognitive learning** refers to understanding, knowing, anticipating, or otherwise making use of information-rich higher mental processes. Cognitive learning extends beyond basic conditioning into the realms of memory, thinking, problem solving, and language. Since these topics are covered in later chapters, our discussion here is limited to a first look at learning beyond conditioning.

Cognitive Maps

How do you navigate around the town you live in? Is it fair to assume that you have simply learned to make a series of right and left turns to get from one point to another? It is far more likely that you have an overall mental picture of how

It's easy to get lost when visiting a new city if you don't have a cognitive map of the area. Printed maps help, but they may still leave you puzzled until you begin to form a mental representation of major landmarks and directions.

Spencer Grant/PhotoEdit

Cognitive learning Higher-level learning involving thinking, knowing, understanding, and anticipation.

© Ed Arno/Science 80

the town is laid out. This *cognitive map* acts as a guide even when you must detour or take a new route. A **cognitive map** is an internal representation of an area, such as a maze, city, or campus. Even the lowly rat—not exactly a mental giant—learns *where* food is found in a maze, not just which turns to make to reach the food (Tolman et al., 1946). If you have ever learned your way through the "locations" found in many video games, you will have a good idea of what a cognitive map is. In a sense, cognitive maps also apply to other kinds of knowledge. For instance, it could be said that you have been developing a "map" of psychology while reading this book. That's why students sometimes find it helpful to draw pictures or diagrams of how they envision concepts fitting together.

Latent Learning

Cognitive learning is also revealed by latent (hidden) learning. **Latent learning** occurs without obvious reinforcement and remains hidden until reinforcement is provided. Here's an example from a classic animal study: Two groups of rats were allowed to explore a maze. The animals in one group found food at the far end of the maze. Soon, they learned to rapidly make their way through the maze when released. Rats in the second group were unrewarded and showed no signs of learning. But later, when the "uneducated" rats were given food, they ran the maze as quickly as the rewarded group (Tolman & Honzik, 1930). Although there was no outward sign of it, the unrewarded animals had learned their way around the maze. Their learning, therefore, remained latent at first (◆Fig. 6.23).

◆**FIGURE 6.23** *Latent learning.* (a) *The maze used by Tolman and Honzik to demonstrate latent learning by rats.* (b) *Results of the experiment. Notice the rapid improvement in performance that occurred when food was made available to the previously unreinforced animals. This indicates that learning had occurred but that it remained hidden or unexpressed.* (Adapted from Tolman & Honzik, 1930.)

How did they learn if there was no reinforcement? Just satisfying curiosity can be enough to reward learning (Harlow & Harlow, 1962). In humans, latent learning is related to higher-level abilities, such as anticipating future reward. For example, if you give an attractive classmate a ride home, you may make mental notes about how to get to his or her house, even if a date is only a remote future possibility.

Discovery Learning

Much of what is meant by cognitive learning is summarized by the word *understanding*. Each of us has, at times, learned ideas by **rote** (repetition and memorization). Although rote learning is efficient, many psychologists believe that learning is more lasting and flexible when people *discover* facts and principles on their own. In **discovery learning,** skills are gained by insight and understanding instead of by rote (de Jong & van Joolingen, 1998).

As long as learning occurs, what difference does it make if it is by discovery or by rote? ◆Figure 6.24 illustrates the difference. Two groups of students were taught to calculate the

Cognitive map Internal images or other mental representations of an area (maze, city, campus, and so forth) that underlie an ability to choose alternative paths to the same goal.

Latent learning Learning that occurs without obvious reinforcement and that remains unexpressed until reinforcement is provided.

Rote learning Learning that takes place mechanically, through repetition and memorization, or by learning rules.

Discovery learning Learning based on insight and understanding.

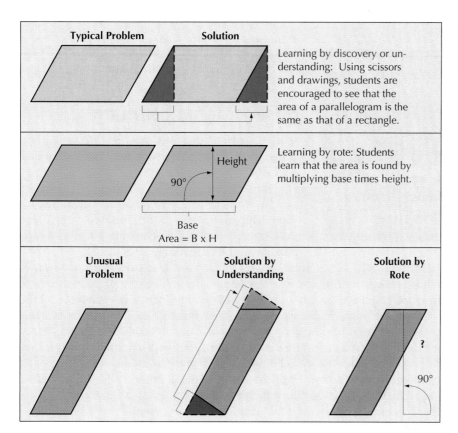

area of a parallelogram by multiplying the height by the length of the base. Some were encouraged to see that a "piece" of a parallelogram could be "moved" to create a rectangle. Later, they were better able to solve unusual problems in which the height times base formula didn't seem to work. Students who simply memorized a rule were confused by the same problems (Wertheimer, 1959). As this implies, discovery leads to a better understanding of new or unusual problems. When possible, people should try new strategies and discover new solutions during learning (McDaniel & Schlager, 1990). (Insightful problem solving, which is related to discovery learning, is discussed in Chapter 10.) Best of all, perhaps, is guided discovery, in which students who are solving problems are given enough freedom to actively think about them and enough guidance so that they gain useful knowledge (Mayer, 2004).

MODELING—DO AS I DO, NOT AS I SAY

] SURVEYQUESTION *Does learning occur by imitation?*

The class watches intently as a skilled potter pulls a spinning ball of clay into the form of a vase. There is little doubt that many skills are learned by what Albert Bandura (1971) calls *observational learning,* or *modeling.* **Observational learning** is achieved by watching and imitating the actions of another person or by noting the consequences of the person's actions. In other words, modeling is any process in which information is imparted by example, before direct practice is allowed (Rosenthal & Steffek, 1991).

The value of learning by observation is obvious: Imagine trying to *tell* someone how to tie a shoe, do a dance step, crochet, or play a guitar. Bandura believes that anything that can be learned from direct experience can be learned by observation. Often, this allows a person to skip the tedious trial-and-error stage of learning.

Observational learning Learning achieved by watching and imitating the actions of another or noting the consequences of those actions.

Observational learning often imparts large amounts of information that would be difficult to obtain by reading instructions or memorizing rules.

Observational Learning

It seems obvious that we learn by observation, but how does it occur? By observing a **model** (someone who serves as an example), a person may (1) learn new responses, (2) learn to carry out or avoid previously learned responses (depending on what happens to the model for doing the same thing), or (3) learn a general rule that can be applied to various situations.

For observational learning to occur, several things must take place. First, the learner must pay *attention* to the model and *remember* what was done. (A beginning auto mechanic might be interested enough to watch an entire tune-up, but unable to remember all the steps.) Next, the learner must be able to *reproduce* the modeled behavior. (Sometimes this is a matter of practice, but it may be that the learner will never be able to perform the behavior. I may admire the feats of world-class gymnasts, but with no amount of practice could I ever reproduce them.) If a model is *successful* at a task or *rewarded* for a response, the learner is more likely to imitate the behavior. In general, models who are attractive, trustworthy, capable, admired, powerful, or high in status also tend to be imitated (Bandura & Walters, 1963b; Brewer & Wann, 1998). Finally, once a new response is tried, *normal reinforcement determines whether it will be repeated thereafter.* (Notice the similarity to latent learning, described earlier.)

Imitating Models

Modeling has a powerful effect on behavior. In a classic experiment, children watched an adult attack a large blowup "Bo-Bo the Clown" doll. Some children saw an adult sit on the doll, punch it, hit it with a hammer, and kick it around the room. Others saw a movie of these actions. A third group saw a cartoon version of the aggression. Later, the children were frustrated by having some attractive toys taken away from them. Then, they were allowed to play with the Bo-Bo doll. Most imitated the adult's attack (◆Fig. 6.25). Some even added new aggressive acts of their own! Interestingly, the cartoon was only slightly less effective in encouraging aggression than the live adult model and the filmed model (Bandura et al., 1963).

Then do children blindly imitate adults? No. Remember that observational learning only prepares a person to duplicate a response. Whether it is actually imitated depends on whether the model was rewarded or punished for what was done. Nevertheless, when parents tell a child to do one thing but model a completely different response, children tend to imitate what the parents *do,* and *not* what they *say* (Bryan & Walbek, 1970). Thus, through modeling, children learn not only attitudes, gestures, emotions, and personality traits, but

Model A person who serves as an example in observational learning.

◆**FIGURE 6.25** *A nursery school child imitates the aggressive behavior of an adult model he has just seen in a movie. (Photos courtesy of Albert Bandura.)*

fears, anxieties, and bad habits as well. A good example is the children of smokers, who are much more likely to try smoking than children from smoke-free homes (Rowe et al., 1996).

Now, consider a typical situation: Little Shawn-Erin-Ringo-Jeremy Jones has just been interrupted at play by his younger brother, Mildew. Angry and frustrated, he screams at Mildew. This behavior interrupts his father's TV watching. Father promptly spanks little Shawn-Erin-Ringo-Jeremy, saying, "This will teach you to hit your little brother." And it will. Because of modeling effects, it is unrealistic to expect a child to "Do as I say, not as I do." The message the father has given the child is clear: "You have frustrated me; therefore, I will hit you." The next time little Shawn-Erin-Ringo-Jeremy is frustrated, it won't be surprising if he imitates his father and hits his brother.

Modeling and Television

Does television promote observational learning? The impact of TV can be found in these figures: By the time the average person has graduated from high school, she or he will have viewed some 15,000 hours of TV, compared with only 11,000 hours spent in the classroom. In that time, viewers will have seen some 18,000 murders and countless acts of robbery, arson, bombing, torture, and beatings. Children watching Saturday morning cartoons see a chilling 26 or more violent acts each hour (Pogatchnik, 1990). Even G-rated cartoons average 10 minutes of violence per hour (Yokota & Thompson, 2000). In short, typical TV viewers are exposed to a massive dose of media violence, which tends to promote observational learning of aggression (Bushman & Anderson, 2001).

Life before and after TV

What effect does the North American penchant for TV watching have on behavior? To answer this question, a team of researchers found a town in northwestern Canada that did not receive TV broadcasts. Discovering that the town was about to get TV, the team seized a rare opportunity. Tannis Williams and her colleagues carefully tested residents of the town just before TV arrived and again 2 years later. This natural experiment revealed that after the tube came to town:

- Reading development among children declined (Corteen & Williams, 1986).
- Children's scores on tests of creativity dropped (Harrison & Williams, 1986).
- Children's perceptions of sex roles became more stereotyped (Kimball, 1986).
- There was a significant increase in both verbal and physical aggression (◆Fig. 6.26). This occurred for both boys and girls, and it applied equally to children who were high or low in aggression before they began watching TV (Joy et al., 1986).

Televised Aggression

The last finding comes as no surprise. Studies show conclusively that if large groups of children watch a great deal of televised violence, they will be more prone to behave aggressively (Bushman & Anderson, 2001; Hughes & Hasbrouck, 1996). In other words, not all children will become more aggressive, but many will. Especially during adolescence, viewing lots of violence on television is associated with actual increases in aggression against others (Johnson et al., 2002). It's little wonder that a large panel of medical and psychological experts recently concluded that media violence is a serious threat to public health (Bushman & Anderson, 2001).

Does the same conclusion apply to video games? See "Violent Video Games—Toxic Kombat?" for some recent evidence.

Is it fair to say, then, that televised violence causes aggression in viewers, especially children? Fortunately, that would be an exaggeration. Televised violence can make aggression more *likely*, but it does not invariably "cause" it to occur for any given child. Many other factors affect the chances that hostile thoughts will be turned into actions. Among children, one such factor is the extent to which a child *identifies* with aggressive characters (Huesmann et al., 1983). That's why it is so sad to find TV *heroes* behaving aggressively, as well as villains.

Televised violence may promote observational learning of aggression. In addition to providing poor behavioral models, constant exposure to aggressive imagery can lower viewers' emotional sensitivity to violence.

◆**FIGURE 6.26** *This graph shows the average number of aggressive acts per minute before and after television broadcasts were introduced into a Canadian town. The increase in aggression after television watching began was significant. Two other towns that already had television were used for comparison. Neither showed significant increases in aggression during the same time period. (Data compiled from Joy et al., 1986.)*

TV heroes can act as powerful models for observational learning of aggression.

A case in point is the popular *Power Rangers* TV programs for children. In each episode, the Power Rangers "morph" into superheroes who use karate and other violent actions to conquer monsters. After watching an episode of the *Power Rangers,* a group of 7-year-old children committed seven times more aggressive acts than a control group that didn't watch. The aggressive children hit, kicked, and karate-chopped their peers, often directly imitating the Power Rangers (Boyatzis, Matillo, & Nesbitt, 1995). Younger children, in particular, are more likely to be influenced by such programs because they don't fully recognize that the characters and stories are fantasies (McKenna & Ossoff, 1998).

Youngsters who believe that aggression is an acceptable way to solve problems, who believe that TV violence is realistic, and who identify with TV characters are most likely to copy televised aggression (Huesmann, Moise, & Podolski, 1997). In view of such findings, it is understandable that Canada, Norway, and Switzerland have restricted the amount of permissible violence on television. Should all countries do the same?

A Look Ahead

Conditioning principles are often derived from animal experiments. However, it should be apparent that the same principles apply to human behavior. Perhaps the best way to appreciate this fact is to observe how reinforcement affects your own behavior. With this in mind, the upcoming Psychology in Action section proposes a personal experiment in operant conditioning. Don't miss this coming attraction!

CRITICAL THINKING Violent Video Games—Toxic Kombat?

As media violence becomes more realistic, kids can experience more gore in a day than most people would experience in a lifetime, even during military combat. For example, in one popular video game you can kill an entire marching band with a flame-thrower. Some of your victims won't die right away. They will just writhe in pain, begging you to finish them off. What effects do such experiences have on people who play violent video games? Recent reviews of a large number of studies lead to the unmistakable conclusion that violent video games increase aggressive behavior in children and young adults (Anderson & Bushman, 2001). As with TV, young children are especially susceptible to fantasy violence in video games (Bensley & Van Eenwyk, 2001; Griffiths, 1999).

A recent study illustrates the impact of video game violence. First, college students played a very violent video game (*Mortal*

Kombat) or a nonviolent one (*PGA Tournament Golf*). Next, they competed with another student (actually an actor) in a task that allowed aggression and retaliation to take place. Students who played *Mortal Kombat* were much more likely to aggress by punishing their competitor (Bartholow & Anderson, 2002). (Don't mess with someone who just played *Mortal Kombat!*)

The new generation of virtual reality and Internet-based games allow players to stalk and attack each other. By practicing violence against other people, players may learn to be aggressive in real life (Unsworth & Ward, 2001). A case in point may be the mass murder at Columbine High School in Littleton, Colorado. Dylan Klebold and Eric Harris, who killed 12 students and a teacher before committing suicide, were avid fans of violent video games.

STUDYBREAK ◆ *Cognitive Learning and Imitation*

RELATE

Try to think of at least one personal example of each of these concepts: cognitive map, latent learning, discovery learning.

Describe a skill you have learned primarily through observational learning. How did modeling help you learn?

What entertainment or sports personalities did you identify with when you were a child? How did it affect your behavior?

LEARNING CHECK

1. An internal representation of relationships is referred to as a _____ _____.

2. Learning that suddenly appears when a reward or incentive for performance is given is called
   a. discovery learning b. latent learning c. rote learning
   d. reminiscence

3. Psychologists use the term _____ to describe observational learning.

4. If a model is successful, rewarded, attractive, or high in status, his or her behavior is
   a. difficult to reproduce   b. less likely to be attended to
   c. more likely to be imitated   d. subject to positive transfer

5. Children who observed a live adult behave aggressively became more aggressive; those who observed movie and cartoon aggression did not. T or F?

6. Children are most likely to imitate TV characters with whom they identify, but this applies primarily to characters who are nonviolent. T or F?

7. Psychological research indicates that televised violence causes aggressive behavior in children. T or F?

Critical Thinking

8. Draw a map of your school's campus as you picture it now. Draw a map of the campus as you pictured it after your first visit. Why do the maps differ?

9. Children who watch many aggressive programs on television tend to be more aggressive than average. Why doesn't this observation prove that televised aggression causes aggressive behavior?

ANSWERS

1. cognitive map 2. b 3. modeling 4. c 5. F 6. F 7. F 8. F. Your cognitive map of the campus has undoubtedly become more accurate and intricate over time as you have added details to it. Your drawings should reflect this change. 9. Because the observation is based on a correlation. Children who are already aggressive may choose to watch more aggressive programs, rather than being made aggressive by them. It took experimental studies to verify that televised aggression promotes aggression by viewers.

Psychology in Action

Behavioral Self-Management—A Rewarding Project

] **SURVEYQUESTION** *How does conditioning apply to practical problems?*

This discussion could be the start of one of the most personal applications of psychology in this book. Many people have learned to use reinforcement to alter or manage their own behavior (Watson & Tharp, 2001). This, then, is an invitation to carry out a self-management project of your own. Would you like to increase the number of hours you spend studying each week? Would you like to exercise more, attend more classes, concentrate longer, or read more books? All of these activities and many others can be improved by following the rules described here.

Self-Managed Behavior

The principles of operant conditioning can be adapted to manage your own behavior. Here's how:

1. **Choose a target behavior.** Identify the activity you want to change.
2. **Record a baseline.** Record how much time you currently spend performing the target activity or count the number of desired or undesired responses you make each day.
3. **Establish goals.** Remember the principle of shaping, and set realistic goals for gradual improvement on each successive week. Also, set daily goals that add up to the weekly goal.

4. **Choose reinforcers.** If you meet your daily goal, what reward will you allow yourself? Daily rewards might be watching television, eating a candy bar, socializing with friends, playing a musical instrument, or whatever you enjoy. Also establish a weekly reward. If you reach your weekly goal, what reward will you allow yourself? A movie? A dinner out? A weekend hike?

5. **Record your progress.** Keep accurate records of the amount of time spent each day on the desired activity or the number of times you make the desired response.

6. **Reward successes.** If you meet your daily goal, collect your reward. If you fall short, be honest with yourself and skip the reward. Do the same for your weekly goal.

7. **Adjust your plan as you learn more about your behavior.** Overall progress will reinforce your attempts at self-management.

If you have trouble finding rewards, or if you don't want to use the entire system, remember that anything done often can serve as reinforcement. This is known as the *Premack principle.* It is named after David Premack, a psychologist who popularized its use. For example, if you watch television every night and want to study more, make it a rule not to turn on the set until you have studied for an hour (or whatever length of time you choose). Then lengthen the requirement each week. Here is a sample of one student's plan:

1. *Target behavior:* number of hours spent studying for school.
2. *Recorded baseline:* an average of 25 minutes per day for a weekly total of 3 hours.
3. *Goal for the first week:* an increase in study time to 40 minutes per day; weekly goal of 5 hours total study time. *Goal for second week:* 50 minutes per day and 6 hours per week. *Goal for third week:* 1 hour per day and 7 hours per week. *Ultimate goal:* to reach and maintain 14 hours per week study time.
4. *Daily reward for reaching goal:* 1 hour of guitar playing in the evening; no playing if the goal is not met. *Weekly reward for reaching goal:* going to a movie or buying a compact disc.

Self-Recording Even if you find it difficult to give and withhold rewards, you are likely to succeed. Simply knowing that you are reaching a desired goal can be reward enough. The key to any self-management program, therefore, is **self-recording** (keeping records of response frequencies). The concept is demonstrated by students in a psychology course. Some of the students recorded their study time and graphed their daily and weekly study behavior. Even though no extra rewards were offered, these students earned better grades than others who were not required to keep records (Johnson & White, 1971).

As discussed earlier, feedback is also valuable for changing personal behavior. Feedback can help you decrease bad habits as well as increase desirable responses. Keep track of the number of times daily that you arrive late to class, smoke a cigarette, watch an hour of TV, drink a cup of coffee, bite your fingernails, swear, or whatever you are interested in changing. A simple tally on a piece of paper will do, or you can get a small mechanical counter like those used to keep golf scores or count calories. Record keeping helps break patterns, and the feedback can be motivating as you begin to make progress.

Good Ways to Break Bad Habits

How can I use learning principles to break a bad habit? By using the methods we have discussed, you can reinforce yourself for *decreasing* unwanted behaviors, such as swearing, biting your nails, criticizing others, smoking, drinking coffee, watching TV too much, or any

Tony Freeman/PhotoEdit

Self-recording Self-management based on keeping records of response frequencies.

other behavior you choose to target. However, breaking bad habits may require some additional techniques. Here are four strategies to help you change bad habits.

Alternate Responses A good strategy for change is to try to get the same reinforcement with a new response.

Example: Marta often tells jokes at the expense of others. Her friends sometimes feel hurt by her sharp-edged humor. Marta senses this and wants to change. What can she do? Usually, Marta's joke telling is reinforced by attention and approval. She could just as easily get the same reinforcement by giving other people praise or compliments. Making a change in her behavior should be easy because she will continue to receive the reinforcement she seeks.

Extinction Try to discover what is reinforcing an unwanted response and remove, avoid, or delay the reinforcement (Ferster et al., 1962).

Example: Tiffany has developed a habit of taking longer and longer "breaks" to watch TV when she should be studying. Obviously, TV watching is reinforcing her break taking. To improve her study habits, Tiffany could delay reinforcement by studying at the library or some other location a good distance from her TV.

Response Chains Break up response chains that precede an undesired behavior. The key idea is to scramble the chain of events that leads to an undesired response (Watson & Tharp, 2001).

Example: Almost every night Steve comes home from work, turns on the TV, and eats a whole bag of cookies or chips. He then takes a shower and changes clothes. By dinner time he has lost his appetite. Steve realizes he is substituting junk food for dinner. Steve could solve the problem by breaking the response chain that precedes dinner. For instance, he could shower immediately when he gets home, or he could avoid turning on the television until after dinner.

Cues and Antecedents Try to avoid, narrow down, or remove stimuli that elicit the bad habit.

Example: Raul wants to cut down on smoking. He has taken many smoking cues out of his surroundings by removing ashtrays, matches, and extra cigarettes from his house, car, and office. This is a good first step. Drug cravings are strongly related to cues conditioned to the drug, such as the odor of cigarettes (Lazev et al., 1999). Raul should try narrowing antecedent stimuli even more. He could begin by smoking only in the lounge at work, never in his office or in his car. He could then limit his smoking to home. Then to only one room at home. Then to one chair at home. If he succeeds in getting this far, he may want to limit his smoking to only one unpleasant place, such as a bathroom, basement, or garage (Goldiamond, 1971).

Contracting If you try the techniques described here and have difficulty sticking with them, you may want to try behavioral contracting. In a **behavioral contract,** you state a specific problem behavior you want to control or a goal you want to achieve. Also state the rewards you will receive, privileges you will forfeit, or punishments you must accept. The contract should be typed and signed by you and a person you trust.

A behavioral contract can be quite motivating, especially when mild punishment is part of the agreement. Here's an example reported by Nurnberger and Zimmerman (1970): A student working on his Ph.D. had completed all requirements but his dissertation, yet for 2 years had not written a single page. A contract was drawn up for him in which he agreed to meet weekly deadlines on the number of pages he would complete. To make sure he would meet the deadlines, he wrote postdated checks. These were to be forfeited if he failed to reach his goal for the week. The checks were made out to organizations he despised (the Ku Klux Klan and American Nazi Party). From the time he signed the contract until he finished his degree, the student's work output was greatly improved.

Behavioral contract A formal agreement stating behaviors to be changed and consequences that apply.

Getting Help

Attempting to manage or alter your own behavior may be more difficult than it sounds. If you feel you need more information, consult either of the books listed below. You will also find helpful advice in the Psychology in Action section of Chapter 17. If you do try a self-modification project but find it impossible to reach your goals, be aware that professional advice is available.

Where to Obtain More Information

Watson, D. L., & Tharp, R. G. (2001). *Self-directed behavior.* Belmont, CA: Wadsworth.

Williams, R. L., & Long, J. D. (1991). *Toward a self-managed life style.* Boston: Houghton Mifflin.

STUDYBREAK *Behavioral Self-Management*

RELATE

Even if you don't expect to carry out a self-management project right now, outline a plan for changing your own behavior. Be sure to describe the behavior you want to change, set goals, and identify reinforcers.

LEARNING CHECK

1. After a target behavior has been selected for reinforcement, it's a good idea to record a baseline so that you can set realistic goals for change. T or F?
2. Self-recording, even without the use of extra rewards, can bring about desired changes in target behaviors. T or F?
3. The Premack principle states that behavioral contracting can be used to reinforce changes in behavior. T or F?
4. A self-management plan should make use of the principle of shaping by setting a graduated series of goals. T or F?

5. Eleni ends up playing dozens of Solitaire games on her computer each time she tries to work on a term paper for her history class. Eventually she does get to work on the paper, but only after a long delay. To break this bad habit, Eleni removes the Solitaire icon from her computer screen so that she won't see it when she begins work. Eleni has used which strategy for breaking bad habits?
   a. alternate responses   b. extinction   c. avoid cues
   d. contracting

Critical Thinking

6. How does setting daily goals in a behavioral self-management program help maximize the effects of reinforcement?

ANSWERS

1. T 2. T 3. F 4. T 5. c 6. Daily performance goals and rewards reduce the delay of reinforcement, which maximizes its impact.

CHAPTER IN REVIEW

Major Points

- Conditioning is a fundamental type of learning that affects many aspects of daily life.
- In classical conditioning, a neutral stimulus is repeatedly paired with a stimulus that reliably provokes a response. By association, the neutral stimulus also begins to elicit a response.
- In operant conditioning, responses that are followed by reinforcement occur more frequently.
- To understand why people behave as they do, it is important to identify how their responses are being reinforced.

- Cognitive learning involves acquiring higher level information, rather than just linking stimuli and responses.
- We also learn by observing and imitating the actions of others.
- Behavioral principles can be used to manage one's own behavior.

Summary

What is learning?

- Learning is a relatively permanent change in behavior due to experience. Learning resulting from conditioning depends on reinforcement. Reinforcement increases the probability that a particular response will occur.

- Classical, or respondent, conditioning and instrumental, or operant, conditioning are two basic types of learning.
- In classical conditioning, a previously neutral stimulus begins to elicit a response through association with another stimulus.
- In operant conditioning, the frequency and pattern of voluntary responses are altered by their consequences.

How does classical conditioning occur?

- Classical conditioning, studied by Pavlov, occurs when a neutral stimulus (NS) is associated with an unconditioned stimulus (US).
- The US causes a reflex called the unconditioned response (UR). If the NS is consistently paired with the US, it becomes a conditioned stimulus (CS) capable of producing a response by itself. This response is a conditioned (learned) response (CR).
- When the conditioned stimulus is followed by the unconditioned stimulus, conditioning is reinforced (strengthened).
- From an informational view, conditioning creates expectancies, which alter response patterns. In classical conditioning, the CS creates an expectancy that the US will follow.
- Higher order conditioning occurs when a well-learned conditioned stimulus is used as if it were an unconditioned stimulus, bringing about further learning.
- When the CS is repeatedly presented alone, conditioning is extinguished (weakened or inhibited). After extinction seems to be complete, a rest period may lead to the temporary reappearance of a conditioned response. This is called spontaneous recovery.
- Through stimulus generalization, stimuli similar to the conditioned stimulus will also produce a response. Generalization gives way to stimulus discrimination when an organism learns to respond to one stimulus, but not to similar stimuli.

Does conditioning affect emotions?

- Conditioning applies to visceral or emotional responses as well as simple reflexes. As a result, conditioned emotional responses (CERs) also occur.
- Irrational fears called phobias may be CERs. Conditioning of emotional responses can occur vicariously (secondhand) as well as directly.

How does operant conditioning occur?

- Operant conditioning occurs when a voluntary action is followed by a reinforcer. Reinforcement in operant conditioning increases the frequency or probability of a response. This result is based on the law of effect.

- Complex operant responses can be taught by reinforcing successive approximations to a final desired response. This is called shaping. It is particularly useful in training animals.
- If an operant response is not reinforced, it may extinguish (disappear). But after extinction seems complete, it may temporarily reappear (spontaneous recovery).

Are there different kinds of operant reinforcement?

- In positive reinforcement, reward or a pleasant event follows a response. In negative reinforcement, responses that end discomfort tend to be repeated.
- Primary reinforcers are "natural," physiologically based rewards. Intra-cranial stimulation of "pleasure centers" in the brain can also serve as a primary reinforcer.
- Secondary reinforcers are learned. They typically gain their reinforcing value by direct association with primary reinforcers or because they can be exchanged for primary reinforcers. Tokens and money gain their reinforcing value in this way.
- Feedback, or knowledge of results, aids learning and improves performance. It is most effective when it is immediate, detailed, and frequent.
- Programmed instruction breaks learning into a series of small steps and provides immediate feedback. Computer-assisted instruction (CAI) does the same, but has the added advantage of providing alternative exercises and information when needed. Four variations of CAI are drill and practice, instructional games, educational simulations, and interactive multimedia instruction.

How are we influenced by patterns of reward?

- Delay of reinforcement greatly reduces its effectiveness, but long chains of responses may be built up so that a single reinforcer maintains many responses.
- Superstitious behaviors often become part of response chains because they *appear* to be associated with reinforcement.
- Reward or reinforcement may be given continuously (after every response) or on a schedule of partial reinforcement. Partial reinforcement produces greater resistance to extinction.
- The four most basic schedules of reinforcement are fixed ratio, variable ratio, fixed interval, and variable interval. Each produces a distinct pattern of responding.
- Stimuli that precede a reinforced response tend to control the response on future occasions (stimulus control). Two aspects of stimulus control are generalization and discrimination.

- In generalization, an operant response tends to occur when stimuli similar to those preceding reinforcement are present.
- In discrimination, responses are given in the presence of discriminative stimuli associated with reinforcement (S+) and withheld in the presence of stimuli associated with non-reinforcement (S–).

What does punishment do to behavior?

- Punishment decreases responding. Punishment occurs when a response is followed by the onset of an aversive event or by the removal of a positive event (response cost).
- Punishment is most effective when it is immediate, consistent, and intense. Mild punishment tends to only temporarily suppress responses that are also reinforced or were acquired by reinforcement.
- The undesirable side effects of punishment include the conditioning of fear to punishing agents and situations associated with punishment, the learning of escape and avoidance responses, and the encouragement of aggression.

What is cognitive learning?

- Cognitive learning involves higher mental processes, such as understanding, knowing, or anticipating. Even in relatively simple learning situations, animals and people seem to form cognitive maps (internal representations of relationships).
- In latent learning, learning remains hidden or unseen until a reward or incentive for performance is offered.
- Discovery learning emphasizes insight and understanding, in contrast to rote learning.

Does learning occur by imitation?

- Much human learning is achieved through observation, or modeling. Observational learning is influenced by the personal characteristics of the model and the success or failure of the model's behavior. Studies have shown that aggression is readily learned and released by modeling.
- Television characters can act as powerful models for observational learning. Televised violence increases the likelihood of aggression by viewers.

How does conditioning apply to practical problems?

- Operant principles can be readily applied to manage behavior in everyday settings. When managing one's own behavior, self-reinforcement, self-recording, feedback, and behavioral contracting are all helpful.
- Four strategies that can help change bad habits are reinforcing alternative responses, promoting extinction, breaking response chains, and avoiding antecedent cues.

Interactive Learning

Internet addresses frequently change. To find the sites listed here, visit www.psychology. wadsworth.com/coon_journey2e for an updated list of Internet addresses and direct links to relevant sites.

PSYCHOLOGY: A JOURNEY COMPANION WEB SITE Online quizzes, flash cards, and other helpful study aids for this text. *www.psychology.wadsworth.com/coon_journey2e*

ANIMAL TRAINING AT SEA WORLD Explains how marine mammals are trained at Sea World.

MEMORY A short tutorial on classical conditioning, operant conditioning, and cognitive learning.

METHODS FOR CHANGING BEHAVIOR Teaches you how to modify your own behavior.

OBSERVATIONAL LEARNING Presents Bandura's original work on modeling, with graphs.

OPPATOONS Cartoons of rats undergoing conditioning.

STUDYING TELEVISION VIOLENCE An article on television violence.

INFOTRAC COLLEGE EDITION For recent articles related to the impact of television, use Key Words search for VIOLENCE ON TELEVISION.

PSYCHNOW! 5a. Classical conditioning, 5b. Operant conditioning, 5c. Observational learning.

Test Your Knowledge: Conditioning and Learning

The questions that follow are only a sample of what you need to know. If you miss any of the items, you should review the entire chapter and get more practice with *WebTutor* or the *Practice Quizzes* that came with this book. Another way to prepare for tests is to use the printed *Study Guide* that is available for this text.

1. The concept of reinforcement applies to both
   A. antecedents and consequences   B. neutral stimuli and rewards   C. classical and operant conditioning   D. acquisition and spontaneous recovery

2. You smell the odor of cookies being baked and your mouth waters. Apparently, the odor of cookies is a _____ and your salivation is a _____.
   A. CR, CS   B. CS, CR   C. consequence, neutral stimulus   D. reflex, CS

3. According to the informational view, classical conditioning creates new
   A. expectancies   B. unconditioned responses   C. unconditioned stimuli   D. generalizations

4. After you have acquired a conditioned response, it may be weakened by
   A. spontaneous recovery   B. stimulus generalization   C. removing reinforcement   D. following the CS with a US

5. At least some phobias can be thought of as
   A. NS-CR connections   B. desensitization gradients   C. extinction responses   D. CERs

6. When a person is in the early stages of dementia, eye-blink conditioning
   A. occurs more slowly   B. occurs more quickly   C. is no longer susceptible to extinction   D. becomes an operant response

7. Three-year-old Josh sees his five-year-old sister get chased by a neighbor's dog. Now Josh is as afraid of the dog as his sister is. Josh's fear is a result of
   A. stimulus discrimination   B. vicarious conditioning   C. spontaneous recovery   D. higher order conditioning

8. The law of effect defines the role of _____ in learning.
   A. antecedent stimuli   B. stimulus generalization   C. operant reinforcers   D. stimulus approximations

9. Operant reinforcement works best when it is
   A. delayed   B. an antecedent   C. response contingent   D. aversive

10. Negative reinforcement _____ responding.
    A. increases   B. decreases   C. reverses   D. extinguishes

11. Response cost is one form of
    A. discrimination conditioning   B. generalization   C. higher order conditioning   D. punishment

12. Which is a correct match?
    A. social reinforcer–primary reinforcement   B. token reinforcer–secondary reinforcement   C. ICS–secondary reinforcement   D. negative reinforcer–punishment

13. CAI is based on the same principles as
    A. negative reinforcement   B. programmed instruction   C. higher order conditioning   D. stimulus generalization

14. Moderate response rates that are marked by spurts of activity and periods of inactivity are characteristic of
    A. FR schedules   B. VR schedules   C. FI schedules   D. VI schedules

15. The "sniffer" dogs who locate drugs and explosives at airports learn to identify contraband through _____ _____ training.
    A. classical extinction   B. classical desensitization   C. vicarious feedback   D. operant discrimination

16. Punishment tends to encourage escape learning, avoidance learning, and
    A. rapid extinction   B. aggression   C. correct responses   D. the partial reinforcement effect

17. Discovery learning is often superior to its opposite:
    A. rote learning   B. negative reinforcement   C. observational learning   D. cognitive learning

18. Children who watch a great deal of televised violence are more prone to be aggressive, an effect that is best explained by
    A. negative reinforcement   B. shaping and successive approximations   C. observational learning   D. vicarious classical conditioning

19. As a behavioral management strategy, self-recording applies _____ to change personal habits.
    A. vicarious conditioning   B. feedback   C. behavioral contracting   D. the Premack principle

20. Bad habits can be altered by finding ways to remove, avoid, or delay the reinforcement that follows unwanted responses. This strategy is best described as
    A. seek alternate responses   B. use operant extinction   C. break up response chains   D. narrow cues and antecedents

Memory

Has Anyone Seen My MemSave?

Cef-Wol is a typical inhabitant of the planet Gex. For hundreds of years, the Gex endured high levels of industrial pollution. They've cleaned up now, but many Gex suffer from memory impairments caused by their exposure to toxic chemicals. Being a technologically advanced society, the Gex issued small, hand-held memory devices to all affected individuals. Cef-Wol, like many other Gex, now relies on her MemSave to get through the day. But she hates the endless chore of entering information into her MemSave, hour by hour, day after day. Cef-Wol also has another problem—when she needs information she has stored in her MemSave, Cef-Wol sometimes forgets that she *has* a MemSave.

Cef-Wol may be a fictional character, but her plight is not entirely fanciful. Consider Kate, who suffers from a rare brain disorder that makes it nearly impossible for her to remember day-to-day events. Kate gets lost in familiar buildings, misses appointments, and quickly forgets recent conversations, messages, and visitors. Because of Kate's memory handicap, her parents must constantly supervise her—even though she is an adult (Vargha-Khadem et al., 1997).

Other types of memory loss can be even more devastating. For instance, when victims of total amnesia look in a mirror, a stranger stares back at them. Imagine the terror of having all of your memories wiped out. You would have no identity, no knowledge, and no life history. You wouldn't recognize friends or family members. Clearly, a life without memory would be meaningless.

Recently, Cef-Wol visited Earth to find out how human memory works. Perhaps by reading this chapter you can do the same.

Survey Questions

- Is there more than one type of memory?
- What are the features of each type of memory?
- Is there more than one type of long-term memory?
- How is memory measured?
- What are "photographic" memories?
- What causes forgetting?
- How accurate are everyday memories?
- What happens in the brain when memories are formed?
- How can I improve my memory?

STAGES OF MEMORY—DO YOU HAVE A MIND LIKE A STEEL TRAP? OR A SIEVE?

] SURVEYQUESTION *Is there more than one type of memory?*

Do you remember what you had for breakfast this morning? Or what happened on September 11, 2001? Of course you do. But how is it possible for us to travel back in time? Let's begin with a look at basic memory systems. An interesting chain of events must occur before you can say "I remember."

Many people think memory is "a dusty storehouse of facts." In reality, **memory** is an active system that stores, organizes, alters, and recovers information (Baddeley, 1996). In some ways memory acts like a computer (◆Fig. 7.1). Incoming information is first **encoded,** or changed into a usable form. This step is like typing data into a computer (or Cef-Wol's MemSave). Next, information is **stored** in the system. (As we will see in a moment, human memory can be pictured as three separate storage systems.) Finally, memories must be **retrieved,** or taken out of storage, to be useful. If you're going to remember all of the 9,856 new terms on your next psychology exam, you must successfully encode, store, and retrieve them.

What are the three separate memory systems just mentioned? Psychologists have identified three stages of memory. Information we want to store for a long time must pass through all three stages (◆Fig. 7.2).

Sensory Memory

Let's say a friend asks you to pick up several things at a market. How will you remember them? Information first enters **sensory memory,** which can hold an exact copy of what you see or hear, for a few seconds or less. For instance, look at a flower and then close your eyes. An **icon** (EYE-kon), or fleeting mental image, of the flower will persist for about one-half second. Similarly, when you hear information, sensory memory stores it as an *echo* for up to 2 seconds (Schweickert, 1993). (An **echo** is a brief flurry of activity in the auditory system.) In general, sensory memory holds information just long enough to move it to the second memory system (Neath, 2002).

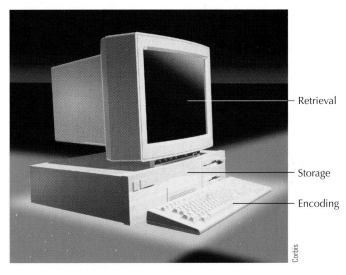

Retrieval

Storage

Encoding

Corbis

◆**FIGURE 7.1** *In some ways, a computer acts like a mechanical memory system. Both systems process information, and both allow encoding, storage, and retrieval of data.*

Memory The mental system for receiving, encoding, storing, organizing, altering, and retrieving information.

Encoding Converting information into a form in which it will be retained in memory.

Storage Holding information in memory for later use.

Retrieval Recovering information from storage in memory.

Sensory memory The first stage of memory, which holds an exact record of incoming information for a few seconds or less.

Icon A mental image or visual representation.

Echo A brief continuation of sensory activity in the auditory system after a sound is heard.

Short-Term Memory

Not everything we see or hear stays in memory. Imagine that a radio is playing in the background as your friend reads her shopping list. Will you remember what the announcer says, too? Probably not, because *selective attention* (focusing on a selected portion of sensory input) controls what information moves on to short-term memory. **Short-term memory (STM)** holds small amounts of information for relatively brief periods. By paying attention to your friend, you will place her shopping list in short-term memory (while you ignore the voice on the radio saying, "Buy Burpo Butter").

How are short-term memories encoded?   Short-term memories can be stored as images. But more often they are stored *phonetically* (by sound), especially in recalling words and letters (Neath, 2002). If you are introduced to Tim at a party and you forget his name, you are more likely to call him by a name that sounds like Tim (Jim, Kim, or Slim, for instance) rather than a name that sounds different, such as Bob or Mike. Your friend with the shopping list may be lucky if you don't bring home jam instead of ham and soap instead of soup!

Short-term memory is a temporary storehouse for small amounts of information. When you dial a phone number or briefly remember a shopping list, you are using STM. Notice that information is quickly "dumped" from STM and forever lost. Short-term memory prevents our minds from storing useless names, dates, telephone numbers, and other trivia.

At the same time, it provides an area of **working memory** where we do much of our thinking. Your working memory acts as a sort of "mental scratchpad." It briefly holds information while you carry out other mental activities, such as doing mental arithmetic (Tuholski, Engle, & Baylis, 2001).

As you may have noticed when dialing a telephone, STM is very sensitive to *interruption,* or *interference.* You've probably had something like this happen: Someone leaves a phone number on your answering machine. You repeat the number to yourself as you start to dial. Then the doorbell rings and you rush to see who is there. When you return to the phone, you have completely forgotten the number. You listen to the message again and memorize the number. This time as you begin to dial, someone asks you a question. You answer, turn to the phone, and find that you have forgotten the number. Notice again that human working memory can handle only small amounts of information. It is very difficult to do more than one task at a time in STM (Miyake, 2001).

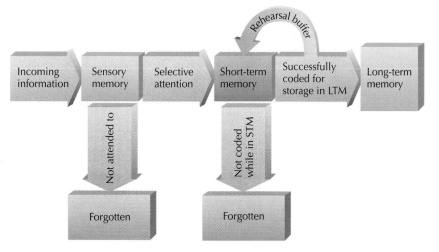

✦FIGURE 7.2 *Remembering is thought to involve at least three steps. Incoming information is first held for a second or two by sensory memory. Information selected by attention is then transferred to temporary storage in short-term memory. If new information is not rapidly encoded, or rehearsed, it is forgotten. If it is transferred to long-term memory, it becomes relatively permanent, although retrieving it may be a problem. The preceding is a useful* model *of memory; it may not be literally true of what happens in the brain (Eysenck & Keane, 1995).*

Long-Term Memory

If short-term memory is brief, easily interrupted, and limited in "size," how do we remember for longer periods of time?   Information that is important or meaningful is transferred to **long-term memory (LTM)**, which acts as a lasting storehouse for knowledge. LTM contains everything you know about the world—from aardvark to zucchini, math to *Myst,* facts to fantasy. And yet, there appears to be no danger of running out of room. LTM can hold nearly limitless amounts of information. In fact, the more you know, the easier it becomes to add new information to memory. This is the reverse of what we would expect if LTM could be "filled up" (Eysenck & Keane, 1995). It is also one of many reasons for getting an education.

Are long-term memories encoded as sounds?   They can be. But typically, information in LTM is stored on the basis of *meaning* and importance, not by sound. If you make an error in LTM, it will probably be related to meaning. For example, if you are trying to recall the word *barn* from a memorized list, you are more likely to mistakenly say *shed* or *farm* than

Short-term memory (STM) The memory system used to hold small amounts of information for relatively brief time periods.

Working memory Another name for short-term memory, especially as it is used for thinking and problem solving.

Long-term memory (LTM) The memory system used for relatively permanent storage of meaningful information.

yarn. If you can link information in STM to knowledge you have already stored in LTM, it gains meaning. This makes it easier to remember. As an example, try to memorize this story:

> With hocked gems financing him, our hero bravely defied all scornful laughter. "Your eyes deceive," he had said. "An egg, not a table, correctly typifies this unexplored planet." Now three sturdy sisters sought proof. Forging along, days became weeks as many doubters spread fearful rumors about the edge. At last from nowhere welcome winged creatures appeared, signifying momentous success. (Adapted from Dooling & Lachman, 1971.)

This odd story emphasizes the impact of meaning on memory. People given the title of the story were able to remember it far better than those not given a title. See if the title helps you as much as it did them. The title is "Columbus Discovers America."

Dual Memory

Most of our daily memory chores are handled by STM and LTM. To summarize their connection, picture short-term memory as a small desk at the front of a huge warehouse full of filing cabinets (LTM). As information enters the warehouse, it is first placed on the desk. Because the desk is small, it must be quickly cleared off to make room for new information. Unimportant items are simply tossed away. Meaningful or important information is placed in the files (LTM).

When we want to use knowledge from LTM to answer a question, the information is returned to STM. Or, in our analogy, a folder is taken out of the files (LTM) and moved to the desk (STM), where it can be used. Now that you have a general picture of memory, it is time to explore STM and LTM in more detail. But first, here's a chance to rehearse what you've learned.

STUDYBREAK *Memory Systems*

RELATE

Wave a pencil back and forth in front of your eyes while focusing on something in the distance. The pencil's image looks transparent. Why? (Because sensory memory briefly holds an image of the pencil. This image persists after the pencil passes by.)

Think of a time today when you used short-term memory (such as briefly remembering a phone number, an Internet address, or someone's name). How long did you retain the information? How did you encode it? How much do you remember now?

How is long-term memory helping you read this sentence? If the words weren't already stored in LTM, could you read at all? How else have you used LTM today?

LEARNING CHECK

Match: A. Sensory memory B. STM C. LTM

1. _____ Working memory
2. _____ Holds information for a few seconds or less
3. _____ Stores an icon or echo
4. _____ Permanent, unlimited capacity
5. _____ Temporarily holds small amounts of information
6. _____ Selective attention determines its contents
7. STM is improved by interruption, or interference, because attention is more focused at such times. T or F?

Critical Thinking

8. Why is sensory memory important to filmmakers?

ANSWERS

1. B 2. A 3. A 4. C 5. B 6. B 7. F 8. Without sensory memory, a movie would look like a series of still pictures. The split-second persistence of visual images helps blend one motion-picture frame into the next.

SHORT-TERM MEMORY—DO YOU KNOW THE MAGIC NUMBER?

] SURVEYQUESTION *What are the features of each type of memory?*

To make good use of your memory, it is valuable to know more about STM and LTM. It's time to dig deeper into our primary memory systems.

How much information can be held in short-term memory? For an answer, read the following numbers once. Then close the book and write as many as you can in the correct order.

8 5 1 7 4 9 3

This is called a digit-span test. It is a measure of attention and short-term memory. If you were able to correctly repeat 7 digits, you have an average short-term memory. Now try to memorize the following list, reading it only once.

7 1 8 3 5 4 2 9 1 6 3

This series was probably beyond your short-term memory capacity. Psychologist George Miller found that short-term memory is limited to the "magic number" 7 (plus or minus 2) **information bits** (Miller, 1956). A bit is a single meaningful "piece" of information, such as a digit. It is as if short-term memory has 7 "slots" or "bins" into which separate items can be placed. Actually, a few people can remember up to 9 bits, and for some types of information 5 bits is the limit. Thus, an *average* of 7 information bits can be held in short-term memory (Neath, 2002).

When all of the "slots" in STM are filled, there is no room for new information. Picture how this works at a party: Let's say your hostess begins introducing everyone who is there, "Chun, Dasia, Marco, Roseanna, Cholik, Shawn, Kyrene . . . ." "Stop," you think to yourself. But she continues, "Nelia, Jay, Efren, Frank, Marietta, Jorge, Patty, Amit, Ricky." The hostess leaves, satisfied that you have met everyone. And you spend the evening talking with Chun, Dasia, and Ricky, the only people whose names you remember!

Recoding Information

Before we continue, try your short-term memory again, this time on letters. Read the following letters once, then look away and try to write them in the proper order.

T V I   B M U S   N Y   M C A

Notice that there are 12 letters, or "bits" of information. This should be beyond the 7-item limit of STM. However, since the letters are in four groups, or *chunks* of information, many students are able to memorize them. **Information chunks** are made up of bits of information grouped into larger units.

How does chunking help? Chunking *recodes* (reorganizes) information into units that are already in LTM. For example, you may have noticed that NY is the abbreviation for New York. If so, the two bits N and Y became one chunk. In an experiment that used lists like this one, people remembered best when the letters were read as familiar meaningful chunks: TV, IBM, USN, YMCA (Bower & Springston, 1970). If you recoded the letters this way, you probably remembered the entire list.

Chunking suggests that STM holds about 5 to 7 of whatever units we are using. A single chunk could be made up of numbers, letters, words, phrases, or familiar sentences (Barsalou, 1992). Picture STM as a small desk again. Through chunking, we combine several items into one "stack" of information. This allows us to place 7 stacks on the desk, where before there was only room for 7 separate items. While you are studying, try to find ways to link 2, 3, or more separate facts or ideas into larger chunks, and your memory will improve. Psychologist Nelson Cowan (2001) believes that STM may actually hold only 4 items, unless some chunking has occurred. The clear message is that creating information chunks is the key to making good use of your short-term memory.

Rehearsing Information

How long do short-term memories last? They disappear very rapidly. However, you can prolong a memory by silently repeating it, a process called **maintenance rehearsal.** You have probably briefly remembered an address or telephone number this way. The more times a short-term memory is rehearsed, the greater its chances of being stored in LTM (Barsalou, 1992). In a sense, rehearsing information allows you to "see" it many times, not just once (Nairne, 2002).

What if rehearsal is prevented, so a memory cannot be recycled or moved to LTM? Without maintenance rehearsal, STM is incredibly brief. In one experiment, subjects heard meaningless syllables like XAR followed by a number like 67. As soon as subjects heard the number, they began counting backward by threes (to prevent them from re-

Information bits Meaningful units of information, such as numbers, letters, words, or phrases.
Information chunks Information bits grouped into larger units.
Maintenance rehearsal Silently repeating or mentally reviewing information to hold it in short-term memory.

peating the syllable). After a delay of only 18 seconds, their memory scores fell to zero (Peterson & Peterson, 1959).

After *18 seconds* without rehearsal, the short-term memories were gone forever! Keep this in mind when you get only one chance to hear information you want to remember. If you are introduced to someone and the name slips out of STM, it is gone forever. To escape this awkward situation, you might try saying something like, "I'm curious, how do you spell your name?" Unfortunately, the response is often an icy reply like, "B-O-B S-M-I-T-H, it's really not too difficult." To avoid embarrassment, pay careful attention to the name, repeat it to yourself several times, and try to use it in the next sentence or two—before you lose it (Neath, 2002).

Elaborative rehearsal, which makes information more meaningful, is a far better way to create lasting memories. Elaborative rehearsal links new information to memories that are already in LTM. When you are studying, you will remember more if you elaborate, extend, and think about information. As you read, try to frequently ask yourself "why" questions, such as "Why would that be true?" Also, try to relate new ideas to your own experiences and knowledge (Hartlep & Forsyth, 2000).

LONG-TERM MEMORY— WHERE THE PAST LIVES

An electrode was placed at location number 11 on the patient's brain. She immediately said, "Yes, sir, I think I heard a mother calling her little boy somewhere. It seemed to be something happening years ago. It was somebody in the neighborhood where I live." A short time later the electrode was applied to the same spot. Again the patient said, "Yes, I hear the same familiar sounds, it seems to be a woman calling, the same lady" (Penfield, 1958). These statements were made by a woman undergoing brain surgery. Only local anesthetics were used (there are no pain receptors in the brain), so the patient was awake as her brain was electrically stimulated (✦Fig. 7.3). When activated, some brain areas seemed to produce vivid memories of long-forgotten events.

Permanence

Is every experience permanently recorded in memory? Results like those described led neurosurgeon Wilder Penfield to claim that the brain records the past like a "continuous strip of movie film, complete with sound track" (Penfield, 1957). But as you know, this is an exaggeration. Many events never get past short-term memory. Also, brain stimulation produces memory-like experiences in only about 3 percent of cases. Most reports resemble dreams more than memories, and many are clearly imaginary. Memory experts now believe that long-term memories are only *relatively* permanent (Barsalou, 1992; Loftus & Loftus, 1980). Perfect, indelible, eternal memories are a myth.

✦**FIGURE 7.3** *Exposed cerebral cortex of a patient undergoing brain surgery. Numbers represent points that reportedly produced "memories" when electrically stimulated. A critical evaluation of such reports suggests that they are more like dreams than memories. This fact raises questions about claims that long-term memories are permanent. (From Wilder Penfield,* The Excitable Cortex in Conscious Man, *1958. Courtesy of the author and Charles C Thomas, Publisher, Springfield, Illinois.)*

TRY IT YOURSELF: HOW'S YOUR MEMORY?

In order to better appreciate the next topic, pause for a moment and read the words you see here. Read through the list once. Then continue reading the next section of this chapter.

    bed dream blanket doze pillow nap snore mattress alarm
       clock rest slumber nod sheet bunk cot cradle groggy

Constructing Memories

There is another reason to doubt Penfield's claim. As new long-term memories are formed, older memories are often updated, changed, lost, or *revised* (Baddeley, 1990, 1996). To illustrate this point, Elizabeth Loftus and John Palmer (1974) showed people a filmed auto-

Elaborative rehearsal Rehearsal that links new information with existing memories and knowledge.

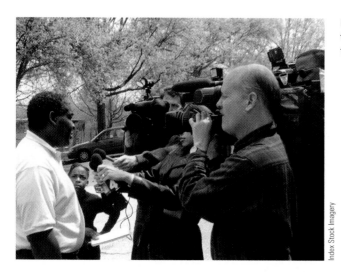

Index Stock Imagery

Eyewitness memories are notoriously inaccurate. By the time witnesses are asked to testify in court, information they learned after an incident may blend into their original memories.

mobile accident. Afterward, some participants were asked to estimate how fast the cars were going when they "smashed" into each other. For others the words "bumped," "contacted," or "hit" replaced "smashed." One week later, each person was asked, "Did you see any broken glass?" Those asked earlier about the cars that "smashed" into each other were more likely to say yes. (No broken glass was shown in the film.) The new information ("smashed") was included in memories and altered them.

TRY IT YOURSELF: OLD OR NEW?

Now, without looking back to the list of words you read a moment ago, see if you can tell which of the following are "old" words (items from the list you read) and which are "new" words (items that weren't on the list). Mark each of the following words as old or new:

sofa   sleep   lamp   kitchen

Updating memories is called **constructive processing.** Gaps in memory, which are common, may be filled in by logic, guessing, or new information (Schacter, Norman, & Koutstaal, 1998). Indeed, it is possible to have "memories" for things that never happened (such as remembering broken glass at an accident when there was none) (Loftus, 2003). In one fascinating study, people who had visited a Disney resort were shown several fake ads for Disney that featured Bugs Bunny. Later, about 16 percent of the people who saw these fake ads claimed that they had met Bugs at Disneyland. This is impossible, of course, because Bugs Bunny is a Warner Brothers character who would never be found at Disneyland (Braun, Ellis, & Loftus, 2002).

TRY IT YOURSELF: AND NOW, THE RESULTS

Return now and look at the labels you wrote on the "old or new" word list. Contrary to what you may think you "remembered," all of the listed words are "new." None was on the original list! If you thought you remembered that sleep was on the original list, you had a false memory. The word *sleep* is associated with most of the words on the original list, which creates a strong impression that you saw it before (Roediger & McDermott, 1995).

As the preceding examples show, thoughts, inferences, and mental associations may be mistaken for true memories. People in Elizabeth Loftus's experiments who had these *pseudo-memories* (false memories) were often quite upset to learn they had given false "testimony" (Loftus & Ketcham, 1991).

False long-term memories are a common problem in police work. For example, a witness may select a photo of a suspect from police files or see a photo in the news. Later, the witness identifies the suspect in a lineup or in court. Did the witness really remember the suspect from the scene of the crime? Or was it from the more recently seen photograph? Under some circumstances, innocent people have been "remembered" and named as criminals (Schachter, 2001).

Does the new information "overwrite" the original memory?   No, the real problem is that we often can't remember the *source* of a memory. This can lead witnesses to "remember" a face that they actually saw somewhere other than the crime scene (Schacter, Norman, & Koutstaal, 1998). Many tragic cases of mistaken identity occur this way.

Couldn't hypnosis be used to avoid such problems?   News stories often give the impression that it can. Is this true? "Hypnosis, Imagination, and Memory" examines research done on this intriguing question.

Constructive processing Reorganizing or updating memories on the basis of logic, reasoning, or the addition of new information.

CRITICAL THINKING Hypnosis, Imagination, and Memory

In 1976, near Chowchilla, California, 26 children were abducted from a school bus and held captive for ransom. Under hypnosis, the bus driver recalled the license plate number of the kidnappers' van. This memory helped break the case and led to the children's rescue. Such successes seem to imply that hypnosis can improve memory. But does it? Read on, and judge for yourself.

Research has shown that a hypnotized person is more likely than normal to use imagination to fill in gaps in memory. Also, when hypnotized persons are given false information, they tend to weave it into their memories (Sheehan & Statham, 1989). Even when a memory is completely false, the hypnotized person's confidence in it can be unshakable (Burgess & Kirsch, 1999). Most telling of all is the fact that hypnosis increases false memories more than it does true ones. Eighty percent of the new mem-

ories produced by hypnotized subjects in one experiment were *incorrect* (Dywan & Bowers, 1983). The worst situation of all occurs when hypnosis is combined with misleading or suggestive questions. Under these conditions, false memories are almost guaranteed (Scoboria et al., 2002). Overall, it can be concluded that hypnosis does not greatly improve memory (Burgess & Kirsch, 1999).

Then why did it help in the Chowchilla case? It is true that hypnosis sometimes uncovers more information, as it did in Chowchilla (Schreiber & Schreiber, 1999). However, when it does, there is no sure way to tell which memories are true and which are false (Perry et al., 1996). Clearly, hypnosis is not the "magic bullet" against forgetting that some police investigators hoped it would be (Newman & Thompson, 2001).

To summarize, forming and using memories is an active, creative, and highly personal process. Our memories are colored by emotions, judgments, and quirks of personality. If you and a friend were lashed together, and you went through life side by side, you would still have different memories. What we remember depends on what we pay attention to, what we regard as meaningful or important, and what we feel strongly about (Schacter, 1996).

Organizing Memories

Long-term memory stores a seemingly limitless amount of information in a lifetime. How is it possible to quickly find specific memories? The answer is that each person's "memory index" is highly organized.

Do you mean that information is arranged alphabetically, as in a dictionary? Not a chance! If I ask you to name a black-and-white animal that lives on ice, is related to a chicken, and cannot fly, you don't have to go from aardvark to zebra to find the answer. You will probably only think of black-and-white birds living in the Antarctic. Which of these cannot fly? *Voilà,* the answer is penguin.

Information in LTM may be arranged according to rules, images, categories, symbols, similarity, formal meaning, or personal meaning (Baddeley, 1990, 1996). In recent years, psychologists have begun to develop a picture of the *structure,* or organization, of memories. *Memory structure* refers to the pattern of associations among items of information. For example, assume that you are given two statements to which you must answer yes or no: (1) *A canary is an animal.* (2) *A canary is a bird.* Which do you answer more quickly? For most people, *A canary is a bird* produces a faster yes than *A canary is an animal* (Collins & Quillian,1969). Why should this be so? Psychologists believe that a **network model** of memory explains why. According to this view, LTM is organized as a network of linked ideas (◆Fig. 7.4). When ideas are "farther" apart, it takes a longer chain of associations to connect them. The more two items are separated, the longer it takes to answer. In terms of information links, *canary* is probably "close" to *bird* in your "memory files." *Animal* and *canary* are farther apart. Remember though, this has nothing to do with alphabetical order. We are talking about organization based on linked meanings.

Redintegrative Memories

Networks of associated memories may help explain a common experience: Imagine finding a picture taken on your sixth birthday or tenth Christmas. As you look at the photo, one memory leads to another, which leads to another, and another. Soon you have unleashed a flood of seemingly forgotten details. This process is called redintegration (ruh-DIN-tuh-GRAY-shun).

Network model A model of memory that views it as an organized system of linked information.

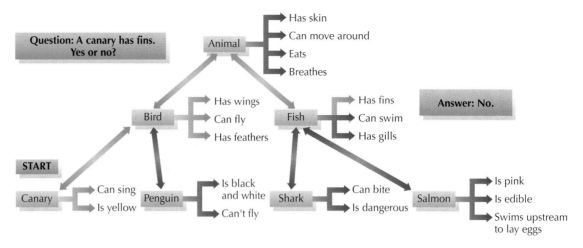

◆FIGURE 7.4 *A hypothetical network of facts about animals shows what is meant by the structure of memory. Small networks of ideas such as this are probably organized into larger and larger units and higher levels of meaning. (Adapted from Collins & Quillian, 1969.)*

Redintegrative memories seem to spread through the "branches" of memory networks. Many people find that such memories are also touched off by distinctive odors out of the past—from a farm visited in childhood, Grandma's kitchen, the seashore, a doctor's office, the perfume or aftershave of a former lover, and so on. The key idea in redintegration is that one memory serves as a cue to trigger another. As a result, an entire past experience may be reconstructed from one small recollection.

How many types of long-term memory are there?   It is becoming clear that more than one type of long-term memory exists. Let's probe a little farther into the mysteries of memory.

Skill Memory and Fact Memory

] SURVEYQUESTION *Is there more than one type of long-term memory?*

A curious thing happens to many people who develop amnesia. Amnesic patients may be unable to learn a telephone number, an address, or a person's name. And yet, the same patients can learn to solve complex puzzles in a normal amount of time (Squire & Zola-Morgan, 1988) (◆Fig. 7.5). These and other observations have led many psychologists to conclude that long-term memories fall into at least two categories. One is called *procedural memory* (or skill memory). The other is *declarative memory* (also sometimes called fact memory).

Skills

Procedural memory includes basic conditioned responses and learned actions, such as those involved in typing, driving, or swinging a golf club. Memories such as these can be fully expressed only as actions (or "know-how"). It is likely that skill memories register in "lower" brain areas, especially the cerebellum. They represent the more basic "automatic" elements of conditioning, learning, and memory (Gabrieli, 1998).

Facts

Declarative memory stores specific factual information, such as names, faces, words, dates, and ideas. Declarative memories are expressed as words or symbols. For example, knowing that Steven Spielberg directed both *Close Encounters of the Third Kind* and *Jurassic Park* is a declarative memory. This is the type of memory that a person with amnesia lacks and that most of us take for granted. Many psychologists believe that declarative memory can be further divided into *semantic memory* and *episodic memory* (Nyberg & Tulving, 1996).

Semantic Memory

Most of our basic factual knowledge about the world is almost totally immune to forgetting. The names of objects, the days of the week or months of the year, simple math skills, the seasons, words and language, and other general facts are all quite lasting. Such impersonal

◆FIGURE 7.5 *The tower puzzle. In this puzzle, all the colored disks must be moved to another post, without ever placing a larger disk on a smaller one. Only one disk may be moved at a time, and a disk must always be moved from one post to another (it cannot be held aside). An amnesic patient learned to solve the puzzle in 31 moves, the minimum possible. Even so, each time he began, he protested that he did not remember ever solving the puzzle before and that he did not know how to begin. Evidence like this suggests that skill memory is distinct from fact memory.*

Redintegrative memories Memories that are reconstructed or expanded by starting with one memory and then following chains of association to other, related memories.

Procedural memory Long-term memories of conditioned responses and learned skills.

Declarative memory That part of long-term memory containing specific factual information.

facts make up a part of LTM called **semantic memory.** Semantic memory serves as a mental dictionary or encyclopedia of basic knowledge.

Episodic Memory

Semantic memory has no connection to times or places. It would be rare, for instance, to remember when and where you first learned the names of the seasons. In contrast, **episodic** (ep-ih-SOD-ik) **memory** is an "autobiographical" record of personal experiences. It stores life events (or "episodes") day after day, year after year. Can you remember your seventh birthday? Your first date? An accident you witnessed? The first day of college? What you did yesterday? All are episodic memories. Note that episodic memories are about the "what," "where," and "when" of our lives. They are more than a simple ability to store information. They make it possible for us to mentally travel back in time and *re-experience* events (Tulving, 2002).

Are episodic memories as lasting as semantic memories? In general, episodic memories are more easily forgotten than semantic memories. This is because new information constantly pours into episodic memory. Stop for a moment and remember where and when you first met your best friend. That was an episodic memory. Notice that you now remember that you just remembered something. You have a new episodic memory in which you remember that you remembered while reading this text! It's easy to see how much we ask of our memory.

Do you remember Kate, who was described at the beginning of this chapter? Her specific problem is an inability to form episodic memories. Over the years, she has been able to store enough information in semantic memory to get through school. However, her impaired episodic memory makes daily life a struggle (Vargha-Khadem et al., 1997).

How Many Types of Memory?

In summary, it is very likely that three kinds of long-term memories exist: procedural, semantic, and episodic (Mitchell, 1989; Squire et al., 1993) (◆Fig. 7.6). While other types of memory may be discovered, it appears that some pieces of the puzzle are falling into place.

◆**FIGURE 7.6** *In the model shown here, long-term memory is divided into procedural memory (learned actions and skills) and declarative memory (stored facts). Declarative memories can be either semantic (impersonal knowledge) or episodic (personal experiences associated with specific times and places).*

Semantic memory A subpart of declarative memory that records impersonal knowledge about the world.
Episodic memory A subpart of declarative memory that records personal experiences that are linked with specific times and places.

MEASURING MEMORY—THE ANSWER IS ON THE TIP OF MY TONGUE

] **SURVEYQUESTION** *How is memory measured?*

You either remember something or you don't, right? Wrong. Partial memories are common. For instance, imagine that a clerk helps you at a clothing store. Will you remember her 6 months later? Probably not—unless you happen to see her again at the mall. If you remember her then, you will have used a form of partial memory called *recognition*.

Partial memory is also demonstrated by the **tip-of-the-tongue (TOT) state.** This is the feeling that a memory is available, but not quite retrievable. It is as if an answer or a memory is just out of reach—on the "tip of your tongue." For instance, in one study, people listened to theme music from popular TV shows. Then they tried to name the program the tune came from. This produced TOT experiences for about 1 out of 5 tunes (Riefer, Keveri, & Kramer, 1995).

In another TOT study, university students read the definitions of words such as *sextant, sampan,* and *ambergris.* Students who "drew a blank" and couldn't name a defined word were asked to give whatever other information they could. Often, they could accurately guess the first and last letter and even the number of syllables of the word they were seeking. They also gave words that sounded like or meant the same thing as the defined word (Brown & McNeill, 1966).

Closely related to the TOT state is the fact that people can often tell beforehand if they are likely to remember something. This is called the *feeling of knowing* (Nelson, 1987). Feeling-of-knowing reactions are easy to observe on television game shows, where they occur just before contestants are allowed to answer.

Because memory is not an all-or-nothing event, there are several ways of measuring it. Three commonly used memory tasks (tests of memory) are *recall, recognition,* and *relearning.* Let's see how they differ.

Recalling Information

What is the name of the first song on your favorite compact disc? Who won the World Series last year? Who wrote *Hamlet?* If you can answer these questions you are using **recall,** a direct retrieval of facts or information. Tests of recall often require *verbatim* (word-for-word) memory. If you study a poem until you can recite it without looking at it, you are recalling it. If you complete a fill-in-the-blank question, you are using recall. When you answer an essay question by providing facts and ideas, you are also using recall, even though you didn't learn your essay verbatim.

The order in which information is memorized has an interesting effect on recall. To experience it, try to memorize the following list, reading it only once:

> bread, apples, soda, ham, cookies, rice, lettuce, beets,
> mustard, cheese, oranges, ice cream, crackers, flour, eggs

If you are like most people, it will be hardest for you to recall items from the middle of the list. ✦Figure 7.7 shows the results of a similar test. Notice that most errors occur with middle items of an ordered list. This is the **serial position effect.** You can remember the last items on a list because they are still in STM. The first items are also remembered well because they entered an "empty" short-term memory. This allows you to rehearse the items so they move into long-term memory (Medin & Ross, 1992). The middle items are neither held in short-term memory nor moved to long-term memory, so they are often lost.

Recognizing Information

Try to write down everything you can remember learning from a class you took last year. (You have 3 minutes, which should be more than enough time!) If you actually did this, you might conclude that you had learned very little. However, a more sensitive test based on

Tip-of-the-tongue state The feeling that a memory is available but not quite retrievable.

Recall To supply or reproduce memorized information with a minimum of external cues.

Serial position effect The tendency to make the most errors in remembering the middle items of an ordered list.

recognition could be used. In **recognition memory,** previously learned material is correctly identified. For instance, you could take a multiple-choice test on facts and ideas from the course. Since you would only have to recognize correct answers, we would probably find that you had learned a lot.

Recognition memory can be amazingly accurate for pictures, photographs, or other visual input. One investigator showed people 2,560 photographs at a rate of one every 10 seconds. Each person was then shown 280 pairs of photographs. Each pair included an "old" picture (from the first set of photos) and a similar "new" image. Subjects could tell 85 to 95 percent of the time which photograph they had seen before (Haber, 1970). This finding may explain why people so often say, "I may forget a name, but I never forget a face." (It's also why we rarely need to see our friends' vacation photos more than once.)

Recognition is usually superior to recall. That's why police departments use photographs or a lineup to identify criminal suspects. Witnesses who disagree when they try to recall a suspect's height, weight, age, or eye color often agree completely when recognition is all that is required.

Is recognition always superior? It depends greatly on the kind of *distractors* used. These are false items included with an item to be recognized. If distractors are very similar to the correct item, memory may be poor. A reverse problem occurs when only one choice looks like it could be correct. This can produce a *false positive*, or false sense of recognition, like the false memory you had earlier when you thought you remembered seeing the word *sleep.*

There have been instances in which witnesses described a criminal as black, tall, or young. Then a lineup was held in which a suspect was the only African American among whites, the only tall suspect, or the only young person. In such cases, a false identification is very likely. A better method is to have *all* the distractors look like the person witnesses described. Also, witnesses should be warned that the culprit *may not be present.* This reduces false positives and increases accurate identifications (Wells et al., 1999). The worst situation occurs when only one person is presented as a suspect. In that case, false identifications of look-alike innocent persons are a real danger (Yarmey, Yarmey, & Yarmey, 1996). Indeed, many hundreds of people have been put in jail on the basis of mistaken eyewitness memories. To avoid tragic mistakes, it's far better to show witnesses one photo at a time (a sequential lineup). For each photo, the witness must decide whether the person is the culprit before another photo is shown (Wells, 2001).

◆FIGURE 7.7 *The serial position effect. The graph shows the percentage of subjects correctly recalling each item in a 15-item list. Recall is best for the first and last items. (Data from Craik, 1970.)*

Police lineups make use of the sensitivity of recognition memory. However, unless great care is taken, false identifications are still possible (Naka, 1998).

Relearning Information

In a classic experiment, a psychologist read a short passage in Greek to his son. He did this each day when the boy was between 15 months and 3 years of age. At age 8, the boy was asked if he remembered the Greek passage. He showed no evidence of recall. He was then shown selections from the passage he heard and selections from other Greek passages. Could he recognize the one he heard as an infant? "It's all Greek to me!" he said, indicating a lack of recognition (and drawing a frown from everyone in the room).

Had the psychologist stopped, he might have concluded that no memory of the Greek remained. However, the child was then asked to memorize the original quotation and others of equal difficulty. This time his earlier learning became evident. The boy memorized the passage he had heard in childhood 25 percent faster than the others (Burtt, 1941). As this experiment suggests, **relearning** is typically the most sensitive measure of memory.

Recognition memory An ability to correctly identify previously learned information.
Relearning Learning again something that was previously learned. Used to measure memory of prior learning.

When a person is tested by relearning, how do we know a memory still exists?   As with the boy described, relearning is measured by a *savings score* (the amount of time saved when relearning information). Let's say it takes you 1 hour to memorize all the names in a telephone book. (It's a small town.) Two years later you relearn them in 45 minutes. Because you "saved" 15 minutes, your savings score would be 25 percent (15 divided by 60 times 100). Savings of this type are a good reason for studying a wide range of subjects. It may seem that learning algebra, history, or a foreign language is wasted if you don't use the knowledge immediately. But when you do need such information, you will be able to relearn it quickly.

Implicit and Explicit Memories

Many memories remain outside of conscious awareness. For example, if you know how to type, it is apparent that you know where the letters are on the keyboard. But how many typists could correctly label blank keys in a drawing of a keyboard? Many people find that they cannot directly remember such information, even though they "know" it.

Who were the last three presidents of the United States? What did you have for breakfast today? What is the title of Aaliyah's best-selling album? Explicit memory is used in answering each of these questions. **Explicit memories** are past experiences that are consciously brought to mind. Recall, recognition, and the tests you take in school rely on explicit memories. In contrast, **implicit memories** lie outside of awareness (Roediger, 1990). That is, we are not aware that a memory exists. Nevertheless, implicit memories—such as unconsciously knowing where the letters are on a keyboard—greatly influence our behavior (Neath, 2002).

Can you label the letter keys on this blank keyboard? If you can, you probably used implicit memory to do it.

Priming

How is it possible to show that a memory exists if it lies outside of awareness?   Psychologists first noticed implicit memory while studying memory loss caused by brain injuries. Let's say, for example, that a patient is shown a list of common words, such as *chair, tree, lamp, table,* and so on. A few minutes later, the patient is asked to recall words from the list. Sadly, he has no memory of the words.

Now, instead of asking the patient to explicitly recall the list, we could "prime" his memory by giving him the first two letters of each word. "We'd like you to say a word that begins with these letters," we tell him. "Just say whatever comes to mind." Of course, many words could be made from each pair of letters. For example, the first item (from chair) would be the letters CH. The patient could say "child," "chalk," "chain," "check," or many other words. Instead, he says "chair," a word from the original list. The patient is not aware that he is remembering the list, but as he gives a word for each letter pair, almost all are from the list. Apparently, the letters **primed** (activated) hidden memories, which then influenced his answers.

Similar effects have been found for people with normal memories. As the preceding example implies, implicit memories are often revealed by giving a person limited cues, such as the first letter of words or partial drawings of objects. Typically, the person believes that he or she is just saying whatever comes to mind. Nevertheless, information previously seen or heard affects the person's answers (Roediger, 1990). Some nutritionists like to say, "You are what you eat." In the realm of memory it appears that we are what we experience—to a far greater degree than once realized.

Explicit memory A memory that a person is aware of having; a memory that is consciously retrieved.

Implicit memory A memory that a person does not know exists; a memory that is retrieved unconsciously.

Priming Facilitating the retrieval of an implicit memory by using cues to activate hidden memories.

Internal images Mental images or visual depictions used in memory and thinking.

EXCEPTIONAL MEMORY—WIZARDS OF RECALL

] SURVEYQUESTION *What are "photographic" memories?*

Can you remember how many doors there are in your house or apartment? To answer a question like this, many people form **internal images** (mental pictures) of each room and count the doorways they visualize. As this example implies, many memories are stored as mental images (Dewhurst & Conway, 1994).

(a)

(b)

◆FIGURE 7.8 (a) *"Treasure map" similar to the one used by Kosslyn, Ball, and Reiser (1978) to study images in memory.* (b) *This graph shows how long it took subjects to move a visualized spot various distances on their mental images of the map. (See text for explanation.)*

Stephen Kosslyn, Thomas Ball, and Brian Reiser (1978) found an interesting way to show that memories do exist as images. People first memorized a sort of treasure map similar to the one shown in ◆Figure 7.8 *a*. They were then asked to picture a black dot moving from one object, such as one of the trees, to another, such as the hut at the top of the island. Did participants really form an image to do this task? It seems they did. As shown in Figure 7.8 *b*, the time it took to "move" the dot was directly related to actual distances on the map.

Is the "treasure map" task an example of photographic memory? In some ways, internal memory images do have "photographic" qualities. However, the term *photographic memory* is more often used to describe eidetic imagery.

Eidetic Imagery

Eidetic (eye-DET-ik) **imagery** occurs when a person has visual images clear enough to be "scanned" or retained for at least 30 seconds. Internal memory images can be "viewed" mentally with the eyes closed. In contrast, eidetic images are "projected" out in front of a person. That is, they are best "seen" on a plain surface, such as a blank piece of paper. In this respect, eidetic images are somewhat like the after-images you might have after looking at a flashbulb or a brightly lit neon sign (Kunzendorf, 1989).

Eidetic memory occurs most often in childhood, with about 8 children out of 100 having eidetic images. In one series of tests, children were shown a picture from *Alice's Adventures in Wonderland* (◆Fig. 7.9). To test your eidetic imagery, look at the picture and read the instructions there.

Now, let's see how much you remember. Can you say (without looking again) which of Alice's apron strings is longer? Are the cat's front paws crossed? How many stripes are on the cat's tail? After the picture was removed from view, one 10-year-old boy was asked what he saw. He replied, "I see the tree, gray tree with three limbs. I see the cat with stripes around its tail." Asked to count the stripes, the boy replied, "There are about 16" (a correct count!). The boy then went on to describe the remainder of the picture in striking detail (Haber, 1969).

◆FIGURE 7.9 *Test picture like that used to identify children with eidetic imagery. To test your eidetic imagery, look at the picture for 30 seconds. Then look at a blank surface and try to "project" the picture on it. If you have good eidetic imagery, you will be able to see the picture in detail. Return now to the text and try to answer the questions there. (Redrawn from an illustration in Lewis Carroll's* Alice's Adventures in Wonderland.*)*

Eidetic imagery The ability to retain a "projected" mental image long enough to use it as a source of information.

Don't be disappointed if you didn't do too well when you tried your eidetic skills. Most eidetic imagery disappears during adolescence and becomes rare by adulthood (Kunzendorf, 1989). Actually, this may not be much of a loss. The majority of eidetic memorizers have no better long-term memory than average.

Exceptional Memory

Let's return now to the concept of internal memory images. In rare instances, such images may be so vivid that it is reasonable to say that a person has "photographic memory." A notable example was reported by Aleksandr Luria (1968) in his book, *The Mind of a Mnemonist.* Luria studied a man he called Mr. S who had practically unlimited memory for visual images. Mr. S could remember almost everything that ever happened to him with incredible accuracy. Luria tried to test Mr. S's memory by using longer and longer lists of words or numbers. However, he soon discovered that no matter how long the list, Mr. S was able to recall it without error. Mr. S could memorize, with equal ease, strings of digits, meaningless consonants, mathematical formulas, and poems in foreign languages. His memory was so powerful that he had to devise ways to *forget*—such as writing information on a piece of paper and then burning it.

© Tribune Media Services, Inc. All rights reserved. Reprinted by permission.

Mr. S's abilities seemed fantastic to Cef-Wol (our visitor from the planet Gex), just as they might to any student of memory. However, Mr. S remembered so much that he couldn't separate important facts from trivia or facts from fantasy (Neath, 2002). For instance, if you asked him to read this chapter, he might remember every word. Yet, he might also recall all the images each word made him think of and all the sights, sounds, and feelings that occurred as he was reading. Therefore, finding the answer for a specific question, writing a logical essay, or even understanding a single sentence was very difficult for him. If you didn't have selective memory you would recall all the ingredients on your cereal box, every street number you've seen, and countless other scraps of information.

Few people in history have possessed memory abilities like Mr. S's. Nonetheless, you probably know at least one person who has an especially good memory. Is superior memory a biological gift? Or do excellent memorizers merely make better-than-average use of normal memory capacities? Let's investigate further.

Strategies for Remembering

At first, a student volunteer named Steve could remember 7 digits—a typical score for a college student. Could he improve with practice? For 20 months, Steve practiced memorizing ever-longer lists of digits. Ultimately, he was able to memorize around 80 digits, like this sample:

92842048050842268953990190252912807999970
6606574717310601080585269726026357332135

How did Steve reach such lofty heights of memory? Basically, he worked by chunking digits into meaningful groups containing 3 or 4 digits each. Steve's avid interest in long-distance running helped greatly. For instance, to him the first three digits above represented 9 minutes and 28 seconds, a good time for a 2-mile run. When running times wouldn't work, Steve used other associations, such as ages or dates, to chunk digits (Ericsson & Chase, 1982). It seems apparent that Steve's success was based on learned strategies. By using similar memory systems, other people have trained themselves to equal Steve's feat (Bellezza, Six, & Phillips, 1992).

Psychologist Anders Ericsson believes that exceptional memory is merely a learned extension of normal memory. As evidence, he notes that Steve's short-term memory did not improve during months of practice. For example, Steve could still memorize only 7 consonants. Steve's phenomenal memory for numbers grew as he figured out new ways to encode digits and store them in LTM. Steve began with a normal memory for digits. He extended his memory by diligent practice. Clearly, exceptional memory can be learned (Neath, 2002). However, we still have to wonder, do some people have naturally superior memories?

Memory Champions

Each year the World Memory Championship is held in England. There, a variety of mental athletes compete to see who has the best memory. To remain in the running, each contestant has to rapidly memorize daunting amounts of information, such as long lists of unrelated words and numbers. Psychologists John Wilding and Elizabeth Valentine saw this event as an opportunity to study exceptional memory and persuaded the contestants to take some additional memory tests. These ranged from ordinary (recall a story), to challenging (recall the telephone numbers of 6 different people), to diabolical (recall 48 numerals arranged in rows and columns; recognize 14 previously seen pictures of snowflakes among 70 new photos) (Wilding & Valentine, 1994a).

Wilding and Valentine found that exceptional memorizers:

- Use memory strategies and techniques
- Have specialized interests and knowledge that make certain types of information easier to encode and recall
- Have naturally superior memory abilities, often including vivid mental images

The first two points confirm what we learned from Steve's acquired memory ability. Many of the contestants, for example, actively used memory strategies called *mnemonics* (nee-MON-iks). Specialized interests and knowledge also helped for some tasks. For example, one contestant, who is a mathematician, was exceedingly good at memorizing numbers (Wilding & Valentine, 1994a).

Several of the memory contestants were able to excel on tasks that prevented the use of learned strategies and techniques. This observation implies that superior memory ability can be a "gift" as well as a learned skill. Wilding and Valentine conclude that exceptional memory may be based on either natural ability or learned strategies. Usually it requires both. In fact, most super memorizers use strategies to augment their natural talents, whenever possible. Some of their strategies are described in this chapter's Psychology in Action section. Please do remember to read it.

```
8 7 3 7 9 2 6 8
2 0 1 1 7 4 9 5
0 1 7 5 8 7 8 3
1 9 4 7 6 0 6 9
3 6 1 6 8 1 5 4
4 5 2 4 0 2 9 7
```

This number matrix is similar to the ones contestants in the World Memory Championship had to memorize. To be scored as correct, digits had to be recalled in their proper positions (Wilding & Valentine, 1994a).

STUDYBREAK ⅄ *Measuring Memory and Exceptional Memory*

RELATE

Have you experienced the TOT state recently? Were you able to retrieve the word you were searching for? If not, what could you remember about it?

Do you prefer tests based primarily on recall or recognition? Have you observed a savings effect while relearning information you studied in the past (such as in high school)?

Can you think of things you do that are based on implicit memories? For instance, how do you know which way to turn various handles in your house, apartment, or dorm? Do you have to explicitly think, "Turn it to the right" before you act?

What kinds of information are you good at remembering? Why do you think your memory is better for those topics?

LEARNING CHECK

Unless you have a memory like Mr. S's, it might be a good idea to see if you can answer these questions before reading on.
1. Four techniques for measuring or demonstrating memory are

_____   _____

_____   _____

2. Essay tests require _____ of facts or ideas.
3. As a measure of memory, a savings score is associated with
   a. recognition b. eidetic images c. relearning
   d. reconstruction
4. Tests of _____ memory are designed to reveal the influences of information that is stored but remains unconscious.
5. Children with eidetic imagery typically have no better than average long-term memory. T or F?
6. In order to perform well on tests of memory, one must be born with naturally superior memory abilities. T or F?

Critical Thinking

7. Mr. S had great difficulty remembering faces. Can you guess why?

ANSWERS

1. recall, recognition, relearning, priming 2. recall 3. c 4. implicit 5. T 6. F 7. Mr. S's memory was so specific that faces seemed different and unfamiliar if he saw them from a new angle or if a face had a different expression on it than when Mr. S last saw it.

FORGETTING—WHY WE, UH, LET'S SEE; WHY WE, UH . . . FORGET!

] **SURVEYQUESTION** *What causes forgetting?*

Why are some memories lost so quickly? For example, why is it hard to remember facts you learned for a test just a week or two later? Forgetting is one of the more vexing aspects of memory. Why do we forget? Again, the more you know about how we "lose" memories, the better you will be able to hang on to them.

Most forgetting tends to occur immediately after memorization. In a famous set of experiments, Herman Ebbinghaus (1885) tested his own memory at various times after learning. Ebbinghaus wanted to be sure he would not be swayed by prior learning, so he memorized *nonsense syllables.* These are meaningless three-letter words such as CEF, WOL, and GEX. The importance of using meaningless words is shown by the fact that VEL, FAB, and DUZ are no longer used on memory tests. Subjects who recognize these words as detergent names find them very easy to remember. This is another reminder that memory is improved by relating new information to what you already know. (Cef-Wol, from the planet Gex, thought that VEL, FAB, and DUZ were hard to remember, but CEF, WOL, and GEX, were quite a bit easier for her.)

By waiting various lengths of time before testing himself, Ebbinghaus plotted a **curve of forgetting.** This graph shows the amount of information remembered after varying lengths of time (✦Fig. 7.10). Because Ebbinghaus took great care in his work, his findings remain valid today. Notice that forgetting is rapid at first and is then followed by a slow decline. The same applies to meaningful information, but the forgetting curve is stretched over a longer time. As you might expect, recent events are recalled more accurately than those from the remote past (O'Conner et al., 2000). Thus, you are more likely to remember that *Gladiator* won the "Best Picture" Academy Award in 2000 than you are to remember that *Unforgiven* won it in 1992.

As a student, you should note that forgetting is minimized by a short delay between studying and taking a test. However, this is no reason for cramming. The error most students make is to cram *only.* If you cram, you don't have to remember for very long, but you may not learn enough in the first place. If you use short, daily study sessions and review intensely before a test, you will get the benefit of good preparation and a minimum time lapse.

The Ebbinghaus curve shows less than 30 percent remembered only 2 days after learning. Is forgetting really that rapid? No, not always. Meaningful information is not lost nearly as quickly as nonsense syllables. For example, it took students who completed a university psychology course about 3 years to forget 30 percent of the facts they had learned. After that, little more forgetting occurred (Conway et al., 1992). In fact, as learning grows stronger, some knowledge may become nearly permanent. Semantic memories and implicit memories (both mentioned earlier) appear to be very lasting (Bower, 1990).

"I'll never forget old, old . . . oh, what's his name?" Forgetting is both frustrating and embarrassing. Why *do* we forget? The Ebbinghaus curve gives a general picture of forgetting, but it doesn't explain it. To understand forgetting, we must search further.

✦**FIGURE 7.10** *The curve of forgetting. This graph shows the amount remembered (measured by relearning) after varying lengths of time. Notice how rapidly forgetting occurs. The material learned was nonsense syllables. Forgetting curves for meaningful information also show early losses followed by a long gradual decline, but overall, forgetting occurs much more slowly. (After Ebbinghaus, 1885.)*

When Encoding Fails

Whose head is on a U.S. penny? Which way is it facing? What is written at the top of a penny? Can you accurately draw and label a penny? In an interesting experiment, Ray Nickerson and Marilyn Adams (1979) asked a large group of students to draw a penny. Few could. Well then, could the students at least recognize a drawing of a real penny among fakes? (See ✦Fig. 7.11.) Again, few could.

Curve of forgetting A graph that shows the amount of memorized information remembered after varying lengths of time.

(a) (b) (c) (d) (e)

(f) (g) (h) (i) (j)

✦FIGURE 7.11 *Some of the distractor items used in a study of recognition memory and encoding failure. Penny A is correct but was seldom recognized. Pennies G and J were popular wrong answers. (Adapted from Nickerson & Adams, 1979.)*

HUMAN DIVERSITY   College Students—They're All Alike!

Imagine yourself in this situation: As you are walking on campus, a young man, who looks like a college student, approaches you and asks for directions. While you are talking, two workers carrying a door pass between you and the young man. While your view is blocked by the door, another man takes the place of the first. Now you are facing a different person than the one who was there just seconds earlier. If this happened to you, do you think you would notice the change? Remarkably, only half of the people tested in this way noticed the switch (Simons & Levin, 1998)!

How could anyone fail to notice that one stranger had been replaced by another? The people who didn't remember the first man were all older adults. College students weren't fooled by the switch. The authors of this study, Daniel Simons and Daniel Levin, believe that older adults encoded the first man in very general terms as a "college student." As a result, that's all they remembered about

him. Because his replacement also looked like a college student, they thought he was the same person (Simons & Levin, 1998).

Actually, such memory failures are not as surprising as they might seem. We all tend to categorize strangers according to the groups they belong to: Is the person young or old, male or female, a member of my ethnic group or another? This tendency to encode only general information about strangers is one reason why eyewitnesses are better at identifying members of their own ethnic group than they are at identifying people from other groups (Kassin et al., 2001). It may seem harsh to say so, but when social contacts are brief or superficial, people really do act like members of other ethnic groups "all look alike." Of course, this bias disappears when we get to know specific members of other groups. Then, we encode more details about each person, which allows us to recognize and appreciate them as individuals.

The most obvious reason for forgetting is also the most commonly overlooked. In many cases we "forget" because of **encoding failure.** That is, a memory was never formed in the first place. Obviously, few of us ever encode the details of a penny. If you are bothered by frequent forgetting, it is wise to ask yourself, "Have I been storing the information in the first place?" If you tend to be absent-minded, encoding failure is probably to blame (Schachter, 1999). (Encoding failures also affect our memories of people. See "College Students—They're All Alike!")

When 140 college professors were asked what strategies they use to improve their memory, the favorite technique was to *write things down* (Park et al., 1990). Making notes or using a handheld personal organizer ensures that information will not be lost from short-term memory before you can review it and store it more permanently.

Memory Decay

One view of forgetting holds that **memory traces** (changes in nerve cells or brain activity) **decay** (fade or weaken) over time. Decay appears to be a factor in the loss of sensory memories. Such fading also applies to short-term memory. Information stored in STM seems to initiate a brief flurry of activity in the brain that quickly dies out. Short-term memory, therefore, operates like a "leaky bucket": New information constantly pours in, but it rapidly

Encoding failure Failure to store sufficient information to form a useful memory.

Memory traces Physical changes in nerve cells or brain activity that take place when memories are stored.

Memory decay The fading or weakening of memories assumed to occur when memory traces become weaker.

fades away and is replaced by still newer information. Let's say that you are trying to remember a short list of letters, numbers, or words after seeing or hearing them once. If it takes you more than 4 to 6 seconds to repeat the list, you will forget some of the items (Dosher & Ma, 1998).

Disuse

Is it possible that the decay of memory traces also explains long-term forgetting? That is, could long-term memory traces fade from **disuse** (infrequent retrieval) and eventually become too weak to retrieve? There is evidence that memories not retrieved and "used" or rehearsed become weaker over time (Schachter, 1999). However, disuse alone cannot fully explain forgetting.

Disuse doesn't seem to account for our ability to recover seemingly forgotten memories through redintegration, relearning, and priming. It also fails to explain why some unused memories fade, while others are carried for life. A third contradiction will be recognized by anyone who has spent time with the elderly. People growing senile may become so forgetful that they can't remember what happened a week ago. Yet at the same time your Uncle Oscar's recent memories are fading, he may have vivid memories of trivial and long-forgotten events from the past. "Why, I remember it as clearly as if it were yesterday," he will say, forgetting that the story he is about to tell is one he told earlier the same day. In short, disuse offers no more than a partial explanation of long-term forgetting.

If decay and disuse don't fully explain forgetting, what does?   Let's briefly consider some additional possibilities.

Cue-Dependent Forgetting

Often, memories appear to be *available,* but not *accessible.* An example is having an answer on the "tip of your tongue." You know the answer is there, but it remains just "out of reach." This suggests that many memories are "forgotten" because **memory cues** (stimuli associated with a memory) are missing when the time comes to retrieve information. For example, if you were asked, "What were you doing on Monday afternoon of the third week in March 2 years ago?" your reply might be, "Come on. How should I know?" However, if you were reminded, "That was the day the courthouse burned," or "That was the day Stacy had her automobile accident," you might remember immediately.

The presence of appropriate cues almost always enhances memory (Nairne, 2002). In theory, for instance, memory will be best if you study in the same room where you will be tested. Because this is often impossible, when you study, try to visualize the room where you will be tested. Doing so can enhance memory later (Jerabek & Standing, 1992). A similar finding is that people remember better if the same odor (such as lemon or lavender) is present when they study and are tested (Parker, Ngu, & Cassaday, 2001). If you wear a particular perfume or cologne while you prepare for a test, it might be wise to wear it when you take the test.

Disuse Theory that memory traces weaken when memories are not periodically used or retrieved.

Memory cue Any stimulus associated with a particular memory. Memory cues usually enhance retrieval.

External cues like those found in a photograph, a scrapbook, or during a walk through an old neighborhood often aid recall of seemingly lost memories. For many veterans, finding a familiar name engraved in the Vietnam Veterans Memorial unleashes a flood of memories.

State-Dependent Learning

Have you heard the story about the drunk who misplaced his wallet and had to get drunk again to find it? Although this tale is often told as a joke, it is not too farfetched. The bodily state that exists during learning can be a strong cue for later memory, an effect known as **state-dependent learning** (Neath, 2002). Being very thirsty, for instance, might prompt you to remember events that took place on another occasion when you were thirsty. Because of such effects, information learned under the influence of a drug is best remembered when the drugged state occurs again (Slot & Colpaert, 1999).

A similar effect applies to emotional states (Eich, 1995). For instance, Gordon Bower (1981) found that people who learned a list of words while in a happy mood recalled them better when they were again happy. People who learned while they felt sad remembered best when they were sad (◆Fig. 7.12). Similarly, if you are in a happy mood you are more likely to remember recent happy events (Salovey & Singer, 1989). If you are in a bad mood you will tend to have unpleasant memories (Eich et al., 1990). Such links between emotional cues and memory could explain why couples who quarrel often end up remembering—and rehashing—old arguments.

Interference

Further insight into forgetting comes from a classic experiment in which college students learned lists of nonsense syllables. After studying, students in one group slept for 8 hours and were then tested for memory of the lists. A second group stayed awake for 8 hours and went about business as usual. When members of the second group were tested, they remembered *less* than the group that slept (◆Fig. 7.13). This difference is based on the fact that new learning can interfere with previous learning. **Interference** refers to the tendency for new memories to impair retrieval of older memories (and the reverse). It seems to apply to both short-term and long-term memory (Lustig, May, & Hasher, 2001; Nairne, 2002).

It is not completely clear if new memories alter existing memory traces or if they make it harder to "locate" (retrieve) earlier memories. In any case, there is no doubt that interference is a major cause of forgetting (Neath, 2002). College students who memorized 20 lists of words (one list each day) were able to recall only 15 percent of the last list. Students who learned only one list remembered 80 percent (Underwood, 1957) (◆Fig. 7.14).

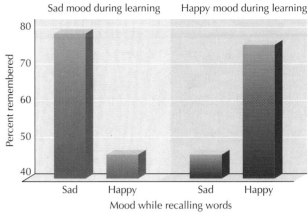

◆**FIGURE 7.12** *The effect of mood on memory. Subjects best remembered a list of words when their mood during testing was the same as their mood was when they learned the list. (Adapted from Bower, 1981.)*

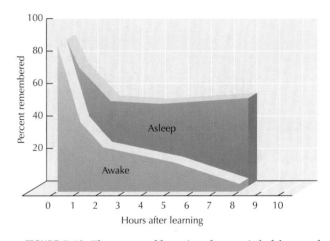

◆**FIGURE 7.13** *The amount of forgetting after a period of sleep or of being awake. Notice that sleep causes less memory loss than activity that occurs while one is awake. (After Jenkins & Dallenbach, 1924.)*

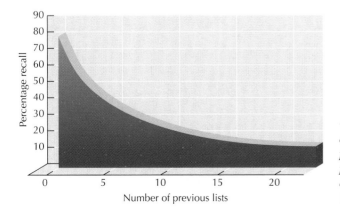

◆**FIGURE 7.14** *Effects of interference on memory. A graph of the approximate relationship between percentage recalled and number of different word lists memorized. (Adapted from Underwood, 1957.)*

State-dependent learning Memory influenced by one's bodily state at the time of learning and at the time of retrieval. Improved memory occurs when the bodily states match.

Interference The tendency for new memories to impair retrieval of older memories, and the reverse.

How could anyone lose something as large as a car? If you park your car in a different place every day, you may have experienced forgetting caused by interference. Today's memory about your car's location is easily confused with memories from yesterday, and the day before, and the day before that.

Order Effects

The sleeping college students remembered more because retroactive (RET-ro-AK-tiv) interference was held to a minimum. **Retroactive interference** refers to the tendency for new learning to impair retrieval of old learning. Avoiding new learning prevents retroactive interference. Of course, this doesn't mean you need to hide in a closet after you study for a test. However, you should avoid studying other subjects until after the exam. Sleeping after studying can help you retain memories, and reading, writing, or even watching TV may cause interference.

Retroactive interference is easily demonstrated in the laboratory by this arrangement:

Experimental group:	Learn A	Learn B	Test A
Control group:	Learn A	Rest	Test A

Imagine yourself as a member of the experimental group. In task A, you learn a list of telephone numbers. In task B, you learn a list of Social Security numbers. How do you score on a test of task A (the telephone numbers)? If you do not remember as much as the control group that learns *only* task A, then retroactive interference has occurred. The second thing learned has interfered with memory of the first thing learned; the interference went "backward," or was "retroactive" (◆Fig. 7.15).

Proactive (pro-AK-tiv) interference is a second basic source of forgetting. **Proactive interference** occurs when prior learning impairs the retrieval of later learning. A test for proactive interference would take this form:

Experimental group:	Learn A	Learn B	Test B
Control group:	Rest	Learn B	Test B

Let's assume that the experimental group remembers less than the control group on a test of task B. In that case, learning task A interfered with memory for task B.

Then proactive interference goes "forward"?   Yes. For instance, if you cram for a psychology exam and then later the same night cram for a history exam, your memory for the second subject studied (history) will be less accurate than if you had studied only history. (Because of retroactive interference, your memory for psychology would probably also suffer.) The greater the similarity in the two subjects studied, the more interference takes place. The moral, of course, is don't procrastinate in preparing for exams. The more you can avoid competing information, the more likely you are to recall what you want to remember (Anderson & Bell, 2001).

◆FIGURE 7.15 *Retroactive and proactive interference. The order of learning and testing shows whether interference is retroactive (backward) or proactive (forward).*

Retroactive interference The tendency for new memories to interfere with the retrieval of old memories.

Proactive interference The tendency for old memories to interfere with the retrieval of newer memories.

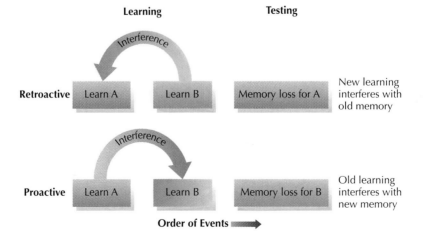

REPRESSION AND SUPPRESSION OF MEMORIES

] **SURVEYQUESTION** *How accurate are everyday memories?*

Take a moment and scan over the events of the last few years of your life. What kinds of things most easily come to mind? Many people remember happy, positive events better than disappointments and irritations (Linton, 1979). A clinical psychologist would call this tendency **repression,** or motivated forgetting. Through repression, painful, threatening, or embarrassing memories are held out of consciousness. An example is provided by soldiers who have repressed some of the horrors they saw during combat (Karon & Widener, 1997, 1998).

The forgetting of past failures, upsetting childhood events, the names of people you dislike, or appointments you don't want to keep may reveal repression. People prone to repression tend to be hyper-sensitive to emotional events. As a result, they use repression to protect themselves from threatening thoughts (Mendolia, Moore, & Tesser, 1996).

It's possible that some adults who were sexually abused as children have repressed memories of their mistreatment. It's also possible that such memories may surface during psychotherapy or other circumstances. However, caution is required any time accusations are made on the basis of seemingly "recovered" memories. In what appeared to be an extreme case of repression, Eileen Franklin testified in court in 1990 that her father, George Franklin, abducted, raped, and killed 8-year-old Susan Nason in 1969. Eileen testified that the memory surfaced one day as she looked into the eyes of her own young daughter. Her father was convicted solely on the basis of her "repressed" memory. However, the conviction was overturned when DNA tests cleared her father of a second murder she also accused him of committing. As the Franklin case illustrates, trying to separate true memories from fantasies is a major headache for psychologists and the courts. See "The Recovered Memory/False Memory Debate" for further cautions.

If I try to forget a test I failed, am I repressing it? No. An active, conscious attempt to put something out of mind is called **suppression.** By not thinking about the test, you have merely suppressed a memory. If you choose to, you can remember the test. Clinicians consider true repression an *unconscious* event. When a memory is repressed we are unaware that forgetting has even occurred. (See Chapter 11 for more information on repression.)

Recently, some psychologists have questioned whether repression exists (Court & Court, 2001). However, there is evidence that we can choose to actively avoid remembering upsetting information (Anderson, 2001). If you have experienced a painful emotional event, you will probably avoid all thoughts associated with it. This tends to keep cues out of mind that could trigger a painful memory. In time, your active suppression of the memory may become true repression (Anderson & Green, 2001; Bowers & Farvolden, 1996).

✦**FIGURE 7.16** *Eileen Franklin's father was convicted on the basis of her "repressed" memories. He was later cleared by DNA testing.*

Flashbulb Memories

Why are some traumatic events vividly remembered while others are repressed? Psychologists use the term **flashbulb memories** to describe images that seem to be frozen in memory at times of personal tragedy, accident, or other emotionally significant events (Finkenauer, 1998).

Depending on your age, you may have a "flashbulb" memory for the Pearl Harbor attack, the assassinations of John F. Kennedy and Martin Luther King, the *Challenger* space shuttle disaster, or the terrorist attack on the World Trade Center in New York. Flashbulb memories are most often formed when an event is surprising, important, or emotional (Rubin, 1985). They are frequently associated with public tragedies, but memories of positive events may also have "flashbulb" clarity.

Repression Unconsciously pushing unwanted memories out of awareness.

Suppression A conscious effort to put something out of mind or to keep it from awareness.

Flashbulb memories Memories created at times of high emotion that seem especially vivid.

CLINICAL FILE The Recovered Memory/False Memory Debate

Many sexually abused children develop problems that persist into adulthood. In some instances, they repress all memory of the abuse. According to some psychologists, uncovering these hidden memories can be an important step toward regaining emotional health.

While the preceding may be true, the search for repressed memories of sexual abuse has itself been a problem. Cases have surfaced in which families were torn apart by accusations of sexual abuse that later turned out to be completely false.

Certainly, some memories of abuse that return to awareness are genuine and must be dealt with. However, in the absence of firm supporting evidence, there is no way to tell if a memory is real or not. No matter how real a recovered memory may seem, it could be false, unless it can be verified by others, or by court or medical records.

Why would anyone have false memories about such disturbing events? Several popular books and a few misguided therapists have actively encouraged people to find repressed memories of abuse. Hypnosis, guided visualization, suggestion, age regression, and similar techniques can elicit fantasies that are mistaken for real memories. False allegations of sexual abuse create a living nightmare for the accused. For example, Gary Ramona lost his marriage and his $400,000-a-year job when his daughter Holly alleged that he molested her throughout her childhood. Ramona sued Holly's therapists, claiming that they had been irresponsible. To prove to Holly that her memories were true, the therapists gave her the drug Amytal and told her that it was a "truth drug." (Amytal is a hypnotic drug that induces a twilight state of consciousness. People do not automatically tell the truth while under its influence.) After reviewing the evidence for 2 months, a jury awarded Gary Ramona $500,000 in damages. In a way, Gary Ramona was lucky. Most people who are falsely accused have no way to prove their innocence.

To summarize, some memories of abuse that return to awareness appear to be genuine. However, there is little doubt that some "recovered" memories are pure fantasy. Researchers have identified many instances in which "recovered" traumatic memories were absolutely false.

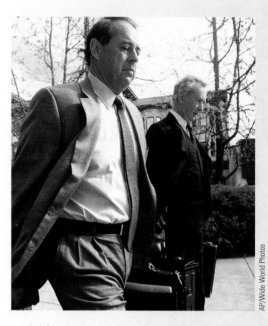

Gary Ramona's life was shattered by "recovered" memories that turned out to be false.

A few years ago, an "epidemic" of recovered memories took place. It subsided as psychologists developed new guidelines for therapists to minimize the risk of influencing clients' memories. Today, both recovered memories and false accusations are relatively uncommon. Nevertheless, false claims about childhood abuse still occasionally make the news. The saddest thing about such claims is that they deaden public sensitivity to actual abuse. Childhood sexual abuse is widespread. Awareness of its existence must not be repressed.

(Sources: Byrd, 1994; Courtois, 1999; Goldstein, 1997; Lindsay, 1998; Loftus, 2003; Palm & Gibson, 1998; Pendergast, 1995; Reisner, 1996; Schacter, 1999.)

Flashbulb memories seem to be very detailed. Often, they focus primarily on how you reacted to the event. ▲Table 7.1 lists some memories that had "flashbulb" clarity for at least 50 percent of a group of college students. How vivid are the memories they trigger for you? (Note again that both positive and negative events are listed.)

▲*TABLE 7.1* **Bright Flashes of Memory**	
MEMORY CUE	PERCENTAGE OF STUDENTS WITH FLASHBULB MEMORIES
A car accident you were in or witnessed	85
When you first met your college roommate	82
The night of your high school graduation	81
The night of your senior prom (if you went or not)	78
An early romantic experience	77
A time you had to speak in front of an audience	72
When you first got your college admissions letter	65
Your first date—the moment you met him/her	57

(From Rubin, 1985.)

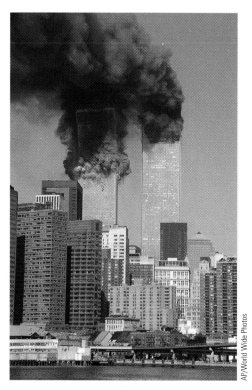

It is highly likely that you have a flashbulb memory about where you were when you first learned about the terrorist attack on the World Trade Center in New York. If someone alerted you about the news, you will remember that person's call, and you will have clear memories about how you reacted to seeing the collapse of the towers.

The term *flashbulb memories* was first used to describe recollections that seemed to be unusually vivid and permanent. It has become clear, however, that flashbulb memories are not always accurate (Harsch & Neisser, 1989). More than anything else, what sets flashbulb memories apart is that we tend to place great *confidence* in them— even when they are wrong (Weaver, 1993). Perhaps that's because we review emotionally charged events over and over and tell others about them. Also, public events such as wars, earthquakes, and assassinations reappear many times in the news, which highlights them in memory (Wright, 1993). Over time, flashbulb memories tend to crystallize into consistent, if not entirely accurate, landmarks in our lives (Schmolck, Buffalo, & Squire, 2000; Winningham, Hyman, & Dinnel, 2000).

MEMORY FORMATION—SOME "SHOCKING" FINDINGS

] SURVEYQUESTION *What happens in the brain when memories are formed?*

One possibility overlooked in our discussion of forgetting is that memories may be lost as they are being formed. For example, a head injury may cause a "gap" in memories preceding the accident. *Retrograde amnesia,* as this is called, involves forgetting events that occurred before an injury or trauma. In contrast, *anterograde amnesia* involves forgetting events that follow an injury or trauma. (An example of this type of amnesia is discussed in a moment.)

Consolidating Memories

Retrograde amnesia can be understood if we assume that it takes a certain amount of time to move information from short-term to long-term memory. The forming of a long-term memory is called **consolidation** (Squire et al., 1993). You can think of consolidation as being somewhat like writing your name in wet concrete. Once the concrete is set, the information (your name) is fairly lasting. But while it is setting, it can be wiped out (amnesia) or scribbled over (interference).

Consider a classic experiment on consolidation, in which a rat is placed on a small platform. The rat steps down to the floor and receives a painful electric shock. After one shock, the rat can be returned to the platform repeatedly, but it will not step down. Obviously, the rat remembers the shock. Would it remember if consolidation were disturbed?

Interestingly, one way to prevent consolidation is to give a different kind of shock called electroconvulsive shock (ECS) (Jarvik, 1964). ECS is a mild electric shock to the

Consolidation Process by which relatively permanent memories are formed in the brain.

brain. It does not harm the animal, but it does destroy any memory that is being formed. If each painful shock (the one the animal remembers) is followed by ECS (which wipes out memories during consolidation), the rat will step down over and over. Each time, ECS will erase the memory of the painful shock. (ECS is employed as a psychiatric treatment for severe depression in humans.)

What would happen if ECS were given several hours after the learning? Recent memories are more easily disrupted than older memories (Gold, 1987). If enough time is allowed to pass between learning and ECS, the memory will be unaffected because consolidation is already complete. That's why people with mild head injuries only lose memories from just before the accident, while older memories remain intact (Baddeley, 1990). Likewise, you would forget more if you studied, stayed awake 8 hours, and then slept 8 hours than you would if you studied, slept 8 hours, and were awake for 8 hours. Either way, 16 hours would pass. However, less forgetting would occur in the second instance, because more consolidation would occur before interference begins (Nesca & Koulack, 1994).

Where does consolidation take place in the brain? Actually, many parts of the brain are responsible for memory, but the **hippocampus** is particularly important. The hippocampus acts as a sort of "switching station" between short-term and long-term memory (Gabrieli, 1998). The hippocampus does this, in part, by growing new neurons. New neurons probably store information by making new connections within the brain (Macklis, 2001).

Humans who have hippocampal damage usually show a striking inability to store new memories (Bigler et al., 1996). A patient described by Brenda Milner provides a vivid example. Two years after an operation damaged his hippocampus, a 29-year-old patient continued to give his age as 27. He also reported that it seemed as if the operation had just taken place (Milner, 1965). His memory of events before the operation remained clear, but he found forming new long-term memories almost impossible. When his parents moved to a new house a few blocks away on the same street, he could not remember the new address. Month after month, he read the same magazines over and over without finding them familiar. If you were to meet this man, he would seem fairly normal because he still has short-term memory. But if you were to leave the room and return 15 minutes later, he would act as if he had never seen you before. Years ago his favorite uncle died, but he suffers the same grief anew each time he is told of the death. Lacking the ability to form new lasting memories, he lives eternally in the present (Hilts, 1995).

The Brain and Memory

Somewhere within the 3-pound mass of the human brain lies all we know: ZIP codes, faces of loved ones, history, favorite melodies, the taste of an apple, and much, much more. Where is this information? Karl Lashley, a pioneering brain researcher, set out in the 1920s to find an **engram,** or memory trace. Lashley taught animals to run mazes and then removed parts of their brains to see how memory of the maze changed. After 30 years he had to concede defeat: Engrams are not located in any one area of the brain. It mattered little which part of the brain's cortex he removed. Only the *amount* removed correlated to memory loss.

Lashley's conclusion remains true for specific memories. However, some areas of the cerebral cortex *are* more important to memory than others. Patterns of blood flow in the cerebral cortex (the wrinkled outer layer of the brain) can be used to map brain activity. ✦Figure 7.17 shows the results of measuring blood flow while people were thinking about a semantic memory *(a)* or an episodic memory *(b)*. In the map, green indicates areas that are more active during semantic thinking. Reds show areas of greater activity during episodic thinking. The brain in view *c* shows the difference in activity between views *a* and *b*. The resulting pattern indicates that the front of the cortex is related to episodic memory. Back areas are more associated with semantic memory (Tulving, 1989, 2002).

To summarize (and simplify greatly), the hippocampus handles memory consolidation. Once long-term memories are formed, they appear to be stored in the cortex of the brain (Gabrieli, 1998; Teng & Squire, 1999).

Hippocampus A brain structure associated with emotion and the transfer of information from short-term memory to long-term memory.
Engram A "memory trace" in the brain.

✦**FIGURE 7.17** *Patterns of blood flow in the cerebral cortex associated with semantic memories and episodic memories.*

How are memories recorded in the cortex? Scientists are beginning to identify the exact ways in which nerve cells record information. For example, Eric Kandel and his colleagues have studied learning in the marine snail *aplysia* (ah-PLEEZ-yah). Kandel found that learning in *aplysia* occurs when certain nerve cells in a circuit alter the amount of transmitter chemicals they release (Kandel, 1999). Learning also alters the activity, structure, and chemistry of brain cells. Such changes determine which connections get stronger and which become weaker. This "reprograms" the brain and records information (Abel & Lattal, 2001; Klintsova & Greenough, 1999).

Scientists continue to study various chemicals, especially neurotransmitters, that affect memory. If their research succeeds, it may be possible to help the millions of persons who suffer from memory impairment (Eli & Nathan, 2001). Will researchers ever produce a "memory pill" to enhance normal memory? Neuroscientists are confident that memory can be and will be artificially enhanced. However, the possibility of something like a "physics pill" or a "math pill" seems remote.

An *aplysia*. The relatively simple nervous system of this sea animal allows scientists to study memory as it occurs in single nerve cells.

STUDYBREAK Forgetting

RELATE

Which of the following concepts best explain why you have missed some answers on psychology tests: encoding failure, decay, disuse, memory cues, interference?

Do you know someone whose name you have a hard time remembering? Do you like or dislike that person? Do you think your difficulty is an instance of repression? Suppression? Interference? Encoding failure?

Have you had a flashbulb memory? How vivid is the memory today? How accurate do you think it is?

Here's a mnemonic tip: Elephants are supposed to have good memories, but a *hippo campus* is the place to go if you want to learn to consolidate memories.

LEARNING CHECK

1. According to the Ebbinghaus curve of forgetting, we forget slowly at first and then a rapid decline occurs. T or F?
2. Which explanation seems to account for the loss of short-term memories?
   a. decay b. disuse c. repression d. interference
3. When memories are available but not accessible, forgetting may be cue dependent. T or F?

4. When learning one thing makes it more difficult to recall another, forgetting may be caused by _____.
5. You are asked to memorize long lists of telephone numbers. You learn a new list each day for 10 days. When tested on list 3, you remember less than a person who only learned the first three lists. Your larger memory loss is probably caused by
   a. disuse b. retroactive interference c. regression
   d. proactive interference
6. Repression is thought of as a type of motivated forgetting. T or F?
7. Retrograde amnesia results when consolidation is speeded up. T or F?

Critical Thinking

8. Based on state-dependent learning, why do you think that music often strongly evokes memories?
9. You must study French, Spanish, psychology, and biology in one evening. What do you think would be the best order in which to study these subjects so as to minimize interference?
10. There may be another way to explain why flashbulb memories are so long lasting. Can you think of one?

ANSWERS 1. F 2. a and d 3. T 4. interference 5. b 6. T 7. F 8. Music tends to affect the mood that a person is in, and moods tend to affect memory (Balch & Lewis, 1996). 9. Any order that separates French from Spanish and psychology from biology would work (for instance: French, psychology, Spanish, biology). 10. Memories of emotionally significant events may be unusually strong because such memories are rehearsed more frequently. People usually mentally review emotionally charged events many times.

IMPROVING MEMORY—KEYS TO THE MEMORY BANK

] SURVEYQUESTION *How can I improve my memory?*

No matter how good your memory may be, there are probably times when you wish it were better. While we're waiting around for the arrival of a memory pill, this section describes some ways to immediately improve your memory skills.

Knowledge of Results

Learning proceeds best when feedback, or knowledge of results, allows you to check your progress. Feedback can help you identify ideas that need extra practice. In addition, knowing that you have remembered or answered correctly is rewarding. A prime way to provide feedback for yourself while studying is *recitation.*

Recitation

If you are going to remember something, eventually you will have to retrieve it. *Recitation* refers to summarizing aloud while you are learning. Recitation forces you to practice retrieving information. When you are reading a text, you should stop frequently and try to remember what you have just read by restating it in your own words. In one experiment, the best memory score was earned by a group of students who spent 80 percent of their time reciting and only 20 percent reading (Gates, 1958). Maybe students who talk to themselves aren't crazy after all.

Rehearsal

The more you *rehearse* (mentally review) information as you read, the better you will remember it. But remember that maintenance rehearsal alone is not very effective. Elaborative rehearsal, in which you look for connections to existing knowledge, is far better. Thinking about facts helps link them together in memory. To learn college-level information, you must make active use of rehearsal strategies (Nist, Sharman, & Holschuh, 1996).

Selection

The Dutch scholar Erasmus said that a good memory should be like a fish net: It should keep all the big fish and let the little ones escape. If you boil down the paragraphs in most textbooks to one or two important terms or ideas, your memory chores will be more manageable. Practice very selective marking in your texts and use marginal notes to further summarize ideas. Most students mark their texts too much instead of too little. If everything is underlined, you haven't been selective. And, very likely, you didn't pay much attention in the first place (Peterson, 1992).

Organization

Assume that you must memorize the following list of words: north, man, red, spring, woman, east, autumn, yellow, summer, boy, blue, west, winter, girl, green, south. This rather difficult list could be reorganized into *chunks* as follows: north-east-south-west, spring-summer-autumn-winter, red-yellow-green-blue, man-woman-boy-girl. This simple reordering made the second list much easier to learn when college students were tested on both lists (Deese & Hulse, 1967). Organizing class notes and summarizing chapters can be quite helpful (Dickinson & O'Connell, 1990). You may even want to summarize your summaries, so that the overall network of ideas becomes clearer and simpler. Summaries improve memory by encouraging better encoding of information (Hadwin, Kirby, & Woodhouse, 1999).

Whole versus Part Learning

If you have to memorize a speech, is it better to try to learn it from beginning to end? Or in smaller parts like paragraphs? Generally it is better to practice whole packages of information rather than smaller parts (*whole learning*). This is especially true for fairly short, organized information. An exception is that learning parts may be better for extremely long, complicated information. In *part learning*, subparts of a larger body of information are studied (such as sections of a textbook chapter). To decide which approach to use, remember to study the *largest meaningful amount of information* you can at one time.

For very long or complex material, try the *progressive part method*, by breaking a learning task into a series of short sections. At first, you study part A until it is mastered. Next, you study parts A and B; then A, B, and C; and so forth. This is a good way to learn the lines of a play, a long piece of music, or a poem (Ash & Holding, 1990). After the material is learned, you should also practice by starting at points other than A (at C, D, or B, for example). This helps prevent getting "lost" or going blank in the middle of a performance.

Serial Position

Whenever you must learn something in *order*, be aware of the serial position effect. As you will recall, this is the tendency to make the most errors in remembering the middle of a list. If you are introduced to a long line of people, the names you are likely to forget will be those in the middle, so you should make an extra effort to attend to them. You should also give extra practice to the middle of a list, poem, or speech. Try to break long lists of information into short sub-lists, and make the middle sub-lists the shortest of all.

Memory Cues

The best memory cues (stimuli that aid retrieval) are those that were present during encoding (Reed, 1996). For example, students in one study had the daunting task of trying to recall a list of 600 words. As they read the list (which they did not know they would be tested on), the students gave three other words closely related in meaning to each listed word. In a test given later, the words each student supplied were used as cues to jog memory. The students recalled an astounding 90 percent of the original word list (Mantyla, 1986).

The preceding example shows, once again, that it often helps to *elaborate* information as you learn. When you study, try to use new names, ideas, or terms in several sentences. Also, form images that include the new information, and relate it to knowledge you already have (Pressley et al., 1988). Your goal should be to knit meaningful cues into your memory code to help you retrieve information when you need it (✦Fig. 7.18).

Over-learning

Numerous studies have shown that memory is greatly improved when you *over-learn*. That is, when study is continued beyond initial mastery of information. After you have learned material well enough to remember it once without error, you should continue studying. Over-learning is your best insurance against going blank on a test because of being nervous.

Spaced Practice

To keep boredom and fatigue to a minimum, try alternating short study sessions with brief rest periods. This pattern, called **spaced practice,** is generally superior to **massed practice,** in which little or no rest is given between learning sessions. By improving attention and consolidation, three 20-minute study sessions can produce more learning than 1 hour of continuous study. There's an old joke that goes, "How do you get to Carnegie Hall?" The answer is, "Practice, practice, practice." A better answer would be "Practice, wait awhile, practice, wait awhile, practice" (Neath, 2002).

Perhaps the best way to make use of spaced practice is to *schedule* your time. To make an effective schedule, designate times during the week before, after, and between

✦**FIGURE 7.18** *Actors can remember large amounts of complex information for many months, even when learning new roles in between. During testing, they remember their lines best when they are allowed to move and gesture as they would when performing. Apparently, their movements supply cues that aid recall (Noice & Noice, 1999).*

Robbie Jack/Corbis

Spaced practice A practice schedule that alternates study periods with brief rests.

Massed practice A practice schedule in which studying continues for long periods, without interruption.

classes when you will study particular subjects. Then treat these times just as if they were classes you had to attend.

Sleep and Memory

Remember that sleeping after study reduces interference. However, unless you are a "night person," late evening may not be a very efficient time for you to study. Also, you obviously can't sleep after every study session or study everything just before you sleep. That's why your study schedule (see "Spaced Practice") should include ample breaks between subjects. Using your breaks and free time in a schedule is as important as living up to your study periods.

Hunger and Memory

People who are hungry almost always score lower on memory tests. So Mother was right: It's a good idea to make sure you've had a good breakfast or lunch before you take tests at school (Martin & Benton, 1999; Smith, Clark, & Gallagher, 1999).

Extend How Long You Remember

When you are learning new information, test yourself repeatedly. As you do, gradually lengthen the amount of time that passes before you test yourself again. For example, if you are studying German words on flashcards, look at the first card and then move it a few cards back in the stack. Do the same with the next few cards. When you get to the first "old" card, test yourself on it and check the answer. Then, move it farther back in the stack. Do the same with other "old" cards as they come up. When "old" cards come up for the third time, put them clear to the back of the stack (Cull, Shaughnessy, & Zechmeister, 1996).

Review

If you have spaced your practice and over-learned, review will be like icing on your study cake. Reviewing shortly before an exam cuts down the time during which you must remember details that may be important for the test. When reviewing, hold the amount of new information you try to memorize to a minimum. It may be realistic to take what you have actually learned and add a little more to it at the last minute by cramming. But remember that more than a little new learning may interfere with what you already know.

Using a Strategy to Aid Recall

Successful recall is usually the result of a planned *search* of memory (Reed, 1996). For example, one study found that students were most likely to recall names that eluded them if they made use of partial information (Reed & Bruce, 1982). The students were trying to answer questions such as, "He is best remembered as the scarecrow in the Judy Garland movie *The Wizard of Oz*." (The answer is Ray Bolger.) Partial information that helped students remember included impressions about the length of the name, letter sounds within the name, similar names, and related information (such as the names of other characters in the movie). A similar helpful strategy is to go through the alphabet, trying each letter as the first sound of a name or word you are seeking.

Using a variety of cues, even partial ones, opens more paths to a memory. "Memory Detectives" gives further hints for recapturing context and jogging memories. After that, the Psychology in Action section covers some of the most powerful memory techniques of all.

Memory in Perspective

Tatiana Cooley won a national memory contest held in New York. To win, she had to memorize long lists of words and numbers, the order of the cards in a shuffled deck, a 54-line poem, and 100 names and faces. Tatiana thinks that memorization is fun. You might expect that she would also be good at everyday memory chores. On the contrary, Tatiana describes herself as "incredibly absent-minded." When asked how many brothers and sisters she has, she replies, "Six, er seven, er six." The year she graduated from high school? She pauses for several seconds, "1990." The elementary school grade she was in when she won a regional spelling bee? She can't remember. Ever fearful of forgetting, Tatiana keeps a daily to-do list and surrounds herself with a thicket of Post-it notes (Levinson, 1999).

USING PSYCHOLOGY   Memory Detectives

You may not think of yourself as a "memory detective," but active probing often helps improve recall. A case in point is the **cognitive interview,** a technique used to jog the memory of eyewitnesses. The cognitive interview was created by R. Edward Geiselman and Ron Fisher to help police detectives. When used properly, it produces 35 percent more correct information than standard questioning (Geiselman et al., 1986). This improvement comes without adding to the number of false memories elicited, as occurs with hypnosis, and it is effective in actual police work (Ginet & Py, 2001; Kebbell & Wagstaff, 1998).

By following four simple steps, you can apply cognitive principles to your own memory. The next time you are searching for a "lost" memory—one that you know is in there somewhere—try the following search strategies.

1. Say or write down *everything* you can remember that relates to the information you are seeking. Don't worry about how trivial any of it seems; each bit of information you remember can serve as a cue to bring back others.
2. Try to recall events or information in different orders. Let your memories flow out backward or out of order, or start with whatever impressed you the most.
3. Recall from different viewpoints. Review events by mentally standing in a different place. Or try to view information as another person would remember it. When taking a test, for instance, ask yourself what other students or your professor would remember about the topic.
4. Mentally put yourself back in the situation where you learned the information. Try to mentally recreate the learning environment or relive the event. As you do, include sounds, smells, details of weather, nearby objects, other people present, what you said or thought, and how you felt as you learned the information (Fisher & Geiselman, 1987).

These strategies help recreate the context in which information was learned, and they provide multiple memory cues. If you think of remembering as a sort of "treasure hunt," you might even learn to enjoy the detective work.

Some police detectives, following the advice of psychologists, re-create crime scenes to help witnesses remember what they saw. Typically, people return to the scene at the time of day the crime occurred. They are also asked to wear the same clothing they wore and go through the same motions as they did before the crime. With so many memory cues available, witnesses sometimes remember key items of information they hadn't recalled before.

What can we learn about memory from Tatiana? First, we should all be more tolerant of occasional memory lapses. Even memory champions have less than perfect memories! As we have seen throughout this chapter, memory is not like a tape recorder or a video camera. Information is frequently lost, and memories change as they are stored and retrieved. This can be frustrating at times, but it's also a good thing. The flexibility of human memory allows us to focus on what's important and meaningful, even though it also contributes to some inaccuracies. A person with total recall would probably be very literal, like a computer. If you type the name of a computer file and leave out one letter, a computer will essentially say, "I'm sorry, I've never heard of that file." A person would say, "That's misspelled, but I think I remember where it is."

Tatiana's success as a "memory athlete" also suggests that making full use of memory requires effort and practice. With that in mind, here are some parting words from our fictional companion, Cef-Wol, spoken just before she departed for Gex: "I didn't appreciate memories until I began to lose them. In a very real sense, we are our memories. You must remember this!"

A Look Ahead

Psychologists still have much to learn about the nature of memory and how to improve it. For now, one thing stands out clearly: People who have good memories excel at organizing information and making it meaningful. With this in mind, the Psychology in Action discussion for this chapter tells how you can combine organization and meaning into a powerful method for improving memory.

Cognitive interview Use of various cues and strategies to improve the memory of eyewitnesses.

RELATE

Return to the topic headings in the preceding pages that list techniques for improving memory. Place a check mark next to those that you have used recently. Review any you didn't mark, and think of a specific example of how you could use each technique at school, at home, or at work.

LEARNING CHECK

1. To improve memory, it is reasonable to spend as much or more time reciting as reading. T or F?
2. Organizing information while studying has little effect on memory because long-term memory is already highly organized. T or F?

3. The progressive part method of study is best suited to long and complex learning tasks. T or F?
4. Sleeping immediately after studying is highly disruptive to the consolidation of memories. T or F?
5. As new information is encoded and rehearsed, it is helpful to elaborate on its meaning and connect it to other information. T or F?

Critical Thinking

6. What advantages would there be to taking notes as you read a textbook, as opposed to underlining words in the text?

ANSWERS

1. T 2. F 3. T 4. F 5. T 6. Note-taking is a form of recitation, it encourages elaborative rehearsal, facilitates the organization and selection of important ideas, and your notes can be used for review.

Psychology in Action

Mnemonics—Memory Magic

] **SURVEYQUESTION** *How can I improve my memory?*

Some stage performers use memory as part of their acts. Do they have eidetic imagery?   Various "memory experts" entertain by memorizing the names of everyone at a banquet, the order of all the cards in a deck, long lists of words, or other seemingly impossible amounts of information. Such feats may seem like magic, but if they are, you can have a magic memory, too. These tricks are performed through the use of *mnemonics* (Wilding & Valentine, 1994b). A **mnemonic** is any kind of memory system or aid. In some cases, mnemonic strategies increase recall 10-fold (Patten, 1990).

Some mnemonic systems are so common that almost everyone knows them. If you are trying to remember how many days there are in a month, you may find the answer by reciting, "Thirty days hath September . . . ." Physics teachers often help students remember the colors of the spectrum by giving them the mnemonic "Roy G. Biv": **R**ed, **O**range, **Y**ellow, **G**reen, **B**lue, **I**ndigo, **V**iolet. The budding sailor who has trouble telling port from starboard may remember that port and left both have four letters or may remind herself, "I *left* port." And what beginning musician hasn't remembered the notes represented by the lines and spaces of the musical staff by learning "F-A-C-E" and "**E**very **G**ood **B**oy **D**oes **F**ine"?

Mnemonic techniques are ways to avoid *rote* learning (learning by simple repetition). The superiority of mnemonic learning as opposed to rote learning has been demonstrated many times. For example, Bower (1973) asked college students to study 5 different lists of 20 unrelated words. At the end of a short study session, subjects tried to recall all 100 items. People using mnemonics remembered an average of 72 items, whereas members of a control group using rote learning remembered an average of 28.

Stage performers rarely have naturally superior memories. Instead, they make extensive use of memory systems to perform their feats (Wilding & Valentine, 1994b). Few of these systems are of practical value to you as a student, but the principles underlying mnemonics are. By practicing mnemonics, you should be able to greatly improve your memory with little effort (Dretzke & Levin, 1996).

Here, then, are the basic principles of mnemonics.

1. **Use mental pictures.** Visual pictures, or images, are generally easier to remember than words. Turning information into mental pictures is therefore very helpful. Make these images as vivid as possible (Campos & Perez, 1997).

Mnemonic Any kind of memory system or aid.

2. **Make things meaningful.** Transferring information from short-term to long-term memory is aided by making it meaningful. If you encounter technical terms that have little or no immediate meaning for you, *give them meaning*, even if you have to stretch the term to do so. (This point is clarified by the examples following this list.)

3. **Make information familiar.** Connect it to what you already know. Another way to get information into long-term memory is to connect it to information already stored there. If some facts or ideas in a chapter seem to stay in your memory easily, associate other more difficult facts with them.

4. **Form bizarre, unusual, or exaggerated mental associations.** Forming images that make sense is better in most situations. However, when associating two ideas, terms, or especially mental images, you may find that the more outrageous and exaggerated the association, the more likely you are to remember. Bizarre images make stored information more *distinctive* and therefore easier to retrieve (Worthen & Marshall, 1996). Imagine, for example, that you have just been introduced to Mr. Rehkop. To remember his name, you could picture him wearing a police uniform. Then replace his nose with a ray gun. This bizarre image will provide two hints when you want to remember Mr. Rehkop's name: *ray* and *cop* (Carney, Levin, & Stackhouse, 1997).

Ulrike Welsch

Mnemonics can be an aid in preparing for tests. However, because mnemonics help most in the initial stages of storing information, it is important to follow through with other elaborative learning strategies.

Bizarre images mainly help improve immediate memory, and they work best for fairly simple information (Robinson-Riegler & McDaniel, 1994). Nevertheless, they can be a first step toward learning.

A sampling of typical applications of mnemonics should make these four points clear to you.

Example 1 Let's say you have 30 new vocabulary words to memorize in Spanish. You can proceed by rote memorization (repeat them over and over until you begin to get them), or you can learn them with little effort by using the keyword method (Pressley, 1987). In the **keyword method,** a familiar word or image is used to link two other words or items. To remember that the word *pájaro* (pronounced PAH-hah-ro) means "bird," you can link it to a "key" word in English: *Pájaro* (to me) sounds like "parked car-o." Therefore, to remember that *pájaro* means bird, I will visualize a parked car jam-packed full of birds. I will try to make this image as vivid and exaggerated as possible, with birds flapping and chirping and feathers flying everywhere. Similarly, for the word *carta* (which means "letter"), I will imagine a shopping *cart* filled with postal letters.

If you link similar keywords and images for the rest of the list, you may not remember them all, but you will get most without any more practice. As a matter of fact, if you have formed the *pájaro* and *carta* images just now, it is going to be almost impossible for you to see these words anytime during the next few days without remembering what they mean.

What about a year from now? How long do keyword memories last? Mnemonic memories work best in the short run. Later, they may be more fragile than conventional memories. That's why it's usually best to use mnemonics during the initial stages of learning (Carney & Levin, 1998). To create more lasting memories, you'll need to use the techniques discussed earlier in this chapter.

Example 2 Let's say you have to learn the names of all the bones and muscles in the human body for biology. You are trying to remember that the jawbone is the *mandible*. This one is easy because you can associate it to a *man nibbling,* or maybe you can

Exaggerated mental images can link two words or ideas in ways that aid memory. Here, the keyword method is used to link the English word *letter* with the Spanish word *carta.*

Keyword method As an aid to memory, using a familiar word or image to link two items.

picture a *man dribbling* a basketball with his jaw (make this image as ridiculous as possible). If the muscle name *latissimus dorsi* gives you trouble, familiarize it by turning it into *"the ladder misses the door, sigh."* Then picture a ladder glued to your back where the muscle is found. Picture the ladder leading up to a small door at your shoulder. Picture the ladder missing the door. Picture the ladder sighing like an animated character in a cartoon.

This seems like more to remember, not less; and it seems like it would cause you to misspell things. Mnemonics are not a complete substitute for normal memory; they are an aid to normal memory. Mnemonics are not likely to be helpful unless you make extensive use of *images* (Willoughby et al., 1997). Your mental pictures will come back to you easily. As for misspellings, mnemonics can be thought of as a built-in hint in your memory. Often, when taking a test, you will find that the slightest hint is all you need to remember correctly. A mnemonic image is like having someone leaning over your shoulder who says, "Psst, the name of that muscle sounds like 'ladder misses the door, sigh.'" If misspelling continues to be a problem, try to create memory aids for spelling, too.

Here are two more examples to help you appreciate the flexibility of a mnemonic approach to studying.

Example 3 Your art history teacher expects you to be able to name the artist when you are shown slides as part of exams. You have seen many of the slides only once before in class. How will you remember them? As the slides are shown in class, make each artist's name into an object or image. Then picture the object *in* the paintings done by the artist. For example, you can picture van Gogh as a *van* (automobile) *going* through the middle of each van Gogh painting. Picture the van running over things and knocking things over. Or, if you remember that van Gogh cut off his ear, picture a giant bloody ear in each of his paintings.

Example 4 If you have trouble remembering history, try to avoid thinking of it as something from the dim past. Picture each historical personality as a person you know right now (a friend, teacher, parent, and so on). Then picture these people doing whatever the historical figures did. Also, try visualizing battles or other events as if they were happening in your town or make parks and schools into countries. Use your imagination.

How can mnemonics be used to remember things in order? Here are three techniques that are helpful.

1. **Form a story or a chain.** To remember lists of ideas, objects, or words in order, try forming an exaggerated association (mental image) connecting the first item to the second, then the second to the third, and so on. To remember the following short list in order—elephant, doorknob, string, watch, rifle, oranges—picture a full-sized *elephant* balanced on a *doorknob* playing with a *string* tied to him. Picture a *watch* tied to the string, and a *rifle* shooting *oranges* at the watch. This technique can be used quite successfully for lists of 20 or more items. In a one test, people who used a linking mnemonic did much better at remembering lists of 15 and 22 errands (Higbee et al., 1990). Try it next time you go shopping and leave your list at home. Another helpful strategy is to make up a short story that links all of the items on a list you want to remember (McNamara & Scott, 2001).

2. **Take a mental walk.** Ancient Greek orators had an interesting way to remember ideas in order when giving a speech. Their method was to take a mental walk along a familiar path. As they did, they associated topics with the images of statues found along the walk. You can do the same thing by "placing" objects or ideas along the way as you mentally take a familiar walk (Neath, 2002).

3. **Use a system.** Many times, the first letters or syllables of words or ideas can be formed into another word that will serve as a reminder of order. "Roy G. Biv" is an example. As an alternative, learn the following: 1 is a bun, 2 is a shoe, 3 is a tree, 4 is a door, 5 is a hive, 6 is sticks, 7 is heaven, 8 is a gate, 9 is a line, 10 is a hen. To remember a list in order, form an image associating bun with the first item on your list. For example, if the first item is *frog,* picture a "frog-burger" on a bun to remember it. Then, associate shoe with the second item, and so on.

If you have never used mnemonics, you may still be skeptical, but give this approach a fair trial. Most people find they can greatly extend their memory through the use of mnemonics. But remember, like most things worthwhile, remembering takes effort.

RELATE

As an exercise, see if you can create mnemonics for the words *icon, implicit memory,* and *mnemonic.* The best mnemonics are your own, but here are some examples to help you get started. An icon is a visual image: Picture an *eye* in a *can* to remember that icons store visual information. Implicit memories are "hidden": Picture an *imp* hiding in memory. A mnemonic is a memory aid: Imagine writing a phone number on your knee to remember it. Imagine your *knee moaning,* "Ick, you shouldn't write on me."

Now, go through the glossary items in this chapter and make up mnemonics for any terms you have difficulty remembering.

LEARNING CHECK

1. Memory systems and aids are referred to as _____.

2. Which of the following is least likely to improve memory?
   a. using exaggerated mental images
   b. forming a chain of associations
   c. turning visual information into verbal information
   d. associating new information to information that is already known or familiar
3. Bizarre images make stored information more distinctive and therefore easier to retrieve. T or F?
4. Bower's 1973 study showed that, in general, mnemonics only improve memory for related words or ideas. T or F?

Critical Thinking

5. How are elaborative rehearsal and mnemonics alike?

ANSWERS

1. mnemonics 2. c 3. T 4. F 5. Both attempt to relate new information to information stored in LTM that is familiar or already easy to retrieve.

CHAPTER IN REVIEW

Major Points

- Remembering is an active process. Our memories are frequently lost, altered, revised, or distorted.
- The best way to remember depends, to an extent, on which memory system you are using.
- Remembering is not an all-or-nothing process. Even when you think you can't recall anything, some information may continue to exist in memory.
- Understanding how and why forgetting occurs will allow you to make better use of your memory.
- Some people have naturally superior memories, but everyone can learn to improve his or her memory.
- Memory systems (mnemonics) greatly improve immediate memory. However, conventional learning tends to create the most lasting memories.

Summary

Is there more than one type of memory?

- Memory is an active, computer-like system that encodes, stores, and retrieves information.
- Humans appear to have three interrelated memory systems. These are sensory memory, short-term memory (STM, also called working memory), and long-term memory (LTM).

What are the features of each type of memory?

- Sensory memory is exact but very brief. Through selective attention, some information is transferred to STM.

- STM has a capacity of about 5 to 7 bits of information, but this can be extended by chunking, or recoding. Short-term memories are brief and very sensitive to interruption, or interference; however, they can be prolonged by maintenance rehearsal.
- LTM functions as a general storehouse of information, especially meaningful information. Elaborative rehearsal helps transfer information from STM to LTM. Long-term memories are relatively permanent, or lasting. LTM seems to have an almost unlimited storage capacity.
- LTM is subject to constructive processing, or ongoing revision and updating. LTM is highly organized to allow retrieval of needed information. The pattern, or structure, of memory networks is the subject of current memory research.
- Redintegrative memories are reconstructed as each memory provides a cue for the next memory.

Is there more than one type of long-term memory?

- Within long-term memory, declarative memories for facts seem to differ from procedural memories for skills.
- Declarative memories may be further categorized as semantic memories or episodic memories.

How is memory measured?

- The tip-of-the-tongue state shows that memory is not an all-or-nothing event. Memories may therefore be revealed by recall, recognition, relearning, or priming.

- In recall, memory proceeds without explicit cues, as in an essay exam. Recall of listed information often reveals a serial position effect (middle items on the list are most subject to errors).
- A common test of recognition is the multiple-choice question.
- In relearning, "forgotten" material is learned again, and memory is indicated by a savings score.
- Recall, recognition, and relearning mainly measure explicit memories. Other techniques, such as priming, are necessary to reveal implicit memories.

What are "photographic" memories?

- Eidetic imagery (photographic memory) occurs when a person is able to project an image onto a blank surface.
- Eidetic imagery is rarely found in adults. However, many adults have internal memory images, which can be very vivid.
- Exceptional memory can be learned by finding ways to directly store information in LTM.
- Learning has no effect on the limits of STM. Some people may have exceptional memories that exceed what can be achieved through learning.

What causes forgetting?

- Forgetting and memory were extensively studied by Herman Ebbinghaus. His work shows that forgetting is most rapid immediately after learning (the curve of forgetting).
- Failure to encode information is a common cause of "forgetting."
- Forgetting in sensory memory and STM probably reflects decay of memory traces in the nervous system. Decay or disuse of memories may also account for some LTM loss.
- Often, forgetting is cue dependent. The power of cues to trigger memories is revealed by state-dependent learning and the link between moods and memory.
- Much forgetting in both STM and LTM can be attributed to interference.
- When recent learning interferes with retrieval of prior learning, retroactive interference has occurred.
- If old learning interferes with new learning, proactive interference has occurred.

How accurate are everyday memories?

- Repression is the forgetting of painful, embarrassing, or traumatic memories.
- Repression is thought to be unconscious, in contrast to suppression, which is a conscious attempt to avoid thinking about something.

What happens in the brain when memories are formed?

- Retrograde amnesia and the effects of electroconvulsive shock (ECS) may be explained by the concept of consolidation.
- Consolidation theory holds that engrams (permanent memory traces) are formed during a critical period after learning. Until they are consolidated, long-term memories are easily destroyed.
- The hippocampus is a brain area that has been linked with consolidation of memories. Once memories are consolidated, they appear to be stored in the cortex of the brain.
- The search within the brain for engrams has now settled on changes in nerve cells and how they interconnect.

How can memory be improved?

- Memory can be improved by using feedback, recitation, and rehearsal; by selecting and organizing information; and by using the progressive part method, spaced practice, over-learning, and active search strategies. Effects of serial position, sleep, review, cues, and elaboration should also be kept in mind when studying or memorizing.
- Mnemonic systems use mental images and unusual associations to link new information with familiar memories already stored in LTM. Such strategies give information personal meaning and make it easier to recall.

Interactive Learning

Internet addresses frequently change. To find the sites listed here, visit www.psychology.wadsworth.com/coon_journey2e for an updated list of Internet addresses and direct links to relevant sites.

PSYCHOLOGY: A JOURNEY COMPANION WEB SITE Online quizzes, flash cards, and other helpful study aids for this text. *www.psychology.wadsworth.com/coon_journey2e*

ACTIVE BRAIN AREAS IN WORKING MEMORY A three-dimensional MRI reconstruction of a person's brain while holding letters in working memory.

EXPLORATORIUM: MEMORY Demonstrations and articles related to memory from an exceptional science museum.

FALSE-MEMORY TEST Use the materials in this site to induce false memories in others (for demonstration purposes).

MEMORIES ARE MADE OF . . . Article from *Scientific American* discusses memory-enhancing drugs for Alzheimer's patients.

MEMORY TECHNIQUES AND MNEMONICS Links to information on mnemonics.

QUESTIONS AND ANSWERS ABOUT MEMORIES OF CHILDHOOD ABUSE From APA, a summary of the repressed memory issue.

REPRESSED AND RECOVERED MEMORIES Site devoted to the recovered memory controversy; has links to both sides of the controversy.

THE MACHINERY OF THOUGHT *Scientific American* article describes research on the physiology of memory.

THE MAGICAL NUMBER SEVEN, PLUS OR MINUS TWO Full text of George Miller's original article.

INFOTRAC COLLEGE EDITION For recent articles on the Psychology in Action feature, use Key Words search for MNEMONICS.

PSYCHNOW! 5d. Memory systems, 5e. Forgetting.

Test Your Knowledge: Memory

The questions that follow are only a sample of what you need to know. If you miss any of the items, you should review the entire chapter and get more practice with *WebTutor* or the *Practice Quizzes* that came with this book. Another way to prepare for tests is to use the printed *Study Guide* that is available for this text.

1. The first step in forming a memory is
   A. retrieval   B. storage   C. rehearsal   D. encoding
2. Storing information as an icon or an echo is most characteristic of
   A. sensory memory   B. short-term memory
   C. long-term memory   D. procedural memory
3. Selective attention controls which information moves from sensory memory to
   A. phonetic memory   B. iconic memory   C. STM
   D. LTM
4. Information in LTM is stored mainly on the basis of
   A. meaning   B. sounds and phonetics   C. icons and echoes   D. how it will be retrieved
5. The digit-span test is primarily a measure of
   A. LTM   B. elaborative rehearsal   C. recoding   D. STM
6. Elaborative rehearsal is especially useful for forming
   A. memory icons   B. long-term memories   C. skill memories   D. retroactive memories
7. The existence of redintegrative memories is best explained by _____ models of memory.
   A. network   B. TOT   C. implicit   D. eidetic
8. Which of the following is a type of skill memory?
   A. semantic memory   B. declarative memory
   C. episodic memory   D. procedural memory
9. The two most sensitive tests of memory are
   A. recall and redintegration   B. recall and relearning
   C. recognition and relearning   D. recognition and digit-span
10. Which type of memory test would be most likely to reveal a serial position effect?
    A. recall   B. recognition   C. relearning   D. implicit
11. Priming is used to reveal which type of memories?
    A. explicit   B. sensory   C. skill   D. implicit
12. For most people, having an especially good memory is based on
    A. maintenance rehearsal   B. constructive processing
    C. phonetic imagery   D. learned strategies

13. Decay of memory traces appears to apply most to the forgetting of
    A. sensory and short-term memories   B. procedural memories   C. semantic memories   D. state-dependent memories
14. A saxophone player learns three new pieces of music, one after the other, in a single afternoon. The next day he is least able to remember the third piece because of
    A. state-dependent learning   B. the time decay of memory traces   C. proactive interference   D. disuse of memory cues
15. If you consciously succeed at putting a painful memory out of mind, you have used
    A. redintegration   B. suppression   C. negative rehearsal   D. repression
16. Flashbulb memories could be thought of as the reverse of
    A. repressed memories   B. proactive memories
    C. retroactive memories   D. episodic memories
17. Memory consolidation would most likely be disrupted by
    A. rehearsal   B. ECS   C. over-learning   D. sleep
18. Which of the following is BAD advice for improving memory?
    A. Use spaced practice.   B. Over-learn.   C. Study when you are hungry.   D. Sleep after you study.
19. The cognitive interview helps people remember more by providing
    A. memory cues   B. a serial position effect   C. phonetic priming   D. massed practice
20. The keyword method is a commonly used
    A. cognitive interviewing technique   B. massed practice strategy   C. mnemonic technique   D. first step in the progressive-part method

ANSWERS   1. d 2. a 3. c 4. a 5. d 6. b 7. a 8. d 9. c 10. a 11. d 12. d 13. a 14. c 15. b 16. a 17. b 18. c 19. a 20. c

Cognition, Intelligence, and Creativity

Gizmos and Doohickeys

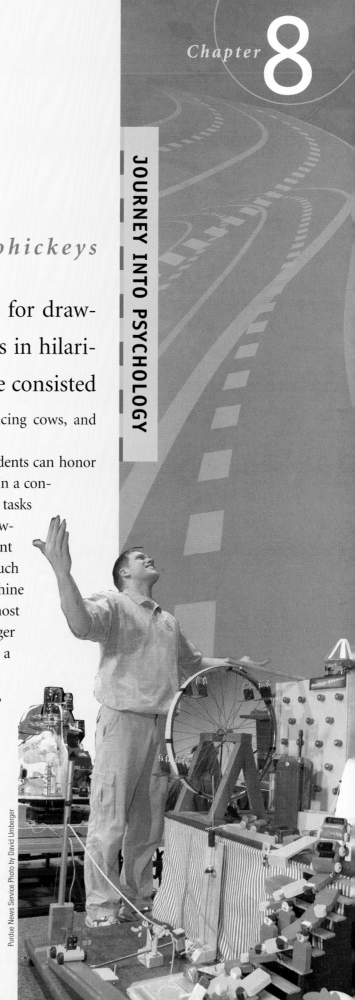

Purdue News Service Photo by David Umberger

Cartoonist Rube Goldberg was famous for drawing wacky machines that did simple tasks in hilarious ways. A typical Rube Goldberg device consisted of pulleys, switches, levers, mousetraps, balloons, fans, dancing cows, and other strange items.

Today, thanks to the Theta Tau engineering fraternity, students can honor Goldberg's zany inspiration while testing their own creativity. In a contest held at Purdue University, students invent machines to do tasks such as sticking a stamp on a letter, teeing up a golf ball, or screwing a lightbulb into a socket. Of course, any engineering student worth his or her calculator could easily create a machine to do such things. The real challenge in the National Rube Goldberg Machine Contest is to build a gadget that does something simple in the most complicated way imaginable. For instance, Doug Shoenenberger and Paul Calhoun won with a contraption that loads a disc into a CD player in 35 mind-boggling steps.

Students like Doug and Paul obviously enjoy complexity, novelty, and problem solving. At higher levels, these are the same qualities that define many of history's geniuses, such as Einstein, Darwin, Mozart, Newton, Michelangelo, Galileo, Madame Curie, Edison, Martha Graham, and others (Michalko, 1998).

Like all creative activities, the Rube Goldberg contest raises questions about human cognition. How do we think? How are we able to solve problems? How do people create works of art, science, and literature? How many engineering students does it take to screw in a lightbulb? For some preliminary answers, we will investigate thinking, problem solving, intelligence, and creativity in the pages that follow.

Survey Questions

- What is the nature of thought?
- In what ways are images related to thinking?
- How do we learn concepts?
- What is the role of language in thinking?
- Can animals be taught to use language?
- What do we know about problem solving?
- What is artificial intelligence?
- How is human intelligence defined and measured?
- How do IQ scores relate to achievement and thinking ability?
- What is creative thinking?
- How accurate is intuition?
- What can be done to improve thinking and promote creativity?

WHAT IS THINKING?—IT'S ALL IN YOUR HEAD!

] SURVEYQUESTION *What is the nature of thought?*

Humans are highly adaptable creatures. We live in deserts, jungles, mountains, frenzied cities, placid retreats, and recently, in space stations. Unlike other species, our success owes more to intelligence and thinking abilities than it does to innate behaviors. Let's see how concepts, language, and mental images make thinking possible.

Cognition refers to mentally processing information. Our thoughts take many forms, including daydreaming, problem solving, and reasoning (to name but a few). Although thinking is not limited to humans, imagine trying to teach an animal to equal Shakuntala Devi's "world record" for mental calculation. Devi once multiplied two 13-digit numbers (7,686,369,774,870 times 2,465,099,745,779) in her head, giving the answer in 28 seconds. (That's 18,947,668,104,042,434,089,403,730 if you haven't already figured it out.)

Investigating our ability to think is similar to figuring out how a computer works by asking, "I wonder what would happen if I did this?" But in cognitive psychology (the study of human information processing) the "computer" is the brain, and thinking is the "programming" we seek to understand.

Some Basic Units of Thought

At its most basic, thinking is an *internal representation* (mental expression) of a problem or situation. (Picture a chess player who mentally tries out several moves before actually touching a chess piece.) The power of being able to mentally represent problems is dramatically illustrated by chess grand master Miguel Najdorf, who once simultaneously played 45 chess games—while blindfolded. How did Najdorf do it? Like most people, he used the

The power of thought is beautifully expressed by Stephen W. Hawking, a theoretical physicist and one of the best-known scientific minds of modern times. Hawking has suffered since age 13 from Lou Gehrig's disease. Today, he can only control his left hand, and he cannot speak. Nevertheless, his brain remains fiercely active. With courage and determination, he has used his intellect to advance our understanding of the universe.

Cognition The process of thinking or mentally processing information (images, concepts, words, rules, and symbols).

basic units of thought: images, concepts, and language (or symbols). **Images** are picture-like mental representations. **Concepts** are generalized ideas that represent a class of objects or events. **Language** consists of words or symbols, and rules for combining them. Thinking often involves all three units. For example, blindfolded chess players rely on visual images, concepts ("Game 2 begins with a strategy known as an English opening"), and the special notational system, or "language," of chess.

In a moment, we will delve further into imagery, concepts, and language. Be aware, however, that thinking involves attention, pattern recognition, memory, decision making, intuition, knowledge, and more. This chapter is only a sample of what cognitive psychology is about.

MENTAL IMAGERY—DOES A FROG HAVE LIPS?

] SURVEYQUESTION *In what ways are images related to thinking?*

Ninety-seven percent of us have visual images, and 92 percent have auditory images. More than 50 percent have imagery for movement, touch, taste, smell, and pain. Thus, mental images can be more than just "pictures." For example, your image of a bakery may also include its delicious odor. Despite such variations, it is generally accepted that most of us use images to think, remember, and solve problems. Here are some ways in which we use mental images (Kosslyn et al., 1990):

- To make a decision or solve a problem (choosing what clothes to wear, figuring out how to arrange furniture in a room).
- To change feelings (thinking of pleasant images to get out of a bad mood, imagining yourself as thin to stay on a diet).
- To improve a skill or to prepare for some action (using images to improve a swimming stroke, mentally rehearsing how you will ask for a raise).
- To aid memory (picturing Mr. Cook wearing a chef's hat so you can remember his name).

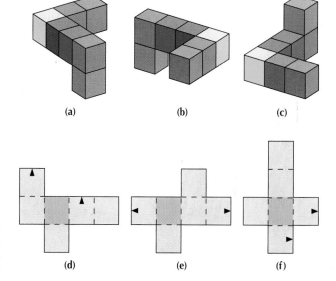

(a)   (b)   (c)

(d)   (e)   (f)

The Nature of Mental Images

Mental images are not flat, like photographs. Researcher Stephen Kosslyn showed this by asking people, Does a frog have lips and a stubby tail? Unless you often kiss frogs, you will probably tackle this question by using mental images. Most people picture a frog, "look" at its mouth, then mentally "rotate" the frog in mental space to check its tail (Kosslyn, 1983). Mental rotation is partly based on imagined movements (◆Fig. 8.1). That is, we mentally "pick up" an object and turn it around (Richter et al., 2000; Wexler, Kosslyn, & Berthoz, 1998).

"Reverse Vision"

What happens in the brain when a person has visual images? Seeing something in your "mind's eye" is similar to seeing real objects. Information from the eyes normally activates the brain's primary visual area, creating an image (◆Fig. 8.2). Other brain areas then help us recognize the image by relating it to stored knowledge. When you form a mental image, the system works in reverse. Brain areas where memories are stored send signals back to the visual cortex, where once again, an image is created (Farah et al., 1989; Kosslyn, Thompson, & Alpert, 1995). For example, if you visualize a friend's face right now, the area of your brain that specializes in perceiving faces will become more active (O'Craven & Kanwisher, 2000).

◆FIGURE 8.1 *Imagery in thinking. (Top) Subjects were shown a drawing similar to (a) and drawings of how (a) would look in other positions, such as (b) and (c). Subjects could recognize (a) after it had been "rotated" from its original position. However, the more (a) was rotated in space, the longer it took to recognize it. This result suggests that people actually formed a three-dimensional image of (a) and rotated the image to see if it matched. (Shepard, 1975.) (Bottom) Try your ability to manipulate mental images: Picture each of these shapes as a piece of paper that can be folded to make a cube. After they have been folded, on which cubes do the arrow tips meet? (After Kosslyn, 1985.)*

Image Most often, a mental representation that has picture-like qualities; an icon.

Concept A generalized idea representing a class of related objects or events.

Language Words or symbols, and rules for combining them, that are used for thinking and communication.

Vision

Frontal lobe

Parietal lobe

Occipital lobe

Temporal lobe

Cerebellum

Visual Image

Frontal lobe

Parietal lobe

Occipital lobe

Temporal lobe

Cerebellum

✦FIGURE 8.2 *When you see a flower, its image is represented by activity in the primary visual area of the cortex, at the back of the brain. Information about the flower is also relayed to other brain areas. If you form a mental image of a flower, information follows a reverse path. The result, once again, is activation of the primary visual area.*

Using Mental Images

How are images used to solve problems? We use *stored images* (information from memory) to apply past experiences to problem solving. Let's say you are asked, "How many ways can you use an empty egg carton?" You might begin by picturing uses you have already seen, such as sorting buttons into a carton. To give more original answers, you will probably need to use *created* images. A *created image* is assembled or invented, rather than simply remembered. Thus, an artist may completely picture a proposed sculpture before beginning work. People with good imaging abilities tend to score higher on tests of creativity (Morrison & Wallace, 2001). In fact, Albert Einstein, Thomas Edison, Lewis Carroll, and many other of history's most original intellects relied heavily on imagery (West, 1991).

Does the "size" of a mental image affect thinking? To find out, first picture a cat sitting beside a housefly. Now try to "zoom in" on the cat's ears so you see them clearly. Next, picture a rabbit sitting beside an elephant. How quickly can you "see" the rabbit's front feet? Did it take longer than picturing the cat's ears?

When a rabbit is pictured with an elephant, the rabbit's image must be small because the elephant is large. Using such tasks, Stephen Kosslyn found that the smaller an image is, the harder it is to "see" its details. To put this finding to use, try forming over-sized images of things you want to think about. For example, to understand electricity, picture the wires as large pipes with electrons the size of golf balls moving through them; to understand the human ear, explore it (in your mind's eye) like a large cave; and so forth.

Kinesthetic Imagery

How do muscular responses relate to thinking? In a sense, we think with our bodies as well as our heads. *Kinesthetic images* are created from produced, remembered, or imagined muscular sensations (Oyama & Ichikawa, 1990). Such images help us think about movements and actions.

Kinesthetic imagery arises from sensations in the muscles and joints. As you think and talk, these sensations tend to guide the flow of ideas. For example, if you try to tell a friend how to make bread, you may move your hands in as if kneading the dough. Or, try answering this question: Which direction do you turn the hot-water handle in your kitchen to shut off the water? Most people haven't simply memorized the words "Turn it clockwise," or "Turn it counterclockwise." Instead you will probably "turn" the faucet in your imagination before answering. You may even make a turning motion with your hand before answering.

Kinesthetic images are especially important in music, sports, dance, skateboarding, martial arts, and other movement-oriented skills. People with good kinesthetic imagery learn such skills faster than those with poor imagery (Glisky, Williams, & Kihlstrom, 1996).

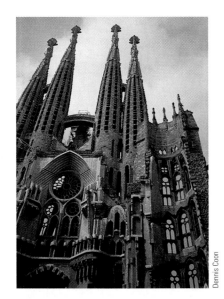

Dennis Coon

The Church of the Sacred Family in Barcelona, Spain, was designed by Antonio Gaudi. Could a person lacking mental imagery design such a masterpiece? Three people out of 100 find it impossible to produce mental images, and 3 out of 100 have very strong imagery. Most artists, architects, designers, sculptors, and film makers have excellent visual imagery.

John Elk III, Stock, Boston/PictureQuest

A study found that rock climbers use kinesthetic imagery to learn climbing routes and to plan their next few moves (Smyth & Waller, 1998).

CONCEPTS—I'M POSITIVE, IT'S A WHATCHAMACALLIT

] SURVEYQUESTION *How do we learn concepts?*

A **concept** is an idea that represents a class of objects or events. Concepts are powerful tools because they allow us to think more *abstractly.* Concepts also help us identify important features of objects or events. That's why experts in various areas of knowledge are good at classifying objects. Bird watchers, tropical fish fanciers, 5-year-old dinosaur enthusiasts, and other experts all learn to look for identifying details that beginners tend to miss. If you are knowledgeable about a topic, such as horses, flowers, or football, you literally see things differently than less well-informed people do (Johnson & Mervis, 1997).

Forming Concepts

How are concepts learned? **Concept formation** is the process of classifying the world into meaningful categories. At its most basic, concept formation is based on *positive* and *negative* *instances* (examples that belong, or do not belong, to the concept class). However, concept formation is not as simple as it might seem. Imagine a child learning the concept of *dog.*

> **ĐOG ĐAZE**
>
> A child and her father go for a walk. At a neighbor's house, they see a medium-sized dog. The father says, "See the dog." As they pass the next yard, the child sees a cat and says, "Dog!" Her father corrects her, "No, that's a *cat.*" The child now thinks, "Aha, dogs are large and cats are small." In the next yard, she sees a Pekingese and says, "Cat!" "No, that's a dog," replies her father.

The child's confusion is understandable. At first she might even mistake a Pekingese for a dust mop. However, with more positive and negative instances, the child will eventually recognize everything from Great Danes to Chihuahuas as members of the same category—dogs.

As adults, we often acquire concepts by learning or forming rules. A **conceptual rule** is a guideline for deciding whether objects or events belong to a concept class. For example, a triangle must be a closed shape with three sides made of straight lines. Rules are an efficient way to learn concepts, but examples remain important. It's unlikely that memorizing rules would allow a new listener to accurately categorize *punk, hip-hop, fusion, salsa, heavy metal, grunge rock,* and *rap* music.

Types of Concepts

Are there different kinds of concepts? Yes, **conjunctive concepts** or "and concepts" are defined by the presence of two or more features. In other words, an item must have "this feature *and* this feature *and* this feature." For example, a *motorcycle* must have two wheels *and* an engine *and* handlebars.

Relational concepts are based on how an object relates to something else, or how its features relate to one another. All of the following are relational concepts: *larger, above, left, north,* and *upside down.* Another example is *sister,* which is defined as "a female considered in her relation to another person having the same parents."

Disjunctive concepts have at *least one* of several possible features. These are "either/or" concepts. To belong to the category, an item must have "this feature *or* that feature *or* another feature." For example, in baseball, a *strike* is *either* a swing and a miss *or* a pitch down the middle *or* a foul ball. The either/or quality of disjunctive concepts makes them hard to learn.

Prototypes

When you think of the concept *bird,* do you mentally list the features that birds have? Probably not. In addition to rules and features, we use **prototypes,** or ideal models, to identify concepts (Rosch, 1977; Smith, 1989). A robin, for example, is a model bird; an

Concept formation The process of classifying information into meaningful categories.

Conceptual rule A formal rule for deciding if an object or event is an example of a particular concept.

Conjunctive concept A class of objects that have two or more features in common. (For example, to qualify as an example of the concept an object must be both red *and* triangular.)

Relational concept A concept defined by the relationship between features of an object or between an object and its surroundings (for example, "greater than," "lopsided").

Disjunctive concept A concept defined by the presence of at least one of several possible features. (For example, to qualify an object must be either blue *or* circular.)

Prototype An ideal model used as a prime example of a particular concept.

◆FIGURE 8.3 *When does a cup become a bowl or a vase? Deciding if an object belongs to a conceptual class is aided by relating it to a prototype, or ideal example. Subjects in one experiment chose number 5 as the "best" cup. (After Labov, 1973.)*

ostrich is not. In other words, some items are better examples of a concept than others are. Which is the example of a cup in ◆Figure 8.3? At some point, as a cup grows taller or wider it becomes a vase or a bowl. To decide if an object is a cup, vase, or bowl, we mentally compare them to an "ideal" cup, like number 5. That's why it's hard to identify concepts when we can't think of a relevant prototype. What, for example, are the objects shown in ◆Figure 8.4? As you can see, prototypes are especially helpful when we try to categorize complex stimuli (Minda & Smith, 2001).

◆FIGURE 8.4 *Use of prototypes in concept identification. Even though its shape is unusual, item (a) can be related to a model (an ordinary set of pliers) and thus recognized. But what are items (b) and (c)? If you don't recognize them, look ahead to ◆Figure 8.6. (After Bransford & McCarrell, 1977.)*

Connotative Meaning

Generally speaking, concepts have two types of meaning. The **denotative meaning** of a word or concept is its exact definition. The **connotative meaning** is its emotional or personal meaning. The word *naked* denotes the same thing (having no clothes) for a nudist, a priest, or a movie censor. However, we could expect their connotations to be quite different. Such differences can influence how we think about important issues. For example, the term *enhanced radiation device* has a more positive connotation than *neutron bomb* does (Gruner & Tighe, 1995).

Can you clarify what a connotative meaning is? Yes, connotative meaning can be measured with a technique called the *semantic differential*, as shown in ◆Figure 8.5. When we rate words or concepts, most of their connotative meaning boils down to the dimensions *good/bad, strong/weak,* and *active/passive.* (Sounds like a good movie title, doesn't it: *My Good and Bad, Strong and Weak, Active and Passive, Big Greek Wedding.*) These dimensions give words very different connotations, even when their denotative meanings are similar. For example, I am *conscientious;* you are *careful;* he is *nitpicky!*

Faulty Concepts

Using inaccurate concepts often leads to thinking errors. For example, *social stereotypes* are oversimplified concepts of groups of people. Stereotypes about men, African Americans, women, conservatives, liberals, police officers, or other groups often muddle thinking about members of the group. A related problem is *all-or-nothing thinking* (one-dimensional thought). In this case, we classify things as absolutely right or wrong, good or bad, fair or unfair, black or white, honest or dishonest. Thinking this way prevents us from appreciating the subtleties of most life problems.

Rate this word: **JAZZ**

Rounded						Angular
Strong						Weak
Smooth						Rough
Passive						Active
Large						Small
Hot						Cold
Bad						Good
Relaxed						Tense
Dry						Wet
Stale						Fresh

◆FIGURE 8.5 *This is an example of Osgood's semantic differential. The connotative meaning of the word jazz can be established by rating it on the scales. Mark your own rating by placing dots or X's in the spaces. Connect the marks with a line; then have a friend rate the word and compare your responses. It might be interesting to do the same for* rock and roll, classical, *and* rap. *You also might want to try the word* psychology. *(From Psychological Bulletin, Vol. 49, No. 3, May 1952.)*

✦FIGURE 8.6 *Context can substitute for a lack of appropriate prototypes in concept identification.*

LANGUAGE—DON'T LEAVE HOME WITHOUT IT

] **SURVEYQUESTION** *What is the role of language in thinking?*

As we have seen, thinking may occur without language. Everyone has searched for a word to express an idea, an image, or a feeling. Nevertheless, most thinking relies heavily on language, because words *encode* (translate) the world into mental symbols that are easy to manipulate (✦Fig. 8.7).

The study of meaning in language is known as **semantics.** It is here that the link between words and thinking becomes most evident. Suppose, on an intelligence test, you were asked to circle the word that does not belong in this series:

SKYSCRAPER   CATHEDRAL   TEMPLE   PRAYER

If you circled *prayer,* you answered as most people do. Now try another problem, again circling the odd item:

CATHEDRAL   PRAYER   TEMPLE   SKYSCRAPER

Did you circle *skyscraper* this time? The new order subtly alters the meaning of the last word (Mayer, 1995). This occurs because words get much of their meaning from *context.* For example, the word *shot* means different things when we are thinking of marksmanship, bartendending, medicine, photography, or golf (Miller, 1999).

Likewise, the words we use can greatly affect our thinking: Has one country's army "invaded" another or "liberated" it? Is the city reservoir "half full" or "half empty"? Would you rather eat "prime beef" or "dead cow"?! More subtle effects also occur. For example, most people have difficulty quickly naming the color of the ink used to print the words in the bottom two rows of ✦Figure 8.8. The word meanings are just too strong to ignore.

Translating languages may also cause a rash of semantic problems. Perhaps the San Jose, California, public library can be excused for displaying a large banner that was supposed to say "You are welcome" in a native Philippine language. The banner actually said "You are circumcised." Likewise, we may forgive Pepsi for translating "Come alive, you Pepsi

✦FIGURE 8.7 *Wine tasting illustrates the encoding function of language. To communicate their experiences to others, wine connoisseurs must put taste sensations into words. The wine you see here is "Marked by deeply concentrated nuances of plum, blackberry, and currant, with a nice balance of tannins and acid, building to a spicy oak finish." (Don't try this with a Pop-tart!)*

PURPLE   BLUE   GREEN   GREEN
RED   PURPLE   RED   GREEN

✦FIGURE 8.8 *The Stroop interference task. Test yourself by naming the colors in the top two rows as quickly as you can. Then name the colors of the ink used to print the words in the bottom two rows (do not read the words themselves). Was it harder to name the ink colors in the bottom rows? (After Tzeng & Wang, 1983.)*

Semantics The study of meanings in language.

generation," into Thai as "Pepsi brings your ancestors back from the dead." However, in more important situations, such as in international diplomacy, avoiding semantic confusion can be vital.

The Structure of Language

What does it take to make a language?   First of all, a language must provide *symbols* that stand for objects and ideas. The symbols we call words are built out of **phonemes** (FOE-neems: basic speech sounds) and **morphemes** (MOR-feems: speech sounds collected into meaningful units, such as syllables or words). For instance, in English the sounds *m, b, w,* and *a* cannot form a syllable *mbwa.* In Swahili, they can. (Also, see ✦Figure 8.9.)

Next, a language must have a **grammar,** or set of rules for making sounds into words and words into sentences. One part of grammar, known as **syntax,** concerns rules for word order. Syntax is important because rearranging words almost always changes the meaning of a sentence: "Dog bites man" versus "Man bites dog."

Traditional grammar is concerned with "surface" language—the sentences we actually speak. Linguist Noam Chomsky has focused instead on the unspoken rules we use to change core ideas into various sentences. Chomsky (1986) believes that we do not learn all the sentences we might ever say. Rather, we actively *create* them by applying **transformation rules** to universal, core patterns. We use these rules to change simple a declarative sentence to other voices or forms (past tense, passive voice, and so forth). For example, the core sentence "Dog bites man" can be transformed to these patterns (and others as well):

> **Past:** The dog bit the man.
> **Passive:** The man was bitten by the dog.
> **Negative:** The dog did not bite the man.
> **Question:** Did the dog bite the man?

Children seem to be using transformation rules when they say things such as "I runned home." That is, the child applied the normal past tense rule to the irregular verb *to run.*

A true language is also *productive*—it can generate new thoughts or ideas. In fact, words can be rearranged to produce a nearly infinite number of sentences. Some are silly: "Please don't feed me to the goldfish." Some are profound: "We hold these truths to be self-evident, that all men are created equal." In either case, the productive quality of language makes it a powerful tool for thinking.

Gestural Languages

It is common to think of language only as a system of spoken sounds and written symbols. However, language is not limited to speech. Consider the case of Ildefonso, a young man who was born deaf. At age 24, Ildefonso had never communicated with another human, except by mime. Then at last, Ildefonso had a breakthrough: After much hard work with a sign language teacher, he understood the link between a cat and the gesture for it. At that magic moment, he grasped the idea that "cat" could be communicated to another person, just by signing the word.

Ildefonso's long-awaited breakthrough was made possible by American Sign Language (ASL), a gestural language. ASL is not pantomime or a code. It is a true language, like German, Spanish, or Japanese. In fact, ASL is not un-

Albanian	mak, mak
Chinese	gua, gua
Dutch	rap, rap
English	quack, quack
French	coin, coin
Italian	qua, qua
Spanish	cuá, cuá
Swedish	kvack, kvack
Turkish	vak, vak

✦**FIGURE 8.9** *Animals around the world make pretty much the same sounds. Notice, however, how various languages use slightly different phonemes to express the sound a duck makes.*

Phonemes The basic speech sounds of a language.

Morphemes The smallest meaningful units in a language, such as syllables or words.

Grammar A set of rules for combining language units into meaningful speech or writing.

Syntax Rules for ordering words when forming sentences.

Transformation rules Rules by which a simple declarative sentence may be changed to other voices or forms (past tense, passive voice, and so forth).

Infants can express the idea "pick me up" in gestures before they can make the same request in words. Their progression from gestures to speech may mirror the evolution of human language abilities (Stokoe, 2001).

Look at   **Stare**

✦**FIGURE 8.10** *ASL has only 3,000 root signs, compared with roughly 600,000 words in English. However, variations in signs make ASL a highly expressive language. For example, the sign LOOK-AT can be varied in ways to make it mean look at me, look at her, look at each, stare at, gaze, watch, look for a long time, look at again and again, reminisce, sightsee, look forward to, predict, anticipate, browse, and many more variations.*

derstood by those who use other gestural languages, such as French Sign, Chinese Sign, Yiddish Sign, or Old Kentish Sign.

Both speech and signing follow similar universal language patterns. Of course, ASL has a *spatial* grammar, syntax, and semantics all its own (✦Fig. 8.10). Just the same, signing children pass through the stages of language development at about the same age as speaking children do. Some psychologists now believe that speech evolved from gestures, far back in human history (Corballis, 2002). Do you ever make hand gestures when you are speaking on the phone? If so, you may be displaying a remnant of the gestural origins of language. Perhaps that's also why the same brain areas become more active when a person speaks or signs (Emmorey et al., 2003).

Sign languages naturally arise out of a need to communicate visually. Sign is the true voice of the deaf and hearing impaired. Those who "speak" sign share not just a language, but a rich culture as well (Kemp, 1998; Meier, 1991; Sacks, 1990; Schaller, 1991).

The Animal Language Debate

] SURVEYQUESTION *Can animals be taught to use language?*

Do animals use language?   Animals do communicate. They react immediately to cries, gestures, and mating calls made by other members of their species. For the most part, however, natural animal communication is quite limited. Even apes and monkeys make only a few dozen distinct cries, which carry messages such as "attack," "flee," or "food here." More important, animal communication is not productive. When a monkey gives an "eagle distress call," it means something like, "I see an eagle." The monkey has no way of saying, "I don't see an eagle," or "Thank heavens that wasn't an eagle," or "That sucker I saw yesterday was some huge eagle" (Glass et al., 1979). Let's explore some successes and failures in trying to teach animals to use language.

Talking Chimps

Early attempts to teach chimps to talk were a dismal failure. The world record was held by Viki, a chimp who could say only four words (*mama, papa, cup,* and *up*) after 6 years of intensive training (Fleming, 1974; Hayes, 1951). (Actually, all four words sounded something like a belch.) Then there was a breakthrough. Beatrix Gardner and Allen Gardner used operant conditioning and imitation to teach a female chimp named Washoe to use American Sign Language. Washoe's "vocabulary" grew rapidly. Soon she began to put together primitive sentence strings like "Come-gimme sweet," "Out please," "Gimme tickle," and "Open food drink." At her peak, Washoe could construct six-word sentences and use about 240 signs (Gardner & Gardner, 1989).

A chimp named Sarah was another well-known language pupil. David Premack taught Sarah to use 130 "words" consisting of plastic chips arranged on a magnetized board (✦Fig. 8.11). From the beginning, Sarah was required to use proper word order. She learned to answer questions; to label things "same" or "different"; to classify objects by

Nouns		Verbs		Concepts Conditionals		Adjectives (Colors)	
Sarah	Chocolate	Is	Give	Same	Different	Red	Yellow

FIGURE 8.11 *Here is a sample of some of the word symbols that Sarah the chimpanzee used to communicate with humans. (After Premack & Premack, 1972.)*

FIGURE 8.12 *After reading the message "Sarah insert apple pail banana dish" on the magnetic board, Sarah performed the actions as directed. (From "Teaching Language to an Ape" by Ann J. Premack and David Premack. Copyright © 1972 by Scientific American, Inc. Reprinted by permission of Eric Mose, Jr.)*

color, shape, and size; and to form compound sentences (Premack & Premack, 1983). One of Sarah's top achievements was her ability to use conditional sentences. A *conditional statement* contains a qualification, often in the if/then form: "If Sarah take apple, then Mary give Sarah chocolate." "If Sarah take banana, then Mary no give Sarah chocolate" (Fig. 8.12).

Can it be said with certainty that the chimps understand such interchanges? Most researchers working with chimps believe that they have indeed communicated with them. Especially striking are the chimps' spontaneous responses. Washoe once "wet" on psychologist Roger Fouts' back while riding on his shoulders. When Fouts asked, with some annoyance, why she had done it, Washoe signed, "It's funny!"

Criticisms

Such interchanges are impressive. But communication and real language usage are different things. Even untrained chimps use simple gestures to communicate with humans. For example, a chimp will point at a banana that is out of reach, while glancing back and forth between the banana and a person standing nearby (Leavens & Hopkins, 1998). (The meaning of the gesture is clear. The meaning of the exasperated look on the chimp's face is less certain, but it probably means, "Yes, give me the banana, you idiot.")

Some psychologists doubt that apes can really use language. For one thing, chimps rarely "speak" without prompting from humans. Also, the apes may be simply performing operant responses to get food, play, or other "goodies" (Hixon, 1998). By using such responses, the apes then manipulate their trainers to get what they want.

You might say the critics believe the apes have made monkeys out of their trainers. However, psychologists Roger and Debbi Fouts studied some 6,000 conversations between chimps. Only 5 percent had anything to do with food (Fouts et al., 1984). Another study found that chimps hold real conversations, even when people are not around to cue them (Greenfield & Savage-Rumbaugh, 1993). In signed interchanges with humans, chimps reply in patterns that are similar to conversations with young children (Jensvold & Gardner, 2000), so, maybe the chimps will make monkeys out of the critics.

Problems with Syntax

At this point, numerous chimps, a gorilla named Koko, and an assortment of dolphins and sea lions have learned to communicate with word symbols of various kinds. Yet, even if some criticisms can be answered, linguists such as Noam Chomsky remain unconvinced that animals can truly use language. The core issue is that problems with syntax (word order) have plagued almost all animal language studies. For example, when a chimp named Nim Chimpsky (no relation to Chomsky) wanted an orange, he would typically signal a grammarless string of words: "Give orange me give eat orange me eat orange give me eat orange give me you." This might be communication, but it is not language.

Lexigrams

More recently, the flames of controversy were fanned again by Kanzi, a pygmy chimpanzee studied by Duane Rumbaugh and Sue Savage-Rumbaugh. Kanzi communicates using gestures and push buttons on a computer keyboard. Each of the 250 buttons is marked with a *lexigram,* or geometric word-symbol (✦Fig. 8.13). Using the lexigrams on a computer or on a chart, Kanzi can create primitive sentences several words long. He can also understand about 650 spoken sentences. During testing, Kanzi hears spoken words over headphones, so his caretakers cannot visually prompt him (Savage-Rumbaugh et al., 1990; Savage-Rumbaugh & Lewin, 1996).

Kanzi's sentences consistently follow correct word order. Like a child learning language, Kanzi picked up some rules from his caregivers (Savage-Rumbaugh & Lewin, 1996). However, he has developed other patterns on his own. For example, Kanzi usually places action symbols in the order he wants to carry them out, such as "chase tickle" or "chase hide." In this respect, Kanzi's use of grammar is on a par with that of a 2-year-old child (Savage-Rumbaugh et al., 1993).

Kanzi's ability to invent a simple grammar may help us better understand the roots of human language. It is certainly the strongest answer yet to the critics. On the other hand, Chomsky insists that if chimps were biologically capable of language, they would use it on their own. Although the issue is far from resolved, such research may unravel the mysteries of language learning. In fact, it has already been helpful for teaching language to children with serious language impairments.

✦**FIGURE 8.13** *Kanzi's language learning has been impressive. He can comprehend spoken English words. He can identify lexigram symbols when he hears corresponding words. He can use lexigrams when the objects they refer to are absent, and he can, if asked, lead someone to the object. All of these skills were acquired through observation, not conditioning (Savage-Rumbaugh et al., 1990).*

STUDYBREAK *Imagery, Concepts, and Language*

RELATE

Name some ways in which you have used imagery in the thinking you have done today.

Write a conceptual rule for the following idea: *unicycle.* Were you able to define the concept with a rule? Would positive and negative instances help make the concept clearer for others?

A true sports car has two seats, a powerful engine, good brakes, and excellent handling. What kind of a concept is the term *sports car*? What do you think of as a prototypical sports car?

Here's some mnemonic help: You use a *phone* to send *phonemes*. To *morph* them into words, you have to hit them with a *grammar*. What wrong is with sentence this? (The answer is not a *sin tax*, but it still may tax you.)

You must learn to communicate with an alien life-form whose language cannot be reproduced by the human voice. Do you think it would be better to use a gestural language or lexigrams? Why?

LEARNING CHECK

1. List three primary units of thought:
   _____
   _____
   _____

2. Our reliance on imagery in thinking means that problem solving is impaired by the use of language or symbols. T or F?

3. Humans appear capable of forming three-dimensional images that can be moved or rotated in mental space. T or F?

4. A *mup* is defined as anything that is small, blue, and hairy. *Mup* is a _____ concept.

5. The connotative meaning of the word *naked* is "having no clothes." T or F?

6. True languages are _____ because they can be used to generate new possibilities.

7. The basic speech sounds are called _____; the smallest meaningful units of speech are called _____.

Critical Thinking

8. A Democrat and a Republican are asked to rate the word *democratic* on the semantic differential. Under what conditions would their ratings be most alike?

9. Chimpanzees and other apes are intelligent and entertaining animals. If you were doing language research with a chimp, what major problem would you have to guard against?

ANSWERS

1. images, concepts, language or symbols (others could be listed) 2. F 3. T 4. conjunctive 5. F 6. productive 7. phonemes, morphemes 8. If they both assume the word refers to a form of government, not a political party or a candidate. 9. The problem of anthropomorphizing (ascribing human characteristics to animals) is especially difficult to avoid when researchers spend many hours "conversing" with chimps.

PROBLEM SOLVING—GETTING AN ANSWER IN SIGHT

] SURVEYQUESTION *What do we know about problem solving?*

A good way to start a discussion of problem solving is to solve a problem. Give this one a try.

> A famous ocean liner (the *Queen Ralph*) is steaming toward port at 20 miles per hour. It is 50 miles from shore when a sea gull takes off from its deck and flies toward port. At the same instant, a speedboat leaves port at 30 miles per hour. The bird flies back and forth between the speedboat and the *Queen Ralph* at a speed of 40 miles per hour. How far will the bird have flown when the two boats pass?

If you don't immediately see the answer to this problem, read it again. (The answer is revealed in "Insightful Solutions.")

We all solve many problems every day. Problem solving can be as commonplace as figuring out how to make a non-poisonous meal out of leftovers or as significant as finding a cure for cancer. How do we solve such problems?

Mechanical Solutions

For routine problems, a **mechanical solution** may be adequate. Mechanical solutions are achieved by trial and error or by rote. If I forget the combination to my bike lock, I may be able to discover it by trial and error. In an era of high-speed computers, many trial-and-error solutions are best left to machines. A computer could generate all possible combinations of the five numbers on my lock in a split second. (Of course, it would take me a long time to try them all.) When a problem is solved by *rote*, thinking is guided by an **algorithm,** or learned set of rules that always leads to a correct solution. A simple example of an algorithm is the steps needed to divide one number into another (by doing arithmetic, not by using a calculator).

If you have a good background in math, you may have solved the problem of the bird and the boats by rote. (I hope you didn't. There is an easier solution.)

Solutions by Understanding

Many problems cannot be solved mechanically. In that case, **understanding** (deeper comprehension of a problem) is necessary. Try this problem:

> A person has an inoperable stomach tumor. A device is available that produces rays that at high intensity will destroy tissue (both healthy and diseased). How can the tumor be destroyed without damaging surrounding tissue? (See the sketch in ✦Figure 8.14.)

What does this problem show about problem solving? German psychologist Karl Duncker did a classic series of studies in which he gave college students this problem. Duncker asked them to think aloud as they worked. He found that successful students first had to discover the *general properties* of a correct solution. A **general solution** defines the requirements for success, but not in enough detail to guide further action. This phase was

Mechanical solution A problem solution achieved by trial and error or by a fixed procedure based on learned rules.

Algorithm A learned set of rules that always leads to the correct solution of a problem.

Understanding In problem solving, a deeper comprehension of the nature of the problem.

General solution A solution that correctly states the requirements for success but not in enough detail for further action.

✦FIGURE 8.14 *A schematic representation of Duncker's tumor problem. The dark spot represents a tumor surrounded by healthy tissue. How can the tumor be destroyed without injuring surrounding tissue? (After Duncker, 1945.)*

complete when students realized that the intensity of the rays had to be lowered on their way to the tumor. Then, in the second phase, they proposed a number of **functional** (workable) **solutions** and selected the best one (Dunker, 1945). (One solution is to focus weak rays on the tumor from several angles. Another is to rotate the person's body, so exposure of healthy tissue is minimized.)

It might help to summarize with a more familiar example. Almost everyone who has tried the Rubik's cube puzzle begins at the mechanical, *trial-and-error level.* If you want to take the easy route, printed instructions are available that give the steps for a *rote* solution. In time, those who persist begin to *understand* the *general properties* of the puzzle. After that, they can solve it consistently.

Heuristics

"You can't get there from here." Or so it may seem when we face a problem. Solving problems often requires a strategy. If the number of alternatives is small, a **random search strategy** might work. This is another example of trial-and-error thinking in which all possibilities are tried, more or less randomly. Imagine, for example, that you are traveling and decide to look up an old friend, J. Smith, in a city you are visiting. You open the phone book and find 47 J. Smiths listed. Of course, you could dial each number until you find the right one. "Forget it," you say to yourself. "Is there any way I can narrow the search?" "Oh, yeah! I remember hearing that Janet lives by the beach." Then you take out a map and call only the numbers with addresses near the waterfront (Ellis & Hunt, 1992).

The approach used in this example is a **heuristic** (hew-RIS-tik: a strategy for identifying and evaluating problem solutions). Typically, a heuristic is a "rule of thumb" that *reduces the number of alternatives* thinkers must consider. This raises the odds of success, although it does not guarantee a solution, as an algorithm does. Here are some heuristic strategies that often work:

- Try to identify how the current state of affairs differs from the desired goal. Then find steps that will reduce the difference.
- Try working backward from the desired goal to the starting point or current state.
- If you can't reach the goal directly, try to identify an intermediate goal or subproblem that at least gets you closer.
- Represent the problem in other ways, with graphs, diagrams, or analogies, for instance.
- Generate a possible solution and test it. Doing so may eliminate many alternatives, or it may clarify what is needed for a solution.

Insightful Solutions

A thinker who suddenly solves a problem has usually experienced **insight.** Most insights are so rapid and clear that we wonder why we didn't see the solution sooner. Insight is usually based on reorganizing a problem. This allows us to see problems in new ways and makes their solutions seem obvious (Durso, Rea, & Dayton, 1994).

Let's return now to the problem of the boats and the bird. The best way to solve it is by insight. Because the boats will cover the 50-mile distance in exactly 1 hour, and the bird flies 40 miles per hour, the bird will have flown 40 miles when the boats meet. No math is necessary if you have insight into this problem. ✦Figure 8.15 lists some additional insight problems you may want to try.

In an interesting study, college students rated how "warm" (close to an answer) they felt while solving insight problems. Those who had insights usually jumped directly from "cold" to the correct answer. Students who only got "warmer" usually produced wrong answers (Metcalfe, 1986). Thus, you may be headed for a mistake if an insight is *not* rapid. Real insight tends to be an all-or-nothing event (Smith & Kounios, 1996).

Functional solution A detailed, practical, and workable solution.

Random search strategy Trying possible solutions to a problem in a more or less random order.

Heuristic Any strategy or technique that aids problem solving, especially by limiting the number of possible solutions to be tried.

Insight A sudden mental reorganization of a problem that makes the solution obvious.

Water lilies

Problem: Water lilies growing in a pond double in area every 24 hours. On the first day of spring, only one lily pad is on the surface of the pond. Sixty days later, the pond is entirely covered. On what day is the pond half-covered?

Twenty dollars

Problem: Jessica and Blair both have the same amount of money. How much must Jessica give Blair so that Blair has $20 more than Jessica?

How many pets?

Problem: How many pets do you have if all of them are birds except two, all of them are cats except two, and all of them are dogs except two?

Between 2 and 3

Problem: What one mathematical symbol can you place between 2 and 3 that results in a number greater than 2 and less than 3?

One word

Problem: Rearrange the letters NEWDOOR to make one word.

Solutions to these problems are listed in ◆ *Table 8.1.*

◆FIGURE 8.15

The Nature of Insight

Psychologists Robert Sternberg and Janet Davidson (1982) believe that insight involves three abilities. The first is *selective encoding,* which refers to selecting information that is relevant to a problem, while ignoring distractions. For example, consider the following problem:

> If you have white socks and black socks in your drawer, mixed in the ratio of 4 to 5, how many socks will you have to take out to make sure of having a pair of the same color?

A person who fails to recognize that "mixed in a ratio of 4 to 5" is irrelevant will be less likely to come up with the correct answer of 3 socks.

Insight also relies on *selective combination,* or bringing together seemingly unrelated bits of useful information. Try this sample problem:

> With a 7-minute hourglass and an 11-minute hourglass, what is the simplest way to time the boiling of an egg for 15 minutes?

The answer requires using both hourglasses in combination. First, the 7-minute and the 11-minute hourglasses are started running. When the 7-minute hourglass runs out, it's time to begin boiling the egg. At this point, 4 minutes remain on the 11-minute hourglass. Thus, when it runs out, it is simply turned over. When it runs out again, 15 minutes will have passed.

A third source of insights is *selective comparison.* This is the ability to compare new problems with old information or with problems already solved. A good example is the hat rack problem, in which subjects must build a structure that can support an overcoat in the middle of a room. Each person is given only two long sticks and a C-clamp to work with. The solution, shown in ◆Figure 8.16, is to clamp the two sticks together so that they are wedged between the floor and ceiling. If you

◆FIGURE 8.16 *Solution to the hat rack problem.*

were given this problem, you would be more likely to solve it if you first thought of how pole lamps are wedged between floor and ceiling.

Fixations

One of the most important barriers to problem solving is **fixation,** the tendency to get "hung up" on wrong solutions or to become blind to alternatives. Usually this occurs when we place unnecessary restrictions on our thinking (Isaak & Just, 1995). How, for example, could you plant four small trees so that each is an equal distance from all the others? (The answer is shown in ✦Figure 8.17.)

A prime example of restricted thinking is **functional fixedness.** This is an inability to see new uses (functions) for familiar objects or for things that were used in a particular way. If you have ever used a dime as a screwdriver, you've overcome functional fixedness.

How does functional fixedness affect problem solving? Karl Duncker illustrated the effects of functional fixedness by asking students to mount a candle on a vertical board so the candle could burn normally. Duncker gave each student three candles, some matches, some cardboard boxes, some thumbtacks, and other items. Half of Duncker's subjects received these items *inside* the cardboard boxes. The others were given all the items, including the boxes, spread out on a tabletop.

Duncker found that when the items were in the boxes, solving the problem was very difficult. Why? If students saw the boxes as *containers,* they didn't realize the boxes might be part of the solution. (If you haven't guessed the solution, check ✦Figure 8.18.) Undoubtedly, we could avoid many fixations by being more flexible in categorizing the world (Langer, 2000). For instance, creative thinking could be facilitated in the container problem by saying "This *could be* a box," instead of "This *is* a box." When tested with the candle problem, 5-year-old children show no signs of functional fixedness. Apparently, this is because they have had less experience with the use of various objects. To be more creative, perhaps we should try to see the world without preconceptions, as if through the eyes of a child (German & Defeyter, 2000).

Common Barriers to Problem Solving

Functional fixedness is just one of the mental blocks that prevent insight. Here's an example of another: A $5 bill is placed on a table, and a stack of objects is balanced precariously on top of the bill. How can the bill be removed without touching or moving the objects? A good answer is to split the bill on one of its edges. Gently pulling from opposite ends will tear the bill in half and remove it without toppling the objects. Many people fail to see this solution because they have learned not to destroy money (Adams, 1988). Notice again the impact of placing something in a category, in this case, "things of value" (which should not be destroyed). Other common mental blocks can hinder problem solving, too, as listed here.

1. **Emotional barriers:** inhibition and fear of making a fool of oneself, fear of making a mistake, inability to tolerate ambiguity, excessive self-criticism
   Example: An architect is afraid to try an unconventional design because she fears that other architects will think it is frivolous.
2. **Cultural barriers:** values that hold that fantasy is a waste of time; that playfulness is for children only; that reason, logic, and numbers are good; that feelings, intuitions, pleasure, and humor are bad or have no value in the serious business of problem solving
   Example: A corporate manager wants to solve a business problem but becomes stern and angry when members of his marketing team joke playfully about possible solutions.
3. **Learned barriers:** conventions about uses (functional fixedness), meanings, possibilities, taboos
   Example: A cook doesn't have any clean mixing bowls and fails to see that he could use a frying pan as a bowl.

✦**FIGURE 8.17** *Four trees can be placed equidistant from one another by piling dirt into a mound. Three of the trees are planted equal distances apart around the base of the mound. The fourth tree is planted on the top of the mound. If you were fixated on arrangements that involve level ground, you may have been blind to this three-dimensional solution.*

(a)   (b)   (c)

✦**FIGURE 8.18** *Materials for solving the candle problem were given to subjects in boxes* (a) *or separately* (b)*. Functional fixedness caused by condition* (a) *interfered with solving the problem. The solution to the problem is shown in* (c)*.*

Fixation The tendency to repeat wrong solutions or faulty responses, especially as a result of becoming blind to alternatives.

Functional fixedness A rigidity in problem solving caused by an inability to see new uses for familiar objects.

▲ *TABLE 8.1*	**Solutions to Insight Problems**

Water lilies: Day 59
Twenty dollars: $10
How many pets?: Three (one bird, one cat, and one dog)
Between 2 and 3: A decimal point
One word: ONE WORD (You may object that the answer is two words, but the problem called for the answer to be "one word," and it is.)

4. **Perceptual barriers:** habits leading to a failure to identify important elements of a problem
Example: A beginning artist concentrates on drawing a vase of flowers without seeing that the "empty" spaces around the vase are part of the composition, too.

Much of what we know about thinking comes from direct studies of how people solve problems. Yet, surprisingly, much can also be learned from machines. As the next section explains, computerized problem solving provides a fascinating "laboratory" for testing ideas about how you and I think.

ARTIFICIAL INTELLIGENCE— I COMPUTE, THEREFORE I AM

] SURVEYQUESTION *What is artificial intelligence?*

It's been a long time since Johann Sebastian Bach, the eighteenth-century German composer, last wrote any music. But listeners sometimes mistake music created by Kemal Ebcioglu for Bach's work. Ebcioglu wrote a computer program that creates harmonies remarkably similar to Bach's. By analyzing Bach's music, Ebcioglu came up with 350 rules that govern harmonization. The result is a program that displays *artificial intelligence.*

Artificial intelligence (**AI**) refers to computer programs capable of doing things that require intelligence when done by people (Best, 1999). Artificial intelligence is based on the fact that many tasks—from harmonizing music to medical diagnosis—can be reduced to a set of rules applied to a body of information. AI is valuable in situations where speed, vast memory, and persistence are required. In fact, AI programs are better at some tasks than humans are. An example is world chess champion Garry Kasparov's loss, in 1997, to a computer called Deep Blue.

Two composers. The one on the left was a genius who wrote sublime, multi-voiced harmonies. The one on the right has created reasonably good, if uninspired, music. Computer models of thought can approximate intelligent human behavior. However, rule-based computer "thinking" still lacks the flexibility, creativity, and common sense of human intelligence.

AI and Cognition

Artificial intelligence provides a way to probe how we comprehend language, make decisions, and solve problems. Increasingly, AI is being used as a research tool in computer simulations and expert systems.

Computer simulations are programs that attempt to duplicate human behavior, especially thinking, decision making, or problem solving. Here, the computer acts as a "laboratory" for testing models of cognition. If a computer program behaves as humans do (including making the same errors), then the program may be a good model of how we think.

Expert systems are computer programs that respond as a human expert would. They have demystified some human abilities by converting complex skills into clearly stated rules a computer can follow. Expert systems can predict the weather, analyze geological formations, diagnose disease, play chess, read, tell when to buy or sell stocks, and do many other tasks.

Experts and Novices

Working with artificial intelligence has helped especially to clarify how novices differ from experts. Research on chess masters, for example, shows that their skills are based on specific *organized knowledge* (systematic information) and *acquired strategies* (learned tactics). In other words, becoming a star performer does not come from some general strengthening of the mind. Master chess players don't necessarily have better memories than beginners (except for realistic chess positions) (Gobet & Simon, 1996). (See ✦Fig. 8.19.) And, typically, they don't explore more moves ahead than lesser players.

What does set master players apart is their ability to recognize *patterns* that suggest the best lines of play (Best, 1999). This helps eliminate a large number of possibilities. The chess

Artificial intelligence Any artificial system (often a computer program) that is capable of human-like problem solving or intelligent responding.

master, therefore, doesn't waste time exploring bad moves. Experts are better able to see the true nature of problems and relate them to general principles (Anderson, 1995).

The Future of AI

AI may lead to robots that recognize voices and that speak and act "intelligently." But cognitive scientists realize that machine "intelligence" is ultimately "blind" outside its underlying set of rules. In contrast, human cognition is much more flexible. For example, u cann understnd wrds thet ar mizpeld. Computers are very literal and easily stymied by such errors. Let's say you are exchanging instant messages with a computer in another room and can ask it questions. If the machine can "fool" you into thinking it is a human, it could be argued that it is intelligent. To date, no machine has come close to passing this test (Moor, 2001). Although Bach might have been fascinated by AI, it is doubtful that his musical magic will be eclipsed by a machine. The next two sections, therefore, are devoted to a discussion of human intelligence and creativity.

Real Game
Black

Random Placement

White

◆**FIGURE 8.19** *The left chessboard shows a realistic game. The right chessboard is a random arrangement of pieces. Expert chess players can memorize the left board at a glance, yet they are no better than beginners at memorizing the random board (Saariluoma, 1994). Expert performance at most thinking tasks is based on acquired strategies and knowledge. If you would like to excel at a profession or a mental skill, plan on adding to your knowledge every day (Holyoak, 1990).*

STUDYBREAK ❖ *Problem Solving and Artificial Intelligence*

RELATE

Identify at least one problem you have solved mechanically or by rote. Now identify a problem you solved by understanding. Did the second problem involve finding a general solution or a functional solution? Or both? What heuristics did you use to solve the problem?

What is the best insightful solution you've ever come up with? Did it involve selective encoding, combination, or comparison?

Can you think of time when you overcame functional fixedness to solve a problem?

LEARNING CHECK

1. Insight refers to rote, or trial-and-error, problem solving. T or F?
2. The first phase in problem solving by understanding is to discover the general properties of a correct solution. T or F?
3. Problem-solving strategies that guide the search for solutions are called _____.

4. A common element underlying insight is that information is encoded, combined, and compared
   a. mechanically   b. by rote   c. functionally   d. selectively
5. The term *fixation* refers to the point at which a helpful insight becomes fixed in one's thinking. T or F?
6. Two aspects of artificial intelligence are computer simulations and automated creativity. T or F?

Critical Thinking

7. Do you think that it is true that "a problem clearly defined is a problem half solved"?
8. Sea otters select suitably sized rocks and use them to hammer shellfish loose for eating. They then use the rock to open the shell. Does this qualify as thinking?
9. Is it ever accurate to describe a machine as "intelligent"?

ANSWERS

1. F 2. T 3. heuristics 4. d 5. F 6. F 7. Although this might be an overstatement, it is true that clearly defining a starting point and the desired goal can serve as a heuristic in problem solving. 8. Psychologist Donald Griffin (1992) believes it does because thinking is implied by actions that appear to be planned with an awareness of likely results. 9. Rule-driven expert systems may appear "intelligent" within a narrow range of problem solving. However, they are "stone stupid" at everything else. This is usually not what we have in mind when discussing human intelligence.

HUMAN INTELLIGENCE—THE IQ AND YOU

] SURVEYQUESTION *How is human intelligence defined and measured?*

Thinking and problem solving are closely related to intelligence. Like many important concepts in psychology, intelligence cannot be observed directly. Nevertheless, we feel certain it exists. Let's compare two children:

> When she was 14 months old, Anne H. wrote her own name. She taught herself to read at age 2. At age 5, she astounded her kindergarten teacher by bringing a

notebook computer to class—on which she was reading an encyclopedia. At 10, she breezed through an entire high school algebra course in 12 hours.

Billy A., who is 10 years old, can write his name and can count, but he has trouble with simple addition and subtraction problems and finds multiplication impossible. He has been held back in school twice and is still incapable of doing the work his 8-year-old classmates find easy.

Anne is considered a genius; Billy, a slow learner. There seems little doubt that they differ in intelligence.

Wait! Anne's ability is obvious, but how do we know that Billy isn't just lazy? This is the same question that Alfred Binet faced in 1904. The minister of education in Paris had asked Binet to find a way to distinguish slower students from the more capable (or the capable but lazy). In a flash of brilliance, Binet and an associate created a test made up of "intellectual" questions and problems. Next, they learned which questions an average child could answer at each age. By giving children the test, they could tell if a child was performing up to his or her potential (Kaufman, 2000).

Defining Intelligence

Is there an accepted definition of intelligence? In general, **intelligence** is the global capacity to act purposefully, to think rationally, and to deal effectively with the environment. Intelligence also involves abstract thinking, reasoning, problem-solving ability, a capacity to acquire knowledge, memory, and adaptation to one's surroundings (Snyderman & Rothman, 1987). Beyond this there is much disagreement. In fact, many psychologists simply accept an *operational definition* of intelligence. (A concept is defined operationally by specifying what procedures we will use to measure it.) Thus, by selecting test items, a psychologist is saying in a very direct way, "This is what I mean by intelligence." A test that measures memory, reasoning, and verbal fluency offers a very different definition of intelligence than one that measures strength of grip, shoe size, length of the nose, or the person's best *Super Mario Brothers* video game score.

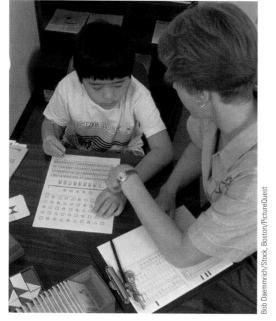
Bob Daemmrich/Stock, Boston/PictureQuest

Modern intelligence tests are widely used to measure intellectual abilities. When properly administered, such tests provide an operational definition of intelligence.

Intelligence Tests

American psychologists quickly saw the value of Alfred Binet's test. In 1916, Lewis Terman and others at Stanford University revised it for use in North America. After more revisions, the *Stanford-Binet Intelligence Scales, Fifth Edition,* continues to be widely used. The original Stanford-Binet assumed that a child's intellectual abilities improve with each passing year. Today, the Stanford-Binet (or SB5) is still primarily made up of age-ranked questions. Naturally, these questions get a little harder at each age level. The SB5 is appropriate for people from age 2 to 90 years, and test scores are very reliable (Roid, 2003).

The SB5 measures five cognitive factors (types of mental abilities) that make up general intelligence. These are *fluid reasoning, knowledge, quantitative reasoning, visual-spatial processing,* and *working memory.* Each factor is measured with verbal questions (those involving words and numbers) and non-verbal questions (items that use pictures and objects). Let's see what each factor looks like.

Fluid Reasoning
This factor tests reasoning ability with questions like the following:

How are an apple, a plum, and a banana different from a beet?
An apprentice is to a master as a novice is to an _____.
"I knew my bag was going to be in the last place I looked, so I looked there first."
    What is silly or impossible about that?

Intelligence An overall capacity to think rationally, act purposefully, and deal effectively with the environment.

Other items ask people to fill in the missing shape in a group of shapes, and to tell a story that explains what's going on in a series of pictures.

Knowledge

This factor assesses the person's knowledge about a wide range of topics.

> Why is yeast added to bread dough?
> What does cryptic mean?
> What is silly or impossible about this picture? (For example, a bicycle has square wheels.)

Quantitative Reasoning

Test items for this factor measure a person's ability to solve problems involving numbers. Here are some samples:

> If I have six marbles and you give me another one, how many marbles will I have?
> Given the numbers 3, 6, 9, 12, what number would come next?
> If a shirt is being sold for 50 percent of the normal price, and the price tag is $60, what is the cost of the shirt?

Visual-Spatial Processing

People who have visual-spatial skills are good at putting picture puzzles together and copying geometric shapes (such as triangles, rectangles, and circles). Other questions ask test takers to reproduce patterns of blocks and choose pictures that show how a piece of paper would look if it were folded or cut. Verbal questions can also require visual-spatial abilities:

> Suppose that you are going east, then turn right, then turn right again, then turn left. In what direction are you facing now?

Working Memory

This part of the SB5 measures the ability to use short-term memory. Some typical memory tasks include:

> Correctly remember the order of colored beads on a stick.
> After hearing several sentences, name the last word from each sentence.
> Repeat a series of digits (forward or backward) after hearing them once.
> After seeing several objects, point to them in the same order as they were presented.

> If you were to take the SB5, it would yield a score for general intelligence, verbal intelligence, non-verbal intelligence, and each of the five cognitive factors (Roid, 2003).

Intelligence Quotients

A child named Yuan can answer intelligence test questions that an average 7-year-old can answer. How smart is she? Actually, we can't say yet, because we don't know how old Yuan is. If she is 10, she's not very smart. If she's 5, she is very bright. Thus, to estimate Yuan's intelligence we need to know both her **chronological age** (age in years) and her **mental age** (actual intellectual performance).

Mental age is based on the level of age-ranked questions a person can answer. For example, at age 8 or 9, very few children can define the word *connection*. At age 10, 10 percent can. At age 13, 60 percent can. Thus, a 13-year-old of average ability can define *connection*. If we had only this one item to test children with, those who answered correctly would be given a mental age of 13. When scores from many such items are combined, a child's overall mental age can be found. ▲Table 8.2 is a sample of items that persons of average intelligence can answer at various ages.

Mental age is a good measure of actual ability. But mental age says nothing about whether your overall intelligence is high or low, compared with other people of the same age. To find out what a particular mental age means, we must also consider a person's

Chronological age A person's age in years.
Mental age The average mental ability people display at a given age.

▲TABLE 8.2	Sample Items from the Stanford-Binet Intelligence Scale
2 years old	On a large paper doll, points out the hair, mouth, feet, ears, nose, hands, and eyes.
	When shown a tower built of four blocks, builds one like it.
3 years old	When shown a bridge built of three blocks, builds one like it.
	When shown a drawing of a circle, copies it with a pencil.
4 years old	Fills in the missing word when asked, "Brother is a boy; sister is a _____."
	"In daytime it is light; at night it is _____."
	Answers correctly when asked, "Why do we have houses?" "Why do we have books?"
5 years old	Defines *ball, hat,* and *stove.*
	When shown a drawing of a square, copies it with a pencil.
9 years old	Answers correctly when examiner says, "In an old graveyard in Spain they have discovered a small skull which they believe to be that of Christopher Columbus when he was about 10 years old. What is foolish about that?"
	Answers correctly when asked, "Tell me the name of a color that rhymes with head." "Tell me a number that rhymes with tree."
Adult	Can describe the difference between laziness and idleness, poverty and misery, character and reputation.
	Answers correctly when asked, "Which direction would you have to face so your right hand would be toward the north?"

(Terman & Merill, 1960.)

David Horan/Index Stock Photography

✦FIGURE 8.20 *With a score of 230, Marilyn vos Savant has the highest IQ ever officially recorded. When she was only 7 years and 9 months old, vos Savant could answer questions that the average 13-year-old can answer. At ages 8, 9, and 10, she got perfect scores on the Stanford-Binet scale. Now in her 40s, she is capitalizing on her celebrity by giving lectures and writing books.*

Intelligence quotient (IQ) An index of intelligence defined as a person's mental age divided by his or her chronological age and multiplied by 100.

Deviation IQ An IQ obtained statistically from a person's relative standing in his or her age group; that is, how far above or below average the person's score was relative to other scores.

chronological age. Then we can relate mental age to actual age. This yields an **IQ,** or **intelligence quotient.** A quotient results from dividing one number into another. When the Stanford-Binet was first used, IQ was defined as mental age (MA) divided by chronological age (CA) and multiplied by 100. (Multiplying by 100 changes the IQ into a whole number, rather than a decimal.)

$$\frac{MA}{CA} \times 100 = IQ$$

An advantage of the original IQ is that intelligence could be compared among children with different chronological and mental ages. For instance, 10-year-old Justin has a mental age of 12. Thus, his IQ is 120:

$$\frac{(MA)\ 12}{(CA)\ 10} \times 100 = 120\ (IQ)$$

Justin's friend Suke also has a mental age of 12. However, Suke's chronological age is 12, so his IQ is 100:

$$\frac{(MA)\ 12}{(CA)\ 12} \times 100 = 100\ (IQ)$$

The IQ shows that 10-year-old Justin is brighter than his 12-year-old friend Suke, even though their intellectual skills are about the same. Notice that a person's IQ will be 100 when mental age equals chronological age. An IQ score of 100 is therefore defined as average intelligence.

Then does a person with an IQ score below 100 have below average intelligence? Not unless the IQ is well below 100. An IQ of 100 is the *mathematical* average (or mean) for such scores. However, average intelligence is usually defined as any score from 90 to 109. The important point is that IQ scores will be greater than 100 when mental age is higher than age in years (✦Fig. 8.20). IQ scores below 100 occur when a person's age in years exceeds his or her mental age. An example of the second situation would be a 15-year-old with an MA of 12:

$$\frac{12}{15} \times 100 = 80\ (IQ)$$

Deviation IQs

The preceding examples may give you insight into IQ scores. However, it's no longer necessary to directly calculate IQs. Instead, modern tests use **deviation IQs.** These scores are based on a person's relative standing in his or her age group. That is, they tell how far above or below average the person's score falls. (For more information, see the Statistics appendix

▲TABLE 8.3	Sample Items Similar to Those Used on the WAIS-III

VERBAL SUBTESTS	SAMPLE ITEMS
Information	How many wings does a bird have? Who wrote *Paradise Lost?*
Digit span	Repeat from memory a series of digits, such as 3 1 0 6 7 4 2 5, after hearing it once.
General Comprehension	What is the advantage of keeping money in the bank? Why is copper often used in electrical wires?
Arithmetic	Three men divided 18 golf balls equally among themselves. How many golf balls did each man receive? If 2 apples cost 15¢ what will be the cost of a dozen apples?
Similarities	In what way are a lion and a tiger alike? In what way are a saw and a hammer alike?
Vocabulary	The test consists simply of asking, "What is a _____?" or "What does _____ mean?" The words cover a wide range of difficulty or familiarity.

PERFORMANCE SUBTESTS	DESCRIPTION OF ITEM
Picture arrangement	Arrange a series of cartoon panels to make a meaningful story.
Picture completion	What is missing from these pictures?
Block design	Copy designs with blocks (as shown at right).
Object assembly	Put together a jigsaw puzzle.
Digit symbol	Fill in the symbols:

1	2	3	4
X	III	I	0

3	4	1	3	4	2	1	2

(Courtesy of The Psychological Corporation.)

near the end of this book.) Tables supplied with the test are then used to convert a person's relative standing in the group to an IQ score (Neisser et al., 1996). For example, if you score at the 50th percentile, half the people your age who take the test score higher than you and half score lower. In this case, your IQ score is 100. If you score at the 84th percentile, your IQ score is 115. If you score at the 97th percentile, your IQ score is 130.

The Wechsler Tests

Is the Stanford-Binet the only intelligence test? A widely used alternative is the *Wechsler Adult Intelligence Scale—Third Edition,* or WAIS-III. A version for children is called the *Wechsler Intelligence Scale for Children—Third Edition* (WISC-III).

The Wechsler tests are similar to the Stanford-Binet, but different in important ways. For one thing, the WAIS-III was specifically designed to test adult intelligence. The original Stanford-Binet was better suited for children and adolescents. The latest Stanford-Binet (the SB5) can now be used for all ages, but the WAIS was the first "adult" IQ test. Like the Stanford-Binet, the Wechsler tests yield a single overall IQ. In addition, the WAIS and WISC give separate scores for **performance** (non-verbal) **intelligence** and **verbal** (language- or symbol-oriented) **intelligence.** (Note that this feature was also recently added to the SB5.) The abilities measured by the Wechsler tests and some sample test items are listed in ▲Table 8.3.

Culture-Fair Tests

Intelligence tests may not be equally valid for all groups. As Jerome Kagan says, "If the Wechsler and Binet scales were translated into Spanish, Swahili, and Chinese and given to every 10-year-old in Latin America, East Africa, or China, the majority would obtain IQ scores in the mentally retarded range."

Performance intelligence Intelligence measured by solving puzzles, assembling objects, completing pictures, and other non-verbal tasks.

Verbal intelligence Intelligence measured by answering questions involving vocabulary, general information, arithmetic, and other language- or symbol-oriented tasks.

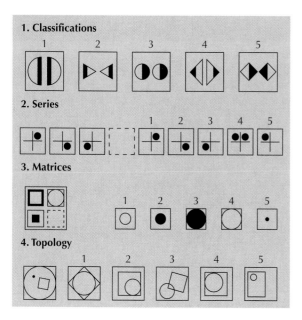

1. Classifications
2. Series
3. Matrices
4. Topology

◆FIGURE 8.21 *Sample items from a culture-fair test. 1. Which pattern is different from the remaining four? (Number 3.) 2. Which of the five figures on the right would properly continue the three on the left—that is, fill the blank? (Number 5.) 3. Which of the figures on the right should go in the square on the left to make it look right? (Number 2.) 4. At left, the dot is outside the square and inside the circle. In which of the figures on the right could you put a dot outside the square and inside the circle? (Number 3.) (Courtesy of R. B. Cattell.)*

Certainly, children of different cultures aren't all retarded. The fault must lie in tests that are designed for Western cultures (Neisser et al., 1996; Nixon, 1990). To avoid this problem, **culture-fair tests** attempt to measure intelligence without being affected by a person's verbal skills, cultural background, and educational level. (For a sample of culture-fair test items, see ◆Figure 8.21.) Culture-fair tests are also useful for testing children who come from poor communities, rural areas, or ethnic minority families (Stephens et al., 1999).

Group Tests

The SB5 and the Wechsler scales are **individual intelligence tests,** which must be given to a single person by a trained specialist. In contrast, **group intelligence tests** can be taken by large groups of people with minimal supervision. Group tests usually require people to solve problems of logic, reasoning, mathematics, or spatial skills. If you're wondering if you have ever taken an intelligence test, the answer is probably yes. The well-known *Scholastic Assessment Test* (SAT) measures aptitudes for language, math, and reasoning. The SAT is designed to predict your chances for success in college. Because it measures a variety of mental aptitudes, it can also be used to estimate general intelligence.

Variations in Intelligence

] SURVEYQUESTION *How do IQ scores relate to achievement and thinking ability?*

IQ scores are classified as shown in ▲Table 8.4. Notice that the distribution (or scattering) of IQ scores approximates a **normal** (bell-shaped) **curve.** That is, most scores fall close to the average and very few are found at the extremes. ◆Figure 8.22 shows this characteristic of measured intelligence.

▲*TABLE 8.4*	Distribution of Adult IQ Scores on WAIS-III	
IQ	**DESCRIPTION**	**PERCENT**
Above 130	Very superior	2.2
120–129	Superior	6.7
110–119	Bright normal	16.1
90–109	Average	50.0
80–89	Dull normal	16.1
70–79	Borderline	6.7
Below 70	Mentally retarded	2.2

Culture-fair test A test (such as an intelligence test) designed to minimize the importance of skills and knowledge that may be more common in some cultures than in others.

Individual intelligence test A test of intelligence designed to be given to a single individual by a trained specialist.

Group intelligence test Any intelligence test that can be administered to a group of people with minimal supervision.

Normal curve A bell-shaped curve characterized by a large number of scores in a middle area, tapering to very few extremely high and low scores.

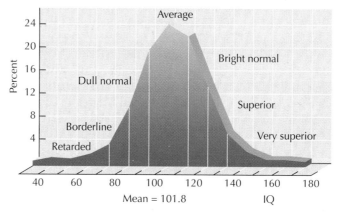

◆FIGURE 8.22 *Distribution of Stanford-Binet Intelligence Test scores for 3,184 children. (After Terman & Merrill, 1960.)*

IQ and Achievement

How do IQ scores relate to success in school, jobs, and other endeavors? The correlation between IQ scores and school grades is .50, a sizable association. The link would be even stronger, but motivation, special talents, off-campus learning, and many other factors also affect grades. The same is true of "real-world" achievements. IQ is not at all good at predicting success in art, music, writing, dramatics, science, and leadership. Creativity is much more strongly related to doing well in these areas (Neisser et al., 1996; Wallach, 1985).

Sex and Intelligence

On the average, do males and females differ in intelligence? IQ scores cannot answer this question because test items were selected to be equally difficult for both sexes. However, men and women do not differ in overall intelligence. Most male-female performance gaps can be traced to *social* differences in the opportunities given to men and women (Tavris, 1992).

When IQs are extreme—below 70 or above 140—differences in a person's potential for success become unmistakable. Only about 3 percent of all people are found in these ranges. Nevertheless, millions of people have exceptionally high or low IQs. Discussions of the mentally gifted and mentally retarded follow.

The Mentally Gifted

How high is the IQ of a genius? Only 2 people out of 100 score above 130 on IQ tests. These bright individuals are usually described as "gifted." Less than one-half of 1 percent of the population scores above 140. These people are certainly gifted or perhaps even "geniuses." However, some experts reserve the term *genius* for people with even higher IQs or those who are exceptionally creative (Kamphaus, 1993).

Gifted Children

Do high IQ scores in childhood predict later ability? To directly answer this question, Lewis Terman selected 1,500 children with IQs of 140 or more. Starting in the 1920s, Terman followed this gifted group (the "Termites" as he called them) into adulthood and found that most were quite successful. A majority finished college, earned advanced degrees, or held professional positions, and many had written books or scientific articles (Terman & Oden, 1959). As we have noted, IQ scores are not very good predictors of real-world success. However, when people score in the gifted range, their chances for high achievement do seem to rise (Shurkin, 1992).

Were all of the gifted children superior as adults? No. Some had committed crimes, were unemployable, or were emotionally troubled. Remember that a high IQ reveals *potential*. It does not guarantee success. Marilyn vos Savant, with an IQ of 230, has contributed little to science, literature, or art. Nobel prize–winning physicist Richard Feynman, whom many regarded as a genius, had an IQ of 122 (Michalko, 1998).

How did Terman's more successful subjects differ from the less successful? Most of them had educated parents who taught them to value learning. They also had *intellectual determination,* which is a desire to know, to excel, and to persevere (Tomlinson-Keasey & Little, 1990). Thus, successful gifted persons tend to be persistent and motivated to learn. As one educator put it, "No one is paid to sit around being capable of achievement—what you do is always more important than what you should be able to do" (Whimbey, 1980). A lot of people with high IQs have accomplished very little. Actually, talents of all kinds are most likely to blossom when they are combined with support, encouragement, education, and effort (Freeman, 1995).

Identifying Gifted Children

How might a parent spot an unusually bright child? Early signs of giftedness are not always purely "intellectual." **Giftedness** can be either a high IQ or having special talents or aptitudes. The following signs may reveal that a child is gifted: a tendency to seek out older children and adults; an early fascination with explanations and problem solving; talking in complete sen-

Giftedness Either the possession of a high IQ or special talents or aptitudes.

Dan McCoy/Rainbow

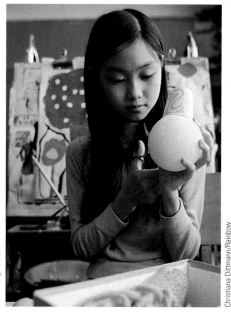

Christiana Dittmann/Rainbow

It is wise to remember that there are many ways in which a child may be gifted. Many schools now offer Gifted and Talented Education programs for students with a variety of special abilities—not just for those who score well on IQ tests.

tences as early as 2 or 3 years of age; an unusually good memory; precocious talent in art, music, or number skills; an early interest in books, early reading (often by age 3); showing of kindness, understanding, and cooperation toward others (Alvino, 1996).

Notice that this list goes beyond straight "academic" intelligence. In fact, if artistic talent, mechanical aptitude, musical aptitude, athletic potential, and so on were considered, 19 out of 20 children could be labeled as having a special "gift" of some sort. Limiting giftedness to high IQ can shortchange children with special talents (see "Frames of Mind—Eight Intelligences?"). This is especially true of ethnic minority children, who may be the victims of subtle biases in standardized intelligence tests. These children, as well as children with disabilities, are less likely to be recognized as gifted (Robinson & Clinkenbeard, 1998).

Mental Retardation

Mental retardation The presence of a developmental disability, a formal IQ score below 70, or a significant impairment of adaptive behavior.

A person with mental abilities far below average is **mentally retarded** or **developmentally disabled.** Retardation begins at an IQ of approximately 70 or below. However, a person's ability to perform *adaptive behaviors* (basic skills such as dressing, eating, communicating, shop-

USING PSYCHOLOGY Frames of Mind—Eight Intelligences?

At an elementary school, a student who is two grades behind in reading shows his teacher how to solve a difficult computer software problem. In a nearby room, one of his classmates, who is poor in math, plays intricate music on a piano. Both of these children show clear signs of intelligence. And yet, each might score below average on a traditional IQ test. Such observations have convinced many psychologists that it is time to define intelligence more broadly. Their basic goal is to better predict real-world success—not just the likelihood of success in school (Sternberg, 1996).

One such psychologist is Howard Gardner of Harvard University. Gardner (1993) theorizes that there are actually eight different kinds of intelligence. These are different mental "languages" that people use for thinking. Each is listed below, with examples of pursuits that make use of them.

1. *language* (linguistic abilities)—writer, lawyer, comedian
2. *logic and math* (numeric abilities)—scientist, accountant, programmer
3. *visual and spatial thinking* (pictorial abilities)—engineer, inventor, artist
4. *music* (musical abilities)—composer, musician, music critic
5. *bodily-kinesthetic skills* (physical abilities)—dancer, athlete, surgeon

6. *intrapersonal skills* (self-knowledge)—poet, actor, minister
7. *interpersonal skills* (social abilities)—psychologist, teacher, politician
8. *naturalist skills* (an ability to understand the natural environment)—biologist, medicine man, organic farmer

To simplify greatly, people can be "word smart," "number smart," "picture smart," "musically smart," "body smart," "self smart," "people smart," and "nature smart." Most of us are probably strong in only a few types of intelligence. In contrast, geniuses like Albert Einstein seem to be able to use all of the intelligences to solve problems.

If Gardner's theory of *multiple intelligences* is correct, traditional IQ tests measure only a part of real-world intelligence—namely, linguistic, logical-mathematical, and spatial abilities. A further implication is that our schools may be wasting a lot of human potential. For example, some children might find it easier to learn math or reading if these topics were tied into art, music, dance, drama, and so on.

Not all psychologists agree with Gardner's broader definition of intelligence. But whether or not he is right, it seems likely that in the future intelligence will not be so strongly equated with IQ. Already, many schools are using Gardner's theory to cultivate a wider range of skills and talents.

▲TABLE 8.5	Levels of Mental Retardation		
IQ RANGE	DEGREE OF RETARDATION	EDUCATIONAL CLASSIFICATION	REQUIRED LEVEL OF SUPPORT
50–55 to 70	Mild	Educable	Intermittent
35–40 to 50–55	Moderate	Trainable	Limited
20–25 to 35–40	Severe	Dependent	Extensive
Below 20–25	Profound	Life support	Pervasive

(DSM-IV-TR, 2000; Hodapp, 1994.)

ping, and working) also figures into evaluating retardation (DSM-IV-TR, 2000; Kamphaus, 1993) (see ▲Table 8.5).

It's important to realize that developmentally disabled persons have no handicap where feelings are concerned. They are easily hurt by rejection, teasing, or ridicule. Likewise, they respond warmly to love and acceptance. Mentally retarded persons have a right to self-respect and a place in the community. This is especially important during childhood, when support from others adds greatly to the person's chances of becoming a well-adjusted member of society.

Causes of Retardation

What causes mental retardation?   About half of all cases of mental retardation are *organic,* or related to physical disorders. Typical problems include birth injuries (such as a lack of oxygen) and fetal damage (from disease, infection, or the mother's abuse of drugs or alcohol). Metabolic disorders also cause retardation. These are problems with the rate of energy production and use in the body. Some forms of retardation are linked to genetic abnormalities, including missing genes, extra genes, or defective genes. Malnutrition and exposure to lead, PCBs, and other toxins early in childhood can also cause organic retardation (Bryant & Maxwell, 1999).

In 30 to 40 percent of cases, no known biological problem can be identified. In many such instances, retardation is mild, in the 50 to 70 IQ range. Quite often, other family members are also mildly retarded. *Familial retardation,* as this is called, occurs mostly in very poor households. In some of these homes, nutrition, medical care, intellectual stimulation, and emotional support are inadequate. This suggests that familial retardation is based largely on an impoverished environment. Thus, many cases of retardation might be prevented by better nutrition, education, and early childhood enrichment programs (Hunt, 1995; Zigler, 1995).

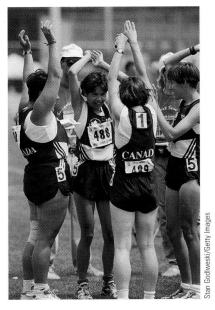

These youngsters are participants in the Special Olympics—an athletic event for the mentally retarded. It is often said of the Special Olympics that "everyone is a winner—participants, coaches, and spectators."

Heredity, Environment, and Intelligence

Is intelligence inherited?   Most people are aware that there is a moderate similarity in the intelligence of parents and their children, or between brothers and sisters. As ✦Figure 8.23 shows, the similarity in IQ scores among relatives grows in proportion to how close they are on the family tree.

Does that indicate that intelligence is hereditary?   Not necessarily. Brothers, sisters, and parents share similar environments as well as similar heredity. To separate nature and nurture, **twin studies** may be done. Such studies compare the IQs of twins who were raised together or separated at birth. This allows us to estimate how much heredity and environment affect intelligence.

Twin Studies

Notice in Figure 8.23 that the IQs of fraternal twins are more alike than the IQs of ordinary siblings. Fraternal twins come from two separate eggs fertilized at the same time. Genetically, they are no more alike than ordinary siblings. Why, then, should the twins' IQs be more similar? The reason is environmental: Parents treat twins more alike than ordinary siblings, resulting in a closer match in IQs.

Twin study A comparison of the characteristics of twins who were raised together or separated at birth; used to identify the relative impact of heredity and environment.

◆FIGURE 8.23 *Approximate correlations between IQ scores for persons with varying degrees of genetic and environmental similarity. Notice that the correlations grow smaller as the degree of genetic similarity declines. Also note that a shared environment increases the correlation in all cases. (Estimates from Bouchard, 1983; Henderson, 1982.)*

Identical twins, who develop from a single egg and have identical genes, are even more alike. At the top of Figure 8.23 you can see that identical twins who grow up in the same family have highly correlated IQs. This is what we would expect with identical heredity and very similar environments. Now, let's consider what happens when identical twins are reared apart. As you can see, the correlation drops, but only from .86 to .72. Psychologists who emphasize genetics believe these figures show that adult intelligence is roughly 50 percent hereditary (Casto, DeFries, & Fulker, 1995; Neisser et al., 1996; Plomin & Rende, 1991).

How do environmentalists interpret the figures? They point out that the IQs of some separated twins differ by as much as 20 points. Such IQ gaps occur when the twins grow up with big educational and environmental differences. It is more common for separated twins to be placed in homes socially and educationally similar to their biological parents. This fact would tend to inflate apparent genetic effects by making the separated twins' IQs more alike. Another frequently overlooked fact is that twins grow up in the same environment *before birth* (in the womb). If we take such environmental similarities into account, intelligence would seem to be less than 50 percent hereditary (Devlin, Daniels, & Roeder, 1997).

◆FIGURE 8.24 *Comparison of an adopted child and a biological child reared in the same family. (After Kamin, 1981.)*

Environmental Influences

Strong evidence concerning the impact of environment on intelligence comes from families that have one adopted child and one biological child. As ◆Figure 8.24 shows, parents contribute genes *and* environment to their biological child. With an adopted child, they contribute only environment. If intelligence is highly genetic, the IQs of biological children should be more like their parents' IQs than are the IQs of adopted children. However, children reared by the same mother tend to resemble her IQ to the same degree. It does not matter whether or not they share her genes (Horn et al., 1979; Kamin, 1981; Weinberg, 1989). (Also see "The Bell Curve: Race, Culture, and IQ.")

HUMAN DIVERSITY The Bell Curve: Race, Culture, and IQ

African-American children in the United States score an average of about 15 points lower on standardized IQ tests than white children. As a group, Japanese-American children score above average in IQ. Could such differences be genetic?

In 1994, Richard Herrnstein and Charles Murray, in a highly controversial book titled *The Bell Curve*, proclaimed that IQ is largely dictated by heredity (Herrnstein & Murray, 1994).

Were they right? Are ethnic group differences in IQ based on genetics? No. Herrnstein and Murray misused statistics and ignored the effects of culture and environment. For example, as a group, African Americans in the United States are more likely to live in environments that are educationally disadvantaged. Japanese-American culture, on the other hand, tends to place a high value on educational achievement. Such differences can significantly af-

fect how people score on IQ tests. When unequal education is part of the equation, IQs tell us little about how heredity affects intelligence (Neisser et al., 1996).

A distinguished group of psychologists evaluated the claims made in *The Bell Curve*. There is no scientific evidence, they concluded, that group differences in average IQ are based on genetics. In fact, studies that used actual blood-group testing found no significant correlations between ethnic ancestry and IQ scores. The conclusions that Herrnstein and Murray drew in *The Bell Curve* reflect their political beliefs and biases, not scientific facts. Group differences in IQ scores are based on cultural and environmental differences, not on heredity (Alva, 1993; Caplan et al., 1992; Neisser et al., 1996; Yee et al., 1993).

IQ and Environment

How much can environment alter intelligence?   In one study, striking increases in IQ occurred in 25 children who were moved from an orphanage to more stimulating environments. The children, all considered mentally retarded, were moved to a setting where they received personal attention from adults. Later, these supposedly retarded children were adopted by parents who gave them love, a family, and a stimulating environment. The children's IQs gained an average of 29 points. For one child, the increase was an amazing 58 points. A second group of initially less "retarded" children who remained in the orphanage *lost* an average of 26 IQ points (Skeels, 1966)! Another study found that average IQs have gone up 15 points in 14 nations during the last 30 years (Flynn, 1987; Horgan, 1995). These IQ boosts seem to reflect improved education or other advantages. In fact, the longer children stay in school, the more their IQ scores rise (Perkins, 1995). This is another encouraging sign that intelligence can be raised by an improved environment and by learning how to think more clearly (Kozulin, 1999; Skuy et al., 2002; Tzuriel & Shamir, 2002).

Summary

To sum up, both heredity and environment affect intelligence. Estimates of the impact of each factor continue to vary. But ultimately, most experts agree that improving social conditions and education can raise intelligence. There is probably no limit to how far *down* intelligence can go in an extremely poor environment. On the other hand, heredity does seem to impose upper limits on IQ, even under ideal conditions. It is telling, nevertheless, that gifted children tend to have parents who spend time with them, answer their questions, and encourage intellectual curiosity (Snowden & Christian, 1999). The fact that intelligence is partly determined by heredity tells us little of any real value. Genes are fixed at birth. Improving the environments in which children learn and grow is the main way in which we can assure that they reach their full potential (Turkheimer, 1998).

As a final summary, it might help to think of inherited intellectual potential as a rubber band that is stretched by outside forces. A long rubber band may be stretched more easily, but a shorter one can be stretched to the same length if enough force is applied. In the final analysis, intelligence reflects development as well as potential, nurture as well as nature (Rose, 1995; Weinberg, 1989).

STUDYBREAK **Y** *Intelligence*

RELATE

If you were going to write an intelligence test, what kinds of questions would you include? How much would they resemble the questions found on the SB5, the WAIS-III, or culture-fair tests?

How has your understanding of the following concepts changed: IQ, giftedness, mental retardation?

A friend says to you, "I think intelligence is entirely inherited from parents." What could you tell your friend to make sure she or he is better informed?

LEARNING CHECK

1. The first successful intelligence test was developed by

   _____.

2. If we define intelligence by writing a test, we are using an _____ definition.

3. IQ was originally defined as _____ × 100.

4. The WAIS-III is a group intelligence test. T or F?

5. The distribution of IQs approximates a _____ (bell-shaped) curve.

6. Only about 6 percent of the population scores above 140 on IQ tests. T or F?

7. Many cases of mental retardation without known organic causes appear to be _____.

8. Most psychologists believe that intelligence is 90 percent hereditary. T or F?

Critical Thinking

9. How rare are high IQ scores? If you were to meet 50 people at random, how many would you expect to have an IQ score above 130 (based on Table 8.4)?

10. Some people treat IQ as if it were a fixed number, permanently stamped on the forehead of each child. Why is this view in error?

ANSWERS
1. Alfred Binet 2. operational 3. MA/CA 4. F 5. normal 6. F 7. familial 8. F 9. Approximately 1 person in 50 or 2 out of 100. 10. Because one's IQ depends on the intelligence test used to measure it: Change the test, and you will change the score. Also, heredity establishes a range of possibilities; it does not automatically preordain a person's intellectual capacities.

CREATIVE THINKING—DOWN ROADS LESS TRAVELED

] SURVEYQUESTION *What is creative thinking?*

Original ideas have changed the course of human history. Much of what we now take for granted in art, medicine, music, technology, and science was once regarded as radical or impossible. How do creative thinkers achieve the breakthroughs that carry us into new realms? Creativity is elusive. Nevertheless, psychologists have learned a great deal about how creativity occurs and how to promote it.

We have seen that problem solving may be mechanical, insightful, or based on understanding. To this we can add that thinking may be **inductive** (going from specific facts or observations to general principles) or **deductive** (going from general principles to specific situations). Thinking may also be **logical** (proceeding from given information to new conclusions on the basis of explicit rules) or **illogical** (intuitive, associative, or personal).

What distinguishes creative thinking from more routine problem solving? Creative thinking involves all of these thinking styles, plus *fluency, flexibility,* and *originality.* Let's say that you would like to find creative uses for the millions of automobile tires discarded each year. The creativity of your suggestions could be rated in this way: **Fluency** is defined as the total number of suggestions you are able to make. **Flexibility** is the number of times you shift from one class of possible uses to another. **Originality** refers to how novel or unusual your ideas are. By counting the number of times you showed fluency, flexibility, and originality, we could rate your creativity, or capacity for *divergent thinking* (Baer, 1993).

In routine problem solving or thinking, there is one correct answer, and the problem is to find it. This leads to **convergent thinking** (lines of thought converge on the answer). **Divergent thinking** is the reverse, in which many possibilities are developed from one starting point (Baer, 1993). (See ▲Table 8.6 for some examples.) Rather than repeating learned solutions, creative thinking produces new answers, ideas, or patterns (Michalko, 1998).

Fluency is an important part of creative thinking. Mozart produced more than 600 pieces of music. Picasso (shown here) created more than 20,000 artworks. Shakespeare wrote 154 sonnets. Not all of these works were masterpieces. However, a fluent outpouring of ideas fed the creative efforts of each of these geniuses.

The first paper clip was patented in 1899. Competition for sales, combined with divergent thinking, has resulted in a remarkable array of alternative designs. These are drawings of just a few of the variations that have appeared over the years. (After Kim, 2000.)

Inductive thought Thinking in which a general rule or principle is gathered from a series of specific examples; for instance, inferring the laws of gravity by observing many falling objects.

Deductive thought Thought that applies a general set of rules to specific situations; for example, using the laws of gravity to predict the behavior of a single falling object.

Logical thought Drawing conclusions on the basis of formal principles of reasoning.

Illogical thought Thought that is intuitive, haphazard, or irrational.

Fluency In tests of creativity, fluency refers to the total number of solutions produced.

Flexibility In tests of creativity, flexibility is indicated by the number of different types of solutions produced.

Originality In tests of creativity, originality refers to how novel or unusual solutions are.

Convergent thinking Thinking directed toward discovery of a single established correct answer; conventional thinking.

Divergent thinking Thinking that produces many ideas or alternatives; a major element in original or creative thought.

▲TABLE 8.6	Convergent and Divergent Problems

CONVERGENT PROBLEMS

- What is the area of a triangle that is 3 feet wide at the base and 2 feet tall?
- Erica is shorter than Zoey but taller than Carlo, and Carlo is taller than Jared. Who is the second tallest?
- If you simultaneously drop a baseball and a bowling ball from a tall building, which will hit the ground first?

DIVERGENT PROBLEMS

- What objects can you think of that begin with the letters BR?
- How could discarded aluminum cans be put to use?
- Write a poem about fire and ice.

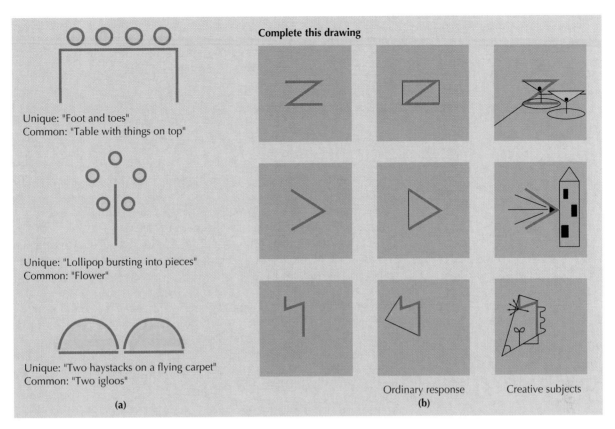

Complete this drawing

Unique: "Foot and toes"
Common: "Table with things on top"

Unique: "Lollipop bursting into pieces"
Common: "Flower"

Unique: "Two haystacks on a flying carpet"
Common: "Two igloos"

(a)

Ordinary response   Creative subjects

(b)

◆**FIGURE 8.25** *Some tests of divergent thinking. Creative responses are more original and more complex. [*(a) *adapted from Wallach & Kogan, 1965;* (b) *adapted from Barron, 1958.]*

Tests of Creativity

There are several ways to measure divergent thinking. In the *Unusual Uses Test,* you would be asked to think of as many uses as possible for some object, such as the tires mentioned earlier. In the *Consequences Test,* you would list the consequences that would follow a basic change in the world. For example, you might be asked "What would happen if everyone suddenly lost the sense of balance and could no longer stay upright?" People try to list as many reactions as possible. If you were to take the *Anagrams Test,* you would be given a word such as *creativity* and asked to make as many new words as possible by rearranging the letters. Each of these tests can be scored for fluency, flexibility, and originality. (For an example of other tests of divergent thinking, see ◆Figure 8.25.) Tests of divergent thinking seem to tap something quite different from intelligence. Generally, there is little correlation between creativity tests and IQ test scores (Wallach, 1985).

Creativity tests have been useful, but they are not the whole story. If you want to predict whether a person will be creative in the future, it helps to look at two more kinds of information (Feldhusen & Goh, 1995):

- The *products* of creative thinking (such as essays, poems, drawings, or constructed objects) are often more informative than test results. When creative people are asked to actually produce something, others tend to judge their work as creative. (The Rube Goldberg machines described earlier are a good example.)
- A simple listing of a person's *past creative activities and achievements* is an excellent guide to the likelihood that she or he will be creative in the future.

Isn't creativity more than divergent thought? What if a person comes up with a large number of useless answers to a problem? A good question. Divergent thinking is an important part of creativity, but there is more to it. To be creative, the solution to a problem must be

Hat-tipping device. According to the patent, it is for "automatically effecting polite salutations by the elevation and rotation of the hat on the head of the saluting party when said person bows to the person or persons saluted." In addition to being original or novel, a creative solution must fit the demands of the problem. Is this a creative solution to the "problem" of hat tipping?

more than novel, unusual, or original. It must also be *practical* if it is an invention and *sensible* if it is an idea. This is the dividing line between a "harebrained scheme" and a "stroke of genius." In other words, the creative person brings reasoning and critical thinking to bear on new ideas once they are produced (Feldhusen, 1995).

Stages of Creative Thought

Is there any pattern to creative thinking?   Typically, five stages occur during creative problem solving:

1. **Orientation.** As a first step, the person defines the problem and identifies its most important dimensions.
2. **Preparation.** In the second stage, creative thinkers saturate themselves with as much information about the problem as possible.
3. **Incubation.** Most major problems produce a period during which all attempted solutions will be futile. At this point, problem solving may proceed on a subconscious level: While the problem seems to have been set aside, it is still "cooking" in the background.
4. **Illumination.** The stage of incubation is often ended by a rapid insight or series of insights. These produce the "Aha!" experience, often depicted in cartoons as a lightbulb appearing over the thinker's head.
5. **Verification.** The final step is to test and critically evaluate the solution obtained during the stage of illumination. If the solution proves faulty, the thinker reverts to the stage of incubation.

Of course, creative thought is not always so neat. Nevertheless, the stages listed are a good summary of the most typical sequence of events.

You may find it helpful to relate the stages to the following more or less true story. Legend has it that the king of Syracuse (a city in ancient Greece) once suspected that his goldsmith had substituted cheaper metals for some of the gold in a crown and kept the extra gold. Archimedes, a famous mathematician and thinker, was given the problem of discovering whether the king had been cheated.

Archimedes began by defining the problem *(orientation):* "How can I tell what metals have been used in the crown without damaging it?" He then checked all known methods of analyzing metals *(preparation).* All involved cutting or melting the crown, so he was forced to temporarily set the problem aside *(incubation).* Then one day as he stepped into his bath, Archimedes suddenly knew he had the solution *(illumination).* He was so excited he is said to have run naked through the streets shouting, "Eureka, eureka!" (I have found it, I have found it!).

On observing his own body floating in the bath, Archimedes realized that different metals of equal weight would displace different amounts of water. A pound of brass, for example, occupies more space than a pound of gold, which is denser. All that remained was to test the solution *(verification).* Archimedes placed an amount of gold (equal in weight to that given the goldsmith) in a tub of water. He marked the water level and removed the gold. He then placed the crown in the water. Was the crown pure gold? If it was, it would raise the water to exactly the same level. Unfortunately, the purity of the crown and the fate of the goldsmith are to this day unknown!

The preceding account is a good general description of creative thinking. However, creative thinking can be highly complex. Some authors believe that truly exceptional creativity requires a rare combination of thinking skills, personality, and a supportive social environment. This mix, they believe, accounts for creative giants such as Edison, Freud, Mozart, Picasso, Tolstoy, and others (Tardif & Sternberg, 1988).

The Creative Personality

What makes a person creative?   According to the popular stereotype, highly creative people are eccentric, introverted, neurotic, socially inept, unbalanced in their interests, and on the edge of madness. Although some artists and musicians cultivate this public

CLINICAL FILE Madness and Creativity

You've probably heard that "genius is next to insanity." Is there really any link between madness and creativity? Generally, the answer is no. The vast majority of creative people do not suffer from mental disorders. (The jury is out on Ozzy Osbourne, however.) And, most people who are mentally ill are not especially creative (Ghadirian, Gregoire, & Kosmidis, 2001).

A notable exception to the preceding conclusion concerns mood disorders. A person with a mood disorder may be manic (agitated, elated, and hyperactive), depressed, or both. (See Chapter 12 for more information.) Many of history's renowned artists, writers, poets, and composers apparently suffered from mood disorders (Jamison, 1999). For example, the composer Robert Schumann wrote most of his music during several "high" periods when he was mildly manic. When he was depressed, his output plunged. Similar patterns marked the work of Vincent van Gogh, Edgar Allan Poe,

Emily Dickinson, Ernest Hemmingway, and many others (Jamison, 1999; McDermott, 2001).

The connection between mood swings and creativity may be mainly a matter of productivity. It's easy to understand why creative persons would more actively paint, write, or compose when they are manic and have boundless energy. Also, people who are manic tend to have illogical thoughts. Such thinking can enhance creativity by promoting unusual connections among ideas (Anderegg & Gartner, 2001).

Again, it is important to emphasize that most creative people are not mentally disturbed, and most mentally disturbed people are not creative. Nevertheless, a few talented (and often miserable) individuals do appear to ride an emotional roller coaster to highs and lows of creativity (Kaufman, 2001).

image, there is little truth in it. Direct studies of creative individuals paint a very different picture. (However, read "Madness and Creativity" to learn about an important exception.)

1. For people of normal intelligence, there is a small positive correlation between creativity and IQ. In other words, smarter people have a slight tendency to be more creative. But, for the most part, at any given level of IQ, some people are creative and some are not. An average IQ is 100. The average college graduate has an IQ of 120. This is more than high enough to allow a person to write novels, do scientific research, or pursue other creative work (Finke, 1990). IQs above 120 do not seem to add anything more to creative ability (Sternberg & Lubart, 1995).

2. Creative people usually have a greater-than-average range of knowledge and interests, and they are more fluent in combining ideas from various sources. They are also good at using mental images and metaphors in thinking (Riquelme, 2002).

3. Creative people are open to a wide variety of experiences. They accept irrational thoughts and are uninhibited about their feelings and fantasies (McCrae, 1987). They tend to use broad categories, to question assumptions, to break mental sets, and they find order in chaos. They also experience more unusual states of consciousness, such as vivid dreams and mystical experiences (Ayers, Beaton, & Hunt, 1999).

4. Creative people enjoy symbolic thought, ideas, concepts, and possibilities. They tend to be interested in truth, form, and beauty, rather than in fame or success. Their creative work is an end in itself (Sternberg & Lubart, 1995).

5. Highly creative people value their independence and prefer complexity. However, they are unconventional and nonconforming primarily in their work; otherwise they do not have unusual, outlandish, or bizarre personalities.

Could Steven Spielberg manage the Yankees? Probably not. It is widely accepted that people tend to be creative in particular skills or pursuits. For example, a person who is a creative writer might be an uncreative artist or businessperson. Perhaps this is because creativity favors a prepared mind. Those who are creative in a particular field often build on a large store of existing knowledge (Kaufman & Baer, 2002). Yoshiro NakaMats, a Japanese inventor who holds more than 2,000 patents, sees such preparation as a way to gain the freedom to think creatively.

Can creativity be learned?   It is beginning to look as if some creative thinking skills can be taught. In particular, you can become more creative by practicing divergent thinking and by taking risks, analyzing ideas, and seeking unusual connections between ideas (Baer, 1993; Sternberg, 2001).

INTUITIVE THOUGHT—MENTAL SHORTCUT? OR DANGEROUS DETOUR?

] SURVEYQUESTION *How accurate is intuition?*

At the same time that irrational, intuitive thought may contribute to creative problem solving, it can also lead to thinking errors. To see how this can happen, try the following problems.

> *Problem 1* An epidemic breaks out, and 600 people are about to die. Doctors have two choices. If they give drug A, 200 lives will be saved. If they give drug B, there is a one-third chance that 600 people will be saved, and a two-thirds chance that none will be saved. Which drug should they choose?

> *Problem 2* Again, 600 people are about to die, and doctors must make a choice. If they give drug A, 400 people will die. If they give drug B, there is a one-third chance that no one will die, and a two-thirds chance that 600 will die. Which drug should they choose?

Most people choose drug A for the first problem and drug B for the second. This is fascinating because the two problems are identical. The only difference is that the first is stated in terms of lives saved, the second in terms of lives lost. Yet, even people who realize that their answers are contradictory find it difficult to change them (Kahneman & Tversky, 1972, 1973).

Intuition

As the example shows, we often make decisions intuitively, rather than logically or rationally. **Intuition** is quick, impulsive thought. It may provide fast answers, but it can also be misleading and sometimes disastrous. Two noted psychologists, Daniel Kahneman (KON-eh-man) and Amos Tversky (tuh-VER-ski) (1937–1996), have studied how we make decisions in the face of uncertainty. They have found that human judgment is often seriously flawed (Kahneman et al., 1982). Let's explore some common intuitive thinking errors, so you will be better prepared to avoid them.

Representativeness

One very common pitfall in judgment is illustrated by the question, Which is more probable?

> A. Venus Williams will lose the first set of a tennis match but win the match.
> B. Venus Williams will lose the first set.

Tversky and Kahneman (1982) found that most people regard statements like A as more probable than B. However, this intuitive answer overlooks an important fact: The likelihood of two events occurring together is lower than the probability of either one alone. (For example, the probability of getting one head when flipping a coin is one half, or .5. The probability of getting two heads when flipping two coins is one fourth, or .25.) Therefore, A is less likely to be true than B.

According to Tversky and Kahneman, such faulty conclusions are based on the **representativeness heuristic.** That is, we tend to give a choice greater weight if it seems to be representative of what we already know. Thus, you probably compared the information about Venus Williams with your mental model of what a tennis pro's behavior should be like. Answer A seems to better represent the model. Therefore, it seems more likely than answer B, even though it isn't. In courtrooms, jurors are more likely to think a defendant is guilty if the person appears to fit the profile of a person likely to commit a crime (Davis & Follette, 2002). For example, a young single male from a poor neighborhood would be more likely to be judged guilty of theft than a middle-aged married father from an affluent suburb.

Intuition Quick, impulsive thought that does not make use of formal logic or clear reasoning.

Representativeness heuristic A tendency to select wrong answers because they seem to match pre-existing mental categories.

Underlying Odds

A second common error involves ignoring the **base rate,** or underlying probability of an event. In one experiment, subjects were told they would receive descriptions of 100 people—70 lawyers and 30 engineers. Subjects were then asked to guess, without knowing anything about a person, whether she or he was an engineer or a lawyer. All correctly stated the probabilities as 70 percent for lawyer and 30 percent for engineer. Participants were then given this description:

> Dick is a 30-year-old man. He is married with no children. A man of high ability and high motivation, he promises to be quite successful in his field. He is well liked by his colleagues.

Notice that the description gives no new information about Dick's occupation. He could still be either an engineer or a lawyer. Therefore, the odds should again be estimated as 70–30. However, most people changed the odds to 50–50. Intuitively it seems that Dick has an equal chance of being either an engineer or a lawyer. But this guess completely ignores the underlying odds.

Perhaps it is fortunate that we do at times ignore underlying odds. Were this not the case, how many people would get married when the divorce rate is 50 percent? Or how many would start high-risk businesses? On the other hand, people who smoke, drink and then drive, or skip wearing auto seat belts ignore rather high odds of injury or illness. In many high-risk situations, ignoring base rates is the same as thinking you are an exception to the rule.

Framing

The most general conclusion about intuition is that the way a problem is stated, or **framed,** affects decisions (Tversky & Kahneman, 1981). As the first example in this discussion revealed, people often give different answers to the same problem if it is stated in slightly different ways. To gain some added insight into framing, try another thinking problem:

> A couple are divorcing. Both parents seek custody of their only child, but custody can be granted to just one parent. If you had to make a decision based on the following information, to which parent would you award custody of the child?

> **Parent A:** average income, average health, average working hours, reasonable rapport with the child, relatively stable social life.

> **Parent B:** above-average income, minor health problems, lots of work-related travel, very close relationship with the child, extremely active social life.

Most people choose to award custody to Parent B, the parent who has some drawbacks but also several advantages (such as above-average income). That's because people tend to look for *positive qualities* that can be *awarded* to the child. However, how would you choose if you were asked this question: Which parent should be denied custody? In this case, most people choose to deny custody to Parent B. Why is Parent B a good choice one moment and a poor choice the next? It's because the second question asked who should be *denied* custody. To answer this question, people tend to look for *negative qualities* that would *disqualify* a parent. As you can see, the way a question is framed can channel us down a narrow path so we attend to only part of the information provided, rather than weighing all the pros and cons (Shafir, 1993).

Usually, the *broadest* way of framing or stating a problem produces the best decisions. However, people often state problems in increasingly narrow terms until a single, seemingly "obvious" answer emerges. For example, to select a career, it would be wise to consider pay, working conditions, job satisfaction, needed skills, future employment outlook, and many other factors. Instead, such decisions are often narrowed to thoughts such as, "I like to write, so I'll be a journalist," "I want to make good money, and law pays well," or "I can be creative in photography." Framing decisions so narrowly greatly increases the risk of making a poor choice. If you would like to think more critically and analytically, it is important to pay attention to how you are defining problems before you try to solve them. Remember, short-cuts to answers often short-circuit clear thinking.

Base rate The basic rate at which an event occurs over time; the basic probability of an event.

Framing In thought, the terms in which a problem is stated or the way that it is structured.

page/image shows text

Wisdom

People can be intelligent without being wise. For example, a person who does well in school and on IQ tests may make a total mess of her life. Likewise, people can be intelligent without being creative, and clear, rational thinking can lead to correct, but uninspired, answers (Sternberg, 2001). In many areas of human life, wisdom represents a mixture of convergent thinking, intelligence, and reason, spiced with creativity and originality. People who are wise approach life with openness and tolerance (Helson & Srivastava, 2002).

STUDYBREAK *Creative Thinking and Intuition*

RELATE

Make up a question that would require convergent thinking to answer. Now do the same for divergent thinking.

Which of the tests of creativity described in the text do you think you would do best on? (Look back if you can't remember them all.)

To better remember the stages of creative thinking, make up a short story that includes these words: *orient, prepare, in Cuba, illuminate, verify*.

Explain in your own words how representativeness and base rates contribute to thinking errors.

LEARNING CHECK

1. Fluency, flexibility, and originality are characteristics of
   a. convergent thought   b. deductive thinking   c. creative thought   d. trial-and-error solutions
2. List the typical stages of creative thinking in the correct order.
   _____ _____ _____
   _____ _____

3. Reasoning and critical thinking tend to block creativity; these are non-creative qualities. T or F?
4. To be creative, an original idea must also be practical or feasible. T or F?
5. Intelligence and creativity are highly correlated; the higher a person's IQ, the more likely he or she is to be creative. T or F?
6. Kate is single, outspoken, and very bright. As a college student, she was deeply concerned with discrimination and other social issues and participated in several protests. Which statement is more likely to be true?
   a. Kate is a bank teller.   b. Kate is a bank teller and a feminist.

Critical Thinking

7. A coin is flipped four times with one of the following results: *(a)* H T T H, *(b)* T T T T, *(c)* H H H H, *(d)* H H T H. Which sequence would most likely precede getting a head on the fifth coin flip?

ANSWERS

1. c 2. orientation, preparation, incubation, illumination, verification 3. F 4. T 5. F 6. a 7. The chance of getting a head on the fifth flip is the same in each case. Each time you flip a coin, the chance of getting a head is 50 percent, no matter what happened before. However, many people intuitively think that *b* is the answer because a head is "overdue," or that *c* is correct because the coin is "on a roll" for heads.

Psychology in Action

Enhancing Creativity—Brainstorms

] SURVEYQUESTION *What can be done to improve thinking and promote creativity?*

Thomas Edison once explained his creativity by saying, "Genius is 1 percent inspiration and 99 percent perspiration." Many studies of creativity show that "genius" and "eminence" owe as much to persistence and dedication as they do to inspiration (Ericsson & Charness, 1994). A recent study of creative artists revealed that many regard creativity as "hard work" (Glueck, Ernst, & Unger, 2002).

Once it is recognized that creativity can be hard work, then something can be done to enhance it. Here are some suggestions on how to begin.

1. Break mental sets and challenge assumptions.

A **mental set** is the tendency to perceive a problem in a way that blinds us to possible solutions. Mental sets are a major barrier to creative thinking. Usually, they lead us to see a problem in preconceived terms that impede our problem-solving attempts. (Fixations and functional fixedness, which were described earlier, are specific types of mental sets.)

Try the problems pictured in ✦Figure 8.26. If you have difficulty, try asking yourself what assumptions you are making. The problems are designed to demonstrate the limiting effects of a mental set. (The answers to these problems, along with an explanation of the sets that prevent their solution, are found in ✦Figure 8.27.)

Now that you have been forewarned about the danger of faulty assumptions, see if you can correctly answer the following questions.

1. A farmer had 19 sheep. All but 9 died. How many sheep did the farmer have left?
2. It is not unlawful for a man living in Winston-Salem, North Carolina, to be buried west of the Mississippi River. T or F?
3. Some months have 30 days, some have 31. How many months have 28 days?
4. I have two coins that together total 30 cents. One of the coins is not a nickel. What are the two coins?
5. If there are 12 one-cent candies in a dozen, how many two-cent candies are there in a dozen?

✦**FIGURE 8.26** (a) *Nine dots are arranged in a square. Can you connect them by drawing four continuous straight lines without lifting your pencil from the paper?* (b) *Six matches must be arranged to make four triangles. The triangles must be the same size, with each side equal to the length of one match. (The solutions to these problems appear in Figure 8.27.)*

These questions are designed to cause thinking errors. Here are the answers:
1. Nineteen—9 alive and 10 dead. 2. F. It is against the law to bury a living person anywhere. 3. All of them. 4. A quarter and a nickel. One of the coins is not a nickel, but the other one is! 5. 12.

If you got caught on any of the questions, consider it an additional reminder of the value of actively challenging the assumptions you are making in any instance of problem solving.

2. Define problems broadly.

An effective way to break mental sets is to enlarge the definition of a problem. For instance, assume your problem is: Design a better doorway. This is likely to lead to ordinary solutions. Why not change the problem to: Design a better way to get through a wall? Now your solutions will be more original. Best of all might be to state the problem as: Find a better way to define separate areas for living and working. This could lead to truly creative solutions (Adams, 1988).

Let's say you are leading a group that's designing a new can opener. Wisely, you ask the group to think about *opening* in general, rather than about can openers. This was just the approach that led to the pop-top can. As the design group discussed the concept of opening, one member suggested that nature has its own openers, like the soft seam on a pea pod. Instead of a new can-opening tool, the group invented the self-opening can (Stein, 1974).

3. Restate the problem in different ways.

Stating problems in novel ways also tends to produce more creative solutions. See if you can cross out six letters to make a single word out of the following:

C S R I E X L E A T T T E R E S

If you're having difficulty, it may be that you need to restate the problem. Were you trying to cross out 6 letters? The real solution is to cross out the letters in the words "six letters," which yields the word CREATE.

One way to restate a problem is to imagine how another person would view it. What would a child, engineer, professor, mechanic, artist, psychologist, judge, or minister ask about the problem? Also, you should almost always ask the following questions:

What information do I have?
What don't I know?
What can I extract from the known information?
Have I used all of the information?

What additional information do I need?
What are the parts of the problem?
How are the parts related?
How could the parts be related?
Is this in any way like a problem I've solved before?

Remember, to think more creatively you must find ways to jog yourself out of mental sets and habitual modes of thought (Michalko, 1998).

4. Allow time for incubation.

Trying to hurry or to force a solution may simply encourage fixation on a dead end. Creativity takes time. You need to be able to revise or embellish initial solutions, even those based on rapid insight. If you are feeling hurried by a sense of time pressure, you are much less likely to think creatively (Amabile, Hadley, & Kramer, 2002).

Incubation is especially fruitful when you are exposed to external cues that relate to the problem (remember Archimedes' bath?). For example, Johannes Gutenberg, creator of the printing press, realized while at a wine harvest that the mechanical pressure used to crush grapes could also be used to imprint letters on paper (Dorfman, Shames, & Kihlstrom, 1996).

5. Seek varied input.

Remember, creativity requires divergent thinking. Rather than digging deeper with logic, you are attempting to shift your mental "prospecting" to new areas. As an example of this strategy, Edward de Bono (1992) recommends that you randomly look up words in the dictionary and relate them to the problem. Often the words will trigger a fresh perspective or open a new avenue. For instance, let's say you are asked to come up with new ways to clean oil off a beach. Following de Bono's suggestion, you would read the following randomly selected words, relate each to the problem, and see what thoughts are triggered: *weed, rust, poor, magnify, foam, gold, frame, hole, diagonal, vacuum, tribe, puppet, nose, link, drift, portrait, cheese, coal.* You may get similar benefits from relating various objects to a problem. Or, take a walk, skim through a newspaper, or look through a stack of photographs to see what thoughts they trigger (Michalko, 1998). Exposing yourself to a wide variety of information is a good way to encourage divergent thinking (Clapham, 2001).

6. Look for analogies.

Many "new" problems are really old problems in new clothing (Siegler, 1989). Representing a problem in a variety of ways is often the key to solution. Most problems become easier to solve when they are effectively represented. For example, consider this problem:

> Two backpackers start up a steep trail at 6 A.M. They hike all day, resting occasionally, and arrive at the top at 6 P.M. The next day they start back down the trail at 6 A.M. On the way down they stop several times and vary their pace. They arrive back at 6 P.M. On the way down, one of the hikers, who is a mathematician, tells the other that she has realized that they will pass a point on the trail at exactly the same time as they did the day before. Her non-mathematical friend finds this hard to believe, since on both days they have stopped and started many times and changed their pace. The problem: Is the mathematician right?

Perhaps you will see the answer to this problem immediately. If not, think of it this way: What if there were two pairs of backpackers, one going up the trail, the second coming down, and both hiking on the *same day?* It becomes obvious that the two pairs of hikers will pass each other at some point on the trail. Therefore, they will be at the same place at the same time. The mathematician was right.

7. Take sensible risks.

A willingness to go against the crowd is a key element in doing creative work. Unusual and original ideas may be rejected at first by conventional thinkers. Often, creative individuals must persevere and take some risks before their ideas are widely accepted. For example,

Post-it notes were invented by an engineer who accidentally created a weak glue. Rather than throw the mixture out, the engineer put it to a highly creative new use. However, it took him some time to convince others that a "bad" adhesive could be a useful product. Today, stick-on notepapers are one of the 3-M Company's most successful products (Sternberg & Lubart, 1995).

8. Delay evaluation.

Various studies suggest that people are most likely to be creative when they are given the freedom to play with ideas and solutions without having to worry about whether they will be evaluated. In the first stages of creative thinking, it is important to avoid criticizing your efforts. Worrying about the correctness of solutions tends to inhibit creativity (Basadur, Runco, & Vega, 2000). This idea is expanded in the discussion that follows.

An alternative approach to enhancing creativity is called *brainstorming*. Although brainstorming is a group technique, it can be applied to individual problem solving as well.

Brainstorming

The essence of **brainstorming** is that producing and evaluating ideas are kept separate. In group problem solving, each person is encouraged to produce as many ideas as possible without fear of criticism (Buyer, 1988). This encourages divergent thinking. Some of the most successful brainstorming takes place on computer networks, where each person's fears of being evaluated are minimized (Siau, 1996).

Only at the end of a brainstorming session are ideas reconsidered and evaluated. As ideas are freely generated, an interesting **cross-stimulation effect** takes place in which one participant's ideas trigger ideas from others (Brown et al., 1998).

The basic rules for successful brainstorming are:

1. Criticism of ideas is absolutely barred. Defer evaluation until later in the session.
2. Modification or combination with other ideas is encouraged. Don't worry about giving credit for ideas or keeping them neat. Mix them up!
3. Quantity of ideas is sought. In the early stages of brainstorming, quantity is more important than quality. Try to generate lots of ideas.
4. Unusual, remote, or wild ideas are sought. Let your imagination run amok!
5. Record ideas as they occur.
6. Elaborate or improve on the most promising ideas (Michalko, 1998).

It is important to be persistent when you are brainstorming. Most groups give up too soon, usually when the flow of new ideas begins to slow (Nijstad, Stroebe, & Lodewijkx, 1999).

How is brainstorming applied to individual problem solving? The essential point to remember is to *suspend judgment.* Ideas should first be produced without regard for logic, organization, accuracy, practicality, or any other evaluation. In writing an essay, for instance, you would begin by writing ideas in any order, the more the better, just as they occur to you. Later you would go back and reorganize, rewrite, and criticize your efforts.

As an aid to following rules 2, 3, and 4 of the brainstorming method, you might find this checklist helpful for encouraging original thought. It can be used to see if you have overlooked a possible solution.

CREATIVITY CHECKLIST

1. **Redefine.** Consider other uses for all elements of the problem. (This is designed to alert you to fixations that may be blocking creativity.)
2. **Adapt.** How could other objects, ideas, procedures, or solutions be adapted to this particular problem?
3. **Modify.** Imagine changing anything and everything that could be changed.
4. **Magnify.** Exaggerate everything you can think of. Think on a grand scale.

◆FIGURE 8.27 *Problem solutions.* (a) *The dot problem can be solved by extending the lines beyond the square formed by the dots. Most people assume incorrectly that they may not do this.* (b) *The match problem can be solved by building a three-dimensional pyramid. Most people assume that the matches must be arranged on a flat surface. If you remembered the four-tree problem from earlier in the chapter, the match problem may have been easy to solve.*

Brainstorming Method of creative thinking that separates the production and evaluation of ideas.

Cross-stimulation effect In group problem solving, the tendency of one person's ideas to trigger ideas from others.

5. **Minify.** What if everything were scaled down? What if all differences were reduced to zero? "Shrink" the problem down to size.
6. **Substitute.** How could one object, idea, or procedure be substituted for another?
7. **Rearrange.** Break the problem into pieces and shuffle them.
8. **Reverse.** Consider reverse orders and opposites, and turn things inside out.
9. **Combine.** This one speaks for itself.

By making a habit of subjecting a problem to each of these procedures, you should be able to greatly reduce the chances that you will overlook a useful, original, or creative solution.

Living More Creatively

Many people who think in conventional ways live intelligent, successful, and fulfilling lives. Just the same, creative thinking can add spice to life and lead to exciting personal insights. Psychologist Mihalyi Csikszentmihalyi (sik-sent-me-HALE-yee) (1997) makes these recommendations about how to become more creative:

- Find something that surprises you every day.
- Try to surprise at least one person every day.
- If something sparks your interest, follow it.
- Make a commitment to doing things well.
- Seek challenges.
- Take time for thinking and relaxing.
- Start doing more of what you really enjoy and less of what you dislike.
- Try to look at problems from as many viewpoints as you can.

Even if you don't become more creative by following these suggestions, they are still good advice. Life is not a standardized test with a single set of correct answers. It is much more like a blank canvas on which you can create designs that uniquely express your talents and interests. To live more creatively, you must be ready to seek new ways of doing things. Try to surprise at least one person today—yourself, if no one else.

STUDYBREAK ◆Y *Enhancing Creativity*

RELATE

Review the preceding pages and note which methods you could use more often to improve the quality of your thinking. Now mentally summarize the points you especially want to remember.

LEARNING CHECK

1. Fixations and functional fixedness are specific types of mental sets. T or F?
2. The incubation period in creative problem solving usually lasts just a matter of minutes. T or F?

3. Exposure to creative models has been shown to enhance creativity. T or F?
4. In brainstorming, each idea is critically evaluated as it is generated. T or F?
5. Defining a problem broadly produces a cross-stimulation effect that can inhibit creative thinking. T or F?

Critical Thinking

6. What mode of thinking does the "Creativity Checklist" (redefine, adapt, modify, magnify, and so forth) encourage?

ANSWERS

1. T 2. F 3. T 4. F 5. F 6. Divergent thinking.

CHAPTER IN REVIEW

Major Points

- Thinking, problem solving, language, and creativity are the origins of intelligent behavior.
- Thinking is influenced by the form in which information is represented—as images, concepts, or symbols.
- Language is an especially powerful way to encode information and manipulate ideas.
- Understanding problem solving can make you more effective at finding solutions.
- Expert problem solving is based on acquired knowledge and strategies.
- Intelligence tests only estimate real world intelligence. A high IQ does not automatically lead to high achievement.
- Creative thinking is novel, divergent, and tempered with a dash of practicality.
- Some thinking errors can be avoided if you know the pitfalls of intuitive thought.
- Creativity can be enhanced by strategies that promote divergent thinking.

Summary

What is the nature of thought?

- Thinking is an internal representation of external stimuli or situations.
- Three basic units of thought are images, concepts, and language (or symbols).

In what ways are images related to thinking?

- Images may be stored in memory or created to solve problems.
- Images can be three-dimensional, they can be rotated in space, and their size may change.
- Kinesthetic images are used to represent movements and actions. Kinesthetic sensations help structure the flow of thoughts for many people.

How do we learn concepts?

- A concept is a generalized idea of a class of objects or events.
- Concept formation may be based on positive and negative instances or rule learning.
- In practice, concept identification frequently makes use of prototypes, or ideal models.
- Concepts may be conjunctive ("and" concepts), disjunctive ("either/or" concepts), or relational.
- The denotative meaning of a word or concept is its dictionary definition. Connotative meaning is per-

sonal or emotional. Connotative meaning can be measured with the semantic differential.

What is the role of language in thinking?

- Language allows events to be encoded into symbols for easy mental manipulation. The study of meaning in language is called *semantics.*
- Language carries meaning by combining a set of symbols according to a set of rules (grammar), which includes rules about word order (syntax).
- True languages are productive and can be used to generate new ideas or possibilities.
- Complex gestural systems, such as American Sign Language, are true languages.

Can animals be taught to use language?

- Animal communication is relatively limited because it lacks symbols that can be rearranged easily.
- Chimpanzees and other primates have been taught American Sign Language and similar systems. This suggests to some that primates are capable of very basic language use. Others question this conclusion. Studies that make use of lexigrams provide the best evidence to date of animal language use.

What do we know about problem solving?

- The solution to a problem may be arrived at mechanically (by trial and error or by rote application of rules), but mechanical solutions are often inefficient.
- Solutions by understanding usually begin with discovery of the general properties of an answer. Next comes the proposal of a functional solution.
- Problem solving is frequently aided by heuristics, which narrow the search for solutions.
- When understanding leads to a rapid solution, insight has occurred. Three elements of insight are selective encoding, selective combination, and selective comparison.
- Insight and other problem solving can be blocked by fixations. Functional fixedness is a common fixation, but emotional blocks, cultural values, learned conventions, and perceptual habits are also problems.

What is artificial intelligence?

- Artificial intelligence refers to any artificial system that can perform tasks that require intelligence when done by people.
- Two principal areas of artificial intelligence research are computer simulations and expert systems.
- Expert human problem solving is based on organized knowledge and acquired strategies, rather than some general improvement in thinking ability.

How is human intelligence defined and measured?

- Intelligence refers to the general capacity to act purposefully, think rationally, and deal effectively with the environment. In practice, intelligence is operationally defined by intelligence tests.

- The first practical intelligence test was assembled by Alfred Binet. A modern version of Binet's test is the *Stanford-Binet Intelligence Scale.*

- A second major intelligence test is the *Wechsler Adult Intelligence Scale* (WAIS). The WAIS measures both verbal and performance intelligence. Culture-fair and group intelligence tests are also available.

- Intelligence is expressed as an intelligence quotient (IQ), defined as mental age divided by chronological age and then multiplied by 100. The distribution of IQ scores approximates a normal curve.

How do IQ scores relate to achievement and thinking ability?

- IQ is related to achievement in school, but many other factors are also important. Outside school, the connection between IQ and achievement is even weaker.

- As a group, males and females do not differ in overall IQ. Also, their intellectual strengths and educational goals are becoming more alike.

- People with IQs in the gifted or "genius" range of above 140 tend to be superior in many respects. However, by criteria other than IQ, many children can be considered gifted or talented in one way or another.

- The terms *mentally retarded* and *developmentally disabled* are applied to those whose IQ falls below 70 or who lack various adaptive behaviors.

- About 50 percent of the cases of mental retardation are organic. The remaining cases are of undetermined cause. Many of these cases are thought to reflect familial retardation.

- Intelligence is partially determined by heredity. However, environment is also important, as revealed by IQ increases induced by education and stimulating environments.

What is creative thinking?

- To be creative, a solution must be practical and sensible as well as original. Creative thinking requires divergent thought, characterized by fluency, flexibility, and originality. Tests of creativity measure these qualities.

- Five stages often seen in creative problem solving are orientation, preparation, incubation, illumination, and verification. Not all creative thinking fits this pattern.

- Studies suggest that the creative personality has a number of characteristics, most of which contradict popular stereotypes. There is only a very small correlation between IQ and creativity.

How accurate is intuition?

- Intuitive thinking often leads to errors. Wrong conclusions may be drawn when an answer seems highly representative of what we already believe is true.

- A second problem is ignoring the base rate (or underlying probability) of an event.

- Clear thinking is usually aided by stating or framing a problem in broad terms.

What can be done to improve thinking and promote creativity?

- Various strategies that promote divergent thinking tend to enhance creative problem solving.

- In group situations, brainstorming may lead to creative solutions. The principles of brainstorming can also be applied to individual problem solving.

Interactive Learning

Internet addresses frequently change. To find the sites listed here, visit www.psychology. wadsworth.com/coon_journey2e for an updated list of Internet addresses and direct links to relevant sites.

PSYCHOLOGY: A JOURNEY COMPANION WEB SITE Online quizzes, flash cards, and other helpful study aids for this text. *www.psychology.wadsworth.com/coon_journey2e*

CREATIVITY WEB Multiple links to resources on creativity.

THE PSYCHOLOGY OF INVENTION An exploration of how invention and discovery happen.

THE QUESTION OF PRIMATE LANGUAGE This article from the National Zoo discusses primate communication and intelligence.

BE CAREFUL OF HOW YOU DEFINE INTELLIGENCE An article about cross-cultural differences in intelligence.

HELPING YOUR HIGHLY GIFTED CHILD Advice for parents of gifted children.

INTRODUCTION TO MENTAL RETARDATION Answers to basic questions about mental retardation.

IQ TESTS Provides links to a number of IQ tests.

THE BELL CURVE FLATTENED An article that summarizes objections to *The Bell Curve.*

THE KNOWNS AND UNKNOWNS OF INTELLIGENCE From the APA, what is known about intelligence and intelligence tests.

INFOTRAC COLLEGE EDITION For recent articles on "talking" chimps, use Key Words search for ANIMAL LANGUAGE. For more information on the controversy concerning the book *The Bell Curve,* use Key Words search for BELL CURVE.

PSYCHNOW! 5f. Cognition and Language, 5g. Problem Solving and Creativity.

Test Your Knowledge: Cognition, Intelligence, and Creativity

The questions that follow are only a sample of what you need to know. If you miss any of the items, you should review the entire chapter and get more practice with *WebTutor* or the *Practice Quizzes* that came with this book. Another way to prepare for tests is to use the printed *Study Guide* that is available for this text.

1. Concepts are
   A. picture-like mental representations   B. generalized ideas of a class of objects or events   C. symbols and rules for combining them   D. symbolic notational systems

2. A person doing mental rotation would need to use which basic unit of thought?
   A. concepts   B. language   C. images   D. symbols

3. Our ability to think about movements and actions is aided by
   A. kinesthetic imagery   B. rotational concepts
   C. mental calculation   D. relational concepts

4. A triangle must be a closed shape and have three sides, and the sides must be straight lines. *Triangle* is a
   A. conjunctive concept   B. relational concept
   C. disjunctive concept   D. connotative concept

5. When you are trying to categorize complex stimuli _____ are especially helpful.
   A. kinesthetic images   B. connotative concepts
   C. denotative concepts   D. prototypes

6. Which of the following is NOT an element of spoken language?
   A. grammar   B. syntax   C. phonemes   D. lexigrams

7. Noam Chomsky believes that we use _____ to change core declarative sentences into other voices and forms.
   A. phonemes   B. transformation rules   C. conditional statements   D. conjunctive encoding

8. Which statement is the best summary of animal language research with chimpanzees?
   A. Chimps can learn to use signs, but they can't make word sounds.   B. Chimps can learn to communicate with signs.   C. Chimps who learn signs use language on a par with 5-year-old children.   D. Because of serious problems with syntax, chimps have been unable to communicate with humans.

9. After you find a general solution to a problem, you must usually also find a
   A. heuristic   B. search strategy   C. fixation
   D. functional solution

10. Functional fixedness is a major barrier to
    A. insightful problem solving   B. using random search strategies   C. mechanical problem solving   D. achieving fixations through problem solving

11. Computer simulations and expert systems are primary research tools in
    A. psycholinguistics   B. the field of AI   C. studies of divergent thinking   D. studies of the semantic differential

12. Which modern intelligence test originated with attempts to measure the mental abilities of children in Paris?
    A. SB5   B. WAIS   C. SAT   D. WISC

13. By definition, a person has average intelligence when
    A. $MA = CA$ B. $CA = 100$ C. $MA = 100$
    D. $MA \times CA = 100$

14. One thing that the mentally gifted and the developmentally disabled have in common is that both have
    A. a tendency to suffer from metabolic disorders   B. to be tested with the WAIS, rather than the SB5   C. MAs that are higher than their CAs   D. extreme IQ scores

15. Which is NOT one of the eight types of intelligence identified by Howard Gardner?
    A. cyber skills   B. music skills   C. visual and spatial skills   D. naturalist skills

16. From a practical point of view, adult intelligence can most readily be increased by
    A. genetics   B. teaching adaptive behaviors   C. stimulating environments   D. applying deviation IQs

17. A test scored for fluency and flexibility is obviously designed to measure
    A. intuitive thinking   B. convergent thinking
    C. divergent thinking   D. algorithms

18. The stage of creative thinking that corresponds to insightful problem solving is
    A. verification   B. incubation   C. induction
    D. illumination

19. Our decisions are greatly affected by the way a problem is stated, a process called
    A. framing   B. base rating   C. induction   D. selective encoding

20. By seeking varied information, delaying evaluation, and looking for analogies, you should be able to increase
    A. intuitive thinking   B. convergent thinking
    C. divergent thinking   D. functional fixedness

ANSWERS   1. b 2. c 3. a 4. a 5. d 6. d 7. b 8. b 9. d 10. a 11. b 12. a 13. a 14. d 15. a 16. c 17. c 18. d 19. a 20. c

Motivation and Emotion

The Sun Sets Twice in Utah

My wife Sevren and I had been backpacking for more than a week in the rugged Unitas mountains of central Utah. Other than having to fend off mosquitoes the size of hummingbirds, we had a glorious time in the wilderness. Every day, we explored new trails, lakes, and streams and enjoyed inspiring vistas, fresh air, and lots of wildlife. Best of all, neither of us wore a watch.

After a long hike one day, we reached a small lake just as it began to get dark. The light was fading quickly, so we set up our tent, cooked dinner, and prepared to eat. Neither of us was very hungry, but we didn't want to spend the night with empty stomachs, so we ate anyway. Then we washed dishes, cleaned the campsite, and climbed into our tent. We talked for a while, then tried to get to sleep. That's when the sun came up.

Pulling back the tent flap, we looked around in amazement to discover bright sunshine. It was late afternoon. We had *hours* of daylight left before nightfall!

Heavy, dark clouds had covered most of the western sky when we first arrived at the lake. Apparently, an approaching storm blocked the sun, reducing the forest to twilight. When the storm retreated, the sun came out again. No wonder we weren't hungry or sleepy. Fortunately, no one else was at the lake to laugh at us—although we did have a good laugh ourselves.

This chapter is about the motives and emotions that underlie human behavior. As my lakeside experience suggests, even "simple" motives such as hunger are not solely under the control of the body. In many instances, external cues, learning, expectations, cultural values, and other factors influence our motives and goals.

Let's begin with basic motives, such as hunger and thirst, and then explore how emotions affect us. While emotions can be the spice of life, they are sometimes the spice of death as well. Read on to find out why.

Survey Questions

- What is motivation? Are there different types of motives?
- What causes hunger? Overeating? Eating disorders?
- Is there more than one type of thirst? In what ways are pain avoidance and the sex drive unusual?
- What are the typical patterns of human sexual response?
- How does arousal relate to motivation?
- What are social motives? Why are they important?
- Are some motives more basic than others?
- What happens during emotion? Can "lie detectors" really detect lies?
- How accurately are emotions expressed by "body language" and the face?
- How do psychologists explain emotions?
- What factors contribute most to a happy and fulfilling life?

MOTIVATION—FORCES THAT PUSH AND PULL

] SURVEYQUESTIONS *What is motivation? Are there different types of motives?*

What are your goals? Why do you pursue them? How vigorously do you try to reach them? When are you satisfied? When do you give up? **Motivation** refers to the dynamics of behavior—the ways in which our actions are *initiated, sustained, directed,* and *terminated* (Petri, 2003).

Can you clarify that? Yes. Imagine that a student named Marcy is studying psychology in the library. She begins to feel hungry and can't concentrate. Her stomach growls. She grows restless and decides to buy an apple from a vending machine. The machine is empty, so she goes to the cafeteria. Closed. Marcy drives home, where she cooks a meal and eats it. At last her hunger is satisfied, and she resumes studying. Notice how Marcy's food seeking was *initiated* by a bodily need. Her search was *sustained* because her need was not immediately met, and her actions were *directed* by possible sources of food. Finally, her food seeking was *terminated* by achieving her goal.

A Model of Motivation

Many motivated activities begin with a **need,** or internal lack or deficiency. The need that initiated Marcy's food search was a shortage of key substances in her body. Needs cause a **drive** (an energized motivational state) to develop. The drive was hunger, in Marcy's case. Drives activate a **response** (an action or series of actions) designed to attain a **goal** (the "target" of motivated behavior). Reaching a goal that satisfies the need will end the chain of events. Thus, a simple model of motivation can be shown in this way:

```
┌─► NEED ──► DRIVE ──► RESPONSE ──► GOAL ─┐
│            (NEED REDUCTION) ◄───────────┘
```

Aren't needs and drives the same thing? No, because the strength of needs and drives can differ. If you begin fasting today, your bodily need for food will increase every day. However, you would probably feel less "hungry" on the seventh day of fasting than you did on the first. While your need for food steadily increases, the hunger drive comes and goes.

Motivation Internal processes that initiate, sustain, and direct activities.

Need An internal deficiency that may energize behavior.

Drive The psychological expression of internal needs or valued goals. For example, hunger, thirst, or a drive for success.

Response Any action, glandular activity, or other identifiable behavior.

Goal The target or objective of motivated behavior.

(a) High-incentive value goal

(b) Low-incentive value goal

◆FIGURE 9.1 *Needs and incentives interact to determine drive strength* (above). *(a) Moderate need combined with a high-incentive goal produces a strong drive. (b) Even when a strong need exists, drive strength may be moderate if a goal's incentive value is low. It is important to remember, however, that incentive value lies "in the eye of the beholder" (photo). No matter how hungry, few people would be able to eat the pictured grubworms.*

Now let's observe Marcy again. It's Saturday night: For dinner, Marcy has soup, salad, a large steak, a baked potato, four pieces of bread, two pieces of cheesecake, and three cups of coffee. After dinner, she complains that she is "too full to move." Soon after, Marcy's roommate arrives with a strawberry pie. Marcy exclaims that strawberry pie is her favorite dessert, and she eats three large pieces! Is this hunger? Certainly, Marcy's dinner satisfied her biological needs for food.

How does that change the model of motivation? Marcy's "pie lust" illustrates that motivated behavior can be energized by the "pull" of external stimuli, as well as by the "push" of internal needs.

Incentives

We call the "pull" of a goal its **incentive value** (the goal's appeal beyond its ability to fill a need). Some goals are so desirable (strawberry pie, for example) that they can motivate behavior in the absence of an internal need. Other goals are so low in incentive value that they may be rejected even if they meet the internal need. Fresh, live grubworms, for instance, are highly nutritious. However, I doubt that you would choose to eat one, no matter how hungry you might be.

David Austen/Woodfin Camp & Associates

Usually, our actions are energized by a mixture of internal needs *and* external incentives. That's why a strong need may change an unpleasant incentive into a desired goal. Perhaps you've never eaten a grubworm, but I'll bet you've eaten some pretty horrible leftovers when the refrigerator was empty. The incentive value of goals also helps explain motives that don't seem to come directly from internal needs, such as drives for success, status, or approval (◆Fig. 9.1).

Types of Motives

For our purposes, motives can be divided into three major categories:

1. **Primary motives** are based on biological needs that we must meet to survive. The most important primary motives are hunger, thirst, pain avoidance, and needs for air, sleep, elimination of wastes, and regulation of body temperature. Primary motives are innate.
2. **Stimulus motives** express our needs for stimulation and information. Examples include activity, curiosity, exploration, manipulation, and physical contact. While such motives also appear to be innate, they are not strictly necessary for survival.
3. **Secondary motives** are based on learned needs, drives, and goals. Learned motives help explain many human activities, such as making music, creating a Web page, or trying to win the skateboarding finals in the X Games. Many secondary motives are related to learned needs for power, affiliation (the need to be with others), approval, status, security, and achievement. Fear and aggression also appear to be greatly affected by learning.

Incentive value The value of a goal above and beyond its ability to fill a need.
Primary motives Innate motives based on biological needs.
Stimulus motives Innate needs for stimulation and information.
Secondary motives Motives based on learned needs, drives, and goals.

Primary Motives and Homeostasis

How important is food in your life? Water? Sleep? Air? Temperature regulation? Finding a public restroom? For most of us, satisfying biological needs is so routine that we tend to overlook how much of our behavior they direct. But exaggerate any of these needs through famine, shipwreck, poverty, near drowning, bitter cold, or drinking 10 cups of coffee, and their powerful grip on behavior becomes evident. We are, after all, still animals in many ways.

Biological drives are essential because they maintain *homeostasis* (HOE-me-oh-STAY-sis), or bodily equilibrium (Cannon, 1932).

What is homeostasis? The term **homeostasis** means "standing steady" or "steady state." Optimal levels exist for body temperature, for chemicals in the blood, for blood pressure, and so forth. When the body deviates from these "ideal" levels, automatic reactions begin to restore the internal balance. Thus, it might help to think of homeostasis as being similar to a thermostat set at a particular temperature.

A (VERY) SHORT COURSE ON THERMOSTATS

When room temperature falls below the level set on a thermostat, the heat is automatically turned on to warm the room. When the heat equals or slightly exceeds the ideal temperature, it is automatically turned off. In this way, room temperature is kept in a state of equilibrium hovering around the ideal level.

The first reactions to disequilibrium in the human body are also automatic. For example, if you become too hot, more blood will flow through your skin and you will begin to perspire, thus lowering body temperature. Usually, we are not aware of such changes, unless continued disequilibrium drives us to seek shade, warmth, food, or water.

STUDYBREAK ◆ *Overview of Motivation*

RELATE

Motives help explain why we do what we do. See if you can think of something you do that illustrates the concepts of need, drive, response, and goal. Does the goal in your example vary in incentive value? What effects do high- and low-incentive-value goals have on your behavior?

Mentally list some primary motives you have satisfied today. Some stimulus motives. Some secondary motives. How did each influence your behavior?

LEARNING CHECK

1. Motives _____, sustain, _____, and terminate activities.
2. Needs provide the _____ of motivation, whereas incentives provide the _____.

Classify the following needs or motives by placing the correct letter in the blank.

A. Primary motive   B. Stimulus motive   C. Secondary motive

3. _____ curiosity
4. _____ status
5. _____ sleep
6. _____ thirst
7. _____ achievement
8. _____ physical contact

9. Maintaining bodily equilibrium is called thermostasis. T or F?
10. A goal high in incentive value may create a drive in the absence of any internal need. T or F?

Critical Thinking

11. There's an old saying that "You can lead a horse to water, but you can't make him drink." Can you restate this in motivational terms?
12. Many people mistakenly believe that they suffer from "hypoglycemia" (low blood sugar), which is often blamed for fatigue, difficulty concentrating, irritability, and other symptoms. Why is it unlikely that many people actually have hypoglycemia?

ANSWERS 1. initiate, direct 2. push, pull 3. B 4. C 5. A 6. A 7. A 8. B 9. F 10. T 11. Providing an incentive (water) will not automatically lead to drinking in the absence of an internal need. 12. Because of homeostasis: Blood sugar is normally maintained within narrow bounds. While blood sugar levels fluctuate enough to affect hunger, true hypoglycemia is an infrequent medical problem.

HUNGER—PARDON ME, THAT'S JUST MY HYPOTHALAMUS GROWLING

] **SURVEYQUESTIONS** *What causes hunger? Overeating? Eating disorders?*

You get hungry, you find food, you eat: Hunger might seem like a "simple" motive, but only recently have we begun to understand it. Hunger provides a good model of how internal and external factors direct our behavior.

Homeostasis A steady state of bodily equilibrium.

Record of stomach contractions

Time record in minutes

Record of hunger pangs

Record of breathing

Gastric balloon

✦**FIGURE 9.2** *In Walter Cannon's early study of hunger, a simple apparatus was used to simultaneously record hunger pangs and stomach contractions. (After Cannon, 1934.)*

What causes hunger? When you feel hungry, you probably think of your stomach. That's why Walter Cannon and A. L. Washburn decided to see if stomach contractions cause hunger. In an early study, Washburn trained himself to swallow a balloon, which could be inflated through an attached tube. This allowed Cannon to record the movements of Washburn's stomach (✦Fig. 9.2). When Washburn's stomach contracted, he said that he felt "hunger pangs." In view of this, the two scientists concluded that hunger is nothing more than the contractions of an empty stomach (Cannon & Washburn, 1912). (Unfortunately, this proved to be an inflated conclusion.)

For many people, hunger produces an overall feeling of weakness or shakiness, rather than a "growling" stomach. Of course, eating *is* limited when the stomach is stretched or distended (full). (Remember last Thanksgiving?) However, we now know that the stomach is not essential for feeling hunger. For medical reasons, many people have had their stomachs removed. Despite this, they continue to feel hungry and eat regularly (Woods et al., 2000).

Then what does cause hunger? One important signal for hunger is lowered levels of glucose (sugar) in the blood (Campfield et al., 1996). Strange as it may seem, the liver also affects hunger.

The liver? Yes, the liver responds to a lack of bodily "fuel" by sending nerve impulses to the brain. These "messages" contribute to a desire to eat (Woods et al., 2000).

Brain Mechanisms

What part of the brain controls hunger? When you are hungry, many parts of the brain are affected, so no single "hunger center" exists. However, a small area called the **hypothalamus** (HI-po-THAL-ah-mus) regulates many motives, including hunger, thirst, and the sex drive (✦Fig. 9.3).

The hypothalamus is sensitive to levels of sugar in the blood (and other substances described in a moment). It also receives messages from the liver and the stomach. When combined, these signals regulate hunger (Woods et al., 2000).

One part of the hypothalamus acts as a feeding system that initiates eating. If the *lateral hypothalamus* is "turned on" with an electrified probe, even a well-fed animal will immediately begin eating. (The term *lateral* simply means the sides of the hypothalamus. See ✦Figure 9.4.) If the same area is destroyed, an animal will never eat again.

A second area in the hypothalamus is part of a satiety system, or "stop mechanism" for eating. If the *ventromedial hypothalamus* (VENT-ro-MEE-dee-al) is destroyed, dramatic overeating results. (*Ventromedial* refers to the bottom middle of the hypothalamus.) Rats with such damage will eat until they balloon up to weights of 1,000 grams or more (✦Fig. 9.5). A normal rat weighs about 180 grams. To put this weight gain in human terms, picture someone you know who weighs 180 pounds growing to a weight of 1,000 pounds.

The *paraventricular nucleus* (PAIR-uh-ven-TRICK-you-ler) of the hypothalamus also affects hunger (Fig. 9.4). This area helps keep blood sugar levels steady. As a result, it is involved in both starting and stopping eating. The paraventricular nucleus is very sensitive to a substance called neuropeptide Y (NPY). If NPY is present in large amounts, an animal will eat until it cannot hold another bite (Woods et al., 2000). Incidentally, the hypothalamus also responds to a chemical in marijuana, which can produce intense hunger (the "munchies") (Di Marzo et al., 2001).

Hypothalamus

✦**FIGURE 9.3** *Location of the hypothalamus in the human brain.*

Hypothalamus A small area at the base of the brain that regulates many aspects of motivation and emotion, especially hunger, thirst, and sexual behavior.

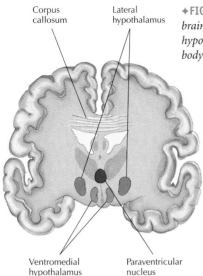

Corpus
callosum

Lateral
hypothalamus

Ventromedial
hypothalamus

Paraventricular
nucleus

✦**FIGURE 9.4** *This is a cross section through the middle of the brain (viewed from the front of the brain). Indicated areas of the hypothalamus are associated with hunger and the regulation of body weight.*

How do we know when to stop eating? A chemical called glucagon-like peptide 1 (GLP-1) causes eating to cease. GLP-1 is released by the intestines after you eat a meal. From there, it travels in the bloodstream to the brain. When enough GLP-1 arrives, your desire to eat ends (Nori, 1998; Turton et al., 1996). It takes about 10 minutes for the hypothalamus to respond after you begin eating. That's why you are less likely to overeat if you eat slowly, which gives your brain time to get the message that you've had enough (Liu et al., 2000).

The substances we have reviewed are only some of the chemical signals that start and stop eating. Others continue to be discovered. In time, they may make it possible to artificially control hunger. If so, better treatments for extreme obesity and self-starvation could follow (Batterham et al., 2003; Woods et al., 2000).

✦**FIGURE 9.5** *Damage to the hunger satiety system in the hypothalamus can produce a very fat rat, a condition called hypothalamic hyperphagia (Hi-per-FAGE-yah: overeating). This rat weighs 1,080 grams. (The pointer has gone completely around the dial and beyond.) (Photo courtesy of Neal E. Miller, Rockefeller University.)*

Set Point

In addition to knowing when to start eating and when a meal is over, your body needs to regulate weight over longer periods of time. This is done by monitoring the amount of fat stored in the body (Woods, Seeley, & Porte, 1998). Basically, your body has a **set point** for the proportion of fat it maintains. The set point acts like a "thermostat" for fat levels. Your own set point is the weight you maintain when you are making no effort to gain or lose weight. When your body goes below its set point, you will feel hungry most of the time. On the other hand, fat cells release a substance called *leptin* when your "spare tire" is well inflated. Leptin is carried in the bloodstream to the brain, where it tells us to eat less (Considine et al., 1996; Mercer et al., 1998).

Set points are only one piece in a complex puzzle that's worth solving. Obesity is a major health risk and, for many, a source of social stigma and low self-esteem.

Obesity

Why do people overeat? If internal needs alone controlled eating, fewer people would overeat. However, most of us are also sensitive to *external eating cues*. These are signs and signals linked with food. Do you tend to eat more when food is attractive, highly visible, and easy to get? If so, then external cues affect your food intake. In cultures like ours, where food is plentiful, eating cues add greatly to the risk of overeating (Woods et al., 2000). For example, many college freshmen gain weight rapidly during their first 3 months on campus. All-you-can-eat dining halls in the dorms and night-time snacking appear to be the culprits (Levitsky et al., 2003).

Is it true that people also overeat when they are emotionally upset? Yes. People with weight problems are just as likely to eat when they are anxious, angry, or sad as when hungry (Schotte, Cools, & McNally, 1990). Furthermore, the obese are often unhappy in our fat-conscious culture. The result is overeating that leads to emotional distress and still more overeating. This makes weight control extremely difficult (Rutledge & Linden, 1998).

Diet

A diet is not just a way to lose weight. Your current diet is defined by the types and amounts of food you regularly eat. Some diets actually encourage overeating. For instance, placing animals on a "supermarket" diet leads to gross obesity. In one experiment, rats were given meals

The mouse on the left has a genetic defect that prevents its fat cells from producing normal amounts of leptin. Without this chemical signal, the mouse's body acts as if its set point for fat storage is, shall we say, rather high.

John Sholtis, The Rockefeller University

Set point The proportion of body fat that tends to be maintained by changes in hunger and eating.

of chocolate chip cookies, salami, cheese, bananas, marshmallows, milk chocolate, peanut butter, and fat. These pampered rodents gained almost three times as much weight as rats that ate only laboratory chow (Sclafani & Springer, 1976). (Rat chow is a dry mixture of several bland grains. If you were a rat, you'd probably eat more cookies than rat chow, too.)

People are also sensitive to dietary content. In general, *sweetness,* high *fat content,* and *variety* tend to encourage overeating (Lucas & Sclafani, 1990). Sadly, our culture provides the worst kinds of foods for people who suffer from obesity. An added problem faced by people who want to control their weight concerns "yo-yo" dieting.

The Paradox of Yo-Yo Dieting

If dieting works, why are hundreds of "new" diets published each year? The answer is that while dieters do lose weight, most regain it soon after they stop dieting. In fact, many people end up weighing even more than before. Why should this be so? Dieting (starving) slows the body's rate of metabolism (the rate at which energy is used up). In effect, a dieter's body becomes highly efficient at *conserving* calories and storing them as fat (Leibel, Rosenbaum, & Hirsch, 1995).

"Yo-yo dieting," or repeatedly losing and gaining weight, is especially dangerous. Frequent changes in weight can dramatically slow the body's metabolic rate. This makes it harder to lose weight each time a person diets and easier to regain weight when the diet ends. Frequent weight changes also increase the risk of heart disease and premature death (Brownell & Rodin, 1994; Lissner et al., 1991).

Apparently, evolution prepared us to save energy when food is scarce and to stock up on fat when food is plentiful. Briefly starving yourself, therefore, may have little lasting effect on weight. The best way to avoid bouncing between feast and famine is to permanently change your eating habits and exercise levels—a topic we will return to soon.

To summarize, overeating is related to internal and external influences, diet, emotions, genetics, exercise, and many other factors. To answer the question we began with, people become obese in different ways and for different reasons. Clearly, scientists are still a long way from winning the "battle of the bulge." Nevertheless, many people have learned to take control of eating by applying psychological principles. See "Behavioral Dieting" for more information.

Fans cheered as daytime TV host Oprah Winfrey lost 67 pounds on a commercial diet. Over the next year, viewers watched in morbid fascination as Oprah regained all of the weight she had lost. Oprah's rebound was no surprise. Numerous studies show that you can lose weight on almost any diet. However, you will almost certainly gain it back in a few years. Oprah was finally able to stabilize her weight through exercise and revised eating habits (Seligman, 1994).

Other Factors in Hunger

As research on overeating suggests, "hunger" is affected by more than just bodily needs for food. Let's consider some additional factors.

Cultural Factors

Learning to think of some foods as desirable and others as revolting has a large impact on what we eat. In North America we would never consider eating the eyes out of the steamed head of a monkey, but in some parts of the world they are considered a delicacy. By the same token, vegans and vegetarians think it is barbaric to eat any kind of meat. In short, cultural values greatly affect the *incentive value* of foods. (Cultural values are widely held beliefs about the desirability of various objects and activities.)

Taste

Even tastes for "normal" foods vary considerably. For example, if you are well fed, leptin dulls the tongue's sensitivity to sweet tastes (Kawai et al., 2000). If you have noticed that you lose your "sweet tooth" when you are full, you may have observed this effect. Actually, if you eat too much of any particular food, it will become less appealing. This probably helps us maintain variety in our diets. However, it also encourages obesity in societies where tasty foods are plentiful. If you overdose on fried chicken or french fries, moving on to some cookies or chocolate cheesecake certainly won't do your body much good (Pinel, Assanand, & Lehman, 2000).

USING PSYCHOLOGY **Behavioral Dieting**

As we have noted, dieting is usually followed by rapid weight gains (Walsh & Flynn, 1995). If you really want to lose weight you must overhaul your eating habits, an approach called **behavioral dieting.** Here are some helpful behavioral techniques.

1. **Get yourself committed to weight loss.** Involve other people in your efforts. Programs such as Overeaters Anonymous or Take Off Pounds Sensibly can be a good source of social support (Foreyt, 1987).
2. **Exercise.** No diet can succeed for long without an increase in exercise, because exercise lowers the body's set point. Stop saving steps and riding elevators. Add activity to your routine in every way you can think of. To lose weight, you must use more calories than you take in. Burning just 200 extra calories a day can help prevent rebound weight gains (Wadden et al., 1998). The more frequently and vigorously you exercise, the more weight you will lose (Jeffery & Wing, 2001).
3. **Learn your eating habits by observing yourself and keeping a "diet diary."** Begin by making a complete, 2-week record of when and where you eat, what you eat, and the feelings and events that occur just before and after eating. Is a roommate, relative, or spouse encouraging you to overeat? What are your most "dangerous" times and places for overeating?
4. **Learn to weaken your personal eating cues.** When you have learned when and where you do most of your eating, avoid these situations. Try to restrict your eating to one room, and do not read, watch TV, study, or talk on the phone while eating. Require yourself to interrupt what you are doing in order to eat.
5. **Count calories, but don't starve yourself.** To lose, you must eat less, and calories allow you to keep a record of your food intake. If you have trouble eating less every day, try dieting 4 days a week. People who diet intensely every other day lose as much as those who diet moderately every day (Viegener et al., 1990).

6. **Develop techniques to control the act of eating.** Begin by taking smaller portions. Carry to the table only what you plan to eat. Put all other food away before leaving the kitchen. Eat slowly, sip water between bites of food, leave food on your plate, and stop eating before you are completely full. Be especially wary of the extra-large servings at fast-food restaurants. Saying "super-size me" too often can, indeed, leave you super-sized (Murray, 2001).
7. **Avoid snacks.** It is generally better to eat several small meals a day than three large ones (Assanand, Pinel, & Lehman, 1998). However, high-calorie snacks tend to be eaten *in addition to* meals. If you have an impulse to snack, set a timer for 20 minutes and see if you are still hungry then. Delay the impulse to snack several times if possible. Dull your appetite by filling up on raw carrots, bouillon, water, coffee, or tea.
8. **Chart your progress daily.** Record your weight, the number of calories eaten, and whether you met your daily goal. Set realistic goals by cutting down calories gradually. Losing about a pound per week is realistic, but remember, you are changing habits, not just dieting. Diets don't work!
9. **Set a "threshold" for weight control.** Maintaining weight loss can be even more challenging than losing weight. A study found that people who successfully maintained weight losses had a regain limit of 3 pounds or less. In other words, if they gained more than 2 or 3 pounds, they immediately began to make corrections in their eating habits and amount of exercise (Brownell et al., 1986).

Be patient with this program. It takes years to develop eating habits. You can expect it to take at least several months to change them. If you are unsuccessful at losing weight with these techniques, you might find it helpful to seek the aid of a psychologist familiar with behavioral weight-loss techniques.

It is easy to acquire a **taste aversion,** or active dislike, for a particular food. This can happen if a food causes sickness or if it is merely associated with nausea (Jacobsen et al., 1993). Not only do we learn to avoid such foods, but they too can become nauseating. A friend of the author's, who once became ill after eating a cheese Danish (well, actually, *several*), has never again been able to come face to face with this delightful pastry.

If getting sick occurs long after eating, how does it become associated with a particular food? A good question. Taste aversions are a type of classical conditioning. As stated in Chapter 6, a long delay between the CS and US usually prevents conditioning. However, psychologists theorize that we have a biological tendency to associate an upset stomach with foods eaten

Behavioral dieting Weight reduction based on changing exercise and eating habits, rather than temporary self-starvation.

Taste aversion An active dislike for a particular food.

earlier. Such learning is usually protective. Yet, sadly, many cancer patients suffer taste aversions long after the nausea of their drug treatments has passed (Stockhorst et al., 1998).

Taste aversions may also help people avoid severe nutritional imbalances. For example, if you go on a fad diet and eat only grapefruit, you will eventually begin to feel ill. In time, associating your discomfort with grapefruit may create an aversion to it and restore some balance to your diet.

Eating Disorders

Under the sheets of her hospital bed, Krystal looks like a skeleton. If her **anorexia nervosa** (AN-uh-REK-see-yah ner-VOH-sah: self-starvation) cannot be stopped, Krystal may die of malnutrition. Victims of anorexia, who are mostly adolescent females (5 to 10 percent are male), suffer devastating weight losses from severe, self-inflicted dieting (Polivy & Herman, 2002).

Do anorexics lose their appetite? No, many continue to feel hungry, yet struggle to starve themselves to excessive thinness. A compulsive attempt to lose weight causes them to lose their appetite (they do not seek or desire food). However, their active avoidance of food does not prevent them from feeling physical hunger. Often, anorexia starts with "normal" dieting that slowly begins to dominate the person's life. In time, anorexics suffer debilitating health problems. Five to 8 percent (more than 1 in 20) die of malnutrition (Polivy & Herman, 2002). ▲ Table 9.1 lists the symptoms of anorexia nervosa.

Bulimia nervosa (bue-LIHM-ee-yah) is a second major eating disorder. Bulimic persons gorge on food, then vomit or take laxatives to avoid gaining weight (see Table 9.1). Like anorexia, most victims of bulimia are girls or women. Approximately 5 percent of college women are bulimic, and as many as 61 percent have milder eating problems. Bingeing and purging can seriously damage health. Typical risks include sore throat, hair loss, muscle spasms, kidney damage, dehydration, tooth erosion, swollen salivary glands, menstrual irregularities, loss of sex drive, and even heart attack.

Causes

What causes anorexia and bulimia? Women who suffer from eating disorders are extremely dissatisfied with their bodies. Usually, they have distorted views of themselves and exaggerated fears of becoming fat. Many overestimate their body size by 25 percent or more. As a result, they think they are disgustingly "fat" when they are actually wasting away

Anorexia is more dangerous than many people realize. This haunting photo shows singer Karen Carpenter shortly before her death. Carpenter died of starvation-induced heart failure. Carpenter was the first celebrity to publicly reveal her eating disorder. Many others have followed, including Paula Abdul, Fiona Apple, Victoria Beckham (Posh Spice), Princess Diana, Kate Dillon, Calista Flockhart, Janet Jackson, Alanis Morrisette, and many more.

▲ TABLE 9.1	**Recognizing Eating Disorders**

ANOREXIA NERVOSA
- Body weight below 85 percent of normal for one's height and age.
- Refusal to maintain body weight in normal range.
- Intense fear of becoming fat or gaining weight, even though underweight.
- Disturbance in one's body image or perceived weight.
- Self-evaluation is unduly influenced by body weight.
- Denial of seriousness of abnormally low body weight.
- Absence of menstrual periods.
- Purging behavior (vomiting or misuse of laxatives or diuretics).

BULIMIA NERVOSA
- Normal or above-normal weight.
- Recurring binge eating.
- Eating within an hour or two an amount of food that is much larger than most people would consume.
- Feeling a lack of control over eating.
- Purging behavior (vomiting or misuse of laxatives or diuretics).
- Excessive exercise to prevent weight gain.
- Fasting to prevent weight gain.
- Self-evaluation is unduly influenced by body weight.

(DSM-IV-TR, 2000.)

less than 1%

Anorexia nervosa Active self-starvation or a sustained loss of appetite that has psychological origins.

Bulimia nervosa Excessive eating (gorging) usually followed by self-induced vomiting and/or taking laxatives.

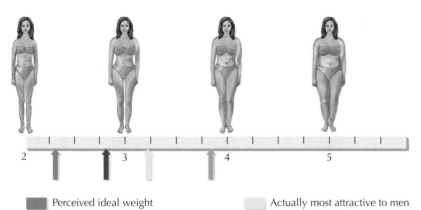

◆FIGURE 9.6 *Women with abnormal eating habits were asked to rate their body shape on a scale similar to the one you see here. As a group, they chose ideal figures much thinner than what they thought their current weights were. (Most women say they want to be thinner than they currently are, but to a lesser degree than women with eating problems.) Notice that women with eating problems chose an ideal weight that was even thinner than what they thought men prefer. This is not typical of most women. Only women with eating problems wanted to be thinner than what they thought men find attractive (Zellner, Harner, & Adler, 1989).*

■ Perceived ideal weight   ■ Actually most attractive to men

■ Perceived as most attractive to men   ■ Perceived current weight

(◆Fig. 9.6) (Gardner & Bokenkamp, 1996; Polivy & Herman, 2002). Many of these problems are related to harmful messages in the media. Girls who spend a lot of time reading teen magazines are likely to develop distorted body images and unrealistic ideas about how they compare with others (Martinez-Gonzalez et al., 2003).

Anorexic teens are usually described as "perfect" daughters—helpful, considerate, conforming, and obedient. Many seem to be seeking perfect control in their lives by being perfectly slim (Pliner & Haddock, 1996). People suffering from bulimia are also concerned with control. Typically, they are obsessed with thoughts of weight, food, eating, and ridding themselves of food. As a result, they feel guilt, shame, self-contempt, and anxiety after a binge. Vomiting reduces their anxiety, which makes purging highly reinforcing (Powell & Thelen, 1996).

Treatment

People who have eating disorders need professional help. Treatment for anorexia usually begins with a medical diet to restore weight and health. Next, a counselor may help patients work on the emotional conflicts that led to weight loss. For bulimia, behavioral counseling may include self-monitoring of food intake. The urge to vomit can be treated with extinction training. A related cognitive-behavioral approach focuses on changing the thinking patterns and beliefs about weight and body shape that perpetuate eating disorders (Whittal, Agras, & Gould, 1999).

Most people suffering from eating disorders will not seek help on their own. Typically, it takes strong urging by family or friends to get victims into treatment.

PRIMARY MOTIVES REVISITED— THIRST, SEX, AND PAIN

] SURVEYQUESTIONS *Is there more than one type of thirst? In what ways are pain avoidance and the sex drive unusual?*

Most biological motives work in ways that are similar to hunger. For example, thirst is only partially controlled by dryness of the mouth. If you were to take a drug that made your mouth constantly wet, or dry, your water intake would remain normal. Like hunger, thirst is regulated by separate *thirst* and *thirst satiety* systems in the hypothalamus. Also like hunger, thirst is strongly affected by learning and cultural values.

Thirst

You may not have noticed, but there are actually two kinds of thirst. **Extracellular thirst** occurs when fluids surrounding the cells of your body lose water. Bleeding, vomiting, diarrhea, sweating, and drinking alcohol cause this type of thirst (Petri, 2003). If a person loses

The relentless parade of atypically thin models in the media contributes to eating disorders. People with eating disorders are much more likely to report being influenced by unrealistic body ideals in the media (Murray, Touyz, & Beumont, 1996).

Extracellular thirst Thirst caused by a reduction in the volume of fluids found between body cells.

Gary Conner/PhotoEdit

It may seem contradictory, but thirst caused by perspiring is best quenched by slightly salty liquids. The salty snacks offered at taverns are intended to increase beer sales, but they also appeal to people who have perspired heavily at work or play.

water and minerals in any of these ways—especially by perspiration—a slightly salty liquid may be more satisfying than plain water.

Why would a thirsty person want to drink salty water?   Before the body can retain water, it must replace minerals lost through perspiration (mainly salt). In lab tests, animals greatly prefer drinking saltwater after salt levels in their bodies are lowered (Strickler & Verbalis, 1988). Similarly, some nomadic peoples of the Sahara Desert prize blood as a beverage, probably because of its saltiness. (Maybe they should try Gatorade?)

A second type of thirst occurs when you eat a salty meal. In this instance your body does not lose fluid. Instead, excess salt causes fluid to be drawn out of cells. As the cells "shrink," **intracellular thirst** is triggered. Thirst of this type is best quenched by plain water.

The drives for food, water, air, sleep, and elimination are all similar in that they are generated by a combination of activities in the body and the brain, and they are influenced by various external factors. However, the sex drive and the drive to avoid pain are more unusual.

Tolerance for pain and the strength of a person's motivation to avoid discomfort are greatly affected by cultural practices and beliefs.

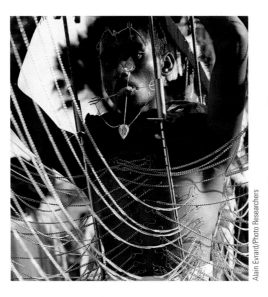

Alain Evrard/Photo Researchers

Pain

How is the drive to avoid pain different?   Hunger, thirst, and sleepiness come and go in a fairly regular cycle each day. Pain avoidance, by contrast, is an **episodic drive** (ep-ih-SOD-ik). That is, it occurs in distinct episodes when bodily damage takes place or is about to occur. Most drives prompt us to actively seek a desired goal (food, drink, warmth, and so forth). Pain prompts us to *avoid* or *eliminate* sources of discomfort.

Some people feel they must be "tough" and not show any distress. Others complain loudly at the smallest ache or pain. The first attitude raises pain tolerance, and the second lowers it. As this suggests, the drive to avoid pain is partly learned. That's why members of some societies endure cutting, burning, whipping, tattooing, and piercing of the skin that would agonize most people (but apparently not devotees of piercing and "body art"). In general, we learn how to react to pain by observing family members, friends, and other role models (Rollman, 1998).

Intracellular thirst Thirst triggered when fluid is drawn out of cells due to an increased concentration of salts and minerals outside the cell.

Episodic drive A drive that occurs in distinct episodes.

Sex drive The strength of one's motivation to engage in sexual behavior.

Estrus Changes in the sexual drives of animals that create a desire for mating; particularly used to refer to females in heat.

Estrogen Any of a number of female sex hormones.

The Sex Drive

Many psychologists do not think of sex as a primary motive, because sex (contrary to anything your personal experience might suggest) is not necessary for *individual* survival. It is necessary, of course, for *group* survival.

The term **sex drive** refers to the strength of one's motivation to engage in sexual behavior. In lower animals the sex drive is directly related to hormones. Most female mammals (other than humans) are interested in mating only when their fertility cycles are in the stage of **estrus,** or "heat." Estrus is caused by a release of **estrogen** (a female sex hormone) into the bloodstream. Hormones are important in males as well. In most animals, castration will abolish the sex drive. But in contrast to females, the normal male animal is almost always ready to mate. His sex drive is primarily aroused by the behavior and scent of a receptive female. Therefore, in many species mating is closely tied to female fertility cycles.

How much do hormones affect human sex drives? Hormones affect the human sex drive, but not as directly as in animals. The sex drive in men is related to the amount of **androgens** (male hormones) provided by the testes. When the supply of androgens dramatically increases at puberty, so does the male sex drive. Likewise, the sex drive in women is related to their estrogen levels (Graziottin, 1998). However, "male" hormones also affect the female sex drive. In addition to estrogen, a woman's body produces small amounts of androgens. When their androgen levels increase, many women experience a corresponding increase in sex drive (Van Goozen et al., 1995). Testosterone levels decline with age, and various medical problems can lower sexual desire. In some instances, taking testosterone supplements can restore the sex drive in both men and women (Crooks & Baur, 2002).

Does alcohol increase the sex drive? In general, no. Alcohol is a *depressant.* As such, it may, in small doses, stimulate erotic desire by lowering inhibitions. This effect no doubt accounts for alcohol's reputation as an aid to seduction. (Humorist Ogden Nash once summarized this bit of folklore by saying "Candy is dandy, but liquor is quicker.") However, in larger doses alcohol suppresses orgasm in women and erection in men. Getting drunk *decreases* sexual desire, arousal, pleasure, and performance (Crowe & George, 1989).

Numerous other drugs are reputed to be aphrodisiacs (af-ruh-DEEZ-ee-aks: substances that increase sexual desire or pleasure). However, like alcohol, a long list of other drugs actually impai sexual response, rather than enhance it. Some examples are amphetamines, amyl nitrite, barbiturates, cocaine, Ecstasy, LSD, and marijuana. As one expert observed, "Love, however you define it, seems to be the best aphrodisiac of all" (Crooks & Baur, 2002).

Perhaps the most interesting fact about the sex drive is that it is largely *non-homeostatic* (relatively independent of bodily need states). In humans, the sex drive can be aroused at virtually any time by almost anything. It therefore shows no clear relationship to deprivation (the amount of time since the drive was last satisfied). Certainly, an increase in desire may occur as time passes. But recent sexual activity does not prevent sexual desire from occurring again. Notice, too, that people may seek to arouse the sex drive as well as to reduce it. This unusual quality may explain why sex is used to sell almost everything imaginable.

The sex drive affects the lives of most people. Let's explore human sexuality in a little more detail.

SEXUAL BEHAVIOR—MAPPING THE EROGENOUS ZONE

] SURVEYQUESTION *What are the typical patterns of human sexual response?*

Human sexual arousal is complex. It may, of course, be produced by direct stimulation of the body's **erogenous zones** (eh-ROJ-eh-nus: productive of pleasure or erotic desire). Human erogenous zones include the genitals, mouth, breasts, ears, anus, and to a lesser degree, the entire surface of the body. It is clear, however, that more than physical contact is involved: A urological or gynecological exam rarely results in any sexual arousal. Likewise, an unwanted sexual advance may produce only revulsion. Human sexual arousal obviously includes a large mental element.

Sexual Scripts

In a restaurant we commonly expect certain things to occur. It could even be said that each of us has a restaurant "script" that defines a plot, dialogue, and actions that should take place. Researcher John Gagnon (1977) points out that, similarly, we learn a variety of **sexual scripts,** or unspoken mental plans that guide our sexual behavior. Such scripts deter-

Androgen Any of a number of male sex hormones, especially testosterone.

Erogenous zones Areas of the body that produce pleasure and/or provoke erotic desire.

Sexual script An unspoken mental plan that defines a "plot," dialogue, and actions expected to take place in a sexual encounter.

◆FIGURE 9.7 *These graphs show the frequency of sexual intercourse for American adults. To generalize, about one third of the people surveyed have sex twice a week or more, one third a few times a month, and one third a few times a year or not at all. The overall average is about once a week (Laumann et al., 1994).*

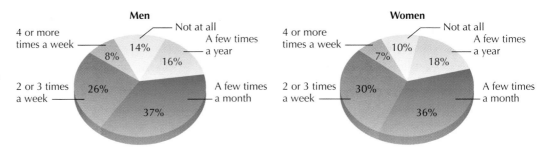

mine when and where we are likely to express sexual feelings, and with whom. They provide a "plot" for the order of events in lovemaking, and they outline "approved" actions, motives, and outcomes.

When two people follow markedly different scripts, misunderstandings are almost sure to occur. Consider, for instance, what happens when a woman acting out a "friendly-first-date" script is paired with a man following a "seduction" script: The result is often anger, hurt feelings, or worse. Even newlyweds may find that their sexual "agendas" differ. In such cases, considerable "rewriting" of scripts is often needed for sexual compatibility. For humans the mind (or brain) is the ultimate erogenous zone.

Sexual Arousal

Are men more easily sexually aroused than women? Overall, women and men have equal potential for sexual arousal, and women are no less *physically* responsive than men. However, women tend to place more emphasis on emotional closeness with a lover than men do (Laan et al., 1995).

Based on the frequency of orgasm (from masturbation or intercourse), the peak of male sexual activity is at age 18. The peak rate of female sexual activity appears to occur a little later (Janus & Janus, 1993). However, male and female sexual patterns are rapidly becoming more alike (Oliver & Hyde, 1993). ◆Figure 9.7 shows the results of a major survey of sexual behavior among American adults. As you can see, the frequency of sexual intercourse is very similar for men and women (Laumann et al., 1994). Exaggerating the differences between male and female sexuality is not only inaccurate, it can also create artificial barriers to sexual satisfaction (Wiederman, 2001). For example, assuming that men should always initiate sex denies the fact that women have comparable sexual interests and needs.

Sexual Orientation

Sexual behavior and romantic relationships are strongly influenced by a person's sexual orientation. **Sexual orientation** refers to your degree of emotional and erotic attraction to members of the same sex, opposite sex, or both sexes. *Heterosexual* people are romantically and erotically attracted to members of the opposite sex. Those who are *homosexual* are attracted to people whose sex matches their own. A person who is *bisexual* is attracted to both men and women. In short, sexual orientation answers these questions: Who are you attracted to? Who do you have erotic fantasies about? Do you love men, or women, or both (Garnets, 2002)?

Sexual orientation is a deep part of personal identity. Starting with their earliest erotic feelings, most people remember being attracted to either the opposite sex or the same sex. The chances are practically zero of an exclusively heterosexual or homosexual person being "converted" from one orientation to the other. If you are heterosexual, you are probably certain that nothing could ever make you have homoerotic feelings. If so, then you know how homosexual persons feel about the prospects for changing *their* sexual orientation (Seligman, 1994).

What determines a person's sexual orientation? Research suggests that a combination of hereditary, biological, social, cultural, and psychological influences combine to produce one's sexual orientation (Garnets, 2002; Van Wyk & Geist, 1995). Evidence also suggests

Sexual orientation One's degree of emotional and erotic attraction to members of the same sex, opposite sex, or both sexes.

that sexual orientation is at least partly hereditary. Some researchers now estimate that sexual orientation is from 30 to 70 percent genetic (Bailey et al., 1993; Bailey & Pillard, 1991).

How could genes affect sexual orientation? Possibly, heredity affects areas of the brain that orchestrate sexual behavior. In support of this idea, scientists have shown that various brain structures differ in heterosexuals and homosexuals (LeVay, 1993).

Homosexuality is not caused by hormone imbalances (Banks & Gartrell, 1995). It is also a mistake to think that parenting makes children homosexual. There is little difference in the development of children with gay or lesbian parents and those who have heterosexual parents (Chan, Raboy, & Patterson, 1998; Parks, 1998). It appears that nature strongly prepares people to be either homosexual or heterosexual. In view of this, discriminating against homosexuals is much like rejecting a person for being blue-eyed or left-handed (Hamill, 1995).

Homosexual people are found in all walks of life, at all social and economic levels, and in all cultural groups (Garnets, 2002). Perhaps as more people come to see gay and lesbian people in terms of their humanity, rather than their sexuality, the prejudices they have faced will wane.

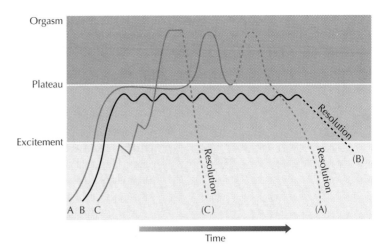

◆FIGURE 9.8 *Female sexual response cycle. The green line shows that sexual arousal rises through the excitement phase and levels off for a time during the plateau phase. Arousal peaks during orgasm and then returns to pre-excitement levels. In pattern A, arousal rises from excitement, through the plateau phase, and peaks in orgasm. Resolution may be immediate, or it may first include a return to the plateau phase and a second orgasm (dotted line). In pattern B, arousal is sustained at the plateau phase and slowly resolved without sexual climax. Pattern C shows a fairly rapid rise in arousal to orgasm. Little time is spent in the plateau phase, and resolution is fairly rapid. (From Frank A. Beach [ed.],* Sex and Behavior, *NY: John Wiley & Sons, Inc., 1965.)*

Human Sexual Response

In a pioneering series of studies, William Masters and Virginia Johnson directly studied sexual intercourse in nearly 700 males and females. The objective information they gained has given us a much clearer picture of human sexuality (Masters & Johnson, 1966, 1970). According to Masters and Johnson, sexual response can be divided into four phases: (1) *excitement,* (2) *plateau,* (3) *orgasm,* and (4) *resolution* (◆Fig. 9.8 and ◆Fig. 9.9). These four phases can be described as follows:

Excitement phase The first level of sexual response, indicated by initial signs of sexual arousal.

Plateau phase The second level of sexual response, during which physical arousal intensifies.

Orgasm A climax and release of sexual excitement.

Resolution The final phase of sexual response, involving a return to lower levels of sexual tension and arousal.

The four phases are the same for people of all sexual orientations (Garnets & Kimmel, 1991).

Female Response

In women, the excitement phase is marked by a complex pattern of changes in the body. The vagina is prepared for intercourse, the nipples become erect, pulse rate rises, and the skin may become flushed or reddened. If sexual stimulation ends, the excitement phase will gradually subside. If a woman moves into the plateau phase, physical changes and subjective feelings of arousal become more intense. Sexual arousal that ends during this phase tends to ebb more slowly, which may produce considerable frustration. Occasionally, women skip the plateau phase (Fig. 9.8). For some women, this is almost always the case.

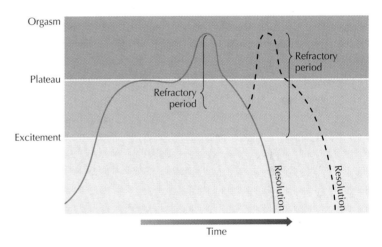

◆FIGURE 9.9 *Male sexual response cycle. The green line shows that sexual arousal rises through the excitement phase and levels off for a time during the plateau phase. Arousal peaks during orgasm and then returns to pre-excitement levels. During the refractory period, immediately after orgasm, a second sexual climax is typically impossible. However, after the refractory period has passed, there may be a return to the plateau phase, followed by a second orgasm (dotted line). (From Frank A. Beach [ed.],* Sex and Behavior, *NY: John Wiley & Sons, Inc., 1965.)*

Excitement phase The first phase of sexual response, indicated by initial signs of sexual arousal.

Plateau phase The second phase of sexual response during which physical arousal is further heightened.

Orgasm A climax and release of sexual excitement.

Resolution The fourth phase of sexual response, involving a return to lower levels of sexual tension and arousal.

Orgasm is usually followed by resolution, a return to lower levels of sexual tension and arousal. After orgasm, about 15 percent of all women return to the plateau phase and may have one or more additional orgasms.

Male Response

Sexual arousal in the male is signaled by erection of the penis during the excitement phase. There is also a rise in heart rate, increased blood flow to the genitals, enlargement of the testicles, erection of the nipples, and numerous other bodily changes. As is true of female sexual response, continued stimulation moves the male into the plateau phase. Again, physical changes and subjective feelings of arousal become more intense. Further stimulation during the plateau phase brings about a reflex release of sexual tension, resulting in orgasm.

In the mature male, orgasm is usually accompanied by ejaculation (release of sperm and seminal fluid). Afterward, it is followed by a short *refractory period* during which a second orgasm is impossible. Only rarely is the male refractory period immediately followed by a second orgasm. Both orgasm and resolution in the male usually do not last as long as they do for females.

Comparing Male and Female Responses

Male and female sexual responses are generally quite similar. However, the differences that do exist can affect sexual compatibility. For example, women typically go through the sexual phases more slowly than men do. However, during masturbation, 70 percent of females reach orgasm in 4 minutes or less. This is quite comparable to male response times. It suggests again that women are no less physically responsive than men.

In one regard, women are clearly more responsive. Only about 5 percent of males are capable of multiple orgasm (and then only after an unavoidable refractory period). Most men are limited to a second orgasm at best. In contrast, Masters and Johnson's findings suggest that most women who regularly experience orgasm are capable of multiple orgasm. According to one survey, 48 percent of all women have had multiple orgasms (Darling et al., 1992). Remember though, that only about 15 percent regularly have multiple orgasms. A woman should not automatically assume that something is wrong if she isn't orgasmic or multi-orgasmic. Many women have satisfying sexual experiences even when orgasm is not involved. (For information about common sexual complaints, see "Sexual Problems—When Pleasure Fades.")

CLINICAL FILE Sexual Problems—When Pleasure Fades

Sexual dysfunctions are far more common than many people realize. Most people who seek sexual counseling have one or more of the following types of problems (DSM-IV-TR, 2000):

Desire Disorders: The person has little or no sexual motivation or desire.
Arousal Disorders: The person desires sexual activity but does not become sexually aroused.
Orgasm Disorders: The person does not have orgasms or experiences orgasm too soon or too late.
Sexual Pain Disorders: The person experiences pain that makes lovemaking uncomfortable or impossible.

There was a time when people suffered such problems in silence. However, in recent years effective treatments have been found for many complaints.

Medical treatments or drugs (such as Viagra and Cialis for men) may be helpful for sexual problems that clearly have physical causes. In other cases, counseling or psychotherapy may be the best approach. For example, many patients benefit from a technique called *sensate focus*. In sensate focus, distressed couples begin by taking turns caressing each other in non-sexual ways. They are told to concentrate on giving pleasure and on signaling what feels good to them. This relieves the pressure to perform and it builds communication skills. Slowly, the couple moves on to mutually satisfying lovemaking, as natural arousal begins to replace fear and anger. Similar solutions exist for many sexual problems. In most communities, professional help can be obtained from appropriately trained psychologists, physicians, or counselors.

Healthy Sexual Relationships

As a shared pleasure, a form of intimacy, a means of communication, and a haven from everyday tensions, a positive sexual relationship can do much to enhance a couple's mutual understanding and caring. People are most likely to value their sexuality when they develop a respectful, trusting, and intimate relationship with their partner. A sense of closeness helps maintain sexual interest and mutually satisfying lovemaking, especially in long-term relationships (McCarthy, 1995).

STUDYBREAK Y *Hunger, Thirst, Pain, and Sex*

RELATE

Think of the last meal you ate. What caused you to feel hungry? What internal signals told your body to stop eating? How sensitive are you to external eating cues? Have you developed any taste aversions?

A friend of yours seems to be engaging in yo-yo dieting. Can you explain to her or him why such dieting is ineffective?

Even if you're not overweight, reread each of the weight control techniques listed in the Using Psychology box and visualize how you would carry out the suggested behaviors.

If you wanted to provoke extracellular thirst in yourself, what would you do? How could you make intracellular thirst occur?

In what ways are sexual responses of members of the opposite sex similar to your own? In what ways are they different?

LEARNING CHECK

1. The hunger satiety system in the hypothalamus signals the body to start eating when it receives signals from the liver or detects changes in blood sugar. T or F?
2. People who diet frequently tend to benefit from practice: They lose weight more quickly each time they diet. T or F?

3. Anorexia nervosa is also known as the binge-purge syndrome. T or F?
4. In addition to burning calories, physical exercise can lower the body's set point. T or F?
5. Thirst may be either intracellular or _____.
6. Pain avoidance is an _____ drive.
7. Sexual behavior in animals is largely controlled by estrogen levels in the female and the occurrence of estrus in the male. T or F?
8. List the four phases of sexual response identified by Masters and Johnson:
_____ _____ _____
_____

Critical Thinking

9. Kim, who is overweight, is highly sensitive to external eating cues. How might her wristwatch contribute to her overeating?
10. Charting weight loss makes use of a behavioral principle discussed in Chapter 6, "Conditioning and Learning." Can you name it?

ANSWERS

1. F 2. F 3. F 4. T 5. extracellular 6. episodic 7. F 8. excitement, plateau, orgasm, resolution 9. The time of day can influence eating, especially for externally cued eaters, who tend to get hungry at mealtimes, irrespective of their internal needs for food. 10. Feedback.

STIMULUS DRIVES—SKYDIVING, HORROR MOVIES, AND THE FUN ZONE

] SURVEYQUESTION *How does arousal relate to motivation?*

Are you full of energy right now? Are you feeling tired? Clearly, your current level of arousal is closely linked with your motivation. Are there ideal levels of arousal for different people and different activities? Let's find out.

Most people enjoy a steady "diet" of new movies, novels, tunes, fashions, games, news, Web sites, and adventures. Yet stimulus drives, which reflect needs for information, exploration, manipulation, and sensory input, go beyond mere entertainment. Stimulus drives also help us survive. As we scan our surroundings, we constantly identify sources of food, danger, shelter, and other key details. Stimulus drives are readily apparent in animals as well as humans. For example, monkeys will quickly learn to solve a mechanical puzzle made up of interlocking metal pins, hooks, and latches (Butler, 1954) (◆Fig. 9.10). No food treats or other external rewards are needed to get them to explore and manipulate their surroundings. The monkeys seem to work for the sheer fun of it.

✦FIGURE 9.10 *Monkeys happily open locks that are placed in their cage. Since no reward is given for this activity, it provides evidence for the existence of stimulus needs. (Photo courtesy of Harry F. Harlow, University of Wisconsin Primate Laboratory.)*

Arousal Theory

Are stimulus drives homeostatic?   Yes. According to a perspective called **arousal theory,** ideal levels of activation exist for various activities. Additionally, we try to keep arousal near these optimal levels (Hebb, 1966). In other words, when your level of arousal is too low, stimulus seeking helps to raise it.

What do you mean by arousal?   Arousal refers to the overall level of activation of the body and the nervous system. Arousal is zero at death; it is low during sleep; it is moderate during normal daily activities; and it is high at times of excitement, emotion, or panic. Arousal theory assumes that we become uncomfortable when arousal is too low ("I'm bored") or when it is too high, as in fear, anxiety, or panic ("The dentist will see you now"). Most adults vary their activities to maintain a comfortable level of activation. We combine music, parties, sports, conversation, sleep, surfing the Net, and the like to keep arousal at moderate levels. The right mix of activities prevents boredom *and* overstimulation.

Sensation Seekers

Do people vary in their needs for stimulation?   Picture a city dweller who is visiting the country. Very soon, she complains that it is "too quiet" and seeks some "action." Now imagine a country dweller who is visiting the city. Very soon, she finds the city "overwhelming" and seeks peace and quiet. These examples are extremes, but arousal theory also suggests that people learn to seek particular levels of arousal. Marvin Zuckerman (1990) has devised a test to measure such differences. The *Sensation-Seeking Scale* (SSS), as he calls it, includes statements like the samples shown here (from Zuckerman, 1996; Zuckerman et al., 1978):

THRILL AND ADVENTURE SEEKING

- I would like to try parachute jumping.
- I think I would enjoy the sensations of skiing very fast down a high mountain slope.

EXPERIENCE SEEKING

- I like to explore a strange city or section of town myself, even if it means getting lost.
- I like to try new foods that I have never tasted before.

DISINHIBITION

- I like wild, "uninhibited" parties.
- I often like to get high (drinking liquor or smoking marijuana).

BOREDOM SUSCEPTIBILITY

- I can't stand watching a movie that I've seen before.
- I like people who are sharp and witty, even if they do sometimes insult others.

Arousal theory Assumes that people prefer to maintain ideal, or comfortable, levels of arousal.

Sensation seeking is a trait of people who prefer high levels of stimulation. Whether you are high or low in sensation seeking is probably based on how your body responds to new, unusual, or intense stimulation (Zuckerman, 1990). People who score high on the SSS tend to be bold, independent individuals who value change. They also report more sexual partners than low scorers; they are more likely to smoke, and they prefer spicy, sour, and crunchy foods over bland foods. Low sensation seekers are orderly, nurturant, and giving, and they enjoy the company of others. Which are you? (Most people fall somewhere between the extremes.)

Thrill seeking is an element of the sensation-seeking personality.

Levels of Arousal

Is there an ideal level of arousal for peak performance? If we set aside individual differences, most people perform best when their arousal level is *moderate.* Let's say that you have to take an essay exam. If you are sleepy or feeling lazy (arousal level too low), your performance will suffer. If you are in a state of anxiety or panic about the test (arousal level too high), you will also perform below par. Thus, the relationship between arousal and performance forms an *inverted U function* (a curve in the shape of an upside-down U) (◆Fig. 9.11) (Anderson, 1990).

The inverted U tells us that at very low levels of arousal you're not sufficiently energized to perform well. Performance will improve as your arousal level increases, up to the middle of the curve. Then it begins to drop off, as you become emotional, frenzied, or disorganized. For example, imagine trying to start a car stalled on a railroad track, with a speeding train bearing down on you. That's what the high-arousal end of the curve feels like.

Is performance always best at moderate levels of arousal? No, the ideal level of arousal depends on the complexity of a task. If a task is relatively simple, it is best for arousal to be high. When a task is more complex, the best performance occurs at lower levels of arousal. This relationship is called the **Yerkes-Dodson law** (Fig. 9.11). It applies to a wide variety of tasks and to measures of motivation other than arousal.

Some examples of the Yerkes-Dodson law might be helpful. At a track meet, it is almost impossible for sprinters to get too aroused for a race. Their task is direct and uncomplicated: Run as fast as possible for a short distance. On the other hand, a basketball player making a game-deciding free throw faces a more sensitive and complex task. Excessive arousal is almost certain to hurt his or her performance. In school, most students have had "test anxiety," a familiar example of how too much arousal can lower performance.

Then is it true that by learning to calm down, a person would do better on tests? Usually, but not always. Studies show that students are most anxious when they don't know the material. If this is the case, calming down simply means you will remain calm while failing. (See "Coping with Test Anxiety" to learn how to avoid excessive arousal.)

Yerkes-Dodson law A summary of the relationships among arousal, task complexity, and performance.

(a) Inverted U function

(b) Simple task

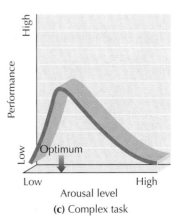
(c) Complex task

◆FIGURE 9.11 (a) *The general relationship between arousal and efficiency can be described by an inverted U curve. The optimal level of arousal or motivation is higher for a simple task (b) than for a complex task (c).*

Coping with Test Anxiety

Would you like to win a million dollars on a game show? Or would you merely like do well on classroom tests? In either case, your ability to answer questions will be impaired if you are too nervous. Test anxiety is a combination of *heightened physiological arousal* (nervousness, sweating, pounding heart) and *excessive worry*. This combination—worry plus arousal—tends to distract students with a rush of upsetting thoughts and feelings (Gierl & Rogers, 1996). Let's see what you can do to alleviate test anxiety.

PREPARATION

The most direct antidote for test anxiety is *hard work*. Many test-anxious students simply study too little, too late. That's why improving your study skills is a good way to reduce test anxiety (Jones & Petruzzi, 1995). The best solution is to *overprepare* by studying long before the "big day." Students who are well prepared score higher, worry less, and are less likely to panic (Zohar, 1998).

RELAXATION

Learning to relax is another way to lower test anxiety (Ricketts & Galloway, 1984). You can learn self-relaxation skills by looking at Chapter 13, where a relaxation technique is described. Emotional support can also help you relax (Sarason, 1981). If you are test anxious, discuss the problem with your professors or study for tests with a supportive classmate.

REHEARSAL

To reduce your nervousness during tests, rehearse how you will cope with upsetting events. Before taking a test, imagine yourself going blank, running out of time, or feeling panicked. Then calmly plan how you will handle each situation—by keeping your attention on the task, by focusing on one question at a time, and so forth (Watson & Tharp, 2001).

RESTRUCTURING THOUGHTS

Many test-anxious students benefit from listing the distracting and upsetting thoughts they typically have during exams. They then learn to combat their worries with calming, rational replies (Jones & Petruzzi, 1995). (These are called *coping statements;* see Chapter 11 for more information.) Let's say you think, "I'm going to fail this test, and everybody will think I'm stupid." A good reply to this upsetting thought would be to say, "If I prepare well and control my worries, I will probably pass the test. Even if I don't, it won't be the end of the world. My friends will still like me, and I can try to improve on the next test."

Students who cope well with exams usually try to do the best they can, even under trying circumstances. Becoming a more confident test taker can actually increase your scores, because it helps you remain calm. With practice, most people can learn to be less testy at test-taking time (Smith, 2002; Zeidner, 1995).

Circadian Rhythms

We have seen that moment-to-moment changes in activation have a major impact on us. What about longer cycles of arousal? Do they affect energy levels, motivation, and performance? Scientists have long known that the bodily activity is guided by internal "biological clocks." Every 24 hours, your body undergoes a cycle of changes called **circadian** (SUR-kay-dee-AN) **rhythms** (*circa*: about; *diem*: a day) (Orlock, 1993). Throughout the day, activities in the liver, kidneys, and endocrine glands undergo large changes. Body temperature, blood pressure, and amino acid levels also shift from hour to hour. These activities, and many others, peak once a day (◆Fig. 9.12). People are usually more energetic and alert at the high point of their circadian rhythms (Natale & Cicogna, 1996).

Circadian rhythms Cyclical changes in bodily functions and arousal levels that vary on a schedule approximating a 24-hour day.

Shift Work and Jet Lag

Circadian rhythms are most noticeable after a major change in time schedules. Businesspersons, athletes, and other time zone travelers tend to perform poorly when their body rhythms are disturbed. If you travel great distances east or west, the peaks and valleys of your circadian rhythms will be out of phase with the sun and clocks. For example, you might be wide awake at midnight and feel like you're sleepwalking during the day (return to Figure 9.12). Shift work has the same effect, causing fatigue, irritability, upset stomach, and depression (Akerstedt, 1990).

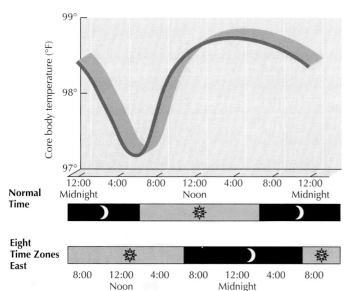

◆FIGURE 9.12 *Core body temperature follows a circadian rhythm. Most people reach a low point 2 to 3 hours before the time they normally wake up. It's no wonder that both the Chernobyl and Three-Mile Island nuclear power plant accidents occurred around 4 A.M. Rapid travel to a different time zone, shift work, depression, and illness can disrupt the body's core rhythm, with disturbing effects (Hauri & Linde, 1990).*

How fast do people adapt to rhythm changes? For major time zone shifts (5 hours or more), it can take from several days to 2 weeks to resynchronize. Adjusting to jet lag is slowest when you stay indoors, where you can sleep and eat on "home time." Getting outdoors, where you must sleep, eat, and socialize on the new schedule, speeds adaptation. A 5-hour dose of bright sunlight early each day is particularly helpful for resetting your circadian rhythm (Czeisler et al., 1989). The *direction* of travel also affects adaptation (Harma et al., 1994). If you fly west, adapting is relatively easy, taking an average of 4 to 5 days. If you fly east, adapting takes 50 percent longer, or more (✦Fig. 9.13).

Why is there a difference? When you fly east, the sun comes up *earlier* relative to your "home" time. Let's say that you live in Los Angeles and fly to New York. If you get up at 7 A.M. in New York, it's 4 A.M. back in Los Angeles—and your body knows it. If you fly west, the sun comes up later. In this case, it is easier for people to "advance" (stay up later and sleep in) than it is to shift backward.

How does this affect those of us who are not world travelers? Most college students have "pulled an all-nighter," especially for final exams. At such times it is wise to remember that departing from your regular schedule usually costs more than it's worth. Often, you can do as much during 1 hour in the morning as you could have done in 3 hours of work after midnight. You might just as well go to sleep 2 hours earlier.

In general, if you can anticipate an upcoming body rhythm change, it is best to preadapt to your new schedule. *Preadaptation* refers to gradually matching your sleep-waking cycle to a new time schedule. Before traveling, for instance, you should go to sleep 1 hour later (or earlier) each day until your sleep cycle matches the time at your destination. If you are unable to do that, it helps to fly early in the day when you fly east. When you fly west, it is better to fly late. (Remember, the *E* in *east* matches the *E* in *early*.)

✦**FIGURE 9.13** *Time required to adjust to air travel across six time zones. The average time to resynchronize was shorter for westbound travel than for eastbound flights. (Data from Beljan et al., 1972; cited by Moore-Ede et al., 1982.)*

LEARNED MOTIVES—IN PURSUIT OF EXCELLENCE

] SURVEYQUESTIONS *What are social motives? Why are they important?*

Some of your friends are more interested than others in success, achievement, competition, money, possessions, status, love, approval, grades, dominance, power, or belonging to groups—all of which are *social motives* or goals. We acquire **social motives** in complex ways, through socialization and cultural conditioning. The behavior of outstanding artists, scientists, athletes, educators, and leaders is best understood in terms of such learned needs, particularly the need for achievement.

The Need for Achievement

To many people, being "motivated" means being interested in achievement. In a later chapter we will investigate aggression, helping, affiliation, seeking approval, and other social motives. For now, let us focus on the **need for achievement** (**nAch**), which is a desire to meet an internal standard of excellence (McClelland, 1961). People with high needs for achievement strive to do well any time they are evaluated.

Is that like the aggressive businessperson who strives for success? Not necessarily. Needs for achievement may lead to wealth and prestige, but people who are high achievers in art, music, science, or amateur sports may excel without seeking riches. Such people typically enjoy challenges and they relish a chance to test their abilities (Puca & Schmalt, 1999).

Social motives Learned motives acquired as part of growing up in a particular society or culture.

Need for achievement The desire to excel or meet some internalized standard of excellence.

Power

The need for achievement is not the same as the **need for power,** which is a desire to have impact or control over others (McClelland, 1975). People with strong needs for power want their importance to be visible: They buy expensive possessions, wear prestigious clothes, and exploit other people. In some ways, seeking power and financial success is the dark side of the American dream. People whose main goal in life is to make lots of money tend to be poorly adjusted and unhappy (Kasser & Ryan, 1996).

Characteristics of Achievers

David McClelland (1917–1998) and others have probed the need for achievement. Using a simple measure, McClelland found that he could predict the behavior of high and low achievers in many situations. For instance, McClelland compared people's occupations with scores on an achievement test they took as college sophomores. Fourteen years later, those who scored high in nAch tended to have jobs that involved risk and responsibility (McClelland, 1965).

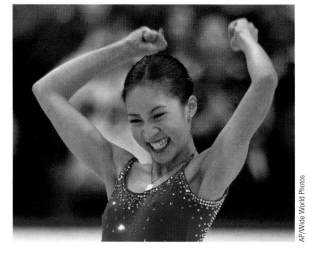

The person with high needs for achievement strives to do well in any situation in which evaluation takes place.

Here's a test: In front of you are five targets, each a little farther from you than the preceding target. You are given a beanbag to toss at the target of your choice. Target A, anyone can hit; target B, most people can hit; target C, some people can hit; target D, very few people can hit; target E is rarely if ever hit. If you hit A, you will receive $2; B, $4; C, $8; D, $16; and E, $32. You get only one toss. Which one would you choose? McClelland's research suggests that if you have a high need for achievement, you will select C or perhaps D. Those high in nAch are *moderate* risk takers. When faced with a problem or a challenge, persons high in nAch avoid goals that are too easy.

Why do they pass up sure success? They do it because easy goals offer no sense of satisfaction. They also avoid long shots because there is either no hope of success, or "winning" will be due to luck rather than skill. Persons low in nAch select sure things or impossible goals. Either way, they don't have to take any responsibility for failure.

Desires for achievement and calculated risk taking lead to success in many situations. People high in nAch tend to complete difficult tasks, they earn better grades, and they excel in their occupations. College students high in nAch attribute success to their own ability and failure to insufficient effort. Thus, high nAch students are more likely to renew their efforts when they perform poorly. When the going gets tough, high achievers get going.

In college, a great deal of importance is placed on academic achievement. In light of this, it is understandable that students are sometimes tempted to buy self-help tapes that promise to improve their motivation to study. Such tapes are aggressively advertised and available in many campus bookstores. However, if you're ever tempted to buy one of these tapes, you should ask a crucial question: Do they work? Read "Mail-Order Motivation?" to find out.

 Need for power The desire to have social impact and control over others.

CRITICAL THINKING   Mail-Order Motivation?

Each year, consumers spend millions of dollars on so-called "subliminal" self-help audiotapes. These tapes supposedly contain "subliminal messages" embedded in relaxing music or the soothing sounds of ocean waves. The tapes purportedly influence "subconscious motivation" to help listeners lose weight, relieve pain, find romance, succeed financially, improve grades, and so forth. Do the tapes work? Tanya Russell, Wayne Rowe, and Albert Smouse (1991) decided to test them under controlled conditions.

Russell, Rowe, and Smouse obtained the tapes *Improve Study Habits* and *Passing Exams* from the largest U.S. manufacturer of subliminal audiotapes. Three groups of university students took part in a 10-week evaluation. An "active treatment group" listened

to tapes containing subliminal suggestions. An "inactive treatment group" listened to placebo tapes with ocean wave sounds but no subliminal messages. Students in a control group didn't listen to any tapes.

The results of the experiment were certainly not subliminal. The message came through loud and clear: Average final exam grades and semester grade point averages for all three groups were the same (Russell, Rowe, & Smouse, 1991). People who think they have been helped by subliminal tapes have experienced nothing more than a placebo effect (Benoit & Thomas, 1992; Froufe & Schwartz, 2001; Merikle & Skanes, 1992; Moore, 1995; Staum & Brotons, 1992).

The Key to Success

What does it take to achieve extraordinary success? Psychologist Benjamin Bloom did an interesting study of America's top concert pianists, Olympic swimmers, sculptors, tennis players, mathematicians, and research neurologists. Bloom (1985) found that drive and determination, not great natural talent, led to exceptional success.

The first steps toward high achievement began when parents exposed their children to music, swimming, scientific ideas, and so forth "just for fun." At first, many of the children had very ordinary skills. One Olympic swimmer, for instance, remembers repeatedly losing races as a 10-year-old. At some point, however, the children began to actively cultivate their abilities. Before long, parents noticed the child's rapid progress and found an expert instructor or coach. After more successes, the youngsters began "living" for their talent and practiced many hours daily. This continued for many years before they reached truly outstanding heights of achievement.

The upshot of Bloom's work is that talent is nurtured by dedication and hard work. It is most likely to blossom when parents actively support a child's special interests and emphasize doing your best at all times. Studies of child prodigies and eminent adults also show that intensive practice and expert coaching are common ingredients of high achievement. Elite performance typically requires at least 10 years of dedicated practice (Ericsson & Charness, 1994). The old belief that talent will emerge on its own is largely a myth.

Self-confidence

Achieving elite performance may be reserved for the dedicated few. Nevertheless, you may be able to improve everyday motivation by increasing your self-confidence. People with self-confidence believe they can successfully carry out an activity or reach a goal. To enhance self-confidence, it is wise to do the following (Druckman & Bjork, 1994):

- Set goals that are specific and challenging, but attainable.
- Advance in small steps.
- When you first acquire a skill, your goal should be to make progress in learning. Later, you can concentrate on improving your performance, compared with other people.
- Get expert instruction that helps you master the skill.
- Find a skilled model (someone good at the skill) to emulate.
- Get support and encouragement from an observer.
- If you fail, regard it as a sign that you need to try harder, not that you lack ability.

Self-confidence affects motivation by influencing the challenges you will undertake, the effort you will make, and how long you will persist when things don't go well. You can be confident that self-confidence is worth cultivating.

MOTIVES IN PERSPECTIVE— A VIEW FROM THE PYRAMID

] SURVEYQUESTION *Are some motives more basic than others?*

What motivates people who live fully and richly?   As you may recall from Chapter 1, Abraham Maslow called the full use of personal potential *self-actualization*. Maslow also described a **hierarchy of human needs,** in which some needs are more basic or powerful than others. Think about the needs that influence your own behavior. Which seem strongest? Which do you spend the most time and energy satisfying? Now look at Maslow's hierarchy (◆Fig. 9.14). Note that physiological needs are at the base of the pyramid. Because these needs must be met if we are to survive, they tend to be *prepotent,* or dominant over the higher needs. It could be said, for example, that "to a starving person, food is god."

Hierarchy of human needs Abraham Maslow's ordering of needs, based on their presumed strength or potency.

◆FIGURE 9.14 *Maslow believed that lower needs in the hierarchy are dominant. Basic needs must be satisfied before growth motives are fully expressed. Desires for self-actualization are reflected in various meta-needs (see text).*

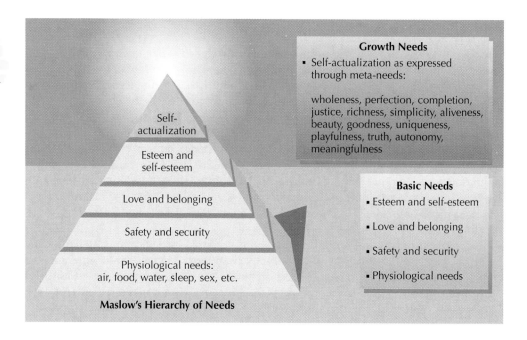

Growth Needs
- Self-actualization as expressed through meta-needs:

  wholeness, perfection, completion, justice, richness, simplicity, aliveness, beauty, goodness, uniqueness, playfulness, truth, autonomy, meaningfulness

Basic Needs
- Esteem and self-esteem
- Love and belonging
- Safety and security
- Physiological needs

Self-actualization

Esteem and self-esteem

Love and belonging

Safety and security

Physiological needs: air, food, water, sleep, sex, etc.

Maslow's Hierarchy of Needs

Maslow believed that higher, more fragile needs are expressed only after we satisfy our physiological needs. This is also true of needs for safety and security. Until they are met, we may have little interest in higher pursuits. A person who is extremely thirsty, for instance, might have little interest in writing poetry or even talking with friends. For this reason, Maslow described the first four levels of the hierarchy as **basic needs.** Other basic needs include love and belonging (family, friendship, caring) and needs for esteem and self-esteem (recognition and self-respect).

All of the basic needs are *deficiency* motives. That is, they are activated by a *lack* of food, water, security, love, esteem, or other basic needs. At the top of the hierarchy we find **growth needs,** which are expressed as a need for self-actualization. The need for self-actualization is not based on deficiencies. Rather, it is a positive, life-enhancing force for personal growth. Like other humanistic psychologists, Maslow believed that people are basically good. If our basic needs are met, he said, we will tend to move on to actualizing our potentials.

How are needs for self-actualization expressed? Maslow called the less powerful but humanly important actualization motives **meta-needs** (Maslow, 1970). Meta-needs are an expression of tendencies to fully development your personal potentials. The meta-needs are:

1. Wholeness (unity)
2. Perfection (balance and harmony)
3. Completion (ending)
4. Justice (fairness)
5. Richness (complexity)
6. Simplicity (essence)
7. Aliveness (spontaneity)
8. Beauty (rightness of form)
9. Goodness (benevolence)
10. Uniqueness (individuality)
11. Playfulness (ease)
12. Truth (reality)
13. Autonomy (self-sufficiency)
14. Meaningfulness (values)

According to Maslow, we tend to move up through the hierarchy of needs, toward the meta-needs. When the meta-needs are unfulfilled, people fall into a "syndrome of decay" marked by despair, apathy, and alienation.

Maslow's point is that mere survival or comfort is usually not enough to make a full and satisfying life. It's interesting to note, in this regard, that college students who are

Basic needs The first four levels of needs in Maslow's hierarchy; lower needs tend to be more potent than higher needs.

Growth needs In Maslow's hierarchy, the higher level needs associated with self-actualization.

Meta-needs In Maslow's hierarchy, needs associated with impulses for self-actualization.

primarily concerned with money, personal appearance, and social recognition score lower than average in vitality, self-actualization, and general well-being (Kasser & Ryan, 1996).

Maslow's hierarchy is not well documented by research, and parts of it are questionable. How, for instance, do we explain the actions of a person who fasts as part of a social protest? How can the meta-need for justice overcome the more basic need for food? (Perhaps the answer is that fasting is temporary and self-imposed.) Despite such objections, Maslow's views are a good way to understand and appreciate the rich interplay of human motives.

Are many people motivated by meta-needs? Maslow estimated that few people are primarily motivated by needs for self-actualization. Most of us are more concerned with esteem, love, or security. Perhaps this is because rewards in our society tend to encourage conformity, uniformity, and security in schools, jobs, and relationships. When was the last time you met a meta-need?

Wheelchair athletes engage in vigorous competition. Maslow considered such behavior an expression of the need for self-actualization.

Intrinsic and Extrinsic Motivation

Some people cook for a living and consider it hard work. Others cook for pleasure and dream of opening a restaurant. For some people, carpentry, gardening, writing, photography, or making jewelry is fun. For others, the same activities are drudgery they must be paid to do. How can the same activity be "work" for one person and "play" for another?

When you do something for enjoyment, to show your ability, or to gain skill, your motivation is usually *intrinsic.* **Intrinsic motivation** occurs when we act without any obvious external rewards. We simply enjoy an activity, see it as a challenge, want to enhance our abilities, or seek to explore and learn. In contrast, **extrinsic motivation** stems from obvious external factors, such as pay, grades, rewards, obligations, and approval. Most of the activities we think of as "work" are extrinsically rewarded (Ryan & Deci, 2000).

Turning Play into Work

Don't extrinsic incentives strengthen motivation? Yes they can, but not always. In fact, *excessive* rewards can decrease intrinsic motivation and spontaneous interest (Lepper, Keavney, & Drake, 1996; Tang & Hall, 1995). For instance, children who were lavishly rewarded for drawing with felt-tip pens later showed little interest in playing with the pens again (Greene & Lepper, 1974). Apparently, "play" can be turned into "work" by *requiring* people to do something they would otherwise enjoy. When we are coerced or "bribed" to act, we tend to feel as if we are "faking it." Employees who lack initiative and teenagers who reject school and learning are good examples of such reactions (Ryan & Deci, 2000).

Creativity

You are more likely to be creative when you are intrinsically motivated. On the job, salaries and bonuses may increase how much work people do. However, work quality and creativity are tied more to intrinsic factors, such as interest, freedom to choose, and useful feedback (Lewis et al., 1995). When a person is intrinsically motivated, a dash of challenge, surprise, and complexity makes a task rewarding. When extrinsic motivation is stressed, people are less likely to solve tricky problems and come up with innovative ideas (Amabile, Hadley, & Kramer, 2002).

How can the concept of intrinsic motivation be applied? Both types of motivation are necessary. But extrinsic motivation shouldn't be overused, especially with children. To summarize: (1) If there's no intrinsic interest in an activity to begin with, you have nothing to lose by using extrinsic rewards; (2) if basic skills are lacking, extrinsic rewards may be necessary at first; (3) extrinsic rewards can focus attention on an activity so real interest will

Intrinsic motivation Motivation that comes from within, rather than from external rewards; motivation based on personal enjoyment of a task or activity.

Extrinsic motivation Motivation based on obvious external rewards, obligations, or similar factors.

People who are intrinsically motivated feel free to explore creative solutions to problems.

Margaret Miller/Photo Researchers, Inc.

develop; (4) if extrinsic rewards are used, they should be small and phased out as soon as possible (Greene & Lepper, 1974). It also helps to tell children they seem to be *really interested* in drawing, playing the piano, learning a language, or whatever activity you are rewarding (Cialdini et al., 1998).

At work, it is valuable for managers to find out what each employee's interests and career goals are. People are not solely motivated by money. A chance to do challenging, interesting, and intrinsically rewarding work is often just as important (Campion & McClelland, 1993). In many situations it is important to encourage intrinsic motivation, especially when children are learning new skills.

STUDYBREAK *Stimulus Motives, Learned Motives, Maslow, and Intrinsic Motivation*

RELATE

Does arousal theory seem to explain any of your own behavior? Think of at least one time when your performance was impaired by arousal that was too low or too high. Now think of some personal examples that illustrate the Yerkes-Dodson law.

In situations involving risk and skill, do you like to "go for broke"? Or do you prefer sure things? Do you think you are high, medium, or low in nAch?

Which levels of Maslow's hierarchy of needs occupy most of your time and energy?

Name an activity you do that is intrinsically motivated and one that is extrinsically motivated. How do they differ?

LEARNING CHECK

1. Exploration, manipulation, and curiosity provide evidence for the existence of _____ drives.
2. People who score high on the SSS tend to be extroverted, independent, and individuals who value change. T or F?
3. When a task is complex, the ideal level of arousal is _____; when a task is simple, the optimal level of arousal is _____.

4. Two key elements of test anxiety that must be controlled are _____ and excessive _____.
5. People with high nAch are attracted to "long shots" and "sure things." T or F?
6. According to Maslow, meta-needs are the most basic and prepotent sources of human motivation. T or F?
7. Intrinsic motivation is often undermined in situations in which obvious external rewards are applied to a naturally enjoyable activity. T or F?

Critical Thinking

8. More than 75 percent of all U.S. college freshmen say that "being well-off financially" is an essential life goal. Seventy-three percent indicate that "making more money" was a very important factor in their decision to attend college. Which meta-needs are fulfilled by "making more money"?

ANSWERS

1. stimulus 2. T 3. low, high 4. arousal, worry 5. F 6. F 7. T 8. None of them.

INSIDE AN EMOTION—HOW DO YOU FEEL?

] SURVEYQUESTIONS *What happens during emotion? Can lie detectors really detect lies?*

Picture the faces of terrified people fleeing the collapse of the World Trade Center towers in New York, and it's easy to see that motivation and emotion are closely related. Emotions shape our relationships and color our daily activities. What are the basic parts of an emotion? How does your body respond to emotions?

Emotion is characterized by physiological arousal and changes in facial expressions, gestures, posture, and subjective feelings. The word *emotion* means "to move," and emotions do indeed move us. First, your body is physically aroused during emotion. Such bodily stirrings are what cause us to say we were "moved" by a play, a funeral, or an act of kindness.

Emotion A state characterized by physiological arousal, changes in facial expression, gestures, posture, and subjective feelings.

Second, we are often motivated, or moved to take action, by emotions such as fear, anger, or joy. Many of the goals we seek make us feel good. Many of the activities we avoid make us feel bad. We feel happy when we succeed and sad when we fail (Oatley & Jenkins, 1992).

Emotions are linked to many basic **adaptive behaviors,** such as attacking, fleeing, seeking comfort, helping others, reproducing, and the like. Such behaviors help us survive and adjust to changing conditions (Plutchik, 2001). However, it is also apparent that emotions can have negative effects. Stage fright or "choking up" in sports can spoil performances. Hate, anger, contempt, disgust, and fear disrupt behavior and relationships. But more often, emotions aid survival.

A pounding heart, sweating palms, "butterflies" in the stomach, and other bodily reactions are a major element of fear, anger, joy, and other emotions. Typical **physiological changes** include alterations in heart rate, blood pressure, perspiration, and other bodily stirrings. Most are caused by activity in the sympathetic nervous system and by the hormone *adrenaline,* which the adrenal glands release into the bloodstream.

Emotional expressions, or outward signs of what a person is feeling, are another ingredient of emotion. For example, when you are intensely afraid, your hands tremble, your face contorts, your posture becomes tense and defensive, and your voice changes. In general, these expressions tell others what emotions we are experiencing. **Emotional feelings** (a person's private emotional experience) are the third element of emotion. This is the part of emotion with which we are usually most familiar.

Primary Emotions

Are some emotions more basic than others? Yes, Robert Plutchik (2001) has identified eight **primary emotions.** These are fear, surprise, sadness, disgust, anger, anticipation, joy, and trust (acceptance). If the list seems too short, it's because each emotion can vary in *intensity.* When you're angry, for instance, you may feel anything from rage to simple annoyance (✦Fig. 9.15).

As shown in Figure 9.15, each adjacent pair of primary emotions can be mixed to yield a third, more complex emotion. Other mixtures are also possible. For example, 5-year-old Shannon feels both joy and fear as she eats a stolen cookie. The result? Guilt—as you may recall from your own childhood. Likewise, jealousy could be a mixture of love, anger, and fear.

A *mood* is the mildest form of emotion (✦Fig. 9.16). Moods are low-intensity emotional states that can last for many hours, or even days. Moods often affect day-to-day behavior by preparing us to act in certain ways. For example, when your neighbor Roseanne is in an irritable mood, she may react angrily to almost anything

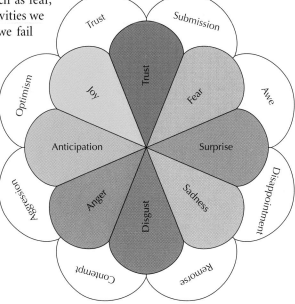

Less intense	Primary emotion	More intense
Interest	Anticipation	Vigilance
Serenity	Joy	Ecstasy
Acceptance	Trust	Admiration
Apprehension	Fear	Terror
Distraction	Surprise	Amazement
Pensiveness	Sadness	Grief
Boredom	Disgust	Loathing
Annoyance	Anger	Rage

✦**FIGURE 9.15** *Primary and mixed emotions. In Robert Plutchik's model, there are eight primary emotions, as listed in the inner areas. Adjacent emotions may combine to give the emotions listed around the perimeter. Mixtures involving more widely separated emotions are also possible. For example, fear plus anticipation produces anxiety. (Adapted from Plutchik, 2001.)*

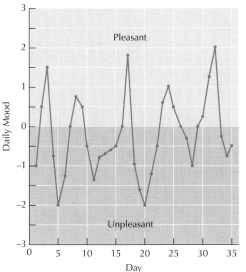

✦**FIGURE 9.16** *Folklore holds that people who work or attend school on a weekly schedule experience their lowest moods on "Blue Monday." Actually, moods tend to be generally lower for most weekdays than they are on weekends. The graph shown here plots the average daily moods of a group of college students over a 5-week period. As you can see, many people find that their moods rise and fall on a 7-day cycle. For most students, a low point tends to occur around Monday or Tuesday and a peak on Friday or Saturday. (Adapted from Larsen & Kasimatis, 1990.) In other words, moods are shaped by weekly schedules.*

Adaptive behaviors Actions that aid attempts to survive and adapt to changing conditions.

Physiological changes (in emotion) Alterations in heart rate, blood pressure, perspiration, and other involuntary responses.

Emotional expression Outward signs that an emotion is occurring.

Emotional feelings The private, subjective experience of having an emotion.

Primary emotions According to Robert Plutchik's theory, the most basic emotions are fear, surprise, sadness, disgust, anger, anticipation, joy, and acceptance.

you say. When she is in a happy mood, she can easily laugh off an insult (Oatley & Jenkins, 1992). Our moods are closely tied to circadian rhythms. When your body temperature is at its daily low point, you are more likely to feel "down" emotionally. When body temperature is at its peak, your mood is likely to be positive—even if you missed a night of sleep (Boivin, Czeisler, & Waterhouse, 1997).

The Brain and Emotion

Emotions can be either positive or negative. Ordinarily, we might think that positive and negative emotions are opposites. But this is not the case. As Shannon's "cookie guilt" implies, it is possible to have positive and negative emotions at the same time. How is that possible? Recordings of brain activity show that positive emotions are processed mainly in the left hemisphere of the brain. In contrast, negative emotions are processed in the right hemisphere. The fact that positive and negative emotions are based on activity in different brain areas helps explain why we can feel happy and sad at the same time (Canli, 1998).

Later we will attempt to put all of the elements of emotion together into a single picture. But first, we need to look more closely at physiological arousal and emotional expressions.

PHYSIOLOGY AND EMOTION—AROUSAL, SUDDEN DEATH, AND LYING

An African Bushman frightened by a lion and a city dweller frightened by a prowler will react in much the same way (Mesquita & Frijda, 1992). Such encounters usually produce muscle tension, a pounding heart, irritability, dryness of the throat and mouth, sweating, butterflies in the stomach, frequent urination, trembling, restlessness, sensitivity to loud noises, and numerous other bodily changes. These reactions are nearly universal because they are innate. Specifically, they are caused by the **autonomic nervous system** (**ANS;** the neural system that connects the brain with internal organs and glands). As you may recall from Chapter 2, activity of the ANS is *automatic,* rather than voluntary.

Fight or Flight

The ANS has two divisions, the sympathetic branch and the parasympathetic branch. The two branches are active at all times. Whether you are relaxed or aroused at any moment depends on the combined activity of both branches.

What does the ANS do during emotion?   In general, the **sympathetic branch** activates the body for emergency action—for "fighting or fleeing." It does this by arousing some bodily systems and inhibiting others (◆Fig. 9.17). These changes have a purpose. Sugar is released into the bloodstream for quick energy, the heart beats faster to supply blood to the muscles, digestion is slowed, blood flow in the skin is restricted to reduce bleeding, and so forth. Such reactions improve the chances of surviving an emergency.

The **parasympathetic branch** reverses emotional arousal by calming and relaxing the body. After a period of high emotion, the heart is slowed, the pupils return to normal size, blood pressure drops, and so forth. In addition to restoring balance, the parasympathetic system helps build up and conserve bodily energy.

The parasympathetic system responds much more slowly than the sympathetic system does. That's why a pounding heart, muscle tension, and other signs of arousal don't fade for 20 or 30 minutes after you feel an intense emotion, such as fear. Moreover, after a strong emotional shock, the parasympathetic system may overreact and lower blood pressure too much. This can cause people to become dizzy or faint after seeing something shocking, such as a horrifying accident.

Autonomic nervous system (ANS) The system of nerves that connects the brain with the internal organs and glands.
Sympathetic branch A part of the ANS that activates the body at times of stress.
Parasympathetic branch A part of the autonomic system that quiets the body and conserves energy.

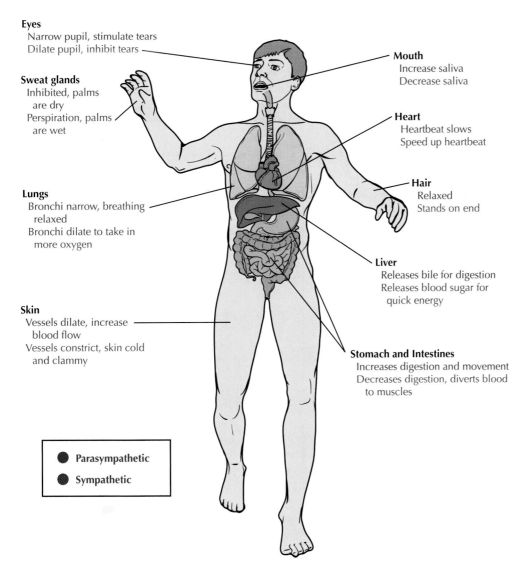

Eyes
Narrow pupil, stimulate tears
Dilate pupil, inhibit tears

Sweat glands
Inhibited, palms
are dry
Perspiration, palms
are wet

Lungs
Bronchi narrow, breathing
relaxed
Bronchi dilate to take in
more oxygen

Skin
Vessels dilate, increase
blood flow
Vessels constrict, skin cold
and clammy

Mouth
Increase saliva
Decrease saliva

Heart
Heartbeat slows
Speed up heartbeat

Hair
Relaxed
Stands on end

Liver
Releases bile for digestion
Releases blood sugar for
quick energy

Stomach and Intestines
Increases digestion and movement
Decreases digestion, diverts blood
to muscles

- ● Parasympathetic
- ● Sympathetic

◆**FIGURE 9.17** *The parasympathetic branch of the ANS calms and quiets the body. The sympathetic branch arouses the body and prepares it for emergency action. (Based on "Anatomy of Fear," by Don Foley, in* Discover *[March 2003], p. 36.)*

Sudden Death

An overreaction to intense emotion is called a **parasympathetic rebound.** If the rebound is severe, it can sometimes cause death. In times of war, for instance, combat can be so savage that some soldiers literally die of fear (Moritz & Zamchech, 1946). Apparently, such deaths occur because the parasympathetic nervous system slows the heart to a stop. Even in civilian life this is possible. In one case, a terrified young woman was admitted to a hospital because she felt she was going to die. A midwife had predicted that the woman's two sisters would die before their 16th and 21st birthdays. Both died as predicted. The midwife also predicted that this woman would die before her 23rd birthday. She was found dead in her hospital bed the day after she was admitted. It was 2 days before her 23rd birthday (Seligman, 1989). The woman was an apparent victim of her own terror.

Is the parasympathetic nervous system always responsible for such deaths? Probably not. For older persons or those with heart problems, sympathetic effects may be enough to bring about heart attack and collapse. For example, five times more people than usual died of heart attacks on the day of a major 1994 earthquake in Los Angeles (Leor, Poole, & Kloner, 1996). In Asia, the number 4 is considered unlucky, and more heart patients die on the fourth day of the month than any other day. Because they fear they will die on an "unlucky day," their chance of dying actually increases (Phillips et al., 2001).

Parasympathetic rebound Excess activity in the parasympathetic nervous system following a period of intense emotion.

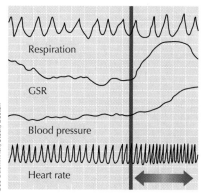

FIGURE 9.18 (left) *A typical polygraph measures heart rate, blood pressure, respiration, and galvanic skin response. Pens mounted on the top of the machine record bodily responses on a moving strip of paper.* (right) *Changes in the area marked by the arrow indicate emotional arousal. If such responses appear when a person answers a question, he or she may be lying, but arousal may have other causes.*

Lie Detectors

Did O. J. do it? Did Monica Lewinsky tell the whole truth? Has a trusted employee been stealing from the business? The most popular method for detecting lies measures the bodily changes that accompany emotion. However, the accuracy of "lie detector" tests is doubtful, and they can be a serious invasion of privacy (Lykken, 1998; National Academy of Sciences, 2003).

What is a lie detector? Do lie detectors really detect lies?   The lie detector is more accurately called a *polygraph*, a word that means "many writings" (Fig. 9.18). A typical **polygraph** records changes in heart rate, blood pressure, breathing, and the galvanic skin response. The galvanic skin response (GSR) is recorded from the hand by electrodes that measure skin conductance or, more simply, sweating.

The polygraph is popularly known as a lie detector because it is used by the police. In reality, the polygraph is not a lie detector at all. The device only records *general emotional arousal*—it can't tell the difference between lying and fear, anxiety, or excitement (Lykken, 1998).

When trying to detect a lie, the polygraph operator begins by asking irrelevant (neutral, non-emotional) questions such as, "Is your name (person's name)?" "Did you eat lunch today?" and so forth. This establishes a "baseline" for normal emotional responses. Then the examiner asks relevant questions: "Did you murder Hensley?" Presumably, only a guilty person will become anxious or emotional if they lie when answering relevant questions.

Wouldn't a person be nervous just from being questioned?   Yes, but to minimize this problem, skilled polygraph examiners ask a series of questions with critical items mixed among them. An innocent person may respond emotionally to the whole procedure, but only a guilty person is supposed to react to key questions. For example, a suspected bank robber might be shown several pictures and asked, "Was the teller who was robbed this person? Was it this person?"

As an alternative, subjects may be asked **control questions,** which are designed to make almost anyone anxious: "Have you ever stolen anything from your place of work?" Typically, such questions are very difficult to answer truthfully with an unqualified no. In theory, they show how a person reacts to doubt or misgivings. The person's reaction to critical questions can then be compared with responses to control questions.

Even when questioning is done properly, lie detection may be inaccurate (Dawson, 1990). For example, a man named Floyd Fay was convicted of murdering his friend Fred Ery. To prove his innocence, Fay volunteered to take a lie detector test, which he failed. Fay spent 2 years in prison before the real killer confessed to the crime. Psychologist David Lykken (1998) has documented many such cases in which innocent people were jailed after being convicted on the basis of polygraph evidence.

If Floyd Fay was innocent, why did he fail the test?   Put yourself in his place, and it's easy to see why. Imagine the examiner asking, "Did you kill Fred?" Since you knew Fred, and you are a suspect, it's no secret that this is a critical question. What would happen to *your* heart rate, blood pressure, breathing, and perspiration under such circumstances?

Proponents of lie detection claim it is 95 percent accurate. But in one study, accuracy was dramatically lowered when people thought about past emotional experiences as they answered irrelevant questions (Ben-Shakhar & Dolev, 1996). Similarly, the polygraph may be thrown off by self-inflicted pain, by tranquilizing drugs, or by people who can lie without anxiety (Waid & Orne, 1982). Worst of all, the test is much more likely to label an innocent person guilty, rather than a guilty person innocent. In studies involving real crimes, an average of 1 innocent person in 5 was rated as guilty by the lie detector (Lykken, 1998; Patrick & Iacono, 1989; Saxe et al., 1985).

Despite the lie detector's flaws, you may be tested for employment or for other reasons. Should this occur, the best advice is to remain calm; then actively challenge the results if the machine wrongly questions your honesty.

Polygraph A device for recording heart rate, blood pressure, respiration, and galvanic skin response; commonly called a "lie detector."

Control questions In a polygraph exam, questions that almost always provoke anxiety.

STUDYBREAK *Emotion and Physiological Arousal*

RELATE

How did your most emotional moment of the past week affect your behavior, expressions, feelings, and bodily state? Could you detect both sympathetic and parasympathetic effects?

Make a list of the emotions you consider to be most basic. To what extent do they agree with Plutchik's list?

What did you think about the lie detector test before reading this chapter? What do you think now?

LEARNING CHECK

1. Many of the physiological changes associated with emotion are caused by secretion of which hormone?
   a. atropine   b. adrenaline   c. attributine   d. amoduline
2. Emotional _____ often serve to communicate a person's emotional state to others.

3. Awe, remorse, and disappointment are among the primary emotions listed by Robert Plutchik. T or F?
4. Emotions are closely related to activity of the _____ nervous system.
5. The sympathetic system prepares the body for "fight or flight" by activating the parasympathetic system. T or F?
6. The parasympathetic system inhibits digestion and raises blood pressure and heart rate. T or F?
7. What bodily changes are measured by a polygraph?
   _____

Critical Thinking

8. Can you explain why people "cursed" by shamans or "witch doctors" sometimes actually die?

ANSWERS

1. b 2. expressions 3. F 4. autonomic 5. F 6. F 7. heart rate, blood pressure, breathing rate, galvanic skin response 8. In cultures where there is deep belief in magic or voodoo, a person who thinks that she or he has been cursed may become uncontrollably emotional. After several days of intense terror, a parasympathetic rebound is likely. If the rebound is severe enough, it can lead to physical collapse and death.

EXPRESSING EMOTIONS—MAKING FACES AND TALKING BODIES

] SURVEYQUESTION *How accurately are emotions expressed by "body language" and the face?*

Next to our own feelings, the expressions of others are the most familiar part of emotion. Are emotional expressions a carryover from human evolution? Charles Darwin thought so. Darwin (1872) observed that angry tigers, monkeys, dogs, and humans all bare their teeth in the same way. Psychologists believe that emotional expressions evolved to communicate our feelings to others, which aids survival. Such messages give valuable hints about what other people are likely to do next (Ekman & Rosenberg, 1997). For instance, in a recent study, people were able to detect angry and scheming faces faster than happy, sad, or neutral faces (✦Fig. 9.19). Presumably, we are especially sensitive to threatening faces because they warn us of possible harm (Oehman, 2002; Tipples, Atkinson, & Young, 2002).

Angry   Sad   Happy   Scheming   Neutral

✦FIGURE 9.19 *When shown groups of simplified faces (without labels), the angry and scheming faces "jumped out" at people faster than sad, happy, or neutral faces. An ability to rapidly detect threatening expressions probably helped our ancestors survive. (Adapted from Tipples, Atkinson, & Young, 2002.)*

The expression of emotion is strongly influenced by learning. As you have no doubt observed, women cry more often, longer, and more intensely than men do. Men begin learning early in childhood to suppress crying—possibly to the detriment of their emotional health (Lynch et al., 2001). Halle Berry wept as she accepted an Academy Award. How many men allowed themselves to cry at the ceremonies?

✦FIGURE 9.20 *Is anger expressed the same way in different cultures? Masks that are meant to be frightening or threatening are strikingly similar around the world. Most have an open, downward-curved mouth and diagonal or triangular eyes, eyebrows, nose, cheeks, and chin. (Keep this list in mind next Halloween.) Obviously, the pictured mask is not meant to be warm and cuddly. Your ability to "read" its emotional message suggests that basic emotional expressions have universal biological roots (Aronoff, Barclay, & Stevenson, 1988).*

Facial Expressions

Are emotional expressions the same for all people?   The most basic expressions are fairly universal (✦Fig. 9.20). Children who are born blind can't learn emotional expressions from others. Even so, they display joy, sadness, fear, anger, and disgust in the same way as sighted people do (Galati, Scherer, & Ricci-Bitti, 1997).

Some facial expressions are shaped by learning and may be found only in specific cultures. Among the Chinese, for example, sticking out the tongue is a gesture of surprise, not of disrespect or teasing. If a person comes from another culture, it is wise to remember that you may easily misunderstand his or her expressions. At such times, knowing the social *context* in which an expression occurs helps clarify its meaning (Carroll & Russell, 1996; Ekman, 1993). (Also, see "Cultural Differences in Emotion.")

Despite cultural differences, facial expressions of *fear, anger, disgust, sadness,* and *happiness* (enjoyment) are recognized around the world. *Contempt, surprise,* and *interest* may also be universal, but researchers are less certain of these expressions (Ekman, 1993). Notice that this list covers most of the primary emotions described earlier. It's also nice to note that a smile is the most universal and easily recognized facial expression of emotion.

Body Language

If a friend walked up to you and said, "Hey, ugly, what are you doing?" would you be offended? Probably not, because such remarks are usually delivered with a big grin. The facial and bodily gestures of emotion speak a language all their own and add to what a person says.

 ## HUMAN DIVERSITY   Cultural Differences in Emotion

How many times have you been angry this week? Once? Twice? Several times? If it was more than once, you're not unusual. Anger is a very common emotion in Western cultures. Very likely this is because our culture emphasizes personal independence and a free expression of individual rights and needs. In North America, anger is widely viewed as a "natural" reaction to feeling that you have been treated unfairly.

On the opposite side of the globe, many Asian cultures place a high value on group harmony. In Asia, expressing anger in public is less common, and anger is regarded as less "natural." The reason for this is that anger tends to separate people. Thus, being angry is at odds with a culture that values cooperation.

It is common to think of emotion as an individual event. However, as you can see, emotion is shaped by cultural ideas, values, and practices (Markus, Kitayama, & VandenBos, 1996).

GENDER AND EMOTION

Women have a reputation for being "more emotional" than men. Are they?   There is little reason to think that men and women differ in their private experiences of emotion. However, in Western cultures women do tend to be more emotionally expressive (Kring & Gordon, 1998). Why should this be so? The answer again lies in learning: As they are growing up, boys learn to suppress their emotional expressions; girls tend to increase theirs (Polce-Lynch et al., 1998). For many men, an inability to express feelings is a major barrier to having close, satisfying relationships with others (Bruch, Berko, & Haase, 1998). It may even contribute to tragedies like the mass murders at Columbine High School in Littleton, Colorado. For many young males, anger is the only emotion they can freely express.

Kinesics (kih-NEEZ-iks) is the study of communication through body movement, posture, gestures, and facial expressions. Informally, we call it body language. To see a masterful use of body language, turn off the sound on a television and watch a popular entertainer or politician at work.

What kinds of messages are sent with body language?   Again, it is important to realize that cultural learning affects the meaning of gestures. What, for instance, does it mean if you touch your thumb and first finger together to form a circle? In North America it means "Everything is fine" or "A-okay." In France and Belgium it means "You're worth zero." In southern Italy it means "You're an ass!" Thus, when the layer of culturally defined meanings is removed, it is more realistic to say that body language reveals an overall emotional tone (underlying emotional state).

Your face can produce some 20,000 different expressions, which makes it the most expressive part of your body. Most of these are *facial blends* (a mixture of two or more basic expressions). Imagine, for example, that you just received an F on an unfair test. Quite likely, your eyes, eyebrows, and forehead would reveal anger, while your mouth would be turned downward in a sad frown.

Most of us believe we can fairly accurately tell what others are feeling by observing their facial expressions. If thousands of facial blends occur, how do we make such judgments? The answer is that facial expressions can be boiled down to three basic dimensions: *pleasantness-unpleasantness, attention-rejection,* and *activation* (or arousal) (Schlosberg, 1954). By smiling when you give a friend a hard time, you add an emotional message of acceptance to the verbal insult, which changes its meaning. As they say in movie Westerns, it makes a big difference to "Smile when you say that, partner."

Other feelings are telegraphed by the body. The most general "messages" involve *relaxation* or *tension* and *liking* or *disliking*. Relaxation is expressed by casually positioning the arms and legs, leaning back (if sitting), and spreading the arms and legs. Liking is expressed mainly by leaning toward a person or object. Thus, body positioning can reveal feelings that would normally be concealed. Who do you "lean toward"?

Emotions are often unconsciously revealed by gestures and body positioning.

THEORIES OF EMOTION—SEVERAL WAYS TO FEAR A BEAR

] SURVEYQUESTION *How do psychologists explain emotions?*

Is it possible to explain what takes place during emotion? How are arousal, behavior, cognition, expressions, and feelings interrelated?   Theories of emotion offer different answers to these questions. Let's explore four views. Each appears to have a part of the truth, so we will try to put them all together in the end.

The James-Lange Theory (1884–1885)

You're hiking in the woods when a bear suddenly steps out onto the trail. What will happen next? Common sense tells us that we see a bear, feel fear, become aroused, and run (and sweat and yell). But is this the correct order of events? In the 1880s, William James and Carl Lange (LON-geh) proposed that common sense had it backward. According to James and Lange, bodily arousal (such as a rapidly beating heart) does not *follow* a feeling such as fear. Instead, they argued, *emotional feelings follow bodily arousal.* Thus, we see a bear, run, are aroused, and *then* feel fear as we become aware of our bodily reactions (◆Fig. 9.21).

To support his ideas, James pointed out that we often do not experience an emotion until after reacting. For example, imagine that you are driving. Suddenly a car pulls out in front of you. You swerve and skid to an abrupt halt at the side of the road. Only after you have come to a stop do you notice your pounding heart, rapid breathing, and tense muscles—and recognize your fear.

Kinesics Study of the meaning of body movements, posture, hand gestures, and facial expressions; commonly called body language.

James-Lange theory States that emotional feelings follow bodily arousal and come from awareness of such arousal.

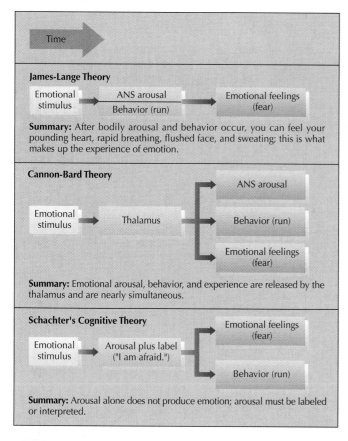

+FIGURE 9.21 *Theories of emotion.*

The Cannon-Bard Theory (1927)

Walter Cannon (1932) and Phillip Bard disagreed with the James-Lange theory. According to them, emotional feelings and bodily arousal *occur at the same time.* Cannon and Bard believed that seeing a bear activates the thalamus in the brain. The thalamus, in turn, alerts the cortex and the hypothalamus for action. The cortex produces our emotional feelings and emotional behavior. The hypothalamus triggers a chain of events that arouses the body. Thus, if you see a dangerous-looking bear, brain activity will simultaneously produce bodily arousal, running, and the feeling we call fear (Fig. 9.21).

Schachter's Cognitive Theory of Emotion (1971)

The previous theories mostly explain our physical responses. Stanley Schachter realized that cognitive (mental) factors also enter into emotion. According to Schachter, emotion occurs when we apply a particular *label* to general physical *arousal.* Schachter believed that when we are aroused, we need to interpret our feelings. Assume, for instance, that someone sneaks up behind you on a dark street and says, "Boo!" No matter who the person is, your body will be aroused (pounding heart, sweating palms, and so on). If the person is a total stranger, you might interpret this arousal as fear; if the person is a close friend, the arousal may be labeled as surprise or delight. The label (such as anger, fear, or happiness) you apply to bodily arousal is influenced by your past experiences, the situation, and the reactions of others (Fig. 9.21).

Support for the cognitive theory of emotion comes from an experiment in which people watched a slapstick movie (Schachter & Wheeler, 1962). Before viewing the movie, one third of the people received an arousing injection of adrenaline, one third got a placebo (salt water) injection, and everyone else was given a tranquilizer. People who received the adrenaline rated the movie funniest and laughed the most while watching it. In contrast, those given the tranquilizer were least amused. The placebo group fell in between.

According to the cognitive theory of emotion, individuals who received adrenaline had a stirred-up body but no explanation for what they were feeling. Consequently, they became happy when the movie implied that their arousal was due to amusement. This and similar

Cannon-Bard theory States that activity in the thalamus causes emotional feelings and bodily arousal to occur simultaneously.
Schachter's cognitive theory States that emotions occur when physical arousal is labeled or interpreted on the basis of experience and situational cues.

Which theory of emotion best describes the reactions of these people? Given the complexity of emotion, each theory appears to possess an element of truth.

experiments make it clear that emotion is much more than just an agitated body. Perception, experience, attitudes, judgment, and many other mental factors also affect the emotions we feel. Schachter's theory would predict, then, that if you met a bear, you would be aroused. If the bear seemed unfriendly, you would interpret your arousal as fear, and if the bear offered to shake your "paw," you would be happy, amazed, and relieved!

Attribution

We now move from slapstick movies and fear of bear bodies to an appreciation of bare bodies. Researcher Stuart Valins (1967) added an interesting wrinkle to Schachter's theory of emotion. According to Valins, arousal can be attributed to various sources—a process that alters our perceptions of emotion. To demonstrate **attribution,** Valins (1966) showed male college students slides of nude females. While viewing the photographs, each subject heard an amplified heartbeat that he believed was his own. In reality, students were listening to a recorded heartbeat carefully designed to beat *louder* and *stronger* when some (but not all) of the slides were shown.

After watching the slides, each student was asked to say which was most attractive. Students who heard the false heartbeat consistently rated slides paired with a "pounding heart" as the most attractive. In other words, when a student saw a slide and heard his heart beat louder, he attributed his "emotion" to the slide. His interpretation seems to have been, "Now that one I like!" His next reaction, perhaps, was "But why?" Later research suggests that subjects persuaded themselves that the slide really was more attractive in order to explain their apparent arousal (Truax, 1983).

That seems somewhat artificial. Does it really make any difference what arousal is attributed to? Yes. To illustrate attribution in the "real world," consider what happens when parents interfere with the budding romance of a son or daughter. Often, trying to separate a young couple *intensifies* their feelings. Meddling parents add frustration, anger, and fear or excitement (as in seeing each other "on the sly") to the couple's feelings. Since they already care for each other, they are likely to attribute all this added emotion to "true love" (Walster, 1971).

Attribution theory predicts that you are most likely to "love" someone who gets you stirred up emotionally (Foster et al., 1998). This is true even when fear, anger, frustration, or rejection is part of the formula. Thus, if you want to successfully propose marriage, take your intended to the middle of a narrow, windswept suspension bridge over a deep chasm and look deeply into his or her eyes. As your beloved's heart pounds wildly (from being on the bridge, not from your irresistible charms), say, "I love you." Attribution theory predicts that your companion will conclude, "Oh wow, I must love you too."

The preceding is not as farfetched as it may seem. In an ingenious study, a female psychologist interviewed men in a park. Some were on a swaying suspension bridge 230 feet above a river. The rest were on a solid wooden bridge just 10 feet above the ground. After the interview, the psychologist gave each man her telephone number, so he could "find out about the results" of the study. Men interviewed on the suspension bridge were much more likely to give the "lady from the park" a call (Dutton & Aron, 1974). Apparently, these men experienced heightened arousal, which they interpreted as attraction to the experimenter—a clear case of love at first fright!

The Facial Feedback Hypothesis

Schachter added thinking and interpretation (cognition) to our view of emotion, but the picture still seems incomplete. What about expressions? How do they influence emotion? As Charles Darwin observed, the face is very central to emotion—certainly it must be more than just an "emotional billboard."

Psychologist Carrol Izard (1977, 1990) was among the first to suggest that the face does, indeed, affect emotion. According to Izard and others, emotions cause innately programmed changes in our facial expressions. Sensations from the face then provide cues to the brain that help us tell what emotion we are feeling. This idea is known as the **facial feedback hypothesis** (Adelmann & Zajonc, 1989). Stated another way, it says that having facial

Attribution The mental process of assigning causes to events. In emotion, the process of attributing arousal to a particular source.

Facial feedback hypothesis States that sensations from facial expressions help define what emotion a person feels.

◆FIGURE 9.22 *Facial feedback and emotion. Participants in Ekman's study formed facial expressions like those normally observed during emotion. When they did this, emotion-like changes took place in their bodily activity. (After Ekman et al., 1983.)*

expressions and becoming aware of them is what produces our private emotional experiences. Exercise, for instance, arouses the body, but this arousal is not experienced as emotion because it does not trigger emotional expressions.

Let's take this idea one step further. Paul Ekman believes that "making faces" can actually cause emotion (Ekman, 1993). In one study, people were guided as they arranged their faces, muscle by muscle, into expressions of surprise, disgust, sadness, anger, fear, and happiness (◆Fig. 9.22). At the same time, each person's bodily reactions were monitored.

Contrary to what you might expect, "making faces" can affect the autonomic nervous system, as shown by changes in heart rate and skin temperature. In addition, each facial expression produces a different pattern of activity. An angry face, for instance, raises heart rate and skin temperature, whereas disgust lowers both (Ekman et al., 1983). Other studies have confirmed that posed expressions alter emotions and bodily activity (Duclos & Laird, 2001; Soussignan, 2002).

In a fascinating experiment on facial feedback, people rated how funny they thought cartoons were while holding a pen crosswise in their mouths. Those who held the pen in their teeth thought the cartoons were funnier than did people who held the pen in their lips. Can you guess why? The answer is that if you hold a pen with your teeth, you are forced to form a smile. Holding it with the lips makes a frown. As predicted by the facial feedback hypothesis, emotional experiences were influenced by the facial expressions that people made (Strack, Martin, & Stepper, 1988). Next time you're feeling sad, bite a pen!

It appears, then, that not only do emotions influence expressions, but expressions influence emotions, as shown here (Adelmann & Zajonc, 1989; Duclos & Laird, 2001).

CONTRACTED FACIAL MUSCLES	FELT EMOTION
Forehead	Surprise
Brow	Anger
Mouth (down)	Sadness
Mouth (smile)	Joy

This could explain an interesting effect you have probably observed. When you are feeling "down," forcing yourself to smile will sometimes be followed by an actual improvement in your mood (Kleinke, Peterson, & Rutledge, 1998).

A Contemporary Model of Emotion

To summarize, James and Lange were right that feedback from arousal and behavior adds to our emotional experiences. Cannon and Bard were right about the timing of events. Schachter showed us that cognition is important. In fact, psychologists are increasingly aware that how you *appraise* a situation greatly affects your emotions (Strongman, 1996). **Emotional appraisal** refers to evaluating the personal meaning of a stimulus: Is it good/bad, threatening/supportive, relevant/irrelevant, and so on?

Emotional appraisal Evaluating the personal meaning of a stimulus or situation.

In recent years, many new theories of emotion have appeared. Rather than pick one theory, let's put the best points of several together in a single model of emotion (◆Fig. 9.23).

Imagine that a large, snarling dog lunges at you with its teeth bared. A modern view of your emotional reactions goes something like this: An *emotional stimulus* (the dog) is *appraised* (judged) as a threat or other cause for emotion (▲Table 9.2). (You think to yourself, "Uh oh, big trouble!") Your appraisal gives rise to *ANS arousal* (your heart pounds and your body becomes stirred up). The appraisal also releases *innate emotional expressions* (your face twists into a mask of fear and your posture becomes tense). At the same time, your appraisal leads to *adaptive behavior* (you run from the dog). It also causes a change in consciousness that you recognize as the subjective experience of fear. (The intensity of this *emotional feeling* is directly related to the amount of ANS arousal taking place in your body.)

Each element of emotion—ANS arousal, adaptive behavior, subjective experience, and your emotional expressions—may further alter your appraisal of the situation, as well as your thoughts, judgments, and perceptions. Such changes affect each of the other reactions, which again alters your appraisal and interpretation of events. Thus, emotion may blossom, change course, or diminish as it proceeds. Note too that the original emotional stimulus can be external, like the attacking dog, or internal, such as a memory of being chased by a dog, rejected by a lover, or praised by a friend. That's why mere thoughts and memories can make us fearful, sad, or happy (Strongman, 1996).

Our discussion suggests that emotion is greatly influenced by how you think about an event. For example, if another driver "cuts you off" on the highway, you could become very angry. But if you do, you will add 15 minutes of emotional upset to your day. By changing your appraisal, you could just as easily choose to laugh at the other driver's childish behavior—and minimize the emotional wear-and-tear (Gross, 2001).

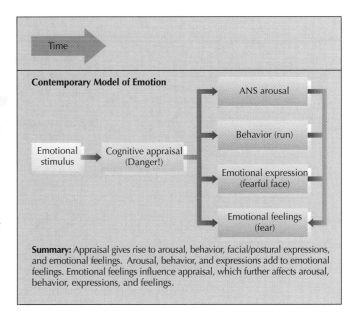

A contemporary model of emotion.

Emotional Intelligence

The Greek philosopher Aristotle had a recipe for handling relationships smoothly. You must be able, he said, "to be angry with the right person, to the right degree, at the right time, for the right purpose, and in the right way." Psychologists Peter Salovey and John Mayer call such self-control **emotional intelligence** (Salovey & Mayer, 1997).

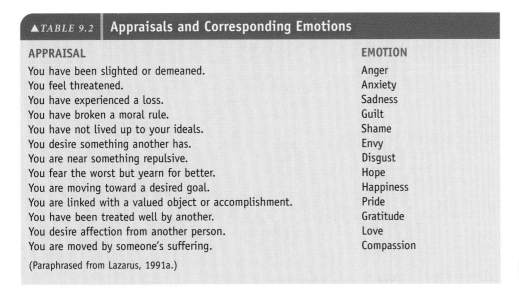

▲*TABLE 9.2*	Appraisals and Corresponding Emotions
APPRAISAL	**EMOTION**
You have been slighted or demeaned.	Anger
You feel threatened.	Anxiety
You have experienced a loss.	Sadness
You have broken a moral rule.	Guilt
You have not lived up to your ideals.	Shame
You desire something another has.	Envy
You are near something repulsive.	Disgust
You fear the worst but yearn for better.	Hope
You are moving toward a desired goal.	Happiness
You are linked with a valued object or accomplishment.	Pride
You have been treated well by another.	Gratitude
You desire affection from another person.	Love
You are moved by someone's suffering.	Compassion

(Paraphrased from Lazarus, 1991a.)

Emotional intelligence Emotional competence, including empathy, self-control, self-awareness, and other skills.

What does it mean to be emotionally intelligent? Many elements contribute to emotional intelligence (Mayer et al., 2001). A list of some of the most important skills follows.

Self-awareness: Emotionally intelligent people are tuned in to their own feelings.

Empathy: Empathetic people accurately perceive emotions in others and sense what others are feeling. They are good at "reading" facial expressions, tone of voice, and other signs of emotion.

Managing emotions: Emotional intelligence involves an ability to manage your own emotions and those of others. For example, you know how to calm down when you are angry, and you also know how to calm others.

Understanding emotions: Emotions contain useful information. For instance, anger is a cue that something is wrong; anxiety indicates uncertainty; embarrassment communicates shame; depression means we feel helpless; enthusiasm tells us we're excited.

Using emotion: People who are emotionally intelligent use their feelings to enhance thinking and decision making.

People who excel in life tend to be emotionally intelligent (Fisher & Ashanasy, 2000; Mehrabian, 2000). Indeed, the costs of poor emotional skills can be high. They range from problems in marriage and parenting to poor physical health. A lack of emotional intelligence can ruin careers and sabotage achievement. Perhaps the greatest toll falls on children and teenagers. For them, having poor emotional skills can contribute to depression, eating disorders, unwanted pregnancy, aggression, and violent crime.

Understandably, many psychologists believe that schools should promote emotional competence as well as intellectual skills. The result, they feel, would be greater self-control, altruism, and compassion—all basic capacities needed if our society is to thrive (Goleman, 1995). On a personal level, emotional intelligence is as important as IQ in many life circumstances (Dulewicz & Higgs, 2000).

There are many valuable lessons to learn from paying close attention to your emotions and the emotions of others. It's a good bet that many of the people you admire the most are not just smart, but also emotionally smart. They are people who know how to offer a toast at a wedding, tell a joke at a roast, comfort the bereaved at a funeral, add to the fun at a party, or calm a frightened child. These are skills worth cultivating.

STUDYBREAK *Emotional Expression and Theories of Emotion*

RELATE

Write a list of emotions that you think you can accurately detect from facial expressions. Does your list match Paul Ekman's? Would you be more confident in rating pleasantness-unpleasantness, attention-rejection, and activation? Why?

Which theory seems to best explain your own emotional experiences? Try frowning or smiling for 5 minutes. Did facial feedback have any effect on your mood? Cover the left column of Table 9.2. Read each emotional label in the right column. What appraisal do you think would lead to the listed emotion? Do the appraisals in the table match your predictions?

LEARNING CHECK

1. Charles Darwin held that emotional expressions aid survival for animals. T or F?
2. A formal term for "body language" is _____.
3. Which three dimensions of emotion are communicated by facial expressions?
   a. pleasantness-unpleasantness   d. anger
   b. complexity   e. curiosity-disinterest
   c. attention-rejection   f. activation

4. According to the James-Lange theory, emotional experience precedes physical arousal and emotional behavior. (We see a bear, are frightened, and run.) T or F?
5. The Cannon-Bard theory of emotion says that bodily arousal and emotional experience occur _____.
6. According to Schachter's cognitive theory, bodily arousal must be labeled or interpreted for an emotional experience to occur. T or F?
7. Subjects in Valin's false heart rate study attributed increases in their heart rate to the action of a placebo. T or F?
8. As you try to wiggle your ears, you keep pulling the corners of your mouth back into a smile. Each time you do, you find yourself giggling. Which of the following provides the best explanation for this reaction?
   a. attribution   b. the Cannon-Bard theory   c. appraisal
   d. facial feedback

Critical Thinking

9. People with high spinal injuries may feel almost no signs of physiological arousal from their bodies. Nevertheless, they still feel emotion, which can be intense at times. What theory of emotion does this observation contradict?

ANSWERS

1. T 2. kinesics 3. a, c, f 4. F 5. simultaneously 6. T 7. F 8. d 9. The James-Lange theory and Schachter's cognitive theory. The facial feedback hypothesis also helps explain the observation.

Psychology in Action

Well-Being and Happiness—What Makes a Good Life?

] SURVEYQUESTION *What factors contribute most to a happy and fulfilling life?*

What makes you happy? Love? Money? Music? Sports? Partying? Religion? Clearly, there is no simple, universal formula for happiness. And what does it mean to have a good life? Is it a matter of health? Achievement? Friendship? Leisure? Personal growth? Again, there is no simple answer. Both happiness and living a "good life" depend greatly on personal needs, goals, and values. Nevertheless, psychologists are starting to understand what it means to be happy and live well.

Happiness

To study happiness, psychologist Ed Diener and his associates have focused on what they call **subjective well-being** (**SWB**). According to them, feelings of well-being, or happiness, occur when we are satisfied with our lives, have frequent positive emotions, and have relatively few negative emotions (Diener et al., 1999).

You are probably satisfied with your life if you agree that "The conditions of my life are excellent." However, day-to-day emotions are also important. Even our best days involve a mixture of positive and negative emotions. That's why happiness is not just a matter of having good feelings. The happiest people are those who have many positive emotional experiences and relatively few negative experiences (Diener et al., 1999).

Life Events

Then do good and bad events dictate if a person is happy? Happiness is related to good and bad life events, but the impact is smaller than you might imagine. The reason for this is that happiness tends to come from within a person. Subjective well-being is affected by your goals, choices, emotions, values, and personality. The way you appraise, interpret, and manage events is as important as the nature of the events themselves. People who are good at dodging life's hard knocks tend to create their own "luck." As a result, they are happier and seem to navigate life's demands more smoothly (Eronen & Nurmi, 1999).

Personal Factors

What about factors such as income, age, or marital status? Are they related to happiness? Personal characteristics have only a small connection with overall happiness. Let's see why.

Wealth

It is tempting to think that wealth brings happiness. Does it? To a small degree, wealthier people are happier than poorer people. However, the overall association between money and happiness is weak. Basically, money can't buy happiness (King and Napa, 1998).

Education

Well-educated people tend to be a little happier than the less educated. However, this is most likely just another way of saying that there is a small connection between wealth and happiness. Higher education generally results in higher income and more social status.

Marriage

Married people report greater happiness than people who are divorced, separated, or single. It could be that happier people are simply more likely to get married. But a better explanation is that marriage partners can act as emotional and economic buffers against the hardships of life.

Esbin-Anderson/The Image Works

Subjective well-being General life satisfaction combined with frequent positive emotions and relatively few negative emotions.

Religion

There is a small but positive association between happiness and holding spiritual beliefs. Religious beliefs may add to feelings of purpose and meaning in life, resulting in greater happiness. Another possibility is that church membership may simply provide social support that softens the impact of life's negative events.

Age

The stereotype of the crotchety old person who is dissatisfied with everything is inaccurate. Life satisfaction and happiness generally *do not* decline with age. People are living longer and staying healthier, which has greatly delayed age-related declines. When declines do occur, older people today seem better able to cope with them.

Sex

Overall, men and women do not differ in happiness. However, women do have a tendency to experience higher emotional highs and lower lows than men do. Thus, more women are found among those rare individuals who are extremely happy or unhappy.

Work

People who are satisfied with their jobs tend to be happier, but the association is weak. In fact, it probably just reflects the fact that job satisfaction is a large part of greater life satisfaction.

Personality

With respect to happiness and personality, it may be fair to paraphrase the movie character Forest Gump and say that "Happy is as happy does." To a degree, some people are more temperamentally disposed to be happy, regardless of life events. In general, happier people also tend to be extroverted (outgoing), optimistic, and worry-free. This combination probably influences the balance of positive and negative emotions that people feel (Diener et al., 1999).

Goals and Happiness

The preceding account gives some insight into who is happy, but we can learn more by examining people's goals. To know if someone is happy, it is helpful to ask, "What is this person trying to do in life? How well is she or he succeeding at it?"

Do you want to be healthy and physically fit? To do well in school? To be liked by friends? To own a shopping mall? To drive a Ferrari? The goals people choose vary widely. Nevertheless, people tend to be happy if they are meeting their personal goals. This is especially true if you feel you are making progress, on a day-to-day basis, on smaller goals that relate to long-term, life goals (King, Richards, & Stemmerich, 1998; McGregor & Little, 1998).

It seems that people who attain their goals are sometimes no happier than before. If making progress toward one's goals brings happiness, how could that be?

Meaning and Integrity

Canadian psychologists Ian McGregor and Brian Little believe they can explain why reaching one's goals doesn't always lead to happiness. Picture a highly successful person who is absorbed in her accomplishments. All it may take is a crisis, like a child's illness or the death of a friend, to make life seem meaningless. But if she begins to act with integrity, her life will regain meaning and the crisis will subside. Thus, McGregor and Little believe that the best lives involve *integrity* as well as an ability to reach goals. "Doing well," they say, brings happiness. "Being yourself" makes life meaningful. The goals we pursue must express our true interests. This is crucial, because overall well-being is a combination of happiness and meaning. Pursuing goals that are inconsistent with personal interests and values can leave people feeling uneasy, bothered, and uncomfortable (McGregor & Little, 1998).

Conclusion

In summary, happier persons tend to be married, comfortable with their work, extroverted, spiritual, optimistic, and generally satisfied with their lives. They are also making progress toward their goals (Diener et al., 1999). However, attaining goals that do not match your deeper interests and values may add little to happiness (Sheldon & Elliot, 1999).

What, then, makes a good life?   As we have seen, a good life is one that is happy *and* meaningful (McGregor & Little, 1998). "To thine own self be true" may seem like a cliché, but it's actually not a bad place to begin a search for happiness. The goals you pursue in coming years will have a major impact on how you spend your time and energy. Be sure to choose wisely—and make sure your goals truly reflect your interests and values.

STUDYBREAK   **Y**   *Well-being and Happiness*

RELATE

How do you think you would rate in SWB? What other factors discussed in this section are related to your own level of happiness?

It is common for students to pursue goals and personal projects that are imposed on them. Which of your activities do you regard as most meaningful? How do they relate to your personal beliefs and values?

LEARNING CHECK

1. Subjective well-being consists of a mixture of _____ _____, positive emotions, and negative emotions.
2. People who experience many positive emotions are, by definition, very happy. T or F?

3. Happiness has only a small positive correlation with wealth. T or F?
4. Single persons are generally happier than those who are married. T or F?
5. Making progress day-by-day toward important _____ _____ is a major source of happiness.

Critical Thinking

6. Under what circumstances would you expect having money to be more strongly associated with happiness?

ANSWERS

1. life satisfaction 2. F 3. T 4. F 5. life goals 6. In poorer countries where life can be harsh, the association between material wealth and happiness is stronger than it is in North America.

CHAPTER IN REVIEW

Major Points

- Motives and goals greatly influence what we do and how we expend our energies.
- The brain monitors various internal signals to control basic motives, such as hunger and thirst.
- Motivated behavior is also influenced by learned habits, external cues, and cultural values.
- Many activities are related to needs for stimulation and our efforts to maintain desired levels of arousal.
- Many needs, goals, and drives are learned.
- Emotions can be disruptive, but overall they help us to adapt and survive.
- Personal well-being is a combination of happiness and meaning in life.

Summary

What is motivation? Are there different types of motives?

- Motives initiate, sustain, and direct activities. Motivation typically involves the sequence: need, drive, goal, and goal attainment (need reduction).
- Behavior can be activated either by needs (push) or by goals (pull).

- The attractiveness of a goal and its ability to initiate action are related to its incentive value.
- Three principal types of motives are primary motives, stimulus motives, and secondary motives.
- Most primary motives operate to maintain homeostasis.

What causes hunger? Overeating? Eating disorders?

- Hunger is influenced by a complex interplay between fullness of the stomach, blood sugar levels, metabolism in the liver, and fat stores in the body.
- The most direct control of eating comes from the hypothalamus, which is sensitive to both neural and chemical messages that affect eating.
- Other factors influencing hunger are the body's set point, external eating cues, the attractiveness and variety of diet, emotions, learned taste preferences and aversions, and cultural values.
- Obesity is the result of internal and external influences, diet, emotions, genetics, and exercise.
- Behavioral dieting is based on techniques that change eating patterns and exercise habits.
- Anorexia nervosa and bulimia nervosa are two prominent eating disorders. Both tend to involve conflicts about self-image, self-control, and anxiety.

Is there more than one type of thirst? In what ways are pain avoidance and the sex drive unusual?

- Like hunger, thirst and other basic motives are primarily under the central control of the hypothalamus. Thirst may be either intracellular or extracellular.
- Pain avoidance is episodic as opposed to cyclic. Pain avoidance and pain tolerance are partially learned.
- The sex drive is unusual because it is non-homeostatic.

What are the typical patterns of human sexual response?

- Sexual arousal is related to the body's erogenous zones, but mental and emotional reactions are the ultimate source of sexual responsiveness.
- Sexual orientation refers to one's degree of emotional and erotic attraction to members of the same sex, opposite sex, or both sexes.
- A combination of hereditary, biological, social, and psychological influences combine to produce one's sexual orientation.
- Human sexual response can be divided into four phases: excitement, plateau, orgasm, and resolution.
- Overall, male and female sexual responses are similar. However, males experience a refractory period after orgasm, and only 5 percent of men are multi-orgasmic. Fifteen percent of women are multi-orgasmic.

How does arousal relate to motivation?

- The stimulus drives reflect needs for information, exploration, manipulation, and sensory input.
- Arousal theory states that an ideal level of bodily arousal will be maintained if possible.
- Optimal performance usually occurs at *moderate* levels of arousal, as described by an inverted U function. The Yerkes-Dodson law further states that for simple tasks the ideal arousal level is higher, and for complex tasks it is lower.
- Circadian rhythms are closely tied to sleep, activity, and energy cycles. Time zone travel and shift work can seriously disrupt sleep and bodily rhythms.

What are social motives? Why are they important?

- Social motives are learned through socialization and cultural conditioning.
- Such motives account for much of the diversity of human motivation.
- A high need for achievement (nAch) is correlated with success in many situations, with career choice, and with *moderate* risk taking.
- Self-confidence greatly affects motivation in everyday life.

Are some motives more basic than others?

- Maslow's hierarchy of motives categorizes needs as either basic or growth oriented. Lower needs are assumed to be prepotent (dominant) over higher needs. Self-actualization, the highest and most fragile need, is reflected in meta-needs.
- Meta-needs are closely related to intrinsic motivation. In some situations, external rewards can undermine intrinsic motivation, enjoyment, and creativity.

What happens during emotion? Can "lie detectors" really detect lies?

- Emotions are linked to many basic adaptive behaviors. Three major elements of emotion are physiological changes in the body, emotional expressions, and emotional feelings.
- The primary emotions are fear, surprise, sadness, disgust, anger, anticipation, joy, and acceptance. Other emotions are mixtures of these primaries.
- Physical changes associated with emotion are caused by the hormone adrenaline and by activity in the autonomic nervous system (ANS).
- The sympathetic branch of the ANS is primarily responsible for arousing the body, the parasympathetic branch for quieting it.
- The polygraph, or "lie detector," measures emotional arousal by monitoring heart rate, blood pressure, breathing rate, and the galvanic skin response (GSR).
- The accuracy of the lie detector can be disturbingly low.

How accurately are emotions expressed by "body language" and the face?

- Basic emotional expressions, such as smiling or baring one's teeth when angry, appear to be unlearned. Facial expressions appear to be central to emotion.
- Body gestures and movements (body language) also express feelings, mainly by communicating emotional tone rather than specific universal messages.
- Three dimensions of facial expressions are pleasantness-unpleasantness, attention-rejection, and activation. The formal study of body language is known as kinesics.
- Lying can sometimes be detected from changes in illustrators and from signs of general arousal.

How do psychologists explain emotions?

- The James-Lange theory says that emotional experience follows bodily reactions. In contrast, the Cannon-Bard theory says that bodily reactions and emotional experiences occur simultaneously.
- Schachter's cognitive theory emphasizes the labels we apply to feelings of bodily arousal. In addition, emotions are affected by attribution (ascribing bodily arousal to a particular source).

- The facial feedback hypothesis holds that facial expressions help define the emotions we feel.
- Contemporary views of emotion emphasize the effects of cognitive appraisals. Also, all of the elements of emotion are seen as interrelated and interacting.

What factors contribute most to a happy and fulfilling life?

- Subjective well-being (happiness) is related to general life satisfaction and to having more positive emotions than negative ones.
- Life events and various demographic factors have relatively little influence on happiness.
- People with extroverted (outgoing), optimistic, and worry-free personalities tend to be happier.
- Making progress toward one's goals is associated with happiness.
- Overall well-being is a combination of happiness and meaning in life.

Interactive Learning

Internet addresses frequently change. To find the sites listed here, visit www.psychology. wadsworth.com/coon_journey2e for an updated list of Internet addresses and direct links to relevant sites.

PSYCHOLOGY: A JOURNEY COMPANION WEB SITE Online quizzes, flash cards, and other helpful study aids for this text. *www.psychology.wadsworth.com/coon_journey2e*

CONTROLLING ANGER Discusses anger and some strategies for its control.

EATING DISORDERS WEB SITE Home page of a self-help group for those afflicted with eating disorders.

EMOTIONS AND EMOTIONAL INTELLIGENCE Discusses emotional intelligence.

GESTURES AROUND THE WORLD A description of body language practices in a variety of cultures.

RESEARCH ON HUMAN EMOTIONS Links to a variety of sources on emotion.

THE VALIDITY OF POLYGRAPH EXAMINATIONS Information about the doubtful validity of polygraph examinations.

WHAT'S YOUR EMOTIONAL INTELLIGENCE QUOTIENT? Visitors may take an online quiz about their E-IQ.

INFOTRAC COLLEGE EDITION For recent articles on lie detection, use Key Words search for POLYGRAPH.

PSYCHNOW! 6a. Motivation, 6b. Emotion.

Test Your Knowledge: Motivation and Emotion

The questions that follow are only a sample of what you need to know. If you miss any of the items, you should review the entire chapter and get more practice with *WebTutor* or the *Practice Quizzes* that came with this book. Another way to prepare for tests is to use the printed *Study Guide* that is available for this text.

1. Human needs for activity and exploration are an expression of
   A. secondary motives   B. primary motives   C. incentive values   D. stimulus motives

2. Desirable goals are motivating because they are high in
   A. secondary value   B. stimulus value   C. homeostatic value   D. incentive value

3. A feeding system exists in the _____ _____ of the brain.
   A. medial leptothalamus   B. ventral paraventriculum   C. lateral hypothalamus   D. leptothalamic nucleus

4. Maintaining your body's set point for fat is closely linked with the amount of _____ in the bloodstream.
   A. hypothalamic factor-1   B. ventromedial peptide-1   C. NPY   D. leptin

5. Bingeing and purging are most characteristic of people who have
   A. taste aversions   B. anorexia   C. bulimia   D. strong sensitivity to external eating cues

6. In addition to changing eating habits, a key element of behavioral dieting is
   A. exercise   B. well-time snacking   C. better eating cues   D. commitment to "starving" every day

7. One thing that men and women have in common is that their sex drive is
   A. affected by androgens   B. extracellular   C. controlled by estrogen   D. homeostatic and episodic

8. A cancer patient has little appetite for food several weeks after the nausea caused by chemotherapy has ended. Her loss of appetite is probably best explained by
   A. increased NPY in the brain   B. a conditioned taste aversion   C. the after effects of yo-yo dieting   D. a loss of extracellular hunger

9. The typical phases of human sexual arousal are
   A. estrus, refractory period, orgasm, resolution
   B. excitement, orgasm, resolution, refractory period
   C. estrus, orgasm, plateau, resolution   D. excitement, plateau, orgasm, resolution

10. Sensate focus is a technique used to treat
    A. estrus disorders in men   B. bulimia nervosa   C. excessive weight cycling   D. sexual disorders

11. Which of the following is NOT a characteristic of people who score high on the *Sensation-Seeking Scale?*
    A. boredom susceptibility   B. experience seeking   C. inhibition   D. thrill seeking

12. Complex tasks, such as taking a classroom test, tend to be disrupted by high levels of arousal, an effect predicted by
    A. the Sensation-Seeking Scale   B. the Yerkes-Dodson law   C. studies of circadian arousal patterns   D. studies of the need for achievement

13. The term *jet lag* is commonly used to refer to disruptions of
    A. the inverted U function   B. circadian rhythms   C. any of the episodic drives   D. the body's set point

14. People high in nAch
    A. prefer long shots   B. prefer sure things   C. are moderate risk takers   D. prefer change and high levels of stimulation

15. The highest level of Maslow's hierarchy of motives involves
    A. meta needs   B. needs for safety and security   C. needs for love and belonging   D. extrinsic needs

16. Polygraph operators try to use which component of emotion to detect deception?
    A. adaptive behaviors   B. physiological changes   C. emotional expressions   D. the parasympathetic rebound

17. Preparing the body for "fighting or fleeing" is largely the job of the
    A. paraventricular nucleus   B. sympathetic branch   C. GSR   D. androgens

18. The idea that labeling arousal helps define what emotions we experience is associated with
    A. the James-Lange theory   B. Schachter's cognitive theory   C. the Cannon-Bard theory   D. Darwin's theory of innate emotional expressions

19. Holding a pen crosswise in your mouth is likely to improve your mood, a result predicted by
    A. the Cannon-Bard theory   B. attribution theory   C. the facial-feedback hypothesis   D. Schachter's cognitive theory

20. People tend to be happy if they are meeting personal goals that
    A. satisfy extrinsic needs   B. are personally meaningful   C. lead to celebrity and wealth   D. satisfy most of the deficiency motives

ANSWERS 1. d 2. d 3. c 4. d 5. c 6. a 7. a 8. b 9. d 10. d 11. c 12. b 13. b 14. c 15. a 16. b 17. b 18. b 19. c 20. b

Personality

The Essence of Annette

Rural Colorado. Our car banged over one last, brain-jarring rut and lurched toward the dilapidated farmhouse. Annette was on the porch, hooting and whooping and obviously happy to see old friends arrive.

If anyone was suited for a move to the "wilds" of Colorado, it was Annette, a strong and resourceful woman. Still, it was hard to imagine a more radical change. After separating from her husband, she had traded a comfortable life in the city for hard times in the high country. Annette was working as a ranch hand and a lumberjack (lumberjill?), trying to make it through some hard winters.

So radical were the changes in Annette's life, I worried that she might be entirely different. She was, on the contrary, more her "old self" than ever.

Perhaps you have had a similar experience. After several years of separation, it is always intriguing to see an old friend. At first, you may be struck by how the person has changed. ("Where did you get that haircut!?") Soon, however, you will probably be delighted to discover that the semi-stranger before you is still the person you once knew. It is exactly this core of consistency that psychologists have in mind when they use the term *personality*.

Without doubt, personality touches our daily lives. Falling in love, choosing friends, getting along with co-workers, voting for a president, or coping with your zaniest relatives all raise questions about personality.

What is personality? How does it differ from temperament, character, or attitudes? Is it possible to measure personality? We'll address these questions and more in this chapter.

Survey Questions

- How do psychologists use the term *personality?*
- What core concepts make up the psychology of personality?
- Are some personality traits more basic or important than others?
- How do psychodynamic theories explain personality?
- What do behaviorists emphasize in their approach to personality?
- How do humanistic theories differ from other perspectives?
- How do psychologists measure personality?
- What causes shyness? What can be done about it?

THE PSYCHOLOGY OF PERSONALITY— DO YOU HAVE PERSONALITY?

] SURVEYQUESTIONS *How do psychologists use the term* personality? *What core concepts make up the psychology of personality?*

It can be fascinating to get to know someone well. As a psychologist, I would like to better understand Annette's personality. What models and concepts can I use?

"Annette has a very optimistic personality." "Ramiro's not handsome, but he has a great personality." "My father's business friends think that he's a nice guy. They should see him at home, where his real personality comes out." "It's hard to believe Tanya and Nikki are sisters. They have such opposite personalities."

It's obvious that we all frequently use the term *personality.* But if you think that personality means "charm," "charisma," or "style," you have misused the term. Psychologists regard **personality** as a person's unique pattern of thinking, emotions, and behavior (Funder, 2001). In other words, personality refers to the consistency in who you are, have been, and will become. It also refers to the special blend of talents, values, hopes, loves, hates, and habits that makes each of us a unique person.

How is that different from the way most people use the term? Many people confuse personality with *character.* The term **character** implies that a person has been evaluated, not just described (Skipton, 1997). If, by saying that Annette has "personality," I mean that she is friendly, outgoing, and attractive, I am actually referring to what we regard as good character in our culture. But in some cultures it is deemed good for people to be fierce, warlike, and cruel. So, while everyone in a particular culture has personality, not everyone has character—or at least not good character. (Do you know any good characters?)

Personality is also distinct from *temperament,* the "raw material" from which personalities are formed. **Temperament** refers to the hereditary aspects of your personality, such as your sensitivity, irritability, distractibility, and typical mood (Kagan, 1989). Judging from Annette's adult personality, I would guess that she was an active, happy baby.

Psychologists use a large number of terms to explain personality. It might be wise, therefore, to start with a few key concepts. These ideas should help you keep your bearings as you read this chapter.

Personality A person's unique and relatively stable behavior patterns.

Character Personal characteristics that have been judged or evaluated; a person's desirable or undesirable qualities.

Temperament The hereditary aspects of personality, including sensitivity, activity levels, prevailing mood, irritability, and adaptability.

Neal Preston/Corbis

Does this man have personality? Do you?

Traits

We use the idea of traits every day to talk about personality. For instance, my friend Dan is *sociable, orderly,* and *intelligent.* His sister Kayla is *shy, sensitive,* and *creative.* In general, **personality traits** like these are stable qualities that a person shows in most situations. Typically, traits are inferred from behavior. If you see Dan talking to strangers—first at a supermarket and later at a party—you might deduce that he is "sociable." Once personality traits are identified, they can be used to predict future behavior. For example, noting that Dan is outgoing might lead you to predict that he will be sociable at school or at work. In fact, such consistencies can span many years. A study of women who appeared to be happy in their college yearbook photos (they had genuine smiles) found that most were still happy people 30 years later (Harker & Keltner, 2001).

As I observed in my reunion with Annette, personality traits are usually quite stable (Gustavsson et al., 1997). Think about how little the traits of your best friends have changed in the last 5 years. It would be strange indeed to feel like you were talking with a different person every time you met a friend or an acquaintance.

At what age are personality traits firmly established? During the 20s, personality slowly begins to harden as people become more emotionally mature. By age 30, personality has usually stabilized. The person you are at age 30 is, for the most part, the person you will be at age 60 (Costa & McCrae, 1992; Roberts, Caspi, & Moffitt, 2001). However, some extreme experiences do have the capacity to alter personality. "Near-Death Experiences—A Fresh Look at Life" provides an example.

Psychologists and employers are especially interested in the personality traits of individuals who hold high-risk, high-stress positions involving public safety, such as police, air-traffic controllers, and nuclear power plant employees.

Types

Have you ever asked the question, "What type of person is she (or he)?" A **personality type** refers to people who have *several traits in common* (Potkay & Allen, 1986). Informally, your own thinking might include categories such as the executive type, the athletic type, the motherly type, the hip-hop type, the techno geek, and so forth. If I asked you to define these informal types, you would probably list a different collection of traits for each one.

How valid is it to speak of personality "types"? Over the years, theorists have proposed many ways to categorize personalities into types. For example, Swiss psychiatrist Carl Jung (yoong), proposed that people are either *introverts* or *extroverts.* An **introvert** is a shy, egocentric person whose attention is focused inward. An **extrovert** is a bold, outgoing person whose attention is directed outward. These terms are so widely used that you may think of yourself and your friends as being one type or the other. However, the wildest, wittiest, most

Personality trait A stable, enduring quality that a person shows in most situations.
Personality type A style of personality defined by a group of related traits.
Introvert A person whose attention is focused inward; a shy, reserved, self-centered person.
Extrovert A person whose attention is directed outward; a bold, outgoing person.

 CLINICAL FILE Near-Death Experiences—A Fresh Look at Life

The emergency room doctors work feverishly over a heart attack victim. "I think we've lost him," says one of the doctors. The patient, who appears to have died, hears the doctor's words, then a buzzing sound. From somewhere above, he sees his own lifeless body on the table. Then he enters a dark tunnel and passes into an area of bright light, where he watches a rapid playback of his entire life. At some point he reaches a barrier. He is completely at peace and feels engulfed by love, but he knows he must go back. Suddenly, he is in his body again. One of the doctors exclaims, "Look, his heart's beating!" The patient recovers. For the rest of his life, he is deeply affected by his journey to the threshold of death and back.

The preceding description contains all the core elements of a *near-death experience* (NDE) (a pattern of experiences that may occur when a person is clinically dead and then resuscitated). Some people regard NDEs as spiritual events. In contrast, medical explanations attribute NDEs to the physiological reactions of an oxygen-starved brain (Wettach, 2000). In any case, one thing is certain: Near-death experiences can profoundly change personality and life goals. Many near-death survivors claim that they are no longer motivated by greed, competition, or material success. Instead, they become more concerned about the needs of other people (Groth-Marnat & Summers, 1998; Kinnier et al., 2001). Apparently, death can be an excellent yardstick for measuring what is really important in life.

THE FAR SIDE® By GARY LARSON

The four basic personality types

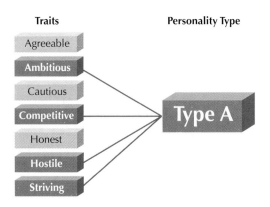

Traits   Personality Type

Agreeable
Ambitious
Cautious
Competitive
Honest
Hostile
Striving

Type A

◆**FIGURE 10.1** *Personality types are defined by the presence of several specific traits. For example, several possible personality traits are shown in the left column. A person who has a Type A personality typically possesses all or most of the highlighted traits. Type A persons are especially prone to heart disease (see Chapter 11).*

party-loving "extrovert" you know is introverted at times. Likewise, extremely introverted persons are assertive and sociable in some situations. In short, two categories (or even several) often fail to fully capture personality differences. That's why rating people on a list of traits tends to be more informative than classifying them into two or three types.

Even though types tend to oversimplify personality, they do have value. Most often, types are a shorthand way of labeling people who have several key traits in common. For example, in the next chapter we will discuss Type A personalities. These are people who have personality traits that increase their chance of suffering a heart attack (◆Fig. 10.1). Similarly, you will read in Chapter 12 about unhealthy personality types such as the paranoid personality, the dependent personality, and the antisocial personality. Each is defined by a specific group of maladaptive traits.

Self-Concept

Self-concepts provide another way of understanding personality. The rough outlines of your self-concept could be revealed by this request: "Please tell us about yourself." In other words, your **self-concept** consists of all your ideas, perceptions, and feelings about who you are. It is the mental "picture" you have of your personality.

We creatively build our self-concepts out of daily experiences. Then we slowly revise them as we have new experiences. Once a stable self-concept exists, it tends to guide what we pay attention to, remember, and think about. Because of this, self-concepts can greatly affect our behavior and personal adjustment—especially when they are inaccurate (Potkay & Allen, 1986). For instance, Alesha is a student who

Self-concepts can be remarkably consistent. In an interesting study, very old people were asked how they had changed over the years. Almost all thought they were essentially the same person they were when they were young (Troll & Skaff, 1997).

Self-concept A person's perception of his or her own personality traits.

HUMAN DIVERSITY Self-Esteem and Culture—Hotshot or Team Player?

You and some friends are playing volleyball. Your team wins, in part because you make some good plays. After the game, you bask in the glow of having performed well. You don't want to brag about being a hotshot, but your self-esteem gets a boost from your personal success.

In Japan, Shinobu and some of his friends are playing volleyball. His team wins, in part because he makes some good plays. After the game Shinobu is happy because his team did well. However, Shinobu also dwells on the ways in which he let his team down. He thinks about how he could improve, and he resolves to be a better team player.

These sketches illustrate a basic difference in Eastern and Western psychology. In individualistic cultures such as the United States, self-esteem is based on personal success and outstanding performance. For us, the path to higher self-esteem lies in self-

enhancement. We are pumped up by our successes and tend to downplay our faults and failures.

Japan and other Asian cultures place a greater emphasis on collectivism or interdependence among people. For them, self-esteem is based on a secure sense of belonging to social groups. As a result, people in Asian cultures are more apt to engage in self-criticism. By correcting personal faults, they add to the well-being of the group. And, when the *group* succeeds, individual members feel better about themselves, which raises their self-esteem.

Perhaps self-esteem is still based on success in both Eastern and Western cultures. However, it is fascinating that cultures define success in such different ways. The North American emphasis on winning is not the only way to feel good about yourself. (Sources: Heine & Lehman, 1999; Kitayama et al., 1997; Lay & Verkuyten, 1999; Markus & Kitayama, 1998.)

thinks she is stupid, worthless, and a failure, despite getting good grades. With such an inaccurate self-concept, she tends to be depressed regardless of how well she does.

Self-Esteem

Note that in addition to having an inaccurate self-concept, Alesha has low **self-esteem** (a negative self-evaluation). A person with high self-esteem is confident, proud, and self-respecting. One who has low self-esteem is insecure, lacking in confidence, and self-critical. Like Alesha, people with low self-esteem are usually anxious and unhappy.

Self-esteem tends to rise when we experience success or praise. A person who is competent and capable and who is loved, admired, and respected will almost always have high self-esteem (Baumeister, 1994). (The reasons for having high self-esteem can vary in different cultures. See "Self-Esteem and Culture—Hotshot or Team Player?" for more information.)

What if you "think you're hot," but you're not? Genuine self-esteem is based on an accurate appraisal of your strengths and weaknesses. A positive self-evaluation that is bestowed too easily may not be healthy (Twenge & Campbell, 2001). People who think very highly of themselves (and let others know it) may at first seem confident, but their arrogance quickly turns off other people (Paulhus, 1998).

Personality Theories

It would be easy to get lost without a framework for understanding personality. How do our thoughts, actions, and feelings relate to one another? How does personality develop? Why do some people suffer from psychological problems? How can they be helped? To answer such questions, psychologists have created a dazzling array of theories. A **personality theory** is a system of concepts, assumptions, ideas, and principles proposed to explain personality (◆Fig. 10.2). In this chapter, we can only explore a few of the many personality theories. The five major perspectives we will consider are:

1. **Trait theories** attempt to learn what traits make up personality and how they relate to actual behavior.
2. **Psychodynamic theories** focus on the inner workings of personality, especially internal conflicts and struggles.
3. **Behavioristic theories** place importance on the external environment and on the effects of conditioning and learning.
4. **Social learning theories** attribute differences in personality to socialization, expectations, and mental processes.
5. **Humanistic theories** stress private, subjective experience and personal growth.

Now that you are oriented, let's take a deeper look at personality.

Self-esteem Regarding oneself as a worthwhile person; a positive evaluation of oneself.

Personality theory A system of concepts, assumptions, ideas, and principles used to understand and explain personality.

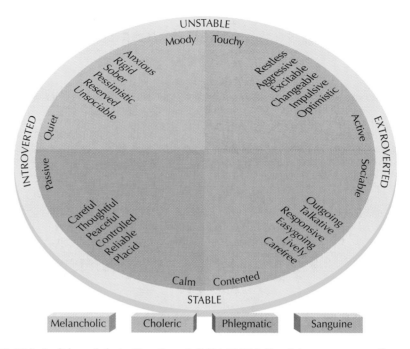

♦FIGURE 10.2 *English psychologist Hans Eysenck (1916–1997) believed that many personality traits are related to whether you are mainly introverted or extroverted and whether you tend to be emotionally stable or unstable (highly emotional). These characteristics, in turn, are related to four basic types of temperament first recognized by the early Greeks. The types are:* melancholic *(sad, gloomy),* choleric *(hot-tempered, irritable),* phlegmatic *(sluggish, calm), and* sanguine *(cheerful, hopeful). (Adapted from Eysenck, 1981.)*

THE TRAIT APPROACH—DESCRIBE YOURSELF IN 18,000 WORDS OR LESS

] SURVEYQUESTION *Are some personality traits more basic or important than others?*

How many words can you think of to describe the personality of a close friend? Your list might be long: More than 18,000 English words refer to personal characteristics. As we have noted, traits are stable qualities that a person shows in most situations. For example, if you are usually friendly, optimistic, and cautious, these qualities are traits of your personality.

What if I am sometimes shy, pessimistic, or uninhibited? The original three qualities are still traits as long as they are most *typical* of your behavior. Let's say my friend Annette approaches most situations with optimism, but tends to expect the worst each time she applies for a job. If her pessimism is limited to this situation or just a few others, it is still accurate and useful to describe her as an optimistic person.

Predicting Behavior

Earlier you learned that separating people into broad types, such as "introvert" or "extrovert," may oversimplify personality. However, introversion/extroversion can also be thought of as a trait. Knowing how you rate on this personality trait would allow us to predict how you will behave in a variety of settings. Where, for example, do you prefer to study in the library? Researchers have found that students high in the trait of extroversion study in noisy locations where there's a good chance of seeing and talking with others (Campbell & Hawley, 1982). In the library at Colgate University (where the study was done), you can find extroverted students in the second floor lounge. Or, if you prefer, more introverted students are in the cubicles on the first and third floors!

Other interesting links exist between traits and behavior. Peter Rentfrow and Samuel Gosling recently found that the types of music that people prefer tend to be associated with their personality characteristics. See if your musical tastes match their findings (Rentfrow & Gosling, 2003).

WHAT'S YOUR MUSICAL PERSONALITY?

- People who value aesthetic experiences, have good verbal abilities, are liberal, and tolerant of others tend to like music that is reflective and complex (blues, jazz, classical, and folk music).
- People who are curious about new experiences, enjoy taking risks, and are physically active prefer intense, rebellious music (rock, alternative, and heavy metal music).
- People who are cheerful, conventional, extroverted, reliable, helpful, and conservative tend to enjoy upbeat conventional music (country, sound track, religious, and pop music).
- People who are talkative, full of energy, forgiving, physically attractive, and who reject conservative ideals tend to prefer energetic, rhythmic music (rap/hip-hop, soul/funk, and electronic/dance music).

Unmistakably, personality traits affect our everyday behavior.

An analysis of former U.S. President Bill Clinton's personality traits showed that he is self-assertive, self-promoting, extroverted, and sociable. These traits probably helped Clinton maintain a surprisingly high degree of public approval during the "Monicagate" scandal (Immelman, 1998).

Describing People

In general, psychologists try to identify traits that best describe a person. Take a moment to check the traits in ▲ Table 10.1 that describe your personality. Are the traits you checked of equal importance? Are some stronger or more basic than others? Do any overlap? For example, if you checked "dominant," did you also check "confident" and "bold"? Answers to these questions would interest a trait theorist. To better understand personality, **trait theorists** attempt to analyze, classify, and interrelate traits.

▲*TABLE 10.1*	**Trait Checklist**

Check the traits you feel are characteristic of your personality. Are some more basic than others?

aggressive	organized	ambitious	clever
confident	loyal	generous	calm
warm	bold	cautious	reliable
sensitive	mature	talented	jealous
sociable	honest	funny	religious
dominant	dull	accurate	nervous
humble	uninhibited	visionary	cheerful
thoughtful	serious	helpful	emotional
orderly	anxious	conforming	good-natured
liberal	curious	optimistic	kind
meek	neighborly	passionate	compulsive

Classifying Traits

Are there different types of traits? Yes, psychologist Gordon Allport (1961) identified several kinds. **Common traits** are shared by most members of a culture. Common traits tell us how people from a particular nation or culture are similar, or which traits a culture emphasizes. In the United States, for example, competitiveness is a fairly common trait. However, among the Hopi of Northern Arizona, it is relatively rare.

Of course, common traits don't tell us much about individuals. While many people are competitive in American culture, various people you know may rate high, medium, or low in this trait. Usually we are also interested in these **individual traits,** which describe a person's unique qualities.

Trait theorist A psychologist interested in classifying, analyzing, and interrelating traits to understand personality.

Common traits Personality traits that are shared by most members of a particular culture.

Individual traits Personality traits that define a person's unique individual qualities.

Here's an analogy to help you separate common traits from individual traits: If you decide to buy a pet dog, you will want to know the general characteristics of the dog's breed (its common traits). In addition, you will want to know about the "personality" of a specific dog (its individual traits) before you decide to take it home.

Allport also made distinctions between *cardinal traits, central traits,* and *secondary traits.* **Cardinal traits** are so basic that all of a person's activities can be traced to the trait. For instance, compassion was an overriding trait of Mother Teresa's personality. Likewise, Abraham Lincoln's personality was dominated by the cardinal trait of honesty. According to Allport, few people have cardinal traits.

Central Traits

How do central and secondary traits differ from cardinal traits? **Central traits** are the basic building blocks of personality. A surprisingly small number of central traits can capture the essence of a person. For instance, just six traits would provide a good description of Annette's personality: dominant, sociable, honest, cheerful, intelligent, and optimistic. When college students were asked to describe a person they knew well, they mentioned an average of just seven central traits (Allport, 1961).

Secondary traits are more superficial personal qualities, such as food preferences, attitudes, political opinions, musical tastes, and so forth. In Allport's terms, a personality description might therefore include the following items.

> **Name:** Jane Doe
> **Age:** 22
> **Cardinal traits:** None
> **Central traits:** Possessive, autonomous, artistic, dramatic, self-centered, trusting
> **Secondary traits:** Prefers colorful clothes, likes to work alone, politically liberal, always late

Source Traits

How can you tell if a personality trait is central or secondary? Raymond B. Cattell (1906–1998) tried to answer this question by directly studying the traits of a large number of people. Cattell began by measuring visible features of personality, which he called **surface traits.** Soon, Cattell noticed that these surface traits often appeared together in groups. In fact, some traits appeared together so often that they seemed to represent a single, more basic trait. Cattell called these deeper characteristics **source traits** (Cattell, 1965). They are the core of each individual's personality.

How do source traits differ from Allport's central traits? Allport classified traits subjectively, and it's possible that he was wrong at times. Cattell used a statistical technique called *factor analysis* to look for connections among traits. For example, he found that imaginative people are almost always *inventive, original, curious, creative, innovative,* and *ingenious.* Thus, *imaginative* is a source trait. If you are an imaginative person, we automatically know a that you have several other traits, too.

Cattell identified 16 source traits. According to him, all 16 are needed to fully describe a personality. Source traits are measured by a test called the *Sixteen Personality Factor Questionnaire* (often referred to as the 16 PF). Like many personality tests, the 16 PF can be used to produce a **trait profile,** or graph of a person's score on each trait. Trait profiles draw a "picture" of individual personalities, which makes it easier to compare them (◆Fig. 10.3).

The Big Five

Noel is outgoing and friendly, conscientious, emotionally stable, and smart. His brother Joel is introverted, hostile, irresponsible, emotionally unpredictable, and disinterested in ideas (stupid). You will be spending a week in a space capsule with either Noel or Joel. Who would you choose? If the answer seems obvious, it's because Noel and Joel were described with the **five-factor model,** a system that identifies the five most basic dimensions of personality.

Cardinal trait A personality trait so basic that all of a person's activities relate to it.
Central traits The core traits that characterize an individual personality.
Secondary traits Traits that are inconsistent or relatively superficial.
Surface traits The visible or observable traits of one's personality.
Source traits Basic underlying traits of personality; each source trait is reflected in a number of surface traits.
Trait profile A graph of the scores obtained on several personality traits.
Five-factor model Proposes that there are five universal dimensions of personality.

The "Big Five" factors listed in ✦Figure 10.4 are based on attempts to further reduce Cattell's 16 factors to just five universal dimensions (Digman, 1990; Goldberg, 1993). The Big Five may be the best answer of all to the question, What is the essence of human personality? (De Raad, 1998; McCrae & Costa, 1997).

Five Key Dimensions

If you would like to compare the personalities of two people, try rating them on the five dimensions shown in Figure 10.4. For factor 1, *extroversion,* rate how introverted or extroverted each person is. Factor 2, *agreeableness,* refers to how friendly, nurturant, and caring a person is, as opposed to cold, indifferent, self-centered, or spiteful. A person who is *conscientious* (factor 3) is self-disciplined, responsible, and achieving. People low on this factor are irresponsible, careless, and undependable. Factor 4, *neuroticism,* refers to negative, upsetting emotions. People who are high in neuroticism tend to be anxious, emotionally "sour," irritable, and unhappy. Finally, people who rate high on factor 5, *openness to experience,* are intelligent and open to new ideas (Digman, 1990). The beauty of this model is that almost any trait you can name will be related to one of the five factors. If you were selecting a college roommate, hiring an employee, or answering a singles ad, you would probably like to know all of the personal dimensions covered by the Big Five.

Before you read the next section, take a moment to answer the questions that follow. Doing so will add to your understanding of a long-running controversy in the psychology of personality.

RATE YOURSELF: HOW DO YOU VIEW PERSONALITY?

1. My friends' actions are fairly consistent from day to day and in different situations. T or F?
2. Whether a person is honest or dishonest, kind or cruel, a hero or a coward depends mainly on circumstances. T or F?
3. Most people I have known for several years have pretty much the same personalities now as they did when I first met them. T or F?
4. The reason that people in some professions (such as teachers, lawyers, or doctors) seem so much alike is because their work requires that they act in particular ways. T or F?
5. One of the first things I would want to know about a potential roommate is what the person's personality is like. T or F?
6. I believe that immediate circumstances usually determine how people act at any given time. T or F?
7. To be comfortable in a particular job, a person's personality must match the nature of the work. T or F?
8. Almost anyone would be polite at a wedding reception; it doesn't matter what kind of personality the person has. T or F?

Now count the number of times you marked true for the odd-numbered items. Do the same for the even-numbered items.

If you agreed with most of the odd-numbered items, you tend to view behavior as strongly influenced by personality traits or lasting personal dispositions.

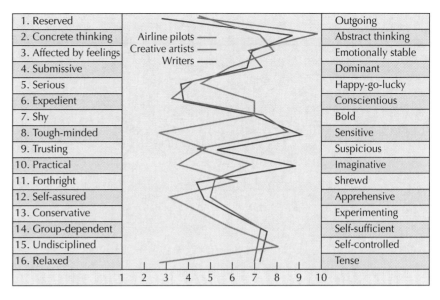

✦**FIGURE 10.3** *The 16 source traits measured by Cattell's 16 PF are listed beside the graph. Scores can be plotted as a profile for an individual or a group. The profiles shown here are group averages for airline pilots, creative artists, and writers. Notice the similarity between artists and writers and the difference between these two groups and pilots. (After Cattell, 1973.)*

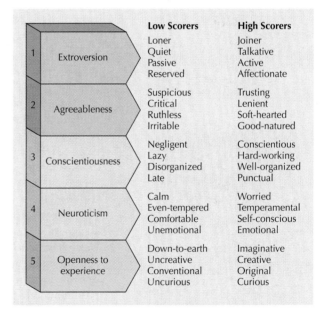

✦**FIGURE 10.4** *The Big Five. According to the five-factor model, basic differences in personality can be "boiled down" to the dimensions shown here. The five-factor model answers these essential questions about a person: Is she or he extroverted or introverted? Agreeable or difficult? Conscientious or irresponsible? Emotionally stable or unstable? Smart or unintelligent? These questions cover a large measure of what we might want to know about someone's personality. (Trait descriptions adapted from McCrae & Costa, 1990.)*

Knowing where a person stands on the "Big Five" personality factors helps predict his or her behavior. For example, people who score high on conscientiousness tend to be safe drivers who are unlikely to have automobile accidents (Arthur & Graziano, 1996).

If you agreed with most of the even-numbered items, you view behavior as strongly influenced by external situations and circumstances.

What if I answered true about equally for odd and even items? Then you place equal weight on traits and situations as ways to explain behavior. This is the view now held by many personality psychologists (Funder, 2001; Mischel & Shoda, 1998).

✦FIGURE 10.5 *Reunited identical twins Terry and Margaret undergo lung function tests at the University of Minnesota. Researchers collected a wide range of medical and psychological data for each set of twins.*

Trait-situation interaction The influence that external settings or circumstances have on the expression of personality traits.

Behavioral genetics The study of inherited behavioral traits and tendencies.

Traits, Consistency, and Situations

To predict how a person will act, is it better to focus on personality traits or external circumstances?   Actually, it's best to take both into account. Personality traits are quite consistent. As we have seen, they can predict such things as job performance, dangerous driving, or success in marriage (Funder, 2001). Yet, *situations* also greatly influence our behavior. For instance, it would be unusual for you to dance at a movie or read a book at a football game. Likewise, few people sleep in roller coasters or tell off-color jokes at funerals. However, your personality traits may predict whether you choose to read a book, go to a movie, or attend a football game in the first place. Typically, traits *interact* with situations to determine how we will act (Sheldon et al., 1997).

In a **trait-situation interaction,** external circumstances influence the expression of a personality trait. For instance, imagine what would happen if you moved from a church to a classroom to a party to a football game. As the setting changed, you would probably become louder and more boisterous. This change would demonstrate situational effects on behavior. At the same time, your personality traits would also be apparent: If you were quieter than average in class, you would probably be quieter than average in the other settings, too. Where do such differences come from? The next section explores one source of personality traits.

Do We Inherit Personality?

How much does heredity affect personality traits?   Some breeds of dogs have reputations for being friendly, aggressive, intelligent, calm, or emotional. Such differences fall in the realm of **behavioral genetics,** the study of inherited behavioral traits. We know that facial features, eye color, body type, and many other physical characteristics are inherited. So are many of our behavioral tendencies (Rose, 1995). Genetic studies have shown that intelligence, some mental disorders, temperament, and other complex qualities are influenced by heredity. In view of such findings, we also might wonder, Do genes affect personality?

Wouldn't comparing the personalities of identical twins help answer the question?   It would indeed—especially if the twins were separated at birth or soon after.

Twins and Traits

For two decades, psychologists at the University of Minnesota have been studying identical twins who grew up in different homes. Medical and psychological tests reveal that reunited twins are very much alike, even when they are reared apart (✦Fig. 10.5) (Bouchard et al., 1990; Lykken et al., 1992). Typically, they are astonishingly similar in appearance, voice quality, facial gestures, hand movements, and nervous tics, such as nail biting. Separated twins also tend to have similar talents. If one twin excels at art, music, dance, drama, or athletics, the other is likely to as well—despite wide differences in childhood environment. However, as the highlight titled "The Minnesota Twins" explains, it's wise to be cautious about some reports of extraordinary similarities in reunited twins.

CRITICAL THINKING   The Minnesota Twins

Many reunited twins in the Minnesota study have displayed similarities far beyond what would be expected on the basis of heredity. A good example is provided by the "Jim twins," James Lewis and James Springer. Both Jims had married and divorced women named Linda. Both had undergone police training. Both had named their firstborn sons James Allan. Both drove Chevrolets and vacationed at the same beach each summer. Both listed carpentry and mechanical drawing among their hobbies. Both had built benches around trees in their yards. And so forth (Holden, 1980).

Does heredity actually control such details of our lives? Are there child-naming genes and bench-building genes? Of course, the idea is preposterous. How, then, do we explain the eerie similarities in separated twins' lives?

The astute reader will realize that completely unrelated persons can also share "amazing" similarities. One study, for instance, compared twins to unrelated pairs of students. The unrelated pairs, who were the same age and sex, were almost as alike as the twins.

They had highly similar political beliefs, musical interests, religious preferences, job histories, hobbies, favorite foods, and so on (Wyatt et al., 1984). Why were the unrelated students so similar? Basically, it's because people of the same age and sex live in the same historical times and select from similar societal options.

Imagine that you were separated at birth from a twin brother or sister. If you were reunited with your twin today, what would you do? Quite likely, you would spend the next several days comparing every imaginable detail of your lives. Under such circumstances it is virtually certain that you and your twin would compile a long list of similarities. ("Wow! I use the same brand of toothpaste you do!") Yet, two unrelated persons of the same age, sex, and race could probably rival your list—*if* they were as motivated to find similarities.

To summarize, many of the seemingly "astounding" coincidences shared by reunited twins may be a special case of the fallacy of positive instances, described in Chapter 1. Similarities blaze brightly in the memories of reunited twins, while differences are ignored.

Summary

Studies of twins make it clear that heredity has a sizable effect on each of us. All told, it seems reasonable to conclude that heredity is responsible for about 25 to 50 percent of the variation in many personality traits (Jang & Livesley, 1998; Loehlin et al., 1998). Notice, however, that the same figures imply personality is shaped as much, or more, by environment as it is by heredity (Gatz, 1990).

Each personality is a unique blend of heredity and environment, biology and culture. We are not—thank goodness—genetically programmed robots whose behavior and personality traits are "wired in" for life. Where you go in life is the result of the choices you make. To a degree, these choices are influenced by inherited tendencies (Saudino et al., 1997). However, they are not merely a product of your genes (Funder, 2001; Rose, 1995).

STUDY BREAK ❦ *Personality and Trait Theories*

RELATE

See if you can define or describe the following terms in your own words: *personality, character, temperament, trait, type, self-concept, self-esteem.*

List six or seven traits that best describe your personality. Which system of traits seems to best match your list, Allport's, Cattell's, or the Big Five?

Choose a prominent trait from your list. Does its expression seem to be influenced by specific situations? Do you think that heredity contributed to the trait?

LEARNING CHECK

1. _____ refers to the hereditary aspects of a person's emotional nature.
2. The term _____ refers to the presence or absence of desirable personal qualities.
   a. personality   b. source trait   c. character
   d. temperament
3. A system that classifies all people as either introverts or extroverts is an example of a _____ approach to personality.

4. An individual's perception of his or her own personality constitutes that person's _____.
5. Central traits are those shared by most members of a culture. T or F?
6. Cattell believes that clusters of _____ traits reveal the presence of underlying _____ traits.
7. Which of the following is *not* one of the Big Five personality factors?
   a. submissiveness   b. agreeableness   c. extroversion
   d. neuroticism
8. To understand personality, it is wise to remember that traits and situations _____ to determine our behavior.

Critical Thinking

9. In what way would memory contribute to the formation of an accurate or inaccurate self-image?
10. Are situations equally powerful in their impact on behavior?

ANSWERS

1. Temperament 2. c 3. type 4. self-concept 5. F 6. surface, source 7. a 8. interact 9. As discussed in Chapter 9, memory is highly selective, and long-term memories are often distorted by recent information. Such properties add to the moldability of self-concept. 10. No. Circumstances can have a strong or weak influence. In some situations, almost everyone will act the same, no matter what their personality traits may be. In other situations, traits may be of greater importance.

PSYCHOANALYTIC THEORY—ID CAME TO ME IN A DREAM

] SURVEYQUESTION *How do psychodynamic theories explain personality?*

Psychodynamic theorists are not content with studying traits. Instead, they try to probe under the surface of personality—to learn what drives, conflicts, and energies animate us. Psychodynamic theorists believe that many of our actions are based on hidden, or unconscious, needs.

Psychoanalytic theory, the best-known psychodynamic approach, grew out of the work of Sigmund Freud, a Viennese physician. As a doctor, Freud was fascinated by patients whose problems seemed to be more emotional than physical. From about 1890 until he died in 1939, Freud evolved a theory of personality that deeply influenced modern thought. Let's consider some of its main features.

The Structure of Personality

How did Freud view personality?   Freud's model portrays personality as a dynamic system directed by three mental structures, the **id,** the **ego,** and the **superego.** According to Freud, most behavior involves activity of all three systems. (Freud's theory includes a large number of concepts. For your convenience, they are defined in ▲Table 10.2 rather than in page margins.)

"All Is Vanity" by Allan Gilbert

Freud considered personality an expression of two conflicting forces, life instincts and the death instinct. Both are symbolized in this drawing by Allan Gilbert. (If you don't immediately see the death symbolism, stand farther from the drawing.)

The Id

The id is made up of innate biological instincts and urges. It is self-serving, irrational, impulsive, and totally unconscious. The id operates on the **pleasure principle.** That is, it seeks to freely express pleasure-seeking urges of all kinds. If we were solely under control of the id, the world would be chaotic beyond belief.

The id acts as a well of energy for the entire **psyche** (sie-KEY), or personality. This energy, called **libido** (lih-BEE-doe), flows from the **life instincts** (or **Eros**). According to Freud, libido underlies our efforts to survive, as well as our sexual desires and pleasure seeking. Freud also described a **death instinct. Thanatos,** as he called it, produces aggressive and destructive urges. Freud offered humanity's long history of wars and violence as evidence of such urges. Most id energies, then, are aimed at discharging tensions related to sex and aggression.

The Ego

The ego is sometimes described as the "executive," because it directs energies supplied by the id. The id is like a blind king or queen whose power is awesome but who must rely on others to carry out orders. The id can only form mental images of things it desires. The ego wins power to direct behavior by relating the desires of the id to external reality.

Are there other differences between the ego and the id?   Yes. Recall that the id operates on the pleasure principle. The ego, in contrast, is guided by the **reality principle.** That is, the ego delays action until it is practical or appropriate. The ego is the system of thinking, planning, problem solving, and deciding. It is in conscious control of the personality.

The Superego

What is the role of the superego?   The superego acts as a judge or censor for the thoughts and actions of the ego. One part of the superego, called the **conscience,** reflects actions for which a person has been punished. When standards of the conscience are not met, you are punished internally by *guilt* feelings.

A second part of the superego is the **ego ideal.** The ego ideal reflects all behavior one's parents approved of or rewarded. The ego ideal is a source of goals and aspirations. When its standards are met, we feel *pride.*

 Psychoanalytic theory Freudian theory of personality that emphasizes unconscious forces and conflicts.

Ego is caught between id + superego

▲ *TABLE 10.2*	**Key Freudian Concepts**	

Anal stage The psychosexual stage corresponding roughly to the period of toilet training (ages 1 to 3).

Anal-expulsive personality A disorderly, destructive, cruel, or messy person.

Anal-retentive personality A person who is obstinate, stingy, or compulsive, and who generally has difficulty "letting go."

Conscience The part of the superego that causes guilt when its standards are not met.

Conscious Region of the mind that includes all mental contents a person is aware of at any given moment.

Ego The executive part of personality that directs rational behavior.

Ego ideal The part of the superego representing ideal behavior; a source of pride when its standards are met.

Electra conflict A girl's sexual attraction to her father and feelings of rivalry with her mother.

Erogenous zone Any body area that produces pleasurable sensations.

Eros Freud's name for the "life instincts."

Fixation A lasting conflict developed as a result of frustration or over-indulgence.

Genital stage Period of full psychosexual development, marked by the attainment of mature adult sexuality.

Id The primitive part of personality that remains unconscious, supplies energy, and demands pleasure.

Latency According to Freud, a period in childhood when psychosexual development is more or less interrupted.

Libido In Freudian theory, the force, primarily pleasure oriented, that energizes the personality.

Moral anxiety Apprehension felt when thoughts, impulses, or actions conflict with the superego's standards.

Neurotic anxiety Apprehension felt when the ego struggles to control id impulses.

Oedipus conflict A boy's sexual attraction to his mother, and feelings of rivalry with his father.

Oral stage The period when infants are preoccupied with the mouth as a source of pleasure and means of expression.

Oral-aggressive personality A person who uses the mouth to express hostility by shouting, cursing, biting, and so forth. Also, one who actively exploits others.

Oral-dependent personality A person who wants to passively receive attention, gifts, love, and so forth.

Phallic personality A person who is vain, exhibitionistic, sensitive, and narcissistic.

Phallic stage The psychosexual stage (roughly ages 3 to 6) when a child is preoccupied with the genitals.

Pleasure principle A desire for immediate satisfaction of wishes, desires, or needs.

Preconscious An area of the mind containing information that can be voluntarily brought to awareness.

Psyche The mind, mental life, and personality as a whole.

Psychosexual stages The oral, anal, phallic, and genital stages, during which various personality traits are formed.

Reality principle Delaying action (or pleasure) until it is appropriate.

Superego A judge or censor for thoughts and actions.

Thanatos The death instinct postulated by Freud.

Unconscious The region of the mind that is beyond awareness, especially impulses and desires not directly known to a person.

The superego acts as an "internalized parent" to bring behavior under control. In Freudian terms, a person with a weak superego will be a delinquent, criminal, or antisocial personality. In contrast, an overly strict or harsh superego may cause inhibition, rigidity, or unbearable guilt.

The Dynamics of Personality

How do the id, ego, and superego interact?   Freud didn't picture the id, ego, and superego as parts of the brain or as "little people" running the human psyche. Instead, they are conflicting mental processes. Freud theorized a delicate balance of power among the three. For example, the id's demands for immediate pleasure often clash with the superego's moral restrictions. Perhaps an example will help clarify the role of each part of the personality.

FREUD IN A NUTSHELL

Let's say you are sexually attracted to an acquaintance. The id clamors for immediate satisfaction of its sexual desires but is opposed by the superego (which finds the very thought of sex shocking). The id says, "Go for it!" The superego icily replies, "Never even think that again!" And what does the ego say? The ego says, "I have a plan!"

Of course, this is a drastic simplification, but it does capture the core of Freudian thinking. To reduce tension, the ego could begin actions leading to friendship, romance, courtship, and marriage. If the id is unusually powerful, the ego may give in and attempt a seduction. If the superego prevails, the ego may be forced to *displace* or *sublimate* sexual energies to other activities (sports, music, dancing, push-ups, cold showers). According to Freud, internal struggles and rechanneled energies typify most personality functioning.

Is the ego always caught in the middle?   Basically yes, and the pressures on it can be intense. In addition to meeting the conflicting demands of the id and superego, the overworked ego must deal with external reality.

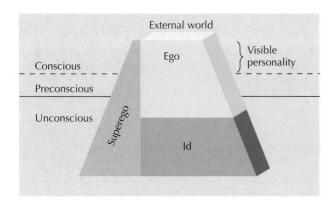

◆**FIGURE 10.6** *The approximate relationship between the id, ego, and superego, and the levels of awareness.*

According to Freud, you feel anxiety when your ego is threatened or overwhelmed. Impulses from the id cause **neurotic anxiety** when the ego can barely keep them under control. Threats of punishment from the superego cause **moral anxiety.** Each person develops habitual ways of calming these anxieties, and many resort to using *ego-defense mechanisms* to lessen internal conflicts. Defense mechanisms are mental processes that deny, distort, or otherwise block out sources of threat and anxiety. (The ego defense mechanisms that Freud identified are used as a form of protection against stress, anxiety, and threatening events. See Chapter 11.)

Levels of Awareness

Like other psychodynamic theorists, Freud believed that our behavior often expresses unconscious (or hidden) internal forces. The **unconscious** holds repressed memories and emotions, plus the instinctual drives of the id. Interestingly, modern scientists have found that the brain's limbic system does, in fact, seem to trigger unconscious emotions and memories (LeDoux, 1996).

Even though they are beyond awareness, unconscious thoughts, feelings, or urges may slip into behavior in disguised or symbolic form. For example, if you meet someone you would like to know better, you may unconsciously leave a book or a jacket at that person's house to ensure another meeting.

Earlier you said that the id is completely unconscious. Are the actions of the ego and superego unconscious? At times, yes, but they also operate on two other levels of awareness (◆Fig. 10.6). The **conscious** level includes everything you are aware of at a given moment, including thoughts, perceptions, feelings, and memories. The **preconscious** contains material that can be easily brought to awareness. If you stop to think about a time when you felt angry or rejected, you will be moving this memory from the preconscious to the conscious level of awareness.

The superego's activities also reveal differing levels of awareness. At times we consciously try to live up to moral codes or standards. Yet, at other times a person may feel guilty without knowing why. Psychoanalytic theory credits such guilt to unconscious workings of the superego. Indeed, Freud believed that the unconscious origins of many feelings cannot be easily brought to awareness.

Personality Development

How does psychoanalytic theory explain personality development? Freud theorized that the core of personality is formed before age 6 in a series of **psychosexual stages.** Freud believed that erotic childhood urges have lasting effects on development. As you might expect, this is a controversial idea. However, Freud used the terms *sex* and *erotic* very broadly to refer to many physical sources of pleasure.

A Freudian Fable?

Freud identified four psychosexual stages, the **oral, anal, phallic,** and **genital.** (He also described a period of "latency" between the phallic and genital stages. Latency is explained in a moment.) At each stage, a different part of the body becomes a child's primary **erogenous zone** (an area capable of producing pleasure). Each area then serves as the main source of pleasure, frustration, and self-expression. Freud believed that many adult personality traits can be traced to **fixations** in one or more of the stages.

What is a fixation? A fixation is an unresolved conflict or emotional hang-up caused by overindulgence or by frustration. As we describe the psychosexual stages you'll see why Freud considered fixations important.

The Oral Stage

During the first year of life, most of an infant's pleasure comes from stimulation of the mouth. If a child is overfed or frustrated, oral traits may be created. Adult expressions of oral needs include gum chewing, nail biting, smoking, kissing, overeating, and alcoholism.

What if there is an oral fixation? Fixation early in the oral stage produces an **oral-dependent** personality. Oral-dependent persons are gullible (they swallow things easily!) and passive and need lots of attention (they want to be mothered and showered with gifts). Frustrations later in the oral stage may cause aggression, often in the form of biting. Fixations here create cynical, **oral-aggressive** adults who exploit others. They also like to argue ("biting sarcasm" is their forte!).

The Anal Stage

Between the ages of 1 and 3, the child's attention shifts to the process of elimination. When parents attempt toilet training, the child can gain approval or express rebellion or aggression by "holding on" or by "letting go." Therefore, harsh or lenient toilet training can cause an anal fixation that may lock such responses into personality. Freud described the **anal-retentive** (holding-on) personality as obstinate, stingy, orderly, and compulsively clean. The **anal-expulsive** (letting-go) personality is disorderly, destructive, cruel, or messy.

The Phallic Stage

Adult traits of the **phallic personality** are vanity, exhibitionism, sensitive pride, and narcissism (self-love). Freud theorized that phallic fixations develop between the ages of 3 and 6. At this time, increased sexual interest causes the child to be physically attracted to the parent of the opposite sex. In males this attraction leads to an **Oedipus conflict,** in which the boy feels a rivalry with his father for the affection of his mother. Freud believed that the male child feels threatened by the father (specifically, the boy fears castration). To ease his anxieties, the boy must **identify** with the father. Their rivalry ends when the boy seeks to become more like his father. As he does, he begins to accept the father's values and forms a conscience.

What about the female child? Girls experience an **Electra conflict.** In this case, the girl loves her father and competes with her mother. However, according to Freud, the girl identifies with the mother more gradually.

Freud believed that females already feel castrated. Because of this, they are less driven to identify with their mothers than boys are with their fathers. This, he said, is less effective in creating a conscience. This particular part of Freudian thought has been thoroughly (and rightfully) rejected by modern feminists. It is probably best understood as a reflection of the male-dominated times in which Freud lived.

Latency

According to Freud, there is a period of *latency* from age 6 to puberty. Latency is not actually a stage. Rather, it is a quiet time during which psychosexual development is dormant. Freud's belief that psychosexual development is "on hold" at this time is hard to accept. Nevertheless, Freud saw latency as a relatively quiet time compared to the stormy first 6 years of life.

The Genital Stage

At puberty an upswing in sexual energies activates all the unresolved conflicts of earlier years. This upsurge, according to Freud, is the reason why adolescence can be filled with emotion and turmoil. The genital stage begins at puberty. It is marked, during adolescence, by a growing capacity for responsible social-sexual relationships. The genital stage ends with a mature capacity for love and the realization of full adult sexuality.

Critical Comments

As bizarre as Freud's theory might seem, it has been influential for several reasons. First, it pioneered the idea that the first years of life help shape adult personality. Second, it identified feeding, toilet training, and early sexual experiences as critical events in personality formation. Third, Freud was among the first to propose that development proceeds through a series of stages. (Erik Erikson's psycho*social* stages, which cover development from birth to old age, are a modern offshoot of Freudian thinking. See Chapter 3.)

Is the Freudian view of development widely accepted? Few psychologists wholeheartedly embrace Freud's theory today. In some cases Freud was clearly wrong. His portrayal of

Bettmann/Corbis

Was Freud's ever-present cigar a sign of an oral fixation? Was it a phallic symbol? Was it both? Or was it neither? An inability to say for sure is one of the shortcomings of psychoanalytic theory.

the elementary school years (latency) as free from sexuality and unimportant for personality development is hard to believe. His idea of the role of a stern or threatening father in the development of a strong conscience in males has also been challenged. Studies show that a son is more likely to develop a strong conscience if his father is affectionate and accepting, rather than stern and punishing. Freud also overemphasized sexuality in personality development. Other motives and cognitive factors are of equal importance.

Recently, Freud has been criticized for his views of patients who believed they were sexually molested as children. Freud assumed that such events were merely childhood fantasies. This view led to a long-standing tendency to disbelieve children who have been molested and women who have been raped (Brannon, 1996).

Another important criticism is that Freud's concepts are almost impossible to verify scientifically. The theory provides numerous ways to explain almost any thought, action, or feeling *after* it has occurred. However, it leads to few predictions, which makes its claims difficult to test. Although more criticisms of Freud could be listed, the fact remains that there is an element of truth to much of what he said. Because of this, some clinical psychologists continue to regard Freudian theory as a useful way to think about human problems.

STUDYBREAK *Psychodynamic Theory*

RELATE

Try to think of at least one time when your thoughts, feelings, or actions seemed to reflect the workings of each of the following: the id, the ego, and the superego.

Do you know anyone who seems to have oral, anal, or phallic personality traits? Do you think Freud's concept of fixation explains their characteristics?

Do any of your personal experiences support the existence of an Oedipus conflict or an Electra conflict? If not, is it possible that you have repressed feelings related to these conflicts?

LEARNING CHECK

1. List the three divisions of personality postulated by Freud.

   _____ _____ _____

2. Which division is totally unconscious? _____
3. Which division is responsible for moral anxiety? _____

4. Freud proposed the existence of a life instinct known as Thanatos. T or F?
5. Freud's view of personality development is based on the concept of _____ stages.
6. Arrange these stages in the proper order: phallic, anal, genital, oral.

   _____ _____
   _____ _____

7. Freud considered the anal-retentive personality to be obstinate and stingy. T or F?

Critical Thinking

8. Many adults would find it embarrassing or humiliating to drink from a baby bottle. Can you explain why?

ANSWERS

1. id, ego, superego 2. id 3. superego 4. F 5. psychosexual 6. oral, anal, phallic, genital 7. T 8. A psychoanalytic theorist would say that it is because the bottle rekindles oral conflicts and feelings of vulnerability and dependence.

LEARNING THEORIES OF PERSONALITY— HABIT I SEEN YOU BEFORE?

] SURVEYQUESTION *What do behaviorists emphasize in their approach to personality?*

After exploring psychoanalytic theory, you might be relieved to know that behavioral theorists explain personality through straightforward concepts, such as learning, reinforcement, and imitation. Behavioral and social learning theories are based on scientific research, which makes them powerful ways of looking at personality.

How do behaviorists approach personality? According to some critics, as if people are robots like R2D2 of *Star Wars* fame. Actually, the behaviorist position is not nearly that mechanistic, and its value is well established. Behaviorists have shown repeatedly that children can *learn* things like kindness, hostility, generosity, or destructiveness. What does this have to do with personality? Everything, according to the behavioral viewpoint.

Behavioral personality theories emphasize that personality is no more (or less) than a collection of learned behavior patterns. Personality, like other learned behavior, is acquired through classical and operant conditioning, observational learning, reinforcement, extinction, generalization, and discrimination. When Mother says, "It's not nice to make mud pies with Mommy's blender. If we want to grow up to be a big girl, we won't do it again, will we?" she serves as a model and in other ways shapes her daughter's personality.

Strict learning theorists reject the idea that personality is made up of traits. They would say, for instance, that there is no such thing as a trait of "honesty" (Bandura, 1973; Mischel, 1968).

Certainly some people are honest while others are not. How can honesty not be a trait? Learning theorists recognize that some people are honest *more often* than others. But knowing this does not allow us to predict whether a person will be honest in a specific situation. It would not be unusual, for example, to find that a person honored for returning a lost wallet had cheated on a test, bought a term paper, or broken the speed limit. If you were to ask a learning theorist, "Are you an honest person?" the reply might be, "In what situation?"

A good example of how situations influence behavior is shown by a study in which people were overpaid for doing a task. Under normal circumstances, 80 percent kept the extra money without saying a word about it. But as few as 17 percent were dishonest if the situation was restructured. For instance, if people thought the money was coming out of the pocket of the person doing the study, far fewer were dishonest (Bersoff, 1999).

As you can see, learning theorists are especially interested in the **situational determinants** (external causes) of our actions. However, this does not entirely remove the person from the equation. Situations always interact with our prior learning history to activate behavior.

Situations vary greatly in their impact. Some are powerful. Others are trivial and have little effect on behavior. The more powerful the situation, the easier it is to see what is meant by situational determinants. For example, each of the following situations would undoubtedly have a strong influence on behavior: an armed terrorist walks into a supermarket; you accidentally sit on a lighted cigarette; you find your lover in bed with your best friend. Yet even these situations could provoke very different reactions from different personalities. That's why behavior is always a product of both prior learning and the situations in which we find ourselves (Mischel & Shoda, 1998).

As discussed earlier, trait theorists also believe that situations affect behavior. But in their view, situations interact with *traits*, rather than a person's learning history. So, in essence, learning theorists favor replacing "traits" with "prior learning" to explain behavior.

Personality = Behavior

How do learning theorists view the structure of personality? The behavioral view of personality can be illustrated with an early theory proposed by John Dollard and Neal Miller (1950). In their view, *habits* (learned behavior patterns) make up the structure of personality. As for the dynamics of personality, habits are governed by four elements of learning: *drive, cue, response,* and *reward.* A *drive* is any stimulus strong enough to spur a person to action (such as hunger, pain, lust, frustration, or fear). *Cues* are signals from the environment. These signals guide *responses* (actions) so that they are most likely to bring about *reward* (positive reinforcement).

How does that relate to personality? Let's say a child named Kindra is frustrated by her older brother Kelvin, who takes a toy from her. Kindra could react in several ways: She could throw a temper tantrum, hit Kelvin, tell Mother, and so forth. The response she chooses is guided by available cues and the previous effects of each response. If telling Mother has paid

Freud believed that aggressive urges are "instinctual." In contrast, behavioral theories assume that personal characteristics such as aggressiveness are learned. Is this boy's aggression the result of observational learning, harsh punishment, or prior reinforcement?

Seventy-five percent of American college students admit that they have been academically dishonest in one way or another. What can be done about these high rates of dishonesty? The behavioral perspective holds that honesty is determined as much by circumstances as it is by personality. In line with this, simple measures like announcing in classes that integrity codes will be enforced can significantly reduce cheating. Using multiple forms of exams and educating students about plagiarism also tends to deter dishonesty (Altschuler, 2001).

Behavioral personality theory Any model of personality that emphasizes learning and observable behavior.
Situational determinants External conditions that strongly influence behavior.

off in the past, and the mother is present, telling again may be her immediate response. If a different set of cues exists (if Mother is absent or if Kelvin looks particularly menacing), Kindra may select some other response. To an outside observer, Kindra's actions seem to reflect her personality. To a learning theorist, they simply express the combined effects of drive, cue, response, and reward.

Doesn't this analysis leave out a lot? Yes. At first, learning theorists wanted to provide a simple, clear model of personality. But in recent years they have had to face a fact that they originally overlooked. The fact is: People think. The new breed of behavioral psychologists—who include perception, thinking, expectations, and other mental events in their views—are called social learning theorists. Learning principles, modeling, thought patterns, perceptions, expectations, beliefs, goals, emotions, and social relationships are combined in **social learning theory** to explain personality (Mischel & Shoda, 1998).

Social Learning Theory

The "cognitive behaviorism" of social learning theory can be illustrated by three concepts proposed by Julian Rotter. They are: the *psychological situation, expectancy,* and *reinforcement value* (Rotter & Hochreich, 1975). Let's examine each.

Someone trips you. How do you react? Your response probably depends on whether you think it was planned or an accident. It is not enough to know the setting in which a person responds. We also need to know the person's **psychological situation** (how the person interprets or defines the situation). As another example, let's say you score low on an exam. Do you consider it a challenge to work harder, a sign that you should drop the class, or an excuse to get drunk? Again, your interpretation is important.

Our actions are affected by an **expectancy,** or anticipation, that making a response will lead to reinforcement. To continue the example, if working harder has paid off in the past, it is a likely reaction to a low test score. But to predict your response, we would also have to know if you *expect* your efforts to pay off in the present situation. In fact, expected reinforcement may be more important than actual past reinforcement. And what about the *value* you attach to grades, school success, or personal ability? Rotter's third concept, **reinforcement value,** states that we attach different subjective values to various activities or rewards. This, too, must be taken into account to understand personality.

Self-Efficacy

An ability to control your own life is the essence of what it means to be human. Because of this, Albert Bandura believes that one of the most important expectancies we develop concerns **self-efficacy** (EF-ih-keh-see: a capacity for producing a desired result). You're attracted to someone in your anthropology class. Will you ask him or her out? You're thinking about learning to snow board. Will you try it this winter? You're beginning to consider a career in psychology. Will you take the courses you need to get into graduate school? You'd like to exercise more on the weekends. Will you join a hiking club? In these, and countless other situations, efficacy beliefs play a key role in shaping our lives by influencing the activities and environments we choose to get into (Bandura, 2001).

Self-Reinforcement

One more idea deserves mention. At times, we all evaluate our actions and may reward ourselves with special privileges or treats for "good behavior." With this in mind, social learning theory adds the concept of self-reinforcement to the behavioristic view. **Self-reinforcement** refers to praising or rewarding yourself for having made a particular response (such as completing a school assignment). Thus, habits of self-praise and self-blame become an important part of personality. In fact, self-reinforcement can be thought of as the social learning theorist's counterpart to the superego.

Social learning theory An explanation of personality that combines learning principles, cognition, and the effects of social relationships.

Psychological situation A situation as it is perceived and interpreted by an individual, not as it exists objectively.

Expectancy Anticipation about the effect a response will have, especially regarding reinforcement.

Reinforcement value The subjective value a person attaches to a particular activity or reinforcer.

Self-efficacy Belief in your capacity to produce a desired result.

Self-reinforcement Praising or rewarding oneself for having made a particular response (such as completing a school assignment).

Through self-reinforcement, we reward ourselves for personal achievements and other "good" behavior.

Self-reinforcement is closely related to high self-esteem. The reverse is also true: Mildly depressed college students tend to have low rates of self-reinforcement. It is not known if low self-reinforcement leads to depression, or the reverse. In either case, self-reinforcement is associated with less depression and greater life satisfaction (Seybolt & Wagner, 1997; Wilkinson, 1997). From a behavioral viewpoint, there is value in learning to be "good to yourself."

Behavioristic View of Development

How do learning theorists account for personality development?   Many of Freud's ideas can be restated in terms of learning theory. Miller and Dollard (1950) agree with Freud that the first 6 years are crucial for personality development, but for different reasons. Rather than thinking in terms of psychosexual urges and fixations, they ask, "What makes early learning experiences so lasting in their effects?" Their answer is that childhood is a time of urgent drives, powerful rewards and punishments, and crushing frustrations. Also important is *social reinforcement,* which is based on praise, attention, or approval from others. These forces combine to shape the core of personality.

Critical Situations

Miller and Dollard believe that during childhood four **critical situations** are capable of leaving a lasting imprint on personality. These are (1) feeding, (2) toilet or cleanliness training, (3) sex training, and (4) learning to express anger or aggression.

Why are these of special importance?   Feeding serves as an illustration. If children are fed when they cry, it encourages them to actively manipulate their parents. The child allowed to cry without being fed learns to be passive. Thus, a basic active or passive orientation toward the world may be created by early feeding experiences. Feeding can also affect later social relationships because the child learns to associate people with pleasure or with frustration and discomfort.

Toilet and cleanliness training can be a particularly strong source of emotion for both parents and children. Rashad's parents were aghast the day they found him smearing feces about with joyful abandon. They reacted with sharp punishment, which frustrated and confused Rashad. Many attitudes toward cleanliness, conformity, and bodily functions are formed at such times. Studies also show that severe, punishing, or frustrating toilet training can have undesirable effects on personality development (Sears et al., 1957). Because of this, toilet and cleanliness training demand patience and a sense of humor.

What about sex and anger?   When, where, and how a child learns to express anger and sexual feelings can leave an imprint on personality. Specifically, permissiveness for sexual and aggressive behavior in childhood is linked to adult needs for power (McClelland & Pilon, 1983). This link probably occurs because permitting such behaviors allows children to get pleasure from asserting themselves. Sex training also involves learning socially defined "male" and "female" gender roles—which also affect personality.

Becoming Male or Female

From birth onward, children are labeled as boys or girls and encouraged to learn sex-appropriate behavior (Witt, 1997). According to social learning theory, identification and imitation contribute greatly to personality development and to sex training. **Identification** refers to the child's emotional attachment to admired adults, especially those who provide love and care. Identification typically encourages **imitation,** a desire to act like the admired person. Many "male" or "female" traits come from children's attempts to imitate a same-sex parent with whom they identify.

If children are around parents of both sexes, why don't they imitate behavior typical of the opposite sex as well as of the same sex?   Recall from Chapter 6 that learning takes place vicariously as well as directly. This means that we can learn by observing and remembering the actions of others. But the actions we choose to imitate depend on their outcomes. For example, boys and girls have equal chances to observe people acting aggressively. However, girls are less likely than boys to imitate aggressive behavior because they rarely see female aggression rewarded or approved. Thus, many arbitrary "male" and "female" qualities are passed on at the same time that sexual identity is learned.

Critical situations Situations during childhood that are capable of leaving a lasting imprint on personality.

Identification Feeling emotionally connected to a person and seeing oneself as like him or her.

Imitation An attempt to match one's own behavior to another person's behavior.

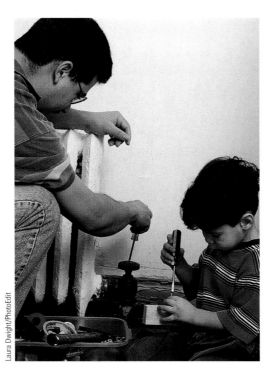

Adult personality is influenced by identification with parents and imitation of their behavior.

Laura Dwight/PhotoEdit

A study of preschool teachers found that they are three times more likely to pay attention to aggressive or disruptive boys than to girls acting the same way. Boys who hit other students or broke things typically got loud scoldings. This made them the center of attention for the whole class. In contrast, disruptive girls were given brief, soft rebukes that others couldn't hear (Serbin & O'Leary, 1975). We know that attention of almost any kind reinforces children's behavior. Therefore, it is clear that boys were encouraged to be active and aggressive. Girls got the most attention when they were within arm's reach, more or less clinging to the teacher.

The pattern just described grows stronger throughout elementary school. In all grades, boys are louder, faster, and more boisterous than girls. Day after day, boys receive a disproportionate amount of the teacher's attention (Sadker & Sadker, 1994). It's easy to see that teachers unwittingly encourage girls to be submissive, dependent, and passive. Similar differences in reinforcement probably explain why males are responsible for more aggression than females are. Among adults, rates of murder and assault are consistently higher for men. The roots of this difference appear to lie in childhood.

Personality and Gender

Overall, parents and other adults tend to encourage boys to engage in **instrumental** (goal-directed) **behaviors,** to be aggressive, to hide their emotions, and to prepare for the world of work. Girls, on the other hand, are encouraged in **expressive** (emotion-oriented) **behaviors** and, to a lesser degree, are socialized for motherhood. From an early age, males and females tend to grow up in different, gender-defined cultures (Martin & Fabes, 2001). What effects do such differences have on adult behavior? To find out, let's explore what it means to have a "masculine" or "feminine" personality.

ANDROGYNY—ARE YOU MASCULINE, FEMININE, OR ANDROGYNOUS?

Are you aggressive, ambitious, analytical, assertive, athletic, competitive, decisive, dominant, forceful, independent, individualistic, self-reliant, and willing to take risks? If so, you are quite "masculine." Are you affectionate, cheerful, childlike, compassionate, flatterable, gentle, gullible, loyal, sensitive, shy, soft-spoken, sympathetic, tender, understanding, warm, and yielding? If so, then you are quite "feminine." What if you have characteristics from both lists? In that case, you may be androgynous (an-DROJ-ih-nus).

Instrumental behaviors Behaviors directed toward the achievement of some goal; behaviors that are instrumental in producing some effect.

Expressive behaviors Behaviors that express or communicate emotion or personal feelings.

Androgyny The presence of both "masculine" and "feminine" traits in a single person (as masculinity and femininity are defined within one's culture).

The two lists you just read are from the work of psychologist Sandra Bem. By combining 20 "masculine" traits (self-reliant, assertive, and so forth), 20 "feminine" traits (affectionate, gentle), and 20 neutral traits (truthful, friendly), Bem created the *Bem Sex Role Inventory* (BSRI). People who take the BSRI are asked to say whether each trait applies to them. Of those surveyed, 50 percent fall into traditional feminine or masculine categories; 15 percent score higher on traits of the opposite sex; and 35 percent are androgynous, getting high scores on both feminine and masculine items.

The word *androgyny* (an-DROJ-ih-nee) literally means "man-woman." Psychologically, it refers to having both feminine and masculine traits. Bem is convinced that our complex society requires flexibility about gender-related traits. It is necessary, she believes, for

Androgynous individuals adapt easily to both traditionally "feminine" and "masculine" situations.

men to be gentle, compassionate, sensitive, and yielding, and for women to be forceful, self-reliant, independent, and ambitious—*as the situation requires*. In short, Bem feels that more people should be androgynous.

Adaptability

Bem has shown that androgynous individuals are more adaptable because they are less hindered by narrow images of "feminine" or "masculine" behavior. For example, in one study, people were given the choice of doing either a "masculine" activity (oil a hinge, nail boards together, and so forth) or a "feminine" activity (prepare a baby bottle, wind yarn into a ball, and so on). Masculine men and feminine women consistently chose to do gender-appropriate activities, even when the opposite choice paid more!

It appears that having rigid gender traits can seriously restrict behavior, especially for men (Bem, 1975a, 1981). Masculine males tend to have great difficulty expressing warmth, playfulness, and concern—even when they are appropriate. Masculine men, it seems, view such feelings as too "feminine." Masculine men also find it hard to accept emotional support from others, particularly from women (Ashton & Fuehrer, 1993). Highly feminine women face opposite problems. For them, being independent and assertive is difficult, even when these qualities are desirable.

Gender in Perspective

Androgyny has been hotly debated over the years. Now, as the dust begins to settle, the picture looks like this:

- Having "masculine" traits primarily means that a person is independent and assertive. Scoring high in "masculinity" is related to high self-esteem and to success in many situations.
- Having "feminine" traits primarily means that a person is nurturant and interpersonally oriented. People who score high in "femininity" tend to experience greater social closeness with others and more happiness in marriage.

In sum, there are advantages to possessing both "feminine" and "masculine" traits. In general, androgynous persons are more flexible when it comes to coping with difficult situations (Jurma & Powell, 1994; Spangenberg & Lategan, 1993) (see ◆Fig. 10.7). Androgynous

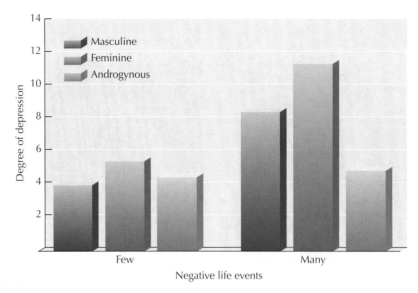

◆**FIGURE 10.7** *Another indication of the possible benefits of androgyny is found in a study of reactions to stress. When confronted with an onslaught of negative events, strongly masculine or feminine persons become more depressed than androgynous individuals do. (Adapted from Roos & Cohen, 1987.)*

persons also tend to be more satisfied with their lives. Apparently, they can use both instrumental and emotionally expressive capacities to enhance their lives and relationships (Dean-Church & Gilroy, 1993; Ramanaiah, Detwiler, & Byravan, 1995).

It is worth saying again that many people remain comfortable with traditional views of gender. Nevertheless, "feminine" traits and "masculine" traits can readily exist in the same person, and androgyny can be a highly adaptive balance.

STUDYBREAK *Behavioral and Social Learning Theories*

RELATE

What are your favorite foods? Can you relate Miller and Dollard's concepts of habit, drive, cue, response, and reward to explain your preference?

Some people love to shop. Others hate it. How have the psychological situation, expectancy, and reinforcement value affected your willingness to "shop 'til you drop"?

Who did you identify with as a child? What aspects of that person's behavior did you imitate?

Think of three people you know, one who is androgynous, one who is traditionally feminine, and one who is traditionally masculine. What advantages and disadvantages do you see in each collection of traits? How do you think you would be classified if you took the BSRI?

LEARNING CHECK

1. Learning theorists believe that personality "traits" really are _____ acquired through prior learning. They also emphasize _____ determinants of behavior.
2. Dollard and Miller consider cues the basic structure of personality. T or F?

3. To explain behavior, social learning theorists include mental elements, such as _____ (the anticipation that a response will lead to reinforcement).
4. Self-reinforcement is to behavioristic theory as superego is to psychoanalytic theory. T or F?
5. Which of the following is *not* a "critical situation" in the behaviorist theory of personality development?
   a. feeding   b. sex training   c. language training
   d. anger training
6. In addition to basic rewards and punishments, a child's personality is also shaped by _____ reinforcement.
7. Social learning theories of development emphasize the impact of identification and _____.
8. A person who is aggressive, ambitious, analytical, assertive would be rated as androgynous on the BSRI. T or F?

Critical Thinking

9. Julian Rotter's concept of *reinforcement value* is closely related to a motivational principle discussed in Chapter 9. Can you name it?

ANSWERS

1. habits, situational 2. F 3. expectancies 4. T 5. c 6. social 7. imitation 8. F 9. incentive value

HUMANISTIC THEORY—PEAK EXPERIENCES AND PERSONAL GROWTH

At the beginning of this chapter you met Annette, an interesting personality. A few years ago, Annette and her husband spent a year riding mules across the country as a unique way to see America and get to know themselves better. Where do such desires for personal growth come from? Humanistic theories pay special attention to the fuller use of human potentials, and they help bring balance to our overall views of personality.

Humanism focuses on human experience, problems, potentials, and ideals. It is a reaction to the rigidity of traits, the pessimism of psychoanalytic theory, and the mechanical nature of learning theory. At its core is a positive image of what it means to be human. Humanists reject the Freudian view of personality as a battleground for instincts and unconscious forces. Instead, they view human nature as inherently good. (Human nature consists of the traits, qualities, potentials, and behavior patterns most characteristic of the human species.) Humanists also oppose the machine-like overtones of behaviorism. We are not, they say, merely a bundle of moldable responses. Rather, we are creative beings capable of *free choice* (an ability to choose that is not controlled by genetics, learning, or unconscious forces). In short, humanists seek ways to encourage our potentials to blossom.

To a humanist, the person you are today is largely the product of all the choices you have made. Humanists also emphasize immediate *subjective experience* (private perceptions of reality), rather than prior learning. They believe that there are as many "real worlds" as there are people. To understand behavior, we must learn how a person subjectively views the world—what is "real" for her or him.

Who are the major humanistic theorists? Many psychologists have added to the humanistic tradition. Of these, the best known are Carl Rogers (1902–1987) and Abraham Maslow (1908–1970). Since Maslow's idea of self-actualization was introduced in Chapter 1, let's begin with a more detailed look at his thinking.

Maslow and Self-Actualization

Abraham Maslow became interested in people who were living unusually effective lives. How were they different? To find an answer, Maslow began by studying some of history's great men and women, such as Albert Einstein, William James, Jane Addams, Eleanor Roosevelt, Abraham Lincoln, John Muir, and Walt Whitman. From there he moved on to directly study living artists, writers, poets, and other creative individuals.

Along the way, Maslow's thinking changed radically. At first he studied only people of obvious creativity or high achievement. However, it eventually became clear that a housewife, clerk, student, or someone like my friend Annette could live a rich, creative, and satisfying life. Maslow referred to the process of fully developing personal potentials as **self-actualization** (Maslow, 1954). The heart of self-actualization is a continuous search for personal fulfillment (Sumerlin, 1997).

Characteristics of Self-Actualizers

A *self-actualizer* is a person who is living creatively and fully using his or her potentials. In his studies, Maslow found that self-actualizers share many similarities. Whether famous or unknown, well schooled or uneducated, rich or poor, self-actualizers tend to fit the following profile.

1. **Efficient perceptions of reality.** Self-actualizers are able to judge situations correctly and honestly. They are very sensitive to the fake and dishonest.
2. **Comfortable acceptance of self, others, nature.** Self-actualizers accept their own human nature with all its flaws. The shortcomings of others and the contradictions of the human condition are accepted with humor and tolerance.
3. **Spontaneity.** Maslow's subjects extended their creativity into everyday activities. Actualizers tend to be unusually alive, engaged, and spontaneous.

Humanism An approach that focuses on human experience, problems, potentials, and ideals.

Self-actualization The process of fully developing personal potentials.

4. **Task centering.** Most of Maslow's subjects had a mission to fulfill in life or some task or problem outside of themselves to pursue. Humanitarians such as Albert Schweitzer and Mother Teresa represent this quality.

5. **Autonomy.** Self-actualizers are free from reliance on external authorities or other people. They tend to be resourceful and independent.

6. **Continued freshness of appreciation.** The self-actualizer seems to constantly renew appreciation of life's basic goods. A sunset or a flower will be experienced as intensely time after time as it was at first. There is an "innocence of vision," like that of an artist or child.

7. **Fellowship with humanity.** Maslow's subjects felt a deep identification with others and the human situation in general.

8. **Profound interpersonal relationships.** The interpersonal relationships of self-actualizers are marked by deep, loving bonds.

9. **Comfort with solitude.** Despite their satisfying relationships with others, self-actualizing persons value solitude and are comfortable being alone (Sumerlin & Bundrick, 1996).

10. **Non-hostile sense of humor.** This refers to the wonderful capacity to laugh at oneself. It also describes the kind of humor a man like Abraham Lincoln had. Lincoln probably never made a joke that hurt anybody. His wry comments were a gentle prodding of human shortcomings.

11. **Peak experiences.** All of Maslow's subjects reported the frequent occurrence of *peak experiences* (temporary moments of self-actualization). These occasions were marked by feelings of ecstasy, harmony, and deep meaning. Self-actualizers reported feeling at one with the universe, stronger and calmer than ever before, filled with light, beautiful and good, and so forth.

In summary, self-actualizers feel safe, calm, accepted, loved, loving, and alive.

Maslow's choice of self-actualizing people for study seems pretty subjective. Is it really a fair representation of self-actualization? Although Maslow tried to investigate self-actualization empirically, his choice of people for study was subjective. Undoubtedly, there are many ways to make full use of one's potentials. Maslow's primary contribution was to draw our attention to the possibility of lifelong personal growth.

What steps can be taken to promote self-actualization? Maslow offered little guidance about how to proceed. Nevertheless, several helpful ideas can be gleaned from his writings (Maslow, 1954, 1967, 1971). See "Steps Toward Self-Actualization" for some specific suggestions.

Carl Rogers' Self Theory

Carl Rogers, another well-known humanist, based his theory on clinical experience with unhappy people. Nevertheless, he emphasized the human capacity for inner peace and happiness. The *fully functioning person,* he said, lives in harmony with his or her deepest feelings and impulses. Such people are open to their experiences, and they trust their inner urges and intuitions (Rogers, 1961). Rogers believed that this attitude is most likely to occur when a person receives ample amounts of love and acceptance from others.

Personality Structure and Dynamics

Rogers' theory emphasizes the **self,** a flexible and changing perception of personal identity. Much behavior can be understood as an attempt to maintain consistency between our *self-image* and our actions. (Your **self-image** is a total subjective perception of your body and personality.) For example, people who think of themselves as kind tend to be considerate in most situations.

Let's say I know a person who thinks she is kind, but she really isn't. How does that fit Rogers' theory? According to Rogers, we allow experiences that match our self-image into awareness, where they gradually change the self. Information or feelings inconsistent with the self-image are said to be incongruent. Thus, a person who thinks she is kind, but really isn't, is in a state of **incongruence.** In other words, there is a discrepancy between her experiences and her self-image. As another example, it would be incongruent to believe that you are a person who "never gets angry" if you spend much of each day seething inside.

Self A continuously evolving conception of one's personal identity.

Self-image Total subjective perception of one's body and personality (another term for self-concept).

Incongruence State that exists when there is a discrepancy between one's experiences and self-image or between one's self-image and ideal self.

USING PSYCHOLOGY Steps Toward Self-Actualization

There is no magic formula for leading a more creative life. Self-actualization is primarily a *process,* not a goal or an end point. As such, it requires hard work, patience, and commitment. Here are some ways to begin.

1. **Be willing to change.** Begin by asking yourself, "Am I living in a way that is deeply satisfying to me and that truly expresses me?" If not, be prepared to make changes in your life. Indeed, ask yourself this question often and accept the need for continual change.
2. **Take responsibility.** You can become an architect of self by acting as if you are personally responsible for every aspect of your life. Shouldering responsibility in this way helps end the habit of blaming others for your own shortcomings.
3. **Examine your motives.** Self-discovery involves an element of risk. If your behavior is restricted by a desire for safety or security, it may be time to test some limits. Try to make each life decision a choice for growth, not a response to fear or anxiety.
4. **Experience honestly and directly.** Wishful thinking is another barrier to personal growth. Self-actualizers trust themselves enough to accept all kinds of information without distorting it to fit their fears and desires. Try to see yourself as others do. Be willing to admit, "I was wrong," or "I failed because I was irresponsible."

5. **Make use of positive experiences.** Maslow considered peak experiences temporary moments of self-actualization. Therefore, you might actively repeat activities that have caused feelings of awe, amazement, exaltation, renewal, reverence, humility, fulfillment, or joy.
6. **Be prepared to be different.** Maslow felt that everyone has a potential for "greatness," but most fear becoming what they might. As part of personal growth, be prepared to trust your own impulses and feelings; don't automatically judge yourself by the standards of others. Accept your uniqueness.
7. **Get involved.** With few exceptions, self-actualizers tend to have a mission or "calling" in life. For these people, "work" is not done just to fill deficiency needs, but to satisfy higher yearnings for truth, beauty, community, and meaning. Get personally involved and committed. Turn your attention to problems outside yourself.
8. **Assess your progress.** There is no final point at which one becomes self-actualized. It's important to gauge your progress frequently and to renew your efforts. If you feel bored at school, at a job, or in a relationship, consider it a challenge. Have you been taking responsibility for your own personal growth? Almost any activity can be used as a chance for self-enhancement if it is approached creatively.

Experiences seriously incongruent with the self-image can be threatening. Because of this, we often distort or deny such experiences, which prevents the self from changing. In time, a gulf develops between the self-image and reality. As the self-image grows more inaccurate and unrealistic, the **incongruent person** becomes confused, vulnerable, dissatisfied, or seriously maladjusted (◆Fig. 10.8). Interestingly, a study of college students confirmed that being *authentic* is vital for healthy functioning. Basically, to be happy, we need to feel that our behavior accurately expresses who we are (Sheldon et al., 1997). Please note, however, that being authentic doesn't mean you can do whatever you want. Being true to yourself is no excuse for acting irresponsibly or ignoring the feelings of others.

When your self-image is consistent with what you really think, feel, do, and experience, you are best able to actualize your potentials. Rogers also considered it essential to have congruence between the self-image and the **ideal self.** The ideal self is similar to Freud's ego ideal. It is an image of the person you would most like to be.

Humanists consider self-image a central determinant of behavior and personal adjustment.

◆**FIGURE 10.8** *Incongruence occurs when there is a mismatch between any of these three entities: the ideal self (the person you would like to be), your self-image (the person you think you are), and the true self (the person you actually are). Self-esteem suffers when there is a large difference between one's ideal self and self-image. Anxiety and defensiveness are common when the self-image does not match the true self.*

Incongruence

Ideal self

Self-image   True self

Congruence

Ideal self
Self-image
True self

Incongruent person A person who has an inaccurate self-image or whose self-image differs greatly from the ideal self.

Ideal self An idealized image of oneself (the person one would like to be).

USING PSYCHOLOGY   Possible Selves—Trying on a Self for Size

My friend Annette, who was described earlier, is an interesting personality, to say the least. Annette is one of those people who seems to have lived many lives in the time that most of us manage only one. Like Annette, you may have pondered many possible personal identities. Psychologists Hazel Markus and Paula Nurius (1986) believe that each of us harbors images of various *possible selves* (persons one could become). These selves include the person we would most like to be (the ideal self), as well as other selves we could become or are afraid of becoming.

Possible selves translate our hopes, fears, fantasies, and goals into specific images of who we *could* be. Thus, a beginning law student might picture herself as a successful attorney; an enterprising college student might imagine himself as a dot.com entrepreneur; and a person on a diet might imagine both slim and grossly obese possible selves. Such images tend to direct our future behavior.

Of course, almost everyone over age 30 has probably felt the anguish of realizing that some cherished possible selves will never be realized. Nevertheless, there is value in asking yourself not just "Who am I?" but also "Who would I like to become?" As you do, remember Maslow's advice that everyone has a potential for "greatness," but most fear becoming what they might.

Is it really incongruent not to live up to your ideal self?   Rogers was aware that we never fully attain our ideals. Nevertheless, the larger the gap between the way you see yourself and the way you would like to be, the more tension and anxiety you will experience.

To maximize our potentials, we must accept information about ourselves as honestly as possible. In accord with this, researchers have found that people with a close match between their self-image and ideal self tend to be socially poised, confident, and resourceful. Those with a poor match tend to be depressed, anxious, and insecure (Alfeld-Liro & Sigelman, 1998; Scott & O'Hara, 1993). (See "Possible Selves—Trying on a Self for Size" for another perspective on the ways in which self-image can influence our behavior.)

Humanistic View of Development

Why do mirrors, photographs, video cameras, and the reactions of others hold such fascination and threat for many people? Carl Rogers' theory suggests it is because they provide information about one's self. The development of a self-image depends greatly on information from the environment. It begins in infancy and childhood with a sorting of perceptions and feelings: my body, my toes, my nose, I want, I like, I am, and so on. Soon, it expands to include self-evaluation: I am a good person, I did something bad just now, and so forth.

How does development of the self contribute to later personality functioning?   Rogers believed that positive and negative evaluations by others cause children to develop internal standards of evaluation called **conditions of worth.** In other words, we learn that some actions win our parents' love and approval, whereas others are rejected. More important, parents may label some *feelings* as bad or wrong. For example, a child might be told that it is wrong to feel angry toward a brother or sister—even when anger is justified. Likewise, a little boy might be told that he must not cry or show fear, two very normal emotions.

Learning to evaluate some experiences or feelings as "good" and others as "bad" is directly related to a later capacity for self-esteem, positive self-evaluation, or **positive self-regard,** to use Rogers' term. To think of yourself as a good, lovable, worthwhile person, your behavior and experiences must match your internal conditions of worth. The problem is that this can cause incongruence by leading to the denial of many true feelings and experiences.

To put it simply, Rogers blamed many adult emotional problems on attempts to live by the standards of others. He believed that congruence and self-actualization are encouraged by replacing conditions of worth with **organismic valuing** (a natural, undistorted, full-body reaction to an experience). Organismic valuing is a direct, gut-level response to life that avoids the filtering and distortion of incongruence. It involves trusting one's own feelings and perceptions. Organismic valuing is most likely to develop, Rogers felt, when children (or adults) receive **unconditional positive regard** (unshakable love and approval) from others. That is, when they are "prized" as worthwhile human beings, just for being themselves, without any conditions or strings attached. Although this may be a luxury few people enjoy, we are more likely to move toward our ideal selves if we receive affirmation and support from a close partner (Drigotas et al., 1999).

Conditions of worth Internal standards used to judge the value of one's thoughts, actions, feelings, or experiences.

Positive self-regard Thinking of oneself as a good, lovable, worthwhile person.

Organismic valuing A natural, undistorted, full-body reaction to an experience.

Unconditional positive regard Unshakable love and approval given without qualification.

RELATE

How do your views of human nature and free choice compare with those of the humanists?

Do you know anyone who seems to be making especially good use of their personal potentials? Does that person fit Maslow's profile of a self-actualizer?

How much difference do you think there is between your self-image, your ideal self, and your true self? Do you think Rogers is right about the effects of applying conditions of worth to your perceptions and feelings?

LEARNING CHECK

1. Humanists view human nature as basically good, and they emphasize the effects of subjective learning and unconscious choice. T or F?
2. Maslow used the term _____ to describe the tendency of certain individuals to fully use their talents and potentials.

3. According to Rogers, a close match between the self-image and the ideal self creates a condition called incongruence. T or F?
4. Rogers' theory considers acceptance of conditions of _____ a troublesome aspect of development of the self.
5. According to Maslow, a preoccupation with one's own thoughts, feelings, and needs is characteristic of self-actualizing individuals. T or F?
6. Maslow regarded _____ experiences as times of temporary self-actualization.

Critical Thinking

7. What role has your self-image played in your choice of a college major?

ANSWERS 1. F 2. self-actualization 3. F 4. worth 5. F 6. peak 7. Career decisions almost always involve, in part, picturing oneself occupying various occupational roles. Such "future selves" play a role in many of the major decisions we make (Markus & Nurius, 1986).

PERSONALITY THEORIES—OVERVIEW AND COMPARISON

Which personality theory is right? Each theory has added to our understanding by organizing observations of human behavior. Nevertheless, theories can never be fully proved or disproved. We can only ask, Does the evidence tend to support this theory or disconfirm it? Yet, while theories are neither true nor false, their implications or predictions may be. The best way to judge a theory, then, is in terms of its *usefulness*. Does the theory adequately explain behavior? Does it stimulate new research? Does it suggest how to treat psychological disorders? Each theory has fared differently in these areas.

In the final analysis, we need all four major perspectives to explain personality. Each provides a sort of lens through which human behavior can be viewed. In many instances, a balanced picture emerges only when each theory is considered. ▲Table 10.3 provides a final overview of the four principal approaches to personality.

▲*TABLE 10.3*	**Comparison of Four Views of Personality**			
	TRAIT THEORIES	**PSYCHOANALYTIC THEORY**	**BEHAVIORISTIC THEORY**	**HUMANISTIC THEORY**
View of human nature	neutral	negative	neutral	positive
Is behavior free or determined?	determined	determined	determined	free choice
Principal motives	depends on one's traits	sex and aggression	drives of all kinds	self-actualization
Personality structure	traits	id, ego, superego	habits	self
Role of unconscious	minimized	maximized	practically nonexistent	minimized
Conception of conscience	traits of honesty, etc.	superego	self-reinforcement punishment history	ideal self, valuing process
Developmental emphasis	combined effects of heredity and environment	psychosexual stages	critical learning situations identification and imitation	development of self-image
Barriers to personal growth	unhealthy traits	unconscious conflicts, fixations	maladaptive habits; unhealthy environment	conditions of worth; incongruence

PERSONALITY ASSESSMENT—PSYCHOLOGICAL YARDSTICKS

] SURVEYQUESTION *How do psychologists measure personality?*

Measuring personality can help predict how people will behave at work, at school, and in therapy. However, painting a detailed picture can be a challenge. Capturing a personality as unique as Annette's might take all of the techniques in this chapter!

How is personality "measured"?   Psychologists use interviews, observation, questionnaires, and projective tests to assess personality. Each method has strengths and limitations. For this reason, they are often used in combination.

Formal personality measures are refinements of more casual ways of judging a person. At one time or another, you have probably "sized up" a potential date, friend, or roommate by engaging in conversation (interview). Perhaps you have asked a friend, "When I am delayed I get angry. Do you?" (questionnaire). Maybe you watch your professors when they are angry or embarrassed to learn what they are "really" like when they're caught off-guard (observation). Or possibly you have noticed that when you say, "I think people feel . . .," you may be expressing your own feelings (projection). Let's see how psychologists apply each of these methods to probe personality.

The Interview

In an **interview,** direct questioning is used to learn about a person's life history, personality traits, or current mental state. In an *unstructured interview,* conversation is informal and topics are taken up freely as they arise. In a *structured interview,* information is gathered by asking a planned series of questions.

How are interviews used?   Interviews are used to identify personality disturbances; to select people for jobs, college, or special programs; and to study the dynamics of personality. Interviews also provide information for counseling or therapy. For instance, a counselor might ask a depressed person, "Have you ever contemplated suicide? What were the circumstances?" The counselor might then follow by asking, "How did you feel about it?" or "How is what you are now feeling different from what you felt then?"

In addition to providing information, interviews make it possible to observe a person's tone of voice, hand gestures, posture, and facial expressions. Such "body language" cues are important because they may radically alter the message sent, as when a person claims to be "completely calm" but trembles uncontrollably.

Limitations

Interviews give rapid insight into personality, but they have limitations. For one thing, interviewers can be swayed by preconceptions. A person identified as a "housewife," "college student," "high school athlete," "punk," "computer nerd," or "ski bum" may be misjudged because of an interviewer's personal biases. Second, an interviewer's own personality, or even gender, may influence a client's behavior. When this occurs, it can accentuate or distort the person's apparent traits (Pollner, 1998). A third problem is that people sometimes try to deceive interviewers. For example, a person accused of a crime might try to avoid punishment by pretending to be mentally disabled.

A fourth problem is the **halo effect,** which is the tendency to generalize a favorable or unfavorable first impression to an entire personality. Because of the halo effect, a person who is likable or physically at-

Interview (personality) A face-to-face meeting held for the purpose of gaining information about an individual's personal history, personality traits, current psychological state, and so forth.

Halo effect The tendency to generalize a favorable or unfavorable first impression to unrelated details of personality.

What is your initial impression of the person wearing the gray jacket? If you think that she looks friendly, attractive, or neat, your subsequent perceptions might be altered by a positive first impression. Interviewers are often influenced by the halo effect (see text).

Bob Daemmrich/The Image Works

tractive may be rated more mature, intelligent, or mentally healthy than she or he actually is. The halo effect is something to keep in mind at job interviews. First impressions do make a difference (Lance, LaPointe, & Stewart, 1994).

Even with their limitations, interviews are a respected method of assessment. In many cases, interviews are the first step in evaluating personality and an essential prelude to therapy. Nevertheless, interviews often may not be enough. Usually, they must be supplemented by other measures and tests (Meyer et al., 2001).

Direct Observation and Rating Scales

Are you fascinated by airports, bus depots, parks, taverns, subway stations, or other public places? Many people relish a chance to observe the actions of others. As an assessment procedure, **direct observation** (looking at behavior) is a simple extension of this natural interest in "people watching." For instance, a psychologist might arrange to watch a disturbed child as she plays with other children. Is the child withdrawn? Does she become hostile or aggressive without warning? By careful observation, the psychologist will identify personality traits and clarify the nature of the child's problems.

Wouldn't observation be subject to the same problems of misperception as an interview? Yes. Misperceptions can be a problem. A solution is to use **rating scales** to evaluate a person. A rating scale is a list of personality traits or specific aspects of behavior (◆Fig. 10.9). Rating scales reduce the risk that some traits will be overlooked while others are exaggerated (Merenda, 1996). Perhaps they should be a standard procedure for choosing a roommate, spouse, or lover!

An alternative approach is to do a **behavioral assessment** by counting the frequency of specific behaviors. In this case, observers record *actions,* not what traits they think a person has. For example, a psychologist working with hospitalized mental patients might note the frequency of a patient's aggression, self-care, speech, and unusual behaviors. Behavioral assessments can also be used to probe thought processes. In one study, for example, students high in math anxiety were asked to think aloud while doing math problems. Later, their thoughts were analyzed to pinpoint why they had math fears (Blackwell et al., 1985).

Direct observation Assessing behavior through direct surveillance.

Rating scale A list of personality traits or aspects of behavior on which a person is rated.

Behavioral assessment Recording the frequency of various behaviors.

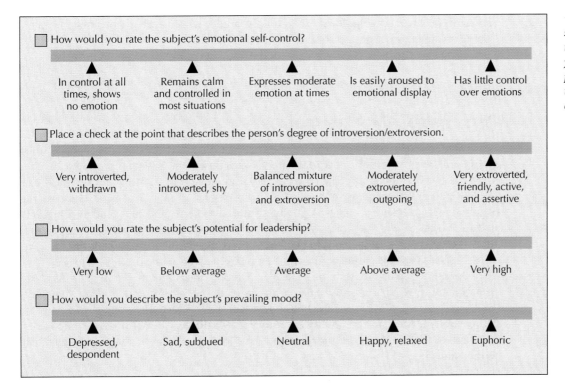

◆**FIGURE 10.9** *Sample rating scale items. To understand how the scale works, imagine someone you know well. Where would you place check marks on each of the scales to rate that person's characteristics?*

How would you rate the subject's emotional self-control?

| In control at all times, shows no emotion | Remains calm and controlled in most situations | Expresses moderate emotion at times | Is easily aroused to emotional display | Has little control over emotions |

Place a check at the point that describes the person's degree of introversion/extroversion.

| Very introverted, withdrawn | Moderately introverted, shy | Balanced mixture of introversion and extroversion | Moderately extroverted, outgoing | Very extroverted, friendly, active, and assertive |

How would you rate the subject's potential for leadership?

| Very low | Below average | Average | Above average | Very high |

How would you describe the subject's prevailing mood?

| Depressed, despondent | Sad, subdued | Neutral | Happy, relaxed | Euphoric |

Situational Testing

In **situational testing,** real-life conditions are simulated so that a person's spontaneous reactions can be observed. Such tests assume that the best way to learn how people react is to put them in realistic situations and watch what happens. In a situational test, you might be exposed to frustration, temptation, pressure, boredom, or other conditions that reveal personality characteristics (Weekley & Jones, 1997). Some of the recently popular "reality TV" programs, such as *Survivor,* bear some similarity to situational tests—which may account for their ability to attract millions of viewers.

How are situational tests done?   An interesting example of situational testing is the judgmental firearms training provided by many police departments. At times, police officers must make split-second decisions about using their weapons. A mistake could be fatal. In a typical shoot–don't shoot test, actors play the part of armed criminals. As various high-risk scenes are acted out live or on videotape, officers must decide to shoot or hold fire. A newspaper reporter who once took the test (and failed it) gives this account (Gersh, 1982):

> I judged wrong. I was killed by a man in a closet, a man with a hostage, a woman interrupted when kissing her lover, and a man I thought was cleaning a shotgun. . . . I shot a drunk who reached for a comb, and a teenager who pulled out a black water pistol. Looked real to me.

A police officer undergoes judgmental firearms training. Variations on this situational test are used by a growing number of police departments. All officers must score a passing grade.

In addition to the training it provides, situational testing uncovers police cadets who lack the good judgment needed to carry a gun out on the street.

To evaluate job applicants, situational tests stage difficult work situations (Borman et al., 1997). For example, in one exercise, people are given an *in-basket test* that simulates executive decision making. The test consists of a basket full of memos, requests, and typical business problems. Each applicant is asked to quickly read all of the materials and take appropriate action. In another, more stressful test, applicants take part in a *leaderless group discussion* that requires group decisions and problem solving. While the group grapples with a realistic business problem, "clerks" bring in price changes, notices about delayed supplies, and so forth. By observing job candidates, it is possible to evaluate their leadership skills and to see how they cope with stress.

Personality Questionnaires

Situational test Simulating real-life conditions so that a person's reactions may be directly observed.

Personality questionnaire A paper-and-pencil test consisting of questions that reveal aspects of personality.

Reliability The ability of a test to yield nearly the same score each time it is given to the same person.

Validity The ability of a test to measure what it purports to measure.

Minnesota Multiphasic Personality Inventory-2 (MMPI-2) One of the best-known and most widely used objective personality questionnaires.

Personality questionnaires are paper-and-pencil tests that reveal personality characteristics. Questionnaires are more objective than interviews or observation. (An objective test gives the same score when different people correct it.) Questions, administration, and scoring are all standardized so that scores are unaffected by any biases an examiner may have. However, this is not enough to ensure accuracy. A good test must also be reliable and valid. A test is **reliable** if it yields close to the same score each time it is given to the same person. A test has **validity** if it measures what it claims to measure. Unfortunately, many personality tests you will encounter, such as those in magazines or on the Internet, have little or no validity.

Dozens of personality tests are available, including the *Guilford-Zimmerman Temperament Survey,* the *California Psychological Inventory,* the *Allport-Vernon Study of Values,* the 16 PF, and many more. One of the best known and most widely used objective tests is the **Minnesota Multiphasic Personality Inventory-2** (**MMPI-2**). The MMPI-2 is composed of 567 items to which a test taker must respond "true" or "false." Items include statements such as the following.

Everything tastes the same.
There is something wrong with my mind.
I enjoy animals.
Whenever possible I avoid being in a crowd.
I have never indulged in any unusual sex practices.
Someone has been trying to poison me.
I daydream often.*

How can these items show anything about personality? For instance, what if a person has a cold so that "everything tastes the same"? For an answer (and a little bit of fun), read the following items. Answer "Yes," "No," or "Don't bother me, I can't cope!"

I would enjoy the work of a chicken flicker.
My eyes are always cold.
Frantic screaming makes me nervous.
I believe I smell as good as most people.
I use shoe polish to excess.
The sight of blood no longer excites me.
As an infant I had very few hobbies.
Dirty stories make me think about sex.
I stay in the bathtub until I look like a raisin.
I salivate at the sight of mittens.
I never finish what I

These items were written by humorist Art Buchwald (1965) and psychologist Carol Sommer to poke fun at personality questionnaires. Such questions may seem ridiculous, but they are not very different from the real thing. How, then, do the items on tests such as the MMPI-2 reveal anything about personality? The answer is that a single item tells little about personality. For example, a person who agrees that "Everything tastes the same" might simply have a cold. It is only through *patterns* of response that personality dimensions are revealed.

Items on the MMPI-2 were selected for their ability to correctly identify people with particular psychological problems. For instance, if a series of items is consistently answered in a particular way by depressed persons, we can assume that others who answer the same way are also prone to depression. As silly as the gag items might seem, it is possible that some could actually work in a legitimate test. But before an item could be part of a test, it would have to correlate highly with some trait or dimension of personality.

The MMPI-2 measures 10 major aspects of personality (listed in ▲Table 10.4). After the MMPI-2 is scored, results are charted graphically as an **MMPI-2 profile** (◆Fig. 10.10).

▲*TABLE 10.4*	**MMPI-2 Basic Clinical Subscales**

1. **Hypochondriasis** (HI-po-kon-DRY-uh-sis). Exaggerated concern about one's physical health.
2. **Depression.** Feelings of worthlessness, hopelessness, and pessimism.
3. **Hysteria.** The presence of physical complaints for which no physical basis can be established.
4. **Psychopathic deviate.** Emotional shallowness in relationships and a disregard for social and moral standards.
5. **Masculinity/femininity.** One's degree of traditional "masculine" aggressiveness or "feminine" sensitivity.
6. **Paranoia.** Extreme suspiciousness and feelings of persecution.
7. **Psychasthenia** (sike-as-THEE-nee-ah). The presence of obsessive worries, irrational fears (phobias), and compulsive (ritualistic) actions.
8. **Schizophrenia.** Emotional withdrawal and unusual or bizarre thinking and actions.
9. **Mania.** Emotional excitability, manic moods or behavior, and excessive activity.
10. **Social introversion.** One's tendency to be socially withdrawn.

---

*Excerpt from Minnesota Multiphasic Inventory 2 (MMPI-2) is reprinted by permission of the University of Minnesota Press. Copyright © 1989 by the University of Minnesota Press.

MMPI-2 profile A graphic representation of an individual's scores on each of the primary scales of the MMPI-2.

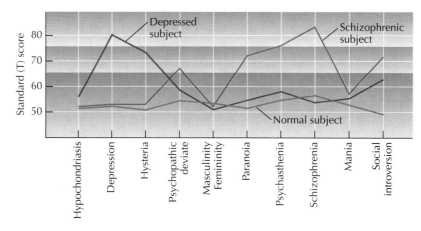

✦**FIGURE 10.10** *An MMPI-2 profile showing hypothetical scores indicating normality, depression, and psychosis. High scores begin at 66 and very high scores at 76. An unusually low score (40 and below) may also reveal personality characteristics or problems.*

By comparing a person's profile to scores produced by normal adults, a psychologist can identify various personality disorders. Additional scales identify substance abuse, eating disorders, Type A (heart-attack prone) behavior, repression, anger, cynicism, low self-esteem, family problems, inability to function in a job, and other difficulties (Hathaway & McKinley, 1989).

How accurate is the MMPI-2?   Personality questionnaires are only accurate if people tell the truth about themselves. Because of this, the MMPI-2 has additional **validity scales** that reveal whether a person's scores should be discarded. The validity scales detect attempts by test takers to "fake good" (make themselves look good) or "fake bad" (make it look like they have problems). Other scales uncover defensiveness or tendencies to exaggerate short-comings and troubles. When taking the MMPI-2, it is best to answer honestly, without try-ing to second-guess the test.

A clinical psychologist trying to decide if a person has emotional problems would be wise to take more than the MMPI-2 into account. Test scores are informative, but they can incorrectly label some people (Cronbach, 1990). ("Honesty Tests—Do They Tell the Truth?" discusses a related problem.) Fortunately, clinical judgments usually rely on information from interviews, tests, and other sources. Also, despite their limitations, it is reassuring to note that psychological assessments are at least as accurate as commonly used medical tests (Meyer et al., 2001).

Validity scales Scales that tell whether test scores should be invalidated for lying, inconsistency, or "faking good."

Honesty test A paper-and-pencil test de-signed to detect attitudes, beliefs, and be-havior patterns that predispose a person to dishonest behavior.

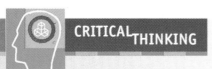

CRITICAL THINKING   Honesty Tests—Do They Tell the Truth?

Each year, millions of anxious job seekers take paper-and-pencil honesty tests given by companies that hope to avoid hiring dis-honest workers. **Honesty tests** (also known as integrity tests) as-sume that poor attitudes toward dishonest acts predispose a per-son to dishonest behavior. Examples include attitudes toward taking office supplies home or leaving work early. Most of the tests also ask people how honest they think the average person is and how honest they are in comparison. Surprisingly, many job appli-cants willingly rate their own honesty as below average (Neuman & Baydoun, 1998). (You have to admire them for being honest about it!) Honesty tests also ask about prior brushes with the law, past acts of theft or deceit, and attitudes toward alcohol and drug use.

Is honesty testing valid?   This question is still very much in dis-pute. Some psychologists believe that the best honesty tests are sufficiently valid to be used for making hiring decisions (Ones &

Viswesvaran, 2001). Others, however, remain unconvinced. Most studies have failed to demonstrate that honesty tests can accu-rately *predict* if a person will be a poor risk on the job (Saxe, 1991). Psychologists are also concerned because honesty tests are often administered by untrained people. Yet another cause for con-cern is the fact that 96 percent of test takers who fail are *falsely labeled* as dishonest (Camara & Schneider, 1994). In North America alone, that means well over a million workers a year are wrongly accused of being dishonest (Rieke & Guastello, 1995).

Some states have banned the use of honesty tests as the sole basis for deciding whether to hire a person. Yet, it's easy to under-stand why employers want to do whatever they can to reduce theft and dishonesty in the workplace. The pressures to use honesty tests are intense. No doubt, the debate about honesty testing will continue. Honest.

PROJECTIVE TESTS OF PERSONALITY— INKBLOTS AND HIDDEN PLOTS

Projective tests take a different approach to personality. Interviews, observation, rating scales, and inventories try to directly identify overt, observable traits (Vane & Guarnaccia, 1989). By contrast, projective tests seek to uncover deeply hidden or *unconscious* wishes, thoughts, and needs.

As a child, you may have delighted in finding faces and objects in cloud formations. Or perhaps you have learned something about your friends' personalities from their reactions to movies or paintings. If so, you will have some insight into the rationale for projective tests. In a **projective test,** a person is asked to describe ambiguous stimuli or make up stories about them. Describing an unambiguous stimulus (a picture of an automobile, for example) tells little about your personality. But when you are faced with an unstructured stimulus, you must organize what you see in terms of your own life experiences. Everyone sees something different in a projective test, and what is perceived can reveal the inner workings of personality.

Projective tests have no right or wrong answers, which makes them difficult to fake (Vane & Guarnaccia, 1989). Moreover, projective tests can be a rich source of information, since responses are not restricted to simple true/false or yes/no answers.

The Rorschach Inkblot Test

Is the inkblot test a projective technique?   The inkblot test, or **Rorschach Technique** (ROR-shock), is one of the oldest and most widely used projective tests. Developed by Swiss psychologist Hermann Rorschach in the 1920s, it consists of 10 standardized inkblots. These vary in color, shading, form, and complexity.

How does the test work?   First, a person is shown each blot and asked to describe what she or he sees in it (✦Fig. 10.11). Later, the psychologist may return to a blot, asking the person to identify specific sections of it, to expand previous descriptions, or to give new impressions about what it contains. Obvious differences in content—such as "blood dripping from a dagger" versus "flowers blooming in a field"—are important for identifying personal conflicts and fantasies. But surprisingly, content is less important than what parts of the inkblot are used to organize images. These factors allow psychologists to detect emotional disturbances by observing how a person perceives the world. The Rorschach is especially good at detecting psychosis, one of the most serious of all mental disorders (Ganellen, 1996).

Projective tests Psychological tests making use of ambiguous or unstructured stimuli.
Rorschach Technique A projective test comprised of 10 standardized inkblots.

✦**FIGURE 10.11** *Inkblots similar to those used on the Rorschach. What do you see?*

The Thematic Apperception Test

Another popular projective test is the **Thematic Apperception Test** (TAT) developed by personality theorist Henry Murray (1893–1988).

How does the TAT differ from the Rorschach? The TAT consists of 20 sketches depicting various scenes and life situations (◆Fig. 10.12). During testing, a person is shown each sketch and asked to make up a story about the people in it. Later, the person looks at each sketch a second or a third time and elaborates on previous stories or creates new stories.

To score the TAT, psychologists analyze the content of the stories. Interpretations focus on how people feel, how they interact, what events led up to the incidents depicted in the sketch, and how the story will end. For example, TAT stories told by bereaved college students typically include themes of death, grief, and coping with loss (Balk et al., 1998).

A psychologist might also count the number of times the central figure in a TAT story is angry, overlooked, apathetic, jealous, or threatened. Here is a story written by a student to describe Figure 10.12:

> The girl has been seeing this guy her mother doesn't like. The mother is telling her that she better not see him again. The mother says, "He's just like your father." The mother and father are divorced. The mother is smiling because she thinks she is right. But she doesn't really know what the girl wants. The girl is going to see the guy again, anyway.

As this example implies, the TAT is especially good at revealing feelings about a person's social relationships (Alvarado, 1994).

Limitations of Projective Testing

Although projective tests have been popular, their validity is considered lowest among tests of personality (Lilienfeld, 1999). Objectivity and reliability (consistency) are also low for different users of the TAT and Rorschach. Note that after a person interprets an ambiguous stimulus, the scorer must interpret the person's (sometimes) ambiguous responses. In a sense, the interpretation of a projective test may be a projective test for the scorer!

Despite their drawbacks, projective tests still have value (Weiner, 1997). This is especially true when they are used as part of a *test battery* (collection of assessment devices and interviews). In the hands of a skilled clinician, projective tests can be a good way to detect major conflicts, to get clients to talk about upsetting topics, and to set goals for therapy (O'Roark, 2001).

◆**FIGURE 10.12** *This is a picture like those used for the Thematic Apperception Test. If you wish to simulate the test, tell a story that explains what led up to the pictured situation, what is happening now, and how the action will end.*

SUDDEN MURDERERS—A RESEARCH EXAMPLE

Personality assessments provide us with clues to some of the most perplexing human events. Consider Fred Cowan, a model student in school and described by those who knew him as quiet, gentle, and a man who loved children. Despite his size (6 feet tall, 250 pounds), Fred was described by a co-worker as "someone you could easily push around."

Fred Cowan represents a puzzling phenomenon: We occasionally read in the news about sudden murderers—gentle, quiet, shy, good-natured people who explode without warning into violence (Lee et al., 1977). Two weeks after he was suspended from his job, Fred returned to work, determined to get even with his supervisor. Unable to find the man, he killed four co-workers and a policeman before taking his own life.

Isn't such behavior contrary to the idea of personality traits? It might seem that sudden murderers are newsworthy simply because they are unlikely candidates for violence. On the contrary, research conducted by Melvin Lee, Philip Zimbardo, and Minerva Bertholf suggests that sudden murderers explode into violence *because* they are shy, restrained, and in-

Thematic Apperception Test (TAT)
A projective test consisting of 20 different scenes and life situations about which respondents make up stories.

expressive, not in spite of it. These researchers studied prisoners at a California prison. Ten were inmates whose homicide was an unexpected first offense. Nine were criminals with a record of habitual violence prior to murder. Sixteen were inmates convicted of nonviolent crimes.

Did the inmates differ in personality makeup? Each of the inmates took a battery of tests, including the MMPI, a measure of shyness, and an adjective checklist. Personal interviews were also done with each inmate. As expected, the sudden murderers were passive, shy, and overcontrolled (restrained) individuals. The habitually violent inmates were "masculine" (aggressive), undercontrolled (impulsive), and viewed themselves as less shy than the average person (Lee et al., 1977).

Psychologists have learned that quiet, overcontrolled individuals are likely to be especially violent if they ever lose control. Their attacks are usually triggered by a minor irritation or frustration, but the attack reflects years of unexpressed feelings of anger and belittlement. When sudden murderers finally release the strict controls they have maintained on their behavior, a furious and frenzied attack ensues. Usually it is totally out of proportion to the offense against them, and many have amnesia for their violent actions.

In comparison, the previously violent murderers showed very different reactions. Although they killed, their violence was moderate—usually only enough to do the necessary damage. Typically, they felt they had been cheated or betrayed and that they were doing what was necessary to remedy the situation or maintain their manhood (Lee et al., 1977).

A Look Ahead

The preceding example illustrates how some of the concepts and techniques discussed in this chapter can be applied to further our understanding. The Psychology in Action section that follows should add balance to your view of personality. Don't be shy. Read on!

STUDYBREAK Y *Personality Assessment*

RELATE

How do *you* assess personality? Do you informally make use of any of the methods described in this chapter?

You are a candidate for a desirable job. Your personality is going to be assessed by a psychologist. What method (or methods) would you prefer that she or he use? Why?

LEARNING CHECK

1. The halo effect is the tendency of an interviewer to influence what is said by the interviewee. T or F?
2. Which of the following is considered the most objective measure of personality?
   a. rating scales   b. personality questionnaires   c. projective tests   d. TAT
3. Situational testing allows direct _____ of personality characteristics.
4. A psychotic person would probably score highest on which MMPI-2 scale?
   a. depression   b. hysteria   c. schizophrenia   d. mania

5. The use of ambiguous stimuli is most characteristic of
   a. interviews   b. projective tests   c. personality inventories   d. direct observation
6. The content of one's responses to the MMPI-2 is considered an indication of unconscious wishes, thoughts, and needs. T or F?
7. Doing a behavioral assessment requires direct observation of the person's actions or a direct report of the person's thoughts. T or F?
8. A surprising finding is that sudden murderers are usually undercontrolled, very masculine, and more impulsive than average. T or F?
9. A test is considered valid if it consistently yields the same score when the same person takes it on different occasions. T or F?

Critical Thinking

10. Can you think of one more reason why personality traits may not be accurately revealed by interviews?
11. Projective testing would be of greatest interest to which type of personality theorist?

ANSWERS

1. F 2. b 3. observation 4. c 5. b 6. F 7. T 8. F 9. F 10. Because of trait-situation interactions, a person may not behave in a normal fashion while being evaluated in an interview. 11. Psychodynamic: Because projective testing is designed to uncover unconscious thoughts, feelings, and conflicts.

Psychology in Action

Barriers and Bridges—Understanding Shyness

] **SURVEYQUESTION** *What causes shyness? What can be done about it?*

As a personality trait, **shyness** refers to a tendency to avoid others, as well as feelings of social inhibition (uneasiness and strain when socializing) (Buss, 1980). Shy persons fail to make eye contact, retreat when spoken to, speak too quietly, and display little interest or animation in conversations. Do you:

- Find it hard to talk to strangers?
- Lack confidence with people?
- Feel uncomfortable in social situations?
- Feel nervous with people who are not close friends?

If so, you may be part of the *50 percent* of college students who consider themselves shy (Carducci & Stein, 1988). Mild shyness may be no more than a nuisance. However, extreme shyness is often associated with depression, loneliness, fearfulness, social anxiety, inhibition, and low self-esteem (Henderson, 1997; Jackson et al., 2002).

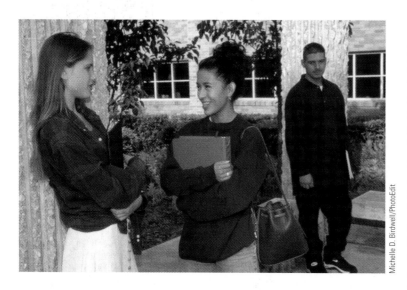

Michelle D. Birdwell/PhotoEdit

Elements of Shyness

What causes shyness?   To begin with, shy persons often lack *social skills* (proficiency at interacting with others). Many simply have not learned how to meet people or how to start a conversation and keep it going. **Social anxiety** (a feeling of apprehension in the presence of others) is also a factor in shyness. Almost everyone feels nervous in some social situations (such as meeting an attractive stranger). Typically, this is a reaction to evaluation fears (fears of being inadequate, embarrassed, ridiculed, or rejected). Although fears of rejection are common, they are much more frequent or intense for shy persons (Jackson, Towson, & Narduzzi, 1997). A third problem for shy persons is a self-defeating bias (distortion) in their thinking. Specifically, shy persons almost always blame themselves when a social encounter doesn't go well. They are unnecessarily self-critical in social situations (Lundh et al., 2002).

Situational Causes of Shyness

Shyness is most often triggered by *novel* or *unfamiliar* social situations. A person who does fine with family or close friends may become shy and awkward when meeting a stranger. Shyness is also magnified by formality, by meeting someone of higher status, by being noticeably different from others, or by being the focus of attention (as in giving a speech) (Buss, 1980).

Don't most people become cautious and inhibited in such circumstances?   Yes. That's why we need to see how the personalities of shy and non-shy persons differ.

Dynamics of the Shy Personality

There is a tendency to think that shy persons are wrapped up in their own feelings and thoughts. But surprisingly, researchers Jonathan Cheek and Arnold Buss (1979) found no connection between shyness and **private self-consciousness** (attention to inner feelings, thoughts, and fantasies). Instead, they discovered that shyness is linked to **public self-consciousness** (acute awareness of oneself as a social object).

Shyness A tendency to avoid others plus uneasiness and strain when socializing.

Social anxiety A feeling of apprehension in the presence of others.

Private self-consciousness Preoccupation with inner feelings, thoughts, and fantasies.

Public self-consciousness Intense awareness of oneself as a social object.

Persons who rate high in public self-consciousness are intensely concerned about what others think of them (Buss, 1980). They worry about saying the wrong thing or appearing foolish. In public, they may feel "naked" or as if others can "see through them." Such feelings trigger anxiety or outright fear during social encounters, leading to awkwardness and inhibition (Buss, 1986). The shy person's anxiety, in turn, often causes her or him to misperceive others in social situations (Schroeder, 1995).

As mentioned, almost everyone feels anxious in at least some social situations. But there is a key difference in the way shy and non-shy persons *label* this anxiety. Shy persons tend to consider their social anxiety a *lasting personality trait.* Shyness, in other words, becomes part of their self-concept. In contrast, non-shy persons believe that *external situations* cause their occasional feelings of shyness. When non-shy persons feel anxiety or "stage fright," they assume that almost anyone would feel as they do under the same circumstances (Zimbardo et al., 1978).

Labeling is important because it affects *self-esteem.* In general, non-shy persons tend to have higher self-esteem than shy persons. This is because non-shy persons give themselves credit for their social successes, and they recognize that failures are often due to circumstances. In contrast, shy people blame themselves for social failures, never give themselves credit for successes, and expect to be rejected (Buss, 1980; Jackson et al., 2002).

Shy Beliefs

What can be done to reduce shyness?   While directing a shyness clinic, psychologist Michel Girodo (1978) observed that shyness is often maintained by unrealistic or self-defeating beliefs. Here's a sample of such beliefs.

1. *If you wait around long enough at a social gathering, something will happen.*
   Comment: This is really a cover-up for fear of starting a conversation. For two people to meet, at least one has to make an effort, and it might as well be you.
2. *Other people who are popular are just lucky when it comes to being invited to social events or asked out.*
   Comment: Except for times when a person is formally introduced to someone new, this is false. People who are more active socially typically make an effort to meet and spend time with others. They join clubs, invite others to do things, strike up conversations, and generally leave little to luck.
3. *The odds of meeting someone interested in socializing are always the same, no matter where I am.*
   Comment: This is another excuse for inaction. It pays to seek out situations that have a higher probability of leading to social contact, such as clubs, teams, and school events.
4. *If someone doesn't seem to like you right away, they really don't like you and never will.*
   Comment: This belief leads to much needless shyness. Even when a person doesn't show immediate interest, it doesn't mean the person dislikes you. Liking takes time and opportunity to develop.

Unproductive beliefs like the preceding can be replaced with statements such as the following.

1. I've got to be active in social situations.
2. I can't wait until I'm completely relaxed or comfortable before taking a social risk.
3. I don't need to pretend to be someone I'm not; it just makes me more anxious.
4. I may think other people are harshly evaluating me, but actually I'm being too hard on myself.
5. I can set reasonable goals for expanding my social experience and skills.
6. Even people who are very socially skillful are never successful 100 percent of the time. I shouldn't get so upset when an encounter goes badly. (Adapted from Girodo, 1978.)

Social Skills

Learning social skills takes practice. There is nothing "innate" about knowing how to meet people or start a conversation. Social skills can be directly practiced in a variety of ways. It can be helpful, for instance, to get a tape recorder and listen to several of your conversations. You may be surprised by the way you pause, interrupt, miss cues, or seem disinterested. Similarly, it can be useful to look at yourself in a mirror and exaggerate facial expressions of surprise, interest, dislike, pleasure, and so forth. By such methods, most people can learn to put more animation and skill into their self-presentation. (For a discussion of related skills, see the section on self-assertion in Chapter 14.)

Conversation

One of the simplest ways to make better conversation is by learning to ask questions. A good series of questions shifts attention to the other person and shows you are interested. Nothing fancy is needed. You can do fine with questions such as, "Where do you (work, study, live)? Do you like (dancing, travel, music)? How long have you (been at this school, worked here, lived here)?" After you've broken the ice, the best questions are often those that are *open ended* (they can't be answered yes or no):

"What parts of the country have you seen?" (as opposed to: "Have you ever been to Florida?")

"What's it like living on the west side?" (as opposed to: "Do you like living on the west side?")

"What kinds of food do you like?" (as opposed to: "Do you like Chinese cooking?")

It's easy to see why open-ended questions are helpful. In replying to open-ended questions, people often give "free information" about themselves. This extra information can be used to ask other questions or to lead into other topics of conversation.

This brief sampling of ideas is no substitute for actual practice. Overcoming shyness requires a real effort to learn new skills and test old beliefs and attitudes. It may even require the help of a counselor or therapist. At the very least, a shy person must be willing to take social risks. Breaking down the barriers of shyness will always include some awkward or unsuccessful encounters. Nevertheless, the rewards are powerful: human companionship and personal freedom.

STUDYBREAK *Understanding Shyness*

RELATE

If you are shy, see if you can summarize how social skills, social anxiety, evaluation fears, self-defeating thoughts, and public self-consciousness contribute to your social inhibition. If you're not shy, imagine how you would explain these concepts to a shy friend.

LEARNING CHECK

1. Surveys show that 14 percent of American college students consider themselves shy. T or F?
2. Social anxiety and evaluation fears are seen almost exclusively in shy individuals; the non-shy rarely have such experiences. T or F?

3. Unfamiliar people and situations most often trigger shyness. T or F?
4. Public self-consciousness plus a tendency to label oneself as shy are major characteristics of the shy personality. T or F?
5. Changing personal beliefs and practicing social skills can be helpful in overcoming shyness. T or F?

Critical Thinking

6. Shyness is a trait of Vonda's personality. Like most shy people, Vonda is most likely to feel shy in unfamiliar social settings. Vonda's shy behavior demonstrates that the expression of traits is governed by what concept?

ANSWERS

1. F 2. F 3. T 4. T 5. T 6. trait-situation interactions

CHAPTER IN REVIEW

Major Points

- Each of us displays consistent behavior patterns that define our own personalities and allow us to predict how other people will act.
- Personality can be understood by identifying traits, by probing mental conflicts and dynamics, by noting the effects of prior learning and situations, and by knowing how people perceive themselves.
- Psychologists use interviews, direct observation, questionnaires, and projective tests to measure and assess personality.
- Shyness is related to public self-consciousness and other psychological factors that can be altered, which makes it possible for some people to overcome shyness.

Summary

How do psychologists use the term personality?

- Personality is made up of one's unique and enduring behavior patterns.
- Character is personality evaluated, or the possession of desirable qualities.
- Temperament refers to the hereditary and physiological aspects of one's emotional nature.

What core concepts make up the psychology of personality?

- Personality traits are lasting personal qualities that are inferred from behavior.
- Personality types group people into categories on the basis of shared traits.
- Behavior is influenced by self-concept, which is a perception of one's own personality traits.
- A positive self-evaluation leads to high self-esteem. Low self-esteem is associated with stress, unhappiness, and depression.
- Personality theories combine interrelated assumptions, ideas, and principles to explain personality.

Are some personality traits more basic or important than others?

- Trait theories identify qualities that are most lasting or characteristic of a person.
- Allport made useful distinctions between common traits and individual traits and among cardinal, central, and secondary traits.
- Cattell's theory attributes visible surface traits to the existence of 16 underlying source traits.
- Source traits are measured by the *Sixteen Personality Factor Questionnaire* (16 PF).

- The five-factor model identifies five universal dimensions of personality: extroversion, agreeableness, conscientiousness, neuroticism, and openness to experience.
- Traits interact with situations to explain our behavior.
- Behavioral genetics and studies of identical twins suggest that heredity contributes significantly to adult personality traits.

How do psychodynamic theories explain personality?

- Like other psychodynamic approaches, Sigmund Freud's psychoanalytic theory emphasizes unconscious forces and conflicts within the personality.
- In Freud's theory, personality is made up of the id, ego, and superego.
- Libido, derived from the life instincts, is the primary energy running the personality. Conflicts within the personality may cause neurotic anxiety or moral anxiety and motivate us to use ego-defense mechanisms.
- The personality operates on three levels: the conscious, preconscious, and unconscious.
- The Freudian view of personality development is based on a series of psychosexual stages: the oral, anal, phallic, and genital stages. Fixation at any stage can leave a lasting imprint on personality.

What do behaviorists emphasize in their approach to personality?

- Behavioral theories of personality emphasize learning, conditioning, and immediate effects of the environment (situational determinants).
- Learning theorists Dollard and Miller consider habits the basic core of personality. Habits express the combined effects of drive, cue, response, and reward.
- Social learning theory adds cognitive elements to the behavioral view of personality. Examples include the psychological situation, expectancies, and reinforcement value.
- The behavioristic view of personality development holds that social reinforcement in four situations is critical. The situations are feeding, toilet or cleanliness training, sex training, and anger or aggression training.
- Identification and imitation are of particular importance in learning to be "male" or "female."
- Psychological androgyny is related to greater behavioral adaptability and flexibility.

How do humanistic theories differ from other perspectives?

- Humanistic theory emphasizes subjective experience and needs for self-actualization.

- Abraham Maslow found that self-actualizers share characteristics that range from efficient perceptions of reality to frequent peak experiences.
- Carl Rogers viewed the self as an entity that emerges from personal experience. We tend to become aware of experiences that match our self-image, while excluding those that are incongruent with it.
- The incongruent person has a highly unrealistic self-image and/or a mismatch between the self-image and the ideal self. The congruent or fully functioning person is flexible and open to experiences and feelings.
- As parents apply conditions of worth to children's behavior, thoughts, and feelings, children begin to do the same. Internalized conditions of worth then contribute to incongruence that disrupts the organismic valuing process.

How do psychologists measure personality?

- Techniques typically used for personality assessment are interviews, observation, questionnaires, and projective tests.
- Structured and unstructured interviews provide much information, but they are subject to interviewer bias and misperceptions. The halo effect may also lower the accuracy of an interview.
- Direct observation, sometimes involving situational tests, behavioral assessment, or the use of rating scales, allows evaluation of a person's actual behavior.
- Personality questionnaires, such as the *Minnesota Multiphasic Personality Inventory-2* (MMPI-2), are objective and reliable, but their validity is open to question.
- Projective tests ask a person to project thoughts or feelings to an ambiguous stimulus or unstructured situation.
- The *Rorschach Technique,* or inkblot test, is a well-known projective technique. A second is the *Thematic Apperception Test* (TAT).
- Projective tests are low in validity and objectivity. Nevertheless, they are considered useful by many clinicians, particularly as part of a test battery.

What causes shyness? What can be done about it?

- Shyness is a mixture of social inhibition and social anxiety. It is marked by heightened public self-consciousness and a tendency to regard one's shyness as a lasting trait.
- Shyness can be lessened by changing self-defeating beliefs and by improving social skills.

 Interactive Learning

Internet addresses frequently change. To find the sites listed here, visit www.psychology.wadsworth.com/coon_journey2e for an updated list of Internet addresses and direct links to relevant sites.

PSYCHOLOGY: A JOURNEY COMPANION WEB SITE Online quizzes, flash cards, and other helpful study aids for this text. *www.psychology.wadsworth.com/coon_journey2e*

ABOUT HUMANISTIC PSYCHOLOGY Discusses the history and future of humanistic psychology.

FAQ ABOUT PSYCHOLOGICAL TESTS Answers to commonly asked questions about tests and testing.

FREUD NET Offers links to information on Freud and psychoanalysis.

PERSONALITY AND IQ TESTS Multiple links to personality tests and IQ tests that are scored on-line.

INFOTRAC COLLEGE EDITION For recent articles related to heritability of personality traits, use Key Words search for TWIN STUDIES.

PSYCHNOW! 7a. Theories of Personality, 7e. Assessment.

Test Your Knowledge: Personality

The questions that follow are only a sample of what you need to know. If you miss any of the items, you should review the entire chapter and get more practice with *WebTutor* or the *Practice Quizzes* that came with this book. Another way to prepare for tests is to use the printed *Study Guide* that is available for this text.

1. When someone's personality has been evaluated, we are making a judgment about his or her
   A. temperament   B. character   C. extroversion
   D. self-esteem

2. A personality type is usually defined by the presence of
   A. all five personality dimensions   B. a stable self concept
   C. several specific traits   D. a source trait

3. Personality theorist Raymond Cattell used factor analysis to identify 16
   A. common traits   B. source traits   C. cardinal traits
   D. trait-situation interactions

4. Which of the following is NOT one of the Big Five personality dimensions?
   A. extroversion   B. agreeableness   C. neuroticism
   D. androgyny

5. The research methods of _____ have been used to study the extent to which we inherit personality characteristics.
   A. behavioral genetics   B. social learning theory
   C. factor analysis   D. trait profiling

6. According to Freud, which division of personality is governed by the reality principle?
   A. ego   B. id   C. ego ideal   D. superego

7. Freud stated that the mind functions on three levels: the conscious, unconscious, and the
   A. psyche   B. preconscious   C. superego   D. subconscious

8. Freudian theory states that a person who is passive, dependent, and needs lots of attention has a fixation in the
   A. oral stage   B. superego   C. Oedipal stage   D. genital stage

9. The situational determinants of our actions are of special interest and importance to
   A. psychodynamic theorists   B. humanistic theorists
   C. learning theorists   D. behavioral geneticists

10. Which of the following is NOT a concept of social learning theory?
   A. incongruence   B. expectancy   C. self-efficacy
   D. reinforcement value

11. Maslow thought of peak experiences as temporary moments of
   A. congruence   B. positive self-regard   C. self-actualization
   D. self-reinforcement

12. Carl Rogers believed that personal growth is encouraged when conditions of worth are replaced by
   A. self-efficacy   B. instrumental worth   C. latency
   D. organismic valuing

13. The halo effect can be a serious problem in accurate personality assessment that is based on
   A. projective testing   B. behavioral recording
   C. interviewing   D. the TAT

14. Situational testing is primarily an example of using _____ to assess personality.
   A. direct observation   B. structured interviewing
   C. cardinal traits   D. projective techniques

15. Which of the following items DOES NOT belong with the others?
   A. Rorschach Technique   B. TAT   C. MMPI-2
   D. projective testing

16. By definition, a test that measures what it claims to measure is
   A. valid   B. situational   C. objective   D. reliable

17. Which of the following is an objective personality questionnaire?
   A. the TAT   B. the *In-basket Test*   C. the NDE-16
   D. the MMPI-2

18. Which MMPI-2 scale is designed to detect phobias and compulsive actions?
   A. Hysteria   B. Paranoia   C. Psychasthenia   D. Mania

19. Contrary to what many people think, shyness is NOT related to
   A. private self-consciousness   B. social anxiety
   C. self-esteem   D. blaming oneself for social failures

20. Shy persons tend to consider their social anxiety to be a
   A. situational reaction   B. personality trait
   C. public efficacy   D. habit

ANSWERS   1. b, 2. c, 3. b, 4. d, 5. a, 6. a, 7. b, 8. a, 9. c, 10. a, 11. c, 12. d, 13. c, 14. a, 15. c, 16. a, 17. d, 18. c, 19. a, 20. b

Health, Stress, and Coping

Taylor's (Not So Very) Fine Adventure

Somehow, Taylor had managed to survive the rush of make-or-break term papers, projects, and classroom speeches. Then it was on to finals, where his tests seemed perfectly timed to inflict as much suffering as possible. His two hardest exams fell on the same day! Great. What luck!

On the last day of finals, Taylor got caught in a traffic jam on his way to school. Two drivers cut him off, and another gave him a one-finger salute. When Taylor finally got to campus, the parking lot was swarming with frantic students. Most of them, like him, were within minutes of missing a final exam. At last, Taylor spied an empty space. As he started toward it, a Volkswagen darted around the corner and into "his" place. The driver of the car behind him began to honk impatiently. For a moment, Taylor was seized by a colossal desire to run over anything in sight.

Finally, after a week and a half of stress, pressure, and frustration, Taylor's finals were over. Sleep deprivation, gallons of coffee, junk food, and equal portions of cramming and complaining had carried him through. He was off for the summer. At last, he could kick back, relax, and have some fun. Or could he? Just 4 days after the end of school, Taylor got a bad cold, followed by bronchitis that lasted for nearly a month.

Taylor's experience illustrates what happens when stress, emotion, personal habits, and health collide. While the timing of his cold might have been a coincidence, odds are it wasn't. Periods of stress are frequently followed by illness (Biondi & Zannino, 1997).

In the first part of this chapter we will explore a variety of behavioral health risks. Then we will look more closely at what stress is and how it affects us. After that, we will stress ways of coping with stress, so you can do a better job of staying healthy than Taylor did.

Image Source/PictureQuest

Survey Questions

- ○ What is health psychology? How does behavior affect health?
- ○ What is stress? What factors determine its severity?
- ○ What causes frustration, and what are typical reactions to it?
- ○ Are there different types of conflict? How do people react to conflict?
- ○ What are defense mechanisms?
- ○ What do we know about coping with feelings of helplessness and depression?
- ○ How is stress related to health and disease?
- ○ What are the best strategies for managing stress?
- ○ How can sexually transmitted diseases be prevented?

HEALTH PSYCHOLOGY—HERE'S TO YOUR GOOD HEALTH

] SURVEYQUESTIONS *What is health psychology? How does behavior affect health?*

Most people agree that health is important—especially their own. Yet, almost one half of all deaths in North America are primarily due to unhealthy behavior. **Health psychology** aims to do something about such deaths by using behavioral principles to promote health and prevent illness (Terborg, 1998). Psychologists working in the allied field of **behavioral medicine** apply psychology to manage medical problems, such as diabetes or asthma. Their interests include pain control, helping people cope with chronic illness, stress-related diseases, self-screening for diseases (such as breast cancer), and similar topics.

Behavioral Risk Factors

One hundred years ago, people primarily died from infectious diseases and accidents. Today, people generally die from **lifestyle diseases,** or health-damaging personal habits. Examples include heart disease, stroke, and lung cancer (◆Fig. 11.1). Clearly, some lifestyles promote health, whereas others lead to illness and death. As one observer put it, "We have met the enemy, and he is us."

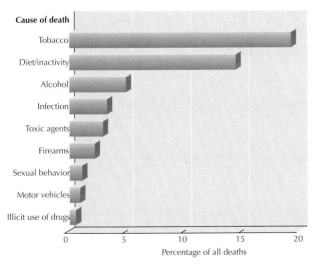

◆FIGURE 11.1 *The nine leading causes of death in the United States are shown in this graph. As you can see, eight of the top nine causes are directly related to behavioral risk factors (infection is the exception). At least 45 percent of all deaths can be traced to unhealthful behavior. The percentage of day-to-day health problems related to unhealthful behavior is even higher. (Data from McGinnis & Foege, 1993.)*

Health psychology Study of the ways in which behavioral principles can be used to prevent illness and promote health.

Behavioral medicine The study of behavioral factors in medicine, physical illness, and medical treatment.

Lifestyle disease A disease related to health-damaging personal habits.

What kinds of behavior are you referring to as unhealthy?   Some causes of illness are beyond our control, but many behavioral risks can be reduced. **Behavioral risk factors** are actions that increase the chances of disease, injury, or early death. For example, being overweight *doubles* the chance of dying from cancer or heart disease. Roughly 60 percent of all American adults are overweight. As a result, obesity may soon overtake smoking as the main cause of preventable deaths. Being fat is not just a matter of fashion—in the long run it could kill you. A person who is overweight at age 20 can expect to lose 5 to 20 years of life expectancy (Fontaine et al., 2003).

Each of the following factors is a major behavioral risk (Baum & Posluszny, 1999; Groth-Marnat & Schumaker, 1995):

- High levels of stress
- Untreated high blood pressure
- Cigarette smoking
- Abuse of alcohol or other drugs
- Overeating
- Inadequate exercise
- Unsafe sexual behavior
- Exposure to toxic substances
- Violence
- Excess sun exposure
- Driving at high speeds
- Disregarding personal safety (accidents)

Seventy percent of all medical costs are related to just six of the listed factors—smoking, alcohol and drug abuse, poor diet, insufficient exercise, and risky sexual practices (Orleans, Gruman, & Hollendonner, 1999). (Unsafe sex is discussed later, in this chapter's Psychology in Action section.)

▲Table 11.1 shows how many high school students in the United States engage in risky behaviors of the kind listed here. The health habits you have by the time you are 18 or 19 greatly affect your health, happiness, and life expectancy years later (Vaillant & Mukamal, 2001).

Specific risk factors are not the only concern. Some people have a general **disease-prone personality** that leaves them depressed, anxious, hostile, and . . . frequently ill. In contrast, people who are intellectually resourceful, compassionate, optimistic, and non-hostile tend to enjoy good health (Taylor et al., 2000). Depression, in particular, is likely to damage health. People who are depressed eat poorly, sleep poorly, rarely exercise, fail to use seat belts in cars, smoke more, and so on (Allgower, Wardle, Steptoe, 2001).

Lifestyle

In your mind's eye, fast-forward an imaginary film of your life all the way to old age. Do it twice—once with a lifestyle including a large number of behavioral risk factors and again without them. It should be obvious that many small risks can add up, dramatically raising

Behavioral risk factors Behaviors that increase the chances of disease, injury, or premature death.

Disease-prone personality A personality type associated with poor health; marked by persistent negative emotions, including anxiety, depression, and hostility.

▲*TABLE 11.1*	Percentage of U.S. High School Students Who Engaged in Health-Endangering Behaviors
RISKY BEHAVIOR	**PERCENTAGE**
Rode with drinking driver (previous month)	35
Were in a physical fight (previous year)	42
Carried a weapon (previous month)	22
Had five or more drinks on one occasion (previous month)	30
Have used marijuana	33
Have engaged in sexual intercourse	53
Did not use condom during last sexual intercourse	47
Smoked cigarettes (previous month)	31
Ate high-fat food (previous day)	34
No vigorous exercise (previous week)	34

(Source: Kolbe, Collins, & Cortese, 1997.)

In the long run, behavioral risk factors and lifestyles do make a difference in health and life expectancy.

the chance of illness. If stress is a frequent part of your life, visualize your body seething with emotion, day after day. If you smoke, picture a lifetime's worth of cigarette smoke blown through your lungs in a week. If you drink, take a lifetime of alcohol's assaults on the brain, stomach, and liver and squeeze them into a month. Your body would be poisoned, ravaged, and soon dead. If you eat a high-fat, high-cholesterol diet, fast-forward a lifetime of heart-killing plaque clogging your arteries.

This discussion is not meant to be a sermon. It is merely a reminder that risk factors do make a difference. To make matters worse, unhealthy lifestyles almost always create multiple risks. That is, people who smoke are also likely to drink excessively. Those who overeat usually do not get enough exercise, and so on (Emmons et al., 1998).

Health-Promoting Behaviors

To prevent disease, health psychologists first try to remove behavioral risk factors. All the medicine in the world may not be enough to restore health without changes in behavior. We all know someone who has had a heart attack or lung disease who couldn't change the habits that led to their illness.

Beyond this, psychologists are also interested in getting people to increase behaviors that promote health. Health-promoting behaviors include such obvious practices as getting regular exercise, controlling smoking and alcohol use, maintaining a balanced diet, getting good medical care, and managing stress (Glik, Kronenfeld, & Jackson, 1996). Even something as simple as using seat belts in a car greatly ups life expectancy.

Healthy behaviors *should* extend a person's life. But do they? A major study done in Alameda County in California provides an answer (Belloc, 1973; Belloc & Breslow, 1972; Breslow & Enstrom, 1980). Nearly 7,000 people filled out a detailed questionnaire about their health practices. In ensuing years, researchers kept a close watch on the medical and death records of these people. Before we discuss the results, you might find it interesting to check the items listed here that apply to you.

1. I get 7 to 8 hours of sleep a night.
2. I am currently at or near the ideal weight for my height.
3. I have never smoked cigarettes.
4. I use alcohol moderately or not at all.
5. I get regular physical exercise.

Men who engaged in all five practices had a death rate almost four times lower than men who engaged in zero to three practices. The death rate was two times lower for women

	SOURCE	DESIRABLE BEHAVIORS
	Nutrition	Eating a balanced, low-fat diet; appropriate caloric intake; maintenance of healthy body weight
	Exercise	At least 30 minutes of aerobic exercise, 5 days per week
	Blood pressure	Lower blood pressure with diet and exercise or medicine if necessary
	Alcohol and drugs	No more than two drinks per day; abstain from using drugs
	Tobacco	Do not smoke; do not use smokeless tobacco
	Sleep and relaxation	Avoid sleep deprivation; provide for periods of relaxation every day
	Sex	Practice safer sex; avoid unplanned pregnancy
	Injury	Curb dangerous driving habits, use seat belts; minimize sun exposure; forgo dangerous activities
	Stress	Learn stress management; lower hostility

▲*TABLE 11.2* **Major Health-Promoting Behaviors**

who engaged in all five practices. (Please note that these are not the only elements of a healthy lifestyle. They are just the ones investigated in this study.)

Do healthy behaviors seem burdensome? They don't have to be. For instance, to benefit from physical activity, you don't need to exercise like an Olympic athlete. All you need is 15 to 20 minutes of exercise (the equivalent of a brisk walk) 3 to 4 times a week. Almost everyone can fit such "lifestyle physical activity" into his or her schedule (Pescatello, 2001).

In some cases, diseases can be treated or prevented by making relatively minor but very specific changes in behavior. For example, hypertension (high blood pressure) can be deadly. Yet, for some people simple lifestyle changes will fend off this "silent killer." Here's the recipe for lower blood pressure: Lose weight, consume less sodium (salt), use alcohol sparingly, and get more exercise (Georgiades et al., 2000).

To summarize, a small number of behavioral patterns accounts for many common health problems. ▲Table 11.2 lists several major ways to promote good health.

Early Prevention

Smoking is the largest preventable cause of death and the single most lethal behavioral risk factor (McGinnis & Foege, 1993). As such, it shows the prospect for preventing illness.

What have health psychologists done to lessen the risks? Attempts to "immunize" youths against pressures to start smoking are a good example. The smoker who says, "Quitting is easy, I've done it dozens of times," states a basic truth—only 1 smoker in 10 has long-term success at quitting. Thus, the best way to deal with smoking is to prevent it before it becomes a lifelong habit. For example, school-based prevention programs have used quizzes about smoking, anti-smoking art contests, poster and T-shirt giveaways, anti-smoking pamphlets for parents, and questions for students to ask their parents (Biglan et al., 1996). Such efforts are designed to persuade kids that smoking is dangerous and "uncool."

Some of the best anti-smoking programs include **refusal skills training.** In this case, youths learn to resist pressures to begin smoking (or using other drugs). For example, junior high students can role-play ways to resist smoking pressures from peers, adults, and

Refusal skills training Program that teaches youths how to resist pressures to begin smoking. (Can also be applied to other drugs and health risks.)

cigarette ads. Similar methods can be applied to other health risks, such as sexually transmitted diseases and teen pregnancy (Wandersman & Florin, 2003).

The latest health programs also teach students general life skills. The idea is to give kids skills that will help them cope with day-to-day stresses. That way, they will be less tempted to escape problems through drug use or other destructive behaviors. **Life skills training** includes practice in stress reduction, self-protection, decision making, goal setting, self-control, and social skills (Tobler et al., 2000).

HEALTH AND WELLNESS— JOB NUMBER ONE

In addition to the prevention efforts described earlier, health psychologists have had some success with **community health campaigns.** These are community-wide education projects designed to lessen major risk factors. Health campaigns inform people of risks such as stress, alcohol abuse, high blood pressure, high cholesterol, smoking, STDs, or excessive sun exposure. This is followed by efforts to motivate people to change their behavior. Campaigns sometimes provide *role models* (positive examples) who show people how to improve their own health. They also direct people to services for health screening, advice, and treatment (Cheadle et al., 1992–93). Health campaigns may reach people through the mass media, public schools, health fairs, their work, or self-help programs (Calvert & Cocking, 1992; Schooler et al., 1993).

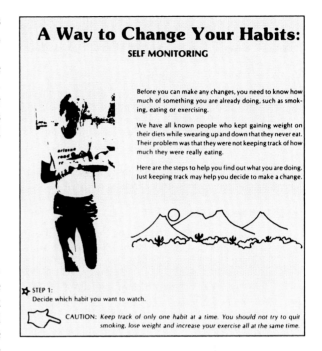

A Way to Change Your Habits:
SELF MONITORING

Before you can make any changes, you need to know how much of something you are already doing, such as smoking, eating or exercising.

We have all known people who kept gaining weight on their diets while swearing up and down that they never eat. Their problem was that they were not keeping track of how much they were really eating.

Here are the steps to help you find out what you are doing. Just keeping track may help you decide to make a change.

STEP 1:
Decide which habit you want to watch.

CAUTION: *Keep track of only one habit at a time. You should not try to quit smoking, lose weight and increase your exercise all at the same time.*

The page shown here is reproduced from a booklet prepared as part of a public health campaign conducted in southern Arizona. Such campaigns promote health by calling attention to psychological risk factors and by telling what to do about them. (From Marques et al., 1982.)

A Model Program

A good example of a community health campaign in action is the Stanford Heart Disease Prevention Program (Meyer et al., 1980). In the Stanford project, a media campaign about risk factors in heart disease—smoking, diet, and exercise—was combined with special group "workshops" for high-risk individuals. After the program had run for 2 years, smokers decreased by 17 percent in two test communities. Compare this figure with the 12 percent *increase* in similar, untreated communities.

Such progress may seem modest, but it is clearly worthwhile. Similar projects have lowered the risk of heart disease in target communities by at least 15 percent (Farquhar et al., 1984; 1997). All you have to do is picture someone you love staying healthy or living longer to appreciate the value of such efforts.

Wellness

Health is not just an absence of disease. People who are truly healthy enjoy a positive state of **wellness** or well-being. Maintaining wellness is a life-long pursuit and, hopefully, a labor of love. People who attain optimal wellness are both physically and psychologically healthy. They are happy, optimistic, self-confident individuals who can bounce back emotionally from adversity (Lightsey, 1996).

People who enjoy a sense of well-being also have supportive relationships with others, they do meaningful work, and they live in a clean environment. Many of these aspects of wellness are addressed in other chapters of this book. In this chapter we will give special attention to the effect that stress has on health and sickness. As stated earlier, stress management is a major activity of health psychologists. Understanding stress and learning to control it can improve not only your health, but the quality of your life as well (Suinn, 2001). For these reasons, a discussion of stress and stress management follows.

Life skills training A program that teaches stress reduction, self-protection, decision making, self-control, and social skills.

Community health campaign A community-wide education program that provides information about how to lessen risk factors and promote health.

Wellness A positive state of good health; more than the absence of disease.

STUDYBREAK ◆ Y *Health Psychology*

RELATE

If you were to work as a health psychologist, would you be more interested in preventing disease or managing it?

Make a list of the major behavioral risk factors that apply to you. Are you laying the foundation for a lifestyle disease?

Which of the health-promoting behaviors listed in Table 11.2 would you like to increase?

If you were designing a community health campaign, who would you use as role models of healthful behavior?

LEARNING CHECK

1. Adjustment to chronic illness and the control of pain are topics that would more likely be of interest to a specialist in _____ _____ rather than a health psychologist.
2. With respect to health, which of the following is *not* a major behavioral risk factor?
   a. over-exercise   b. cigarette smoking   c. stress   d. high blood pressure

3. According to a major health study, eating breakfast almost every day and rarely eating between meals are the two most important health-promoting behaviors. T or F?
4. Health psychologists tend to prefer _____ rather than modifying habits (like smoking) that become difficult to break once they are established.
5. The disease-prone personality is marked by _____, anxiety, and hostility.

Critical Thinking

6. The general public is increasingly well informed about health risks and healthful behavior. Can you apply the concept of reinforcement to explain why so many people fail to act on this information?

ANSWERS

1. behavioral medicine 2. a 3. F 4. prevention 5. depression 6. Many health payoffs are delayed by months or years, greatly lessening the immediate rewards for healthful behavior.

STRESS—THRILL OR THREAT?

] SURVEYQUESTIONS *What is stress? What factors determine its severity?*

Stress can be dangerous if it is prolonged or severe. Yet, stress isn't always bad. As stress researcher Hans Selye (SEL-yay) (1976) observed, "To be totally without stress is to be dead." That's because **stress** is the mental and physical condition that occurs when we adjust or adapt to the environment. Unpleasant events such as work pressures, marital problems, or financial woes naturally produce stress. But so do travel, sports, a new job, mountain climbing, dating, and other positive activities. Even if you aren't a thrill seeker, a healthy lifestyle may include a fair amount of *eustress* (good stress). Activities that provoke "good stress" are usually challenging, rewarding, and energizing.

A **stress reaction** begins with the same autonomic nervous system arousal that occurs during emotion. Imagine you are standing at the top of a wind-whipped ski jump for the first time. Internally, there would be a rapid surge in your heart rate, blood pressure, respiration, muscle tension, and other ANS responses. *Short-term* stresses of this kind can be uncomfortable, but they rarely do any damage. (Your landing might be another matter, however.) Later we will describe the *long-term* physical impact of prolonged stress—which can do harm (Sternberg, 2000). For now, here's a list of some of the typical signs or symptoms of on-going stress (Doctor & Doctor, 1994).

Emotional signs: Anxiety, apathy, irritability, mental fatigue
Behavioral signs: Avoidance of responsibilities and relationships, extreme or self-destructive behavior, self-neglect, poor judgment
Physical signs: Excessive worry about illness, frequent illness, exhaustion, overuse of medicines, physical aliments and complaints

Other than when it is long lasting, why is stress sometimes damaging and sometimes not? Stress reactions are complex. Let's examine some of the factors that determine whether or not stress is harmful.

Stress The mental and physical condition that occurs when a person must adjust or adapt to the environment.

Stress reaction The physical response to stress, consisting mainly of bodily changes related to autonomic nervous system arousal.

When Is Stress a Strain?

It goes almost without saying that some events are more likely to cause stress than others. A **stressor** is a condition or event that challenges or threatens a person. Police officers, for instance, suffer from a high rate of stress-related diseases. The threat of injury or death, plus occasional confrontations with angry, drunk, or hostile citizens, takes a toll. A major factor is the *unpredictable* nature of police work. An officer who stops a car to issue a traffic ticket never knows if a cooperative citizen or an armed gang member is waiting inside.

A revealing study shows how unpredictability adds to stress. In a series of one-minute trials, college students breathed air through a mask. On some trials, the air contained 20 percent more carbon dioxide (CO_2) than normal. If you were to inhale this air, you would feel anxious, stressed, and a little like you were suffocating. Students tested this way hated the "surprise" doses of CO_2. They found it much less stressful to be told in advance which trials would include a choking whiff of CO_2 (Lejuez, 2000).

Pressure is another element of stress, especially job stress. **Pressure** occurs when a person must meet *urgent* external demands or expectations (Weiten, 1998). For example, we feel pressured when activities must be speeded up, when deadlines must be met, when extra work is added unexpectedly, or when we must work near maximum capacity for long periods. Most students who have survived final exams are familiar with the effects of pressure.

What if I set deadlines for myself? Does it make a difference where the pressure comes from? Yes. People generally feel more stress in situations over which they have little or no control (Taylor et al., 2000). Consider, for example, a study in which college students tried to avoid electric shocks. During testing, some students were allowed to select their own rest periods; others were told when they could rest. Students allowed to control their own rest periods had lower stress levels (as measured by blood pressure) than those who were given no choice (DeGood, 1975).

To summarize, when emotional "shocks" are *intense* or *repeated, unpredictable, uncontrollable,* and linked to *pressure,* stress will be magnified and damage is likely to result. At work, people face many of these sources of stress every day. In fact, chronic job stress sometimes results in *burnout,* a pattern of emotional exhaustion.

Job Burnout

Margo, a young nurse, realizes with dismay that she has "lost all patience with her patients" and wishes they would "go somewhere else to be sick." Margo's feelings are a clear sign of job **burnout,** a condition in which workers are physically, mentally, and emotionally drained. Burnout has three aspects (Maslach, Schaufeli, & Leiter, 2001).

- **Emotional exhaustion:** Affected persons are fatigued, tense, apathetic, and suffer from physical ailments. They feel "used up" and "empty."
- **Cynicism or detachment:** Burned-out workers have an "I don't give a damn anymore" attitude, and they treat clients coldly, as if they were objects.
- **Feelings of reduced personal accomplishment:** Burned-out workers do poor work and feel helpless, hopeless, or angry.

Burnout may occur in any job, but it is a special problem in emotionally demanding helping professions, such as nursing, teaching, social work, child care, counseling, or police work. Often, the most idealistic and caring workers are the ones who burn out. As some say, "You have to be on fire to burn out" (Maslach, Schaufeli, & Leiter, 2001).

Although it may not seem so, assembly line work can be quite stressful because of the lack of control employees have over the pace of work.

The helping professions require empathy, caring, and emotional involvement. As a result, caregivers risk depleting their emotional resources and ability to cope. Over time, this can lead to burnout.

Stressor A specific condition or event in the environment that challenges or threatens a person.

Pressure A stressful condition that occurs when a person must meet urgent external demands or expectations.

Burnout A job-related condition of mental, physical, and emotional exhaustion.

If we wish to keep caring people in the helping professions, it may be necessary to adjust workloads, rewards, and the amount of control people have in their jobs (Maslach, Schaufeli, & Leiter, 2001). Better social support systems at work would also be valuable. For example, support groups help caregivers deal with stress by allowing them to talk about their feelings and problems at work (Greenglass, Burke, & Konarski, 1998).

Appraising Stressors

It might seem that stressful events "happen to" us. Sometimes this is true, but as noted in Chapter 9, our emotions are greatly affected by how we appraise situations. That's why some people are distressed by events that others view as a thrill or a challenge (eustress). Ultimately, stress depends on how you perceive a situation. I have a friend who would find it stressful to listen to five of his son's rap CDs in a row. His son would find it stressful to listen to *one* of his father's opera CDs. To know if you are stressed, we must know what meaning you place on events. As we will see in a moment, whenever a stressor is appraised as a *threat* (potentially harmful), a powerful stress reaction follows (Lazarus, 1991a).

"Am I Okay or in Trouble?"

Situation: You have been selected to give a speech to 300 people. Or, a doctor tells you that you must undergo a dangerous and painful operation. Or, the one true love of your life walks out the door. What would your emotional response to these events be? How do you cope with an emotional threat?

According to Richard Lazarus (1991a), there are two important steps in managing a threat. The first is a **primary appraisal,** in which you decide if a situation is relevant or irrelevant, positive or threatening. In essence, this step answers the question, "Am I okay or in trouble?" Then you make a **secondary appraisal,** in which you assess your resources and choose a way to meet the threat or challenge. ("What can I do about this situation?") Thus, the way a situation is "sized up" greatly affects our ability to cope with it (◆Fig. 11.2). Public speaking, for instance, can be appraised as an intense threat or as a chance to perform. Emphasizing the threat—by imagining failure, rejection, or embarrassment—obviously invites disaster (Lazarus, 1993).

The Nature of Threat

What does it mean to feel threatened by a stressor? Certainly in most day-to-day situations it doesn't mean you think your life is in danger. (Unless, of course, you owe money to "Eddie The Enforcer.") Threat has more to do with the idea of control. We are particularly prone to feel stressed when we can't—or think we can't—control our immediate environment. In short, a *perceived* lack of control is just as threatening as an actual lack of control (DasGupta, 1992). If your answer to the question "What can I do about this situation?" is "nothing," you will feel emotionally stressed.

A sense of control also comes from believing you can reach desired goals. It is threatening to feel that we lack *competence* to cope with life's demands (Bandura, 2001). Because of this, the intensity of your body's stress reaction often depends on what you think and tell yourself about a stressor. That's why it's valuable to learn to think in ways that ward off the body's stress response. (Some strategies for controlling upsetting thoughts are described later in "Stress Management.")

Coping with Threat

You have appraised a situation as threatening. What will you do next? There are two major choices. **Problem-focused coping** is aimed at managing or altering the distressing situation itself. In **emotion-focused coping,** we try to control our emotional reactions to the situation (Lazarus, 1993).

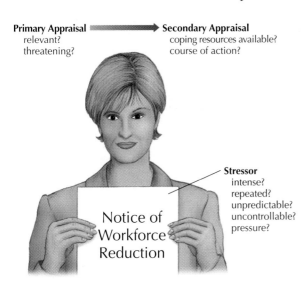

Primary Appraisal
relevant?
threatening?

→ **Secondary Appraisal**
coping resources available?
course of action?

Stressor
intense?
repeated?
unpredictable?
uncontrollable?
pressure?

Notice of Workforce Reduction

◆**FIGURE 11.2** *Stress is the product of an interchange between a person and the environment.*

Primary appraisal Deciding if a situation is relevant to oneself and if it is a threat.

Secondary appraisal Deciding how to cope with a threat or challenge.

Problem-focused coping Directly managing or remedying a stressful or threatening situation.

Emotion-focused coping Managing or controlling one's emotional reaction to a stressful or threatening situation.

CLINICAL FILE September 11th and Traumatic Stress

Traumatic experiences produce psychological injury or intense emotional pain. Victims of **traumatic stresses** such as war, torture, rape, assassination, plane crashes, natural disasters, or street violence, may suffer from nightmares, flashbacks, insomnia, irritability, nervousness, grief, emotional numbing, and depression. There's little doubt that the tragedy of September 11th had these effects. Like most traumatic stresses, the attack on the World Trade Center in New York was sudden, unexpected, and overwhelming.

People who personally witness or survive a disaster are most affected by traumatic stress. Twenty percent of the people who lived close to Ground Zero in New York suffered serious stress disorders. Yet, even those who experience horror at a distance may be traumatized. Among U.S. adults who only saw the September 11th terrorist attacks on television, 44 percent had at least some stress symptoms.

Traumatic stress produces feelings of helplessness and vulnerability. Victims realize that disaster could strike again without warning. In addition to feeling threatened, many victims sense that they are losing control of their lives.

What can people do about such reactions? Psychologists recommend the following:

- Identify what you are feeling and talk to others about your fears and concerns.
- Think about the skills that have helped you overcome adversity in the past and apply them to the present situation.
- Continue to do the things that you enjoy and that make life meaningful.
- Get support from others. This is a major element in recovery from all traumatic events.
- Give yourself time to heal. Fortunately, most people are more resilient than they think.

When traumatic stresses are severe or repeated, some people have even more serious symptoms. They suffer from crippling anxiety or emotional numbing. Typically, they can't stop thinking about the disturbing event; they anxiously avoid anything associated with the event; and they are constantly fearful or nervous. (These are the symptoms of *stress disorders*, which are discussed in Chapter 12.) Such reactions can leave victims emotionally handicapped for months or years after a disaster. If you feel that you are having trouble coping with a severe emotional shock, consider seeking help from a psychologist or other professional. (Sources: Fields & Margolin, 2001; Galea et al., 2002; LeDoux & Gorman, 2001; Pfefferbaum et al., 2001; Schuster et al., 2001; Scurfield, 2002; Tucker et al., 2000; Wilson et al., 2000; Wilson, Meyers, & Gilbert, 2001.)

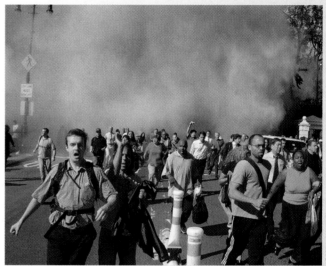

There can be little doubt that the terrorist attack on the World Trade Center was a traumatically stressful event. Even people who merely witnessed the disaster on television suffered from stress symptoms.

Couldn't both types of coping occur together? Yes. Sometimes the two types of coping aid one another. Say, for example, that a woman feels anxious as she steps to the podium to give a speech. If she does some deep breathing to reduce her anxiety (emotion-focused coping), she will be better able to glance over her notes to improve her delivery (problem-focused coping).

It is also possible for coping efforts to clash. For instance, if you have to make a difficult decision, you may suffer intense emotional distress. In such circumstances there is a temptation to make a quick, ill-advised choice, just to end the suffering. Doing so may allow you to cope with your emotions, but it shortchanges problem-focused coping.

In general, problem-focused coping tends to be especially useful when you are facing a controllable stressor—that is, a situation you can actually do something about. Emotion-focused efforts are best suited to managing stressors you cannot control (Lazarus, 1993). To improve your chances of coping effectively, the stress-fighting strategies described in this chapter include a mixture of both techniques.

So far, our discussion has focused on everyday stresses. How do people react to the extreme stresses imposed by war, violence, or disaster? The highlight "September 11th and Traumatic Stress" discusses this important topic.

We will soon return to another look at stress and its effects. But first, let's examine two major (and all too familiar) causes of stress: frustration and conflict.

Traumatic stresses Extreme events that cause psychological injury or intense emotional pain.

FRUSTRATION—BLIND ALLEYS AND LEAD BALLOONS

] **SURVEYQUESTION** *What causes frustration, and what are typical reactions to it?*

Do you remember how frustrated Taylor was when he couldn't find a parking place? **Frustration** is a negative emotional state that occurs when people are prevented from reaching desired goals. In Taylor's case, the goal of finding a parking space was blocked by another car.

Obstacles of many kinds cause frustration. A useful distinction can be made between external and personal sources of frustration. *External frustration* is based on conditions outside a person that impede progress toward a goal. All of the following are external frustrations: getting stuck with a flat tire; having a marriage proposal rejected; finding the cupboard bare when you go to get your poor dog a bone; finding the refrigerator bare when you go to get your poor tummy a T-bone; finding the refrigerator gone when you return home; being chased out of the house by your starving dog. In other words, external frustrations are based on *delays, failure, rejection, loss,* and other direct blocking of motivated behavior.

Notice that external obstacles can be either *social* (slow drivers, tall people in theaters, people who cut into lines) or *non-social* (stuck doors, a dead battery, rain on the day of the game). If you ask ten of your friends what has frustrated them recently, most will probably mention someone's behavior ("My sister wore one of my dresses when I wanted to wear it," "My supervisor is unfair," "My history teacher grades too hard"). As social animals, we humans are highly sensitive to social sources of frustration (Peeters, Buunk, & Schaufeli, 1995). That's probably why unfair treatment associated with racial or ethnic prejudice is a major source of frustration and stress in the lives of many African Americans and other minority group members (Clark, Anderson, Clark, & Williams, 1999).

Frustration usually increases as the *strength, urgency,* or *importance* of a blocked motive increases. Taylor was especially frustrated in the parking lot because he was late for an exam. Likewise, an escape artist submerged in a tank of water and bound with 200 pounds of chain would become *quite* frustrated if a trick lock jammed. Remember, too, that motivation becomes stronger as we near a goal. As a result, frustration is more intense when a person runs into an obstacle very close to a goal. If you've ever missed an A grade by 5 points, you were probably very frustrated. If you've missed an A by 1 point—well, frustration builds character, right?

A final factor affecting frustration is summarized by the old phrase "the straw that broke the camel's back." The effects of *repeated* frustrations can accumulate until a small irritation sets off an unexpectedly violent response. A case in point is the fact that people with long daily commutes are more likely to display "road rage" (angry, aggressive driving) (Harding et al., 1998).

Personal frustrations are based on personal characteristics. If you are 4 feet tall and aspire to be a professional basketball player, you very likely will be frustrated. If you want to go to medical school but can earn only D grades, you will likewise be frustrated. In both examples, frustration is actually based on personal limitations. Yet, failure may be *perceived* as externally caused. We will return to this point in a discussion of stress management. In the meantime, let's look at some typical reactions to frustration.

Reactions to Frustration

Aggression is any response that is made with the aim of doing harm. It is one of the most persistent and frequent responses to frustration (Berkowitz, 1988). The frustration-aggression link is so common, in fact, that experiments are hardly necessary to show it. A glance at almost any newspaper will provide examples like the one that follows.

Frustration A negative emotional state that occurs when one is prevented from reaching a goal.

Aggression Any response made with the intent of causing harm.

BURIEN, WASHINGTON (AP)—Barbara Smith committed the assault, but police aren't likely to press charges. Her victim was an old Oldsmobile which failed once too often to start.

When Officer Jim Fuda arrived at the scene, he found one beat-up car, a broken baseball bat, and a satisfied 23-year-old Seattle woman.

"I feel good," Ms. Smith reportedly told the officer. "That car's been giving me misery for years, and I killed it."

Does frustration always cause aggression? Aren't there other reactions? Although the connection is strong, frustration does not always incite aggression. More often, frustration is met first with *persistence,* often in the form of more vigorous efforts and varied responses (◆Fig. 11.3). For example, if you put your last quarter in a vending machine and pressing the button has no effect, you will probably press harder and faster (vigorous effort). Then you will press all the other buttons (varied response). Persistence may help you reach your goal by getting *around* a barrier. However, if the machine *still* refuses to deliver or return your quarter, you may become aggressive and kick the machine (or at least tell it what you think of it).

Persistence can be very adaptive. Overcoming a barrier ends the frustration and allows the need or motive to be satisfied. The same is true of aggression that removes or destroys a barrier. Picture a small band of nomadic humans, parched by thirst but separated from a water hole by a menacing animal. It is easy to see that attacking the animal may ensure their survival. In modern society such direct aggression is seldom acceptable. If you find a long line at the drinking fountain, aggression is hardly appropriate. Because direct aggression is discouraged, it is frequently *displaced.*

How is aggression displaced? Does displaced aggression occur often? Directing aggression toward a source of frustration may be impossible, or it may be too dangerous. If you are frustrated by your boss at work or by a teacher at school, the cost of direct aggression may be too high (losing your job or failing a class). Instead, the aggression may be displaced, or redirected, toward whomever or whatever is available. Targets of **displaced aggression** tend to be safer, or less likely to retaliate, than the original source of frustration.

Sometimes long *chains* of displacement occur, in which one person displaces aggression to the next. For instance, a businesswoman who is frustrated by high taxes reprimands an employee, who swallows his anger until he returns home and then yells at his wife, who in turn yells at the children, who then tease the dog. The dog chases the cat, who later knocks over the canary cage.

Psychologists attribute much hostility and violence to displaced aggression. A disturbing example is the finding that when unemployment increases, so does child abuse (Steinberg et al., 1981). In a pattern known as **scapegoating,** a person or a group is blamed for conditions not of their making. A *scapegoat* is a person who has become a habitual target of displaced aggression. Despite recent progress, many minority groups continue to suffer from hostility based on scapegoating. Think, for example, about the hostility expressed toward recent immigrants during times of economic hardship. In many communities, layoffs and

◆**FIGURE 11.3** *Frustration and common reactions to it.*

Bumper cars seem to bring out aggressive impulses in many drivers. Wild smash-ups are part of the fun, but are some drivers displacing aggressive urges related to frustration in other areas of their lives?

Displaced aggression Redirecting aggression to a target other than the actual source of one's frustration.

Scapegoating Blaming a person or a group of people for conditions not of their making.

job losses continue to be associated with increased violence (Catalano, Novaco, & McConnell, 1997). Or think about the hostility expressed toward anyone in the United States who looked even vaguely "foreign" after the September 11th terrorist attacks.

I have a friend who dropped out of school to hitchhike around the country. He seemed very frustrated before he quit. What type of response to frustration is that?   Another major reaction to frustration is escape or withdrawal. It is stressful and unpleasant to be frustrated. If other reactions do not reduce frustration, a person may try to escape. **Escape** may mean actually leaving a source of frustration (dropping out of school, quitting a job, leaving an unhappy marriage), or it may mean psychologically escaping. Two common forms of psychological escape are apathy (pretending not to care) and the use of drugs such as cocaine, alcohol, marijuana, or narcotics. (See Figure 11.3 for a summary of common reactions to frustration.)

Coping with Frustration

In a classic experiment, a psychologist studying frustration placed rats on a small platform at the top of a tall pole. Then he forced them to jump off the platform toward two elevated doors, one locked and the other unlocked. If the rat chose the correct door, it swung open, and the rat landed safely on another platform. Rats who chose the locked door bounced off it and fell into a net far below.

The problem of choosing the open door was made unsolvable and very frustrating by randomly alternating which door was locked. After a time, most rats adopted a stereotyped response. That is, they chose the same door every time. This door was then permanently locked. All the rat had to do was to jump to the other door to avoid a fall, but time after time the rat bounced off the locked door (Maier, 1949).

Isn't that an example of persistence?   No. Persistence that is *inflexible* can turn into "stupid," stereotyped behavior like that of a rat on a jumping stand. When dealing with frustration, you must know when to quit and establish a new direction. Here are some suggestions to help you avoid needless frustration.

1. Try to identify the source of your frustration. Is it external or personal?
2. Is the source of frustration something that can be changed? How hard would you have to work to change it? Is it under your control at all?
3. If the source of your frustration can be changed or removed, are the necessary efforts worth it?

The answers to these questions help determine if persistence will be futile. There is value in learning to accept gracefully those things that cannot be changed.

It is also important to distinguish between *real* barriers and *imagined* barriers. All too often we create our own imaginary barriers. For example, Anita wants a part-time job to earn extra money. At the first place she applied, she was told that she didn't have enough "experience." Now she complains of being frustrated because she wants to work but cannot. She needs "experience" to work but can't get experience without working. She has quit looking for a job.

Is Anita's need for experience a real barrier? Unless she applies for *many* jobs, it is impossible to tell if she has overestimated its importance. For her the barrier is real enough to prevent further efforts, but with persistence she might locate an "unlocked door." If a reasonable amount of effort does show that experience is essential, it might be obtained in other ways—through temporary volunteer work, for instance.

CONFLICT—YES, NO, YES, NO, YES, NO, WELL, MAYBE

] **SURVEYQUESTIONS** *Are there different types of conflict? How do people react to conflict?*

Conflict occurs whenever a person must choose between contradictory needs, desires, motives, or demands. Choosing between college and work, marriage and single life, or study and failure are common conflicts. There are four general forms of conflict. As we will see, each has its own properties (✦Fig. 11.4 and ✦Fig. 11.5).

Escape Reducing discomfort by leaving frustrating situations or by psychologically withdrawing from them.

Conflict A stressful condition that occurs when a person must choose between incompatible or contradictory alternatives.

✦**FIGURE 11.4** *The three most basic forms of conflict. For this woman, choosing between pie and ice cream is a minor approach-approach conflict; deciding whether to take a job that will require weekend work is an approach-avoidance conflict; and choosing between paying higher rent and moving is an avoidance-avoidance conflict.*

Approach-Approach Conflicts

A simple **approach-approach conflict** comes from having to choose between two positive, or desirable, alternatives. Choosing between tutti-frutti-coconut-mocha-champagne ice and orange-marmalade-peanut butter-coffee swirl at the ice cream parlor may throw you into a temporary conflict. However, if you really like both choices, your decision will be quickly made. Even when more important decisions are at stake, approach-approach conflicts tend to be the easiest to resolve. The old fable about the mule that died of thirst and starvation while standing between a bucket of water and a bucket of oats is obviously unrealistic. When both options are positive, the scales of decision are easily tipped one direction or the other.

Avoidance-Avoidance Conflicts

Being forced to choose between two negative, or undesirable, alternatives creates an **avoidance-avoidance conflict.** A person in an avoidance conflict is caught between "the devil and the deep blue sea," "the frying pan and the fire," or "a rock and a hard place." In real life, double-avoidance conflicts involve dilemmas such as choosing between unwanted pregnancy and abortion, the dentist and tooth decay, a monotonous job and poverty, or dorm food and starvation.

Suppose I don't object to abortion. Or suppose that I consider any pregnancy sacred and not to be tampered with? Like many other stressful situations, these examples can be defined as conflicts only on the basis of personal needs and values. If a woman wants to end a pregnancy and does not object to abortion, she experiences no conflict. If she would not consider abortion under any circumstances, there is no conflict.

Avoidance conflicts often have a "damned if you do, damned if you don't" quality. In other words, both choices are negative, but *not choosing* may be impossible or equally undesirable. To illustrate, imagine the plight of a person trapped in a hotel fire 20 stories from the ground. Should she jump from the window and almost surely die on the pave-

Approach-approach conflict Choosing between two positive, or desirable, alternatives.
Avoidance-avoidance conflict Choosing between two negative, undesirable alternatives.

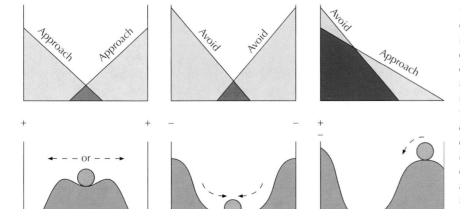

✦**FIGURE 11.5** *Conflict diagrams. As shown by the colored areas in the graphs, desires to approach and to avoid increase near a goal. The effects of these tendencies are depicted below each graph. The "behavior" of the ball in each example illustrates the nature of the conflict above it. An approach conflict (left) is easily decided. Moving toward one goal will increase its attraction (graph) and will lead to a rapid resolution. (If the ball moves in either direction, it will go all the way to one of the goals.) In an avoidance conflict (center), tendencies to avoid are deadlocked, resulting in inaction. In an approach-avoidance conflict (right), approach proceeds to the point where desires to approach and avoid cancel each other. Again, these tendencies are depicted (below) by the action of the ball. (Graphs after Miller, 1944.)*

ment? Or should she try to dash through the flames and almost surely die of smoke inhalation and burns? When faced with a choice such as this, it is easy to see why people often *freeze*, finding it impossible to decide or take action. A trapped individual may first think about the window, approach it, and then back away after looking down 20 stories. Next, she may try the door and again back away as heat and smoke billow in. In actual disasters of this sort, people are often found dead in their rooms, victims of an inability to take action.

Indecision, inaction, and freezing are not the only reactions to double-avoidance conflicts. Since avoidance conflicts are stressful and rarely solved, people sometimes pull out of them entirely. This reaction, called *leaving the field*, is another form of escape. It may explain the behavior of a student who could not attend school unless he worked. However, if he worked he could not earn passing grades. His solution after much conflict and indecision? He joined the navy.

Approach-Avoidance Conflicts

Approach-avoidance conflicts are also difficult to resolve. In some ways they are more troublesome than avoidance conflicts because people seldom escape them. A person in an **approach-avoidance conflict** is "caught" by being attracted to, and repelled by, the same goal or activity. Attraction keeps the person in the situation, but its negative aspects cause turmoil and distress. For example, a high school student arrives to pick up his date for the first time. He is met at the door by her father, who is a professional wrestler—7 feet tall, 300 pounds, and entirely covered with hair. The father gives the boy a crushing handshake and growls that he will break him in half if the girl is not home on time. The student considers the girl attractive and has a good time. But does he ask her out again? It depends on the relative strength of his attraction and his fear. Almost certainly he will feel *ambivalent* about asking her out again, knowing that another encounter with her father awaits him.

Ambivalence (mixed positive and negative feelings) is a central characteristic of approach-avoidance conflicts. Ambivalence is usually translated into *partial approach* (Miller, 1944). Since our student is still attracted to the girl, he may spend time with her at school and elsewhere. But he may not actually date her again. Some more realistic examples of approach-avoidance conflicts are planning to marry someone your parents strongly disapprove of, wanting to be in a play but suffering stage fright, wanting to buy a car but not wanting to make monthly payments, and wanting to eat when you're already overweight. Many of life's important decisions have approach-avoidance dimensions.

Multiple Conflicts

Aren't real-life conflicts more complex than the ones described here? Yes. Conflicts are rarely as clear-cut as those described. People in conflict are usually faced with several dilemmas at once, so several types of conflict may be intermingled. The fourth type of conflict moves us closer to reality. In a **double approach-avoidance conflict** each alternative has both positive and negative qualities. For example, you are offered two jobs: One has good pay but poor hours and dull work; the second has interesting work and excellent hours but low pay. Which do you select? This situation is more typical of the choices we must usually make. It offers neither completely positive nor completely negative options.

As with single approach-avoidance conflicts, people faced with double approach-avoidance conflicts feel ambivalent about each choice. This causes them to *vacillate,* or waver between the alternatives. Just as you are about to choose one such alternative, its undesirable aspects tend to loom large. So, what do you do? You swing back toward the other choice. If you have ever been romantically attracted to two people at once—each having qualities you like and dislike—then you have probably experienced vacillation. Another example that may be familiar is trying to decide between two college majors, each with advantages and disadvantages.

In real life it is common to face **multiple approach-avoidance conflicts** in which several alternatives each have positive and negative features. An example would be trying to choose which automobile to buy among several brands. On a day-to-day basis, most multiple approach-avoidance conflicts are little more than an annoyance. When they involve ma-

Approach-avoidance conflict Being attracted to and repelled by the same goal or activity.

Double approach-avoidance conflict Being simultaneously attracted to and repelled by each of two alternatives.

Multiple approach-avoidance conflict Being simultaneously attracted to and repelled by each of several alternatives.

jor life decisions, such as choosing a career, a school, a mate, or a job, they can add greatly to the amount of stress we experience.

Managing Conflicts

How can I handle conflicts more effectively?   Most of the suggestions made earlier concerning frustration also apply to conflicts. However, here are some additional things to remember when you are in conflict or must make a difficult decision.

1. Don't be hasty when making important decisions. Take time to collect information and to weigh pros and cons. Hasty decisions are often regretted. Even if you do make a faulty decision, it will trouble you less if you know that you did everything possible to avoid a mistake.
2. Try out important decisions *partially* when possible. If you are thinking about moving to a new town, try to spend a few days there first. If you are choosing between colleges, do the same. If classes are in progress, sit in on some. If you want to learn to scuba dive, rent equipment for a reasonable length of time before buying.
3. Look for workable compromises. Again it is important to get all available information. If you think that you have only one or two alternatives and they are undesirable or unbearable, seek the aid of a teacher, counselor, minister, or social service agency. You may be overlooking possible alternatives these people will know about.
4. When all else fails, make a decision and live with it. Indecision and conflict exact a high cost. Sometimes it is best to select a course of action and stick with it unless it is very obviously wrong after you have taken it.

Conflicts are a normal part of life. With practice you can learn to manage many of the conflicts you will face.

 STUDYBREAK   *Stress, Frustration, and Conflict*

RELATE

What impact did pressure, control, predictability, repetition, and intensity have on your last stress reaction?

  What type of coping do you tend to use when you face a stressor such as public speaking or taking an important exam?

  Think of a time when you were frustrated. What was your goal? What prevented you from reaching it? Was your frustration external or personal?

  Have you ever displaced aggression? Why did you choose another target for your hostility?

  Review the major types of conflict and think of a conflict you have faced that illustrates each type. Did your reactions match those described in the text?

LEARNING CHECK

1. Emotional exhaustion, depersonalization, and reduced accomplishment are characteristics of job _____.
2. Stress tends to be greatest when a situation is appraised as a _____ and a person does not feel _____ to cope with the situation.
3. According to Lazarus, coping with threatening situations can be both problem focused and _____ focused.

4. Which of the following is *not* a common reaction to frustration?
    a. ambivalence   b. aggression   c. displaced aggression
    d. persistence
5. Sampson Goliath is 7 feet tall and weighs 300 pounds. He has failed miserably in his aspirations to become a jockey. The source of his frustration is mainly _____.
6. Inaction and freezing are most characteristic of avoidance-avoidance conflicts. T or F?
7. Approach-avoidance conflicts produce mixed feelings called _____.

Critical Thinking

8. Which do you think would produce more stress: (a) Appraising a situation as mildly threatening but feeling like you are totally incompetent to cope with it? Or, (b) appraising a situation as very threatening but feeling that you have the resources and skills to cope with it?
9. Being frustrated is unpleasant. If some action, including aggression, ends frustration, why might we expect the action to be repeated on other occasions?

ANSWERS

1. burnout 2. threat, competent 3. emotion 4. a 5. personal 6. T 7. ambivalence 8. There is no correct answer here because individual stress reactions vary greatly. However, the secondary appraisal of a situation often determines just how stressful it is. Feeling incapable of coping is very threatening. 9. If a response ends discomfort, the response has been negatively reinforced. This makes it more likely to occur in the future (see Chapter 6).

PSYCHOLOGICAL DEFENSE—MENTAL KARATE?

] SURVEYQUESTION *What are defense mechanisms?*

Threatening situations tend to produce **anxiety.** A person who is anxious feels tense, uneasy, apprehensive, worried, and vulnerable. This can lead to emotion-focused coping that is *defensive* in nature (Lazarus, 1991b). Since anxiety is unpleasant and uncomfortable, we are usually motivated to avoid it. Psychological defense mechanisms allow us to reduce feelings of anxiety caused by stressful situations or by our shortcomings.

What are psychological defense mechanisms, and how do they reduce anxiety? A **defense mechanism** is any mental process used to avoid, deny, or distort sources of threat or anxiety, including threats to one's self-image. Many of the defenses were first identified by Sigmund Freud, who assumed they operate *unconsciously.* Often, defense mechanisms create large blind spots in awareness. For instance, I know an extremely stingy person who is completely unaware that he is a tightwad.

Everyone has at one time or another used defense mechanisms. Let's consider some of the most common. (A more complete listing is given in ▲Table 11.3.)

Denial

One of the most basic defenses is **denial** (protecting oneself from an unpleasant reality by refusing to accept it or believe it). Denial is closely linked with death, illness, and similar painful and threatening events. For instance, if you were told that you had only 3 months to live, how would you react? Your first thoughts might be "Aw, come on, someone must have mixed up the x-rays" or "The doctor must be mistaken" or simply "It can't be true!" Similar denial and disbelief are common reactions to the unexpected death of a friend or relative: "It's just not real. I don't believe it. I just don't believe it!"

Repression

Freud noticed that his patients had tremendous difficulty recalling shocking or traumatic events from childhood. It seemed that powerful forces were holding these painful memories from awareness. Freud called this **repression.** He believed that we protect ourselves by repressing threatening thoughts and impulses. Feelings of hostility toward a family member, the names of people we dislike, and past failures are common targets of repression.

Reaction Formation

In a **reaction formation,** impulses are not just repressed; they are also held in check by exaggerating opposite behavior. For example, a mother who unconsciously resents her children may, through reaction formation, become absurdly overprotective and overindulgent. Her real thoughts of "I hate them" and "I wish they were gone" are replaced by "I love them" and "I don't know what I would do without them." The mother's hostile impulses are traded for "smother" love so that she won't have to admit she hates her children. Thus, the basic idea in a reaction formation is that the individual acts out an opposite behavior to block threatening impulses or feelings.

Regression

In its broadest meaning, **regression** refers to any return to earlier, less demanding situations or habits. Most parents who have a second child have to put up with at least some regression by the older child. Threatened by a new rival for affection, an older child may regress

Anxiety Apprehension, dread, or uneasiness similar to fear but based on an unclear threat.

Defense mechanism A habitual and often unconscious psychological process used to reduce anxiety.

JUMP START reprinted by permission of United Features Syndicate, Inc.

▲*TABLE 11.3*	**Psychological Defense Mechanisms**	
Compensation Counteracting a real or imagined weakness by emphasizing desirable traits or seeking to excel in the area of weakness or in other areas.	**Intellectualization** Separating emotion from a threatening or anxiety-provoking situation by talking or thinking about it in impersonal "intellectual" terms.	**Reaction formation** Preventing dangerous impulses from being expressed in behavior by exaggerating opposite behavior.
Denial Protecting oneself from an unpleasant reality by refusing to perceive it.	**Isolation** Separating contradictory thoughts or feelings into "logic-tight" mental compartments so that they do not come into conflict.	**Regression** Retreating to an earlier level of development or to earlier, less demanding habits or situations.
Fantasy Fulfilling unmet desires in imagined achievements or activities.	**Projection** Attributing one's own feelings, shortcomings, or unacceptable impulses to others.	**Repression** Unconsciously preventing painful or dangerous thoughts from entering awareness.
Identification Taking on some of the characteristics of an admired person, usually as a way of compensating for perceived personal weaknesses or faults.	**Rationalization** Justifying your behavior by giving reasonable and "rational," but false, reasons for it.	**Sublimation** Working off unmet desires, or unacceptable impulses, in activities that are constructive.

to childish speech, bed-wetting, or infantile play after the new baby arrives. If you've ever seen a child get homesick at summer camp or on a vacation, you've observed regression. The child wants to go home, where it's "safe." An adult who throws a temper tantrum or a married adult who "goes home to mother" is also regressing.

Projection

Projection is an unconscious process that protects us from the anxiety we would feel if we were to discern our faults. A person who is projecting tends to see his or her own feelings, shortcomings, or unacceptable impulses in others. **Projection** lowers anxiety by exaggerating negative traits in others. This justifies one's own actions and directs attention away from personal failings.

Your author once worked for a greedy shop owner who cheated many of his customers. This same man considered himself a pillar of the community and a good Christian. How did he justify to himself his greed and dishonesty? He believed that everyone who entered his store was bent on cheating *him* any way they could. In reality, few, if any, of his customers shared his motives, but he projected his own greed and dishonesty onto them.

Rationalization

Every teacher is familiar with this strange phenomenon: On the day of an exam, an incredible wave of disasters sweeps through the city. Mothers, fathers, sisters, brothers, aunts, uncles, grandparents, friends, relatives, and pets become ill or die. Motors suddenly fall out of cars. Books are lost or stolen. Alarm clocks go belly-up and ring no more.

The making of excuses comes from a natural tendency to explain our behavior. **Rationalization** refers to justifying personal actions by giving "rational" but false reasons for them. When the explanation you give for your behavior is reasonable and convincing—but not the real reason—you are *rationalizing*. For example, Taylor failed to turn in an assignment made at the beginning of the semester in one of his classes. Here's the explanation he gave his professor:

> My car broke down 2 days ago, and I couldn't get to the library until yesterday. Then I couldn't get all the books I needed because some were checked out, but I wrote what I could. Then last night, as the last straw, the ink cartridge in my printer ran out, and since all the stores were closed, I couldn't finish the paper on time.

When asked why he left the assignment until the last minute (the real reason it was late), Taylor offered another set of rationalizations. Like many people, Taylor had difficulty seeing himself without the protection of his rationalizations.

All of the defense mechanisms described seem pretty undesirable. Do they have a positive side? People who overuse defense mechanisms become less adaptable, because they consume great amounts of emotional energy to control anxiety and maintain an unrealistic self-image. Defense mechanisms do have value, though. Often, they help keep us from being overwhelmed by immediate threats. This can provide time for a person to learn to cope in a more effective, problem-focused manner. If you recognize some of your own behavior in the

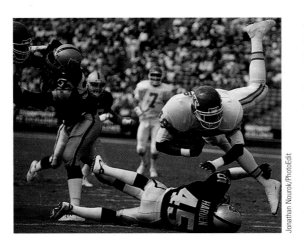

For some players—and fans—football probably allows sublimation of aggressive urges. *Mortal Kombat* and similar computer games may serve the same purpose.

Jonathan Nourok/PhotoEdit

descriptions here, it is hardly a sign that you are hopelessly defensive. As noted earlier, most people occasionally use defense mechanisms.

Two defense mechanisms that have a decidedly more positive quality are compensation and sublimation.

Compensation

Compensatory reactions are defenses against feelings of inferiority. A person who has a defect or weakness (real or imagined) may go to unusual lengths to overcome the weakness or to *compensate* for it by excelling in other areas. One of the pioneers of "pumping iron" in America is Jack LaLanne. LaLanne made a successful career out of body building in spite of the fact that he was thin and sickly as a young man. Or perhaps it would be more accurate to say *because* he was thin and sickly. There are dozens of examples of **compensation** at work. A childhood stutterer may excel in debate at college. As a child, Helen Keller was unable to see or hear, but she became an outstanding thinker and writer. Doc Watson, Ray Charles, Stevie Wonder, and a number of other well-known musicians are blind.

Sublimation

The defense called **sublimation** (sub-lih-MAY-shun) is defined as working off frustrated desires (especially sexual desires) through socially acceptable activities. Freud believed that art, music, dance, poetry, scientific investigation, and other creative activities can serve to rechannel sexual energies into productive behavior. Freud also felt that almost any strong desire can be sublimated. For example, a very aggressive person may find social acceptance as a professional soldier, boxer, or football player. Greed may be refined into a successful business career. Lying may be sublimated into storytelling, creative writing, or politics.

Sexual motives appear to be the most easily and widely sublimated. Freud would have had a field day with such modern pastimes as surfing, motorcycle riding, drag racing, and dancing to or playing rock music, to name but a few. People enjoy each of these activities for a multitude of reasons, but it is hard to overlook the rich sexual symbolism apparent in each.

LEARNED HELPLESSNESS—IS THERE HOPE?

] SURVEYQUESTION *What do we know about coping with feelings of helplessness and depression?*

What would happen if a person's defenses failed or if the person appraised a threatening situation as hopeless? Martin Seligman studied the case of a young marine who seemed to have adapted to the stresses of being held prisoner during the Vietnam War. The marine's health was related to a promise made by his captors: If he cooperated, they said, he would be released on a certain date. As the date approached, his spirits soared. Then came a devastating blow. He had been deceived. His captors had no intention of ever releasing him. He immediately lapsed into a deep depression, refused to eat or drink, and died shortly thereafter.

That seems like an extreme example. Does anything similar occur outside of concentration camps? Apparently so. For example, researchers in Finland found that even in everyday life, people who feel a sense of hopelessness die at elevated rates (Everson, Goldberg, & Salonen, 1996).

How can we explain such patterns? Psychologists have focused on the concept of learned helplessness (Seligman, 1989). **Learned helplessness** is an acquired inability to overcome obstacles and avoid aversive stimuli. To observe learned helplessness, let's see what happens when animals are tested in a shuttle box (◆Fig. 11.6). If placed in one side of

Learned helplessness A learned inability to overcome obstacles or to avoid punishment; learned passivity and inaction to aversive stimuli.

a divided box, dogs will quickly learn to leap to the other side to escape an electric shock. If they are given a warning before the shock occurs (for example, a light that dims), most dogs learn to avoid the shock by leaping the barrier before the shock arrives. This is true of most dogs, but not those who have learned to feel helpless (Overmier & LoLordo, 1998).

How is a dog made to feel helpless? Before being tested in the shuttle box, a dog can be placed in a harness (from which the dog cannot escape). The dog is then given several painful shocks. The animal is helpless to prevent these shocks. When placed in the shuttle box, dogs trained this way react to the first shock by crouching, howling, and whining. None of them try to escape. They helplessly resign themselves to their fate. After all, they have already learned that there is nothing they can do about shock.

As the shuttle box experiments suggest, helplessness is a psychological state that occurs when events *appear to be uncontrollable* (Seligman, 1989). Helplessness also afflicts humans. It is a common reaction to repeated failure and to unpredictable or unavoidable punishment. A prime example is college students who feel helpless about their school work. Such students tend to procrastinate and give up easily (McKean, 1994).

✦FIGURE 11.6 *In the normal course of escape and avoidance learning, a light dims shortly before the floor is electrified* (a). *Since the light does not yet have meaning for the dog, the dog receives a shock (non-injurious, by the way) and leaps the barrier* (b). *Dogs soon learn to watch for the dimming of the light* (c) *and to jump before receiving a shock* (d). *Dogs made to feel "helpless" rarely even learn to escape shock, much less to avoid it.*

Where humans are concerned, attributions (discussed in Chapter 9) have a large effect on helplessness. Persons who are made to feel helpless in one situation are more likely to act helpless in other situations if they attribute their failure to *lasting, general* factors. An example would be concluding "I must be stupid" after doing poorly on a test in a biology class. In contrast, attributing a low score to specific factors in the situation ("I'm not too good at the type of test my biology professor uses" or "I'm not very interested in biology") tends to prevent learned helplessness from spreading (Alloy et al., 1984; Anderson et al., 1984).

Depression

Seligman and others have pointed out the similarities between learned helplessness and **depression.** Both are marked by feelings of despondency, powerlessness, and hopelessness. "Helpless" animals become less active and less aggressive, and they lose their appetite and sex drive. Humans suffer from similar effects and also tend to see themselves as failing, even when they're not (Seligman, 1989).

Depression is one of the most widespread emotional problems, and it undoubtedly has many causes. However, learned helplessness seems to explain many cases of depression and hopelessness. For example, Seligman (1972a) describes the fate of Archie, a 15-year-old boy. For Archie, school is an unending series of shocks and failures. Other students treat him as if he's stupid; in class he rarely answers questions because he doesn't know some of the words. He feels knocked down everywhere he turns. These may not be electric shocks, but they are certainly emotional "shocks," and Archie has learned to feel helpless to prevent them. When he leaves school his chances of success will be poor. He has learned to passively endure whatever shocks life has in store for him. Archie is not alone in this regard. Hopelessness is almost always a major element of depression (Alloy & Clements, 1998; Ciarrochi, Dean, & Anderson, 2002).

Hope

Does Seligman's research give any clues about how to "unlearn" helplessness? With dogs, an effective technique is to forcibly drag them away from shock into the "safe" compartment. After this is done several times, the animals regain "hope" and feelings of control over the environment. Just how this can be done with humans is a question psychologists are exploring.

Depression A state of despondency marked by feelings of powerlessness and hopelessness.

Mastery training can occur informally when people learn to cope with challenges. For example, 18- to 21-year-old trainees on a transatlantic sailing voyage showed marked improvements in their ability to cope with stress (Norris & Weinman, 1996).

Stephen Rose/Rainbow

It seems obvious, for instance, that someone like Archie would benefit from an educational program that would allow him to "succeed" repeatedly.

In **mastery training,** responses are reinforced that lead to mastery of a threat or control over one's environment. Animals who undergo such training become more resistant to learned helplessness (Volpicelli et al., 1983). For example, animals that first learn to escape shock become more persistent in trying to flee inescapable shock. In effect, they won't give up, even when the situation really is "hopeless."

Such findings suggest that we might be able to "immunize" people against helplessness and depression by allowing them to master difficult challenges. The Outward Bound schools, in which people pit themselves against the rigors of mountaineering, white-water canoeing, and wilderness survival, might serve as a model for such a program.

The value of hope should not be overlooked. As fragile as this emotion seems to be, it is a powerful antidote to depression and helplessness. As an individual, you may find hope in religion, nature, human companionship, or even technology. Wherever you find it, remember its value: Hope is among the most important of all human emotions. Having positive beliefs, such as optimism, hope, and a sense of meaning and control is closely related to overall well-being (Lachman & Weaver, 1998; Taylor et al., 2000).

Why Students Get the Blues

During the school year, nearly 80 percent of all college students suffer some symptoms of depression. At any given time, from 16 to 30 percent of the student population is depressed (McLennan, 1992; Wong & Whitaker, 1993). Why should so many students be "blue"? Various problems contribute to depressive feelings. Here are some of the most common:

1. Stresses from college work and pressures to choose a career can leave students feeling that they are missing out on fun or that all their hard work is meaningless.
2. Isolation and loneliness are common when students leave their support groups behind. In the past, family, a circle of high school friends, and often a boyfriend or girlfriend could be counted on for support and encouragement.
3. Problems with studying and grades frequently trigger depression. Many students start college with high aspirations and little prior experience with failure. At the same time, many lack basic skills necessary for academic success.
4. Depression can be triggered by the breakup of an intimate relationship, either with a former boyfriend or girlfriend or with a newly formed college romance.
5. Students who find it difficult to live up to their idealized images of themselves are especially prone to depression (Scott & O'Hara, 1993).
6. An added danger is that depressed students are more likely to abuse alcohol, which is a depressant (Camatta & Nagoshi, 1995).

Barbara Stitzer/PhotoEdit

Mastery training Reinforcement of responses that lead to mastery of a threat or control over one's environment.

In a survey, college students reported that they were depressed from one to two times a month. These episodes lasted from a few hours to several days.

USING PSYCHOLOGY Coping with Depression

If you don't do well on a test or a class assignment, how do you react? If you see it as a small, isolated setback, you probably won't feel too bad. However, if you feel like you have "blown it" in a big way, depression may follow. Students who strongly link everyday events to long-term goals (such as a successful career or high income) tend to overreact to day-to-day disappointments (McIntosh, Harlow, & Martin, 1995).

What does the preceding tell us about the college blues? The implication is that it's important to take daily tasks one step at a time and chip away at them. That way, you are less likely to feel overwhelmed, helpless, or hopeless. Beck and Greenberg (1974) suggest that when you feel "blue," you should make a *daily schedule* for yourself. Try to schedule activities to fill up every hour during the day. It is best to start with easy activities and progress to more difficult tasks. Check off each item as you complete it. That way, you will begin to break the self-defeating cycle of feeling

helpless and falling further behind. (Depressed students spend much of their time sleeping.) A series of small accomplishments, successes, or pleasures may be all that you need to get going again. However, if you are lacking skills needed for success in college, ask for help in getting them. Don't remain "helpless."

Feelings of worthlessness and hopelessness are usually supported by self-critical or negative thoughts. Beck and Greenberg recommend writing down such thoughts as they occur, especially those that immediately precede feelings of sadness. After you have collected these thoughts, write a rational answer to each. For example, the thought "No one loves me" should be answered with a list of those who do care. (See Chapter 13 for more information.) One more point to keep in mind is this: When events begin to improve, try to accept it as a sign that better times lie ahead. Positive events are most likely to end depression if you view them as stable and continuing, rather than temporary and fragile (Needles & Abramson, 1990).

Recognizing Depression

Most people know, obviously enough, when they are "down." Aaron Beck, an authority on depression, suggests you should assume that more than a minor fluctuation in mood is involved when five conditions exist:

1. You have a consistently negative opinion of yourself.
2. You engage in frequent self-criticism and self-blame.
3. You place negative interpretations on events that usually wouldn't bother you.
4. The future looks bleak and negative.
5. You feel that your responsibilities are overwhelming.

What can be done to combat depression?   Bouts of the college blues are closely related to stressful events. Learning to manage college work and to challenge self-critical thinking can help alleviate mild school-related depression. See "Coping with Depression" for some helpful suggestions.

Attacks of the college blues are common and should be distinguished from more serious cases of depression. Severe depression is a serious problem that can lead to suicide or a major impairment of emotional functioning. In such cases it would be wise to seek professional help.

STUDYBREAK   *Defense Mechanisms, Helplessness, and Depression*

RELATE

We tend to be blind to our own reliance on defense mechanisms. Return to the definitions in Table 11.3 and see if you can think of one example of each defense that you have observed someone else using.

Have you ever felt helpless in a particular situation? What caused you to feel that way? Does any part of Seligman's description of learned helplessness match your own experience?

Imagine that a friend of yours is suffering from the college blues. What advice would you give your friend?

LEARNING CHECK

1. Fulfilling frustrated desires in imaginary achievements or activities defines the defense mechanism of
   a. compensation   b. isolation   c. fantasy   d. sublimation

2. Of the defense mechanisms, two that are considered relatively constructive are
   a. compensation   b. denial   c. isolation   d. projection
   e. regression   f. rationalization   g. sublimation

3. Depression in humans is similar to _____ _____ observed in animal experiments.

4. At any given time, over one half of the college student population suffers symptoms of depression. T or F?

5. Countering negative, self-critical thoughts only calls attention to them and makes depression worse. T or F?

Critical Thinking

6. Learned helplessness is closely related to which of the factors that determine the severity of stress?

ANSWERS   1. c 2. a, g 3. learned helplessness 4. F 5. F 6. Feelings of incompetence and lack of control.

STRESS AND HEALTH—UNMASKING A HIDDEN KILLER

] **SURVEYQUESTION** *How is stress related to health and disease?*

Disaster, depression, and sorrow often precede illness. As Taylor (our intrepid student) learned after finals week, stressful events reduce the body's natural defenses against disease. More surprising is the finding that *life changes*—both good and bad—can increase susceptibility to accidents or illness. Major changes in our surroundings or routines require us to be vigilant, on guard, and ready to react. Over long time periods, this can be quite stressful (Sternberg, 2000).

Life Events and Stress

How can I tell if I am subjecting myself to too much stress? Dr. Thomas Holmes and his associates developed the first rating scale to estimate the health hazards we face when stresses add up (Holmes & Masuda, 1972). More recently, Mark Miller and Richard Rahe updated the scale for use today. The **Social Readjustment Rating Scale** (**SRRS**) is reprinted in ▲Table 11.4. Notice that the impact of life events is expressed in **life change units** (**LCUs**) (numerical values assigned to each life event).

As you read the scale, notice again that positive life events may be as costly as disasters. Marriage rates 50 life change units, even though it is usually a happy event. You'll also see many items that read "Change in . . . ." This means that improved life conditions can be as costly as declines. A stressful adjustment may be necessary in either case.

To use the scale, add up the LCUs for all life events you have experienced during the last year and compare the total to the following standards.

> 0–150: No significant problems
> 150–199: Mild life crisis (33 percent chance of illness)
> 200–299: Moderate life crisis (50 percent chance of illness)
> 300 or more: Major life crisis (80 percent chance of illness)

According to Holmes, there is a high chance of illness or accident when your LCU total exceeds 300 points. A more conservative rating of stress can be obtained by totaling LCU points for only the previous 6 months.

Many of the listed life changes don't seem relevant to young adults or college students. Does the SRRS apply to them? The SRRS tends to be more appropriate for older, more established adults. However, the health of college students is also affected by stressful events, such as entering college, changing majors, or the breakup of a steady relationship (Crandall, Preisler, & Aussprung, 1992). (For a student-oriented rating of stress, see Table 11.7 in "Stress Management.")

Evaluation

People differ greatly in their reactions to the same event. For such reasons, the SRRS is at best a rough index of stress. Nevertheless, it's hard to ignore a study in which people were deliberately exposed to the virus that causes common colds. The results were nothing to sneeze at: If a person had a high stress score, she or he was much more likely to actually get a cold (Cohen et al., 1993). In view of such findings, a high LCU score should be taken seriously. If your score goes much over 300, an adjustment in your activities or lifestyle may be needed. Remember, "To be forewarned is to be forearmed."

The Hazards of Hassles

There must be more to stress than major life changes. Isn't there a link between ongoing stresses and health? In addition to having a direct impact, major life events spawn countless daily frustrations and irritations (Pillow, Zautra, & Sandler, 1996). Also, many of us face ongoing

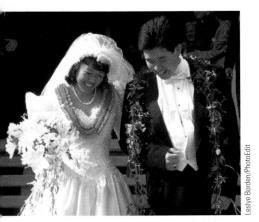

Leslye Borden/PhotoEdit

Marriage is usually a positive life event. Nevertheless, the many changes it brings can be stressful.

Social Readjustment Rating Scale (SRRS) A scale that rates the impact of various life events on the likelihood of illness.

Life change units (LCUs) Numerical values assigned to each life event on the SRRS.

▲ TABLE 11.4	Social Readjustment Rating Scale					
RANK	LIFE EVENT	LIFE CHANGE UNITS	RANK	LIFE EVENT	LIFE CHANGE UNITS
1	Death of spouse or child	119	22	Child leaving home	44
2	Divorce	98	23	Mortgage or loan greater than $10,000	44
3	Death of close family member	92	24	Change in responsibilities at work	43
4	Marital separation	79	25	Change in living conditions	42
5	Fired from work	79	26	Change in residence	41
6	Major personal injury or illness	77	27	Begin or end school	38
7	Jail term	75	28	Trouble with in-laws	38
8	Death of close friend	70	29	Outstanding personal achievement	37
9	Pregnancy	66	30	Change in work hours or conditions	36
10	Major business readjustment	62	31	Change in schools	35
11	Foreclosure on a mortgage or loan	61	32	Christmas	30
12	Gain of new family member	57	33	Trouble with boss	29
13	Marital reconciliation	57	34	Change in recreation	29
14	Change in health or behavior of family member	56	35	Mortgage or loan less than $10,000	28
15	Change in financial state	56	36	Change in personal habits	27
16	Retirement	54	37	Change in eating habits	27
17	Change to different line of work	51	38	Change in social activities	27
18	Change in number of arguments with spouse	51	39	Change in number of family get-togethers	26
19	Marriage	50	40	Change in sleeping habits	26
20	Spouse begins or ends work	46	41	Vacation	25
21	Sexual difficulties	45	42	Change in church activities	22
			43	Minor violations of the law	22

(Source: Reprinted from M. A. Miller & R. H. Rahe, "Life changes scaling for the 1990s" in *Journal of Psychosomatic Research,* 43(3), 1997, 279–292, Table II, p. 282, copyright © 1997, with permission from Elsevier.)

stresses at work or at home that do not involve major life changes. In view of these facts, psychologist Richard Lazarus and his associates studied the impact of minor but frequent stresses. Lazarus (1981) calls such distressing daily annoyances **hassles,** or **microstressors** (see ▲ Table 11.5).

In a year-long study, 100 men and women recorded the hassles they endured. Participants also reported on their physical and mental health. As Lazarus suspected, frequent and severe hassles turned out to be better predictors of day-to-day health than major life events were. However, major life events did predict changes in health 1 or 2 years after the events took place. It appears that daily hassles are closely linked to immediate health and psychological well-being (Johnson & Sherman, 1997; Treharne, Lyons, & Tupling, 2001). Major life changes have more of a long-term impact.

▲ TABLE 11.5	Examples of Daily Hassles	
Too many responsibilities or commitments	Physical illness, symptoms, complaints
Problems with work, boss, or co-workers	Concerns about weight, appearance
Unexpected house guests	Frustrations with daily chores
Inconsiderate neighbors	Delays, transportation problems
Noisy, messy, or quarreling children	Paperwork, filling out forms
Regrets over past decisions	Misplacing or losing things
Having trouble making decisions	Noise, pollution, deteriorating neighborhoods
Money worries or concerns	Bad weather
Not enough time for family, relaxation, entertainment	Crime, disturbing news events
Loneliness, social isolation, separation from family	

Microstressor Any distressing, day-to-day annoyance; also called a *hassle.*

What can be done about a high LCU score or feeling excessively hassled? A good response is to use stress management skills. For serious problems, stress management should be learned directly from a therapist or a stress clinic. When ordinary stresses are involved, there is much you can do on your own. An upcoming discussion of stress management will give you a start. In the meantime, take it easy!

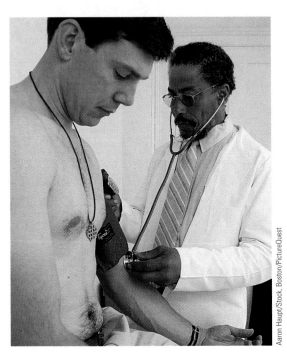

It is estimated that at least half of all patients who see a doctor have a psychosomatic disorder or an illness that is complicated by psychosomatic symptoms.

Aaron Haupt/Stock, Boston/PictureQuest

Psychosomatic Disorders

As we have seen, chronic or repeated stress can damage physical health, as well as upset emotional well-being. Prolonged stress reactions are closely related to a large number of psychosomatic (SIKE-oh-so-MAT-ik) illnesses. In **psychosomatic disorders** (*psyche:* mind; *soma:* body), psychological factors contribute to actual bodily damage or to damaging changes in bodily functioning. Psychosomatic problems, therefore, are *not* the same as hypochondria. **Hypochondriacs** (HI-po-KON-dree-aks) imagine that they have diseases. There is nothing imaginary about asthma, a migraine headache, or high blood pressure. Severe psychosomatic disorders can be fatal. The person who says, "Oh it's *just* psychosomatic" misunderstands how serious stress-related diseases really are.

The most common psychosomatic problems are gastrointestinal and respiratory (stomach pain and asthma, for example), but many others exist. Typical problems include eczema (skin rash), hives, migraine headaches, rheumatoid arthritis, hypertension (high blood pressure), colitis (ulceration of the colon), and heart disease. Actually, these are only the major problems. Many lesser health complaints are also stress related. Typical examples include sore muscles, headaches, neckaches, backaches, indigestion, constipation, chronic diarrhea, fatigue, insomnia, premenstrual problems, and sexual dysfunctions (De Benedittis et al., 1990). For some of these problems biofeedback may be helpful. The next section explains how.

Biofeedback

Psychologists have discovered that people can learn to control bodily activities once thought to be involuntary. This is done by applying informational feedback to bodily control, a process called **biofeedback.** If I were to say to you, "Raise the temperature of your right hand," you probably couldn't, because you wouldn't know if you were succeeding. To make your task easier, we could attach a sensitive thermometer to your hand. The thermometer could be wired so that an increase in temperature would activate a signal light. Then, all you would have to do is try to keep the light on as much as possible. With practice and the help of biofeedback, you could learn to raise your hand temperature at will.

Biofeedback holds promise as a way to treat some psychosomatic problems (◆Fig. 11.7). For instance, people have been trained to prevent migraine headaches with biofeedback. Sensors are taped to patients' hands and foreheads. Patients then learn to redirect blood flow away from the head to their extremities. Since migraine headaches involve excessive blood flow to the head, biofeedback helps patients reduce the frequency of their headaches (Gauthier et al., 1994; Kropp et al., 1997).

Early successes led many to predict that biofeedback would offer a cure for psychosomatic illnesses, anxiety, phobias, drug abuse, and a long list of other problems. In reality, biofeedback has proved helpful but not an instant cure (Amar, 1993). Biofeedback can relieve muscle-tension headaches, migraine headaches, and chronic pain (Arena et al., 1995; Buckelew et al., 1998; Gauthier et al., 1994). It shows promise for lowering blood pressure and controlling heart rhythms (Blanchard et al., 1996; Lal et al., 1998). The technique has been used with some success to control epileptic seizures and hyperactivity in children (Potashkin & Beckles, 1990; Sterman, 1996). Insomnia also responds to biofeedback therapy (Barowsky et al., 1990).

Psychosomatic disorders Illnesses in which psychological factors contribute to bodily damage or to damaging changes in bodily functioning.

Hypochondriac A person who complains about illnesses that appear to be imaginary.

Biofeedback Information given to a person about his or her ongoing bodily activities; aids voluntary regulation of bodily states.

◆**FIGURE 11.7** *In biofeedback training, bodily processes are monitored and processed electronically. A signal is then routed back to the patient through headphones, signal lights, or other means. This information helps the patient alter bodily activities not normally under voluntary control.*

How does biofeedback help?   Some researchers believe that many of its benefits arise from *general relaxation*. Others emphasize that there is no magic in biofeedback. The method simply acts as a "mirror" to help a person perform tasks involving *self-regulation*. Just as a mirror does not comb your hair, biofeedback does not do anything by itself. It can, however, help people make desired changes in their behavior (Amar, 1993; Weems, 1998).

The Cardiac Personality

It would be a mistake to assume that stress is the sole cause of psychosomatic diseases. Genetic differences, organ weaknesses, and learned reactions to stress combine to do damage. Personality also enters the picture. As mentioned earlier, a general disease-prone personality type exists. To a degree, there are also "headache personalities," "asthma personalities," and so on. The best documented of such patterns is the "cardiac personality"— a person at high risk for heart disease.

Two cardiologists, Meyer Friedman and Ray Rosenman, offer a glimpse at how some people create stress for themselves. In a landmark study of heart problems, Friedman and Rosenman (1983) classified people as either **Type A personalities** (those who run a high risk of heart attack) or **Type B personalities** (those who are unlikely to have a heart attack). Then they did an 8-year follow-up, finding more than twice the rate of heart disease in Type A's than in Type B's (Rosenman et al., 1975).

Type A

What is the Type A personality like?   Type A people are hard driving, ambitious, highly competitive, achievement oriented, and striving. Type A people believe that with enough effort they can overcome any obstacle, and they "push" themselves accordingly.

Perhaps the most telltale signs of a Type A personality are *time urgency* and chronic *anger* or *hostility*. Type A's seem to chafe at the normal pace of events. They hurry from one activity to another, racing the clock in self-imposed urgency. As they do, they feel a constant sense of frustration and anger. Feelings of anger and hostility, in particular, are strongly related to increased risk of heart attack (Miller et al., 1996). One study found that 15 percent of a group of 25-year-old doctors and lawyers who scored high on a hostility test were dead by age 50. The most damaging pattern may occur in hostile persons who keep their anger "bottled up." Such people seethe with anger but don't express it outwardly. This increases their pulse rate and blood pressure and puts a tremendous strain on the heart (Bongard, al'Absi, & Lovallo, 1998).

To summarize, there is growing evidence that anger or hostility may be the core lethal factor of Type A behavior (Krantz & McCeney, 2002; Niaura et al., 2002). To date, hundreds of studies have supported the validity of the Type A concept. In view of this, Type A's would be wise to take their increased health risks seriously.

How are Type A people identified?   Characteristics of Type A people are summarized in the short self-identification test presented in ▲Table 11.6. If most of the list applies to

Individuals with Type A personalities feel a continuous sense of anger, irritation, and hostility.

Type A personality A personality type with an elevated risk of heart disease; characterized by time urgency, anger, and hostility.

Type B personality All personality types other than Type A; a low cardiac-risk personality.

▲TABLE 11.6	Characteristics of the Type A Person

Check the items that apply to you. Do you:

_____ Have a habit of explosively accentuating various key words in ordinary speech even when there is no need for such accentuation?

_____ Finish other persons' sentences for them?

_____ *Always* move, walk, and eat rapidly?

_____ Quickly skim reading material and prefer summaries or condensations of books?

_____ Become easily angered by slow-moving lines or traffic?

_____ Feel an impatience with the rate at which most events take place?

_____ Tend to be unaware of the details or beauty of your surroundings?

_____ Frequently strive to think of or do two or more things simultaneously?

_____ Almost always feel vaguely guilty when you relax, vacation, or do absolutely nothing for several days?

_____ Tend to evaluate your worth in quantitative terms (number of A's earned, amount of income, number of games won, and so forth)?

_____ Have nervous gestures or muscle twitches, such as grinding your teeth, clenching your fists, or drumming your fingers?

_____ Attempt to schedule more and more activities into less time and in so doing make fewer allowances for unforeseen problems?

_____ Frequently think about other things while talking to someone?

_____ Repeatedly take on more responsibilities than you can comfortably handle?

Shortened and adapted from Meyer Friedman and Ray H. Rosenman, *Type A Behavior and Your Heart* (New York: Knopf, 1983).

you, you might be a Type A. However, confirmation of your type would require more powerful testing methods. Also, remember that the original definition of Type A behavior was probably too broad. The key psychological factors that increase heart disease risk appear to be anger, hostility, and mistrust (Krantz. & McCeney, 2002). Also, while Type A behavior appears to promote heart disease, depression or distress may be what finally triggers a heart attack (Denollet & Van Heck, 2001; Dinan, 2001).

Because our society places a premium on achievement, competition, and mastery, it is not surprising that many people develop Type A personalities. The best way to avoid the self-made stress this causes is to adopt behavior that is the opposite of that listed in Table 11.6 (Karlberg, Krakau, & Unden, 1998). It is entirely possible to succeed in life without sacrificing your health or happiness in the process. People who frequently feel angry and hostile toward others may benefit from the advice of Redford Williams, a physician interested in Type A behavior. "Strategies for Reducing Hostility" summarizes his advice.

The Hardy Personality

How do Type A people who do not develop heart disease differ from those who do? Psychologists Salvatore Maddi and others have studied people who have a **hardy personality.** Such people seem to be unusually resistant to stress. The first study of hardiness began with two groups of managers at a large utility company. All of the managers held high-stress positions. Yet, some tended to get sick after stressful events, while others were rarely ill. How did the people who were thriving differ from their "stressed-out" colleagues? Both groups seemed to have traits typical of the Type A personality, so that wasn't the explanation. They were also quite similar in most other respects. The main difference was that the hardy group seemed to hold a world view that consisted of three traits (Maddi, Kahn, & Maddi, 1998):

1. They had a sense of personal *commitment* to self, work, family, and other stabilizing values.
2. They felt that they had *control* over their lives and their work.
3. They had a tendency to see life as a series of *challenges*, rather than as a series of threats or problems.

Hardy personality A personality style associated with superior stress resistance.

USINGPSYCHOLOGY Strategies for Reducing Hostility

According to Redford Williams, reducing hostility involves three goals. First, you must stop mistrusting the motives of others. Second, you must find ways to reduce how often you feel anger, indignation, irritation, and rage. Third, you must learn to be kinder and more considerate. Based on his clinical experience, Williams (1989) recommends 12 strategies for reducing hostility and increasing trust.

1. Become aware of your angry, hostile, and cynical thoughts by logging them in a notebook. Record what happened, what you thought and felt, and what actions you took. Review your hostility log at the end of each week.
2. Admit to yourself and to someone you trust that you have a problem with excessive anger and hostility.
3. Interrupt hostile, cynical thoughts whenever they occur. (The Psychology in Action section of Chapter 13 explains a thought-stopping method you can use for this step.)
4. When you have an angry, hostile, or cynical thought about someone, silently look for the ways in which it is irrational or unreasonable.
5. When you are angry, try to mentally put yourself in the other person's shoes.
6. Learn to laugh at yourself and use humor to defuse your anger.
7. Learn reliable ways to relax. Two methods are described in this chapter's Psychology in Action section. Another can be found in the Psychology in Action discussion of Chapter 13.
8. Practice trusting others more. Begin with situations where no great harm will be done if the person lets you down.
9. Make an effort to listen more to others and to really understand what they are saying.
10. Learn to be assertive, rather than aggressive, in upsetting situations. (See Chapter 14 for information about self-assertion skills.)
11. Rise above small irritations by pretending that today is the last day of your life.
12. Rather than blaming people for mistreating you and becoming angry over it, try to forgive them. We all have shortcomings.

How do such traits protect people from the effects of stress? Persons strong in *commitment* find ways of turning what they are doing into something that seems interesting and important. They get involved rather than feeling alienated.

Persons strong in *control* believe that they can influence the course of events around them. This prevents them from passively seeing themselves as victims of circumstance.

Finally, people strong in *challenge* find fulfillment in continual growth. They seek to learn from their experiences, rather than accepting easy comfort, security, and routine (Maddi, Kahn, & Maddi, 1998). Indeed, many "negative" experiences can actually enhance personal growth—if you have support from others and the skills needed to cope with challenge (Armeli, Gunthert, & Cohen, 2001).

Hardiness and Happiness

Good and bad events occur in all lives. What separates happy people from those who are unhappy is largely a matter of attitude. Happy people tend to see their lives in more positive terms, even when trouble comes their way. For example, happier people tend to find humor in disappointments. They look at setbacks as challenges. They are strengthened by losses (Lyubomirsky & Tucker, 1998). In short, happiness tends to be related to hardiness (Brebner, 1998). Why is there a connection? As psychologist Barbara Fredrickson has pointed out, positive emotions tend to broaden our mental focus. Emotions such as joy, interest, and contentment create an urge to play, to be creative, to explore, to savor life, to seek new experiences, to integrate, and to grow. When you are stressed, experiencing positive emotions can make it more likely that you will find creative solutions to your problems. Positive emotions also tend to reduce the bodily arousal that occurs when we are stressed, possibly limiting stress-related damage (Fredrickson, 2003).

The General Adaptation Syndrome

At this point we have left a very basic issue unexplained: How does stress, and our response to it, translate into disease? The answer seems to lie in the body's defenses against stress, a pattern known as the general adaptation syndrome.

The **general adaptation syndrome (G.A.S.)** is a series of bodily reactions to prolonged stress. Canadian physiologist Hans Selye (1976) noticed that the first symptoms of almost any disease or trauma (poisoning, infection, injury, or stress) are almost identical. Selye's

General adaptation syndrome (G.A.S.)
A series of bodily reactions to prolonged stress; occurs in three stages: alarm, resistance, and exhaustion.

studies showed that the body responds in the same way to any stress, be it infection, failure, embarrassment, a new job, trouble at school, or a stormy romance.

What pattern does the body's response to stress take? The G.A.S. consists of three stages: an alarm reaction, a stage of resistance, and a stage of exhaustion (Selye, 1976).

In the **alarm reaction,** your body mobilizes its resources to cope with added stress. The pituitary gland signals the adrenal glands to produce more adrenaline, noradrenaline, and cortisol. As these stress hormones are dumped into the bloodstream, some bodily processes are speeded up and others are slowed. This allows bodily resources to be applied where they are needed (Haddy & Clover, 2001).

We should all be thankful that our bodies automatically respond to emergencies. But brilliant as this emergency system is, it can also cause problems. In the first phase of the alarm reaction, people have such symptoms as headache, fever, fatigue, sore muscles, shortness of breath, diarrhea, upset stomach, loss of appetite, and a lack of energy. Notice that these are also the symptoms of being sick, of stressful travel, of high-altitude sickness, of final exams week, and (possibly) of falling in love!

During the **stage of resistance,** bodily adjustments to stress stabilize. As the body's defenses come into balance, symptoms of the alarm reaction disappear. Outwardly, everything seems normal. However, this appearance of normality comes at a high cost. The body is better able to cope with the original stressor, but its resistance to other stresses is lowered (◆Fig. 11.8). For example, animals placed in extreme cold become more resistant to the cold but more susceptible to infection. It is during the stage of resistance that the first signs of psychosomatic disorders begin to appear.

Continued stress leads to the **stage of exhaustion** in which the body's resources are drained and stress hormones are depleted. Unless a way of relieving stress is found, the result will be a psychosomatic disease, a serious loss of health, or complete collapse.

The G.A.S. may sound melodramatic if you are young and healthy or if you've never endured prolonged stress. However, stress should not be taken lightly. When Selye examined animals in the later stages of the G.A.S., he found that their adrenal glands were enlarged and discolored. There was intense shrinkage of internal organs, such as the thymus, spleen, and lymph nodes, and many animals had stomach ulcers. In addition to such direct effects, stress can disrupt the body's immune system, as described next.

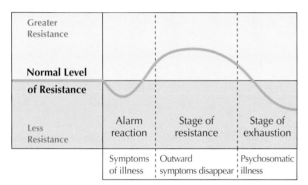

◆FIGURE 11.8 *The General Adaptation Syndrome. During the initial alarm reaction to stress, resistance falls below normal. It rises again as bodily resources are mobilized, and it remains high during the stage of resistance. Eventually, resistance falls again as the stage of exhaustion is reached. (From* The Stress of Life *by Hans Selye. Copyright © 1976 by Hans Selye. Used by permission of McGraw-Hill Book Company.)*

Stress, Illness, and Your Immune System

How else might stress affect health? An answer can be found in your body's immune system, which mobilizes defenses (such as white blood cells) against invading microbes and other disease agents. The immune system is regulated, in part, by the brain. Because of this link, stress and upsetting emotions can affect the immune system in ways that increase susceptibility to disease (Miller, Cohen, & Ritchey, 2002). (By the way, the study of links among behavior, stress, disease, and the immune system is called **psychoneuroimmunology** [Kiecolt-Glaser et al., 2002]. Try dropping that into a conversation sometime if you want to see a stress reaction!)

Studies show that the immune system is weakened in students during major exam times. Immunity is also lowered by divorce, bereavement, a troubled marriage, job loss, depression, and similar stresses (Gilbert et al., 1996; Herbert & Cohen, 1993; Stein et al., 1990). Lowered immunity explains why the "double whammy" of getting sick when you are trying to cope with

Alarm reaction First stage of the G.A.S., during which bodily resources are mobilized to cope with a stressor.

Stage of resistance Second stage of the G.A.S., during which bodily adjustments to stress stabilize, but at a high physical cost.

Stage of exhaustion Third stage of the G.A.S., at which time the body's resources are exhausted and serious health consequences occur.

Psychoneuroimmunology Study of the links among behavior, stress, disease, and the immune system.

Stress and negative emotions lower immune system activity and increase inflammation. This, in turn, raises our vulnerability to infection, worsens illness, and delays recovery.

prolonged or severe stress is so common (Biondi & Zannino, 1997). Stress causes the body to release substances that increase inflammation. This is part of the body's self-protective response to threats, but it can prolong infections and delay healing (Kiecolt-Glaser et al., 2002).

Could reducing stress help prevent illness? Yes. Various psychological approaches, such as support groups, relaxation exercises, guided imagery, and stress management training can actually boost immune system functioning (Kiecolt-Glaser & Glaser, 1992). By doing so, they help promote and restore health. For example, stress management reduced the severity of cold and flu symptoms in a group of university students (Reid, Mackinnon, & Drummond, 2001). It's also worth noting again the value of positive emotions. Happiness, laughter, and delight tend to strengthen immune system response. Doing things that make you happy can protect your health (Rosenkranz et al., 2003).

There is even evidence that stress management positive emotions can improve the chances of survival following life-threatening diseases, such as cancer, heart disease, and HIV/AIDS (Schneiderman et al., 2001). With some successes to encourage them, psychologists are now searching for the best combination of treatments to help people resist disease (Miller & Cohen, 2001). No one is immune to stress. Nevertheless, it's reassuring to know that managing stress may help to protect your immune system and your health. In the discussion that follows, we will look at what you can do to better cope with stress. But first, the following questions may help you maintain a healthy grade on your next psychology test.

STUDYBREAK *Stress and Health*

RELATE

Pick a year from your life that was unusually stressful. Use the SRRS to find your LCU score for that year. Do you think there was a connection between your LCU score and your health? Or have you observed more of a connection between microstressors and your health?

Mindy complains about her health all the time, but she actually seems to be just fine. An acquaintance of Mindy's dismisses her problems by saying, "Oh, she's not really sick. It's just psychosomatic." What's wrong with this use of the term *psychosomatic*?

Do you think you are basically a Type A or a Type B personality? To what extent do you possess traits of the hardy personality?

Can you say *psychoneuroimmunology*? Have you impressed anyone with the word yet?

LEARNING CHECK

1. Holmes's SRRS appears to predict long-range changes in health, whereas the frequency and severity of daily microstressors is closely related to immediate ratings of health. T or F?
2. Ulcers, migraine headaches, and hypochondria are all frequently psychosomatic disorders. T or F?

3. Which of the following is *not* classified as a psychosomatic disorder?
a. hypertension b. colitis c. eczema d. thymus
4. Two major elements of biofeedback training appear to be relaxation and self-regulation. T or F?
5. Evidence suggests that the most important feature of the Type A personality is a sense of time urgency rather than feelings of anger and hostility. T or F?
6. A sense of commitment, challenge, and control characterizes the hardy personality. T or F?
7. The first stage of the G.A.S. is called the _____ reaction.
8. Whereas stressful incidents suppress the immune system, stress management techniques have almost no effect on immune system functioning. T or F?

Critical Thinking

9. People with a hardy personality type appear to be especially resistant to which of the problems discussed earlier in this chapter?

ANSWERS

1. T 2. F 3. d 4. T 5. F 6. T 7. alarm 8. F 9. Learned helplessness.

STRESS MANAGEMENT—
WINNING THE STRESS GAME

] SURVEYQUESTION *What are the best strategies for managing stress?*

Stress management is the use of behavioral strategies to reduce stress and improve coping skills. As promised, this section describes strategies for managing stress. Before you continue reading, you may want to assess your level of stress again, this time using a scale developed

Stress management The application of behavioral strategies to reduce stress and improve coping skills.

▲TABLE 11.7	College Life Stress Inventory

Circle the "stress rating" number for any item that has happened to you in the last year, then add them.

EVENT	STRESS RATING	EVENT	STRESS RATING
Being raped	100	Lack of sleep	69
Finding out that you are HIV-positive	100	Change in housing situation (hassles, moves)	69
Being accused of rape	98	Competing or performing in public	69
Death of a close friend	97	Getting in a physical fight	66
Death of a close family member	96	Difficulties with a roommate	66
Contracting a sexually transmitted disease (other than AIDS)	94	Job changes (applying, new job, work hassles)	65
Concerns about being pregnant	91	Declaring a major or concerns about future plans	65
Finals week	90	A class you hate	62
Concerns about your partner being pregnant	90	Drinking or use of drugs	61
Oversleeping for an exam	89	Confrontations with professors	60
Flunking a class	89	Starting a new semester	58
Having a boyfriend or girlfriend cheat on you	85	Going on a first date	57
Ending a steady dating relationship	85	Registration	55
Serious illness in a close friend or family member	85	Maintaining a steady dating relationship	55
Financial difficulties	84	Commuting to campus or work or both	54
Writing a major term paper	83	Peer pressures	53
Being caught cheating on a test	83	Being away from home for the first time	53
Drunk driving	82	Getting sick	52
Sense of overload in school or work	82	Concerns about your appearance	52
Two exams in one day	80	Getting straight A's	51
Cheating on your boyfriend or girlfriend	77	A difficult class that you love	48
Getting married	76	Making new friends; getting along with friends	47
Negative consequences of drinking or drug use	75	Fraternity or sorority rush	47
Depression or crisis in your best friend	73	Falling asleep in class	40
Difficulties with parents	73	Attending an athletic event (e.g., football game)	20
Talking in front of a class	72		

(Source: From M. J. Renner & R. S. Mackin, "A life stress instrument for classroom use," *Teaching of Psychology*, 25(1), 1998, p. 47. Reprinted by permission of Lawrence Erlbaum Associates, Inc., and the author.)

for undergraduate students (see ▲Table 11.7). Like the SRRS, high scores on the *College Life Stress Inventory* suggest that you have been exposed to health-threatening levels of stress (Renner & Mackin, 1998).

The *College Life Stress Inventory* is scored by adding the ratings for all of the items that have happened to you in the last year. The scale below is an approximate guide to the meaning of your score. But remember, stress is an internal state. If you are good at coping with stressors, a high score may not be a problem for you.

2351+	Extremely high
1911–2350	Very high
1471–1910	High
1031–1470	Average
591–1030	Below average
151–590	Low
0–150	Very low

Now that you have a picture of your current level of stress, what can you do about it? The simplest way of coping with stress is to modify or remove its source—by leaving a stressful job, for example. Obviously this is often impossible, which is why learning to manage stress is so important.

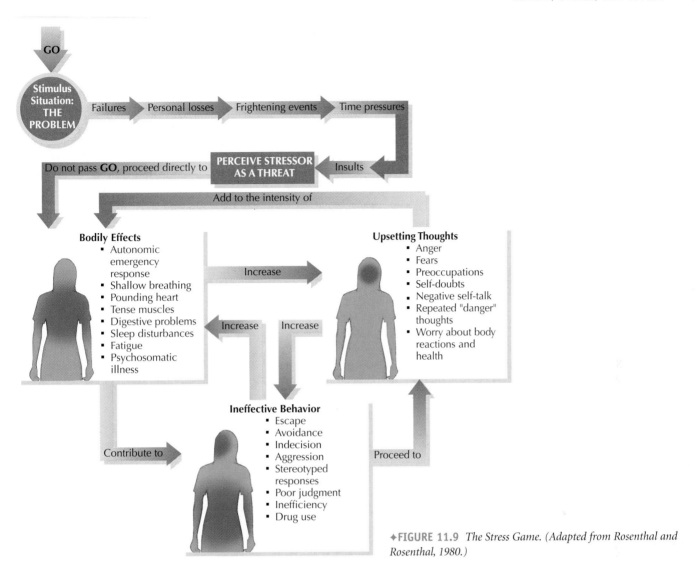

◆**FIGURE 11.9** *The Stress Game. (Adapted from Rosenthal and Rosenthal, 1980.)*

As shown in ◆Figure 11.9, stress triggers *bodily effects, upsetting thoughts,* and *ineffective behavior.* Also shown is the fact that each element worsens the others in a vicious cycle. Indeed, the basic idea of the "Stress Game" is that once it begins, *you lose*—unless you take action to break the cycle. The information that follows tells how.

Managing Bodily Reactions

Much of the immediate discomfort of stress is caused by fight-or-flight emotional responses. The body is ready to act, with tight muscles and a pounding heart. If action is prevented, we merely remain "uptight." A sensible remedy is to learn a reliable, drug-free way of relaxing.

Exercise

Stress-based arousal can be dissipated by using the body. Any full-body exercise can be effective. Swimming, dancing, jumping rope, yoga, most sports, and especially walking are valuable outlets. Regular exercise alters hormones, circulation, muscle tone, and a number of other aspects of physical functioning. Together, such changes can reduce anxiety and lower the risks for disease (Baum & Posluszny, 1999; Salmon, 2001).

Be sure to choose activities that are vigorous enough to relieve tension yet enjoyable enough to be done repeatedly. Exercising for stress management is most effective when it is done daily. As little as 30 minutes of total exercise per day, even if it occurs in short 10 to 20 minute sessions, can improve mood and energy (Hansen, Stevens, & Coast, 2001).

Meditation

Many stress counselors recommend *meditation* for quieting the body and promoting relaxation. Meditation and its effects were discussed in Chapter 5. Here, it is enough to restate that meditation is easy to learn—taking an expensive commercial course is unnecessary.

Meditation is one of the most effective ways to relax (Deckro et al., 2002). But be aware that listening to or playing music, taking nature walks, enjoying hobbies, and the like can be meditations of sorts. Anything that reliably interrupts upsetting thoughts and promotes relaxation can be helpful.

Progressive Relaxation

It is possible to relax systematically, completely, and by choice. To learn the details of how this is done, consult Chapter 13 of this book. The basic idea of **progressive relaxation** is to tighten all the muscles in a given area of your body (the arms, for instance) and then voluntarily relax them. By first tensing and relaxing each area of the body, you can learn what muscle tension feels like. Then when each area is relaxed, the change is more noticeable and more controllable. In this way it is possible, with practice, to greatly reduce tension.

Guided Imagery

In a technique called **guided imagery,** people visualize images that are calming, relaxing, or beneficial in other ways. Relaxation, for instance, can be promoted by visualizing peaceful scenes. Pick several places where you feel safe, calm, and at ease. Typical locations might be a beach or lake, the woods, floating on an air mattress in a warm pool, or lying in the sun at a quiet park. To relax, vividly imagine yourself in one of these locations. In the visualized scene, you should be alone and in a comfortable position. It is important to visualize the scene as realistically as possible. Try to feel, taste, smell, hear, and see what you would actually experience in the calming scene. Practice forming such images several times a day for about 5 minutes each time. When your scenes become familiar and detailed, they can be used to reduce anxiety and encourage relaxation (Rosenthal, 1993).

Modifying Ineffective Behavior

Stress is often made worse by our misguided responses to it. The following suggestions may help you deal with stress more effectively.

Slow Down

Remember that stress can be self-generated. Try to deliberately do things at a slower pace—especially if your pace has speeded up over the years. Tell yourself, "What counts most is not if I get there first, but if I get there at all" or "My goal is distance, not speed."

Organize

Disorganization creates stress. Try to take a fresh look at your situation and get organized. Setting priorities can be a real stress fighter. Ask yourself what's really important and concentrate on the things that count. Learn to let go of trivial but upsetting irritations. And above all, when you are feeling stressed, remember to K.I.S.: **K**eep **I**t **S**imple. (Some people prefer K.I.S.S.: Keep It Simple, Stupid.)

Strike a Balance

Work, school, family, friends, interests, hobbies, recreation, community, church—there are many important elements in a satisfying life. Damaging stress often comes from letting one element—especially work or school—get blown out of proportion. Your goal should be quality in life, not quantity. Try to strike a balance between challenging "good stress" and relaxation. Remember, when you are "doing nothing," you are actually doing something very

Progressive relaxation A method for producing deep relaxation of all parts of the body.

Guided imagery Intentional visualization of images that are calming, relaxing, or beneficial in other ways.

important: Set aside time for "me acts" such as loafing, browsing, puttering, playing, and napping.

Recognize and Accept Your Limits

Many of us set unrealistic and perfectionistic goals. Given that no one can ever be perfect, this attitude leaves many people feeling inadequate, no matter how well they have performed. Set gradual, achievable goals for yourself. Also, set realistic limits on what you try to do on any given day. Learn to say no to added demands or responsibilities.

Seek Social Support

Social support (close, positive relationships with others) facilitates good health and morale. People with close, supportive relationships have better immune responses and better health (Kiecolt-Glaser et al., 2002). Apparently, support from family and friends serves as a buffer to cushion the impact of stressful events.

Women tend to make better use of social support than men do. Women who are stressed seek support and nurture others. Men are more likely to become aggressive or to withdraw emotionally (Taylor et al., 2000). This may be why "manly men" won't ask for help, whereas women in trouble call their friends! Where stress is concerned, many men could benefit from adopting women's tendency to tend and befriend others.

Write About Your Feelings

If you don't have someone you can talk to about stressful events, you might try expressing your thoughts and feelings in writing. Several studies have found that students who write about their upsetting experiences, thoughts, and feelings are better able to cope with stress. They also experience fewer illnesses, and they get better grades (Esterling et al., 1999; Pennebaker & Francis, 1996). Writing about your feelings tends to leave your mind clearer. This makes it easier to pay attention to life's challenges and come up with effective coping strategies (Klein & Boals, 2001a, 2001b). Thus, after you write about your feelings, it helps to make specific plans for coping with upsetting experiences (Cameron & Nicholls, 1998).

Avoiding Upsetting Thoughts

Assume you are taking a test. Suddenly you realize that you are running short of time. If you say to yourself, "Oh no, this is terrible, I've blown it now," your body's response will probably be sweating, tenseness, and a knot in your stomach. On the other hand, if you say, "I should have watched the time, but getting upset won't help, I'll just take one question at a time," your stress level will be much lower.

As stated earlier, stress is greatly affected by the views we take of events. Physical symptoms and a tendency to make poor decisions are increased by negative thoughts or "self-talk." In many cases what you say to yourself can be the difference between coping and collapsing (Matheny et al., 1996).

Coping Statements

Psychologist Donald Meichenbaum has popularized a technique called **stress inoculation.** In it, clients learn to fight fear and anxiety with an internal monologue of positive coping statements. First, clients learn to identify and monitor **negative self-statements** (self-critical thoughts that increase anxiety). Negative thoughts are a problem because they tend to directly elevate physical arousal. To counter this effect, clients learn to replace negative statements with coping statements from a supplied list. Eventually they are encouraged to make their own lists (Saunders et al., 1996).

How are coping statements applied? **Coping statements** are reassuring and self-enhancing. They are used to block out, or counteract, negative self-talk in stressful situations. Before giving a short speech, for instance, you would replace "I'm scared," "I can't do this," "My mind will go blank and I'll panic," or "I'll sound stupid and boring" with "I'll give my speech on something I like," or "I'll breathe deeply before I start my speech," or "My

Social support Close, positive relationships with other people.

Stress inoculation Use of positive coping statements to control fear and anxiety.

Negative self-statements Self-critical thoughts that increase anxiety and lower performance.

Coping statements Reassuring, self-enhancing statements that are used to stop self-critical thinking.

pounding heart just means I'm psyched up to do my best." Additional examples of coping statements follow.

PREPARING FOR STRESSFUL SITUATION

I'll just take things one step at a time.
If I get nervous I'll just pause a moment.
Tomorrow I'll be through it.
I've managed to do this before.
What exactly do I have to do?

CONFRONTING THE STRESSFUL SITUATION

Relax now, this can't really hurt me.
Stay organized, focus on the task.
There's no hurry, take it step by step.
Nobody's perfect, I'll just do my best.
It will be over soon, just be calm.

Meichenbaum cautions that saying the "right" things to yourself may not be enough to improve stress tolerance. You must practice this approach in actual stress situations. Also, it is important to develop your own personal list of coping statements by finding what works for you. Ultimately, the value of learning this, and other stress management skills, ties back into the idea that much stress is self-generated. Knowing that you can manage a demanding situation is in itself a major antidote for stress. In a recent study, college students who learned stress inoculation not only had less anxiety and depression, but better self-esteem, as well (Schiraldi & Brown, 2001).

Lighten Up

Humor is worth cultivating as a way to reduce stress. A good sense of humor can lower your distress/stress reaction to difficult events (Lefcourt & Thomas, 1998). In addition, an ability to laugh at life's ups and downs is associated with better immunity to disease (McClelland & Cheriff, 1997). Don't be afraid to laugh at yourself and at the many ways in which we humans make things difficult for ourselves. You've probably heard the following advice about everyday stresses: "Don't sweat the small stuff," and "It's all small stuff." Humor is one of the best antidotes for anxiety and emotional distress because it helps put things into perspective (Cann, Holt, & Calhoun, 1999; Henman, 2001). The vast majority of events are only as stressful as you allow them to be. Have some fun. It's perfectly healthy.

A Look Ahead

The ideas we have reviewed here make it clear that each of us has a personal responsibility for maintaining and promoting health. In the Psychology in Action section that follows, we will return to the topic of unsafe sex. This is one risk factor that can be almost completely eliminated by relatively small changes in behavior.

STUDYBREAK   Y   *Coping with Stress*

RELATE

If you were going to put together a "tool kit" for stress management, what items would you include?

LEARNING CHECK

1. Exercise, meditation, and progressive relaxation are considered effective ways of countering negative self-statements. T or F?
2. Research shows that social support from family and friends has little effect on the health consequences of stress. T or F?

3. One element of stress inoculation is training in the use of positive coping statements. T or F?
4. People who write about their feelings tend to dwell on stressful events, which reduces their ability to meet life challenges. T or F?

Critical Thinking

5. Steve always feels extremely pressured when the due date arrives for his major term papers. How could he reduce stress in such instances?

ANSWERS

1. F 2. F 3. T 4. F 5. The stress associated with doing term papers can be almost completely eliminated by making a long-term assignment into many small daily or weekly assignments. Students who habitually procrastinate are often amazed at how pleasant college work can be once they renounce "brinkmanship."

Psychology in Action

STDs and Safer Sex—Risk and Responsibility

] SURVEYQUESTION *How can sexually transmitted diseases be prevented?*

It's difficult to change eating or exercise habits or to quit smoking. Avoiding risky sex should be far easier. However, a surprisingly large number of people continue to play Russian roulette with their health. With this in mind, let's briefly address the topic of safer sex.

Sexually Transmitted Diseases

A **sexually transmitted disease** (**STD**) is an infection passed from one person to another by intimate physical contact. Sexually active people run a high risk of getting chlamydia (klah-MID-ee-ah), gonorrhea, hepatitis B, herpes, syphilis, and other STDs. Many people who carry STDs remain *asymptomatic* (a-SIMP-teh-mat-ik: lacking obvious symptoms). It is easy to have an infection without knowing it. Likewise, it is often impossible to tell if a sexual partner is infectious. Thus, risky sex is a serious hazard. A recent study of sexually active teenage girls engaging in risky sex is a case in point. Nearly 90 percent of the girls thought that they had virtually no chance of getting an STD. In reality, over the next 18 months 1 in 4 got chlamydia or gonorrhea (Ethier et al., 2003).

For many sexually active people, the human immunodeficiency virus (HIV) has added a new threat. HIV is a sexually transmitted disease that disables the immune system. Whereas most other STDs are treatable, HIV infections can be lethal. Check your knowledge about HIV against the following summary.

The AIDS Memorial Quilt was begun in 1985 to commemorate those who have died from AIDS. Today, the quilt has grown to immense size, symbolizing the extent of the AIDS epidemic. Originally the quilt memorialized only homosexual victims. It now includes heterosexual men, women, and children, signifying that AIDS respects no boundaries.

Leonard Lessin/Photo Researchers

HIV/AIDS

Acquired immune deficiency syndrome (AIDS) is caused by an HIV infection. As the immune system weakens, other "opportunistic" diseases invade the body. Most AIDS victims eventually die of multiple infections (although a new three-drug therapy has greatly improved the odds of survival). The first symptoms of AIDS may show up as little as 2 months after infection, but they typically don't appear for 10 years. Because of this long incubation period, infected persons often pass the AIDS virus on to others without knowing it. Medical testing can detect an HIV infection. However, for at least the first 6 months after becoming infected, a person can test negative while carrying the virus. A negative test result, therefore, is no guarantee that a person is a "safe" sex partner.

HIV infections are spread by direct contact with body fluids—especially blood, semen, and vaginal secretions. The AIDS virus cannot be transmitted by casual contact. People do not get AIDS from shaking hands, touching or using objects touched by an AIDS patient, eating food prepared by an infected person, or from social kissing, sweat or tears, sharing drinking glasses, sharing towels, and so forth.

AIDS can be spread by all forms of sexual intercourse, and it has affected persons of all sexual orientations. One in 75 men and 1 in 700 women in North America are now infected with HIV. As a result, people who engage in unsafe sex are gambling with their lives—at very poor odds (◆Fig. 11.10). HIV infection is the leading cause of death among women and

Sexually transmitted disease (STD) A disease that is typically passed from one person to the next by intimate physical contact; a venereal disease.

◆FIGURE 11.10 *Popular professional basketball star Earvin "Magic" Johnson stunned fans when he announced that he had tested positive for HIV. Johnson, who is heterosexual, emphasized that his infection is a warning that anyone who is sexually active can contract the AIDS virus if they don't follow safe sex practices. Johnson further stressed that abstinence is the surest way to prevent AIDS. Johnson's infection increased public awareness about AIDS. Unfortunately, though, it has resulted in little real change in risky behavior (Brown et al., 1996).*

men between the ages of 25 and 44 (Gayle, 2000). Worldwide, three million people die each year from HIV/AIDS and 5 million new infections occur.

Behavioral Risk Factors

Sexually active people can do much to protect their own health. The behaviors listed here are risky when performed with an infected person.

RISKY BEHAVIORS

- Sharing drug needles and syringes
- Anal sex, with or without a condom
- Vaginal or oral sex with someone who injects drugs or engages in anal sex
- Sex with someone you don't know well or with someone you know has had several partners
- Unprotected sex (without a condom) with an infected partner
- Having two or more sex partners (additional partners further increase the risk)

In the United States, between 2 and 4 of every 100 adults put themselves at high risk by engaging in the behaviors just listed (Gayle, 2000). For many, drinking alcohol greatly increases the likelihood that they will take sexual risks (Corbin & Fromme, 2002).

It's important to remember that you can't tell from appearance if a person is infected. Many people would be surprised to learn that their partners have engaged in behavior that places them both at risk (Seal & Palmer-Seal, 1996).

The preceding high-risk behaviors can be contrasted with the following list of safer sexual practices. Note, however, that unless a person completely abstains, sex can be made safer, but not risk-free.

SAFER SEX PRACTICES

- Not having sex
- Sex with one mutually faithful, uninfected partner
- Not injecting drugs
- Discussing contraception with partner
- Being selective regarding sexual partners
- Reducing the number of sexual partners
- Discussing partner's sexual health prior to engaging in sex
- Not engaging in sex while intoxicated
- Using a condom

Sexually active persons should practice safer sex until their partner's sexual history and/or health has been clearly established. A study of heterosexually active adults found that 62 percent did not practice safer sex with their last partner. Most of these "gamblers" knew too little about their partners to be assured that they were not taking a big risk. The most common excuses they gave for engaging in risky sex were (Kusseling et al., 1996):

REASONS FOR NOT HAVING SAFER SEX	PERCENTAGE GIVING EXCUSE
Condom not available	20
Didn't want to use a condom	19
"Couldn't stop ourselves"	15
Partner didn't want to use a condom	14
Alcohol or drug use	11

One chilling study of HIV patients—who knew they were infectious—found that 41 percent of those who were sexually active did not always use condoms (Sobel et al., 1996)! Thus, responsibility for "safer sex" rests with each sexually active person. It is unwise to count on a sexual partner for protection against HIV infection or any STD, for that matter. Over the next 15 years, 65 million more people will die of AIDS unless prevention efforts are greatly expanded (Altman, 2002).

Isn't it possible that practicing safer sex would be interpreted as a sign that you mistrust your lover?   Actually, taking precautions could, instead, be defined as a way of showing that you really care about the welfare of your partner (Hammer et al., 1996). As is the case with other behavioral risk factors, it's certainly a way of showing that you care about your own health.

STUDYBREAK ◆ *STDs and Safer Sex*

RELATE

As a counselor, you are working with a young person who seems to be sexually active. What can you tell this person about STDs and safer sex practices?

LEARNING CHECK

1. For at least the first 6 months after becoming infected with HIV, a person can test negative while carrying the virus. T or F?
2. Because HIV is spread by direct contact with body fluids, it can be transmitted by social kissing or contact with food or dishes handled by an AIDS patient. T or F?

3. In the United States, at least 2 of every 100 adults engage in high risk sexual behavior. T or F?
4. If people know they have STDs, it is extremely rare for them to engage in unprotected sex. T or F?

Critical Thinking

5. Of the following reasons that teenage boys and girls give for engaging in sex: love, curiosity, sexual gratification, peer pressure, and "everyone's doing it," which do you think they rank first, and which last?

ANSWERS

1. T 2. F 3. T 4. F 5. Peer pressure ranks first (cited by 30 percent of those surveyed) and love ranked last (cited by 8 percent) ("Teen sex," 1989).

CHAPTER IN REVIEW

Major Points

- A variety of personal habits and behavior patterns affect health.
- Maintaining good health is a personal responsibility, not a matter of luck. Wellness is based on minimizing risk factors and engaging in health-promoting behaviors.
- Stress is a normal part of life; however, it is also a major risk factor for illness and disease.

- While some events are more stressful than others, stress always represents an interaction between people and the environments in which they live.
- Personality characteristics affect the amount of stress a person experiences and the subsequent risk of illness.
- The body's reactions to stress can directly damage internal organs and stress impairs the body's immune system, increasing susceptibility to disease.

- The damaging effects of stress can be reduced with stress management techniques.

Summary

What is health psychology? How does behavior affect health?

- Health psychologists are interested in behavior that helps maintain and promote health.
- Studies of health and illness have identified a number of behavioral risk factors and health-promoting behaviors.
- Health psychologists have pioneered efforts to prevent the development of unhealthy habits and to improve well-being through community health campaigns.

What is stress? What factors determine its severity?

- Stress occurs when demands are placed on an organism to adjust or adapt.
- Stress is more damaging in situations involving pressure, a lack of control, unpredictability of the stressor, and intense or repeated emotional shocks.
- Stress is intensified when a situation is perceived as a threat and when a person does not feel competent to cope with it.
- In work settings, prolonged stress can lead to burnout.
- The primary appraisal of a situation greatly affects our emotional response to it.
- During a secondary appraisal, a problem-focused or emotion-focused way of coping is selected.

What causes frustration, and what are typical reactions to it?

- Frustration is the negative emotional state that occurs when progress toward a goal is blocked.
- External frustrations are based on delay, failure, rejection, loss, and other direct blocking of motives. Personal frustration is related to personal characteristics over which one has little control.
- Frustrations of all types become more intense as the strength, urgency, or importance of the blocked motive increases.
- Major behavioral reactions to frustration include persistence, more vigorous responding, circumvention, direct aggression, displaced aggression (including scapegoating), and escape or withdrawal.

Are there different types of conflict? How do people react to conflict?

- Conflict occurs when one must choose between contradictory alternatives.
- Five major types of conflict are approach-approach, avoidance-avoidance, approach-avoidance, double approach-avoidance, and multiple approach-avoidance.

- Approach-approach conflicts are usually the easiest to resolve.
- Avoidance conflicts are difficult to resolve and are characterized by inaction, indecision, freezing, and a desire to escape.
- People usually remain in approach-avoidance conflicts but fail to fully resolve them, which leads to ambivalence and partial approach.
- Vacillation is a common reaction to double approach-avoidance conflicts.

What are defense mechanisms?

- Anxiety, threat, or feelings of inadequacy frequently lead to the use of defense mechanisms that reduce anxiety.
- Many defense mechanisms have been identified, including compensation, denial, fantasy, intellectualization, isolation, projection, rationalization, reaction formation, regression, repression, and sublimation.

What do we know about coping with feelings of helplessness and depression?

- Learned helplessness has been used as a model for understanding depression. Mastery training acts as an antidote to helplessness.
- Depression is a major, and surprisingly common, emotional problem. Actions and thoughts that reverse feelings of helplessness tend to reduce depression.
- The college blues are a relatively mild form of depression. Learning to manage college work and to challenge self-critical thinking can help cure the college blues.

How is stress related to health and disease?

- Work with the *Social Readjustment Rating Scale* indicates that multiple life changes tend to increase long-range susceptibility to accident or illness.
- Immediate psychological and mental health is more closely related to the intensity and severity of daily hassles (microstressors).
- Intense or prolonged stress may cause damage in the form of psychosomatic problems.
- During biofeedback training, bodily processes are monitored and converted to a signal that tells what the body is doing. This allows people to control some bodily activities and alleviate some psychosomatic illnesses.
- People with Type A personalities are competitive, striving, hostile, and impatient. These characteristics—especially hostility—double the risk of heart attack.
- People who have traits of the hardy personality seem to be unusually resistant to stress.
- The body reacts to stress in a series of stages called the general adaptation syndrome (G.A.S.).

- The stages of the G.A.S. are alarm, resistance, and exhaustion. The G.A.S. appears to explain how psychosomatic disorders develop.
- Studies of psychoneuroimmunology show that stress also lowers the body's immunity to disease.

What are the best strategies for managing stress?

- A sizable number of coping skills can be applied to manage stress. Most of these focus on one of three areas: bodily effects, ineffective behavior, and upsetting thoughts.

How can sexually transmitted diseases be prevented?

- Many sexually active people continue to take unnecessary risks with their health by failing to follow safer sex practices.
- Safe-sex practices help protect your own health and they show that you care about the welfare of your partner.

Interactive Learning

Internet addresses frequently change. To find the sites listed here, visit www.psychology. wadsworth.com/coon_journey2e for an updated list of Internet addresses and direct links to relevant sites.

PSYCHOLOGY: A JOURNEY COMPANION WEB SITE Online quizzes, flash cards, and other helpful study aids for this text. *www.psychology.wadsworth.com/coon_journey2e*

BURNOUT TEST A short questionnaire on job burnout.

COPING WITH TERRORISM Information about emotional reactions to terrorism; provided by the American Psychological Association.

FOCUS ON STRESS A series of articles about stress.

HEALTHYWAY A set of pages on health, nutrition, addictions, disabilities, sexuality, fitness, and much more.

PREVENTIVE HEALTH CENTER A general source of information on how to maintain health and prevent disease.

STRESS MANAGEMENT: REVIEW OF PRINCIPLES Links to articles on stress management.

STRESS, ANXIETY, FEARS, AND PSYCHOSOMATIC DISORDERS A comprehensive source on stress, anxiety, and related disorders.

TYPE A BEHAVIOR Describes Type A behavior, with links to an on-line test and related sites.

INFOTRAC COLLEGE EDITION For recent articles related to the college blues and more serious forms of depression, use Key Words search for MENTAL DEPRESSION.

PSYCHNOW! 6c. Coping with Emotion 6d. Stress and Health.

Test Your Knowledge: Health, Stress, and Coping

The questions that follow are only a sample of what you need to know. If you miss any of the items, you should review the entire chapter and get more practice with *WebTutor* or the *Practice Quizzes* that came with this book. Another way to prepare for tests is to use the printed *Study Guide* that is available for this text.

1. Lifestyle diseases related to just six behaviors account for 70 percent of all medical costs. The behaviors are smoking, alcohol and drug abuse, poor diet, insufficient exercise, and A. driving too fast   B. excessive sun exposure   C. unsafe sex   D. exposure to toxins

2. People who have a disease-prone personality style are anxious and hostile. These traits can also be observed in the _____ personality.
   A. emotion-focused   B. problem-focused
   C. SSRS-prone   D. Type A

3. Health promoting behaviors that combat hypertension include the following: lose weight, consume less sodium, use alcohol sparingly, and get more
   A. sleep   B. exercise   C. LCUs   D. cholesterol

4. Which of the following is NOT an STD?
   A. herpes   B. eczema   C. chlamydia   D. hepatitis B

5. For the first _____ after infection, a negative test result for the HIV virus is no guarantee that a person is a "safe" sex partner.
   A. 3 weeks   B. 6 weeks   C. 6 months   D. 3 years

6. A good indication that stress is a normal part of life is provided by the existence of
   A. learned helplessness   B. hypochondria   C. sublimation
   D. eustress

7. According to Richard Lazarus, choosing a way to meet a threat or challenge takes place during the
   A. primary stress reaction   B. secondary stress reaction
   C. primary appraisal   D. secondary appraisal

8. Aggression is an especially common reaction to
   A. frustration   B. scapegoating   C. approach conflicts
   D. ambivalence

9. Displaced aggression is closely related to the pattern of behavior known as
   A. scapegoating   B. leaving the field   C. stereotyped responding   D. burnout

10. You would be most likely to experience vacillation if you found yourself in
    A. an approach-approach conflict   B. an avoidance-avoidance conflict   C. a double approach-avoidance conflict   D. the condition called emotion-focused coping

11. Justifying your actions by making excuses that appear to explain your behavior is called
    A. sublimation   B. reaction formation   C. compensation
    D. rationalization

12. Learned helplessness tends to occur when events appear to be
    A. frustrating   B. in conflict   C. uncontrollable
    D. problem focused

13. Ratings on the SRRS are based on the total number of _____ a person has for the preceding year.
    A. hassles   B. LCUs   C. STDs   D. psychosomatic illnesses

14. Anger, hostility, and mistrust appear to be the core lethal factors in
    A. hypochondria   B. learned helplessness   C. the G.A.S.
    D. Type A behavior

15. In many ways, a person who has a hardy personality is the opposite of a person who has
    A. a high STD score   B. a low LCU score   C. Type A traits   D. Type B traits

16. The first signs of psychosomatic disorders begin to appear during the stage of
    A. alarm   B. exhaustion   C. resistance   D. appraisal

17. Students taking stressful final exams are more susceptible to the cold virus, a pattern best explained by the concept of
    A. the disease-prone personality   B. psychoneuroimmunology   C. emotion-focused coping   D. reaction formation

18. A person using progressive relaxation for stress management is most likely trying to control which component of stress?
    A. bodily reactions   B. upsetting thoughts   C. ineffective behavior   D. the primary appraisal

19. Exercise, meditation, progressive relaxation, and guided imagery would be least likely to help a person who is in the G.A.S. stage of
    A. alarm   B. resistance   C. exhaustion   D. adaptation

20. While taking a stressful classroom test you say to yourself, "Stay organized, focus on the task." It's obvious that you are using
    A. guided imagery   B. coping statements   C. LCUs
    D. guided relaxation

ANSWERS   1. c 2. d 3. b 4. b 5. c 6. d 7. d 8. a 9. a 10. c 11. d 12. c 13. b 14. d 15. c 16. c 17. b 18. a 19. c 20. b

Psychological Disorders

Beware the Helicopters

"The helicopters. Oh no, not the helicopters. Have come to tear the feathers out of my frontal lobes. Help me, nurse, help me, can't you hear them?

Gotta get back into my body to save it . . . . The doctor is thinking I would make good glue."

These are the words of Carol North, a psychiatrist who survived schizophrenia. In addition to being plagued by hallucinated helicopters, Carol heard voices that said: "Be good," "Do bad," "Stand up," "Sit down," "Collide with the other world," "Do you want a cigar?" (North, 1987).

Carol North's painful journey into the shadows of madness left her incapacitated for nearly 20 years. Her case is but one hint of the magnitude of mental health problems. Here are the facts on psychological disorders:

- 1 out of every 100 persons will become so severely disturbed as to require hospitalization at some point in his or her lifetime.
- Some 3 to 6 percent of the aged suffer from organic psychoses.
- 7 percent of the population has an anxiety-related disorder.
- 1 out of every 8 school-age children is seriously maladjusted.
- 10 to 20 percent or more of all adults suffer a major depression in their lifetime.
- Each year in North America, more than 2 million people are admitted for psychiatric treatment in general hospitals.

What does it mean to be "crazy"? A hundred years ago, doctors and non-professionals alike used terms such as "crazy," "insane," "cracked," and "lunatic" quite freely. The "insane" were thought of as bizarre and definitely different from you or me. Today, our understanding of psychological disorders is more sophisticated. To draw the line between normal and abnormal, we must weigh some complex issues. We'll explore some of them in this chapter, as well as an array of psychological problems.

Royalty-Free/Corbis

Survey Questions

- How is normality defined, and what are the major psychological disorders?
- What is a personality disorder?
- What problems result when a person suffers high levels of anxiety?
- How do psychologists explain anxiety-based disorders?
- What are the general characteristics of psychotic disorders?
- What is the nature of a delusional disorder?
- What forms does schizophrenia take? What causes it?
- What are mood disorders? What causes depression?
- Why do people commit suicide? Can suicide be prevented?

NORMALITY—WHAT IS NORMAL?

] SURVEYQUESTION *How is normality defined, and what are the major psychological disorders?*

Deciding if a person's behavior is abnormal is harder than it might seem. The conservative, church-going housewife down the street might be flagrantly psychotic and a lethal danger to her children. The reclusive eccentric who hangs out at the park could be the most sane person in town. Let's begin our discussion with some basic factors that affect judgments of normality.

"That guy is really wacko. His porch lights are dimming." "Yeah, the butter's sliding off his waffle. I think he's ready to go postal." Informally, it's tempting to make snap judgments about mental health. However, to seriously classify people as psychologically unhealthy raises complex and age-old issues. The scientific study of mental, emotional, and behavioral disorders is known as **psychopathology.** The term also refers to mental disorders themselves, such as schizophrenia or depression, and to behavior patterns that make people unhappy and impair their personal growth (Butcher, Mineka, & Hooley, 2004).

Defining abnormality can be tricky. We might begin by saying that psychopathology is characterized by *subjective discomfort* (private feelings of discomfort, unhappiness, or emotional distress) like Carol North endured.

But couldn't a person be seriously disturbed without feeling discomfort?   Yes. Psychopathology doesn't always cause personal anguish. A person suffering from mania might feel elated and "on top of the world." Also, a *lack* of discomfort may reveal a problem. For example, if you showed no signs of grief after the death of a close friend, we might suspect psychopathology. In practice, subjective discomfort explains most instances in which people voluntarily seek professional help.

Some psychologists use statistics to define normality more objectively. **Statistical abnormality** refers to scoring very high or low on some dimension, such as intelligence, anxiety, or depression. Anxiety, for example, is a feature of several psychological disorders. To measure it, we could create a test to learn how many people show low, medium, or high levels of anxiety. Usually, the results of such tests will form a *normal* (bell-shaped) *curve*. (*Normal* in this case refers only to the *shape* of the curve.) Notice that most people score near the middle of a normal curve; very few have extremely high and low scores (◆Fig. 12.1). A person who deviates from the average by being anxious all the time (high anxiety) might be abnormal. So, too, might a person who never feels anxiety.

Then statistical abnormality tells us nothing about the meaning of deviations from the norm?   Right. It is as statistically "abnormal" (unusual) for a person to score above 145 on an IQ test as it is to score below 55. However, only the lower score is regarded as "abnormal" or undesirable (Wakefield, 1992).

Psychopathology The scientific study of mental, emotional, and behavioral disorders; also, abnormal or maladaptive behavior.

Statistical abnormality Abnormality defined on the basis of an extreme score on some dimension, such as IQ or anxiety.

Statistical definitions also can't tell us *where to draw the line* between normality and abnormality. To take a new example, we could obtain the average frequency of sexual intercourse for persons of a particular age, sex, sexual orientation, and marital status. Clearly, a person who feels driven to have sex dozens of times a day has a problem. But as we move back toward the norm we face the problem of drawing lines. How often does a normal behavior have to occur before it becomes abnormal? As you can see, statistical boundary lines tend to be somewhat arbitrary (Widiger & Trull, 1991).

Atypical behavior or nonconformity may underlie some disorders. **Social nonconformity** refers to disobeying public standards for acceptable conduct. Extreme nonconformity can lead to destructive or self-destructive behavior. (Think, for instance, of a drug abuser or a prostitute.) However, we must be careful to separate unhealthy nonconformity from creative lifestyles. Many eccentric "characters" are charming and emotionally stable. Note, too, that strictly following social norms is no guarantee of mental health. In some cases, psychopathology involves rigid conformity.

A young woman ties a thick rubber cord around her ankles, screams hysterically, and jumps head-first off a bridge. Twenty years ago, the woman's behavior might have seemed completely crazy. Today, it is a routine form of entertainment. Before any behavior can be defined as abnormal, we must consider the *situational context* (social situation, behavioral setting, or general circumstances) in which it occurs. Is it normal to stand outside and water a lawn with a hose? It depends on whether it is raining. Is it abnormal for a grown man to remove his pants and expose himself to another man or woman in a place of business? It depends on whether the other person is a bank clerk or a doctor!

Almost any imaginable behavior can be considered normal in some contexts. In mid-October 1972, an airplane carrying a rugby team crashed in the snow-capped Andes of South America. Incredibly, 16 of the 45 people onboard survived 73 days in deep snow and subfreezing temperatures. They were forced to use extremely grim measures to do so—they ate the bodies of those who died in the crash.

As implied by our earlier discussion of social norms, culture is one of the most influential contexts in which any behavior is judged. In some cultures it is considered normal to defecate or urinate in public or to appear naked in public. In our culture such behaviors would be considered unusual or abnormal. In Muslim cultures, women who remain completely housebound are considered normal or even virtuous. In western cultures they might be diagnosed as suffering from a disorder called agoraphobia (Widiger & Sankis, 2000). (Agoraphobia is described later in this chapter.)

Thus, *cultural relativity* (the idea that judgments are made relative to the values of one's culture) can affect the diagnosis of psychological disorders. (See "The Politics of Madness.") Still, *all* cultures classify people as abnormal if they fail to communicate with others or are consistently unpredictable in their actions.

Number of cases (y-axis) / *Characteristic level of anxiety* (x-axis): Extremely low — Low — Moderate — High — Extremely high; "Abnormal?" regions at both extremes.

✦**FIGURE 12.1** *The number of people displaying a personal characteristic may help define what is statistically abnormal.*

Social nonconformity does not automatically indicate psychopathology.

Core Features of Disordered Behavior

If abnormality is so hard to define, how are judgments of psychopathology made? It's clear that all of the standards we have discussed are *relative.* However, abnormal behavior does have two core features. First, it is **maladaptive.** Rather than helping people cope successfully, abnormal behavior makes it more difficult for them to cope with day-to-day life. Second, people suffering from psychological disorders *lose the ability to control* their thoughts, behaviors, or feelings adequately. For example, gambling is not a problem if a person bets for entertainment and can maintain self-control. However, compulsive gam-

Social nonconformity Failure to conform to societal norms or the usual minimum standards for social conduct.

Maladaptive behavior Behavior that makes it difficult to adapt to the environment and meet the demands of day-to-day life.

The year is 1840. You are a slave who has tried repeatedly to escape from a cruel and abusive master. An expert is consulted about your "abnormal" behavior. His conclusion? You are suffering from "drapetomania," a mental "disorder" that causes slaves to run away (Wakefield, 1992).

As this example suggests, psychiatric terms are easily abused. Historically, some have been applied to culturally disapproved behaviors that are not really disorders. For example, all of the following were once considered disorders: drapetomania, childhood masturbation, lack of vaginal orgasm, self-defeating personality (applied mainly to women), homosexuality, and nymphomania (a woman with a healthy sexual appetite) (Wakefield, 1992). Even today, race, gender, and social class continue to affect the diagnosis of various disorders (Nathan & Langenbucher, 1999).

Gender is probably the most common source of bias in judging normality because standards tend to be based on males (Hartung

& Widiger, 1998). According to psychologist Paula Caplan (1995) and others, women are penalized both for conforming to female stereotypes and for ignoring them. If a woman is independent, aggressive, and unemotional, she may be considered "unhealthy." Yet at the same time, a woman who is vain, emotional, irrational, and dependent on others (all "feminine" traits in our culture) may be classified as a histrionic, or dependent personality (Bornstein, 1996). Indeed, a majority of persons classified as having dependent personality disorder are women. In view of this, Paula Caplan asks, Why isn't there a category called "delusional dominating personality disorder" for obnoxious men (Caplan, 1995)?

The differences we have reviewed illustrate the subtle influence that culture can have on perceptions of disorder and normality. Be cautious before you leap to conclusions about the mental health of others (DSM-IV-TR, 2000).

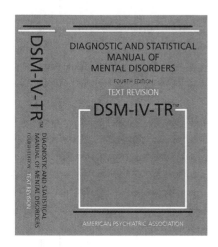

DSM-IV-TR is not the only system for classifying mental disorders. Nevertheless, most activities in mental health settings—from diagnosis to therapy to billing of insurance companies—are influenced by the DSM. DSM-IV-TR is both a scientific document and a social one. Major disorders are well-documented problems. Some problems, however, have little to do with "mental illness." Instead, they are primarily socially disapproved behaviors. (Reprinted with permission from the *Diagnostic and Statistical Manual of Mental Disorders, Fourth Edition, Text Revision,* copyright 2000. American Psychiatric Association.)

Mental disorder A significant impairment in psychological functioning.

Psychotic disorder A severe mental disorder characterized by a retreat from reality, by hallucinations and delusions, and by social withdrawal.

bling is a sign of psychopathology. The voices that Carol North kept hearing are a prime example of what it means to lose control of one's thoughts. In extreme cases, people become a danger to themselves or others, which is clearly maladaptive (Widiger & Sankis, 2000).

In practice, deciding that a person needs help usually occurs when the person *does something* (hits a person, hallucinates, stares into space, collects rolls of toilet paper, and so forth) that *annoys* or *gains the attention* of a person in a *position of power* in the person's life (an employer, teacher, parent, spouse, or the person himself or herself). That person then *does something* about it. (A police officer may be called, the person may be urged to see a psychologist, a relative may start commitment proceedings, or the person may voluntarily seek help.)

CLASSIFYING MENTAL DISORDERS— PROBLEMS BY THE BOOK

Psychological problems are classified by using the *Diagnostic and Statistical Manual of Mental Disorders* (DSM-IV-TR, 2000). The DSM helps psychologists correctly identify mental disorders and select the best therapies to treat them (Nathan & Langenbucher, 1999).

A **mental disorder** is a serious impairment in psychological functioning. If you were to glance through the DSM, you would see many disorders described, including those in ▲Table 12.2 (on page 466). It's impossible here to discuss all of these problems. Major disorders are listed in Table 12.2 so you can see what types of problems the DSM covers. (You don't need to memorize all of them.) The descriptions that follow will give you an overview of some selected problems.

An Overview of Psychological Disorders

People suffering from **psychotic disorders** have "retreated from reality." That is, they suffer from hallucinations and delusions, and they are socially withdrawn. Psychotic disorders are severely disabling and often lead to hospitalization. Typically, psychotic patients cannot control their thoughts and actions. For example, a college student who became psychotic told his father: "It's the strangest thing. I hear voices, hundreds of them, telling me that everyone wants me dead. It's like all the radios of the world blaring all the stations at once, and it doesn't stop. It jams my brain . . ." (Weisburd, 1990). Psychotic symptoms occur in schizophrenia, delusional disorders, and some mood disorders. Also, psychosis may be related to medical problems, drug abuse, and other conditions. (▲Table 12.1 provides a simplified list of major disorders.)

Organic mental disorders involve brain pathology related to diseases, brain injuries, drug use, poisons, and so on (◆Fig. 12.2). A person with an organic disorder may have disturbed emotions, impaired thinking, memory loss, personality changes, delirium, or psychotic symptoms. Actually, almost all mental disorders are partly biological (Widiger & Sankis, 2000). That's why you won't find "organic mental disorders" in Table 12.2. Nevertheless, several problems in the DSM are closely related to brain damage. These include delirium, dementia, amnesia, cognitive impairments, and substance related disorders (drug abuse).

One of the more common organic problems is *Alzheimer's disease* (ALLS-hi-merz), which leads to impaired memory and a loss of mental abilities. Alzheimer's victims slowly lose the ability to work, cook, drive, read, write, or do arithmetic. Eventually they are mute and bedridden. Alzheimer's disease appears to be caused by unusual webs and tangles in the brain that damage areas important for memory and learning (Ingram, 2003).

Mood disorders are primarily defined by the presence of extreme, intense, and long-lasting emotions. Afflicted persons may be *manic,* meaning agitated, elated, and hyperactive, or they may be *depressed.* Some people with mood disorders cycle between mania and depression, and they may have psychotic symptoms as well.

Anxiety disorders are marked by fear, apprehension, or anxiety and distorted behavior. Some anxiety disorders involve feelings of panic. Others take the form of phobias (irrational fears) or just overwhelming anxiety. Two additional anxiety disorders are post-traumatic stress disorder and acute stress disorder. Obsessive-compulsive behavior patterns are also associated with high anxiety. (These problems are described later in this chapter.)

Somatoform disorders (so-MAT-oh-form) occur when a person has physical symptoms that mimic disease or injury (paralysis, blindness, illness, or chronic pain, for example) for which there is no identifiable physical cause. In such cases, psychological factors appear to underlie the symptoms.

A person with a **dissociative disorder** may have temporary amnesia or multiple personalities. Also included in this category are frightening episodes of depersonalization, in

◆**FIGURE 12.2** *This MRI scan of a human brain (viewed from the top) reveals a tumor (dark spot). Mental disorders sometimes have organic causes of this sort. However, in many instances no organic damage can be found.*

Scott Camazine/Photo Researchers, Inc.

The self-portraits shown here were painted by Andy Wilf between 1978 and 1981. During that time, Wilf is said to have increasingly abused drugs and alcohol. This dramatic series of images is a record of his self-destructive descent into a private hell. The third painting shows a shrouded skull—and foretells the artist's fate. Wilf died of a drug overdose. Drug abuse is but one of the many psychopathologies, or "problems in living," psychologists seek to alleviate. (Courtesy of Ulrike Kantor, Ulrike Kantor Gallery.)

Organic mental disorder A mental or emotional problem caused by brain diseases or injuries. *Alzheimers*

Mood disorder A major disturbance in mood or emotion, such as depression or mania. *Bipolar*

Anxiety disorder Disruptive feelings of fear, apprehension, or anxiety, or distortions in behavior that are anxiety related. *Obsessive Compulsive*

Somatoform disorder Physical symptoms that mimic disease or injury for which there is no identifiable physical cause.

Dissociative disorder Temporary amnesia, multiple personality, or depersonalization.

▲ TABLE 12.1	Some Selected Categories of Psychopathology	
PROBLEM	**PRIMARY SYMPTOM**	**TYPICAL SIGNS OF TROUBLE**
Psychotic disorders	Loss of contact with reality	You hear or see things that others don't; your mind has been playing tricks on you
Mood disorders	Mania or depression	You feel sad and hopeless, or you talk too loud and too fast and have a rush of ideas and feelings that others think are unreasonable
Anxiety disorders	High anxiety or anxiety-based distortions of behavior	You have anxiety attacks and feel like you are going to die; or you are afraid to do things that most people can do; or you spend unusual amounts of time doing things like washing your hands or counting your heartbeats
Somatoform disorders	Bodily complaints without an organic (physical) basis	You feel physically sick, but your doctor says nothing is wrong with you; or you suffer from pain that has no physical basis; or you are preoccupied with thoughts about being sick
Dissociative disorders	Amnesia, feelings of unreality, multiple identities	There are major gaps in your memory of events; you feel like you are a robot or a stranger to yourself; others tell you that you have done things that you don't remember doing
Personality disorders	Unhealthy personality patterns	Your behavior patterns repeatedly cause problems at work, school, and in your relationships with others
Sexual and gender identity disorders	Disturbed gender identity, deviant sexual behavior, problems in sexual adjustment	You feel that you are a man trapped in a woman's body (or the reverse); or you can only gain sexual satisfaction by engaging in highly atypical sexual behavior; or you have problems with sexual desire, arousal, or performance
Substance related disorders	Disturbances related to drug abuse or dependence	You have been drinking too much, using illegal drugs, or taking prescription drugs more often than you should

[Handwritten margin notes:]

DSM-IV

AXIS 1 - Clinical Disorders
AXIS 2 - Personality Disorders + Mental Retardation
AXIS 3 - General Medical Disorders
AXIS 4 - Psychological + Environmental Factors
AXIS 5 - Global Assessment of Functioning

*all individualized

Personality disorder A maladaptive personality pattern.

Sexual and gender identity disorders Any of a wide range of difficulties with sexual identity, deviant sexual behavior, or sexual adjustment.

Substance related disorder Abuse of or dependence on a mood- or behavior-altering drug.

Neurosis An outdated term once used to refer, as a group, to anxiety disorders, somatoform disorders, dissociative disorders, and some forms of depression.

which people feel like they are outside of their bodies, are behaving like a robot, or are lost in a dream world.

Personality disorders are deeply ingrained, unhealthy personality patterns. Such patterns usually appear by adolescence and continue through much of adult life. They include paranoid (overly suspicious), narcissistic (self-loving), dependent, borderline, and antisocial personality types, as well as others.

Sexual and gender identity disorders include any of a wide range of difficulties with sexual identity, deviant sexual behavior, or sexual adjustment. In gender identity disorders, sexual identity does not match a person's physical sex and the person may seek a sex-change operation. Deviations in sexual behavior known as *paraphilias* include exhibitionism, fetishism, voyeurism, and so on. Also found in this category are a variety of *sexual dysfunctions* (problems in sexual desire, arousal, or response).

Substance related disorders involve abuse of, or dependence on, psychoactive drugs. Typical culprits include alcohol, barbiturates, opiates, cocaine, amphetamines, hallucinogens, marijuana, and nicotine. A person with a substance disorder cannot stop using the drug and may also suffer from withdrawal symptoms, delirium, dementia, amnesia, psychosis, emotional outbursts, sexual problems, and sleep disturbances. (Problems related to drug abuse are discussed in Chapter 5.)

Shouldn't neurosis be listed here? Neurosis was once a recognized mental disorder. However, it is no longer in the DSM because the term *neurosis* is too imprecise. Behavior that psychologists used to call "neurotic" is now a part of anxiety, somatoform, or dissociative disorders. Even though **neurosis** is an outdated term, you may hear it used to loosely refer to problems involving excessive anxiety.

In addition to the mental disorders we have reviewed, many cultures have names for "unofficial" psychological "disorders." See "Running Amok with Cultural Maladies" for some samples.

Running Amok with Cultural Maladies

Every culture recognizes the existence of psychopathology, and most have at least a few folk names for afflictions you won't find in DSM-IV-TR. Here are some examples from around the world:

- **Amok** Men in Malaysia, Laos, the Philippines, and Polynesia who believe they have been insulted are sometimes known to go amok. After a period of brooding, they erupt into an outburst of violent, aggressive, or homicidal behavior randomly directed at people and objects.
- **Ataque de nervios** Among Latinos from the Caribbean, the symptoms of an *ataque de nervios* (attack of nerves) include shouting, crying, trembling, aggression, threats of suicide, and seizures or fainting. *Ataques de nervios* frequently occur after a stressful event, such as the death of a close relative, divorce, or an accident involving a family member.
- **Ghost sickness** Among many American Indian tribes, people who become preoccupied with death and the deceased are said to suffer from ghost sickness. The symptoms of ghost sickness include bad dreams, weakness, loss of appetite, fainting, dizziness, fear, anxiety, hallucinations, loss of consciousness, confusion, feelings of futility, and a sense of suffocation.
- **Koro** In south and east Asia, a man may experience sudden and intense anxiety that his penis (or, in females, the vulva

and nipples) will recede into the body. In addition to the terror this incites, victims also believe that advanced cases of *koro* can cause death.
- **Locura** Latinos in the United States and Latin America use the term *locura* to refer to people who suffer from chronic psychotic symptoms such as incoherence, agitation, auditory and visual hallucinations, inability to follow social rules, unpredictability, and violence.
- **Zar** In North African and Middle Eastern societies, *zar* is said to occur when spirits possess an individual. *Zar* is marked by shouting, laughing, hitting the head against a wall, singing, or weeping. Victims may become apathetic or withdrawn and may refuse to eat or carry out daily tasks.

It's clear that people have a need to label and categorize disturbed behavior. As you can see, however, folk terminology tends to be vague. The terms listed here provide little guidance about the true nature of a person's problems or the best ways to treat them. That's why the DSM is based on empirical data and clinical observations. Otherwise, psychologists and psychiatrists would be no better than folk healers when making diagnoses. (Sources: "Outline for Cultural," 2000; Regeser López & Guarnaccia, 2000.)

General Risk Factors

What causes mental and psychological disorders like those listed in Table 12.1? We will soon explore the causes of some specific problems. For now, it is worth noting that a variety of risks contribute to psychopathology, including the following factors.

- **Social conditions:** poverty, stressful living conditions, homelessness, social disorganization, overcrowding
- **Family factors:** parents who are immature, mentally disturbed, criminal, or abusive; severe marital strife; extremely poor child discipline; disordered family communication patterns
- **Psychological factors:** stress, low intelligence, learning disorders, lack of control or mastery
- **Biological factors:** genetic defects or inherited vulnerabilities, poor prenatal care, very low birth weight, chronic physical illness or disability, exposure to toxic chemicals or drugs, head injuries

Insanity

Which of the mental disorders causes insanity? None. **Insanity** is a legal term. It refers to an inability to manage one's affairs or foresee the consequences of one's actions. People who are declared insane are not legally responsible for their actions. If necessary, they can be involuntarily committed to a mental hospital.

Legally, insanity is established by testimony from expert witnesses (psychologists and psychiatrists). An *expert witness* is a person recognized by a court of law as being qualified to give opinions on a specific topic. People who are involuntarily committed are usually judged to be a danger to themselves or to others, or they are severely mentally disabled. Involuntary commitments happen most often when people are brought to emergency rooms. Then, if two doctors agree that the person will either commit suicide or hurt someone else, she or he is put into the hospital (Gorman, 1996).

Insanity Plea - less than 1% of all criminal cases + only 1/4 are found not guilty

Insanity A legal term that refers to a mental inability to manage one's affairs or to be aware of the consequences of one's actions.

| ▲ *TABLE 12.2* | **Major DSM-IV-TR Categories** |

*DISORDERS USUALLY FIRST DIAGNOSED IN INFANCY, CHILDHOOD, OR ADOLESCENCE

Mental retardation
Example: Mild mental retardation
Learning disorders
Example: Reading disorder
Motor skills disorder
Example: Developmental coordination disorder
Pervasive developmental disorders
Example: Autistic disorder
Disruptive behavior and attention-deficit disorders
Example: Attention-deficit/hyperactivity disorder
Feeding and eating disorders of infancy or early childhood
Example: Pica
Tic disorders
Example: Transient tic disorder
Communication disorders
Example: Stuttering
Elimination disorders
Example: Enuresis (bedwetting)
Other disorders of infancy, childhood, or adolescence
Example: Separation anxiety disorder

*DELIRIUM, DEMENTIA, AMNESTIC, AND OTHER COGNITIVE DISORDERS

Delirium
Example: Delirium due to a general medical condition
Dementia
Example: Dementia of the Alzheimer's type
Amnestic disorders (memory loss)
Example: Amnestic disorder due to a general medical condition
Cognitive disorder not otherwise specified

*MENTAL DISORDERS DUE TO A GENERAL MEDICAL CONDITION NOT ELSEWHERE CLASSIFIED

Catatonic disorder due to a general medical condition
Personality change due to a general medical condition
Mental disorder not otherwise specified due to a general medical condition

*SUBSTANCE RELATED DISORDERS

Example: Cocaine use disorders

*SCHIZOPHRENIA AND OTHER PSYCHOTIC DISORDERS

Schizophrenia
Example: Schizophrenia, paranoid type
Schizophreniform disorder
Schizoaffective disorder
Delusional disorder
Example: Delusional disorder, grandiose type
Brief psychotic disorder
Shared psychotic disorder (folie à deux)
Psychotic disorder due to a general medical condition
Substance-induced psychotic disorder
Psychotic disorder not otherwise specified

*MOOD DISORDERS
Depressive disorders
Example: Major depressive disorder
Bipolar disorders
Example: Bipolar I disorder
Mood disorder due to a general medical condition
Substance-induced mood disorder
Mood disorder not otherwise specified

*ANXIETY DISORDERS
Example: Panic disorder

*SOMATOFORM DISORDERS
Example: Conversion disorder

*FACTITIOUS DISORDERS (FAKED DISABILITY OR ILLNESS)
Example: Factitious disorder

*DISSOCIATIVE DISORDERS
Example: Dissociative identity disorder

*SEXUAL AND GENDER IDENTITY DISORDERS
Sexual dysfunctions
Example: Sexual arousal disorders
Paraphilias
Example: Voyeurism
Sexual disorder not otherwise specified
Gender identity disorders
Example: Gender identity disorder

*EATING DISORDERS
Example: Anorexia nervosa

*SLEEP DISORDERS
Primary sleep disorders
Dyssomnias
Example: Primary insomnia
Parasomnias
Example: Sleep terror disorder
Sleep disorders related to another mental disorder
Example: Insomnia related to post-traumatic stress disorder
Other sleep disorders
Example: Substance-induced sleep disorder

*IMPULSE CONTROL DISORDERS NOT ELSEWHERE CLASSIFIED
Example: Kleptomania

*ADJUSTMENT DISORDERS
Example: Adjustment disorder

*PERSONALITY DISORDERS
Example: Antisocial personality disorder

In upcoming sections we will explore some selected problems in more detail, beginning with personality disorders. Before we do, here's a Study Break to help you diagnose your grasp of psychopathology.

STUDYBREAK Y *Normality and Psychopathology*

RELATE

Think of an instance of abnormal behavior you have witnessed. By what formal standards would the behavior be regarded as abnormal? In what way was the behavior maladaptive?

What disorders would the following sentences help you remember? An anxious psychotic in a bad mood asked for an organic substance. "First you have to fill out a somato form and tell us what sex or gender you are," he was told. "Don't diss my personality," he replied.

LEARNING CHECK

1. Statistical definitions of abnormality successfully avoid the limitations of other approaches. T or F?
2. One of the most powerful contexts in which judgments of normality and abnormality are made is
   a. the family b. occupational settings c. religious systems d. culture
3. Amnesia, multiple identities, and depersonalization are possible problems in
   a. mood disorders b. somatoform disorders c. psychosis d. dissociative disorders
4. Which among the following is *not* a major psychological problem listed in DSM-IV-TR?
   a. mood disorders c. insanity b. personality disorders d. anxiety disorders

5. A major difference between psychotic disorders and anxiety disorders (or other milder problems) is that in psychosis the individual has lost contact with reality as shown by the presence of _____ or _____.
6. Which of the following is NOT a term used by folk healers to label or categorize disturbed behavior?
   a. amok b. delirium c. locura d. koro
7. Someone who engages in one of the paraphilias has what type of disorder?
   a. dissociative b. somatoform c. substance d. sexual

Critical Thinking

8. Brian, a fan of grunge rock, occasionally wears a skirt in public. Does Brian's cross-dressing indicate that he has a mental disorder?
9. Many states began to restrict use of the insanity defense after John Hinkley, Jr., who tried to murder former U.S. President Ronald Reagan, was acquitted by reason of insanity. What does this trend reveal about insanity?

ANSWERS

1. F 2. d 3. d 4. c 5. delusions, hallucinations 6. b 7. d 8. Probably not. Undoubtedly, Brian's cross-dressing is socially disapproved by many people. Nevertheless, to be classified as a mental disorder it must cause him to feel disabling shame, guilt, depression, or anxiety. The cultural relativity of behavior like Brian's is revealed by the fact that it is fashionable and acceptable for women to wear men's clothing. 9. It emphasizes that insanity is a legal concept, not a psychiatric diagnosis. Laws reflect community standards. When those standards change, lawmakers may seek to alter definitions of legal responsibility.

PERSONALITY DISORDERS—BLUEPRINTS FOR MALADJUSTMENT

] **SURVEYQUESTION** *What is a personality disorder?*

"Get out of here and leave me alone so I can die in peace," Judy screamed at her nurses in the seclusion room of the psychiatric hospital. On one of her arms, long dark red marks mingled with the scars of previous suicide attempts. Judy once bragged that her record was 67 stitches. Today, the nurses had to strap her into restraints to keep her from gouging her own eyes. She was given a sedative and slept for 12 hours. She woke calmly and asked for her therapist—even though her latest outburst began when he canceled a morning appointment and changed it to afternoon.

Judy has a condition called *borderline personality disorder*. Although she is capable of working, Judy has repeatedly lost jobs because of her turbulent relationships with other people. At times she can be friendly and a real charmer. At other times she is extremely unpredictable, moody, and even suicidal. Being a friend to Judy can be a fearsome challenge. Canceling an appointment, forgetting a special date, using a wrong turn of phrase—these and similar small incidents may trigger Judy's anger or a suicide attempt. Like other people with borderline personality disorder, Judy is extremely sensitive to ordinary criticism, which leaves her feeling rejected and abandoned. Typically, she reacts with rage, self-hatred, and impulsive behavior. These "emotional storms" damage her personal relationships and leave her confused about who she is (Siever & Koenigsberg, 2000).

Maladaptive Personality Patterns

As stated earlier, a person with a personality disorder has a maladaptive personality pattern. For example, people with a paranoid personality disorder are suspicious, hypersensitive, and wary of others. Narcissistic persons need constant admiration, and they are lost in fantasies of power, wealth, brilliance, beauty, or love. The dependent personality suffers from extremely low self-confidence. Dependent persons allow others to run their lives, and they place everyone else's needs ahead of their own. People with a histrionic personality disorder constantly seek attention by dramatizing their emotions and actions.

Typically, patterns like the ones just described begin during adolescence or even childhood. The list of personality disorders is long (▲Table 12.3), so we will focus on a single frequently misunderstood problem, the antisocial personality.

Antisocial Personality

What are the characteristics of an antisocial personality? A person with an **antisocial personality** lacks a conscience. Such people are impulsive, selfish, dishonest, emotionally shallow, and manipulative. Antisocial persons, who are sometimes called *sociopaths* or *psychopaths,* are poorly socialized and seem to be incapable of feeling guilt, shame, fear, loyalty, or love (DSM-IV-TR, 2000).

Are sociopaths dangerous? Sociopaths tend to have a long history of conflict with society. Many are delinquents or criminals who may be a threat to the general public (Rice, 1997). However, sociopaths are rarely the crazed murderers you may have seen portrayed on TV and in movies. In fact, many sociopaths are "charming" at first. Their "friends" only gradually become aware of the sociopath's lying and self-serving manipulation. Many successful businesspersons, entertainers, politicians, and other seemingly normal people have psychopathic leanings. Basically, antisocial persons coldly use others and cheat their way through life (Rice, 1997). A recent study found that psychopaths are "blind" to signs of disgust in others. This

▲TABLE 12.3	**Personality Disorders and Typical Degree of Impairment**

MODERATE IMPAIRMENT

Dependent   Unhealthy submissiveness and dependence on others (clinging)
Histrionic   Excessive emotion and attention-seeking behavior
Narcissistic   Exaggerated self-importance and desire for constant admiration
Antisocial   Irresponsible and antisocial behavior, such as aggression, deceit, recklessness, and lack of remorse

HIGH IMPAIRMENT

Obsessive-compulsive   Traits of orderliness, perfectionism, and rigid routine
Schizoid   Limited emotion and a lack of interest in close personal relationships with others
Avoidant   Discomfort in social situations, fear of evaluation, timidity

SEVERE IMPAIRMENT

Borderline   Unstable self-image, relationships, moods, and impulses; extreme sensitivity to perceived rejection by others
Paranoid   A deep distrust and suspiciousness of the motives of others, which are seen as demeaning or threatening
Schizotypal   Social isolation, extremely odd behavior, and disturbed thought patterns, but not actively psychotic

(From DSM-IV-TR, 2000; Millon, 1981.)

Antisocial personality A person who lacks a conscience, is emotionally shallow, impulsive, selfish, and tends to manipulate others.

Sociopaths &
Psychopaths

may add to their capacity for cruelty and their ability to use others (Kosson et al., 2002).

Causes

What causes sociopathy? Typically, people with antisocial personalities were emotionally deprived, neglected, and physically abused as children (Pollock et al., 1990). Adult sociopaths also display subtle neurological problems (✦Fig. 12.3). For example, they have unusual brain-wave patterns that suggest under-arousal of the brain. This may explain why sociopaths tend to be thrill seekers. Quite likely, they are searching for stimulation strong enough to overcome their chronic under-arousal and feelings of "boredom" (Hare, 1996).

In a revealing study, psychopaths were shown extremely grisly and unpleasant photographs of mutilations. The photos were so upsetting that normal people were visibly startled by them. The psychopaths, however, showed no startle response to the photos (Levenston et al., 2000). (They didn't "bat an eyelash.") Those with antisocial personalities might therefore be described as *emotionally cold.* They simply do not feel normal pangs of conscience, guilt, or anxiety (Hare, 1996). Again, this coldness seems to account for an unusual ability to calmly lie, cheat, steal, or take advantage of others.

Can sociopathy be treated? Antisocial personality disorders are rarely treated with success. All too often, sociopaths manipulate therapy, just like any other situation. If it is to their advantage to act "cured," they will do so. However, they return to their former behavior patterns as soon as possible. On a more positive note, however, antisocial behavior does tend to decline somewhat after age 40, even without treatment.

An individual with an antisocial personality feels very little anxiety. At the other end of the scale, people who have lots of anxiety also suffer from debilitating problems, as described next.

Studies show that more than 65 percent of all persons with antisocial personalities have been arrested, usually for crimes such as robbery, vandalism, or rape.

✦**FIGURE 12.3** *Using PET scans, Canadian psychologist Robert Hare found that the normally functioning brain (left) lights up with activity when a person sees emotion-laden words such as "maggot" or "cancer." But the brain of a psychopath (right) remains inactive, especially in areas associated with feelings and self-control. When Dr. Hare showed the right image to several neurologists, one asked, "Is this person from Mars?" (Images courtesy of Robert Hare.)*

ANXIETY-BASED DISORDERS— WHEN ANXIETY RULES

] SURVEYQUESTION *What problems result when a person suffers high levels of anxiety?*

Imagine that you are waiting to take a very important test for which you are unprepared or waiting to give a speech to a large audience of strangers. You've almost certainly felt *anxiety* in one of these situations. If you have, then you will understand why anxiety-based disorders are so debilitating. People who suffer from extreme anxiety are miserable, and their behavior becomes distorted and self-defeating.

Anxiety refers to feelings of apprehension, dread, or uneasiness. We all feel anxiety, but anxiety that is out of proportion to a situation may reveal a problem. An example is a college student named Jian, who became unbearably anxious when he took exams. By the time Jian went to see a counselor, he had skipped several tests and was in danger of dropping out of school. In general, anxiety-related problems like Jian's involve:

- High levels of anxiety and/or restrictive, self-defeating behavior patterns
- A tendency to use elaborate defense mechanisms or avoidance responses to get through the day
- Pervasive feelings of stress, insecurity, inferiority, and dissatisfaction with life

People with anxiety-related problems feel threatened, but they don't do anything constructive about it. They struggle to control themselves, but they remain ineffective and unhappy (Zinbarg et al., 1992). On any given day, roughly 7 percent of the adult population is suffering from an anxiety disorder.

If anxiety is normal, when does it signify a problem? A problem exists when intense anxiety prevents you from doing what you want or need to do. Also, your anxieties will be out of control—you simply can't stop worrying.

Adjustment Disorders

Do such problems cause a "nervous breakdown"? People suffering from anxiety-based problems may be miserable, but they rarely experience a "breakdown." Actually, the term *nervous breakdown* has no formal meaning. Nevertheless, a problem known as an *adjustment disorder* does come close to being something of a "breakdown."

Adjustment disorders occur when ordinary stresses push people beyond their ability to cope with life. Examples of such stresses are the loss of a job, intense marital strife, and chronic physical illness. People suffering from an adjustment disorder may be extremely irritable, anxious, apathetic, or depressed. They also have trouble sleeping, lose their appetite, and suffer from various physical complaints. Often, their problems can be relieved by rest, sedation, supportive counseling, and a chance to "talk through" their fears and anxieties (DSM-IV-TR, 2000).

How is an adjustment disorder different from an anxiety disorder? The outward symptoms are similar. However, adjustment disorders disappear when a person's life circumstances improve. People suffering from anxiety disorders seem to generate their own misery, regardless of what's happening around them. They feel that they must be on guard against *future* threats that *could happen* at any time (Barlow, 2000).

Anxiety Disorders

In most anxiety disorders, distress seems greatly out of proportion to a person's circumstances. For example, consider the following description of Ethel B:

> She was never completely relaxed, and complained of vague feelings of restlessness, and a fear that something was "just around the corner." Although she felt that she had to go to work to help pay the family bills, she could not bring herself to start anything new for fear that something terrible would happen on the job. She had experienced a few extreme anxiety attacks during which she felt "like I couldn't breathe, like I was sealed up in a transparent envelope. I thought I was going to have a heart attack. I couldn't stop shaking." (Suinn, 1975*)

Distress like Ethel B's is a key ingredient in anxiety disorders. Many psychologists believe it also underlies dissociative and somatoform disorders, where maladaptive behavior serves to reduce anxiety and discomfort. To deepen your understanding, let's first examine the anxiety disorders themselves (▲Table 12.4). Then we will see how anxiety contributes to other closely related problems.

Generalized Anxiety Disorder

A person with a **generalized anxiety disorder** has been extremely anxious and worried for at least 6 months. Sufferers typically complain of sweating, a racing heart, clammy hands, dizziness, upset stomach, rapid breathing, irritability, and poor concentration. Overall, more women than men have these symptoms (Brawman-Mintzer & Lydiard, 1996).

Was Ethel B's problem a generalized anxiety disorder? No, her *anxiety attacks* reveal that she suffered from panic disorder.

▲*TABLE 12.4*	**Anxiety Disorders**

Generalized anxiety disorder
Panic disorder
  Without agoraphobia
  With agoraphobia
Agoraphobia (without a history of panic disorder)
Specific phobia
Social phobia
Obsessive-compulsive disorder
Post-traumatic stress disorder
Acute stress disorder

(DSM-IV-TR, 2000.)

Adjustment disorder An emotional disturbance caused by on-going stressors within the range of common experience.

Generalized anxiety disorder The person is in a chronic state of tension and worries about work, relationships, ability, or impending disaster.

*From *Fundamentals of Behavior Pathology* by R. M. Suinn. Copyright © 1975. Reprinted by permission of John Wiley & Sons, Inc. Additional Suinn quotes in this chapter are from the same source.

Panic Disorder (without Agoraphobia)

In a **panic disorder (without agoraphobia)** people are highly anxious and also feel sudden, intense, unexpected panic. During a panic attack, victims experience chest pain, a racing heart, dizziness, choking, feelings of unreality, trembling, or fears of losing control. Many believe that they are having a heart attack, are going insane, or are about to die. Needless to say, this pattern leaves victims unhappy and uncomfortable much of the time. Again, the majority of people who suffer from panic disorder are women (Sansone, Sansone, & Righter, 1998).

To get an idea of how a panic attack feels, imagine that you are trapped in your state-room on a sinking ocean liner (the *Titanic?*). The room fills with water. When only a small air space remains near the ceiling and you are gasping for air, you'll know what a panic attack feels like.

Panic Disorder (with Agoraphobia)

In a **panic disorder (with agoraphobia)** people suffer from chronic anxiety and sudden panic. In addition, they have **agoraphobia** (ah-go-rah-FOBE-ee-ah), which is an intense, irrational *fear that a panic attack will occur* in a public place or unfamiliar situation. That is, agoraphobics intensely fear leaving their home and familiar surroundings. Typically, they find ways of avoiding places that frighten them—such as crowds, open roads, supermarkets, automobiles, and so on. As a result, some agoraphobics are prisoners in their own homes (DSM-IV-TR, 2000).

Agoraphobia

The problem known as **agoraphobia** can also occur without panic. In this case, people *fear that something extremely embarrassing will happen* if they leave home or enter an unfamiliar situation. For example, an agoraphobic person may refuse to go outside because he or she fears having a sudden attack of dizziness or diarrhea or shortness of breath. Going outside the home alone, being in a crowd, standing in line, crossing a bridge, or riding in a car can be impossible for an agoraphobic person (DSM-IV-TR, 2000). About 7 percent of all adults suffer from agoraphobia (with or without panic) during their lifetime (Magee et al., 1996).

Specific Phobia

As we noted earlier, phobias are intense, irrational fears that a person cannot shake off, even when there is no real danger. In a **specific phobia,** the person's fear, anxiety, and avoidance are focused on particular objects, activities, or situations. People affected by phobias recognize that their fears are unreasonable, but they cannot control them. Specific phobias can be linked to nearly any object or situation. Many have been given names, such as these:

Acrophobia	fear of heights
Astraphobia	fear of storms, thunder, lightning
Arachnophobia	fear of spiders
Aviophobia	fear of airplanes
Claustrophobia	fear of closed spaces
Hematophobia	fear of blood
Microphobia	fear of germs
Nyctophobia	fear of darkness
Pathophobia	fear of disease
Pyrophobia	fear of fire
Xenophobia	fear of strangers
Zoophobia	fear of animals

By combining the appropriate root word with the word *phobia*, any number of unlikely fears can be named. Some are *acarophobia*, a fear of itching; *zemmiphobia*, fear of the great mole rat; *phobosophobia*, fear of fear; *arachibutyrophobia*, fear of peanut butter sticking to the roof of the mouth, and *hippopotomonstrosesquipedaliophobia*, fear of long words!

Almost everyone has a few mild phobias, such as fearing heights, closed spaces, or bugs and crawly things. A phobic disorder differs from such garden-variety fears in that it pro-

Panic disorder (without agoraphobia) The person is in a chronic state of anxiety and also has brief moments of sudden, intense, unexpected panic.

Panic disorder (with agoraphobia) A chronic state of anxiety and brief moments of sudden panic. The person fears that these panic attacks will occur in public places or unfamiliar situations.

Agoraphobia (without panic) The person fears that something extremely embarrassing will happen to them if they leave the house or enter unfamiliar situations.

Specific phobia An intense, irrational fear of specific objects, activities, or situations.

For a person with a strong fear of snakes (ophidiophobia), merely looking at this picture may be unsettling.

duces overwhelming fear. True phobias may lead to vomiting, wild climbing and running, or fainting. For a phobic disorder to exist, the person's fear must disrupt his or her daily life. Phobic persons are so threatened that they will go to almost any length to avoid the feared object or situation, such as driving 50 miles out of the way to avoid crossing a bridge. About 11 percent of all adults have phobic disorders during their lifetime (Magee et al., 1996).

Social Phobia

In a **social phobia,** people fear situations in which they can be observed, evaluated, embarrassed, or humiliated by others. This leads them to avoid certain social situations, such as eating, writing, using the restroom, or speaking in public. When such situations cannot be avoided, people endure them with intense anxiety or distress. It is common for them to have uncomfortable physical symptoms, such as a pounding heart, shaking hands, sweating, diarrhea, mental confusion, and blushing. Social phobias greatly impair a person's ability to work, attend school, and form personal relationships (DSM-IV-TR, 2000). About 13 percent of all adults are affected by social phobias at one time or another (Fones et al., 1998).

Obsessive-Compulsive Disorder

People who suffer from **obsessive-compulsive disorder** are preoccupied with certain distressing thoughts and feel compelled to perform certain behaviors. You have probably experienced a mild obsessional thought, such as a song or stupid commercial jingle that repeats over and over in your mind. This may be irritating, but it's usually not terribly disturbing. True obsessions are images or thoughts that force their way into awareness against a person's will. They are so disturbing that they cause intense anxiety. The most common obsessions are about violence or harm (such as poisoning one's spouse or being hit by a car), about being "dirty" or "unclean," about whether one has performed some action (such as turning off the stove), and about committing immoral acts.

Obsessions usually give rise to compulsions. These are irrational acts that a person feels driven to repeat. Often, compulsive acts help control or block out anxiety caused by an obsession. For example, a minister who finds profanities popping into her mind might start compulsively counting her heartbeat. Doing this would prevent her from thinking "dirty" words.

Social phobia An intense, irrational fear of being observed, evaluated, embarrassed, or humiliated by others in social situations.

Obsessive-compulsive disorder An extreme preoccupation with certain thoughts and compulsive performance of certain behaviors.

The severe obsessions and compulsions of billionaire Howard Hughes led him to live as a recluse for over 20 years. Hughes had an intense fear of contamination. He constructed sterile environments in which his contact with people and objects was strictly limited by complicated rituals. For instance, before handling a spoon Hughes had the handle wrapped in tissue paper and sealed with tape. A second piece of tissue had to be wrapped around the first before he would touch it. A spoon prepared as Hughes required is shown at right.

Many compulsive people are *checkers* or *cleaners.* For instance, a young mother who repeatedly pictures a knife plunging into her baby might check once an hour to make sure all the knives in her house are locked away. Doing so may reduce her anxieties, but it will probably also take over her life. Likewise, a person who feels "contaminated" from touching ordinary objects because "germs are everywhere" may be driven to wash his hands hundreds of times a day. Typically, such compulsive behavior will continue even after the person's hands become raw and painful (Tallis, 1996).

Of course, not all obsessive-compulsive disorders are so dramatic. Many simply involve extreme orderliness and rigid routine. Compulsive attention to detail and rigidly following rules helps keep activities totally under control and makes the highly anxious person feel more secure. (Notice that if such patterns are long-standing, but less intense, they are classified as a personality disorder.)

Stress Disorders

What happens when people endure sudden disasters, such as floods, tornadoes, earthquakes, or horrible accidents? Often, psychological damage follows such events. **Stress disorders** occur when people experience stresses outside the range of normal human experience. They affect many political hostages, combat veterans, prisoners of war, and victims of terrorism, torture, violent crime, child molestation, rape, domestic violence, or people who have witnessed a death or serious injury (Creamer et al., 2001; Jones et al., 2001).

Symptoms of stress disorders include repeatedly reliving the traumatic event, avoiding reminders of the event, and blunted emotions. Also common are insomnia, nightmares, wariness, poor concentration, irritability, and explosive anger or aggression. If such reactions last *less* than a month after a traumatic event, the problem is called an **acute stress disorder.** If they last *more* than a month, the person is suffering from **post-traumatic stress disorder** (**PTSD**) (Shalev, 2001).

Distress, anxiety, and fear are related to our basic survival instincts. Such emotions help us avoid dangerous situations in the future. However, victims of PTSD fail to recover from these reactions (Breslau, 2001b; Yehuda, 2002). Military combat is especially likely to cause PTSD. The constant threat of death and the gruesome sights and sounds of war take a terrible toll. A recent study found that 8 percent of military veterans still had symptoms of PTSD 40 years after they were in combat (Dirkzwager et al., 2001). Even among the general population, nearly 1 adult out of 12 has suffered from post-traumatic stress at some time (Kessler, Sonnega, & Nelson, 1995). Events like the September 11th terrorist attacks in the United States and the return of soldiers from Iraq will undoubtedly add to the number of PTSD cases.

Dissociative Disorders

In dissociative reactions we see striking episodes of *amnesia, fugue,* or *multiple identity.* **Dissociative amnesia** is an inability to recall one's name, address, or past. **Dissociative fugue** (sounds like "fewg") involves sudden, unplanned travel away from home and confusion about personal identity. Dissociations are often triggered by highly traumatic events (Lipschitz et al., 1996). In such cases, forgetting personal identity and fleeing unpleasant situations appear to be defenses against intolerable anxiety.

A person suffering from a **dissociative identity disorder** has two or more separate identities or personality states. (Note that identity disorders are not the same as schizophrenia. Schizophrenia, which is a psychotic disorder, is discussed later in this chapter.) A dramatic example of multiple identity is described in the book *Sybil* (Schreiber, 1973). Sybil reportedly had 16 different personality states. Each identity had a distinct voice, vocabulary, and posture. One personality could play the piano (not Sybil), but the others could not.

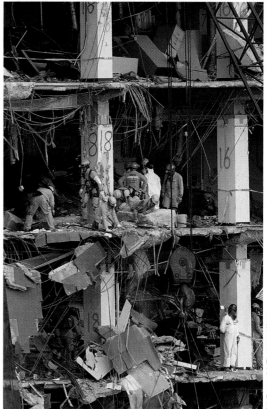

Bob Daemmrich/The Image Works

A terrorist bomb destroyed the Alfred P. Murrah Building in Oklahoma City on April 19, 1995. The bomb killed 169 people and left over 600 injured. In the aftermath of such disasters, many survivors suffer from acute stress reactions. For some, the flare-up of anxiety and distress occurs months or years after the stressful event, an example of a post-traumatic stress reaction.

Stress disorder A significant emotional disturbance caused by stresses outside the range of normal human experience.

Acute stress disorder A psychological disturbance lasting up to 1 month following stresses that would produce anxiety in anyone who experienced them.

Post-traumatic stress disorder A psychological disturbance lasting more than 1 month following stresses that would produce anxiety in anyone who experienced them.

Dissociative amnesia Loss of memory (partial or complete) for important information related to personal identity.

Dissociative fugue Sudden travel away from home, plus confusion about one's personal identity.

Dissociative identity disorder The presence of two or more distinct personalities (multiple personality).

When an identity other than Sybil was in control, Sybil experienced a "time lapse," or memory blackout. Sybil's amnesia and alternate identities first appeared during childhood. As a girl she was beaten, locked in closets, perversely tortured, sexually abused, and almost killed. Sybil's first dissociations allowed her to escape by creating another person who would suffer torture in her place. Identity disorders often begin with unbearable childhood experiences, like Sybil endured. A history of childhood trauma, especially sexual abuse, is found in over 95 percent of persons whose personalities split into multiple identities (Scroppo et al. 1998; Tutkun, Yargic, & Sar, 1995).

Flamboyant cases like Sybil's have led some experts to question the existence of multiple personalities (Casey, 2001). However, a majority of psychologists continue to believe that multiple identity is a real, if rare, problem (Cormier & Thelen, 1998).

Therapy for dissociative identity disorders may make use of hypnosis, which allows contact with the various personality states. The goal of therapy is *integration* and *fusion* of the identities into a single, balanced personality. Fortunately, multiple identity disorders are far rarer in real life than they are in TV dramas!

Somatoform Disorders

Have you ever known someone who appeared to be healthy but seemed to constantly worry about disease? These people are preoccupied with bodily functions, such as their heartbeat or breathing or digestion. Minor physical problems—even a small sore or an occasional cough—may convince them that they have cancer or some other dreaded disease. Typically, they can't give up their fears of illness, even if doctors can find no medical basis for their complaints.

Are you describing hypochondria?   Yes. In **hypochondriasis** (HI-po-kon-DRY-uh-sis), people interpret normal bodily sensations as proof that they have a terrible disease. In a related problem called **somatization disorder** (som-ah-tuh-ZAY-shun), people express their anxieties through various bodily complaints. That is, they suffer from problems such as vomiting or nausea, shortness of breath, difficulty swallowing, or painful menstrual periods. Typically, the person feels ill much of the time and visits doctors repeatedly. Most sufferers take medicines or other treatments, but no physical cause can be found for their distress. Similarly, a person with **pain disorder** is disabled by pain that has no identifiable physical basis.

A rarer somatoform disorder ("body-form" disorder) is called a *conversion reaction*. In a **conversion disorder,** severe emotional conflicts are "converted" into symptoms that actually disturb physical functioning or closely resemble a physical disability. For instance, a soldier might become deaf or lame or develop "glove anesthesia" just before a battle.

What is "glove anesthesia"?   "Glove anesthesia" is a loss of sensitivity in the areas of the skin that would normally be covered by a glove. Glove anesthesia shows that conversion symptoms often contradict known medical facts. The system of nerves in the hands does not form a glove-like pattern and could not cause such symptoms (◆Fig. 12.4).

If symptoms disappear when a victim is asleep, hypnotized, or anesthetized, a conversion

Uncontrollable sneezing, which is often a conversion disorder, may continue for days or weeks. In such cases, sneezing is abnormal in rate and rhythm. In addition, the person's eyes do not close during a sneeze and sneezing does not occur during sleep. (A normal sneeze is shown here.) All of these signs suggest that the cause of the sneezing is psychological, not physical (Fochtmann, 1995).

Hypochondriasis A preoccupation with fears of having a serious disease. Ordinary physical signs are interpreted as proof that the person has a disease, but no physical disorder can be found.

Somatization disorder Afflicted persons have numerous physical complaints. Typically, they have consulted many doctors, but no organic cause for their distress can be identified.

Pain disorder Pain that has no identifiable physical cause and appears to be of psychological origin.

Conversion disorder A bodily symptom that mimics a physical disability but is actually caused by anxiety or emotional distress.

Bruce Ayres/Getty Images

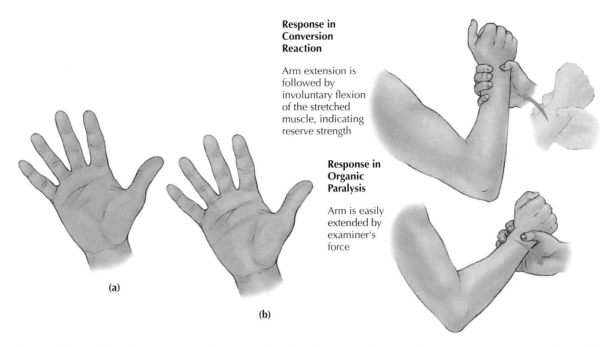

Response in Conversion Reaction

Arm extension is followed by involuntary flexion of the stretched muscle, indicating reserve strength

Response in Organic Paralysis

Arm is easily extended by examiner's force

(a)

(b)

◆**FIGURE 12.4** (left) *"Glove" anesthesia is a conversion reaction involving loss of feeling in areas of the hand that would be covered by a glove* (a). *If the anesthesia were physically caused, it would follow the pattern shown in* (b). *(right) To test for organic paralysis of the arm, an examiner can suddenly extend the arm, stretching the muscles. A conversion reaction is indicated if the arm pulls back involuntarily. (Adapted from Weintraub, 1983.)*

reaction must be suspected (Russo et al., 1998). Another sign to watch for is that victims of conversion reactions are strangely unconcerned about suddenly being disabled.

ANXIETY AND DISORDER—FOUR PATHWAYS TO TROUBLE

] SURVEYQUESTION *How do psychologists explain anxiety-based disorders?*

What causes the problems described in the preceding discussion? Because we are both biological and social creatures, it is not surprising that susceptibility to anxiety-based disorders appears to be partly inherited. Studies show that being high strung, nervous, or emotional runs in families. For example, 60 percent of children born to parents suffering from panic disorder have a fearful, inhibited temperament. Such children are irritable and wary as infants, shy and fearful as toddlers, and quiet and cautious introverts in elementary school. By the time they reach adulthood, they are at high risk for anxiety problems, such as panic attacks, in adulthood (Barlow, 2000).

At least four major perspectives on the causes of dissociative, anxiety, and somatoform disorders exist. These are (1) the *psychodynamic* approach, (2) the *humanistic-existential* approach, (3) the *behavioral* approach, and (4) the *cognitive* approach.

Psychodynamic Approach

The term *psychodynamic* refers to internal motives, conflicts, unconscious forces, and other dynamics of mental life. Freud was the first to propose a psychodynamic explanation for what he called "neurosis." According to Freud, disturbances like those we have described represent a raging conflict among subparts of the personality—the id, ego, and superego.

Freud emphasized that intense anxiety can be caused by forbidden id impulses for sex or aggression that threaten to break through into behavior. The person constantly fears doing something "crazy" or forbidden. She or he may also be tortured by guilt, which the superego uses to suppress forbidden impulses. Caught in the middle, the ego is eventually overwhelmed. This forces the person to use rigid defense mechanisms and misguided, inflexible behavior to prevent a disastrous loss of control (see Chapter 11).

Humanistic-Existential Approaches

Humanistic theories emphasize subjective experience, human problems, and personal potentials. Humanistic psychologist Carl Rogers regarded emotional disorders as the end product of a faulty self-image or self-concept (Rogers, 1959). Rogers believed that anxious individuals have built up unrealistic mental images of themselves. This leaves them vulnerable to contradictory information. Let's say, for example, that an essential part of Carli's self-image is the idea that she is highly intelligent. If Carli does poorly in school, she may deny or distort her perceptions of herself and the situation. Should Carli's anxiety become severe, she may resort to using defense mechanisms. A conversion reaction, anxiety attacks, or similar symptoms could also result from threats to her self-image. These symptoms, in turn, would become new threats that provoke further distortions. Soon, she would fall into a vicious cycle of maladjustment and anxiety that feeds on itself once started.

Existentialism focuses on the elemental problems of existence, such as death, meaning, choice, and responsibility. Psychologists who take a more existential view stress that unhealthy anxiety reflects a loss of *meaning* in one's life. According to them, we must show *courage* and *responsibility* in our choices if life is to have meaning. Too often, they say, we give in to "existential anxiety" and back away from life-enhancing choices. Existential anxiety is the unavoidable anguish that comes from knowing we are personally responsible for our lives. Hence, we have a crushing need to choose wisely and courageously as we face life's empty and impersonal void.

From the existential view, people who are unhappy and anxious are living in "bad faith." That is, they have collapsed in the face of the awesome responsibility to choose a meaningful existence. In short, they have lost their way in life. From this point of view, making choices that don't truly reflect what you value, feel, and believe can make you sick.

Behavioral Approach

Behavioristic approaches emphasize overt, observable behavior and the effects of learning and conditioning. Behaviorists assume that the "symptoms" we have discussed are learned, just as other behaviors are. You might recall from Chapter 6, for instance, that phobias can be acquired through classical conditioning. Similarly, anxiety attacks may reflect conditioned emotional responses that generalize to new situations. As another example, the hypochondriac's "sickness behavior" may be reinforced by the sympathy and attention he or she gets.

One point that all theorists agree on is that disordered behavior is ultimately self-defeating and paradoxical. A paradox is a contradiction. The contradiction in self-defeating behavior is that it makes the person more miserable in the long run, even though it temporarily lowers anxiety.

But if the person becomes more miserable in the long run, how does the pattern get started? The behavioral explanation is that self-defeating behavior begins with avoidance learning (described in Chapter 6). Avoidance learning occurs when making a response delays or prevents the onset of a painful or unpleasant stimulus. Here's a quick review to refresh your memory:

> An animal is placed in a special cage. After a few minutes a light comes on, followed a moment later by a painful shock. Quickly, the animal escapes into a second chamber. After a few minutes, a light comes on in this chamber, and the shock is repeated. Soon the animal learns to avoid pain by moving before the shock occurs. Once an animal learns to avoid the shock, it can be turned off altogether. A well-trained animal may avoid the nonexistent shock indefinitely.

The same analysis can be applied to human behavior. A behaviorist would say that the powerful reward of immediate relief from anxiety keeps self-defeating avoidance behaviors alive. This view, known as the **anxiety reduction hypothesis,** seems to explain why the behavior patterns we have discussed often look very "stupid" to outside observers.

Cognitive Approach

The cognitive view is that distorted thinking causes people to magnify ordinary threats and failures, which leads to distress (Foa et al., 1996). For example, Terrie, who is socially phobic, constantly has upsetting thoughts about being evaluated. One reason for this is that people with social phobias tend to be perfectionists. Like other social phobics, Terrie is excessively concerned about mistakes. She also perceives criticism where none exists (Juster et al., 1996). Terrie tends to focus too much attention on herself, which intensifies her anxiety in social situations (Woody, 1996). Even when socially phobic persons are successful, distorted thinking leads them to think they have failed (Alden & Wallace, 1995). In short, changing the thinking patterns of anxious individuals like Terrie can greatly lessen their fears (Poulton & Andrews, 1996).

Summary

There is probably a core of truth to all four psychological explanations. For this reason, understanding anxiety-based disorders may be aided by combining parts of each perspective. Each viewpoint also suggests a different approach to treatment. Because there are many possibilities, therapy is discussed later, in Chapter 13.

Anxiety reduction hypothesis Explains the self-defeating nature of avoidance responses as a result of the reinforcing effects of relief from anxiety.

PSYCHOTIC DISORDERS—LIFE IN THE SHADOW OF MADNESS

] SURVEYQUESTION *What are the general characteristics of psychotic disorders?*

Imagine that a member of your family has been hearing voices, is talking strangely, has covered her head with aluminum foil, and believes that houseflies are speaking to her in code. If you observed such symptoms, would you be concerned? Of course you would, and rightly so. Psychotic disorders are among the most serious of all mental problems.

A person who is psychotic undergoes a number of striking changes in thinking, behavior, and emotion. Basic to all of these changes is the fact that **psychosis** reflects a loss of contact with shared views of reality (psycho*sis,* singular; psycho*ses,* plural). The following comments, made by two psychotic patients, illustrate what is meant by a "split" from reality (Torrey, 1988).

> Everything is in bits. You put the picture up bit by bit into your head. It's like a photograph that's torn in bits and put together again. If you move it's frightening.

> Last week I was with a girl and suddenly she seemed to get bigger and bigger, like a monster coming nearer and nearer.

The Nature of Psychosis

What are the major features of psychotic disorders? Delusions and hallucinations are core features, but there are others as well.

People who suffer from **delusions** hold false beliefs that they insist are true, regardless of the facts. An example is a 43-year-old schizophrenic man who was sure he was pregnant (Mansouri & Adityanjee, 1995).

Are there different types of delusions? Yes, some common types of delusions are: (1) *depressive* delusions, in which people feel that they have committed horrible crimes or sinful deeds; (2) *somatic* delusions, such as believing your body is "rotting away" or that it is emitting foul odors; (3) delusions of *grandeur,* in which people think they are extremely important; (4) delusions of *influence,* in which people feel they are being controlled or influenced by others or by unseen forces; (5) delusions of *persecution,* in which people believe that others are "out to get them"; and (6) delusions of *reference,* in which people assign great personal meaning to unrelated events. For instance, delusional persons might think that a television program is giving them a special private message (DSM-IV-TR, 2000).

Hallucinations are imaginary sensations, such as seeing, hearing, or smelling things that don't exist in the real world. The most common psychotic hallucination is hearing voices, like the voice that told Carol North to "Collide with the world." Sometimes these voices command patients to hurt themselves. Unfortunately, many people obey (Kasper, Rogers, & Adams, 1996). More rarely, psychotic people may feel "insects crawling under their skin," taste "poisons" in their food, or smell "gas" their "enemies" are using to "get" them. Sensory changes, such as anesthesia (numbness, or a loss of sensation) or extreme sensitivity to heat, cold, pain, or touch, can also occur.

During a psychotic episode, emotions are often severely disturbed. For instance, the psychotic person may be wildly elated, depressed, hyper-emotional, or apathetic. Sometimes psychotic patients display *flat affect,* a condition in which the face is frozen in a blank expression. However, behind their "frozen masks," psychotic people continue to feel emotions just as strongly as ever (Sison et al., 1996).

Some psychotic symptoms can be thought of as a primitive type of communication. That is, many patients can only use their actions to say "I need help," or "I can't handle it any more." Disturbed verbal communication is a nearly universal symptom of psychosis. In fact, psychotic speech tends to be so garbled and chaotic that it sometimes sounds like a "word salad."

Major disturbances such as those just described—as well as added problems with thinking, memory, and attention—bring about personality disintegration and a

Psychosis A withdrawal from reality marked by hallucinations and delusions, disturbed thought and emotions, and by personality disorganization.

Delusion A false belief held against all contrary evidence.

Hallucination An imaginary sensation, such as seeing, hearing, or smelling things that don't exist in the real world.

▲*TABLE 12.5*	**Warning Signs of Psychotic Disorders and Major Mood Disorders**

- You express bizarre thoughts or beliefs that defy reality.
- You have withdrawn from family members and other relationships.
- You hear unreal voices or see things others don't.
- You are extremely sad, persistently despondent, or suicidal.
- You are excessively energetic and have little need for sleep.
- You lose your appetite, sleep excessively, and have no energy.
- You exhibit extreme mood swings.
- You believe someone is trying to get you.
- You have engaged in anti-social, destructive, or self-destructive behavior.

(Sources: Harvey et al., 1996; Sheehy & Cournos, 1992.)

break with reality. *Personality disintegration* occurs when a person's thoughts, actions, and emotions are no longer coordinated. When psychotic disturbances and a fragmented personality are evident for weeks or months, the person has suffered a psychosis (DSM-IV-TR, 2000). (See ▲Table 12.5.)

Organic Psychosis

As we will see later, psychotic disorders appear to involve physical changes in the brain. In a sense, then, all psychoses are partly organic. However, the general term *organic psychosis* is usually reserved for problems involving clear-cut brain injuries or diseases. For example, poisoning by lead or mercury can damage the brain and cause hallucinations, delusions, and a loss of emotional control (◆Fig. 12.5). A particularly dangerous situation is found in old buildings that contain leaded paints. Lead tastes sweet. Thus, young children may be tempted to eat leaded paint flakes as if they were candy. Children who eat leaded paint can become psychotic or retarded (Mielke, 1999).

Leaded paints also release powdered lead into the air. Children may breathe the powder or eat it after handling contaminated toys. Other sources of lead are soldered water pipes, old lead-lined drinking fountains, lead-glazed pottery, and lead deposited years ago from automobile exhaust. On a much larger scale, "poisoning" of another type, in the form of drug abuse, can also produce psychotic symptoms (DSM-IV-TR, 2000).

Benelux Press/Getty Images

A scene in a state mental hospital.

Bettmann/Corbis

◆**FIGURE 12.5** *The Mad Hatter, from Lewis Carroll's* Alice's Adventures in Wonderland. *History provides numerous examples of psychosis caused by toxic chemicals. Carroll's Mad Hatter character is based on an occupational disease of the eighteenth and nineteenth centuries. In that era, hatmakers were heavily exposed to mercury used in the preparation of felt. Consequently, many suffered brain damage and became psychotic, or "mad" (Kety, 1979).*

Joe Sohm/The Image Works

The soil and dust in cities and near busy streets is often heavily contaminated with lead. This lead came from automobile exhaust before leaded gasoline was banned. Young children frequently put objects and their hands in their mouths. As a result, dust is a major source of childhood lead poisoning. Paving play areas or covering them with clean soil can greatly reduce lead exposure (Mielke, 1999).

Are there specific kinds of psychotic disorders?   Two major types of psychosis are *delusional disorders* and *schizophrenia*. As you will recall, mood disorders mainly involve emotional extremes. Nevertheless, psychotic symptoms can also occur in some mood disorders. You'll find information on each of these problems in upcoming discussions.

DELUSIONAL DISORDERS—AN ENEMY BEHIND EVERY TREE

] SURVEYQUESTION *What is the nature of a delusional disorder?*

People with delusional disorders usually do not suffer from hallucinations, emotional excesses, or personality disintegration. Even so, their break with reality is unmistakable. The main feature of **delusional disorders** is the presence of deeply held false beliefs, which may take the following forms (DSM-IV-TR, 2000):

* **Erotomanic type** In this disorder, people have erotic delusions that they are loved by another person, especially by someone famous or of higher status.
* **Grandiose type** In this case, people suffer from the delusion that they have some great, unrecognized talent, knowledge, or insight. They may also believe that they have a special relationship with an important person or with God or that they are a famous person. (If the famous person is alive, the deluded person regards her or him as an imposter.)
* **Jealous type** An example of this type of delusion would be having an all-consuming, but unfounded, belief that your spouse or lover is unfaithful.
* **Persecutory type** Delusions of persecution involve belief that you are being conspired against, cheated, spied on, followed, poisoned, maligned, or harassed.
* **Somatic type** People suffering from somatic delusions typically believe that their bodies are diseased or rotting, or infested with insects or parasites, or that parts of their bodies are defective.

Although they are false, and sometimes far-fetched, all of these delusions are about experiences that could occur in real life (Manschreck, 1996). In other types of psychosis, delusions tend to be more bizarre. For example, a person with schizophrenia might believe that space aliens have replaced all of his internal organs with electronic monitoring devices. In contrast, people with ordinary delusions merely believe that someone is trying to steal their invention, that they are being deceived by a lover, that the FBI is watching them, and the like (DSM-IV-TR, 2000).

Paranoid Psychosis

The most common delusional disorder, often called **paranoid psychosis,** centers on delusions of persecution. Many self-styled reformers, crank letter writers, conspiracy theorists, "UFO abductees," and the like, suffer paranoid delusions. Paranoid individuals often believe that they are being cheated, spied on, followed, poisoned, harassed, or plotted against. Usually they are intensely suspicious, believing they must be on guard at all times.

The evidence such people find to support their beliefs usually fails to persuade others. Every detail of the paranoid person's existence is woven into a private version of "what's really

Delusional disorder A psychosis marked by severe delusions of grandeur, jealousy, persecution, or similar preoccupations.
Paranoid psychosis A delusional disorder centered especially on delusions of persecution.

going on." Buzzing on a telephone may be interpreted as "someone listening"; a stranger doing a survey may be seen as "really trying to get information for government agents"; and so forth.

People suffering paranoid delusions are rarely treated. It is almost impossible for them to accept that they need help. Anyone who suggests that they have a problem simply becomes part of the "conspiracy" to "persecute" them.

Paranoid people frequently lead lonely, isolated, and humorless lives dominated by constant suspicion and hostility. While they are not necessarily dangerous to others, they can be. People who believe that the Mafia, "government agents," terrorists, or a street gang is slowly closing in on them may be moved to violence by their irrational fears. Imagine that a stranger comes to the door to ask a paranoid person for directions. If the stranger has his hand in his coat pocket, he could become the target of a paranoid attempt at "self-defense."

Delusional disorders are rare. By far, the most common form of psychosis is schizophrenia. Let's explore schizophrenia in more detail and see how it differs from a delusional disorder.

SCHIZOPHRENIA—SHATTERED REALITY

] SURVEYQUESTION *What forms does schizophrenia take? What causes it?*

Schizophrenia (SKIT-soh-FREE-nee-uh) is marked by delusions, hallucinations, apathy, thinking abnormalities, and a "split" between thought and emotion. In schizophrenia, emotions may become blunted or very inappropriate. For example, if a person with schizophrenia is told his mother just died, he might smile or giggle or show no emotion at all. Schizophrenic delusions may include the idea that the person's thoughts and actions are being controlled, that thoughts are being broadcast (so others can hear them), that thoughts have been "inserted" into the person's mind, or that thoughts have been removed. In addition, schizophrenia involves withdrawal from contact with others, a loss of interest in external activities, a breakdown of personal habits, and an inability to deal with daily events. One person in 100 will become schizophrenic, and roughly half of all the people admitted to mental hospitals are schizophrenic (DSM-IV-TR, 2000).

Remember the person with psychosis who said, "Everything is in bits. . . . It's like a photograph that's torn in bits and put together again"? Many schizophrenic symptoms appear to be related to problems with *selective attention*. In other words, it is hard for people with schizophrenia to focus on one item of information at a time. Having an impaired "sensory filter" in their brains may be why they are overwhelmed by a jumble of thoughts, sensations, images, and feelings (Heinrichs, 2001).

Is there more than one type of schizophrenia? Schizophrenia appears to be a group of related disturbances. It has four major subtypes:

- **Disorganized type** Schizophrenia marked by incoherence, grossly disorganized behavior, bizarre thinking, and flat or grossly inappropriate emotions.
- **Catatonic type** Schizophrenia marked by stupor, rigidity, unresponsiveness, posturing, mutism, and, sometimes, agitated, purposeless behavior.
- **Paranoid type** Schizophrenia marked by a preoccupation with delusions or by frequent auditory hallucinations related to a single theme, especially grandeur or persecution.
- **Undifferentiated type** Schizophrenia in which there are prominent psychotic symptoms, but none of the specific features of catatonic, disorganized, or paranoid types.

Disorganized Schizophrenia

The disorder known as disorganized schizophrenia (sometimes called hebephrenic schizophrenia) comes close to matching the stereotyped images of "madness" seen in movies. In **disorganized schizophrenia,** personality disintegration is nearly complete: Emotions,

Schizophrenia A psychosis characterized by delusions, hallucinations, apathy, and a "split" between thought and emotion.

Disorganized schizophrenia Schizophrenia marked by incoherence, grossly disorganized behavior, bizarre thinking, and flat or grossly inappropriate emotions.

In disorganized schizophrenia, behavior is marked by silliness, laughter, and bizarre or obscene behavior.

speech, and behavior are all highly disorganized. The result is silliness, laughter, and bizarre or obscene behavior, as shown by this intake interview of a patient named Edna:

DR. I am Dr. _____. I would like to know something more about you.
PATIENT You have a nasty mind. Lord! Lord! Cat's in a cradle.
DR. Tell me, how do you feel?
PATIENT London's bell is a long, long dock. Hee! Hee! (Giggles uncontrollably.)
DR. Do you know where you are now?
PATIENT D_____n! S_____t on you all who rip into my internals! The grudgerometer will take care of you all! (Shouting) I am the Queen, see my magic, I shall turn you all into smidgelings forever!
DR. Your husband is concerned about you. Do you know his name?
PATIENT (Stands, walks to and faces the wall) Who am I, who are we, who are you, who are they, (turns)
I . . . I . . . I . . . I! (Makes grotesque faces.)

> Edna was placed in the women's ward where she proceeded to masturbate. Occasionally, she would scream or shout obscenities. At other times she giggled to herself. She was known to attack other patients. She began to complain that her uterus was attached to a "pipeline to the Kremlin" and that she was being "infernally invaded" by Communism. (Suinn, 1975)

Disorganized schizophrenia typically develops in adolescence or young adulthood. Chances of improvement are limited, and social impairment is usually extreme (DSM-IV-TR, 2000).

Catatonic Schizophrenia

Can the catatonic's rigid postures and stupor be understood in terms of abnormal body chemistry? Environment? Heredity? As is true of other forms of schizophrenia, the answer appears to be all three factors.

The catatonic person seems to be in a state of total panic. **Catatonic schizophrenia** brings about a stuporous condition in which odd positions may be held for hours or even days. These periods of rigidity may be similar to the tendency to "freeze" at times of great emergency or panic. Catatonic individuals appear to be struggling desperately to control their inner turmoil. One sign of this is the fact that stupor may occasionally give way to agitated outbursts or violent behavior. The following excerpt describes a catatonic episode.

> Manuel appeared to be physically healthy upon examination. Yet he did not regain his awareness of his surroundings. He remained motionless, speechless, and seemingly unconscious. One evening an aide turned him on his side to straighten out the sheet, was called away to tend another patient, and forgot to return. Manuel was found the next morning, still on his side, his arm tucked under his body, as he had been left the night before. His arm was turning blue from lack of circulation, but he seemed to be experiencing no discomfort. (Suinn, 1975)

Notice that Manuel did not speak. *Mutism*, along with a lack of responsiveness, makes the catatonic patient difficult to "reach." Fortunately, this bizarre form of schizophrenia has become rare in Europe and North America (DSM-IV-TR, 2000).

Paranoid Schizophrenia

Catatonic schizophrenia Schizophrenia marked by stupor, rigidity, unresponsiveness, posturing, mutism, and, sometimes, agitated, purposeless behavior.

Paranoid schizophrenia Schizophrenia marked by a preoccupation with delusions or by frequent auditory hallucinations related to a single theme, especially grandeur or persecution.

Paranoid schizophrenia is the most common schizophrenic disorder. As in paranoid delusional disorders, **paranoid schizophrenia** centers around delusions of grandeur and persecution. However, paranoid schizophrenics also hallucinate, and their delusions are more bizarre and unconvincing than those in a delusional disorder.

Thinking that their minds are being controlled by God, the government, or "cosmic rays from space" or that someone is trying to poison them, people suffering from paranoid schizophrenia may feel forced into violence to "protect" themselves. An example is James Huberty, who brutally murdered 21 people at a McDonald's restaurant in San Ysidro, Cali-

CRITICAL THINKING Are the Mentally Ill Prone to Violence?

News reports and television programs tend to exaggerate the connection between mental illness and violence (Diefenbach, 1997). In reality, research on this question leads to these conclusions:

• Only persons who are *actively psychotic* are more violence prone than non-patients. That is, if a person is experiencing delusions and hallucinations, the risk of violence is elevated. Other mental problems are unrelated to violence.

• Only persons *currently* experiencing psychotic symptoms are at increased risk for violence. Violent behavior is not related to having been a mental patient in the past or having had psychotic symptoms in the past.

Thus, most news stories give a false impression. Even when we consider people who are actively psychotic, we find that the vast majority are not violent. The risk of violence from mental patients is actually many times lower than that from persons who have the following attributes: young, male, poor, and intoxicated.

Beliefs about mental disorders are important because they affect laws and personal attitudes toward the mentally ill. People who strongly believe that the mentally ill are prone to violence are typically afraid to have former mental patients as neighbors, co-workers, or friends. But as you can see, only a small minority of the actively mentally ill pose an increased risk. Former mental patients, in particular, are no more likely to be violent than people in general. No matter how disturbed a person may have been, she or he merits respect and compassion. Remember, the overwhelming majority of violent crimes are committed by people who are not mentally ill. (Sources: Monahan, 1992; Noble, 1997; Rice, 1997; Teplin, Abram, & McClelland, 1994.)

Curt Borgwardt/Sygma/Corbis

News stories give the impression that the mentally ill are dangerous. Consider, for example, the ghastly case of Jeffrey Dahmer, who killed, sexually molested, and then ate his victims. Like Dahmer, most of the mentally disordered persons who make the evening news have committed a horrible crime. This tends to give the impression that the mentally ill are violent and dangerous. Yet in reality, only a tiny percentage of all mentally disordered persons are more violent than average.

fornia. Huberty was a paranoid schizophrenic who felt persecuted and cheated by life. Shortly before he announced to his wife that he was "going hunting humans," Huberty had been hearing hallucinated voices (◆Fig. 12.6).

How dangerous are the mentally ill? Depictions in the news certainly give the impression that practically everyone who is mentally ill is dangerous. But are they? You might be surprised by the answer, found in "Are the Mentally Ill Prone to Violence?"

The Causes of Schizophrenia

Former British Prime Minister Winston Churchill once described a question that perplexed him as "a riddle wrapped in a mystery inside an enigma." The same words might describe the causes of schizophrenia.

Environment

What causes schizophrenia? An increased risk of developing schizophrenia may begin at birth or even before. Women who are exposed to the influenza (flu) virus or to rubella (German measles) during the middle of pregnancy have children who are more likely to become schizophrenic (Brown et al., 2001). Malnutrition during pregnancy and complications at the time of birth can have a similar impact. Possibly, such events disturb brain development, leaving people more vulnerable to a psychotic break with reality (Cannon, 1998).

Early **psychological trauma** (a psychological injury or shock) may also add to the risk. Often, the victims of schizophrenia were exposed to violence, sexual abuse, death, divorce, separation, or other stresses in childhood (Mirsky & Duncan, 1986). Living in a troubled

Bruce Ely/Getty Images

◆**FIGURE 12.6** *Over a period of years, Theodore Kaczynski mailed bombs to unsuspecting victims, many of whom were maimed or killed. As a young adult, Kaczynski was a brilliant mathematician. At the time of his arrest, he had become the Unabomber—a reclusive "loner" who deeply mistrusted other people and modern technology. After his arrest, Kaczynski was judged to be suffering from paranoid schizophrenia.*

Psychological trauma A psychological injury or shock, such as that caused by violence, abuse, neglect, separation, and so forth.

family is a related risk factor. In a disturbed family environment, stressful relationships, communication patterns, and negative emotions prevail. For example, a 15-year study found that the chance of developing schizophrenia is related to deviant communication within families (Goldstein, 1985). Deviant communication patterns cause anxiety, confusion, anger, conflict, and turmoil. Typically, disturbed families interact in ways that are laden with guilt, prying, criticism, negativity, and emotional attacks (Bressi, Albonetti, & Razzoli, 1998; Docherty et al., 1998).

Although they are attractive, environmental explanations alone are not enough to account for schizophrenia (Fowles, 1992). For example, when the children of schizophrenic parents are raised away from their chaotic home environment, they are still more likely to become psychotic.

Does that mean that heredity affects the risk of developing schizophrenia?

Heredity

There is now little doubt that heredity is a factor in schizophrenia. It appears that some individuals inherit a *potential* for developing schizophrenia. They are, in other words, more *vulnerable* to the disorder than others are (Cannon et al., 1998; Fowles, 1992).

How has that been shown? If one identical twin becomes schizophrenic (remember, identical twins have identical genes), then the other twin has a *48 percent* chance of also becoming schizophrenic (Lenzenweger & Gottesman, 1994). The figure for twins can be compared to the risk of schizophrenia for the population in general, which is 1 percent. (See ◆Figure 12.7 for other relationships.) In general, schizophrenia is clearly more common among close relatives and it tends to run in families (Plomin & Rende, 1991). There's even a case on record of *four* identical quadruplets *all* developing schizophrenia. In light of such evidence, researchers are now beginning to search for specific genes related to schizophrenia.

A problem exists with current genetic explanations of schizophrenia: Very few people with schizophrenia have children. How could a genetic defect be passed from one generation to the next if afflicted people don't reproduce? One possible answer is suggested by the fact that the older a man is when he fathers a child, the more likely it is that the child will develop schizophrenia. Apparently, genetic mutations occur in aging male reproductive cells and increase the risk of schizophrenia (as well as other medical problems) (Malaspina, 2001; Malaspina et al., 2001).

Brain Chemistry

How could someone inherit a susceptibility to schizophrenia? Amphetamine, LSD, PCP ("angel dust"), and similar drugs produce effects that partially mimic the symptoms of schizophrenia. Also, the same drugs (phenothiazines) used to treat LSD overdoses tend to alleviate

◆FIGURE 12.7 *Lifetime risk of developing schizophrenia is associated with how closely a person is genetically related to a schizophrenic person. A shared environment also increases the risk. (Estimates from Lenzenweger & Gottesman, 1994.)*

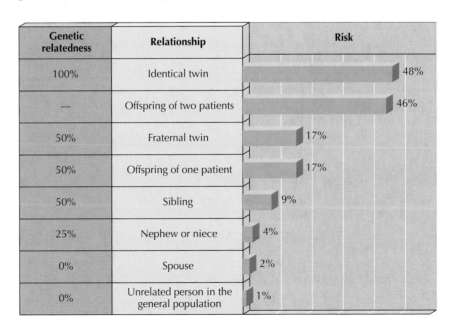

Genetic relatedness	Relationship	Risk
100%	Identical twin	48%
—	Offspring of two patients	46%
50%	Fraternal twin	17%
50%	Offspring of one patient	17%
50%	Sibling	9%
25%	Nephew or niece	4%
0%	Spouse	2%
0%	Unrelated person in the general population	1%

This series of paintings by Louis Wain reflects a troubled personality. Wain was a British illustrator who became schizophrenic in middle age. As Wain's psychosis progressed, his cat paintings became highly abstract and fragmented. In many ways, Wain's paintings resemble the perceptual changes caused by psychedelic drugs such as mescaline and LSD. Recent research suggests that psychosis may, in fact, be the result of mind-altering changes in brain chemistry. (Derik Bayes/Courtesy Guttman-Maclay *Life* Picture Service.)

psychotic symptoms. Facts such as these suggest that biochemical abnormalities (disturbances in brain chemicals or neurotransmitters) may occur in schizophrenic people. It is possible that the schizophrenic brain produces some substance similar to a *psychedelic* (mind-altering) drug. At present, one likely candidate is dopamine (DOPE-ah-meen), an important chemical messenger found in the brain.

Many researchers believe that schizophrenia is related to overactivity in brain dopamine systems (Abi-Dargham et al., 1998). Another possibility is that dopamine receptors become super-responsive to normal amounts of dopamine (Port & Seybold, 1995). Dopamine appears to trigger a flood of unrelated thoughts, feelings, and perceptions, which may account for the voices, hallucinations, and delusions of schizophrenia. The implication is that schizophrenic people may be on a sort of drug trip caused by their own bodies (◆Fig. 12.8). In short, most evidence suggests that schizophrenia is a brain disease.

Dopamine is not the only brain chemical that has caught scientists' attention. For instance, the neurotransmitter glutamate also appears to be related to schizophrenia (Belsham, 2001). People who take the hallucinogenic drug PCP, which affects glutamate, have symptoms that closely mimic schizophrenia (Murray, 2002). This occurs because glutamate influences brain activity in areas that control emotions and sensory information (Tsai & Coyle, 2002). Another tantalizing connection is the fact that stress alters glutamate levels, which in turn alter dopamine systems (Moghaddam, 2002). The story is far from complete, but it appears that dopamine, glutamate, and other brain chemicals partly explain the devastating symptoms of schizophrenia (Sawa & Snyder, 2002).

◆FIGURE 12.8 *Dopamine normally crosses the synapse between two neurons, activating the second cell. Antipsychotic drugs bind to the same receptor sites as dopamine does, blocking its action. In people suffering from schizophrenia, a reduction in dopamine activity can quiet a person's agitation and psychotic symptoms.*

The Schizophrenic Brain

Medical researchers have long hoped for a way to directly observe the schizophrenic brain. Three medical techniques are now making it possible. One, called a *CT scan,* provides an X-ray picture of the brain. (CT stands for computed tomography, or computer-enhanced X-ray images.) ◆Figure 12.9 shows a CT scan of the brain of John Hinkley, Jr., who shot former U.S. President Ronald Reagan and three other men in 1981. In the ensuing trial, Hinkley was declared insane. As you can see, his brain differed from the norm. Specifically, it had wider surface fissuring.

Dennis Brack/Black Star

✦FIGURE 12.9 *The CT scan on the left shows the brain of would-be presidential assassin John Hinkley, Jr., when he was 25. Notice how wide the fissures are in the wrinkled surface of Hinkley's brain. A CT scan of a normal 25-year-old's brain is pictured on the right. As you can see, in most young adults the surface folds of the brain are tightly pressed together. Pronounced brain fissuring in a young adult may be a sign of schizophrenia, chronic alcoholism, or other problems.*

MRI scans (magnetic resonance imaging) are allowing researchers to peer inside the schizophrenic brain. What they find is that schizophrenic people tend to have enlarged ventricles (fluid-filled spaces within the brain) (Sharma et al., 1998). Other brain regions also appear to be abnormal. It is telling that the affected areas are crucial for regulating motivation, emotion, perception, actions, and attention (Degreef et al., 1992; Frazier et al., 1996; Gur et al., 1998).

A third technique, called a *PET scan* (positron emission tomography), provides an image of brain activity. To make a PET scan, a radioactive sugar solution is injected into a vein. When the sugar reaches the brain, an electronic device measures how much is used in each area. These data are then translated into a color map, or scan, of brain activity (✦Fig. 12.10). Researchers are finding patterns in such scans that are consistently linked with schizophrenia, affective disorders, and other problems. For instance, activity tends to be abnormally low in the frontal lobes of the schizophrenic brain (Velakoulis & Pantelis, 1996). In the future, PET scans may be used to accurately diagnose schizophrenia. For now, PET scans show that there is a clear difference in schizophrenic brain activity.

NORMAL   SCHIZOPHRENIC   MANIC-DEPRESSIVE

The Brookhaven National Laboratory

✦FIGURE 12.10 *Positron emission tomography produces PET scans of the human brain. In the scans shown here, red, pink, and orange indicate lower levels of brain activity; white and blue indicate higher activity levels. Notice that activity in the schizophrenic brain is quite low in the frontal lobes (top area of each scan) (Velakoulis & Pantelis, 1996). Activity in the manic-depressive brain is low in the left brain hemisphere and high in the right brain hemisphere. The reverse is more often true of the schizophrenic brain. Researchers are trying to identify consistent patterns like these to help them diagnosis mental disorders.*

Implications

In summary, the emerging picture of psychotic disorders such as schizophrenia takes this form: Anyone subjected to enough stress may be pushed to a psychotic break. (Battlefield psychosis is an example.) However, some people inherit a difference in brain chemistry or brain structure that makes them more susceptible—even to normal life stresses.

Thus, the right mix of inherited potential and environmental stress brings about mind-altering changes in brain chemicals and brain structure. This explanation is called a

The Stress-Vulnerability Model

Vulnerability ☐
Stress ☐

Low   Medium   High
Degree of psychopathology

◆**FIGURE 12.11** *A combination of vulnerability and stress may produce psychological problems. The top bar shows low vulnerability and low stress. The result? No problem. The same is true of the next bar down, where low vulnerability is combined with moderate stress. Even high vulnerability (third bar) may not lead to problems if stress levels remain low. However, when high vulnerability combines with moderate or high stress (bottom two bars) the person "crosses the line" and suffers from psychopathology.*

stress-vulnerability model. It attributes psychotic disorders to a blend of environmental stress and inherited susceptibility. The model seems to apply to other forms of psychopathology as well, such as depression (◆Fig. 12.11).

Despite advances in our understanding, psychosis remains "a riddle wrapped in a mystery inside an enigma." Let us hope that recent progress toward a cure for schizophrenia will continue.

STUDYBREAK *Psychosis, Delusional Disorders, and Schizophrenia*

RELATE

What did you think psychosis was like before you read about it? How has your understanding changed? If you were writing a "recipe" for psychosis, what would the main "ingredients" be?

If you were asked to play the role of a paranoid person for a theater production, what symptoms would you emphasize?

You have been asked to explain the causes of schizophrenia to the parents of a schizophrenic teenager. What would you tell them?

LEARNING CHECK

1. Carol wrongly believes that her body is "rotting away." She is suffering from
   a. depressive hallucinations   b. a delusion   c. flat affect
   d. Alzheimer's disease
2. Colin, who has suffered a psychotic break, is hearing voices. This symptom is referred to as
   a. flat affect   b. hallucination   c. a word salad   d. organic delusions
3. A psychosis caused by lead poisoning would be regarded as an organic disorder. T or F?

4. Hallucinations and personality disintegration are the principal features of paranoid psychosis. T or F?
5. Environmental explanations of schizophrenia emphasize emotional trauma and
   a. manic parents   b. schizoaffective interactions   c. psychedelic interactions   d. disturbed family relationships
6. The _____ _____ of a schizophrenic person runs a 48 percent chance of also becoming psychotic.
7. Enlarged surface fissures and ventricles, as revealed by CT scans, are found only in the brains of chronic schizophrenics. T or F?

Critical Thinking

8. Researchers have found nearly double the normal number of dopamine receptor sites in the brains of schizophrenics. Why might that be important?
9. Enlarged surface fissures and ventricles are frequently found in the brains of chronic schizophrenics. Why is it a mistake to conclude that such features cause schizophrenia?

ANSWERS with schizophrenia. They could be additional symptoms, rather than causes, of the disorder. levels of dopamine in the brain. 9. Because correlation does not confirm causation. Structural brain abnormalities are merely *correlated* 1. b 2. b 3. T 4. F 5. d 6. identical twin 7. F 8. Because of the extra receptors, schizophrenics may get psychedelic effects from normal

MOOD DISORDERS—PEAKS AND VALLEYS

] SURVEYQUESTIONS *What are mood disorders? What causes depression?*

For some people, minor bouts of depression are as common as colds. But extreme swings of mood can be as disabling as a serious physical illness. In fact, depression can be deadly, because depressed persons may be suicidal. It is difficult to imagine how bleak and hopeless

Stress-vulnerability model Attributes psychosis to a combination of environmental stress and inherited susceptibility.

▲ TABLE 12.6	DSM-IV-TR Classification of Mood Disorders	
PROBLEM	**PRIMARY SYMPTOM**	**TYPICAL SIGNS OF TROUBLE**
Depressive Disorders		
Major depressive disorder	Extreme emotional depression for at least 2 weeks	You feel extremely sad, worthless, fatigued, and empty; you are unable to feel pleasure; you are having thoughts of suicide.
Dysthymic disorder	Moderately depressed mood on most days during the last 2 years.	You feel down and depressed more days than not; your self-esteem and energy levels have been low for many months.
Bipolar Disorders		
Bipolar I disorder	Extreme mania and depression	At times you have little need for sleep, can't stop talking, your mind races, and everything you do is of immense importance; at other times you feel extremely sad, worthless, and empty.
Bipolar II disorder	Emotional depression and at least one episode of mild mania	Most of the time you feel extremely sad, worthless, fatigued and empty; however, at times you feel unusually good, cheerful, energetic, or "high."
Cyclothymic disorder	Periods of moderate depression and moderate mania for at least 2 years	You have been experiencing upsetting emotional ups and downs for many months.

the world looks to a person who is deeply depressed, or how "crazy" it can be to ride a wave of mania. Let's explore mood disorders and their causes.

Nobody loves you when you're down and out—or so it seems. Psychologists have come to realize that **mood disorders** (major disturbances in emotion) are among the most serious of all. Two general types of mood disorder are depressive disorders and bipolar disorders (see ▲ Table 12.6). In **depressive disorders,** sadness and despondency are exaggerated, prolonged, or unreasonable. Signs of a depressive disorder are dejection, hopelessness, and an inability to feel pleasure or to take interest in anything. Other common symptoms are fatigue, disturbed sleep and eating patterns, feelings of worthlessness, a very negative self-image, and thoughts of suicide. In **bipolar disorders,** people go both "up" and "down" emotionally (DSM-IV-TR, 2000).

In Europe and North America, between 10 and 20 percent of the adult population has had a major depressive episode at some time (DSM-IV-TR, 2000). At any given time, roughly 5 percent of the population is suffering from a mood disorder.

Some mood disorders are long-lasting but relatively moderate problems. If a person is mildly depressed for at least 2 years, the problem is called a **dysthymic disorder** (dis-THY-mik). If depression alternates with periods when the person's mood is cheerful, expansive, or irritable, the problem is a **cyclothymic disorder** (SIKE-lo-THY-mik). Even at this level, mood disorders can be debilitating. However, major mood disorders are much more damaging.

Mood disorder Major disturbances in mood or emotion, such as depression or mania.

Depressive disorders Emotional disorders primarily involving sadness, despondency, and depression.

Bipolar disorders Emotional disorders involving both depression and mania or hypomania.

Dysthymic disorder Moderate depression that persists for 2 years or more.

Cyclothymic disorder Moderate manic and depressive behavior that persists for 2 years or more.

Major mood disorders Disorders marked by lasting extremes of mood or emotion and sometimes accompanied by psychotic symptoms.

Major depressive disorder A mood disorder in which the person has suffered one or more intense episodes of depression.

Bipolar I disorder A mood disorder in which a person has episodes of mania (excited, hyperactive, energetic, grandiose behavior) and also periods of deep depression.

Bipolar II disorder A mood disorder in which a person is mostly depressed (sad, despondent, guilt ridden) but has also had one or more episodes of mild mania (hypomania).

Major Mood Disorders

Major mood disorders are characterized by emotional extremes. The person who only goes "down" emotionally suffers from a **major depressive disorder.** During major depressive episodes everything looks bleak and hopeless. The person has feelings of failure, sinfulness, worthlessness, and total despair. Suffering is intense, and the person may become extremely subdued, withdrawn, or intensely suicidal. Severe depression is a serious threat. Suicide attempted during a major depression is rarely a "plea for help." Usually, the person intends to succeed and may give no prior warning.

In a **bipolar I disorder,** people experience both extreme mania and deep depression. During manic episodes, the person is loud, elated, hyperactive, grandiose, and energetic. Manic patients may go bankrupt in a matter of days, get arrested, or go on a binge of promiscuous sex. During periods of depression, the person is deeply despondent and possibly suicidal.

In a **bipolar II disorder** the person is mostly sad and guilt ridden but has had one or more mildly manic episodes (called *hypomania*). That is, in a bipolar II disorder, both elation and depression occur, but the person's mania is not as extreme as in a bipolar I disorder. Bipolar II patients who are hypomanic usually just manage to irritate everyone around them. They are excessively cheerful, aggressive, or irritable, and they may brag, talk too fast, interrupt conversations, or spend too much money (Gorman, 1996).

In serious cases of depression it is impossible for a person to function at work or at school. Sometimes, depressed individuals cannot even feed or dress themselves. In cases of depression and/or mania that are even more severe, the person may also lose touch with reality and display psychotic symptoms. About 14 percent of patients in mental hospitals have major mood disorders.

How do major mood disorders differ from dysthymic and cyclothymic disorders?   As mentioned, the major mood disorders involve more extreme emotional changes. Also, major mood disorders more often appear to be **endogenous** (en-DOJ-eh-nus: produced from within) rather than a reaction to external events.

In major depressive disorders, suicidal impulses can be intense and despair total.

What Causes Mood Disorders?

Depression and other mood disorders have resisted adequate explanation and treatment. Some scientists are focusing on the biology of mood changes. They are interested in brain chemicals and transmitter substances, especially serotonin, noradrenaline, and dopamine levels. Their findings are incomplete, but progress has been made. For example, the chemical *lithium carbonate* can be effective for treating some cases of bipolar depression.

Other researchers seek psychological explanations. Psychoanalytic theory, for instance, holds that depression is caused by repressed anger. This rage is displaced and turned inward as self-blame and self-hate. As discussed in Chapter 11, behavioral theories of depression emphasize learned helplessness (Seligman, 1989). Cognitive psychologists believe that self-criticism and negative, distorted, or self-defeating thoughts underlie many cases of depression. (This view is discussed in Chapter 13.) Clearly, life stresses trigger many mood disorders (Kessler, 1997). This is especially true for people who have personality traits and thinking patterns that make them vulnerable to depression (Franche & Dobson, 1992; Gatz, 1990; Miranda, 1992).

Overall, women are twice as likely as men to experience depression (Culertson, 1997). Authorities believe that social and environmental conditions are the main reason for this difference. Factors that contribute to women's greater risk of depression include conflicts about birth control and pregnancy, work and parenting, and the strain of providing emotional support for others. Marital strife, sexual and physical abuse, and poverty are also factors. Nationwide, women and children are most likely to live in poverty. As a result, poor women frequently suffer the stresses associated with single parenthood, loss of control over their lives, poor housing, and dangerous neighborhoods (Russo, 1990). A recent study found that women in the United States were most likely to be depressed if they had these characteristics: low education, unmarried, Latina, high stress levels, and feelings of hopelessness (Meyers et al., 2002).

Does the fact that major mood disorders appear to be endogenous imply that heredity is involved?   Yes, especially in bipolar disorders (Gershon et al., 1998). As a case in point, if one identical twin is depressed, the other has an 80 percent chance of suffering depression, too. For non-twin siblings the probability is 35 percent. This difference may be related to the recent finding that people who have a particular version of a gene are more likely to become depressed when they are stressed (Caspi et al., 2003). As we have noted, psychological causes are important in many cases of depression. But for major mood disorders, biological factors seem to play a larger role. Surprisingly, one source of depression is related to the seasons.

Seasonal Affective Disorder

Unless you have experienced a winter of "cabin fever" in the far north, you may be surprised to learn that the rhythms of the seasons underlie some depressions. Researcher Norman Rosenthal has found that some people suffer from **seasonal affective disorder** (**SAD**), or depression that only occurs during the fall and winter months. Almost anyone can get a little depressed when days are short, dark, and cold. But when a person's symptoms are last-

Endogenous depression Depression that appears to be produced from within (perhaps by chemical imbalances in the brain), rather than as a reaction to life events.

Seasonal affective disorder Depression that occurs only during fall and winter; presumably related to decreased exposure to sunlight.

ing and disabling, the problem may be SAD. Here are some of the major symptoms of SAD (Rosenthal, 1993):

- **Oversleeping and difficulty staying awake:** Your sleep patterns may be disturbed and waking very early in the morning is common.
- **Fatigue:** You feel too tired to maintain a normal routine.
- **Craving:** You hunger for carbohydrates and sweets, leading to overeating and weight gain.
- **Inability to cope:** You feel irritable and stressed.
- **Social withdrawal:** You become unsocial in the winter but are socially active during other seasons.

Starting in the fall, people with SAD sleep longer but more poorly. During the day they feel tired and drowsy, and they tend to overeat. With each passing day they become more sad, anxious, irritable, and socially withdrawn.

Although their depressions are not severe, many victims of SAD face each winter with a sense of foreboding. SAD is especially prevalent in northern latitudes, where days are very short during the winter (Booker & Hellekson, 1992) (◆Fig. 12.12). For instance, one study found that 13 percent of college students living in northern New England showed signs of suffering from SAD (Low & Feissner, 1998). The students most likely to be affected were those who had moved from the south to attend college!

Seasonal depressions are related to the release of more melatonin during the winter. This hormone, which is secreted by the pineal gland in the brain, regulates the body's response to changing light conditions (Wehr et al., 2001). That's why 80 percent of SAD patients can be helped by extra doses of bright light, a remedy called phototherapy (◆Fig. 12.13). **Phototherapy** involves exposing SAD patients to one or more hours of very bright fluorescent light each day (Lewy et al., 1998). This is best done early in the morning, where it simulates dawn in the summer (Avery et al., 2001). For many SAD sufferers a hearty dose of morning "sunshine" appears to be the next best thing to vacationing in the tropics.

Rates of seasonal affective disorder, by latitude

◆**FIGURE 12.12** *Seasonal affective disorder appears to be related to reduced exposure to daylight during the winter. SAD affects 1 to 2 percent of Florida's population, about 6 percent of the people living in Maryland and New York City, and nearly 10 percent of the residents of New Hampshire and Alaska (Booker & Hellekson, 1992).*

◆**FIGURE 12.13** *An hour or more of bright light a day can dramatically reduce the symptoms of seasonal affective disorder. Treatment is usually necessary from fall through spring. Light therapy typically works best when it is used early in the morning (Lewy et al., 1998).*

DISORDERS IN PERSPECTIVE— PSYCHIATRIC LABELING

As we conclude our survey of psychological disorders, a caution is in order. The terms we have reviewed in this chapter aid communication about human problems. But if used carelessly, they can hurt people. Everyone has felt or acted "crazy" during brief periods of stress or high emotion. People with psychological disorders have problems that are more severe or long-lasting than most of us experience. Otherwise, they may not be that different from you or me.

A fascinating study done by psychologist David Rosenhan illustrates the impact of psychiatric labeling. Rosenhan and several colleagues had themselves committed to mental hospitals with a diagnosis of "schizophrenia" (Rosenhan, 1973). After being admitted, each of these "pseudo-patients" dropped all pretense of mental illness. Yet, even though they acted com-

Phototherapy A treatment for seasonal affective disorder that involves exposure to bright, full-spectrum light.

pletely normal, none of the researchers was ever recognized by hospital *staff* as a phony patient. Real patients were not so easily fooled. It was not unusual for a patient to say to one of the researchers, "You're not crazy, you're checking up on the hospital!" or, "You're a journalist."

To record his observations, Rosenhan took notes by carefully jotting things on a small piece of paper hidden in his hand. However, he soon learned that stealth was totally unnecessary. Rosenhan simply walked around with a clipboard, recording observations. No one questioned this behavior. Rosenhan's note-taking was just regarded as a symptom of his "illness." This observation clarifies why staff members failed to detect the fake patients. Because they were in a mental ward and because they had been *labeled* schizophrenic, anything the pseudo-patients did was seen as a symptom of psychopathology.

As Rosenhan's study shows, it is far better to label *problems* than to label people. Think of the difference in impact between saying, "You are experiencing a serious psychological disorder" and saying, "You're a schizophrenic." Which statement would you prefer to have said about yourself?

Social Stigma

An added problem with psychiatric labeling is that it frequently leads to prejudice and discrimination. That is, the mentally ill in our culture are often *stigmatized* (rejected and disgraced). People who have been labeled mentally ill (at any time in their lives) are less likely to be hired. They also tend to be denied housing, and they are more likely to be falsely accused of crimes. Thus, people who are grappling with mental illness may be harmed as much by social stigma as they are by their immediate psychological problems (Corrigan & Penn, 1999).

A Look Ahead

Treatments for psychological problems range from counseling and psychotherapy to mental hospitalization and drug therapy. Because they vary greatly, a complete discussion of therapies is found in the next chapter. For now, it's worth noting that many milder mental disorders can be treated successfully. Even major disorders may respond well to drugs and other techniques. It is wrong to fear "former mental patients" or to exclude them from work, friendships, and other social situations. A struggle with major depression or a psychotic episode does not inevitably lead to lifelong dysfunction. Too often, however, they lead to unnecessary rejection based on groundless fears (Monahan, 1992).

Let's conclude with a look at a widely misunderstood problem: By the time you finish reading this page, someone in the United States will have attempted suicide. What can be done about suicide? The upcoming Psychology in Action provides some answers.

STUDYBREAK *Mood Disorders*

RELATE

On a piece of paper write "Bipolar Disorders" and "Depressive Disorders." How much of Table 12.6 can you fill in under these headings? Keep reviewing until you can recreate the table (in your own words).

How are the mentally ill stigmatized in movies and television dramas? How do you think such portrayals affect attitudes about mental disorders?

LEARNING CHECK

1. Dysthymic disorder is to depression as cyclothymic disorder is to manic-depression. T or F?
2. Major mood disorders, especially bipolar disorders, often appear to be endogenous. T or F?

3. Learned helplessness is emphasized by _____ theories of depression.
   a. humanistic b. biological c. behavioristic d. psychoanalytic
4. The drug lithium carbonate has been shown to be an effective treatment for anxiety disorders. T or F?
5. The acronym SAD stands for schizotypal affective disorder. T or F?

Critical Thinking

6. How might relationships contribute to the higher rates of depression experienced by women?

ANSWERS

1. T 2. T 3. c 4. F 5. F 6. Women tend to be more focused on relationships than men are. When listing the stresses in their lives, depressed women consistently report higher rates of relationship problems, such as loss of a friend, spouse, or lover, problems getting along with others, and illnesses suffered by people they care about. Depressed men tend to mention issues such as job loss, legal problems, or work problems (Kendler, Thornton, & Prescott, 2001).

Psychology in Action

Suicide—Lives on the Brink

] **SURVEYQUESTIONS** *Why do people commit suicide? Can suicide be prevented?*

"Suicide: A permanent solution to a temporary problem."

Suicide ranks as the seventh cause of death in North America. Roughly 1 person out of 100 attempts suicide during his or her life. We tend to be very concerned about the high rates of murder in North America. However, for every 2 people who die by homicide, 3 will kill themselves. Sooner or later you are likely to be affected by the suicide attempt of someone you know. Check your knowledge of suicide against the following information.

What factors affect suicide rates?   Suicide rates vary greatly, but some general patterns do emerge.

Season

Contrary to popular belief, suicide rates are lower than average between Thanksgiving and Christmas (Phillips & Wills, 1987). On the other hand, more suicides take place at New Year's than on any other day. A "Monday effect" also exists, with higher suicide rates occurring on the first day of the week (McCleary et al., 1991).

Sex

Men have the questionable honor of being better at suicide than women. Three times as many men as women *complete* suicide, but women make more attempts. Male suicide attempts are more lethal because men typically use a gun or an equally fatal method (Garland & Zigler, 1993). Women most often attempt a drug overdose, so there's a better chance of help arriving before death occurs. Sadly, women are beginning to use more deadly methods and may soon equal men in their risk of death by suicide.

Tony Freeman/PhotoEdit

Age

Age is also a factor in suicide. Suicide rates gradually rise during adolescence. They then sharply increase during young adulthood (ages 20–24). From then until age 84 the rate continues to gradually rise with advancing age. As a result, more than half of all suicide victims are over 45 years old. White males 65 years and older are particularly at risk.

In recent years there has been a steady increase in the suicide rates for adolescents and young adults (Diekstra & Garnefski, 1995) (◆Fig. 12.14). Among college students, suicide is the second leading cause of death (Jamison, 2001). School is a factor in some suicides but only in the sense that suicidal students were not living up to their own extremely high standards. Many were good students. Other important factors in student suicide are chronic health problems (real or imagined) and interpersonal difficulties (some suicides are rejected lovers, but others are simply withdrawn and friendless people).

Income

Some professions, such as medicine and psychiatry, have higher than average suicide rates. Overall, however, suicide is equally a problem for the rich and the poor.

Marital Status

Marriage (when successful) may be the best natural guard against suicidal impulses. The highest suicide rates are found among the divorced, the next-highest rates occur among the widowed, lower rates are recorded for single persons, and married individuals have the lowest rates of all.

Immediate Causes of Suicide

Why do people try to kill themselves? The best explanation for suicide may simply come from a look at the conditions that precede it. The following are all major *risk factors* for suicide (Gould et al., 1998; Hall, Platt, & Hall, 1999):

- Drug or alcohol abuse
- A prior suicide attempt
- Depression or other mood disorder
- Feelings of hopelessness, worthlessness
- Anti-social, impulsive, or aggressive behavior
- Severe anxiety, panic attacks
- Family history of suicidal behavior
- Shame, humiliation, failure, or rejection
- Availability of a firearm

Suicidal people usually have a history of trouble with family, a lover, or a spouse. Often they have drinking or drug abuse problems, sexual adjustment problems, or job difficulties. Depression is a factor in 70 percent of all suicides (Lecomte & Fornes, 1998). Factors such as these lead to a preoccupation with death as a way to end the person's suffering.

Typically, suicidal people isolate themselves from others, feel worthless, helpless, and misunderstood, and want to die. An extremely negative self-image and severe feelings of *hopelessness* are warnings that the risk of suicide is very high (Beck et al., 1990; Boergers, Spirito, & Donaldson, 1998). A long history of such conditions is not always necessary to produce a desire for suicide. Anyone may temporarily reach a state of depression severe enough to attempt suicide. Most dangerous for the average person are times of divorce, separation, rejection, failure, and bereavement. Each situation can seem intolerable and motivate an intense desire to die, to escape, or to obtain relief (Boergers, Spirito, & Donaldson, 1998). For young people, feelings of anger and hostility add to the danger. When the impulse to harm others is turned inward, the risk of suicide increases dramatically (Jamison, 2001).

Preventing Suicide

Is it true that people who talk about or threaten suicide are rarely the ones who try it? No, this is a major fallacy. Of every 10 potential suicides, 8 give warning beforehand. A person who threatens suicide should be taken seriously (see ✦Fig. 12.15). A suicidal person may say nothing more than "I feel sometimes like I'd be better off dead." Warnings may also come indirectly. If a friend gives you a favorite ring and says, "Here, I won't be needing this anymore," or comments, "I guess I won't get my watch fixed—it doesn't matter anyway," it may be a plea for help. The warning signs in the list that follows—especially if they are observed in combination—can signal an impending suicide attempt (Leenaars, 1995; Slaby, Garfinkel, & Garfinkel, 1994).

- Withdrawal from contact with others
- Sudden swings in mood
- Recent occurrence of life crisis or emotional shock
- Personality change
- Gift giving of prized possessions
- Depression/hopelessness
- Aggression and/or risk taking
- Single-car accident
- Preoccupation with death
- Drug use
- Death imagery in art
- Direct threats to commit suicide

Is it true that suicide can't be prevented, that the person will find a way to do it anyway? No. Suicide attempts usually come when a person is alone, depressed, and unable to view matters objectively. You *should* intervene if someone seems to be threatening suicide.

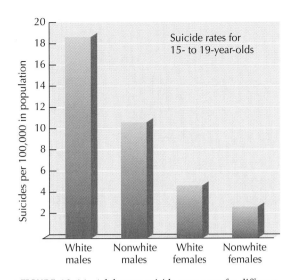

✦**FIGURE 12.14** *Adolescent suicide rates vary for different racial and ethnic groups. Higher rates occur among whites than among non-whites. White male adolescents run the highest risk of suicide. Considering gender alone, it is apparent that more male than female adolescents commit suicide. This is the same as the pattern observed for adults.*

✦**FIGURE 12.15** *Suicidal behavior usually progresses from suicidal thoughts, to threats, to attempts. A person is unlikely to make an attempt without first making threats. Thus, suicide threats should be taken seriously (Garland & Zigler, 1993).*

It is estimated that about two thirds of all suicide attempts fall in the "to be" category. That is, they are made by people who do not really want to die. Almost a third more are characterized by a "to be or not to be" attitude. These people are *ambivalent* or undecided about dying.

Only 3 to 5 percent of suicide cases involve people who really want to die. Most people, therefore, are relieved when someone comes to their aid. Remember that suicide is almost always a cry for help and that you *can* help. As suicide expert Edwin Shneidman (1987a) puts it, "Suicidal behavior is often a form of communication, a cry for help born out of pain, with clues and messages of suffering and anguish and pleas for response."

How You Can Help

What is the best thing to do if someone hints they are thinking about suicide?   It helps to know some of the common characteristics of suicidal thoughts and feelings. Edwin Shneidman (1987b) has identified several.

1. **Escape.** Everyone at times feels like running away from an upsetting situation. Running away from home, quitting school, abandoning a marriage—these are all departures. Suicide, of course, is the ultimate escape. It helps when suicidal persons see that the natural wish for escape doesn't have to be expressed by ending it all.
2. **Unbearable psychological pain.** Emotional pain is what the suicidal person is seeking to escape. A goal of anyone hoping to prevent suicide should be to reduce the pain in any way possible. Ask the person, "Where does it hurt?"
3. **Frustrated psychological needs.** Often, suicide can be prevented if a distressed person's frustrated needs can be identified and eased. Is the person deeply frustrated in his or her search for love, achievement, trust, security, or friendship?
4. **Constriction of options.** The suicidal person feels helpless and decides that death is the *only* solution. The person has narrowed all his or her options solely to death. The rescuer's goal, then, is to help broaden the person's perspective. Even when all the choices are unpleasant, suicidal persons can usually be made to see that their *least unpleasant option* is better than death.

Knowing these patterns will give some guidance in talking to a suicidal person. In addition, your most important task may be to establish *rapport* (a harmonious connection) with the person. You should offer support, acceptance, and legitimate caring.

Remember that a suicidal person feels misunderstood. Try to accept and understand the feelings the person is expressing. Acceptance should also extend to the idea of suicide itself. It is completely acceptable to ask, "Are you thinking of suicide?"

Establishing communication with suicidal persons may be enough to carry them through a difficult time. You may also find it helpful to get day-by-day commitments from them to meet for lunch, share a ride, and the like. Let the person know you *expect* her or him to be there. Such commitments, even though small, can be enough to tip the scales when a person is alone and thinking about suicide.

Don't end your efforts too soon. A dangerous time for suicide is when a person suddenly seems to get better after a severe depression. This often means the person has finally decided to end it all. The improvement in mood is deceptive because it comes from an anticipation that suffering is about to end.

Crisis Intervention

Most cities have mental health crisis intervention teams or centers for suicide prevention. Both have staff members trained to talk with suicidal persons over the phone. Give a person who seems to be suicidal the number of one of these services. Urge the person to call you or the other number if she or he becomes frightened or impulsive. Or better yet, help the person make an appointment to get psychological treatment (Garland & Zigler, 1993).

The preceding applies mainly to persons who are having mild suicidal thoughts. If a person actually threatens suicide, you must act more quickly. Ask how the person plans to carry out the suicide. A person who has a *specific, workable plan,* and the means to carry it out, should be asked to accompany you to the emergency ward of a hospital.

If a person seems on the verge of attempting suicide, don't worry about overreacting. Call the police, crisis intervention, or a rescue unit. Needless to say, you should call immediately if a person is in the act of attempting suicide or if a drug has already been taken. The majority of suicide attempts come at temporary low points in a person's life and may never be repeated. Get involved—you may save a life! But remember, if a suicide attempt seems to be imminent, don't hesitate to immediately seek professional assistance.

STUDYBREAK *Suicide and Suicide Prevention*

RELATE

You're working a suicide hotline, and you take a call from a very distressed young man. What risk factors will you look for as he tells you about his anguish?

What are the common characteristics of suicidal thoughts and feelings identified by Edwin Shneidman? If a friend of yours were to express any of these thoughts or feelings, how would you respond?

LEARNING CHECK

1. More women than men use guns in their suicide attempts. T or F?

2. While the overall suicide rate has remained about the same, there has been a decrease in adolescent suicides. T or F?
3. Suicide is equally a problem of the rich and the poor. T or F?
4. The highest suicide rates are found among the divorced. T or F?
5. The majority (two thirds) of suicide attempts fall in the "to be" category. T or F?

Critical Thinking

6. If you follow popular music, see if you can answer this question: What two major risk factors contributed to the 1994 suicide of Kurt Cobain, lead singer for the rock group Nirvana?

ANSWERS   1. F 2. F 3. T 4. T 5. T 6. Drug or alcohol abuse and availability of a firearm.

CHAPTER IN REVIEW

Major Points

- Judgments of normality are relative, but psychological disorders clearly exist and need to be classified, explained, and treated.
- Psychopathology, which involves identifying, classifying, and explaining psychological disorders, is worthwhile and necessary.
- Psychologically unhealthy behavior is maladaptive and involves a loss of adequate control over thoughts, feelings, and actions.
- Maladaptive behavior patterns, unhealthy personality types, and excessive levels of anxiety underlie many mental disorders.
- The most severe forms of psychopathology involve emotional extremes and/or a break with reality.
- Psychological disorders are complex and have multiple causes.
- Suicide is a relatively frequent cause of death that can, in many cases, be prevented.

Summary

How is normality defined, and what are the major psychological disorders?

- Psychopathology refers to maladaptive behavior and to the scientific study of mental disorders.
- Definitions of normality usually take into account the following: subjective discomfort, statistical abnormality, social nonconformity, and the cultural or situational context of behavior.
- Two key elements in judgments of disorder is that a person's behavior must be maladaptive and it must involve a loss of control.
- Major mental disorders include psychotic disorders, dementia, substance related disorders, mood disorders, anxiety disorders, somatoform disorders, dissociative disorders, personality disorders, and sexual or gender identity disorders.
- Insanity is a legal term defining whether a person may be held responsible for his or her actions. Sanity is determined in court on the basis of testimony by expert witnesses.

What is a personality disorder?

- Personality disorders are deeply ingrained maladaptive personality patterns.
- Sociopathy is a common personality disorder. Antisocial persons seem to lack a conscience. They are emotionally unresponsive, manipulative, shallow, and dishonest.

What problems result when a person suffers high levels of anxiety?

- Anxiety disorders, dissociative disorders, and somatoform disorders are characterized by high levels of anxiety, rigid defense mechanisms, and self-defeating behavior patterns.
- The term *nervous breakdown* has no formal meaning. However, "emotional breakdowns" do correspond somewhat to the occurrence of an adjustment disorder.
- Anxiety disorders include generalized anxiety disorder, panic disorder with or without agoraphobia, agoraphobia (without panic), specific phobias, social phobia, obsessive-compulsive disorders, post-traumatic stress disorder, and acute stress disorder.
- Dissociative disorders may take the form of dissociative amnesia, dissociative fugue, or dissociative identity disorder.
- Somatoform disorders center on physical complaints that mimic disease or disability. Four examples of somatoform disorders are hypochondriasis, somatization disorder, somatoform pain disorder, and conversion disorders.

How do psychologists explain anxiety-based disorders?

- The psychodynamic approach emphasizes unconscious conflicts as the cause of disabling anxiety.
- The humanistic approach emphasizes the effects of a faulty self-image.
- The behaviorists emphasize the effects of previous learning, particularly avoidance learning.
- Cognitive theories of anxiety focus on distorted thinking, judgment, and attention.

What are the general characteristics of psychosis?

- Psychosis is a break in contact with reality that is marked by delusions, hallucinations, sensory changes, disturbed emotions, disturbed communication, and personality disintegration.
- An organic psychosis is based on known injuries or diseases of the brain, including damage caused by poisoning and drug abuse.

What is the nature of a delusional disorder?

- Delusional disorders are almost totally based on the presence of delusions of grandeur, persecution, infidelity, romantic attraction, or physical disease.

- The most common delusional disorder is paranoid psychosis. Paranoid persons may be violent if they believe they are threatened.

What forms does schizophrenia take? What causes it?

- Schizophrenia involves a split between thought and emotion, delusions, hallucinations, and communication difficulties.
- Disorganized schizophrenia is marked by extreme personality disintegration and silly, bizarre, or obscene behavior. Social impairment is usually extreme.
- Catatonic schizophrenia is associated with stupor, mutism, and odd postures. Sometimes violent and agitated behavior also occurs.
- In paranoid schizophrenia (the most common type), outlandish delusions of grandeur and persecution are coupled with psychotic symptoms and personality breakdown.
- Current explanations of schizophrenia emphasize a combination of early trauma, environmental stress, inherited susceptibility, and abnormalities in the brain.
- Environmental factors that increase the risk of schizophrenia include viral infection or malnutrition during the mother's pregnancy, birth complications, early psychological trauma, and a disturbed family environment.
- Heredity is a major factor in schizophrenia.
- Recent biochemical studies have focused on the brain transmitter dopamine and its receptor sites.
- The dominant explanation of schizophrenia, and other problems as well, is the stress-vulnerability model.

What are mood disorders? What causes depression?

- Mood disorders primarily involve disturbances of mood or emotion, producing manic or depressive states.
- Depression that is long-lasting, though relatively moderate, is called a dysthymic disorder. Chronic, though moderate, swings in mood between depression and elation are called a cyclothymic disorder.
- Bipolar disorders combine mania and depression. In a bipolar I disorder, the person swings between mania and depression. In a bipolar II disorder, the person is mostly depressed but has had periods of mild mania.
- A major depressive disorder involves extreme sadness and despondency but no evidence of mania.
- Seasonal affective disorder (SAD), which occurs during the winter months, is another common form of depression. SAD is typically treated with phototherapy.
- Biological, psychoanalytic, cognitive, and behavioral theories of depression have been proposed. Heredity is clearly a factor in susceptibility to mood disorders. Research on the causes and treatment of depression continues.

Why do people commit suicide? Can suicide be prevented?

- Suicide is statistically related to such factors as age, sex, and marital status.
- In individual cases, the potential for suicide is best identified by a desire to escape, unbearable psychological pain, frustrated psychological needs, and a constriction of options.
- Suicide can often be prevented by the efforts of family, friends, and mental health professionals.

Interactive Learning

Internet addresses frequently change. To find the sites listed here, visit www.psychology.wadsworth.com/coon_journey2e for an updated list of Internet addresses and direct links to relevant sites.

PSYCHOLOGY: A JOURNEY COMPANION WEB SITE Online quizzes, flash cards, and other helpful study aids for this text. *www.psychology.wadsworth.com/coon_journey2e*

A GUIDE TO DEPRESSIVE AND MANIC DEPRESSIVE ILLNESS A complete overview of mood disorders.

ANXIETY DISORDERS Information and links to sites about anxiety disorders.

DEPRESSION AFTER DELIVERY A site devoted to providing information about postpartum depression.

DSM-IV QUESTIONS AND ANSWERS Answers to common questions about the DSM-IV.

INTERNET MENTAL HEALTH Comprehensive page on mental health, with links to many other sites.

NATIONAL ALLIANCE FOR THE MENTALLY ILL Home page of the group, with links.

NATIONAL INSTITUTE OF MENTAL HEALTH Links to public information, news and events, and research activities.

PERSONALITY DISORDERS Multiple links to information on personality disorders and their treatment.

UNDERSTANDING SCHIZOPHRENIA An extensive look at schizophrenia.

INFOTRAC COLLEGE EDITION For recent articles related to the Psychology in Action feature, use Key Words search for SUICIDE PREVENTION.

PSYCHNOW! 7c. Abnormality and Psychopathology, 7d. Non-psychotic, Psychotic, and Affective Disorders.

Test Your Knowledge: Psychological Disorders

The questions that follow are only a sample of what you need to know. If you miss any of the items, you should review the entire chapter and get more practice with *WebTutor* or the *Practice Quizzes* that came with this book. Another way to prepare for tests is to use the printed *Study Guide* that is available for this text.

1. The core feature of abnormal behavior is that it is
   A. statistically unusual   B. maladaptive   C. socially non-conforming   D. a source of subjective discomfort

2. In North America, the most widely used standard for classifying mental disorders is the
   A. PTSD   B. *Schedule of Personality Dysfunctions*   C. DSM   D. *Psychiatrist's Desk Reference*

3. People are said to have "retreated from reality" when they suffer from
   A. psychotic disorders   B. mood disorders   C. somatoform disorders   D. personality disorders

4. A person who has periods of extreme mania suffers from
   A. a somatoform disorder   B. a mood disorder   C. an anxiety disorder   D. a neurosis

5. Koro and locura are
   A. somatoform disorders   B. forms of psychosis   C. folk terminology   D. organic mental disorders

6. Which of the following is a *legal* concept?
   A. neurosis   B. psychosis   C. drapetomania   D. insanity

7. Which of the following is NOT a type of personality disorder?
   A. schizoid   B. borderline   C. neurotic   D. dependent

8. A person who is impulsive, dishonest, emotionally cold, and manipulative may suffer from
   A. anti-social personality disorder   B. histrionic personality disorder   C. dependent personality disorder   D. obsessive-compulsive personality disorder

9. When prolonged unemployment, a bad marriage, or physical illness pushes a person beyond his or her ability to cope, it is most likely that which of the following problems will occur?
   A. a dissociative disorder   B. agoraphobia   C. an adjustment disorder   D. a conversion disorder

10. Agoraphobia is most often a feature of
    A. adjustment disorder   B. panic disorder   C. DSM   D. obsessive-compulsive disorder

11. According to the _____ view, anxiety disorders are the end result of a faulty self-image.
    A. psychodynamic   B. humanistic   C. behavioristic   D. cognitive

12. Delusions and hallucinations are most characteristic of
    A. neurosis   B. psychosis   C. Alzheimer's disease   D. dysthymic disorder

13. Paranoid psychosis is the most common type of
    A. catatonic schizophrenia   B. delusional disorder   C. personality disorder   D. dementia

14. Which of the following is NOT one of the subtypes of schizophrenia?
    A. erotomanic type   B. catatonic type   C. paranoid type   D. disorganized type

15. Biochemical explanations of schizophrenia have focused on excessive amounts of _____ in the brain.
    A. radioactive sugar   B. webs and tangles   C. PCP   D. dopamine and glutamate

16. The stress-vulnerability model of psychosis explains mental disorders as a product of environmental stresses and
    A. psychological trauma   B. deviant communication   C. exposure to the flu virus during pregnancy   D. heredity

17. Bipolar disorders that are not too severe are called
    A. endogenous disorders   B. cyclothymic disorders   C. seasonal affective disorders   D. dysthymic disorders

18. The fact that lithium carbonate is effective in treating some cases of bipolar depression suggests that the causes of bipolar disorders are at least partly _____.
    A. biological   B. existential   C. environmental   D. neurotic

19. Depression that occurs only in the winter is likely to be classified as
    A. SAD   B. PTSD   C. bipolar   D. endogenous

20. The risk that a person may attempt suicide is greatest if the person has
    A. a concrete, workable plan   B. had a recent life crisis   C. withdrawn from contact with others   D. frustrated psychological needs

ANSWERS   1. b 2. c 3. a 4. b 5. c 6. d 7. c 8. a 9. c 10. b 11. b 12. b 13. b 14. a 15. d 16. d 17. b 18. a 19. a 20. a

Therapies

Cold Terror on a Warm Afternoon

The warm Arizona sun was shining brightly. Outside my office window an assortment of small birds sang sweetly. I could hear them between Susan's frightened sobs.

As a psychologist, I meet many students with personal problems. Still, I was surprised to see Susan at my office door. Her excellent work in class and her healthy, casual appearance left me unprepared for her first words. "I feel like I'm losing my mind," she said. "Can I talk to you?"

In the next hour, Susan described her own personal hell. Her calm appearance hid a world of crippling fear, anxiety, and depression. At work, she was deathly afraid of talking to co-workers and customers. Her social phobia led to frequent absenteeism and embarrassing behavior. At each job she held, it was only a matter of time until she got fired.

At school, Susan felt "different" and was sure that other students could tell she was "weird." Several disastrous romances had left her terrified of men. Lately she had been so depressed that she thought of suicide. Often, she became terrified for no apparent reason. Each time, her heart pounded wildly, and she felt that she was about to completely lose control.

Susan's visit to my office was an important turning point. Emotional conflicts had made her existence a nightmare. At a time when she was becoming her own worst enemy, Susan realized she needed help from another person. In Susan's case, that person was a talented psychologist to whom I referred her. With psychotherapy, the psychologist was able to help Susan come to grips with her emotions and regain her balance.

This chapter discusses methods used to alleviate problems like Susan's. First, we will describe therapies that emphasize the value of gaining *insight* into personal problems. Then, we will focus on *behavior therapies* and *cognitive therapies*, which directly change troublesome actions and thoughts. Later, we will conclude with *medical therapies*, which are based on psychiatric drugs and other physical treatments.

Roger Allyn Lee/SuperStock

Survey Questions

- How do psychotherapies differ? How did psychotherapy originate?
- Is Freudian psychoanalysis still used?
- What are the major humanistic therapies?
- What is behavior therapy?
- How is behavior therapy used to treat phobias, fears, and anxieties?
- What role does reinforcement play in behavior therapy?
- Can therapy change thoughts and emotions?
- Can psychotherapy be done with groups of people?
- What do various therapies have in common?
- How do psychiatrists treat psychological disorders?
- How are behavioral principles applied to everyday problems?
- How could a person find professional help?

PSYCHOTHERAPY—GETTING BETTER BY THE HOUR

] SURVEYQUESTIONS *How do psychotherapies differ? How did psychotherapy originate?*

Fortunately, the odds are that you will *not* experience an emotional problem like Susan's. But if you did, what help is available? **Psychotherapy** refers to any psychological technique that can bring about positive changes in personality, behavior, or personal adjustment. In most cases, psychotherapy is based on a dialogue between a therapist and his or her client. Some therapists also use learning principles to directly alter troublesome behaviors.

Psychotherapists have many approaches to choose from: psychoanalysis, desensitization, Gestalt therapy, client-centered therapy, cognitive therapy, and behavior therapy—to name but a few. As we will see, the concepts and methods emphasized by each therapy vary greatly. For this reason, the best approach for a particular person or problem may also vary.

Dimensions of Therapy

The terms listed below describe basic aspects of various therapies. Notice that more than one term may apply to a particular therapy. For example, it is possible to have a directive, action-oriented group therapy or a non-directive, individual, insight-oriented therapy.

- **Individual therapy** A therapy involving only one client and one therapist.
- **Group therapy** A therapy session in which several clients participate at the same time.
- **Insight therapy** Any psychotherapy whose goal is to lead clients to a deeper understanding of their thoughts, emotions, and behavior.
- **Action therapy** Any therapy designed to bring about direct changes in troublesome thoughts, habits, feelings, or behavior, without seeking insight into their origins or meanings.
- **Directive therapy** Any approach in which the therapist provides strong guidance.
- **Non-directive therapy** A style of therapy in which clients assume responsibility for solving their own problems; the therapist assists, but does not guide or give advice.
- **Time-limited therapy** Any therapy begun with the expectation that it will last only a limited number of sessions.
- **Supportive therapy** An approach in which the therapist's goal is to offer support, rather than to promote personal change. A person trying to get through an emotional crisis or one who wants to solve day-to-day problems may benefit from supportive therapy.

Psychotherapy Any psychological technique used to facilitate positive changes in a person's personality, behavior, or adjustment.

Myths

Psychotherapy has been depicted as a complete personal transformation—a sort of "major overhaul" of the psyche. But therapy is *not* equally effective for all problems. Chances of improvement are fairly good for phobias, low self-esteem, some sexual problems, and marital conflicts. More complex problems can be difficult to solve. For many people, the major benefit of therapy is that it provides comfort, support, and a way to make constructive changes (Hellerstein et al., 1998).

In short, it is often unrealistic to expect psychotherapy to undo a person's entire past history. Yet even when problems are severe, therapy may help a person gain a new perspective or learn behaviors to better cope with life. Psychotherapy can be hard work for both clients and therapists. But when it succeeds, few activities are more worthwhile.

It's also a mistake to think that psychotherapy is only used to solve problems or end a crisis. Even if a person is already doing well, therapy can be a way to promote personal growth (Buck, 1990). ▲Table 13.1 lists some of the elements of positive mental health that therapists seek to restore or promote.

ORIGINS OF THERAPY—BORED SKULLS AND HYSTERIA ON THE COUCH

Early treatments for mental problems give good reasons to appreciate modern therapies. Archaeological findings dating to the Stone Age suggest that most primitive approaches were marked by fear and superstitious belief in demons, witchcraft, and magic. One of the more dramatic "cures" practiced by primitive "therapists" was a process called *trepanning* (treh-PAN-ing; also sometimes spelled *trephining*). In modern usage, trepanning is any surgical procedure in which a hole is bored in the skull. In the hands of primitive therapists it meant boring, chipping, or bashing holes into a patient's head. Presumably, this was done to relieve pressure or release evil spirits (✦Fig. 13.1). Actually, many "patients" didn't survive the "treatment," which suggests that trepanning may have simply been an excuse to kill people who were unusual.

During the Middle Ages, treatments for mental illness in Europe focused on **demonology,** the study of demons and persons plagued by spirits. Medieval "therapists" commonly blamed abnormal behavior on supernatural forces, such as possession by the devil, or on curses from witches and wizards. As a cure, they used exorcism to "cast out evil spirits." For the fortunate, exorcism was a religious ritual. More often, physical torture was used to make the body an inhospitable place for the devil to reside.

One reason for the rise of demonology may lie in *ergotism* (AIR-got-ism), a psychotic-like condition caused by ergot poisoning. In the Middle Ages, rye (grain) fields were often infested with ergot fungus. Ergot, we now know, is a natural source of LSD and other mind-altering chemicals. Eating tainted bread could have caused symptoms that were easily mistaken for bewitchment or madness. Pinching sensations, muscle twitches, facial spasms, delirium, and hallucinations are all signs of ergot poisoning (Kety, 1979; Matossian, 1982). Thus, many people "treated" by demonologists may have been doubly victimized.

✦**FIGURE 13.1** *Primitive "treatment" for mental disorders sometimes took the form of boring a hole in the skull. This example shows signs of healing, which means the patient survived the treatment. Many didn't.*

(left) Supernatural explanations attributed abnormal behavior to the work of the devil or "possession" by demons. A modern analysis of "demonic possession" suggests that some victims were suffering from dissociative disorders (van der Hart, Lierens, & Goodwin, 1996). *(right)* Many other cases of "possession" in medieval Europe and "bewitchment" in colonial New England may be explained by the psychedelic effects of ergot fungus. An ear of rye infested with the fungus (dark areas) is shown here.

▲*TABLE 13.1* | **Elements of Positive Mental Health**

- Personal autonomy and independence
- A sense of identity
- Feelings of personal worth
- Skilled interpersonal communication
- Sensitivity, nurturance, and trust
- Genuine and honest with self and others
- Self-control and personal responsibility
- Committed and loving personal relationships
- Capacity to forgive others and oneself
- Personal values and a purpose in life
- Self-awareness and motivation for personal growth
- Adaptive coping strategies for managing stresses and crises
- Fulfillment and satisfaction in work
- Good habits of physical health

(Adapted from Bergin, 1991.)

Demonology In medieval Europe, the study of demons and the treatment of persons "possessed" by demons.

(left) Many early asylums were no more than prisons with inmates held in chains. *(right)* One late nineteenth-century "treatment" was based on swinging the patient in a harness—presumably to calm the patient's nerves.

It wasn't until 1793 that the emotionally disturbed were regarded as "mentally ill" and given compassionate treatment. That was the year a French doctor named Philippe Pinel changed the Bicêtre Asylum in Paris from a squalid "madhouse" into a mental hospital by unchaining the inmates. Although it has been over 200 years since Pinel began humane treatment, the process of improving psychiatric care continues today.

When was psychotherapy developed? The first true psychotherapy was developed about 100 years ago by Sigmund Freud. As a physician in Vienna, Freud was intrigued by cases of *hysteria.* People suffering from hysteria have physical symptoms (such as paralysis or numbness) for which no physical causes can be found. (Such problems are now called somatoform disorders.) Slowly, Freud became convinced that hysteria was related to deeply hidden unconscious conflicts. Based on this insight, Freud developed a therapy called psychoanalysis. Since it is the "granddaddy" of more modern therapies, let us examine psychoanalysis in some detail.

PSYCHOANALYSIS—EXPEDITION INTO THE UNCONSCIOUS

] SURVEYQUESTION *Is Freudian psychoanalysis still used?*

Isn't psychoanalysis the therapy where the patient lies on a couch? Freud's patients usually reclined on a couch during therapy, while Freud sat out of sight taking notes and offering interpretations. This arrangement was supposed to encourage a free flow of thoughts and images from the unconscious. However, it is the least important feature of psychoanalysis, and many modern analysts have abandoned it.

Pioneering psychotherapist Sigmund Freud in his office.

How did Freud treat emotional problems? Freud's theory stressed that "neurosis" and "hysteria" are caused by repressed memories, motives, and conflicts—particularly those stemming from instinctual drives for sex and aggression. Although they are hidden, these forces remain active in the personality where they cause some people to develop rigid ego-defenses and compulsive, self-defeating behavior. Thus, the main goal of **psychoanalysis** is to reduce internal conflicts that lead to emotional suffering (Wolitzky, 1995).

Freud relied on four basic techniques to uncover the unconscious roots of neurosis (Freud, 1949). These are *free association, dream analysis, analysis of resistance,* and *analysis of transference.*

Free Association

Saying whatever comes to mind is the basis for **free association.** Patients must speak without worrying whether ideas are painful, embarrassing, or illogical. Thoughts are simply allowed to move freely from one idea to the next, without self-censorship. The purpose of free association is to lower defenses so that unconscious thoughts and feelings can emerge (Wolitzky, 1995).

Psychoanalysis A Freudian therapy that emphasizes the use of free association, dream interpretation, resistances, and transference to uncover unconscious conflicts.

Free association In psychoanalysis, the technique of having a client say anything that comes to mind, regardless of how embarrassing or unimportant it may seem.

Dream Analysis

Freud believed that dreams provide a "royal road to the unconscious" because they freely express forbidden desires and unconscious feelings. Such feelings are found in the **latent content** (hidden, symbolic meaning) of dreams. Normally, we only remember a dream's **manifest content** (obvious, visible meaning), which tends to disguise information from the unconscious.

Freud was especially interested in unconscious messages revealed by **dream symbols** (images that have personal or emotional meanings). Let's say a young man reports a dream in which he pulls a pistol from his waistband and aims at a target while his wife watches. The pistol repeatedly fails to discharge, and the man's wife laughs at him. Freud might have seen this as an indication of repressed feelings of sexual impotence, with the gun serving as a disguised image of the penis.

Analysis of Resistance

When free associating or describing dreams, patients may *resist* talking about or thinking about certain topics. Such **resistances** (blockages in the flow of ideas) reveal particularly important unconscious conflicts. As analysts become aware of resistances, they bring them to the patient's awareness so the patient can deal with them realistically (Wolitzky, 1995). Rather than being roadblocks in therapy, resistances can be challenges and guides (May, 1996).

Analysis of Transference

Transference is the tendency to "transfer" feelings to a therapist that match those the patient had for important persons in his or her past. At times, the patient may act as if the analyst is a rejecting father, an unloving or overprotective mother, or a former lover. As the patient re-experiences repressed emotions, the therapist can help the patient recognize and understand them. Troubled persons often provoke anger, rejection, boredom, criticism, and other negative reactions from others. Effective therapists learn to avoid reacting as others do and playing the patient's habitual "games." This, too, contributes to therapeutic change.

Psychoanalysis Today

What is the status of psychoanalysis today?   Traditional psychoanalysis called for three to five therapy sessions a week, often for many years. Today, most patients are only seen once or twice per week, but treatment may still go on for years (Friedman et al., 1998). Because of the huge amounts of time and money this requires, psychoanalysts have become relatively rare. Nevertheless, psychoanalysis made a major contribution to modern therapies by highlighting the importance of unconscious conflicts (Rangell, 2002).

Many therapists have switched to doing **brief psychodynamic therapy,** which uses direct questioning to reveal unconscious conflicts (Book & Luborsky, 1998). Modern therapists also actively provoke emotional reactions that will lower defenses and provide insights (Davanloo, 1995). Interestingly, brief therapy can speed recovery. Patients seem to realize that they need to get to the heart of their problems quickly (Reynolds et al., 1996).

The development of newer, more streamlined dynamic therapies is in part due to questions about whether traditional psychoanalysis "works." One critic, Hans J. Eysenck (1967, 1994), suggested that psychoanalysis simply takes so long that patients experience a *spontaneous remission* of symptoms (improvement due to the mere passage of time). How could we tell if a particular therapy or the passage of time is responsible for a person's improvement? Typically, some patients are randomly assigned for treatment, while others are placed on a waiting list. If members of this *waiting-list control group,* who receive no treatment, improve at the same rate as those in therapy, the therapy may be of little value.

How seriously should the possibility of spontaneous remission be taken?   It's true that problems ranging from hyperactivity to anxiety improve with the passage of time. However, researchers have confirmed psychoanalysis does, in fact, produce improvement in a majority of patients (Doidge, 1997).

Latent dream content The hidden or symbolic meaning of a dream, as revealed by dream interpretation and analysis.

Manifest dream content The surface, "visible" content of a dream; dream images as they are remembered by the dreamer.

Dream symbols Images in dreams whose personal or emotional meanings differ from their literal meanings.

Resistance A blockage in the flow of free association; topics the client resists thinking or talking about.

Transference The tendency of patients to transfer feelings to a therapist that correspond to those the patient had for important persons in his or her past.

Brief psychodynamic therapy A modern therapy based on psychoanalytic theory but designed to produce insights more quickly.

The real value of Eysenck's critique is that it encouraged psychologists to try new ideas and techniques. Researchers began to ask: "When psychoanalysis works, why does it work? What parts of it are essential and which are unnecessary?" Modern therapists have given surprisingly varied answers to these questions. Upcoming sections will acquaint you with some of the therapies currently in use.

STUDYBREAK   *Psychotherapy and Psychoanalysis*

RELATE

How has your understanding of psychotherapy changed? How many types of therapy can you name?

Make a list describing what you think it means to be mentally healthy. How well does your list match the items in Table 13.1?

The use of trepanning, demonology, and exorcism all implied that the mentally ill are "cursed." To what extent are the mentally ill rejected and stigmatized today?

Try to free associate (aloud) for 10 minutes. How difficult was it? Did anything interesting surface?

Can you explain, in your own words, the role of dream analysis, resistances, and transference in psychoanalysis?

LEARNING CHECK

Match:

_____ 1. Directive therapies
_____ 2. Action therapies
_____ 3. Insight therapies
_____ 4. Non-directive therapies

A. Change behavior
B. Place responsibility on the client
C. The client is guided strongly
D. Seek understanding

5. Pinel is famous for his use of exorcism. T or F?
6. In psychoanalysis, what is an emotional attachment to the therapist by the patient called?
a. free association   b. manifest association   c. resistance   d. transference

Critical Thinking

7. Waiting-list control groups help separate the effects of therapy from improvement related to the mere passage of time. What other type of control group might be needed to learn if therapy is truly beneficial?

ANSWERS

1. C 2. A 3. D 4. B 5. F 6. d 7. Placebo therapy is sometimes used to assess the benefits of real therapy. Placebo therapy superficially resembles the real thing but lacks key elements that are thought to be therapeutic.

HUMANISTIC THERAPIES—RESTORING HUMAN POTENTIAL

] **SURVEYQUESTION** *What are the major humanistic therapies?*

As stated earlier, insight therapists help clients gain a deeper understanding of their thoughts, emotions, and behavior. Better self-knowledge was also the goal of traditional psychoanalysis. However, Freud claimed that his patients could expect only to change their "hysterical misery into common unhappiness"! Humanistic therapies are more optimistic. Most assume that it is possible for people to use their potentials fully and live rich, rewarding lives. Psychotherapy is seen as a way to give mental health a chance to emerge.

Client-Centered Therapy

What is client-centered therapy? How is it different from psychoanalysis?   Psychoanalysts delve into the unconscious. Psychologist Carl Rogers (1902–1987) found it more beneficial to explore *conscious* thoughts and feelings. The psychoanalyst tends to take a position of authority, stating what dreams, thoughts, or memories "mean." In contrast, Rogers believed that what is right or valuable for the therapist may be wrong for the client. (Rogers preferred the term *client* to *patient* because "patient" implies a person is "sick" and needs to be "cured.") Consequently, the client determines what will be discussed during each session. Thus, **client-centered therapy** (also called **person-centered therapy**) is non-directive and based on insights from conscious thoughts and feelings (Bohart, 1995).

Client-centered (or person-centered) therapy A non-directive therapy based on insights gained from conscious thoughts and feelings; emphasizes accepting one's true self.

If the client runs things, what does the therapist do? The therapist's job is to create an "atmosphere of growth." The therapist provides opportunities for change, but the client must actively seek to solve his or her problems. The therapist cannot "fix" the client (Bohart & Tallman, 1996).

Health-Promoting Conditions

Rogers believed that effective therapists maintain four basic conditions. First, the therapist offers the client **unconditional positive regard** (unshakable personal acceptance). The therapist refuses to react with shock, dismay, or disapproval to anything the client says or feels. Total acceptance by the therapist is the first step to self-acceptance by the client.

Second, the therapist attempts to achieve genuine **empathy** by trying to see the world through the client's eyes and feeling some part of what the client is feeling.

As a third essential condition, the therapist strives to be **authentic** (genuine and honest). The therapist must not hide behind a professional role. Rogers believed that phony fronts destroy the growth atmosphere sought in client-centered therapy.

Fourth, the therapist does not make interpretations, propose solutions, or offer advice. Instead, the therapist **reflects** (rephrases, summarizes, or repeats) the client's thoughts and feelings. This allows the therapist to act as a psychological "mirror" so clients can see themselves more clearly. Rogers theorized that a person armed with a realistic self-image and greater self-acceptance will gradually discover solutions to life's problems.

Psychotherapist Carl Rogers, who originated client-centered therapy.

Existential Therapy

According to the existentialists, "being in the world" (existence) creates deep conflicts. Each of us must deal with the realities of death. We must face the fact that we create our private world by making choices. We must overcome isolation on a vast and indifferent planet. Most of all, we must confront feelings of meaninglessness.

What do these concerns have to do with psychotherapy? **Existential therapy** focuses on the problems of existence, such as meaning, choice, and responsibility. Like client-centered therapy, it promotes self-knowledge and self-actualization. However, there are important differences. Client-centered therapy seeks to uncover a "true self" hidden behind a screen of defenses. In contrast, existential therapy emphasizes free will, the human ability to make choices. Accordingly, existential therapists believe you can *choose to become* the person you want to be.

Existential therapists try to give clients the *courage* to make rewarding and socially constructive choices. Typically, therapy focuses on *death, freedom, isolation,* and *meaninglessness,* the "ultimate concerns" of existence (Yalom, 1980). These universal human challenges include: an awareness of one's mortality, the responsibility that comes with freedom to choose, being alone in your own private world, and the need to create meaning in your life.

What does the existential therapist do? The therapist helps clients discover self-imposed limitations in personal identity. To be successful, the client must fully accept the challenge of changing his or her life (Bugental & Sterling, 1995). A key aspect of existential therapy is *confrontation,* in which clients are challenged to examine their values and choices and to take responsibility for the quality of their existence (Gerwood, 1998).

An important part of confrontation is the unique, intense, here-and-now *encounter* between two human beings. When existential therapy is successful, it brings about a renewed sense of purpose and a reappraisal of what's important in life. Some clients even experience an emotional rebirth, as if they had survived a close brush with death. As Marcel Proust wrote, "The real voyage of discovery consists not in seeing new landscapes but in having new eyes."

Gestalt Therapy

Gestalt therapy is based on the idea that perception, or *awareness,* is disjointed and incomplete in maladjusted persons. The German word *Gestalt* means "whole," or "complete." **Gestalt therapy** helps people rebuild thinking, feeling, and acting into connected wholes.

Unconditional positive regard An unqualified, unshakable acceptance of another person.

Empathy A capacity for taking another's point of view; the ability to feel what another is feeling.

Authenticity In Carl Rogers's terms, the ability of a therapist to be genuine and honest about his or her own feelings.

Reflection In client-centered therapy, the process of rephrasing or repeating thoughts and feelings expressed by clients so they can become aware of what they are saying.

Existential therapy An insight therapy that focuses on the elemental problems of existence, such as death, meaning, choice, and responsibility; emphasizes making courageous life choices.

Gestalt therapy An approach that focuses on immediate experience and awareness to help clients rebuild thinking, feeling, and acting into connected wholes; emphasizes the integration of fragmented experiences.

This is achieved by expanding personal awareness; by accepting responsibility for one's thoughts, feelings, and actions; and by filling in gaps in experience (Yontef, 1995).

What do you mean by gaps in experience? Gestalt therapists believe that we often shy away from expressing or "owning" upsetting feelings. This creates a gap in self-awareness that may become a barrier to personal growth. For example, a person who feels anger after the death of a parent might go for years without fully expressing it. This and similar threatening gaps may impair emotional health.

The Gestalt approach is more directive than client-centered or existential therapy, and it emphasizes immediate experience. Working either one-to-one or in a group setting, the Gestalt therapist encourages clients to become more aware of their moment-to-moment thoughts, perceptions, and emotions (Cole, 1998). Rather than discussing *why* clients feel guilt, anger, fear, or boredom, they are encouraged to have these feelings in the "here and now" and become fully aware of them. The therapist promotes awareness by drawing attention to a client's posture, voice, eye movements, and hand gestures. Clients may also be asked to exaggerate vague feelings until they become clear. Gestalt therapists believe that expressing such feelings allows people to "take care of unfinished business" and break through emotional impasses.

Gestalt therapy is most often associated with the work of Frederick (Fritz) Perls (1969). In all his writings, Perls' basic message comes through clearly: Emotional health comes from knowing what you *want* to do, not dwelling on what you *should* do, *ought* to do, or *should want* to do. Another way of stating this idea is that emotional health comes from taking full responsibility for one's feelings and actions. For example, it means changing "I can't," to "I won't," or "I must" to "I choose to."

How does Gestalt therapy help people discover their real wants? Above all else, Gestalt therapy emphasizes *present* experience. Clients are urged to stop intellectualizing and talking *about* feelings. Instead, they learn to live now; live here; stop imagining; experience the real; stop unnecessary thinking; taste and see; express rather than explain, justify, or judge; give in to unpleasantness and pain just as to pleasure; and surrender to being as you are (Naranjo, 1970). Gestalt therapists believe that, paradoxically, the best way to change is to become who you really are (Yontef, 1995).

Because of their emphasis on verbal interaction, humanistic therapies may be conducted at a distance, by telephone or e-mail. Let's investigate this possibility.

PSYCHOTHERAPY AT A DISTANCE— PSYCH JOCKEYS AND CYBERTHERAPY

How valid are psychological services offered over the phone and on the Internet? For better or worse, psychotherapy and counseling are rapidly entering the electronic age. Today, psychological services are available through radio, telephone, videoconferencing, e-mail, and Internet chat rooms. What are the advantages and disadvantages of getting help "online"? What are the risks and possible benefits?

Media Psychologists

By now, you have probably heard a phone-in radio psychologist. On a typical program, callers describe problems arising from child abuse, loneliness, love affairs, phobias, sexual adjustment, or depression. The radio psychologist then offers reassurance, advice, or suggestions for getting help. Talk-radio psychology and similar TV programs may seem harmless, but they raise some important questions. For instance, is it reasonable to give advice without knowing anything about a person's background? Could the advice do harm? What good can a psychologist do in 3 minutes?

In defense of themselves, media psychologists point out that listeners may learn solutions to their problems by hearing others talk. Many also stress that their work is educational, not therapeutic. Nevertheless, the question arises, When does advice become therapy? The American Psychological Association urges media psychologists to discuss problems only of a general nature, instead of actually counseling anyone. For example, if a caller complains about insomnia, the radio psychologist should talk about insomnia in general, not probe the caller's personal life.

By giving information, advice, and social support, media psychologists probably do help some people. Even so, a good guide for anyone tempted to call a radio psychologist might be "let the consumer beware."

Media psychologists have been urged to educate without actually doing therapy on the air. Some overstep this boundary, however.

Telephone Therapists

The same caution applies to telephone therapists. These "counselors" can be reached through 900-number services for $3 to $4 per minute. To date, there is no evidence that commercial telephone counseling is effective. Successful face-to-face therapy is based on a continuing *relationship* between two people. Telephone therapy is also seriously limited by a lack of visual cues, such as facial expressions and body language (Haas, Benedict, & Kobos, 1996).

It's important to note that legitimate therapists occasionally use the phone to calm, console, or advise clients between therapy sessions. Others are experimenting with actually doing therapy by telephone. For example, after the bombing of the World Trade Center towers, many rescue personnel needed counseling. To fill the need, a phone network was created to link emergency workers with psychologists all over the country (Murray, 2001; Shore, 2003). Under the right circumstances, telephone therapy can be as successful as face-to-face therapy (X Day & Schneider, 2002). Likewise, using the telephone for suicide hotlines and crisis counseling is well established. Nevertheless, it's worth saying again that the value of commercial telephone therapists is questionable. Consumers might well ask themselves, How much confidence would I place in a physician who would make a diagnosis over the phone? Many telephone "therapists" actually may be just untrained operators (Newman, 1994).

Cybertherapy

You can find almost anything on the Internet. Recently, "cybertherapy," psychological advice, support groups, and self-help magazines have been added to the list. Some services, such as support groups, are free. Online counseling or advice, in contrast, is typically offered for a fee. Some online therapists will "discuss" problems with you through e-mail messages. Others merely answer questions or give advice concerning specific problems.

Online counseling and advice services do have some advantages. For one thing, clients can remain anonymous. Thus, a person who might hesitate to see a psychologist can seek help privately, online. Likewise, the Internet can link people who live in rural areas with psychologists living in large cities. And, compared with traditional office visits, cybertherapy is less expensive.

As with radio talk shows and telephone counselors, many objections can be raised about online psychological services. Clearly, brief e-mail messages are no way to make a diagnosis. And forget about facial expressions or body language—not even tone of voice reaches the cybertherapist. Typing little smiley faces or frowns is a poor substitute for real human interaction. Another problem is that e-mail counseling may not be completely confidential. In some cases, highly personal messages could be intercepted and misused. Of special concern is the fact that "cybershrinks" may or may not be trained professionals (Bloom, 1998). And even if they are, questions exist about whether a psychologist licensed in one state can legally do therapy in another state, via the Internet. Despite such objections, psychologists are actively exploring the possibility of providing therapy over the Internet, at least for certain types of problems (Lange et al., 2001).

Telehealth

Many of the drawbacks we have discussed can be solved with videoconferencing. In this approach, therapists provide services to people who live too far away to be seen in person. A two-way audio-video link allows the client and therapist to see one another on TV screens and to talk via speakerphones. Doing therapy this way still lacks the close personal contact of face-to-face interaction. However, it does remove many of the objections to doing therapy at a distance. It's very likely that "telehealth" services will become a major source of mental health care in coming years (Jerome et al., 2000).

Summary

As you can see, psychological services that rely on electronic communication may serve some useful purposes. However, the effectiveness of therapy offered by commercial telephone "counselors" and Internet "therapists" remains questionable. The very best advice given by media psychologists, telephone counselors, or cybertherapists may be, "You should consider discussing this problem with a psychologist or counselor in your own community" (Hannon, 1996; Sleek, 1995; Zgodzinski, 1996).

STUDYBREAK ⓨ *Insight Therapies*

RELATE

Here's a mnemonic for the elements of client-centered therapy: Picture a therapist saying "I ear u" to a client. The E stands for empathy, A for authenticity, R for reflection, and U for unconditional positive regard.

What would an existential therapist say about the choices you have made so far in your life? Should you be choosing more "courageously"?

You are going to play the role of a therapist for a classroom demonstration. How would you act if you were a client-centered therapist? An existential therapist? A Gestalt therapist?

A neighbor of yours is thinking about getting counseling on the Internet. What would you tell her about the pros and cons of distance therapy?

LEARNING CHECK

Match:

_____ 1. Client-centered therapy	A. Electronic advice
_____ 2. Gestalt therapy	B. Unconditional positive regard
_____ 3. Existential therapy	C. Gaps in awareness
_____ 4. Cybertherapy	D. Choice and becoming

5. The Gestalt therapist tries to *reflect* a client's thoughts and feelings. T or F?
6. Client-centered therapy is directive. T or F?
7. Confrontation and encounter are concepts of existential therapy. T or F?

Critical Thinking

8. How might using the term *patient* affect the relationship between an individual and a therapist?

ANSWERS

1. B 2. C 3. D 4. A 5. F 6. F 7. T 8. The terms *doctor* and *patient* imply a large gap in status and authority between the individual and his or her therapist. Client-centered therapy attempts to narrow this gap by making the person the final authority concerning solutions to his or her problems. Also, the word *patient* implies that a person is "sick" and needs to be "cured." Many regard this as an inappropriate way to think about human problems.

BEHAVIOR THERAPY—HEALING BY LEARNING

] **SURVEYQUESTION** *What is behavior therapy?*

Five times a day, for several days, Brooks Workman stopped what she was doing and vividly imagined opening a soft-drink can. She then pictured herself bringing the can to her mouth and placing her lips on it. Just as she was about to drink, hordes of roaches poured out of the can and scurried into her mouth—writhing, twitching, and wiggling their feelers (Williams & Long, 1991).

Why would anyone imagine such a thing? Brooks Workman's behavior is not as strange as it may seem. Her goal was self-control: Brooks was drinking too many colas and she wanted to cut down. The method she chose (called *covert sensitization*) is a form of behavior therapy (Cautela & Kearney, 1986). **Behavior therapy** is the use of learning principles to make constructive changes in behavior. Behavioral approaches include behavior modification, aversion therapy, desensitization, token economies, and other techniques.

Behavior therapists believe that deep insight into one's problems is often unnecessary for improvement. Instead, they try to directly alter troublesome thoughts and actions.

Behavior therapy Any therapy designed to actively change behavior.

Brooks Workman didn't need to probe into her past or her emotions and conflicts; she simply wanted to break her habit of drinking too many colas. Even when more serious problems are at stake, techniques like the one she used are valuable.

In general, how does behavior therapy work? Behavior therapists assume that people have *learned* to be the way they are. If they have learned responses that cause problems, then they can change them by *relearning* more appropriate behaviors. Broadly speaking, **behavior modification** refers to any use of classical or operant conditioning to directly alter human behavior (Spiegler & Guevremont, 2003).

How does classical conditioning work? I'm not sure I remember. Classical conditioning is a form of learning in which simple responses (especially reflexes) are associated with new stimuli. Perhaps a brief review would be helpful. In classical conditioning, a neutral stimulus is followed by an *unconditioned stimulus* (*US*) that consistently produces an unlearned reaction, called the *unconditioned response* (*UR*). Eventually, the previously neutral stimulus begins to produce this response directly. The response is then called a *conditioned response* (*CR*), and the stimulus becomes a *conditioned stimulus* (*CS*). Thus, for a child the sight of a hypodermic needle (CS) is followed by an injection (US), which causes anxiety or fear (UR). Eventually the sight of a hypodermic (the conditioned stimulus) may produce anxiety or fear (a conditioned response) *before* the child gets an injection.

What does classical conditioning have to do with behavior modification? Classical conditioning can be used to associate discomfort with a bad habit, as Brooks Workman did. More powerful versions of this approach are called aversion therapy.

Aversion Therapy

Imagine that you are eating an apple. Suddenly you discover that you just bit a large green worm in half. You vomit. Months pass before you can eat an apple again without feeling ill. It's apparent that you have developed a conditioned aversion to apples. (A *conditioned aversion* is a learned dislike or negative emotional response to some stimulus.)

How are conditioned aversions used in therapy? In **aversion therapy,** an individual learns to associate a strong aversion to an undesirable habit such as smoking, drinking, or gambling. Aversion therapy has been used to cure hiccups, sneezing, stuttering, vomiting, nail-biting, bed-wetting, compulsive hair-pulling, alcoholism, and the smoking of tobacco, marijuana, or crack cocaine. (To learn how aversion therapy can help people quit smoking, see "Puffing Up an Aversion.") Actually, aversive conditioning happens everyday. For example, not many physicians who treat lung cancer are smokers, nor do many emergency room doctors drive without using their seat belts (Rosenthal & Steffek, 1991).

Behavior modification The application of learning principles to change human behavior, especially maladaptive behavior.

Aversion therapy Suppressing an undesirable response by associating it with aversive (painful or uncomfortable) stimuli.

USING PSYCHOLOGY Puffing Up an Aversion

The fact that nicotine is toxic makes it easy to create an aversion to smoking. Behavior therapists have found that electric shock, nauseating drugs, and similar aversive stimuli are not required to make smokers uncomfortable. All that is needed is for the smoker to smoke—rapidly and for a long time.

Rapid smoking (prolonged smoking at a forced pace) is the most widely used aversion therapy for smoking. In this method, clients are told to smoke continuously, taking a puff every 6 to 8 seconds. Rapid smoking continues until the smoker is miserable and can stand it no more. By then, most people are thinking, "I never want to see another cigarette for the rest of my life."

Studies suggest that rapid smoking is one of the most effective behavior therapies for smoking (Tiffany et al., 1986). Nevertheless, anyone tempted to try rapid smoking should realize that it is very unpleasant. Without the help of a therapist, most people quit too

soon for the procedure to succeed. In addition, rapid smoking can be dangerous. It should only be done with professional supervision. (An alternative method that is more practical is described in the Psychology in Action section of this chapter.)

A problem with rapid smoking—as with other stop-smoking methods—is that about one half of those who quit smoking begin again. During at least the first year after quitting, there is no "safe point" after which relapse becomes less likely (Swan & Denk, 1987).

Because the "evil weed" calls so strongly to former smokers, support from a stop-smoking group or a close, caring person can make a big difference. Former smokers who get encouragement from others are much more likely to stay smoke free (Gruder et al., 1993). Those whose social groups include many smokers are more likely to begin smoking again (Mermelstein, 1986).

Aversion therapy for drinking. The sights, smells, and tastes of drinking are associated with unpleasant electric shocks applied to the hand.

An excellent example of aversion therapy is provided by the work of Roger Vogler and his associates (1977). Vogler works with alcoholics who were unable to stop drinking. For many clients, aversion therapy is a last chance. While drinking an alcoholic beverage, clients receive a painful (although non-injurious) electric shock to the hand. Most of the time, these shocks occur as the client is beginning to take a drink of alcohol.

These *response-contingent shocks* (shocks that are linked to a response) obviously take the pleasure out of drinking. Shocks also cause the alcohol abuser to develop a conditioned aversion to drinking. Normally, the misery caused by alcohol abuse comes long after the act of drinking—too late to have much effect. But if alcohol can be linked with *immediate* discomfort, then drinking will begin to make the individual very uncomfortable.

Is it really acceptable to treat clients this way?   People are often disturbed (shocked?) by such methods. However, clients usually *volunteer* for aversion therapy because it helps them overcome a destructive habit. Indeed, commercial aversion programs for overeating, smoking, and alcohol abuse have attracted many willing customers. And more important, aversion therapy can be justified by its long-term benefits. As behaviorist Donald Baer put it, "A small number of brief, painful experiences is a reasonable exchange for the interminable pain of a lifelong maladjustment."

DESENSITIZATION

] SURVEYQUESTION *How is behavior therapy used to treat phobias, fears, and anxieties?*

Assume that you are a swimming instructor who wants to help a child named Jamie overcome fear of the high diving board. How might you proceed? Directly forcing Jamie off the high board could be a psychological disaster. Obviously, a better approach would be to begin by teaching her to dive off the edge of the pool. Then she could be taught to dive off the low board, followed by a platform 6 feet above the water and then an 8-foot platform. As a last step, Jamie could try the high board.

Who's Afraid of a Hierarchy?

This rank-ordered series of steps is called a **hierarchy.** The hierarchy allows Jamie to undergo *adaptation.* Gradually, she adapts to the high dive and overcomes her fear. When Jamie has conquered her fear, we can say that *desensitization* (dee-SEN-sih-tih-ZAY-shun) has occurred (Spiegler & Guevremont, 2003).

Desensitization is also based on **reciprocal inhibition** (using one emotional state to block another) (Wolpe & Plaud, 1997). For instance, it is impossible to be anxious and relaxed at the same time. If we can get Jamie onto the high board in a relaxed state, her anxiety and fear will be inhibited. Repeated visits to the high board should cause fear in this situation to disappear. Again we would say that Jamie has been desensitized. Typically, **systematic desensitization** (a guided reduction in fear, anxiety, or aversion) is attained by gradually approaching a feared stimulus while maintaining relaxation.

What is desensitization used for?   Desensitization is primarily used to help people unlearn phobias (intense, unrealistic fears) or strong anxieties. For example, each of these people might be a candidate for desensitization: a teacher with stage fright, a student with test anxiety, a salesperson who fears people, or a newlywed with an aversion to sexual intimacy.

Performing Desensitization

How is desensitization done?   First, the client and the therapist *construct a hierarchy.* This is a list of fear-provoking situations, arranged from least disturbing to most frightening. Second, the client is taught *exercises that produce deep relaxation.* (These are de-

Hierarchy A rank-ordered series of higher and lower amounts, levels, degrees, or steps.

Reciprocal inhibition The presence of one emotional state can inhibit the occurrence of another, such as joy preventing fear or anxiety inhibiting pleasure.

Systematic desensitization A reduction in fear, anxiety, or aversion brought about by planned exposure to aversive stimuli.

scribed in this chapter's Psychology in Action section.) Once the client is relaxed, she or he proceeds to the third step by trying to *perform the least disturbing item* on the list. For a fear of heights (acrophobia), this might be: "(1) Stand on a chair." The first item is repeated until no anxiety is felt. Any change from complete relaxation is a signal that clients must relax again before continuing. Slowly, clients move up the hierarchy: "(2) Climb to the top of a small stepladder"; "(3) Look down a flight of stairs"; and so on, until the last item is performed without fear: "(20) Fly in an airplane."

For many phobias, desensitization works best when people are directly exposed to the stimuli and situations they fear (Oest et al., 2001). For something like a simple spider phobia, this exposure can even be done in groups (Oest, 1996). Also, for some fears (such as fear of riding an elevator) desensitization may be completed in a single session (Sturges & Sturges, 1998).

Vicarious Desensitization

I understand how some fears could be desensitized by gradual approach—as in the case of the child on the high dive. But what if it's not practical to directly act out the steps of a hierarchy? For a fear of heights, the steps of the hierarchy might be acted out. However, if this is impractical the problem can be handled by having clients observe *models* who are performing the feared behavior (Rosenthal & Steffek, 1991) (✦Fig. 13.2). A model is a person (either live or filmed) who serves as an example for observational learning. If such **vicarious desensitization** (secondhand learning) can't be used, there is yet another option. Fortunately, desensitization works almost as well when a person *vividly imagines* each step in the hierarchy (Deffenbacher & Suinn, 1988). If the steps can be visualized without anxiety, fear in the actual situation is reduced. Because imagining feared stimuli can be done at a therapist's office, it is the most common way of doing desensitization.

Programs for treating fears of flying combine relaxation, systematic desensitization, group support, and lots of direct exposure to airliners. Many such programs conclude with a brief flight, so that participants can "test their wings" (Roberts, 1989).

✦FIGURE 13.2 *Treatment of a snake phobia by vicarious desensitization. The photographs show models interacting with snakes. To overcome their own fears, phobic subjects observed the models (Bandura et al., 1969). (Photos courtesy of Albert Bandura.)*

Vicarious desensitization A reduction in fear or anxiety that takes place vicariously ("second hand") when a client watches models perform the feared behavior.

✦FIGURE 13.3 (left) *Dr. Barbara Rothbaum and Dr. Larry Hodges show how a virtual reality system is used to expose people to feared stimuli. Many patients would rather face feared stimuli in a virtual environment than in a real physical environment.* (right) *A computer image from a virtual elevator. Over an 8-week period, patients who suffered from acrophobia "rode" in the elevator. Each session took them to greater heights. (Image courtesy of Larry Hodges, Thomas Meyer, and Rob Kooper.)*

Virtual Reality Exposure

Desensitization is an *exposure therapy.* Like other such therapies, it involves exposing people to feared stimuli until their fears extinguish. In an important new development, psychologists are beginning to use virtual reality to treat phobias. Virtual reality is a computer-generated, three-dimensional "world" that viewers enter by wearing a head-mounted video display. **Virtual reality exposure** presents computerized fear stimuli to patients in a controlled fashion. It has already been used to treat acrophobia (fear of heights), fears of flying and driving and public speaking, spider phobias, and claustrophobia (Botella et al., 1998; Lee et al., 2002; Rothbaum et al., 1996; Rothbaum, Hodges, & Kooper, 1997; Wald and Taylor, 2000) (✦Fig. 13.3).

Desensitization has been one of the most successful behavior therapies. A second new technique may provide yet another way to lower fears, anxieties, and psychological pain.

Eye Movement Desensitization

Traumatic events produce painful memories. Victims of accidents, disasters, molestations, muggings, rapes, or emotional abuse are often haunted by disturbing flashbacks. Recently, Dr. Francine Shapiro developed **eye movement desensitization and reprocessing** (**EMDR**) to help ease traumatic memories and post-traumatic stress.

In a typical EMDR session, the client is asked to visualize the images that most upset her or him. At the same time, a pencil (or other object) is moved rapidly from side to side in front of the person's eyes. Watching the moving object causes the person's eyes to dart swiftly back and forth. Shapiro believes that rapid eye movements generate brain activity that helps restructure painful memories. After about 30 seconds, patients describe any memories, feelings, and thoughts that emerged and discuss them with the therapist. These steps are repeated until troubling thoughts and emotions no longer surface (Shapiro, 1995).

A number of studies suggest that EMDR lowers anxieties and takes the pain out of traumatic memories (Carlson et al., 1998; Lazgrove et al., 1998; Scheck, Schaeffer, & Gillette, 1998). However, EMDR is highly controversial. Some studies, for example, have found that eye movements add nothing to the treatment. The apparent success of EMDR may simply be based on gradual exposure to upsetting stimuli, like in other forms of desensitization (Cahill, Carrigan, & Frueh, 1999; Davidson & Parker, 2001). On the other hand, some researchers continue to find that EMDR is superior to traditional therapies (Ironson et al., 2002; Rogers & Silver, 2002).

Is EMDR a breakthrough? Or will it prove to be a case of wishful thinking? Given the frequency of traumas in modern society, it shouldn't be long before we find out.

Virtual reality exposure Use of computer-generated images to present fear stimuli. The virtual environment responds to a viewer's head movements and other inputs.

Eye movement desensitization and reprocessing (EMDR) A technique for reducing fear or anxiety; based on holding upsetting thoughts in mind while rapidly moving the eyes from side to side.

STUDYBREAK ❖ *Behavior Therapy*

RELATE

Can you describe three problems for which you think behavior therapy would be an appropriate treatment?

A friend of yours has a dog that goes berserk during thunderstorms. You own an audio tape of a thunderstorm. How could you use the tape to desensitize the dog? (Hint: The tape-player has a volume control.)

Have you ever become naturally desensitized to a stimulus or situation that at first made you anxious (for instance, heights, public speaking, or driving on freeways)? How would you explain your reduced fear?

LEARNING CHECK

1. What two types of conditioning are used in behavior modification? _____ and _____

2. Shock, pain, and discomfort play what role in conditioning an aversion?
   a. conditioned stimulus   b. unconditioned response
   c. unconditioned stimulus   d. conditioned response

3. If shock is used to control drinking, it must be _____ contingent.

4. What two principles underlie systematic desensitization? _____ and _____

5. When desensitization is carried out through the use of live or filmed models, it is called
   a. cognitive therapy   b. flooding   c. covert desensitization
   d. vicarious desensitization

6. The three basic steps in systematic desensitization are: construct a hierarchy, flood the person with anxiety, and imagine relaxation. T or F?

7. In EMDR therapy, computer-generated virtual reality images are used to expose patients to fear-provoking stimuli. T or F?

Critical Thinking

8. Alcoholics who take a drug called Antabuse become ill after drinking alcohol. Why, then, don't they develop an aversion to drinking?

9. A natural form of desensitization often takes place in hospitals. Can you guess what it is?

ANSWERS 1. classical (or respondent), operant 2. c 3. response 4. adaptation, reciprocal inhibition 5. d 6. F 7. F 8. Their discomfort is delayed enough to prevent it from being closely associated with drinking. Fortunately, there are safer, better ways to do aversion therapy (Wilson, 1987). 9. Doctors and nurses learn to relax and remain calm at the sight of blood because of their frequent exposure to it.

OPERANT THERAPIES—ALL THE WORLD IS A SKINNER BOX?

] **SURVEYQUESTION** *What role does reinforcement play in behavior therapy?*

Aversion therapy and desensitization are based on classical conditioning. Where does operant conditioning fit in? As you may recall, *operant conditioning* refers to learning based on the consequences of making a response. The operant principles most often used by behavior therapists to deal with human behavior are:

1. **Positive reinforcement.** Responses that are followed by reward tend to occur more frequently. If children whine and get attention, they will whine more frequently. If you get A's in your psychology class, you may become a psychology major.

2. **Non-reinforcement.** A response that is not followed by reward will occur less frequently.

3. **Extinction.** If a response is not followed by reward after it has been repeated many times, it will go away. After winning three times, you pull the handle on a slot machine 30 times more without a payoff. What do you do? You go away. So does the response of handle pulling (for that particular machine, at any rate).

4. **Punishment.** If a response is followed by discomfort or an undesirable effect, the response will be suppressed (but not necessarily extinguished).

5. **Shaping.** Shaping means rewarding actions that are closer and closer approximations to a desired response. For example, if I want to reward a retarded child for saying "ball," I may begin by rewarding the child for saying anything that starts with a *b* sound.

6. **Stimulus control.** Responses tend to come under the control of the situation in which they occur. If I set my clock 10 minutes fast, I can get to work on time in

the morning. My departure is under the stimulus control of the clock, even though I know it is fast.

7. **Time out.** A time-out procedure usually involves removing the individual from a situation in which reinforcement occurs. Time out is a variation of non-reinforcement: It prevents reward from following an undesirable response. For example, children who fight with each other can be sent to separate rooms and allowed out only when they are able to behave more calmly. (For a more thorough review of operant learning, return to Chapter 6.)

As simple as these principles may seem, they have been used very effectively to overcome difficulties in work, home, school, and industrial settings. Let's see how.

Non-Reinforcement and Extinction

An extremely overweight mental patient had a persistent and disturbing habit: She stole food from other patients. No one could persuade her to stop stealing or to diet. For the sake of her health, a behavior therapist assigned her a special table in the ward dining room. If she approached any other table, she was immediately removed from the dining room. Since her attempts to steal food went unrewarded, they rapidly disappeared. Additionally, any attempt to steal from others caused the patient to miss her own meal (Ayllon, 1963).

What operant principles did the therapist in this example use? The therapist used *non-reward* to produce *extinction*. The most frequently occurring human behaviors lead to some form of reward. An undesirable response can be eliminated by *identifying* and *removing* the rewards that maintain it. But people don't always do things for food, money, or other obvious rewards. Most of the rewards maintaining human behavior are more subtle. *Attention, approval,* and *concern* are common yet powerful reinforcers for humans (◆Fig. 13.4).

Non-reward and extinction can eliminate many problem behaviors, especially in schools, hospitals, and institutions. Often, difficulties center around a limited number of particularly disturbing responses. Time out is a good way to remove such responses, usually by refusing to pay attention to a person who is misbehaving. For example, 14-year-old Zeke periodically appeared in the nude in the activity room of a training center for disturbed

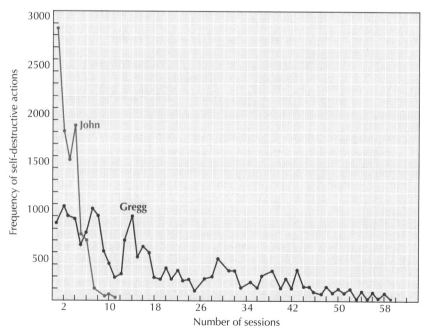

◆**FIGURE 13.4** *This graph shows extinction of self-destructive behavior in two autistic boys. Before extinction began, the boys received attention and concern from adults for injuring themselves. During extinction, the adults were taught to ignore the boys' self-damaging behavior. As you can see, the number of times that the boys tried to injure themselves declined rapidly. (Adapted from Lovaas & Simons, 1969.)*

adolescents. This behavior always generated a great deal of attention from staff and other patients. Usually Zeke was returned to his room and confined there. During this "confinement," he often missed doing his usual chores. As an experiment he was placed on time out. The next time he appeared nude, counselors and other staff members greeted him normally and then ignored him. Attention from other patients rapidly subsided. Sheepishly, he returned to his room and dressed.

Reinforcement and Token Economies

A distressing problem therapists sometimes face is how to break through to severely disturbed patients who won't talk. Conventional psychotherapy offers little hope of improvement for such patients.

What can be done for them? One widely used approach is based on *tokens* (symbolic rewards, such as plastic chips, that can be exchanged for real rewards). Tokens may be printed slips of paper, check marks, points, or gold stars. Whatever form they take, tokens serve as rewards because they may be exchanged for candy, food, cigarettes, recreation, or privileges, such as private time with a therapist, outings, or watching TV. Tokens are used in mental hospitals, half-way houses, schools for the retarded, programs for delinquents, and ordinary classrooms. They usually produce dramatic improvements in behavior (Foxx, 1998; Mohanty, Pati, & Kumar, 1998; Truchlicka, McLaughlin, & Swain, 1998).

By using tokens, a therapist can *immediately reward* positive responses. For maximum impact, therapists select specific *target behaviors* (actions or other behaviors the therapist seeks to modify). Target behaviors are then reinforced with tokens. For example, a mute mental patient might first be given a token each time he or she says a word. Next, tokens may be given for speaking a complete sentence. Later, the patient could gradually be required to speak more often, then to answer questions, and eventually to carry on a short conversation in order to receive tokens. In this way, deeply withdrawn patients have been returned to the world of normal communication.

Full-scale use of tokens in an institutional setting produces a *token economy*. In a **token economy,** patients are rewarded with tokens for a wide range of socially desirable or productive activities (Spiegler & Guevremont, 2003). They must *pay* tokens for privileges and for engaging in problem behaviors (✦Fig. 13.5). For example, tokens are given to patients who get out of bed, dress themselves, take required medication, arrive for meals on time, and so on. Constructive activities, such as gardening, cooking, or cleaning, may also earn tokens. Patients must *exchange* tokens for meals and private rooms, movies, passes, off-ward activities, and other privileges. They are *charged* tokens for staying in bed, disrobing in public, talking to themselves, fighting, crying, and similar target behaviors (Morisse et al., 1996).

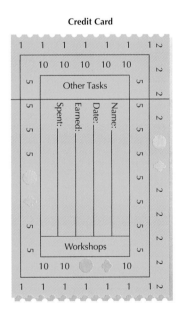

✦FIGURE 13.5 *Shown here is a token used in one token economy system. In this instance the token is a card that records the number of credits eared by a patient. Also pictured is a list of credit values for various activities. Tokens may be exchanged for items or for privileges listed on the board. (After photographs by Robert P. Liberman.)*

Token economies can radically change a patient's overall adjustment and morale. Patients are given an incentive to change, and they are held responsible for their actions. The use of tokens may seem manipulative, but it actually empowers patients. Many "hopelessly" retarded, mentally ill, and delinquent people have been returned to productive lives by means of token economies (Corrigan, 1997).

Token economy A therapeutic program in which desirable behaviors are reinforced with tokens that can be exchanged for goods, services, activities, and privileges.

By the time they are ready to leave, patients may be earning tokens on a weekly basis for maintaining sane, responsible, and productive behavior (Binder, 1976). Typically, the most effective token economies are those that gradually switch from tokens to *social rewards* such as praise, recognition, and approval. Such rewards are what patients will receive when they return to family, friends, and community.

COGNITIVE THERAPY—THINK POSITIVE!

] SURVEYQUESTION *Can therapy change thoughts and emotions?*

How would a behavior therapist treat a problem like depression? None of the techniques described seem to apply.   As we have discussed, behavior therapists usually try to change troublesome actions. However, in recent years cognitive therapists have become interested in what people think, believe, and feel, as well as how they act. In general, **cognitive therapy** helps clients change thinking patterns that lead to troublesome emotions or behaviors (Freeman & Reinecke, 1995). For example, compulsive hand-washing can be greatly reduced just by changing a client's thoughts and beliefs about dirt and contamination (Jones & Menzies, 1998). Cognitive therapy is used as a remedy for many problems, but it has been especially successful in treating depression (Chambless & Ollendick, 2001).

Cognitive Therapy for Depression

Cognitive therapy has been especially effective for treating depression. As you may recall from Chapter 12, Aaron Beck (1991) believes that negative, self-defeating thoughts underlie depression. According to Beck, depressed persons see themselves, the world, and the future in negative terms. Beck believes this occurs because of major distortions in thinking. The first is **selective perception,** which refers to perceiving only certain stimuli in a larger array. If five good things happen during the day and three bad things, depressed people focus only on the bad. A second thinking error in depression is **overgeneralization,** the tendency to let upsetting events affect unrelated situations. An example would be considering yourself a total failure or completely worthless if you were to lose a part-time job or fail a test. To complete the picture, depressed persons tend to magnify the importance of undesirable events by engaging in **all-or-nothing thinking.** That is, they see events as completely good or bad, right or wrong, and themselves as either successful or failing miserably (Beck, 1985).

How do cognitive therapists alter such patterns?   Cognitive therapists make a step-by-step effort to correct negative thoughts that lead to depression or similar problems. At first, clients are taught to recognize and keep track of their own thoughts. The client and therapist then look for ideas and beliefs that cause depression, anger, and avoidance. For example, here's how a therapist might challenge all-or-nothing thinking (Burns & Persons, 1982):

PATIENT: I'm feeling even more depressed. No one wants to hire me, and I can't even clean up my apartment. I feel completely incompetent!
THERAPIST: I see. The fact that you are unemployed and have a messy apartment proves that you are completely incompetent?
PATIENT: Well . . . I can see that doesn't add up.

Next, clients are asked to gather information to test their beliefs. For instance, a depressed person might list his or her activities for a week. The list is then used to challenge all-or-nothing thoughts, such as "I had a terrible week" or "I'm a complete failure." With more coaching, clients learn to alter their thoughts in ways that improve their moods, actions, and relationships.

Cognitive therapy is as effective as drugs for treating many cases of depression. More important, people who have adopted new thinking patterns are less likely to become depressed again—a benefit that drugs can't impart (Fava et al., 1998; Gloaguen et al., 1998).

Cognitive therapy A therapy directed at changing the maladaptive thoughts, beliefs, and feelings that underlie emotional and behavioral problems.

Selective perception Perceiving only certain stimuli among a larger array of possibilities.

Overgeneralization Blowing a single event out of proportion by extending it to a large number of unrelated situations.

All-or-nothing thinking Classifying objects or events as absolutely right or wrong, good or bad, acceptable or unacceptable, and so forth.

USING PSYCHOLOGY   Ten Irrational Beliefs—Which Do You Hold?

Rational-emotive behavior therapists have identified numerous beliefs that commonly lead to emotional upsets and conflicts. See if you recognize any of the following irrational beliefs:

1. I must be loved and approved by almost every significant person in my life, or it's awful and I'm worthless.
   Example: "One of my roommates doesn't seem to like me. I must be a total zero."
2. I should be completely competent and achieving in all ways to be a worthwhile person.
   Example: "I don't understand my chemistry class. I guess I really am a stupid person."
3. Certain people I must deal with are thoroughly bad and should be severely blamed and punished for it.
   Example: "The old man next door is such a pain. I'm going to play my stereo even louder the next time he complains."
4. It is awful and upsetting when things are not the way I would very much like them to be.
   Example: "I should have gotten a B in that class. The teacher is unfair."
5. My unhappiness is always caused by external events; I cannot control my emotional reactions.
   Example: "You make me feel awful. I would be happy if it weren't for you."
6. If something unpleasant might happen, I should keep dwelling on it.
   Example: "I'll never forget the time my boss insulted me. I think about it every day at work."
7. It is easier to avoid difficulties and responsibilities than to face them.
   Example: "I don't know why my wife seems angry. Maybe it will just pass by if I ignore it."
8. I should depend on others who are stronger than I am.
   Example: "I couldn't survive if he left me."
9. Because something once strongly affected my life, it will do so indefinitely.
   Example: "My girlfriend dumped me during my junior year in college. I don't know if I can ever trust a woman again."
10. There is always a perfect solution to human problems, and it is awful if this solution is not found.
    Example: "I'm so depressed about politics in this country. It all seems hopeless."
    (Adapted from Rohsenow & Smith, 1982.)

If any of the listed beliefs sound familiar, you may be creating unnecessary emotional distress for yourself by holding on to unrealistic expectations.

In an alternate approach, cognitive therapists look for an *absence* of effective coping skills and thinking patterns, not for the *presence* of self-defeating thoughts (Freeman & Reinecke, 1995). The aim is to teach clients how to cope with anger, depression, shyness, stress, and similar problems. Stress inoculation, which was described in Chapter 11, is a good example of this approach.

Cognitive therapy is a rapidly expanding specialty. Before we leave the topic, let's explore another widely used cognitive therapy.

Rational-Emotive Behavior Therapy

Rational-emotive behavior therapy (**REBT**) attempts to change irrational beliefs that cause emotional problems. According to Albert Ellis (1973, 1995), the basic idea of rational-emotive behavior therapy is as easy as A-B-C. Ellis assumes that people become unhappy and develop self-defeating habits because they have unrealistic or faulty *beliefs*.

How are beliefs important? Ellis analyzes problems in this way: The letter A stands for an *activating experience,* which the person assumes to be the cause of C, an *emotional consequence.* For instance, a person who is rejected (the activating experience) feels depressed, threatened, or hurt (the consequence). Rational-emotive behavior therapy shows the client that the real problem is what comes between A and C: In between is B, the client's irrational and unrealistic *beliefs.* In this example, an unrealistic belief leading to unnecessary suffering is: "I must be loved and approved by almost everyone at all times." REBT holds that events do not *cause* us to have feelings. We feel as we do because of our beliefs (Kottler & Brown, 1999). (For some examples, see "Ten Irrational Beliefs—Which Do You Hold?")

Ellis (1979, 1987) says that most irrational beliefs come from three core ideas, each of which is unrealistic:

1. I *must* perform well and be approved of by significant others. If I don't, then it is awful, I cannot stand it, and I am a rotten person.
2. You *must* treat me fairly. When you don't, it is horrible, and I cannot bear it.
3. Conditions *must* be the way I want them to be. It is terrible when they are not, and I cannot stand living in such an awful world.

Rational-emotive behavior therapy (REBT) An approach that states that irrational beliefs cause many emotional problems and that such beliefs must be changed or abandoned.

It's easy to see that such beliefs can lead to much grief and needless suffering in a less than perfect world. Rational-emotive behavior therapists are very directive in their attempts to change a client's irrational beliefs and "self-talk." The therapist may directly attack clients' logic, challenge their thinking, confront them with evidence contrary to their beliefs, and even assign "homework." Here, for instance, are some examples of statements that dispute irrational beliefs (after Kottler & Brown, 1999):

- "Where is the evidence that you are a loser just because you didn't do well this one time?"
- "Who said the world should be fair? That's your rule."
- "What are you telling yourself to make yourself feel so upset?"
- "Is it really terrible that things aren't working out as you would like? Or is it just inconvenient?"

Many of us would probably do well to give up our irrational beliefs. Improved self-acceptance and a better tolerance of daily annoyances are the benefits of doing so.

The value of cognitive approaches is further illustrated by three techniques (*covert sensitization, thought stopping,* and *covert reinforcement*) described in this chapter's Psychology in Action section. A little later you can see what you think of them.

STUDYBREAK ▼ *Operant Therapies and Cognitive Therapies*

RELATE

See if you can give a personal example of how the following principles have affected your behavior: positive reinforcement, extinction, punishment, shaping, stimulus control, and time out.

You are setting up a token economy for troubled elementary school children. What target behaviors will you attempt to reinforce? For what behaviors will you charge tokens?

We all occasionally engage in negative thinking. Can you remember a time recently when you engaged in selective perception? Over-generalization? All-or-nothing thinking?

Which of REBT's irrational beliefs have affected your feelings? Which beliefs would you like to change?

LEARNING CHECK

1. Behavior modification programs aimed at extinction of an undesirable behavior typically make use of what operant principles?
   a. punishment and stimulus control   b. punishment and shaping   c. non-reinforcement and time out   d. stimulus control and time out

2. Attention can be a powerful _____ for humans.
3. Token economies depend on the time-out procedure. T or F?
4. Tokens basically allow the operant shaping of desired responses or "target behaviors." T or F?
5. According to Beck, selective perception, overgeneralization, and _____ thinking are cognitive habits that underlie depression.
6. REBT teaches people to change the antecedents of irrational behavior. T or F?

Critical Thinking

7. In Aaron Beck's terms, a belief such as "I must perform well or I am a rotten person" involves two thinking errors. These are:

ANSWERS

1. c 2. reinforcer 3. F 4. T 5. all-or-nothing 6. F 7. Over-generalization and all-or-nothing thinking.

GROUP THERAPY—PEOPLE WHO NEED PEOPLE

] SURVEYQUESTION *Can psychotherapy be done with groups of people?*

To complete our look at psychotherapies, we will begin with group therapy. Group therapy has certain advantages, not the least of which is reduced cost. After that, we will identify the core features and helping skills that make psychotherapy "work." To conclude, we will explore medical approaches to treating mental disorders.

Group therapy is psychotherapy done with more than one person. Most of the therapies we have discussed can be adapted for use in groups. Psychologists first tried working with groups because there was a shortage of therapists. Surprisingly, group therapy has

Group therapy Psychotherapy conducted in a group setting to make therapeutic use of group dynamics.

turned out to be just as effective as individual therapy and it has some special advantages (McRoberts, Burlingame, & Hoag, 1998).

What are the advantages? In group therapy, a person can *act out* or directly experience problems. Doing so often produces insights that might not occur from merely talking about an issue. In addition, other group members with similar problems can offer support and useful input. Group therapy is especially good for helping people understand their personal relationships (McCluskey, 2002). For reasons such as these, a number of specialized groups have emerged. Because they range from Alcoholics Anonymous to Marriage Encounter, we will sample only a few examples.

Psychodrama

One of the first groups was developed by Jacob L. Moreno (1953), who called his technique psychodrama. In **psychodrama,** clients act out personal conflicts with others who play supporting roles. Through role-playing, the client re-enacts incidents that cause problems in real life. For example, Don, a disturbed teenager, might act out a typical family fight, with the therapist playing his father and with other clients playing his mother, brothers, and sisters. Moreno believed that insights gained in this way transfer to real-life situations.

Therapists using psychodrama often find that role reversals are helpful. A **role reversal** involves taking the part of another person to learn how he or she feels. For instance, Don might role-play his father or mother to better understand their feelings. A related method is the **mirror technique,** in which clients observe another person re-enact their behavior. Thus, Don might briefly join the audience and watch as another group member plays his role. This would allow him to see himself as others do. Later, the group may summarize what happened and reflect on its meaning (Turner, 1997).

A group therapy session. Group members offer mutual support while sharing problems and insights.

Family Therapy

Family relationships are the source of great pleasure, and all too often, of great pain. In **family therapy,** husband, wife, and children work as a group to resolve the problems of each family member. Family therapy tends to be brief and focused on specific problems, such as frequent fights or a depressed teenager. For some types of problems, family therapy may be superior to other approaches (Pinsof, Wynne, & Hambright, 1996).

Family therapists believe that a problem experienced by one family member is really the whole family's problem. If the entire pattern of behavior in a family doesn't change, improvements in any single family member may not last. Thus, family members work together to improve communication, to change destructive patterns, and to see themselves and each other in new ways. This helps them reshape distorted perceptions and interactions directly, with the very persons with whom they have troubled relationships (Goldfried, Greenberg, & Marmar, 1990).

Does the therapist work with the whole family at once? Family therapists treat the family as a unit, but they may not meet with the entire family at each session. If a family crisis is at hand, the therapist may first try to identify the most resourceful family members who can help solve the immediate problem. The therapist and family members may then work on resolving more basic conflicts and on improving family relationships (Dies, 1995).

Group Awareness Training

Thirty years ago, the human potential movement led many people to seek personal growth experiences. Often, their interest was expressed by participation in sensitivity training or encounter groups.

Psychodrama A therapy in which clients act out personal conflicts and feelings in the presence of others who play supporting roles.
Role reversal Taking the role of another person to learn how one's own behavior appears from the other person's perspective.
Mirror technique Observing another person re-enact one's own behavior, like a character in a play; designed to help persons see themselves more clearly.
Family therapy Technique in which all family members participate, both individually and as a group, to change destructive relationships and communication patterns.

What is the difference between sensitivity and encounter groups? Sensitivity groups tend to be less confrontational than encounter groups. Participants in **sensitivity groups** take part in exercises that gently enlarge self-awareness and sensitivity to others. For example, in a "trust walk," participants expand their confidence in others by allowing themselves to be led around while blindfolded.

Encounter groups are based on an honest expression of feelings, and intensely personal communication may take place. Typically, the emphasis is on tearing down defenses and false fronts. Because there is a danger of hostile confrontation, participation is safest when members are carefully screened and a trained leader guides the group. Encounter group "casualties" are rare, but they do occur (Shaffer & Galinsky, 1989).

In business settings, psychologists still use the basic principles of sensitivity and encounter groups—truth, self-awareness, and self-determination—to improve employee relationships. Specially designed encounter groups for married couples are also widely held.

There has also been much public interest in various forms of large-group awareness training. **Large-group awareness training** refers to programs that claim to increase self-awareness and facilitate constructive personal change. Lifespring, Actualizations, the Forum, and similar commercial programs are examples. Like the smaller groups that preceded them, large-group trainings combine psychological exercises, confrontation, new viewpoints, and group dynamics to promote personal change.

Are sensitivity, encounter, and awareness groups really psychotherapies? These experiences tend to be positive, but they produce only moderate benefits (Faith, Wong, & Carpenter, 1995). Moreover, many of the claimed benefits may simply result from a kind of **therapy placebo effect,** in which improvement is based on a client's belief that therapy will help. Positive expectations, a break in daily routine, and an excuse to act differently can have quite an impact. Also, less ambitious goals may be easier to attain. For example, one recent program succeeded in teaching stress-management techniques in a large group setting (Timmerman, Emmelkamp, & Sanderman, 1998). Because of their versatility, groups undoubtedly will continue to be a major tool for solving problems and improving lives.

PSYCHOTHERAPY—AN OVERVIEW

] SURVEYQUESTION *What do various therapies have in common?*

How effective is psychotherapy? Judging the outcome of therapy is tricky. Nevertheless, there is ample evidence that therapy is beneficial. Hundreds of studies show a strong pattern of positive effects for psychotherapy and counseling (Lambert & Cattani-Thompson, 1996; Lipsey & Wilson, 1993). Even more convincing, perhaps, are the findings of a national survey. Nearly 9 out of 10 people who have sought mental health care say their lives improved as a result of the treatment (Consumer, 1995; Kotkin, Daviet, & Gurin, 1996).

In general, then, psychotherapy works (Kopta et al., 1999). Of course, results vary in individual cases. For some people therapy is immensely helpful; for others it is unsuccessful; overall it is effective for more people than not. Speaking more subjectively, a real success, in which a person's life is changed for the better, can be worth the disappointment of several cases in which little progress is made.

It is common to think of therapy as a long, slow process. But this is not always the case. Research shows that about 50 percent of all patients feel better after only 8 therapy sessions. After 26 sessions, roughly 75 percent have improved (Howard et al., 1986) (◆Fig. 13.6). The typical "dose" of therapy is one hourly session per week. This means that the majority of patients improve after 6 months of therapy and half feel better in just 2 months. Keep in mind that people often suffer for several years before seeking help. In view of this, such rapid improvement is impressive.

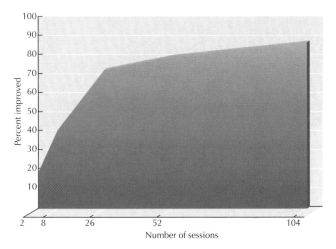

◆FIGURE 13.6 *The dose-improvement relationship in psychotherapy. This graph shows the percentage of patients who improved after varying numbers of therapy sessions. Notice that the most rapid improvement took place during the first 6 months of once-a-week sessions. (From Howard et al., 1986.)*

Sensitivity group A group experience consisting of exercises designed to increase self-awareness and sensitivity to others.

Encounter group A group experience that emphasizes intensely honest interchanges among participants regarding feelings and reactions to one another.

Large-group awareness training Any of a number of programs (many of them commercialized) that claim to increase self-awareness and facilitate constructive personal change.

Therapy placebo effect Improvement caused not by the actual process of therapy but by a client's expectation that therapy will help.

▲*TABLE 13.2*	**Comparison of Psychotherapies**			
	INSIGHT OR ACTION?	**DIRECTIVE OR NON-DIRECTIVE?**	**INDIVIDUAL OR GROUP?**	**THERAPY'S STRENGTH***
Psychoanalysis	Insight	Directive	Individual	Searching honesty
Brief psychodynamic therapy	Insight	Directive	Individual	Productive use of conflict
Client-centered therapy	Insight	Non-directive	Both	Acceptance, empathy
Existential therapy	Insight	Both	Individual	Personal empowerment
Gestalt therapy	Insight	Directive	Both	Focus on immediate awareness
Behavior therapy	Action	Directive	Both	Observable changes in behavior
Cognitive therapy	Action	Directive	Individual	Constructive guidance
Rational-emotive behavior therapy	Action	Directive	Individual	Clarity of thinking and goals
Psychodrama	Insight	Directive	Group	Constructive re-enactments
Family therapy	Both	Directive	Group	Shared responsibility for problems

*This column based in part on Andrews (1989).

Core Features of Psychotherapy

What do psychotherapies have in common?   We have sampled only a few of the many therapies in use today. For a summary of major differences among psychotherapies, see ▲Table 13.2. To add to your understanding, let's see what all techniques have in common.

Psychotherapies of various types share all or most of these goals: restoring hope, courage, and optimism; gaining insight; resolving conflicts; improving one's sense of self; changing unacceptable patterns of behavior; finding purpose; mending interpersonal relations; and learning to approach problems rationally (Seligman, 1998). To accomplish these goals, psychotherapies offer the following.

1. Therapy provides a *caring relationship* between the client and therapist, called a **therapeutic alliance.** Emotional rapport, warmth, friendship, understanding, acceptance, and empathy are the basis for this relationship. The therapeutic alliance unites the client and therapist as they work together to solve the client's problems. The strength of this alliance has a major impact on whether therapy succeeds (Kozart, 2002; Martin et al., 2000; Stiles et al., 1998).
2. Therapy offers a *protected setting* in which emotional *catharsis* (release) can take place. Therapy is a sanctuary in which the client is free to express fears, anxieties, and personal secrets without fearing rejection or loss of confidentiality (Weiss, 1990).
3. All therapies to some extent offer an *explanation* or *rationale* for the client's suffering. Additionally, they propose a line of action that will end this suffering.
4. Therapy provides clients with a *new perspective* about themselves and their situations and a chance to practice *new behaviors* (Crencavage & Norcross, 1990).

If you recall that our discussion began with trepanning and demonology, it is clear that psychotherapy has come a long way. Still, the search for ways to improve psychotherapy remains an urgent challenge for those who devote their lives to helping others.

Therapeutic alliance A caring relationship that unites a therapist and a client in working to solve the client's problems.

The Future of Psychotherapy

What will psychotherapy look like in the near future? A group of experts predicted the following (Norcross, Hedges, & Prochaska, 2002):

- There will be an increase in the use of short-term therapy and solution-focused, problem solving approaches.
- More therapy will be provided by master's-level practitioners (counselors, social workers, and psychiatric nurses).
- The use of lower-cost Internet services, telephone counseling, paraprofessionals, and self-help groups will grow.
- The use of psychiatrists and psychoanalysis will decrease.

As you might guess, many of these predicted changes are based on pressures to reduce the cost of mental health services. Another interesting cost-saving measure is the idea that computers may be able to treat some relatively minor problems. In a recent study, clients worked through 10 computer-guided sessions that helped them identify a problem, form a plan of action, and work through carrying out the plan. Most were satisfied with the help they received (Jacobs et al., 2001).

Basic Counseling Skills

A number of general helping skills can be distilled from the various approaches to therapy. These are points to keep in mind if you would like to comfort a person in distress, such as a troubled friend or relative (▲Table 13.3).

Active Listening

People frequently talk "at" each other without really listening. A person with problems needs to be heard. Make a sincere effort to listen to and understand the person. Try to accept the person's message without judging it or leaping to conclusions. Let the person know you are listening, through eye contact, posture, your tone of voice, and your replies (Kottler & Brown, 1999).

Clarify the Problem

People who have a clear idea of what is wrong in their lives are more likely to discover solutions. Try to understand the problem from the person's point of view. As you do, check your understanding often. For example, you might ask, "Are you saying that you feel depressed just at school? Or in general?" Remember, a problem well defined is often half solved.

▲*TABLE 13.3*	**Helping Behaviors**

To help another person gain insight into a personal problem, it is valuable to keep the following comparison in mind.

BEHAVIORS THAT HELP	BEHAVIORS THAT HINDER
Active listening	Probing painful topics
Acceptance	Judging/moralizing
Reflecting feelings	Criticism
Open-ended questioning	Threats
Supportive statements	Rejection
Respect	Ridicule/sarcasm
Patience	Impatience
Genuineness	Placing blame
Paraphrasing	Opinionated statements

(Adapted from Kottler & Brown, 1999.)

Focus on Feelings

Feelings are neither right nor wrong. By focusing on feelings you can encourage the outpouring of emotion that is the basis for catharsis. Passing judgment on what is said just makes people defensive. For example, a friend confides that he has failed a test. Perhaps you know that he studies very little. If you say, "Just study more and you would do better," he will probably become defensive or hostile. Much more can be accomplished by saying, "You must feel very frustrated" or simply, "How do you feel about it?" (Ivey & Galvin, 1984).

Teams of psychologists and counselors are often assembled to provide support to victims of major accidents and natural disasters. Because their work is stressful and often heart wrenching, relief workers also benefit from on-site counseling. Expressing emotions and talking about feelings are major elements of disaster counseling.

Gilles Mingasson/Getty Images

Avoid Giving Advice

Many people mistakenly think that they must solve problems for others. Remember that your goal is to provide understanding and support, not solutions. Of course, it is reasonable to give advice when you are asked for it, but beware of the trap of the "Why don't you . . . ? Yes, but . . ." game. According to psychotherapist Eric Berne (1964), this "game" follows a pattern: Someone says, "I have this problem." You say, "Why don't you do thus and so?" The person replies, "Yes, but . . ." and then tells you why your suggestion won't work. If you make a new suggestion, the reply will once again be, "Yes, but . . ." Obviously, the person either knows more about his or her personal situation than you do or he or she has reasons for avoiding your advice. The student described earlier knows he needs to study. His problem is to understand why he doesn't *want* to study.

Accept the Person's Frame of Reference

W. I. Thomas said, "Things perceived as real are real in their effects." Try to resist imposing your views on the problems of others. Since we all live in different psychological worlds, there is no "correct" view of a life situation. A person who feels that his or her viewpoint has been understood feels freer to examine it objectively and to question it. (Accepting and understanding the perspective of another person can be especially difficult when cultural differences exist. See "Cultural Issues in Counseling and Psychotherapy.")

Culturally skilled therapist A therapist who has the awareness, knowledge, and skills necessary to treat clients from diverse cultural backgrounds.

 HUMANDIVERSITY **Cultural Issues in Counseling and Psychotherapy**

When a client and therapist come from different cultural backgrounds, misunderstandings are common (Storck, 1997). For example, in most Native American cultures, one of the ways you show respect is by not making eye contact. Looking a therapist in the eye would be a challenge to his or her authority. But if the therapist doesn't understand this, lack of eye contact looks like a textbook case of poor self-esteem (Heinrich, Corbine, & Thomas, 1990). Misunderstanding such non-verbal communication can lead to serious mistakes by therapists (Singh, McKay, & Singh, 1998).

Culturally skilled therapists are skilled at working with clients from various cultural backgrounds. To be culturally skilled, a counselor must be able to do all of the following (Lee, 1991):

- Be aware of his or her own cultural values and biases
- Establish rapport with a person from a different cultural background

- Adapt traditional theories and techniques to meet the needs of clients from non-European ethnic or racial groups
- Be sensitive to cultural differences without resorting to stereotypes
- Treat members of racial or ethnic communities as individuals
- Be aware of a client's ethnic identity and degree of acculturation to the majority society
- Use existing helping resources within a cultural group to support efforts to resolve problems

Cultural awareness has helped broaden our ideas about mental health and optimal development (Lee, 1991). It is also worth remembering that cultural barriers apply to communication in all areas of life, not just therapy. While such differences can be challenging, they are also frequently enriching (Sue, 1998).

Reflect Thoughts and Feelings

One of the best things you can do when offering support to another person is to give feedback by simply restating what is said. This is also a good way to encourage a person to talk. If your friend seems to be at a loss for words, *restate* or *paraphrase* his or her last sentence. Here's an example.

FRIEND: I'm really down about school. I can't get interested in any of my classes. I flunked my Spanish test, and somebody stole my notebook for psychology.

YOU: You're really upset about school, aren't you?

FRIEND: Yeah, and my parents are hassling me about my grades again.

YOU: You're feeling pressured by your parents?

FRIEND: Yeah, damn.

YOU: It must make you angry to be pressured by them.

As simple as this sounds, it is very helpful to someone trying to sort out feelings. Try it. If nothing else, you'll develop a reputation as a fantastic conversationalist!

Silence

Studies show that counselors tend to wait longer before responding than do people in everyday conversations. Pauses of 5 seconds or more are not unusual, and interrupting is rare. Listening patiently lets the person feel unhurried and encourages her or him to speak freely (Goodman, 1984).

Questions

Because your goal is to encourage free expression, *open questions* tend to be the most helpful (Goodman, 1984). A *closed question* is one that can be answered yes or no. Open questions call for an open-ended reply. Say, for example, that a friend tells you, "I feel like my boss has it in for me at work." A closed question would be, "Oh yeah? So, are you going to quit?" Open questions, such as, "Do you want to tell me about it?" or "How do you feel about it?" are more likely to be helpful.

Maintain Confidentiality

Your efforts to help will be wasted if you fail to respect the privacy of someone who has confided in you. Put yourself in the person's place. Don't gossip.

These guidelines are not an invitation to play "junior therapist." Professional therapists are trained to approach serious problems with skills far exceeding those described here. However, the points made help define the qualities of a therapeutic relationship. They also emphasize that each of us can supply two of the greatest mental health resources available at any cost: friendship and honest communication.

MEDICAL THERAPIES—PSYCHIATRIC CARE

] SURVEYQUESTION *How do psychiatrists treat psychological disorders?*

Psychotherapy may be applied to anything from a brief crisis to a full-scale psychosis. However, most psychotherapists *do not* treat patients with major depressive disorders, schizophrenia, or other severe conditions. Major mental disorders are more often treated medically (Kopta et al., 1999).

Three main types of **somatic** (bodily) **therapy** are *pharmacotherapy, electroconvulsive therapy,* and *psychosurgery.* Somatic therapy is often done in the context of psychiatric hospitalization. All the somatic approaches have a strong medical slant, and they are typically administered by psychiatrists.

Drug Therapies

The atmosphere in psychiatric wards and mental hospitals changed radically in the mid-1950s with the widespread adoption of pharmacotherapy (FAR-meh-koe-THER-eh-pea). **Pharmacotherapy** refers to the use of drugs to treat emotional disturbances. Drugs may re-

Somatic therapy Any bodily therapy, such as drug therapy, electroconvulsive therapy, or psychosurgery.
Pharmacotherapy The use of drugs to alleviate the symptoms of emotional disturbance.

▲*TABLE 13.4*	Commonly Prescribed Psychiatric Drugs	
CLASS	**EXAMPLES (TRADE NAMES)**	**EFFECTS**
Anxiolytics (anti-anxiety drugs)	Ativan, Halcion, Librium, Restoril, Valium, Xanax	Reduce anxiety, tension, fear
Antidepressants	Anafranil, Elavil, Nardil, Norpramin, Parnate, Paxil, Prozac, Tofranil, Zoloft	Counteract depression
Antipsychotics (major tranquilizers)	Clozaril, Haldol, Mellaril, Navane, Risperdal, Thorazine	Reduce agitation, delusions, hallucinations, thought disorders

lieve the anxiety attacks and other discomforts of milder psychological disorders. More often, however, they are used to combat schizophrenia and major mood disorders.

What sorts of drugs are used in pharmacotherapy? Three major types of drugs are used. **Anxiolytics** (such as Valium) produce relaxation or reduce anxiety. **Antidepressants** are mood-elevating drugs that combat depression. **Antipsychotics** (also called **major tranquilizers**) have tranquilizing effects and, in addition, reduce hallucinations and delusions. (See ▲ Table 13.4 for examples of each class of drugs.)

Are drugs a valid approach to treatment? Drugs have shortened hospital stays and greatly improved the chances that people will recover from major psychological disorders. Drug therapy has also made it possible for many people to return to the community, where they can be treated on an out-patient basis.

Limitations of Drug Therapy

Drugs do have drawbacks. For example, 15 percent of patients taking major tranquilizers for long periods develop a neurological disorder that causes rhythmic facial and mouth movements (Chakos et al., 1996). Newer drugs are often hailed as medical "miracles." However, all drugs involve a trade-off between benefits and risks. For example, the drug Clozaril (clozapine) can relieve the symptoms of schizophrenia in some previously "hopeless" cases (Buchanan et al., 1998). But Clozaril is nearly as dangerous as it is helpful: Two out of 100 patients taking the drug suffer from a potentially fatal blood disease.

Is the risk worth it? Many experts think it is, because chronic schizophrenia robs people of almost everything that makes life worth living. It's possible, of course, that newer drugs will improve the risk-benefit ratio in the treatment of severe problems like schizophrenia. For example, the drug Risperdal (risperidone) appears to be as effective as Clozaril, without the lethal risk. But, even the best new drugs are not cure-alls. They help some people and relieve some problems, but not all. It is noteworthy that for serious mental disorders a combination of medication and psychotherapy almost always works better than drugs alone. Nevertheless, where schizophrenia and major mood disorders are concerned, drugs will undoubtedly remain the primary mode of treatment (Thase & Kupfer, 1996).

Electroshock

In **electroconvulsive therapy** (**ECT**) a 150-volt electrical current is passed through the brain for slightly less than a second. This rather drastic medical treatment for depression triggers a convulsion and causes the patient to lose consciousness for a short time. Muscle relaxants and sedative drugs are given with ECT to soften its impact. Treatments are given in a series of six to eight sessions spread over 3 to 4 weeks.

How does shock help? Actually, it is the seizure activity that is believed to be helpful. Proponents of ECT claim that shock-induced seizures alter the biochemical and hormonal balance in the brain and body, bringing an end to severe depression and suicidal behavior (Fink, 2000). Others have charged that ECT works only by confusing patients so they can't remember why they were depressed.

Anxiolytics Drugs (such as Valium) that produce relaxation or reduce anxiety.

Antidepressants Mood-elevating drugs.

Antipsychotics Drugs that, in addition to having tranquilizing effects, also tend to reduce hallucinations and delusional thinking. (Also called **major tranquilizers.**)

Electroconvulsive therapy (**ECT**) A treatment for severe depression, consisting of an electric shock passed directly through the brain, which induces a convulsion.

In electroconvulsive therapy, electrodes are attached to the head, and a brief electrical current is passed through the brain. ECT is used in the treatment of severe depression.

The ECT Debate

Not all professionals support the use of ECT. However, most experts seem to agree on the following: (1) At best, ECT produces only temporary improvement—it gets the patient out of a bad spot, but it must be combined with other treatments; (2) ECT can cause memory losses in some patients; (3) ECT should be used only after other treatments have failed; and (4) to lower the chance of a relapse, ECT should be followed by antidepressant drugs (Sackeim et al., 2001). All told, ECT is considered by many to be a valid treatment for selected cases of depression—especially when it rapidly ends wildly self-destructive or suicidal behavior (Kellner, 1998). It's interesting to note that most ECT patients feel that the treatment helped them. Most, in fact, would have it done again (Bernstein et al., 1998).

Psychosurgery

The most extreme medical treatment is **psychosurgery** (any surgical alteration of the brain). The best-known psychosurgery is the lobotomy. In the *prefrontal lobotomy,* the frontal lobes were surgically disconnected from other brain areas. This procedure was supposed to calm persons who didn't respond to any other type of treatment.

When the lobotomy was first introduced in the 1940s, there were enthusiastic claims for its success. But later studies suggested that some patients were calmed, some showed no change, and some became mental "vegetables." Lobotomies also produced a high rate of undesirable side effects, such as seizures, blunted emotions, major personality changes, and stupor. At about the same time that such problems became apparent, the first antipsychotic drugs became available. Soon after, the lobotomy was abandoned (Pressman, 1998; Swayze, 1995).

To what extent is psychosurgery used now? Psychosurgery is still considered valid by many neurosurgeons. However, most now use *deep lesioning,* in which small target areas are destroyed in the brain's interior. The appeal of deep lesioning is that it can have fairly specific effects. For instance, patients suffering from a severe type of obsessive-compulsive disorder may be helped by psychosurgery (Cumming et al., 1995).

It is worth remembering that psychosurgery cannot be reversed. A drug can be given or taken away. You can't take back psychosurgery. Many critics argue that psychosurgery should be banned altogether. Others continue to report success with brain surgery. All things considered, it is perhaps most accurate, even after decades of use, to describe psychosurgery as an experimental technique. Nevertheless, it may have value as a remedy for some very specific disorders (Fenton, 1998).

Hospitalization

Mental hospitalization for major mental disorders involves placing a person in a protected setting where medical therapy is provided. Hospitalization, by itself, can be a form of treatment. Staying in a hospital takes patients out of situations that may be sustaining their problems. For example, people with drug addictions may find it nearly impossible to resist the temptations for drug abuse in their daily lives. Hospitalization can help them make a clean break from their self-destructive behavior patterns (Gorman, 1996).

At their best, hospitals are sanctuaries that provide diagnosis, support, refuge, and therapy. This is generally true of psychiatric units in general hospitals and private psychiatric hospitals. At worst, confinement to an institution can be a brutal experience that leaves people less prepared to face the world than when they arrived. This is more often the case in large state mental hospitals (Gorman, 1996).

In most instances, hospitals are best used as a last resort for treatment. If hospitalization does prove to be necessary, most psychiatric patients do as well with short-term stays

Psychosurgery Any surgical alteration of the brain designed to bring about desirable behavioral or emotional changes.

Mental hospitalization Placing a person in a protected, therapeutic environment staffed by mental health professionals.

as they do with longer ones. For this reason, patients now spend an average of 20 days in psychiatric hospitals, rather than 3 to 4 months, as they did 20 years ago.

A new trend in treatment is **partial hospitalization.** In this approach, some patients spend their days in the hospital, but go home at night. Others attend therapy sessions during the evening. A major advantage of partial hospitalization is that patients can go home and practice what they've been learning. Eventually, most return to normal life. Overall, partial hospitalization is as effective as full hospitalization (Sledge et al., 1996).

Deinstitutionalization

In the last 30 years the population in large mental hospitals has dropped by two thirds. This is largely a result of **deinstitutionalization,** or reduced use of full-time commitment to mental institutions. Long-term "institutionalization" can lead to dependency, isolation, and continued emotional disturbance (Chamberlin & Rogers, 1990). Deinstitutionalization was meant to remedy this problem.

How successful has deinstitutionalization been? In truth, its success has been limited. Many states reduced mental hospital populations primarily as a way to save money. The upsetting result is that many chronic patients have been discharged to hostile communities without adequate care. Many former patients have joined the ranks of the homeless. Others are repeatedly jailed for minor crimes. Sadly, patients who trade hospitalization for unemployment, homelessness, and social isolation all too often end up rehospitalized or in jail (Goldman, 1998).

Large mental hospitals may no longer be warehouses for society's unwanted, but many former patients are no better off in bleak nursing homes, single-room hotels, board-and-care homes, shelters, or jails. Over 2 million Americans who are in jail or prison are mentally ill—three times the number who are in mental hospitals ("Ill-equipped," 2003). These figures suggest that jails are replacing mental hospitals as our society's "solution" for mental illness. Yet, ironically, high-quality care is available in almost every community. As much as anything, a simple lack of money prevents large numbers of people from getting the help they need (Torrey, 1996).

Half-way houses may be a better way to ease a patient's return to the community (Anthony, Cohen, & Kennard, 1990). **Half-way houses** are short-term group living facilities for people making the transition from an institution (mental hospital, prison, and so forth) to independent living. Typically, they offer supervision and support, without being as restricted and medically oriented as hospitals. They also keep people near their families. Most important, half-way houses can reduce a person's chances of being readmitted to a hospital (Coursey, Ward-Alexander, & Katz, 1990).

Depending on the quality of the institution, hospitalization may be a refuge or a brutalizing experience. Many state "asylums" or mental hospitals are antiquated and in need of drastic improvement.

Community Mental Health Programs

Community mental health centers are a bright spot in the area of mental health care. **Community mental health centers** offer a wide range of mental health services and psychiatric care. Such centers try to help people avoid hospitalization and find answers to mental health

A well-run half-way house can be a humane and cost-effective way to ease former mental patients back into the community (Coursey, Ward-Alexander, & Katz, 1990).

Partial hospitalization An approach in which patients receive treatment at a hospital during the day, but return home at night.

Deinstitutionalization Reduced use of full-time commitment to mental institutions to treat mental disorders.

Half-way house A community-based facility for individuals making the transition from an institution (mental hospital, prison, and so forth) to independent living.

Community mental health center A facility offering a wide range of mental health services, such as prevention, counseling, consultation, and crisis intervention.

problems. Typically, they do this by providing short-term treatment, counseling, outpatient care, emergency services, and suicide prevention.

If it is like most, the primary aim of the mental health center in your community is to directly aid troubled citizens. Its second goal is likely to be *prevention*. Consultation, education, and **crisis intervention** (skilled management of a psychological emergency) are used to prevent problems before they become serious. Also, some centers attempt to raise the general level of mental health in a community by combating unemployment, delinquency, and drug abuse (Levine et al., 1993).

How have community mental health centers done in meeting their goals? In practice, they have concentrated much more on providing clinical services than they have on preventing problems. This appears to be primarily the result of wavering government support (translation: money). Overall, community mental health centers have succeeded in making psychological services more accessible than ever before. Many of their programs rely on **paraprofessionals** (individuals who work in a near-professional capacity under the supervision of more highly trained staff). Some paraprofessionals are ex-addicts, ex-alcoholics, or ex-patients who have "been there." Many more are persons (paid or volunteer) who have skills in tutoring, crafts, or counseling or who are simply warm, understanding, and skilled at communication. Often, paraprofessionals are more approachable than "doctors." This encourages people to seek mental health services that they might otherwise be reluctant to use (Everly, 2002).

A Look Ahead

In the Psychology in Action section that follows, we will return briefly to behavioral approaches. There you will find a number of useful techniques that you may be able to apply to your own behavior. You'll also find a discussion of when to seek professional help and how to find it. Here's your author's professional advice: This is information you won't want to skip.

Crisis intervention Skilled management of a psychological emergency.

Paraprofessional An individual who works in a near-professional capacity under the supervision of a more highly trained person.

STUDYBREAK ⓨ *Group Therapies, Psychotherapy Skills, and Medical Therapies*

RELATE

Would you rather participate in individual therapy or group therapy? What advantages and disadvantages do you think each has?

Based on your own experience, how valid do you think it is to say that within families "a problem for one is a problem for all"?

What lies at the "heart" of psychotherapy? How would you describe it to a friend?

Which of the basic counseling skills do you already use? Which would improve your ability to help a person in distress?

If a family member of yours became severely depressed, what therapies would be available to him or her? What are the pros and cons of each choice?

LEARNING CHECK

1. In psychodrama, people attempt to form meaningful wholes out of disjointed thoughts, feelings, and actions. T or F?
2. Most large-group awareness trainings make use of Gestalt therapy. T or F?
3. Which therapy places great emphasis on role-playing?
   a. psychodrama b. awareness training c. family therapy
   d. encounter

4. Emotional _____ (release) in a protected setting is an element of most psychotherapies.
5. To aid a troubled friend, you should focus on facts rather than feelings, and you should critically evaluate what the person is saying to help him or her grasp reality. T or F?
6. ECT is a modern form of pharmacotherapy. T or F?
7. Currently, the frontal lobotomy is the most widely used form of psychosurgery. T or F?

Critical Thinking

8. In your opinion, do psychologists have a duty to protect others who may be harmed by their clients? For example, if a patient has homicidal fantasies about his ex-wife, should she be informed?
9. Residents of Berkeley, California, voted on a referendum to ban the use of ECT within city limits. Do you think that the use of certain psychiatric treatments should be controlled by law?

ANSWERS

1. F 2. F 3. a 4. catharsis 5. F 6. F 7. F 8. According to the law, there is a duty to protect others where a therapist could, with little effort, prevent serious harm. However, this duty can conflict with a client's rights to confidentiality and with client-therapist trust. Therapists often must make difficult choices in such situations. 9. The question of who can prescribe drugs, do surgery, and administer ECT is controlled by law. However, psychiatrists strongly object to residents, city councils, or government agencies making *medical* decisions.

Psychology in Action

Self-Management and Seeking Professional Help

] **SURVEYQUESTION** *How are behavioral principles applied to everyday problems?*

"Throw out the snake oil, ladies and gentlemen, and throw away your troubles. Doctor B. Havior Modification is here to put an end to all human suffering."

True? Well, not quite. Behavior therapy is not a cure-all. Its use is often quite complicated and requires a great deal of expertise. Still, behavior therapy offers a straightforward solution to many problems.

As mentioned elsewhere in this book, you should seek professional help when a significant problem exists. For lesser difficulties, you may want to try applying behavioral principles yourself. Let us see how this might be done.

Covert Reward and Punishment—Boosting Your "Willpower"

"Have you ever decided to quit smoking cigarettes, watching television too much, eating too much, drinking too much, or driving too fast?"

"Well, one of those applies. I have decided several times to quit smoking."

"When have you decided?"

"Usually after I am reminded of how dangerous smoking is—like when I heard that my uncle had died of lung cancer. He smoked constantly."

"If you have decided to quit 'several times,' I assume you haven't succeeded."

"No, the usual pattern is for me to become upset about smoking and then to cut down for a day or two."

"You forget the disturbing image of your uncle's death, or whatever, and start smoking again."

"Yes, I suppose if I had an uncle die every day or so, I might actually quit!"

The use of electric shock to condition an aversion seems remote from everyday problems. Even naturally aversive actions are difficult to apply to personal behavior. As mentioned earlier, for instance, rapid smoking is difficult for most smokers to carry out on their own. And what about a problem like overeating? It would be difficult indeed to eat enough to create a lasting aversion to overeating. (Although it's sometimes tempting to try.)

Bob Daemmrich/Stock, Boston

In view of such limitations, psychologists have developed an alternative procedure that can be used to curb smoking, overeating, and other habits (Cautela & Bennett, 1981; Cautela & Kearney, 1986).

Covert Sensitization

In **covert sensitization,** aversive imagery is used to reduce the occurrence of an undesired response. Here's how it's done: Obtain six 3×5 cards and on each write a brief description of a scene related to the habit you wish to control. The scene should be so *disturbing* or *disgusting* that thinking about it would temporarily make you very uncomfortable about indulging in the habit. For smoking, the cards might read:

- I am in a doctor's office. The doctor looks at some reports and tells me I have lung cancer. She says a lung will have to be removed and sets a date for the operation.
- I am in bed under an oxygen tent. My chest feels caved in. There is a tube in my throat. I can barely breathe.
- I wake up in the morning and smoke a cigarette. I begin coughing up blood.
- My lover won't kiss me because my breath smells bad.
- Other cards would continue along the same line.

Covert sensitization Use of aversive imagery to reduce the occurrence of an undesired response.

For overeating the cards might read:

- I am at the beach. I get up to go for a swim, and I overhear people whispering to each other, "Isn't that fat disgusting?"
- I am at a store buying clothes. I try on several things that are too small. The only things that fit look like rumpled sacks. Salespeople are staring at me.
- Other cards would continue along the same line.

The trick, of course, is to get yourself to imagine or picture vividly each of these disturbing scenes *several times* a day. Imagining the scenes can be accomplished by placing them under *stimulus control*. Simply choose something you do *frequently* each day (such as getting a cup of coffee or getting up from your chair). Next make a rule: Before you can get a cup of coffee or get up from your chair, or whatever you have selected as a cue, you must take out your cards and *vividly picture* yourself engaging in the action you wish to curb (eating or smoking, for example). Then *vividly picture* the scene described on the top card. Imagine the scene for 30 seconds.

After visualizing the top card, move it to the bottom so the cards are rotated. Make up new cards each week. The scenes can be made much more upsetting than the samples given here. The samples are toned down to keep you from being "grossed out."

Covert sensitization can also be used directly in situations that test your self-control. If you are trying to lose weight, for instance, you might be able to turn down a tempting dessert in this way: As you look at the dessert, visualize maggots crawling all over it. If you make this image as vivid and nauseating as possible, losing your appetite is almost a certainty. If you want to apply this technique to other situations, be aware that vomiting scenes are especially effective. Covert sensitization may sound as if you are "playing games with yourself," but it can be a great help if you want to cut down on a bad habit (Cautela & Kearney, 1986). Try it!

Thought Stopping

As discussed earlier, behavior therapists accept that thoughts, like visible responses, can also cause trouble. Think of times when you have repeatedly "put yourself down" mentally or when you have been preoccupied by needless worries, fears, or other negative and upsetting thoughts. If you would like to gain control over such thoughts, thought stopping may help you do it.

In **thought stopping,** aversive stimuli are used to interrupt or prevent upsetting thoughts. The simplest thought-stopping technique makes use of mild punishment to suppress upsetting mental images and internal "talk." Simply place a large, flat rubber band around your wrist. As you go through the day, apply this rule: Each time you catch yourself thinking the upsetting image or thought, pull the rubber band away from your wrist and snap it. You need not make this terribly painful. Its value lies in drawing your attention to how often you form negative thoughts and in interrupting the flow of thoughts. Strong punishment is not required.

It seems like this procedure might be abandoned rapidly. Is there an alternative? A second thought-stopping procedure requires only that you interrupt upsetting thoughts each time they occur. Begin by setting aside time each day during which you will deliberately think the unwanted thought. As you begin to form the thought, shout "Stop!" aloud, with conviction. (Obviously, you should choose a private spot for this part of the procedure!)

Repeat the thought-stopping procedure 10 to 20 times for the first 2 or 3 days. Then switch to shouting "Stop!" covertly (to yourself) rather than aloud. Thereafter, thought stopping can be carried out throughout the day whenever upsetting thoughts occur (Williams & Long, 1991). After several days of practice, you should be able to stop unwanted thoughts whenever they occur.

Covert Reinforcement

Earlier we discussed how punishing images can be used to decrease undesirable responses, such as smoking or overeating. Many people also find it helpful to covertly *reinforce* desired actions. **Covert reinforcement** is the use of positive imagery to reinforce desired behavior.

Thought stopping Use of aversive stimuli to interrupt or prevent upsetting thoughts.
Covert reinforcement Using positive imagery to reinforce desired behavior.

For example, suppose your target behavior is, once again, not eating dessert. If this were the case, you could do the following (Cautela & Bennett, 1981; Cautela & Kearney, 1986):

> Imagine that you are standing at the dessert table with your friends. As dessert is passed, you politely refuse and feel good about staying on your diet.

These images would then be followed by imagining a pleasant, reinforcing scene:

> Imagine that you are your ideal weight. You look really slim in your favorite color and style. Someone you like says to you, "Gee, you've lost weight. I've never seen you look so good."

For many people, of course, actual direct reinforcement (as described in the Psychology in Action section of Chapter 6) is the best way to alter behavior. Nevertheless, covert or "visualized" reinforcement can have similar effects. To make use of covert reinforcement, choose one or more target behaviors and rehearse them mentally. Then follow each rehearsal with a vivid, rewarding image.

Self-Directed Desensitization—Overcoming Common Fears

You have prepared for 2 weeks to give a speech in a large class. As your turn approaches, your hands begin to tremble. Your heart pounds and you find it difficult to breathe. You say to your body, "Relax!" What happens? Nothing!

Relaxation

The key to desensitization is relaxation. To inhibit fear, one must *learn* to relax. Here is a description of how the **tension-release method** can be used to achieve deep-muscle relaxation.

> Tense the muscles in your right arm until they tremble. Hold them tight for about 5 seconds and then let go. Allow your hand and arm to go limp and to relax completely. Repeat the procedure. Releasing tension two or three times will allow you to feel whether or not your arm muscles have relaxed. Repeat the tension-release procedure with your left arm. Compare it with your right arm. Repeat until the left arm is equally relaxed. Apply the tension-release technique to your right leg, to your left leg, to your abdomen, to your chest and shoulders. Clench and release your chin, neck, and throat. Wrinkle and release your forehead and scalp. Tighten and release your mouth and face muscles. As a last step, curl your toes and tense your feet. Then release.

Practice the tension-release method until you can achieve complete relaxation quickly (5 to 10 minutes).

After you have practiced relaxation once a day for a week or two, you will begin to be able to tell when your body (or a group of muscles) is tense. Also, you will begin to be able to relax on command. As an alternative, you might want to try imagining a very safe, pleasant, and relaxing scene. Some people find such images as relaxing as the tension-release method (Rosenthal, 1993b). Once you have learned to relax, the next step is to identify the fear you would like to control and construct a hierarchy.

Procedure for Constructing a Hierarchy

Make a list of situations (related to the fear) that make you anxious. Try to list at least 10 situations. Some should be very frightening and others only mildly frightening. Write a short description of each situation on a separate 3×5 card. Place the cards in order from the least disturbing situation to the most disturbing. Here is a sample hierarchy for a student afraid of public speaking:

1. Being given an assignment to speak in class
2. Thinking about the topic and the date the speech must be given
3. Writing the speech; thinking about delivering the speech
4. Watching other students speak in class the week before the speech date
5. Rehearsing the speech alone; pretending to give it to the class

Tension-release method A procedure for systematically achieving deep relaxation of the body.

6. Delivering the speech to my roommate; pretending my roommate is the teacher
7. Reviewing the speech on the day it is to be presented
8. Entering the classroom; waiting and thinking about the speech
9. Being called; standing up; facing the audience
10. Delivering the speech

Using the Hierarchy

When you have mastered the relaxation exercises and have the hierarchy constructed, set aside time each day to work on reducing your fear. Begin by performing the relaxation exercises. When you are completely relaxed, visualize the scene on the first card (the least frightening scene). If you can *vividly* picture and imagine yourself in the first situation twice *without a noticeable increase in muscle tension,* proceed to the next card. Also, as you progress, relax yourself between cards.

Each day, stop when you reach a card that you cannot visualize without becoming tense in three attempts. Each day, begin one or two cards before the one on which you stopped the previous day. Continue to work with the cards until you can visualize the last situation without experiencing tension (techniques are based on Wolpe, 1974).

By using this approach you should be able to reduce the fear or anxiety associated with things such as public speaking, entering darkened rooms, asking questions in large classes, heights, talking to members of the opposite sex, and taking tests. Even if you are not always able to reduce a fear, you will have learned to place relaxation under voluntary control. This alone is valuable because controlling unnecessary tension can increase energy and efficiency.

Seeking Professional Help—When, Where, and How?

] SURVEYQUESTION *How could a person find professional help?*

How would I know if I should seek professional help at some point in my life?   Although there is no simple answer to this question, the following guidelines may be helpful.

1. If your level of psychological discomfort (unhappiness, anxiety, or depression, for example) is comparable to a level of physical discomfort that would cause you to see a doctor or dentist, you should consider seeing a psychologist or a psychiatrist.
2. Another signal to watch for is significant changes in behavior, such as the quality of your work (or schoolwork), your rate of absenteeism, your use of drugs (including alcohol), or your relationships with others.
3. Perhaps you have urged a friend or relative to seek professional help and were dismayed because he or she refused to do so. If *you* find friends or relatives making a similar suggestion, recognize that they may be seeing things more clearly than you are.
4. If you have persistent or disturbing suicidal thoughts or impulses, you should seek help immediately.

Locating a Therapist

If I wanted to talk to a therapist, how would I find one?   Here are some suggestions that could help you get started.

1. *The yellow pages.* Psychologists are listed in the telephone book under "Psychologist" or in some cases under "Counseling Services." Psychiatrists are generally listed as a subheading under "Physicians." Counselors are usually found under the heading "Marriage and Family Counselors." These listings will usually put you in touch with individuals in private practice.
2. *Community or county mental health centers.* Most counties and many cities offer public mental health services. (These are listed in the phone book.) Public mental health centers usually provide counseling and therapy services directly, and they can refer you to private therapists.

3. *Mental health associations.* Many cities have mental health associations organized by concerned citizens. Groups such as these usually keep listings of qualified therapists and other services and programs in the community.
4. *Colleges and universities.* If you are a student, don't overlook counseling services offered by a student health center or special student counseling facilities.
5. *Newspaper advertisements.* Some psychologists advertise their services in newspapers. Also, low-cost "outreach" clinics occasionally try to make their presence known to the public by advertising. In either case, you should carefully inquire into a therapist's training and qualifications. Without the benefit of a referral from a trusted person, it is wise to be cautious.
6. *Crisis hotlines.* The typical crisis hotline is a telephone service staffed by community volunteers. These people are trained to provide information concerning a wide range of mental health problems. They also have lists of organizations, services, and other resources in the community where you can go for help.

▲Table 13.5 summarizes all of the sources for psychotherapy, counseling, and referrals we have discussed, as well as some additional possibilities.

Options How would I know what kind of a therapist to see? How would I pick one? The choice between a psychiatrist and a psychologist is somewhat arbitrary. Both are trained to do psychotherapy. While a psychiatrist can administer somatic therapy and prescribe drugs, a psychologist can work in conjunction with a physician if such services are needed. Psychologists and psychiatrists are equally effective as therapists (Consumer, 1995; Seligman, 1995).

Fees for psychiatrists are usually higher, averaging about $115 an hour. Psychologists average about $85 an hour. Counselors and social workers typically charge about $70 per hour. Group therapy averages only about $40 an hour because the therapist's fee is divided among several people.

With fees in mind, be aware that most health insurance plans will pay for psychological services. If fees are a problem, keep in mind that many therapists charge on a sliding scale, or ability-to-pay basis, and that community mental health centers almost always charge on a sliding scale. In one way or another, help is almost always available for anyone who needs it.

Some communities and college campuses have counseling services staffed by sympathetic paraprofessionals or peer counselors. These services are free or very low cost. As mentioned earlier, paraprofessionals are people who work in a near-professional capacity under professional supervision. **Peer counselors** are non-professional persons who have learned basic counseling skills. There is a natural tendency, perhaps, to doubt the abilities of paraprofessionals. However, many studies have shown that paraprofessional counselors are often as effective as professionals (Christensen & Jacobson, 1994).

Also, don't overlook self-help groups, which can add valuable support to professional treatment. Members of a self-help group typically share a particular type of problem, such as eating disorders or coping with an alcoholic parent. **Self-help groups** offer members mutual support and a chance to discuss problems. In many instances helping others also serves as therapy for those who give help (Levine, Toro, & Perkins, 1993). For some problems, self-help groups may be the best choice of all (Christensen & Jacobson, 1994; Fobair, 1997).

Qualifications You can usually find out about a therapist's qualifications simply by asking. A reputable therapist will be glad to reveal his or her background. If you have any doubts, credentials may be checked and other helpful information can be obtained from local branches of any of the following organizations. You can also write to the addresses listed here.

American Family Therapy Association
2020 Pennsylvania Ave. N.W., Suite 273
Washington, DC 20006

▲TABLE 13.5 **Mental Health Resources**

- Family doctors (for referrals to mental health professionals)
- Mental health specialists, such as psychiatrists, psychologists, social workers, or mental health counselors
- Health maintenance organizations
- Community mental health centers
- Hospital psychiatry departments and outpatient clinics
- University- or medical school-affiliated programs
- State hospital outpatient clinics
- Family service/social agencies
- Private clinics and facilities
- Employee assistance programs
- Local medical, psychiatric, or psychological societies

(Source: National Institute of Mental Health)

Peer counselor A non-professional person who has learned basic counseling skills.
Self-help group A group of people who share a particular type of problem and provide mutual support to one another.

American Psychiatric Association
1400 K Street N.W.
Washington, DC 20005

American Psychological Association
750 1st Street N.E.
Washington, DC 20002

American Association of Humanistic Psychology
7 Hartwood Dr.
Amherst, NY 14226

Canadian Psychiatric Association
200-237 Argyle
Ottawa, ONT K2P1B8

National Mental Health Association
1021 Prince St.
Alexandria, VA 22314

The question of how to pick a particular therapist remains. The best way is to start with a short consultation with a respected psychiatrist, psychologist, or counselor. This will allow the person you consult to evaluate your difficulty and recommend a type of therapy or a therapist who is likely to be helpful. As an alternative, you might ask the person teaching this course for a referral.

Evaluating a Therapist   *How would I know whether or not to quit or ignore a therapist?* A balanced look at psychotherapies suggests that all *techniques* are about equally successful (Wampold et al., 1997). However, all *therapists* are not equally successful. Far more important than the approach used are the therapist's personal qualities (Luborsky et al., 1997). The most consistently successful therapists are those who are willing to use whatever method seems most helpful for a client. They are also marked by personal characteristics of warmth, integrity, sincerity, and empathy (Jennings & Skovholt, 1999).

It is perhaps most accurate to say that at this stage of development, psychotherapy is an art, not a science. The *relationship* between a client and therapist is the therapist's most basic tool (Hubble, Duncan, & Miller, 1999). This is why you must trust and easily relate to a therapist for therapy to be effective. Here are some danger signals to watch for in psychotherapy:

- Sexual advances by therapist
- Therapist makes repeated verbal threats or is physically aggressive
- Therapist is excessively blaming, belittling, hostile, or controlling
- Therapist makes excessive small talk; talks repeatedly about his/her own problems
- Therapist encourages prolonged dependence on him/her
- Therapist demands absolute trust or tells client not to discuss therapy with anyone else

Clients who like their therapist are generally more successful in therapy (Talley et al., 1990). An especially important part of the therapeutic alliance is agreement about the goals of therapy. It is therefore a good idea to think about what you would like to accomplish by entering therapy. Write down your goals and discuss them with your therapist during the first session. Your first meeting with a therapist should also answer all of the following questions (Somberg et al., 1993):

- Will the information I reveal in therapy remain completely confidential?
- What risks do I face if I begin therapy?
- How long do you expect treatment to last?
- What form of treatment do you expect to use?
- Are there alternatives to therapy that might help me as much or more?

It's always tempting to avoid facing up to personal problems. With this in mind, you should give a therapist a fair chance and not give up too easily. But don't hesitate to change therapists or to terminate therapy if you lose confidence in the therapist or if you don't relate well to the therapist as a person.

STUDYBREAK *Self-Management and Finding Professional Help*

RELATE

How could you use covert sensitization, thought stopping, and covert reinforcement to change your behavior? Try to apply each technique to a specific example.

Just for practice, make a fear hierarchy for a situation you find frightening. Does vividly picturing items in the hierarchy make you tense or anxious? If so, can you intentionally relax using the tension-release method?

Assume that you want to seek help from a psychologist or other mental health professional. How would you proceed? Take some time to actually find out what mental health services are available to you.

LEARNING CHECK

1. Covert sensitization and thought stopping combine aversion therapy and cognitive therapy. T or F?
2. Like covert aversion conditioning, covert reinforcement of desired responses is also possible. T or F?

3. Exercises that bring about deep-muscle relaxation are an essential element in covert sensitization. T or F?
4. Items in a desensitization hierarchy should be placed in order from the least disturbing to the most disturbing. T or F?
5. The first step in desensitization is to place the visualization of disturbing images under stimulus control. T or F?
6. Persistent emotional discomfort is a clear sign that professional psychological counseling should be sought. T or F?
7. Community mental health centers rarely offer counseling or therapy themselves; they only do referrals. T or F?
8. In many instances, a therapist's personal qualities have more of an effect on the outcome of therapy than does the type of therapy used. T or F?

Critical Thinking

9. Would it be acceptable for a therapist to urge a client to break all ties with a troublesome family member?

ANSWERS

1. T 2. T 3. F 4. T 5. F 6. T 7. F 8. T 9. Such decisions must be made by clients themselves. Therapists can help clients evaluate important decisions and feelings about significant persons in their lives. However, actively urging a client to sever a relationship borders on unethical behavior.

CHAPTER IN REVIEW

Major Points

- Psychotherapy facilitates positive changes in personality, behavior, or adjustment.
- Before the development of modern therapies, superstition dominated attempts to treat psychological problems.
- Five major categories of psychotherapy are psychodynamic, insight, behavioral, cognitive, and group therapies.
- Psychotherapy is generally effective, although no single form of therapy is superior to others.
- All medical treatments for psychological disorders have pros and cons. Overall, however, their effectiveness is improving.
- Some personal problems can be successfully treated using self-management techniques.
- Everyone should know how to obtain high-quality mental health care in his or her community.

Summary

How do psychotherapies differ? How did psychotherapy originate?

- Psychotherapies may be classified as insight, action, directive, non-directive, or supportive therapies, and combinations of these.
- Therapies may be conducted either individually or in groups, and they may be time limited.
- Primitive approaches to mental illness were often based on belief in supernatural forces.
- Demonology attributed mental disturbance to demonic possession and prescribed exorcism as the cure.
- In some instances, the actual cause of bizarre behavior may have been ergot poisoning.
- More humane treatment began in 1793 with the work of Philippe Pinel in Paris.

Is Freudian psychoanalysis still used?

- Freud's psychoanalysis was the first formal psychotherapy. Psychoanalysis seeks to release repressed thoughts and emotions from the unconscious.
- The psychoanalyst uses free association, dream analysis, and analysis of resistance and transference to reveal health-producing insights.
- Some critics argue that traditional psychoanalysis receives credit for spontaneous remissions of symptoms. However, psychoanalysis is successful for many patients.
- Brief psychodynamic therapy (which relies on psychoanalytic theory but is brief and focused) is as effective as other major therapies.

What are the major humanistic therapies?

- Client-centered (or person-centered) therapy is nondirective and is dedicated to creating an atmosphere of growth.
- Unconditional positive regard, empathy, authenticity, and reflection are combined to give the client a chance to solve his or her own problems.
- Existential therapies focus on the end result of the choices one makes in life. Clients are encouraged through confrontation and encounter to exercise free will and to take responsibility for their choices.
- Gestalt therapy emphasizes immediate awareness of thoughts and feelings. Its goal is to rebuild thinking, feeling, and acting into connected wholes and to help clients break through emotional blockages.
- Media psychologists, telephone counselors, and cybertherapists may, on occasion, do some good. However, each has serious drawbacks, and the effectiveness of telephone counseling and cybertherapy has not been established.
- Therapy by videoconferencing shows more promise as a way to provide mental health services at a distance.

What is behavior therapy?

- Behavior therapists use various behavior modification techniques that apply learning principles to change human behavior.
- In aversion therapy, classical conditioning is used to associate maladaptive behavior (such as smoking or drinking) with pain or other aversive events in order to inhibit undesirable responses.

How is behavior therapy used to treat phobias, fears, and anxieties?

- Classical conditioning also underlies systematic desensitization, a technique used to overcome fears and anxieties. In desensitization, gradual adaptation and reciprocal inhibition break the link between fear and particular situations.

- Typical steps in desensitization are: Construct a fear hierarchy; learn to produce total relaxation; and perform items on the hierarchy (from least to most disturbing).
- Desensitization may be carried out with real settings, or it may be done by vividly imagining the fear hierarchy or by watching models perform the feared responses.
- In some cases, virtual reality exposure can be used to present fear stimuli in a controlled manner.
- A new technique called eye movement desensitization and reprocessing (EMDR) shows promise as a treatment for traumatic memories and stress disorders. At present, however, EMDR is highly controversial.

What role does reinforcement play in behavior therapy?

- Behavior modification also makes use of operant principles, such as positive reinforcement, non-reinforcement, extinction, punishment, shaping, stimulus control, and time out. These principles are used to extinguish undesirable responses and to promote constructive behavior.
- Non-reward can extinguish troublesome behaviors. Often this is done by simply identifying and eliminating reinforcers, particularly attention and social approval.
- To apply positive reinforcement and operant shaping, tokens are often used to reinforce selected target behaviors.
- Full-scale use of tokens in an institutional setting produces a token economy. Toward the end of a token economy program, patients are shifted to social rewards such as recognition and approval.

Can therapy change thoughts and emotions?

- Cognitive therapy emphasizes changing thought patterns that underlie emotional or behavioral problems. Its goals are to correct distorted thinking and/or teach improved coping skills.
- In a variation of cognitive therapy called rational-emotive behavior therapy (REBT), clients learn to recognize and challenge their own irrational beliefs.

Can psychotherapy be done with groups of people?

- Group therapy may be a simple extension of individual methods, or it may be based on techniques developed specifically for groups.
- In psychodrama, individuals enact roles and incidents resembling their real-life problems. In family therapy, the family group is treated as a unit.
- Although they are not literally psychotherapies, sensitivity and encounter groups attempt to encourage positive personality change. In recent years, commercially offered large-group awareness trainings have become popular. However, the therapeutic benefits of such programs are questionable.

What do various therapies have in common?

- To alleviate personal problems, all psychotherapies offer a caring relationship, emotional rapport, a protected setting, catharsis, explanations for the client's problems, a new perspective, and a chance to practice new behaviors.
- Many basic counseling skills underlie a variety of therapies. These include listening actively, helping to clarify the problem, focusing on feelings, avoiding the giving of unwanted advice, accepting the person's perspective, reflecting thoughts and feelings, being patient during silences, using open questions when possible, and maintaining confidentiality.
- The culturally skilled counselor must be able to establish rapport with a person from a different cultural background and adapt traditional theories and techniques to meet the needs of clients from non-European ethnic or racial groups.

How do psychiatrists treat psychological disorders?

- Three medical, or somatic, approaches to treatment are pharmacotherapy, electroconvulsive therapy (ECT), and psychosurgery. All three techniques are controversial to a degree because of questions about effectiveness and side effects.
- Community mental health centers seek to avoid or minimize mental hospitalization. They also seek to prevent mental health problems through education, consultation, and crisis intervention.

How are behavioral principles applied to everyday problems?

- Cognitive techniques can be an aid to managing personal behavior.
- In covert sensitization, aversive images are used to discourage unwanted behavior.
- Thought stopping uses mild punishment to prevent upsetting thoughts.
- Covert reinforcement is a way to encourage desired responses by mental rehearsal.
- Desensitization pairs relaxation with a hierarchy of upsetting images in order to lessen fears.

How could a person find professional help?

- In most communities, a competent and reputable therapist can be located with public sources of information or through a referral.
- Practical considerations such as cost and qualifications enter into choosing a therapist. However, the therapist's personal characteristics are of equal importance.

Interactive Learning

Internet addresses frequently change. To find the sites listed here, visit www.psychology.wadsworth.com/coon_journey2e for an updated list of Internet addresses and direct links to relevant sites.

PSYCHOLOGY: A JOURNEY COMPANION WEB SITE Online quizzes, flash cards, and other helpful study aids for this text. *www.psychology.wadsworth.com/coon_journey2e*

BASICS OF COGNITIVE THERAPY An overview of cognitive therapy, with suggested readings.

HOW TO FIND HELP FOR LIFE'S PROBLEMS Provides information on psychotherapy and advice on how to choose a psychotherapist.

NETPSYCHOLOGY Explores the delivery of psychological services on the Internet.

PSYCHOLOGICAL SELF-HELP An online book about self-improvement.

SCIENCE AND PSEUDOSCIENCE REVIEW IN MENTAL HEALTH A review of therapies that are considered to be scientifically dubious.

THE EFFECTIVENESS OF PSYCHOTHERAPY A summary of the *Consumer Reports* survey on the effectiveness of psychotherapy.

TYPES OF THERAPIES Describes four different approaches to therapy. Also has information about choosing a therapist.

WEB COUNSELOR Typical personal problems are presented along with examples of advice.

INFOTRAC COLLEGE EDITION For more information about topics in the Psychology in Action feature, use Key Words search for PSYCHOTHERAPY.

PSYCHNOW! 7b. Major psychological therapies.

Test Your Knowledge: Therapies

The questions that follow are only a sample of what you need to know. If you miss any of the items, you should review the entire chapter and get more practice with *WebTutor* or the *Practice Quizzes* that came with this book. Another way to prepare for tests is to use the printed *Study Guide* that is available for this text.

1. An approach that is incompatible with insight therapy is
   A. individual therapy   B. action therapy   C. non-directive therapy   D. group therapy

2. Which type of therapy is LEAST likely to bring about personal change?
   A. non-directive therapy   B. supportive therapy   C. time-limited therapy   D. group therapy

3. A scientific explanation of Medieval "possessions" by "demons" is related to the effects of
   A. ergot poisoning   B. trepanning   C. exorcism   D. unconscious transference

4. Which of the following is NOT a psychoanalytic concept?
   A. free association   B. resistance   C. transference   D. trepanning

5. When evaluating a therapy, one way to avoid being mislead by a spontaneous remission of symptoms is to use a _____ control group.
   A. non-directive   B. latent   C. psychodynamic   D. waiting-list

6. Carl Rogers did not believe in using _____ in therapy.
   A. empathy   B. authenticity   C. reflection   D. confrontation

7. Filling in gaps in immediate self-awareness is one of the principal goals of
   A. REBT   B. existential therapy   C. person-centered therapy   D. Gestalt therapy

8. To date, the most acceptable type of "distance therapy" is
   A. media psychology   B. commercial telephone counseling   C. Internet-based cybertherapy   D. telehealth

9. Classical conditioning principles are the basis for
   A. aversion therapy   B. time-out   C. token economies   D. EMDR

10. Reciprocal inhibition is an important principle in
    A. EMDR   B. REBT   C. desensitization   D. the design of a token economy

11. A psychologist who is interested in overgeneralization and irrational beliefs is obviously a proponent of
    A. exposure therapy   B. token economies   C. systematic desensitization   D. cognitive therapy

12. The B in the A-B-C of REBT stands for
    A. behavior   B. belief   C. being   D. backward

13. The mirror technique is frequently used in
    A. exposure therapy   B. psychodrama   C. family therapy   D. EMDR

14. Research shows that about half of all patients feel better after their first _____ therapy sessions.
    A. 8   B. 16   C. 24   D. 26

15. Emotional rapport, warmth, understanding, acceptance, and empathy are the core of
    A. the therapeutic alliance   B. large-group awareness training   C. role reversals   D. action therapies

16. Culturally skilled therapists do all but one of the following; which does NOT apply?
    A. Be aware of the client's degree of acculturation.
    B. Use helping resources within the client's cultural group.
    C. Adapt standard techniques to match cultural stereotypes
    D. Be aware of their own cultural values.

17. Major tranquilizers are also known as
    A. anxiolytics   B. antipsychotics   C. antidepressants   D. prefrontal sedatives

18. ECT is classified as a type of
    A. somatic therapy   B. pharmacotherapy   C. psychosurgery   D. deep lesioning

19. Mild punishment is used in which self-management technique?
    A. thought stopping   B. desensitization   C. REBT   D. time out

20. The tension-release method is an important part of
    A. covert reinforcement   B. thought stopping   C. desensitization   D. peer counseling

---

ANSWERS   1. b 2. b 3. a 4. d 5. d 6. d 7. d 8. d 9. a 10. c 11. d 12. b 13. b 14. a 15. a 16. c 17. b 18. a 19. a 20. c

Social Behavior

We Are Social Animals

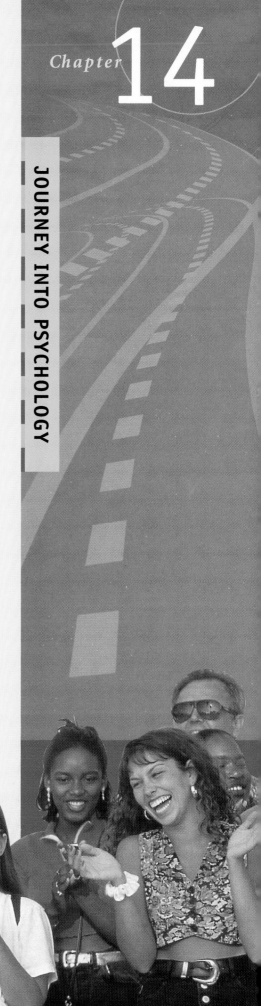

Survivor and other "reality" programs on television have offered an interesting, if voyeuristic, look at some of the best and worst aspects of human behavior.

However, such programs have nothing over the most revealing experiments in social psychology. For example, a classic study done by Phil Zimbardo and his students at Stanford University showed dramatically how social settings influence our behavior.

In the study, normal, healthy, male college students were paid to serve as "inmates" and "guards" in a simulated prison (Zimbardo et al., 1973). After just 2 days in "jail," the inmates grew restless and defiant. When they staged a disturbance, the guards unmercifully suppressed the rebellion. Over the next few days, the guards clamped down with increasing brutality. In a surprisingly short time, the sham convicts looked like real prisoners: They were dejected, traumatized, passive, and dehumanized. Four of them had to be released because they were crying, confused, or severely depressed. Each day, the guards tormented the prisoners with more commands, insults, and demeaning tasks. After 6 days the experiment was halted.

What had happened? Apparently, the assigned social roles—prisoner and guard—were so powerful that in just a few days the experiment became "reality" for those involved. Afterward, it was difficult for many of the guards to believe their own behavior. As one recalls, "I was surprised at myself. I made them call each other names and clean toilets out with their bare hands. I practically considered the prisoners cattle" (Zimbardo, 1973). We tend to think of people as inherently good or bad. But students in the Stanford prison study were randomly assigned to be prisoners or guards. Clearly, we are greatly influenced by the social environments in which we find ourselves.

Social behavior has been the target of an immense amount of study—too much, in fact, for us to cover in detail. Therefore, this chapter is a social psychology "sampler." I hope that the topics I have selected for this final chapter will prove to be interesting and thought provoking.

David Young-Wolff/PhotoEdit

Survey Questions

- Why do people affiliate? What factors influence interpersonal attraction?
- How does group membership affect our behavior?
- What have social psychologists learned about conformity, obedience, compliance, and self-assertion?
- How are attitudes acquired and changed?
- Under what conditions is persuasion most effective?
- Is brainwashing actually possible? How are people converted to cult membership?
- What causes prejudice and intergroup conflict?
- How do psychologists explain human aggression?
- Why are bystanders so often unwilling to help in an emergency?
- What can be done to avoid prejudice and promote social harmony?

AFFILIATION AND ATTRACTION— COME TOGETHER

] SURVEYQUESTIONS *Why do people affiliate? What factors influence interpersonal attraction?*

Social psychology is the scientific study of how people behave, think, and feel in social situations (that is, in the presence, actual or implied, of others) (Baron & Byrne, 2002). Each of us is immersed in a complex social world of families, teams, crowds, tribes, companies, parties, troops, bands, sects, gangs, crews, clans, communities, and nations. But what brings us together in the first place? The *need to affiliate* (associate with other people) is based on basic human desires for approval, support, friendship, and information. We also seek the company of others to alleviate fear or anxiety. An experiment in which college women were threatened with electric shock illustrates this point.

ZILSTEIN'S SHOCK SHOP

A man introduced as Dr. Gregor Zilstein ominously explained to arriving participants, "We would like to give each of you a series of electric shocks . . . these shocks will hurt, they will be painful." In the room was a frightening electrical device that seemed to verify Zilstein's plans. While waiting to be shocked, each woman was given a choice of waiting alone or with other participants. Women frightened in this way more often chose to wait with others; those who expected the shock to be "a mild tickle or tingle" were more willing to wait alone (Schachter, 1959).

Apparently, the frightened women found it comforting to be with others. Should we conclude that "misery loves company"? Actually, this is not entirely correct. In a later study, women who expected to be shocked were given the choice of waiting with other shock recipients, with women waiting to see their college advisors, or alone. Most women chose to wait with other future "victims." In short, misery seems to love miserable company! In general, we prefer to be with people in circumstances similar to our own (Gump & Kulik, 1997).

Is there a reason for that? Yes. Other people provide information that helps us evaluate our own reactions. When a situation is threatening or unfamiliar or when we are in doubt, *social comparisons* tend to guide our behavior (Banaji & Prentice, 1994).

Social psychology The scientific study of how individuals behave, think, and feel in social situations.

Social Comparison Theory

If I want to know how tall I am, I can get out a tape measure. But how do I know if I am a good athlete, guitarist, worker, parent, or friend? How do I know if my views on politics, religion, or grunge rock are unusual or widely shared? When there are no objective standards, the only available yardstick is provided by comparing yourself to others (Festinger, 1954).

Social psychologist Leon Festinger (1919–1989) theorized that belonging to groups fills our needs for **social comparison** (comparing our own actions, feelings, opinions, or abilities to those of others). Have you ever "compared notes" with other students after taking an exam? ("How did you do?" "Wasn't that last question hard?") If you have, you were satisfying needs for social comparison.

Typically, we don't make social comparisons randomly or on some ultimate scale. Meaningful evaluations are based on comparing ourselves with people of similar backgrounds, abilities, and circumstances (Miller, Turnbull, & McFarland, 1988). To illustrate, let's ask a student named Wendy if she is a good tennis player. If Wendy compares herself to a professional, the answer will be no. But this tells us little about her *relative* ability. Within her tennis group, Wendy is regarded as an excellent player. On a fair scale of comparison, Wendy knows she is good, and she takes pride in her tennis skills. In the same way, thinking of yourself as successful, talented, responsible, or fairly paid depends entirely on whom you choose for comparison. Thus, a desire for social comparison provides a motive for associating with others and influences which groups we join.

Don't people also affiliate out of attraction for one another? They do, of course. Let's see why.

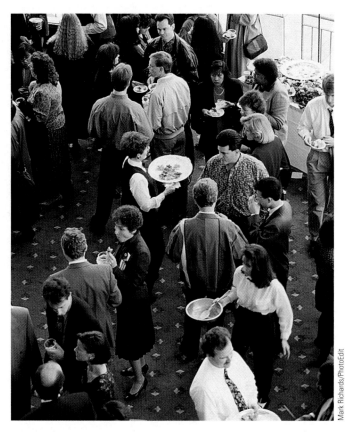

High school class reunions are notorious for the rampant social comparison they often encourage. Apparently it's hard to resist comparing yourself to former classmates to see how you are doing in life.

Interpersonal Attraction

"Birds of a feather flock together." "Familiarity breeds contempt." "Opposites attract." "Absence makes the heart grow fonder." Are these statements true? Actually, the folklore about friendship is, at best, a mixture of fact and fiction.

What does attract people to each other? **Interpersonal attraction** (affinity to another person) is the basis for most voluntary social relationships. As you might expect, we look for friends and lovers who are kind and understanding, who have attractive personalities, and who like us in return (Sprecher, 1998). In addition, several less obvious factors influence attraction.

Physical Proximity

Our choice of friends (and even lovers) is based more on *physical proximity* (nearness) than we might care to believe. For example, the closer people live to each other, the more likely they are to become friends. Likewise, lovers like to think they have found the "one and only" person in the universe for them. In reality, they have probably found the best match in a 5-mile radius—or at least within driving distance (Buss, 1985)! Marriages are not made in heaven—they are made in schools, businesses, and neighborhoods.

Proximity promotes attraction by increasing the *frequency of contact* between people. In general, we are attracted to people we see often. (If you have a reluctant sweetheart, be careful not to send too many love letters—she or he might run off with the letter carrier!) Notice that frequent contact can now occur through Internet chat rooms and e-mail, which can lead to romance at a distance.

What attracts people to each other? Proximity and frequency of contact have a surprisingly large impact.

Social comparison Making judgments about ourselves through comparison with others.

Interpersonal attraction Social attraction to another person.

542   PSYCHOLOGY: A JOURNEY

Physical beauty can be socially advantageous because of the widespread belief that "what is beautiful is good." However, physical beauty is generally unrelated to actual personal traits and talents.

Physical Attractiveness

People who are *physically attractive* are regarded as good-looking by other members of their culture. Beautiful people are generally rated as more appealing than average-looking people. This is due to the *halo effect,* a tendency to extend a limited impression to other personal characteristics. Because of it, we assume that beautiful people are also likable, intelligent, warm, witty, mentally healthy, and socially skilled. However, physical attractiveness actually has almost *no* connection to intelligence, talents, or abilities (Feingold, 1992). Perhaps that's why beauty mainly affects our initial interest in getting to know others (Keller & Young, 1996). Later, more meaningful qualities gain in importance (Berscheid, 1994).

Competence

People who are *competent* have knowledge, ability, or proficiency. All other things being equal, we are more attracted to people who are talented or competent. However, there's an interesting twist to this. In a revealing study, college students listened to audio tapes of candidates for a "College Quiz Bowl." Two of the candidates seemed to be highly intelligent. The other two were of average ability. In addition, one "intelligent" candidate and one "average" candidate clumsily spilled coffee on himself. Later, students rated the intelligent candidate who blundered as *most* attractive. The *least* attractive person was the candidate who was average and clumsy (Aronson, 1969). Thus, the superior but clumsy person was more attractive than the person who was only superior. Apparently, we like people who are competent but imperfect—which makes them more "human."

Similarity

Take a moment to make a list of your closest friends. What do they have in common (other than the joy of knowing you)? It is likely that most are close to you in age and of the same sex and ethnicity as you are. There will be exceptions, of course. But similarity on these three dimensions is the general rule for friendships.

Similarity refers to how alike you are to another person in background, age, interests, attitudes, beliefs, and so forth. In everything from marriage to casual acquaintance, similar people are attracted to each other (Carli et al., 1991). And why not? It's reinforcing to see our beliefs and attitudes shared by others. It shows we are "right" and reveals that they are clever people as well (Alicke et al., 1996)!

In choosing a mate, we tend to marry someone who is like us in almost every way, a pattern called *homogamy* (huh-MOG-ah-me) (Caspi & Herbener, 1990). Studies show that married couples are highly similar in age, education, race, religion, and ethnic background. To a lesser

In college dormitories, roommates who are similar in personality and physical attractiveness tend to be more satisfied with their relationship (Carli, Ganley, & Pierce-Otay, 1991).

degree, they are also similar in attitudes and opinions, mental abilities, socioeconomic status, height, weight, and eye color. In case you're wondering, homogamy also applies to unmarried couples who are living together (Blackwell & Lichter, 2000).

Homogamy is probably a good thing. The risk of divorce is highest among couples with sizable differences in age and education (Tzeng, 1992). Most dangerous of all are "fatal attractions," in which qualities that originally made a partner appealing later come to be disliked. Fatal attractions are likely when you are drawn to someone who seems "different," "unique," or "extreme." In the long run, lovers who are similar are less likely to become disenchanted with one another (Felmlee, 1998).

Self-Disclosure

How do people who are not yet friends learn if they are similar? To get acquainted, you must be willing to talk about more than just the weather, sports, or nuclear physics. At some point you must begin to share private thoughts and feelings and reveal yourself to others. This process, which is called **self-disclosure,** is essential for developing close relationships. Lack of self-disclosure is associated with anxiety, unhappiness, and loneliness (Meleshko & Alden, 1993; Mikulincer & Nachshon, 1991).

We more often reveal ourselves to persons we like than to those we find unattractive. Disclosure also requires a degree of trust. Many people play it safe, or "close to the vest," with people they do not know well. Indeed, self-disclosure is governed by unspoken rules about what's acceptable. Moderate self-disclosure leads to *reciprocity* (a return in kind). *Overdisclosure,* however, gives rise to suspicion and reduces attraction. Overdisclosure exceeds what is appropriate for a relationship or social situation. For example, imagine standing in line at a market and having the stranger in front of you say, "Lately I've been thinking about how I really feel about myself. I think I'm pretty well adjusted, but I occasionally have some questions about my sexual adequacy."

When self-disclosure proceeds at a moderate pace, it builds trust, intimacy, reciprocity, and positive feelings. When it is too rapid or inappropriate, we are likely to "back off" and wonder about the person's motives. Thus, as friends talk, they influence each other in ways that gradually deepen the level of liking, trust, and self-disclosure (Levesque et al., 2002).

Excessive self-disclosure is a staple of many television talk shows. Guests frequently reveal intimate details about their personal lives, including private family matters, sex and dating, physical or sexual abuse, major embarrassments, and criminal activities. Viewers probably find such intimate disclosures entertaining, rather than threatening, because they don't have to reciprocate.

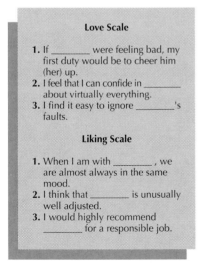

Love Scale

1. If _____ were feeling bad, my first duty would be to cheer him (her) up.
2. I feel that I can confide in _____ about virtually everything.
3. I find it easy to ignore _____'s faults.

Liking Scale

1. When I am with _____, we are almost always in the same mood.
2. I think that _____ is unusually well adjusted.
3. I would highly recommend _____ for a responsible job.

Loving and Liking— Dating, Rating, Mating

How does romantic attraction differ from interpersonal attraction? **Romantic love** is based on interpersonal attraction, but it also involves high levels of emotional arousal and/or sexual desire (Regan, 1998). To investigate love, psychologist Zick Rubin (1973) chose to think of it as an attitude we hold toward another person. This allowed him to develop "liking" and "love" scales to measure each "attitude" (see ✦Fig. 14.1). Next, he asked dating couples to complete the scales twice, once with their lover in mind and once for a close friend of the same sex.

✦FIGURE 14.1 *Sample love-scale and liking-scale items. Each scale consists of 13 items similar to those shown. Scores on these scales correspond to other indications of love and liking. (From Zick Rubin, "Measurement of Romantic Love,"* Journal of Personality and Social Psychology, *1970, pp. 265–273. Copyright © 1970 Zick Rubin. Reprinted by permission of the author.)*

Self-disclosure The process of revealing private thoughts, feelings, and one's personal history to others.

Romantic love Love that is associated with high levels of interpersonal attraction, heightened arousal, mutual absorption, and sexual desire.

▲TABLE 14.1	Average Love and Liking Scores for Date and Same-Sex Close Friend

ATTITUDE TOWARD DATING PARTNER

	Love score	Liking score
Women	89.5	88.5
Men	89.4	84.7

ATTITUDE TOWARD CLOSE FRIEND

	Love score	Liking score
Women	65.3	80.5
Men	55.0	79.1

(Source: From Zick Rubin, "Measurement of Romantic Love," *Journal of Personality and Social Psychology,* 1970, pp. 265–273. Copyright © 1970 Zick Rubin. Reprinted by permission of the author.)

What were the results? Love for partners and friends differed more than liking did (▲ Table 14.1). (**Liking** is affection without passion or deep commitment.) Basically, dating couples like *and* love their partners, but mostly they just like their friends. Women, however, were a little more "loving" of their friends than men were. Does this reflect real differences in the strength of male friendships and female friendships? Maybe not, since it is more acceptable in our culture for women to express love for one another than it is for men. Nevertheless, another study confirmed that dating couples feel a mixture of love and friendship for their partners. In fact, 44 percent of a group of dating persons named their romantic partner as their closest friend (Hendrick & Hendrick, 1993).

Love and friendship differ in another interesting way. Romantic love, in contrast to simple liking, usually involves deep *mutual absorption.* In other words, lovers (unlike friends) pay attention almost exclusively to one another. It's not surprising then, that couples scoring high on Rubin's Love Scale spend more time looking into each other's eyes than low-scoring couples do. And what do lovers see when they gaze into each other's eyes? Generally, romantic partners tend to idealize each other, which helps keep relationships going, despite the fact that nobody's perfect (Murray, Holmes, & Griffin, 1996).

Evolution and Mate Selection

Evolutionary psychology is the study of the evolutionary origins of human behavior patterns. Many psychologists believe that evolution left an imprint on men and women that has influenced everything from sexual attraction and infidelity to jealousy and divorce. According to David Buss, the key to understanding human mating patterns is to understand how evolved behavior patterns guide our choices (Buss, 1994).

In a study of 37 cultures on six continents, Buss found the following patterns: Compared with women, men are more interested in casual sex; they prefer younger, more physically attractive partners; and they get more jealous over real or imagined sexual infidelities than they do over a loss of emotional commitment. Compared with men, women prefer slightly older partners who appear to be industrious, higher in status, or economically successful; women are more upset by a partner who becomes emotionally involved with someone else, rather than one who is sexually unfaithful (Buss, 1994; Townsend & Wasserman, 1998) (✦Fig. 14.2).

✦FIGURE 14.2 *What do people look for when considering potential dating partners? Here are the results of a study in which personal ads were placed in newspapers. As you can see, men were more influenced by looks, and women by success (Goode, 1996).*

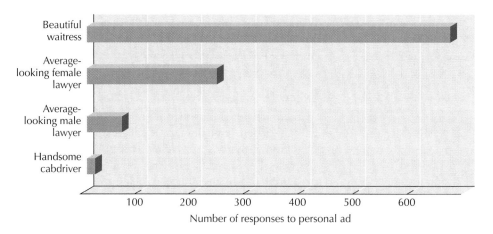

Why do such differences exist? Buss and others believe that mating preferences evolved in response to the differing reproductive challenges faced by men and women. As a rule, women must invest more time and energy in reproduction and nurturing children than men do. Consequently, women evolved an interest in whether their partners will stay with them and whether their mates have the resources to provide for their children (Archer, 1996; Regan et al., 2000).

Liking A relationship based on intimacy, but lacking passion and commitment.

Evolutionary psychology Study of the evolutionary origins of human behavior patterns.

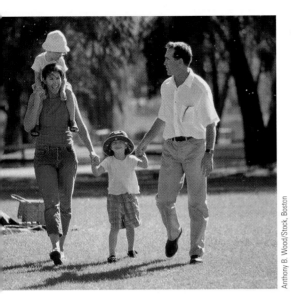

According to evolutionary psychologists, women tend to be concerned with whether mates will devote time and resources to a relationship. Men place more emphasis on physical attractiveness and sexual fidelity.

In contrast, the reproductive success of men depends on their mates' fertility. Men, therefore, tend to look for health, youth, and beauty in a prospective mate, as signs of suitability for reproduction (Regan et al., 2000). This preference, perhaps, is why some older men abandon their first wives in favor of young, beautiful "trophy wives." Evolutionary theory further explains that the male emphasis on their mates' sexual fidelity is based on concerns about the paternity of offspring. From a biological perspective, men do not benefit from investing resources in children they did not sire (Schmitt & Buss, 1996).

A sizable body of evidence supports the evolutionary view of mating. However, it is important to remember that evolved mating tendencies are subtle at best and easily overruled by other factors. Some mating patterns may simply reflect the fact that men still tend to control the power and resources in most societies (Feingold, 1992). Most important of all, remember that kindness and intelligence rate highest when men and women choose mates (Regan et al., 2000). They are love's greatest allies.

Needs for affiliation and interpersonal attraction inevitably bring people together in groups. In the next section we will explore several interesting aspects of group membership. But first, here's a chance to review what you have learned.

STUDYBREAK Affiliation, Friendship, and Love

RELATE

How has social comparison affected your behavior? Has it influenced who you associate with?

Think of three close friends. Which of the attraction factors described earlier apply to your friendships?

To what extent do Rubin's findings about love and liking match your own experiences?

LEARNING CHECK

1. Women threatened with electric shock in an experiment generally chose to wait alone or with other women not taking part in the experiment. T or F?
2. Interpersonal attraction is increased by all but one of the following. (Which does not fit?)
   a. physical proximity   b. competence   c. similarity
   d. overdisclosure
3. High levels of self-disclosure are reciprocated in most social encounters. T or F?
4. Women rate their friends higher on the Love Scale than do men. T or F?
5. The most striking finding about marriage patterns is that most people choose mates whose personalities are quite unlike their own. T or F?
6. Compared with men, women tend to be more upset by sexual infidelity than by a loss of emotional commitment on the part of their mates. T or F?

Critical Thinking

7. How have contemporary communications networks altered the effects of proximity on interpersonal attraction?

ANSWERS

1. F 2. d 3. F 4. T 5. F 6. F 7. As mentioned earlier, it is now possible to interact with another person by telephone, fax, short-wave radio, modem, or similar means. This makes actual physical proximity less crucial in interpersonal attraction, because frequent contact is possible even at great distances. Internet romances are a good example of this possibility.

LIFE IN GROUPS—PEOPLE, PEOPLE, EVERYWHERE

] **SURVEYQUESTION** *How does group membership affect our behavior?*

We all belong to many overlapping social groups, and in each, we occupy a *position* in the *structure* of the group. **Social roles** are patterns of behavior expected of persons in various social positions. For instance, playing the role of mother, boss, or student involves different sets of behaviors and expectations. Some roles are *ascribed* (they are assigned to a person or are not under personal control): male or female, son, adolescent, inmate. *Achieved roles* are voluntarily attained by special effort: spouse, teacher, scientist, band leader.

Roles have a powerful impact on social behavior. What kinds of behavior do you expect from your teachers? What behaviors do they expect from you? What happens if either of you fails to match the other's expectations?

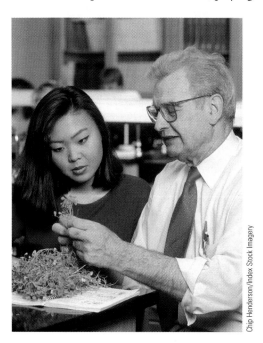

Chip Henderson/Index Stock Imagery

What effect does role-playing have on behavior? Roles streamline daily interactions by allowing us to anticipate the behavior of others. When a person is acting as a doctor, mother, clerk, or police officer, we expect certain behaviors. However, roles have a negative side too. Many people experience **role conflicts,** in which two or more roles make conflicting demands on them. Consider, for example, a teacher who must flunk a close friend's daughter; a mother who has a full-time job; and a soccer coach whose son is on the team but isn't a very skilled player. Likewise, the clashing demands of work, family, and school create role conflicts for many students (Hammer, Grigsby, & Woods, 1998).

Group Structure, Cohesion, and Norms

Are there other dimensions of group membership? Two important dimensions of any group are its structure and cohesiveness. **Group structure** consists of the network of roles, communication pathways, and power in a group. Organized groups such as an army or an athletic team have a high degree of structure. Informal friendship groups may or may not be very structured.

Group cohesiveness is basically the degree of attraction among group members or their commitment to remaining in the group. Members of cohesive groups literally stick together: They tend to stand or sit close together, they pay more attention to one another, and they show more signs of mutual affection. Also, their behavior tends to be closely coordinated (Levine & Moreland, 1990). Cohesiveness is the basis for much of the power that groups exert over us. Therapy groups, businesses, sports teams, and the like seek to increase cohesion because it helps people work together better (Craig & Kelly, 1999).

In-Groups

Cohesiveness is particularly strong for **in-groups** (groups with which a person mainly identifies). Very likely, your own in-group is defined by a combination of prominent social dimensions, such as nationality, ethnicity, age, education, religion, income, political values, gender, sexual orientation, and so forth. In-group membership helps define who we are socially. Predictably, we tend to attribute positive characteristics to our in-group and negative qualities to **out-groups** (groups with which we do not identify). We also tend to exaggerate differences between members of out-groups and our own group. This sort of "us-and-them" thinking seems to be a basic fact of social life. It also sets the stage for conflict between groups and for racial and ethnic prejudice—topics we will explore later in this chapter.

Social role Expected behavior patterns associated with particular social positions (such as daughter, worker, student).

Role conflict Trying to occupy two or more roles that make conflicting demands on behavior.

Group structure The network of roles, communication pathways, and power in a group.

Group cohesiveness The degree of attraction among group members or their commitment to remaining in the group.

In-group A group with which a person identifies.

Out-group A group with which a person does not identify.

Status

In addition to defining roles, a person's social position within groups determines his or her **status,** or level of social power and importance. In most groups, higher status bestows special privileges and respect. For example, in a classic experiment, researchers left dimes in phone booths. When people entered the booths, a researcher approached and said, "Excuse me, I think I left a dime in this phone booth a few minutes ago. Did you find it?" Seventy-seven percent of the people returned the money when the researcher was well dressed. Only 38 percent returned it to poorly dressed researchers (Bickman, 1974). You don't have to be in a phone booth for this to work. In most situations, we are more likely to comply with a request made by a high-status (well-dressed) person (Gueguen, 2002). Perhaps the better treatment given "higher-status" persons explains some of our society's preoccupation with expensive clothes, cars, and other status symbols.

Norms

We are also greatly affected by group norms. A **norm** is a widely accepted (but often unspoken) standard for appropriate behavior. If you have the slightest doubt about the power of norms, try this test: Walk into a crowded supermarket, get in a checkout line, and begin singing loudly in your fullest voice. Probably only 1 person in 100 could actually carry out these instructions.

The impact of norms is shown by an interesting study of littering. The question was, Does the amount of trash in an area affect whether people will add to the litter? To find out, people were given handbills as they walked into a public parking garage. As you can see in ✦Figure 14.3, the more litter there was on the floor, the more likely people were to add to it by dropping their handbill. Apparently, seeing that others had already littered implied a lax norm about whether littering is acceptable. The moral? The cleaner a public area is kept, the less likely people are to "trash" it (Cialdini, Reno, & Kallgren, 1990).

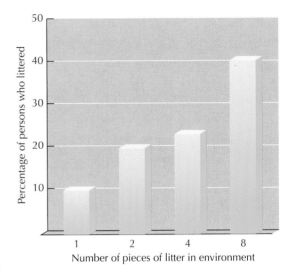

✦**FIGURE 14.3** *Results of an experiment on norms concerning littering. The prior existence of litter in a public setting implies that littering is acceptable. This encourages others to "trash" the area. (From Cialdini, Reno, & Kallgren, 1990.)*

Making Attributions

Every day we must form impressions of people from only the smallest shreds of evidence. We do this through a process called **attribution.** As we observe others, we tend to make inferences about them. Why did Vonda insult Sutchai? Why did Nick change his college major? Why does Kirti talk so fast when she's around men? In answering such questions we *attribute* people's behavior to various causes. Whether we are right or wrong about the causes of behavior, our conclusions affect how we act. To learn how we fill in the "person behind the mask," let's explore the making of attributions.

Two people enter a restaurant and order different meals. Nell tastes her food, then salts it. Bert salts his food before he tastes it. How would you explain their behavior? In Nell's case, you might assume that the *food* needed salt. If so, you have attributed her actions to an *external cause* (one that lies outside a person). With Bert, you might be more inclined to conclude that he must really *like* salt. If so, the cause of his behavior is internal. *Internal causes,* such as needs, personality traits, and Bert's taste for salt, lie within the person.

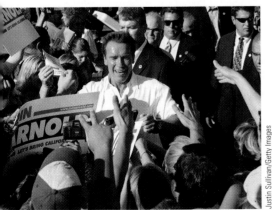

During his run for governor of California in 2003, Arnold Schwarzenegger was accused by several women of sexual harassment and sexual assault. Soon after, Schwarzenegger publicly apologized to anyone he might have offended in the past. Did you attribute his apology to sincere regret? Or did you attribute it to political self-interest? Such attributions affect how we perceive and respond to the behavior of others.

Status An individual's position in a social structure, especially with respect to power, privilege, or importance.

Norm A widely accepted standard of conduct for appropriate behavior.

Attribution The process of making inferences about the causes of one's own behavior and that of others.

What effects do such interpretations have? To fully understand your social behavior, we need to know about the attributions you have made. For instance, let's say that at the last five parties you've been to, you've seen a woman named Macy. Based on this, you assume that Macy likes to socialize. You see Macy at yet another gathering and mention that she seems to like parties. She says, "Actually, I hate these parties, but I get invited to play my tuba at them. My music teacher says I need to practice in front of an audience, so I keep attending these dumb events. Want to hear a Sousa march?"

We seldom know the real reasons for others' actions. That is why we tend to infer causes from *circumstances.* However, in doing so, we often make mistakes like the one with Macy. The most common error is to attribute the actions of others to internal causes (Jones & Nisbett, 1971). This mistake is called the **fundamental attributional error.** We tend to think the actions of others have internal causes even if they are actually caused by external forces or circumstances.

Where our own behavior is concerned, we are more likely to think that external causes explain our actions. In other words, there is an **actor-observer bias** in how we explain behavior. As *observers,* we attribute the behavior of others to their wants, motives, and personality traits (this is the fundamental attributional error). As *actors,* we tend to find external explanations for our own behavior (Krueger, Ham, & Linford, 1996). No doubt you chose your major in school because of what it has to offer. Other students choose *their* majors because of the kind of people they are. Other people who don't leave tips in restaurants are cheapskates. If you don't leave a tip, it's because the service was bad. And, of course, other people are always late because they are irresponsible. I am late because I was held up by events beyond my control.

Ye Old Double Standard

Attributions reveal an interesting double standard regarding the abilities of men and women. In a study, people overheard a male or female doing extremely well on a perception task. Each person then rated whether the test taker's success was due to ability, luck, or some combination of the two. Both men and women attributed male success mainly to skill and women's performances mainly to luck! This was true even though male and female performances were identical (Deaux & Emswiller, 1974).

As early as *kindergarten,* boys tend to take credit for successes. Girls tend to discount their own performances ("put themselves down") (Burgner & Hewstone, 1993). In general, there is a strong tendency to assume, "He's skilled, she's lucky," when judging men and women (Swim & Sanna, 1996). Throughout life, such attributions no doubt dog the heels of many talented and successful women.

Social Influence—Follow the Leader

] SURVEYQUESTION *What have social psychologists learned about conformity, obedience, compliance, and self-assertion?*

No topic lies nearer the heart of social psychology than **social influence** (changes in behavior induced by the actions of others). When people interact, they almost always affect one another's behavior (Crano, 2000). For example, in a sidewalk experiment, various numbers of people stood on a busy New York City street. On cue they all looked at a sixth-floor window across the street. A camera recorded how many passersby also stopped to stare. The larger the influencing group, the more people were swayed to join in staring at the window (Milgram et al., 1969).

Are there different kinds of social influence? Social influence ranges from simple suggestion to intensive indoctrination (brainwashing). Daily behavior is probably most influenced by group pressures for **conformity** (bringing your behavior into agreement with the actions, norms, or values of others) (Baron & Byrne, 2002). We all conform to a degree. In fact, some uniformity is a necessity. Imagine being totally unable to anticipate the actions of others. In stores, schools, and homes, this would be frustrating and disturbing. On the highways, it would be lethal.

Fundamental attributional error The tendency to attribute the behavior of others to internal causes (personality, likes, and so forth).

Actor-observer bias The tendency to attribute the behavior of others to internal causes while attributing one's own behavior to external causes (situations and circumstances).

Social influence Changes in a person's behavior induced by the presence or actions of others.

Conformity Bringing one's behavior into agreement or harmony with norms or with the behavior of others in a group.

Conformity is a subtle dimension of daily life. Notice the similarities in clothing and hairstyles among these couples.

Conformity

When John first started working at the Fleegle Flange Factory, he found it easy to process 300 flanges an hour. Others around him averaged only 200. John's co-workers told him to slow down and take it easy. "I get bored," he said and continued to do 300 flanges an hour. At first John was welcomed, but now conversations broke up when he approached. Other workers laughed at him or ignored him when he spoke. Although he never made a conscious decision to conform, in another week John's output had slowed to 200 flanges an hour. Perhaps the most basic of all group norms is, as John discovered, "Thou shalt conform." Like it or not, life is filled with instances of conformity.

The Asch Experiment

How strong are group pressures for conformity? One of the first experiments on conformity was staged by Solomon Asch (1907–1996). To fully appreciate it, imagine yourself as a subject. Assume that you are seated at a table with six other students. Your task is actually quite simple. On each trial you are shown three lines. Your job is to select the line that matches a "standard" line (◆Fig. 14.4).

As the testing begins, each person announces an answer for the first card. When your turn comes, you agree with the others. "This isn't hard at all," you say to yourself. For several more trials your answers agree with those of the group. Then comes a shock. All six people announce that line 1 matches the standard, and you were about to say line 2 matches. Suddenly you feel alone and upset. You nervously look at the lines again. The room falls silent. Everyone seems to be staring at you. The experimenter awaits your answer. Do you yield to the group?

In this study the other "students" were all actors who gave the wrong answer on about a third of the trials to create group pressure (Asch, 1956). Real students conformed to the group on about one third of the critical trials. Of those tested, 75 percent yielded at least once. People tested alone erred in less than 1 percent of their judgments. Clearly, those who yielded to group pressures were denying what their eyes told them.

Are some people more susceptible to group pressures than others? People with high needs for structure or certainty are more likely to conform. So are people who are anxious, low in self-confidence, or concerned with the approval of others. People who live in cultures that emphasize group cooperation (such as many Asian cultures) are also more likely to conform (Bond & Smith, 1996).

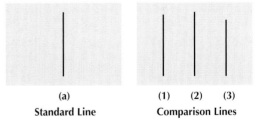

(a)
Standard Line

(1) (2) (3)
Comparison Lines

◆**FIGURE 14.4** *Stimuli used in Solomon Asch's conformity experiments.*

USING PSYCHOLOGY Groupthink—Agreement at Any Cost

What happens when people in positions of power fall prey to pressures for conformity? To find out, Yale psychologist Irving Janis (1918–1990) analyzed a series of disastrous decisions made by government officials. His conclusion? Many such fiascoes are the result of **groupthink**—a compulsion by decision makers to maintain each other's approval, even at the cost of critical thinking (Janis, 1989).

Groupthink has been blamed for many embarrassments, such as the *Columbia* space shuttle disaster in 2003, and the loss, in 1999, of the $165 million *Mars Climate Orbiter*. An analysis of 19 international crises found that groupthink contributed to most (Schafer & Crichlow, 1996).

The core of groupthink is misguided loyalty. Group members are hesitant to "rock the boat" or question sloppy thinking. This self-censorship leads people to believe they agree more than they actually do (Bernthal & Insko, 1993; Esser, 1998).

To prevent groupthink, group leaders should take the following steps:

* Define each group member's role as a "critical evaluator."
* Avoid revealing any personal preferences in the beginning.
* State the problem factually, without bias.
* Invite a group member or outside person to play devil's advocate.
* Make it clear that group members will be held accountable for decisions.
* Encourage open inquiry and a search for alternate solutions (Chen et al., 1996; Kroon et al., 1992).

In addition, Janis suggested that there should be a "second-chance" meeting to re-evaluate important decisions. That is, each decision should be reached twice.

In an age clouded by the threat of war, meltdowns, and similar disasters, even stronger solutions to the problem of groupthink would be welcome. Perhaps we should form a group to think about it?

In addition to personal characteristics, certain situations tend to encourage conformity—sometimes with disastrous results. "Groupthink—Agreement at Any Cost" offers a prime example.

Group Factors in Conformity

How do groups enforce norms?   In most groups, we have been rewarded with acceptance and approval for conformity and threatened with rejection or ridicule for non-conformity. These reactions are called *group sanctions*. Negative sanctions range from laughter, staring, or social disapproval to complete rejection or formal exclusion. If you've ever felt the sudden chill of disapproval by others, you will understand the power of group sanctions.

Wouldn't the effectiveness of group sanctions depend on the importance of the group? Yes. The more important group membership is to a person, the more he or she will be influenced by other group members. The risk of being rejected can be a threat to our sense of personal identity (Crano, 2000). That's why the Asch experiments are impressive. Since these were only temporary groups, sanctions were informal and rejection had no lasting importance. Just the same, the power of the group was evident.

What other factors, besides importance of the group, affect the degree of conformity?   In the sidewalk experiment described earlier, we noted that large groups had more influence. In Asch's face-to-face groups the size of the majority also made a difference, but a surprisingly small one. In other studies, the number of people who conformed increased dramatically as the majority grew from two to three people. However, a majority of three produced about as much yielding as a majority of eight. The next time you want to talk someone into (or out of) something, take two friends along and see what a difference it makes! (Sometimes it helps if the two are large and mean-looking.)

Even more important than the size of the majority is its *unanimity* (total agreement). Having at least one person in your corner can greatly reduce pressures to conform. When Asch gave subjects an ally (who also opposed the majority by giving the correct answer), conformity was lessened. In terms of numbers, a unanimous majority of three is more powerful than a majority of eight with one dissenting. Perhaps this accounts for the rich diversity of human attitudes, beliefs, opinions, and lifestyles. If you can find at least one other person who sees things as you do (no matter how weird), you can be relatively secure in your opposition to other viewpoints. Incidentally, the Internet is a perfect way to find that other person (McKenna & Bargh, 1998)!

Groupthink A compulsion by members of decision-making groups to maintain agreement, even at the cost of critical thinking.

STUDYBREAK   *Groups, Attribution, and Conformity*

RELATE

What are the most prominent roles you play? Which are achieved, and which are ascribed? How do they affect your behavior? What conflicts do they create?

Do you commit the fundamental attributional error? Try to think of a specific example that illustrates the concept.

Identify a recent time when you conformed in some way. How did norms, group pressure, sanctions, and unanimity contribute to your tendency to conform?

LEARNING CHECK

1. Status refers to a set of expected behaviors associated with a social position. T or F?
2. The fundamental attributional error is to attribute the actions of others to internal causes. T or F?

3. The effect one person's behavior has on another is called

_____ _____.
4. Subjects in Solomon Asch's conformity study yielded on about 75 percent of the critical trials. T or F?
5. Non-conformity is punished by negative group

_____.
6. Janis used the term _____ to describe a compulsion among decision-making groups to maintain an illusion of unanimity.

Critical Thinking

7. Would it be possible to be completely non-conforming (that is, to not conform to some group norm)?

ANSWERS

1. F 2. T 3. social influence 4. F 5. sanctions 6. groupthink 7. A person who did not follow at least some norms concerning normal social behavior would very likely be perceived as extremely bizarre, disturbed, or psychotic.

OBEDIENCE—WOULD YOU ELECTROCUTE A STRANGER?

A person who has social power in one situation may have very little in another. In those situations where a person has power, she or he is described as an *authority*. Let's investigate **obedience,** a special type of conformity to the demands of an authority.

The question is this: If ordered to do so, would you shock a man with a heart condition who is screaming and asking to be released? Certainly, few people would obey. Or would they? In Nazi Germany, obedient soldiers (once average citizens) helped slaughter over 6 million people in concentration camps. Do such inhumane acts reflect deep character flaws? Are they the acts of heartless psychopaths or crazed killers? Or are they simply the result of obedience to authority? What are the limits of obedience? These are questions that puzzled social psychologist Stanley Milgram (1965) when he began a provocative series of studies on obedience.

How did Milgram study obedience?   As was true of the Asch experiments, Milgram's research is best appreciated by imagining yourself as a subject. Place yourself in the following situation.

Milgram's Obedience Studies

Imagine answering a newspaper ad to take part in a "learning" experiment at Yale University. When you arrive, a coin is flipped and a second person, a pleasant-looking man in his 50s, is designated the "learner." By chance you have become the "teacher."

Your task is to read a list of word pairs. The learner's task is to memorize them. You are to punish him with an electric shock each time he makes a mistake. The learner is taken to an adjacent room and you watch as he is seated in an "electric chair" apparatus. Electrodes are attached to his wrists. You are then escorted to your position in front of a "shock generator." On this device is a row of 30 switches marked from 15 to 450 volts. Corresponding labels range from "Slight Shock" to "Extreme Intensity Shock" and finally "Danger Severe Shock." You are instructed to shock the learner each time he makes a mistake. You must begin with 15 volts and then move one switch (15 volts) higher for each additional mistake (◆Fig. 14.5).

Obedience Conformity to the demands of an authority.

✦**FIGURE 14.5** *Scenes from Stanley Milgram's study of obedience: the "shock generator," strapping a "learner" into his chair, and a "teacher" being told to administer a severe shock to the learner. (Scenes from the film "Obedience" by Stanley Milgram, The Pennsylvania State University, Audio Visual Services. Used by permission.)*

✦**FIGURE 14.6** *Results of Milgram's obedience experiment. Only a minority of subjects refused to provide shocks, even at the most extreme intensities. The first substantial drop in obedience occurred at the 300-volt level (Milgram, 1963).*

The experiment begins, and the learner soon makes his first error. You flip a switch. More mistakes. Rapidly you reach the 75-volt level. The learner moans after each shock. At 100 volts he complains that he has a heart condition. At 150 volts he says he no longer wants to continue and demands to be released. At 300 volts he screams and says he can no longer give answers.

At some point during the experiment, you begin to protest to the experimenter. "That man has a heart condition," you say; "I'm not going to kill that man." The experimenter says, "Please continue." Another shock and another scream from the learner and you say, "You mean I've got to keep going up the scale? No, sir. I'm not going to give him 450 volts!" The experimenter says, "The experiment requires that you continue." For a time the learner refuses to answer any more questions and screams with each shock (Milgram, 1965). Then he falls chillingly silent for the rest of the experiment.

It's hard to believe many people would do this. What happened? Milgram also doubted that many people would obey his orders. When he polled a group of psychiatrists before the experiment, they predicted that less than 1 percent of those tested would obey. The astounding fact is that 65 percent obeyed completely by going all the way to the 450-volt level. Virtually no one stopped short of 300 volts ("Severe Shock") (✦Fig. 14.6).

Was the learner injured? The time has come to reveal that the "learner" was actually an actor who turned a tape recorder on and off in the shock room. No shocks were ever administered, but the dilemma for the "teacher" was quite real. Subjects protested, sweated, trembled, stuttered, bit their lips, and laughed nervously. Clearly they were disturbed by what they were doing. Nevertheless, most obeyed the experimenter's orders.

Milgram's Follow-Up

Why did so many people obey? Some have suggested that the prestige of Yale University added to subjects' willingness to obey. Could it be that they assumed the professor running the experiment would not really allow anyone to be hurt? To test this possibility, the study was rerun in a shabby office building in nearby Bridgeport, Connecticut. Under these conditions fewer people obeyed (48 percent), but the reduction was minor.

Milgram was disturbed by the willingness of people to knuckle under to authority and senselessly shock someone. In later experiments, he tried to reduce obedience. He found that the distance between the teacher and the learner was important. When subjects were in the *same room* as the learner, only 40 percent obeyed fully. When they were *face to face* with the learner and required to force his hand down on a simulated "shock plate," only 30 percent obeyed (✦Fig. 14.7). Distance from the authority also had an effect. When the experimenter gave his orders over the phone, only 22 percent obeyed. You may doubt that Milgram's study of obedience applies to you. If so, take a moment to read the following description:

QUACK LIKE A DUCK

The demonstration described here has become a favorite of many psychology teachers (Halonen, 1986). Imagine your response to the following events. On the first day of class, your professor begins to establish the basic rules of behavior for the course. Seats are assigned and you must move to a new location. You are told not to talk during class. Your professor tells you that you must have permission to leave early. You are told to bring your textbook to class at all times. Up to this point you might not have any difficulty obeying your professor's orders. Then the demands become less reasonable. The professor says, "Use only a pencil for taking notes. Borrow one if you must." "Take off your watch." "Keep both hands on your desktop at all times." "All students who are freshmen stand at the back of the class." The demonstration is capped by orders that you cannot follow without looking silly: "Stick two fingers up your nose and quack like a duck."

Where do you think you would draw the line in obeying such orders? In reality, you might find yourself obeying a legitimate authority long after that person's demands had become unreasonable. What would happen, though, if a few students resisted orders early in the sequence? Would that help free others to disobey? For an answer, let's return to some final remarks on Milgram's experiment.

Implications

Milgram's research raises nagging questions about our willingness to commit antisocial or inhumane acts commanded by a "legitimate authority." The excuse so often given by war criminals—"I was only following orders"—takes on new meaning in this light. Milgram suggested that when directions come from an authority, people rationalize that they are not personally responsible for their actions. In locales as diverse as Vietnam, Rwanda, Bosnia, South Africa, Nicaragua, Sri Lanka, and Laos, the tragic result has been "sanctioned massacres" of chilling proportions. Even in everyday life, crimes of obedience are common. In order to keep their jobs, many people obey orders to do things that they know are dishonest, unethical, or harmful (Hamilton & Sanders, 1995).

Let us end on a more positive note. In one of his experiments, Milgram found that group support can greatly reduce destructive obedience. When real subjects saw two other "teachers" (both actors) resist orders and walk out of the experiment, only 10 percent continued to obey. Thus, a personal act of courage or moral fortitude by one or two members of a group may free others to disobey misguided or unjust authority.

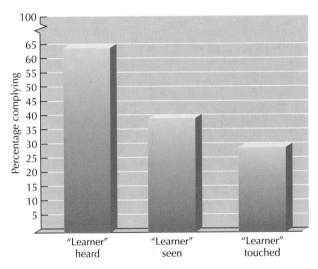

FIGURE 14.7 *Physical distance from the "learner" had a significant effect on the percentage of subjects obeying orders.*

Obedience to authority is often necessary and reasonable; however, it can also be destructive.

COMPLIANCE—A FOOT IN THE DOOR

Pressures to "fit in" and conform are usually indirect. When an authority commands obedience the pressure is direct and difficult to resist. There is a third possibility. The term **compliance** refers to situations in which one person bends to the requests of another person who has little or no authority. Pressures to comply are quite common. For example, a stranger might ask you to yield a phone booth so he can make a call; a saleswoman might suggest that you buy a more expensive watch than you had planned on; or a co-worker might ask you for a dollar to buy a cup of coffee.

What determines whether a person will comply with a request?   Many factors could be listed, but three stand out as especially interesting. Let's consider each.

The Foot-in-the-Door Effect

People who sell door-to-door have long recognized that once they get a foot in the door, a sale is almost a sure thing. To state the **foot-in-the-door principle** more formally, a person who first agrees to a small request is later more likely to comply with a larger demand (Dillard, 1991). For instance, if someone asked you to put a large, ugly sign in your front yard to promote safe driving, you would probably refuse. If, however, you had first agreed to put a small sign in your window, you would later be much more likely to allow the big sign in your yard (Freedman & Fraser, 1966).

Apparently, the foot-in-the-door effect is based on observing one's own behavior. Seeing yourself agree to a small request helps convince you that you didn't mind doing what was asked. After that, you are more likely to comply with a larger request (Dillard, 1991).

The Door-in-the-Face Effect

Let's say that a neighbor comes to your door and asks you to feed his dogs, water his plants, and mow his yard while he is out of town for a month. This is quite a major request—one that most people would probably turn down. Feeling only slightly guilty, you tell your neighbor that you're sorry but you can't help him. Now, what if the same neighbor returns the next day and asks if you would at least pick up his mail while he is gone. Chances are very good that you would honor this request, even if you might have resisted it otherwise.

Psychologist Robert Cialdini coined the term **door-in-the-face effect** to describe the tendency for a person who has refused a major request to agree to a smaller request (Cialdini et al., 1975). In other words, after a person has turned down a major request ("slammed the door in your face"), he or she may be more willing to comply with a lesser demand. This strategy works because a person who abandons a large request appears to have given up something. In response, many people feel that they must repay her or him by giving in to the smaller request (Dillard, 1991). In fact, a good way to get another person to comply with a request is to first do a small favor for the person (Whatley et al., 1999).

Calvin and Hobbes © Watterson. Reprinted by permission of Universal Press Syndicate.

Compliance Bending to the requests of a person who has little or no authority or other form of social power.

Foot-in-the-door effect The tendency for a person who has first complied with a small request to be more likely later to fulfill a larger request.

Door-in-the-face effect The tendency for a person who has refused a major request to subsequently be more likely to comply with a minor request.

Low-ball technique A strategy in which commitment is gained first to reasonable or desirable terms, which are then made less reasonable or desirable.

The Low-Ball Technique

Anyone who has purchased an automobile will recognize a third way of inducing compliance. Automobile dealers are notorious for convincing customers to buy cars by offering "low-ball" prices that undercut the competition. The dealer first gets the customer to agree to buy at an attractively low price. Then, once the customer is committed, various techniques are used to bump the price up before the sale is concluded.

The **low-ball technique** consists of getting a person committed to act and then making the terms of acting less desirable. Here's another example: A fellow student asks to borrow $25 for a day. This seems reasonable and you agree. However, once you have given your classmate the money, he explains that it would be easier to repay you after payday, in

2 weeks. If you agree, you've succumbed to the low-ball technique. Here's another example: Let's say you ask someone to give you a ride to school in the morning. Only after the person has agreed do you tell her that you have to be there at 6 A.M.

Passive Compliance

Complying with requests is a normal part of life. At times, however, a willingness to comply can exceed what is reasonable. Researcher Thomas Moriarty (1975) demonstrated excessive, passive compliance under realistic conditions. *Passive compliance* refers to quietly bending to unreasonable demands or unacceptable conditions. Moriarty observed that many people will put up with almost anything to avoid a confrontation. For example, he and his students staged loud conversations behind people in movie theaters or people studying in a library. Very few protested. In other experiments, people were accosted in phone booths. The experimenter explained that he had left a ring in the booth and asked if the person had found it. When subjects said no, the experimenter demanded that they empty their pockets. Most did.

In these and similar situations, people passively accepted having their personal rights trampled, even when objecting was no threat to their safety (◆Fig. 14.8). Overly passive women, in particular, tend to be ripe targets for exploitation, especially by men (Richards, Rollerson, & Phillips, 1991). Have we become "a nation of willing victims"? Certainly, we hope not. Let's see how assertive people handle difficult social situations.

◆**FIGURE 14.8** *In an experiment done at an airport, a smoker intentionally sat or stood near non-smokers. Only 9 percent of the non-smokers asked the smoker to stop smoking, even when no-smoking signs were clearly visible nearby (Gibson & Werner, 1994).*

Assertiveness Training

Have you ever done any of the following?

- Hesitated to question an error on a restaurant bill because you were afraid of making a scene?
- Backed out of asking for a raise or a change in working conditions?
- Said yes when you wanted to say no?
- Been afraid to question a grade that seemed unfair?

If you've ever had trouble with similar situations, *assertiveness training* (instruction in how to be self-assertive) may offer a solution. In assertiveness training, people learn assertive behavior through group exercises, videotapes, and staged conflicts. They also learn to practice honesty, disagreeing, questioning authority, and assertive postures and gestures. As their self-confidence improves, non-assertive clients are taken on "field trips" to shops and restaurants where they practice what they have learned.

The first step in assertiveness training is to convince yourself of three basic rights: You have the right to refuse, to request, and to right a wrong. **Self-assertion** involves standing up for these rights by speaking out in your own behalf.

Is self-assertion just getting things your own way? Not at all. A basic distinction can be made between *self-assertion* and *aggressive* behavior. Self-assertion is a direct, honest expression of feelings and desires. It is not exclusively self-serving. People who are non-assertive are usually patient to a fault. Sometimes their pent-up anger explodes with unexpected fury, which can damage relationships. In contrast to assertive behavior, **aggression** involves hurting another person or achieving one's goals at the expense of another. Aggression does not take into account the feelings or rights of others. It is an attempt to get one's own way no matter what. Assertion techniques emphasize firmness, not attack (▲Table 14.2).

The basic idea in assertiveness training is that each assertive action is practiced until it can be repeated even under stress. For example, let's say it really angers you when a store clerk waits on several people who arrived after you did. To improve your assertiveness in this situation, you would begin by *rehearsing* the dialogue, posture, and gestures you would use to confront the clerk or the other customer. Working in front of a mirror can be very helpful. If

Self-assertion A direct, honest expression of feelings and desires.
Aggression Hurting another person or achieving one's goals at the expense of another person.

▲ TABLE 14.2	Comparison of Assertive, Aggressive, and Non-assertive Behavior	
	ACTOR	**RECEIVER OF BEHAVIOR**
Non-assertive behavior	Self-denying, inhibited, hurt, and anxious; lets others make choices; goals not achieved	Feels sympathy, guilt, or contempt for actor; achieves goals at actor's expense
Aggressive behavior	Achieves goals at others' expense; expresses feelings, but hurts others; chooses for others or puts them down	Feels hurt, defensive, humiliated, or taken advantage of; does not meet own needs
Assertive behavior	Self-enhancing; acts in own best interests; expresses feelings; respects rights of others; goals usually achieved, self-respect maintained	Needs respected and feelings expressed; may achieve goal; self-worth maintained

possible, you should *role-play* the scene with a friend. Be sure to have your friend take the part of a really aggressive or irresponsible clerk, as well as a cooperative one. Rehearsal and role-playing should also be used when you expect a possible confrontation with someone—for example, if you are going to ask for a raise, challenge a grade, or confront a landlord.

Self-assertion does not supply instant poise, confidence, or self-assurance. However, it is a way of combating anxieties associated with life in an impersonal and sometimes intimidating society. If you are interested in more information, you can consult a book entitled *Your Perfect Right* by Alberti and Emmons (1995).

STUDYBREAK *Social Power, Obedience, and Compliance*

RELATE

Are you surprised that so many people obeyed orders in Milgram's experiments? Do you think you would have obeyed? How actively do you question authority?

You would like to persuade people to donate to a deserving charity. How, specifically, could you use compliance techniques to get people to donate?

Pick a specific instance when you could have been more assertive. How would you handle the situation if it occurs again? Think of a specific instance when you were angry and acted aggressively. How could you have handled the situation through self-assertion, instead of aggression?

LEARNING CHECK

1. The term *compliance* refers to situations in which a person complies with commands made by a person who has authority. T or F?
2. Obedience in Milgram's experiments was related to
   a. distance between learner and teacher
   b. distance between experimenter and teacher
   c. obedience of other teachers
   d. all of these
3. By repeating his obedience experiment in a downtown office building, Milgram demonstrated that the prestige of Yale University was the main reason for subjects' willingness to obey in the original experiment. T or F?
4. The research of Thomas Moriarty and others has highlighted the problem of _____ _____, rather than obedience to authority.
5. In assertiveness training, people learn techniques for getting their way in social situations and angry interchanges. T or F?
6. Non-assertive behavior causes hurt, anxiety, and self-denial in the actor and sympathy, guilt, or contempt in the receiver. T or F?

Critical Thinking

7. Modern warfare allows killing to take place impersonally and at a distance. How does this relate to Milgram's experiments?

ANSWERS

1. F 2. d 3. F 4. passive compliance 5. F 6. T 7. There is a big difference between killing someone in hand-to-hand combat and killing someone by lining up images on a video screen. Milgram's research suggests that it is easier for a person to follow orders to kill another human when the victim is at a distance and removed from personal contact.

ATTITUDES—DOOMSDAY FOR THE SEEKERS

] **SURVEYQUESTION** *How are attitudes acquired and changed?*

Hardly a year passes without a doomsday group of one kind or another making the news. In a classic example of such groups, a woman named Mrs. Keech claimed she was receiving messages from alien beings on a planet called Clarion. The aliens told Mrs. Keech that they had detected a fault in the Earth's crust that would plunge North America into the ocean, causing an unimaginable disaster. The tragedy would occur on December 21. However, Mrs. Keech and her band of followers, who called themselves the Seekers, had no fear: On December 20 they expected to be met at midnight by a flying saucer and taken to safety in outer space.

The night of December 20 arrived, and the Seekers gathered at Mrs. Keech's house. Many had given up their jobs and possessions to prepare for departure. Expectations were high and commitment was total. But as midnight passed, the world continued to exist. It was a bitter and embarrassing disappointment for the Seekers.

Did the group break up then?   Our story now takes an amazing twist—one that intrigued social psychologists. Instead of breaking up, the Seekers became *more* convinced than ever before that they had been right. At about 5 A.M. Mrs. Keech announced she had received a message explaining that the Seekers had saved the world.

Before December 20, the Seekers were uninterested in persuading other people that the world was coming to an end. Now they called newspapers and radio stations to convince others of their accomplishment.

How do we explain this strange turn in behavior? An answer may lie in the concept of *cognitive dissonance,* which also helps explain many aspects of attitude change. We will return to cognitive dissonance in a moment, but first let's answer some basic questions about attitudes.

Belief + Emotion + Action

What is your attitude toward affirmative action, euthanasia, environmental groups, the death penalty, legalized abortion, junk food, psychology? The answers can have far-reaching effects on your behavior. Attitudes are intimately woven into our actions and views of the world. Our tastes, friendships, votes, preferences, and goals are all touched by attitudes.

What specifically is an attitude?   An **attitude** is a mixture of belief and emotion that predisposes a person to respond to other people, objects, or groups in a positive or negative way. Attitudes summarize your *evaluation* of objects (Petty, Wegener, & Fabrigar, 1997). As a result, they predict and direct many of our actions.

"Your attitude is showing," is sometimes said. Actually, attitudes are expressed through beliefs, emotions, and actions. The *belief component* of an attitude is what you believe about a particular object or issue. The *emotional component* consists of your feelings toward the attitudinal object. The *action component* refers to your actions toward various people, objects, or institutions. Consider, for example, your attitude toward gun control. You will have beliefs about whether gun control would affect rates of crime or violence. You will respond emotionally to guns, finding them either attractive and desirable or threatening and destructive. And you will have a tendency to seek out or avoid gun ownership. The action component of your attitude will probably also include support of organizations that urge or oppose gun control. As you can see, attitudes orient us to the social world. In doing so, they prepare us to act in certain ways (Ajzen, 2001). (For another example, please see ✦Figure 14.9.)

Attitude A learned tendency to respond to people, objects, or institutions in a positive or negative way.

Issue: Affirmative Action

Belief component
Restores justice
Provides equal opportunity

Emotional component
Optimism

Action component
Vote for affirmative action
Donate to groups that support affirmative action

Belief component
Unfair to majority
Reverse discrimination

Emotional component
Anger

Action component
Vote against affirmative action
Donate to groups that oppose affirmative action

✦FIGURE 14.9 *Elements of positive and negative attitudes toward affirmative action.*

© Lynn Johnson Productions, Inc./Dist. by United Feature Syndicate, Inc. Reprinted by permission.

Forming Attitudes

How do people acquire attitudes?   Attitudes are acquired in several basic ways. Sometimes, attitudes come from *direct contact* (personal experience) with the object of the attitude—such as opposing pollution when a nearby factory ruins your favorite river. Attitudes are also learned through *interaction with others;* that is, through discussion with people holding a particular attitude. For instance, if three of your friends are volunteers at a local recycling center and you talk with them about their beliefs, you will probably come to favor recycling, too. More generally, there is little doubt that many of our attitudes are influenced by *group membership.* In most groups, pressures to conform shape our attitudes, just as they do our behavior. *Child rearing* (the effects of parental values, beliefs, and practices) also affects attitudes. For example, if both parents belong to the same political party, chances are 2 out of 3 that their children will belong to that party as adults.

There can be no doubt that attitudes are influenced by the *mass media* (all media, such as magazines and television, that reach large audiences). Every day we are coaxed, persuaded, and skillfully manipulated by messages in the mass media. Ninety-nine percent of North American homes have a television set, which is on an average of over 7 hours a day. The information thus channeled into homes has a powerful impact. For instance, frequent viewers mistrust others and overestimate their own chances of being harmed. This suggests that a steady diet of TV violence leads some people to develop a *mean world view,* in which they regard the world as a dangerous and threatening place (Heath & Gilbert, 1996).

Some attitudes are simply formed through *chance conditioning* (learning that takes place by chance or coincidence) (Olson & Zanna, 1993). Let's say, for instance, that you have had three encounters in your lifetime with psychologists. If all three were negative, you might take an unduly dim view of psychology. In the same way, people often develop strong attitudes toward cities, foods, or parts of the country on the basis of one or two unusually good or bad experiences.

Attitudes and Behavior

Why are some attitudes acted on, while others are not?   To answer this question, let's consider an example. Assume that a woman named Lorraine knows that automobiles add to air pollution, and she hates smog. Why would Lorraine continue to drive to work every day? Probably it is because the *immediate consequences* of our actions weigh heavily on the choices we make. No matter what Lorraine's attitude may be, it is difficult for her to resist the immediate convenience of driving. Our expectations of how *others will evaluate* our actions are also important. By taking this factor into account, researchers have been able to predict family planning choices, alcohol use by teenagers, re-enlistment in the National Guard, voting on a nuclear power plant initiative, and so forth (Cialdini et al., 1981). Finally, we must not overlook the effects of long-standing *habits* (Petty, Wegener, & Fabrigar, 1997). Let's say that a "male chauvinist" boss vows to change his sexist attitudes toward female employees. Two months later, it would not be unusual for his behavior to show the effects of habit rather than his good intentions.

In short, there are often large differences between attitudes and behavior—particularly between privately held attitudes and public behavior. However, barriers to action typically fall when a person holds an attitude with *conviction.* If you have *conviction* about an issue it evokes strong feelings, you think about it and discuss it often, and you are knowledgeable about it. Attitudes held with passionate conviction often lead to major changes in personal behavior (Petty, Wegener, & Fabrigar, 1997).

ATTITUDE CHANGE—WHY THE "SEEKERS" WENT PUBLIC

] **SURVEYQUESTION** *Under what conditions is persuasion most effective?*

Although attitudes are fairly stable, they do change. Some attitude change can be understood in terms of **reference groups** (any group a person uses as a standard for social comparison). It is not necessary to have face-to-face contact with other people for them to be a reference group. It depends instead on whom you identify with or whose attitudes and values you care about (Ajzen, 2001).

In the 1930s, Theodore Newcomb studied real-life attitude change among students at Bennington College. Most students came from conservative homes, but Bennington was a very liberal school. Newcomb found that most students shifted significantly toward more liberal attitudes during their 4 years at Bennington. Those who didn't change kept their parents and hometown friends as primary reference groups. This is typified by a student who said, "I decided I'd rather stick to my father's ideas." Those who did change identified primarily with the campus community. Notice that all students could count the college and their families as *membership* groups. However, one group or the other tended to become their point of reference.

Do you exercise regularly? Like students in the Bennington study, your intentions to exercise are probably influenced by the exercise habits of your reference groups (Terry & Hogg, 1996).

Persuasion

What about advertising and other direct attempts to change attitudes? Are they effective? **Persuasion** is any deliberate attempt to change attitudes or beliefs through information and arguments. Businesses, politicians, and others who seek to persuade us obviously believe that attitudes can be changed. Over $15 billion is spent yearly on television advertising in the United States and Canada alone. Persuasion can range from the daily blitz of media commercials to personal discussion among friends. In most cases, the success or failure of persuasion can be understood if we consider the *communicator,* the *message,* and the *audience.*

At a community meeting, let's say you have a chance to promote an issue important to you (for or against building a nuclear power plant nearby, for instance). Whom should you choose to make the presentation, and how should that person present it? Research suggests that attitude change is encouraged when the following conditions are met.

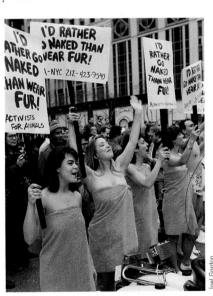

Persuasion. Would you be likely to be swayed by this group's message? Successful persuasion is related to characteristics of the communicator, the message, and the audience.

1. The communicator is likable, expressive, trustworthy, an expert on the topic, and similar to the audience in some respect.
2. The message appeals to emotions, particularly to fear or anxiety.
3. The message also provides a clear course of action that will, if followed, reduce fear or produce personally desirable results.
4. The message states clear-cut conclusions.
5. The message is backed up by facts and statistics.
6. Both sides of the argument are presented in the case of a well-informed audience.
7. Only one side of the argument is presented in the case of a poorly informed audience.
8. The persuader appears to have nothing to gain if the audience accepts the message.
9. The message is repeated as frequently as possible (Aronson, 1992; Petty et al., 1997).

You should have little trouble seeing how these principles are applied to sell everything from underarm deodorants to presidents.

Reference group Any group that an individual uses as a standard for social comparison.

Persuasion A deliberate attempt to change attitudes or beliefs with information and arguments.

▲*TABLE 14.3*	**Strategies for Reducing Cognitive Dissonance**

Celia, who is a college student, has always thought of herself as an environmental activist. Recently, Celia "inherited" a car from her parents, who were replacing the family "barge." In the past, Celia biked or used public transportation to get around. Her parent's old car is an antiquated gas-guzzler, but she has begun to drive it every day. How might Celia reduce the cognitive dissonance created by the clash between her environmentalism and her use of an inefficient automobile?

STRATEGY	EXAMPLE
Change your attitude	"Cars are not really a major environmental problem."
Add consonant thoughts	"This is an old car, so keeping it on the road makes good use of the resources consumed when it was manufactured."
Change the importance of the dissonant thoughts	"It's more important for me to support the environmental movement politically than it is to worry about how I get to school and work."
Reduce the amount of perceived choice	"My schedule has become too hectic, I really can't afford to bike or take the bus anymore."
Change your behavior	"I'm only going to use the car when it's impossible to bike or take the bus."

(After Franzoi, 2000.)

Cognitive Dissonance Theory

Cognitions are thoughts. Dissonance means clashing. The influential theory of **cognitive dissonance** states that contradicting or clashing thoughts cause discomfort. That is, we have a need for *consistency* in our thoughts, perceptions, and images of ourselves (Festinger, 1957; Thibodeau & Aronson, 1992).

What happens if people act in ways that are inconsistent with their attitudes or self-images? Typically, the contradiction makes them uncomfortable. Such discomfort can motivate people to make their thoughts or attitudes agree with their actions (Petty et al., 1997). For example, smokers are told on every pack that cigarettes endanger their lives. They light up and smoke anyway. How do they resolve the tension between this information and their actions? They could quit smoking, but it may be easier to convince themselves that smoking is not really so dangerous. To do this, many smokers seek examples of heavy smokers who have lived long lives; they spend their time with other smokers; and they avoid information about the link between smoking and cancer. According to cognitive dissonance theory, we also tend to reject new information that contradicts ideas we already hold. We're all guilty of this "don't bother me with the facts, my mind is made up" strategy at times.

Now recall Mrs. Keech and her doomsday group. Why did their belief in Mrs. Keech's messages *increase* after the world failed to end? Why did the group suddenly become interested in convincing others that they were right? Cognitive dissonance theory explains that after publicly committing themselves to their beliefs, they had a strong need to maintain consistency. In effect, convincing others was a way of adding proof that they were correct (▲Table 14.3).

Acting contrary to one's attitudes doesn't always bring about change. How does cognitive dissonance account for that? The amount of justification for acting contrary to your attitudes and beliefs affects how much dissonance you feel. (*Justification* is the degree to which a person's actions are explained by rewards or other circumstances.) In a classic study, college students did an extremely boring task (turning wooden pegs on a board), for a *long* time. Afterward, they were asked to help lure others into the experiment by pretending that the task was interesting and enjoyable. Students paid $20 for lying to others did not change their own negative opinion of the task: "That was *really* boring!" Those who were paid only $1 later rated the task as "pleasant" and "interesting." How can we explain these results? Apparently, students paid $20 experienced no dissonance. These students could reassure themselves that anybody would tell a little white lie for $20. Those paid $1 were faced with the conflicting thoughts: "I lied," and " I had no good reason to do it." Rather than admit to themselves that they had lied, these students changed their attitude toward what they had done (Festinger & Carlsmith, 1959) (◆Fig. 14.10).

We are especially likely to experience dissonance after we cause an event to occur that we wish hadn't taken place (Cooper & Fazio, 1984). Let's say that you agree to help a friend

Cognitive dissonance An uncomfortable clash between self-image, thoughts, beliefs, attitudes, or perceptions and one's behavior.

move to a new apartment. The big day arrives and you feel like staying in bed. Actually, you wish you hadn't promised to help. To reduce dissonance, you may convince yourself that the work will actually be "good exercise," "sort of fun," or that your friend really deserves the help. We often make such adjustments in attitudes to minimize cognitive dissonance.

Before we leave the topic of attitudes, let's see what psychologists have learned about brainwashing and other high-pressure attempts to change attitudes.

FORCED ATTITUDE CHANGE— BRAINWASHING AND CULTS

] SURVEYQUESTIONS *Is brainwashing actually possible? How are people converted to cult membership?*

It you're a history enthusiast, you may associate *brainwashing* with techniques used by the Communist Chinese on prisoners during the Korean War. Through various types of "thought reform," the Chinese were able to coerce 16 percent of these prisoners to sign false confessions. More recently, the mass murder/suicide at Jonestown, the Branch Davidian tragedy at Waco, the Heaven's Gate group suicide in San Diego, and Osama bin Laden's al-Qaeda movement have heightened public interest in forced attitude change.

How does it differ from other persuasive techniques? Brainwashing, or forced attitude change, requires a captive audience. If you are offended by a television commercial, you can tune it out. Prisoners in the POW camps are completely at the mercy of their captors. Complete control over the environment allows a degree of psychological manipulation that would be impossible in a normal setting.

Brainwashing

How does captivity facilitate persuasion? Brainwashing typically begins by making the target person feel completely helpless. Physical and psychological abuse, lack of sleep, humiliation, and isolation from others serve to *unfreeze,* or loosen, former values and beliefs. When exhaustion, pressure, and fear become unbearable, *change* occurs as the person begins to abandon former beliefs. Prisoners who reach the breaking point sign a false confession or cooperate to gain relief. When they do, they are suddenly rewarded with praise, privileges, food, or rest. From that point on, a mixture of hope and fear, plus pressures to conform, serves to *refreeze* (solidify) new attitudes (Schein et al., 1961).

How permanent are changes caused by brainwashing? In most cases, the dramatic shift in attitudes brought about by brainwashing is temporary. Most "converted" prisoners who returned to the United States after the Korean War eventually reverted to their original beliefs. Nevertheless, brainwashing can be powerful, as shown by the success of cults in recruiting new members.

Cults

Exhorted by their leader, some 900 members of the Reverend Jim Jones' People's Temple picked up paper cups and drank purple Kool-Aid laced with the deadly poison cyanide. Psychologically, the mass suicide at Jonestown in 1978 is not so incredible as it might seem. The inhabitants of Jonestown were isolated in the jungles of Guyana, intimidated by guards, and lulled with sedatives. They were also cut off from friends and relatives and totally accustomed to obeying rigid rules of conduct, which primed them for Jones' final "loyalty test." Of greater psychological interest is the question of how people reach such a state of commitment and dependency.

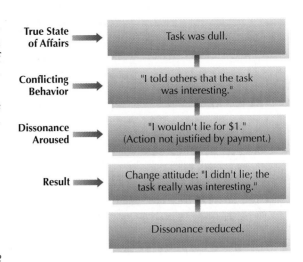

◆FIGURE 14.10 *Summary of the Festinger and Carlsmith (1959) study from the viewpoint of a person experiencing cognitive dissonance.*

In the tragic fire at the Branch Davidian compound near Waco, Texas, some members paid with their lives for giving total allegiance to cult leader David Koresh.

Why do people join groups such as the People's Temple? The People's Temple was a classic example of a *cult*. A *cult* is a group in which the leader's personality is more important than the beliefs she or he preaches. Cult members give their allegiance to this person, who is regarded as infallible, and they follow his or her dictates without question. Almost always, cult members are victimized by their leaders in one way or another. For example, in April 1993, David Koresh and members of his Branch Davidian group perished in an inferno at their Waco, Texas, compound. Authorities believe the fire was set by a cult member, under the direction of Koresh. Like Jim Jones had done years before in Jonestown, Koresh took nearly total control of his followers' lives. He told them what to eat, dictated sexual mores, and directed the paddling of errant followers. Followers were persuaded to surrender money, property, and even their children and wives. Like Jones, Koresh also took mistresses and had children out of wedlock. Like other cult leaders, Jones and Koresh demanded absolute loyalty and obedience, with tragic results (Reiterman, 1993).

Psychologist Margaret Singer has studied and aided hundreds of former cult members. Her interviews reveal that in recruiting new members, cults use a powerful blend of guilt, manipulation, isolation, deception, fear, and escalating commitment. In this respect, cults employ high-pressure indoctrination techniques not unlike those used in brainwashing (Singer & Addis, 1992). In the United States alone, an estimated 2 to 5 million people have succumbed to the lure of cults (Robinson, Frye, & Bradley, 1997).

Recruitment

Some people studied by Singer were seriously distressed when they joined a cult. Most, however, were simply undergoing a period of mild depression, indecision, or alienation from family and friends (Hunter, 1998). Cult members try to catch potential converts at a time of need—especially when a sense of belonging will be attractive to converts. For instance, many people were approached just after a romance had broken up, or when they were struggling with exams, or were trying to become independent from their families (Sirkin, 1990). At such times, people are easily persuaded that joining the group is all they need to do to be happy again (Hunter, 1998; Schwartz, 1991).

Conversion

How is conversion achieved? Often it begins with intense displays of affection and understanding ("love bombing"). Next comes isolation from non-cult members and drills, discipline, and rituals (all-night meditation or continuous chanting, for instance). These rituals wear down physical and emotional resistance, discourage critical thinking, and generate feelings of commitment (Galanti, 1993).

Many cults make clever use of the foot-in-the-door technique, described earlier. At first, recruits make small commitments (to stay after a meeting, for example). Then, larger commitments are encouraged (to stay an extra day, to call in sick at work, and so forth). Making a major commitment is usually the final step. The new devotee signs over a bank account or property to the group, moves in with the group, and so forth. Making such major public commitments creates a powerful cognitive dissonance effect. Before long, it becomes virtually impossible for converts to admit they have made a mistake.

Once in the group, members are cut off from family and friends (former reference groups), and the cult can control the flow and interpretation of information to them. Members are isolated from their former value systems and social structures. Conversion is complete when they come to think of themselves more as group members than as individuals. At this point obedience is nearly total (Schwartz, 1991; Wexler, 1995).

Implications

Behind the "throne" from which Jim Jones ruled Jonestown was a sign bearing these words: "Those who do not remember the past are condemned to repeat it." Sadly, another cult-related tragedy occurred in 2001. The terrorist attacks on the United States were carried out by followers of cult leader Osama bin Laden. At his direction, they learned hatred and contempt for everyone outside their band of true believers. If there is a lesson to be learned from such destructive cults, it is this: All true spiritual leaders have taught love and compassion. They also encourage followers to question their beliefs and to reach their own conclusions about how to live. In contrast, destructive cults show that it is dangerous to trade personal independence and critical thinking for security (Goldberg, 2001).

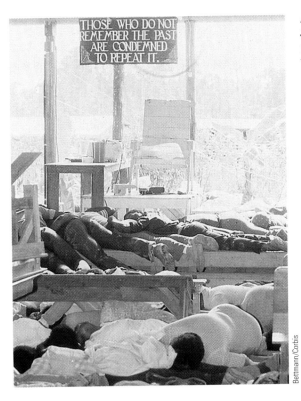

THOSE WHO DO NOT REMEMBER THE PAST ARE CONDEMNED TO REPEAT IT.

Bettmann/Corbis

Aftermath of the mass suicide at Jonestown. Cult-like groups use powerful psychological manipulation to recruit new devotees.

STUDYBREAK *Attitudes and Persuasion*

RELATE

Describe an attitude that is important to you. What are its three components?

Which of the various sources of attitudes best explain your own attitudes?

Who belongs to your most important reference group?

Imagine that you would like to persuade voters to support an initiative to preserve a small wilderness area by converting it to a park. Using research on persuasion as a guide, what could you do to be more effective?

How would you explain cognitive dissonance theory to a person who knows nothing about it?

LEARNING CHECK

1. Attitudes have three parts: a _____ component, an _____ component, and an _____ component.
2. Which of the following is associated with attitude formation?
   a. group membership   b. mass media   c. chance conditioning
   d. child rearing   e. all of the preceding   f. a and d only
3. In presenting a persuasive message, it is best to give both sides of the argument if the audience is already well informed on the topic. T or F?

4. Much attitude change is related to a desire to avoid clashing or contradictory thoughts, an idea summarized by _____ _____ theory.
5. Brainwashing differs from other persuasive attempts in that brainwashing requires a _____.
6. Which statement about brainwashing is *false?*
   a. The target person is isolated from others.
   b. Attitude changes brought about by brainwashing are usually permanent.
   c. The first step is unfreezing former values and beliefs.
   d. Cooperation with the indoctrinating agent is rewarded.

Critical Thinking

7. Students entering a college gym are asked to sign a banner promoting water conservation. Later, the students shower at the gym. What effect would you expect signing the banner to have on how long students stay in the showers?
8. Cognitive dissonance theory predicts that false confessions obtained during brainwashing are not likely to bring about lasting changes in attitudes. Why?

ANSWERS

1. belief, emotional, action 2. e 3. T 4. cognitive dissonance theory 6. b 7. Cognitive dissonance theory predicts that students who sign the banner will take shorter showers, to be consistent with their publicly expressed support of water conservation. This is exactly the result observed in a study done by social psychologist Elliot Aronson. 8. Because there is strong justification for such actions. As a result, little cognitive dissonance is created when a prisoner makes statements that contradict his or her beliefs.

PREJUDICE—ATTITUDES THAT INJURE

] **SURVEYQUESTION** *What causes prejudice and intergroup conflict?*

Love and friendship bind people together. Prejudice, which is marked by suspicion, fear, or hatred, has the opposite effect. **Prejudice** is a negative emotional attitude held toward members of a specific social group. Prejudices may be reflected in the policies of schools, businesses, police departments, or governments. In such cases, prejudice is referred to as *racism, sexism, ageism,* or *heterosexism,* depending on the group affected. Because it is so prevalent and damaging, let's focus on racism.

Both racial prejudice and racism lead to **discrimination,** or unequal treatment of people who should have the same rights as others. Discrimination prevents people from doing things they should be able to do, such as buying a house, getting a job, or attending a high-quality school. For example, in many cities, African Americans have been the target of "racial profiling" in which they are stopped by police without reason. Sometimes, they are merely questioned, but many are cited for minor infractions, such as a cracked taillight or an illegal lane change. For many law-abiding citizens, being detained in this manner is a rude awakening (Harris, 1999). It's also one reason why many Blacks and other persons of color in America distrust police and the legal system (Dovido et al., 2002).

Becoming Prejudiced

How do prejudices develop?   One major theory suggests that prejudice is a form of *scapegoating* (blaming a person or a group for the actions of others or for conditions not of their making). Scapegoating, you may recall, is a type of *displaced aggression* in which hostilities triggered by frustration are redirected at "safe" targets. One interesting test of this hypothesis was conducted at a summer camp for young men. The men were given a difficult test they were sure to fail. Additionally, completing the test caused them to miss a trip to the movies, which was normally the high point of their weekly entertainment. Attitudes toward Mexicans and Japanese were measured before the test and after the men had failed the test and missed the movie. Subjects in this study, all European Americans, consistently rated members of the two ethnic groups lower after being frustrated (Miller & Bugelski, 1970). This effect was easy to observe after the September 11, 2001, terrorist attack in the United States, when people who looked "foreign" became targets for displaced anger and hostility.

At times, the development of prejudice (like other attitudes) can be traced to direct experiences with members of the rejected group. A child who is repeatedly bullied by members of a particular ethnic group might develop a lifelong dislike for all members of the group. The tragedy is that once prejudices are established, they prevent us from accepting more positive experiences that could reverse the damage (Wilder, Simon, & Faith, 1996).

Distinguished psychologist Gordon Allport (1958) concluded that there are two important sources of prejudice. *Personal prejudice* occurs when members of another ethnic group are perceived as a threat to one's own interests. For example, members of another group may be viewed as competitors for jobs. *Group prejudice* occurs when a person conforms to group norms. Let's say, for instance, that you have no personal reason for disliking out-group members. Nevertheless, your friends, acquaintances, or co-workers expect it of you.

The Prejudiced Personality

Prejudice A negative emotional attitude held against members of a particular group of people.

Discrimination Treating members of various social groups differently in circumstances where their rights or treatment should be identical.

Other research suggests that prejudice can be a general personality characteristic. Theodore Adorno and his associates (1950) carefully probed what they called the *authoritarian personality* (ah-thor-ih-TARE-ee-un). These researchers started out by studying anti-Semitism. In the process, they found that people who are prejudiced against one group tend to be prejudiced against *all* out-groups (Perreault & Bourhis, 1999).

What are the characteristics of the prejudice-prone personality?   The **authoritarian personality** is marked by rigidity, inhibition, prejudice, and over-simplification (black-and-white thinking). Authoritarians also tend to be very *ethnocentric*. **Ethnocentrism** refers to placing one's own group "at the center," usually by rejecting all other groups. Put more simply, authoritarians consider their own ethnic group superior to others. In fact, authoritarians think they are superior to everyone who is different, not just other ethnic groups (Whitley, 1999).

In addition to rejecting out-groups, authoritarians are overwhelmingly concerned with power, authority, and obedience. To measure these qualities, the *F scale* was created (the *F* stands for "fascism"). This scale is made up of statements such as the ones that follow—to which authoritarians readily agree (Adorno et al., 1950).

AUTHORITARIAN BELIEFS

- Obedience and respect for authority are the most important virtues children should learn.
- People can be divided into two distinct classes: the weak and the strong.
- If people would talk less and work more, everybody would be better off.
- What this country needs most, more than laws and political programs, is a few courageous, tireless, devoted leaders, in whom the people can put their faith.
- Nobody ever learns anything really important except through suffering.
- Every person should have complete faith in some supernatural power whose decisions are obeyed without question.
- Certain religious sects that refuse to salute the flag should be forced to conform to such patriotic action or else be abolished.

As you can see, authoritarians are rather close-minded (Butler, 2000). As children, authoritarians were usually severely punished. Most learned to fear authority (and to covet it) at an early age. Authoritarians are not happy people.

Even if we discount the obvious bigotry of the authoritarian personality, racial prejudice runs deep in many nations. Let's probe deeper into the roots of such prejudiced behavior.

INTERGROUP CONFLICT—THE ROOTS OF PREJUDICE

An unfortunate by-product of group membership is that it often limits contact with people in other groups. Additionally, groups themselves may come into conflict. Both events tend to foster hatred and prejudice toward the out-group. The bloody clash of opposing forces in Israel, Ireland, Africa, and Hometown, USA, are reminders that intergroup conflict is widespread. Daily, we read of jarring strife between political, religious, or ethnic groups.

Shared beliefs concerning *superiority, injustice, vulnerability,* and *distrust* are common triggers for hostility between groups. Pick almost any group in conflict with others, and you will find people thinking along these lines: "We are special people who are superior to other groups, but we have been unjustly exploited, wronged, or humiliated [superiority and injustice]. Other groups are a threat to us [vulnerability]. They are dishonest and have repeatedly betrayed us [distrust]. Naturally, we are hostile toward them. They don't deserve our respect or cooperation" (Eidelson & Eidelson, 2003).

In addition to hostile beliefs about other groups, conflicts are almost always amplified by stereotyped images of out-group members (Bar-Tal & Labin, 2001).

What exactly is a stereotype?   **Social stereotypes** are oversimplified images of people in various groups. There is a good chance that you have stereotyped images of some of the following categories: redneck, politician, show-off, do-gooder, juvenile delinquent, business executive, housewife, snob, playboy, teenager, slob, spoiled brat, billionaire. In general, the top three categories on which most stereotypes are based are sex, age, and race (Fiske, 1993a).

Authoritarian personality A personality pattern characterized by rigidity, inhibition, prejudice, and an excessive concern with power, authority, and obedience.

Ethnocentrism Placing one's own group or race at the center—that is, tending to reject all other groups but one's own.

Social stereotypes Oversimplified images of the traits of individuals who belong to a particular social group.

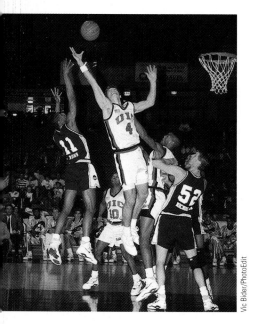

Vic Bider/PhotoEdit

◆**FIGURE 14.11** *Racial stereotypes are common in sports. For example, a study confirmed that many people actually do believe that "White men can't jump." This stereotype implies that Black basketball players are naturally superior in athletic ability. White players, in contrast, are falsely perceived as smarter and harder working than Blacks. Such stereotypes set up expectations that distort the perceptions of fans, coaches, and sportswriters. The resulting misperceptions, in turn, help perpetuate the stereotypes (Stone, Perry, & Darley, 1997).*

Symbolic prejudice Prejudice that is expressed in disguised fashion.

Stereotypes tend to simplify people into "us" and "them" categories. Actually, aside from the fact that they always oversimplify, stereotypes may be either *positive* or *negative* (◆Fig. 14.11). ▲Table 14.4 shows stereotyped images of various national and ethnic groups and their changes over a 34-year period. Notice that many of the qualities listed are desirable. Note too, that while the overall trend was a decrease in negative stereotypes, belief in the existence of some negative traits increased.

Even though stereotypes sometimes include positive traits, they are mainly used to control people. When a person is stereotyped, the easiest thing for her or him to do is to abide by others' expectations—even if they are demeaning. That's why no one likes to be stereotyped. Being forced into a small, distorted social "box" is limiting and insulting. Without stereotypes there would be far less hate, prejudice, exclusion, and conflict (Fiske, 1993b).

When a prejudiced person meets a pleasant or likable member of a rejected group, the out-group member tends to be perceived as "an exception to the rule," not as evidence against the stereotype. This prevents prejudiced persons from changing their stereotyped beliefs (Wilder et al., 1996). In addition, some elements of prejudice are unconscious, which makes them difficult to change (Dovido et al., 2002).

Today's racism is often disguised by **symbolic prejudice.** That is, many people realize that crude and obvious racism is socially unacceptable. However, this may not stop them from expressing prejudice in thinly veiled forms when they state their opinions about affirmative action, busing, immigration, crime, and so on. In effect, modern racists find ways to rationalize their prejudice so that it seems to be based on issues other than raw racism. For instance, a Black candidate and a White candidate apply for a job. Both are only moderately qualified for the position. If the person making the hiring decision is White, who gets the job? As you might guess, the White candidate is much more likely to be hired. In other words, the White candidate will be given "the benefit of the doubt" about his or her abilities, whereas the Black candidate won't. People making such decisions often believe that they aren't being prejudiced, but they unconsciously discriminate against minorities (Dovido et al., 2002).

Two experiments, both in unlikely settings and both using children, offer some additional insights into how stereotypes and intergroup tensions develop.

Experiments in Prejudice

What is it like to be discriminated against? In a unique experiment, elementary school teacher Jane Elliot sought to give her pupils direct experience with prejudice. On the first day of the experiment, Elliot announced that brown-eyed children were to sit in the back of

▲*TABLE 14.4*	University Students' Characterizations of Ethnic Groups, 1933 and 1967							
Trait	PERCENT CHECKING TRAIT *1933*	*1967*	*Trait*	PERCENT CHECKING TRAIT *1933*	*1967*	*Trait*	PERCENT CHECKING TRAIT *1933*	*1967*
Americans			**Italians**			**Jews**		
Industrious	48	23	Artistic	53	30	Shrewd	79	30
Intelligent	47	20	Impulsive	44	28	Mercenary	49	15
Materialistic	33	67	Musical	32	9	Grasping	34	17
Progressive	27	17	Imaginative	30	7	Intelligent	29	37
Germans			**Irish**			**Blacks**		
Scientific	78	47	Pugnacious	45	13	Superstitious	84	13
Stolid	44	9	Witty	38	7	Lazy	75	26
Methodical	31	21	Honest	32	17	Ignorant	38	11
Efficient	16	46	Nationalistic	21	41	Religious	24	8

Source: M. Karlins, T. L. Coffman, and G. Walters, "On the fading of social stereotypes: Studies in three generations of college students," *Journal of Personality and Social Psychology* 13 (1969): 1–16.

the room and that they could not use the drinking fountain. Blue-eyed children were given extra recess time and got to leave first for lunch. At lunch, brown-eyed children were told not to take second helpings because they would "just waste it." Brown-eyed and blue-eyed children were kept from mingling, and the blue-eyed children were praised for being "cleaner" and "smarter" (Peters, 1971).

Eye color might seem like a trivial basis for creating prejudices. However, people primarily use skin color to make decisions about the race of another person (Brown, Dane, & Durham, 1998). Surely, this is just as superficial a way of judging people as eye color is.

At first, Elliot made an effort to constantly criticize and belittle the brown-eyed children. To her surprise, the blue-eyed children rapidly joined in and were soon outdoing her in the viciousness of their attacks. The blue-eyed children began to feel superior, and the brown-eyed children felt just plain awful. Fights broke out. Test scores of the brown-eyed children fell.

How lasting were the effects of this experiment?   The effects were short lived, because two days later the children's roles were reversed. Before long, the same destructive effects occurred again, but this time in reverse. The implications of this experiment are unmistakable. In less than one day it was possible to get children to hate each other because of eye color and *status inequalities* (differences in power, prestige, or privileges). Certainly the effects of a lifetime of real racial or ethnic prejudice are infinitely more powerful and destructive (Clark et al., 1999).

Ethnic pride is slowly replacing stereotypes and discrimination. For example, the African-American festival of Kwanzaa, a holiday celebrated late in December, emphasizes commitment to family, community, and African culture. However, despite affirmations of ethnic heritage, the problem of prejudice is far from solved.

Equal-Status Contact

What can be done to combat prejudice?   Several lines of thought suggest that equal-status contact between groups in conflict can reduce prejudice and stereotyping (Olson & Zanna, 1993). *Equal-status contact* is social interaction that occurs on an equal footing, without obvious differences in power or status. In various studies, mixed-race groups have been formed at work, in the laboratory, and at schools. The conclusion from such research is that personal contact with a disliked group tends to induce friendly behavior, respect, and liking. However, these benefits occur only when personal contact is cooperative and on an equal footing (Grack & Richman, 1996).

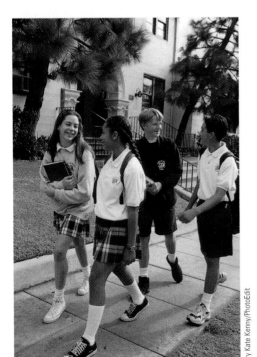

Superordinate Goals

Let us now consider a revealing study done with 11-year-old boys. When the boys arrived at a summer camp, they were split into two groups and housed in separate cabins. At first the groups were kept apart to build up in-group friendships. Soon each group had a flag and a name (the "Rattlers" and the "Eagles") and each had staked out its territory. At this time the two groups were placed in competition with each other. After a number of clashes, disliking between the

Many school districts in the United States have begun requiring students to wear uniforms. Appearance (including gang colors) is one of the major reasons why kids treat each other differently. Uniforms help minimize status inequalities and in-group/out-group distinctions. In Long Beach, California, a switch to uniforms was followed by a 91 percent drop in student assaults, thefts, vandalism, and weapons and drug violations (Ritter, 1998).

groups bordered on hatred: The boys baited each other, started fights, and raided each other's cabins (Sherif et al., 1961).

Were they allowed to go home hating each other? As an experiment in reducing intergroup conflict, and to prevent the boys from remaining enemies, various strategies to reduce tensions were tried. Holding meetings between group leaders did nothing. When the groups were invited to eat together, the event turned into a free-for-all. Finally, emergencies that required *cooperation* among members of both groups were staged at the camp. For example, the water supply was damaged so that all the boys had to work together to repair it. Creating this and other *superordinate goals* helped restore peace between the two groups. (A **superordinate goal** exceeds or overrides other lesser goals.)

Cooperation and shared goals seem to help reduce conflict by encouraging people in opposing groups to see themselves as members of a single, larger group (Gaertner et al., 2000). Superordinate goals, in other words, have a "we're all in the same boat" effect on perceptions of group membership. The power of superordinate goals can be seen in the unity that prevailed in the United States for months after the September 11 terrorist attacks. Can such goals exist on a global scale? One example might be a desire to avoid nuclear holocaust. Another that comes to mind is the need to preserve the natural environment on a global scale. Still another is the continuing threat posed by terrorism and religious extremism. Politically, such goals may be far from universal. But their superordinate quality is clearly evident.

Jonathan Nourok/PhotoEdit

In a "jigsaw" classroom, children help each other prepare for tests. As they teach each other what they know, the children learn to cooperate and to respect the unique strengths of each individual.

"Jigsaw" Classrooms

Contrary to the hopes of many, integrated public schools often have little positive effect on racial prejudice. In fact, prejudice may be made worse, and the self-esteem of minority students frequently decreases (Aronson, 1992).

If integrated schools provide equal-status contact, shouldn't prejudice be reduced? Theoretically, yes. But in practice, minority group children often enter schools unprepared to compete on an equal footing. The competitive nature of schools almost guarantees that children will *not* learn to like and understand each other.

With the preceding in mind, social psychologist Elliot Aronson pioneered a way to apply superordinate goals to ordinary classrooms. According to Aronson, such goals are effective because they create **mutual interdependence.** That is, people must depend on one another to meet each person's goals. When individual needs are linked, cooperation is encouraged (Deutsch, 1993).

How has that idea been applied? Aronson has successfully created "jigsaw" classrooms that emphasize cooperation rather than competition. The term *jigsaw* refers to the pieces of a jigsaw puzzle. In a **jigsaw classroom,** each child is given a "piece" of the information needed to complete a project or prepare for a test.

In a typical session, children are divided into groups of five or six and given a topic to study for a later exam. Each child is given his or her "piece" of information and asked to learn it. For example, one child might have information on Thomas Edison's invention of the light bulb; another, facts about his invention of the long-playing phonograph record; and a third, information about Edison's childhood. After the children have learned their parts, they teach them to others in the group. Even the most competitive children quickly realize that they cannot do well without the aid of everyone in the group. Each child makes a unique and essential contribution, so the children learn to listen to and respect each other.

Does the jigsaw method work? Compared to children in traditional classrooms, children in jigsaw groups are less prejudiced, they like their classmates more, they have more positive attitudes toward school, their grades improve, and their self-esteem increases (Walker & Crogan, 1998; Webb & Farivar, 1994). Such results are quite encouraging. As distinguished African-American psychologist Kenneth Clark said, "Racial prejudice ... debases all human beings—those who are its victims, those who victimize, and in quite subtle ways, those who are merely accessories."

Superordinate goal A goal that exceeds or overrides all others; a goal that renders other goals relatively less important.

Mutual interdependence A condition in which people must depend on one another to meet each person's goals.

Jigsaw classroom A method of reducing prejudice; each student receives only part of the information needed to complete a project or prepare for a test.

To summarize, prejudice will be reduced when:

- Members of different groups have equal status *within the situation* that brings them together.
- Members of all groups seek a common goal.
- Group members must cooperate to reach the goal.
- Group members spend enough time together for cross-group friendships to develop (Pettigrew, 1998).

Sports teams are an excellent example of a situation in which all of these conditions apply. The close contact and interdependent effort required in team sports often creates life-long friendships and breaks down the walls of prejudice.

STUDY BREAK ⓨ *Prejudice and Intergroup Conflict*

RELATE

Mentally scan over the events of the last week. How would they have changed if prejudices of all types ceased to exist?

Think of the most rigid person you know. Does he or she match the profile of the authoritarian personality?

Stereotypes exist for many social categories, even ordinary ones such as "college student" or "unmarried young adult." What stereotypes do you think you face in daily life?

The director of a youth recreation center is concerned about the amount of conflict she is seeing between boys and girls from different racial and ethnic groups. What advice can you give the director?

LEARNING CHECK

1. As a basis for prejudice, _____ is frequently related to frustration and displaced _____.
2. The authoritarian personality tends to be prejudiced against all out-groups, a quality referred to as _____.

3. The stereotypes underlying racial and ethnic prejudice tend to evolve from the superordinate goals that often separate groups. T or F?
4. The term *symbolic prejudice* refers to racism or prejudice that is expressed in disguised or hidden form. T or F?
5. Jane Elliot's classroom experiment in prejudice showed that children could be made to dislike one another by frustrating the students. T or F?
6. Research suggests that prejudice and intergroup conflict may be reduced by _____ interaction and _____ goals.

Critical Thinking

7. In court trials, defense lawyers sometimes try to identify and eliminate prospective jurors who have authoritarian personality traits. Can you guess why?

ANSWERS

1. scapegoating, aggression 2. ethnocentrism 3. F 4. T 5. F 6. equal-status, superordinate 7. Because authoritarians tend to believe that punishment is effective, they are more likely to vote for conviction.

AGGRESSION—THE WORLD'S MOST DANGEROUS ANIMAL

] SURVEY QUESTION *How do psychologists explain human aggression?*

"I know not with what weapons World War III will be fought, but World War IV will be fought with sticks and stones." Albert Einstein

For a time, the City Zoo of Los Angeles, California, had on display two examples of the world's most dangerous animal—the only animal capable of destroying the Earth and all other animal species. Perhaps you have already guessed which animal it was. In the cage were two college students, representing the species *Homo sapiens!*

The human capacity for aggression is staggering. It has been estimated that during the 125-year period ending with World War II, 58 million humans were killed by other humans (an average of nearly one person per minute). War, homicide, riots, family violence, assassination, rape, assault, forcible robbery, and other violent acts offer sad testimony to the realities of human aggression.

What causes aggression? **Aggression** refers to any action carried out with the intention of harming another person. The complexity of aggression has given rise to many potential explanations for its occurrence. Brief descriptions of some of the major possibilities follow.

Aggression Any action carried out with the intention of harming another person.

Ritualized human aggression. Violent and aggressive behavior is so commonplace it may be viewed as entertainment. How "natural" is aggressive behavior?

Instincts

Some theorists argue we are naturally aggressive creatures, having inherited a "killer instinct" from our animal ancestors. Ethologists theorize that aggression is a biologically rooted behavior observed in all animals, including humans. (An *ethologist* is a person who studies the natural behavior patterns of animals.) Noted ethologist Konrad Lorenz (1966, 1974) also believed that humans lack certain innate patterns that inhibit aggression in animals. For example, in a dispute over territory, two wolves may growl, lunge, bare their teeth, and fiercely threaten each other. In most instances, though, neither is killed or even wounded. One wolf, recognizing the dominance of the other, will typically bare its throat in a gesture of submission. The dominant wolf could kill in an instant, but it is inhibited by the submissive gesture. In contrast, human confrontations of equal intensity almost always end in injury or death.

The idea that humans are "naturally" aggressive has an intuitive appeal, but many psychologists question it. Many of Lorenz's "explanations" of aggression are little more than loose comparisons between human and animal behavior. Just labeling a behavior as "instinctive" does little to explain it. More important, we are left with the question of why some individuals or human groups (the Arapesh, the Senoi, the Navajo, the Eskimo, and others) show little hostility or aggression. And, thankfully, the vast majority of humans *do not* kill or harm others.

Biology

Despite problems with the instinctive view, aggression may have a biological basis. Physiological studies have shown that some brain areas are capable of triggering or ending aggressive behavior. Also, researchers have found a relationship between aggression and such physical factors as low blood sugar, allergy, and specific brain injuries and diseases. For both men and women, higher levels of the hormone testosterone are associated with more aggressive behavior (Banks & Dabbs, 1996; Harris et al., 1996). Perhaps because of their higher testosterone levels, men are 10 times more likely to commit murder than women are (Anderson & Bushman, 2002). However, none of these biological factors can be considered a direct *cause* of aggression. Instead, they probably lower the threshold for aggression, making hostile behavior more likely to occur (Baron & Richardson, 1994).

The effects of alcohol and other drugs provide another indication of the role of the brain and biology in aggression. Alcohol is involved in large percentages of murders and violent crimes. Like the conditions already noted, intoxicating drugs seem to lower inhibitions to act aggressively—often with tragic results (Anderson & Bushman, 2002; Ito et al., 1996).

To summarize, the fact that we are biologically *capable* of aggression does not mean that aggression is inevitable or "part of human nature." Twenty eminent scientists who studied the question concluded that, "Biology does not condemn humanity to war . . . . Violence is neither in our evolutionary legacy nor in our genes. The same species that invented war is capable of inventing peace" (Scott & Ginsburg, 1994; UNESCO, 1990). Humans are fully capable of learning to inhibit aggression. For example, American Quakers, who live in this country's increasingly violent culture, adopt non-violence as a way of life (Bandura, 2001).

Frustration

Step on a dog's tail and you may get nipped. Frustrate a human and you may get insulted. The **frustration-aggression hypothesis** states that frustration tends to lead to aggression.

Does frustration always produce aggression? Although the connection is strong, a moment's thought will show that frustration does not *always* lead to aggression. Frustration, for instance, may lead to stereotyped responding or perhaps to a state of "learned helplessness" (see Chapter 11). Also, aggression can occur in the absence of frustration. This is il-

Frustration-aggression hypothesis States that frustration tends to lead to aggression.

Road rage and some freeway shootings may be a reaction to the frustration of traffic congestion. The fact that automobiles provide anonymity, or a loss of personal identity, may also encourage aggressive actions that would not otherwise occur.

lustrated by sports spectators who start fights, throw bottles, tear down goal posts, and so forth after their team has *won*.

Aversive Stimuli

Frustration probably encourages aggression because it makes us uncomfortable. Various *aversive stimuli*, which produce discomfort or displeasure, can heighten hostility and aggression (Anderson, Anderson, & Deuser, 1996; Berkowitz, 1990) (◆Fig. 14.12). Examples include insults, high temperatures, pain, and even disgusting scenes or odors. Such stimuli probably raise overall arousal levels so that we become more sensitive to *aggression cues* (signals that are associated with aggression) (Carlson, Marcus-Newhall, & Miller, 1990). Aversive stimuli also tend to activate ideas, memories, and expressions associated with anger and aggression (Berkowitz, 1990).

Some cues for aggression are internal (angry thoughts, for instance). Many are external: Certain words, actions, and gestures made by others are strongly associated with aggressive responses. A raised middle finger, for instance, is an almost universal invitation to aggression in North America. Weapons serve as particularly strong cues for aggressive behavior (Berkowitz, 1968). The implication of this *weapons effect* seems to be that the symbols and trappings of aggression encourage aggression. A prime example is the fact that murders are almost 3 times more likely to occur in homes where guns are kept. Nearly 80 percent of the victims in such homes are killed by a family member or acquaintance. Only 4 percent are murdered by strangers (Kellermann et al., 1993).

Social Learning

One of the most widely accepted explanations of aggression is also the simplest. Social learning theory holds that we learn to be aggressive by observing aggression in others (Bandura, 1973). **Social learning theory** combines learning principles with cognitive processes, socialization, and modeling to explain behavior. According to this view, there is no instinctive human programming for fist-fighting, pipe-bombing, knife wielding, gun loading, 95-mile-an-hour "bean balls," or other violent or aggressive behaviors. Hence, aggression must be learned (◆Fig. 14.13).

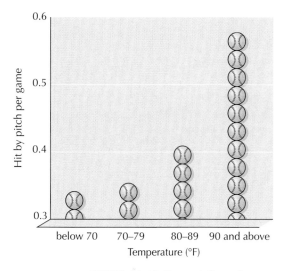

◆**FIGURE 14.12** *Personal discomfort caused by aversive (unpleasant) stimuli can make aggressive behavior more likely. For example, studies of crime rates show that the incidence of highly aggressive behavior, such as murder, rape, and assault, rises as the air temperature goes from warm to hot to sweltering (Anderson, 1989). The results you see here further confirm the heat-aggression link. The graph shows that there is a strong association between the temperatures at major league baseball games and the number of batters hit by a pitch during those games. When the temperature goes over 90°, watch out for that fastball (Reifman, Larrick, & Fein, 1991)!*

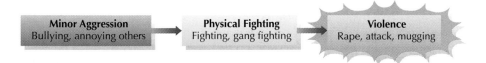

◆**FIGURE 14.13** *Violent behavior among delinquent boys doesn't appear overnight. Usually, their capacity for violence develops slowly, as they move from minor aggression to increasingly brutal acts. Overall aggression increases dramatically in early adolescence as boys gain physical strength and more access to weapons (Loeber & Hay, 1997).*

Social learning theory Combines learning principles with cognitive processes, socialization, and modeling, to explain behavior.

Social learning theorists predict that people growing up in non-aggressive cultures will themselves be non-aggressive. Those raised in a culture with aggressive models and heroes will learn aggressive responses (Bandura, 2001). Considered in such terms, it is no wonder that America has become one of the most violent of all countries. It is estimated that a violent crime occurs every 54 seconds in the United States. Approximately 40 percent of the population owns firearms. Nationally, 70 percent agree that "When a boy is growing up, it is very important for him to have a few fist-fights." Children and adults are treated to an almost non-stop parade of aggressive models, in the media as well as in actual behavior. We are, without a doubt, an aggressive culture.

Televised Violence

Every day, TV provides an endless stream of bad models, especially concerning violence. In the United States there are nearly 200 hours of violent programs per week. Eighty-one percent of all programs contain violence, which is often quite unrealistic. For instance, an astounding 73 percent of violent characters go unpunished, and 58 percent of violent acts don't lead to painful results. Only 16 percent of all programs show any realistic long-term consequences for violence. For children's programs the rate falls to just 5 percent (*National Television Violence Study,* 1995–1996).

How much does TV violence affect children?   As Albert Bandura showed in his studies of imitation (Chapter 6), children may learn new aggressive actions by watching violent or aggressive behavior, or they may learn that violence is "okay." Either way, they are more likely to act aggressively. Heroes on TV are as violent as the villains, and they usually receive praise for their violence. There is now little doubt that widespread exposure to media violence contributes to aggression (Bushman & Huesmann, 2001). Boys and girls who watch a lot of violence on television are much more likely to be aggressive as adults (Huesmann et al., 2003).

In addition to teaching new antisocial actions, television may disinhibit dangerous impulses that viewers already have. *Disinhibition* (the removal of inhibition) results in acting out behavior that normally would be restrained. For example, many TV programs give the message that violence is acceptable behavior that leads to success and popularity. For some people, this message can lower inhibitions against acting out hostile feelings (Berkowitz, 1984).

Another effect of TV violence is that it tends to lower sensitivity to violent acts. As anyone who has seen a street fight or a mugging can tell you, TV violence is sanitized and unrealistic. The real thing is gross, ugly, and gut wrenching. Even when it is graphic, TV violence is viewed in the relaxed and familiar setting of the home. For at least some viewers, this combination diminishes emotional reactions to violent scenes. When Victor Cline and his associates showed a bloody fight film to a group of boys, they found that heavy TV viewers (averaging 42 hours a week) showed much less emotion than those who watched little or no TV (Cline et al., 1972). Television, it seems, can cause a *desensitization* (reduced emotional sensitivity) to violence (Huesmann et al., 2003).

Preventing Aggression

What can be done about aggression?   Social learning theory implies that "aggression begets aggression." For example, children who are physically abused at home, those who suffer severe physical punishment, and those who merely witness violence in the community are more likely to be involved in fighting, aggressive play, and antisocial behavior at school (Macmillan, 2001; Margolin & Gordis, 2000).

According to social learning theorists, watching a prizefight, sporting event, or violent television program may increase aggression, rather than drain off aggressive urges. A case in point is provided by psychologist Leonard Eron, who spent 22 years following over 600 children into adulthood. Eron (1987) observes, "Among the most influential models for children were those observed on television. One of the best predictors of how aggressive a young man would be at age 19 was the violence of the television programs he preferred when he was 8 years old" (♦Fig. 14.14). According to Eron, children learn aggressive strate-

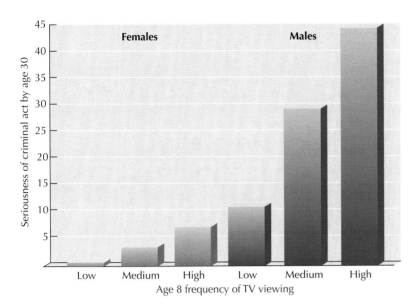

◆**FIGURE 14.14** *Although TV violence does not cause aggression, it can encourage it. The likelihood of committing criminal acts by age 30 is related to the amount of TV watching a person did when she or he was a child (Eron, 1987). (From L. D. Eron, "The Development of Aggressive Behavior from the Perspective of a Developing Behaviorism,"* American Psychologist, *May 1987, pp. 435–442. Copyright © 1987 American Psychological Association. Reprinted with permission of the publisher and author.)*

gies and actions from TV violence. Because of this, they are more prone to aggress when they face frustrating situations or cues. Others have found that viewers who watch violent videotapes have more aggressive thoughts. As we have noted, violent thoughts often precede violent actions (Bushman & Geen, 1990). Thus, the spiral of aggression might be broken if we did not so often portray it, reward it, and glorify it (Hughes & Hasbrouck, 1996).

Parents as TV Guides

As the preceding studies show, reduced TV watching is one way to lower aggression. However, other than pulling the plug, what can parents do about television's negative effects on children? Actually, quite a lot. Children typically model parents' TV viewing habits, and they are guided by parents' reactions to programs. Parents can make a big difference if they do the following (Eron, 1986; Frydman, 1999; Schneider, 1987).

1. Limit total viewing time so that television does not dominate your child's view of the world. If necessary, set schedules for when watching TV is allowed. Don't use television as a babysitter.
2. Closely monitor what your child does watch. Change channels or turn off the TV if you object to a program. Be prepared to offer games and activities that stimulate your child's imagination and creativity.
3. Actively seek programs your child will enjoy, especially those that model positive behavior and social attitudes.
4. Watch television with your child so that you can counter what is shown. Help your child distinguish between reality and TV fantasies. Reply to distortions and stereotypes as they appear on screen.
5. Discuss the social conflicts and violent solutions shown on television. Ask your child in what ways the situations are unrealistic and why the violence shown would not work in the real world. Encourage the child to propose more mature, realistic, and positive responses to situations.
6. Show by your own disapproval that violent TV heroes are not the ones to emulate. Remember, children who identify with TV characters are more likely to be influenced by televised aggression.

By following these guidelines you can help children learn to enjoy television without being overly influenced by programs and advertisers. A recent study found that elementary school children become less aggressive when they decrease the amount of time they spend watching TV and playing video games (Robinson et al., 2001). (Also see "School Violence— Warning Signs and Remedies" for more information on what individuals can do to prevent violence.)

CLINICAL FILE School Violence—Warning Signs and Remedies

Fortunately, school shootings are relatively rare. Nevertheless, they represent the tip of a growing problem of school violence. In 1998, for example, 15-year-old Kip Kinkel murdered his father and mother and then opened fire on classmates in Springfield, Oregon, murdering two and injuring 25. Many people close to Kip never noticed his potential for violence.

What are the warning signs for school violence? The following points can help friends, family members, and teachers identify children at risk. A student who is prone to violence:

- Consistently does not listen to adults and rejects authority
- Has trouble paying attention and concentrating
- Does poorly in school, is disruptive, and skips class
- Frequently gets in fights, may join a gang, or is involved in stealing or destroying property
- Is easily frustrated and reacts with extreme anger to criticism or disappointments
- Feels that life is unfair and blames others or seeks revenge
- Watches many violent television shows and movies or plays a lot of violent video games
- Has few friends and is often publicly rejected or teased by others
- Has friends who are unruly or aggressive
- Is cruel or violent toward pets or other animals
- Drinks alcohol and/or uses inhalants or drugs

One of the best antidotes to youth violence is a warm and loving family. Depression, pain, hate, and violence often originate in dysfunctional families. To minimize anger, aggression, and violence, parents should:

- Make sure their children are supervised.
- Show by example how children should act.
- Teach children non-aggressive ways to solve problems.
- Avoid hitting their children.
- Be consistent about rules and discipline.
- Make sure children do not have access to guns.
- Try to keep children from seeing violence at home, in the media, or in the community.

Healthy communities also discourage violence. Parents should get involved in the community and get to know their neighbors. Children benefit from participating in groups that build pride in the community, such as those that organize clean-ups of litter or graffiti. Such groups provide a great opportunity for parents, children, and neighbors to spend time together in rewarding activities. (Sources: Pollack, 2001; "Warning Signs," 2000.)

Beyond this, the question remains, How shall we tame the world's most dangerous animal? There is no easy answer. For the immediate future, it is clear that we need more people who are willing to engage in helpful, altruistic, **prosocial behavior** (actions that are constructive, altruistic, or helpful to others). In the next section we will examine some of the forces that prevent people from helping others and how to encourage prosocial behavior.

PROSOCIAL BEHAVIOR—HELPING OTHERS

] SURVEYQUESTION *Why are bystanders so often unwilling to help in an emergency?*

Late one night, tenants of a Queens, New York, apartment building watched and listened in horror as a young woman named Kitty Genovese was murdered on the sidewalk outside. From the safety of their rooms, no fewer than 38 people heard the agonized screams as her assailant stabbed her, was frightened off, and returned to stab her again.

Kitty Genovese's murder took over 30 minutes, but none of her neighbors tried to help. None even called the police until after the attack had ended. Perhaps it is understandable that no one wanted to get involved. After all, it could have been a violent lovers' quarrel. Or helping might have meant risking personal injury. But what prevented these people from at least calling the police?

Isn't this an example of the alienation of city life? News reports treated this incident as evidence of a breakdown in social ties caused by the impersonality of the city. While it is true that urban living can be dehumanizing, this does not fully explain such *bystander apathy* (unwillingness of bystanders to offer help during emergencies). According to psychologists Bibb Latané and John Darley, failure to help is related to the number of people present. Over the years many studies have shown that the *more* potential helpers present, the *lower* the chances that help will be given (Latané et al., 1981).

Why would people be less willing to help when others are present? In Kitty Genovese's case, the answer is that everyone thought *someone else* would help. The dynamics of this effect are easily illustrated: Suppose that two motorists have stalled at roadside, one on a

Prosocial behavior Behavior toward others that is helpful, constructive, or altruistic.

sparsely traveled country road and the other on a busy freeway. Who gets help first?

On the freeway, where hundreds of cars pass every minute, each driver can assume that someone else will help. Personal responsibility for helping is spread so thin that no one takes action. On the country road, one of the first few people to arrive will probably stop, since the responsibility is clearly theirs. In general, Latané and Darley assume that bystanders are not apathetic or uncaring; they are inhibited by the presence of others.

Bystander Intervention

People must pass through four decision points before giving help. First they must notice that something is happening. Next they must define the event as an emergency. Then they must take responsibility. Finally, they must select a course of action (✦Fig. 14.15). Laboratory experiments have shown that each step can be influenced by the presence of other people.

Noticing

What would happen if you fainted and collapsed on the sidewalk? Would someone stop to help? Would people think you were drunk? Would they even notice you? Latané and Darley suggest that if the sidewalk is crowded, few people will even see you. This has nothing to do with people blocking each other's vision. Instead, it is related to widely accepted norms against staring at others in public. People in crowds typically "keep their eyes to themselves."

Is there any way to show that this is a factor in bystander apathy?   To test this idea, students were asked to fill out a questionnaire either alone or in a room full of people. While the students worked, a thick cloud of smoke was blown into the room through a vent.

Most students left alone in the room noticed the smoke immediately. Few of the people in groups noticed the smoke until it actually became difficult to see through it. Subjects working in groups politely kept their eyes on their papers and avoided looking at others (or the smoke). In contrast, those who were alone scanned the room from time to time.

Defining an Emergency

The smoke-filled room also shows the influence others have on defining a situation as an emergency. When subjects in groups finally noticed the smoke, they cast sidelong glances at others in the room. Apparently, they were searching for clues to help interpret what was happening. No one wanted to overreact or act like a fool if there was no emergency. However, as subjects coolly surveyed the reactions of others, they were themselves being watched. In real emergencies, people sometimes "fake each other out" and underestimate

Does the person lying on the ground need help? What factors determine whether a person in trouble will receive help in an emergency? Surprisingly, more potential helpers tend to lower the chances that help will be given.

Joel Gordon

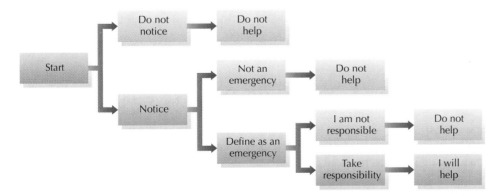

✦**FIGURE 14.15** *This decision tree summarizes the steps a person must take before making a commitment to offer help, according to Latané and Darley's model.*

the need for action because each person attempts to appear calm. In short, until someone acts, no one acts.

Taking Responsibility

Perhaps the most crucial step in helping is assuming responsibility. In this case, groups limit helping by causing a *diffusion of responsibility* (spreading responsibility among several people).

Is that like the unwillingness of drivers to offer help on a crowded freeway? Exactly. It is the feeling that no one is personally responsible for helping. This problem was demonstrated in an experiment in which students took part in a group discussion over an intercom system. Actually, there was only one real subject in each group; the others were tape-recorded actors. Each subject was placed in a separate room (supposedly to maintain confidentiality), and discussions of college life were begun. During the discussion, one of the "students" simulated an epileptic-like seizure and called out for help. In some cases, subjects thought they were alone with the seizure victim. Others believed they were members of three- or six-person groups.

Subjects who thought they were alone with the "victim" of this staged emergency reported it immediately or tried to help. Some subjects in the three-person groups failed to respond, and those who did were slower. In the six-person groups, over a third of the subjects took no action at all. People in this experiment were obviously faced with a conflict like that in many real emergencies: Should they be helpful and responsible, or should they mind their own business? Many were influenced toward inaction by the presence of others.

People do help in some emergencies. How are these different? It is not always clear what makes the difference. Helping behavior is complex and influenced by many variables. One naturalistic experiment staged in a New York City subway gives a hint of the kinds of things that may be important. When a "victim" (actor) "passed out" in a subway car, he received more help when carrying a cane than when carrying a liquor bottle. More important, however, was the fact that most people were willing to help in either case (Piliavin et al., 1969).

To better answer the question we need to consider some factors not included in Latané and Darley's account of helping.

Who Will Help Whom?

Many studies suggest that when we see a person in trouble, it tends to cause *heightened arousal* (Dovidio, 1984). This aroused, keyed-up feeling can motivate us to give aid, but only if the rewards of helping outweigh the costs. Higher costs (such as great effort, personal risk, or possible embarrassment) almost always decrease helping (Foss, 1986). In addition to general arousal, potential helpers may also feel **empathic arousal.** This means they empathize with the person in need or feel some of the person's pain, fear, or anguish. Helping is much more likely when we are able to take the perspective of others and feel sympathy for their plight (Eisenberg, 1991).

Empathic arousal is especially likely to motivate helping when the person in need seems to be similar to ourselves (Eisenberg & Miller, 1987). In fact, a feeling of connection to the victim may be one of the most important factors in helping. This, perhaps, is why being in a good mood also increases helping. When we are feeling successful, happy, or fortunate, we may also feel more connected to others (Dovidio, 1984). In summary, there is a strong **empathy-helping relationship:** We are most likely to help someone in need when we "feel for" that person and experience emotions such as empathy, sympathy, and compassion (Batson, 1990).

Is there anything that can be done to encourage prosocial behavior? People who see others helping are more likely to offer help themselves. Also, persons who give help in one situation tend to perceive themselves as helpful people. This change in self-image encourages them to help in other situations. One more point is that norms of fairness encourage us to help others who have helped us (Dovidio, 1984). For all these reasons, helping others not only assists them directly, it encourages others to help, too.

Empathic arousal Emotional arousal that occurs when you feel some of another person's pain, fear, or anguish.

Empathy-helping relationship Observation that we are most likely to help someone else when we feel emotions such as empathy and compassion.

"De-Victimize" Yourself

If you should find yourself in need of help during an emergency, what can you do to avoid being a victim of bystander apathy? The work we have reviewed here suggests that you should make sure that you are noticed, that people realize there's an emergency, and that they need to take action. Being noticed can be promoted in some situations by shouting "Fire!" Bystanders who might run away from a robbery or an assault may rush to see where the fire is. At the very least, remember not to just scream. Instead, you should call out "Help," or "I need help right now." Whenever possible, define your situation for bystanders. Say, for instance, "I'm being attacked, call the police." Or, "Stop that man, he has my purse." You can also directly assign responsibility to a bystander by pointing to someone and saying, "You, call the police" or "I'm injured, I need you to call an ambulance" (Cummins, 1995).

A Look Ahead

The Psychology in Action section of this chapter returns to the topic of prejudice for some further thoughts about how to promote tolerance. Don't miss this interesting conclusion to our discussion of social psychology.

STUDYBREAK Aggression and Prosocial Behavior

RELATE

Most people have been angry enough at some time to behave aggressively. Which concepts or theories do you think best explain your own aggressive actions?

An elderly woman is at the side of the road, trying to change a flat tire. She obviously needs help. You are approaching her in your car. What must happen before you are likely to stop and help her?

LEARNING CHECK

1. The position of ethologists is that there is no biological basis for aggression. T or F?
2. Higher levels of testosterone are associated with more aggressive behavior. T or F?
3. Frustration and aversive stimuli are more likely to produce aggression when cues for aggressive behavior are present. T or F?

4. Social learning theory holds that exposure to aggressive models helps drain off aggressive energies. T or F?
5. Heavy exposure to television results in lowered emotional sensitivity to violence. T or F?
6. _____ behavior refers to actions that are constructive, altruistic, or helpful to others.
7. Seeing that a person in need is similar to ourselves tends to increase empathic arousal and the likelihood that help will be given. T or F?

Critical Thinking

8. If televised violence contributes to aggressive behavior in our society, do you think it is possible that television could also promote prosocial behavior?

ANSWERS

1. F 2. T 3. T 4. F 5. T 6. Prosocial 7. T 8. Yes. TV could be used to promote helping, cooperation, charity, and brotherhood in the same way that it has encouraged aggression. Numerous studies show that prosocial behavior on TV increases prosocial behavior by viewers.

Psychology in Action

Multiculturalism—Living with Diversity

] SURVEYQUESTION *What can be done to avoid prejudice and promote social harmony?*

Today's society is more like a "tossed salad" than a cultural "melting pot." Rather than expecting everyone to be alike, psychologists believe that we must learn to respect and appreciate our differences. **Multiculturalism,** as this is called, gives equal status to different ethnic, racial, and cultural groups. It is a recognition and acceptance of human diversity (Fowers & Richardson, 1996).

Breaking the Prejudice Habit

Most people publicly support policies of equality and fairness. Yet, many still have lingering biases and negative images of Blacks, Latinos, Asians, and other ethnic minorities. How can we make sense of such conflicting attitudes? Patricia Devine, a social psychologist, has

Multiculturalism Giving equal status, recognition, and acceptance to different ethnic and cultural groups.

shown that a decision to forsake prejudice does not immediately eliminate prejudiced thoughts and feelings. People who are not prejudiced may continue to respond emotionally to members of other ethnic groups. Quite likely this reflects lingering stereotypes and prejudices learned in childhood (Devine et al., 1991).

For many people, becoming less prejudiced begins with sincerely accepting values of tolerance and equality. People who value tolerance feel pangs of guilt or self-criticism when they have intolerant thoughts or feelings (Zuwerink et al., 1996). This motivates them to try to alter their own biased reactions (Dovidio & Gaertner, 1999). But doing so is not easy. Typically, it requires repeated efforts to learn to think, feel, and act differently. Nevertheless, many people have succeeded in overcoming the "prejudice habit" (Devine et al., 1991). If you would like to be more tolerant, the following points may be helpful to you.

Beware of Stereotyping

Stereotypes make the social world more manageable. But placing people in categories almost always causes them to appear more similar than they really are. As a result, we tend to see out-group members as very much alike, even when they are as varied as our friends and family. People who are not prejudiced work hard to actively inhibit stereotyped thoughts and to emphasize fairness and equality (Devine, 1990). A good way to tear down stereotypes is to get to know individuals from various ethnic and cultural groups.

Seek Individuating Information

When are we most tempted to apply stereotypes? Typically it is when we only have minimal information about a person. Stereotypes help us guess what a person is like and how she or he will act. Unfortunately, these inferences are usually wrong.

One of the best antidotes for stereotypes is **individuating information** (information that helps us see a person as an individual, rather than as a member of a group) (Click, Zion, & Nelson, 1988). Anything that keeps us from placing a person in a particular social category tends to negate stereotyped thinking. When you meet individuals from various backgrounds, focus on the *person,* not the *label* attached to her or him.

A good example of the effects of individuating information comes from a study in Canada of English-speaking students in a French language program. Students who were "immersed" (spent most of their waking hours with French Canadians) became more positive toward them. Immersed students were more likely to say they had come to appreciate and like French Canadians; they were more willing to meet and interact with them; and they saw themselves as less different from French Canadians (Lambert, 1987). In fact, with more subtle kinds of symbolic prejudice, such contact may be the best way to reduce intergroup conflict (Dovidio & Gaertner, 1999).

Don't Fall Prey to Just-World Beliefs

Do you believe that the world is basically fair? Even if you don't, you may believe that the world is sufficiently just so that people generally get what they deserve. It may not be obvious, but such beliefs can directly increase prejudiced thinking.

As a result of discrimination, social conditions, and circumstances (such as recent immigration), minorities may occupy lower socio-economic positions. **Just-world beliefs** (belief that people generally get what they deserve) can lead us to assume that minority group members wouldn't be in such positions if they weren't inferior in some way. This bit of faulty thinking amounts to blaming people who are *victims* of prejudice and discrimination for their plight. For example, assuming that a poor person is lazy may overlook the fact that discrimination in hiring has made it very difficult for him or her to find a job.

Be Aware of Self-Fulfilling Prophecies

You may recall from Chapter 1 that people tend to act in accordance with the behavior expected by others. If you hold strong stereotypes about members of various groups, a vicious cycle can occur. When you meet someone who is different from yourself, you may treat her or him in a way that is consistent with your stereotypes. If the other person is influenced by your behavior, she or he may act in ways that seem to match your stereotype. For example, a person who believes that members of another ethnic group are hostile and unfriendly will prob-

Individuating information Information that helps define a person as an individual rather than as a member of a group or social category.

Just-world beliefs Belief that people generally get what they deserve.

ably treat people in that group in ways that provoke hostile and unfriendly response. This creates a self-fulfilling prophecy and reinforces belief in the stereotype. (A **self-fulfilling prophecy** is an expectation that prompts people to act in ways that make the expectation come true.)

Remember, Different Does Not Mean Inferior

Some conflicts between groups cannot be avoided. What *can* be avoided is unnecessary **social competition** (rivalry among groups, each of which regards itself as superior to others). The concept of social competition refers to the fact that some individuals seek to enhance their self-esteem by identifying with a group. However, this works only if the group can be seen as superior to others. Because of social competition, groups tend to view themselves as better than their rivals (Baron & Byrne, 2002). In a survey, every major ethnic group in the United States rated itself as better than any other group (Njeri, 1991). This is a little like the fabled town of Lake Woebegone, where all the children are above average.

A person who has high self-esteem does not need to treat others as inferior in order to feel good about himself or herself. Similarly, it is not necessary to degrade other groups in order to feel positive about one's own group identity (Messick & Mackie, 1989). In fact, each ethnic group has strengths that members of other groups could benefit from emulating. For instance, African Americans, Asians, and Latinos emphasize family networks that help buffer them from some of the stresses of daily life (Suinn, 1999).

Understand that Race Is a Social Construction

From the viewpoint of modern genetics, the concept of race has absolutely no meaning. Members of various groups are so varied genetically and human groups have intermixed for so many centuries, that it is impossible to tell, biologically, to what "race" any given individual belongs. Thus, race is an illusion based on superficial physical differences and learned ethnic identities. Certainly people *act as if* different races exist. But this is a matter of social labeling, not biological reality. To assume that any human group is biologically superior or inferior is simply wrong. In fact, the best available evidence suggests that all people are descended from the same ancient ancestors. The origins of our species lie in Africa, about 100,000 years ago. Among early human populations, darker skin is a protective adaptation to sun exposure near the equator (Jablonski & Chaplin, in press). Biologically, we are all brothers and sisters under the skin (Graves, 2001; Segall, Lonner, & Berry, 1998).

Look for Commonalities

We live in a society that puts a premium on competition and individual effort. One problem with this is that competing with others fosters desires to demean, defeat, and vanquish them. When we cooperate with others we tend to share their joys and suffer when they are in distress (Lanzetta & Englis, 1989). If we don't find ways to cooperate and live in greater harmony, everyone will suffer. That, if nothing else, is one thing that we all have in common. Everyone knows what it feels like to be different. Greater tolerance comes from remembering those times.

Set an Example for Others

People who act in a tolerant fashion can serve as models of tolerance for others. An example is the use of newsletters to promote understanding at an ethnically diverse high school in Houston, Texas. Students wrote stories for the newsletter about situations in which cooperation led to better understanding. For instance, a story about an Hispanic-Anglo friendship in a sports team had this headline: "Don't judge somebody until you know them. The color of the skin doesn't matter." Other stories emphasized the willingness of students to get acquainted with people from other ethnic groups and the new perceptions they had of their abilities. After just 5 months of modeling tolerance, hostility between campus ethnic groups was significantly reduced (McAlister et al., 2000).

Tolerance and Cultural Awareness

Living comfortably in a multicultural society means getting to know a little about other groups. Getting acquainted with a person whose cultural background is different from your own can be a wonderful learning experience. No one culture has all the answers or the best

Self-fulfilling prophecy An expectation that prompts people to act in ways that make the expectation come true.

Social competition Rivalry among groups, each of which regards itself as superior to others.

ways of doing things. Multicultural populations enrich a community's food, music, arts, and philosophy. Likewise, learning about different racial, cultural, and ethnic groups can be personally rewarding.

The importance of cultural awareness often lies in subtleties and details. For example, in large American cities, many small stores are owned by Korean immigrants. Some of these Korean-American merchants have been criticized for being cold and hostile to their customers. Refusing to place change directly in customers' hands, for instance, helped trigger an African-American boycott of Korean grocers in New York City. The core of the problem was a lack of cultural awareness on both sides.

In America, if you walk into a store, you expect the clerk to be courteous to you. One way of showing politeness is by smiling. But in the Confucian-steeped Korean culture, a smile is reserved for family members and close friends. If a Korean or Korean American has no reason to smile, he or she just doesn't smile. There's a Korean saying: "If you smile a lot, you're silly." Expressions such as "thank you" and "excuse me" are also used sparingly and strangers rarely touch each other—not even to return change.

Here's another example of how ignorance of cultural practices can lead to needless friction and misunderstanding: An African-American woman who wanted to ease racial tensions took a freshly baked pie to her neighbors across the way, who were Orthodox Jews. At the front door the woman extended her hand, not knowing that Orthodox Jews don't shake women's hands, unless the woman is a close family member. Once she was inside, she picked up a kitchen knife to cut the pie, not knowing the couple kept a kosher household and used different knives for different foods. The woman's well-intentioned attempt at neighborliness ended in an argument! Knowing a little more about each other's cultures could have prevented both of the conflicts just described.

If the Earth's population could be condensed to just 100 people, with all of the current human ratios maintained, it would look like this:

- There would be 57 Asians, 21 Europeans, 14 from the Western Hemisphere, including North and South America, and 8 from Africa.
- Seventy would be non-white, while 30 would be white.
- Sixty-six would be non-Christian and 33 Christian.
- Half of the entire village's wealth would be in the hands of only six people, all of them U.S. citizens.
- Half the people in the village would suffer from malnutrition.
- Within the village are enough nuclear weapons to blow everyone to smithereens many times over.

When you consider the world from such a compressed perspective, the need for tolerance and understanding becomes readily apparent.

The Journey Continues—Psychology and You

The technological advances of the last 20 years have dramatically changed what is humanly possible. Yet, as a species we still have much in common with people who lived many hundreds of years ago. Although we might like to think otherwise, we cannot count on technology to solve all of our problems. The threat of war, social conflict, crime, prejudice, infectious disease, over-population, environmental damage, famine, homicide, economic disaster—these and most other major dilemmas facing us are *behavioral*. Will the human family endure? It's a psychological question.

At the beginning of this book I described psychology as a journey of self-discovery. It is my sincere hope that you have found enough relevance and value here to spark a lifelong interest in psychology. As your personal journey continues, one thing is certain: Many of your greatest challenges and most treasured moments will involve other people. You would be wise to continue adding to your understanding of human behavior. Psychology's future looks exciting. What role will it play in your life?

RELATE

Which strategies for breaking the prejudice habit do you already use? How could you apply the remaining strategies to become more tolerant?

LEARNING CHECK

1. Multiculturalism refers to the belief that various subcultures and ethnic groups should be blended into a single emergent culture. T or F?
2. Patricia Devine found that many people who hold non-prejudiced beliefs still have prejudiced thoughts and feelings in the presence of minority group individuals. T or F?

3. Individuating information tends to be a good antidote for stereotypes. T or F?
4. Just-world beliefs are the primary cause of social competition. T or F?

Critical Thinking

5. Why is it valuable to learn the terms by which members of various groups prefer to be addressed (for example, Mexican-American, Latino [or Latina], Hispanic, or Chicano [Chicana])?

ANSWERS

1. F 2. T 3. T 4. F 5. Because labels might have negative meanings that are not apparent to persons outside the group. People who are culturally aware allow others to define their own identities, rather than imposing labels on them.

CHAPTER IN REVIEW

Major Points

- Social psychology studies how we behave, think, and feel in social situations.
- We are attracted to other people for reasons that are fairly universal.
- To understand social behavior we must know what roles people play, their status, the norms they follow, and the attributions they make.
- Everyone is affected by pressures to conform, obey, and comply. There are times when it is valuable to resist such pressures.
- Attitudes subtly affect nearly all aspects of social behavior.
- To persuade others, you must be aware of your role as a communicator, the nature of the audience, and messages that will appeal to them.
- Prejudice is reduced by equal-status contact and mutual interdependence.
- Aggression is a fact of life, but humans are not inevitably aggressive.
- We can encourage helping and altruism by removing barriers to prosocial behavior.
- Multicultural harmony can be attained through conscious efforts to be more tolerant of others.

Summary

Why do people affiliate? What factors influence interpersonal attraction?

- Affiliation is tied to needs for approval, support, friendship, and information. Also, affiliation can reduce anxiety.

- Social comparison theory holds that we affiliate to evaluate our actions, feelings, and abilities.
- Interpersonal attraction is increased by proximity, frequent contact, beauty, competence, and similarity.
- Mate selection is characterized by a large degree of similarity on many dimensions.
- Self-disclosure follows a reciprocity norm: Low levels of self-disclosure are met with low levels in return; moderate self-disclosure elicits more personal replies.
- In comparison with liking, romantic love involves higher levels of emotional arousal and is accompanied by mutual absorption between lovers.
- Evolutionary psychology attributes human mating patterns to the differing reproductive challenges faced by men and women since the dawn of time.

How does group membership affect our behavior?

- Social roles are particular behavior patterns associated with social positions.
- Higher status within groups is associated with special privileges and respect.
- Group structure refers to roles, communication pathways, and power within a group. Group cohesiveness is the degree of attraction among group members.
- Norms are standards of conduct enforced (formally or informally) by groups.
- Attribution theory describes how we perceive the causes of behavior.
- The fundamental attributional error is to think that internal causes explain the actions of other people. In contrast, we tend to attribute our own behavior to external causes.

What have social psychologists learned about conformity, obedience, compliance, and self-assertion?

- Social influence refers to alterations in behavior brought about by the behavior of others.
- The famous Asch experiments demonstrated that various group pressure and group sanctions encourage conformity.
- Groupthink refers to compulsive conformity in group decision making.
- Obedience to authority in Milgram's studies decreased when the "teacher" and "learner" were close to one another, when the authority was absent, and when others refused to obey.
- Three strategies for gaining compliance are the foot-in-the-door technique, the door-in-the-face approach, and the low-ball technique.
- Many people show a surprising level of passive compliance to unreasonable requests.
- Self-assertion, as opposed to aggression, involves clearly stating one's wants and needs to others.

How are attitudes acquired and changed?

- Attitudes are learned dispositions made up of a belief component, an emotional component, and an action component.
- Attitudes may be formed by direct contact, interaction with others, child-rearing practices, and group pressures. Peer group influences, reference group membership, the mass media, and chance conditioning also appear to be important in attitude formation.
- Effective persuasion occurs when characteristics of the communicator, the message, and the audience are well matched.
- In general, a likable and believable communicator who repeats a credible message that arouses emotion in the audience and states clear-cut conclusions will be persuasive.
- Maintaining and changing attitudes is closely related to cognitive dissonance and our needs to be consistent in our thoughts and actions.

Is brainwashing actually possible? How are people converted to cult membership?

- Brainwashing is a form of forced attitude change. It depends on control of the target person's total environment.
- Three steps in brainwashing are unfreezing, changing, and refreezing attitudes and beliefs.
- Many cults recruit new members with high-pressure indoctrination techniques involving isolation, displays of affection, rituals, intimidation, and escalating commitment.

What causes prejudice and intergroup conflict?

- Prejudice is a negative attitude held toward members of various out-groups. One theory attributes prejudice to scapegoating. A second account says that prejudices may be held for personal reasons (personal prejudice) or simply through adherence to group norms (group prejudice).
- Prejudiced individuals tend to have an authoritarian personality.
- Intergroup conflict gives rise to hostility and the formation of social stereotypes. Status inequalities tend to build prejudice. Equal-status contact tends to reduce it.
- Superordinate goals are a key to reducing intergroup conflict.
- On a smaller scale, jigsaw classrooms (which encourage cooperation through mutual interdependence) have been shown to combat prejudice.

How do psychologists explain human aggression?

- Ethological explanations of aggression attribute it to inherited instincts. Biological explanations emphasize brain mechanisms and physical factors related to thresholds for aggression.
- According to the frustration-aggression hypothesis, frustration and aggression are closely linked.
- Frustration is only one of many aversive stimuli that can arouse a person and make aggression more likely. Aggression is especially likely to occur when aggression cues are present.
- Social learning theory has focused attention on the role of aggressive models in the development of aggressive behavior.

Why are bystanders so often unwilling to help in an emergency?

- Four decision points that must be passed before a person gives help are: noticing, defining an emergency, taking responsibility, and selecting a course of action.
- Helping is less likely at each point when other potential helpers are present.
- Helping is encouraged by general arousal, empathic arousal, being in a good mood, low effort or risk, and perceived similarity between the victim and the helper.
- For several reasons, giving help tends to encourage others to help, too.

What can be done to avoid prejudice and promote social harmony?

- Multiculturalism is an attempt to give equal status to different ethnic, racial, and cultural groups.

- Greater tolerance can be encouraged by neutralizing stereotypes with individuating information; by looking for commonalities with others; and by avoiding the effects of just-world beliefs, self-fulfilling prophecies, and social competition.
- Cultural awareness is a key element in promoting greater social harmony.

Interactive Learning

Internet addresses frequently change. To find the sites listed here, visit www.psychology. wadsworth.com/coon_journey2e for an updated list of Internet addresses and direct links to relevant sites.

PSYCHOLOGY: A JOURNEY COMPANION WEB SITE Online quizzes, flash cards, and other helpful study aids for this text. *www.psychology.wadsworth.com/coon_journey2e*

SOCIAL PSYCHOLOGY NETWORK A comprehensive site with many links to information about social psychology.

IN YOUR FACE Discusses research on facial attractiveness.

CENTER FOR EVOLUTIONARY PSYCHOLOGY A primer on evolutionary psychology, a reading list, and links.

PREVENTING GROUPTHINK Offers five ways to prevent groupthink.

INFORMATION ABOUT CULTS AND PSYCHOLOGICAL MANIPULATION

IMPLICIT ASSOCIATION TEST Online tests that purportedly reveal the unconscious roots of prejudice.

VIOLENCE ON TELEVISION Discusses research and implications of watching violence on television.

INFOTRAC COLLEGE EDITION For recent articles on the Psychology in Action feature, use Key Words search for ASSERTIVENESS. For recent articles on coercive attitude change, use Key Words search for CULTS and BRAINWASHING.

PSYCHNOW! 8a. Helping Others, 8b. Attribution, 8c. Social Influence, 8d. Attitudes and Prejudice, 8e. Aggression, 8g. Gender and Stereotyping.

Test Your Knowledge: Social Behavior

The questions that follow are only a sample of what you need to know. If you miss any of the items, you should review the entire chapter and get more practice with *WebTutor* or the *Practice Quizzes* that came with this book. Another way to prepare for tests is to use the printed *Study Guide* that is available for this text.

1. The pattern known as homogamy shows the powerful effect that _____ has on interpersonal attraction.
   A. physical beauty   B. similarity   C. competence   D. physical proximity

2. The fact that men tend to prefer younger, more physically attractive partners is predicted by
   A. evolutionary psychology   B. the overdisclosure hypothesis   C. social comparison theory   D. Rubin's studies of mutual absorption

3. Away from the office, Jan has become friends with Fran, a woman she supervises at work. Jan must do an evaluation of Fran, who hasn't been very efficient lately. It is most likely that Jan will experience
   A. groupthink   B. role conflict   C. group sanctions   D. overdisclosure

4. A common error we all make is to attribute the actions of others to internal causes. This is known as the fundamental
   A. reciprocity norm   B. role conflict   C. social comparison   D. attributional error

5. In Solomon Asch's conformity experiment, subjects yielded to group pressure on about _____ of the critical trials.
   A. 1 percent   B. 10 percent   C. one third   D. two thirds

6. Groupthink is an example of the danger that lies in powerful pressures for group
   A. cohesion   B. conformity   C. attribution   D. reciprocity

7. In Milgram's experiments, the lowest level of obedience occurred when subjects
   A. saw another person refuse to obey   B. were in the same room with the "learner"   C. were face to face with the "learner"   D. received orders over the phone

8. Which compliance technique involves getting a person committed to act and then making the terms of acting less desirable?
   A. foot in the door   B. low ball   C. door in the face   D. groupthink

9. "Achieving one's goals without taking into account the rights of others." This statement describes
   A. self-assertion   B. overdisclosure   C. cognitive dissonance   D. aggression

10. The three parts of an attitude are
    A. internal, external, group   B. conviction, attribution, absorption   C. status, norm, cohesion   D. belief, emotion, action

11. Which of the following is NOT one of the factors that typically determines whether our attitudes are expressed as actions?
    A. empathic arousal   B. existing habits   C. immediate consequences   D. anticipated evaluations by others

12. If you are trying to persuade a well-informed audience, it is usually best to present
    A. one side of the argument   B. both sides of the argument   C. the unfreezing, change, refreezing cycle   D. negative sanctions

13. The amount of cognitive dissonance a person feels is related to how much _____ exists for his or her actions.
    A. reciprocity   B. justification   C. chance conditioning   D. reference

14. Some expressions of prejudice can be thought of as scapegoating or
    A. displaced aggression   B. empathic arousal   C. reference group reversal   D. external attribution

15. One of the reasons that superordinate goals tend to reduce prejudice is that they require cooperation and
    A. social stereotyping   B. ethnocentrism   C. unfreezing   D. equal-status contact

16. Jigsaw classrooms use _____ to create mutual interdependence.
    A. social competition   B. just world beliefs   C. self-fulfilling prophecies   D. superordinate goals

17. The *weapons effect* refers to impact that _____ have on behavior.
    A. just world beliefs   B. aggression cues   C. self-fulfilling prophecies   D. televised models

18. The point of view most at odds with the idea that humans are instinctively aggressive is
    A. social learning theory   B. the frustration-aggression hypothesis   C. ethology   D. the aversive stimuli effect

19. People are more likely to help another who is in trouble if
    A. many other helpers are present   B. a diffusion of responsibility occurs   C. they experience empathic arousal   D. desensitization has taken place

20. One of the best antidotes for stereotypes is
    A. accepting just-world beliefs   B. individuating information   C. accepting self-fulfilling prophecies   D. honest social competition

Behavioral Statistics

Statistics from "Heads" to "Tails"

Let's say a friend of yours invites you to try your hand at a "game of chance." He offers to flip a coin and pay you a dollar if the coin comes up heads.

If the coin shows tails, you must pay him a dollar. He flips the coin: tails—you pay him a dollar. He flips it again: tails. Again: tails. And again: tails. And again: tails.

At this point you are faced with a choice. Should you continue the game in an attempt to recoup your losses? Or should you assume that the coin is biased and quit before you really get "skinned"? Taking out a pocket calculator (and the statistics book you carry with you at all times), you compute the odds of obtaining 5 tails in a row from an unbiased coin. The probability is 0.031 (roughly 3 times out of 100).

If the coin really is honest, 5 consecutive tails is a rare event. Wisely, you decide that the coin is probably biased and refuse to play again. (Unless, of course, your "friend" is willing to take "tails" for the next 5 tosses!)

Perhaps a decision could have been made in this hypothetical example without using statistics. But notice how much clearer the situation becomes when it is expressed statistically.

Psychologists try to extract and summarize useful information from the observations they make. To do so, they use two major types of statistics. **Descriptive statistics,** summarize or "boil down" numbers so they become more meaningful and easier to communicate to others. In comparison, **inferential statistics** are used for decision making, for generalizing from small samples, and for drawing conclusions. As was the case in the coin-flipping example, psychologists must often base decisions on limited data. Such decisions are much easier to make with the help of inferential statistics. Let's see how statistics are used in psychology.

Dennis Coon

$$r = \frac{\Sigma XY - \frac{(\Sigma X)(\Sigma Y)}{N}}{\sqrt{\left[\Sigma X^2 - \frac{(\Sigma X)^2}{N}\right]\left[\Sigma Y^2 - \frac{(\Sigma Y)^2}{N}\right]}}$$

$$\bar{X} = \frac{\Sigma X}{N}$$

Survey Questions

- What are descriptive statistics?
- How are statistics used to identify an average score?
- What statistics do psychologists use to measure how much scores differ from one another?
- What are inferential statistics?
- How are correlations used in psychology?

DESCRIPTIVE STATISTICS—PSYCHOLOGY BY THE NUMBERS

Let's say that you have completed a study on human behavior. The results seem interesting, but can you really tell what your data reveal, just by looking at a jumble of numbers? To get a clear picture of how people behaved, you will probably turn to descriptive statistics. By summarizing the results of your study, statistics will help you draw valid conclusions about what you observed.

Statistics bring greater clarity and precision to psychological thought and research. To see how, let's begin by considering three basic types of descriptive statistics: *graphical statistics,* measures of *central tendency,* and measures of *variability.* Let's start with **graphical statistics,** which present numbers pictorially, so they are easier to visualize.

Graphical Statistics

▲Table A.1 shows simulated scores on a test of hypnotic susceptibility given to 100 college students. With such disorganized data, it is hard to form an overall "picture" of the differences in hypnotic susceptibility. But by using a *frequency distribution,* large amounts of information can be neatly organized and summarized. A **frequency distribution** is made by breaking down the entire range of possible scores into classes of equal size. Next, the number of scores falling into each class is recorded. In ▲Table A.2, the raw data from Table A.1 have been condensed into a frequency distribution. Notice how much clearer the pattern of scores for the entire group becomes.

Frequency distributions are often shown *graphically* to make them more "visual." A **histogram,** or graph of a frequency distribution, is made by labeling class intervals on the *abscissa* (horizontal line) and frequencies (the number of scores in each class) on the *ordinate* (vertical line). Next, bars are drawn for each class interval; the height of each bar is de-

Descriptive statistics Mathematical tools used to describe and summarize numeric data.

Inferential statistics Mathematical tools used for decision making, for generalizing from small samples, and for drawing conclusions.

Graphical statistics Techniques for presenting numbers pictorially, often by plotting them on a graph.

Frequency distribution A table that divides an entire range of scores into a series of classes and then records the number of scores that fall into each class.

Histogram A graph of a frequency distribution in which the number of scores falling in each class is represented by vertical bars.

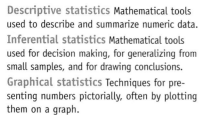

▲TABLE A.1		Raw Scores of Hypnotic Susceptibility							
55	86	52	17	61	57	84	51	16	64
22	56	25	38	35	24	54	26	37	38
52	42	59	26	21	55	40	59	25	57
91	27	38	53	19	93	25	39	52	56
66	14	18	63	59	68	12	19	62	45
47	98	88	72	50	49	96	89	71	66
50	44	71	57	90	53	41	72	56	93
57	38	55	49	87	59	36	56	48	70
33	69	50	50	60	35	67	51	50	52
11	73	46	16	67	13	71	47	25	77

termined by the number of scores in each class (◆Fig. A.1). An alternate way of graphing scores is the more familiar **frequency polygon** (◆Fig. A.2). Here, points are placed at the center of each class interval to indicate the number of scores. Then the dots are connected by straight lines.

▲TABLE A.2	Frequency Distribution of Hypnotic Susceptibility Scores

CLASS INTERVAL	NUMBER OF PERSONS IN CLASS
0–19	10
20–39	20
40–59	40
60–79	20
80–99	10

◆FIGURE A.1 *Frequency histogram of hypnotic susceptibility scores contained in Table A.2.*

◆FIGURE A.2 *Frequency polygon of hypnotic susceptibility scores contained in Table A.2.*

Measures of Central Tendency

Notice in Table A.2 that more scores fall in the range 40–59 than elsewhere. How can we show this fact? A measure of **central tendency** is simply a number describing a "typical score" around which other scores fall. A familiar measure of central tendency is the mean, or "average." But as we shall see in a moment, there are other types of "averages" that can be used. To illustrate each we need an example: ▲Table A.3 shows the raw data for an imaginary experiment in which two groups of subjects were given a test of memory. Assume that one group was given a drug that might improve memory (let's call the drug Rememberine). The second group received a placebo. Is there a difference in memory scores between the two groups? It's difficult to tell without computing an average.

The Mean

As one type of "average," the **mean** is calculated by adding all the scores for each group and then dividing by the total number of scores. Notice in Table A.3 that the means reveal a difference between the two groups.

Frequency polygon A graph of a frequency distribution in which the number of scores falling in each class is represented by points on a line.

Central tendency The tendency for a majority of scores to fall in the midrange of possible values.

Mean A measure of central tendency calculated by adding a group of scores and then dividing by the total number of scores.

▲TABLE A.3	Raw Scores on a Memory Test for Subjects Taking Rememberine or a Placebo	
SUBJECT	GROUP 1 REMEMBERINE	GROUP 2 PLACEBO
1	65	54
2	67	60
3	73	63
4	65	33
5	58	56
6	55	60
7	70	60
8	69	31
9	60	62
10	68	61
Sum	650	540
Mean	65	54
Median	66	60

$$\text{Mean} = \frac{\Sigma X}{N} \text{ or } \frac{\text{Sum of all scores, X}}{\text{number of scores}}$$

$$\text{Mean Group 1} = \frac{65 + 67 + 73 + 65 + 58 + 55 + 70 + 69 + 60 + 68}{10}$$

$$= \frac{650}{10} = 65$$

$$\text{Mean Group 2} = \frac{54 + 60 + 63 + 33 + 56 + 60 + 60 + 31 + 62 + 61}{10}$$

$$= \frac{540}{10} = 54$$

Median = the middle score or the mean of the two middle scores*

Median Group 1 = 55 58 60 65 [65 67] 68 69 70 73

$$= \frac{65 + 67}{2} = 66$$

Median Group 2 = 31 33 54 56 [60 60] 60 61 62 63

$$= \frac{60 + 60}{2} = 60$$

* ☐ indicates middle score(s)

The mean is sensitive to extremely high or low scores in a distribution. For this reason, it is not always the best measure of central tendency. (Imagine how distorted it would be to calculate average yearly incomes from a small sample of people that happened to include a multimillionaire.) In such cases, the middle score in a group of scores—called the *median*—is used instead.

The Median

The **median** is found by arranging scores from the highest to the lowest and selecting the score that falls in the middle. In other words, half the values in a group of scores fall below the median, and half fall above. Consider, for example, the following weights obtained from a small class of college students: 105, 111, 123, 126, 148, 151, 154, 162, 182. The median for the group is 148, the middle score. Of course, if there is an even number of scores, there will be no "middle score." This problem is handled by averaging the two scores that "share" the middle spot. This procedure yields a single number to serve as the median (see the bottom panel of Table A.3).

The Mode

A final measure of central tendency is the *mode.* The **mode** is simply the most frequently occurring score in a group of scores. If you were to take the time to count the scores in Table A.3, you would find that the mode of Group 1 is 65, and the mode of Group 2 is 60. The mode is usually easy to obtain. However, the mode can be an unreliable measure, especially in a small group of scores. The mode's advantage is that it gives the score actually obtained by the greatest number of people.

Measures of Variability

Let's say a researcher discovers two drugs that lower anxiety in agitated patients. However, let's also assume that one drug consistently lowers anxiety by moderate amounts, whereas the second sometimes lowers it by large amounts, sometimes has no effect, or may even increase anxiety in some patients. Overall, there is no difference in the *average* (mean) amount of anxiety reduction. Even so, an important difference exists between the two drugs. As this example shows, it is not enough to simply know the average score in a distribution. Usually, we would also like to know if scores are grouped closely together or scattered widely.

Measures of **variability** provide a single number that tells how "spread out" scores are. When the scores are widely spread, this number gets larger. When they are close together, it gets smaller. If you look again at the example in Table A.3, you will notice that the scores within each group vary widely. How can we show this fact?

The Range

The simplest way would be to use the **range,** which is the difference between the highest and lowest scores. In Group 1 of our experiment, the highest score is 73, and the lowest is 55; thus, the range is 18 (73 − 55 = 18). In Group 2, the highest score is 63, and the lowest is 31; this makes the range 32. Scores in Group 2 are more spread out than those in Group 1.

Median A of central tendency found by arranging scores from the highest to the lowest and selecting the score that falls in the middle. That is, half the values in a group of scores fall above the median and half fall below.

Mode A measure of central tendency found by identifying the most frequently occurring score in a group of scores.

Variability The tendency for a group of scores to differ in value. Measures of variability indicate the degree to which a group of scores differ from one another.

Range The difference between the highest and lowest scores in a group of scores.

The Standard Deviation

A better measure of variability is the **standard deviation** (an index of how much a typical score differs from the mean of a group of scores). To obtain the standard deviation, we find the deviation (or difference) of each score from the mean and then square it (multiply it by itself). These squared deviations are then added and averaged (the total is divided by the number of deviations). Taking the square root of this average yields the standard deviation (▲Table A.4). Notice again that the variability for Group 1 (5.4) is smaller than that for Group 2 (where the standard deviation is 11.3).

Standard Scores

A particular advantage of the standard deviation is that it can be used to "standardize" scores in a way that gives them greater meaning. For example, John and Susan both took psychology midterms but in different classes. John earned a score of 118, and Susan scored 110. Who did better? It is impossible to tell without knowing what the average score was on each test, and whether John and Susan scored at the top, middle, or bottom of their classes. We would like to have one number that gives all this information. A number that does this is the *z-score*.

To convert an original score to a **z-score,** we subtract the mean from the score. The resulting number is then divided by the standard deviation for that group of scores. To illustrate, Susan had a score of 110 in a class with a mean of 100 and a standard deviation of 10. Therefore, her z-score is +1.0 (▲Table A.5). John's score of 118 came from a class having a mean of 100 and a standard deviation of 18; thus his z-score is also +1.0 (Table A.5). Originally, it looked as if John did better on his midterm than Susan did. But we now see that relatively speaking, their scores were equivalent. Compared to other students, each was an equal distance above average.

The Normal Curve

When chance events are recorded, we find that some outcomes have a high probability and occur very often; others have a low probability and occur infrequently; still others have little probability and occur rarely. As a result, the distribution (or tally) of chance events typically resembles a *normal curve* (◆Fig. A.3). A **normal curve** is bell-shaped, with a large number of scores in the middle, tapering to very few extremely high and low scores. Most psychological traits or events are determined by the action of a large number of factors. Therefore, like chance events, measures of psychological variables tend to roughly match a normal curve. For example, direct measurement has shown such characteristics as height, memory span, and intelligence to be distributed approximately along a normal curve. In other words, many people have average height, memory ability, and intelligence. However, as we move above or below average, fewer and fewer people are found.

It is very fortunate that so many psychological variables tend to form a normal curve, because much is known about the curve. One valuable property concerns the rela-

▲*TABLE A.4*	Computation of the Standard Deviation

GROUP 1 MEAN = 65

SCORE MEAN	DEVIATION (d)	DEVIATION SQUARED (d²)
65 − 65 =	0	0
67 − 65 =	2	4
73 − 65 =	8	64
65 − 65 =	0	0
58 − 65 =	−7	49
55 − 65 =	−10	100
70 − 65 =	5	25
69 − 65 =	4	16
60 − 65 =	−5	25
68 − 65 =	3	9
		292

$$SD = \sqrt{\frac{\text{sum of d}^2}{n}} = \sqrt{\frac{292}{10}} = \sqrt{29.2} = 5.4$$

GROUP 2 MEAN = 54

SCORE MEAN	DEVIATION (d)	DEVIATION SQUARED (d²)
54 − 54 =	0	0
60 − 54 =	6	36
63 − 54 =	9	81
33 − 54 =	−21	441
56 − 54 =	2	4
60 − 54 =	6	36
60 − 54 =	6	36
31 − 54 =	−23	529
62 − 54 =	8	64
61 − 54 =	7	49
		1276

$$SD = \sqrt{\frac{\text{sum of d}^2}{n}} = \sqrt{\frac{1276}{10}} = \sqrt{127.6} = 11.3$$

▲*TABLE A.5*	Computation of a z-score

$$z = \frac{X - \bar{X}}{SD} = \text{ or } \frac{\text{score} - \text{mean}}{\text{standard deviation}}$$

Susan:
$$z = \frac{110 - 100}{10} = \frac{+10}{10} = +1.0$$

John:
$$z = \frac{118 - 100}{18} = \frac{+18}{18} = +1.0$$

Standard deviation An index of how much a typical score differs from the mean of a group of scores.

z-score A number that tells how many standard deviations above or below the mean a score is.

Normal curve A bell-shaped distribution, with a large number of scores in the middle, tapering to very few extremely high and low scores.

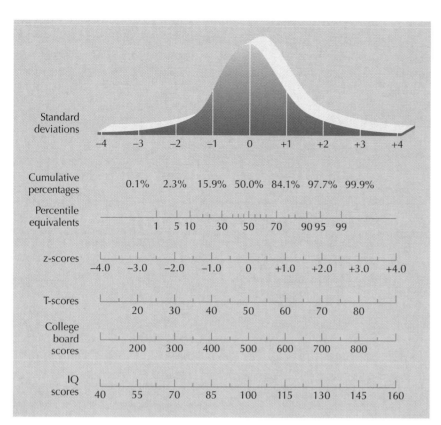

FIGURE A.3 *The normal curve. The normal curve is an idealized mathematical model. However, many measurements in psychology closely approximate a normal curve. The scales you see here show the relationship of standard deviations, z-scores, and other measures to the curve.*

tionship between the standard deviation and the normal curve. Specifically, the standard deviation measures off set proportions of the curve above and below the mean. For example, in ✦Figure A.4, notice that roughly 68 percent of all cases (IQ scores, memory scores, heights, or whatever) fall between one standard deviation above and below the mean (± 1 SD); 95 percent of all cases fall between ± 2 SD; and 99 percent of the cases can be found between ± 3 SD from the mean.

▲Table A.6 gives a more complete account of the relationship between z-scores and the percentage of cases found in a particular area of the normal curve. Notice, for example, that 93.3 percent of all cases fall below a z-score of +1.5. A z-score of 1.5 on a test (no matter what the original, or "raw," score was) would be a good performance, since roughly 93 percent of all scores fall below this mark. Relationships between the standard deviation (or z-scores) and the normal curve do not change. This makes it possible to compare various tests or groups of scores if they come from distributions that are approximately normal.

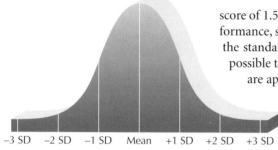

FIGURE A.4 *Relationship between the standard deviation and the normal curve.*

▲TABLE A.6	Area Under the Normal Curve as a Percentage of Total Area for a Variety of z-Scores	
Z-SCORE	PERCENTAGE OF AREA TO THE LEFT OF THIS VALUE	PERCENTAGE OF AREA TO THE RIGHT OF THIS VALUE
−3.0 SD	00.1	99.9
−2.5 SD	00.6	99.4
−2.0 SD	02.3	97.7
−1.5 SD	06.7	93.3
−1.0 SD	15.9	84.1
−0.5 SD	30.9	69.1
0.0 SD	50.0	50.0
+0.5 SD	69.1	30.9
+1.0 SD	84.1	15.9
+1.5 SD	93.3	06.7
+2.0 SD	97.7	02.3
+2.5 SD	99.4	00.6
+3.0 SD	99.9	00.1

STUDYBREAK Y *Descriptive Statistics*

RELATE

Let's say you ask 100 people how long they sleep each night and record their answers. How could you show these scores graphically?

To find the average amount of sleep for your subjects, would you prefer to know the most frequent score (the mode), the middle score (the median), or the arithmetic average (the mean)?

How could you determine how much sleep times vary? That is, would you prefer to know the highest and lowest scores (the range), or the average amount of variation (the standard deviation)?

How would you feel about receiving your scores on classroom tests in the form of z-scores?

Do you think the distribution of scores in your study of sleep would form a normal curve? Why or why not?

LEARNING CHECK

1. _____ statistics summarize numbers so they become more meaningful or easier to communicate; _____ statistics are used for decision making, generalizing, or drawing conclusions.

2. Histograms and frequency polygons are graphs of frequency distributions. T or F?

3. Three measures of central tendency are the mean, the median, and the _____.

4. If scores are placed in order, from the smallest to the largest, the median is defined as the middle score. T or F?

5. As a measure of variability, the standard deviation is defined as the difference between the highest and lowest scores. T or F?

6. A z-score of −1 tells us that a score fell one standard deviation below the mean in a group of scores. T or F?

7. In a normal curve, 99 percent of all scores can be found between +1 and −1 standard deviations from the mean. T or F?

ANSWERS

1. Descriptive, inferential 2. T 3. mode 4. T 5. F 6. T 7. F

INFERENTIAL STATISTICS— SIGNIFICANT NUMBERS

You would like to know if boys are more aggressive than girls. You observe a group of 5-year-old boys and girls on a playground. After collecting data for a week, you find that the boys committed more aggressive acts than the girls. Could this difference just be a meaningless fluctuation in aggression? Or does it show conclusively that boys are more aggressive than girls? Inferential statistics were created to answer just such questions.

As stated earlier, **inferential statistics** are techniques that allow us to make inferences. That is, they allow us to generalize from the behavior of small groups of subjects to that of the larger groups they represent. For example, let's say that a researcher studies the effects of a new therapy on a small group of depressed individuals. Is she or he interested only in these particular individuals? Usually not, since except in rare instances, psychologists seek to discover general laws of behavior that apply widely to humans and animals. Undoubtedly the researcher would like to know if the therapy holds any promise for all depressed people.

Samples and Populations

In any scientific study, we would like to observe the entire set, or **population,** of subjects, objects, or events of interest. However, this is usually impossible or impractical. Observing all Catholics, all cancer patients, or all mothers-in-law could be both impractical (since all are large populations) and impossible (since people change denominations, may be unaware of having cancer, and change their status as relatives). In such cases, **samples** (smaller cross sections of a population) are selected, and observations of the sample are used to draw conclusions about the entire population.

For any sample to be meaningful, it must be **representative.** That is, the sample group must truly reflect the membership and characteristics of the larger population. In our earlier hypothetical study of a memory drug, it would be essential for the sample of 20 people to be representative of the general population. A very important aspect of representative samples is that their members are chosen at **random.** In other words, each member of the population must have an equal chance of being included in the sample.

Population An entire group of animals, people, or objects belonging to a particular category (for example, all college students or all married women).

Sample A smaller subpart of a population.

Representative sample A small, randomly selected part of a larger population that accurately reflects characteristics of the whole population.

Random selection Choosing a sample so that each member of the population has an equal chance of being included in the sample.

Significant Differences

In our imaginary drug experiment, we found that the average memory score was higher for the group given the drug than it was for persons who didn't take the drug (the placebo group). Certainly this result is interesting, but could it have occurred by chance? If two groups were repeatedly tested (with neither receiving any drug), their average memory scores would sometimes differ. How much must two means differ before we can consider the difference "real" (not due to chance)?

Notice that the question is similar to one discussed earlier: How many tails in a row must we obtain when flipping a coin before we can conclude that the coin is biased? In the case of the coin, we noted that obtaining 5 tails in a row is a rare event. Thus, it became reasonable to assume that the coin was biased. Of course, it is possible to get 5 tails in a row when flipping an honest coin. But since this outcome is unlikely, we have good reason to suspect that something other than chance (a loaded coin, for instance) caused the results. Similar reasoning is used in tests of statistical significance.

Tests of **statistical significance** provide an estimate of how often experimental results could have occurred by chance alone. The results of a significance test are stated as a probability. This probability gives the odds that the observed difference was due to chance. In psychology, any experimental result that could have occurred by chance 5 times (or less) out of 100 (in other words, a probability of .05 or less) is considered *significant*. In our memory experiment, the probability is .025 ($p = .025$) that the group means would differ as they do by chance alone. This allows us to conclude with reasonable certainty that the drug actually did improve memory scores.

CORRELATION—RATING RELATIONSHIPS

Psychologists are very interested in detecting relationships between events: Are children from single-parent families more likely to misbehave at school? Is wealth related to happiness? Is there a relationship between childhood exposure to lead and IQ at age 10? Is the chance of having a heart attack related to having a hostile personality? All of these are questions about correlation.

Many of the statements that psychologists make about behavior do not result from the use of experimental methods. Rather, they come from keen observations and measures of existing phenomena. A psychologist might note, for example, that the higher a couple's socioeconomic and educational status, the smaller the number of children they are likely to have. Or that grades in high school are related to how well a person is likely to do in college. Or even that as rainfall levels increase within a given metropolitan area, crime rates decline. In these instances, we are dealing with the fact that two variables are **co-relating** (varying together in some orderly fashion).

The simplest way of visualizing a correlation is to construct a **scatter diagram**. In a scatter diagram, two measures (grades in high school and grades in college, for instance) are obtained. One measure is indicated by the X axis and the second by the Y axis. The scatter diagram plots the intersection (crossing) of each pair of measurements as a single point. Many such measurement pairs give pictures like those shown in ✦Figure A.5.

(a) r = +1.00
(b) r = 0.91
(c) r = 0.56
(d) r = 0.00
(e) r = −0.66
(f) r = −1.00

✦FIGURE A.5 *Scatter diagrams showing various degrees of relationship for a positive, zero, and negative correlation.*

Statistical significance The degree to which an event (such as the results of an experiment) is unlikely to have occurred by chance alone.

Correlation The existence of a consistent, systematic relationship between two events, measures, or variables.

Scatter diagram A graph that plots the intersection of paired measures; that is, the points at which paired X and Y measures cross.

Relationships

Figure A.5 also shows scatter diagrams of three basic kinds of relationships between variables (or measures). Graphs A, B, and C show *positive relationships* of varying strength. As you can see, in a **positive relationship,** increases in the X measure (or score) are matched by increases on the Y measure (or score). An example would be finding that higher IQ scores (X) are associated with higher college grades (Y). A **zero correlation** suggests that no relationship exists between two measures (see graph D). This might be the result of comparing subjects' hat sizes (X) to their college grades (Y). Graphs E and F both show a **negative relationship** (or correlation). Notice that as values of one measure increase, those of the second become smaller. An example might be the relationship between amount of alcohol consumed and scores on a test of coordination: Higher alcohol levels are correlated with lower coordination scores.

The Correlation Coefficient

The strength of a correlation can also be expressed as a **coefficient of correlation.** This coefficient is simply a number falling somewhere between +1.00 and −1.00. If the number is zero or close to zero, it indicates a weak or non-existent relationship. If the correlation is +1.00, a **perfect positive relationship** exists; if the correlation is −1.00, a **perfect negative relationship** has been discovered. The most commonly used correlation coefficient is called the Pearson *r*. Calculation of the Pearson *r* is relatively simple, as shown in ▲Table A.7. (The numbers shown are hypothetical.)

As stated in Chapter 1, correlations in psychology are rarely perfect. Most fall somewhere between zero and plus or minus 1. The closer the correlation coefficient is to +1.00

▲TABLE A.7	**IQ and Grade Point Average for Computing Pearson *r***				
STUDENT NO.	IQ (X)	GRADE POINT AVERAGE (Y)	X SCORE SQUARED (X²)	Y SCORE SQUARED (Y²)	X TIMES Y (XY)
1	110	1.0	12,100	1.00	110.0
2	112	1.6	12,544	2.56	179.2
3	118	1.2	13,924	1.44	141.6
4	119	2.1	14,161	4.41	249.9
5	122	2.6	14,884	6.76	317.2
6	125	1.8	15,625	3.24	225.0
7	127	2.6	16,124	6.76	330.2
8	130	2.0	16,900	4.00	260.0
9	132	3.2	17,424	10.24	422.4
10	134	2.6	17,956	6.76	348.4
11	136	3.0	18,496	9.00	408.0
12	138	3.6	19,044	12.96	496.8
Total	1503	27.3	189,187	69.13	3488.7

$$r = \frac{\Sigma XY - \frac{(\Sigma X)(\Sigma Y)}{N}}{\sqrt{\left[\Sigma X^2 - \frac{(\Sigma X)^2}{N}\right]\left[\Sigma Y^2 - \frac{(\Sigma Y)^2}{N}\right]}}$$

$$= \frac{3488.7 - \frac{1503(27.3)}{12}}{\sqrt{\left[189,187 - \frac{(1503)^2}{2}\right]\left[69.13 - \frac{(27.3)^2}{12}\right]}}$$

$$= \frac{69.375}{81.088} = 0.856 = 0.86$$

Adapted from Pagano, 1981.

Positive relationship A mathematical relationship in which increases in one measure are matched by increases in the other (or decreases correspond with decreases).

Zero correlation The absence of a (linear) mathematical relationship between two measures.

Negative relationship A mathematical relationship in which increases in one measure are matched by decreases in the other.

Coefficient of correlation A statistical index ranging from −1.00 to +1.00 that indicates the direction and degree of correlation.

Perfect positive relationship A mathematical relationship in which the correlation between two measures is +1.00.

Perfect negative relationship A mathematical relationship in which the correlation between two measures is −1.00.

or −1.00, the stronger the relationship. An interesting example of some typical correlations is provided by a study that compared the IQs of adopted children with the IQs of their biological mothers. At age 4, the children's IQs correlated .28 with their mothers' IQs. By age 7, the correlation was .35. And by age 13, it had grown to .38.

Prediction

Correlations often provide highly useful information. For instance, it is valuable to know that there is a correlation between cigarette smoking and lung cancer rates. Another example is the fact that higher consumption of alcohol during pregnancy is correlated with lower birth weight and a higher rate of birth defects. There is a correlation between the number of recent life stresses experienced and the likelihood of emotional disturbance. Many more examples could be cited, but the point is, correlations help us to identify relationships that are worth knowing.

Correlations are particularly valuable for making *predictions*. If we know that two measures are correlated, and we know a person's score on one measure, we can predict his or her score on the other. For example, most colleges have formulas that use multiple correlations to decide which applicants have the best chances for success. Usually the formula includes such predictors as high school GPA, teacher ratings, extracurricular activities, and scores on the *Scholastic Assessment Test* (SAT) or some similar test. Although no single predictor is perfectly correlated with success in college, together the various predictors correlate highly and provide a useful technique for screening applicants.

There is an interesting "trick" you can do with correlations that you may find useful. It works like this: If you *square* the correlation coefficient (multiply *r* by itself), you will get a number telling the **percent of variance** (amount of variation in scores) accounted for by the correlation. For example, the correlation between IQ scores and college grade point average is .5. Multiplying .5 times .5 gives .25, or 25 percent. This means that 25 percent of the variation in college grades is accounted for by knowing IQ scores. In other words, with a correlation of .5, college grades are "squeezed" into an oval like the one shown in graph C of Figure A.5. IQ scores take away some of the possible variation in corresponding grade point averages. If there were no correlation between IQ and grades, grades would be completely free to vary, as shown in Figure A.5, graph D.

Along the same line, a correlation of +1.00 or −1.00 means that 100 percent of the variation in the Y measure is accounted for by knowing the X measure: If you know a person's X score, you can tell exactly what the Y score is. An example that comes close to this state of affairs is the high correlation (.86) between the IQs of identical twins. In any group of identical twins, 74 percent of the variation in the "Y" twins' IQs is accounted for by knowing the IQs of their siblings (the "X's").

Correlation and Causation

It is very important to recognize that finding a correlation between two measures does not automatically mean that one causes the other: Correlation does not demonstrate causation. When a correlation exists, the best we can say is that two variables are related. Of course, this does not mean that it is impossible for two correlated variables to have a cause-and-effect relationship. Rather, it means that we cannot *conclude*, solely on the basis of correlation, that a causal link exists. To gain greater confidence that a cause-and-effect relationship exists, an experiment must be performed (see Chapter 1).

Often, two correlated measures are related as a result of the influence of a third variable. For example, we might observe that the more hours students devote to studying, the better their grades. Although it is tempting to conclude that more studying produces (causes) better grades, it is possible (indeed, it is probable) that grades and the amount of study time are both related to the amount of motivation or interest a student has.

The difference between cause-and-effect data and data that reveal a relationship of unknown origin is one that should not be forgotten. Since we rarely run experiments in daily life, the information on which we act is largely correlational. This should make us more humble and more tentative in the confidence with which we make pronouncements about human behavior.

Percent of variance A portion of the total amount of variation in a group of scores.

Causation The act of causing some effect.

STUDYBREAK ⓨ *Inferential Statistics*

RELATE

Informally, you have probably inferred something about a population of people based on the small sample you have observed directly. How could statistics improve the accuracy of your inferences?

If you were trying to test whether a drug causes birth defects, what level of statistical significance would you use? If you were doing a psychology experiment, what level would you be comfortable with?

See if you can identify at least one positive relationship and one negative relationship involving human behavior that you have observed. How strong to you think the correlation would be in each case? What correlation coefficient would you expect to see?

A woman you know drinks more coffee in the winter than she does in the summer. She also has more colds in the winter. She decides to reduce the amount of coffee she drinks to help prevent colds. What can you tell her about correlation and causation?

LEARNING CHECK

1. In inferential statistics, observations of a _____ are used to make inferences and draw conclusions about an entire _____.
2. A representative sample can be obtained by selecting members of the sample at _____.
3. If the results of an experiment could have occurred by chance alone less than 25 times out of 100, the result is considered statistically significant. T or F?
4. A scatter diagram can be used to plot and visualize a _____ between two groups of scores.
5. In a negative relationship, increases in X scores correspond to decreases in Y scores. T or F?
6. A perfect positive correlation exists when the correlation coefficient is 0.00. T or F?
7. It is important to remember that correlation does not demonstrate _____.

ANSWERS

1. sample, population 2. random 3. F 4. correlation 5. T 6. F 7. causation

APPENDIX IN REVIEW

Major Points

- The results of psychological studies are often expressed as numbers, which must be summarized and interpreted before they have any meaning.
- Summarizing numbers visually, by using various types of graphs, makes it easier to see trends and patterns in the results of psychological investigations.
- We usually want to know the "average" of a group of scores as well as how much they vary.
- Many psychological measures produce scores that form a normal curve. This is useful because the characteristics of normal curves are well known.
- Some statistical techniques can be used to generalize results from samples to populations, to draw conclusions, and to tell if the results of a study could have occurred by chance.
- When there is a correlation, or consistent relationship, between scores on two measures, knowing a person's score on one measure allows us to predict his or her score on the second measure.

Summary

What are descriptive statistics?

- Descriptive statistics organize and summarize numbers.
- Graphical statistics, such as histograms and frequency polygons, are used to represent numbers pictorially.

How are statistics used to identify an average score?

- Measures of central tendency define the "typical score" in a group of scores.
- The mean is found by adding all the scores in a group and then dividing by the total number of scores.
- The median is found by arranging a group of scores from the highest to the lowest and selecting the middle score.
- The mode is the score that occurs most frequently in a group of scores.

What statistics do psychologists use to measure how much scores differ from one another?

- Measures of variability provide a number that shows how much scores vary.
- The range is the difference between the highest score and the lowest score in a group of scores.
- The standard deviation shows how much, on average, all the scores in a group differ from the mean.
- To change an original score into a standard score (or z-score), you must subtract the mean from the score and then divide the result by the standard deviation.
- Standard scores (z-scores) tell, in standard deviation units, how far above or below the mean a score is. This allows meaningful comparisons between scores from different groups.

- Scores that form a normal curve are easy to interpret because the properties of the normal curve are well known.

What are inferential statistics?

- Inferential statistics are used to make decisions, to generalize from samples, and to draw conclusions.
- Most studies in psychology are based on samples. Findings from representative samples are assumed to also apply to entire populations.
- In psychology experiments, differences in the average performance of groups could occur purely by chance. Tests of statistical significance tell us if the observed differences between groups are common or rare. If a difference is large enough to be improbable, it suggests that the results did not occur by chance alone.

How are correlations used in psychology?

- Pairs of scores that vary together in an orderly fashion are said to be correlated.
- The relationship between two variables or measures can be positive or negative.

- Correlation coefficients tell how strongly two groups of scores are related.
- Correlation alone does not demonstrate cause-and-effect links between variables or measures.

 Interactive Learning

PSYCHOLOGY: A JOURNEY COMPANION WEB SITE Online quizzes, flash cards, and other helpful study aids for this text. *www.psychology.wadsworth.com/coon_journey2e*

STATISTICS TO USE If you enter a series of numbers, this site will calculate basic descriptive statistics and more advanced inferential statistics.

INFOTRAC COLLEGE EDITION For recent articles related to inferential statistics, use Key Words search for NORMAL CURVE.

PSYCHNOW! 1c. Research Methods

Glossary

Ablation Surgical removal of tissue.

Absolute threshold The minimum amount of physical energy necessary to produce a sensation.

Accommodation (perceptual) Changes in the shape of the lens of the eye that serve to focus objects at varying distances.

Accommodation (Piaget) The modification of existing mental patterns to fit new demands.

Acetylcholine The neurotransmitter released by neurons to activate muscles.

Achieved role A role that is assumed voluntarily.

Achievement motivation A need for success or the attainment of excellence.

Acquisition The period in conditioning during which a response is reinforced.

Action component That part of an attitude consisting of how one tends to act toward the object of the attitude.

Action potential The nerve impulse, which is a rapid change in electrical charge across the cell membrane.

Activation As reflected in facial expressions, the degree of arousal experienced by the person making the expression.

Activation-synthesis hypothesis Theory that relates dream content to motor commands in the brain, which are made, but not carried out, during sleep.

Actor In making attributions, the person whose behavior is being interpreted.

Actor-observer bias When making attributions, the tendency to attribute the behavior of others to internal causes while attributing one's own behavior to external causes (situations and circumstances).

Acuity That aspect of visual perception having to do with the sharpness or resolution of images.

Acupuncture The Chinese medical art of relieving pain and treating illness by inserting thin needles at various points on the body.

Acute stress disorder Psychological disturbance lasting up to 1 month following stresses, such as natural disasters or military combat, that would produce anxiety in anyone who experienced them.

Adaptation level An internal or mental "average" or "medium" point that is used to judge amounts.

Adaptive behaviors (emotion) Actions that aid humans and animals in their attempts to survive and adapt to changing conditions.

Adaptive behaviors (retardation) Basic skills and actions considered necessary for self-care and for dealing successfully with the environment.

Addiction Development of physical dependence on a drug such that craving and physical discomfort (withdrawal symptoms) occur in its absence.

Adjustment disorder Emotional disturbance caused by stressors within the range of common experience; stress is ongoing and produces anxiety and physical symptoms.

Adolescence The socially defined period between childhood and adulthood.

Adrenal glands Endocrine glands whose hormones arouse the body, regulate salt balance, adjust the body to stress, and affect sexual functioning.

Adrenaline A hormone produced by the adrenal glands that tends, in general, to arouse the body.

Affect Pertaining to emotion or feelings.

Affectional needs One's emotional needs in general but, especially, needs for love, attention, and affection.

Afterimage A visual sensation that persists after a stimulus is removed.

Ageism Discrimination or prejudice based on a person's age.

Aggression Any action carried out with the intent of harming another person.

Aggression cues Stimuli or signals that are associated with aggression and tend to elicit it.

Agnosia A disturbance in the ability to perceive the meaning of stimuli, such as words, objects, or pictures.

Agoraphobia (without panic) Persons fear that something extremely embarrassing will happen to them if they leave the house or enter unfamiliar situations.

Alarm reaction First stage of the G.A.S., during which bodily resources are mobilized to cope with a stressor.

All-or-nothing thinking Classifying objects or events as absolutely right or wrong, good or bad, acceptable or unacceptable, and so forth.

Altered state of consciousness A condition of awareness distinctly different in quality or pattern from waking consciousness.

Alzheimer's disease An age-related disease characterized by memory loss, mental confusion, and in its later stages, a nearly total loss of mental abilities.

Ambiguous stimuli Patterns that allow more than one perceptual organization.

Ambivalence Mixed positive and negative feelings or simultaneous attraction and repulsion.

Ambivalent attachment An emotional bond marked by conflicting feelings of affection, anger, and emotional turmoil.

American Sign Language A language system of hand gestures used by deaf and hearing-impaired persons.

Ames room An intentionally distorted room that interrupts perceptual constancies.

Amnesia Loss of memory (partial or complete) for past events and, especially, loss of memory for one's identity.

Amphetamines A class of synthetic drugs that have stimulant effects on the nervous system.

Anagrams Test A test of creativity in which subjects try to make as many new words as possible from the letters in a given word.

Anal stage In Freud's theory, the psychosexual stage corresponding roughly to the period of toilet training (age 1 to 3) and characterized by a preoccupation with the process of elimination.

Androgen Any of a number of male sex hormones, especially testosterone.

Androgyny The presence of both "masculine" and "feminine" traits in a single person (as masculinity and femininity are traditionally defined within one's culture).

Animal model In research, an animal whose behavior is used to discover principles that may apply to human behavior.

Anorexia nervosa Active self-starvation or a sustained loss of appetite that has psychological origins.

Anosmia Loss or impairment of the sense of smell.

Antecedents Events that precede a response.

Anterograde amnesia Loss of the ability to form or retrieve memories for events that occur after an injury or trauma.

Anthropomorphic fallacy The error of attributing human thoughts, feelings, or motives to animals.

Antidepressant A mood-elevating drug.

Antipsychotic A drug that, in addition to having tranquilizing effects, also tends to reduce hallucinations and delusional thinking.

Antisocial personality A person who seems to lack a conscience; is emotionally shallow, impulsive, and selfish; and tends to manipulate others; also referred to as a sociopath or psychopath.

Anxiety Apprehension, dread, or uneasiness similar to fear but based on an unclear threat.

Anxiety disorder A disorder characterized by disruptive feelings of fear, apprehension, or anxiety or by distortions in behavior that are anxiety related.

Anxiety reduction hypothesis An explanation of the self-defeating nature of many avoidance responses that emphasizes the immediate reinforcing effects of relief from anxiety.

Aphasia A speech disturbance resulting from damage to language areas on the temporal lobes of the brain.

Apparent distance hypothesis An explanation of the moon illusion stating that the horizon seems more distant than the night sky overhead, because there are more depth cues near the horizon.

Applied psychology The use of psychological principles and research methods to solve practical problems.

Applied research Scientific study undertaken to solve immediate practical problems.

Approach-approach conflict A condition in which a person or animal must choose between two positive, or desirable, alternatives.

Approach-avoidance conflict An unpleasant condition in which a person or animal is simultaneously attracted to and repelled by the same goal.

Arousal The overall level of excitation or activation in a person or animal.

Arousal theory A theory of motivation that assumes people prefer to maintain "ideal," or comfortable, levels of arousal.

Artificial intelligence Any artificial system (often a computer program) that is capable of human-like problem solving or skilled responding.

Ascribed role A role that is assigned to a person; a role one has no choice about playing.

Assertiveness training Instruction in how to be self-assertive.

Assessment Evaluation or measurement.

Assimilation In Piaget's theory, the application of existing mental patterns to new situations (that is, the new situation is assimilated to existing mental schemes).

Association cortex All areas of the cerebral cortex that are not specifically sensory or motor in function.

Astigmatism Defects in the cornea, lens, or eye that cause some areas of vision to be out of focus.

Astrology False system based on the belief that human behavior is influenced by the position of stars and planets.

Attention Orienting toward or focusing on some stimulus.

Attitude A learned tendency to respond to people, objects, or institutions in a positive or negative way.

Attitude scale A collection of attitude statements with which respondents indicate agreement or disagreement.

Attribution The process of making inferences about the causes of one's own behavior and that of others. In emotion, the process of attributing perceived arousal to a particular source.

Auditory area Sites on the temporal lobes where auditory information registers.

Auditory ossicles The three small bones that link the eardrum to the inner ear.

Authenticity In Carl Rogers's terms, the ability of a therapist to be genuine and honest regarding his or her feelings.

Authoritarian parents Parents who enforce rigid rules and demand strict obedience to authority.

Authoritarian personality A personality pattern characterized by rigidity, inhibition, prejudice, and an excessive concern with power, authority, and obedience.

Authoritative parents Parents who supply firm and consistent guidance combined with love and affection.

Autonomic nervous system The neural system that connects the brain with the internal organs and glands.

Autonomy A freedom from dependence on external authority or the opinions of others.

Aversion therapy Suppression of an undesirable response by associating it with aversive (painful or uncomfortable) stimuli.

Aversive stimulus Any stimulus that produces discomfort or displeasure.

Avoidance learning Learning that occurs when making a particular response delays or prevents the onset of a painful or unpleasant stimulus.

Avoidance-avoidance conflict An unpleasant condition requiring a choice between two negative, or mutually undesirable, alternatives.

Avoidant attachment An emotional bond marked by a tendency to resist commitment to others.

Axon A thin fiber that conducts information away from the cell body of a neuron.

Babbling The repetition by infants of meaningless language sounds (including both vowel and consonant sounds).

Bait shyness An unwillingness or hesitation on the part of animals to eat a particular food; often caused by the presence of a taste aversion.

Barbiturate One of a large group of sedative drugs.

Barnum effect The tendency to consider a personal description accurate if it is stated in very general terms.

Base rate The basic rate at which an event occurs over time; the basic probability of an event.

Baseline A record of the initial frequency of a target behavior.

Basic needs The first four levels of needs in Maslow's hierarchy; lower needs tend to be more potent than higher needs.

Basic research Scientific inquiry done to advance basic knowledge, not to solve a practical problem.

Basic suggestion effect The tendency of hypnotized persons to carry out suggested actions as if they were involuntary.

Behavior modification The application of learning principles to change human behavior, especially maladaptive behavior.

Behavior therapy The use of learning principles to make constructive changes in behavior.

Behavioral assessment Recording the frequency of various behaviors.

Behavioral medicine The study of behavioral factors associated with physical illness and its treatment.

Behavioral personality theory Any model of personality that emphasizes observable behavior, stimuli and responses, and the impact of learning.

Behavioral risk factors Behaviors that increase the chances of disease or injury or that shorten life expectancy.

Behaviorism The study of overt, observable behavior.

Bem Sex Role Inventory (BSRI) A list of 60 personal traits including "masculine," "feminine," and "neutral" traits; used to rate one's degree of androgyny.

Beta-endorphin A natural chemical produced by the pituitary gland that is similar in structure and painkilling effect to opiate drugs such as morphine.

Biased sample A sample that does not accurately reflect the population from which it was drawn.

Bibliotherapy Use of books to impart helpful information, either alone or as an adjunct to other forms of therapy.

Binge drinking Consuming five or more drinks in a short time (four drinks for women).

Binocular depth cues Depth cues that function only when both eyes are used.

Biochemical abnormality A disturbance of the body's chemical systems, especially in brain chemicals or neurotransmitters.

Biofeedback Information about bodily activities that aids voluntary regulation of bodily states.

Biological determinism Belief that behavior is controlled by biological processes, such as heredity or evolution.

Biological predisposition The presumed biological readiness of humans to learn certain skills, such as how to use language.

Biological rhythm Any cycle of biological activity, such as sleep and waking cycles or changes in body temperature.

Biopsychologist A psychologist who studies the relationship between behavior and biological processes, especially activity in the nervous system.

Biopsychology The study of biological processes as they relate to behavior.

Bipolar disorders Emotional disorders involving both depression and extremely elevated or manic moods and behavior.

Bipolar I disorder A mood disorder in which a person has episodes of mania and also periods of deep depression.

Bipolar II disorder A mood disorder in which a person is mostly depressed (sad, despondent, guilt ridden) but has also had one or more mildly manic episodes.

Birth injury Any injury or damage that occurs to an infant during delivery.

Bisexual A person romantically and erotically attracted to both men and women.

Blind spot A portion of the retina lacking visual receptors (the point where the optic nerve leaves the eye).

Bottom-up processing Organizing perceptions by beginning with low-level features.

Brain dominance The language-producing cerebral hemisphere.

Brainstem The lowest portions of the brain, including the cerebellum, medulla, and reticular formation.

Brainstorming Method of creative thinking that separates the production and evaluation of ideas.

Brainwashing Engineered or forced attitude change involving a captive audience.

Branching program A computer program that gives learners corrective information and exercises based on the nature of their errors.

Brightness The intensity of light reflected from or emanating from a surface.

Brightness constancy The apparent (or relative) brightness of various objects remains the same as long as each object is illuminated by the same amount of light.

Broca's area A language area in the brain related to grammar and pronunciation.

Bulimia nervosa Excessive eating (gorging) usually followed by self-induced vomiting and/or taking laxatives.

Burnout A job-related condition of mental, physical, and emotional exhaustion.

Caffeine A natural drug with stimulant properties; found in coffee, tea, and chocolate and added to artificial beverages and medicines.

Caffeinism Excessive consumption of caffeine, leading to dependence and a variety of physical and psychological complaints.

Camouflage Designs that break up figure-ground organization, making objects more difficult to see.

Cannabis sativa The hemp plant, from whose leaves and flowers marijuana and hashish are derived.

Cannon-Bard theory According to this theory, emotional feelings and bodily arousal occur simultaneously and both begin with activity in the thalamus.

Cardinal trait A personality trait so basic or powerful that all or most of a person's activities spring from existence of the trait.

Caregiving styles Identifiable patterns of parental caretaking and interaction with children.

Caretaker speech An exaggerated pattern of speech used by adults when talking to infants.

Case study An intensive investigation of the behavior of a single person.

Cataplexy A sudden temporary paralysis of the muscles.

Catatonic episode Period of extreme stupor, immobility, and unresponsiveness.

Catatonic schizophrenia Schizophrenia marked by stupor, rigidity, unresponsiveness, posturing, mutism, and sometimes, agitated, purposeless behavior.

Causation The act of causing some effect.

Central nervous system The brain and spinal cord.

Central traits The core traits that characterize an individual personality.

Cerebellum A cauliflower-shaped projection at the base of the brain that controls posture and coordination.

Cerebral cortex The layer of tissue that forms the outer layer and surface of the cerebrum; the cerebral cortex is responsible for basic sensory and motor functions as well as higher mental processes in humans.

Cerebral hemispheres The right and left halves of the cerebrum.

Cerebrum The two large hemispheres that cover the upper part of the brain.

Character Personal characteristics that have been judged or evaluated; a person's desirable or undesirable qualities.

Chemical senses Senses, such as smell and taste, that respond to chemical molecules.

Chemotherapy Use of psychoactive drugs to treat mental or emotional disturbances.

Chromosomes Thread-like structures ("colored bodies") in the nucleus of each cell that are made up of DNA, which carries the genes. Normal human cells have 23 pairs of chromosomes (46 total).

Chronological age A person's age in years.

Circadian rhythms Cyclical changes in bodily function and arousal that vary on a schedule approximating one 24-hour day.

Clairvoyance The purported ability to perceive events at a distance or through physical barriers.

Classical conditioning A basic form of learning in which existing reflex responses come to be elicited by new stimuli (also known as respondent conditioning).

Client-centered therapy A non-directive therapy based on drawing insights from conscious thoughts and feelings; emphasizes accepting one's true self.

Clinical psychologist A specialist who treats or does research on psychological problems.

Clinical study An intensive investigation of the behavior of a single person, especially one suffering from some injury, disease, or disorder.

Closure Gestalt term for the perceptual tendency to complete figures by "closing" or ignoring small gaps.

Cocaine A crystalline drug derived from coca leaves; used as a central nervous system stimulant and local anesthetic.

Cochlea The snail-shaped organ that makes up the inner ear.

Coefficient of correlation A statistical index ranging from -1.00 to $+1.00$ that indicates the direction and degree of correlation.

Cognition The process of thinking, knowing, or mentally processing information.

Cognitive-behavioral therapy The use of learning principles to change maladaptive thoughts, beliefs, and feelings that underlie emotional and behavioral problems.

Cognitive behaviorism An approach that combines behavioral principles with cognition (perception, thinking, anticipation) to explain behavior.

Cognitive dissonance An uncomfortable clash between self-image, thoughts, beliefs, attitudes, or perceptions and one's behavior.

Cognitive learning Higher-level learning involving thinking, knowing, understanding, and anticipation.

Cognitive map A mental image of an area (building, city, country) that guides movement from one location to another.

Cognitive psychology The study of human thinking, knowing, understanding, and information processing.

Cognitive therapy The use of learning principles and other methods to change maladaptive thoughts, beliefs, and feelings.

Color blindness A total inability to perceive colors.

Color weakness An inability to fully distinguish some colors from others.

Common traits Personality traits that are shared by most members of a particular culture.

Communicator In persuasion, the person presenting arguments or information.

Community health campaign A community-wide education program that provides information about factors that affect health and what to do about them.

Community mental health center A facility offering a wide range of mental health services, such as prevention, counseling, consultation, and crisis intervention.

Community psychology Use of community resources to promote mental health and treat or prevent mental health problems.

Comparative psychology The study and comparison of the behavior of different species, especially animals.

Compensation Counteracting a real or imagined weakness by emphasizing desirable traits or by seeking to excel in other areas.

Competence As a factor in interpersonal attraction, the degree of general ability or proficiency a person displays.

Compliance Bending to the requests of a person who has little or no authority or other form of social power.

Compulsion An act an individual feels driven to repeat, often against his or her will.

Computer simulations Computer programs that mimic some aspect of human thinking, decision making, or problem solving.

Computer-assisted instruction (CAI) Learning aided by computer-presented information and exercises.

Concentrative meditation Mental exercise based on focusing attention on a single target of contemplation.

Concept A generalized idea representing a class of related objects or events.

Concept formation The process of classifying information into meaningful categories by direct experience, rule learning, or exposure to prototypes (idealized models).

Conceptual rule A formal rule by which one may decide whether an object or event is an example of a particular concept.

Concrete operational stage Period of cognitive development during which children become able to use the concepts of time, space, volume, and number, but in ways that remain simplified and concrete.

Condensation Combining several people, objects, or events into a single dream image.

Conditional statement A statement that contains a qualification, often of the *if-then* form.

Conditioned aversion A learned dislike or conditioned negative emotional response to some stimulus.

Conditioned emotional response An emotional response that has been linked to a previously non-emotional stimulus by classical conditioning.

Conditioned response A reflex response linked to a new stimulus through learning.

Conditioned stimulus A previously neutral stimulus that acquires the capacity to evoke a response by being paired with an unconditioned stimulus.

Conditioning chamber An apparatus designed for the study of operant conditioning in animals; a Skinner box.

Conditions of worth Internal standards used to judge the value of one's thoughts, actions, feelings, or experiences.

Conduction deafness Poor transfer of sounds from the eardrum to the inner ear.

Cones Visual receptors for colors and daylight visual acuity.

Conflict A stressful condition that occurs when a person must choose between incompatible or contradictory alternatives.

Conformity Bringing one's behavior into agreement or harmony with norms or with the behavior of others in a group.

Confrontation In existential therapy, the process of confronting clients with their own values and with the need to take responsibility for the quality of their existence.

Congenital problems Problems or defects that originate during prenatal development.

Conjunctive concept A concept defined by the presence of two or more specific features. (For example, to qualify as an example of the concept an object must be both red *and* triangular.)

Connector neuron A nerve cell that serves as a link between two others.

Connotative meaning The subjective, personal, or emotional meaning of a word or concept.

Conscience In Freudian theory, the part of the superego that causes guilt when its standards are not met.

Conscious Region of the mind that includes all mental contents (thoughts, images, feelings, memories, and so on) a person is aware of at any given moment.

Consciousness A person's experience of mental awareness, including current sensations, perceptions, memories, and feelings.

Consensus The degree to which people respond alike. In making attributions, consensus implies that responses are externally caused.

Consequences Effects that follow a response.

Consequences Test A test of creativity based on listing the consequences that would follow a basic change in the world.

Conservation In Piaget's theory, mastery of the concept that the volume of matter remains unchanged (is conserved) even when the shape or appearance of objects changes.

Consistency When making attributions, noticing that a behavior changes very little on different occasions.

Consolidation Process by which relatively permanent memories are formed in the brain.

Constructive processing Reorganizing memories on the basis of logic, inference, or the addition of new information.

Context Information surrounding a stimulus that gives meaning to the stimulus; with regard to behavior, the social situation, behavioral setting, or other surrounding circumstances in which an action takes place.

Continuous reinforcement A schedule of reinforcement in which every correct response is followed by a reinforcer.

Control (experimental) Eliminating, identifying, or equalizing all factors in an experiment that could affect the outcome.

Control (stress) With regard to stress, the ability to exert some influence over one's circumstances.

Control group In an experiment, subjects exposed to all conditions *except* the independent variable.

Control questions In a polygraph exam, questions that almost always provoke anxiety, thus providing a baseline of emotional responsiveness.

Conventional moral reasoning Moral thinking based on a desire to please others or to follow accepted rules and values.

Convergence The simultaneous turning inward of the two eyes as they focus on nearby objects.

Convergent thought Thinking directed toward discovery of a single established correct answer; conventional thinking.

Conversion disorder A symptom or disability that appears to be physical but that actually results from anxiety, stress, or emotional conflict.

Cooing Spontaneous repetition of vowel sounds by infants.

Coping statements Reassuring, self-enhancing statements that are used to stop self-critical thinking.

Corpus callosum The large bundle of fibers connecting the right and left cerebral hemispheres.

Correlation An orderly relationship between two events, measures, or variables.

Correlational study A non-experimental study designed to measure the degree of relationship (if any) between two or more events, measures, or variables.

Corticalization An increase in the relative size of the cerebral cortex.

Counseling psychologist A specialist who treats milder emotional and behavioral disturbances.

Counselor An adviser who helps people solve problems related to marriage, career, schoolwork, or the like.

Counterirritation Using mild pain to block more intense or long-lasting pain.

Courtesy bias The tendency to give "polite" answers to avoid hurting an interviewer's feelings.

Covert behavior A response that is internal or hidden from view.

Covert reinforcement Using positive imagery to reinforce desired behavior.

Covert sensitization Use of aversive imagery to reduce the occurrence of an undesired response.

Cranial nerve One of 12 major nerves that leave the brain without passing through the spinal cord.

Created image A mental image that has been assembled or invented rather than simply remembered.

Critical situations Situations during childhood that are capable of leaving a lasting imprint on personality.

Critical thinking An ability to evaluate, compare, analyze, critique, and synthesize information.

Cross-cultural psychologist A psychologist who studies the ways in which culture affects human behavior.

CT scan Computed tomography scan; a computer-enhanced X-ray image of the brain.

Cue External stimuli or signs that guide responses, especially those that signal the likely presence or absence of reinforcement.

Cult A group that professes great devotion to some person, idea, or thing.

Cultural psychologist A psychologist who studies the ways in which culture affects human behavior.

Cultural relativity Perceptions and judgments made relative to the values of one's culture.

Cultural values The values attached to various objects and activities by people in a given culture.

Culture An ongoing pattern of life, characterizing a society at a particular stage in its development or at a given point in history.

Culture-fair test A test (such as an intelligence test) designed to minimize the importance of skills and knowledge that may be more common in some cultures than in others.

Curare A drug that competes with acetylcholine, causing paralysis.

Curiosity drive A hypothesized drive assumed to underlie a wide range of investigative and stimulus-seeking behaviors.

Curve of forgetting A graph that shows the amount of memorized information remembered after varying lengths of time.

Curvilinear relationship A relationship that forms a curved line when graphed.

Cyclothymic disorder Moderate manic and depressive behavior that persists for 2 years or more.

Dark adaptation The process by which the eye adapts to low illumination and becomes more light sensitive, principally by a shift to rod vision.

Data Observed facts or evidence (*data:* plural; *datum:* singular).

Data reduction system Any system that selects, analyzes, or condenses information.

Daydream A vivid waking fantasy.

Declarative memory That part of long-term memory containing factual information.

Deductive thought Thought that applies a general set of rules to specific situations; for example, using the laws of gravity to predict the behavior of a single falling object.

Deep lesioning Use of an electrode (electrified wire) to destroy small areas deep within the brain.

Deep sleep Stage 4 sleep; the deepest form of normal sleep.

Defense mechanisms Habitual and often unconscious psychological strategies used to avoid or reduce anxiety.

Deinstitutionalization Reduced use of full-time commitment to mental institutions to treat mental disorders.

Delta waves Large, slow brain waves that occur in deeper sleep (stages 3 and 4).

Delusion A false belief held against all contrary evidence.

Delusional disorder A psychosis marked by severe delusions of grandeur, jealousy, persecution, or similar preoccupations.

Demonology In medieval Europe, the study of demons and the treatment of persons "possessed" by demons.

Dendrites Fibers projecting from nerve cells that receive information from other neurons and carry it to the cell body.

Denial Protecting oneself from an unpleasant reality by refusing to perceive it or believe it.

Denotative meaning The exact, dictionary definition of a word or concept; its objective meaning.

Dependent variable In an experiment, the condition (usually a behavior) that reflects the effects of the independent variable.

Depressant A substance that decreases activity in the body and nervous system.

Depression A state of deep despondency marked by apathy, emotional negativity, and behavioral inhibition.

Depressive disorders Emotional disorders primarily involving sadness, despondency, and depression.

Deprivation In development, the loss or withholding of normal stimulation, nutrition, comfort, love, and so forth; a condition of lacking.

Depth cues Perceptual features that impart information about distance and three-dimensional space.

Depth perception The ability to see three-dimensional space and to accurately estimate distances.

Desensitization Reducing fear or anxiety by repeatedly exposing a person to emotional stimuli while the person is deeply relaxed.

Determinism The doctrine that all behavior has prior causes.

Detoxification To remove poison or the effects of poison; in the treatment of alcoholism, the withdrawal of the patient from alcohol.

Developmental level An individual's current state of physical, emotional, and intellectual development.

Developmental milestone A significant turning point or marker in personal development.

Developmental psychologist A psychologist who studies the course of human growth and development.

Developmental psychology The study of progressive changes in behavior and abilities from conception to death.

Developmental task Any skill that must be mastered, or personal change that must take place, for optimal development at a particular life stage.

Deviant communication Patterns of communication that cause guilt, anxiety, confusion, anger, conflict, and emotional turmoil.

Deviation IQ An IQ obtained statistically from a person's relative standing in his or her age group.

Diet The types and amounts of food and drink regularly consumed over a period of time.

Difference threshold The smallest change in stimulus intensity that can be detected by an observer.

Digit-span test A test of attention and short-term memory in which a string of digits is recalled.

Direct instruction Presentation of factual information by lecture, demonstration, and rote practice.

Direct observation (personality) Any observation of a person's behavior in a natural or prearranged situation undertaken to form an impression of his or her personality.

Discounting Downgrading internal explanations of behavior when a person's actions appear to have strong external causes.

Discovery learning Learning based on insight or understanding rather than on mechanical application of rules.

Discrimination Treating members of various social groups differently in circumstances where their rights or treatment should be identical.

Discriminative stimuli Stimuli that precede rewarded and non-rewarded responses in operant conditioning and that come to exert some control over whether the response is made.

Disease-prone personality A personality style associated with poor health; marked by persistent negative emotions, including anxiety, depression, and hostility.

Dishabituation A reversal of habituation.

Disinhibition The removal of inhibition, resulting in the acting out of behavior that normally would be restrained.

Disjunctive concept A concept defined by the presence of at least one of several possible features. (For example, to qualify, an object must be either blue *or* circular.)

Disorganized schizophrenia Schizophrenia marked by incoherence, disorganized behavior, bizarre thinking, and flat or grossly inappropriate emotions.

Displaced aggression Redirecting aggression to a target other than the actual source of one's frustration.

Dissection Separation of tissues into their parts.

Dissociative amnesia Loss of memory (partial or complete) for past events and, especially, loss of memory for one's personal identity.

Dissociative disorder Temporary amnesia, multiple personality, or depersonalization.

Dissociative fugue Fleeing to escape extreme emotional conflict, anxiety, or threat.

Dissociative identity disorder The presence of two or more distinct personalities or personal identities (multiple personality).

Distinctiveness As a basis for making causal attributions, noticing that a behavior occurs only under a specific (distinct) set of circumstances.

Distractors False items included with a correct item to form a test of recognition memory (for example, the wrong answers on a multiple-choice test).

Disuse Theory that memory traces weaken when memories are not periodically used or retrieved.

Divergent thought Thinking that produces many ideas or alternatives; a major element in original or creative thought.

Divided attention Allotting mental space or effort to various tasks or parts of a task.

DNA Deoxyribonucleic acid; a twisted, ladder-like molecular structure containing the chemical code for genetic information.

Dogmatism An unwarranted positiveness or certainty in matters of belief or opinion.

Dominant gene A gene whose influence will be expressed each time the gene is present.

Door-in-the-face effect The tendency for a person who has refused a major request to subsequently be more likely to comply with a minor request.

Dopamine An important transmitter substance found in the brain, especially in the limbic system, an area associated with emotional response.

Double approach-avoidance conflict An unpleasant state in which one is simultaneously attracted to and repelled by each of two alternatives.

Double-blind experiment A test in which neither subjects nor experimenters know which subjects are in the experimental group.

Down syndrome A genetic disorder caused by the presence of an extra chromosome; results in mental retardation.

Dream symbols Images in dreams that serve as visible signs of hidden ideas, desires, impulses, emotions, relationships, and so forth.

Drill and practice A basic computer-assisted learning format, typically consisting of questions and answers.

Drive The psychological expression of a motive; for example, hunger, thirst, or a drive for success.

Drug interaction A combined effect of two drugs that exceeds the addition of one drug's effects to the other.

Drug tolerance A reduction in the body's response to a drug.

Dysthymic disorder A moderate level of depression that has persisted for 2 years or more but has not included periods of severe depression.

Easy child A child who is temperamentally relaxed and agreeable.

Echo A brief continuation of sensory activity in the auditory system after a sound is heard.

Eclectic Selected from many sources.

Educational psychology The study of learning, teaching, and related topics.

Educational simulations Computer programs that simulate real-world settings or situations to promote learning.

Effective parents Parents who supply firm and consistent guidance combined with love and affection.

Effector cells Cells in muscles and glands specialized for the production of responses.

Ego In Freudian theory, the executive part of personality that directs rational, realistic behavior.

Ego ideal In Freudian theory, the part of the superego representing ideal behavior; a source of pride when its standards are met.

Egocentric thought Thought that is self-centered and fails to consider the viewpoints of others.

Eidetic imagery The ability to retain a "projected" mental image long enough to use it as a source of information.

Ejaculation The release of sperm and seminal fluid by the male at the time of orgasm.

Elaborative rehearsal Rehearsal that links new information with existing memories and knowledge.

Electra conflict Freudian concept referring to a girl's sexual attraction to her father and resultant feelings of rivalry with her mother.

Electrical stimulation of the brain (ESB) Direct electrical stimulation and action of brain tissue.

Electroconvulsive therapy (ECT) A medical treatment for severe depression, consisting of an electric shock passed directly through the brain, which produces a convulsion.

Electrode Any wire, needle, or metal plate used to electrically stimulate nerve tissue or to record its activity.

Electroencephalograph (EEG) A device designed to detect, amplify, and record electrical activity in the brain.

Electromagnetic spectrum The full range of electrical and magnetic wavelengths, including X-rays, radio waves, light waves, and so forth.

Emotion A state characterized by physiological arousal, subjective feelings, changes in facial expression, and adaptive behaviors.

Emotion-focused coping Managing or controlling one's emotional reaction to a stressful or threatening situation.

Emotional appraisal Evaluating the personal meaning of a situation; specific emotions are assumed to result from various appraisals, such as an appraisal of threat leading to anxiety.

Emotional attachment A close emotional bond that infants form with their parents, caregivers, or others.

Emotional bonding An especially close emotional bond between infants and their parents, caregivers, or others (another term for attachment).

Emotional component One's feelings toward the object of an attitude.

Emotional expression Any behavior that gives an outward sign of emotion, especially those signs that communicate emotional states to others.

Emotional feelings The private, subjective experience of having an emotion.

Emotional tone The underlying emotional state an individual is experiencing at any given moment.

Empathy A capacity for taking another's point of view; the ability to feel what another is feeling.

Empirical evidence Facts or information gained by direct observation or experience.

Encoding Changing information into a form that allows it to be stored in memory and manipulated in thought.

Encoding failure Failure to store sufficient information to form a useful memory.

Encounter group A group experience based on intensely honest expressions of feelings and reactions of participants to one another.

Endocrine system Glands whose secretions pass directly into the bloodstream or lymph system.

Endogenous depression Depression that appears to be produced from within (perhaps by chemical imbalances in the brain) rather than as a reaction to life events.

Endorphins A class of chemicals produced by the pituitary gland that are similar in structure and painkilling effect to opiate drugs such as morphine.

Energizers Mood-elevating drugs.

Engineering psychology A specialty concerned with the design of machines and work environments so that they are compatible with human perceptual and physical capacities.

Engram Hypothesized physical changes that take place in the brain as it stores information; a memory trace.

Enkephalins Opiate-like brain chemicals that regulate reactions to pain and stress.

Enriched environment An environment deliberately made more novel, complex, and perceptually stimulating.

Enrichment In development, any attempt to make a child's environment more novel, complex, and perceptually or intellectually stimulating.

Environment ("nurture") The sum total of all external conditions affecting development.

Environmental assessment Measurement and analysis of the effects an environment has on the behavior of people within that environment.

Environmental psychology The formal study of how environments affect behavior.

Episodic drive A drive that occurs in distinct episodes associated with particular conditions (for example, pain avoidance, sexual motivation).

Episodic memory A subpart of declarative memory that records personal experiences that are linked with specific times and places.

Equal-status contact Social interaction that occurs on an equal footing, without obvious differences in power or status.

Ergotism A pattern of psychotic-like symptoms that accompanies poisoning by ergot fungus.

Erogenous zone Any body area that produces pleasurable sensations.

Eros Freud's name for the "life instincts" postulated by his theory.

Escape Reducing discomfort by leaving frustrating situations or by psychologically withdrawing from them.

Escape learning Learning to make a response in order to end an aversive (painful or uncomfortable) stimulus.

Estrogen Any of a number of female sex hormones.

Estrus Changes in the reproductive organs and sexual drives of animals that create a desire for mating; particularly used to refer to females in heat.

Ethnocentrism Placing one's own group or race at the center—that is, tending to reject all other groups but one's own.

Ethologist A person who studies the natural behavior patterns of animals.

Evolutionary psychology Study of the evolutionary origins of human behavior patterns.

Excitement General emotional arousal associated with activation of the autonomic nervous system.

Excitement phase The first phase of sexual response, indicated by initial signs of sexual arousal.

Exhibitionism Deriving sexual pleasure from displaying the genitals (usually) to an unwilling viewer ("flashing").

Existential therapy An insight therapy that focuses on the problems of existence, such as death, meaning, choice, and responsibility; emphasizes making courageous life choices.

Exorcism In medieval Europe, the practice of expelling or driving off an "evil spirit," especially one residing in the body of a person who is "possessed."

Expectancy An anticipation concerning future events or relationships.

Experiment A formal trial undertaken to confirm or disconfirm a fact or principle.

Experimental group In a controlled experiment, the group of subjects exposed to the independent variable or experimental manipulation.

Experimental psychologist One who scientifically studies human and animal behavior.

Experimental self-observation Wilhelm Wundt's technique of combining trained introspection with objective measurement.

Experimental subjects Humans or animals whose behavior is investigated in an experiment.

Experimenter effect Changes in subjects' behavior caused by the unintended influence of an experimenter's actions.

Expert systems Computer programs designed to respond as a human expert would; programs based on the knowledge and rules that underlie human expertise in specific topics.

Expert witness A person recognized by a court of law as being qualified to give expert testimony on a specific topic.

Explicit memory A memory that a person is aware of having; a memory that is consciously retrieved.

Exploration drive Drive to investigate unfamiliar areas of the environment.

Expressive behavior Behavior that expresses or communicates emotion.

External cause A cause of behavior that is assumed to lie outside a person.

External eating cue Any external stimulus that tends to encourage hunger or to elicit eating.

Extinction A gradual decrease in the frequency of a non-reinforced response.

Extracellular thirst Thirst caused by a reduction in the volume of fluids found between body cells.

Extraneous variable In an experiment, any condition prevented from influencing the outcome.

Extrasensory perception The purported ability to perceive events in ways that cannot be explained by known capacities of the sensory organs.

Extrinsic motivation Motivation based on obvious external rewards, obligations, or similar factors.

Extrovert A person whose attention is directed outward; a bold, sociable, outgoing person.

Eye movement desensitization A reduction in fear or anxiety that occurs when a person holds upsetting thoughts in mind while rapidly moving the eyes from side to side.

Facial blend A facial gesture that mixes parts of two or more basic facial expressions.

Facial feedback hypothesis Explanation that says facial expressions generate feelings that help define what emotion a person is feeling.

Fact memory That part of long-term memory containing factual information (declarative memory).

Factor analysis A statistical technique used to correlate multiple measurements. Measurements that form "clusters" of correlations are assumed to reflect some general underlying factor.

Fallacy of positive instances The tendency to remember or notice information that fits one's expectations, while forgetting discrepancies.

False positive An erroneous sense of recognition.

Familial retardation Mild mental retardation associated with homes that are intellectually, nutritionally, and emotionally impoverished.

Family therapy Technique in which all family members participate, both individually and as a group, to change destructive relationships and communication patterns.

Fantasy A product of the imagination determined mainly by one's motives or feelings. Fantasy may be used as an escape mechanism.

Feature detector A sensory system highly attuned to a specific stimulus pattern.

Feedback Information on the effects a response has had that is returned to the person performing the response (also known as knowledge of results).

Feeding system Areas on each side of the hypothalamus that initiate eating when stimulated.

Feeling of knowing The ability to predict beforehand whether one will be able to remember something.

Female orgasmic disorder An inability to reach orgasm during intercourse.

Female sexual arousal disorder A lack of physical arousal to sexual stimulation.

Fetal alcohol syndrome A pattern of birth complications and bodily defects in infants caused by consumption of alcohol by the mother during pregnancy.

Fetal damage A congenital problem; that is, damage or injury that occurs to the fetus during prenatal development.

Fetishism Gaining sexual gratification from inanimate objects; especially, an inability to achieve sexual arousal without the object.

Field experiment An experiment conducted in a natural setting.

Figure-ground organization A basic perceptual organization in which part of a stimulus appears to stand out as an object (figure) against a less prominent background (ground).

Five-factor model A model proposing that the five most universal dimensions of personality are extroversion, agreeableness, conscientiousness, neuroticism, and openness to experience.

Fixation (cognition) The tendency to repeat wrong solutions or faulty responses, especially as a result of becoming blind to alternatives.

Fixation (Freudian) In Freudian theory, lasting conflicts developed during a particular psychosexual stage as a result of frustration or overindulgence.

Fixed action pattern (FAP) An instinctual chain of movements found in almost all members of a species.

Fixed interval schedule A pattern in which a reinforcer is given only when a correct response is made after a set amount of time has passed since the last reinforced response. Responses made before the time interval has ended are not reinforced.

Fixed ratio schedule A pattern in which a set number of correct responses must be made to get a reinforcer. For example, a reinforcer is given for every four correct responses.

Flashbulb memories Memories created at times of high emotion that seem especially vivid.

Flat affect An extreme lack of emotion.

Fluency In tests of creativity, fluency refers to the total number of solutions produced.

fMRI scan Functional magnetic resonance imaging that records brain activity.

Foot-in-the-door effect The tendency for a person who has first complied with a small request to be more likely later to fulfill a larger request.

Forcible rape Sexual intercourse carried out against the victim's will, under the threat of force.

Forebrain The highest brain areas, including the hypothalamus, thalamus, corpus callosum, and cerebrum.

Formal operations stage Period of cognitive development marked by a capacity for abstract, theoretical, and hypothetical thinking.

Fovea A small depression at the center of the retina containing only cones and providing the greatest sharpness of vision.

Frame of reference A mental or emotional perspective used for evaluating events.

Framing In thought, the terms in which a problem is stated or the way that it is structured.

Fraternal twins Twins conceived from two separate eggs. Fraternal twins are no more alike genetically than other siblings.

Free association In psychoanalysis, the technique of having a client say anything that comes to mind, regardless of how embarrassing or unimportant it may seem.

Free choice The ability to freely make choices that are not controlled by genetics, learning, or unconscious forces.

Free will The doctrine that human beings are capable of freely making choices.

Free-floating anxiety Anxiety that is very general and pervasive.

Frequency theory Holds that, in hearing, the cochlea converts tones up to about 4,000 hertz into nerve impulses that match the frequency of each tone.

Frontal lobes Areas at the top front of the cerebral cortex that include sites associated with the control of movement, the processing of smell, and higher mental functions.

Frontal lobotomy The destruction of brain tissue in frontal areas of the brain.

Frotteurism Sexually touching or rubbing against a non-consenting person.

Frustration An internal emotional state resulting from interference with satisfaction of a motive or blocking of goal-directed behavior.

Frustration-aggression hypothesis Hypothesis stating that frustration tends to lead to aggression.

Fugue Taking flight to escape extreme emotional conflict, anxiety, or threat.

Fully functioning person Carl Rogers's term for persons living in harmony with their deepest feelings, impulses, and intuitions.

Functional fixedness A rigidity in problem solving caused by an inability to see new uses for familiar objects.

Functional MRI An MRI scan that records brain activity.

Functional solution A detailed, practical, and workable solution.

Functionalism School of psychology concerned with how behavior and mental abilities help people adapt to their environments.

Fundamental attributional error The tendency to attribute the behavior of others to internal causes (personality, likes, and so forth).

Galvanic skin response (GSR) A change in the electrical resistance (or inversely, the conductance) of the skin due to activity in the sweat glands associated with arousal or anxiety.

Ganzfeld A perceptual "blank screen"; usually achieved by creating a uniform white visual field and a neutral auditory tone.

Gate control theory Proposes that pain messages pass through neural "gates" in the spinal cord.

Gender Psychological and social characteristics associated with being male or female; defined especially by one's gender identity and learned gender roles.

Gender bias A tendency for researchers to base conclusions solely on subjects of one sex (usually males).

Gender role socialization The process of learning behaviors considered appropriate for one's sex in a given culture.

Gender role stereotypes Oversimplified and widely held beliefs about the basic characteristics of men and women.

Gender roles Separate patterns of traits, mannerisms, interests, and behaviors that are regarded as "male" and "female" by one's culture.

General adaptation syndrome (G.A.S.) A series of bodily reactions to prolonged stress that occurs in three stages: alarm, resistance, and exhaustion.

General intelligence test A test that measures a wide variety of mental abilities.

General solution A solution that states the requirements for success but not in enough detail for further action.

Generalization Transfer of a learned response from one stimulus situation to other similar situations.

Generalized anxiety disorder The person is in a chronic state of tension and worries about work, relationships, ability, or impending disaster.

Generalized reinforcer A secondary reinforcer that has become independent of direct association with primary reinforcers.

Genome An organism's entire set of genes.

Genes Specific areas on a strand of DNA that carry hereditary information affecting various personal characteristics.

Genetic abnormality Any abnormality in the genes, including missing genes, extra genes, or defective genes.

Genetic sex Sex as indicated by the presence of *XX* (female) or *XY* (male) chromosomes.

Genital sex Sex as indicated by the presence of male or female genitals.

Genital stage In Freud's theory, the culmination of personality development, marked, among other things, by the attainment of mature adult sexuality.

Gerontologist One who scientifically studies aging and its effects.

Gestalt A German word meaning "form," "pattern," or "whole."

Gestalt psychology The school of psychology emphasizing the study of thinking, learning, and perception in whole units, not by analysis into parts.

Gestalt therapy An approach that focuses on immediate experience and awareness to help clients rebuild thinking, feeling, and acting into connected wholes; emphasizes the integration of fragmented experiences.

GHB (gamma-hydroxybutyrate) An illicit central nervous system depressant that produces intoxication and sedation.

Giantism Excessive bodily growth caused by too much growth hormone.

Giftedness Either the possession of a high IQ or special talents or aptitudes.

Glucagon-like peptide 1 A substance in the brain that terminates eating.

Goal The target or objective of a motivated and directed chain of behaviors.

Gonadal sex Sex as indicated by the presence of ovaries (female) or testes (male).

Gonads The primary sex glands—the testes in males and ovaries in females.

Grammar A set of rules for combining language units into meaningful speech or writing.

Graphology False system based on the belief that handwriting can reveal personality traits.

Grasping reflex A neonatal reflex consisting of grasping objects placed in the palms.

Gray matter Areas in the nervous system that have a grayish color due to a high concentration of nerve cell bodies.

Group cohesiveness The degree of attraction among group members or their degree of commitment to remaining in the group.

Group intelligence test Any intelligence test that can be administered to a group of people with minimal supervision.

Group prejudice Prejudice held out of conformity to group views.

Group sanctions Rewards and punishments (such as approval or disapproval) administered by groups to enforce a degree of conformity among members.

Group structure The network of roles, communication pathways, and power in a group.

Group therapy Psychotherapy conducted with a group of people.

Groupthink A compulsion by members of decision-making groups to maintain agreement, even at the cost of critical thinking.

Growth needs In Maslow's hierarchy, the higher-level needs associated with self-actualization (needs that contribute to personal growth and full development of personal potential).

Guided imagery Intentional visualization of images that are calming, relaxing, or beneficial in other ways.

Gustation The sense of taste.

Habit A deeply ingrained, learned pattern of behavior.

Habituation A decrease in perceptual response to a repeated stimulus.

Hair cells Receptor cells within the cochlea that transduce vibrations into nerve impulses.

Halfway house A community-based facility for individuals making the transition from an institution (mental hospital, prison, and so forth) to independent living.

Hallucination An imaginary sensation—such as seeing, hearing, or smelling something that does not exist in the external world.

Hallucinogen Any substance that alters or distorts sensory impressions.

Halo effect The tendency of an interviewer to extend a favorable or unfavorable impression to unrelated aspects of an individual's personality.

Handedness A preference for using the right or left hand in most activities.

Hardy personality A personality style associated with superior stress resistance.

Hassle Any distressing, day-to-day annoyance; also called a microstressor.

Health psychology Study of the ways in which psychological principles can be used to maintain and promote health.

Heredity ("nature") The transmission of physical and psychological characteristics from parents to offspring through genes.

Hertz One cycle (or vibration) per second.

Heterosexism The belief that heterosexuality is better or more natural than homosexuality.

Heterosexual A person romantically and erotically attracted to members of the opposite sex.

Heuristic Any strategy or technique that aids problem solving, especially by limiting the number of possible solutions to be tried.

Hierarchy A rank-ordered series of higher and lower amounts, levels, degrees, or steps.

Hierarchy of needs A rank ordering of needs based on their presumed strength or potency.

Higher order conditioning Classical conditioning in which a conditioned stimulus is used to reinforce further learning; that is, a CS is used as if it were a US.

Hippocampus A structure in the brain associated with the regulation of emotions and the transfer of information from short-term memory to long-term memory.

Homeostasis A steady state of bodily equilibrium normally maintained automatically by various physiological mechanisms.

Homogamy Marriage of two people who are similar to one another.

Homophobia A powerful fear of homosexuality.

Homosexual A person romantically and erotically attracted to same-sex persons.

Honesty test A paper-and-pencil test designed to detect attitudes, beliefs, and behavior patterns that predispose a person to engage in dishonest behavior.

Hormonal sex Sex as indicated by a preponderance of estrogens (female) or androgens (male) in the body.

Hormone A glandular secretion that affects bodily functions or behavior.

Hospice A medical facility or program dedicated to providing optimal care for persons who are dying.

Hue Classification of colors into basic categories of red, orange, yellow, green, blue, indigo, and violet.

Human growth sequence The general pattern of physical development from conception to death.

Human immunodeficiency virus (HIV) The sexually transmitted virus that disables the immune system and causes AIDS.

Human nature Those traits, qualities, potentials, and behavior patterns most characteristic of the human species.

Humanism An approach to psychology that focuses on human experience, problems, potentials, and ideals.

Hyperopia Difficulty focusing nearby objects (farsightedness).

Hypersomnia Extreme daytime sleepiness.

Hyperthyroidism Faster metabolism and excitability caused by an overactive thyroid gland.

Hypnic jerk A reflex muscle twitch throughout the body that often occurs as one is falling asleep.

Hypnagogic images Vivid mental images that may occur just as one enters stage 1 sleep; although somewhat dream-like, the images are usually not associated with REMs.

Hypnosis An altered state of consciousness characterized by narrowed attention and increased suggestibility.

Hypnotic susceptibility scale Any test designed to assess an individual's capacity for becoming hypnotized.

Hypoactive sexual desire A persistent loss of sexual motivation.

Hypochondriac A person who is excessively preoccupied with minor bodily problems or who complains about illnesses that appear to be imaginary.

Hypochondriasis A preoccupation with minor bodily problems and the presence of illnesses that appear to be imaginary.

Hypoglycemia Below-normal blood sugar level.

Hypopituitary dwarfism Shortness and smallness caused by too little growth hormone.

Hypothalamus A small area at the base of the brain that regulates many aspects of motivation and emotion, especially hunger, thirst, and sexual behavior.

Hypothesis The predicted outcome of an experiment or an educated guess about the relationship between variables.

Hypothyroidism Slower metabolism and sluggishness caused by an underactive thyroid gland.

Hysteria Wild emotional excitability sometimes associated with the development of apparent physical disabilities (numbness, blindness, and the like) without known physical cause.

Icon A mental image or representation.

Id According to Freud, the most primitive part of personality, which remains unconscious, supplies energy to other parts of the psyche, and demands immediate gratification.

Ideal self An idealized image of oneself (the person one would like to be).

Identical twins Twins who develop from the same egg and who, therefore, have identical genes.

Identification Incorporating the goals and values of another person into one's own behavior; feeling emotionally connected to a person and wanting to be like him or her.

Illogical thought Thought that is intuitive, invalid, or haphazard.

Illusion A misleading or distorted perception.

Illusory figure An implied shape that is not actually bounded by an edge or an outline.

Image Most often, a mental representation that has picture-like qualities; an icon.

Imitation An attempt to match one's own behavior to another person's behavior.

Immune system System that mobilizes bodily defenses (such as white blood cells) against invading microbes and other disease agents.

Implicit memory A memory that a person does not know exists; a memory that is retrieved unconsciously.

Impossible figure A stimulus pattern that cannot be organized into a stable perception.

Imprinting A rapid and relatively permanent type of learning that occurs during a limited time period early in life.

Inattentional blindness Failure to perceive a stimulus that is in plain view but not the focus of attention.

In-basket test A testing procedure that simulates the individual decision-making challenges that executives face.

Incentive value The value a goal holds for a person or animal above and beyond the goal's ability to fill a need.

Incongruence State that exists when there is a discrepancy between one's experiences and self-image or between one's self-image and ideal self.

Incongruent person A person who has an inaccurate self-image or a person whose self-image differs greatly from the ideal self.

Independent variable In an experiment, the condition being investigated as a possible cause of some change in behavior. The values that this variable takes do not depend on any other condition; they are chosen by the experimenter.

Individual intelligence test A test of intelligence designed for administration to a single individual by a trained specialist.

Individual traits Personality traits that comprise a person's unique individual qualities.

Individuating information Information that helps define a person as an individual rather than as a member of a group or social category.

Inductive thought A type of thinking in which a general rule or principle is inferred from a series of specific examples; for instance, inferring the laws of gravity by observing many falling objects.

Industrial-organizational psychology The psychology of work and organizations, especially with respect to personnel selection, human relations, and management.

Information bits Meaningful units of information, such as numbers, letters, words, or phrases.

Information chunks Information bits grouped into larger units.

Innate behavior Inborn, unlearned behavior.

Insanity Legally, a mental disability shown by an inability to manage one's affairs or to be aware of the consequences of one's actions.

Insecure-ambivalent attachment An anxious emotional bond marked by a desire to be with a parent or caregiver and resistance to being reunited.

Insecure-avoidant attachment An anxious emotional bond marked by a tendency to avoid reunion with a parent or caregiver.

Insight A sudden mental reorganization of a problem that causes the solution to seem self-evident.

Insomnia Difficulty in getting to sleep or staying asleep.

Instructional games Educational computer programs designed to resemble games in order to motivate learning.

Instrumental behavior Behavior directed toward the achievement of some goal; behavior that is instrumental in producing some effect.

Intelligence An overall capacity to think rationally, act purposefully, and deal effectively with the environment.

Intelligence quotient (IQ) An index of intelligence defined as a person's mental age divided by his or her chronological age and multiplied by 100.

Interference The tendency for new memories to impair retrieval of older memories, and the reverse.

Internal cause A cause of behavior that is assumed to lie within a person—for instance, a need, preference, or personality trait.

Internal representation Any image, concept, precept, symbol, or process used to mentally represent information during thought.

Internet A connection of networks that enables computers to communicate with one another, usually through the telephone system.

Interpersonal attraction Social attraction to another person.

Interview (personality) A face-to-face meeting held for the purpose of gaining information about an individual's personal history, personality traits, current psychological state, and so forth.

Intimate distance The most private space immediately surrounding the body (about 18 inches from the skin).

Intracranial stimulation Direct electrical stimulation and activation of brain tissue.

Intracellular thirst Thirst triggered when fluid is drawn out of cells due to an increased concentration of salts and minerals outside the cell.

Intrauterine environment The physical and chemical environment within the uterus during prenatal development.

Intrinsic motivation Motivation that comes from personal enjoyment of an activity rather than from external rewards.

Introspection To look within; to examine one's own thoughts, feelings, or sensations.

Introvert A person whose attention is focused inward; a shy, reserved, self-centered person.

Intuitive thought Quick, impulsive thinking that makes little or no use of formal reasoning and logic.

Inverted U function A curve, roughly in the shape of an upside-down U, that relates the quality of performance to levels of arousal.

Ion An electrically charged molecule.

Ion channels Channels through the axon membrane.

Iris Colored circular muscle of the eye that opens and closes to admit more or less light into the eye.

Irrelevant questions In a polygraph exam, neutral, non-threatening, or non-emotional questions.

Ishihara test A test for color blindness and color weakness.

James-Lange theory According to this theory, emotional feelings follow bodily arousal and come from awareness of such arousal.

Jigsaw classroom A method of reducing prejudice in which each student receives a different part of a body of information needed to complete a project or prepare for a test.

Just noticeable difference The amount of increase or decrease in a stimulus that can be reliably detected as a change in amount, value, or intensity.

Just-world beliefs Belief that people generally get what they deserve.

Justification In cognitive dissonance theory, the degree to which one's actions are justified by rewards or other circumstances.

Keyword method As an aid to memory, using a familiar word or image to link two items.

Kinesics Study of the meaning of body movements, posture, hand gestures, and facial expressions, commonly called body language.

Kinesthetic imagery Images created by produced, remembered, or imagined muscular sensations.

Kinesthetic senses The senses of body movement and positioning.

Knowledge of results During learning, feedback or information provided about the correctness of responses or other aspects of performance.

Language A collection of words or symbols and rules for combining them, which allows them to be used for thinking and communication.

Large-group awareness training Any of a number of programs (many of them commercialized) that claim to increase self-awareness and facilitate constructive personal change.

Latency (Freudian) According to Freud, a period in childhood when psychosexual development is more or less interrupted.

Latency (response) The amount of time that passes between the presentation of a stimulus and the occurrence of a response.

Latent dream content The hidden or symbolic meaning of a dream, as revealed by dream interpretation and analysis.

Latent learning Learning that occurs without obvious reinforcement and that remains unexpressed until reinforcement is provided.

Lateralization Specialization in the abilities of the brain hemispheres.

Law of effect Responses that lead to desirable effects are repeated; those that produce undesirable results are not.

Learned helplessness A learned inability to overcome obstacles or to avoid punishment. A learned state of passivity and inaction in the face of aversive stimuli.

Learning Any relatively permanent change in behavior that can be attributed to experience but not to fatigue, malnutrition, injury, and so forth.

Learning psychologist A psychologist who studies how learning occurs.

Learning theorist A psychologist interested in the ways that learning shapes and explains personality.

Leptin A substance released by fat cells that inhibits eating.

Lesbianism Female homosexuality.

Lexigram A geometric shape used as a symbol for a word.

Libido In Freudian theory, the force, primarily pleasure-oriented, that energizes the subparts of personality.

Life change units (LCUs) Numerical values assigned to each life event on the *Social Readjustment Rating Scale* and used to predict the likelihood of illness.

Life expectancy The average number of years a person of a given sex, race, and nationality can expect to live.

Life stages Widely recognized periods of life corresponding to various ages and broad phases of development.

Light sleep Stage 1 sleep; marked by small, irregular brain waves and some alpha waves.

Limbic system A system of interconnected structures in the forebrain that are closely associated with emotional response.

Limen A threshold or a limit.

Linear relationship A relationship that forms a straight line when graphed.

Lithium carbonate A drug used to lessen mood swings in persons suffering from some types of affective disorders.

Lobes (cerebral cortex) Areas on the cortex bordered by major fissures or associated with particular functions.

Localization of function The principle stating that sensations are determined by the area of the brain that is activated.

Lock and key theory The theory of olfaction that relates odors to the shapes of chemical molecules.

Logical thought Drawing conclusions on the basis of formal principles of reasoning.

Logotherapy A form of existential therapy that emphasizes the need to find and maintain meaning in one's life.

Long-term memory (LTM) The memory system used for relatively permanent storage of meaningful information.

Looking chamber An experimental apparatus used to test infant perception by presenting visual stimuli and observing infant responses.

Loudness The intensity of a sound; determined by the amplitude of sound waves.

Low-ball technique A strategy in which commitment is gained first to reasonable or desirable terms, which are then made less reasonable or desirable.

Lucid dream A dream in which the dreamer feels awake and capable of normal thought and action.

Maintenance rehearsal Silently repeating or mentally reviewing information to hold it in short-term memory.

Major depressive disorder A mood disorder in which the person has suffered one or more intense episodes of depression.

Major mood disorders Disorders marked by lasting extremes of mood or emotion and often accompanied by psychotic symptoms.

Major tranquilizers (antipsychotics) Drugs that, in addition to having tranquilizing effects, also tend to reduce hallucinations and delusional thinking.

Maladaptive behavior Behavior that makes it more difficult for a person to adapt to his or her environment and meet the demands of day-to-day life.

Male erectile disorder An inability to maintain an erection for sexual intercourse.

Male orgasmic disorder An inability to reach orgasm during intercourse.

Manic Extremely excited, hyperactive, or irritable.

Manifest dream content The surface, "visible" content of a dream; dream images as they are remembered by the dreamer.

Manipulation drive Drive to investigate objects by touching and handling them.

Mantra A word or sound used as the focus of attention in concentrative meditation.

Marijuana The leaves and flowers of the hemp plant *Cannabis sativa*.

Masochism Deriving sexual arousal or pleasure from having pain inflicted during the sex act.

Mass media Collectively, all media that reach very large audiences (magazines, for instance, are a medium of mass communication).

Massed practice A practice schedule in which studying continues for long periods, without interruption.

Mastery training Reinforcement of responses that lead to mastery of a threat or control over one's environment.

Masturbation Production of sexual pleasure or orgasm through manipulation of the genitals (other than by intercourse).

Maternal influences The aggregate of all psychological effects mothers have on their children.

Maternity blues A brief and relatively mild state of depression often experienced by mothers 2 or 3 days after giving birth.

Maturation The physical growth and development of the body and nervous system.

Maximum life span The biologically determined maximum number of years humans could live under optimal conditions.

MDMA (methylenedioxymethamphetamine) A stimulant drug closely related to amphetamine and commonly known as Ecstasy.

Mean world view Viewing the world and other people as dangerous and threatening.

Means-ends analysis An analysis of how to reduce the difference between the present state of affairs and a desired goal.

Mechanical solution A problem solution achieved by trial and error or by a fixed procedure based on learned rules.

Meditation A mental technique for quieting the mind and body.

Medulla The enlarged stalk at the base of the brain that connects to the spinal cord and controls vital life functions.

Melatonin A hormone produced by the pineal gland in response to cycles of light and dark.

Memory The mental system for receiving, storing, organizing, altering, and recovering information.

Memory cue Any stimulus associated with a particular memory. The presence of such cues usually enhances memory retrieval.

Memory decay The fading or weakening of memories assumed to occur when memory traces become weaker.

Memory structure The pattern of associations among bits of information stored in memory.

Memory traces Hypothesized physical changes that take place in the brain as it stores information; engrams.

Mental age The average mental ability displayed by people of a given age.

Mental disorder A significant impairment in psychological functioning.

Mental hospitalization Confinement to a protected environment that provides various forms of therapy for mental, emotional, and behavioral problems.

Mental retardation The presence of a developmental disability, a formal IQ score below 70, or a significant impairment of adaptive behavior.

Mental rotation The ability to change the position of an image in mental space to examine it from a new perspective.

Mesmerize To hypnotize.

Meta-analysis A statistical technique for combining the results of many studies on the same subject.

Meta-needs In Maslow's hierarchy, those needs above and beyond the ordinary; needs associated with impulses for self-actualization.

Metabolic disorder Any disorder in metabolism (the rate of energy production and use in the body).

Metabolic rate The rate at which energy is consumed by bodily activity.

Methamphetamine A stimulant drug closely related to amphetamine in structure and effect.

Micro-electrode An electrode small enough to record the activity of a single neuron.

Micromovements Tiny, nearly imperceptible movements associated with changes in muscular tension and activity.

Microsleep A momentary shift in brain-wave patterns to those of sleep.

Microstressor Any distressing, day-to-day annoyance; also called a *hassle.*

Midbrain The area of the brain consisting of structures linking the forebrain and the brainstem.

Mild punishment Punishment that has a relatively weak effect, especially punishment that only temporarily slows responding.

Minimal brain dysfunction (MBD) A hypothesized explanation for hyperactivity, involving a lag in brain development or low-level damage to the brain.

Minnesota Multiphasic Personality Inventory-2 (MMPI-2) The latest version of one of the best-known and most widely used objective personality questionnaires.

Minor tranquilizers Drugs (such as Valium) that produce relaxation or reduce anxiety.

Mirror technique Observing another person reenact one's own behavior, like a character in a play; designed to help persons to see themselves more clearly.

MMPI-2 profile A graphic representation of an individual's scores on each of the primary scales of the MMPI-2.

Mnemonic A memory system or aid.

Model (learning) A person (either live or filmed) who serves as an example for observational learning or vicarious conditioning.

Model (scientific) In research, an animal whose behavior is used to derive principles that may apply to human behavior.

Modeling Any process in which information is imparted by example, before direct practice is allowed.

Monocular depth cues Depth cues that can be sensed with one eye.

Mood A low-intensity, long-lasting emotional state.

Mood disorder A major disturbance in mood or emotion, such as depression or mania.

Moon illusion The apparent change in size that occurs as the moon moves from the horizon (large moon) to overhead (small moon).

Moral anxiety Apprehension felt when one's thoughts, impulses, or actions conflict with standards enforced by the superego.

Moral development The development of values, beliefs, and thinking abilities that act as a guide regarding what is acceptable behavior.

Moro reflex Neonatal reflex evoked by sudden loss of support or the sounding of a loud noise; in response, the arms are extended and then brought toward each other.

Morphemes The smallest meaningful units in a language, such as syllables or words.

Motivation Mechanisms within an organism that initiate, sustain, and direct activities.

Motor cortex An area on the top of the brain directly associated with control of voluntary movements.

Motor neuron A nerve cell that carries motor commands from the central nervous system to muscles and glands.

Motor program A mental plan or model that guides skilled movement.

Motor skill A series of actions molded into a smooth and efficient performance.

MRI scan Magnetic resonance imaging; a computer-enhanced three-dimensional representation of the brain or body, based on the body's response to a magnetic field.

Müller-Lyer illusion A stimulus consisting of two parallel lines tipped with inward or outward pointing V's. Although they are of equal length, one of the lines appears longer than the other.

Multiculturalism Giving equal status, recognition, and acceptance to different ethnic, racial, and cultural groups.

Multiple approach-avoidance conflict Being simultaneously attracted to and repelled by each of several alternatives.

Multiple aptitude test Test that measures two or more aptitudes.

Multiple personality A form of dissociative disorder in which a person develops two or more distinct personalities.

Muscular imagery Any mental representation based on produced, remembered, or imagined muscular sensations; for instance, the images produced when one imagines hammering a nail.

Muscular responses Visible movement of the muscles or unseen changes in their tension, which creates kinesthetic sensations.

Mutual absorption With regard to romantic love, the almost exclusive attention lovers give to one another.

Mutual interdependence A condition in which two or more persons must depend on one another to meet each person's needs or goals.

Myelin A fatty layer coating some axons that increases the rate at which nerve impulses travel along the axon.

Myoclonus Restless spasms of the leg muscles that disturb sleep.

Myopia A visual defect that makes it difficult to focus distant objects (nearsightedness).

Narcolepsy A serious sleep disturbance in which the individual suffers uncontrollable sleep attacks.

Natural clinical test An accident or other natural event that provides psychological data.

Natural selection Darwin's theory that evolution favors those plants and animals best suited to their living conditions.

Natural setting The environment in which an organism typically lives.

Naturalistic observation Observation and recording of naturally occurring behavior that is not manipulated experimentally.

Near-death experience A pattern of experiences that may occur when a person is clinically dead and then resuscitated.

Need An internal deficiency that may energize behavior.

Need for achievement (nAch) The desire to excel or meet some internalized standard of excellence.

Need for power The desire to have social impact and control over others.

Need to affiliate The desire to associate with other people.

Negative after-potential A drop in electrical charge below the resting potential.

Negative attention seeking A pattern, seen especially in children, in which misbehavior is used to gain attention.

Negative instance In concept learning, an object or event that does not belong to the concept class.

Negative reinforcement Occurs when a response is followed with an end to discomfort or with the removal of a negative state of affairs.

Negative relationship A relationship in which increases in one measure correspond to decreases in the other.

Negative self-statements Self-critical thoughts that increase anxiety and lower performance.

Negative transfer Mastery of one task conflicts with learning or performing another.

Neglect Ignoring one side of vision or of the body after damage to a brain hemisphere.

Neo-Freudian A personality theorist who accepts the broad features of Freud's theory but has revised the theory to fit his or her own concepts.

Neonate A newborn infant during the first weeks following birth.

Nerve A bundle of neuron fibers supported by connective tissue; nerves can be seen with the unaided eye; neuron fibers are microscopic projections from single cells.

Nerve deafness Deafness caused by damage to the hair cells or auditory nerve.

Network model A model of memory that views it as an organized system of linked information.

Neurilemma A layer of living cells that encases the axons of some neurons.

Neurogenesis The production of new brain cells.

Neurological soft signs Subtle behavioral signs of brain dysfunction, including clumsiness, an awkward gait, poor hand-eye coordination, and other perceptual and motor problems.

Neurons Individual nerve cells.

Neuropeptide Y A substance in the brain that initiates eating.

Neuropeptides Brain chemicals that regulate the activity of neurons, thereby influencing memory, emotion, pain, hunger, and other behavior.

Neurosis An outdated term once used to refer, as a group, to anxiety disorders, somatoform disorders, dissociative disorders, and some forms of depression.

Neurotic anxiety Apprehension felt when the ego must struggle to maintain control over id impulses.

Neurotransmitter Any of a number of chemical substances secreted by neurons that alter activity in other neurons.

Neutral stimulus A stimulus that fails to elicit a response.

Nicotine A potent stimulant drug found primarily in tobacco; nicotine is a known carcinogen.

Night blindness A visual defect in which daylight vision is normal, but blindness occurs under conditions of low illumination.

Night terror A very frightening NREM sleep episode.

Nightmare An upsetting dream.

Non-homeostatic drive A drive that is relatively independent of physical deprivation cycles or bodily need states.

Non-reinforcement Withholding reinforcement after selected responses (in other words, extinction training).

Nonsense syllables Invented three-letter words used to test learning and memory.

Noradrenaline A hormone produced by the adrenal glands that tends to arouse the body; noradrenaline is associated with anger.

Norm (social) An accepted (but often unspoken) standard of conduct for appropriate behavior.

Norm (testing) An average score for a designated group of people.

Normal curve A bell-shaped curve with a large number of scores in the middle, tapering to very few extremely high and low scores.

NREM sleep Non-rapid eye movement sleep characteristic of stages 2, 3, and 4, and largely dream free.

Obedience Conformity to the demands of an authority.

Object In making attributions, the aim, motive, or target of an action.

Object permanence Concept, gained in infancy, that objects continue to exist even when they are hidden from view.

Objective test A test that gives the same score when different people correct it.

Observation Directly gathering data by recording facts or events.

Observational learning Learning achieved by watching and imitating the actions of another or noting the consequences of those actions.

Observer bias The tendency of an observer to distort observations or perceptions to match his or her expectations.

Observer effect Changes in a person's behavior brought about by an awareness of being observed.

Obsession Recurring irrational or disturbing thoughts or mental images a person cannot prevent.

Obsessive-compulsive disorder An extreme, unavoidable preoccupation with certain thoughts and compulsive performance of certain behaviors.

Occipital lobes Portion at the back of the cerebral cortex that includes areas where vision registers in the brain.

Oedipus conflict Freudian concept referring to a boy's sexual attraction to his mother and feelings of rivalry with his father.

Olfaction The sense of smell.

Olfactory area Sites on the frontal lobes where information on smell registers.

Open-ended interview An interview in which persons are allowed to freely state their views.

Operant conditioning Learning based on the consequences of responding.

Operant extinction The weakening or disappearance of a non-reinforced operant response.

Operant reinforcer Any event that reliably increases the probability or frequency of responses it follows.

Operant shaping Gradually molding responses by rewarding ever-closer approximations to a final desired pattern.

Operant stimulus discrimination The tendency to make a response when stimuli previously associated with reward are present and to withhold the response when stimuli associated with non-reward are present.

Operant stimulus generalization The tendency to respond to stimuli similar to those present when an operant response was acquired.

Operational definition Defining a scientific concept by stating the specific actions or procedures used to measure it. For example, "hunger" might be defined as "the number of hours of food deprivation."

Opponent-process theory (sensation) The theory of color vision stating that three coding systems (red or green, yellow or blue, black or white) are used by the visual system to analyze color information.

Oral stage In Freud's theory, the period early in life when infants are preoccupied with the mouth as a source of pleasure and means of expression.

Organ of Corti Center part of the cochlea, containing hair cells, canals, and membranes.

Organic mental disorder A mental or emotional problem caused by malfunction of the brain.

Organic psychosis A psychosis caused by a known brain injury or disease.

Organismic valuing Placing value on an experience on the basis of how one responds to it as an entire organism; judgment made directly on the basis of one's perceptions and feelings.

Organizational psychology A field that focuses on the psychology of work and on behavior within organizations.

Orgasm A climax and release of sexual excitement.

Orientation response The pattern of changes occurring throughout the body that prepares an organism to receive information from a particular stimulus.

Originality In tests of creativity, originality refers to the degree of novelty or unusualness of the solutions produced.

Otolith organs Vestibular structures sensitive to movement, acceleration, and gravity.

Oval window A membrane on the cochlea connected to the third auditory ossicle.

Overdisclosure Self-disclosure that exceeds what is appropriate for a particular relationship or social situation.

Overeating Eating in excess of one's daily caloric needs.

Overgeneralization Blowing a single event out of proportion by extending it to a large number of unrelated situations.

Overlearning Study or learning that continues after initial mastery of skills or information.

Overly permissive parents Parents who give their children little guidance, allow them too much freedom, or do not require the child to take responsibility for his or her actions.

Overprotection Excessively guarding and shielding a child from possible stresses.

Overt behavior An action or response that is directly observable.

Ovulation The release of an ovum (egg cell) by the ovaries; ova combine with sperm cells to begin the growth of an embryo.

Pain disorder Pain that has no identifiable physical cause and appears to be of psychological origin.

Palmistry False system that claims to reveal personality traits and to predict the future by "reading" lines on the palms of the hands.

Panic disorder (with agoraphobia) The person is in a chronic state of anxiety and also has brief moments of sudden, intense, unexpected panic. In addition, the person fears that these panic attacks will occur in public places or unfamiliar situations.

Panic disorder (without agoraphobia) The person is in a chronic state of anxiety and also has brief moments of sudden, intense, unexpected panic.

Paranoid psychosis A delusional disorder centered especially on delusions of persecution.

Paranoid schizophrenia Schizophrenia marked by a preoccupation with delusions or by frequent auditory hallucinations related to a single theme, especially grandeur or persecution.

Paraphilias Compulsive or destructive deviations in sexual preferences or behavior.

Paraprofessional An individual who works in a near-professional capacity under the supervision of a more highly trained person.

Parapsychology The study of extranormal psychological events, such as extrasensory perception.

Parasympathetic rebound Excess activity in the parasympathetic nervous system following a period of intense emotion.

Parasympathetic system A branch of the autonomic nervous system responsible for quieting the body and conserving energy.

Parietal lobes Area at the top of the brain that includes sites where bodily sensations register in the brain.

Part learning Separately studying subparts of a larger body of information (such as sections of a textbook chapter).

Partial hospitalization Treatment in which patients spend only part of their time at the hospital.

Partial reinforcement A pattern in which only some responses are reinforced (also called intermittent reinforcement).

Partial reinforcement effect Greater resistance to extinction is found in responses acquired on a schedule of partial reinforcement.

Passion The presence of heightened arousal in one's emotional response to another person.

Passive compliance Passively bending to unreasonable demands or circumstances.

Paternal influences The aggregate of all psychological effects fathers have on their children.

Peak experiences Temporary moments of self-actualization, marked by feelings of ecstasy, harmony, and deep meaning.

Peak performance A performance during which physical, mental, and emotional states are harmonious and optimal.

Pedophilia Sex with children, or child molesting.

Peer counselor A non-professional person who has learned basic counseling skills.

Peer group A group of people who share similar social status.

Perception The mental process of organizing sensations into meaningful patterns.

Perceptual category A preexisting class, type, or grouping.

Perceptual defense Resistance to perceiving threatening or disturbing stimuli.

Perceptual expectancy (or set) A readiness to perceive in a particular manner, induced by strong expectations.

Perceptual features Important elements of a stimulus pattern, such as lines, shapes, edges, spots, and colors.

Perceptual habits Established patterns of perceptual organization and attention.

Perceptual hypothesis An initial guess regarding the correct way to organize (perceive) a stimulus pattern.

Perceptual stimulation Varied, patterned, and meaningful sensory input.

Performance intelligence Intelligence measured by solving puzzles, assembling objects, completing pictures, and doing other non-verbal tasks.

Peripheral nervous system All parts of the nervous system lying outside the brain and spinal cord.

Peripheral vision Vision at the periphery (edges) of the visual field.

Personal distance The distance maintained when interacting with close friends (about 18 inches to 4 feet from the body).

Personal frustration A negative emotional state caused by personal characteristics that hinder satisfaction of a motive or that block progress toward a goal.

Personal interview Formal or informal questioning of job applicants to learn their qualifications and to gain an impression of their personalities.

Personal prejudice Prejudicial attitudes held toward persons who are perceived as a direct threat to one's own interests.

Personal space An area immediately surrounding the body that is regarded as private and subject to personal control.

Personality An individual's unique and relatively unchanging psychological characteristics and behavior patterns.

Personality disintegration A shattering of the coordination among thoughts, actions, and emotions normally found in personality.

Personality disorder A deeply ingrained, unhealthy, maladaptive personality pattern.

Personality psychologist A psychologist who studies personality traits and dynamics.

Personality questionnaire A paper-and-pencil test consisting of questions designed to reveal various aspects of the respondent's personality.

Personality theory An interrelated system of concepts and principles used to understand and explain personality.

Personality trait A behavioral characteristic displayed in most situations.

Personality type A style of personality defined by a group of related traits.

Personnel psychology Branch of industrial-organizational psychology concerned with testing, selection, placement, and promotion of employees.

Persuasion A deliberate attempt to change attitudes or beliefs with information and arguments.

PET scan Positron emission tomography; a computer-generated image of brain activity, based on glucose consumption in the brain.

Phallic stage In Freud's theory, the psychosexual stage (roughly age 3 to 6) when a person is preoccupied with the genitals as a source of pleasure.

Phantom limb The illusory sensation that a limb still exists after it is lost through accident or amputation.

Phenylketonuria A genetic disease that allows phenylpyruvic acid to accumulate in the body.

Philosophy The study of knowledge, reality, and human nature.

Phobia An intense and unrealistic fear of some object or situation.

Phobic disorder A type of anxiety disorder in which irrational fears (phobias) are focused on specific objects, activities, or situations.

Phonemes The basic sounds of a language that can be joined into syllables and words.

Photon One quantum of light energy.

Photoreceptor Sensory receptors sensitive to light and specialized for the transduction of light stimuli into neural impulses.

Phototherapy A treatment for seasonal affective disorder that involves exposure to bright, full-spectrum light.

Phrenology False and antiquated system based on the belief that personality traits are revealed by the shape of the skull.

Physical attractiveness A person's degree of physical beauty, as defined by his or her culture.

Physical dependence Physical addiction, as indicated by the presence of drug tolerance and withdrawal symptoms.

Physiological changes in emotion Changes in bodily activities (especially involuntary responses) that accompany emotional states.

Pictorial depth cues Features found in paintings, drawings, and photographs that impart information about space, depth, and distance.

Pineal gland Gland in the brain that helps regulate body rhythms and sleep cycles.

Pitch Higher or lower tones; related to the frequency of sound waves.

Pituitary gland The "master gland" at the base of the brain whose hormones influence the output of other endocrine glands.

Place theory Theory of hearing which says that higher- and lower-frequency tones are detected at specific locations in the cochlea.

Placebo A substance that resembles a drug but has no chemical effect.

Placebo effect Changes in behavior due to expectations that a drug (or other treatment) will have some effect.

Plasticity The brain's capacity for revising its organization.

Plateau phase The second phase of sexual response during which physical arousal is further heightened.

Pleasure principle The principle under which the id operates, consisting of a desire for immediate satisfaction of wishes, desires, or needs.

Polygenic characteristics Personal characteristics that are influenced by a combination of genes.

Polygraph A device for recording several physiological activities, typically including heart rate, blood pressure, respiration, and galvanic skin response; commonly called a "lie detector."

Population An entire group of animals or people belonging to a particular category (for example, all college students or all married women).

Positive instance In concept learning, an object or event that belongs to the concept class.

Positive reinforcement Occurs when a response is followed with a reward or other positive event.

Positive relationship A relationship in which increases in one measure correspond to increases in the other.

Positive self-regard Thinking of oneself as a good, lovable, worthwhile person.

Positive transfer Mastery of one task aids learning or performing another.

Positron emission tomography An image of brain activity based on glucose consumption.

Possible self A collection of thoughts, beliefs, feelings, and images concerning a self one could become.

Posttraumatic stress disorder Psychological disturbance lasting more than 1 month following stresses, such as natural disasters or military combat, that would produce anxiety in anyone who experienced them.

Postconventional moral reasoning Moral thinking based on carefully examined and self-chosen moral principles.

Postpartum depression A mild to moderately severe depression that begins within 3 months following childbirth.

Power assertion The use of physical punishment or coercion to enforce child discipline.

Preadaptation Gradual matching of sleeping-waking cycles to a new time schedule before an anticipated major change in circadian rhythms.

Precognition The purported ability to accurately predict future events.

Preconscious An area of the mind that contains information not currently in consciousness but that can be voluntarily brought to awareness.

Preconventional moral reasoning Moral thinking based on the consequences of one's choices or actions (punishment, reward, or an exchange of favors).

Prefrontal lobotomy An antiquated surgery in which portions of the frontal lobes were destroyed or disconnected from other brain areas.

Prejudice A negative attitude or prejudgment held against members of a particular group of people.

Premack principle Any high-frequency response can be used to reinforce a low-frequency response.

Premature ejaculation Ejaculation that consistently occurs before the man and his partner want it to occur.

Preoperational stage Period of intellectual development during which children begin to use language and think symbolically, yet remain intuitive and egocentric in their thought.

Prepared childbirth Techniques to manage discomfort and facilitate birth with a minimum of painkilling drugs.

Presbyopia Farsightedness caused by a loss of elasticity in the lens due to aging.

Pressure A stressful condition that occurs when a person must respond at, or near, maximum capacity for long time periods.

Primary appraisal The first step in coping with a threatening situation, consisting of deciding whether the situation is indeed a threat.

Primary auditory area Main area on the temporal lobes where hearing registers.

Primary emotions According to Plutchik, the most basic emotions are fear, surprise, sadness, disgust, anger, anticipation, joy, and acceptance.

Primary motives Innate motives based on biological needs.

Primary reinforcers Unlearned reinforcers; usually those that satisfy physiological needs.

Primary sexual characteristics Gender as defined by the genitals and internal reproductive organs.

Primary visual area Main area of the cerebral cortex that processes visual information.

Primate A member of the family of mammals including humans, apes, and monkeys.

Priming Activating implicit (hidden) memories by providing partial information that is linked with them.

Principle of motor primacy Principle that motor, muscular, and physical development must precede the learning of certain skills.

Proactive interference The tendency for old memories to interfere with the retrieval of newer memories.

Proactive maternal involvement Sensitive caregiving in which a mother actively provides her child with educational experiences.

Problem-focused coping Directly managing or remedying a stressful or threatening situation.

Procedural memory That part of long-term memory made up of conditioned responses and learned skills.

Productivity The capacity of language for generating new ideas and possibilities.

Programmed instruction Any learning format that presents information in small amounts, gives immediate practice, and provides continuous feedback to learners.

Progressive relaxation A method for producing deep relaxation of all parts of the body.

Projection Attributing one's own feelings, shortcomings, or unacceptable impulses to others.

Projective tests Psychological tests making use of ambiguous or unstructured stimuli. Subjects are presumed to project their own thoughts and impulses onto these stimuli.

Prosocial behavior Behavior toward others that is helpful, constructive, or altruistic.

Prototype An ideal, or model, used as a prime example of a particular concept.

Proxemics Systematic study of the human use of space, particularly interpersonal space in various social settings.

Pseudo-memories False memories that a person believes are real or accurate.

Pseudo-psychology Any false and unscientific system of beliefs and practices that is offered as an explanation of behavior.

Psi phenomena Events that seem to lie outside the realm of accepted scientific laws.

Psyche The mind, mental life, and personality as a whole.

Psychiatric social worker A professional who applies social science principles to help patients in clinics and hospitals.

Psychiatrist A medical doctor who specializes in treating mental disorders.

Psychoactive drug A substance capable of altering attention, memory, judgment, sense of time, self-control, mood, or perception.

Psychoanalysis A Freudian approach to psychotherapy emphasizing the exploration of unconscious conflicts.

Psychoanalyst A mental health professional (usually a medical doctor) trained to practice psychoanalysis.

Psychoanalytic theory Freudian theory of personality that emphasizes unconscious forces and internal conflicts in its explanations of behavior.

Psychodrama A therapy in which clients act out personal conflicts and feelings in the presence of others who play supporting roles.

Psychodynamic theory Any theory of behavior that emphasizes internal conflicts, motives, and unconscious forces.

Psychokinesis The purported ability to mentally alter or influence objects or events.

Psycholinguist A specialist in the psychology of language and language development.

Psychological dependence Drug dependence that is based primarily on emotional or psychological needs.

Psychological situation A situation as it is perceived and interpreted by an individual, not as it exists objectively.

Psychological trauma A psychological injury or shock, such as that caused by violence, abuse, neglect, separation, and so forth.

Psychologist An individual highly trained in the methods, factual knowledge, and theories of psychology.

Psychology The scientific study of human and animal behavior.

Psychometrics Mental measurement or testing.

Psychoneuroimmunology Study of the links among behavior, disease, and the immune system.

Psychopath An individual who appears to make no distinctions between right and wrong and who feels no guilt about destructive or antisocial behavior.

Psychopathology The scientific study of mental, emotional, and behavioral disorders; also refers to abnormal or maladaptive behavior, itself.

Psychophysics The study of the relationship between physical stimuli and the sensations they evoke in a human observer.

Psychosexual stages In Freud's theory of personality development, the oral, anal, phallic, and genital stages, during which various personality traits are formed.

Psychosis A severe psychological disorder characterized by a retreat from reality, hallucinations and delusions, disturbed emotions, and social withdrawal.

Psychosocial dilemma A conflict, between personal impulses and the social world, that affects development.

Psychosomatic disorder Illness in which psychological factors contribute to bodily damage or to damaging changes in bodily functioning.

Psychosurgery Any surgical alteration of the brain designed to bring about desirable behavioral or emotional changes.

Psychotherapist Anyone who does psychological therapy. Persons who call themselves psychotherapists are not always psychologists.

Psychotherapy Any form of psychological treatment for behavioral or emotional problems.

Psychotic disorder A severe psychological disorder characterized by a retreat from reality, by hallucinations and delusions, and by social withdrawal.

Puberty The biologically defined period during which a person matures sexually and becomes capable of reproduction.

Public distance Distance at which formal interactions, such as giving a speech, occur (about 12 feet or more from the body).

Punisher Any event that decreases the probability or frequency of responses it follows.

Punishment Occurs when a response is followed with pain or an otherwise negative event or when a response is followed with the removal of a positive reinforcer (response cost).

Pupil The dark spot at the front of the eye through which light passes.

Racism Racial prejudice that has become institutionalized (that is, it is reflected in government policy, schools, and so forth) and that is enforced by the existing social power structure.

Random assignment The use of chance (for example, flipping a coin) to assign subjects to experimental and control groups.

Random search strategy Trying possible solutions to a problem in a more or less random sequence.

Rapid eye movements (REMs) Swift eye movements during sleep.

Rating scale A list of various personality traits or aspects of behavior on which a person is rated, during or after observation of the person's behavior.

Rational-emotive behavior therapy (REBT) An approach that attempts to change or remove irrational beliefs that cause emotional problems.

Rationalization Justifying one's own behavior by giving reasonable and "rational" but false reasons for it.

Reaction formation Preventing dangerous or threatening impulses from being expressed by exaggerating opposite behavior.

Readiness Sufficient maturation for rapid acquisition of a skill.

Reality principle The principle by which the ego functions, involving delaying action (or pleasure) until it is appropriate.

Reality testing Obtaining additional information to check on the accuracy of perceptions.

Recall To supply or reproduce memorized information with a minimum of external cues.

Receptive meditation Meditation in which attention is widened to include an awareness of one's total subjective experience.

Receptor sites Areas on the surface of neurons and other cells that are sensitive to neurotransmitters or hormones.

Recessive gene A gene whose influence will be expressed only when it is paired with a second recessive gene (it cannot be expressed when paired with a dominant gene).

Reciprocal inhibition Principle that one emotional state can block another, such as joy preventing fear or anxiety inhibiting pleasure.

Recitation As a memory aid, repeating aloud information one wishes to retain.

Recoding Reorganizing or otherwise transforming information to facilitate storage in memory.

Recognition Memory in which previously learned material is correctly identified as that which was seen before.

Redintegration The process of reconstructing an entire complex memory after observing or remembering only a part of it.

Reference group Any group that an individual identifies with and uses as a standard for social comparison.

Reflection In client-centered therapy, the process of rephrasing or repeating thoughts and feelings so that clients become aware of what they are saying about themselves.

Reflex An innate, automatic response to a stimulus; for example, an eye blink, knee jerk, or dilation of the pupil.

Reflex arc The simplest behavior pattern, involving only three neurons; leads from a stimulus to an automatic response, such as an eye blink or knee jerk.

Refractory period A short time period after orgasm during which males are unable to again reach orgasm.

Refreezing In brainwashing, the process of rewarding and strengthening new attitudes and beliefs.

Refusal skills training Training that teaches youngsters how to resist influences to begin smoking (can also be applied to other drugs, such as alcohol or cocaine).

Regression Any return to an earlier, more infantile behavior pattern.

Rehearsal Silently repeating or mentally reviewing information to hold it in short-term memory or aid its long-term storage.

Reinforcement Any event that brings about learning or increases the probability that a particular response will occur.

Reinforcement value The subjective value a person attaches to a particular activity or reinforcer.

Relational concept A concept defined by the relationship between features of an object or between an object and its surroundings (for example, "greater than," "lopsided").

Relaxation response The pattern of physiological changes that occurs in the body at times of relaxation.

Relearning Learning again something that was previously learned. Used to measure one's memory of prior learning.

Relevant questions In a polygraph exam, questions to which only a guilty person should react.

Reliability The ability of a test to yield the same score, or nearly the same score, each time it is given to the same person.

REM behavior disorder A failure of normal muscle paralysis, leading to violent actions during REM sleep.

REM rebound The occurrence of extra amounts of REM sleep in a person who has been deprived of REM sleep.

REM sleep Sleep marked by rapid eye movements, a return to stage 1 EEG patterns; usually associated with dreaming.

Replicate To reproduce or repeat.

Representative sample A small, randomly selected part of a larger population that accurately reflects characteristics of the whole population.

Representativeness hueristic A tendency to select wrong answers because they seem to match preexisting mental categories.

Repression Unconsciously pushing out or barring from awareness unwanted memories.

Research method A systematic approach to answering scientific questions.

Resistance Blocking that occurs in psychoanalysis during free association; topics the client resists thinking or talking about.

Resolution (sexual) The fourth phase of sexual response, involving a return to lower levels of sexual tension and arousal.

Respondent conditioning Another term for classical conditioning.

Respondent reinforcement In classical conditioning, reinforcement that occurs when the unconditioned stimulus closely follows the conditioned stimulus.

Response Any muscular action, glandular activity, or other identifiable behavior.

Response chaining The assembly of a series of responses into a chain of actions leading to reinforcement.

Response cost Punishment that occurs when a response leads to the removal of a positive reinforcer.

Response-contingent Applying reinforcement, punishment, or other consequences only when a certain response is made.

REST Restricted Environmental Stimulation Therapy.

Resting potential The electrical charge that exists between the inside and outside of a neuron at rest.

Retardation Mental capacity significantly below average; traditionally defined as an IQ score below 70.

Reticular activating system (RAS) A part of the reticular formation that activates the cerebral cortex.

Reticular formation A network of fibers within the medulla associated with attention, alertness, and activation of higher brain areas.

Retina The light-sensitive layer of cells at the back of the eye.

Retinal Part of the chemical compound that makes up rhodopsin (also known as retinene).

Retinal disparity Small discrepancies in the images falling on each retina caused by separation of the eyes.

Retrieval Recovering information from memory.

Retroactive interference The tendency for new memories to interfere with the retrieval of old memories.

Retrograde amnesia Loss of memory for events that preceded a head injury or other amnesia-causing event.

Reversibility of thought Recognition that relationships involving equality or identity can be reversed (for example, if A = B, then B = A).

Reversible figure A stimulus pattern that allows perceivers to reverse figure-ground organization.

Reward Anything that produces pleasure or satisfaction; a positive reinforcer.

Rhodopsin The photosensitive pigment in the rods.

Rods Visual receptors that are responsive to dim light but produce only black and white sensations.

Role conflict An upsetting condition that exists when a person tries to occupy two or more roles that make conflicting demands on behavior.

Role model A person who serves as a positive example of desirable behavior.

Role-playing The dramatic enactment or reenactment of significant life events.

Role reversal Taking the role of another person to learn how one's own behavior appears from the other person's perspective.

Romantic love A combination of intimacy and passion that does not include much commitment.

Rooting reflex Neonatal reflex elicited by a light touch to the cheek, causing the infant to turn toward the object and attempt to nurse.

Rorschach Inkblot Test A projective test comprised of ten standardized inkblots that are described by the person taking the test.

Run of luck A statistically unusual outcome (as in getting five heads in a row when flipping a coin) that could still occur by chance alone.

Sadism Deriving erotic satisfaction by inflicting pain on another; more broadly, love of cruelty.

Sample A subset or portion of a population.

Satiety system Areas on the bottom middle of the hypothalamus that terminate eating.

Saturation That quality of colors related to their being very pure, from a narrow area of the spectrum, or free from mixture with other colors.

Savings score The amount of time saved (expressed as a percentage) when relearning information.

Scaffolding The process of adjusting instruction so that it is responsive to a beginner's behavior and supports the beginner's efforts to understand a problem or gain a mental skill.

Scapegoating Selecting a person or group of people to take the blame for conditions not of their making; habitual redirection of aggression toward some person or group.

Schedule of reinforcement A rule or plan for determining which responses will be reinforced.

Schizophrenia A psychosis characterized by delusions, hallucinations, apathy, and a "split" between thought and emotion.

Schizotypal personality A non-psychotic personality disorder involving withdrawal, social isolation, and odd behavior, but no break with reality.

Science A body of knowledge gained through systematic observation and experimentation.

Scientific Conducted strictly according to the principles of evidence used in the natural sciences.

Scientific method Testing the truth of a proposition through careful measurement and controlled observation.

Scientific observation Orderly observation designed to answer questions about the world.

Scientist-practitioner model Training of clinical psychologists to do both research and therapy.

Seasonal affective disorder (SAD) Depression that occurs during fall and winter; presumably related to decreased exposure to sunlight.

Secondary appraisal Deciding how to cope with a threat or challenge.

Secondary elaboration Making a dream more logical and complete while remembering it.

Secondary motives Motives based on learned psychological needs.

Secondary reinforcer A learned reinforcer; often one that gains reinforcing properties through association with a primary reinforcer.

Secondary sexual characteristics Sexual features other than the genitals and reproductive organs—such as the breasts, body shape, and facial hair.

Secondary traits Personality traits that are inconsistent or relatively superficial.

Secure attachment A stable and positive emotional bond.

Sedative A substance that calms, tranquilizes, or induces sleep by depressing activity in the nervous system.

Selective attention Voluntarily focusing on a selected portion of sensory input, most likely by rerouting messages within the brain.

Selective combination In problem solving, the ability to connect seemingly unrelated items of information.

Selective comparison The ability to relate a present problem to similar problems solved in the past or to prior experience.

Selective encoding The mental ability to select relevant information while ignoring useless or distracting information.

Selective perception Perceiving only certain stimuli among a larger array of possibilities.

Self A continuously evolving conception of one's personal identity.

Self-actualization The ongoing process of fully developing one's personal potential.

Self-assertion A direct, honest expression of feelings and desires.

Self-awareness Consciousness of oneself as a person.

Self-concept Personal perception of one's own personality traits; a collection of beliefs, ideas, and feelings about one's own identity.

Self-disclosure The process of revealing private thoughts, feelings, and personal history to others.

Self-efficacy Belief in your capacity to produce a desired result.

Self-esteem Regarding oneself as a worthwhile person; a positive evaluation of oneself.

Self-evaluation Positive and negative feelings held toward oneself.

Self-fulfilling prophecy A prediction that prompts people to act in ways that make the prediction come true.

Self-handicapping Arranging to perform under conditions that usually lower performance so as to have an excuse available for a poor showing.

Self-help group A group of people who share a particular type of problem and provide mutual support to one another.

Self-hypnosis A state of hypnosis attained without the aid of a hypnotist; autosuggestion.

Self-image Total subjective perception of one's body and personality (another term for self-concept).

Self-recording Self-management based on keeping records of response frequencies.

Self-regulated learning Active, self-guided learning.

Self-reinforcement Praising or rewarding oneself for having made a particular response (such as completing a school assignment).

Self-testing Answering self-administered questions.

Semantic differential A measure of connotative meaning obtained by rating words or concepts on several dimensions.

Semantic memory A subpart of declarative memory that records impersonal knowledge about the world.

Semantics The study of meanings in language.

Semicircular canals Fluid-filled vestibular canals; the sensory organs for balance.

Sensate focus Form of therapy that directs a couple's attention to natural sensations of sexual pleasure.

Sensation The immediate response in the brain caused by excitation of a sensory organ.

Sensation and perception psychologist A psychologist with expert knowledge on the sense organs and the processes involved in perception.

Sensation seeking A personality characteristic of persons who prefer high levels of stimulation.

Sensitive period During development, a period of increased sensitivity to environmental influences. Also, a time during which certain events must take place for normal development to occur.

Sensitivity group A group experience designed to increase self-awareness and sensitivity to others.

Sensorimotor stage Stage of intellectual development during which sensory input and motor responses become coordinated.

Sensory adaptation A decrease in sensory response to an unchanging stimulus.

Sensory analysis The capacity of sensory systems to separate incoming information into important elements.

Sensory coding Various codes used by the sense organs to transmit information to the brain.

Sensory conflict theory Attributes motion sickness to mismatched information from vision, the vestibular system, and kinesthesis.

Sensory deprivation Any major reduction in the amount or variety of sensory stimulation.

Sensory gating Alteration of incoming sensory messages in the spinal cord, before they reach the brain.

Sensory memory The first stage of memory, which holds an explicit and literal record of incoming information for 2 seconds or less.

Sensory neuron A nerve cell that carries information from the senses toward the central nervous system.

Separation anxiety Distress displayed by infants when they are separated from their parents or principal caregivers.

Serial position effect The tendency for the greatest number of memory errors to occur in the middle portion of an ordered list.

Set A predisposition to respond in a certain way.

Set point A theoretical proportion of body fat that tends to be maintained by changes in hunger and eating.

Setting In making attributions, the social and/or physical environment in which an action occurs.

Severe punishment Intense punishment; by definition, punishment capable of suppressing a response for long periods.

Sex One's biological classification as female or male.

Sex drive The strength of one's motivation to engage in sexual behavior.

Sexism Institutionalized prejudice against members of either sex, based solely on their gender.

Sexual and gender identity disorders Any of a wide range of difficulties with sexual identity, deviant sexual behavior, or sexual adjustment.

Sexual aversion Fear, anxiety, or disgust about engaging in sex.

Sexual disorder Any of a wide range of difficulties with sexual identity, sexual behavior, or sexual adjustment.

Sexual masochism Deriving sexual pleasure from having pain inflicted during the sex act.

Sexual orientation One's degree of emotional and erotic attraction to members of the same sex, opposite sex, or both sexes.

Sexual sadism Gaining sexual pleasure by inflicting pain during the sex act.

Sexual script An unspoken mental plan that defines a "plot," dialogue, and actions expected to take place in a sexual encounter.

Sexually transmitted disease A disease that is typically passed from one person to the next through intimate physical contact; a venereal disease.

Shape constancy The perceived shape of objects is unaltered by changes in the shape of their images on the retina.

Shaping Gradually molding responses to a final desired pattern.

Short-term dynamic therapy Modern psychodynamic therapy designed to produce insights within a shorter time than traditional psychoanalysis.

Short-term memory (STM) The memory system used to hold small amounts of information for relatively brief time periods.

Shyness A tendency to avoid others, plus uneasiness and strain when socializing.

Signal In early language development, any behavior, such as touching, vocalizing, gazing, or smiling, that allows non-verbal interaction and turn-taking between parent and child.

Similarity In interpersonal attraction, the extent to which two people are alike in background, age, interests, attitudes, beliefs, and so forth.

Single-blind experiment An arrangement in which subjects remain unaware of whether they are in the experimental group or the control group.

Single-word stage In language development, the period during which a child first begins to use single words.

Situational context The social situation, behavioral setting, or general circumstances in which an action takes place.

Situational demands Unstated expectations that define desirable or appropriate behavior in various settings and social situations.

Situational determinants External conditions that strongly influence behavior.

Situational test Simulating real-life conditions so that a person's reactions may be directly observed.

Size constancy The perceived size of objects remains unchanged despite changes in the size of the images they cast on the retina.

Size-distance invariance The strict relationship that exists between the distance an object lies from the eyes and the size of its image.

Skin receptors Sensory organs for touch, pressure, pain, cold, and warmth.

Skin senses The senses of touch, pressure, pain, heat, and cold.

Sleep apnea Repeated interruption of breathing during sleep.

Sleep deprivation Being deprived of desired or needed amounts of sleep.

Sleep patterns The order and duration of daily sleep and waking periods.

Sleep spindles Distinctive bursts of brain-wave activity that indicate a person is asleep.

Sleep stages Various levels of sleep depth identified by brain-wave patterns and behavioral changes.

Sleep-deprivation psychosis A major disruption of mental and emotional functioning brought about by lack of sleep.

Sleeptalking Speaking while asleep.

Slow-to-warm-up child A child who is temperamentally restrained, unexpressive, or shy.

Social comparison Making judgments about ourselves through comparison with others.

Social development The development of self-awareness, attachment to caregivers, and relationships with other children and adults.

Social distance Distance at which impersonal interaction takes place (about 4 to 12 feet from the body).

Social distance scale An attitude measure that asks people to rate the degree to which they would be willing to have contact with a member of another group.

Social influence Changes in a person's behavior induced by the presence or actions of others.

Social learning theory An approach that combines learning principles with cognitive processes (perception, thinking, anticipation), plus the effects of observational learning, to explain behavior.

Social motives Learned motives acquired as part of growing up in a particular society or culture.

Social nonconformity Failure to conform to societal norms or the usual minimum standards for social conduct.

Social phobia An intense, irrational fear of being observed, evaluated, embarrassed, or humiliated by others in social situations, such as eating, writing, blushing, or speaking in public.

Social power The capacity to control, alter, or influence the behavior of another person.

Social psychology The study of human social behavior (behavior that is influenced by one's relationship with others).

Social Readjustment Rating Scale (SRRS) A scale that rates the impact of various life events on the likelihood of illness.

Social referencing Observing others in social situations to obtain information or guidance.

Social reinforcement Praise, attention, approval, and/or affection from others.

Social role Expected behavior patterns associated with particular social positions (such as daughter, worker, student).

Social stereotypes Oversimplified images of the traits of individuals who belong to a particular social group.

Social support Close, positive relationships with other people.

Socialization The process of learning to live in a particular culture by adopting socially acceptable values and behavior.

Sociopath Another name for the psychopath or antisocial personality.

Soma The main body of a neuron or other cell.

Somatic pain Pain from the skin, muscles, joints, and tendons.

Somatic system The system of nerves linking the spinal cord with the body and sense organs.

Somatic therapy Any bodily therapy, such as drug therapy, electroconvulsive therapy, or psychosurgery.

Somatization disorder Afflicted persons have numerous physical complaints. Typically, they have consulted many doctors, but no organic cause for their distress can be identified.

Somatoform disorder The presence of physical symptoms that mimic disease or injury for which there is no identifiable physical cause.

Somatoform pain Pain that has no identifiable physical cause and appears to be of psychological origin.

Somatosensory area The part of the parietal lobes that serves as a receiving area for bodily sensations.

Somesthetic sense Pertaining to sensations produced by the skin, muscles, joints, viscera, and organs of balance.

Somnambulist One who sleepwalks.

Sound wave A cyclic compression of air molecules.

Source traits Basic underlying traits of personality; each source trait is reflected in a larger number of surface traits.

Spaced practice A practice schedule that alternates study periods with brief rests. (Massed practice, in comparison, continues for long periods, without interruption.)

Spatial neglect A tendency to ignore the left or right side of one's body and the left or right side of visual space after damage to one of the brain hemispheres.

Specific phobia An intense, irrational fear of specific objects, activities, or situations.

Spinal nerve One of 62 major nerves that channel sensory and motor information in and out of the spinal cord.

Split-brain operation A surgical technique in which the corpus callosum is cut, functionally disconnecting the two cerebral hemispheres.

Spontaneous recovery The reappearance of a learned response after its apparent extinction.

Spontaneous remission The disappearance of a psychological disturbance without the aid of therapy.

Sports psychology Study of the psychological and behavioral dimensions of sports performance.

SQ4R method A reading method based on these steps: survey, question, read, recite, relate, and review.

Stage of exhaustion Third stage of the G.A.S., at which time the body's resources are exhausted and serious health consequences occur.

Stage of resistance Second stage of the G.A.S., during which bodily adjustments to stress stabilize but at a high physical cost.

Stanford-Binet Intelligence Scale A widely used individual test of intelligence; a direct descendant of Alfred Binet's first intelligence test.

State-dependent learning Memory influenced by one's bodily state at the time of learning and at the time of retrieval. Improved memory occurs when the bodily states match.

Statistical abnormality Abnormality defined on the basis of an extreme score on some measure or dimension, such as IQ or anxiety.

Statistical significance Experimental results that would rarely occur by chance alone.

Status An individual's position in a group or social structure, especially with respect to power, privilege, importance, and so forth.

Status inequalities Differences in the power, prestige, or privileges of two or more persons or groups.

Stereocilia Bristle-like structures on hair cells.

Stereoscopic vision Perception of space and depth caused chiefly by the fact that the eyes receive different images.

Stereotype An inaccurate, rigid, and oversimplified image of members of a social group, especially an out-group.

Stereotyped response A rigid, repetitive, and non-productive response made mechanically and without regard for its appropriateness.

Stimulant A substance that produces a temporary increase of activity in the body and nervous system.

Stimulation deafness Deafness resulting from damage caused by exposure to excessively loud sounds.

Stimulus Any physical energy sensed by an organism.

Stimulus control The tendency of stimuli present when an operant response is acquired to subsequently control when and where the response is made.

Stimulus discrimination The learned ability to detect differences in stimuli, often produced by reinforcing responses to one stimulus but not another.

Stimulus generalization The tendency to respond to stimuli similar to, but not identical to, a conditioned stimulus.

Stimulus motives Innate needs for stimulation and information.

Stress The condition that occurs when a challenge or a threat forces a person to adjust or adapt to the environment.

Stress inoculation Use of positive coping statements to control fear and anxiety.

Stress management The application of behavioral strategies to reduce stress and improve coping skills.

Stress reaction The physical response to stress, consisting mainly of bodily changes related to autonomic nervous system arousal.

Stressor A specific condition or event in the environment that challenges or threatens a person.

Stroboscopic movement Illusion of movement in which an object is shown in a rapidly changing series of positions.

Structuralism The school of thought in psychology concerned with analyzing sensations and personal experience into basic elements.

Structured interview An interview that follows a prearranged plan, usually defined by asking a series of planned questions.

Subcortex All brain structures below the cerebral cortex.

Subjective discomfort Personal, private feelings of discomfort or unhappiness.

Subjective experience Reality as it is perceived and interpreted, not as it exists objectively; personal, private, non-objective experience.

Sublimation Working off frustrated desires or unacceptable impulses in substitute activities that are constructive or accepted by society.

Subliminal perception Perception of a stimulus presented below the threshold for conscious recognition.

Substance-related disorder Abuse of or dependence on a mood- or behavior-altering drug.

Successive approximations A series of steps that change behavior to a desired response pattern.

Sucking reflex Rhythmic sucking movements elicited by touching the neonate's mouth.

Sudden infant death syndrome (SIDS) The sudden, unexplained death of an apparently healthy infant.

Superego In Freudian theory, an internalization of parental values and societal standards.

Superordinate goal A goal that exceeds or overrides all others; a goal that renders other goals relatively less important.

Superstitious behavior In conditioning, a behavior repeated because it seems to produce reinforcement, even though it is actually unnecessary.

Support group A group formed to provide emotional support for its members through discussion of shared stresses and concerns.

Suppression A conscious effort to not think of something or to keep it from awareness.

Surface traits The visible or observable traits of one's personality.

Survey method The use of public polling techniques to answer psychological questions.

Syllogism A format for analyzing logical arguments.

Symbolic prejudice Prejudice that is expressed in disguised fashion.

Symbolization In Carl Rogers's theory, the process of admitting an experience to awareness.

Sympathetic system A branch of the autonomic system responsible for arousing and activating the body at times of stress.

Synapse The microscopic space, between an axon terminal and another neuron, over which neurotransmitters pass.

Syntax Rules for ordering words when forming sentences.

Systematic desensitization A guided reduction in fear, anxiety, or aversion.

Target behaviors Actions or other behaviors (such as speech) that a behavior therapist seeks to modify.

Task centering Focusing on the task at hand, rather than on one's own feelings or needs.

Taste aversion An active dislike for a particular food; frequently created when the food is associated with illness or discomfort.

Taste bud The receptor organ for taste.

Telepathy The purported ability to directly know another person's thoughts.

Temperament The physical foundation of personality, including emotional and perceptual sensitivity, energy levels, typical mood, and so forth.

Temporal lobes Areas on each side of the cerebral cortex that include the sites where hearing registers in the brain.

Test anxiety High levels of arousal and worry that seriously impair test performance.

Test battery A group of tests and interviews given to the same individual.

Test standardization Establishing standards for administering a test and interpreting scores.

Testosterone Male sex hormone, secreted mainly by the testes and responsible for the development of male sexual characteristics.

Thalamus A structure at the center of the brain that relays sensory information to the cerebral cortex.

Thanatos The death instinct postulated by Freud.

THC Tetrahydrocannabinol, the main active chemical in marijuana.

Thematic Apperception Test (TAT) A projective test consisting of 20 different scenes and life situations about which respondents make up stories.

Theory A system designed to interrelate concepts and facts in a way that summarizes existing data and predicts future observations.

Therapy placebo effect Improvement caused not by the actual process of therapy but by a client's expectation that therapy will help.

Thought stopping Use of aversive stimuli to interrupt or prevent upsetting thoughts.

Threat An event or situation perceived as potentially harmful to one's well-being.

Thyroid gland Endocrine gland whose hormones help regulate metabolism (the production and expenditure of energy within the body).

Time out To produce extinction, removing a person from a situation in which rewards for maladaptive behavior are available; also, the withholding of social reinforcers (attention, approval) when undesirable responses are made.

Tinnitus A ringing or buzzing sensation in the ears not caused by an external stimulus.

Tip-of-the-tongue state The experience of feeling that a memory is available but being unable to retrieve it.

Token economy A therapeutic program in which desirable behaviors are reinforced with tokens that can be exchanged for goods, services, activities, and privileges.

Token reinforcer A tangible secondary reinforcer such as money, gold stars, poker chips, and the like.

Tokens Symbolic rewards, or secondary reinforcers (such as plastic chips, gold stars, or points), that can be exchanged for real reinforcers.

Top-down processing Applying higher-level knowledge to rapidly organize sensory information into a meaningful perception.

Trait profile A graphic representation of the ratings obtained by an individual (or sometimes a group) on each of several personality traits.

Trait theorist A psychologist who is interested in classifying, analyzing, and interrelating traits, and in discovering their origins, to understand and explain personality.

Trait-situation interaction Variations in behavior that occur when the expression of a trait is influenced by settings or circumstances.

Traits (personality) Relatively permanent and enduring qualities of behavior that a person displays in most situations.

Transducer A device that converts energy from one system into energy in another.

Transference In psychoanalysis, the tendency of a client to transfer to the therapist feelings that correspond to those the client had for important persons in his or her past.

Transformation In Piaget's theory, the mental ability to change the shape or form of a substance (such as clay or water) and to perceive that its volume remains the same.

Transformation rules Rules by which a simple declarative sentence may be changed to other voices or forms (past tense, passive voice, and so forth).

Transvestic fetishism Achieving sexual arousal by wearing clothing of the opposite sex.

Traumatic stress A stressful experience that produces psychological injury or intense emotional pain.

Trepanning In modern usage, any surgical procedure in which a hole is bored in the skull; historically, the chipping or boring of holes in the skull to "treat" mental disturbance.

Trichromatic theory The theory of color vision based on the assumption that there are three types of cones, with peak sensitivity to red, green, or blue.

Tryptophan A sleep-promoting amino acid.

Tunnel vision Vision restricted to the center of the visual field.

Turn-taking In early language development, the tendency of parent and child to alternate in the sending and receiving of signals or messages.

Tympanic membrane The eardrum.

Type A personality A personality type with an elevated risk of heart disease; characterized by time urgency, anger, and hostility.

Type B personality All personality types other than Type A; a low-cardiac-risk personality.

Unconditional positive regard Unshakable love and approval given without qualification.

Unconditioned response An innate reflex response elicited by an unconditioned stimulus.

Unconditioned stimulus A stimulus innately capable of eliciting a response.

Unconscious Region of the mind that is beyond awareness, especially impulses and desires not directly known to a person.

Undifferentiated schizophrenia Schizophrenia lacking the specific features of catatonic, disorganized, or paranoid types.

Unfreezing In brainwashing, a loosening of convictions about former values, attitudes, and beliefs.

Unipolar disorder A mood disorder in which a person experiences extended periods of deep depression but has no history of ever having been manic.

Unstructured interview An interview in which conversation is informal and topics are taken up freely as they arise.

Unusual Uses Test A test of creativity in which subjects try to think of new uses for a common object.

Vacillation Wavering in intention or feelings.

Validity The ability of a test to measure what it purports to measure.

Validity scales Scales that tell whether test scores should be invalidated for lying, inconsistency, or "faking good."

Variable Any condition that changes or can be made to change; a measure, event, or state that may vary.

Variable interval schedule A schedule in which a reinforcer is given for the first correct response made after a varied amount of time has passed (measured from the previous reinforced response). Responses made before the time interval has ended are not reinforced.

Variable ratio schedule A pattern in which a varied number of correct responses must be made to get a reinforcer. For example, a reinforcer is given after three to seven correct responses; the actual number changes randomly.

Verbal intelligence Intelligence measured by answering questions involving vocabulary, general information, arithmetic, and other language- or symbol-oriented tasks.

Vestibular senses The senses of balance, body position, and acceleration.

Vicarious classical conditioning Classical conditioning brought about by observing another person react to a particular stimulus.

Vicarious desensitization A reduction in fear or anxiety that takes place vicariously ("secondhand") when a client watches models perform the feared behavior.

Visible spectrum That portion of the electromagnetic spectrum to which the eyes are sensitive.

Visual acuity The clarity or sharpness of visual perception.

Visual cliff An apparatus that looks like the edge of an elevated platform or cliff; used to test for depth perception in infants and baby animals.

Visual pigment A chemical found in the rods and cones that is sensitive to light.

Voyeurism Deriving sexual pleasure from viewing the genitals of others, usually without their knowledge or permission (peeping).

Waiting-list control group A group of people who receive no treatment in experiments designed to test the effectiveness of psychotherapy.

Waking consciousness A state of normal, alert awareness.

Warning system Pain based on large nerve fibers; warns that bodily damage may be occurring.

Weapons effect The observation that weapons serve as strong cues for aggressive behavior; also, the tendency for eyewitnesses to focus almost entirely on an assailant's weapon.

Weber's law States that the just noticeable difference is a constant proportion of the original stimulus intensity; actually applies most accurately to stimuli in the mid-range of intensities.

Wechsler Adult Intelligence Scale-Third Edition (WAIS-III) A widely used adult intelligence test that rates both verbal and performance intelligence.

Wechsler Intelligence Scale for Children-Third Edition (WISC-III) A widely used intelligence test for children that rates both verbal and performance intelligence.

Wellness A positive state of good health; more than the absence of disease.

Wernicke's area An area of the brain related to language comprehension.

White matter Portions of the nervous system that appear white due to the presence of myelin.

Whole learning Studying an entire package of information (such as a complete poem) at once.

Wish fulfillment Freudian belief that the content of many dreams reflects unfulfilled desires that cannot be consciously expressed.

Withdrawal of love Withholding affection to enforce child discipline.

Withdrawal symptoms Physical illness and discomfort that accompany the withdrawal of an addictive drug.

Working memory Another name for short-term memory, especially as it is used for thinking and problem solving.

X chromosome The female chromosome contributed by the mother; produces a female when paired with another *X* chromosome and a male when paired with a *Y* chromosome.

Y chromosome The male chromosome contributed by the father; produces a male when paired with an *X* chromosome. Fathers may give either an *X* or a *Y* chromosome to their offspring.

Yerkes-Dodson law A qualification of the inverted U function that states the relationships among arousal, task complexity, and performance.

Zener cards A deck of 25 cards bearing various symbols and used in early parapsychological research.

Zone of proximal development Refers to the range of tasks a child cannot yet master alone but that she or he can accomplish with the guidance of a more capable partner.

References

Abel, T., & Lattal, K. M. (2001). Molecular mechanisms of memory acquisition, consolidation and retrieval. *Current Opinion in Neurobiology, 11*(2), 180–187.

Abi-Dargham, A., et al. (1998). Increased striatal dopamine transmission in schizophrenia. *American Journal of Psychiatry, 155*(6), 761–767.

Abramson, R. (1993, January 8). EPA officially links passive smoke, cancer. *Los Angeles Times,* A27.

Adams, J. (1988). *Conceptual blockbusting.* New York: Norton.

Adelmann, P. K., & Zajonc, R. B. (1989). Facial efference and the experience of emotion. *Annual Review of Psychology, 40,* 249–280.

Adolph, K. E. (1997). Learning in the development of infant locomotion. *Monographs of the Society for Research in Child Development, 62*(3), 1–140.

Adorno, T. W., Frenkel-Brunswik, E., Levinson, D. J., & Sanford, R. N. (1950). *The authoritarian personality.* New York: Harper.

Ahissar, M. (1999). Perceptual learning. *Current Directions in Psychological Science, 8*(4), 124–128.

Ajzen, I. (2001). Nature and operation of attitudes. *Annual Review of Psychology, 52,* 27–58.

Akerstedt, T. (1990). Psychological and psychophysiological effects of shift work. *Scandinavian Journal of Work, Environment & Health, 16*(Suppl. 1), 67–73.

Akerstedt, T., Hume, K., Minors, D., & Waterhouse, J. (1993). Regulation of sleep and naps on an irregular schedule. *Sleep, 16*(8), 736–743.

Alarcon, R. D. (1995). Culture and psychiatric diagnosis: Impact on DSM-IV and ICD-10. *Psychiatric Clinics of North America, 18*(3), 449–465.

Alberti, R., & Emmons, M. (1995). *Your perfect right.* San Luis Obispo, CA: Impact.

Alberto, P. A., & Troutman, A. C. (1998). *Applied behavior analysis for teachers.* Englewood Cliffs, NJ: Prentice Hall

Alcock, J. E. (1990). *Science and supernature: A critical appraisal of parapsychology.* Buffalo, NY: Prometheus.

Alden, L. E., & Wallace, S. T. (1995). Social phobia and social appraisal in successful and unsuccessful social interactions. *Behaviour Research & Therapy, 33*(5), 497–505.

Alfeld-Liro, C., & Sigelman, C. K. (1998). Sex differences in self-concept and symptoms of depression during the transition to college. *Journal of Youth & Adolescence, 27*(2), 219–244.

Alicke, M. D., Yurak, T. J., & Vredenburg, D. S. (1996). Using personal attitudes to judge others. *Journal of Research in Personality, 30*(1), 103–119.

Allgower, A., Wardle, J., & Steptoe, A. (2001). Depressive symptoms, social support, and personal health behaviors in young men and women. *Health Psychology, 20*(3), 223–227.

Alloy, L. B., & Clements, C. M. (1998). Hopelessness theory of depression. *Cognitive Therapy & Research, 22*(4), 303–335.

Alloy, L. B., Peterson, C., Abramson, L. Y., & Seligman, M. E. (1984). Attributional style and the generality of learned helplessness. *Journal of Personality & Social Psychology, 46,* 681–687.

Allport, G. W. (1958). *The nature of prejudice.* Garden City, NY: Anchor Books, Doubleday.

Allport, G. W. (1961). *Pattern and growth in personality.* New York: Holt, Rinehart, and Winston.

Altman, L. K. (2002). AIDS threatens to claim 65M more lives by '20. *Arizona Daily Star,* July 3, A7.

Altschuler, G. C. (2001, January 7). Battling the cheats. *The New York Times: Education,* 15.

Alva, S. A. (1993). Differential patterns of achievement among Asian-American adolescents. *Journal of Youth and Adolescence, 22*(4), 407–423.

Alvarado, N. (1994). Empirical validity of the Thematic Apperception Test. *Journal of Personality Assessment, 63*(1), 59–79.

Alvino, J., & the Editors of *Gifted Children Monthly.* (1996). *Parents' guide to raising a gifted child.* New York: Ballantine.

Amabile, T., Hadley, C. N., & Kramer, S. J. (2002). Creativity under the gun. *Harvard Business Review, 80*(8), 52–61.

Amar, P. B. (1993). Biofeedback and applied psychophysiology at the crossroads. *Biofeedback & Self-Regulation, 18*(4), 201–209.

Anderegg, D., & Gartner, G. (2001). Manic dedifferentiation and the creative process. *Psychoanalytic Psychology, 18*(2), 365–379.

Anderson, C. A. (1989). Temperature and aggression. *Psychological Bulletin, 106,* 74–96.

Anderson, C. A., Anderson, K. B., & Deuser, W. E. (1996). Examining an affective aggression framework. *Personality & Social Psychology Bulletin, 22*(4), 366–376.

Anderson, C. A., & Bushman, B. J. (2002). Human aggression. *Annual Review of Psychology, 53,* 27–51.

Anderson, J. R. (1995). *Cognitive psychology.* New York: Freeman.

Anderson, K. J. (1990). Arousal and the inverted-U hypothesis. *Psychological Bulletin, 107*(1), 96–100.

Anderson, M. C., & Bell, T. (2001). Forgetting our facts: The role of inhibitory processes in the loss of propositional knowledge. *Journal of Experimental Psychology: General, 130*(3), 544–570.

Anderson, M. C. (2001). Active forgetting: Evidence for functional inhibition as a source of memory failure. *Journal of Aggression, Maltreatment & Trauma, 4*(2), 185–210.

Anderson, M. C., & Green, C. (2001). Suppressing unwanted memories by executive control. *Nature, 410*(6826), 366–369.

Anderson, R. H., Anderson, K., Flemming, D. E., & Kinghorn, E. (1984). A multidimensional test of the attributional reformulation of learned helplessness. *Bulletin of the Psychonomic Society, 22,* 211–213.

Andresen, J. (2000). Meditation meets behavioural medicine: The story of experimental research on meditation. *Journal of Consciousness Studies, 7*(11–12), 17–73.

Annett, M., & Manning, M. (1990). Arithmetic and laterality. *Neuropsychologia, 28*(1), 61–69.

Anthony, W. A., Cohen, M., & Kennard, W. (1990). Understanding the current facts and principles of mental health systems planning. *American Psychologist, 45*(11), 1249–1252.

APA. (1998). *APA directory (draft).* American Psychological Association Research Office. Washington, DC: APA.

Archer, J. (1996). Sex differences in social behavior. *American Psychologist, 51*(9), 909–917.

Arena, J. G., Bruno, G. M., Hannah, S. L., & Meador, K. J. (1995). A comparison of frontal electromyographic biofeedback training, trapezius electromyographic biofeedback training, and progressive muscle relaxation therapy in the treatment of tension headache. *Headache, 35*(7), 411–419.

Arendt, J. (1994). Clinical perspectives for melatonin and its agonists. *Biological Psychiatry, 35*(1), 1–2.

Ariely, D., & Wertenbroch, K. (2002). Procrastination, deadlines, and performance: Self-control by precommitment. *Psychological Science, 13*(3), 219–224.

Armeli, S., Gunthert, K. C., & Cohen, L. H. (2001). Stressor appraisals, coping, and post-event outcomes: The dimensionality and antecedents of stress-related growth. *Journal of Social & Clinical Psychology, 20*(3), 366–395.

Aronoff, J., Barclay, A. M., & Stevenson, L. A. (1988). The recognition of threatening facial stimuli. *Journal of Personality & Social Psychology, 54*(4), 647–655.

Aronson, E. (1969). Some antecedents of interpersonal attraction. In W. J. Arnold & D. Levine (Eds.), *Nebraska Symposium on Motivation.* Lincoln: University of Nebraska Press.

Aronson, E. (1992). *The Social Animal.* San Francisco: W. H. Freeman.

Arthur, W., Jr., & Graziano, W. G. (1996). The five-factor model, conscientiousness, and driving accident involvement. *Journal of Personality, 64*(3), 593–618.

Ary, D. V., Duncan, T. E., Biglan, A., Metzler, C. W., et al. (1999). *Journal of Abnormal Child Psychology, 27*(2), 141–150.

Asch, S. E. (1956). Studies of independence and conformity: A minority of one against a unanimous majority. *Psychological Monographs, 70*(416).

Ash, D. W., & Holding, D. H. (1990). Backward versus forward chaining in the acquisition of a keyboard skill. *Human Factors, 32*(2), 139–146.

Ashton, W. A., & Fuehrer, A. (1993). Effects of gender and gender role identification of participant and type of social support resource on support seeking. *Sex Roles, 28*(7–8), 461–476.

Aslin, R. N., & Smith, L. B. (1988). Perceptual development. *Annual Review of Psychology, 39,* 435–473.

Assanand, S., Pinel, J. P. J., & Lehman, D. R. (1998). Personal theories of hunger and eating. *Journal of Applied Social Psychology, 28*(11), 998–1015.

Attenburrow, M. E. J., Cowen, P. J., & Sharpley, A. L. (1996). Low dose melatonin improves sleep in healthy middle-aged subjects. *Psychopharmacology, 126*(2), 179–181.

Avery, D. H., Eder, D. N., Bolte, M. A., Hellekson, C. J., et al. (2001). Dawn simulation and bright light in the treatment of SAD. *Biological Psychiatry, 50*(3), 205–216.

Ayers, L., Beaton, S., & Hunt, H. (1999). The significance of transpersonal experiences, emotional conflict, and cognitive abilities in creativity. *Empirical Studies of the Arts, 17*(1), 73–82.

Ayllon, T., & Azrin, N. H. (1965). The measurement and reinforcement of behavior of psychotics. *Journal of the Experimental Analysis of Behavior, 8,* 357–383.

Azrin, N. H., Hutchinson, R. R., & McLaughlin, R. (1965). The opportunity for aggression as an operant reinforcer during aversive stimulation. *Journal of Experimental Analysis of Behavior, 8,* 171–180.

Bachman, J. G., & Johnson, L. D. (1979). The freshmen. *Psychology Today, 13,* 78–87.

Baddeley, A. (1990). *Human memory.* Needham Heights, MA: Allyn & Bacon.

Baddeley, A. (1996). *Your memory: A user's guide.* North Pomfret, England: Trafalgar Square.

Baer, J. M. (1993). *Creativity and divergent thinking.* Hillsdale, NJ: Erlbaum.

Bahrke, M. S., Yesalis, C. E., & Brower, K. J. (1998). Anabolic-androgenic steroid abuse and performance-enhancing drugs among adolescents. *Child & Adolescent Psychiatric Clinics of North America, 7*(4), 821–838.

Bailey, J. M., & Pillard, R. C. (1991). A genetic study of male sexual orientation. *Archives of General Psychiatry, 48*(12), 1089–1096.

Bailey, J. M., Pillard, R. C., Neale, M. C., & Agyei, Y. (1993). Heritable factors influence sexual orientation in women. *Archives of General Psychiatry, 50*(3), 217–223.

Baillargeon, R. (1991). Reasoning about the height and location of a hidden object in 4.5– and 6.5–month-old infants. *Cognition, 38*(1), 13–42.

Baillargeon, R., & DeVos, J. (1992). Object permanence in young infants: Further evidence. *Child Development, 62*(6), 1227–1246.

Baillargeon, R., DeVos, J., & Graber, M. (1989). Location memory in 8–month-old infants in a non-search AB task. *Cognitive Development, 4,* 345–367.

Balk, D. E., et al. (1998). TAT results in a longitudinal study of bereaved college students. *Death Studies, 22*(1), 3–21.

Baltes, P. B., Staudinger, U. M., & Lindenberger, U. (1999). Lifespan psychology. *Annual Review of Psychology, 50,* 471–507.

Banaji, M. R., & Prentice, D. A. (1994). The self in social contexts. *Annual Review of Psychology, 45,* 297–332.

Bandura, A. (1971). *Social learning theory.* New York: General Learning Press.

Bandura, A. (1973). *Aggression: A social learning analysis.* Englewood Cliffs, NJ: Prentice-Hall.

Bandura, A. (2001). Social cognitive theory. *Annual Review of Psychology, 52,* 1–26.

Bandura, A., Blanchard, E. B., & Ritter, B. (1969). Relative efficacy of desensitization and modeling approaches for inducing behavioral, affective, and attitudinal changes. *Journal of Personality & Social Psychology, 13*(3), 173–199.

Bandura, A., & Rosenthal, T. L. (1966). Vicarious classical conditioning as a function of arousal level. *Journal of Personality & Social Psychology, 3,* 54–62.

Bandura, A., & Walters, R. (1959). *Adolescent aggression.* New York: Ronald.

Bandura, A., & Walters, R. (1963a). Aggression. In H. W. Stevenson (Ed.), *Child psychology.* Chicago: University of Chicago Press.

Bandura, A., & Walters, R. (1963b). *Social learning and personality development.* New York: Holt.

Banks, A., & Gartrell, N. K. (1995). Hormones and sexual orientation: A questionable link. *Journal of Homosexuality, 28*(3–4), 247–268.

Banks, T., & Dabbs, J. M., Jr. (1996). Salivary testosterone and cortisol in delinquent and violent urban subculture. *Journal of Social Psychology, 136*(1), 49–56.

Barabasz, A. (2000). EEG markers of alert hypnosis. *Sleep & Hypnosis, 2*(4), 164–169.

Barber, T. X. (1970). *Suggested ("hypnotic") behavior: The trance paradigm versus an alternative paradigm.* Harding, MA. Medfield Foundation, Report No. 103.

Bard, C., Fleury, M., & Goulet, C. (1994). Relationship between perceptual strategies and response adequacy in sport situations. *International Journal of Sport Psychology, 25*(3), 266–281.

Barker, E. A. (1993, Spring). Evaluating graphology. *Skeptical Inquirer, 17,* 312–315.

Barlow, D. H. (2000). Unraveling the mysteries of anxiety and its disorders from the perspective of emotion theory. *American Psychologist,* Nov., 1247–1263.

Barnet, A. B., & Barnet, R. J. (1998). *The youngest minds.* New York: Touchstone

Baron, R. A., & Byrne, D. E. (2002). *Social psychology.* Boston: Allyn & Bacon.

Baron, R. A., & Richardson, D. R. (1994). *Human aggression.* New York: Plenum.

Barowsky, E. I., Moskowitz, J., & Zweig, J. B. (1990). Biofeedback for disorders of initiating and maintaining sleep. *Annals of the New York Academy of Sciences, 602,* 97–103.

Barrett, D. (1993). The "committee of sleep": A study of dream incubation for problem solving. *Dreaming, 3*(2), 115–122.

Barrett, R. J. (1985). Behavioral approaches to individual differences in substance abuse. In M. Galizio & S. A. Maisto (Eds.), *Determinants of substance abuse treatment: Biological, psychological, and environmental factors.* New York: Plenum.

Barron, F. (1958). The psychology of imagination. *Scientific American, 199*(3), 150–170.

Barsalou, L. W. (1992). *Cognitive psychology.* Hillsdale, NJ: Lawrence Erlbaum.

Barsky, S. H., Roth, M. D., Kleerup, E. C., et al. (1998). Histopathologic and molecular alterations in bronchial epithelium in habitual smokers of marijuana, cocaine, and/or tobacco. *Journal of the National Cancer Institute, 90*(16), 1198–1205.

Bar-Tal, D., & Labin, D. (2001). The effect of a major event on stereotyping: Terrorist attacks in Israel and Israeli adolescents' perceptions of Palestinians, Jordanians and Arabs. *European Journal of Social Psychology, 31*(3), 265–280.

Bartholow, B. D., & Anderson, C. A. (2002). Effects of violent video games on aggressive behavior. *Journal of Experimental Social Psychology, 38*(3), 283–290.

Bartlett, J. C., & Searcy, J. (1993). Inversion and configuration of faces. *Cognitive Psychology, 25*(3), 281–316.

Bartz, W. R. (1990). The basics of critical thought. Personal communication.

Bartz, W. R. (2002, September/October). Teaching skepticism via the CRITIC acronym. *Skeptical Inquirer,* 42–44.

Basadur, M., Runco, M. A., & Vega, L. A. (2000). Understanding how creative thinking skills, attitudes and behaviors work together. *Journal of Creative Behavior, 34*(2), 77–100.

Batejat, D. M., & Lagarde, D. P. (1999). Naps and modafinil as countermeasures for the effects of sleep deprivation on cognitive performance. *Aviation, Space, & Environmental Medicine, 70*(5), 493–498.

Bath, H. (1996). Everyday discipline or control with care. *Journal of Child & Youth Care, 10*(2), 23–32.

Batson, C. D. (1990). How social an animal? The human capacity for caring. *American Psychologist, 45*(3), 336–346.

Batterman, R. L., Cohen, M. A., Ellis, S. M., Le Roux, C. E., et al. (2003, September 4). Inhibition of food intake in obese subjects by peptide YY3–36. *New England Journal of Medicine 349,* 941–948.

Baum, A., & Posluszny, D. M. (1999). Health psychology. *Annual Review of Psychology, 50,* 137–163.

Baumeister, R. F. (1994). Self-esteem. *Encyclopedia of human behavior, Vol. 4.* San Diego, CA: Academic.

Baumrind, D. (1991). The influence of parenting style on adolescent competence and substance use. *Journal of Early Adolescence, 11*(1), 56–95.

Baumrind, D., Larzelere, R. E., & Cowan, P. A. (2002). Ordinary physical punishment: Is it harmful? *Psychological Bulletin, 128*(4), 580–589.

Beach, F. A. (1975). Behavioral endocrinology: An emerging discipline. *American Scientist, 63,* 178–187.

Beck, A. T. (1985). Cognitive therapy of depression: New perspectives. In P. Clayton (Ed.), *Depression.* New York: Raven.

Beck, A. T. (1991). Cognitive therapy. *American Psychologist, 46*(4), 368–375.

Beck, A. T., & Greenberg, R. L. (1974). *Coping with depression.* Institute For Rational Living.

Beck, A. T., Brown, C., Berchick, R. J., Stewart, B. L., et al. (1990). Relationship between hopelessness and ultimate suicide. *American Journal of Psychiatry, 147*(2), 190–195.

Beck, B. L., Koons, S. R., & Milgrim, D. L. (2000). Correlates and consequences of behavioral procrastination. *Journal of Social Behavior & Personality, 15*(5), 3–13.

Beebe, B., Gerstman, L., Carson, B., Dolins, M., Zigman, A., Rosenweig, H., Faughey K., & Korman, M. (1982). Rhythmic communication in the mother-infant dyad. In M. Davis (Ed.), *Interaction rhythms, periodicity in communicative behavior.* New York: Human Sciences Press.

Beilin, H. (1992). Piaget's enduring contribution to developmental psychology. *Developmental Psychology, 28*(2), 191–204.

Beljan, J. R., Rosenblatt, L. S., Hetherington, N. W., Layman, J., Flaim, S. E. T., Dale, G. T., & Holley, D. C. (1972). *Human performance in the aviation environment.* NASA Contract no. 2–6657, Pt. Ia, 253–259.

Bellezza, F. S., Six, L. S., & Phillips, D. S. (1992). A mnemonic for remembering long strings of digits. *Bulletin of the Psychonomic Society, 30*(4), 271–274.

Bellisle, F. (1999). Glutamate and the UMAMI taste. *Neuroscience & Biobehavioral Reviews, 23*(3), 423–438.

Belloc, N. B., (1973). Relationship of physical health practices and mortality. *Preventive Medicine, 2,* 67–81.

Belloc, N. B., & Breslow, L. (1972). Relationship of physical health status and healthy practices. *Preventive Medicine, 1,* 409–421.

Belsham, B. (2001). Glutamate and its role in psychiatric illness. *Human Psychopharmacology Clinical & Experimental, 16*(2), 139–146.

Belsky, J. (1996). Parent, infant, and social-contextual antecedents of father-son attachment security. *Developmental Psychology, 32*(5), 905–913.

Belsky, J., Gilstrap, B., & Rovine, M. (1984). The Pennsylvania infant and family development project, I: Stability and change in mother-infant and father-infant interactions in a family setting at one, three, and nine months. *Child Development, 55,* 692–705.

Bem, S. L. (1975). Sex-role adaptability: One consequence of psychological androgyny. *Journal of Personality & Social Psychology, 31,* 634–643.

Bem, S. L. (1981). Gender schema theory. A cognitive account of sex typing. *Psychological Review, 88,* 354–364.

Benbow, C. P. (1986). Physiological correlates of extreme intellectual precocity. *Neuropsychologia, 24*(5), 719–725.

Benloucif, S., Bennett, E. L., & Rosenzweig, M. R. (1995). Norepinephrine and neural plasticity: The effects of xylamine on experience-induced changes in brain weight, memory, and behavior. *Neurobiology of Learning & Memory, 63*(1), 33–42.

Benoit, S. C., & Thomas, R. L. (1992). The influence of expectancy in subliminal perception experiments. *Journal of General Psychology, 119*(4), 335–341.

Ben-Shakhar, G., & Dolev, K. (1996). Psychophysiological detection through the guilty knowledge technique: Effect of mental countermeasures. *Journal of Applied Psychology, 81*(3), 273–281.

Ben-Shakhar, G., Bar-Hillel, M., Bilu, Y., Ben-Abba, E., & Flug, A. (1986). Can graphology predict occupational success? Two empirical studies and some methodological ruminations. *Journal of Applied Psychology, 71*(4), 645–653.

Bensley, L., & Van Eenwyk, J. (2001). Video games and real-life aggression. *Journal of Adolescent Health, 29*(4), 244–257.

Benson, H. (1977). Systematic hypertension and the relaxation response. *The New England Journal of Medicine, 296,* 1152–1156.

Bergin, A. E. (1991). Values and religious issues in psychotherapy and mental health. *American Psychologist, 46,* (4), 394–403.

Berkowitz, L. (1968). The frustration-aggression hypothesis revisited. In L. Berkowitz (Ed.), *Roots of aggression: A re-examination of the frustration-aggression hypothesis.* New York: Atherton.

Berkowitz, L. (1984). Some effects of thoughts on anti- and prosocial influences of media events: A cognitive-neoassociation analysis. *Psychological Bulletin, 95,* 410–427.

Berkowitz, L. (1989). Frustrations, appraisals, and aversively stimulated aggression. *Aggressive Behavior, 14*(1), 3–11.

Berkowitz, L. (1990). On the formation and regulation of anger and aggression. *American Psychologist, 45*(4), 494–503.

Berlyne, D. (1966). Curiosity and exploration. *Science, 153,* 25–33.

Berne, E. (1964). *Games people play.* New York: Grove.

Bernstein, H. J., et al., (1998). Patient attitudes about ECT after treatment. *Psychiatric Annals, 28*(9), 524–527.

Bernthal, P. R., & Insko, C. A. (1993). Cohesiveness without groupthink: The interactive effects of social and task cohesion. *Group & Organization Management, 18*(1), 66–87.

Bersheid, E. (1994). Interpersonal relations. *Annual Review of Psychology, 45,* 79–129.

Bersoff, D. M. (1999). Why good people sometimes do bad things: Motivated reasoning and unethical behavior. *Personality & Social Psychology Bulletin, 25*(1), 28–39.

Bertsch, G. J. (1976). Punishment of consummatory and instrumental behavior: A review. *Psychological Record, 26,* 13–31.

Best, J. B. (1999). *Cognitive psychology.* Pacific Grove: Brooks/Cole.

Betancur, C., Velez, A., Cabanieu, G., le Moal, M., et al. (1990). Association between left-handedness and allergy: A reappraisal. *Neuropsychologia, 28*(2), 223–227.

Beyerstein, B. L., & Beyerstein, D. F. (1992). *The write stuff: Evaluations of graphology.* Buffalo, NY: Prometheus.

Bickman, L. (1974, April). Clothes make the person. *Psychology Today,* 48–51.

Bierley, C., McSweeney, F. K., & Vannieuwerk, R. (1985). Classical conditioning of preferences for stimuli. *Journal of Consumer Research, 12,* 316–323.

Biglan, A., Ary, D., Yudelson, H., & Duncan, T. E. (1996). Experimental evaluation of a modular approach to mobilizing antitobacco influences of peers and parents. *American Journal of Community Psychology, 24*(3), 311–339.

Bigler, E. D., Johnson, S. C., Anderson, C. V., & Blatter, D. D. (1996). Traumatic brain injury and memory: The role of hippocampal atrophy. *Neuropsychology, 10*(3), 333–342.

Binder, V. (1976). Behavior modification: Operant approaches to therapy. In V. Binder, A. Binder, & B. Rimland (Eds.), *Modern therapies.* Englewood Cliffs, NJ: Prentice-Hall.

Binks, P. G., Waters, W. F., & Hurry, M. (1999). Short-term total sleep deprivations does not selectively impair higher cortical functioning. *Sleep, 22*(3), 328–334.

Biondi, M., & Zannino, L. (1997). Psychological stress, neuroimmunomodulation, and susceptibility to infectious diseases in animals and man. *Psychotherapy & Psychosomatics, 66*(1), 3–26.

Birch, J., & McKeever, L. M. (1993). Survey of the accuracy of new pseudoisochromatic plates. *Ophthalmic & Physiological Optics, 13*(1), 35–40.

Birnbaum, M. H. (2000). *Introduction to behavioral research on the Internet.* Saddle River, NJ: Prentice-Hall.

Blackmore, S. (1989). What do we really think? A survey of parapsychologists and sceptics. *Journal of the Society for Psychical Research, 55*(814), 251–262.

Blackmore, S. (1991). Lucid dreaming. *Skeptical Inquirer, 15,* 362–370.

Blackmore, S. (2001, March/April). Giving up the ghosts. *Skeptical Inquirer, 25.*

Blackwell, D. L., & Lichter, D. T. (2000). Mate selection among married and cohabiting couples. *Journal of Family Issues, 21*(3), 275–302.

Blackwell, R. T., Galassi, J. P., Galassi, M. D., & Watson, T. E. (1985). Are cognitive assessments equal? A comparison of think aloud and thought listing. *Cognitive Therapy and Research, 9,* 399–413.

Blanchard, E. B., Eisele, G., Vollmer, A., & Payne, A. (1996). Controlled evaluation of thermal biofeedback in treatment of elevated blood pressure in unmedicated mild hypertension. *Biofeedback & Self Regulation, 21*(2), 167–190.

Blood, A. J., & Zatorre, R. J. (2001). Intensely pleasurable responses to music correlate with activity in brain regions implicated in reward and emotion. *Proceedings National Academy of Sciences, 98*(20), 11818–11823.

Bloom, B. (1985). *Developing talent in young people.* New York: Ballantine.

Bloom, J. W. (1998). The ethical practice of WebCounseling. *British Journal of Guidance & Counselling, 26*(1), 53–59.

Blumberg, M. S., & Wasserman, E. A. (1995). Animal mind and the argument from design. *American Psychologist, 50*(3), 133–144.

Boergers, J., Spirito, A., & Donaldson, D. (1998). Reasons for adolescent suicide attempts. *Journal of the American Academy of Child & Adolescent Psychiatry, 37*(12), 1287–1293.

Bohannon, J. N., & Stanowicz, L. B. (1988). The issue of negative evidence: Adult responses to children's language errors. *Developmental Psychology, 24*(5), 684–689.

Bohart, A. C., & Tallman, K. (1996). The active client: Therapy as self-help. *Journal of Humanistic Psychology, 36*(3), 7–30.

Bohart, W. (1995). The person-centered therapies. In A. S. Gurman & S. B. Messer, *Essential Psychotherapies.* New York: Guilford.

Boivin, D. B., Czeisler, C. A., & Waterhouse, J. W. (1997). Complex interaction of the sleep-wake cycle and circadian phase modulates mood in healthy subjects. *Archives of General Psychiatry, 54*(2), 145.

Bolles, R. C. (1979). *Learning theory.* New York: Holt, Rinehart & Winston.

Bond, R., & Smith, P. B. (1996). Culture and conformity: A meta-analysis of studies using Asch's (1952b, 1956) line judgment task. *Psychological Bulletin, 119*(1), 111–137.

Bond, T., & Wooten, V. (1996). The etiology and management of insomnia. *Virginia Medical Quarterly, 123*(4), 254–255.

Bongard, S., al'Absi, M., & Lovallo, W. R. (1998). Interactive effects of trait hostility and anger expression on cardiovascular reactivity in young men. *International Journal of Psychophysiology, 28*(2), 181–191.

Book, H. E., & Luborsky, L. (1998). *Brief psychodynamic psychotherapy.* Washington, DC: American Psychological Association.

Booker, J. M., & Hellekson, C. J. (1992). Prevalence of seasonal affective disorder in Alaska. *American Journal of Psychiatry, 149*(9), 1176–1182.

Bootzin, R. R., & Epstein, D. R. (2000). Stimulus control. In K. L. Lichstein & C. M. Morin. *Treatment of late life insomnia.* Thousand Oaks, CA: Sage.

Borlongan, C. V., Sanberg, P. R., & Freeman, T. B. (1999). Neural transplantation for neurodegenerative disorders. *Lancet, 353*(Suppl 1), S29–30.

Borman, W. C., Hanson, M. A., & Hedge, J. W. (1997). Personnel psychology. *Annual Review of Psychology, 48,* 299–337.

Bornstein, M. H. (1989). Sensitive periods in development: Structural characteristics and causal interpretations. *Psychological Bulletin, 105*(2), 179–197.

Bornstein, M. H. (1995). Parenting infants. In M. H. Bornstein (Ed.), *Handbook of parenting.* Mahwah, NJ: Erlbaum.

Bornstein, M. H., Haynes, O. M., Azuma, H., Galperín, C., et al. (1998). A cross-national study of self-evaluations and attributions in parenting. *Developmental Psychology, 34,* 662–676.

Bornstein, R. F. (1996). Sex differences in dependent personality disorder prevalence rates. *Clinical Psychology: Science & Practice, 3*(1), 1–12.

Borod, J. C., Bloom, R. L., Brickman, A. M., Nakhutina, L., & Curko, E. A. (2002). Emotional processing deficits in individuals with unilateral brain damage. *Applied Neuropsychology, 9*(1), 23–36.

Borod, J. C., Cicero, B. A., Obler, L. K., et al. (1998). Right hemisphere emotional perception. *Neuropsychology, 12*(3), 446–458.

Borrie, R. A. (1990–1991). The use of restricted environmental stimulation therapy in treating addictive behaviors. *International Journal of the Addictions, 25*(7A–8A), 995–1015.

Botella, C., et al. (1998). Virtual reality treatment of claustrophobia. *Behaviour Research & Therapy, 36*(2), 239–246.

Bouchard, T. J. (1983). Twins—Nature's twice-told tale. *Yearbook of science and the future,* 66–81. Chicago: Encyclopedia Britannica.

Bouchard, T. J., Lykken, D. T., McGue, M., Segal, N. L., & Tellegen, A. (1990). Sources of human psychological differences: The Minnesota study of twins reared apart. *Science, 250,* 223–228.

Bower, B. (1990, November 17). Gone but not forgotten. *Science News, 138,* 312–314.

Bower, G. H. (1973, October). How to . . . uh . . . remember. *Psychology Today,* 63–70.

Bower, G. H. (1981). Mood and memory. *American Psychologist, 36,* 129–148.

Bower, G. H., & Springston, F. (1970). Pauses as recoding points in letter series. *Journal of Experimental Psychology, 83,* 421–430.

Bowers, K. S., & Farvolden, P. (1996). Revisiting a century-old Freudian slip—From suggestion disavowed to the truth repressed. *Psychological Bulletin, 119*(3), 355–380.

Bowers, K. S., & Woody, E. Z. (1996). Hypnotic amnesia and the paradox of intentional forgetting. *Journal of Abnormal Psychology, 105*(3), 381–390.

Boyatzis, C. J., Matillo, G. M., & Nesbitt, K. M. (1995). Effects of "The Mighty Morphin Power Rangers" on children's aggression with peers. *Child Study Journal, 25*(1), 45–55.

Bradley, R. H., Caldwell, B. M., Rock, S. L., Ramey, C. T., et al. (1989). Home environment and cognitive development in the first 3 years of life: A collaborative study involving six sites and three ethnic groups in North America. *Developmental Psychology, 25*(2), 217–235.

Braffman, W., & Kirsch, I. (1999). Imaginative suggestibility and hypnotizability. *Journal of Personality & Social Psychology, 77*(3), 578–587.

Brannon, L. (1996). *Gender.* Boston: Allyn & Bacon.

Bransford, J. D., & McCarrell, N. S. (1977). A sketch of cognitive approach to comprehension: Some thoughts about understanding what it means to comprehend. In P. N. Johnson-Laird & P. C. Wason (Eds.), *Thinking: Readings in cognitive science.* Cambridge: Cambridge University Press.

Braun, A. R., Balkin, T. J., & Herscovitch, P. (1998). Dissociated pattern of activity in visual cortices and their projections during human rapid eye movement sleep. *Science, 279*(5347), 91–95.

Braun, K. A., Ellis, R., & Loftus, E. F. (2002). Make my memory: How advertising can change memories of the past. *Psychology and Marketing, 19,* 1–23.

Braun, S. (2001). Seeking insight by prescription. *Cerebrum, 3*(2), 10–21.

Braungart, J. M., Plomin, R., DeFries, J. C., & Fulker, D. W. (1992). Genetic influence on tester-rated infant temperament as assessed by Bayley's Infant Behavior Record. *Developmental Psychology, 28*(1), 40–47.

Brawman-Mintzer, O., & Lydiard, R. B. (1996). Generalized anxiety disorder: issues in epidemiology. *Journal of Clinical Psychiatry, 57*(Suppl. 7), 3–8.

Brebner, J. (1998). Happiness and personality. *Personality & Individual Differences, 25*(2), 279–296.

Brenner, V., & Fox, R. A. (1998). Parental discipline and behavior problems in young children. *Journal of Genetic Psychology, 159*(2), 251–256.

Breslau, N. (2001). Outcomes of posttraumatic stress disorder. Outcomes of post-traumatic stress disorder. *Journal of Clinical Psychiatry, 62*(Suppl. 17), 55–59.

Breslau, N., Johnson, E. O., Hiripi, E., & Kessler, R. (2001). Nicotine dependence in the United States. *Archives of General Psychiatry, 58*(9), 810–816.

Breslow, L., & Enstrom, J. E. (1980). Persistence of health habits and their relationship to mortality. *Preventive Medicine, 9,* 469–483.

Bressi, C., Albonetti, S., & Razzoli, E. (1998). "Communication deviance" and schizophrenia. *New Trends in Experimental & Clinical Psychiatry, 14*(1), 33–39.

Brewer, K. R., & Wann, D. L. (1998). Observational learning effectiveness as a function of model characteristics. *Social Behavior & Personality, 26*(1), 1–10.

Bridges, K. M. B. (1932). Emotional development in early infancy. *Child Development, 3,* 324–334.

Bridgett, D. J., & Cuevas, J. (2000). Effects of listening to Mozart and Bach on the performance of a mathematical test. *Perceptual & Motor Skills, 90*(3, Pt. 2), 1171–1175.

Britton, B. K., & Tesser, A. (1991). Effects of time-management practices on college grades. *Journal of Educational Psychology, 83*(3), 405–410.

Brody, H., & Brody, D. (2000). Three perspectives on the placebo response: Expectancy, conditioning, and meaning. *Advances in Mind-Body Medicine, 16*(3), 216–232.

Brothen, T., & Wambach, C. (2001). Effective student use of computerized quizzes. *Teaching of Psychology, 28*(4), 292–294.

Brown, A. M. (1990). Development of visual sensitivity to light and color vision in human infants: A critical review. *Vision Research, 30*(8), 1159–1188.

Brown, A. S., Cohen, P., Harkavy-Friedman, J., Babulas, V., et al. (2001). Prenatal rubella, premorbid abnormalities, and adult schizophrenia. *Biological Psychiatry, 49*(6), 473–486.

Brown, B. R., Jr., Baranowski, M. D., Kulig, J. W., & Stephenson, J. N. (1996). Searching for the Magic Johnson effect: AIDS, adolescents, and celebrity disclosure. *Adolescence, 31*(122), 253–264.

Brown, G. M. (1994). Light, melatonin and the sleep-wake cycle. *Journal of Psychiatry & Neuroscience, 19*(5), 345–353.

Brown, R., & McNeill, D. (1966). The "tip of the tongue" phenomenon. *Journal of Verbal Learning and Verbal Behavior, 5,* 325–337.

Brown, R. L., Leonard, T., Saunders, L. A., & Papasouiotis, O. (1997). A two-item screening test for alcohol and other drug problems. *Journal of Family Practice, 44*(2), 151–160.

Brown, R. T. (1991). Helping students confront and deal with stress and procrastination. *Journal of College Student Psychotherapy, 6*(2), 87–102.

Brown, S. A., Tapert, S. F., Granholm, E., & Delis, D. C. (2000). Neurocognitive functioning of adolescents: Effects of protracted alcohol use. *Alcoholism: Clinical & Experimental Research, 24*(2), 164–171.

Brown, T. D., Dane, F. C., & Durham, M. D. (1998). Perception of race and ethnicity. *Journal of Social Behavior & Personality, 13*(2), 295–306.

Brownell, K. D., Greenwood, M. R. C., Stellar, E., & Shrager, E. E. (1986). The effects of repeated cycles of weight loss and regain in rats. *Physiology and Behavior, 38,* 459–464.

Brownell, K. D., & Rodin, J. (1994). The dieting maelstrom. *American Psychologist, 49,* 781–791.

Bruch, M. A., Berko, E. H., & Haase, R. F. (1998). Shyness, masculine ideology, physical attractiveness, and emotional inexpressiveness. *Journal of Counseling Psychology, 45*(1), 84–97.

Bruner, J. (1983). *Child's Talk.* New York: Norton.

Bryan, J. H., & Walbek, N. H. (1970). Preaching and practicing generosity: Children's actions and reactions. *Child Development, 41,* 329–353.

Bryant, D. M., & Maxwell, K. L. (1999). The environment and mental retardation. *International Review of Psychiatry, 11*(1) 56–67

Buchanan, R. W., et al. (1998). Positive and negative symptom response to clozapine in schizophrenic patients. *American Journal of Psychiatry, 155*(6), 751–760.

Buchwald, A. (1965, June 20). Psyching out. *The Washington Post.*

Buck, L. A. (1990). Abnormality, normality and health. *Psychotherapy, 27*(2), 187–194.

Buckelew, S. P., et al. (1998). Biofeedback/relaxation training and exercise interventions for fibromyalgia. *Arthritis Care & Research, 11*(3), 196–209.

Buckhout, R. (1974). Eyewitness testimony. *Scientific American, 231,* 23–31.

Budney, A. J., Novy, P. L., & Hughes, J. R. (1999). Marijuana withdrawal among adults seeking treatment for marijuana dependence. *Addiction, 94*(9), 1311–1322.

Bugental, J. F. T., & Sterling, M. M. (1995). Existential-humanistic psychotherapy: New perspectives. In A. S. Gurman & S. B. Messer, *Essential Psychotherapies.* New York: Guilford.

Burchinal, M. R., Roberts, J. E., Riggins, R., Zeisel, S. A., Neebe, E., & Bryant, D. (2000). Relating quality of center-based child care to early cognitive and language development longitudinally. *Child Development, 71*(2), 339–357.

Burgess, C. A., & Kirsch, I. (1999). Expectancy information as a moderator of the effects of hypnosis on memory. *Contemporary Hypnosis, 16*(1), 22–31.

Burgner, D., & Hewstone, M. (1993). Young children's causal attributions for success and failure. *British Journal of Developmental Psychology, 11*(2), 125–129.

Burka, J. B., & Yuen, L. M. (1990). *Procrastination: Why You Do It; What To Do About It.* Cambridge, MA: Perseus Books.

Burns, D. D., & Persons, J. (1982). Hope and hopelessness: A cognitive approach. In L. E. Abt & I. R. Stuart (Eds.), *The newer therapies: A sourcebook.* New York: Van Nostrand Reinhold.

Burtt, H. E. (1941). An experimental study of early childhood memory: Final report. *Journal of General Psychology, 58,* 435–439.

Bushman, B. J., & Anderson, C. A. (2001). Media violence and the American public. *American Psychologist, 56*(6/7), 477–489.

Bushman, B. J., & Geen, R. G. (1990). Role of cognitive-emotional mediators and individual differences in the effects of media violence on aggression. *Journal of Personality & Social Psychology, 58*(1), 156–163.

Bushman, B. J., & Huesmann, L. R. (2001). Effects of televised violence on aggression. In *Handbook of Children and the Media,* D. Singer & J. Singer (Eds.). Thousand Oaks, CA: Sage.

Bushnell, L. W., Sai, F., & Mullin, L. T. (1989). Neonatal recognition of the mother's face. *British Journal of Developmental Psychology, 7*(1), 3–15.

Buss, A. H. (1980). *Self-consciousness and social anxiety.* San Francisco: Freeman.

Buss, A. H. (1986). A theory of shyness. In W. H. Jones, J. M. Cheek, & S. R. Briggs, *Shyness: Perspectives on research and treatment.* New York: Plenum.

Buss, D. M. (1985). Human mate selection. *American Scientist, 73,* 47–51.

Buss, D. M. (1994). *The evolution of desire.* New York: Basic.

Butcher, J. N., Mineka, S., & Hooley, J. (2004). *Abnormal psychology.* Boston: Allyn & Bacon.

Butler, J. C. (2000). Personality and emotional correlates of right-wing authoritarianism. *Social Behavior & Personality,* 28(1), 1–14.

Butler, R. (1954). Curiosity in monkeys. *Scientific American, 190*(18), 70–75.

Buyer, L. S. (1988). Creative problem solving: A comparison of performance under different instructions. *Journal of Creative Behavior, 22*(1), 55–61.

Byrd, K. R. (1994). The narrative reconstructions of incest survivors. *American Psychologist, 49*(5), 439–440.

Cahill, S. P., Carrigan, M. H., & Frueh, B. C. (1999). Does EMDR work? and if so, why? *Journal of Anxiety Disorders, 13*(1–2), 5–33.

Calvert, S. L., & Cocking, R. R. (1992). Health promotion through mass media. *Journal of Applied Developmental Psychology, 13*(2), 143–149.

Camara, W. J., & Schneider, D. L. (1994). Integrity tests. *American Psychologist, 49*(2), 112–119.

Camatta, C. D., & Nagoshi, C. T. (1995). Stress, depression, irrational beliefs, and alcohol use and problems in a college student sample. *Alcoholism: Clinical & Experimental Research, 19*(1), 142–146.

Cameron, L. D., & Nicholls, G. (1998). Expression of stressful experiences through writing. *Health Psychology, 17*(1), 84–92.

Campbell, J. B., & Hawley, C. W. (1982). Study habits and Eysenck's theory of extraversion-introversion. *Journal of Research in Personality, 16*, 139–146.

Campfield, L. A., Smith, F. J., Rosenbaum, M., & Hirsch, J. (1996). Human eating: Evidence for a physiological basis using a modified paradigm. *Neuroscience & Biobehavioral Reviews, 20*(1), 133–137.

Campion, M. A., & McClelland, C. L. (1993). Follow-up and extension of interdisciplinary costs and benefits of enlarged jobs. *Journal of Applied Psychology, 78*(3), 339–351.

Campos, A., & Perez, M. J. (1997). Mnemonic images and associated pair recall. *Journal of Mental Imagery, 21*(3–4), 73–82.

Camras, L. A., Sullivan, J., & Michel, G. (1993). Do infants express discrete emotions? *Journal of Nonverbal Behavior, 17*(3), 171–186.

Canli, T., Desmond, J. E., Zhao, Z., Glover, G., et al. (1998). Hemispheric asymmetry for emotional stimuli detected with fMRI. *Neuroreport, 9*(14), 3233–3239.

Cann, A., Holt, K., & Calhoun, L. G. (1999). The roles of humor and sense of humor in responses to stressors. *Humor: International Journal of Humor Research, 12*(2), 177–193.

Cannon, T. D. (1998). Neurodevelopmental influences in the genesis and epigenesis of schizophrenia. *Applied & Preventive Psychology, 7*(1), 47–62.

Cannon, T. D., et al. (1998). The genetic epidemiology of schizophrenia in a Finnish twin cohort. *Archives of General Psychiatry, 55*(1), 67–74.

Cannon, W. B. (1932). *The wisdom of the body.* New York: Norton.

Cannon, W. B. (1934). Hunger and thirst. In C. Murchinson (Ed.), *Handbook of general experimental psychology.* Worcester, MA: Clark University Press.

Cannon, W. B., & Washburn, A. L. (1912). An exploration of hunger. *American Journal of Physiology, 29*, 441–454.

Caplan, N., Choy, M. H., & Whitmore, J. K. (1992). Indochinese refugee families and academic achievement. *Scientific American*, Feb., 36–42.

Caplan, P. J. (1995). *They say you're crazy.* Reading, MA: Addison-Wesley.

Carducci, B. J., & Stein, N. D. (1988). *The personal and situational pervasiveness of shyness in college students: A nine-year comparison.* Paper presented at the meeting of the Southeastern Psychological Association, New Orleans, April 1988.

Carli, L. L., Ganley, R., & Pierce-Otay, A. (1991). Similarity and satisfaction in roommate relationships. *Personality & Social Psychology Bulletin, 17*(4), 419–426.

Carlson, C. L., Pelham, W. E., Milich, R., & Dixon, J. (1992). Single and combined effects of methylphenidate and behavior therapy on the classroom performance of children with attention-deficit hyperactivity disorder. *Journal of Abnormal Child Psychology, 20*(2), 213–232.

Carlson, J. G., et al. (1998). Eye movement desensitization and reprocessing (EDMR) treatment for combat-related posttraumatic stress disorder. *Journal of Traumatic Stress, 11*(1), 3–24.

Carlson, M., Marcus-Hewhall, A., & Miller, N. (1990). Effects of situational aggression cues: A quantitative review. *Journal of Personality & Social Psychology, 58*(4), 622–633.

Carlson, N. R. (2001). *Physiology of behavior* (7th ed.). Boston: Allyn & Bacon.

Carnegie Corporation of New York. (1994). *Starting points: Meeting the needs of our youngest children.* New York: The Carnegie Corporation.

Carney, R. N., & Levin, J. R. (1998). Do mnemonic memories fade as time goes by? *Contemporary Educational Psychology, 23*(3), 276–297.

Carney, R. N., Levin, J. R., & Stackhouse, T. L. (1997). The face-name mnemonic strategy from a different perspective. *Contemporary Educational Psychology, 22*(3), 399–412.

Carroll, J. M., & Russell, J. A. (1996). Do facial expressions signal specific emotions? Judging emotion from the face in context. *Journal of Personality & Social Psychology, 70*(2), 205–218.

Carter, R. (1998). *Mapping the mind.* Berkeley, CA: University of California Press.

Carter, W. E. (Ed.) (1980). *Cannabis in Costa Rica: A study of chronic marihuana use.* Philadelphia: Institute for the Study of Human Issues.

Cartwright, R., & Lamberg, L. (1992). *Crisis dreaming.* New York: HarperCollins.

Casey, P. (2001). Multiple personality disorder. *Primary Care Psychiatry, 7*(1), 7–11.

Caspi, A., & Herbener, E. S. (1990). Continuity and change: Associative marriage and the consistency of personality in adulthood. *Journal of Personality & Social Psychology, 58*(2), 250–258.

Caspi, A., Sugden, K., Moffitt, T. E., Taylor, A., et al. (2003). Influence of life stress on depression: Moderation by a polymorphism in the 5-HTT gene. *Science, 301*(5631), 386–389.

Casto, S. D., DeFries, J. C., & Fulker, D. W. (1995). Multivariate genetic analysis of Wechsler Intelligence Scale for Children— Revised (WISC–R) factors. *Behavior Genetics, 25*(1), 25–32.

Catalano, R., Novaco, R., & McConnell, W. (1997). A model of the net effect of job loss on violence. *Journal of Personality & Social Psychology, 72*(6), 1440–1447.

Cattell, R. B. (1965). *The scientific analysis of personality.* Baltimore: Penguin.

Cattell, R. B. (1973, July). Personality pinned down. *Psychology Today*, 40–46.

Cautela, J. R., & Bennett, A. K. (1981). Covert conditioning. In R. J. Corsini (Ed.), *Handbook of innovative psychotherapies*, pp. 189–204. New York: Wiley.

Cautela, J. R., & Kearney, A. J. (1986). *The covert conditioning handbook.* New York: Springer.

Cecil, H., Evans, R. J., & Stanley, M. A. (1996). Perceived believability among adolescents of health warning labels on cigarette packs. *Journal of Applied Social Psychology, 26*(6), 502–519.

Chabris, C. F., Steele, K. M., Bella, S. D., et al. (1999). Prelude or requiem for the "Mozart effect"? *Nature, 400*(6747), 826–828.

Chakos, M. H., Alvir, J. M. J., Woerner, M., & Koreen, A. (1996). Incidence and correlates of tardive dyskinesia in first episode of schizophrenia. *Archives of General Psychiatry, 53*(4), 313–319.

Chamberlin, J., & Rogers, J. A. (1990). Planning a community-based mental health system. *American Psychologist, 45*(11), 1241–1244.

Chambers, R. A., Taylor, J. R., & Potenza, M. N. (2003). Developmental neurocircuitry of motivation in adolescence: A critical period of addiction vulnerability. *American Journal of Psychiatry, 160*(6), 1041–1052.

Chambless, D. L., & Ollendick, T. H. (2001). Empirically supported psychological interventions. *Annual Review of Psychology, 52*, 685–716.

Chan, R. W., Raboy, B., & Patterson, C. J. (1998). Psychosocial adjustment among children conceived via donor insemination by lesbian and heterosexual mothers. *Child Development, 69*(2), 443–457.

Chastain, G., & Thurber, S. (1989). The SQ3R study technique enhances comprehension of an introductory psychology textbook. *Reading Improvement, 26*(1), 94.

Cheadle, A., Psaty, B. M., Diehr, P., Koepsell, T., et al. (1992–93). An empirical exploration of a conceptual model for community-based health-promotion. *International Quarterly of Community Health Education, 13*(4), 329–363.

Cheek, J., & Buss, A. H. (1979). Scales of shyness, sociability and self-esteem and correlations among them. Unpublished research, University of Texas. (Cited by Buss, 1980.)

Chen, K., & Kandel, D. B. (1995). The natural history of drug use from adolescence to the mid-thirties in a general population sample. *American Journal of Public Health, 85*(1), 41–47.

Chen, Z., Lawson, R. B., Gordon, L. R., & McIntosh, B. (1996). Groupthink: Deciding with the leader and the devil. *Psychological Record, 46*(4), 581–590.

Cheng, H., Cao, Y., & Olson, L. (1996). Spinal cord repair in adult paraplegic rats: Partial restoration of hind limb function. *Science, 273*(5274), 510.

Chess, S., & Thomas, A. (1986). *Know your child.* New York: Basic.

Chesson, A. L., Anderson, W. M., Littner, M., Davila, D., et al. (1999). Practice parameters for the nonpharmacologic treatment of chronic insomnia. *Sleep, 22*, 1128–33.

Chomsky, N. (1975). *Reflections on language.* New York: Pantheon.

Chomsky, N. (1986). *Knowledge of language.* New York: Praeger.

Christensen, A., & Jacobson, N. S. (1994). Who (or what) can do psychotherapy. *Psychological Science, 5*(1), 8–14.

Christensen, D. (1999). Mind over matter. *Science News, 156*, 142–143.

Christianson, S., Saisa, J., & Silfvenius, H. (1995). The right hemisphere recognises the bad guys. *Cognition & Emotion, 9*(4), 309–324.

Cialdini, R. B., Eisenberg, N., & Green, B. L., et al. (1998). Undermining the undermining effect of reward on sustained interest. *Journal of Applied Social Psychology, 28*(3), 249–263.

Cialdini, R. B., Petty, R. E., & Cacippo, T. J. (1981). Attitude and attitude change. *Annual Review of Psychology, 32*, 357–404.

Cialdini, R. B., Reno, R. R., & Kallgren, C. A. (1990). A focus theory of normative conduct: Recycling the concept of norms to reduce littering in public places. *Journal of Personality & Social Psychology, 58*(6), 1015–1026.

Cialdini, R. B., Vincent, J. E., Lewis, S. K., Catalan, J., Wheeler, D., & Darby, B. L. (1975). A reciprocal concessions procedure for inducing compliance: The door-in-the-face technique. *Journal of Personality & Social Psychology, 21*, 206–215.

Ciarrochi, J., Dean, F. P., & Anderson, S. (2002). Emotional intelligence moderates the relationship between stress and mental health. *Personality & Individual Differences, 32*(2), 197–209.

Cinciripini, P. M., Wetter, D. W., & McClure, J. B. (1997). Scheduled reduced smoking. *Addictive Behaviors, 22*(6), 759–767.

Clapham, M. M. (2001). The effects of affect manipulation and information exposure on divergent thinking. *Creativity Research Journal, 13*(3–4), 335–350.

Clark, R., Anderson, N. B., Clark, V. R., & Williams, D. R. (1999). Racism as a stressor for African Americans. *American Psychologist, 54*(10), 805–816.

Click, P., Zion, C., & Nelson, C. (1988). What mediates sex discrimination in hiring decisions? *Journal of Personality & Social Psychology, 55*(2), 178–186.

Cline, V. B., Croft, R. G., & Courrier, S. (1972). Desensitization of children to television violence. *Journal of Personality & Social Psychology, 27*, 360–365.

Cohen, N. L., Waltzman, S. B., & Fisher, S. G. (1993). A prospective, randomized study of cochlear implants. *New England Journal of Medicine, 328*(4), 233–237.

Cole, J. (1995). *Pride and a daily marathon.* Cambridge, MA: MIT Press.

Cole, P. H. (1998). Affective process in psychotherapy: A *Gestalt* therapist's view. *Gestalt Journal, 21*(1), 49–72.

Colin, A. K., Moore, K., & West, A. N. (1996). Creativity, oversensitivity, and rate of habituation. *EDRA: Environmental Design Research Association, 20*(4), 423–427.

Collins, A. M., & Quillian, M. R. (1969). Retrieval time from semantic memory. *Journal of Verbal Learning and Verbal Behavior, 8*, 240–247.

Collins, W. A., & Gunnar, M. R. (1990). Social and personality development. *Annual Review of Psychology, 41*, 387–416.

Comperatore, C. A., Lieberman, H. R., Kirby, A. W., & Adams, B. (1996). *Melatonin* efficacy in aviation missions requiring rapid deployment and night operations. *Aviation, Space, & Environmental Medicine, 67*(6), 520–524.

Condon, W. S., & Sander, L. W. (1974) Synchrony demonstrated between movements of the neonate and adult speech. *Child Development, 45*(2), 456–462.

Considine, R. V., Sinha, M. K., Heiman, M. L., Kriauciunas, A., et al. (1996). Serum immunoreactive-leptin concentrations in normal-weight and obese humans. *New England Journal of Medicine, 334*(5), 292–295.

Consumer Reports. (1995, November). Mental health: Does therapy help? 734–739.

Conway, A. R. A., Cowan, N., & Bunting, M. F. (2001). The cocktail party phenomenon revisited. *Psychonomic Bulletin & Review, 8*(2), 331–335.

Conway, M. A., Cohen, G., & Stanhope, N. (1992). Very long-term memory for knowledge acquired at school and university. *Applied Cognitive Psychology, 6*(6), 467–482.

Cooper, G. D., Adams, H. B., & Scott, J. C. (1988). Studies in REST: I. Reduced Environmental Stimulation Therapy (REST) and reduced alcohol consumption. *Journal of Substance Abuse Treatment, 5*(2), 61–68.

Cooper, J., & Fazio, R. H. (1984). A new look at dissonance theory. *Advances in Experimental Social Psychology, 17,* 226–229.

Cooper, R. P., Abraham, J., Berman, S., & Staska, M. (1997). The development of infants' preference for motherese. *Infant Behavior and Development, 20*(4), 477–488.

Coopersmith, S. (1968). Studies in self-esteem. *Scientific American, 218,* 96–106.

Corballis, M. C. (2002). *From hand to mouth: The origins of language.* Princeton, NJ: Princeton University Press.

Corbin, W. R., & Fromme, K. (2002). Alcohol use and serial monogamy as risks for sexually transmitted diseases in young adults. *Health Psychology, 21*(3), 229–236.

Cordova, D. I., & Lepper, M. R. (1996). Intrinsic motivation and the process of learning. *Journal of Educational Psychology, 88*(4), 715–730.

Coren, S. (1992). The left-hander syndrome. New York: Free Press.

Coren, S. (1996). *Sleep thieves.* New York: Free Press.

Cormier, J. F., & Thelen, M. H. (1998). Professional skepticism of multiple personality disorder. *Professional Psychology: Research and Practice, 29*(2), 163–167.

Corrigan, P. W. (1997). Behavior therapy empowers persons with severe mental illness. *Behavior Modification, 21*(1), 45–61.

Corteen, R. S., & Williams, T. M. (1986). Television and reading skills. In T. M. Williams (Ed.), *The impact of television: A natural experiment in three communities.* Orlando, FL: Academic.

Costa, P. T., & McCrae, R. R. (1992). Multiple uses for longitudinal personality data. *European Journal of Personality, 6*(2), 85–102.

Coursey, R. D., Ward-Alexander, L., & Katz, B. (1990). Cost-effectiveness of providing insurance benefits for posthospital psychiatric halfway house stays. *American Psychologist, 45*(10), 1118–1126.

Court, J. H., & Court, P. C. (2001). Repression: R. I. P. *Australian Journal of Clinical & Experimental Hypnosis, 29*(1), 8–16.

Courtois, C. A. (1999). *Recollections of sexual abuse.* New York: Norton Professional Books.

Covell, K., Grusec, J. E., & King, G. (1995). The intergenerational transmission of maternal discipline and standards for behavior. *Social Development, 4*(1), 32–43.

Cowan, N. (2001). The magical number 4 in short-term memory. *Behavioral & Brain Sciences, 24*(1), 87–185.

Cowles, J. T. (1937). Food tokens as incentives for learning by chimpanzees. *Comparative Psychology,* Monograph, *14*(5, Whole No. 71).

Cox, W. E. (1994). Exceptional evidence of ESP by a reputed sensitive. *Journal of the Society for Psychical Research, 60*(836), 16–28.

Craig, T. Y., & Kelly, J. R. (1999). Group cohesiveness and creative performance. *Group Dynamics, 3*(4), 243–256.

Craik, F. I. M. (1970). The fate of primary items in free recall. *Journal of Verbal Learning and Verbal Behavior, 9,* 143–148.

Crandall, C. S., Preisler, J. J., & Aussprung, J. (1992). Measuring life event stress in the lives of college students: The Undergraduate Stress Questionnaire (USQ). *Journal of Behavioral Medicine, 15*(6), 627–662.

Crano, W. D. (2000). Milestones in the Psychological Analysis of Social Influence. *Group Dynamics: Theory, Research, and Practice, 4*(1), 68–80.

Cravatt, B. F., Prospero-Garcia O., Siuzdak G., Gilula, N. B., et al. (1995). Chemical characterization of a family of brain lipids that induce sleep. *Science, 268*(5216), 1506–1509.

Crawley, S. B., & Sherrod, K. B. (1984). Parent-infant play during the first year of life. *Infant Behavior & Development, 7,* 65–75.

Creamer, M., Burgess, P., & McFarlane, A. C. (2001). Post-traumatic stress disorder: Findings from the Australian National Survey of Mental Health and Well-Being. *Psychological Medicine, 31*(7), 1237–1247.

Cregler, L. L., & Mark, H. (1985). Medical complications of cocaine abuse. *New England Journal of Medicine, 315*(23), 1495–1500.

Crencavage, L. M., & Norcross, J. C. (1990). Where are the commonalities among the therapeutic common factors? *Professional Psychology: Research & Practice, 21*(5), 372–378.

Cronbach, L. (1990). *Essentials of psychological testing.* Reading, PA: Addison-Wesley.

Crooks, R., & Baur, K. (2002). *Our sexuality.* Belmont, CA: Wadsworth.

Crowe, L. C., & George, W. H. (1989). Alcohol and human sexuality: Review and integration. *Psychological Bulletin, 105*(3), 374–386.

Crown, C. L., Feldstein, S., Jasnow, M. D., Beebe, B., & Jaffe, J. (2002). The cross-modal coordination of interpersonal timing. *Journal of Psycholinguistic Research, 31*(1), 1–23.

Csikszentmihalyi, M. (1997). *Creativity.* New York: HarperCollins.

Culertson, F. M. (1997). Depression and gender. *American Psychologist, 52*(1), 25–31.

Cull, W. L., Shaughnessy, J. J., & Zechmeister, E. B. (1996). Expanding understanding of the expanding-pattern-of-retrieval mnemonic. *Journal of Experimental Psychology: Applied, 2*(4), 365–378.

Cumming, S., Hay, P., Lee, T., & Sachdev, P. (1995). Neuropsychological outcome from psychosurgery for obsessive-compulsive disorder. *Australian & New Zealand Journal of Psychiatry, 29*(2), 293–298.

Cummins, D. D. (1995). *The other side of psychology.* New York: St. Martins.

Czeisler, C. A., Duffy, J. F., Shanahan, T. L., Brown, E. N., et al. (1999). Stability, precision, and near-24-hour period of the human circadian pacemaker. *Science,*

Czeisler, C. A., Kronauer, R. E., Allan, J. S., et al. (1989, June). Bright light induction of strong (Type O) resetting of the human circadian pacemaker. *Science, 244,* 1328–1333.

Czeisler, C. A., Richardson, G. S., Zimmerman, J. C., Moore-Ede, M. C., & Weitzman, E. D. (1981). Entrainment of human circadian rhythms by light-dark cycles: A reassessment. *Photochemistry, Photobiology, 34,* 239–247.

Darley, J. M., & Latane, B. (1968). Bystander intervention in emergencies: Diffusion of responsibility. *Journal of Personality & Social Psychology, 8,* 377–383.

Darling, C. A., Davidson, J. K., & Passarello, L. C. (1992). The mystique of first intercourse among college youth: The role of partners, contraceptive practices, and psychological reactions. *Journal of Youth & Adolescence, 21*(1), 97–117.

Darwin, C. (1872). *The expression of emotion in man and animals.* Chicago: The University of Chicago Press.

DasGupta, B. (1992). Perceived control and examination stress. *Psychology: A Journal of Human Behavior, 29*(1), 31–34.

Davidson, P. R., & Parker, K. C. H. (2001). Eye movement desensitization and reprocessing (EMDR): A meta-analysis. *Journal of Consulting & Clinical Psychology, 69*(2), 305–316.

Davidson, R. J., Kabat-Zinn, J., Schumacher, J., Rosenkranz, M., et al. (2003). Alternations in brain and immune function produced by mindfulness meditation. *Psychosomatic Medicine, 65*(4), 564–570.

Davis, D., & Follette, W. C. (2002). Rethinking the probative value of evidence. *Law & Human Behavior, 26*(2), 133–158.

Daw, J. (2002, April). New Mexico becomes first state to gain Rx privileges. *Monitor on Psychology,* 24–25.

Dawson, M. E. (1990). Where does the truth lie? A review of the polygraph test: Lies, truth, and science. *Psychophysiology, 27*(1), 120–121.

Day, S., & Schneider, P. L. (2002). Psychotherapy using distance technology. *Journal of Counseling Psychology, 49*(4), 499–503.

De Benedittis, G., Lorenzetti, A., & Pieri, A. (1990). The role of stressful life events in the onset of chronic primary headache. *Pain, 40*(1), 65–75.

De Bono, E. (1992). *Serious creativity.* New York: HarperCollins.

de Jong, P. J., & Muris, P. (2002). Spider phobia. *Journal of Anxiety Disorders, 16*(1), 51–65.

de Jong, T., & van Joolingen, W. R. (1998). Scientific discovery learning with computer simulations of conceptual domains. *Review of Educational Research, 68*(2), 179–201.

de las Fuentes, C., & Vasquez, M. J. T. (1999). Immigrant adolescent girls of color. In N. G. Johnson, M. C. Roberts, & J. Worell (Eds.), *Beyond Appearance.* Washington, DC: APA.

de Luccie, M. F., & Davis, A. J. (1991). Father-child relationships from the preschool years through mid-adolescence. *Journal of Genetic Psychology, 152*(2), 225–238.

De Raad, B. (1998). Five big, Big Five issues. *European Psychologist, 3*(2), 113–124.

Dean-Church, L., & Gilroy, F. D. (1993). Relation of sex-role orientation to life satisfaction in a healthy elderly sample. *Journal of Social Behavior & Personality, 8*(1), 133–140.

Deaux, K., & Emswiller, T. (1974). Explanation of successful performance on sex-linked tasks: What is skill for the male is luck for the female. *Journal of Personality & Social Psychology, 29,* 80–85.

Deckro, G. R., Ballinger, K. M., Hoyt, M., Wilcher, M., et al. (2002). The evaluation of a mind/body intervention to reduce psychological distress and perceived stress in college students. *Journal of American College Health, 50*(6), 281–287.

Deese, J., & Hulse, S. J. (1967). *The psychology of learning* (3rd. ed.). New York: McGraw-Hill.

Deffenbacher, J. L., & Suinn, R. M. (1988). Systematic desensitization and the reduction of anxiety. *Counseling Psychologist, 16*(1), 9–30.

DeGood, D. E. (1975). Cognitive factors in vascular stress responses. *Psychophysiology, 12,* 399–401.

Degreef, G., Ashtari, M., Bogerts, B., et al. (1992). Volumes of ventricular system subdivisions measured from magnetic resonance images in first-episode schizophrenic patients. *Archives of General Psychiatry, 49*(7), 531–537.

DeKlyen, M., Biernbaum, M. A., Spelz, M. L., & Greenberg, M. T. (1998). *Developmental Psychology, 34*(2), 264–275.

Delgado, B. M., & Ford, L. (1998). Parental perceptions of child development among low-income Mexican American families. *Journal of Child & Family Studies, 7*(4), 469–481.

Denmark, F. L. (1994). Engendering psychology. *American Psychologist, 49*(4), 329–334.

Denollet, J., & Van Heck, G. L. (2001). Psychological risk factors in heart disease. *Journal of Psychosomatic Research, 51*(3), 465–468.

Derzon, J. H., & Lipsey, M. W. (1999). A synthesis of the relationship of marijuana use with delinquent and problem behaviors. *School Psychology International, 20*(1), 57–68.

Deutsch, M. (1993). Educating for a peaceful world. *American Psychologist, 48*(5), 510–517.

Devine, P. G. (1990). Stereotypes and prejudice: Their automatic and controlled components. *Journal of Personality & Social Psychology, 56*(1), 5–18.

Devine, P. G., Monteith, M. J., Zuerink, J. R., & Elliot, A. J. (1991). Prejudice with and without compunction. *Journal of Personality & Social Psychology, 60*(6), 817–830.

Devlin, B., Daniels, M., & Roeder, K. (1997). The heritability of IQ. *Nature, 388*(6641), 468–471.

Devoto, A., Lucidi, F., Violani, C., & Bertini, M. (1999). Effects of different sleep reductions on daytime sleepiness. *Sleep, 22*(3), 336–343.

Dewhurst, S. A., & Conway, M. A. (1994). Pictures, images, and recollective experience. *Journal of Experimental Psychology: Learning, Memory, and Cognition, 20,* 1088–1098.

Di Marzo, V., Goparaju, S. K., Wang, L., Liu, J., et al. (2001). Leptin-regulated endocannabinoids are involved in maintaining food intake. *Nature, 410*(6830), 822–825.

Dickinson, D. J., & O'Connell, D. Q. (1990). Effect of quality and quantity of study on student grades. *Journal of Educational Research, 83*(4), 227–231.

Diefenbach, D. L. (1997). Portrayal of mental illness on prime-time television. *Journal of Community Psychology, 25*(3), 289–302.

Diekstra, R. F., & Garnefski, N. (1995). On the nature, magnitude, and causality of suicidal behaviors: An international perspective. *Suicide & Life-Threatening Behavior, 25*(1), 36–57.

Diener, E., Suh, E. M., Lucas, R. E., & Smith, H. L. (1999). Subjective well-being: Three decades of progress. *Psychological Bulletin, 125*(2), 276–302.

Dies, R. R. (1995). Group psychotherapies. In A. S. Gurman & S. B. Messer, *Essential Psychotherapies.* New York: Guilford.

Dieter, J. N. I., & Emory, E. K. (1997). Supplemental stimulation of premature infants. *Journal of Pediatric Psychology, 22*(3), 281–295.

Digman, J. M. (1990). Personality structure: Emergence of the five-factor model. *Annual Review of Psychology, 41,* 417–440.

Dinan, T. G. (2001). Stress, depression and cardiovascular disease. *Stress & Health: Journal of the International Society for the Investigation of Stress, 17*(2), 65–66.

Dinkmeyer, D., Sr., McKay, G. D., & Dinkmeyer, D., Jr. (1997). *The parent's handbook.* Circle Pines, MN: American Guidance Service.

Dirkzwager, A. J. E., Bramsen, I., & Van Der Ploeg, H. M. (2001). The longitudinal course of posttraumatic stress disorder symptoms among aging military veterans.

Journal of Nervous & Mental Disease, 189(12), 846–853.

Dobelle, W. H. (2000). Artificial vision for the blind by connecting a television camera to the visual cortex. *American Society of Artificial Internal Organs, 46,* 3–9.

Docherty, N. M., et al. (1998). Communication disturbances and family psychiatric history in parents of schizophrenic patients. *Journal of Nervous & Mental Disease, 186*(12), 761–768.

Doctor, R. M., & Doctor, J. N. (1994). Stress. *Encyclopedia of human behavior, Volume 4,* 311–323. San Diego, CA: Academic.

Doidge, N. (1997). Empirical evidence for the efficacy of psychoanalytic psychotherapies and psychoanalysis. *Psychoanalytic Inquiry, Suppl.,* 102–150.

Dollard, J., & Miller, N. E. (1950). *Personality and psychotherapy: An analysis in terms of learning, thinking and culture.* New York: McGraw-Hill.

Domhoff, G. W. (1999). Drawing theoretical implications from descriptive empirical findings on dream content. *Dreaming: Journal of the Association for the Study of Dreams, 9*(2–3), 201–210.

Domingo, R. A., & Goldstein-Alpern, N. (1999). "What dis?" and other toddler-initiated, expressive language-learning strategies. *Infant-Toddler Intervention, 9*(1), 39–60.

Dooling, D. J., & Lachman, R. (1971). Effects of comprehension on retention of prose. *Journal of Experimental Psychology, 88,* 216–222.

Dorfman, J., Shames, J., & Kihlstrom, J. F. (1996). Intuition, incubation, & insight. In G. Underwood (Ed.), *Implicit cognition.* New York: Oxford University Press.

Dosher, B. A., & Ma, J. (1998). Output loss or rehearsal loop? *Journal of Experimental Psychology: Learning, Memory, & Cognition, 24*(2), 316–335.

Douvan, E. (1997). Erik Erikson: Critical times, critical theory. *Child Psychiatry & Human Development, 28*(1), 15–21.

Dovidio, J. F. (1984). Helping behavior and altruism: An empirical and conceptual overview. In L. Berkowitz (Ed.), *Advances in experimental social psychology, Vol. 17.* New York: Academic.

Dovidio, J. F., & Gaertner, S. L. (1999). Reducing prejudice: Combating intergroup biases. *Current Directions in Psychological Science, 8*(4), 101–105.

Dovidio, J. F., Gaertner, S. L., Kawakami, K., & Hodson, G. (2002). Why can't we just get along? *Cultural Diversity and Ethnic Minority Psychology, 8*(2), 88–102.

Dragoi, V., & Staddon, J. E. R. (1999). The dynamics of operant conditioning. *Psychological Review, 106*(1), 20–61.

Dretzke, B. J., & Levin, J. R. (1996). Assessing students' application and transfer of a mnemonic strategy. *Contemporary Educational Psychology, 21*(1), 83–93.

Drigotas, S. M., Rusbult, C. E., Wieselquist, J., & Whitton, S. W. (1999). Close partner as sculptor of the ideal self: Behavioral affirmation and the Michelangelo phenomenon. *Journal of Personality & Social Psychology, 77*(2), 293–323.

Drolet, G., Dumont, E. C., Gosselin, I., Kinkead, R., et al. (2001). Role of endogenous opioid system in the regulation of the stress response. *Progress in Neuro-Psychopharmacology & Biological Psychiatry, 25*(4), 729–741.

Druckman, D., & Bjork, R. A. (1994). Learning, remembering, believing: Enhancing human performance. Washington, DC: National Academy Press.

DSM-IV-TR: Diagnostic and statistical manual of mental disorders (5th ed.). (2000).

Washington, DC: American Psychiatric Association.

Dubow, E. F., Huesmann, L. R., & Eron, L. D. (1987). Childhood correlates of adult ego development. *Child Development, 58*(3), 859–869.

Duclos, S. E., & Laird, J. D. (2001). The deliberate control of emotional experience through control of expressions. *Cognition and Emotion, 15,* 27–56.

Dulewicz, V., & Higgs, M. (2000). Emotional intelligence. *Journal of Managerial Psychology, 15*(4), 341–372.

Duncan, J., Seitz, R. J., Kolodny, J., et al. (2000). A neural basis for general intelligence. *Science, 289,* 457–460.

Dunker, K. (1945). On problem solving. *Psychological Monographs, 58*(270).

Dunn, B. R., Hartigan, J. A., & Mikulas, W. L. (1999). Concentration and mindfulness meditations: Unique forms of consciousness? *Applied Psychophysiology & Biofeedback, 24*(3), 147–165.

Durham, M. D., & Dane, F. C. (1999). Juror knowledge of eyewitness behavior. *Journal of Social Behavior & Personality, 14*(2), 299–308.

Durso, F. T., Rea, C. B., & Dayton, T. (1994). Graph-theoretic confirmation of restructuring during insight. *Psychological Science, 5*(2), 94–98.

Dutton, D. G., & Aron, A. P. (1974). Some evidence for heightened sexual attraction under conditions of high anxiety. *Journal of Personality & Social Psychology, 30,* 510–517.

Dywan, J., & Bowers, K. S. (1983). The use of hypnosis to enhance recall. *Science, 222,* 184–185.

Ebbinghaus, H. (1885). *Memory: A contribution to experimental psychology.* Translated by H. A. Ruger & C. E. Bussenius, 1913. New York: New York Teacher's College, Columbia University.

Eckerman, D. A. (1999). Scheduling reinforcement about once a day. *Behavioural Processes, 45*(1–3), 101–114.

Edwards, D. J. A. (1998). Types of case study work. *Journal of Humanistic Psychology, 38*(3), 36–70.

Eich, E. (1995). Mood as a mediator of place dependent memory. *Journal of Experimental Psychology: General, 124*(3), 293–308.

Eich, E., Rachman, S., & Lopatka, C. (1990). Affect, pain, and autobiographical memory. *Journal of Abnormal Psychology, 99*(2) 174–178.

Eidelson, R. J., & Eidelson, J. I. (2003). Dangerous ideas. *American Psychologist, 58*(3), 182–192.

Eimas, P. D., Quinn, P. C., & Cowan, P. (1994). Development of exclusivity in perceptually based categories of young infants. *Journal of Experimental Child Psychology, 58*(3), 418–431.

Eisenberg, N. (1991). Meta-analytic contributions to the literature on prosocial behavior. *Personality & Social Psychology Bulletin, 17*(3), 273–282.

Eisenberg, N., & Miller, P. A. (1987). The relation of empathy to prosocial and related behaviors. *Psychological Bulletin, 101*(1), 91–119.

Ekman, P. (1993). Facial expression and emotion. *American Psychologist, 48*(4), 384–392.

Ekman, P., Levenson, R. W., & Friesen, W. V. (1983). Autonomic nervous system activity distinguishes among emotions. *Science, 221,* 1208–1210.

Ekman, P., & Rosenberg, E. (1997). *What the face reveals.* New York: Oxford University Press.

Eliot, L. (1999). *What's going on in there?* New York: Bantam

Elli, K. A., & Nathan, P. J. (2001). The pharmacology of human working memory. *International Journal of Neuropsychopharmacology, 4*(3), 299–313.

Ellis, A. (1973, February). The no cop-out therapy. *Psychology Today, 7,* 56–60, 62.

Ellis, A. (1979). The practice of rational-emotive therapy. In A. Ellis & J. Whiteley (Eds.) *Theoretical and empirical foundations of rational-emotive therapy.* Monterey, CA: Brooks/Cole.

Ellis, A. (1987). A sadly neglected cognitive component in depression. *Cognitive Therapy & Research, 11*(1), 121–145.

Ellis, A. (1995). Changing rational-emotive therapy (RET) to rational emotive behavior therapy (REBT). *Journal of Rational-Emotive & Cognitive Behavior Therapy, 13*(2), 85–89.

Ellis, H. C., & Hunt, R. R. (1992). *Fundamentals of cognitive psychology.* Madison, WI: Brown & Benchmark.

Emmons, K. M., et al. (1998). Predictors of smoking among US college students. *American Journal of Public Health, 88*(1), 104–107.

Emmorey, K., Grabowski, T., McCullough, S., Damasio, H., et al. (2003). Neural systems underlying lexical retrieval for sign language. *Neuropsychologia, 41*(1), 85–95.

Enns, J. T., & Coren, S. (1995). The box alignment illusion. *Perception & Psychophysics, 57*(8), 1163–1174.

Erdelyi, M. H., & Appelbaum, A. G., (1973). Cognitive masking: The disruptive effect of an emotional stimulus upon the perception of contiguous neutral items. *Bulletin of the Psychonomic Society, 1,* 59–61.

Erickson, C. D., & Al-Timimi, N. R. (2001). Providing mental health services to Arab Americans. *Cultural Diversity and Ethnic Minority Psychology, 7*(4), 308–327.

Ericsson, K. A. (2000). How experts attain and maintain superior performance. *Journal of Aging & Physical Activity, 8*(4), 366–372.

Ericsson, K. A., & Charness, N. (1994). Expert performance. *American Psychologist, 49*(8), 725–747.

Ericsson, K. A., & Chase, W. G. (1982). Exceptional memory. *American Scientist, 70,* 607–615.

Erikson, E. H. (1963). *Childhood and society.* New York: Norton.

Ernst, E. (1994). Is acupuncture effective for pain control? *Journal of Pain & Symptom Management, 9*(2), 72–74.

Eron, L. D. (1986). Interventions to mitigate the psychological effects of media violence on aggressive behavior. *Journal of Social Issues, 42*(3), 155–169.

Eron, L. D. (1987). The development of aggressive behavior from the perspective of a developing behaviorism. *American Psychologist, 42,* 435–442.

Eronen, S., & Nurmi, J. (1999). Life events, predisposing cognitive strategies and well-being. *European Journal of Personality, 13*(2), 129–148.

Espie, C. A. (2002). Insomnia. *Annual Review of Psychology, 53,* 215–243.

Espy, K. A., Kaufmann, P. M., & Glisky, M. L. (1999). Neuropsychological function in toddlers exposed to cocaine in utero: A preliminary study. *Developmental Neuropsychology, 15*(3), 447–460.

Esser, J. K. (1998). Alive and well after 25 years: A review of groupthink research. *Organizational Behavior & Human Decision Processes, 73*(2–3), 116–141.

Esterling, B. A., L'Abate, L., Murray, E. J., & Pennebaker, J. W. (1999). Empirical foundations for writing in prevention and psy-

chotherapy: Mental and physical health outcomes. *Clinical Psychology Review, 19*(1), 79–96.

Ethical principles of psychologists and code of conduct (2002). The American Psychological Association. *American Psychologist,57*(12), 1060–1073.

Ethier, K. A., Kershaw, T., Niccolai, L., Lewis, J. B., & Ickovics, J. R. (2003). Adolescent women underestimate their susceptibility to sexually transmitted infections. *Sexually Transmitted Infections, 79,* 408–411.

Everly, G. S. (2002). Thoughts on peer (paraprofessional) support in the provision of mental health services. *International Journal of Emergency Mental Health, 4*(2), 89–92.

Everson, C. A. (1998). Physiological consequences of sleep deprivation. *Journal of Musculoskeletal Pain, 6*(3), 93–101.

Everson, S. A., Goldberg, D. E., & Salonen, J. T. (1996). Hopelessness and risk of mortality and incidence of myocardial infarction and cancer. *Psychosomatic Medicine, 58*(2), 113.

Eyer, D. E. (1994). Mother-infant bonding: A scientific fiction. *Human Nature, 5*(1), 69–94.

Eysenck, H. J. (1994). The outcome problem in psychotherapy: What have we learned? *Behaviour Research & Therapy, 32*(5), 477–495.

Eysenck, H. J. (Ed.). (1981). *A model for personality.* New York: Springer-Verlag.

Eysenck, M. W., & Keane, M. T. (1995). *Cognitive psychology.* Hove, East Sussex, UK: Erlbaum.

Fairclough, S. H., & Graham, R. (1999). Impairment of driving performance caused by sleep deprivation or alcohol. *Human Factors, 41*(1), 118–128.

Faith, M. S., Wong, F. Y., & Carpenter, K. M. (1995). Group sensitivity training: Update, meta-analysis, and recommendations. *Journal of Counseling Psychology, 42*(3), 390–399.

Falkowski, C. (2000). *Dangerous Drugs.* Center City, MN: Hazelden Information Education.

Fantz, R. L. (1961, May). The origin of form perception. *Scientific American,* 71.

Farah, M. J., Weisberg, L. L., Monheit, M. A., & Peronnet, F. (1989). Brain activity underlying mental imagery. *Journal of Cognitive Neuroscience, 1*(4), 302–316.

Farquhar, J. W., et al. (1997). Short- and long-term outcomes of a health promotion program in a small rural community. *American Journal of Health Promotion, 11*(6), 411–414.

Farquhar, J. W., Fortmann, S. P., Maccoby, N., Wood, P. D., et al. (1984). The Stanford Five City Project: An overview. In J. D. Matarazzo, S. M. Weiss, J. A. Herd, N. E. Miller, & S. M. Weiss (Eds.), *Behavioral health: A handbook of health enhancement and disease prevention.* New York: Wiley.

Farrimond, T. (1990). Effect of alcohol on visual constancy values and possible relation to driving performance. *Perceptual & Motor Skills, 70*(1), 291–295.

Farthing, G. W. (1992). The psychology of consciousness. Englewood Cliffs, NJ: Prentice Hall.

Fava, G. A., et al. (1998). Prevention of recurrent depression with cognitive behavioral therapy. *Archives of General Psychiatry, 55*(9), 816–820.

Feingold, A. (1992). Gender differences in mate selection preferences. *Psychological Bulletin, 111,* 304–341.

Feldhusen, J. F., & Goh, B. E. (1995). Assessing and accessing creativity: An integrative review of theory, research, and development. *Creativity Research Journal, 8*(3), 231–247.

Feldman, R. S., & Meyer, J. (1996). *Fundamentals of neuropsychopharmacology.* Sunderland, MA: Sinauer Associates.

Felmlee, D. H. (1998). "Be careful what you wish for . . .": A quantitative and qualitative investigation of "fatal attractions." *Personal Relationships, 5*(3), 235–253.

Fenton, G. W. (1998). Neurosurgery for mental disorder. *Irish Journal of Psychological Medicine, 15*(2), 45–48.

Fernald, A. (1989). Intonation and communicative intent in mothers' speech to infants: Is the melody the message? *Child Development, 60*(6), 1497–1510.

Fernald, A., & Mazzie, C. (1991). Prosody and focus in speech to infants and adults. *Developmental Psychology, 27*(2), 209–221.

Ferrari, J. R., & Scher, S. J. (2000). Toward an understanding of academic and nonacademic tasks procrastinated by students: The use of daily logs. *Psychology in the Schools, 37*(4), 359–366.

Ferster, C. B., Nurnberger, J. I., & Levitt, E. B. (1962). The control of eating. *Journal of Mathematics, 1,* 87–109.

Festinger, L. (1954). A theory of social comparison processes. *Human Relations, 7,* 117–140.

Festinger, L. (1957). *A theory of cognitive dissonance.* Stanford, CA: Stanford University Press.

Festinger, L., & Carlsmith, J. M. (1959). Cognitive consequences of forced compliance. *Journal of Abnormal and Social Psychology, 58,* 203–210.

Fields, R. M., & Margolin, J. (2001). Coping with trauma. Washington, D.C: American Psychological Association.

Fink, M. (2000, March/April). Electroshock revisited. *American Scientist, 88,* 162–167.

Finke, R. (1990). *Creative imagery.* Hillsdale, NJ: Erlbaum.

Finkenauer, C., Luminet, O., Gisle, L., et al. (1998). Flashbulb memories and the underlying mechanisms of their formation. *Memory & Cognition, 26*(3), 516–531.

Fisher, C. D., & Ashanasy, N. M. (2000). The emerging role of emotions in work life. *Journal of Organizational Behavior, 21,* 123–129.

Fisher, R. P., & Geiselman, R. E. (1987). Enhancing eyewitness memory with the cognitive interview. In M. M. Gruneberg, P. E. Morris, & R. N. Sykes (Eds.), *Practical aspects of memory: Current research and issues.* Chinchester, UK: Wiley.

Fisher, S., & Greenberg, R. P. (1996). Freud scientifically reappraised. Hoboken, NJ: Wiley.

Fiske, S. T. (1993a). Social cognition and social perception. In L. W. Porter & M. R. Rosenzweig (Eds.), *Annual Review of Psychology, 44,* 155–194.

Fiske, S. T. (1993b). Controlling other people. *American Psychologist, 48*(6), 621–628.

Flavell, J. H. (1992). Cognitive development: Past, present, and future. *Developmental Psychology, 28*(6), 998–1005.

Flavell, J. H. (1999). Cognitive development: Children's knowledge about the mind. *Annual Review of Psychology, 50,* 21–45.

Fleming, J. (1974, January). Field report: The state of the apes. *Psychology Today,* 46.

Flynn, J. R. (1987). Massive IQ gains in 14 nations: What IQ tests really measure. *Psychological Bulletin, 101*(2), 171–191.

Foa, E. B., Franklin, M. E., Perry, K. J., & Herbert, J. D. (1996). Cognitive biases in generalized social phobia. *Journal of Abnormal Psychology, 105*(3), 433–439.

Fobair, P. (1997). Cancer support groups and group therapies. *Journal of Psychosocial Oncology, 15*(3–4), 123–147.

Fochtmann, L. J. (1995). Intractable sneezing as a conversion symptom. *Psychosomatics, 36*(2), 103–112.

Fones, C. S. L., et al. (1998). Social phobia: An update. *Harvard Review of Psychiatry, 5*(5), 1998, 247–259.

Fontaine, K. R., Redden, D. T., Wang, et al. (2003). Years of life lost due to obesity. *JAMA, 289,* 187–193.

Fontenelle, D. H. (1989). *How to live with your children.* Tucson, AZ: Fisher Books.

Foos, P., & Clark, M. C. (1984). *Human learning, 2*(3).

Foreyt, J. P. (1987a). Behavioral medicine. In G. T. Wilson, C. M. Franks, P. C. Kendall, & J. P. Foreyt (Eds.), *Review of behavior therapy: Theory and practice, Vol. II.* New York: Guilford.

Foreyt, J. P. (1987b). The addictive disorders. In G. T. Wilson, C. M. Franks, P. C. Kendall, & J. P. Foreyt (Eds.), *Review of behavior therapy: Theory and practice, Vol. II.* New York: Guilford.

Forgays, D. G., & Belinson, M. J. (1986). Is flotation isolation a relaxing environment? *Journal of Environmental Psychology, 6*(1), 19–34.

Foss, R. D. (1986). Using social psychology to increase altruistic behavior: Will it help? In M. J. Saks & L. Saxe (Eds.), *Advances in applied social psychology, Vol. 3.* Hillsdale, NJ: Erlbaum.

Fosse, R., Stickgold, R., & Hobson, J. A. (2001). The mind in REM sleep: Reports of emotional experience. *Sleep: Journal of Sleep & Sleep Disorders Research, 24*(8), 947–955.

Foster, C. A., et al. (1998). Arousal and attraction. *Journal of Personality & Social Psychology, 74*(1), 86–101.

Foster, G., & Ysseldyke, J. (1976). Expectancy and halo effects as a result of artificially induced teacher bias. *Contemporary Educational Psychology, 1,* 37–45.

Fouts, R., Fouts, D., & Schoenfield, D. (1984). Sign language conversational interaction between chimpanzees. *Sign Language Studies, 42,* 1–12.

Fowers, B. J., & Reinecke, F. C. (1996). Why is multiculturalism good? *American Psychologist, 51*(6), 609–621.

Fowles, D. C. (1992). Schizophrenia: Diathesis-stress revisited. *Annual Review of Psychology, 43,* 303–336.

Foxhall, K. (2000, January). Suddenly, a big impact on criminal justice. APA Monitor, 36–37.

Foxx, R. M. (1998). A comprehensive treatment program for inpatient adolescents. *Behavioral Interventions, 13*(1), 67–77.

Franche, R., & Dobson, K. S. (1992). Self-criticism and interpersonal dependency as vulnerability factors to depression. *Cognitive Therapy & Research, 16*(4), 419–435.

Frankenburg, W. K., & Dodds, J. B. (1967). The Denver Developmental Screening Test. *The Journal of Pediatrics, 1,* 181–191.

Franzoi, S. L. (2000). *Social psychology.* New York: McGraw-Hill.

Frazier, J. A., Giedd, J. N., Hamburger, S. D., & Albus, K. E. (1996). Brain anatomic magnetic resonance imaging in childhood-onset schizophrenia. *Archives of General Psychiatry, 53*(7), 617–624.

Fredrickson, B. L. (2003). The value of positive emotions. *American Scientist, 91,* 330–335.

Freedman, J. L., & Fraser, S. C. (1966). Compliance without pressure: The foot-in-the-door technique. *Journal of Personality & Social Psychology, 4,* 195–202.

Freeman, A., & Reinecke, M. A. (1995). Cognitive therapy. In A. S. Gurman & S. B. Messer, *Essential Psychotherapies.* New York: Guilford.

Freeman, J. (1995). Recent studies of giftedness in children. *Journal of Child Psychology & Psychiatry & Allied Disciplines, 36*(4), 531–547.

Freeman, W. J. (1991, February). The physiology of perception. *Scientific American,* 78–85.

French, C. C., Fowler, M., McCarthy, K. & Peers, D. (1991). A test of the Barnum effect. *Skeptical Inquirer, 15*(4), 66–72.

Freud, S. (1900). *The interpretation of dreams.* London: Hogarth.

Freud, S. (1949). *An outline of psychoanalysis.* New York: Norton.

Fried, P., Watkinson, B., James, D., & Gray, R. (2002). Current and former marijuana use: preliminary findings of a longitudinal study of effects on IQ in young adults. *Canadian Medical Association Journal, 166,* 887–891.

Fried, P. A., O'Connell, C. M., & Walkinson, B. (1992). 60– and 72–month follow-up of children prenatally exposed to marijuana, cigarettes, and alcohol. *Journal of Developmental & Behavioral Pediatrics, 13*(6), 383–391.

Fried, P.A., & Smith, A. M. (2001) A literature review of the consequences of prenatal marijuana exposure. *Neurotoxicology and Teratology, 23*(1), 1–11.

Friedman, M., & Rosenman, R. (1983). *Type A behavior and your heart.* New York: Knopf.

Friedman, R. C., et al. (1998). Private psychotherapy patients of psychiatrist psychoanalysts. *American Journal of Psychiatry, 155,* 1772–1774.

Froufe, M., & Schwartz, C. (2001). Subliminal messages for increasing self-esteem: Placebo effect. *Spanish Journal of Psychology, 4*(1), 19–25.

Frydman, M. (1999). Television, aggressiveness and violence. *International Journal of Adolescent Medicine & Health, 11*(3–4), 335–344.

Fukuda, K., & Ishihara, K. (2001). Age-related changes of sleeping pattern during adolescence. *Psychiatry & Clinical Neurosciences, 55*(3), 231–232.

Funder, D. C. (2001). Personality. *Annual Review Psychology, 52,* 197–221.

Furumoto, L., & Scarborough, E. (1986). Placing women in the history of psychology. *American Psychologist, 41,* 35–42.

Gabrieli, J. D. E. (1998). Cognitive neuroscience of human memory. *Annual Review of Psychology, 49,* 87–115.

Gaertner, S. L., Dovidio, J. F., Banker, B. S., Houlette, M., et al. (2000). Reducing intergroup conflict: From superordinate goals to decategorization, recategorization, and mutual differentiation. *Group Dynamics, 4*(1), 98–114.

Gagnon, J. H. (1977). *Human sexualities.* Glenview, IL: Scott, Foresman.

Galanti, G. (1993). Cult conversion, deprogramming, and the triune brain. *Cultic Studies Journal, 10*(1), 45–52.

Galati, D., Scherer, K. R., & Ricci-Bitti, P. E. (1997). Voluntary facial expression of emotion: Comparing congenitally blind with normally sighted encoders. *Journal of Personality & Social Psychology, 73*(6), 1363–1379.

Galea, S., Ahern, J., Resnick, H., Kilpatrick, D., Bucuvalas, M., Gold, J., & Vlahov, D. (2002). Psychological sequelae of the September 11 terrorist attacks in New York City. *New England Journal of Medicine, 346*(13), 982–987.

Ganellen, R. J. (1996). Comparing the diagnostic efficiency of the MMPI, MCMI-II, and Rorschach. *Journal of Personality Assessment, 67*(2), 219–243.

Gardner, H. (1993). *Frames of mind.* New York: Basic.

Gardner, R. A., & Gardner, B. T. (1989). *Teaching sign language to chimpanzees.* Albany, NY: State University of New York Press.

Gardner, R. M., & Bokenkamp, E. D. (1996). The role of sensory and nonsensory factors in body size estimations of eating disorders subjects. *Journal of Clinical Psychology, 52*(1), 3–15.

Garland, A. F., & Zigler, E. (1993). Adolescent suicide prevention. *American Psychologist, 48*(2), 169–182.

Garnets, L. D. (2002). Sexual orientation in perspective. *Cultural Diversity and Ethnic Minority Psychology, 8*(2), 115–129.

Garnets, L. D., & Kimmel, D. (1991). Lesbian and gay male dimensions in the psychological study of human diversity. *Psychological perspectives on human diversity in America.* Washington, DC: American Psychological Association.

Gates, A. I. (1958). Recitation as a factor in memorizing. In J. Deese (Ed.), *The psychology of learning.* New York: McGraw-Hill.

Gatz, M. (1990, July/August). Interpreting behavioral genetic results. *Journal of Counseling & Development, 68,* 601–605.

Gauthier, J., Cote, G., & French, D. (1994). The role of home practice in the thermal biofeedback treatment of migraine headache. *Journal of Consulting & Clinical Psychology, 62*(1), 180–184.

Gayle, H. (2000). An overview of the global HIV/AIDS epidemic, with a focus on the United States. *AIDS, 14*(Suppl 2), S8–S17.

Gazzaniga, M. S. (1970). *The bisected brain.* New York: Plenum.

Gazzaniga, M. S. (1995). On neural circuits and cognition. *Neural Computation, 7*(1), 1–12.

Geiger, M. A. (1991) Changing multiple-choice answers: Do students accurately perceive their performance? *Journal of Experimental Education, 59*(3), 250–257.

Geiselman, R. E., Fisher, R. P., MacKinnon, D. P., & Holland, H. L. (1986). Eyewitness memory enhancement with the cognitive interview. *American Journal of Psychology, 99,* 385–401.

Georgiades, A., Serwood, A., et al. (2000). Effects of exercise and weight loss on mental stress-induced cardiovascular responses in individuals with high blood pressure. *Hypertension, 36,* 171–176.

German, T. P., & Defeyter, M. A. (2000). Immunity to functional fixedness in young children. *Psychonomic Bulletin & Review, 7*(4), 707–712.

Gersh, R. D. (1982, June 20). Learning when not to shoot. *Santa Barbara News Press.*

Gershoff, E. T. (2002). Corporal punishment by parents and associated child behaviors and experiences: A meta-analytic and theoretical review. *Psychological Bulletin, 128*(4), 539–579.

Gershon, E. S., et al. (1998). Closing in on genes for manic-depressive illness and schizophrenia. *Neuropsychopharmacology, 18*(4), 233–242.

Gerwood, J. B. (1998). The legacy of Viktor Frankl. *Psychological Reports, 82*(2), 673–674.

Geschwind, N. (1979). Specializations of the human brain. *Scientific American, 241,* 180–199.

Gewirtz, J. C., & Davis, M. (1998). Application of Pavlovian higher-order conditioning to the analysis of the neural substrates of fear conditioning. *Neuropharmacology, 37*(4–5), 453–459.

Ghadirian, A-M., Gregoire, P., & Kosmidis, H. (2001). Creativity and the evolution of psychopathologies. *Creativity Research Journal, 13*(2), 145–148.

Gibson, B., & Werner, C. M. (1994). The airport as a behavior setting: The role of legibility in communicating the setting program. *Journal of Personality and Social Psychology, 66,* 1049–1060.

Gibson, E. J., & Walk, R. D. (1960). The "visual cliff." *Scientific American, 202*(4), 67–71.

Gibson, H. B., & Heap, M. (1991). *Hypnosis in therapy.* Hillsdale, NJ: Erlbaum.

Gibson, K. R. (2002). Evolution of human intelligence: The roles of brain size and mental construction. *Brain, Behavior & Evolution, 59*(1–2), 10–20.

Gierl, M. J., & Rogers, W. T. (1996). A confirmatory factor analysis of the Test Anxiety Inventory using Canadian high school students. *Educational & Psychological Measurement, 56*(2), 315–324.

Gilbert, D. G., Stunkard, M. E., Jensen, R. A., & Detwiler, F. R. J. (1996). Effects of exam stress on mood, cortisol, and immune functioning. *Personality & Individual Differences, 21*(2), 235–246.

Gill, S. T. (1991). Carrying the war into the never-never land of psi. *Skeptical Inquirer, 15*(1), 269–273.

Gillberg, M., & Akerstedt, T. (1998). Sleep loss performance: No "safe" duration of a monotonous task. *Physiology & Behavior, 64*(5), 599–604.

Ginet, M., & Py, J. (2001). A technique for enhancing memory in eyewitness testimonies for use by police officers and judicial officials: The cognitive interview. *Travail Humain, 64*(2), 173–191.

Ginott, H. G. (1965). *Between parent and child: New solutions to old problems.* New York: Macmillan.

Girodo, M. (1978). *Shy? (You don't have to be!).* New York: Pocket Books.

Glass, A. L., Holyoak, K. J., & Santa, J. L. (1979). *Cognition.* Reading, MA: Addison-Wesley.

Glik, D. C., Kronenfeld, J. J., & Jackson, K. (1996). Predictors of well role performance behaviors. *American Journal of Health Behavior, 20*(4), 218–228.

Glisky, M. L., Williams, J. M., & Kihlstrom, J. F. (1996). Internal and external mental imagery perspectives and performance on two tasks. *Journal of Sport Behavior, 19*(1), 3–18.

Gloaguen, V., et al. (1998). A meta-analysis of the effects of cognitive therapy in depressed patients. *Journal of Affective Disorders, 49*(1) 59–72.

Globus, G. (1987). *Dream life, wake life: The human condition through dreams.* Albany, NY: State University of New York Press.

Glueck, J., Ernst, R., & Unger, F. (2002). How creatives define creativity. *Creativity Research Journal, 14*(1), 55–67.

Gobet, F., & Simon, H. A. (1996). Recall of random and distorted chess positions: Implications for the theory of expertise. *Memory & Cognition, 24*(4), 493–503.

Goel, V., & Grafman, J. (1995). Are the frontal lobes implicated in "planning" functions? Interpreting data from the Tower of Hanoi. *Neuropsychologia, 33*(5), 623–642.

Gold, P. E. (1987, March/April). Sweet Memories. *American Scientist, 75,* 151–155.

Goldberg, C. (2001). Of prophets, true believers, and terrorists. *The Dana Forum on Brain Science, 3*(3), 21–24.

Goldberg, L. R. (1993). The structure of phenotypic personality traits. *American Psychologist, 48*(1), 26–34.

Goldfried, M. R., Greenberg, L. S., & Marmar, C. (1990). Individual psychotherapy: Process and outcome. *Annual Review of Psychology, 41,* 659–688.

Goldiamond, I. (1971). Self-control procedures in personal behavior problems. In

M. S. Gazzaniga & E. P. Lovejoy (Eds.), *Good reading in psychology.* Englewood Cliffs, NJ: Prentice-Hall.

Goldman, H. H. (1998). Deinstitutionalization and community care. *Harvard Review of Psychiatry, 6*(4), 219–222.

Goldstein, E. (1997). False memory syndrome. *American Journal of Family Therapy, 25*(4), 307–317.

Goldstein, E. B. (2003). *Sensation and perception.* Belmont, CA: Wadsworth.

Goldstein, M. J. (1985). *The UCLA family project.* Presented at NIMH High-Risk Consortium, San Francisco. Cited by Mirsky & Duncan, 1986.

Goldstone, R. L. (1998). Perceptual learning. *Annual Review of Psychology, 49,* 585–612.

Goleman, D. (1982, March). Staying up: The rebellion against sleep's gentle tyranny. *Psychology Today,* 24–35.

Goleman, D. (1995). *Emotional intelligence.* New York: Bantam.

Good, M. (1995). A comparison of the effects of jaw relaxation and music on post-operative pain. *Nursing Research, 44*(1), 52–57.

Goodall, J. (1990). *Through a window: My thirty years with the chimpanzees of the Gombe.* Boston: Houghton Mifflin.

Goode, E. (1996). Gender and courtship entitlement: Responses to personal ads. *Sex Roles, 34*(3–4), 141–169.

Goodman, G. (1984). SASHA tapes: Expanding options for help-intended communication. In D. Larson (Ed.), *Teaching psychological skills.* Monterey, CA: Brooks/Cole.

Gopnik, A., Meltzoff, A. N., & Kuhl, P. K. (1999). *The scientist in the crib.* New York: William Morrow.

Gordon, T. (1970). *P.E.T. parent effectiveness training: A tested new way to raise children.* New York: Peter H. Wyden.

Gorman, J. M. (1996). The essential guide to mental health. New York: St. Martin's Griffin.

Gottlieb, G. (1998). Normally occurring environmental and behavioral influences on gene activity: From central dogma to probabilistic epigenesis. *Psychological Review, 105*(4), 792–802.

Gould, E., & Gross, C. G. (2002). Neurogenesis in adult mammals: Some progress and problems. *Journal of Neuroscience, 22*(3), 619–623.

Gould, E., Reeves, A. J., & Gross, C. G. (1999). Neurogenesis in the neocortex of adult primates. *Science, 286*(5439), 548.

Gould, M. S., et al. (1998). Psychopathology associated with suicidal ideation and attempts among children and adolescents. *Journal of the American Academy of Child & Adolescent Psychiatry, 37*(9), 915–923.

Grack, C., & Richman, C. L. (1996). Reducing general and specific heterosexism through cooperative contact. *Journal of Psychology & Human Sexuality, 8*(4), 59–68.

Graham, S. (1992). Most of the subjects were White and middle class. *American Psychologist, 47,* 629–639.

Grant, B. F., & Dawson, D. A. (1997). Age at onset of alcohol use and its association with DSM-IV alcohol abuse and dependence. *Journal of Substance Abuse, 9,* 103.

Grant, I., Gonzalez, R., Carey, C., & Natarajan, L. (2001). Long-term neurocognitive consequences of marijuana. In *National Institute on Drug Abuse Workshop on Clinical Consequences of Marijuana,* August 13, 2001, Rockville, MD.

Graves, J. L. (2001). *The emperor's new clothes.* Piscataway, NJ: Rutgers University Press.

Graziottin, A. (1998). The biological basis of female sexuality. *International Clinical Psychopharmacology, 13*(Suppl 6), S15–S22.

Greene, D., & Lepper, M. R. (1974). How to turn play into work. *Psychology Today,* Sept., 49.

Greenfield, P. M., & Savage-Rumbaugh, E. S. (1993). Comparing communicative competence in child and chimp: The pragmatics of repetition. *Journal of Child Language, 20*(1), 1–26.

Greenglass, E. R., Burke, R. J., & Konarski, R. (1998). Components of burnout, resources, and gender-related differences. *Journal of Applied Social Psychology, 28*(12), 1088–1106.

Gregory, R. L. (1990). *Eye and brain: The psychology of seeing.* Princeton, NJ: Princeton University Press.

Griffin, D. R. (1992). *Animal minds.* Chicago: University of Chicago Press.

Griffiths, M. (1999). Violent video games and aggression: A review of the literature. *Aggression & Violent Behavior, 4*(2), 203–212.

Grobstein, P., & Chow, K. L. (1975). Perceptive field development and individual experience. *Science, 190,* 352–358.

Grolnick, W. S., Cosgrove, T. J., & Bridges, L. J. (1996). Age-graded change in the initiative of positive affect. *Infant Behavior & Development, 19*(1), 153–157.

Gross, J. J. (2001). Emotion regulation in adulthood: Timing is everything. *Current Directions in Psychological Science, 10*(6), 214–219.

Groth-Marnat, G., & Schumaker, J. (1995). Psychologists in disease prevention and health promotion: A review of the cost effectiveness literature. *Psychology: A Journal of Human Behavior, 32*(1), 1–10.

Groth-Marnat, G., & Summers, R. (1998). Altered beliefs, attitudes, and behaviors following near-death experiences. *Journal of Humanistic Psychology, 38*(3), 110–125.

Gruder, C. L., Mermelstein, R. J., Kirkendol, S., et al. (1993). Effects of social support and relapse prevention training as adjuncts to a televised smoking-cessation intervention. *Journal of Consulting & Clinical Psychology, 61*(1), 113–120.

Gruner, C. R., & Tighe, M. R. (1995). Semantic differential measurements of connotations of verbal terms and their doublespeak facsimiles in sentence contexts. *Psychological Reports, 77*(3, Pt. 1) 778.

Gueguen, N. (2002). Status, apparel and touch: Their joint effects on compliance to a request. *North American Journal of Psychology, 4*(2), 279–286.

Gump, B. B., & Kulik, J. A. (1997). Stress, affiliation, and emotional contagion. *Journal of Personality & Social Psychology, 72*(2), 305–319.

Gur, R. E., et al. (1998). A follow-up magnetic resonance imaging study of schizophrenia. *Archives of General Psychiatry, 55*(2), 145–152.

Gustavsson, J. P., et al. (1997). Stability and predictive ability of personality traits across 9 years. *Personality & Individual Differences, 22*(6), 783–791.

Haas, L. J., Benedict, J. G., & Kobos, J. C. (1996). Psychotherapy by telephone: Risks and benefits for psychologists and consumers. *Professional Psychology: Research & Practice, 27*(2), 154–160.

Haber, R. N. (1969). Eidetic images; with biographical sketches. *Scientific American, 220*(12), 36–44.

Haber, R. N. (1970, May). How we remember what we see. *Scientific American,* 104–112.

Haddy, R. I., & Clover, R. D. (2001). The biological processes in psychological stress. *Families, Systems & Health, 19*(3), 291–302.

Hadwin, A. F., Kirby, J. R., & Woodhouse, R. A. (1999). Individual differences in notetaking, summarization and learning from lectures. *Alberta Journal of Educational Research, 45*(1), 1–17.

Haier, R. J., Siegel, B. V., Nuechterlein, K. H., Hazlett, E., et al. (1988). Cortical glucose metabolic rate correlates of abstract reasoning and attention studied with positron emission tomography. *Intelligence, 12,* 199–217.

Hall, C. (1966a). *The meaning of dreams.* New York: McGraw-Hill.

Hall, C. (1974a). What people dream about. In R. L. Woods & H. B. Greenhouse (Eds.), *The new world of dreams: An anthology.* New York: Macmillan.

Hall, C., Domhoff, G. W., Blick, K. A., & Weesner, K. E. (1982). The dreams of college men and women in 1950 and 1980: A comparison of dream contents and sex differences. *Sleep, 5*(2), 188–194.

Hall, E. T. (1966b). *The hidden dimension.* Garden City, NY: Doubleday.

Hall, E. T. (1974b). *Handbook for proxemic research.* Washington, DC: Social Anthropology and Visual Communication.

Hall, R. C. W., Platt, D. E., & Hall, R. C. W. (1999). Suicide risk assessment. *Psychosomatics, 40*(1), 18–27.

Halonen, J. S. (1986). *Teaching critical thinking in psychology.* Milwaukee, WI: Alverno Productions.

Hamer, D. H., & Copeland, P. (1998). *Living with our genes.* New York: Anchor.

Hamill, J. A. (1995). Dexterity and sexuality: Is there a relationship? *Journal of Homosexuality, 28*(3–4), 375–396.

Hamilton, V. L., & Sanders, J. (1995). Crimes of obedience and conformity in the workplace. *Journal of Social Issues, 51*(3), 67–88.

Hammer, J. C., Fisher, J. D., Fitzgerald, P., & Fisher, W. A. (1996). When two heads aren't better than one: AIDS risk behavior in college-age couples. *Journal of Applied Social Psychology, 26*(5), 375–397.

Hammer, L. B., Grigsby, T. D., & Woods, S. (1998). The conflicting demands of work, family, and school among students at an urban university. *Journal of Psychology, 132*(2), 220–226.

Haney, M., Ward, A. S., Comer, S. D., Foltin, R. W., & Fischman, M. W. (1999). Abstinence symptoms following oral THC administration to humans. *Psychopharmacology, 141*(4), 385–394.

Hannon, K. (1996, May 13). Upset? Try cybertherapy. *U.S. News and World Report,* 81–83.

Hansel, C. E. M. (1980). *ESP and parapsychology: A critical reevaluation.* Buffalo, NY: Prometheus.

Hansen, C. J., Stevens, L. C., & Coast, J. R. (2001). Exercise duration and mood state. *Health Psychology, 20*(4), 267–275.

Harding, D. J., Fox, C., & Mehta, J. D. (2002). Studying rare events through qualitative case studies. *Sociological Methods & Research, 31*(2), 174–217.

Harding, R. W., et al. (1998). Road rage and the epidemiology of violence. *Studies on Crime & Crime Prevention, 7*(2), 221–238.

Hare, R. D. (1996). Psychopathy: A clinical construct whose time has come. *Criminal Justice and Behavior, 23,* 25–54.

Harker, L., & Keltner, D. (2001). Expressions of positive emotion in women's college yearbook pictures and their relationship to personality and life outcomes across adulthood. *Journal of Personality & Social Psychology, 80*(1), 112–124.

Harlow, H. F., & Harlow, M. K. (1962). Social deprivation in monkeys. *Scientific American, 207,* 136–146.

Harma, M., Laitinen, J., Partinen, M., & Suvanto, S. (1994). The effect of four-day round trip flights over 10 time zones on the circadian variation of salivary melatonin and cortisol in airline flight attendants. *Ergonomics, 37*(9), 1479–1489.

Harris, D. A. (1999). *Driving while black.* American Civil Liberties Union Special Report, June.

Harris, J. A., Rushton, J. P., Hampson, E., & Jackson, D. N. (1996). Salivary testosterone and self-report aggressive and prosocial personality characteristics in men and women. *Aggressive Behavior, 22*(5), 321–331.

Harris, J. R., & Liebert, R. M. (1991). *The child.* Englewood Cliffs, NJ: Prentice Hall.

Harrison, L. F., & Williams, T. M. (1986). Television and cognitive development. In T. M. Williams (Ed.), *The impact of television: A natural experiment in three communities.* Orlando, FL: Academic.

Harsch, N., & Neisser, U. (1989). *Substantial and irreversible errors in flashbulb memories of the* Challenger *explosion.* Poster presented at the meeting of the Psychonomic Society, November 1989, Atlanta, GA.

Hart, B., & Risley, T. R. (1999). *The social world of children learning to talk.* Baltimore, MD: Paul H. Brookes

Hartlep, K. L., & Forsyth, G. A. (2000). The effect of self-reference on learning and retention. *Teaching of Psychology, 27*(4), 269–271.

Hartung, C. M., & Widiger, T. A. (1998). Gender differences in the diagnosis of mental disorders. *Psychological Bulletin, 123*(3), 260–278

Harvey, C. A., Curson, D. A., Pantelis, C., & Taylor, J. (1996). Four behavioural syndromes of schizophrenia. *British Journal of Psychiatry, 168*(5), 562–570.

Harvil, L. M., & Davis, G. (1997). Medical students' reasons for changing answers on multiple-choice tests. *Academic Medicine, 72*(10, Suppl 1), S97–S99.

Hathaway, S. R., & McKinley, J. C. (1989). *MMPI-2: Manual for administration and scoring.* Minneapolis, MN: University of Minnesota Press.

Hauck, F. R., Moore, C. M., Herman, S. M., Donovan, M., et al. (2002). The contribution of prone sleeping position to the racial disparity in sudden infant death syndrome. Pediatrics, 110, 772–780.

Hauri, P., & Linde, S. (1990). *No more sleepless nights.* New York: Wiley.

Hay, I., Ashman, A. F., & Van Kraayenoord, C. E. (1998). Educational characteristics of students with high or low self-concept. *Psychology in the Schools, 35*(4), 391–400.

Hayes, C. (1951). *The ape in our house.* New York: Harper & Row.

Hayne, H., & Rovee-Collier, C. (1995). The organization of reactivated memory in infancy. *Child Development, 66*(3), 893–906.

Heath, D. B. (2001). Culture and substance abuse. *Psychiatric Clinics of North America, 24*(3), 479–496.

Heath, L., & Gilbert, K. (1996). Mass media and fear of crime. *American Behavioral Scientist, 39*(4), 379–386.

Hebb, D. O. (1966). *A textbook of psychology.* Philadelphia: Saunders.

Heckhausen, J. (1987). Balancing for weaknesses and challenging developmental potential. *Developmental Psychology, 23*(6), 762–770.

Heermann, J. A., Jones, L. C., & Wikoff, R. L. (1994). Measurement of parent behavior during interactions with their infants. *Infant Behavior & Development, 17*(3), 311–321.

Heimann, M., & Meltzoff, A. N. (1996, March). Deferred imitation in 9– and 14–month-old infants. *British Journal of Developmental Psychology, 14,* 55–64.

Heine, S. J., & Lehman, D. R. (1999). Culture, self-discrepancies, and self-satisfaction. *Personality & Social Psychology Bulletin, 25*(8), 915–925.

Heinrich, R. K., Corbine, J. L., & Thomas, K. R. (1990, November/December). Counseling Native Americans. *Journal of Counseling and Development, 69,* 128–133.

Heinrichs, R. W. (2001). *In search of madness: Schizophrenia and neuroscience.* New York: Oxford University Press.

Heinze, H. J., Hinrichs, H., Scholz, M., Burchert, W., & Mangun, G. R. (1998). Neural mechanisms of global and local processing. *Journal of Cognitive Neuroscience, 10*(4), 485–498.

Hellerstein, D. J., et al. (1998). A randomized prospective study comparing supportive and dynamic therapies. *Journal of Psychotherapy Practice & Research, 7*(4), 261–271.

Hellige, J. B. (1990). Hemispheric asymmetry. *Annual Review of Psychology, 41,* 55–60.

Hellige, J. B. (1993). *Hemispheric asymmetry.* Cambridge, MA: Harvard University Press.

Helson, R., & Srivastava, S. (2002). Creative and wise people. *Personality & Social Psychology Bulletin, 28*(10), 1430–1440.

Henderson, L. (1997). Mean MMPI profile of referrals to a shyness clinic. *Psychological Reports, 80*(2) 695–702.

Henderson, N. D. (1982). Human behavior genetics. *Annual Review of Psychology, 33,* 403–440.

Hendrick, S. S., & Hendrick, C. (1993). Lovers as friends. *Journal of Social & Personal Relationships, 10*(3), 459–466.

Henman, L. D. (2001). Humor as a coping mechanism. *Humor: International Journal of Humor Research, 14*(1), 83–94.

Henningfield, J. E., & Heishman, S. J. (1995). The addictive role of nicotine in tobacco use. *Psychopharmacology, 117*(1), 11–13.

Hepper, P.G., McCartney, G. R., & Shannon, E. A. (1998). Lateralised behaviour in first trimester human fetuses. *Neuropsychologia, 36*(6), 531–534.

Herbert. T. B., & Cohen, S. (1993). Depression and immunity. *Psychological Bulletin, 113*(3), 472–486.

Hernstein, R., & Murray, C. (1994). *The Bell Curve.* New York: Free Press.

Hersen, M. (2002). Rationale for clinical case studies. *Clinical Case Studies, 1*(1), 3–5.

Herz, R. S. (2001). Ah sweet skunk! *Cerebrum, 3*(4)., 31–47.

Higbee, K. L., Clawson, C., DeLano, L., & Campbell, S. (1990). Using the link mnemonic to remember errands. *Psychological Record, 40*(3), 429–436.

Hilgard, E. R. (1968). *The experience of hypnosis.* New York: Harcourt Brace Jovanovich.

Hill, L. (1990). Effort and reward in college: A replication of some puzzling findings. *Journal of Social Behavior & Personality, 5(4),* 151–161.

Hilts, P. J. (1995). *Memory's ghost.* New York: Simon & Schuster.

Hixon, M. D. (1998). Ape language research: A review and behavioral perspective. *Analysis of Verbal Behavior, 15,* 17–39.

Hobson, J. A. (1999). Order from Chaos. In R. Conlan (Ed.), *States of mind.* New York: Wiley.

Hobson, J. A. (2001). *The dream drugstore.* Cambridge, MA: MIT Press.

Hobson, J. A., Pace-Schott, E. F., & Stickgold, R. (2000). Dream science 2000. *Behavioral & Brain Sciences, 23*(6), 1019–1035; 1083–1121.

Hobson, J. A., Pace-Schott, E. F., Stickgold, R., & Kahn, D. (1998). *Current Opinion in Neurobiology, 8*(2), 239–244.

Hochstenbach, J., Mulder, T., van Limbeek, J., Donders, R., & Schoonderwaldt, H. (1998). Cognitive decline following stroke. *Journal of Clinical & Experimental Neuropsychology, 20*(4), 503–517.

Hodapp, R. M. (1994). Mental retardation. *Encyclopedia of human behavior, Vol 3,* 175–185. San Diego: Academic Press.

Hoffman, D. D. (1999). *Visual intelligence.* New York: Norton.

Holden, C. (1980). Twins reunited. *Science 80,* Nov., 55–59.

Holmes, D. S. (1984). Meditation and somatic arousal reduction: A review of the experimental evidence. *American Psychologist, 39*(1), 1–10.

Holmes, D. S., Solomon, S., Cappo, B. M., & Greenberg, J. L. (1983). Effects of transcendental meditation versus resting on physiological and subjective arousal. *Journal of Personality & Social Psychology, 44,* 1245–1252.

Holmes, T., & Masuda, M. (1972, April). Psychosomatic syndrome. *Psychology Today,* 71.

Holyoak, K. J. (1990). Problem solving. In D. N. Osherson & E. E. Smith, *Thinking,* Cambridge, MA: The MIT Press.

Hopson, J. L. (1986, June). The unraveling of insomnia. *Psychology Today,* 43–49.

Horgan, J. (1995, November). Get smart, take a test: A long-term rise in IQ scores baffles intelligence experts. *Scientific American,* 2–14.

Horn, J. M., Loehlin, J. C., & Willerman, L. (1979). Intellectual resemblance among adoptive and biological relatives: The Texas adoption project. *Behavior Genetics, 9,* 177–207.

Horne, J. A., & Reyner, L. A. (1996). Counteracting driver sleepiness: Effects of napping, caffeine, and placebo. *Psychophysiology, 33*(3), 306–309.

Horne, R. S. C., Andrew, S., Mitchell, K., Sly, D. J., et al. (2001). Apnoea of prematurity and arousal from sleep. *Early Human Development, 61*(2), 119–133.

Horvath, A. O., & Goheen, M. D. (1990). Factors mediating the success of defiance- and compliance-based interventions. *Journal of Counseling Psychology, 37*(4), 363–371.

Hosch, H. M., & Cooper, D. S. (1982). Victimization as a determinant of eyewitness accuracy. *Journal of Applied Psychology, 67,* 649–652.

Howard, A., Pion, G. M., Gottfredson, G. D., Flattau, P. E., et al. (1986a). The changing face of American psychology. *American Psychologist, 41,* 1311–1327.

Howard, K. I., Kopta, S. M., Krause, M. S., & Orlinsky, D. E. (1986b). The dose-effect relationship in psychotherapy. *American Psychologist, 41,* 159–164.

Howes, C. (1997). Children's experiences in center-based child care as a function of teacher background and adult:child ratio. *Merrill-Palmer Quarterly, 43*(3), 404–425.

Hsia, Y., & Graham, C. H. (1997). Color blindness. In: A. Byrne, D. R. Hilbert, et al., (Eds), *Readings on color, Vol. 2: The science of color.* Cambridge, MA: The MIT Press.

Hubble, M.A., Duncan, B. L., and Miller, S. D., (Eds.). (1999). *The heart and soul of change: What works in therapy.* Washington, DC: American Psychological Association.

Hubel, D. H., & Wiesel, T. N. (1979). Brain mechanisms of vision. *Scientific American, 241,* 150–162.

Huebner, R. (1998). Hemispheric differences in global/local processing revealed by same-different judgements. *Visual Cognition, 5*(4), 457–478.

Huesmann, L. R., Eron, L., Klein, L., Brice, P., & Fischer, P. (1983). Mitigating the imitation of aggressive behaviors by changing children's attitudes about media violence. *Journal of Personality & Social Psychology, 44,* 899–910.

Huesmann, L. R., Moise, J. F., & Podolski, C. (1997). The effects of media violence on the development of antisocial behavior. In D. M. Stoff, et al. (Eds.), *Handbook of antisocial behavior.* New York: Wiley.

Huesmann, L. R., Moise-Titus, J., Podolski, C., & Eron, L. D. (2003). Longitudinal relations between children's exposure to TV violence and their aggressive and violent behavior in young adulthood: 1977–1992. *Developmental Psychology, 39*(2), 201–221.

Hughes, J. N., & Hasbrouck, J. E. (1996). Television violence: Implications for violence prevention. *School Psychology Review, 25*(2), 134–151.

Hughes, J. R., Oliveto, A. H., Liguori, A., Carpenter, J., & Howard, T. (1998). Endorsement of DSM-IV dependence criteria among caffeine users. *Drug & Alcohol Dependence, 52*(2), 99–107.

Humphries, S. A., Johnson, M. H., & Long, N. R. (1996). An investigation of the gate control theory of pain using the experimental pain stimulus of potassium iontophoresis. *Perception & Psychophysics, 58*(5), 1996, 693–703.

Hunt E. (1995, July/August). The role of intelligence in modern society. *American Scientist, 83,* 356–368.

Hunter, E. (1998). Adolescent attraction to cults. *Adolescence, 33*(131), 709–714.

Hyman, R. (1996a). Evaluation of the military's twenty-year program on psychic spying. *Skeptical Inquirer, 20*(2), 21–23.

Hyman, R. (1996b). The evidence for psychic functioning: Claims vs. reality. *Skeptical Inquirer, 20*(2), 24–26.

Hyman, S. (1999). Susceptibility and "Second Hits." In R. Conlan (Ed.), *States of mind.* New York: Wiley.

Ill-equipped: U.S. prisons and offenders with mental illness. (2003). New York: Human Rights Watch.

Immelman, A. (1998). The political personalities of 1996 U.S. presidential candidates Bill Clinton and Bob Dole. *Leadership Quarterly, 9*(3), 335–366.

Ingram, V. (2003, July/August). Alzheimer's disease. *American Scientist, 91,* 312–321.

Institute of Medicine. (1990). *Broadening the base of treatment for alcohol problems.* Washington, DC: National Academy Press.

Ironson, G., Freud, B., Strauss, J. L., & Williams, J. (2002). Comparison for two treatments for traumatic stress: A community-based study of EMDR and prolonged exposure. *Journal of Clinical Psychology, 58*(1), 113–128.

Isaak, M. I., & Just, A. (1995). Constraints on thinking in insight and invention. In R. J. Sternberg & J. E. Davidson (Eds.), *The nature of insight.* Cambridge, MA: MIT Press.

Ito, T. A., Miller, N., & Pollock, V. E. (1996). Alcohol and aggression. *Psychological Bulletin, 120*(1), 60–82.

Ivey, A. E., & Galvin, M. (1984). Microcounseling: A metamodel for counseling, therapy, business, and medical interviews. In D. Larson (Ed.), *Teaching psychological skills.* Monterey, CA: Brooks/Cole.

Izard, C. E. (1977). *Human emotions.* New York: Plenum.

Izard, C. E. (1990). Facial expressions and the regulation of emotions. *Journal of Personality & Social Psychology, 58*(3), 487–498.

Izard, C. E., Fantauzzo, C. A., Castle, J. M., Haynes, O. M., Rayias, M. F., & Putnam, P. H. (1995). The ontogeny and significance of infants' facial expressions in the first 9 months of life. *Developmental Psychology, 31*(6), 997–1013.

Jackson, T., Fritch, A., Nagasaka, T., & Gunderson, J. (2002). Towards explaining the association between shyness and loneliness. *Social Behavior & Personality, 30*(3), 263–270.

Jackson, T., Towson, S., & Narduzzi, K. (1997). Predictors of shyness. *Social Behavior & Personality, 25*(2), 149–154.

Jacobs, M. K., Christensen, A., Snibbe, J. R., Dolezal-Wood, S., et al. (2001). A comparison of computer-based versus traditional individual psychotherapy. *Professional Psychology: Research & Practice, 32*(1), 92–96.

Jacobsen, P. B., Bovbjerg, D. H., Schwartz, M. D., et al. (1993). Formation of food aversions in cancer patients receiving repeated infusions of chemotherapy. *Behavior Research & Therapy, 31*(8), 739–748.

Jaffe, J., Beatrice, B., Feldstein, S., Crown, C. L., & Jasnow, M. D. (2001). Rhythms of dialogue in infancy. *Monographs of the Society for Research in Child Development, 66*(2), vi-131.

Jahn, R. G. (1982). The persistent paradox of psychic phenomena. *Proceedings of the IEEE, 70*(2), 136–166.

Jamison, K. R. (1999). A magical orange grove in a nightmare: Creativity and mood disorders. In R. Cohen (Ed.), *States of mind.* New York: Wiley.

Jamison, K. R. (2001). Suicide in the Young: An essay. *Cerebrum, 3*(3), 39–42.

Jang, K. L., & Livesley, W. J. (1998). Support for a hierarchical model of personality. *Journal of Personality and Social Psychology, 74*(6), 1556–1565.

Janis, I. L. (1989). *Crucial decisions.* New York: Free Press.

Janssen, S. A., & Arntz, A. (2001). Real-life stress and opioid-mediated analgesia in novice parachute jumpers. *Journal of Psychophysiology, 15*(2), 106–113.

Janus, S. S., & Janus, C. L. (1993). *The Janus report.* New York: Wiley.

Jarvik, E. M. (1964). Ciba found. In H. Steinberg et al., *Symposium of animal pharmacology drug action.*

Jarvik, M. E. (1995). "The scientific case that nicotine is addictive": Comment. *Psychopharmacology, 117*(1), 18–20.

Jeffery, R. W., & Wing, R. R. (2001). The effects of an enhanced exercise program on long-term weight loss. *Obesity Research, 9*(3), O193.

Jellinik, E. M. (1960). *The disease concept of alcoholism.* New Haven: Hill House.

Jenkins, J. G., & Dallenbach, K. M. (1924). Obliviscence during sleep and waking. *American Journal of Psychology, 35,* 605–612.

Jennings, L., & Skovholt, T. M. (1999). The cognitive, emotional, and relational characteristics of master therapists. *Journal of Counseling Psychology, 46*(1), 3–11.

Jensvold, M. L. A., & Gardner, R. A. (2000). Interactive use of sign language by cross-fostered chimpanzees (Pan troglodytes). *Journal of Comparative Psychology, 114*(4), 335–346.

Jerabek, I., & Standing, L. (1992). Imagined test situations produce contextual memory enhancement. *Perceptual & Motor Skills, 75*(2), 400.

Jerome, L. W., DeLeon, P. H., James, L. C., Folen, R., et al. (2000). The coming of age of telecommunications in psychological research and practice. *American Psychologist, 55*(4), 407–421.

Johnson, J. G., Cohen, P., Smailes, E. M., Kasen, S., & Brook, J. S. (2002). Television viewing and aggressive behavior during adolescence and adulthood. *Science, 295*(5564), 2468–2471.

Johnson, J. G., & Sherman, M. F. (1997). Daily hassles mediate the relationship be-tween major life events and psychiatric symptomatology. *Journal of Social & Clinical Psychology, 16*(4), 389–404.

Johnson, K. E., & Mervis, C. B. (1997). Effects of varying levels of expertise on the basic level of categorization. *Journal of Experimental Psychology: General, 126*(3), 248–277.

Johnson, M. H., Breakwell, G., Douglas, W., & Humphries, S. (1998). The effects of imagery and sensory detection distractors on different measures of pain. *British Journal of Psychology, 37*(2), 141–154.

Johnson, S. M., & White, G. (1971). Self-observation as an agent of behavioral change. *Behavior Therapy, 2,* 488–497.

Johnson, S. P., & Nanez, J. E. (1995). Young infants' perception of object unity in two-dimensional displays. *Infant Behavior & Development, 18*(2), 133–143.

Johnsrude, I. S., Owen, A. M., Zhao, W. V., & White, N. M. (1999). Conditioned preference in humans. *Learning & Motivation, 30*(3), 250–264.

Jones, E. E., & Nisbett, R. E. (1971). The actor and observer: Divergent perceptions of the causes of behavior. In E. E. Jones, D. E. Kanouse, H. H. Kelley, R. E. Nisbett, S. Valins, & B. Weiner (Eds.), *Attribution: Perceiving the causes of behavior.* Morristown, NJ: General Learning Press.

Jones, G. V., & Martin, M. (2001). Confirming the X-linked handedness gene as recessive, not additive. *Psychological Review, 108*(4), 811–813.

Jones, L., Hughes, M., & Unterstaller, U. (2001). Post-traumatic stress disorder (PTSD) in victims of domestic violence. *Trauma Violence & Abuse, 2*(2), 99–119.

Jones, L., & Petruzzi, D. C. (1995). Test anxiety: A review of theory and current treatment. *Journal of College Student Psychotherapy, 10*(1), 3–15.

Jones, M. K., & Menzies, R. G. (1998). Danger ideation reduction therapy (DIRT) for obsessive-compulsive washers. *Behaviour Research & Therapy, 36*(10), 959–970.

Jones, S. S., Collins, K., & Hong, H. W. (1991). An audience effect on smile production in 10–month-old infants. *Psychological Science, 2,* 45–49.

Jourard, S. M. (1974). *Healthy personality.* New York: Macmillan.

Jouvet, M. (1999). The paradox of sleep. Boston, MA: MIT Press.

Joy, L. A., Kimball, M. M., & Zabrack, M. L. (1986). Television and aggressive behavior. In T. M. Williams (Ed.), *The impact of television: A natural experiment involving three towns.* New York: Academic.

Julien, R. M. (1998). *A primer of drug action.* San Francisco: Freeman.

Jurma, W. E., & Powell, M. L. (1994). Perceived gender roles of managers and effective conflict management. *Psychological Reports, 74*(1), 104–106.

Jussim, L., & Eccles, J. S. (1992). Teacher expectations. *Journal of Personality & Social Psychology, 63*(6), 947–961.

Juster, H. R., Heimberg, R. G., Frost, R. O., & Holt, C. S. (1996). Social phobia and perfectionism. *Personality & Individual Differences, 21*(3), 403–410.

Kagan, J. (1989). Temperamental contributions to social behavior. *American Psychologist, 44*(4), 668–674.

Kagan, J. (1991). The theoretical utility of constructs for self. *Developmental Review, 11*(3), 244–250.

Kahneman, D., Slovic, P., & Tversky, A. (1982). *Judgment under uncertainty: Heuristics and biases.* Cambridge: Cambridge University Press.

Kahneman, D., & Tversky, A. (1972). Subjective probability: A judgment of represen-tativeness. *Cognitive Psychology, 3,* 430–454.

Kahneman, D., & Tversky, A. (1973). On the psychology of prediction. *Psychological Review, 80,* 237–251.

Kaitz, M., Zvi, H., Levy, M., Berger, A., et al. (1995). The uniqueness of mother-own-infant interactions. *Infant Behavior & Development, 18*(2), 247–252.

Kalal, D. M. (1999). Critical thinking in clinical practice: Pseudoscience, fad psychology, and the behavioral therapist. *The Behavior Therapist, 22*(4), 81–84.

Kamin, L. J. (1981). *The intelligence controversy.* New York: Wiley.

Kamphaus, R. W. (1993). *Clinical assessment of children's intelligence.* Needham Heights, MA: Allyn and Bacon.

Kandel, E. (1999). Of learning, memory, and genetic switches. In R. Conlan (Ed.), *States of mind.* New York: Wiley.

Kaplan, P. S. (1998). *The human odyssey.* Pacific Grove, CA: Brooks/Cole.

Kaplan, P. S., Goldstein, M. H., Huckeby, E. R., & Cooper, R. P. (1995). Habituation, sensitization, and infants' responses to motherese speech. *Developmental Psychobiology, 28*(1), 45–57.

Kapleau, P. (1966). *The three pillars of Zen.* New York: Harper & Row.

Karlberg, L. Krakau, I., & Unden, A. (1998). Type A behavior intervention in primary health care reduces hostility and time pressure. *Social Science & Medicine, 46*(3), 397–402.

Karon, B. P., & Widener, A. J. (1997). Repressed memories and World War II: Lest we forget! *Professional Psychology: Research & Practice, 28*(4), 338–340.

Karon, B. P., & Widener, A. (1998). Repressed memories: The real story. *Professional Psychology: Research & Practice, 29*(5), 482–487.

Kasper, M. E., Rogers, R., & Adams, P. A. (1996). Dangerousness and command hallucinations. *Bulletin of the American Academy of Psychiatry & the Law, 24*(2), 219–224.

Kasser, T., & Ryan, R. M. (1993). A dark side of the American dream: Correlates of financial success as a central life aspiration. *Journal of Personality & Social Psychology, 65*(2), 410–422.

Kassin, S. M., Tubb, V. A., Hosch, H. M., & Memon, A. (2001). On the "general acceptance" of eyewitness testimony research. *American Psychologist, 56*(5), 405–416.

Kaufman, A. S. (2000). Intelligence tests and school psychology: Predicting the future by studying the past. *Psychology in the Schools, 37*(1), 7–16.

Kaufman, J. C. (2001). The Sylvia Plath effect: Mental illness in eminent creative writers. *Journal of Creative Behavior, 35*(1), 37–50.

Kaufman, J. C., & Baer, J. (2002). Could Steven Spielberg manage the Yankees?: Creative thinking in different domains. *Korean Journal of Thinking & Problem Solving, 12*(2), 5–14.

Kaufman, L., & Kaufman, J. H. (2000). Explaning the moon illusion. *Proceedings of the National Academy of Sciences, 97*(1), 500–505.

Kawai, K., Sugimoto, K., Nakashima, K., Miura, H., & Ninomiya, Y. (2000). Leptin as a modulator of sweet taste sensitivities in mice. *Proceedings: National Academy of Sciences, 97*(20), 11044–11049.

Kazdin, A. E. (1975). *Behavior modification in applied settings.* Homewood, IL: Dorsey Press.

Kebbell, M. R., & Wagstaff, G. F. (1998). Hypnotic interviewing: The best way to interview eyewitnesses? *Behavioral Sciences & the Law, 16*(1), 115–129.

Keller, M. C., & Young, R. K. (1996). Mate assortment in dating and married couples. *Personality & Individual Differences, 21*(2), 217–221.

Kellermann, A. L., Rivara, F. P., Rushforth, N. B., Banton, J. G., et al. (1993). Gun ownership as a risk factor for homicide in the home. *New England Journal of Medicine, 329*(15), 1084–1091.

Kelley, H. H. (1950). The warm-cold variable in first impressions of persons. *Journal of Personality, 18,* 431–439.

Kellner, C. H. (1998). ECT in the media. *Psychiatric Annals, 28*(9), 528–529.

Kelly, I. W. (1998). Why astrology doesn't work. *Psychological Reports, 82,* 527–546.

Kelly, I. W. (1999, November/December). "Debunking the debunkers": A response to an astrologer's debunking of skeptics. *Skeptical Inquirer,* 37–43.

Kelly, I. W., & Saklofske, D. H. (1994). Psychology and pseudoscience. *Encyclopedia of human behavior, 3,* 611–618.

Kelly, T. H., Foltin, R. W., Emurian, C. S., & Fischman, M. W. (1990). Multidimensional behavioral effects of marijuana. *Progress in Neuro-psychopharmacology & Biological Psychiatry, 14*(6), 885–902.

Kemp, M. (1998). Why is learning American Sign Language a challenge? *Accident Analysis & Prevention, 143*(3), 255–259.

Kendler, K. S., Thornton, L. M., & Prescott, C. A. (2001). Gender differences in the rates of exposure to stressful life events and sensitivity to their depressogenic effects. *American Journal of Psychiatry, 158*(4), 587–593.

Kennedy, P. R., & Bakay, R. A. (1998). Restoration of neural output from a paralyzed patient by a direct brain connection. *Neuroreport, 9*(8), 1707–1711.

Kenneth, M., Carpenter, K. M., & Hasin, D. S. (1998). Reasons for drinking alcohol. *Psychology of Addictive Behaviors, 12*(3), 168–184.

Kenrick, D. T., & MacFarlane, S. W. (1986). Ambient temperature and horn honking: A field study of the heat/aggression relationship. *Environment and Behavior, 18*(2), 179–191.

Kessler, R. C. (1997). The effects of stressful life events on depression. *Annual Review of Psychology, 48,* 191–214.

Kessler, R. C., Sonnega, A., & Nelson, C. B. (1995). Posttraumatic stress disorder in the National Comorbidity Survey. *Archives of General Psychiatry, 52*(12), 1048.

Kety, S. S. (1979, September). Disorders of the human brain. *Scientific American, 241,* 202–214.

Kiecolt-Glaser, J. K., & Glaser, R. (1992). Psychoneuroimmunology: Can psychological interventions modulate immunity? *Journal of Consulting & Clinical Psychology, 60*(4), 569–575.

Kiecolt-Glaser, J. K., McGuire, L. Robles, T. F., & Glaser, R. (2002). Emotions, morbidity, and mortality. *Annual Review of Psychology, 53,* 83–107.

Kiewra, K. A., DuBois, N. F., Christian, D., McShane, A., et al. (1991). Note-taking functions and techniques. *Journal of Educational Psychology, 83*(2), 240–245.

Kihlstrom, J. F. (1985). Hypnosis. *Annual Review of Psychology 36,* 385–418.

Killen, J. D., & Fortmann, S. P. (1997). Craving is associated with smoking relapse.

Kim, A., Martin, D., & Martin, M. (1989). Effects of personality on marital satisfaction. *Family Therapy, 16*(3), 243–248.

Kim, S. (2000, December). Bogglers. *Discover,* 98.

Kimball, M. M. (1986). Television and sex-role attitudes. In T. M. Williams (Ed.), *The impact of television: A natural experi-*

ment in three communities. Orlando, FL: Academic.

King, A. (1992). Comparison of self-questioning, summarizing, and notetaking-review as strategies for learning from lectures. *American Educational Research Journal, 29(2),* 303–323.

King, A. (1995). Cognitive strategies for learning from direct teaching. In E. Wood, V. Woloshyn, and T. Willoughby (Eds.), *Cognitive strategy instruction for middle and high schools,* Brookline, Cambridge, MA.

King, L., & Napa, C. (1998). What Makes a Life Good? *Journal of Personality and Social Psychology, 75(1)* 156–165.

King, L. A., Richards, J. H., & Stemmerich, E. (1998). Daily goals, life goals, and worst fears. *Journal of Personality, 66(5),* 713–744.

Kinnier, R. T., Tribbensee, N. E.. Rose, C. A., & Vaughan, S. M. (2001). In the final analysis: More wisdom from people who have faced death. *Journal of Counseling & Development, 79(2),* 171–177.

Kirsch, I., & Lynn, S. J. (1995). The altered state of hypnosis. *American Psychologist, 50(10),* 846–858.

Kirsch, I., Montgomery, G., & Sapirstein, G. (1995). Hypnosis as an adjunct to cognitive behavioral therapy: A meta-analysis. *Journal of Consulting and Clinical Psychology, 63,* 214–220.

Kirsch, I., & Sapirstein, G. (1998, June 26). Listening to Prozac but hearing placebo: A meta-analysis of antidepressant medication. *Prevention & Treatment, 1.*

Kisilevsky, B. S., & Low, J. A. (1998). Human fetal behavior. *Developmental Review, 18(1),* 1–29.

Kitayama, S., Markus, H. R., Matsumoto, H., & Norasakkunkit, V. (1997). Individual and collective processes in the construction of the self. *Journal of Personality & Social Psychology, 72(6),* 1245–1267.

Kjellgren, A., Sundequist, U., Norlander, T., & Archer, T. (2001). Effects of flotation-REST on muscle tension pain. *Pain Research & Management, 6(4),* 181–189.

Klaus, M. H., Kennell, J. H., & Klaus, P. H. (1995). *Bonding.* Reading, MA: Addison-Wesley.

Klebanoff, M. A., Levine, R. J., DerSimonian, R., Clemens, J. D., & Wilkins, D. G. (1999). Maternal serum paraxanthine, a caffeine metabolite, and the risk of spontaneous abortion. *New England Journal of Medicine, 341(22),* 1639–1644.

Klein, K., & Boals, A. (2001a). The relationship of life event stress and working memory capacity. *Applied Cognitive Psychology, 15(5),* 565–579.

Klein, K., & Boals, A. (2001b). Expressive writing can increase working memory capacity. *Journal of Experimental Psychology: General, 130(3),* 520–533.

Klein, S. B., Loftus, J., & Kihlstrom, J. F. (1996). Self-knowledge of an amnesic patient. *Journal of Experimental Psychology: General, 125(3),* 250–260.

Kleinke, C. L., Peterson, T. R., & Rutledge, T. R. (1998). Effects of self-generated facial expressions on mood. *Journal of Personality and Social Psychology, 74(1),* 272–279.

Klintsova, A. Y., & Greenough, W. T. (1999). Synaptic plasticity in cortical systems. *Current Opinion in Neurobiology, 9(2),* 203–208.

Koenig, S. M. (1996). Central sleep apnea. *Virginia Medical Quarterly, 123(4),* 247–250.

Koepke, J. E., & Bigelow, A. E. (1997). Observations of newborn suckling behavior. *Infant Behavior & Development, 20(1),* 93–98.

Kohlberg, L. (1969). The cognitive-developmental approach to socialization. In A. Goslin (Ed.), *Handbook of socialization theory and research.* Chicago: Rand McNally.

Kolb, B., & Whishaw, I. Q. (1998). Brain plasticity and behavior. *Annual Review of Psychology, 49,* 43–64.

Kolbe, L. J., Collins, J., & Cortese, P. (1997). Building the capacity of schools to improve the health of the nation. *American Psychologist, 52(3),* 256–265.

Konner, M. (1991). *Childhood.* Boston: Little, Brown.

Kopta, S. M., et al. (1999). Individual psychotherapy outcome and process research. *Annual Review of Psychology, 50,* 441–469.

Kosslyn, S. M. (1983). *Ghosts in the mind's machine.* New York: Norton.

Kosslyn, S. M. (1985, May). Stalking the mental image. *Psychology Today,* 23–28.

Kosslyn, S. M., et al. (2000). Hypnotic visual illusion alters color processing in the brain. *American Journal of Psychiatry, 157(8),* 1279–1284.

Kosslyn, S. M., Ball, T. M., & Reiser, B. J. (1978). Visual images preserve metric spatial information: Evidence from studies of image scanning. *Journal of Experimental Psychology: Human Perception and Performance, 4,* 47–60.

Kosslyn, S. M., Seger, C., Pani, J. R., & Hillger, L. A. (1990). When is imagery used in everyday life? A diary study. *Journal of Mental Imagery, 14(3–4),* 131–152.

Kosslyn, S. M., Thompson, W. L., & Alpert, N. N. (1995). Topographical representation of mental images in primary visual cortex. *Nature, 378(6556),* 496.

Kosson, D. S., Suchy, Y., Mayer, A. R., & Libby, J. (2002). Facial affect recognition in criminal psychopaths. *Emotion, 2(4),* 398–411.

Kotkin, M., Daviet, C., & Gurin, J. (1996). The Consumer Reports mental health survey. *American Psychologist, 51(10),* 1080–1082.

Kottler, J. A., & Brown, R. W. (1999). *Introduction to therapeutic counseling.* Monterey, CA: Brooks/Cole.

Kozart, M. F. (2002). Understanding efficacy in psychotherapy. *American Journal of Orthopsychiatry, 72(2),* 217–231.

Kozulin, A. (1999). Cognitive learning in younger and older immigrant students. *School Psychology International, 20(2),* 177–190.

Krakow, B., Kellner, R., Pathak, D., & Lambert, L. (1996). Long term reduction of nightmares with imagery rehearsal treatment. *Behavioural & Cognitive Psychotherapy, 24(2),* 135–148.

Krakow, B., & Neidhardt, J. (1992). *Conquering bad dreams and nightmares.* New York: Berkley Books.

Krantz, D. S., & McCeney, M. K. (2002). Effects of psychological and social factors on organic disease. *Annual Review of Psychology, 53,* 341–369.

Kratofil, P. H., Baberg, H. T., & Dimsdale, J. E. (1996). Self-mutilation and severe self-injurious behavior associated with amphetamine psychosis. *General Hospital Psychiatry, 18(2),* 117–120.

Kring, A. M., & Gordon, A. H. (1998). Sex differences in emotion. *Journal of Personality & Social Psychology, 74(3),* 686–703.

Kroon, M. B., Van Kreveld, D., & Rabbie, J. M. (1992). Group versus individual decision making: Effects of accountability and gender on groupthink. *Small Group Research, 23(4),* 427–458.

Kropp, P., et al. (1997) Behavioral treatment in migraine. *Functional Neurology, 12(1),* 17–24.

Krosnick, J. A. (1999). Survey research. *Annual Review of Psychology, 50,* 537–567.

Krueger, J., Ham, J. J., & Linford, K. M. (1996). Perceptions of behavioral consistency: Are people aware of the actor-observer effect? *Psychological Science, 7(5),* 259–264.

Kubovy, M., & Holcombe, A. O. (1998). *On the lawfulness of grouping by proximity.* Cognitive Psychology, 35(1), 71–98.

Kuhn, C. M., & Wilson, W. A. (2001). Our dangerous love affair with Ecstasy. *Cerebrum, 3(2),* 22–33.

Kunkel, M. A. (1993). A teaching demonstration involving perceived lunar size. *Teaching of Psychology, 20(3),* 178–180.

Kunzendorf, R. G. (1989). After-images of eidetic images: A developmental study. *Journal of Mental Imagery, 13(1),* 55–62.

Kusseling, F. S., Shapiro, M. F., Greenberg, J. M., & Wenger, N. S. (1996). Understanding why heterosexual adults do not practice safer sex: A comparison of two samples. *AIDS Education & Prevention, 8(3),* 247–257.

La Berge, S. P. (1981, January). Lucid dreaming: Directing the action as it happens. *Psychology Today,* 48–57.

La Berge, S. P. (1985). *Lucid dreaming.* Los Angeles: Tarcher.

Laan, E., Everaerd, W., van der Velde, J., & Geer, J. H. (1995). Determinants of subjective experience of sexual arousal in women. *Psychophysiology, 32(5),* 444–451.

Laberge, L., Petit, D., Simard, C., Vitaro, F., et al. (2001). Development of sleep patterns in early adolescence. *Journal of Sleep Research, 10(1),* 59–67.

Labov, W. (1973). The boundaries of words and their meanings. In C. J. N. Bailey & R. W. Shuy (Eds.) *New ways of analyzing variation in English.* Washington, DC: Georgetown University Press.

Lacayo, A. (1995). Neurologic and psychiatric complications of cocaine abuse. *Neuropsychiatry, Neuropsychology, & Behavioral Neurology, 8(1),* 53–60.

Lachman, M. E., & Weaver, S. L. (1998). The sense of control as a moderator of social class differences in health and well-being. *Journal of Personality & Social Psychology, 74(3),* 763–773.

Lacks, P., & Morin, C. M. (1992). Recent advances in the assessment and treatment of insomnia. *Journal of Clinical and Consulting Psychology, 60(4),* 586–594.

Lahtinen, V., Lonka, K., & Lindbloom-Ylaenne, S. (1997). Spontaneous study strategies and the quality of knowledge construction. *British Journal of Educational Psychology, 67(1),* 13–24.

Lal, S. K. L., et al. (1998). Effect of feedback signal and psychological characteristics on blood pressure self-manipulation capability. *Psychophysiology, 35(4),* 405–412.

Lamb, M. R., & Yund, E. W. (1996). Spatial frequency and attention. *Perception & Psychophysics, 58(3),* 363–373.

Lambert, M. J. (1999). Are differential treatment effects inflated by researcher therapy allegiance? *Clinical Psychology: Science & Practice, 6(1),* 127–130.

Lambert, M. J., & Cattani-Thompson, K. (1996). Current findings regarding the effectiveness of counseling. *Journal of Counseling & Development, 74(6),* 601–608.

Lambert, W. E. (1987). The effects of bilingual and bicultural experiences on children's attitudes and social perspectives. In P. Homel, M. Palij, & D. Aaronson (Eds.), *Childhood bilingualism.* Hillsdale, NJ: Erlbaum.

Lance, C. E., LaPointe, J. A., & Stewart, A. M. (1994). A test of the context dependency of three causal models of halo rater error.

Journal of Applied Psychology, 79(3), 332–340.

Lange, A., van de Ven, J., Schrieken, B., & Emmelkamp, P. M. G. (2001). *Journal of Behavior Therapy & Experimental Psychiatry, 32(2),* 73–90.

Langer, E. J. (2000). Mindful learning. *Current Directions in Psychological Science, 9(6),* 220–223.

Langer, E. J., & Abelson, R. P. (1974). A patient by any other name: Clinician group difference in labeling bias. *Journal of Consulting and Clinical Psychology, 42(1),* 4–9.

Lanzetta, J. T., & Englis, B. G. (1989). Expectations of cooperation and competition and their effects on observers' vicarious emotional responses. *Journal of Personality & Social Psychology, 56(4),* 543–554.

Larner, A. J., Moss, J., Rossi, M. L., & Anderson, M. (1994). Congenital insensitivity to pain. *Journal of Neurology, Neurosurgery & Psychiatry, 57(8),* 973–974.

Larsen, R. J., & Kasimatis, M. (1990). Individual differences in entrainment of mood to the weekly calendar. *Journal of Personality & Social Psychology, 58(1),* 164–171.

Larson, C. A., & Carey, K. B. (1998). Caffeine. *Professional Psychology: Research & Practice, 29(4),* 373–376.

Latane, L., Nida, S. A., & Wilson, D. W. (1981). The effects of group size on helping behavior. In J. P. Rushton & R. M. Sorrentino (Eds.), *Altruism and helping behavior: Social, personality and developmental perspectives.* Hillsdale, NJ: Erlbaum.

Lattal, K. A., Reilly, M. P., & Kohn, J. P. (1998). Response persistence under ratio and interval reinforcement schedules. *Journal of the Experimental Analysis of Behavior, 70(2),* 165–183.

Laumann, E., Michael, R., Michaels, S., & Gagnon, J. (1994). *The social organization of sexuality.* Chicago: University of Chicago Press.

Lavallee, A. C. (1999). Capuchin (Cebus apella) tool use in a captive naturalistic environment. *International Journal of Primatology, 20(3),* 399–414.

Lavie, P. (2001). Sleep-wake as a biological rhythm. *Annual Review of Psychology, 52,* 277–303.

Lay, C., & Verkuyten, M. (1999). Ethnic identity and its relation to personal self-esteem. *Journal of Social Psychology, 139(3),* 288–299.

Lazar, S. W., Bush, G., Gollub, R. L., Fricchione, G. L., et al. (2000). Functional brain mapping of the relaxation response and meditation. *Neuroreport, 11(7),* 1581–1585.

Lazarus, R. S. (1981, July). Little hassles can be hazardous to health. *Psychology Today,* 12–14.

Lazarus, R. S. (1991a). Progress on a cognitive-motivational-relational theory of emotion. *American Psychologist, 46(8),* 819–834.

Lazarus, R. S. (1991b). Cognition and motivation in emotion. *American Psychologist, 46(4),* 352–367.

Lazarus, R. S. (1993). From psychological stress to the emotions: A history of changing outlooks. In L. W. Porter and M. R. Rosenzweig (Eds.), *Annual Review of Psychology, 44,* 1–21.

Lazev, A. B., Herzog, T. A., & Brandon, T. H. (1999). Classical conditioning of environmental cues to cigarette smoking. *Experimental and Clinical Psychopharmacology, 7(1),* 56–63.

Lazgrove, S., et al. (1998). An open trial for EMDR as treatment for chronic PTSD. *American Journal of Orthopsychiatry, 68(4),* 601–608.

Leavens, D. A., & Hopkins, W. D. (1998). Intentional communication by chimpanzees. *Developmental Psychology, 34*(5), 813–822.

Lecomte, D., & Fornes, P. (1998). Suicide among youth and young adults, 15 through 24 years of age. *Journal of Forensic Sciences, 43*(5), 964–968.

LeDoux, J. (1996). *The emotional brain: The mysterious underpinnings of emotional life.* New York: Simon & Schuster.

LeDoux, J. (1999). The Power of Emotions. In R. Conlan (Ed.), *States of mind.* New York: Wiley.

LeDoux, J. E., & Gorman, J. M. (2001). A call to action: Overcoming anxiety through active coping. *American Journal of Psychiatry. 158*(12), 1953–1955.

Lee, C. C. (1991a). Cultural dynamics. In C. C. Lee & B. L. Richardson (Eds.), *Multicultural issues in counseling.* Alexandria, VA: American Association for Counseling and Development.

Lee, C. C. (1991b). New approaches to diversity. In C. C. Lee & B. L. Richardson (Eds.), *Multicultural issues in counseling.* Alexandria, VA: American Association for Counseling and Development.

Lee, J. M., Ku, J. H., Jang, D. P., Kim, D., et al. (2002). Virtual reality system for treatment of the fear of public speaking using image-based rendering and moving pictures. *CyberPsychology & Behavior, 5*(3), 191–195.

Lee, M., Zimbardo, P. G., & Bertholf, M. (1977, November). Shy murderers. *Psychology Today.*

Lee, T. D., & Carnahan, H. (1990). When to provide knowledge of results during motor learning: Scheduling effects. *Human Performance, 3*(2), 87–105.

Leeming, F. C. (1997). Commitment to study as a technique to improve exam performance. *Journal of College Student Development, 38*(5), 499–507.

Leenaars, A. A. (1995). Suicide. In H. Wass & R. A. Neimeyer (Eds.), *Dying.* Washington, DC: Taylor & Francis.

Leeper, R. W. (1935). A study of a neglected portion of the field of learning: The development of sensory organization. *Pedagogical Seminary and Journal of Genetic Psychology, 46*, 41–75.

Lefcourt, H. M., & Thomas, S. (1998). Humor and stress revisited. In W. Ruch, et al. (Eds.) *The sense of humor.* Berlin, Germany: Walter De Gruyter.

Leibel, R. L., Rosenbaum, M., & Hirsch, J. (1995). Changes in energy expenditure resulting from altered body weight. *New England Journal of Medicine, 332*(10), 621–628.

Lejuez, C. W., Eifert, G. H., Zvolensky, M. J., & Richards, J. B. (2000). Preference between onset predictable and unpredictable administrations of 20% carbon-dioxide-enriched air. *Journal of Experimental Psychology: Applied, 6*(4), 349–358.

Lenzenweger, M. F., & Gottesman, I. I. (1994). Schizophrenia. In V. S. Ramachandran (Ed.), *Encyclopedia of human behavior.* San Diego, CA: Academic.

Leonard, C. M. (1997). Language and the prefrontal cortex. In N. A. Krasnegor, G. R. Lyon, et al. (Eds.) *Development of the prefrontal cortex: Evolution, neurobiology, and behavior.* Baltimore: Paul H. Brookes.

Leor, J., Poole, W. K., & Kloner, R. A. (1996). Sudden cardiac death triggered by earthquake. *The New England Journal of Medicine, 334*(7), 413.

Lepore, F. E. (2002). When seeing is not believing. *Cerebrum, 4*(2), 23–38.

Lepper, M. R., Keavney, M., & Drake, M. (1996). Intrinsic motivation and extrinsic

rewards. *Review of Educational Research, 66*(1), 5–32.

Leslie, K., & Ogilvie, R. (1996). Vestibular dreams: The effect of rocking on dream mentation. Dreaming: *Journal of the Association for the Study of Dreams, 6*(1), 1–16.

Lettvin, J. Y. (1961). Two remarks on the visual system of the frog. In W. Rosenblith (Ed.), *Sensory communication.* Cambridge, MA: MIT Press.

LeVay, S. (1993). *The sexual brain.* Cambridge, MA: The MIT Press.

Levenston, G. K., Patrick, C. J., Bradley, M. M., & Lange, P. J. (2000). The psychopathic observer. *Journal of Abnormal Psychology, 109*, 373–385.

Levesque, M. F., & Neuman, T. (1999). Human trials to begin. *Spinal Cord Society Newsletter, 246*, 3–4.

Levesque, M. J., Steciuk, M., & Ledley, C. (2002). Self-disclosure patterns among well-acquainted individuals. *Social Behavior & Personality, 30*(6), 579–592.

Levi, A. M. (1998). Are defendants guilty if they were chosen in a lineup? *Law & Human Behavior, 22*(4), 389–407.

Levine, J. M., & Moreland, R. L. (1990). Progress in small group research. *Annual Review of Psychology, 41*, 485–634.

Levine, M., Toro, P. A., & Perkins, D. V., (1993). Social and community interventions. In L. W. Porter and M. R. Rosenzweig (Eds.), *Annual Review of Psychology, 44*, 525–558.

Levinson, A. (1999). Memory champ an absent-minded lady. *Tucson Daily Star,* Feb.

Levitsky, D. A., Nussbaum, M., Halbmaier, C.A., Mrdjenovic, G. (2003). The Freshman 15: a model for the study of techniques to curb the 'epidemic' of obesity. Society for the Study of Ingestive Behavior: Annual Meeting, July 15–19, University of Groningen, Haren, The Netherlands.

Levy, J., & Reid, M. (1976). Cerebral organization. *Science,* 337–339.

Lewis, M., & Brooks-Gunn, J. (1979). *Social cognition and the acquisition of self.* New York: Plenum.

Lewis, M. (1995, January/February). Self-conscious emotions. *American Scientist, 83*, 68–78.

Lewis, P. S., Goodman, S. H., & Fandt, P. M. (1995). *Management.* St Paul, MN: West.

Lewy, A. J., et al. (1998). Morning vs evening light treatment of patients with winter depression. *Archives of General Psychiatry, 55*(10), 890–896

Light, P. (1997). Computers for learning. *Journal of Child Psychology & Psychiatry & Allied Disciplines, 38*(5), 497–504.

Lightsey, O. R., Jr. (1996). What leads to wellness? The role of psychological resources in well-being. *Counseling Psychologist, 24*(4), 589–759.

Lilienfeld, S. (1998). Pseudoscience in contemporary clinical psychology. *The Clinical Psychologist, 51*(4), 3–9.

Lilienfeld, S. O. (1999, September/October). Projective measures of personality and psychopathology. *Skeptical Inquirer,* 32–39.

Lindemann, B. (2000). A taste for umami. *Nature Neuroscience, 3*, 99–100.

Lindemann, B. (2001). Receptors and transduction in taste. *Nature, 413*, 219–225.

Lindsay, D. S. (1998). Depolarizing views on recovered memory experiences. In S. J. Lynn, K. M. McConkey, et al. (Eds.), *Truth in memory.* New York: The Guilford Press.

Lindsay, E. W., Mize, J., & Pettit, G. S. (1997). Differential pay patterns of mothers and fathers of sons and daughters. *Sex Roles, 37*(9–10), 643–661.

Linton, M. (1979, July). I remember it well. *Psychology Today,* 81–86.

Lipman, J. J., Miller, B. E., Mays, K. S., Miller, M. N., et al. (1990). Peak B-endorphin concentration in cerebro-spinal fluid: Reduced in chronic pain patients and increased during the placebo response. *Psychopharmacology, 102*(1), 112–116.

Lipschitz, D. S., Kaplan, M. L., Sorkenn, J., & Chorney, P. (1996). Childhood abuse, adult assault, and dissociation. *Comprehensive Psychiatry, 37*(4), 261–266.

Lipsey, M. W., & Wilson, D. B. (1993). The efficacy of psychological, educational, and behavioral treatment. *American Psychologist, 48*(12), 1181–1209.

Lissner, L., Odell, P. M., D'Agostino, R. B., et al. (1991). Variability of body weight and health outcomes in the Farmington population. *The New England Journal of Medicine, 324*(26), 1839–1844.

Liu, X., Matochik, J. A., Cadet, J., et al. (1998). Smaller volume of prefrontal lobe in polysubstance abusers. *Neuropsychopharmacology, 18*(4), 243–252.

Liu, Y., Gao, J., Liu, H., & Fox, P. T. (2000). The temporal response of the brain after eating revealed by functional MRI. *Nature, 405*, 1058–1062.

Lobo, L. L., & Tufik, S. (1997). Effects of alcohol on sleep parameters of sleep-deprived healthy volunteers. *Sleep, 20*(1), 52–59.

Loeber, R., & Hay, D. (1997). Key issues in the development of aggression and violence from childhood to early adulthood. In J. T. Spence (Ed.), *Annual Review of Psychology, 48*, 371–410.

Loehlin, J. C., McCrae, R. R., Costa, P. T., & John, O. (1998). Heritabilities of common and measure-specific components of the Big Five personality factors. *Journal of Research in Personality, 32*(4), 431–453.

Loftus, E. F. (1994). The repressed memory controversy. *American Psychologist, 49*(5), 443–444.

Loftus, E. F. (2003). Make-believe memories. *American Psychologist, 58*(11), 867–873.

Loftus, E., & Ketcham, K. (1991). *Witness for the defense.* New York: St. Martin's Press.

Loftus, E., & Loftus, G. (1980). On the permanence of stored information in the human brain. *American Psychologist, 35*, 409–420.

Loftus, E., & Palmer, J. C. (1974). Reconstruction of automobile destruction: An example of interaction between language and memory. *Journal of Verbal Learning and Verbal Behavior, 13*, 585–589.

Loftus, G. R., & Mackworth, N. H. (1978). Cognitive determinants of fixation location in picture viewing. *Journal of Experimental Psychology: Human Perception and Performance, 4*, 565–572.

Long, D. M. (1991). Fifteen years of transcutaneous electrical stimulation for pain control. *Stereotactic & Functional Neurosurgery, 56*(1), 2–19.

López, S. R., & Guarnaccia, P. J. J. (2000). Cultural psychopathology. *Annual Review of Psychology, 51*, 571–598.

Lorenz, K. (1966). *On aggression.* Translated by M. Kerr-Wilson. New York: Harcourt Brace Jovanovich.

Lorenz, K. (1974). *The eight deadly sins of civilized man.* Translated by M. Kerr-Wilson. New York: Harcourt Brace Jovanovich.

Lovaas, O., & Simmons, J. (1969). Manipulation of self-destruction in three retarded children. *Journal of Applied Behavior Analysis, 2*, 143–157.

Low, K. G., & Feissner, J. M. (1998). Seasonal affective disorder in college students: Prevalence and latitude. *Journal of American College Health, 47*(3), 135–137.

Luborsky, L., et al. (1997). The psychotherapist matters. *Clinical Psychology: Science & Practice, 4*(1), 53–65.

Lucas, F., & Sclafani, A. (1990). Hyperphagia in rats produced by a mixture of fat and sugar. *Physiology & Behavior, 47*(1), 51–55.

Luce, G. G. (1965). *Current research on sleep and dreams.* Health Service Publication, No. 1389. U.S. Department of Health, Education and Welfare.

Luckie, W. R., & Smethurst, W. (1998). *Study power.* Cambridge, MA: Brookline, 1998.

Lundh, L., Berg, B., Johansson, H., Nilsson, L., et al. (2002). Social anxiety is associated with a negatively distorted perception of one's own voice. *Cognitive Behaviour Therapy, 31*(1), 25–30.

Luria, A. R. (1968). *The mind of a mnemonist.* New York: Basic.

Luster, T., & Dubow, E. (1992). Home environment and maternal intelligence as predictors of verbal intelligence. *Merrill-Palmer Quarterly, 38*(2), 151–175.

Lustig, C., May, C. P., & Hasher, L. (2001). Working memory span and the role of proactive interference. *Journal of Experimental Psychology: General, 130*(2), 199–207.

Luxem, M., & Christophersen, E. (1994). Behavioral toilet training in early childhood: Research, practice, and implications. *Journal of Developmental & Behavioral Pediatrics, 15*(5), 370–378.

Lykken, D. T. (1998). *A tremor in the blood: Uses and abuses of the lie detector.* New York: Plenum.

Lykken, D. T., McGue, M., Tellegen, A., & Bouchar, T. J. (1992). Emergenesis. *American Psychologist, 47*, 1565–1567.

Lynch, T. R., Robins, C. J., Morse, J. Q., & MorKrause, E. D. (2001). A mediational model relating affect intensity, emotion inhibition, and psychological distress. *Behavior Therapy, 32*(3), 519–536.

Lyubomirsky, S., & Tucker, K. L. (1998). Implications of individual differences in subjective happiness for perceiving, interpreting, and thinking about life events. *Motivation & Emotion, 22*(2), 155–186.

Lyznicki, J. M., Doege, T. C., Davis, R. M., & Williams, M. A. (1998). Sleepiness, driving, and motor vehicle crashes. *Journal of the American Medical Association, 279*(23), 1908–1913.

Maas, J. (1999). *Power Sleep.* New York: HarperCollins.

Mabry, J. H. (1998). Something for the future. *Analysis of Verbal Behavior, 15*, 129–130.

Mack, A. (2002). Is the visual world a grand illusion? *Journal of Consciousness Studies, 9*(5–6), 102–110.

Mack, A., & Rock, I. (1998). *Inattentional Blindness.* Cambridge, MA: MIT Press.

Macklis, J. D. (2001). New memories from new neurons. *Nature, 410*(6826), 314–315.

Macmillan, R. (2001). Violence and the life course. *Annual Review of Sociology, 27*, 1–22.

Maddi, S. R., Kahn, S., & Maddi, K. L. (1998). The effectiveness of hardiness training. *Consulting Psychology Journal: Practice & Research, 50*(2), 78–86.

Madigan, S., & O'Hara, R. (1992). Short-term memory at the turn of the century. *American Psychologist, 47*(2), 170–174.

Madon, S., Jussim, L., & Eccles, J. (1997). In search of the powerful self-fulfilling prophecy. *Journal of Personality and Social Psychology, 72*, 791–809.

Magee, W. J., Eaton, W. W., & Wittchen, H. (1996). Agoraphobia, simple phobia, and social phobia in the national comorbidity survey. *Archives of General Psychiatry, 53*(2), 159–168.

Maguire, E. A., Frackowiak, R. S. J., & Frith, C. D. (1997). Recalling routes around London: Activation of the hippocampus in taxi drivers. *The Journal of Neuroscience, 17*(8), 7103.

Maier, N. R. F. (1949). *Frustration.* New York: McGraw-Hill.

Malaspina, D. (2001). Paternal factors and schizophrenia risk: De novo mutations and imprinting. *Schizophrenia Bulletin, 27*(3), 379–393.

Malaspina, D., Harlap, S., Fennig, S., Heiman, D., et al. (2001). Advancing paternal age and the risk of schizophrenia. *Archives of General Psychiatry, 58*(4), 361–367.

Malnic, B., Hirono, J., & Buck, L. B. (1999). Combinatorial Receptor Codes for Odors. *Cell, 96*(5), 713.

Mandler, J. M., & McDonough, L. (1998). On developing a knowledge base in infancy. *Developmental Psychology, 34*(6), 1274–1288.

Mangun, G. R. (1995). Neural mechanisms of visual selective attention. *Psychophysiology, 32*(1), 4–18.

Manschreck, T. C. (1996). Delusional disorder: The recognition and management of paranoia. *Journal of Clinical Psychiatry, 57*(3, Suppl.), 32–38.

Mansouri, A., & Adityanjee. (1995). Delusion of pregnancy in males: A case report and literature review. *Psychopathology, 28*(6), 307–311.

Mantyla, T. (1986). Optimizing cue effectiveness: Recall of 600 incidentally learned words. *Journal of Experimental Psychology: Learning, Memory, and Cognition, 12*(1), 66–71.

Margolin, G., & Gordis, E. B. (2000). The effects of family and community violence on children. *Annual Review of Psychology, 51*, 445–479.

Marks, D. F. (1990). Comprehensive commentary, insightful criticism. *Skeptical Inquirer, 14*(3), 413–418.

Marks, D. F. (2000). *The psychology of the psychic.* Buffalo, NY: Prometheus.

Marks, D. F., & Kammann, R. (1979). *The psychology of the psychic.* Buffalo, NY: Prometheus.

Markus, H., & Kitayama, S. (1991). Culture and the self: Implications for cognition, emotion, and motivation. *Psychological Bulletin, 98*, 224–253.

Markus, H. R., & Kitayama, S. (1998). The cultural psychology of personality. *Journal of Cross-Cultural Psychology, 29*(1), 63–87.

Markus, H., Kitayama, S., & VandenBos, G. R. (1996). The mutual interactions of culture and emotion. *Psychiatric Services, 47*(3), 225–226.

Markus, H. R., & Nurius, P. (1986). Possible selves. *American Psychologist, 41*, 954–969.

Marques, P., Bradley, J., Shappee, J., & Marques, C. (1982). *Bienestar: Health, well-being and lifestyle choices for Pinal County.* Tucson, AZ: Project West Pinal, University of Arizona Health Sciences Center.

Martens, R., & Trachet, T. (1998). *Making sense of astrology.* Amherst, MA: Prometheus.

Martin, C. L., & Fabes, R. A. (2001). The stability and consequences of young children's same-sex peer interactions. *Developmental Psychology, 37*(3), 431–446.

Martin, D. J., Garske, J. P., & Davis, M. K. (2000). Relation of the therapeutic alliance with outcome and other variables: A meta-analytic review. *Journal of Consulting & Clinical Psychology, 68*(3), 438–450.

Martin, P. Y., & Benton, D. (1999). The influence of a glucose drink on a demanding working memory task. *Physiology & Behavior, 67*(1), 69–74.

Martin, S. (1995, January). Field's status unaltered by the influx of women. *APA Monitor, 9.*

Martin, W. L. B., & Freitas, M. B. (2002). Mean mortality among Brazilian left- and right-handers: Modification or selective elimination. *Laterality, 7*(1), 31–44.

Martinez-Gonzalez, M. A., Gual, P., Lahortiga, F., Alonso, Y., et al. (2003). Parental factors, mass media influences, and the onset of eating disorders in a prospective population-based cohort. *Pediatrics, 111,* 315–320.

Masi, G., Mucci, M., & Millepiedi, S. (2001). Separation anxiety disorder in children and adolescents. *CNS Drugs, 15*(2), 93–104.

Maslach, C. Schaufeli, W. B., & Leiter, M. P. (2001). Job burnout. *Annual Review of Psychology, 52,* 397–422.

Maslow, A. H. (1954). *Motivation and personality.* New York: Harper.

Maslow, A. H. (1967). Self-actualization and beyond. In J. F. T. Bugental (Ed.), *Challenges of humanistic psychology.* New York: McGraw-Hill.

Maslow, A. H. (1969). *The psychology of science.* Chicago: Henry Regnery.

Maslow, A. H. (1970). *Motivation and personality.* New York: Harper & Row.

Maslow, A. H. (1971). *The farther reaches of human nature.* New York: Viking.

Masse, L. C., & Tremblay, R. E. (1997). Behavior of boys in kindergarten and the onset of substance use during adolescence. *Archives of General Psychiatry, 54*(1), 62.

Masters, W. H., & Johnson, V. E. (1966). *Human sexual response.* Boston: Little, Brown.

Masters, W. H., & Johnson, V. E. (1970). *The pleasure bond: A new look at sexuality and commitment.* Boston: Little, Brown.

Matheny, K. B., Brack, G. L., McCarthy, C. J., & Penick, J. M. (1996). The effectiveness of cognitively-based approaches in treating stress-related symptoms. *Psychotherapy, 33*(2), 305–320.

Matias, R., & Cohn, J. F. (1993). Are max-specified infant facial expressions during face-to-face interaction consistent with differential emotions theory? *Developmental Psychology, 29*(3), 524–531.

Matossian, M. K. (1982). Ergot and the Salem witchcraft affair. *American Scientist, 70,* 355–357.

Matson, J. L., Sevin, J. A., Fridley D., & Love, S. R. (1990). Increasing spontaneous language in three autistic children. *Journal of Applied Behavior Analysis, 23*(2), 223–227.

Matsuda, L. A., Lolait, S. J., Brownstein, M. J., Young, A. C., & Bonner, T. I. (1990). Structure of a cannabinoid receptor and functional expression of the cloned cDNA. *Nature, 346*(6284), 561–564.

Mattson, S. N., Riley, E. P., Gramling, L., et al. (1998). Neuropsychological comparison of alcohol-exposed children with or without physical features of fetal alcohol syndrome. *Neuropsychology, 12*(1), 146–153.

Mauer, M. H., Burnett, K. F., Ouellette, E. A., Ironson, G. H., et al. (1999). Medical hypnosis and orthopedic hand surgery. *International Journal of Clinical & Experimental Hypnosis, 47*(2), 144–161.

May, M. (1996). Resistance: Friend or foe? *American Journal of Psychotherapy, 50*(1), 32–44.

Mayer, J. D., & Hanson, E. (1995). Mood-congruent judgment over time. *Personality & Social Psychology Bulletin, 21*(3), 237–244.

Mayer, J. D., Salovey, P., Caruso, D. R., & Sitarenios, G. (2001). Emotional intelli-gence as standard intelligence. *Emotion, 1*(3), 232–242.

Mayer, R. E. (1995). *Thinking, problem solving, and cognition.* New York: Freeman.

Mayer, R. E. (2004). Should there be a three-strikes rule against pure discovery learning? *American Psychologist, 59*(1), 14–19.

McAlister, A. L., Ama, E., Barroso, C., Peters, R. J., & Kelder, S. (2000). Promoting tolerance and moral engagement through peer modeling. *Cultural Diversity and Ethnic Minority Psychology, 6*(4), 363–373.

McBride, W. J., Murphy, J. M., & Ikemoto, S. (1999). Localization of brain reinforcement mechanisms. *Behavioural Brain Research, 101*(2), 129–152.

McCann, S. L., & Stewin, L. L. (1988). Worry, anxiety, and preferred length of sleep. *Journal of Genetic Psychology, 149*(3), 413–418.

McCarley, R. W. (1998). Dreams: Disguise of forbidden wishes or transparent reflections of a distinct brain state? In R. M. Bilder, F. F. LeFever, et al. (Eds.), *Neuroscience of the mind on the centennial of Freud's Project for a Scientific Psychology.* New York: New York Academy of Sciences.

McCartney, K., Bernieri, F., & Harris, M. J. (1990). Growing up and growing apart: A developmental meta-analysis of twin studies. *Psychological Bulletin, 107*(2), 226–237.

McCarty, R. (1998). Making the case for animal research. *APA Monitor,* Nov., 18.

McCleary, R., Chew, K. S., Hellsten, J. J., & Flynn-Bransford, M. (1991). Age- and sex-specific cycles in United States suicides, 1973 to 1985. *American Journal of Public Health, 81*(11), 1494–1497.

McClelland, D. C. (1961). *The achieving society.* New York: Van Nostrand.

McClelland, D. C. (1965). Achievement and entrepreneurship. *Journal of Personality & Social Psychology, 1,* 389–393.

McClelland, D. C. (1975). *Power: the inner experience.* New York: Irvington.

McClelland, D. C., & Cheriff, A. D. (1997). The immunoenhancing effects of humor on secretory IgA and resistance to respiratory infections. *Psychology & Health, 12*(3), 329–344.

McClelland, D. C., & Pilon, D. A. (1983). Sources of adult motives in patterns of parent behavior in early childhood. *Journal of Personality & Social Psychology, 44,* 564–574.

McCluskey, U. (2002). The dynamics of attachment and systems-centered group psychotherapy. *Group Dynamics, 6*(2), 131–142.

McCrae, R. R. (1987). Creativity, divergent thinking, and openness to experience. *Journal of Personality & Social Psychology, 52*(6), 1258–1265.

McCrae, R. R., & Costa, P. T. (1990). *Personality in adulthood.* New York: Guilford.

McCrae, R. R., & Costa, P. T. (1997). Personality trait structure as a human universal. *American Psychologist, 52*(5), 509–516.

McCutcheon, L. E. (2000). Another failure to generalize the Mozart effect. *Psychological Reports, 87*(1), 325–330.

McDaniel, M. A., & Schlager, M. S. (1990). Discovery learning and transfer of problem-solving skills. *Cognition & Instruction, 7*(2), 129–159.

McDermott, J. F. (2001). Emily Dickinson revisited: A study of periodicity in her work. *American Journal of Psychiatry, 158*(5), 686–690.

McGinnis, J. M., & Foege, W. H. (1993). Actual causes of death in the United States. *Journal of the American Medical Association, 270*(18), 2207–2212.

McGregor, I., & Little, B. R. (1998). Personal Projects, Happiness, and Meaning. *Journal of Personality and Social Psychology, 74*(2), 494–512.

McIntosh, W. D., Harlow, T. F., & Martin, L. L. (1995). Linkers and nonlinkers: Goal beliefs as a moderator of the effects of everyday hassles on rumination, depression, and physical complaints. *Journal of Applied Social Psychology, 25*(14), 1231–1244.

McKean, K. J. (1994). Using multiple risk factors to assess the behavioral, cognitive, and affective effects of learned helplessness. *Journal of Psychology, 128*(2), 177–183.

McKeever, W. F. (2000). A new family handedness sample with findings consistent with X-linked transmission. *British Journal of Psychology, 91*(1), 21–39.

McKeever, W. F., Cerone, L. J., Suter, P. J., & Wu, S. M. (2000). Family size, miscarriage-proneness, and handedness. *Laterality, 5*(2), 111–120.

McKelvie, P., & Low, J. (2002). Listening to Mozart does not improve children's spatial ability. *British Journal of Developmental Psychology, 20*(2), 241–258.

McKenna, K. Y. A., & Bargh, J. A. (1998). Coming out in the age of the Internet: Identity "demarginalization" through virtual group participation. *Journal of Personality & Social Psychology, 75*(3), 681–694.

McKenna, M. W., & Ossoff, E. P. (1998). Age differences in children's comprehension of a popular television program. *Child Study Journal, 28*(1), 52–68.

McKim, W. A. (1997). *Drugs and behavior.* Upper Saddle River, NJ: Prentice Hall.

McLennan, J. (1992). "University blues": Depression among tertiary students during an academic year. *British Journal of Guidance & Counselling, 20*(2), 186–192.

McLoyd, V. (1998). Socioeconomic disadvantage and child development. *American Psychologist, 53*(2), 185–204.

McLoyd, V. C., & Smith, J. (2002). Physical discipline and behavior problems in African American, European American, and Hispanic children: Emotional support as a moderator. *Journal of Marriage & Family, 64*(1), 40–53.

McManus, I. C., Sik, G., Cole, D. R., Muellon, A. F., et al. (1988). The development of handedness in children. *British Journal of Developmental Psychology, 6*(3), 257–273.

McMullan, W. E., & Stocking, J. R. (1978). Conceptualizing creativity in three dimensions. *The Journal of Creative Behavior, 12,* 161–167.

McNamara, D. S., & Scott, J. L. (2001). Working memory capacity and strategy use. *Memory & Cognition, 29*(1), 10–17.

McRoberts, C., Burlingame, G. M., & Hoag, M. J. (1998). Comparative efficacy of individual and group psychotherapy. *Group Dynamics, 2*(2), 101–117.

Meagher, M. W., Arnau, R. C., & Rhudy, J. L. (2001). Pain and emotion. *Psychosomatic Medicine, 63*(1), 79–90.

Medhus, E. (2001). When the bough breaks: The making of a terrorist. www.drmedhus.com.

Medin, D. L., & Ross, B. H. (1992). *Cognitive psychology.* Fort Worth: Harcourt Brace Jovanovich.

Mehrabian, A. (2000). Beyond IQ. *Genetic Social, and General Psychology Monographs, 126,* 133–239.

Mehren, E. (1994, April 8). Study finds most child care lacking. *The Los Angeles Times,* E-5.

Meier, R. P. (1991). Language acquisition by deaf children. *American Scientist, 79*(1), 60–70.

Meleshko, K. G., & Alden, L. E. (1993). Anxiety and self-disclosure. *Journal of Personality & Social Psychology, 64*(6), 1000–1009.

Meltzoff, A. N., & Moore, M. K. (1983). Newborn infants imitate adult facial gestures. *Child Development, 54,* 702–709.

Meltzoff, J. (1998). *Critical thinking about research.* Washington, DC: American Psychological Association.

Melzack, R. (1993). Pain: Past, present and future. *Canadian Journal of Experimental Psychology, 47*(4), 615–629.

Melzack, R., & Wall, P. D. (1996). *The Challenge of Pain.* Harmondworth, UK: Penguin.

Mendolia, M., Moore, J., & Tesser, A. (1996). Dispositional and situational determinants of repression. *Journal of Personality & Social Psychology, 70*(4), 856–867.

Mercer, J. G., Beck, B., Burlet, A., et al. (1998). Leptin (ob) mRNA and hypothalamic NPY in food-deprived/refed Syrian hamsters. *Physiology & Behavior, 64*(2), 191–195.

Merckelbach, H., & Muris, P. (1997). The etiology of childhood spider phobia. *Behaviour Research & Therapy, 35*(11), 1031–1034.

Merenda, P. F. (1996). BASC: Behavior Assessment System for Children. *Measurement & Evaluation in Counseling & Development, 28*(4), 229–232.

Merikle, P. M., & Skanes, H. E. (1992). Subliminal self-help audiotapes: A search for placebo effects. *Journal of Applied Psychology, 77*(5), 772–776.

Mermelstein, R. (1986). Social support and smoking cessation and maintenance. *Journal of Consulting & Clinical Psychology, 54*(4), 447–453.

Merritt, J. M., Stickgold, R., Pace-Schott, E., Williams, J., et al. (1994). Emotion profiles in the dreams of men and women. *Consciousness & Cognition, 3*(1), 46–60.

Mesquita, B., & Frijda, N. H. (1992). Cultural variations in emotions. *Psychological Bulletin, 112*(2), 179–204.

Messick, D. M., & Mackie, D. M. (1989). Intergroup relations. *Annual Review of Psychology, 40,* 45–81.

Metcalfe, J. (1986). Premonitions of insight predict impending error. *Journal of Experimental Psychology: Learning, Memory, and Cognition, 12,* 623–634.

Metzner, R. (1998). Hallucinogenic drugs and plants in psychotherapy and shamanism. *Journal of Psychoactive Drugs, 30*(4), 333–341.

Meyer, A. J., Nash, J. D., McAlister, A. L., Maccoby, N., & Farquhar, J. W. (1980). Skills training in a cardiovascular health education campaign. *Journal of Consulting and Clinical Psychology, 48,* 129–142.

Meyer, G. J., Finn, S. E., Eyde, L. D., Kay, G. G., et al. (2001). Psychological testing and psychological assessment. *American Psychologist, 56*(2) 128–165.

Michalko, M. (1998). *Cracking creativity.* Berkeley, CA: Ten Speed Press.

Michel, D. E., & Chesky, K. S. (1995). A survey of music therapists using music for pain relief. *Arts in Psychotherapy, 22*(1), 49–51.

Michotte, A. (1963). *The perception of causality.* New York: Methuen/Basic.

Mielke, H. W. (1999). Lead in the inner cities. *American Scientist, 87*(Jan.-Feb.), 62–73.

Mikulincer, M., & Nachshon, O. (1991). Attachment styles and patterns of self-disclosure. *Journal of Personality & Social Psychology, 61*(2), 321–331.

Milgram, S. (1963). Behavioral study of obedience. *Journal of Abnormal and Social Psychology, 67,* 371–378.

Milgram, S. (1965). Some conditions of obedience and disobedience to authority. *Human Relations, 18,* 57–76.

Milgram, S., Bickman, L., & Berkowitz, L. (1969). Note on the drawing power of crowds of different size. *Journal of Personality & Social Psychology, 13,* 79–82.

Miller, D. T., Turnbull, W., & McFarland, C. (1988). Particularistic and universalistic evaluation in the social comparison process. *Journal of Personality & Social Psychology, 55*(6), 908–917.

Miller, G. A. (1956). The magical number seven, plus or minus two: Some limits on our capacity for processing information. *Psychological Review, 63,* 81–87.

Miller, G. A. (1999). On knowing a word. *Annual Review of Psychology, 50,* 1–19.

Miller, G. E., & Cohen, S. (2001). Psychological interventions and the immune system. *Health Psychology, 20*(1), 47–63.

Miller, G. E., Cohen, S., & Ritchey, A. K. (2002). Chronic psychological stress and the regulation of pro-inflammatory cytokines. *Health Psychology, 21*(6), 531–541.

Miller, M. A., & Rahe, R. H. (1997). Life changes scaling for the 1990s. *Journal of Psychosomatic Research, 43*(3), 279–292.

Miller, N. E. (1944). Experimental studies of conflict. In J. McV. Hunt (Ed.), *Personality and the behavior disorders,* Vol. I, 431–465. New York: Ronald Press.

Miller, N. E., & Bugelski. R. (1970). The influence of frustration imposed by the ingroup on attitudes expressed toward outgroups. In R. I. Evans & R. M. Rozelle (Eds.), *Social psychology in life.* Boston: Allyn & Bacon.

Miller, T. Q., Smith, T. W., Turner, C. W., & Guijarro, M. L. (1996). Meta-analytic review of research on hostility and physical health. *Psychological Bulletin, 119*(2), 322–348.

Millon, T. (1981) *Disorders of personality: DSM-III: Axis II.* New York: Wiley.

Milner, B. (1965). Memory disturbance after bilateral hippocampal lesions. In P. Milner, & S. Glickman (Eds.), *Cognitive processes and the brain,* pp. 97–111. Princeton, NJ: Van Nostrand.

Milton, J., & Wiseman, R. (1997). *Guidelines for extrasensory perception research.* Hertfordshire, England, UK: University of Hertfordshire Press.

Milton, J., & Wiseman, R. (1999). A meta-analysis of mass-media tests of extrasensory perception. *British Journal of Psychology, 90*(2), 235–240.

Minda, J. P., & Smith, J. D. (2001). Prototypes in category learning. *Journal of Experimental Psychology: Learning, Memory, & Cognition, 27*(3), 775–799.

Mineka, S., & Hamida, S. B. (1998). Observational and nonconscious learning. In W. T. O'Donohue, et al. (Eds.), *Learning and behavior therapy.* Boston: Allyn & Bacon

Minton, H. L. (2000). Psychology and gender at the turn of the century. *American Psychologist, 55*(6), 613–615.

Miotto, K., Darakjian, J., Basch, J., Murray, S., et al. (2001). Gamma-hydroxybutyric acid: Patterns of use, effects and withdrawal. *American Journal on Addictions, 10*(3), 232–241.

Miranda, J. (1992). Dysfunctional thinking is activated by stressful life events. *Cognitive Therapy & Research, 16*(4), 473–483.

Mirsky, A. F., Bieliauskas, L. A., French, L. M., Van Kammen, D. P., et al. (2000). A 39-year followup on the Genain quadruplets. *Schizophrenia Bulletin, 26*(3), 699–708.

Mirsky, A. F., & Duncan, C. C. (1986). Etiology and expression of schizophrenia. *Annual Review of Psychology, 37,* 291–319.

Mischel, W., & Shoda, Y. (1998). Reconciling processing dynamics and personality dispositions. *Annual Review of Psychology, 49,* 229–258.

Mischel, W. (1968). *Personality and assessment.* New York: Wiley.

Mitchell, D. (1987, February). Firewalking cults: Nothing but hot air. *Laser,* 7–8.

Mitchell, D. B. (1989). How many memory systems? Evidence from aging. *Journal of Experimental Psychology: Learning, Memory, and Cognition, 15*(1), 31–49.

Mitru, G., Millrood, D.L., & Mateika, J. H. (2002). The impact of sleep on learning and behavior in adolescents. *Teachers College Record, 104*(4), 704–726.

Miyake, A. (2001). Individual differences in working memory. *Journal of Experimental Psychology: General, 130*(2), 163–168.

Mogg, K., Bradley, B. P., Hyare, H., & Lee, S. (1998). Selective attention to food-related stimuli in hunger. *Behaviour Research & Therapy, 36*(2), 227–237.

Moghaddam, B. (2002). Stress activation of glutamate neurotransmission in the prefrontal cortex. *Biological Psychiatry, 51*(10), 775–787.

Mohanty, S., Pati, N. C., & Kumar, R. (1998). Effects of token economy on the rate of envelope making in the persons with mental retardation. *Social Science International, 14*(1–2), 84–97.

Mombaerts, P. (1999). Molecular biology of odorant receptors in vertebrates. *Annual Review of Neuroscience, 22,* 487–509.

Monahan, J. (1992). Mental disorder and violent behavior. *American Psychologist, 47*(4), 511–521.

Montgomery, G. (1989, March). The mind in motion. *Discover,* 58–68.

Moor, J. H. (2001). The status and future of the Turing test. *Minds & Machines, 11*(1), 77–93.

Moore, T. E. (1995). Subliminal self-help auditory tapes: An empirical test of perceptual consequences. *Canadian Journal of Behavioural Science, 27*(1), 9–20.

Moore-Ede, M. C., Sulzman, F. M., & Fuller, C. A. (1982). *The clocks that time us.* Cambridge, MA: Harvard University Press.

Morelli, G. A., Rogoff, B., Oppenheim, D., & Goldsmith, D. (1992). Cultural variation in infants' sleeping arrangements. *Developmental Psychology, 28*(4), 604–613.

Moreno, J. L. (1953). *Who shall survive?* New York: Beacon.

Morgan, M. J. (2000). Ecstasy (MDMA): A review of its possible persistent psychological effects. *Psychopharmacology, 152,* 230–248.

Morgenstern, J., Labouvie, E., McCrady, B. S., et al. (1997). Affiliation with Alcoholics Anonymous after treatment. *Journal of Consulting & Clinical Psychology, 65*(5), 768–777.

Moriarty, T. (1975, April). A nation of willing victims. *Psychology Today,* 43–50.

Morisse, D., Batra, L., Hess, L., & Silverman, R. (1996). A demonstration of a token economy for the real world. *Applied & Preventive Psychology, 5*(1), 41–46.

Moritz, A. P., & Zamchech, N. (1946). Sudden and unexpected deaths of young soldiers. *American Medical Association Archives of Pathology, 42,* 459–494.

Morrison, R. G., & Wallace, B. (2001). Imagery vividness, creativity and the visual arts. *Journal of Mental Imagery, 25*(3–4), 135–152.

Moss, K. (1989). Performing the light-switch task in lucid dreams: A case study. *Journal of Mental Imagery, 13*(2), 135–137.

Murray, B. (2001, November). "A daunting unbelievable experience." *Monitor on Psychology,* 18.

Murray, J. B. (2002). Phencyclidine (PCP): A dangerous drug, but useful in schizophrenia research. *Journal of Psychology, 136*(3), 319–327.

Murray, S. H., Touyz, S. W., & Beumont, P. J. V. (1996). Awareness and perceived influence of body ideals in the media: A comparison of eating disorder patients and the general community. *Eating Disorders: The Journal of Treatment & Prevention, 4*(1), 33–46.

Murray, S. L., Holmes, J. G., & Griffin, D. W. (1996). The self-fulfilling nature of positive illusions in romantic relationships. *Journal of Personality & Social Psychology, 71*(6), 1155–1180.

Mussen, P. H., Conger, J. J., Kagan, J., & Geiwitz, J. (1979). *Psychological development: A life span approach.* New York: Harper & Row.

Myers, H. F., Lesser, I., Rodriguez, N., Mira, C. B., et al. (2002). Ethnic differences in clinical presentation of depression in adult women. *Cultural Diversity and Ethnic Minority Psychology, 8*(2), 138–156.

Nagy, Z., Esiri, M. M., Jobst, K. A., & Morris, J. H. (1996). Clustering of pathological features in Alzheimer's disease. *Dementia, 7*(3), 121–127.

Nairne, J. S. (2002). Remembering over the short-term. *Annual Review of Psychology, 53,* 53–81.

Naitoh, P., Kelly, T. L., & Englund, C. E. (1989). *Health effects of sleep deprivation.* U.S. Naval Health Research Center Report, No. 89–46.

Naka, M. (1998). The variables affecting the reliability of eyewitness testimony. *Japanese Journal of Psychonomic Science, 16*(2), 100–106.

Nantais, K. M., & Schellenberg, E. G. (1999). The Mozart effect: An artifact of preference. *Psychological Science, 10*(4), 370–373.

Naranjo, C. (1970). Present-centeredness: Technique, prescription, and ideal. In J. Fagan & I. L. Shepherd (Eds.), *What is Gestalt therapy?* New York: Harper & Row.

Natale, V., & Cicogna, P. (1996). Circadian regulation of subjective alertness in morning and evening types. *EDRA: Environmental Design Research Association, 20*(4), 491–497.

Nathan, P. E., & Langenbucher, J. W. (1999). Psycho-pathology. *Annual Review of Psychology, 50,* 79–107.

National Academy of Sciences (2003). *The polygraph and lie detection.* Washington, DC: National Academy of Sciences.

National Institute of Child Health and Human Development (1999). The NICHD Study of Early Child Care.

National television violence study. (1995–96). Studio City, CA: Mediascope, Inc.

Navarro, M. (1995, December 9) Drug sold abroad by prescription becomes widely abused in U.S. *The New York Times,* 1, 9.

Naveh-Benjamin, M. (1990) The acquisition and retention of knowledge: Exploring mutual benefits to memory research and the educational setting. *Applied Cognitive Psychology, 4*(4), 295–320.

Neath, I. (2002). *Human memory.* Belmont, CA: Wadsworth.

Needles, D. J., & Abramson, L. Y. (1990). Positive life events, attributional style, and hopefulness: Testing a model of recovery from depression. *Journal of Abnormal Psychology, 99*(2), 156–165.

Neisser, U., Boodoo, G., Bouchard, T. J., et al, (1996). Intelligence: Knowns and unknowns. *American Psychologist, 51*(2), 77–101.

Nelson, C. A. (1999). How important are the first 3 years of life? *Applied Developmental Science, 3*(4), 235–238.

Nelson, T. O. (1987). Predictive accuracy of the feeling of knowing across different tasks and across different subject populations and individuals. In M. M. Gruneberg, P. E. Morris, & R. N. Sykes (Eds.), *Practical aspects of memory: Current research and issues.* Chinchester, UK: Wiley.

Nesca, M., & Koulack, D. (1994). Recognition memory, sleep and circadian rhythms. *Canadian Journal of Experimental Psychology, 48*(3) 359–379.

Neter, E., & Ben-Shakhar, G. (1989). The predictive validity of graphological inferences: A meta-analytic approach. *Personality and Individual Differences, 10*(7), 737–745.

Neugarten, B. (1971, December). Grow old along with me! The best is yet to be. *Psychology Today,* 45.

Neuman, G. A., & Baydoun, R. (1998). An empirical examination of overt and covert integrity tests. *Journal of Business & Psychology, 13*(1), 65–79.

Newman, A. W., & Thompson, J. W. (2001). The rise and fall of forensic hypnosis in criminal investigation. *Journal of the American Academy of Psychiatry & the Law, 29*(1), 75–84.

Newman, B. M., & Newman, P. R. (1987). The impact of high school on social development. *Adolescence, 22*(87), 525–534.

Newman, R. (1994, August). Electronic therapy raises issues, risks. *APA Monitor,* 25.

Niaura, R., Todaro, J. F., Stroud, L., Spiro, A., et al. (2002). Hostility, the metabolic syndrome, and incident coronary heart disease. *Health Psychology, 21*(6), 588–593.

Nickell, J. (2001, November/December). John Edward: Hustling the bereaved. *Skeptical Inquirer,* 19–22.

Nickerson, R. S., & Adams, M. J. (1979). Long-term memory for a common object. *Cognitive Psychology, 11,* 287–307.

Nielsen, D. M., & Metha, A. (1994). Parental behavior and adolescent self-esteem in clinical and nonclinical samples. *Adolescence, 29*(115), 525–542.

Nijstad, B. A., Stroebe, W., & Lodewijkx, H. F. M. (1999). Persistence of brainstorming groups: How do people know when to stop? *Journal of Experimental Social Psychology, 35*(2), 165–185.

Nikles, C. D., Brecht, D. L., Klinger, E., & Bursell, A. L. (1998). The effects of current-concern- and nonconcern-related waking suggestions on nocturnal dream content. *Journal of Personality & Social Psychology, 75*(1) 242–255.

Nist, S. L., Sharman, S. J., & Holschuh, J. L. (1996). The effects of rereading, self-selected strategy use, and rehearsal on the immediate and delayed understanding of text. *Reading Psychology, 17*(2), 137–157.

Nixon, M. (1990). Professional training in psychology. *American Psychologist, 45*(11), 1257–1262.

Njeri, I. (1991, January 13). Beyond the melting pot. *Los Angeles Times,* E-1, E-8.

Noble, P. (1997). Violence in psychiatric inpatients. *International Review of Psychiatry, 9*(2–3), 207–216.

Noice, H., & Noice, T. (1999). Long-term retention of theatrical roles. *Memory, 7*(3), 357–382.

Norcross, J. C., Hedges, M., & Prochaska, J. O. (2002). The face of 2010: A Delphi poll on the future of psychotherapy. *Professional Psychology: Research & Practice, 33*(3), 316–322.

Nori, G. (1998). Glucagon and the control of meal size. In: G. P. Smith, et al. (Eds.), *Satiation: From gut to brain.* New York: Oxford University Press.

Norlander, T., Anonymous, & Archer, T. (1998). Effects of flotation rest on creative problem solving and originality. *Journal of Environmental Psychology, 18*(4), 399–408.

Norlander, T., Bergman, H., & Archer, T. (1999). Primary process in competitive archery performance: Effects of flotation REST. *Journal of Applied Sport Psychology, 11*(2), 194–209.

Norman, A. D., Ramsay, S. G., Martray, C. R., & Roberts, J. L. (1999). Relationship between levels of giftedness and psychosocial adjustment. *Roeper Review, 22*(1), 5–9.

Norris, R. M., & Weinman, J. A. (1996). Psychological change following a long sail training voyage. *Personality & Individual Differences, 21*(2), 189–194.

North, C. S. (1987). *Welcome silence.* New York: Simon & Schuster.

Nurnberger, J. I., & Zimmerman, J. (1970). Applied analysis of human behaviors: An alternative to conventional motivational inferences and unconscious determination in therapeutic programming. *Behavior Therapy, 1,* 59–69.

Nyberg, L., & Tulving, E. (1996). Classifying human long-term memory: Evidence from converging dissociations. *European Journal of Cognitive Psychology, 8*(2), 163–183.

Oakley, D. A., Whitman, L. G., & Halligan, P. W. (2002). Hypnotic imagery as a treatment for phantom limb pain. *Clinical Rehabilitation, 16*(4), 368–377.

Oatley, K., & Jenkins, J. M. (1992). Human emotions: Function and dysfunction. In M. R. Rosenzweig and L. W. Porter (Eds.), *Annual Review of Psychology, 45,* 55–85.

Obernier, J. A., White, A. M., Swartzwelder, H. S., & Crews, F. T. (2002). Cognitive deficts and CNS damage after a 4–day binge ethanol exposure in rats. *Pharmacology, Biochemistry & Behavior, 72*(3), 521–532.

O'Brien, R. M., Figlerski, R. W., Howard, S. R., & Caggiano, J. (1981). The effects of multi-year, guaranteed contracts on the performance of pitchers in major league baseball. Paper presented at the annual meeting of the American Psychological Association, Los Angeles, August 1981.

O'Conner, T. G., Marvin, R. S., Rutter, M., Olrick, J. T., & Britner, P. A. (2003). Child-parent attachment following early institutional deprivation. *Development & Psychopathology, 15*(1), 19–38.

O'Connor, M. G., Sieggreen, M. A., Bachna, K., Kaplan, B., et al. (2000). Long-term retention of transient news events. *Journal of the International Neuropsychological Society, 6*(1), 44–51.

O'Craven, K. M., & Kanwisher, N. (2000). Mental imagery of faces and places activates corresponding stimulus-specific brain regions. *Journal of Cognitive Neuroscience, 12*(6), 1013–1023.

Oehman, A. (2002). Automaticity and the amygdala: Nonconscious responses to emotional faces. *Current Directions in Psychological Science, 11*(2), 62–66.

Oest, L. (1996). One-session group treatment of spider phobia. *Behaviour Research & Therapy, 34*(9), 707–715.

Oest, L., Svensson, L., Hellstroem, K., & Lindwall, R. (2001). One-session treatment of specific phobias in youths. *Journal of Consulting & Clinical Psychology, 69*(5), 814–824.

Ohayon, M. M., Guilleminault, C., & Priest, R. G. (1999). Night terrors, sleepwalking, and confusional arousals in the general population. *Journal of Clinical Psychiatry, 60*(4), 268–276.

Olds, M. E., & Fobes, J. L. (1981). The central basis of motivation: Intracranial self-stimulation studies. *Annual Review of Psychology, 32,* 523–574.

Oliver, M. B., & Hyde, J. S. (1993). Gender differences in sexuality. *Psychological Bulletin, 114*(1), 29–51.

Oliwenstein, L. (1993, May). The gene with two faces. *Discover,* 26.

Ollendick, T. H., & King, N. J. (1991). Origins of childhood fears. *Behaviour Research & Therapy, 29*(2), 117–123.

Olson, J. M., & Zanna, M. P. (1993). Attitudes and attitude change. In L. W. Porter and M. R. Rosenzweig (Eds.), *Annual Review of Psychology, 44,* 117–154.

Olson, S. L., Bates, J. E., & Kaskie, B. (1992). Caregiver-infant interaction antecedents of children's school-age cognitive ability. *Merrill-Palmer Quarterly, 38*(3), 309–330.

O'Neill, B. (2003). Don't believe everything you read online. BBC News: http://news.bbc.co.uk, March 8.

Ones, D. S., & Viswesvaran, C. (2001). Integrity tests and other criterion-focused occupational personality scales (COPS) used in personnel selection. *International Journal of Selection & Assessment, 9*(1–2), 31–39.

Onwuegbuzie, A. J. (2000). Academic procrastinators and perfectionistic tendencies among graduate students. *Journal of Social Behavior & Personality, 15*(5), 103–109.

Orleans, C. T., Gruman, J., & Hollendonner, J. K. (1999). Rating our progress in population health promotion: Report card on six behaviors. *American Journal of Health Promotion 14*(2), 75–82.

Orlock, C. (1993). *Inner time.* New York: Birch Lane Press.

Ornstein, R. (1997). *The right mind.* San Diego, CA: Harcourt Brace.

Ornstein, R., & Ehrlich, P. (1989). *New world new mind.* New York: Simon & Schuster.

O'Roark, A. M. (2001). Personality assessment, projective methods and a triptych perspective. *Journal of Projective Psychology & Mental Health, 8*(2), 116–126.

Osgood, C. E. (1952). The nature and measurement of meaning. *Psychological Bulletin, 49,* 197–237.

"Outline for cultural formulation and glossary of culture-bound syndromes." (2000). *DSM-IV-TR: Diagnostic and statistical manual of mental disorders* (5th ed.). Washington, DC: American Psychiatric Association.

Overmier, J. B., & LoLordo, V. M. (1998). Learned helplessness. In W. T. O'Donohue, et al. (Eds.), *Learning and behavior therapy.* Boston: Allyn & Bacon.

Oyama, T., & Ichikawa, S. (1990). Some experimental studies on imagery in Japan. *Journal of Mental Imagery, 14*(3–4), 185–195.

Pagano, R. R., & Warrenburg, S. (1983). Meditation. In R J. Davidson, G. E. Schwartz, & D. Shapiro (Eds.), *Consciousness and self-regulation,* pp. 153–210. New York: Plenum.

Palfai, T., & Jankiewicz, H. (1991). *Drugs and human behavior.* Dubuque, IA: Wm. C. Brown.

Palm, K., & Gibson, P. (1998). Recovered memories of childhood sexual abuse: Clinicians' practices and beliefs. *Professional Psychology: Research & Practice, 29*(3), 257–261.

Palmer, S. (1992). Common region: A new principle of perceptual grouping. *Cognitive Psychology, 24*(3), 436–447.

Papa, F. J., Aldrich, D., & Schumacker, R. E. (1999). The effects of immediate online feedback upon diagnostic performance. *Academic Medicine, 74*(Suppl. 10), S16–S18.

Papps, F., Walker, M., Trimboli, A., & Trimboli, C. (1995). Parental discipline in Anglo, Greek, Lebanese, and Vietnamese cultures. *Journal of Cross-Cultural Psychology, 26*(1), 49–64.

Park, D. C., Smith, A. D., & Cavanaugh, J. C. (1990). Metamemories of memory researchers. *Memory & Cognition, 18*(3), 321–327.

Parke, R. D. (1995). Fathers and Families. In M. H. Bornstein (Ed.), *Handbook of parenting, Vol. 3.* Mahwah, NJ: Erlbaum.

Parker, A., Ngu, H., & Cassaday, H. J. (2001). Odour and Proustian memory. *Applied Cognitive Psychology, 15*(2), 159–171.

Parks, C. A. (1998). Lesbian parenthood: A review of the literature. *American Journal of Orthopsychiatry, 68*(3), 376–389.

Patrick, C. J., & Iacono, W. G. (1989). Psychopathy, threat, and polygraph test accuracy. *Journal of Applied Psychology, 74*(2), 347–355.

Patten, B. M. (1990). The history of memory arts. *Neurology, 40*(2), 346–352.

Patterson, G. R. (1982). *Coercive family process.* Eugene, OR: Castilia Press.

Paulhus, D. L. (1998). Interpersonal and intrapsychic adaptiveness of trait self-enhancement. *Journal of Personality and Social Psychology, 74*(5), 1197–1208.

Pavlov, I. P. (1927). *Conditioned reflexes.* Translated by G. V. Anrep. New York: Dover.

Peeters, M. C. W., Buunk, B. P., & Schaufeli, W. B. (1995). A micro-analysis exploration of the cognitive appraisal of daily stressful events at work. *Anxiety, Stress & Coping: An International Journal, 8*(2), 127–139.

Pendergast, M. (1995). *Victims of memory: Incest accusations and shattered lives.* Hinesburg, VT: Upper Access.

Penfield, W. (1957, April 27). Brain's record of past a continuous movie film. *Science News Letter,* 265.

Penfield, W. (1958). *The excitable cortex in conscious man.* Springfield, IL: Charles C Thomas.

Pennebaker, J. W., & Francis, M. E. (1996). Cognitive, emotional, and language processes in disclosure. *Cognition & Emotion, 10*(6), 601–626.

Pepler, D. J., & Craig, W. M. (1995). A peek behind the fence: Naturalistic observations of aggressive children with remote audiovisual recording. *Developmental Psychology, 31*(4), 548–553.

Pepler, D. J., Craig, W. M., & Roberts, W. L. (1998). Observations of aggressive and nonaggressive children on the school playground. *Merrill-Palmer Quarterly, 44*(1), 55–76.

Perin, C. T. (1943). A quantitative investigation of the delay of reinforcement gradient. *Journal of Experimental Psychology, 32,* 37–51.

Perkins, D. (1995). *Outsmarting IQ: The emerging science of learnable intelligence.* New York: Free Press.

Perls, F. (1969). *Gestalt therapy verbatim.* Lafayette, CA: Real People.

Perreault, S., & Bourhis, R. Y. (1999). Ethnocentrism, social identification, and discrimination. *Personality & Social Psychology Bulletin, 25*(1), 92–103.

Perry, C., Orne, M. T., London, R. W., & Orne, E. C. (1996). Rethinking per se exclusions of hypnotically elicited recall as legal testimony. *International Journal of Clinical & Experimental Hypnosis, 44*(1), 66–81.

Perry, D. G., Perry, L. C., & Weiss, R. J. (1989). Sex differences in the consequences that children anticipate for aggression. *Developmental Psychology, 25*(2), 312–319.

Perry, R. P., Hladkyj, S., Pekrun, R. H., & Pelletier, S. T. (2001). Academic control and action control in the achievement of college students: A longitudinal field study. *Journal of Educational Psychology, 93*(4), 776–789.

Perugini, E. M., Kirsch, I., Allen, S. T., et al. (1998). Surreptitious observation of responses to hypnotically suggested hallucinations. *International Journal of Clinical & Experimental Hypnosis, 46*(2), 191–203.

Pescatello, L. S. (2001). Exercising for health. *Western Journal of Medicine, 174*(2), 114–118.

Peters, W. A. (1971). *A class divided.* Garden City, NY: Doubleday.

Peterson, B. E., & Klohnen, E. C. (1995). Realization of generativity in two samples of women at midlife. *Psychology & Aging, 10*(1), 20–29.

Peterson, L. R., & Peterson, M. J. (1959). Short-term retention of individual verbal items. *Journal of Experimental Psychology, 58,* 193–198.

Peterson, S. E. (1992). The cognitive functions of underlining as a study technique. *Reading Research & Instruction, 31*(2), 49–56.

Petri, H. (2003). *Motivation.* Belmont, CA: Wadsworth.

Pettigrew, T. F. (1998). Intergroup contact theory. *Annual Review of Psychology, 49,* 65–85.

Pettit, G. S., Brown, E. G., Mize, J., & Lindsey, E. (1998). Mothers' and fathers' socializing behaviors in three contexts. *Merrill-Palmer Quarterly, 44*(2), 173–193.

Petty, R. E., Wegener, D. T., & Fabrigar, L. R. (1997). Attitudes and attitude change. *Annual Review of Psychology, 48,* 609–647.

Pfefferbaum, B., Nixon, S. J., Tivis, R. D., Doughty, D. E., et al. (2001). Television exposure in children after a terrorist incident. *Psychiatry: Interpersonal & Biological Processes, 64*(3), 202–211.

Phillips, D. P., Liu, G. C., Kwok, K., Jarvinen, J., et al. (2001). The Hound of the Baskervilles effect: Natural experiment on the influence of psychological stress on timing of death. *British Medical Journal, 323*(7311), 1443–1446

Phillips, D. P., & Wills, J. S. (1987). A drop in suicides around major national holidays. *Suicide and Life-Threatening Behavior, 17,* 1–12.

Phillips, J. L. (1969). *Origins of intellect: Piaget's theory.* San Francisco: Freeman.

Piaget, J. (1951, original French, 1945). *The psychology of intelligence.* New York: Norton.

Piaget, J. (1952). *The origins of intelligence in children.* New York: International University Press.

Piccione, C., Hilgard, E. R., & Zimbardo, P. G. (1989). On the degree of stability of measured hypnotizability over a 25–year period. *Journal of Personality & Social Psychology, 56*(2), 289–295.

Pierce, J. P. (1991). Progress and problems in international public health efforts to reduce tobacco usage. *Annual Review of Public Health, 12,* 383–400.

Pierrehumbert, B., Ramstein, T., Karmaniola, A., Miljkovitch, R., & Halfon, O. (2002). Quality of child care in the preschool years. *International Journal of Behavioral Development, 26*(5), 385–396.

Piliavin, I. M., Rodin, J., & Piliavin, J. A. (1969). Good samaritanism: An underground phenomenon? *Journal of Personality & Social Psychology, 13,* 289–299.

Pillow, D. R., Zautra, A. J., & Sandler, I. (1996). Major life events and minor stressors: Identifying mediational links in the stress process. *Journal of Personality & Social Psychology, 70*(2), 381–394.

Pinel, J. P. J., Assanand, S., & Lehman, D. R. (2000). Hunger, eating, and ill health. *American Psychologist, 55*(10), 1105–1116.

Pinsof, W. M., Wynne, L. C., & Hambright, A. B. (1996). The outcomes of couple and family therapy. *Psychotherapy, 33*(2), 321–331.

Pisacreta, R. (1998). Superstitious behavior and response stereotypy prevent the emergence of efficient rule-governed behavior in humans. *Psychological Record, 48*(2), 251–274.

Pliner, P., & Haddock, G. (1996). Perfectionism in weight-concerned and -unconcerned women. *International Journal of Eating Disorders, 19*(4), 381–389.

Plomin, R., & Rende, R. (1991). Human behavioral genetics. In M. R. Rosenzweig & L. W. Porter (Eds.), *Annual Review of Psychology, 42,* 161–190.

Plug, C., & Ross, H. E. (1994). The natural moon illusion: A multifactor angular account. *Perception, 23*(3), 321–333.

Plutchik, R. (2001). The nature of emotions. *American Scientist, 89,* 344–350.

Pogatchnik, S. (1990, January 26). Kids' TV gets more violent, study finds. *The Los Angeles Times,* F-1, F-27.

Polce-Lynch, M., Myers, B. J., Kilmartin, C. T., Forssmann-Falck, R., & Kliewer, W. (1998). Gender and age patterns in emotional expression, body image, and self-esteem. *Sex Roles, 38*(11–12), 1025–1048.

Polemikos, N., & Papaeliou, C. (2000). Sidedness preference as an index of organization of laterality. *Perceptual & Motor Skills, 91*(3, Pt. 2), 1083–1090.

Polivy, J., & Herman, C. P. (2002). Causes of eating disorders. *Annual Review of Psychology, 53,* 187–213.

Pollack, W. S. (2001). Preventing violence through family connection. *The Brown University Child and Adolescent Behavior Letter, 17*(12), 1, 3–4.

Pollner, M. (1998). The effects of interviewer gender in mental health interviews. *Journal of Nervous & Mental Disease, 186*(6), 369–373.

Pollock, V. E., Briere, J., Schneider, L., Knop, J., et al. (1990). Childhood antecedents of antisocial behavior. *American Journal of Psychiatry, 147*(10), 1290–1293.

Pope, H. G., Gruber, A. J., & Yurgelun-Todd, D. (1995). The residual neuropsychological effects of cannabis. *Drug & Alcohol Dependence, 38*(1), 25–34.

Porac, C., Friesen, I. C., Barnes, M. P., & Gruppuso, V. (1998). Illness and accidental injury in young and older adult left- and right-handers: Implications for genetic theories of hand preference. *Developmental Neuropsychology, 14*(1), 157–172.

Port, R. L., & Seybold, K. S. (1995). Hippocampal synaptic plasticity as a biological substrate underlying episodic psychosis. *Biological Psychiatry, 37*(5), 318–324.

Posada, G., Jacobs, A., Richmond, M. K., Carbonell, O. A., et al. (2002). Maternal caregiving and infant security in two cultures. *Developmental Psychology, 38*(1), 67–78.

Potashkin, B. D., & Beckles, N. (1990). Relative efficacy of Ritalin and biofeedback treatments in the management of hyperactivity. *Biofeedback & Self-Regulation, 15*(4), 305–315.

Potkay, C. R., & Allen, B. P. (1986). *Personality: Theory, research, and applications.* Monterey, CA: Brooks/Cole.

Poulton, R. G., & Andrews, G. (1996). Change in danger cognitions in agoraphobia and social phobia during treatment. *Behaviour Research & Therapy, 34*(5–6), 413–421.

Powell, A. L., & Thelen, M. H. (1996). Emotions and cognitions associated with bingeing and weight control behavior in bulimia. *Journal of Psychosomatic Research, 40*(3), 317–328.

Premack, A. J., & Premack, D. (1972, October). Teaching language to an ape. *Scientific American,* 92–99.

Premack, D., & Premack, A. J. (1983). *The mind of an ape.* New York: Norton.

Pressley, M. (1987). Are key-word method effects limited to slow presentation rates? An empirically based reply to Hall and Fuson (1986). *Journal of Educational Psychology, 79*(3), 333–335.

Pressley, M., Symons, S., McDaniel, M. A., Snyder, B., et al. (1988). Elaborative interrogation facilitates acquisition of confusing facts. *Journal of Educational Psychology, 80*(3), 268–278.

Pressman, J. D. (1998). *Last resort: Psychosurgery and the limits of medicine.* New York, NY: Cambridge University Press.

Provins, K. A. (1997). Handedness and Speech. *Psychological Review, 104*(3), 554–571.

Puca, R. M., & Schmalt, H. (1999). Task enjoyment: A mediator between achievement motives and performance. *Motivation & Emotion, 23*(1), 15–29.

Pursch, J. A. (1983, June 12). Cocaine can give you the business. *Los Angeles Times,* VII-12.

Pychyl, T. A., Lee, J. M., Thibodeau, R., & Blunt, A. (2000). Five days of emotion: An experience sampling study of undergraduate student procrastination. *Journal of Social Behavior & Personality, 15*(5), 239–254.

Quinn, P. C., & Bhatt, R. S. (1998). Visual pop-out in young infants. *Infant Behavior & Development, 21*(2), 273–288.

Quitkin, F. M. (1999). Placebos, drug effects, and study design: A clinician's guide. *American Journal of Psychiatry, 156*(6), 829–836.

Rafaeli, A., & Klimoski, R. J. (1983). Predicting sales success through handwriting analysis: An evaluation of the effects of training and handwriting sample content. *Journal of Applied Psychology, 68,* 212–217.

Raison, C. L., Klein, H. M., & Steckler, M. (1999). The moon and madness reconsidered. *Journal of Affective Disorders, 53*(1), 96–106.

Ramachandran, V. S. (1992, May). Blind spots. *Scientific American,* 86–91.

Ramachandran, V. S. (1995). 2–D or not 2–D—that is the question. In R. Gregory, J. Harris, P. Heard, & D. Rose (Eds.), *The artful eye.* Oxford: Oxford University Press.

Ramanaiah, N. V., Detwiler, F. R. J., & Byravan, A. (1995, December). Sex-role orientation and satisfaction with life. *Psychological Reports, 77*(3, Pt. 2), 1260–1262.

Randi, J. (1980). *Flim-flam!* New York: Lippincott & Crowell.

Randi, J. (1983). Science and the chimera. In G. O. Abell & B. Singer (Eds.), *Science and the paranormal.* New York: Scribner's.

Rangell, L. (2002). Mind, body, and psychoanalysis. *Psychoanalytic Psychology, 19*(4), 634–650.

Rauscher, F. H., & Shaw, G. L. (1998). Key components of the Mozart effect. *Perceptual & Motor Skills, 86*(3, Pt. 1), 835–841.

Reed, J. D., & Bruce, D. (1982). Longitudinal tracking of difficult memory retrievals. *Cognitive Psychology, 14,* 280–300.

Reed, S. K. (1996). *Cognition: Theory and applications* (3rd ed.). Pacific Grove, CA: Brooks/Cole.

Regan, P. C. (1998). Of lust and love. *Personal Relationships, 5*(2), 139–157.

Regan, P. C., Levin, L., Sprecher, S., Christopher, F. S., & Cate, R. (2000). Partner preferences: What characteristics do men and women desire in their short-term sexual and long-term romantic partners? *Journal of Psychology & Human Sexuality, 12*(3), 1–21.

Reid, M. R., Mackinnon, L. T., & Drummond, P. D. (2001). The effects of stress management on symptoms of upper respiratory tract infection, secretory immunoglobulin A, and mood in young adults. *Journal of Psychosomatic Research, 51*(6), 721–728.

Reid, P. T. (2002). Multicultural psychology. *Cultural Diversity and Ethnic Minority Psychology, 8*(2), 103–114.

Reiff, S., Katkin, E. S., & Friedman, R. (1999). Classical conditioning of the human blood pressure response. *International Journal of Psychophysiology, 34*(2), 135–145.

Reifman, A. S., Larrick, R. P., & Fein, S. (1991). Temper and temperature on the diamond: The heat-aggression relationship in major league baseball. *Personality & Social Psychology Bulletin, 17*(5), 580–585.

Reisner, A. D. (1996). Repressed memories: True and false. *Psychological Record, 46*(4), 563–579.

Reiss, M., Tymnik, G., Koegler, P., Koegler, W., & Reiss, G. (1999). Laterality of hand, foot, eye, and ear in twins. *Laterality, 4*(3), 287–297.

Reiterman, T. (1993, April 23). Parallel roads led to Jonestown, Waco. *The Los Angeles Times,* A-24.

Renner, M. J., & Mackin, R. S. (1998). A life stress instrument for classroom use. *Teaching of Psychology, 25*(1), 46–48.

Rentfrow, P. J., & Gosling, S. D. (2003). The do re mi's of everyday life: The structure and personality correlates of music preferences. *Journal of Personality & Social Psychology, 84*(6), 1236–1256.

Rescorla, R. A. (1987). A Pavlovian analysis of goal-directed behavior. *American Psychologist, 42,* 119–126.

Restak, R. M. (2001). *The secret life of the brain.* New York: The Dana Press.

Reynolds, S., Stiles, W. B., Barkham, M., & Shapiro, D. A. (1996). Acceleration of changes in session impact during contrasting time-limited psychotherapies. *Journal of Consulting & Clinical Psychology, 64*(3), 577–586.

Reznick, J. S., & Goldfield, B. A. (1992). Rapid change in lexical development in comprehension and production. *Developmental Psychology, 28*(3), 406–413.

Rhine, J. B. (1953). *New world of the mind.* New York: Sloane.

Rice, M. E. (1997). Violent offender research and implications for the criminal justice system. *American Psychologist, 52*(4), 414–423.

Richards, L., Rollerson, B., & Phillips, J. (1991). Perceptions of submissiveness: Implications for victimization. *Journal of Psychology, 125*(4), 407–411.

Richelle, M. N. (1995). *B. F. Skinner: A reappraisal.* Hillsdale: Erlbaum.

Richter, W., Somorjai, R., Summers, R., Jarmasz, M., et al. (2000). Motor area activity during mental rotation studied by time-resolved single-trial fMRI. *Journal of Cognitive Neuroscience, 12*(2), 310–320.

Ricketts, M. S., & Galloway, R. E. (1984). Effects of three different one-hour single-session treatments for test anxiety. *Psychological Reports, 54,* 113–119.

Rideout, B. E., Dougherty, S., & Wernert, L. (1998). Effect of music on spatial performance: A test of generality. *Perceptual & Motor Skills, 86*(2), 512–514.

Rideout, B. E., & Taylor, J. (1997). Enhanced spatial performance following 10 minutes exposure to music: A replication. *Perceptual & Motor Skills, 85*(1), 112–114.

Riefer, D. M., Keveri, M. K., & Kramer, D. L. (1995). Name that tune: Eliciting the tip-of-the-tongue experience using auditory stimuli. *Psychological Reports, 77*(3, Pt. 2), 1379–1390.

Rieke, M. L., & Guastello, S. J. (1995, June). Unresolved issues in honesty and integrity testing. *American Psychologist,* 458–459.

Riquelme, H. (2002). Can people creative in imagery interpret ambiguous figures faster than people less creative in imagery? *Journal of Creative Behavior, 36*(2), 105–116.

Ritter, J. (1998, October 15). Uniforms changing the culture of the nation's classrooms. *USA Today,* 1A, 2A.

Roberts, B. W., Caspi, A., & Moffitt, T. E. (2001). The kids are alright: Growth and stability in personality development from adolescence to adulthood. *Journal of Personality & Social Psychology, 81*(4), 670–683.

Roberts, R. (1989). Passenger fear of flying: Behavioural treatment with extensive *in vivo* exposure and group support. *Aviation, Space, & Environmental Medicine, 60*(4), 342–348.

Roberts, R. E., Phinney, J. S., Masse, L. C., Chen, Y. R., et al. (1999). The structure of ethnic identity of young adolescents from diverse ethnocultural groups. *Journal of Early Adolescence, 19*(3), 301–322.

Robins, R. W., Gosling, S. D., & Craik, K. H. (1998, July/August). Psychological science at the crossroads. *American Scientist, 86,* 310–313.

Robins, R. W., Gosling, S. D., & Craik, K. H. (1999). An empirical analysis of trends in psychology. *American Psychologist, 54*(2), 117–128.

Robinson, A., & Clinkenbeard, P. R. (1998). Giftedness. *Annual Review of Psychology, 49,* 117–139.

Robinson, B., Frye, E. M., & Bradley, L. J. (1997). Cult affiliation and disaffiliation. *Counseling & Values, 41*(2), 166–173.

Robinson, T. N., Wilde, M. L., Navracruz, L. C., Haydel, K. F., & Varady, A. (2001). Effects of reducing children's television and video game use on aggressive behavior. *Archives of Pediatrics and Adolescent Medicine, 155*(1), 17–23.

Robinson-Riegler, B., & McDaniel, M. (1994). Further constraints on the bizarreness effect: Elaboration at encoding. *Memory & Cognition, 22*(6), 702–712.

Robson, C. R. (1984). Prewalking locomotor movements and their use in predicting standing and walking. *Child Care, Health & Development, 10,* 317–330.

Roediger, H. L. (1990). Implicit memory. *American Psychologist, 45*(9), 1043–1056.

Roediger, H. L., & McDermott, K. B. (1995). Creating false memories: Remembering words not presented on lists. *Journal of Experimental Psychology: Learning, Memory, and Cognition, 21*(4), 803–814.

Rogers, C. R. (1959). A theory of therapy, personality, and interpersonal relationships, as developed in the client-centered framework. In S. Koch (Ed.), *Psychology: A study of a science,* Vol. 3. New York: McGraw-Hill.

Rogers, C. R. (1961). *On becoming a person: A therapist's view of psychotherapy.* Boston: Houghton Mifflin.

Rogers, S., & Silver, S. M. (2002). Is EMDR an exposure therapy? A review of trauma protocols. *Journal of Clinical Psychology, 58*(1), 43–59.

Rogerson, J. (1997). Canine fears and phobias; A regime for treatment without recourse to drugs. *Applied Animal Behaviour Science, 52*(3–4), 291–297.

Rohsenow, D. J., & Smith R. E. (1982). Irrational beliefs as predictors of negative affective states. *Motivation and Emotion, 6,* 299–301.

Roid, G. (2003). *Technical manual: Stanford-Binet Intelligence Scales* (5th ed.). Itasca, IL: Riverside.

Rollman, G. B. (1998). Culture and pain. In S. S. Kazarian, et al. (Eds.), *Cultural clinical psychology.* New York: Oxford University Press.

Roos, P. E., & Cohen, L. H. (1987). Sex roles and social support as moderators of life stress adjustment. *Journal of Personality & Social Psychology, 52,* 576–585.

Rosch, E. (1977). Classification of real-world objects: Origins and representations in cognition. In P. N. Johnson-Laird & P. C. Wason (Eds.), *Thinking: Reading in cognitive science.* Cambridge: Cambridge University Press.

Rose, R. J. (1995). Genes and human behavior. *Annual Review of Psychology, 46,* 625–654.

Rosen, L. A., Booth, S. R., Bender, M. E., McGrath, M. L., et al. (1988). Effects of sugar (sucrose) on children's behavior. *Journal of Consulting & Clinical Psychology, 56*(4), 583–589.

Rosenberg, L. B. (1994). The effect of interocular distance upon depth perception when using stereoscopic displays to perform work within virtual and telepresent environments. USAF AMRL Technical Report (Wright-Patterson), Jul., AL/CF-TR-1994-0052.

Rosenkranz, M.A., Jackson, D. C., Dalton, K. M., Dolski, I., et al, (2003). Affective style and *in vivo* immune response: Neurobehavioral mechanisms. *Proceedings of the National Academy of Sciences, 100,* 11148–11152

Rosenman, R. H., Brand, R. J., Jenkins, C. D., Friedman, M., Straus, R., & Wurm, M. (1975). Coronary heart disease in the Western Collaborative Group Study: Final follow-up experience of 8 1/2 years. *Journal of the American Medical Association, 233,* 872–877.

Rosenthal, N. E. (1993). *Winter blues: Seasonal affective disorder.* New York: Guilford Press.

Rosenthal, R. (1965). *Clever Hans: A case study of scientific method.* Introduction to *Clever Hans: (The horse of Mr. Von Osten),* by O. Pfungst. New York: Holt, Rinehart & Winston.

Rosenthal, R. (1973, September). The Pygmalion effect lives. *Psychology Today,* 56–63.

Rosenthal, R. (1994). Science and ethics in conducting, analyzing, and reporting psychological research. *Psychological Science, 5,* 127–34.

Rosenthal, T. L. (1993). To soothe the savage breast. *Behavior Research & Therapy, 31*(5), 439–462.

Rosenthal, T. L., & Rosenthal, R. (1980). The vicious cycle of stress reaction. Copyright, Renate and Ted Rosenthal, Stress Management Clinic, Department of Psychiatry, University of Tennessee College of Medicine, Memphis, Tennessee.

Rosenthal, T. L., & Steffek, B. D. (1991). Modeling methods. In F. H. Kanfer & A. P. Goldstein (Eds.), *Helping people change.* Elmsford, NY: Pergamon.

Rosenzweig, M. R. (1999). Continuity and change in the development of psychology around the world. *American Psychologist, 54*(4), 252–259.

Ross, D. C., Jaffe, J., Collins, R. L., Page, W., & Robinette, D. (1999). Handedness in the NAS/NRC Twin Study. *Laterality, 4*(3), 257–264.

Rossell, S. L., Bullmore, E. T., Williams, S. C. R., & David, A.S. (2002). Sex differences in functional brain activation during a lexical visual field task. *Brain & Language, 80*(1), 97–105.

Rothbaum, B. O., Hodges, L. F., Kooper, R., Opdyke, D., et al. (1995). Effectiveness of computer-generated (virtual reality) graded exposure in the treatment of acrophobia. *American Journal of Psychiatry, 152*(4), 626–628.

Rothbaum, B. O., Hodges, L., Watson, B. A., Kessler, G. D., et al. (1996). Virtual reality exposure therapy in the treatment of fear of flying: A case report. *Behaviour Research & Therapy, 34*(5–6), 477–481.

Rotter, J. B., & Hochreich, D. J. (1975). *Personality.* Glenview, IL: Scott, Foresman.

Rowe, D. C., Chassin, L., Presson, C., & Sherman, S. J. (1996). Parental smoking and the "epidemic" spread of cigarette smoking. *Journal of Applied Social Psychology, 26*(5), 437–454.

Rubin, D. C. (1985, September). The subtle deceiver: Recalling our past. *Psychology Today,* 38–46.

Rubin, V., & Comitas, L. (Eds.). (1975). *Ganja in Jamaica.* The Hague: Mouton.

Rubin, Z. (1970). Measurement of romantic love. *Journal of Personality & Social Psychology, 16,* 265–273.

Rubin, Z. (1973). *Liking and loving: An invitation to social psychology.* New York: Holt.

Russell, T. G., Rowe, W., & Smouse, A. D. (1991, March/April). Subliminal self-help tapes and academic achievement: An evaluation. *Journal of Counseling and Development, 69,* 359–362.

Russo, M. B., et al. (1998). Conversion disorder presenting as multiple sclerosis. *Military Medicine, 163*(10), 709–710.

Russo, N. F. (1990). Forging research priorities for women's mental health. *American Psychologist, 45*(3), 368–373.

Rutledge, T., & Linden, W. (1998). To eat or not to eat: Affective and physiological mechanisms in the stress-eating relationship. *Journal of Behavioral Medicine, 21*(3), 221–240.

Rutter, M. (1995). Maternal deprivation. In M. H. Bornstein (Ed.), *Handbook of parenting, Vol. 4.* Mahwah, NJ: Erlbaum.

Ryan, M. P. (2001). Conceptual models of lecture learning. *Reading Psychology, 22*(4), 289–312.

Ryan, R. M., & Deci, E. L. (2000). Self-determination theory and the facilitation of intrinsic motivation, social development, and well-being. *American Psychologist, 55*(1), 68–78.

Ryff, C. D. (1995). Psychological well-being in adult life. *Current Directions in Psychological Science, 4*(4), 99–104.

Ryff, C. D., & Keyes, C. L. (1995). The structure of psychological well-being revisited. *Journal of Personality & Social Psychology, 69*(4), 719–727.

Ryff, C. D., & Singer, B. (2000). Interpersonal flourishing. *Personality and Social Psychology Review, 4,* 30–44.

Saadeh, W., Rizzo, C. P., & Roberts, D. G. (2002). Spanking. *Clinical Pediatrics, 41*(2), 87–88.

Saariluoma, P. (1994). Location coding in chess. *Quarterly Journal of Experimental Psychology: Human Experimental Psychology, 47A*(3), 607–630.

Sackeim, H. A., Haskett, R. F., Mulsant, B. H., Thase, M. E., et al. (2001). Continuation pharmacotherapy in the prevention of relapse following electroconvulsive therapy. *Journal of the American Medical Association, 285,* 1299–1307.

Sacks, O. (1990). *Seeing voices.* New York: Harper Perennial.

Sadker, M., & Sadker, D. (1994). *Failing at fairness: How America's schools cheat girls.* New York: Scribner's.

Sahelian, R. (1998). *5–HTP.* Wakefield, RI: Moyer Bell.

Salmon, P. (2001). Effects of physical exercise on anxiety, depression, and sensitivity to stress: A unifying theory. *Clinical Psychology Review, 21*(1), 33–61.

Salovey, P., & Mayer, J. (1997). *Emotional development and emotional intelligence.* New York: Basic.

Salovey, P., & Singer, J. A. (1989). Mood congruency effects in recall of childhood versus recent memories. *Journal of Social Behavior & Personality, 4*(2), 99–120.

Sampson, E. E. (1993). Identity politics. *American Psychologist, 48*(12), 1219–1230.

Sansone, R. A., Sansone, L. A., & Righter, E. L. (1998). Panic disorder. *Journal of Women's Health, 7*(8), 983–989.

Sarason, I. G. (1981). Test anxiety, stress, and social support. *Journal of Personality, 49,* 101–114.

Saudino, K. J., et al. (1997). Can personality explain genetic influences on life events? *Journal of Personality & Social Psychology, 72*(1), 196–206.

Saunders, T., Driskell, J. E., Johnston, J. H., & Salas, E. (1996). The effect of stress inoculation training on anxiety and performance. *Journal of Occupational Health Psychology, 1*(2), 170–186.

Savage-Rumbaugh, E. S., Murphy, J., Sevcik, R. A., Brakke, K. E., et al. (1993). Language comprehension in ape and child. *Monographs of the Society for Research in Child Development, 58*(3–4), v-221.

Savage-Rumbaugh, S., & Lewin, R. (1996). *Kanzi.* New York: Wiley.

Savage-Rumbaugh, S., Sevcik, R. A., Brakke, K. E., Rumbaugh, D. M., et al. (1990). Symbols: Their communicative use, comprehension, and combination by bonobos (Pan paniscus). *Advances in Infancy Research, 6,* 221–278.

Sawa, A., & Snyder, S. H. (2002). Schizophrenia: Diverse approaches to a complex disease. *Science, 296*(5568), 692–695.

Saxe, L. (1991). Lying. *American Psychologist, 46*(4), 409–415.

Saxe, L., Dougherty, D., & Cross, T. (1985). The validity of polygraph testing. *American Psychologist, 40,* 355–366.

Scarr, S. (1998). American child care today. *American Psychologist, 53*(2), 95–108.

Schachter, S. (1959). *Psychology of affiliation.* Stanford, CA: Stanford University Press.

Schachter, S., & Wheeler, L. (1962). Epinephrine, chlorpromazine and amusement. *Journal of Abnormal and Social Psychology, 65,* 121–128.

Schacter, D. L. (1996). *Searching for memory.* New York: Basic.

Schacter, D. L. (1999). The seven sins of memory. *American Psychologist, 54*(3), 194–201.

Schacter, D. L. (2001). *The seven sins of memory.* Boston, MA: Houghton Mifflin.

Schacter, D. L., Norman, K. A., & Koutstaal, W. (1998). The cognitive neuroscience of constructive memory. *Annual Review of Psychology, 49,* 289–318.

Schafer, M., & Crichlow, S. (1996). Antecedents of groupthink: A quantitative study. *Journal of Conflict Resolution, 40*(3), 415–435.

Schaie, K. W. (1988). Ageism in psychological research. *American Psychologist, 43*(3), 179–183.

Schaie, K. W. (1994). The course of adult intellectual development. *American Psychologist, 49*(4), 304–313.

Schaller, S. (1991). *A man without words.* New York: Summit.

Scheck, B., Neufeld, P., & Dwyer, J. (2000). *Actual innocence.* New York: Doubleday.

Scheck, M. M., Schaeffer, J. A., & Gillette, C. (1998). Brief psychological intervention with traumatized young women. *Journal of Traumatic Stress, 11*(1) 25–44

Schein, E. H., Schneier, I., & Barker, C. H. (1961). *Coercive persuasion.* New York: Norton.

Schick, T., & Vaughn, L. (1995). How to think about weird things: Critical thinking for a new age. Mountain View, CA: Mayfield.

Schick, T., & Vaughn, L. (2001). How to think about weird things: Critical thinking for a new age. New York: McGraw-Hill.

Schiraldi, G. R., & Brown, S. L. (2001). Primary prevention for mental health: Results of an exploratory cognitive-behavioral college course. *Journal of Primary Prevention, 22*(1), 55–67.

Schlosberg, H. (1954). Three dimensions of emotion. *Psychological Review, 61,* 81–88.

Schmitt, D. P., & , Buss, D. M. (1996). Strategic self-promotion and competitor derogation. *Journal of Personality & Social Psychology, 70*(6), 1185–1204.

Schmitt, E. (2001, April 1). U.S. now more diverse, ethnically and racially. *The New York Times,* A-18.

Schmolck, H., Buffalo, E. A., & Squire, L. R. (2000). Memory distortions develop over time. *Psychological Science, 11*(1), 39–45.

Schneider, C. (1987). *Children's television: The art, the business, and how it works.* Chicago: NTC Business Books.

Schneider, H. G., & Shugar, G. J. (1990). Audience and feedback effects in computer learning. *Computers in Human Behavior, 6*(4), 315–321.

Schneider, K. J., Bugental, J. F. T., & Pierson, J. F. (2001). Introduction. *The Handbook of Humanistic Psychology,* Thousand Oaks, CA: Sage.

Schneiderman, N., Antoni, M. H., Saab, P. G., & Ironson, G. (2001). Health psychology. *Annual Review of Psychology, 52,* 555–580.

Schooler, C., Flora, J. A., & Farquhar, J. W. (1993). Moving toward synergy: Media supplementation in the Stanford Five-City Project. *Communication Research, 20*(4), 587–610.

Schotte, D. E., Cools, J., & McNally, R. J. (1990). Film-induced negative affect triggers overeating in restrained eaters. *Journal of Abnormal Psychology, 99*(3), 317–320.

Schouten, S. A. (1994). An overview of quantitatively evaluated studies with mediums and psychics. *Journal of the American Society for Psychical Research, 88*(3), 221–254.

Schredl, M. (1995). Creativity and dream recall. *Journal of Creative Behavior, 29*(1), 16–24.

Schreiber, E. H., & Schreiber, D. E. (1999). Use of hypnosis with witnesses of vehicular homicide. *Contemporary Hypnosis, 16*(1), 40–44.

Schreiber, F. R. (1973). *Sybil.* Chicago: Regency.

Schroeder, J. E. (1995). Self-concept, social anxiety, and interpersonal perception skills. *Personality & Individual Differences, 19*(6), 955–958.

Schuel, H., Chang, M. C., Burkman, L. J., Picone, R. P., et al. (1999) Cannabinoid receptors in sperm. In G. Nahas, K. M. Sutin, and S. Agurell (Eds.), *Marihuana and medicine.* Totowa, NJ: Humana Press.

Schum, T. R., et al. (2001). Factors associated with toilet training in the 1990s. *Ambulatory Pediatrics, 1*(2), 79–86.

Schunk, D. H. (1990). Goal setting and self-efficacy during self-regulated learning. Special issue: Self-regulated learning and academic achievement. *Educational Psychologist, 25*(1), 71–86.

Schuster, M. A., Stein, B. D., Jaycox, L. H., Collins, R. L., et al. (2001). A national survey of stress reactions after the September 11, 2001, terrorist attacks. *New England Journal of Medicine, 345*(20), 1507–1512.

Schwartz, B., & Robbins, S. J. (1995). *Psychology of learning & behavior.* New York: Norton.

Schwartz, L. L. (1991). The historical dimension of cultic techniques of persuasion and control. *Cultic Studies Journal, 8*(1), 37–45.

Schweickert, R. (1993). A multinomial processing tree model for degradation and redintegration in immediate recall. *Memory & Cognition, 21*(2), 168–175.

Sclafani, A., & Springer, D. (1976). Dietary obesity in adult rats: Similarities to hypothalamic and human obesity syndromes. *Psychology and Behavior, 17,* 461–471.

Scorbia, A., Mazzoni, G., Kirsch, L., and Milling, L. S. (2002). Immediate and persisting effects of misleading questions and hypnosis on memory reports. *Journal of Experimental Psychology: Applied, 8,* 26–32.

Scott, J. P., & Ginsburg, B. E. (1994). The Seville statement on violence revisited. *American Psychologist, 49*(10), 849–850.

Scott, L., & O'Hara, M. W. (1993). Self-discrepancies in clinically anxious and depressed university students. *Journal of Abnormal Psychology, 102*(2), 282–287.

Scroppo, J. C., Drob, S. L., Weinberger, J. L., & Eagle, P. (1998). Identifying dissociative identity disorder: A self-report and projective study. *Journal of Abnormal Psychology, 107*(2), 272–284.

Scurfield, R. M. (2002). Commentary about the terrorist acts of September 11, 2001: Posttraumatic reactions and related social and policy issues. *Trauma Violence & Abuse, 3*(1), 3–14.

Seal, D. W., & Palmer-Seal, D. A. (1996). Barriers to condom use and safer sex talk among college dating couples. *Journal of Community & Applied Social Psychology, 6*(1), 15–33.

Sears, R. R., Maccoby, E. E., & Levin, H. (1957). *Patterns of child rearing.* Evanston, IL: Row, Peterson.

Seckel, A. (2000). *The art of optical illusions.* London: Carlton Books.

Segall, M. H., Lonner, W. J., & Berry, J. W. (1998). Cross-cultural psychology as a scholarly discipline. *American Psychologist, 53*(10), 1101–1110.

Seidman, B. F. (2001, January/February). Medicine wars. *Skeptical Inquirer,* 28–35.

Seligman, M. E. P. (1972). For helplessness: Can we immunize the weak? In *Readings in psychology today* (2nd ed.). Del Mar, CA: CRM.

Seligman, M. E. P. (1989). *Helplessness.* New York: Freeman.

Seligman, M. E. P. (1994). *What you can change and what you can't.* New York: Knopf.

Seligman, M. E. P. (1995). The effectiveness of psychotherapy. *American Psychologist, 50*(12), 965–974.

Seligman, M. E. P. (1998). Why therapy works. *APA Monitor, 29*(12), 2.

Seligman, M. E. P. & Csikszentmihalyi, M. (2000). Positive psychology: An introduction. *American Psychologist, 55,* 5–14.

Selye, H. (1976). *The stress of life.* New York: Knopf.

Senden, M. V. (1960). *Space and sight.* Translated by P. Heath. Glencoe, IL: Free Press.

Serbin, L. A., & O'Leary, K. D. (1975, December). How nursery schools teach girls to shut up. *Psychology Today,* 57–58, 102–103.

Seybolt, D. C., & Wagner, M. K. (1997). Self-reinforcement, gender-role, and sex of participant in prediction of life satisfaction. *Psychological Reports, 81*(2), 519–522.

Shaffer, D. R. (1999). *Developmental psychology.* Pacific Grove, CA: Brooks/Cole.

Shaffer, J. B., & Galinsky, M. D. (1989). *Models of group therapy.* Englewood Cliffs, NJ: Prentice Hall.

Shafir, E. (1993). Choosing versus rejecting: Why some options are both better and worse than others. *Memory and Cognition, 21,* 546–556.

Shafton, A. (1995). *Dream reader.* Albany, NY: SUNY Press.

Shalev, A. Y. (2001). What is posttraumatic stress disorder? *Journal of Clinical Psychiatry, 62*(Suppl. 17), 4–10.

Shapiro, F. (1995). *Eye movement desensitization and reprocessing.* New York: Guilford.

Sharma, T., et al. (1998). Brain changes in schizophrenia. *British Journal of Psychiatry, 173*(Aug.), 132–138.

Shaw, G. L. (1999). *Keeping Mozart in mind.* San Diego, CA: Academic.

Shaywitz, S. E., & Gore, J. C. (1995). Sex differences in functional organization of the brain for language. *Nature, 373*(6515), 607.

Sheehan, P. W., & Statham, D. (1989). Hypnosis, the timing of its introduction, and acceptance of misleading information. *Journal of Abnormal Psychology, 98*(2), 170–176.

Sheehy, M., & Cournos, F. (1992). What Is Mental Illness? In F. I. Kass, J. M. Oldham, & H. Pardes (Eds.), *The Columbia University College of Physicians and Surgeons Complete Home Guide to Mental Health.* New York: Sharpe Communications/Henry Holt.

Sheldon, K. M., & Elliot, A. J. (1999). Goal Striving, Need Satisfaction, and Longitudinal Well-Being. *Journal of Personality and Social Psychology, 76*(3), 482–497.

Sheldon, K. M., Ryan, R. M., Rawsthorne, L. J., & Ilardi, B. (1997). Trait self and true self: Cross-role variation in the Big-Five personality traits and its relations with psychological authenticity and subjective well-being. *Journal of Personality & Social Psychology, 73*(6), 1380–1393.

Shepard, R. N. (1975). Form, formation, and transformation of internal representations. In R. L. Solso (Ed.), *Information processing and cognition: The Loyola Symposium.* Hillsdale, NJ: Erlbaum.

Sherif, M., Harvey, O. J., White, B. J., Hood, W. R., & Sherif, C. W. (1961). *Intergroup conflict and cooperation: The Robbers Cave experiment.* University of Oklahoma, Institute of Group Relations.

Shneidman, E. S. (1987a, March). At the point of no return. *Psychology Today,* 54–58.

Shneidman, E. S. (1987b). Psychological approaches to suicide. In G. R. VandenBos & B. K. Bryant (Eds.), *Cataclysms, crises, and catastrophes: Psychology in action.* Washington, DC: American Psychological Association.

Shore, H. (2003). Personal communication.

Shore, L. A. (1990, Fall). Skepticism in light of scientific literacy. *Skeptical Inquirer, 15,* 3–4.

Shurkin, J. N. (1992). *Terman's kids.* Boston: Little, Brown.

Shweder, R. A. (1999). Why cultural psychology? *Ethos. 27*(1), 62–73.

Siau, K. L. (1996). Group creativity and technology. *Journal of Creative Behavior, 29*(3), 201–216.

Siegler, R. S. (1989). Mechanisms of cognitive development. *Annual Review of Psychology, 40,* 353–379.

Siever, L. J., & Koenigsberg, H. W. (2000). The frustrating no-man's-land of borderline personality disorder. *Cerebrum, 2*(4), 85–99.

Silva, C. E., & Kirsch, I. (1992). Interpretive sets, expectancy, fantasy proneness, and dissociation as predictors of hypnotic response. *Journal of Personality & Social Psychology, 63*(5), 847–856.

Silverman, K., Evans, S. M., Strain, E. C., & Griffiths, R. R. (1992). Withdrawal syndrome after the double-blind cessation of caffeine consumption. *New England Journal of Medicine, 327*(16), 1109–1114.

Simon, A. (1998). Aggression in a prison setting as a function of lunar phases. *Psychological Reports, 82*(3, Pt. 1), 747–752.

Simons, D. J., & Chabris, C. F. (1999). Gorillas in our midst: Sustained inattentional blindness for dynamic events. *Perception, 28,* 1059–1074.

Simons, D. J., & Levin, D. T. (1998). Failure to detect changes to people during a real-world interaction. *Psychonomic Bulletin & Review, 5*(4), 644–649.

Simpson, D. D., Joe, G. W., Fletcher, B. W., Hubbard, R. L, & Anglin, M. D. (1999). A national evaluation of treatment outcomes for cocaine dependence. *Archives of General Psychiatry, 57*(6), 507–514.

Singer, L. T., Arendt, R., Fagan, J., Minnes, S., et al. (1999). Neonatal visual information processing in cocaine-exposed and non-exposed infants. *Infant Behavior & Development, 22*(l), 1–15.

Singer, M. T., & Addis, M. E. (1992). Cults, coercion, and contumely. *Cultic Studies Journal, 9*(2), 163–189.

Singh, N. N., McKay, J. D., & Singh, A. N. (1998). Culture and mental health: Nonverbal communication. *Journal of Child & Family Studies, 7*(4), 403–409.

Sirkin, M. I. (1990). Cult involvement: A systems approach to assessment and treatment. *Psychotherapy, 27*(1), 116–123.

Sison, C. E., Alpert, M., Fudge, R., & Stern, R. M. (1996). Constricted expressiveness and psychophysiological reactivity in schizophrenia. *Journal of Nervous & Mental Disease, 184*(10), 589–597.

Skeels, H. M. (1966). Adult status of children with contrasting early life experiences. *Monograph of the Society for Research in Child Development, 31*(3).

Skinner, B. F. (1938). *The behavior of organisms.* Englewood Cliffs, NJ: Prentice-Hall.

Skipton, L. H. (1997). The many faces of character. *Consulting Psychology Journal: Practice & Research, 49*(4), 235–245

Skrandies, W., Reik, P., & Kunze, C. (1999). Topography of evoked brain activity during mental arithmetic and language tasks: Sex differences. *Neuropsychologia, 37*(4), 421–430.

Skuy, M., Gewer, A., Osrin, Y., Khunou, D., et al. (2002). Effects of mediated learning experience on Raven's matrices scores of African and non-African university students in South Africa. *Intelligence, 30*(3), 221–232.

Slaby, A. E., Garfinkel, B. D., & Garfinkel, L. F. (1994). *No one say my pain.* New York: Norton.

Slater, A., Mattock, A., Brown, E., & Bremner, J. G. (1991). Form perception at birth: Cohen and Younger (1984) revisited. *Journal of Experimental Child Psychology, 51*(3), 395–406.

Sledge, W. H., Tebes, J., Rakfeldt, J., & Davidson, L. (1996). Day hospital/crisis respite care versus inpatient care: I. Clinical outcomes. *American Journal of Psychiatry, 153*(8), 1065–1073.

Sleek, S. (1995, November). Online therapy services raise ethical questions. *APA Monitor, 9*.

Sleek, S. (1998, November). How are psychologists portrayed on screen? *APA Monitor, 11*.

Slot, L. A. B., & Colpaert, F. C. (1999). Recall rendered dependent on an opiate state. *Behavioral Neuroscience, 113*(2), 337–344.

Slotkin, T. A. (1998). Fetal nicotine or cocaine exposure: which one is worse?

Smith, A., Sturgess, W., & Gallagher, J. (1999). Effects of a low dose of caffeine given in different drinks on mood and performance. *Human Psychopharmacology Clinical & Experimental, 14*(7), 473–482.

Smith, C., Carey, S., & Wiser, M. (1985). On differentiation: A case study of the development of the concepts of size, weight, and density. *Cognition, 21*(3), 177–237.

Smith, E. E. (1989). Concepts and induction. In M. I. Posner (Ed.), *Foundations of cognitive science,* Cambridge, MA: The MIT Press.

Smith, K. E., Landry, S. H., & Swank, P. R. (2000). Does the content of mothers' verbal stimulation explain differences in children's development of verbal and nonverbal cognitive skills? *Journal of School Psychology, 38*(1), 27–49.

Smith, L. F. (2002). The effects of confidence and perception of test-taking skills on performance. *North American Journal of Psychology, 4*(1), 37–50.

Smith, R. W., & Kounios, J. (1996). Sudden insight: All-or-none processing revealed by speed-accuracy decomposition. *Journal of Experimental Psychology: Learning, Memory, & Cognition, 22*(6), 1443–1462.

Smith, S. M., McIntosh, W. D., & Bazzini, D. G. (1999). Are the beautiful good in Hollywood? *Basic & Applied Social Psychology, 21*(1), 69–80.

Smith, W. P., Compton, W. C., & West, W. B. (1995). Meditation as an adjunct to a happiness enhancement program. *Journal of Clinical Psychology, 51*(2), 269–273.

Smyth, M. M., & Waller, A. (1998). Movement imagery in rock climbing. *Applied Cognitive Psychology, 12*(2), 145–157.

Snowden, P. L., & Christian, L. G. (1999). Parenting the young gifted child: Supportive behaviors. *Roeper Review, 21*(3), 215–221.

Snyderman, M., & Rothman, S. (1987). Survey of expert opinion on intelligence and aptitude testing. *American Psychologist, 42*(1), 137–144.

Sobel, E., Shine, D., DiPietro, D., & Rabinowitz, M. (1996). Condom use among HIV/infected patients in South Bronx, New York. *AIDS, 10*(2), 235–236.

Solowij, N., Stephens, R. S., Roffman, R. A., et al. (2002). Cognitive functioning of long-term heavy cannabis users seeking treatment. *Journal of the American Medical Association, 287,* 1123–1131.

Somberg, D. R., Stone, G., & Claiborn, C. D. (1993). Informed consent: Therapist's beliefs and practices. *Professional Psychology: Research & Practice, 24*(2), 153–159.

Soussignan, R. (2002). Duchenne smile, emotional experience, and autonomic reactivity. *Emotion, 2*(1), 52–74.

Spangenberg, J. J., & Lategan, T. P. (1993). Coping, androgyny, and attributional style. *South African Journal of Psychology, 23*(4), 195–203.

Sperry, R. W. (1968). Hemisphere deconnection and unity in conscious awareness. *American Psychologist, 23,* 723–733.

Sperry, R. W. (1995). The riddle of consciousness and the changing scientific worldview. *Journal of Humanistic Psychology, 35*(2), 7–33.

Spiegler, M. D., & Guevremont, D. C. (2003). *Contemporary behavior therapy.* Belmont, CA: Wadsworth

Sporer, S. L. (2001). Recognizing faces of other ethnic groups. *Psychology, Public Policy, and Law, 7*(1), 36–97

Sprecher, S. (1998). Insiders' perspectives on reasons for attraction to a close other. *Social Psychology Quarterly, 61*(4), 287–300.

Springer, S. P., & Deutsch, G. (1998). *Left brain, right brain.* New York: Freeman.

Squire, L. R., & Zola-Morgan, S. (1988). Memory: Brain systems and behavior. *Trends in Neurosciences, 11*(4), 170–175.

Squire, L. R., Knowlton, B., & Musen, G., (1993). The structure and organization of memory. In L. W. Porter & M. R. Rosenzweig (Eds.), *Annual Review of Psychology, 44,* 453–495.

Stanovich, K. E. (2001). *How to think straight about psychology.* Boston: Allyn & Bacon.

Staum, M. J., & Brotons, M. (1992). The influence of auditory subliminals on behavior. *Journal of Music Therapy, 29*(3), 130–185.

Steblay, N. M. (1992). A meta-analytic review of the weapon focus effect. *Law and Human Behavior, 16,* 413–424.

Steele, K. M., Bass, K. E., & Crook, M. D. (1999). The mystery of the Mozart effect: Failure to replicate. *Psychological Science, 10*(4), 366–369.

Steele, K. M., Brown, J. D., & Stoecker, J. A. (1999). Failure to confirm the Rauscher and Shaw description of recovery of the Mozart effect. *Perceptual & Motor Skills, 88*(3, Pt. 1), 843–848.

Stefanis, C., Dornbush, R. L., & Fink, M. (1977). *Hashish: A study of long-term use.* New York: Raven.

Stein, M. I. (1974). *Stimulating creativity* (Vol. 1). New York: Academic.

Stein, M., Miller, A. H., & Trestman, R. L. (1990). Depression and the immune system. In R. Ader, N. Cohen, & D. L. Felten (Eds.), *Psychoneuroimmunology II.* New York: Academic Press.

Steinberg, L. D., Catalano, R., & Dooley, P. (1981). Economic antecedents of child abuse and neglect. *Child Development, 52,* 975–985.

Steinhausen, H., & Spohr, H. (1998). Long-term outcome of children with fetal alcohol syndrome. *Alcoholism: Clinical & Experimental Research. 22*(2), 334–338.

Stephan, W., Berscheid, E., & Walster, E. (1971). Sexual arousal and heterosexual perception. *Journal of Personality & Social Psychology, 20*(1), 93–101.

Stephens, K., Kiger, L., Karnes, F. A., & Whorton, J. E. (1999). Use of nonverbal measures of intelligence in identification of culturally diverse gifted students in rural areas. *Perceptual & Motor Skills, 88*(3, Pt. 1), 793–796.

Steriade, M., & McCarley, R. W. (1990). Brainstem control of wakefulness and sleep. New York: Plenum.

Sterman, M. B. (1996). Physiological origins and functional correlates of EEG rhythmic activities: Implications for self-regulation. *Biofeedback & Self Regulation, 21*(1), 3–33.

Stern, D. (1982). Some interactive functions of rhythm changes between mother and infant. In M. Davis (Ed.), *Interaction rhythms, periodicity in communicative behavior.* New York: Human Sciences Press.

Sternberg, E. M. (2000). *The balance within: The science of connecting health with emotions.* New York: Freeman.

Sternberg, R. J., & Davidson, J. D. (1982, June). The mind of the puzzler. *Psychology Today.*

Sternberg, R. J. (1996). *Successful intelligence.* New York: Simon & Schuster.

Sternberg, R. J. (2001). What is the common thread of creativity? *American Psychologist, 56*(4), 360–362.

Sternberg, R. J., & Lubart, T. I. (1995). *Defying the crowd.* New York: The Free Press.

Sternberg, W. F., Bailin, D., Grant, M., & Gracely, R. H. (1998). Competition alters the perception of noxious stimuli in male and female athletes. *Pain, 76*(1–2), 231–238.

Stewart, A. J., & Ostrove, J. M. (1998). Women's personality in middle age. *American Psychologist, 53*(11), 1185–1194.

Stewart, J. V. (1996). *Astrology: What's really in the stars.* Amherst, NY: Prometheus.

Stickgold, R., Hobson, J. A., Fosse, R., & Fosse, M. (2001). Sleep, learning, and dreams: Off-line memory reprocessing. *Science, 294*(5544), 1052–1057.

Stiles, W. B., et al. (1998). Relations of the alliance with psychotherapy outcome. *Journal of Consulting & Clinical Psychology, 66*(5), 791–802.

Stockhorst, U., Klosterhalfen, S., & Steingrueber, H. (1998). Conditioned nausea and further side-effects in cancer chemotherapy. *Journal of Psychophysiology, 12*(Suppl. 1), 14–33.

Stokes, D. M. (2001, May/June). The shrinking filedrawer. *Skeptical Inquirer,* 22–25.

Stokoe, W. C. (2001). *Language in hand: Why sign came before speech.* Washington, DC: Gallaudet University Press.

Stolerman, I. P., & Jarvis, M. J. (1995) The scientific case that nicotine is addictive. *Psychopharmacology, 117*(1), 2–10.

Stone, J., Perry, Z. W., & Darley, J. M. (1997). "White men can't jump." *Basic and Applied Social Psychology, 19*(3), 291–306.

Stoney, S., & Wild, M. (1998). Motivation and interface design: Maximising learning opportunities. *Journal of Computer Assisted Learning, 14*(1), 40–50.

Storck, L. E. (1997). Cultural psychotherapy. *Group, 21*(4), 331–349.

Strack. F., Martin, L. L., & Stepper, S. (1988). Inhibiting and facilitating conditions of facial expressions: A non-obtrusive test of the facial feedback hypothesis. *Journal of Personality & Social Psychology, 54,* 768–777.

Straneva, P. A., Maixner, W., Light, K. C., Pedersen, C. A., et al. (2002). Menstrual cycle, beta-endorphins, and pain sensitivity in premenstrual dysphoric disorder. *Health Psychology, 21*(4), 358–367.

Straus, M. A., & Mouradian, V. E. (1998). Impulsive corporal punishment by mothers and antisocial behavior and impulsiveness of children. *Behavioral Sciences & the Law, 16*(3), 353–374.

Strayer, D. L., Drews, F. A., & Johnston, W. A. (2003). Cell phone-induced failures of visual attention during simulated driving. *Journal of Experimental Psychology: Applied, 9*(1), 23–32.

Strickler, E. M., & Verbalis, J. G. (1988, May/June). Hormones and behavior: The biology of thirst and sodium appetite. *American Scientist,* 261–267.

Strongman, K. T. (1996). *The psychology of emotion.* New York: Wiley.

Strote, J., Lee, J. E., & Wechsler, H. (2002). Increasing MDMA use among college students: Results of a national survey. *Journal of Adolescent Health, 30*(1), 64–72.

Sturges, J. W., & Sturges, L. V. (1998). In vivo systematic desensitization in a single-session treatment of an 11-year old girl's elevator phobia. *Child & Family Behavior Therapy, 20*(4), 55–62.

Sue, S. (1998). In search of cultural competence in psychotherapy and counseling. *American Psychologist, 53*(4), 440–448.

Suedfeld, P. (1990). Restricted environmental stimulation and smoking cessation. *International Journal of Addictions, 25*(8), 861–888.

Suedfeld, P., & Borrie, R. A. (1999). Health and therapeutic applications of chamber and flotation restricted environmental stimulation therapy (REST). *Psychology & Health, 14*(3), 545–566.

Suinn, R. M. (1975). *Fundamentals of behavior pathology* (2nd ed.). New York: Wiley.

Suinn, R. M. (1999, March). Scaling the summit: Valuing ethnicity. *APA Monitor, 2*.

Suinn, R. M. (2001). The terrible twos—Anger and anxiety. *American Psychologist, 56*(1), 27–36.

Sullivan, M. J., Johnson, P. I., Kjelberg, B. J., Williams, J., et al. (1998). Community leadership opportunities for psychologists. *Professional Psychology: Research and Practice, 29*(4), 328–331.

Sumerlin, J. R. (1997). Self-actualization and hope. *Journal of Social Behavior & Personality, 12*(4), 1101–1110.

Sumerlin, J. R., & Bundrick, C. M. (1996). Brief Index of Self-Actualization: A measure of Maslow's model. *Journal of Social Behavior & Personality, 11*(2), 253–271.

Swan, G. E., & Denk, C. E. (1987). Dynamic models for the maintenance of smoking cessation: Event history analysis of late relapse. *Journal of Behavioral Medicine, 10*(6), 527–554.

Swanson, M. W., Streissguth, A. P., Sampson, P.D., & Carmichael-Olson, H. (1999). Prenatal cocaine and neuromotor outcome at four months: Effect of duration of exposure. *Journal of Developmental & Behavioral Pediatrics, 20*(5), 325–334.

Swayze, V. W. (1995). Frontal leukotomy and related psychosurgical procedures in the era before antipsychotics (1935–1954): A historical overview. *American Journal of Psychiatry, 152*(4), 505–515.

Swim, J. K., & Sanna, L. J. (1996). He's skilled, she's lucky: A meta-analysis of observers' attributions for women's and men's successes and failures. *Personality & Social Psychology Bulletin, 22*(5), 507–519.

Talley, P. F., Strupp, H. H., & Morey, L. C. (1990). Matchmaking in psychotherapy: Patient-therapist dimensions and their impact on outcome. *Journal of Consulting & Clinical Psychology, 58*(2), 182–188.

Tallis, F. (1996). Compulsive washing in the absence of phobic and illness anxiety. *Behaviour Research & Therapy, 34*(4), 361–362.

Tamis-LeMonvda, C. S., & Bornstein, M. H. (1994). Specificity in mother-toddler language-play relations across the second year. *Developmental Psychology, 30*(2), 283–292.

Tang, S., & Hall, V. C. (1995). The overjustification effect: A meta-analysis. *Applied Cognitive Psychology, 9*(5), 365–404.

Tanner, J. M. (1973, September). Growing up. *Scientific American,* 34–43.

Taraban, R., Rynearson, K., & Kerr, M. (2000). College students' academic performance and self-reports of comprehension strategy use. *Reading Psychology, 21*(4), 283–308.

Tardif, T. Z., & Sternberg, R. J. (1988). What do we know about creativity? In R. J. Sternberg (Ed.), *The nature of creativity.* Cambridge University Press.

Tart, C. T. (1986). Consciousness, altered states, and worlds of experience. *Journal of Transpersonal Psychology, 18*(2), 159–170.

Tavris, C. (1992). *The mismeasure of woman.* New York: Touchstone/Simon & Schuster.

Taylor, S. E., Kemeny, M. E., Reed, G. M., Bower, J. E., & Gruenewald, T. L. (2000).

Psychological resources, positive illusions, and health. *American Psychologist, 55*(1), 99–109.

Teng, E., & Squire, L. R. (1999). Memory for places learned long ago is intact after hippocampal damage. *Nature, 400*(6745), 675–677.

Teplin, L. A., Abram, K. M., & McClelland. (1994). Does psychiatric disorder predict violent crime among released jail detainees? *American Psychologist, 49*(4), 335–342.

ter Riet, G., de Craen, A. J. M., de Boer, A., & Kessels, A.G. H. (1998). Is placebo analgesia mediated by endogenous opioids? A systematic review. *Pain, 76*(3), 273–275.

Terborg, J. R. (1998). Health psychology in the United States. *Applied Psychology: An International Review, 47*(2), 199–217.

Terman, L. M., & Merrill, M. A. (1937; revised, 1960). *Stanford-Binet Intelligence Scale*. Boston: Houghton Mifflin.

Terman, L. M., & Oden, M. (1959). *The gifted group in mid-life. Vol. 5, Genetic studies of genius*. Stanford, CA: Stanford University Press.

Terry, D. J., & Hogg, M. A. (1996). Group norms and the attitude-behavior relationship. *Personality & Social Psychology Bulletin, 22*(8), 776–793.

Thase, M. E., & Kupfer, D. L. (1996). Recent developments in the pharmacotherapy of mood disorders. *Journal of Consulting & Clinical Psychology, 64*(4), 646–659.

Thelen, E. (1995). Motor development. *American Psychologist, 50*(2), 79–95.

"They'd kill for $1 million." (1991, July 1). *The Los Angeles Times*, A-8.

Thibodeau, R., & Aronson, E. (1992). Taking a closer look: Reasserting the role of self-concept in dissonance theory. *Personality and Social Psychology Bulletin, 18*(5), 591–602.

Thompson, R. A., & Nelson, C. A. (2001). Developmental science and the media. *American Psychologist, 56*(1), 5–15.

Thompson, R. F. (1991). Are memory traces localized or distributed? *Neuropsychologia, 29*(6), 571–582.

Tice, D. M., & Baumeister, R. F. (1997). Longitudinal study of procrastination, performance, stress, and health: The costs and benefits of dawdling. *Psychological Science, 8*(6), 454–458.

Tierny, J. (1987, September/October). Stitches: Good news: Better health linked to sin, sloth. *Hippocrates*, 30–35.

Tiffany, S. T., Martin, E. M., & Baker, T. B. (1986). Treatments for cigarette smoking: An evaluation of the contributions of aversion and counseling procedures. *Behavior Research & Therapy, 24*(4), 437–452.

Till, B. D., & Priluck, R. L. (2000). Stimulus generalization in classical conditioning: An initial investigation and extension. *Psychology & Marketing, 17*(1), 55–72.

Timmerman, I. G. H., Emmelkamp, P. M. G., & Sanderman, R. (1998). The effects of a stress-management training program in individuals at risk in the community at large. *Behaviour Research & Therapy, 36*(9), 863–875.

Tipples, J., Atkinson, A. P., & Young, A. W. (2002). The eyebrow frown: A salient social signal. *Emotion, 2*(3), 288–296.

Tobler, N. S., Roona, M. R., Ocshorn, P., Marshall, D. G., et al. (2000). School-based adolescent drug prevention programs: 1998 meta-analysis. *Journal of Primary Prevention, 20*, 275–337.

Tolman, E. C., & Honzik, C. H. (1930). Introduction and removal of reward and maze performance in rats. *University of California Publications in Psychology, 4*, 257–275.

Tolman, E. C., Ritchie, B. F., & Kalish, D. (1946). Studies in spatial learning: II. Place learning versus response learning. *Journal of Experimental Psychology, 36*, 221–229.

Tomes, H. (1998, December). Diversity: psychology's life depends on it. *APA Monitor*, 28.

Tomlinson-Keasey, C., & Little, T. D. (1990). Predicting educational attainment, occupational achievement, intellectual skill, and personal adjustment among gifted men and women. *Journal of Educational Psychology, 82*(3), 442–455.

Toneatto, T., Sobell, L. C., Sobell, M. B., & Rubel, E. (1999). Natural recovery from cocaine dependence. *Psychology of Addictive Behaviors, 13*(4), 259–268.

Torrance, M., Thomas, Glyn V., & Robinson, E. J. (1991). Strategies for answering examination essay questions: Is it helpful to write a plan? *British Journal of Educational Psychology, 61*(1), 46–54.

Torrey, E. F. (1988). *Surviving schizophrenia: A family manual*. New York: Harper & Row.

Torrey, E. F. (1996). *Out of the shadows*. New York: John Wiley & Sons.

Townsend, J. M., & Wasserman, T. (1998). *Sexual attractiveness. Evolution & Human Behavior, 19*(3), 171–191.

Treharne, G. J., Lyons, A. C., & Tupling, R. E. (2001). The effects of optimism, pessimism, social support, and mood on the lagged relationship between daily stress and symptoms. *Current Research in Social Psychology, 7*(5), 60–81.

Trehub, S. E., Unyk, A. M., & Trainor, L. J. (1993a). Adults identify infant-directed music across cultures. *Infant Behavior & Development, 16*(2), 193–211.

Trehub, S. E., Unyk, A. M., & Trainor, L. J. (1993b). Maternal singing in cross-cultural perspective. *Infant Behavior & Development, 16*(3), 285–295.

Troll, L. E., & Skaff, M. M. (1997). Perceived continuity of self in very old age. *Psychology & Aging, 12*(1), 162–169.

Truax, S. R. (1983). Active search, mediation, and the manipulation of cue dimensions: Emotion attribution in the false feedback paradigm. *Motivation and Emotion, 7*, 41–60.

Truchlicka, M., McLaughlin, T. F., & Swain, J. C. (1998). Effects of token reinforcement and response cost on the accuracy of spelling performance with middle-school special education students with behavior disorders. *Behavioral Interventions, 13*(1), 1–10.

Tsai, G., & Coyle, J. T. (2002). Glutamatergic mechanisms in schizophrenia. *Annual Review of Pharmacology & Toxicology, 42*, 165–179.

Tse, L. (1999). Finding a place to be: Ethnic identity exploration of Asian Americans. *Adolescence, 34*(133), 121–138.

Tucker, P., Pfefferbaum, B., Nixon, S. J., & Dickson, W. (2000). Predictors of post-traumatic stress symptoms in Oklahoma City. *Journal of Behavioral Health Services & Research, 27*(4), 406–416.

Tuholski, S. W., Engle, R. W., & Baylis, G. C. (2001). Individual differences in working memory capacity and enumeration. *Memory & Cognition, 29*(3), 484–492.

Tulley, M., & Chiu, L. H. (1995). Student teachers and classroom discipline. *Journal of Educational Research, 88*(3), 164–171.

Tulving, E. (1989). Remembering and knowing the past. *American Scientist, 77*(4), 361–367.

Tulving, E. (2002). Episodic memory. *Annual Review of Psychology, 53*, 1–25.

Turkheimer, E. (1998). Heritability and biological explanation. *Psychological Review, 105*(4), 782–791.

Turner, S. J. M. (1997). The use of the reflective team in a psychodrama therapy group. *International Journal of Action Methods, 50*(1), 17–26.

Turton, M. D., O'Shea, D., Gunn, I., Beak, S. A., et al. (1996). A role for glucagon-like peptide-1 in the central regulation of feeding. *Nature, 379*(6560), 69–74.

Tutkun, H., Yargic, L. I., & Sar, V. (1995). Dissociative identity disorder. *Dissociation: Progress in the Dissociative Disorders, 8*(1), 3–9.

Tversky, A., & Kahneman, D. (1981). The framing of decisions and the psychology of choice. *Science, 211*, 453–458.

Tversky, A., & Kahneman, D. (1982). Judgments of and by representativeness. In D. Kahneman, P. Slovic, & A. Tversky, *Judgment under uncertainty: Heuristics and biases*. Cambridge: Cambridge University Press.

Twenge, J. M., & Campbell, W. K. (2001). Age and birth cohort differences in self-esteem. *Personality & Social Psychology Review, 5*(4), 321–344.

Tye-Murray, N., Spencer, L., & Woodworth, G. G. (1995). Acquisition of speech by children who have prolonged cochlear implant experience. *Journal of Speech & Hearing Research, 38*(2), 327–337.

Tzeng, M. (1992). The effects of socioeconomic heterogamy and changes on marital dissolution for first marriages. *Journal of Marriage and Family, 54*, 609–619.

Tzeng, O. J., & Wang, W. S. (1983). The first two r's. *American Scientist, 71*(3), 238–243.

Tzuriel, D., & Shamir, A. (2002). The effects of mediation in computer assisted dynamic assessment. *Journal of Computer Assisted Learning, 18*(1), 21–32.

Ulrich, R. E., Stachnik, T. J., & Stainton, N. R. (1963). Student acceptance of generalized personality interpretations. *Psychological Reports, 131*, 831–834.

Underwood, B. J. (1957). Interference and forgetting. *Psychological Review, 64*, 49–60.

UNESCO. (1990). The Seville statement on violence. *American Psychologist, 45*(10), 1167–1168.

Unsworth, G., & Ward, T. (2001). Video games and aggressive behaviour. *Australian Psychologist, 36*(3), 184–192.

Vaillant, G. E. (2002). *Aging well*. Boston: Little, Brown.

Vaillant, G. E., & Mukamal, K. (2001). Successful aging. *American Journal of Psychiatry, 158*(6), 839–847.

Valins, S. (1966). Cognitive effects of false heart-rate feedback. *Journal of Personality & Social Psychology, 4*, 400–408.

Valins, S. (1967). Emotionality and information concerning internal reactions. *Journal of Personality & Social Psychology, 6*, 458–463.

van der Hart, O., Lierens, R., & Goodwin, J. (1996). Jeanne Fery: A sixteenth-century case of dissociative identity disorder. *Journal of Psychohistory, 24*(1), 18–35.

Van Goozen, S. H. M., Cohen-Kettenis, P. T., Gooren, L. J. G., & Frijda, N. H. (1995). Gender differences in behaviour: Activating effects of cross-sex hormones. *Psychoneuroendocrinology, 20*(4), 343–363.

van Lawick-Goodall, J. (1971). *In the shadow of man*. New York: Houghton Mifflin.

van Rooij, J. J. F. (1994). Introversion-extraversion: Astrology versus psychology. *Personality & Individual Differences, 16*(6), 985–988.

Van Wyk, P. H., & Geist, C. S. (1995). Biology of bisexuality: Critique and observations. *Journal of Homosexuality, 28*(3–4), 357–373.

VandenBos, G. R., & Bryant, B. K. (Eds.), *Cataclysms, crises, and catastrophes: Psychology in action*. Washington, DC: American Psychological Association.

Vane, J. R., & Guarnaccia, V. J. (1989). Personality theory and personality assessment measures: How helpful to the clinician? *Journal of Clinical Psychology, 45*(1), 5–19.

Vargha-Khadem, F., Gadian, D. G., Watkins, K. E., Connelly, A., et al. (1997). Differential effects of early hippocampal pathology on episodic and semantic memory. *Science, 277*(5324), 376–380.

Velakoulis, D., & Pantelis, C. (1996). What have we learned from functional imaging studies in schizophrenia? *Australian & New Zealand Journal of Psychiatry, 30*(2), 195–209.

Verkuyten, M., & Lay, C. (1998). Ethnic minority identity and psychological well-being: The mediating role of collective self-esteem. *Journal of Applied Social Psychology, 28*(21), 1969–1986.

Viegener, B. J., Perri, M. G., Nezu, A. M., et al. (1990). Effects of an intermittent, low-fat, low-calorie diet in the behavioral treatment of obesity. *Behavior Therapy, 21*(4), 499–509.

Vogler, R. E., & Bartz, W. R. (1982). *The better way to drink*. New York: Simon & Schuster.

Vogler, R. E., & Bartz, W. R. (1992). *Teenagers and alcohol*. Philadelphia: Charles Press.

Vogler, R. E., Weissbach, T. A., Compton, J. V., & Martin, G. T. (1977). Integrated behavior change techniques for problem drinkers in the community. *Journal of Consulting and Clinical Psychology, 45*, 267–279.

Volkmann, J., Schnitzler, A., Witte, O. W., & Freund, H. J. (1998). Handedness and asymmetry of hand representation in human motor cortex. *Journal of Neurophysiology, 79*(4), 2149–2154.

Volkow, N. D., Gillespie, H., Mullani, N., & Tancredi, L. (1996). Brain glucose metabolism in chronic marijuana users at baseline and during marijuana intoxication. *Psychiatry Research: Neuroimaging, 67*(1), 29–38.

Volpicelli, J. R., Ulm, R. R., Altenor, A., & Seligman, M. E. P. (1983). Learned mastery in the rat. *Learning and Motivation, 14*, 204–222.

Vygotsky, L. S. (1962). *Thought and language*. Cambridge, MA: MIT Press.

Vygotsky, L. S. (1978). *Mind in society*. Cambridge, MA: Harvard University Press.

Wadden, T. A., Vogt, R. A., Foster, G. D., & Anderson, D. A. (1998). Exercise and the maintenance of weight loss. *Journal of Consulting and Clinical Psychology, 66*(2), 429–433.

Waid, W. M., & Orne, M. T. (1982, July/August). The physiological detection of deception. *American Scientist, 70*, 402–409.

Wakefield, J. C. (1992). The concept of mental disorder. *American Psychologist, 47*(3), 373–388.

Wald, J., & Taylor, S. (2000). Efficacy of virtual reality exposure therapy to treat driving phobia. *Journal of Behavior Therapy & Experimental Psychiatry, 31*(3–4), 249–257.

Walker, I., & Crogan, M. (1998). Academic performance, prejudice, and the Jigsaw classroom. *Journal of Community & Applied Social Psychology, 8*(6), 381–393.

Wallach, M. A. (1985). Creativity testing and giftedness. In F. D. Horowitz & M. O'Brien (Eds.), *The gifted and talented: Developmental perspectives*, Washington, DC: American Psychological Association, 99–123.

Wallach, M. A., & Kogan, N. (1965). *Modes of thinking in young children.* New York: Holt.

Walsh, J., & Uestuen, T. B. (1999). Prevalence and health consequences of insomnia. *Sleep, 22*(Suppl. 3), S427–S436.

Walsh, J. K., & Scweitzer, P. K. (1999). Ten-year trends in the pharmacological treatment of insomnia. *Sleep, 22*(3), 371–375.

Walsh, M. F., & Flynn, T. J. (1995). A 54–month evaluation of a popular very low calorie diet program. *Journal of Family Practice, 41*(3), 231–236.

Walster, E. (1971). Passionate love. In B. I. Murstein (Ed.), *Theories of attraction and love.* New York: Springer.

Walton, C. E., Bower, M. L., & Bower, T. G. (1992). Recognition of familiar faces by newborns. *Infant Behavior & Development, 15*(2), 265–269.

Wampold, B. E., et al. (1997). A meta-analysis of outcome studies comparing bona fide psychotherapies. *Psychological Bulletin, 122*(3), 203–215.

Wandersman, A., & Florin, P. (2003). Community interventions and effective prevention. *American Psychologist, 58*(6/7), 441–448.

Warning Signs. (2000). American Psychological Association. Washington, DC: APA.

Warwick-Evans, L. A., Symons, N., Fitch, T., & Burrows, L. (1998). Evaluating sensory conflict and postural instability. Theories of motion sickness. *Brain Research Bulletin, 47*(5), 465–469.

Watson, J. B. (1913). Psychology as the behaviorist views it. *Psychological Review, 20,* 158–177.

Watson, J. B. (1994). Psychology as the behaviorist views it. Special Issue: The centennial issue of the Psychological Review. *Psychological Review, 101*(2), 248–253.

Watson, D. L., & Tharp, R. G. (2001). *Self-directed behavior: Self-modification for personal adjustment,* 8th ed. Belmont, CA: Wadsworth.

Weaver, C. A. (1993). Do you need a "flash" to form a flashbulb memory? *Journal of Experimental Psychology: General, 122*(1), 39–46.

Webb, N. M., & Farivar, S. (1994). Promoting helping behavior in cooperative small groups in middle school mathematics. *American Educational Research Journal, 31*(2), 369–395.

Wechsler, H., Lee, J. E., Kuo, M., Seibring, M., et al. (2002). Trends in college binge drinking during a period of increased prevention efforts. *Journal of American College Health, 50*(5), 203–217.

Wechsler, H., & Wuethrich, B. (2002). *Dying to drink.* Emmaus, PA: Rodale Books.

Weekley, J. A., & Jones, C. (1997). Video-based situational testing. *Personnel Psychology, 50*(1), 25–49.

Weems, C. F. (1998). The evaluation of heart rate biofeedback using a multi-element design. *Journal of Behavior Therapy & Experimental Psychiatry, 29*(2), 157–162.

Wehr, T. A., Duncan, W. C., Sher, L., Aeschbach, D., et al. (2001). A circadian signal of change of season in patients with seasonal affective disorder. *Archives of General Psychiatry, 58*(12), 1108–1114.

Weinberg, R. A. (1989). Intelligence and IQ. *American Psychologist, 44*(2), 98–104.

Weiner, I. B. (1997). Current status of the Rorschach Inkblot Method. *Journal of Personality Assessment, 68*(1), 5–19.

Weintraub, M. I. (1983). *Hysterical conversion reactions.* New York: SP Medical & Scientific Books.

Weintraub, S., Powell, D. H., & Whitla, D. K. (1994). Successful cognitive aging. *Journal of Geriatric Psychiatry, 27*(1), 15–34.

Weisburd, D. E. (1990). Planning a community-based mental health system: Perspective of a family member. *American Psychologist, 45*(11), 1245–1248.

Weiss, B., Dodge, K. A., Bates, J. E., & Pettit, G. S. (1992). Some consequences of early harsh discipline. *Child Development, 63*(6), 1321–1335.

Weiss, J. (1990). Unconscious mental functioning. *Scientific American,* March, 103–109.

Weiten, W. (1998). Pressure, major life events, and psychological symptoms. *Journal of Social Behavior & Personality, 13*(1), 51–68.

Wells, G. L. (1993). What do we know about eyewitness identification? *American Psychologist, 48*(5), 553–571.

Wells, G. L. (2001). Police lineups: Data, theory, and policy. *Psychology, Public Policy, & Law, 7*(4), 791–801.

Wells, G. L., Small, M., Penrod, S., Malpass, R. S., et al. (1999). Eyewitness identification procedures: Recommendations for lineups and photospreads. *Law & Human Behavior, 22*(6), 603–647.

Wells, N. (1994). Perceived control over pain: Relation to distress and disability. *Research in Nursing & Health, 17*(4), 295–302.

Welte, J. W., Barnes, G. M., Hoffman, J. H., & Dintcheff, B.A. (1999). Trends in adolescent alcohol and other substance use. *Substance Use & Misuse, 34*(10), 1427–1449.

Werner, C. M., & Makela, E. (1998). Motivations and behaviors that support recycling. *Journal of Environmental Psychology, 18*(4), 373–386.

Wertheimer, M. (1959). *Productive thinking.* New York: Harper & Row.

West, T. G. (1991). *In the mind's eye.* Buffalo, NY: Prometheus.

Westen, D. (1998). The scientific legacy of Sigmund Freud: Toward a psychodynamically informed psychological science. *Psychological Bulletin, 124*(3), 333–371.

Wettach, G. E. (2000). The near death experience as a product of isolated subcortical brain function. *Journal of Near-Death Studies, 19*(2), 71–90.

Wexler, M. N. (1995). Expanding the groupthink explanation to the study of contemporary cults. *Cultic Studies Journal, 12*(1), 49–71.

Wexler, M., Kosslyn, S. M., & Berthoz, A. (1998). Motor processes in mental rotation. *Cognition, 68*(1), 77–94.

Whatley, M. A., Webster, J. M., Smith, R. H., & Rhodes, A. (1999). The effect of a favor on public and private compliance. *Basic & Applied Social Psychology, 21*(3), 251–259.

Whimbey, A., with Whimbey, L. S. (1980). *Intelligence can be taught.* New York: Dutton.

White, B. L., & Watts, J. C. (1973). *Experience and environment Vol. I.* Englewood Cliffs, NJ: Prentice-Hall.

Whitley, B. E. (1999). Right-wing authoritarianism, social dominance orientation, and prejudice. *Journal of Personality & Social Psychology, 77*(l), 126–134.

Whittal, M. L., Agras, W. S., & Gould, R. A. (1999). Bulimia nervosa: A meta-analysis of psychosocial and pharmacological treatments. *Behavior Therapy, 30*(1), 117–135.

Widiger, T. A., & Sankis, L. M. (2000). Adult psychopathology. *Annual Review of Psychology, 51,* 377–404.

Widiger, T. A., & Trull, T. J. (1991). Diagnosis and clinical assessment. In M. R. Rosenzweig & L. W. Porter (Eds.), *Annual Review of Psychology, 42,* 109–133.

Wiederman, M. W. (2001). Gender differences in sexuality: Perceptions, myths, and realities. *Family Journal-Counseling & Therapy for Couples & Families, 9*(4), 468–471.

Wilder, D. A., Simon, A. F., & Faith, M. (1996). Enhancing the impact of counterstereotypic information. *Journal of Personality & Social Psychology, 71*(2), 276–287.

Wilding, J., & Valentine, E. (1994a). Memory champions. *British Journal of Psychology, 85*(2), 231–244.

Wilding, J., & Valentine, E. (1994b). Mnemonic wizardry with the telephone directory: But stories are another story. *British Journal of Psychology, 85*(4), 501–509.

Wilhelm, J. L. (1976). *The search for superman.* New York: Simon & Schuster.

Wilkinson, B., Piccinelli, M., Roberts, S., Micciolo, R., & Fry, J. (1997). Lunar cycle and consultations for anxiety and depression in general practice. *International Journal of Social Psychiatry, 43*(1), 29–34.

Wilkinson, R. B. (1997). Interactions between self and external reinforcement in predicting depressive symptoms. *Behaviour Research & Therapy, 35*(4), 281–289.

Williams, R. (1989). The trusting heart: Great news about Type A behavior. New York: Random House.

Williams, R. L., & Eggert, A. (2002). Note-taking predictors of test performance. *Teaching of Psychology, 29*(3), 234–236.

Williams, R. L., & Long, J. D. (1991). *Toward a self-managed life style.* Boston: Houghton Mifflin.

Williams, R. L., et al. (1964). Sleep patterns in young adults: An EEG study. *Electroencephalography and Clinical Neurophysiology,* 376–381.

Willoughby, T., Wood, E., Desmarais, S., Sims, S., & Kalra, M. (1997). Mechanisms that facilitate the effectiveness of elaboration strategies. *Journal of Educational Psychology, 89*(4), 682–685.

Wilson, G. T. (1987). Chemical aversion conditioning as a treatment for alcoholism: A re-analysis. *Behaviour Research and Therapy, 25*(6), 503–516.

Wilson, R. R. (1986). *Don't panic: Taking control of anxiety attacks.* New York: Harper & Row.

Wilson, T. D., Meyers, J., & Gilbert, D. T. (2001). Lessons from the past: Do people learn from experience that emotional reactions are short-lived? *Personality & Social Psychology Bulletin, 27*(12), 1648–1661.

Wilson, T. D., Wheatley, T., Meyers, J. M., Gilbert, D. T., & Axsom, D. (2000). Focalism: A source of durability bias in affective forecasting. *Journal of Personality & Social Psychology, 78*(5), 821–836.

Wilson, T. L., & Brown, T. L. (1997). Reexamination of the effect of Mozart's music on spatial-task performance. *Journal of Psychology, 131*(4), 365–370.

Winningham, R. G., Hyman, I. E., & Dinnel, D. L. (2000). Flashbulb memories? The effects of when the initial memory report was obtained. *Memory, 8*(4), 209–216.

Wise, R. A., & Rompre, P. P. (1989). Brain dopamine and reward. *Annual Review of Psychology, 40,* 191–225.

Withers, N. W., Pulvirenti, L., Koob, G. F., & Gillin, J. C. (1995). Cocaine abuse and dependence. *Journal of Clinical Psychopharmacology, 15*(1), 63–78.

Witt, S. D. (1997). Parental influences on children's socialization to gender roles. *Adolescence, 32*(126), 253–259.

Woehr, D. J., & Cavell, T. A. (1993). Self-report measures of ability, effort, and nonacademic activity as predictors of introductory psychology test scores. *Teaching of Psychology, 20*(3), 156–160.

Wolfe, J. B. (1936). Effectiveness of token rewards for chimpanzees. *Comparative Psychology Monographs, 12*(5), Whole No. 60.

Wolitzky, D. L. (1995). The theory and practice of traditional psychoanalytic psychotherapy. In A. S. Gurman & S. B. Messer, *Essential Psychotherapies.* New York: Guilford.

Wolpe, J. (1974). *The practice of behavior therapy* (2nd ed.). New York: Pergamon.

Wolpe, J., & Plaud, J. J. (1997). Pavlov's contributions to behavior therapy. *American Psychologist, 52*(9), 966–972.

Wolpin, M., Marston, A., Randolph, C., & Clothier, A. (1992). Individual difference correlates of reported lucid dreaming frequency and control. *Journal of Mental Imagery, 16*(3–4), 231–236.

Wong, J. L., & Whitaker, D. J. (1993). Depressive mood states and their cognitive and personality correlates in college students. *Journal of Clinical Psychology, 49*(5), 615–621.

Wood, E., & Willoughby, T. (1995). Cognitive strategies for test-taking. In E. Wood, V. Woloshyn, & T. Willoughby (Eds.), *Cognitive strategy instruction for middle and high schools.* Cambridge, MA: Brookline.

Wood, J. M., & Bootzin, R. R. (1990). The prevalence of nightmares and their independence from anxiety. *Journal of Abnormal Psychology, 99*(1), 64–68.

Wood, J. M., Bootzin, R. R., Kihlstrom, J. F., & Schacter, D. L. (1992). Implicit and explicit memory for verbal information presented during sleep. *Psychological Science, 3*(4), 236–239.

Wood, N. L., & Cowan, N. (1995). The cocktail party phenomenon revisited. *Journal of Experimental Psychology: General, 124*(3), 243–262.

Woodruff-Pak, D. S. (2001). Eyeblink classical conditioning differentiates normal aging from Alzheimer's disease. *Integrative Physiological & Behavioral Science, 36*(2), 87–108.

Woods, S. C., Schwartz, M. W, Baskin, D. G., & Seeley, R J. (2000). Food intake and the regulation of body weight. *Annual Review of Psychology. 51,* 255–277.

Woods, S. C., Seeley, R. J., & Porte, D. (1998). Signals that regulate food intake and energy homeostasis. *Science, 280*(5368), 1378–1383.

Woodward, J., & Goodstein, D. (1996). Conduct, misconduct and the structure of science. *American Scientist, 84*(5), 479–490.

Woody, S. R. (1996). Effects of focus of attention on anxiety levels and social performance of individuals with social phobia. *Journal of Abnormal Psychology, 105*(1), 61–69.

Worthen, J. B., & Marshall, P. H. (1996). Intralist and extralist sources of distinctiveness and the bizarreness effect. *American Journal of Psychology, 109*(2), 239–263.

Wright, D. B. (1993). Recall of the Hillsborough disaster over time: Systematic biases of "flashbulb" memories. *Applied Cognitive Psychology, 7*(2), 129–138.

Wulf, G., Shea, C. H., & Matschiner, S. (1998). Frequent feedback enhances complex motor skill learning. *Journal of Motor Behavior, 30*(2), 180–192.

Wyatt, J. W., Posey, A., Welker, W., & Seamonds, C. (1984). Natural levels of similarities between identical twins and between unrelated people. *The Skeptical Inquirer, 9,* 62–66.

Yalom, I. D. (1980). *Existential psychotherapy.* New York: Basic.

Yarmey, A. D., Yarmey, M. J., & Yarmey, A. L. (1996). Accuracy of eyewitness identification in showups and lineups. *Law & Human Behavior, 20*(4), 459–477.

Yee, A. H., Fairchild, H. H., Weizmann, F., & Wyatt, G. E. (1993). Addressing psychology's problems with race. *American Psychologist, 48*(11), 1132–1140.

Yehuda, R. (2002). Post-traumatic stress disorder. *New England Journal of Medicine, 346*(2), 108–114.

Yokota, F., & Thompson, K. M. (2000). Violence in G-rated animated films. *Journal of the American Medical Association, 283*(20), 2716.

Yontef, G. M. (1995). Gestalt therapy. In A. S. Gurman & S. B. Messer, *Essential Psychotherapies.* New York: Guilford.

Yoshida, M. (1993). Three-dimensional electrophysiological atlas created by computer mapping of clinical responses elicited on stimulation of human subcortical structures. *Stereotactic & Functional Neurosurgery, 60*(1–3), 127–134.

Zakzanis, K. K., & Young, D. A. (2001). Memory impairment in abstinent MDMA ("Ecstasy") users: A longitudinal investigation. *Neurology, 56*(7), 966–969.

Zeidner, M. (1995). Adaptive coping with test situations: A review of the literature. *Educational Psychologist, 30*(3), 123–133.

Zellner, D. A., Harner, D. E., & Adler, R. L. (1989). Effects of eating abnormalities and gender on perceptions of desirable body shape. *Journal of Abnormal Psychology, 98*(1), 93–96.

Zemishlany, Z., Aizenberg, D., & Weizman, A. (2001). Subjective effects of MDMA ("Ecstasy") on human sexual function. *European Psychiatry, 16*(2), 127–130.

Zgodzinski, D. (1996, February). Cybertherapy. *Internet World,* 50–53.

Zigler, E. (1995). Can we "cure" mild mental retardation among individuals in the lower socioeconomic stratum? *American Journal of Public Health, 85*(3), 302–304.

Zimbardo, P. G., Haney, C., & Banks, W. C. (1973, April 8). A pirandellian prison. *The New York Times Magazine.*

Zimbardo, P. G., Pilkonis, P. A., & Norwood, R. M. (1978). The social disease called shyness. In *Annual editions, personality and adjustment 78/79.* Guilford CT: Dushkin.

Zimmerman, B. J. (1996a). Enhancing student academic and health functioning: A self-regulatory perspective. *School Psychology Quarterly, 11*(1), 47–66.

Zimmerman, J. D. (1996b). A prosocial media strategy. *American Journal of Orthopsychiatry, 66*(3), 354–362.

Zinbarg, R. E., Barlow, D. H., Brown, T. A., & Hertz, R. M. (1992). Cognitive-behavioral approaches to the nature and treatment of anxiety disorders. In M. R. Rosenzweig & L. W. Porter (Eds.), *Annual Review of Psychology, 43,* 235–267.

Zohar, D. (1998). An additive model of test anxiety: Role of exam-specific expectations.

Zucker, A. (1995). "Rights and the dying." In H. Wass & R. A. Neimeyer (Eds.), *Dying: Facing the facts.* Washington, DC: Taylor & Francis.

Zuckerman, M. (1990). The psychophysiology of sensation seeking. *Journal of Personality, 58*(1), 313–345.

Zuckerman, M. (1996). Item revisions in the Sensation Seeking Scale Form V (SSS-V). *EDRA: Environmental Design Research Association, 20*(4), 515.

Zuckerman, M., Eysenck, S., & Eysenck, H. J. (1978). Sensation seeking in England and America: Cross-cultural, age, and sex comparisons. *Journal of Consulting and Clinical Psychology, 46,* 139–149.

Zuwerink, J. R., Devine, P. G., Monteith, M. J., & Cook, D. A. (1996). Prejudice toward Blacks: With and without compunction? *Basic & Applied Social Psychology, 18*(2), 131–150.

Photo Credits

This page constitutes an extension of the copyright page. We have made every effort to trace the ownership of all copyrighted material and to secure permission from copyright holders. In the event of any question arising as to the use of any material, we will be pleased to make the necessary corrections in future printings. Thanks are due to the following authors, publishers, and agents for permission to use the material indicated.

Introduction. 1, top: Seth Resnick/Stock, Boston **1, bottom:** Charles Gupton/Stock, Boston

Chapter 1. 13: PhotoDisc/Corbis **14, left:** Hank Morgan/Rainbow **14, right:** Jeff Greenberg/PhotoEdit **16, top left:** Mireille Vauier/Woodfin Camp/PictureQuest **16, top right:** Eric A. Wessman/Stock, Boston/ PictureQuest **16, bottom left:** Greg Epperson/Index Stock Imagery **16, bottom right:** Greg Johnston/Lonely Planet Images/PictureQuest **17, top:** Anna Clopet/Corbis **17, bottom:** Charles Gupton/Stock, Boston **18, 19, all:** Archives of the History of American Psychology, University of Akron **20, top:** Neena Leen/*Life Magazine*/Timepix **20, bottom, 21 all:** Archives of the History of American Psychology, University of Akron **22:** Ted Polumbaum **24:** Joseph Sohm/Stock, Boston **25:** Miramax/The Kobal Collection **28:** Dan McCoy/Rainbow **31:** Baron Hugo van Lawick/National Geographic Society **36:** Esbin-Anderson/The Image Works **41:** Bettmann/Corbis **44:** Nancy Richmond/ The Image Works **46:** John Nordell/The Image Works

Chapter 2. 51: Cameron/Corbis **58:** Steve Liss/Getty Images **60:** Charles Gupton/Stock, Boston **61, top:** Huntington Magnetic Resonance Center, Pasadena, CA **61, center, bottom:** Washington University School of Medicine, St. Louis **64:** Courtesy of Richard Haier, University of California, Irvine **66:** Ronald C. James **69:** Shaywitz et al., 1995 NMR Research/Yale Medical School **71:** Rod Planch/Photo Researchers, Inc. **74, top left:** Dan McCoy/Rainbow **74, top right:** Keystone/ The Image Works **74, bottom:** Tom McCarthy/ PhotoEdit **75:** Getty Images **77:** Bob Daemmrich/The Image Works **79:** Custom Medical Stock Photo

Chapter 3. 83: PhotoDisc/Corbis **84:** Bio-photo Associates/Science-Source/Photo Researchers, Inc. **85:** Myrleen Ferguson/ PhotoEdit **87, top:** Petit Format/Photo Researchers, Inc. **87, bottom:** Ted Wood **88:** Anna Kaufman Moon/Stock, Boston **90:** Margaret Miller/Photo Researchers, Inc. **91, top:** From A.N. Meltzoff & M.K. Moore, "Imitation of facial and manual gestures by human neonates," *Science*, 1977,198, 75-78 **91, bottom :** Courtesy of David Linton **93:** Michael Newman/PhotoEdit **95, top:** Chris Lowe/Index Stock Imagery **95, bottom:** David Grossman **98:** D. L. Baldwin/Photo Net-work **105:** Gary Conner/Index Stock Imagery **106:** Tony Freeman/PhotoEdit **107, top:** Yves De Braine/Black Star **107, bottom:** Bob Daemmrich/The Image Works **113, top:** Sarah Putnum/Index Stock Imagery **113, bottom:** Tom McCarthy/PhotoEdit **115:** Jeff Greenberg **116:** AFP/Corbis **118:** SW Production/Index Stock Imagery

Chapter 4. bottom: Stereogram © Anything Enterprises, 1994 **125:** Jay Dickman/Corbis **129:** Omikron/Photo Researchers, Inc. **132, left, center, right:** Michael Newman/ PhotoEdit **134:** Jon L. Barken/Index Stock Imagery **137:** Dr. G. Oran Bredberg/SPL/ Photo Researchers, Inc. **139:** Richard Costana, *Discover Magazine*, 1993 **140:** Omikron/ Photo Researchers, Inc. **142:** Esbin Anderson/ Photo Network/PictureQuest **143, left:** NASA **143, right:** Roger Ressmeyer/Stock, Boston **144:** Bob Daemmrich/The Image Works **145:** Herve Donnezan/Photo Researchers, Inc. **147, top:** Yvaral, © 1990, *Marilyn Numerisee #420*, Courtesy of Circle Gallery **147, bottom right:** Mark Richards/ PhotoEdit **149:** E. R. Degginger/Animals Animals **152:** Bob Western **154:** Collection Haags Gemeente Museum, The Hague. © 1994 M. C. Escher/Cordon Art, Baarn, The Netherlands. All rights reserved. **154, 156:** Dennis Coon **157:** Bettmann/Corbis **158:** Mark McKenna **162:** © Held, Al, "*The Big N*" (1965) synthetic polymer paint on canvas 9'⅜" x 9'. Collection, The Museum of Modern Art, New York, Mrs. Armand P. Bartos fund **164:** Susan Van Etten/PhotoEdit **165, all:** Dennis Coon **167:** AP/Wide World Photo

Chapter 5. 174: Michael A. Keller/Corbis **176, bottom:** Timothy Ross/The Image Works **176, top:** Joel Gordon **179, top:** Yale Joel/TimePix **179, bottom:** Wadsworth/ Thomson Learning **185, top:** Michael Newman/PhotoEdit **185, bottom:** AP/Wide World Photo **186:** AKG Berlin/SuperStock **189:** Dennis Coon **191, left:** Dan Francis/ Mardan Photography **191, right:** Dan Francis/ Mardan Photography **197:** National Library of Medicine **198:** Rod Boren/AP/Wide World Photo **199:** P. Iovino/Archive Photos/ Getty Images **200:** Mark C. Burnett/Stock, Boston **204:** Creasource/Series/PictureQuest **206:** "Marijuana and the Brain," *Science News*, Vol. 143 **208:** A Ramey/PhotoEdit **210:** Courtesy of Maryanne Mott

Chapter 6. 216: PhotoDisc/Corbis **222:** Dan Francis/Mardan Photography **229:** Yale Joel/ *Life Magazine*/TimePix **231:** Chimp-O-Mat, Yukes Regional Primate Research Center, Emory University **235:** Christoph Wilhelm/ Getty Images **238:** Carleton Ray/Photo Researchers, Inc. **239:** Tony Freeman/PhotoEdit **243:** Spencer Grant/PhotoEdit **246, bottom:** Courtesy of Albert Bandura **246, top:** Steve Skjold/PhotoEdit **247:** Tony Freeman/ PhotoEdit **248:** Getty Images **250:** Tony Freeman/PhotoEdit

Chapter 7. 256: PhotoDisc/Corbis **257:** Corbis **261:** From Wilder Penfield, *The Excitable Cortex in Conscious Man*, 1958. Courtesy of the author and Charles C. Thomas, Publisher, Springfield, Illinois **262:** Index Stock Imagery **267:** SW Production/Index Stock Imagery **274:** Paul Conklin/PhotoEdit **276:** Spencer Grant/Photo Researchers, Inc. **277:** Rick Martin/San Jose Mercury News **278:** AP/Wide World Photo **279:** AP/Wide World Photo **281:** © Tulving, E. (1989). Remembering and Knowing the Past. *American Scientist*, 77, (4), 361–367 **283:** Robbie Jack/Corbis **283:** Jeffrey L. Rotman/Corbis **285:** A. Ramey/ PhotoEdit **287:** Ulrike Welsch

Chapter 8. 293: Purdue News Service Photo by David Umberger **294:** James D. Wilson/ Getty Images **296, left:** Dennis Coon **296, right:** John Elk III, Stock, Boston/PictureQuest **299:** Javier Plerin/Latin Stock/The Stock Market/Corbis **300:** Rick Sauders/Index Stock Imagery **303:** Robin Nelson/PhotoEdit **308, left:** Archiv/Photo Researchers, Inc. **308, right:** Courtesy of Cray Computer **310:** Bob Daemmrich/Stock, Boston/ PictureQuest **312:** David Horan/Index Stock Imagery **316, left:** Dan McCoy/Rainbow **316, right:** Christiana Dittmann/Rainbow **317:** Stan Godlweski/Getty Images **320:** Hulton/Getty Images

Chapter 9. 334: Todd Powell/Index Stock Imagery **336:** David Austen/Woodfin Camp & Associates **339, top:** Courtesy of Dr. Neal E. Miller, Rockefeller University **339, bottom:** John Sholtis, The Rockefeller University, New York, NY, © 1995 Amgen, Inc. **340, left:** Theo Westenberger/Archive Photos/Getty Images **340, right:** Arnaldo Magnani/Getty Images **342:** Getty Images **343:** Evan Agostini/Getty Images **344, top:** Gary Conner/PhotoEdit **344, bottom:** Alain Evrard/Photo Researchers, Inc. **350:** Courtesy of Harry F. Harlow, University of Wisconsin Primate Laboratory **351:** Andy Belcher/ImageState/PictureQuest **354:** AP/Wide World Photo **357:** Reuters/Corbis **358:** Margaret Miller/Photo Researchers, Inc. **362:** Bob Daemmrich/Stock, Boston **364, right:** Gary Conner/PhotoEdit **364, left:** AP/Wide World Photo **365:** David Young-Wolff/PhotoEdit **366:** Michael Grecco/Stock, Boston **368:** Dan Francis/Mardan Photography **371:** Esbin-Anderson/The Image Works

Chapter 10. 377: PhotoDisc/Corbis **378:** Neal Preston/Corbis **379:** Michael Newman/ PhotoEdit **380:** Laurence Monneret/Getty Images **383:** Stephen Jaffe/The Image Works **386, top:** Alris Upitis/Black Star **386, top:** Tony Freeman/PhotoEdit **388:** "*All is Vanity*" by Allen Gilbert **391:** Bettmann/ Corbis **393, top:** Bonnie Kamin/PhotoEdit **393, bottom:** Joel Gordon **394:** Bob Daemmrich/The Image Works **396:** Laura Dwight/PhotoEdit **397, left:** Charlie Westerman/Getty Images **397, right:** Gilles Mingasson/Getty Images **401:** Photolibrary/ PictureQuest **404:** Bob Daemmrich/The Image Works **406:** David McNew/ Newsmakers/Getty Images **412:** Michelle D. Birdwell/PhotoEdit

Chapter 11. 418: Image Source/PictureQuest **421, left:** Darren Robb/Getty Images **421, right:** Thomas Hoeffgen/Getty Images **425, top:** David Frazier/Photolibrary/Photo Researchers, Inc. **425, bottom:** Bob Daemmrich/The Image Works **427:** AP/Wide World Photo **429:** Tony Anderson/ Getty Images **431:** Royalty-Free/Corbis **436:** Jonathan Nourok/PhotoEdit **438, top:** Stephen Rose/Rainbow **438, bottom:** Barbara Stitzer/PhotoEdit **440:** Leslye Borden/PhotoEdit **442:** Dan McCoy/ Rainbow **443:** Hisham Ibrahim/Getty Images **446:** Aaron Haupt/Stock, Boston/ PictureQuest **453:** Leonard Lessin/Photo Researchers, Inc. **454:** Diana Walker/Getty Images

Chapter 12. 459: Royalty-Free/Corbis **461:** Naile Goelbasi/Getty Images **463, top:** Scott Camazine/Photo Researchers, Inc. **463, bottom:** Courtesy of Ulrike Kantor Gallery **469, bottom:** Courtesy of Robert Hare **469, top:** Cary Wolinsky/Stock, Boston **472:** Brent Stirton/The Image Bank/Getty Images **472, bottom left:** Bettmann/Corbis **472, bottom right:** Dennis Coon **473:** Bob Daemmrich/The Image Works **474:** Bruce Ayres/Getty Images **479, top:** Benelux Press/ Getty Images **479, bottom:** Bettmann/Corbis **480:** Joe Sohm/The Image Works **482, top:** Peter Granser/Laif/Aurora Photos **482, bottom:** Grunnitis/Photo Researchers, Inc. **483, bottom:** Bruce Ely/Getty Images **483:** Curt Borgwardt/Corbis Sygma **485:** Derik Bayes/ Courtesy Guttman-Maclay Life Picture Service **486, top:** Dennis Brack/Black Star **486, bottom:** The Brookhaven National Laboratory **489:** Darren Robb/Getty Images **490:** Dan McCoy/Rainbow **492:** Tony Freeman/ PhotoEdit

Chapter 13. 499: Roger Allyn Lee/SuperStock **501, top:** Daniele Pellegrini/Photo Researchers, Inc. **501, bottom:** CIMMYT **502, top left:** Mary Evans Picture Library/Photo Researchers, Inc. **502, top right:** Bettmann/ Corbis **502, bottom:** Archiv/Photo Researchers, Inc. **505:** Courtesy of Dr. Natalie Rogers **507:** D. Grecco/The Image Works **510:** Curt Gunther/Camera 5 **511, bottom:** Courtesy of Albert Bandura **511, top:** Teresa Zabula/Uniphoto/Pictor **512, left:** Courtesy of Larry Hodges, Thomas and Rob Kooper **512, right:** Georgia Tech Telephoto **519:** Joel Gordon **523:** Gilles Mingasson/Getty Images **526:** Will & Deni McIntyre/Photo Researchers, Inc. **527, top:** Peter Southwick/Stock, Boston **527, bottom:** Bruce Ayers/Getty Images **529:** Bob Daemmrich/Stock, Boston

Chapter 14. 539: David Young-Wolff/ PhotoEdit **541, top:** Mark Richards/ PhotoEdit **541, bottom:** Jeff Greenberg / Rainbow **542, top:** Joe Sohm/The Image Works **542, bottom:** Frank Siteman/Stock, Boston **543:** Ralf-Finn Hestoft/Corbis **545:** Anthony B. Wood/Stock, Boston **546:** Chip Henderson/Index Stock Imagery **547:** Justin Sullivan/Getty Images **549:** Bill Bachmann/ PhotoEdit **552:** Scenes from the film "*Obedience*" by Stanley Milgram, The Pennsylvania State University, Audio Visual Services. Used by permission. **553:** Billy E. Barnes/ PhotoEdit **555:** Michael Newman/PhotoEdit **559, top:** Bob Llewellen/Pictor International Ltd./PictureQuest **559, bottom:** Joel Gordon **562:** *Dallas Morning News*/Getty Images **563:** Bettmann/Corbis **566:** Vic Bider/PhotoEdit **567, top:** David Young-Wolff/ PhotoEdit **567, bottom:** Mary Kate Denny/PhotoEdit **568:** Jonathan Nourok/PhotoEdit **570:** Duomo/Corbis **571:** Harvey Schwartz/Index Stock Imagery **575:** Joel Gordon

Appendix: A-1: Dennis Coon

Name Index

Subject Index

TO THE OWNER OF THIS BOOK:

I hope that you have found *Psychology: A Journey*, Second Edition, useful. So that this book can be improved in a future edition, would you take the time to complete this sheet and return it? Thank you.

School and address: _____

_____

Department: _____

Instructor's name: _____

1. What I like most about this book is: _____

_____

_____

2. What I like least about this book is: _____

_____

_____

3. My general reaction to this book is: _____

_____

_____

4. The name of the course in which I used this book is: _____

_____

5. Were all of the chapters of the book assigned for you to read? _____

   If not, which ones weren't? _____

6. In the space below, or on a separate sheet of paper, please write specific suggestions for improving this book and anything else you'd care to share about your experience in using this book.

_____

_____

_____

_____

_____

_____

_____

BUSINESS REPLY MAIL
FIRST-CLASS MAIL   PERMIT NO. 102   MONTEREY CA

POSTAGE WILL BE PAID BY ADDRESSEE

Attn: Dennis Coon/Psychology

Wadsworth/Thomson Learning
60 Garden Ct Ste 205
Monterey CA 93940-9967

OPTIONAL:

Your name: _____   Date: _____

May we quote you, either in promotion for *Psychology: A Journey*, Second Edition, or in future publishing ventures?

    Yes: _____   No: _____

    Sincerely yours,

    Dennis Coon